Encyclopedia of

AMERICAN
SOCIAL
HISTORY

Encyclopedia of

AMERICAN SOCIAL HISTORY

MARY KUPIEC CAYTON
ELLIOTT J. GORN
PETER W. WILLIAMS

EDITORS

Volume II

CHARLES SCRIBNER'S SONS / NEW YORK
MAXWELL MACMILLAN CANADA/TORONTO
MAXWELL MACMILLAN INTERNATIONAL/NEW YORK OXFORD SINGAPORE SYDNEY

Copyright © 1993 Charles Scribner's Sons

Library of Congress Cataloging-in-Publication Data

Encyclopedia of American social history / Mary Kupiec Cayton, Elliott
J. Gorn and Peter W. Williams, editors.
    p. cm.—
    Includes bibliographical references and index.
    ISBN 0–684–19246–2
    1. United States—Social conditions—Encyclopedias. 2. United
States—Social life and customs—Encyclopedias. 3. Social history—
Encyclopedias. I. Cayton, Mary Kupiec. II. Gorn, Elliott J.,
1951–   III. Williams, Peter W. IV. Series.
HN57.E58 1992
301′.0973—dc20   92-10577
ISBN 0-684-19246-2 Set   CIP
ISBN 0-684-19455-4 Volume 1
ISBN 0-684-19456-2 Volume 2
ISBN 0-684-19457-0 Volume 3

Published simultaneously in Canada
by Maxwell Macmillan Canada, Inc.

3   4   5   6   7   8   9   10

Printed in the United States of America.

The paper in this book meets the guidelines for permanence and
durability of the Committee on Production Guidelines for Book Longevity
of the Council on Library Resources.

CONTENTS

Volume II

CONTENTS

CONTENTS

vii

CONTENTS

CONTENTS

Part V

ETHNIC AND RACIAL SUBCULTURES

AMERICAN INDIANS OF THE EAST

Daniel H. Usner, Jr.

IN 1820 THE Reverend Jedidiah Morse was commissioned by the United States government to travel across the country and gather information about its American Indian inhabitants. Like so many other documents generated by both attentive and casual observers of Indian societies during this period, Morse's report to the secretary of war contains many interesting details about social life in hundreds of different native communities. At the Onondaga reservation in central New York, he noted the cultivation of various grains, vegetables, and fruits, praised the recent conversion of a few residents to Christianity, and listened to the chiefs plead for stricter laws against the sale of alcohol to their young men. The Ottawas at L'Arbre Croche on the eastern shore of Lake Michigan impressed Morse with the large surpluses of corn that they produced with only hoes and sold in the Mackinaw market. In Mississippi he observed a significant increase in livestock raising and cotton farming by Choctaw households. He also visited the Eliot and Mayhew schools, which had recently been established among the Choctaw towns by the American Board of Commissioners for Foreign Missions.

These informative glimpses into the conditions of Indian life across states and territories east of the Mississippi River were nevertheless tainted by narrow perceptions and purposes, which Morse shared with most agents of government policy. Their vision during the early 1820s focused on signs of reform within Indian societies and on clues to willingness among Indian leaders to move west of the Mississippi. Jeffersonian efforts to engineer change in the name of "civilization" showed mixed and scattered results. Churchmen and officials took credit for favorable shifts in custom and belief, while they discredited changes and continuities that increased resistance to government policy. Morse predicted that New England Indians would object to removal because, "having intermarried with the lowest classes of white people and negroes, and

feeling no sympathy with Indians of pure blood," they "would not be comfortable, or happy, or of wholesome influence, if removed and planted among them." Attempts to teach domestic industry, plow agriculture, and Christianity to the Iroquois communities of New York, the minister had no doubt, were "much obstructed by the influence of low and depraved white people, who have insinuated themselves among these Indians, and whose interest is to keep them ignorant; and whose exertions, of course, would be against all improvements."

The ideological climate of the early nineteenth century locked eastern Indians into a precarious situation and, in the long run, hindered historical understanding of the complicated changes occurring within their societies. Evidence of desirable social change was used to promote removal as a means of expanding public support of directed reform. By relocating Indians tribes west of the Mississippi, the federal government could more efficiently manage the process of "civilization." Evidence of social anomie or resistance, though, was also cited as proof that removal was necessary; Indian societies, it was claimed, needed to be distanced from deleterious and disruptive influences exerted by some whites. Not only did this duplicity misrepresent and manipulate conditions being experienced by Indians at the time, it created a simplistic picture of social change among eastern Indians for generations of historians to come. Indians in the eastern United States faced difficult, but diverse, choices in the early nineteenth century, and their decisions evolved from a long continuum of adaptation and survival that deserves close scrutiny.

Based on statistics assembled by Jedidiah Morse in *A Report to the Secretary of War of the United States, on Indian Affairs* (1822), the Indian population of New England stood at 2,526 people. These included Passamaquoddies and Penobscots in Maine, Martha's Vineyard and Mashpee Wampanoags in Massachusetts, Narragansetts in Rhode Island, and Mohegans and Pequots in Connecticut. New York's Indian population numbered 5,184, mostly Iroquois in the northern and western parts of the state but also Montauks on Long Island. Wyandots, Delawares, Shawnees, Menominees, and Potawatomis were among the 17,006 Indians scattered across Ohio, Indiana, and Illinois. The Michigan Territory was inhabited by 28,380 Indians, mostly Ottawas, Chippewas, and Winnebagos. In the southeastern United States the Cherokees numbered 11,000 people, the Creeks 20,000, the Seminoles 5,000, the Choctaws 25,000, and the Chickasaws 3,625. Nottaways in Virginia and Catawbas in South Carolina were among the smaller communities remaining along the eastern seaboard.

Altogether the American Indian population east of the Mississippi numbered approximately 121,000 people by the early 1820s. An additional 13,000 eastern Indians were living in areas just west of the Mississippi. Groups of Shawnees, Delawares, Peorias, Piankashaws, and Cherokees had recently migrated into Missouri and Arkansas. Over the preceding decades Louisiana and eastern Texas had been settled by such eastern Indian migrants as the Choctaws, Tunicas, Biloxis, Apalachees, and Coushattas. For centuries some American Indian groups had employed migration as a strategic response to external pressure or sudden adversity. The Mississippi River served principally as a channel of communication, crossed for various reasons by eastern Indians living in the Mississippi Valley. Toward the end of the eighteenth century, encroachment on their territory and depletion of game drove more and more groups across the river for seasonal or year-round occupancy. In the early nineteenth century, mounting federal pressure for land cessions and local antagonism against tribal sovereignty made the systematic removal of Indian nations beyond state boundaries a priority in United States Indian affairs; by the 1850s, the policy of removal had uprooted some 100,000 American Indians from their eastern homelands and transplanted them west of the Mississippi.

Social historians of American Indians during the colonial and early national periods are just beginning to make up for years of neglect. Historians of the colonial era certainly have not ignored the presence of native peoples during the early years of European colonization or in the wars of international rivalry. The problem is actually the excessive attention paid to geopolitical events and military conflicts. Literature on the English colo-

nies focuses on seventeenth-century Indian wars, usually depicting coastal tribes in desperate struggle against inevitable destiny. American Indians later reappear in the scholarship only as pawns in the French-British imperial contest. The formative years of the United States make up the final chapter of this tragic story, in which the survivors of the seventeenth- and eighteenth-century conflicts are finally swept away from eastern North America by hordes of American settlers.

This misleading treatment of the role of Indians in early American history is finally being replaced by a new scholarship that strives to improve our knowledge of the complex ways that Indians related to colonial society and to the new nation. Closer examination of Indian life in and around European settlements has become an important angle of revision in colonial history. American Indians interacted with and influenced English colonists in a variety of ways. The causes and consequences of Indian wars are being closely reexamined. Colonial policies and ideologies are being explored in light of Indian initiatives and values. The enduring and wide-ranging presence of Indian people in the colonies—as free and unfree laborers within colonial society or as members of semiautonomous communities—is finally coming into sharper focus. As the smoke screen created by the likes of Jedidiah Morse fades away, it is possible to gain a clearer view of the challenges faced by eastern Indians during the removal era and of the experiences from which they drew their responses.

THE COLONIAL PERIOD

The nearly 135,000 eastern Indians counted in Morse's 1822 report descended from native societies that had been much more numerous and populous at the beginning of European contact. The pre-Columbian eastern Woodlands of North America were inhabited by a diversity of peoples. Muskogean-speaking societies stretched across the Southeast from Florida to Louisiana, with Siouan-speaking groups concentrated on the Carolina piedmont and coast. Algonkian speakers populated most of the Northeast, from the Atlantic coast to the western Great Lakes. Iroquoian-speaking nations, from the Hurons in Canada to the Cherokees in southern Appalachia, occupied much of the interior. In social organization, the Muskogean and Iroquoian peoples were generally of matrilineal descent, while Algonquians and Siouans tended to be patrilineal. Broad categories of language and lineage, however, cannot convey the wide range of social and cultural differences that distinguished one group from another. Societies mixed farming, hunting, gathering, and fishing in various combinations. Coastal peoples of the North Atlantic, like the Micmacs and Penobscots, relied heavily upon fish and game for food, while interior tribes such as the Senecas and Choctaws drew a heavier proportion of their sustenance from corn, beans, and squash. Trade networks and political alliances facilitated exchange of surpluses between the different Indian nations. Diplomacy and warfare generated significant fluidity across territorial boundaries.

The most important sphere of social and economic life among all of these distinct peoples was the local community. At the village or band level everyday life moved through annual cycles of livelihood and ritual. As communities practiced their seasonal subsistence activities—producing food, fuel, clothing, and other material goods from local environments—they followed a calendar of ceremonies deeply integrated with the natural world. Village and band leaders provided the essential leadership in the day-to-day lives of people. Cultural and social ties, of course, extended beyond these small groups to include tribes or nations. Indian nations were based on various forms of political cohesion among culturally related local communities, and nations interacted with each other through dynamic alliances and confederations.

Changes and continuities in eastern Indian societies can best be traced at the local level. The political history of Indian-white relations has naturally focused on tribal and intertribal organizations, which usually forged the alliances and waged the wars. But the social impact of European conquest and colonization was most intimately felt inside native villages. The most enduring strategies of adaptation and resistance were designed within these communities. The most troublesome divisions and fissions also occurred there. The waves of epidemics that began sweeping across North America in the sixteenth century killed millions of Indian people and extinguished scores of Indian polities. In order to maintain social stability and cultural identity in the face of this catastrophe, survivors often had to relocate their communities and even merge with other groups.

As European trade and settlement increased during the seventeenth century, Indian communities experienced a wide range of social and economic changes. Increasing participation in the transatlantic fur trade injected new products into each society's material culture, and competition over access to new trade partners often led to destructive warfare against other Indian tribes and their European allies. For a long time, however, Indian nations managed to stave off complete subordination to the market economy by imposing some of their own conditions upon the exchange of goods. Prices had to be fixed, commerce regulated, and gifts received in order to maintain a reciprocal relationship that tied economic transactions to political obligations. While metalware, firearms, and textiles were adopted into household economies, Indians changed their production activities, cooking methods, and clothing styles very selectively. The most damaging commodity received in exchange for furs was alcohol, which many European traders exploited as a means of inducing Indian hunters to produce larger quantities of beaver pelts or deerskins.

During the seventeenth century, coastal tribes became surrounded by a growing colonial population of Europeans and Africans who valued acquisition of Indian land above access to their trade. As disease and war reduced their numbers, Indians from the Gulf of Maine to the Gulf of Mexico relinquished most of their territory and resorted to village sites interspersed among European settlements. Called mission reserves in New France, praying towns in New England, settlement tribes in the southern Atlantic colonies, and small nations in Louisiana, these Indian enclaves developed close, but not always favorable, relations with surrounding colonial communities. They were highly vulnerable to the debilitating influence of disease and alcohol and frequently subject to legal disputes over land use and property rights. Conflicts over colonists' livestock straying onto Indians' fields occasionally erupted into open conflict, as occurred around New Amsterdam during the 1640s. Foodstuffs, handicrafts, information, and labor regularly provided by these Indian communities, however, did allow them to adjust to a rapidly changing world without losing all of their social autonomy. Indian men on Long Island and in southern New England, for example, became expert crewmen on commercial whaling ships. Peddling certain goods and performing selected services were widespread means of expressing a distinct identity while remaining tied to colonial society.

Throughout most of the colonial period, Indian nations in the interior of eastern North America managed to hold onto their territories and to maintain political leverage between European powers. The social life of these tribes, consequently, remained buffered from the full impact of colonial expansion. By the eighteenth century, the Iroquois nations were able to influence terms of trade because of their advantageous location between New York and New France. In the Southeast, the populous Cherokee and Choctaw nations became valuable trade partners and military allies of English South Carolina and French Louisiana, respectively, while the Creeks employed a policy of neutrality that allowed them to deflect aggressive approaches from English, Spanish, and French colonies alike. Under the watchful eyes of village leaders, European traders and their entourage of packhorsemen, guides, and interpreters had to satisfy Indian customs in order to secure profitable economic relations. In the hundreds of villages across the Great Lakes region, this process involved marriage into Indian families and generated the formation of a sizable population of métis (people of mixed Indian and European descent).

In both coastal and interior regions of eastern North America, outside influence on native society was most intense in those scattered communities that hosted European missionaries. Efforts to convert native Americans to Christianity were very uneven over the colonial period. Along the Saint Lawrence River and the Great Lakes, French Jesuits made some of the deepest inroads into traditional Indian belief patterns by drawing people to mission towns. In the lower Mississippi Valley, however, the French failed to establish a comparable network of missions across Indian country. Spanish Franciscans in Florida actually proselytized the heaviest concentration of American Indians, with Guales, Timucuans, and Apalachees clustered at times into densely populated areas. Indian revolts and English raids, however, caused the collapse of these mission centers by the early eighteenth century. Survivors scattered in different directions as the English captured many as slaves and as refugees migrated to other regions. Missionary efforts by the English took longer to gain momentum, but by the end of the seventeenth century, some ministers had reorganized many survivors of the New England conflicts into so-called praying towns.

The process of conversion itself took many forms. Recent scholarship reveals that the Indian neophytes residing in these different mission communities were able to adopt selectively, and even alter, elements of European religion in ways that frustrated missionaries at the time and eluded his-

torians for generations to come. With outright rejection proving ineffective and total conversion being undesirable, American Indians relied on subtle means of resistance and accommodation to measures intent on undermining their cultures. Iroquois and Algonquian peoples who settled on the mission reserves along the Saint Lawrence River attempted to blend new symbols and rituals into their traditional belief system. Whether in Canada, New England, or Florida, Indians also tried to use their relations with missionaries to some kind of political or economic advantage. Wampanoag communities on Martha's Vineyard and Cape Cod accepted the new faith as an instrument of protection against colonial trespassers. In many cases, Christianity became a new tradition that helped preserve a degree of social autonomy. European efforts to reshape Indian societies and countervailing Indian responses produced mixed results. People in a single community showed varying degrees of Christian faith, and Christianity manifested itself in different forms from tribe to tribe. But overall the scattered Indians who were affected by European missionaries did not allow a new religion to dissolve their cultural identity or political sovereignty.

THE AGE OF REVOLUTION

Geopolitical change that began unfolding in the mid eighteenth century sent a sequence of new pressures and adversities sweeping across eastern Indian societies. The British and French empires came face to face in the Ohio Valley, intensifying the commercial and military contest for Indian allies and quickly involving them in the Seven Years' War (1756–1763). When France withdrew from North America in 1763, northeastern Indians were suddenly enclosed by British possessions in Canada and along the Atlantic seaboard. For some political leverage, southeastern Indian nations could still turn to Spain, which acquired Louisiana from France in 1762. But in the long run, the role of eastern Indians in European international affairs was slipping. By 1783 the success of the American Revolution produced an independent and aggressive new nation in their midst that began to further reduce their military and political power. Indian societies consequently became, more than ever, vulnerable to revolutionary challenges and threats.

The revolutionary war itself proved costly to many American Indians. Tribes allied with Great Britain fought long and hard against the rebellious colonies. The war divided tribes and confederacies, as illustrated by the Oneidas and Tuscaroras, who split from their loyalist brethren in the Iroquois League to assist the patriot cause. Iroquois and Cherokee homelands suffered devastating invasions by the revolutionary armies. American frontiersmen sought vengeance against any and all Indians for losses suffered during the bloody war. In 1782 nearly one hundred Moravian Delawares at the mission town of Gnadenhutten, Ohio—men, women, and children—were killed by an Indian-hating mob. The United States government at first tried to coerce Indian nations into submission with assertions that they were automatically conquered because of Great Britain's defeat. Indian opposition to this stance, through both diplomatic and military resistance, convinced federal officials that negotiation with individual tribes was the better approach to take.

Over the decades following the American Revolution, Indians living in the populous areas of the original states experienced a continuation of familiar patterns of change and continuity. The size of communal and personal landholdings continued to erode. Many men from the enclave communities had fought as volunteers in the Continental army, including thirty Stockbridge soldiers who died at White Plains in 1778. Contribution to the cause of American independence, however, did not guarantee protection against mounting state pressures on Indian lands and resources. Despite their sacrifice during the revolutionary war and the diplomatic and military assistance subsequently provided by chief Hendrick Aupaumut, the Stockbridge people were driven from Massachusetts in 1783 and sought refuge near the Oneida community of Brotherton. Unable to secure land rights in New York and then in Indiana, they purchased in 1822 several thousand acres from the Menominees in Wisconsin. The Catawbas' service and sacrifice during the Revolution won them a somewhat better relationship with their home state. The South Carolina government helped the Catawbas recover from the destruction of their town by the British army and maintained a respectful relationship with them as fellow patriots. Nonetheless, by 1840 the Catawbas were pressured into selling their bountiful land at King's Bottom for money to be used to purchase property elsewhere.

The survival of small Indian communities along the Atlantic seaboard depended on flexible forms of social interaction with neighboring settlements and towns. Work, trade, and amusement regularly brought Indians together with whites and blacks, and intimate relationships naturally occurred between men and women from different cultures. The marriage of non-Indians into Indian communities helped Indian settlements maintain a viable number of residents. This mixing of peoples produced gradual changes in social organization and in cultural tradition but did not significantly weaken the ethnic identity of Indian groups. This pattern of adopting blacks and whites, as well as other Indians, into their communities persisted into the nineteenth century. But as race relations became more tightly regulated and narrowly categorized, especially in the South, the racial identity of many Indian groups was subjected to greater scrutiny and control. Local governments and federal officials insisted on classifying Indians as mulattoes or Negroes. Social and economic relations with African Americans grew more rigid inside the communities as the status of both Indians and free blacks declined in larger society. The Catawbas, Houmas, and other southeastern groups began to scorn intermarriage with non-Indians and to accept dominant attitudes toward blacks.

The interior Indian societies of eastern North America faced a different set of challenges during the late eighteenth and early nineteenth centuries. Continuing wars against the United States kept the Ohio Valley and Great Lakes region in almost constant turmoil. As villages ceded one tract of land after another in an endless string of treaties, refugeeism became a way of life for many Indian families. In the Southeast, a segment of Cherokee nation called the Chickamaugas waged military resistance against encroaching settlements into the 1790s and then began to migrate west of the Mississippi River. Given so much violence and movement, Indian societies managed to maintain a remarkable degree of internal stability, largely because of the resourceful responses they had made to colonial forces in the past.

In addition to treaties and wars, the United States government employed instruments of social change to control Indian life and to acquire Indian land. The Jeffersonian program for "civilizing" American Indians was designed to reform their societies through ideological and technical means. The federal government operated trade houses and located agencies inside Indian country in order to deliver ideas and implements that the government hoped would transform Indians into individual property owners and faithful Christian believers. With increasing financial assistance from the government, religious denominations escalated their missionary efforts among an Indian population beleaguered by deteriorating fur-trade systems, hateful white neighbors, land-hungry officials, and diminishing political options. Conditions were ripe for the infiltration of new values and beliefs.

Indian initiatives and responses were still as pluralistic and dynamic as in former times. Indian societies shared a common desire to preserve political sovereignty over whatever lands they managed to secure, but the social circumstances of this struggle varied from place to place. After the American Revolution, many Iroquois people—Christians and non-Christians—decided to take permanent refuge in British Canada. Segments of other Indian nations likewise chose migration as a strategy of survival. The movement of many Creek Indians into Florida during these years resulted in the formation of a new tribal group called the Seminoles. Sizable groups of Shawnees, Delawares, Cherokees, and Choctaws also sought social and economic security across the Mississippi, on lands offered them by Spanish Louisiana.

Accommodation and resistance to United States policies took a variety of forms inside the different tribes. Many community leaders enthusiastically accepted Christianity, plow agriculture, or schools, or some combination of these new ways. Black Hoof of the Shawnees, James Vann of the Cherokees, and Cornplanter of the Senecas embraced agricultural and educational innovations. Most Indian advocates of change, however, refused to accept the entire cultural package being presented to them by government and religious agents. People who converted to Christianity still resisted efforts to alter their traditional uses of the land. The familiar process of blending new and old beliefs continued to work. Practicing more intensive agriculture with plows and oxen did not usually mean accepting a breakup of community land into privately owned farms. Sending children to mission schools was often a strategy for learning literacy in order to combat more effectively the pressures being exerted on Indian sovereignty and territory.

Handsome Lake of the Senecas redesigned traditional ways to meet new challenges by starting a revitalization movement among the Iroquois people. Suffering from alcohol abuse and physical weakness, Handsome Lake recovered through a sequence of visions that began in 1799. He delivered a message to his people that warned of imminent destruction and prescribed a way to salvation.

Handsome Lake's gospel generally reinforced the ancient beliefs and rituals of the Iroquois but discouraged particular customs such as witchcraft, which he considered detrimental to their social recovery. He encouraged economic adjustments along lines being recommended by Quaker missionaries but strongly opposed any further loss of Indian land and any deeper intervention by whites into Indian life. The cultural renaissance and political fortitude inspired by Handsome Lake greatly bolstered the Iroquois people's determination to endure for generations to come.

By the second decade of the nineteenth century, the clash between United States policies and American Indian objectives climaxed violently in two volatile regions. Seething resentment among Indians in the Ohio Valley over military defeats and territorial losses to the United States was galvanized under the spiritual leadership of the Shawnee Prophet, Tenskwatawa, whose life paralleled that of Handsome Lake in significant ways. Declining rapidly in health and reputation, Tenskwatawa received a visionary message calling for social revitalization and passive resistance. Thousands of Indian people from across the Great Lakes region visited Prophetstown, established in 1808 along the Wabash River, to hear Tenskwatawa preach abstinence from drinking alcohol, restoration of traditional ways, and avoidance of white people. The Shawnee Prophet confounded and infuriated United States officials, who tried to discredit his popular movement. But his brother, Tecumseh, began to translate the spiritual message into political action. He traveled widely across eastern North America to recruit the different Indian nations into a pan-tribal confederacy. Soon war broke out with the United States, and Tecumseh joined the military cause of his people to that of Great Britain in the War of 1812.

A similar process unfolded in the Mississippi Territory. The Creek nation experienced intense pressures on its society and territory in the early nineteenth century. Deepening debt to the United States trade house and to private merchants, caused by declining prices for deerskins, made the Creeks vulnerable to demands for payment with their lands. White settlements along the Tennessee and Alabama rivers began to sprawl around their villages, while a heavy-handed government agent aggressively interfered with tribal politics and culture. A revitalization movement inspired earlier by a number of prophets made many Creeks receptive to Tecumseh's visit in the fall of 1811. What began as a civil war between militant traditionalists and United States sympathizers resulted in a bloody invasion by American troops and militiamen. The war ultimately cost the Creeks some three thousand lives and twenty-two million acres of land.

THE REMOVAL ERA

Social change and continuity among Indians in the United States occurred in ways still largely guided by the Indians' own various priorities and circumstances. Intervention and control by government policymakers proceeded with uneven results. No matter what happened inside native societies in the early nineteenth century, however, Indian lands and governments faced a mounting assault led increasingly by interests and officials at the state level. The official commitment of the federal government was to protect Indian sovereignty from jealous state governments. But the early republic's own incongruities in Indian policy helped undermine some of its good intentions. Reciprocal negotiation between tribes and the nation suffered abuse at the hands of commissioners sent into Indian country to make one treaty after another, all because the national government needed more and more land to raise revenues and to satisfy citizens. In the name of benevolence and goodwill, too many agents from the United States trampled over the values and customs still cherished by Indian people. So when state governments began threatening during the 1820s to dissolve the political independence and territorial integrity of Indians living inside their boundaries, the federal government began seeking an easy way around its legal and moral obligations. By the time Andrew Jackson was elected to the presidency in 1828, the United States was already moving toward a policy of removal.

Dramatic changes in the Cherokee nation during the early nineteenth century illustrate how endurance and resilience in Indian societies, not weakness and inflexibility, actually made them seem more threatening to state interests. The Cherokees recovered remarkably well from the social collapse and military defeat suffered during the American Revolution. Agricultural improvements, livestock raising, mills, roads, and schools spread across the Cherokee landscape. Some households even became prosperous slave-owning plantations.

Missionaries were cautiously welcomed by Cherokee families, who saw the value in reading and writing skills, and the invention of a syllabary by the Cherokee Sequoya advanced Cherokee self-control over literacy. Politically, the Cherokees transformed their tribe into a republic of their own. A full-blown elective government—with executive, legislative, and judicial branches—was operating by the late 1820s. The economic and political development of the Cherokees strengthened their resolve to govern themselves in their own homeland.

Anxious to gain access to Indian lands and resources, Georgia and neighboring states grew intolerant toward Cherokee nationalism and escalated pressures for removal. Other Indian nations managed similar movements toward stronger central governance, thereby alienating their closest white neighbors. State governments began to impose jurisdiction over tribal territory, while Indian leaders appealed to the federal government for protection. Although the Supreme Court, in *Worcester* v. *Georgia* (1832), confirmed the United States's obligation to defend Indian autonomy against state intrusion, the Jackson administration intensified its efforts to cajole and coerce tribes into leaving their homelands for territory west of the Mississippi.

Removal uprooted about one hundred thousand eastern Indians between 1820 and 1850. Many of these people had been on successful paths of social adaptation to the changing world around them. Others were still struggling to find an appropriate balance between tradition and innovation. The federal government's relocation policy imposed new hazards and strains on Indian society. The experience of mass migration itself cost an estimated thirty thousand lives and made recovery in the West a difficult and painful process. For the twenty thousand or so Indians who managed to remain on their eastern lands, year of adversity and neglect would severely test the social fabric of their communities. Most lost their official status as Indian nations. They were cheated out of homesteads promised them by the United States under the removal treaties. They became isolated or invisible communities by the end of the nineteenth century.

In the twentieth century, however, the struggle to endure as Indian peoples brought recognition and recovery to many of these eastern communities. Anthropologists and sociologists took note of the survival of Indian cultures from Maine to Mississippi. State governments established formal relations with Indian groups within their boundaries, while the United States government selectively acknowledged its responsibilities to particular eastern Indian societies. The pursuit of land claims, federal recognition, and economic development has helped forge a common regional identity among Native Americans still living east of the Mississippi River.

BIBLIOGRAPHY

Indians in the Colonial Northeast

Axtell, James. *The Invasion Within: The Contest of Cultures in Colonial North America* (1985).

Calloway, Colin G. *The Western Abenakis of Vermont, 1600–1800: War, Migration, and the Survival of an Indian People* (1990).

Cronon, William. *Changes in the Land: Indians, Colonists, and the Ecology of New England* (1983).

Hauptman, Laurence M., and James D. Wherry, eds. *The Pequots in Southern New England: The Fall and Rise of an American Indian Nation* (1990).

Jennings, Francis. *The Invasion of America: Indians, Colonialism, and the Cant of Conquest* (1975).

Kupperman, Karen Ordahl. *Settling with the Indians: The Meeting of English and Indian Cultures in America, 1580–1640* (1980).

Mancall, Peter C. *Valley of Opportunity: Economic Culture Along the Upper Susquehanna, 1700–1800* (1991).

Salisbury, Neal. *Manitou and Providence: Indians, Europeans, and the Making of New England, 1500–1643* (1982).

Tanner, Helen Hornbeck. *Atlas of Great Lakes Indian History* (1987).

Trigger, Bruce. *The Children of Aataentsic: A History of the Huron People to 1660* (1976).

White, Richard. *The Middle Ground: Indians, Empires, and Republics in the Great Lakes Region, 1650–1815* (1991).

Indians in the Colonial Southeast

Brain, Jeffrey P. *Tunica Archaeology* (1988).

Galloway, Patricia K., ed. *La Salle and His Legacy: Frenchmen and Indians in the Lower Mississippi Valley* (1982).

Goodwin, Gary. *Cherokees in Transition: A Study of Changing Culture and Environment Prior to 1775* (1977).

Hann, John H. *Apalachee: The Land Between the Rivers* (1988).

Merrell, James H. *The Indians' New World: Catawbas and Their Neighbors from European Contact Through the Era of Removal* (1989).

Rountree, Helen C. *Pocahontas's People: The Powhatan Indians of Virginia Through Four Centuries* (1990).

Silver, Timothy. *A New Face on the Countryside: Indians, Colonists, and Slaves in South Atlantic Forests, 1500–1800* (1990).

Usner, Daniel H., Jr. *Indians, Settlers, and Slaves in a Frontier Exchange Economy: The Lower Mississippi Valley Before 1783* (1992).

White, Richard. *The Roots of Dependency: Subsistence, Environment, and Social Change Among the Choctaws, Pawnees, and Navajos* (1983).

Wood, Peter H., Gregory A. Waselkov, and M. Thomas Hatley, eds. *Powhatan's Mantle: Indians in the Colonial Southeast* (1989).

Wright, J. Leitch, Jr. *The Only Land They Knew: The Tragic Story of the American Indians in the Old South* (1981).

From the American Revolution to the Removal Era

Dowd, Gregory Evans. *A Spirited Resistance: The North American Indian Struggle for Unity, 1745–1815* (1991).

Edmunds, R. David. *The Shawnee Prophet* (1983).

———. *Tecumseh and the Quest for Indian Leadership* (1984).

Green, Michael D. *The Politics of Indian Removal: Creek Government and Society in Crisis* (1982).

Henri, Florette. *The Southern Indians and Benjamin Hawkins, 1796–1816* (1986).

McLoughlin, William G. *The Cherokee Ghost Dance: Essays on the Southeastern Indians, 1789–1861* (1984).

———. *Cherokees and Missionaries, 1789–1839* (1984).

———. *Cherokee Renascence in the New Republic* (1986).

Martin, Joel W. *Sacred Revolt: The Muskogees' Struggle for a New World* (1991).

Wallace, Anthony F. C. *The Death and Rebirth of the Seneca* (1970).

Wright, J. Leitch, Jr. *Creeks and Seminoles: Destruction and Regeneration of the Muscogulge People* (1986).

SEE ALSO various essays in the sections "**Periods of Social Change**" and "**Regionalism and Regional Subcultures**."

AMERICAN INDIANS OF THE WEST

Peter Iverson

THE STORY OF AMERICAN INDIANS since the 1840s is told generally in terms of tragedy and loss. Even the much celebrated film of 1990, *Dances with Wolves,* concluded with a note of seemingly inevitable surrender and an impression of finality about the end of an era. Hollywood, history texts, and other media have combined to fashion an image both incomplete and misleading. In the early 1990s a more appropriate and more accurate portrait may yet be drawn. It will be one that does not deny the impact of racism nor the ravages of disease. The history of this nation's first residents must acknowledge that Indians have had to confront bigotry and bias. Their numbers were reduced, their lands lost. And yet the Indians remain in the region and indeed are far more numerous than they were a century ago. Thus our portrait must be more than a delineation of defeat and decay. We must do more than portray Indians as victims. We must also attest to continuity through change, to survival and persistence, to permanence. Although not in the same way that they did in the 1840s, American Indians remain vital and significant participants in the West.

1840–1890

At the beginning of the 1840s, the American Indian world was characterized by migration and adaptation. Indeed, whether one accepts the notion of a migration over thousands of years across the Bering Strait and throughout the Americas, independent origination within the region, or some other theory, American Indian history reflects movement, experimentation, conflict, and discovery. By the mid nineteenth century, there were new forms of immigration. The Cherokees and other great southeastern Indian nations had been forced to move from their homelands to new country in what one day would be called Oklahoma; only remnant enclaves were able to persist in small portions of western Carolina, south Florida, and central Mississippi. Those who came west did not lose hope despite the trauma of being uprooted and the suffering endured along what has been termed The Trail of Tears. Rather, they rebuilt their societies in new surroundings, establishing schools and economies and enjoying considerable prosperity.

Many Indian communities in the region had, of course, not been moved to it. These indigenous groups encompassed a remarkable variety of responses to the varied environments in which they found themselves. In the Northwest Coast area, for example, the rich resources of ocean and land permitted larger numbers of people not merely to live but to prosper. Their rivers teemed with salmon; their magnificent forests offered the materials for substantial houses and imposing boats. By contrast, in more arid regions the harshness of the climate and the limited quantities of food forced small groups of people to travel for hundreds of miles in order to hunt and gather. Such enclaves had little time to create the elaborate works of art for which Northwest Coast peoples became justly famous. However, trade for items used in ceremonials or for foods that could not be grown locally could add diversity to a limited cultural repertoire.

Regardless of their surroundings, Indian peoples emphasized harmony with the world and a sense that a kind of balance within that world had to be achieved. It was a difficult equilibrium to reach, to be sure; it was a fragile business. One had to pray to the gods; one had to live in the right way. But if one did, the chances were good that life would offer you much.

Thus we should not assume that in 1840 Indian communities were universally pessimistic about their future. Indeed, many looked forward to a seemingly bright future. The Navajos in the region today known as the Southwest continued to add to their numbers and their holdings of livestock. They represented an excellent example of a people who

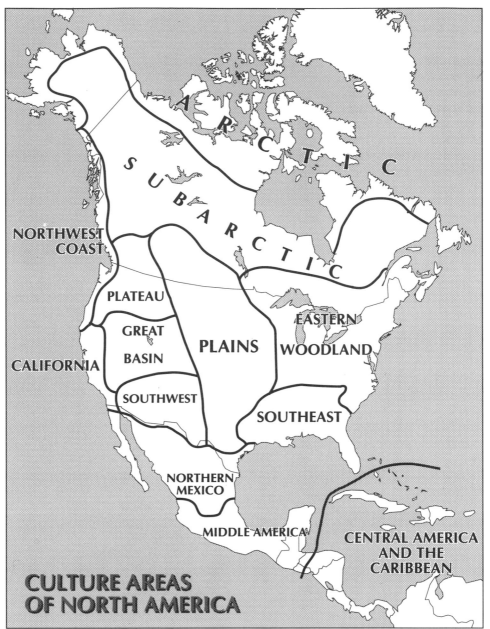

Map 1

Source: Josephy, *Indian Heritage of America*

had actually benefited in some ways from European incursion. They had taken the sheep brought by the Spanish, they had incorporated Pueblo Indian refugees in the wake of the Pueblo revolt of 1680 and the return by the Spaniards in 1692 to the Rio Grande Valley, and they had thus transformed who they were and who they could be. The Navajos illustrated a more general principle that contact with outside peoples, ideas, and institutions does not necessarily lead to decline. Other Indian commu-

nities also exemplified this notion. Horses and rifles allowed one to hunt buffalo more effectively on the plains. The relative newcomers to the northern and central Great Plains, the Lakotas or Sioux, controlled an expanding arc of territory and embraced the Black Hills as sacred ground (see Map 1).

The latter part of the 1840s witnessed a sudden and dramatic change in the map of the West. In 1846 the United States concluded negotiations with Great Britain to accept the forty-ninth parallel as the boundary with Canada west of the Rockies. The Treaty of Guadalupe Hidalgo, which ended the war with Mexico (1848), had as one of its provisions the cession by Mexico of what is now California, Nevada, Utah, and most of New Mexico and Arizona for fifteen million dollars. Mormon migrants to their promised land in the Salt Lake City area and the massive movement accompanying the California gold rush altered the futures of native peoples in northern Utah and all along the routes to the diggings near the Sierra Nevada.

This new map and these new inhabitants of this vast region produced one conflict after another between Indians and non-Indians over control of the land and its resources. Officials of the federal government assessed the situation and called for what one historian has termed an alternative to extinction. Given the history of previous frontiers, Bureau of Indian Affairs personnel knew that even in the vastness of the trans-Mississippi West, Indians would need formal legal protection of their lands. At the same time, in order for Indians to be assimilated into the larger society, they needed time to learn a new language and new values. With prevailing hostility toward Indians and the unwillingness on the part of the non-Indian public to take responsibility for that kind of cultural transformation, American Indians needed some kind of transitional, protected space. Such territory became known, and is still called, a reservation.

The reservation symbolized contradictory American impulses. On the one hand, it represented a concerted attempt to isolate Indians from the rest of the populace, generally on land perceived to be of little value. At the same time, policymakers, educators, missionaries, and other agents of imposed cultural change wanted to transform the Indians. They wanted Indians to farm (although many were indeed already skilled farmers), to speak English, to become Christians, and to embrace the ideals of private property and individualism. Especially for Indian communities that had employed large territories to hunt and gather, reservations represented an unwanted and severe restriction on their freedom. These groups signed treaties under duress and often without accurate translation of the terms under which they now were supposed to live.

As that understanding grew, so did resistance. By the mid 1850s, the Blackfeet of Montana had been forced to the treaty table. So had many of the plains tribes been forced to Fort Laramie, Wyoming, in 1851. Non-Indian Texas had crushed Indian re-

sistance to the point of near annihilation, with reservations in that new state merely a brief and ineffective barrier to Anglo intrusion. In the Northwest, Washington territorial governor Isaac Stevens heard the Suquamish leader Seattle acknowledge the supremacy of the white man, then warn that tribe followed tribe and nation followed nation: "Your time of decay may be distant," he told the governor, "but it will surely come."

In a nation gripped by civil war, wars broke out between Indian communities and their neighbors or the military forces charged with the responsibility for control. The Sioux uprising in southwestern Minnesota in 1862 decimated the Santee Sioux population. Two years later, in the Southwest, Kit Carson somewhat reluctantly helped enforce the whims and dreams of General James Carleton, who determined that the Mescalero Apaches and the Navajos must be moved into exile along the less-than-fertile banks of the Pecos River in east-central New Mexico.

Although the Navajos and the Mescaleros suffered the indignity and the terror of this transfer, they were, in one sense at least, fortunate. Some of them hid in the more distant reaches of their country and thus escaped imprisonment at Fort Sumner. Moreover, when the government negotiated for a more permanent home for them following the undeniable failure of Carleton's brief experiment, during which crops had failed and people had sickened and died, the possibility still remained that they could return to a portion of their homeland. The Mescaleros earlier had gained territory in southern New Mexico where they could live, and the Navajos in 1868 convinced General William Tecumseh Sherman and other federal officials that they did not have to go to Oklahoma. The Navajo leader Barboncito pleaded that his people not be forced to go to any country other than their own. Their treaty of July 1868 allowed them to return to a portion of their cultural homeland. Return to life within boundaries of sacred mountains meant their social system could continue on familiar terms. They were where they belonged.

However, the balance of power in the region was shifting quickly. By 1871 the Congress had declared that the United States would no longer sign treaties with Indian nations. From now on such accords would be labeled agreements. As non-Indian peoples continued to flood into the West and as the United States Army grew in size, extended negotiations or bargaining sessions appeared to be unnecessary. From the perspective of many native communities, the government acted too quickly and too harshly; it asked them to give up too much. And so they fought. In 1868 the allied forces of the Teton Lakotas, Northern Cheyennes, and Northern Arapahoes had won military control over the road the Anglos called the Bozeman Trail. Only after the forts on the trail had been abandoned would Red Cloud, an Oglala (Lakota) Sioux, ride into Fort Laramie to affix his name to another treaty of Fort Laramie (1868) that federal officials had wanted signed for months. It proved a short-lived triumph. Red Cloud had thought the Black Hills were his people's forever. The discovery of gold there changed "forever" to "forfeit" in less than a decade. By means of a shady treaty engineered in 1876, the Black Hills were no longer officially part of the Indian domain.

When one considers the rapid pace of westward expansion—the railroads constructed, the steady decline of the bison herds, the growth of farming and ranching enterprises, the gold and silver rushes and consequent boomtowns—and when one ponders the prospect of a tightly regulated reservation environment that denied both freedom and tribal values, it is not surprising that so many Indians fought desperately in the 1860s, 1870s, and 1880s. That resistance took a number of forms; the fight did not include only military confrontations.

Thus Little Big Horn, the flight of the Nez Perce, the resistance by Geronimo, and the tragedy of Wounded Knee occurred at specific times in specific places for specific reasons. Little Big Horn gained more recognition in white America than in Indian America, although those tribes which combined forces to defeat George Armstrong Custer certainly celebrated and remembered their victory on 25 June 1876 in southeastern Montana. But the United States citizenry to the east were startled by the news of Custer's demise. The totality of the debacle reminded people as they observed the country's centennial that the subjugation of American Indians would not be easily achieved.

There were other reminders in the next decade about the fragility of American dominion. Chief Joseph and other Nez Perce leaders eluded their would-be captors for months and for hundreds of miles before they were finally surprised by Nelson Miles and his men in the Bear Paw Mountains of northern Montana, only thirty miles from the Canadian border. Joseph pledged in 1877 that he "would fight no more forever," but other nations continued their struggles against imprisonment on reservations.

The Hunkpapa leader Sitting Bull led hundreds of followers into Canada in 1876, only to return reluctantly to the United States in 1881, after his food supplies had dwindled and his people's morale had deteriorated. He returned to the Dakota Country in 1883, then traveled for a time with Buffalo Bill Cody's Wild West show. In December 1890 Sitting Bull was shot and killed in a scuffle with tribal policemen who sought to bring the old man into the Standing Rock agency headquarters in connection with the hysteria surrounding the Ghost Dance movement that had swept through Lakota country that year.

Geronimo was another individual who could not tolerate the limitations of the reservation. After the deaths of Cochise (1874) and Victorio (1880), Geronimo rose to prominence among the Chiricahua Apaches of the Southwest. A personal tragedy fueled his wrath against Mexicans and Anglos alike: his wife and children were killed by Mexicans while he and other men were away from their camp in 1858, and the horror and injustice of that day always remained with him. On several occasions he and others bolted from the confines of the San Carlos reservation in Arizona. Geronimo eventually could not use the Mexican border as a shield. Indian scouts helped lead Nelson Miles, by now a general, to his final place of refuge in Sonora. Geronimo's surrender at Skeleton Canyon, Arizona, on 4 September 1886 signaled the end of armed resistance in the Southwest.

1890–1930

Four years later, the 1890 census reflected the end of the American frontier. A tragic clash in December of that year etched another ending point at Wounded Knee Creek, on the Pine Ridge reservation in western South Dakota. Many of the Lakotas had subscribed to their version of the Ghost Dance doctrine of the Paiute visionary Wovoka. The Ghost Dance ritual had promised a new day when the buffalo would return, the dead would be reunited with the living, and the whites would vanish altogether. The fervor which surrounded the Ghost Dance on Pine Ridge and other Sioux reservations prompted fear on the part of Daniel Royer, an inexperienced agent for the Bureau of Indian Affairs. Royer called for troops only days after he had come to Pine Ridge, and the sight of blue coats in the field frightened hundreds of Lakotas into flight.

The men, women, and children brought to Wounded Knee by soldiers of the Seventh Cavalry, the unit that had been decimated at the Little Big Horn, actually had fled from the Cheyenne River reservation and had attempted to hide in the Badlands north of Pine Ridge. As they were being lined up for formal surrender and relinquishment of weapons on the morning of 29 December, an altercation sparked widespread firing by the soldiers who surrounded them. More than two hundred Lakotas died, their bodies left frozen on the ground, covered by a blizzard that swept the earth but could not obliterate the memory of what can only be called a massacre. Seventeen congressional Medals of Honor later awarded further contributed to the legacy of a particularly shameful episode.

Yet Wounded Knee no more marked the end of Indian America than 1890 marked the end of the American West. Well prior to that year American Indian communities were doing their best to confront a variety of nonmilitary challenges and choices. Many of these communities had not fought with the army; some were still trying to achieve permanent homelands in the first years of the new century. The last of the lower forty-eight states to achieve statehood, Arizona, yielded land for several new reservations, including Fort McDowell, Ak-Chin, and Papago (now Tohono O'odham), and new lands for others, such as the Navajo, that were already established.

For most reservations, however, the probability of subtraction rather than addition loomed. Indian reservations were perceived as encompassing more land than their residents truly needed. The combination of pressure from non-Indian land seekers and reformers who believed that tribally held land blocked Indian advancement proved lethal. Passage of the General Allotment Act, also known as the Dawes Act after its congressional sponsor, Senator Henry Dawes of Massachusetts, in 1887 followed years of lobbying for division and reduction of the American Native estate. Through the provisions of the Allotment Act, reservations could be divided into 160-acre (64-hectare) parcels for each family, with parcels as small as forty acres for individuals such as orphans, and remaining "surplus" lands could be sold by the federal government to non-Indians.

Not all Indian reservations were so subdivided. However, the ones that possessed the greatest farming or ranching promise—those in the northern plains—were especially hard hit by the Allotment Act. Disappointed with the relatively slow workings of this piece of legislation, which included twenty-five years of federal guardianship before individual Indian land holdings could be alienated entirely, federal officials tried to accelerate the process. By the early twentieth century it became easier for Indians to lease or sell their lands, and agents such as the ubiquitous James (White Hair) McLaughlin moved around the West following the *Lone Wolf* v. *Hitchcock* decision of 1903, in which the Supreme Court held that Indian approval was not necessary for Congress to act to alter reservation boundaries or eliminate reservations. For every three acres that Indians held in the middle of the 1880s, two were no longer under their control by the late 1920s.

The reduction of Indian lands posed several interrelated problems for Indian societies. The push for individualism worked against the grain of tribal or communal approaches to working and living on the land. Traditional Native American values were generosity, reciprocity, and the extended family. Yet the 160-acre land allotment implicitly argued for saving rather than sharing and for the prosperity of the nuclear family, perhaps at the expense of the extended family. Moreover, the allotment rarely proved large enough, and division among heirs reduced it further for the next generation. Those inadequate acreages promoted leasing or sale and the immediate or eventual displacement of Native American families. Indian communities often tried to develop tribal ranches or community farms. But the costs of mechanization, limited federal support for development of irrigation works, and other problems curtailed many promising initiatives.

Other components of the prevailing federal policy in the period from the 1870s through the 1920s also posed dilemmas for Indian communities. Richard Henry Pratt's Carlisle Indian School in Pennsylvania provided a model for the education of Indian children and young adults. Such boarding schools brought together students from many different tribes in a deliberate effort to discourage the speaking of native languages and to promote the speaking of a common language: English. "The language of the white man and the black man ought to be good enough for the red man," said one commissioner of Indian affairs. Many other boarding schools in the late nineteenth century assembled students far from home. Haskell (Kansas), Chilocco (Oklahoma), Chemawa (Oregon), Sherman (California), Phoenix (Arizona), and Albuquerque (New Mexico) were among the institutions to which thousands of Indian students traveled. Not entirely unlike schools such as Tuskegee or Hampton Institute in the South for African American students, these schools emphasized vocational and technical training, Anglo values echoing themes of social Darwinism, and the general notion that the Indian future lay in assimilation. "Kill the Indian in him and save the man," said Richard Henry Pratt.

Attendance at such schools brought more than homesickness. Students sometimes died from diseases to which they had acquired little immunity. By being away from home, they missed instruction from their elders and were absent from important religious ceremonies. It is not surprising that many mothers and fathers resisted sending their children away nor that many of the students tried to run away from the schools.

Although the U.S. Constitution may have called for the separation of church and state, Christian church representatives worked hand in glove with federal personnel to promote religious conversion. Native ceremonies such as the Sun Dance were outlawed by the government. There were missionaries who eventually gained an appreciation for particular tribal rituals, languages, and customs; the Franciscan fathers at Saint Michaels, Arizona, particularly Father Bernard Haile, did important work in this regard on the Navajo reservation. Most, however, echoed the sentiment on the sign outside one mission hospital: "Tradition is the Enemy of Progress."

This era thus presented enormous problems and caused considerable despair. Tuberculosis and trachoma struck many communities. Traditional healers could not cure these problems, and the government did not provide adequate means, either in terms of trained personnel or sufficient medical facilities, to eradicate them. Loss of land, livelihood, and ways of gaining prestige within the tribe led some individuals to alcoholism. Parents wept as their children left them, often for years at a time, to attend distant schools over which they had no control.

But the record of Indian societies reveals that these communities are resilient and that ill-advised policies may yield unanticipated and occasionally beneficial results. The boarding schools gave Indians a common language, English, which could be used to move people beyond the old divisions among tribes and to hasten a greater degree of commonality. The boarding schools also offered a setting through which new forms of Indian identity could be transplanted. For example, the Native American church filled its ranks with boarding school students and graduates.

The Native American church is but one example of American Indian efforts to accommodate to new times with a blend of old and new elements. The church ritual uses the bud of the peyote cactus, a mildly hallucinogenic substance, which grows primarily in Mexico and in a small stretch of the Southwest. There are local variations of the ritual, but the church inspires a general sense of community and healing. Peyotists preached against the abuse of alcohol, and membership in the Native American church frequently provides a necessary means to assist those struggling with alcoholism. For the Indian men of the plains, the new faith offered a chance to assume leadership roles. Denied the opportunity to lead on the hunt or in war, these men welcomed a new avenue to demonstrate their abilities.

The evolution of the Native American church was part of a larger process of redefining what it meant to be a member of a particular tribe and what it meant to be an Indian. Government agents may have ruled most reservations heavy-handedly, yet they could not stop the people from coming to terms with their surroundings. The reservations were not ideal locations, but they encompassed lands that mattered more with each passing generation. Reservations included lands with short growing seasons, winds that always seemed to blow, temperatures that appeared to vary between freezing and boiling. But to their residents, despite their social problems and struggling economies, they increasingly were defined as home. Thus, reservation residents tried to limit their losses of additional lands (see Map 2). They began to incorporate tribal business committees or tribal councils into the workings of community life. On the national level, new organizations such as the Society of American Indians, founded in 1911, looked with pride at American Indian identity and looked forward to newfound prosperity in the young century.

Nonetheless, it could not be denied that the accumulated pressures of the period since the 1870s had taken an inevitable toll. Finally, in the middle of the 1920s Secretary of the Interior Herbert Work yielded to outcries about the living conditions of many Indians and charged a committee with the responsibility of investigating the subject. Under the leadership of Lewis Meriam, of the Institute for Government Research, the committee published a damning critique of current federal policy in *The Problem of Indian Administration* (1928). The Meriam Report, as it became known, scored

Map 2

the Bureau of Indian Affairs for its handling of Indian lands, education, and health care. This hefty volume yielded a mandate for a change of direction that was partially realized in the Hoover administration and much more fully activated at the start of the New Deal.

1930–1970

The commissioner of Indian affairs for the administration of Franklin D. Roosevelt had gained national attention during the 1920s as an ardent crusader for policy reform. John Collier, a former social worker in New York City, had been dismayed by the costs of industrialization and the cultural sacrifices made by immigrants to the United States. An invitation from a New York acquaintance, Mabel Dodge Luhan, brought him to Taos, New Mexico, in December 1920. Overwhelmed by the beauty of the surroundings, Collier made a deeply felt personal

discovery that guided the remainder of his career. The Pueblo Indians of Taos had managed to combine concern for the individual with concern for the larger community. Pueblo Indian societies, Collier concluded, not only had found answers for themselves but had unearthed what America needed as well. He promptly became involved in defending Pueblo land rights and lobbied through the press and before Congress on the need to alter the course of federal policy. In 1933 he gained what reformers sometimes dread: the opportunity to be in charge of the agency of which he had been so critical.

As the commissioner of Indian affairs who served the longest term, Collier had over a decade to try to achieve his goals. A conservative Congress and the weight of the past half-century of policy prevented improvement past a certain point, yet land allotment was halted, Indian arts and crafts were promoted, native languages were used for instruction in schools, and tribal governments were established. The landmark piece of legislation, the Indian Reorganization Act (Wheeler-Howard Act) of 1934, did not allow for as much Indian self-rule as Collier had hoped, and the fledgling tribal governments often inspired factionalism as much as they did self-determination.

Although Collier recognized the potential and value of Indian societies, he could still impose his own version of proper direction and action. In an era of dust bowls and soil erosion, he became convinced that Indian livestock had overgrazed their range. Collier thus called for tribes such as the Navajos and the Tohono O'odham to reduce their livestock holdings substantially. This well-intentioned but ill-advised directive struck at the heart of these native societies, for their livestock mattered as much socially as they did economically. To the Navajos, for example, sheep figured integrally in the workings of their social order. Herding the sheep taught children responsibility. Weaving the wool from the sheep into beautiful rugs not only supplemented family incomes but also gave women the opportunity to create and to carry on a tradition learned from their mothers and grandmothers. Sheep fed the people who came to a ceremony held to heal a family member; sheep paid the singer who conducted the necessary ritual. Sheep therefore symbolized the vitality of Navajo life, and by taking them away Collier and his associates stirred deep resentment and anger that made Navajos question the value of other initiatives, including the construction of day schools as a partial replacement for boarding schools.

Despite its shortcomings, Collier's "Indian New Deal" did reaffirm the right of Indians to have land bases, to speak their languages, and to practice their religions. The years of World War II overlapped with this New Deal and also brought important changes to Indian individuals and communities. As the nation turned its immediate and full attention to the war effort, the Indian New Deal faded quickly into the background. By the time Collier left his post in 1945, the changing national sentiment already suggested a new course for federal policy.

The war widened the world of many Indians. Thousands served in the armed forces, and thousands more worked in off-reservation war-related industries. Pima marine Ira Hayes helped raise the flag atop Mount Suribachi on Iwo Jima, and Navajo "code talkers" used their linguistic skills to assist with communications in the Pacific. Osage Clarence Finker, a brigadier general, had charge of the Ha-

waiian air force for the army air corps. Indian achievements not only were the source of pride in tribal communities but also caused federal officials to consider the ability of those communities to flourish without federal trusteeship. Passage of the Indian Claims Act in 1946 attested to a national concern for righting old wrongs as well as for setting a new course. Indians deserved some compensation for broken treaties and past injustices; they also merited the chance to be treated like everyone else.

To be treated like everyone else presented the proverbial double-edged sword. On the one hand, Indians wanted the rights and the opportunities of other Americans. They pushed for the right to vote in states such as Arizona and New Mexico and gained that right through court decisions. They could purchase liquor where previously they had not been permitted to do so. Laws originally fashioned to aid public school districts with military dependents were amended to provide districts with funding for construction and maintenance of schools for Indian children. Rather suddenly, many Indian students could now attend public rather than Bureau of Indian Affairs schools. Federal investment after the war brought funds as well for new reservation roads and for the promotion of economic development.

However, such initiatives encouraged the rise of sentiment for termination of federal guardianship. Why should the federal government protect the Indians? Why should reservations keep Indians segregated from the rest of America? Why should the government spend all of this money to promote segregation? In the wake of anticommunist sentiment gripping the country, anticommunalism or antitribalism appeared equally appropriate. In the post-Collier years, Bureau of Indian Affairs officials concurred with congressional proponents of terminating federal responsibilities and protection.

House Concurrent Resolution 108, calling for the government to "free Indians from federal control, and their wardship status and subject them to the same laws and privileges the citizens enjoyed as rapidly as possible," swept through Congress in 1953. Eventually, tribes such as the Klamaths in Oregon and the Menominees in Wisconsin fell victim to the ax of termination. Their loss of reservation status could be blamed on their success; because of their relative prosperity, based largely on timber resources, these tribes were deemed good prospects for "independence." The Menominees gained restoration of reservation status in 1973, but the Klamaths and other terminated tribal communities were not as fortunate. Congress also passed Public Law 280, which permitted Minnesota, Nebraska, Oregon, California, and Wisconsin to take over, for the most part, civil and criminal jurisdiction on Indian reservations within these five states.

In another way, Indians fit into a larger socioeconomic pattern. Americans flocked to the cities from rural areas during the late 1940s and the 1950s in search of better job opportunities. Some Indians voluntarily joined this movement, usually migrating to the nearest urban locations. Despairing of the economic potential of most reservations and perceiving urban relocation as a means for assimilation, the federal government in 1950 created a formal program to place Indians in selected cities. This effort offered transportation along with temporary assistance in employment, housing, and counseling about urban life.

Like the era from the 1870s to the late 1920s, the so-called termination era created many problems for American Indians. Terminated tribes struggled in the wake of the loss of reservation status. Indians who came to the cities frequently confronted discrimination. The promise of redress through the Indian Claims Commission usually proved empty or disappointing. The general assimilationist thrust at the federal level denied pluralism; bilingual, bicultural efforts of the 1930s waned to the point of disappearance. Government economic development programs shortchanged tribal communities through exploitation of mineral resources and Indian labor with minimal returns.

What has been less generally recognized is that the period from 1945 to the beginning of the 1960s also provided a foundation on which contemporary Indian communities would build their efforts toward self-determination. The war altered many Indians' perspectives on the need for education. Schooling for children gained wider support in this less insular age. The formation of the National Congress of American Indians (NCAI) at Denver in November 1944 mirrored the need for a group to speak out for common concerns. NCAI was a leading voice against termination. Termination in turn encouraged Indian communities to form their own courts and improve their tribal councils before they could be absorbed by state entities. As some tribal members left the reservation for the cities, tribal efforts redoubled to gain more returns for their land resources. With the assistance of newly acquired legal counsel, Indian communities began to push for more equitable payments for their mineral resources or grazing lands. And because Indians in the cities tended to be identified as Indians rather than as members of specific tribes, many saw themselves more as Indians than as Hopi or Choctaw. Some of them adopted more militant perspectives, as exemplified by the American Indian Movement.

SINCE 1970

Urbanization has emerged as one of the critical dimensions of modern Indian life. Today more Indians live off reservations than on them; most Native Americans who have moved from reservations have relocated to urban areas, primarily for economic reasons. Such migration may not be permanent, and a move off the reservation does not necessarily mean abandonment of all tribal ties. However, the social consequences of urbanization for Indians of the American West are far-reaching and often are not unrelated to more general American social patterns of migration.

While it is dangerous to generalize about these effects, it may be said that for many western Indians urbanization increases the likelihood of marriage outside of one's tribe. This in turn increases the chances that children from that marriage will grow up speaking English as their first language, especially when schoolmates probably will not speak their native language and older relatives are less likely to be present to reinforce that language. Powwows, Indian centers, colleges and universities, and other institutions are multitribal—again reinforcing Indian rather than tribal identity.

There is another level of urban migration in addition to that from reservation to city. This level encompasses movement from rural reaches of larger reservations to the main towns within them. Schools, jobs, and the other usual forces have drawn people from outlying areas into these towns. Children growing up in such communities may have access to television but not to sheepherding. They will attend public schools rather than boarding schools. It is too soon to calculate what the trade-offs will mean, but it is safe to conclude that the ramifications of this demographic shift are important.

Clearly, many western Indians would prefer to live on reservations rather than off them, and they often make economic sacrifices in order to do so. Family considerations and obligations, and priorities given to ongoing community values, keep a certain percentage of people from moving away. But economic development remains a pressing challenge so that a large and young labor force may not be drawn off in the face of limited job opportunities. In this sense, Indian communities face dilemmas comparable with those of non-Indian rural peoples in forging successful strategies to nurture their economies. In this century the federal government has been a major employer of reservation residents. Especially since World War II, tribal governments and public schools have employed many individuals. Given the relative isolation of most reservations, there are limits to certain forms of economic enterprise.

Limited forms of gambling emerged in the 1980s as one alternative. The 1988 Indian Gaming Regulatory Act called for states and tribes to negotiate over what kinds of gambling would be permitted. As of 1991, reservation gambling existed in seven states: Arizona, California, Michigan, Minnesota, New York, and North and South Dakota. Three others (Connecticut, Washington, and Wisconsin) had scheduled it. The dimensions of gambling on Indian lands remained to be determined, but given the general expansion of state lotteries and other sanctioned forms of gambling, it seemed clear that tribal governments on some reservations would press to expand their operations.

In recent years tribal governments have focused considerable attention on maximizing returns from natural resources and on guaranteeing water rights. Western Indian reservations boast major reserves of oil, uranium, coal, and natural gas. While earlier efforts to exploit such resources were almost always disappointing, more recent ventures have reflected increasing sophistication on the part of tribal negotiators, in part through better legal counsel. Joint ventures, hiring-preference clauses, enhanced royalty provisions, and other features characterized negotiations and actual contracts. Many western reservations have mineral resource exploitation as a vital or potentially vital element in their economies. They include twenty-eight reservations in Montana, North and South Dakota, Wyoming, Utah, Colorado, Arizona, and New Mexico.

The *Winters* v. *United States* decision of the Supreme Court in 1908 theoretically reserved a certain amount of water for Indian reservation communities, but translating the "Winters Doctrine" into acre-feet of water usually became problematic. In the West most delivered water has gone to agricultural interests, although a growing urban population has demanded more water in the past generation. Although Indian water rights form a cat-

egory distinct from the prevailing western method of prior appropriation, Indian communities have had to contend with well-established non-Indian users of this pervious resource. Some tribes have opted to negotiate with the states and federal entities for a guaranteed amount of delivered water to serve present and future needs. Such arrangements may be more feasible for smaller reservations, such as Ak-Chin or Fort McDowell in southern Arizona, than for larger reservations. In any event, access to sufficient water obviously is crucial to Indian agriculture and other economic pursuits.

An activist stance by western tribal governments has been instrumental in the acquisition not only of quantifiable water rights but of other rights as well. In the Northwest, through a decision by U.S. District Court Judge George Boldt, Indian communities have obtained collective rights to almost half of the region's annual salmon harvest. Tribal officials helped push for the passage of the Indian Child Welfare Act of 1978, a landmark piece of legislation designed to limit and review the adoption of Indian children by non-Indian families. The development of tribal courts has been crucial to the functioning of tribal review of such adoption. The U.S. Supreme Court decision of *Oliphant* v. *Suquamish Tribe of Indians* in 1978 has limited for the moment efforts by tribal governments to gain greater jurisdiction on the reservation over non-Indians, but generally vigorous efforts to reinforce and expand tribal sovereignty are anticipated in the future.

The form of tribal councils functioning today on western Indian reservations generally derives from the structure imposed upon the tribes in the 1930s or earlier. In some instances, over time, this form has been incorporated successfully into the workings of an effective tribal political system. In other cases, the tribal government has remained a faction-ridden operation, with limited effectiveness granted to it by the public at large. More traditional communities or elements within a reservation may boycott or deny the legitimacy of some tribal governments. In either instance elected tribal officials face vexing questions, and frequent turnover of top officeholders can usually be anticipated.

One of the most dramatic examples of Native American decision making and socioeconomic challenges has been witnessed in Alaska. Because of the sparse non-Native population in Alaska prior to World War II, Natives (including the groups generally termed in the region "Indian," "Aleut," and "Inuit") were not without conflicts over lands and resources but, comparatively speaking, had fewer problems. Steady increase of the non-Native population led to statehood in 1959. From that point on, state interests and claims conflicted with Native interests and claims. Mineral discoveries and exploitation complicated the picture.

The Alaska Native Claims Settlement Act (ANCSA) of 1971 was widely hailed upon its passage but has come under increasing criticism in recent years. It did give to Native communities a cash settlement of $962.5 million and conveyed to them 44 million acres (17.6 million hectometers) of land. But there were three major trade-offs in the deal. The Natives surrendered future claims of aboriginal land rights. They limited their land occupancy and agreed to have the state divided into twelve regions. Corporations represented these regions and the individual villages. (A thirteenth was later created for nonresident Natives.) The corporations at the village and regional level were established for a period of twenty years.

After 1991, it appeared that under the original terms of ANCSA Native shares in these corporations could be sold. This possibility cast a long shadow over the 1970s and 1980s, for the results of the General Allotment Act in the lower states are well known. Through this legislation, coupled with subsequent acts and administrative decisions, Indians lost about two out of every three acres they held from 1887 until the end of the 1920s. Indian lands were subdivided into individual holdings and were subject to lease or sale. Even though many individuals hoped to hold on to their small amounts of land, they frequently proved unable to stop the forces allied against them.

On 3 February 1988 amendments to ANCSA were adopted that addressed the fears the original act had produced. These additions may make it more difficult for Native lands to be alienated and more possible for the generation born after 1971 to benefit from shares in the corporations. Nonetheless, the 1990s bring great uncertainty to the Native peoples of Alaska. More dependent than their southern counterparts on subsistence hunting and fishing, and more recently emerged from a period of greater isolation, these Native communities indeed confronted central problems in the final decade of the century. Volumes such as Thomas Berger's *Village Journey* (1985) and Indian journals such as *Tundra Times* echoed anxious refrains about what lay ahead after 1991. At the same time,

the negotiations over ANCSA and other subsequent issues helped to develop a seasoned core of Native leaders well qualified to attempt to deal with these difficult matters.

For the Native peoples in Alaska and the rest of the American West, education is generally deemed essential for present and future well-being. Although Indian student dropout rates remain higher than the national average, a growing number of Indian students have enjoyed success within the educational system. Thousands of western Indian men and women have obtained undergraduate and graduate degrees, with a resultant emergence of people trained in a variety of professional fields. Some of these individuals are attracted to higher-paying positions away from reservations or do not hail from reservation communities. Many others have played vital roles in Indian communities as teachers, doctors, attorneys, engineers, and architects, as well as other occupations.

Included in the ranks of talented and dedicated people leaving their marks on contemporary western Indian life are individuals in the creative arts. In 1969 Kiowa writer N. Scott Momaday won the Pulitzer Prize for his novel *House Made of Dawn*. In the generation that has followed, other Indian novelists have gained international acclaim for their work. Among them are the wife-and-husband team of Louise Erdrich (Turtle Mountain Chippewa) and Michael Dorris (Modoc). Each has earned recognition for work published under her (*Love Medicine* and *Tracks*) or his (*A Yellow Raft in Blue Water*) name; in 1991 they published *The Crown of Columbus* together. Other major writers are James Welch (Blackfeet–Gros Ventre), noted for his poetry (*Riding the Earthboy 40*) as well as his novels (*Winter in the Blood* and *Fools Crow*), and Leslie Marmon Silko, a Laguna Pueblo (*Ceremony* and *Storyteller*).

In addition, Indian men and women have contributed their painting, pottery, silversmithing, sculpture, weaving, and other forms of artistic expression. Painters Oscar Howe (Yankton Sioux), Fritz Scholder (Luiseño), Frank LaPena (Wintu), T. C. Cannon (Caddo-Kiowa), Helen Hardin (Santa Clara Pueblo), R. C. Gorman (Navajo), and many others have attracted enthusiastic followings for their work. María Martínez of San Ildefonso helped inspire an awareness of the beauty of Pueblo pottery that benefited many gifted potters from her pueblo as well as Acoma, Hopi, Santa Clara, and other communities. Helen Cordero of Cochiti

Pueblo, for example, created the widely imitated storyteller figure. Today's silversmiths follow in the legacy of or fashion forms different from such major contributors as Kenneth Begay (Navajo) and Charles Loloma (Hopi). Allan Houser (Chiricahua Apache), Willard Stone (Cherokee), Robert Davidson (Haida), and W. Richard West (Cheyenne) figure among prominent stone and wood sculptors. Daisy Tauglechee and Mabel Myers have been followed by a new generation of Navajo weavers, who continue to bring honor to one of the richest of all Indian art forms.

The contemporary Indian social panorama includes evident and serious socioeconomic problems. Yet the 1990 census figures initially available suggest a growing, vital American Indian presence in the West and in the United States. In the 1890s, few observers would have predicted that the Indian population would be growing rather than declining, that dozens of Indian languages would still be spoken, that Indian artistic and cultural expression would be thriving, that Indians would be more clearly understood as permanent rather than vanishing participants in the region and the nation. Native Americans have maintained ties to their lands, to their extended families, and to their heritage. As the twentieth century draws to a close, there is ample reason to be optimistic about their future.

BIBLIOGRAPHY

Bibliographies
Prucha, Francis Paul. *A Bibliographical Guide to the History of Indian-White Relations in the United States* (1977).

———. *Indian-White Relations in the United States: A Bibliography of Works Published in 1975–1980* (1982).

Historiographical Surveys
Calloway, Colin G., ed. *New Directions in American Indian History* (1988). Essays on recent work in quantitative methods, Indian women, métis history, the southern plains, the law, the twentieth century, language study, economics, and religion.

Swagerty, W. R., ed. *Scholars and the Indian Experience: Critical Reviews of Recent Writing in the Social Sciences* (1984). Chapters include work on nineteenth-century Indian-white relations, twentieth-century federal policy, contemporary Indians, Indians and the environment, and tribal history.

Smithsonian Institution Series (*Handbook of North American Indians*)
Damas, David L., ed. Vol. 5, *Arctic* (1985).

D'Azevedo, Warren L., ed. Vol. 11, *Great Basin* (1986).

Heizer, Robert F., ed. Vol. 8, *California* (1978).

Helm, June, ed. Vol. 6, *Subarctic* (1981).

Ortiz, Alfonso, ed. Vol. 9, *Southwest* (1979). Pueblo communities.

———. Vol. 10, *Southwest* (1983). Other Indian communities in the region.

Suttles, Wayne, ed. Vol. 7, *Northwest Coast* (1990).

Washburn, Wilcomb E., ed. Vol. 4, *History of Indian-White Relations* (1988).

Federal Indian Policy
Fixico, Donald L. *Termination and Relocation: Federal Indian Policy, 1945–1960* (1986).

Hoxie, Frederick E. *A Final Promise: The Campaign to Assimilate the Indians, 1880–1920* (1984).

Philp, Kenneth R. *John Collier's Crusade for Indian Reform, 1920–1954* (1977).

Prucha, Francis Paul. *The Great Father: The United States Government and the American Indians.* 2 vols. (1984). Vol. 2 covers 1880–1980.

Indian Education

Szasz, Margaret Connell. *Education and the American Indian: The Road to Self-Determination Since 1928.* 2d ed. (1977).

Trennert, Robert A. *The Phoenix Indian School: Forced Assimilation in Arizona, 1891–1935* (1988).

Western Indians Since 1840

Berger, Thomas. *Village Journey: A Report of the Alaska Native Review Commission* (1985).

Bernstein, Alison R. *American Indians and World War II: Toward a New Era in Indian Affairs* (1991).

Hoxie, Frederick E., ed. *Indians in American History: An Introduction* (1988).

Hurtado, Albert. *Indian Survival on the California Frontier* (1988).

Iverson, Peter, ed. *The Plains Indians of the Twentieth Century* (1985).

Powell, Peter John. *People of the Sacred Mountain: A History of the Northern Cheyenne Chiefs and Warrior Societies, 1830–1879, with an Epilogue, 1969–1974.* 2 vols. (1981).

Spicer, Edward H. *Cycles of Conquest: The Impact of Spain, Mexico, and the United States on the Indians of the Southwest, 1533–1960* (1962).

Stewart, Omer C. *Peyote Religion: A History* (1987).

Utley, Robert. *The Indian Frontier of the American West, 1846–1890* (1984).

Indian Land and Water

Ambler, Marjane. *Breaking the Iron Bonds: Indian Control of Energy Development* (1990). Primary focus is on the 1970s and 1980s.

McCool, Daniel. *Command of the Waters: Iron Triangles, Federal Water Development, and Indian Water* (1987). Emphasis is on the West in the twentieth century since the *Winters* decision.

Indian Governments

Deloria, Vine, Jr., and Clifford M. Lytle. *American Indians, American Justice* (1983). Reviews the evolution of tribal governments, civil and criminal justice systems, Indian judicial systems, the role of attorneys, and other central topics.

Iverson, Peter. *The Navajo Nation* (1981). Examines the efforts of the United States's largest tribe especially since 1945.

O'Brien, Sharon. *American Indian Tribal Governments* (1989). Includes case studies of the Muscogee, Cheyenne River Sioux, Isleta Pueblo, and Yakima tribal governments.

Statistical Surveys

Snipp, C. Matthew. *American Indians: The First of This Land* (1989). Based on the 1980 census, this is a detailed study of the composition and characteristics of Indian populations, including Alaska. Housing, family structure, language use and education, socioeconomic status, migration, and mortality are the major subjects.

Stuart, Paul. *Nations Within a Nation: Historical Statistics of American Indians* (1987). Statistical information relating to land base and climate, population, removal relocation, and urbanization; vital statistics and health, government activities, health care and education, employment, earnings, and income; and Indian resources and economic development.

SEE ALSO **Anthropological Approaches and Studies of Folk Cultures; California; The Great Plains; The Mormon Region; The Mountain West; Native Peoples Prior to European Arrival; The Natural Environment: The West; The Pacific Northwest and Alaska; Rural Life in the West; The Southwest; Texas.**

ENGLISH-SPEAKING PROTESTANTS

James Horn

FOR OVER THREE CENTURIES, beginning in the early seventeenth century, a massive and virtually continuous flow of emigrants left all parts of Britain to settle in the New World. Their contribution to the development of American society is incalculable. During the seventeenth century, colonists (predominantly English) carved out the first permanent European societies in the South, the West Indies, New England, and the Middle Colonies, providing the human resources—settlers, labor, and leadership—as well as the capital for colonization. In the following century they were joined by increasing numbers of Scotch-Irish, Scots, other Europeans (notably German-speaking), and African slaves to create ethnically diverse societies, distinctive from one another and from Britain. Mainland British-America developed as a sprawling conglomeration of dependencies strung along the eastern Atlantic seaboard from Nova Scotia to Florida, linked to the parent society by perduring political, commercial, and social ties.

BACKGROUND TO BRITISH MIGRATION

Emigrants came from rich and variegated provincial cultures in which their accustomed beliefs and patterns of behavior were deeply embedded. It goes without saying that Highland Scots had little in common culturally with their Lowland brethren, much less with English emigrants from south of the River Tees; but even within England regional differences between, for example, the South East and the West Country were considerable, as were the differences between large urban centers such as London and Bristol and small rural communities in wood-pasture and flat, open districts. Emigration must therefore be interpreted as a regional rather than a national, or a subnational (English, Scottish, Irish, or Welsh), phenomenon. Regional as well as national cultural characteristics influenced the trans-ferral of British values and attitudes overseas, and the mixing or the relative isolation of these regional subcultures played an important role in the development of particular colonies and regions in America. These points apply equally to the nineteenth and twentieth centuries. Whereas in the early nineteenth century much emigration took place from depressed rural areas in southern and western counties of England, the Scottish Highlands, and Ireland, later in the century there was a significant increase in emigrants from Britain's principal towns and cities.

Emigration from Britain, in any given period, rarely took the form of a single outpouring of people united by a common goal or vision. More typically, it comprised a *series* of emigrations only loosely related to one another or entirely autonomous. The point should be kept in mind so as not to underestimate the diversity of emigrants' backgrounds and their motives for leaving Britain, or to confuse separate movements. Timing of emigration was crucial. England in the 1660s was very different from what it had been half a century earlier. Just as emigration from Ulster immediately before the American Revolution had a different quality from that of the 1720s. Colonists arriving as indentured servants (laborers who contracted to serve in the colonies usually for four to five years in return for their passage, board and lodging, and various "freedom dues"), who comprised the majority of immigrants before 1800, had virtually dried up by the early nineteenth century. Thereafter most new arrivals paid their own transportation costs and started life in America unfettered by labor contracts. The magnitude and pace of immigration, direction of movement, regional origins of migrants, and motives for emigration were closely related to the changing times: demographic pressures, local and regional recessions, political developments, government policies, changing technologies, and opportunities in the New World.

Studies of immigration have two main facets. First is the context of emigration: the social characteristics of emigrants, their Old World backgrounds, and why they emigrated. Second is immigrants' settlement in America: how they adjusted to their new environment and their long-term impact on the development of society. While the first is reasonably discrete, the latter is highly complex. Some immigrant groups initially established enclaves in America where their distinctive ways of life could be perpetuated. But this was hardly typical. For much of the period from the seventeenth to the twentieth century, most immigrants found themselves rubbing shoulders with people from different regions in England, Britain, Europe, and other parts of the world. The mixing of peoples from different ethnic stocks is seen as one of the cardinal features of American society and a principal ingredient in the formation of American identity. Isolating the contributions of particular groups, such as the English, Scots, Scotch-Irish, or Welsh, to American social development implies unraveling the social fabric and picking out individual threads. Even those who can be identified as descendants of particular ethnic groups on the basis of surname analysis (itself a controversial technique), may well have intermarried or interacted with other ethnic groups over generations. In these circumstances, the rough edges of distinctive Old World regional and national cultures were eroded as second-, third-, and fourth-generation immigrants gradually absorbed the cultural mix around them. Only a general and speculative assessment of the contributions of particular groups from Britain to the evolution of American society can therefore be made. The whole is greater than the sum of its parts.

SEVENTEENTH-CENTURY EMIGRATION

Approximately 400,000 British settlers emigrated to North America and the West Indies in the seventeenth century; a ratio of emigrants to domestic population greater than from any other part of Europe in this period. The majority (at least 70 percent) were English. Scots were accounted foreign nationals before the Union of 1707 and were prohibited from settling in English possessions unless granted special permission. In fact, several thousand (no precise figure is available) went to the colonies as indentured servants and political prisoners during the second half of the century, many of whom ended up in Barbados, where planters pre-

ferred them to Catholic Irish laborers. Additionally, there were a number of small-scale ventures in Nova Scotia (1629), South Carolina (1684), East New Jersey (1685), and New Caledonia at Darien, near Panama (1698), none of which was of lasting significance other than as testimony to the successive failure of Scottish-backed colonization schemes. Several thousand Welsh settlers, many of whom left the towns, valleys, and coastal plain of South Wales and emigrated from Bristol in the third quarter of the century, made their way to the plantation colonies of the Chesapeake and Caribbean. Bristol had close commercial links with the region, particularly Monmouth and Glamorgan. Lastly, large numbers of Catholic Irish (one recent estimate suggests 50,000 to 100,000) were recruited for the West Indies, but relatively few Protestant Irish, or Scotch-Irish, were attracted to America. Large-scale Protestant emigration from Ireland awaited the next century.

Most settlers went to colonies that produced the major staples of colonial trade, tobacco and sugar. Some 225,000 went to the Caribbean (58 percent), 125,000 to the southern colonies, principally Virginia and Maryland (32 percent), compared with about 40,000 to New England and the Middle Colonies (10 percent). In the context of England's emergent transatlantic economy, New England remained a backwater for much of the century; the epicenter of colonial commerce was farther south. The phenomenal growth of the tobacco industry in Virginia and Maryland after 1620 and the start of sugar production in Barbados in the early 1640s created a voracious demand for cheap labor, initially met by indentured servants and then by black slaves. The peak period of immigration occurred within a single generation, between 1630 and 1660, when over half the total number of seventeenth-century British immigrants arrived. It is worth emphasizing, however, that the timing of immigration varied from one part of British-America to another. In New England, the great majority of settlers arrived between 1630 and 1640, and in the West Indies between 1630 and 1660. In the Chesapeake, most arrived between 1630 and the onset of the long depression in tobacco prices in 1680, but there was substantial immigration afterwards. Whereas the white population of the Caribbean began to decline after 1660, and a significant flow of people left New England after 1640, the Chesapeake attracted large numbers of British settlers throughout the century. Over 27,000 arrived in the final two decades alone.

ENGLISH-SPEAKING PROTESTANTS

TABLE 1 Sex Ratios of British Servants Who Immigrated to the West Indies and
Mainland Colonies, 1635–1739

Port of Embarkation	West Indies		North American Mainland	
	Number	Ratio	Number	Ratio
London, 1635	836	1,717.4	2,011	642.1
Bristol, 1654–1680	4,260	366.1	5,081	309.1
London, 1682–1686	703	368.7	838	246.3
London, 1718–1739	1,418	3,732.4	1,334	1,101.8

Sources: London, 1635: Hilary McD. Beckles, *White Servitude and Black Slavery in Barbados, 1627–1715* (1989), table 1.6, p. 34, and James Horn, "Servant Emigration to the Cheaspeake in the Seventeenth Century," in Thad W. Tate and David L. Ammerman, eds., *The Chesapeake in the Seventeenth Century: Essays on Anglo-American Society* (1979), table 3, p. 63. Figures for Bristol, 1654–1689, London, 1682–1686 and 1718–1739, computed from data in Farley Grubb, "The Long-Run Trend in the Value of Indentured Servants: 1654–1831," Working Paper no. 90–25, Department of Economics, University of Delaware (June 1990), Appendix, pp. 44–61.

Different patterns of migration to the plantation colonies and New England is reflected in the social characteristics of settlers and their motives for leaving Britain. Not less than 70 percent of immigrants to the West Indies and the Chesapeake were indentured servants, typically serving four to five years laboring on sugar and tobacco plantations. Most were young, single, and male. The great majority, men and women, emigrated between the ages of fifteen and twenty-five; an age when they might well have been in service of one kind or another in England as domestics, "servants in husbandry," apprentices, or unskilled casual workers. Family emigration among servants was rare; most were below marriageable age when they left England, and merchants and planters were reluctant to engage married couples. Indentured servants were expected to be unencumbered by family responsibilities, and therefore able to devote all their energies to working for their masters. In the early years of settlement, men outnumbered women by a factor of between six and seventeen to one, but as the century progressed the sex ratio became more balanced (Table 1). Nonetheless, both societies experienced a serious shortage of women.

The occupational background of servants who emigrated from Bristol and London between 1654 and 1686, is summarized in Table 2. Notable is the diversity of occupations. Of servants going to the Chesapeake, for example, sixty-six different trades were represented in the Bristol sample and thirty-four by the London group. They ranged from sons

TABLE 2 Occupations of Male Indentured Servants Who Emigrated from Bristol and
London to America, 1654–1686

	Bristol, 1654–1686		London, 1683–1684	
	Number	%	Number	%
Gentry and Professional	44	2.3	28	11.0
Agriculture	910	48.0	59	23.2
Food, Drink, and Supplies	55	2.9	10	3.9
Clothing and Textiles	282	14.9	36	14.2
Leather Trades	101	5.3	14	5.5
Building/Woodwork	125	6.6	22	8.7
Metalwork	62	3.3	17	6.7
Semi- and Unskilled	310	16.4	59	23.2
Miscellaneous	6	0.3	9	3.5
Total	1,895	100.0	254	99.9

Source: Adapted from James Horn, "Servant Emigration to the Chesapeake in the Seventeenth Century," in Thad W. Tate and David L. Ammerman, eds., *The Chesapeake in the Seventeenth Century: Essays on Anglo-American Society* (1979), table 1, p. 58.

of gentry to the unskilled and to petty criminals, from hemp dressers and barber surgeons to buttonmold makers. In both samples, men from agricultural backgrounds, clothing and textile trades, and semi- or unskilled work constituted the majority of recorded occupations. It is evident, however, that a large proportion whose occupation was not registered came from the lower echelons of society and were either unemployed youths, poor migrants, or casual laborers, picking up jobs where they could find them. Probably between one-half and two-thirds of servants leaving England in this period fell into these categories. If indentured servants cannot be characterized as "rogues, whores, and vagabonds," as contemporaries described them, neither were they drawn principally from the middle ranks of English society, as Mildred Campbell argued. Rather, recent research has shown, they came predominantly from a broad spectrum of working people, ranging from the destitute and desperate to the lower middle classes.

Conventionally, historians have stressed the contrasts with New England immigration. Most settlers departing for the northern colonies paid their own passage, left in family groups, were on average considerably older than Chesapeake immigrants, and were much more likely to come from skilled or established trades, particularly artisanal backgrounds. In addition, the sex ratio was more balanced. Of a sample of 679 colonists who left England between 1635 and 1638 studied by Virginia Anderson, 386 (57 percent) were male and 293 (43 percent) female. Migration to New England, it has been argued, "was primarily a transplantation of families." This aspect of immigration has been used, in turn, to explain the orderly settlement and relative social stability of New England compared with the chaotic and conflictual societies to the south, where family formation was retarded by the prevalence of servitude and the skewed sex ratio.

Recent studies have suggested that these generalizations are only partially valid. Based on a large sample of immigrants who arrived between 1620 and 1649, Richard Archer concludes that "historians have exaggerated the importance of the family unit in migration to New England" ("New England Mosaic," p. 487). He found that a third of adult males who immigrated before 1650 were single and without any family connection in the colonies. Many were probably servants (about a fifth of all new arrivals were servants in this period). Most immigrants were young. Well over 40 percent were less than twenty, and 72 percent less than thirty years of age. And male settlers outnumbered females by two to one, a ratio similar to that in parts of the Chesapeake in the second half of the century. In sum, an important, and neglected, element of the New England migratory stream bore a resemblance to their more numerous counterparts who ended up in the plantation colonies to the south. As will be seen later, arguments about the composition of immigrants have an important bearing on the debate about what prompted emigration.

Reasons for Immigration Why people immigrated to America is elusive, involving national (or international) developments, regional and local factors, as well as individual motivations. There is no need to go into detail about the changes that transformed English society in the sixteenth and seventeenth centuries, but it worth highlighting those aspects that had a significant influence on emigration. First and foremost, since so much stemmed from it, was demographic growth. England's population rose by about a third from just over 3 million to 4.2 million between 1551 and 1601, and by another quarter to 5.3 million in 1656. Growth was most obvious in the sprawling slums of the major towns and cities, but in the countryside, especially wood-pasture and forest areas, rapid population increase led to land shortages, deepening poverty, and greater mobility. Contemporaries were perplexed and alarmed. There is "nothing more dangerous to the estate of commonwealths," Robert Gray observed in 1609, "than when the people do increase to a greater multitude and number than may justly parallel with the largeness of the place and country" (*Seventeenth-Century Economic Documents,* p. 75). Authorities condemned the burgeoning armies of "masterless men"—vagrants, the idle and dissolute—which (in their view) infested the highways and swarmed in to towns and villages bringing disease and disorder in their wake. Spiraling food prices and a concomitant decline in real wages after 1550 led to a disastrous drop in the living standards of the poorer sections of society, while recurrent harvest failures and dearth in the 1590s and 1620s to 1650s brought widespread misery as well as sporadic food and enclosure riots throughout southern and central England. By mid century the third world of the poor had risen in some regions, particularly industrial areas, to between a third and a half of the population.

Far-reaching social changes were accompanied by equally important economic changes. One of the most notable was the emergence of an integrated national market for foodstuffs and manufactured goods centered on London. Local markets retained their vitality but producers also looked to more distant horizons and became more closely involved, via provincial capitals, major ports, and London, in national and international trade. The steady advance of commercial agriculture, in pastoral and arable areas, was encouraged by the growing population and expansive metropolitan and overseas markets. Much interest, too, was shown in initiatives to develop industries in the countryside, particularly marginal areas. The growth of domestic manufacturers from the mid sixteenth century eroded England's traditional reliance on foreign imports and provided new avenues of investment. Experiments with "industrial" crops—rape, flax, hemp, woad, and tobacco—promoted enthusiastically by agricultural improvers of the age, were subsequently transferred to the American colonies where efforts were made to establish industries and crops that had already proven promising in England.

The conjunction of these social and economic changes together with a switch in direction of English expansionist policies account for the colonization schemes of the 1560s onward. In previous centuries, English territorial ambitions had been focused on maintaining a presence in France, but with the end of the attempt to retain a beachhead on the Continent after the loss of Calais in 1558, merchants and statesmen began looking westward rather than to Europe for expansion, first to Ireland, then the Caribbean, and then the North American mainland. The two major advantages of American colonization were commercial and social. All kinds of goods and products imported from Europe and Asia could instead, it was argued, be imported cheaply from English colonies in the New World. England's surplus poor, the able-bodied poor and unemployed, an "altogether unprofitable" drain on the country's resources, could be put to work in the colonies to their own and the nation's advantage. Overpopulation would be avoided and the mounting social problems associated with poverty, vagrancy, and underemployment alleviated. The large-scale transfer of poor to America would create an enormous and growing demand for English goods, thereby stimulating industry at home.

Servant immigration to the West Indies and the Chesapeake can be interpreted as a response to demographic and economic pressures in Britain. The great majority came from the towns, cities, and populous lowland regions of southern and central England. Most left their home parishes without the preconceived idea of emigrating and followed the general pattern of migration in this period, moving to neighboring market towns where they expected to find work. Others shifted to industrial areas for the same reason, or sought temporary shelter in forested regions, which were traditional havens of the itinerant poor. After a period of tramping the highways they eventually ended up in one of the major ports that had ready connections to the colonies, London, Bristol, Liverpool, or Plymouth, where some chose or were persuaded to try their luck laboring in the plantations. Poor emigrants were therefore part of a much larger volume of migration in this period. They cannot be distinguished by their vision or enterprise in desiring to leave England from the mass of migrants who, for one reason or another, opted to remain behind. It is not clear whether most servants had anything more than a vague conception of the societies to which they were going.

Settlers who paid their own way to the West Indies and the Chesapeake went primarily to make money, either as sugar or tobacco planters, factors, merchants, and government officials. In the early years of colonization, some gentry were attracted to Virginia by the prospect of easy wealth and military adventure. Exploration and conquest of foreign lands were thought worthy pursuits for gentlemen, especially when allied to the propagation of the Protestant faith. Hopes that Virginia would furnish the fabulous riches associated with the Spanish conquest rapidly faded in the face of the hardships encountered within a few years after the initial settlement in 1607. As it became apparent that the colony was no Mexico or Peru the upper gentry and aristocracy lost interest. The typical free emigrant, insofar as one existed, was not so much the representative of England's landed classes as of the mercantile communities of provincial towns and the major ports. Thousands of small and middling merchants and retailers from London and Bristol moved permanently or temporarily to the Chesapeake during the century.

Religion as a Motive For a minority, making money was not the main motive for emigrating. While British-America did not become a forum for a Protestant (Anglican) crusade, a foil to the Counter-Reformation, the colonies did attract men and women whose religious beliefs were threatened or marginalized in England: Puritans, Catholics, and adherents of new radical sects such as the Quakers. The scale of Puritan migration to the Chesapeake was far smaller than that to New England, but was nonetheless significant. Separatist settlements in Virginia were guided by the same impulses that led the Pilgrims to Plymouth. Like the Pilgrims, early leaders of Virginia's Puritans had been associated with the separatist church in the Netherlands before immigrating to America. Like their New England counterparts they sought to establish a godly community in the New World which would reflect their social as well as religious ideals. By the mid seventeenth century, large numbers of nonconformist congregations were established throughout the Chesapeake tidewater, including Independents, Presbyterians, Anabaptists, and Quakers.

Finally, nonconformists of another kind, political rather than religious, settled in the Chesapeake in the 1640s and 1650s as echoes of the English Civil Wars and the overthrow of the monarchy reached the colonies. Probably no more than a few hundred "cavaliers" immigrated to Virginia in this period, but some established prominent families who had a lasting influence on the political development of the colony for the remainder of the century. Numerically, royalist émigrés were inconsequential, but in local as well as provincial life they exercised an influence wholly disproportionate to their numbers.

Discussions of the settlement of New England have revolved around the relative importance of religious or other motives in generating emigration. The conventional view, reflected in the stress given to the Puritan character of migration, is that religious factors were predominant. It has recently been given renewed emphasis by Virginia Anderson, who argues against an overly economic interpretation. If settlers sought economic opportunities, why did they not go to the Netherlands or to the Chesapeake or Caribbean? And since it was well known by the mid 1630s that New England was no paradise, why did colonists continue to immigrate? Anderson suggests that the major reason was spiritual gain. The "majority of emigrants responded to a common spiritual impulse in moving to New England." They were well aware of the Puritan temperament of the region and chose to move to that part of the New World where they could live according to their religious principles. Nor did the quest for spiritual wealth necessarily imply material ruin. In following their mission, Puritans believed that God would look after His own and grant them, through their own efforts, a modest sufficiency. Some might even improve their economic fortunes, but material gain was perceived as incidental to the religious imperatives which shaped their society.

The emphasis given to religion has been questioned from a number of perspectives. Timothy Breen, Stephen Foster, and David Grayson Allen have argued that religious and economic motives were inextricably interwoven, and that it is impossible to sort the complex admixture of economic distress, religious persecution, local and individual factors into a neat list of discrete influences ranked in order of importance. Rather than trying to "separate the historically inseparable," they favor examining the interrelationships between different motives. Emigrants were not all convinced Puritans. The presence of a sizable group of servants, the majority of whom were young, male, and poor, suggests that similar socioeconomic factors that influenced immigration to the plantation colonies may have operated on a proportion of New England migrants. They may have been more concerned about finding work and having the opportunity to set up for themselves after completing their terms than the well-being of their souls or building a godly commonwealth. Similarly, many free emigrants believed the northern colonies offered bright prospects for commercial agriculture, trade, fishing, and various other profitable enterprises. One cannot rule out that they were influenced by religious factors, but equally one cannot assume that these were primary. A "variety of motives" approach, which blends the "secular and circumstantial" with religious factors, offers a more promising line of inquiry than the insistence given to "Puritan migration," with all that it implies for the subsequent development of New England society.

Within little more than the span of a couple of generations an intense burst of colonizing activity took hundreds of thousands of English emigrants across the Irish Sea to Munster and Ulster and beyond to the Caribbean and the northern mainland. By 1690 approximately 86,000 white settlers lived in New England, 78,000 in the Chesapeake and Carolinas, 32,000 in the Middle Colonies, and 37,000 in the West Indies, the great majority of whom (90 percent in the mainland colonies) were of English descent. As far as white settlement is concerned, the seventeenth century was emphatically the English phase of North American immigration.

EIGHTEENTH-CENTURY IMMIGRATION

Two major developments distinguish eighteenth-century immigration from the earlier period. First, immigrants were from more diverse ethnic backgrounds and, second, the direction of movement changed. Once again, there are few reliable indicators of the size of British migration, but down to the Revolution it was probably of a similar magnitude to that of the seventeenth century; in the range of 380,000 to 400,000. Of these, about 200,000 left Northern Ireland, 50,000 left Scotland, and the remainder left England and Wales. The precipitous decline in English emigration was therefore compensated by large-scale migration from Ulster. "In the 18th century," comments Maldwyn Jones, "Ireland in general—Ulster in particular—was the most important source of bound labor for the American colonies" (*Harvard Encyclopedia*, p. 898). About 95,000 Scotch-Irish arrived between 1783 and 1800, and thousands of Scots went to the United States and Canada. Across the century, four-fifths of immigrants went to the mainland, predominantly to the Chesapeake, the Carolinas, and the Middle Colonies of Pennsylvania and New York. The major receptor of the seventeenth century, the West Indies, received only 20 percent of the migrant flow.

From Scotland to North Ireland Scotch-Irish migration may be interpreted as a drawn-out example (stretching over two centuries) of the "two-stage" migratory process that typified much of the earlier movement to America from England. During the seventeenth century, up to 200,000 Scots, mainly from Galloway in southwest Scotland, the Borders, and the counties around Edinburgh, settled in Ulster. Highlanders were initially excluded from the Six Counties but many from the "inward parts of Scotland," between Aberdeenshire and Inverness, and the Western Isles moved there during the century. The major stimulus to movement was economic. Down to the end of the seventeenth century, economic progress was retarded by generally primitive methods of husbandry, tenure systems that placed little emphasis on the improvement of land, an underdeveloped industrial sector, and a weak and segmented market structure. Scotland was described in a petition to the House of Commons of about 1720 as "a country the most barren of manufactures of any nation in these parts of Europe—they have nothing of their own growth to export, except corn, coals, cattle and some wool; nor nothing to form any manufactures from that which they receive from their neighbours." Including the Western Isles, about half of Scotland is made up of the Highlands, much of which is desolate moor, uninhabitable and uncultivable, and devoid of mineral wealth. The majority of the population, together with coal and iron deposits, and the best farming land were located in the Lowlands below the Forth-Clyde line, and along the coastal plain of eastern Scotland. The Lowland-Highland division represented the fundamental fault line of Scottish society; two distinctive cultures that clashed violently with one another and with an increasingly intrusive metropolitan culture.

In the sixteenth and seventeenth centuries, conditions for smaller tenants and peasants steadily deteriorated owing to population increase, periodic and severe dearth, and the conversion of traditional rents paid in kind to "feu-duty," or a fixed money rent. Feuferme (or feufarm, the practice of renting a farm by the year) gave security of tenure, but introduced a more openly commercial element into the relationship between landowner and tenant. Those who could not pay lost their land and were reduced to the condition of a subtenant or common laborer. Others drifted to the towns where they swelled the growing number of urban poor. The prospect of good, fertile land and cheap rents in Northern Ireland was therefore particularly attractive to struggling farmers and dispossessed tenants who saw no future in Scotland. It was also attractive to cattle thieves and men of violence, "scum ... fleeing from justice" (according to the Calvinist minister Andrew Stewart) in the wake of James I's policy of bringing law and order to the Borders. But a third factor, increasingly important from the 1660s and without which the subsequent history of Ulster would make little sense, was the transplanting of Scottish Presbyterianism. Ulster was Scotland's New England, an asylum from persecution and a forum for the creation of a godly society by a covenanted people. Advocacy of Scottish settlement, based on the premise of a thoroughly Protestant settler population controlling, converting, and in extremis removing the Catholic native Irish, relied on the conviction that the presence of Calvinist settlers would act as a bastion against the resurgence of the Catholic Irish, as the tragic events of 1641 and 1689–1691 were to prove.

In terms of sheer numbers there can be no doubt that Scottish colonization was a success. By 1640, about 50,000 migrants had made the short voyage across the North Channel, and after the turmoil of the 1640s and 1650s tens of thousands more poured into the province down to 1715. They settled predominantly in Antrim and Down, the northern part of Londonderry, and along the Donegal-Tyrone border. Important pockets were also established in the vicinity of the town of Donegal, eastern and southern parts of Tyrone, parts of Armagh, Fermanagh, and Cavan. Ulster society brought together five different cultural groups:

Lowland Scots, smaller numbers of Highlanders, recent English immigrants, the Old English (descendants of Anglo-Norman immigrants), and the native Irish. By the early eighteenth century, Northern Ireland was "a mosaic of discrete districts, easily definable as predominantly, Scottish, English, or Irish" (*Miller, Emigrants and Exiles,* p. 20). Subject to regional variations and despite some intermingling, Ulster Scots kept themselves largely to themselves. Their association with Scotland was maintained throughout the century by the arrival of new settlers and by a steady flow of commerce and information back and forth across the water.

As the century progressed, however, the Scotch-Irish began to shed their cultural dependence on their native land and gradually forged their own distinctive way of life. They adapted farming methods to suit their own purposes, combining practices inherited from their backgrounds with those of the native Irish. A collective identity emerged in part from the rigors of living in a potentially hostile environment, and a resentful Catholic population whose lands they occupied. Castles, bawns (fortified enclosures), and fortified houses dotted across the landscape defending scattered settlements testified to their sense of insecurity, just as the "massacre" of Protestants in 1641 and the Jacobite war of 1689–1691 both confirmed their worst fears of Catholic insurrection and their own role as defenders of the Protestant faith against popery. During the next century, their own brand of Presbyterianism developed a more latitudinarian temperament than the mother Church of Scotland, and was more powerfully influenced by lay initiatives and evangelicalism. Prayer meetings extending over several days conducted by lay preachers before large congregations reflected the centrality of lay involvement and an emotional intensity that became a hallmark of their religion. Ulster Presbyterianism emerged as the most "conspicuous element" of Scotch-Irish identity in Ireland and subsequently in America.

From North Ireland to North America   Five main waves of Scotch-Irish immigration occurred down to the American Revolution: 1717–1720, 1725–1729, 1740–1741, 1754–1755, and 1770–1775. The first migration was caused by the expiration of generous leases granted by landowners in the 1690s to attract emigrants from famine-stricken Scotland. As leases fell in, proprietors consolidated holdings, raised rents, and put farms out to competitive bidding. Rack renting (charging the highest possible rent) combined with four years of

drought, crop failure, cattle disease, and high food prices convinced thousands of settlers that America might offer them better prospects than staying put. Five years later, a similar combination of high rents and disastrous harvests persuaded thousands more to leave. Hugh Boutler, archbishop of Armagh, wrote at the height of the emigration epidemic in 1728, "We have had three bad harvests together. . . . Above 4,200 men, women and children have been shipped off from home . . . 3,100 this last summer. . . . The humour has spread like a contagious distemper, and the people will hardly hear anybody that tries to cure them of their madness" (Leyburn, *The Scotch Irish,* p. 171). Severe food shortages and "dearness of provision" reduced many small farmers and laborers to abject poverty, encouraging thousands to take up indentures for service in America. The doubling of rents and reduction in the length of leases also induced the better off to emigrate. "Ye richer sort," it was reported in 1729, believed "that if they stay in Ireland their children will be slaves and that it is better for them to make money of their leases while they are still worth something to inable them to transport themselves and familys to America" (*Emigrants and Exiles,* p. 153) than be subjected to the same poverty as their undertenants. Numbers of immigrants to Pennsylvania were so great that a contemporary commented that "it looks as if Ireland is to send us all its inhabitants hither."

Continuing efforts by commercially minded landlords to improve their land and rents, together with periodic crop failures, and the ensuing spiraling cost of food created the basic preconditions underlying mass migration throughout the rest of the century. But several new factors surfaced. Letters from settlers who had already emigrated encouraged families, relatives, and friends to follow in their wake. To a degree, emigration became self-sustaining. Some colonies, such as South Carolina and Georgia, offered cheap land and other inducements to immigrants willing to settle in the backcountry. Finally, in addition to the economic problems caused to tenant farmers by rack renting and price rises, slumps in the linen industry had a disastrous effect on thousands of poor cottager-weavers who had multiplied rapidly in the province after 1720. During the climax of emigration between 1770 and 1775, when about 30,000 migrants left Ulster, a severe recession put roughly a third of weavers out of work. Cottager-weavers and smallholders composed the majority of the members of the Hearts of Steel, a loosely coordinated movement which sought to resist excessive rents and wholesale evictions as well as government troops sent to quell the disorders. Subsequent repression led thousands more to emigrate. Across the eighteenth century, "the rapid commercialization of Ulster" caused the emiseration of large numbers of the most vulnerable sections of the working classes in town and country alike, and explains why the bulk of emigrants, the displaced poor condemned by contemporaries as "idle and worthless," could not raise their passage money and went to America as indentured servants or "redemptioners" (servants given the opportunity to buy their freedom by paying the cost of their passage shortly after arrival).

Ulster accounted for about 70 percent of Irish Protestants who emigrated in the eighteenth century and, as Kerby Miller suggests, has tended to overshadow the movement of Anglicans and Dissenters from the southern provinces. As in Ulster, those most likely to emigrate were the poorer elements of the population—smallholders, artisans, and laborers—driven out by rising rents and food prices. They were joined by a miscellany of former Catholics, ex-soldiers, younger sons of gentry and merchants, and colonial officials, all of whom looked forward to the seemingly limitless opportunities that provincial America offered to those with capital and connections. The most important group of Dissenters to emigrate were Quakers. Between 1682 and the Revolution, as many as 3,000 Irish Friends, mostly of English origin, moved to the New World, scattering across the mainland and the West Indies.

Changes in Scotland Significant advances in Scottish agriculture, manufacturing, and trade during the eighteenth century provide the context for the central theme of the period: the increasing polarization of Scottish society between the Lowlands and Highlands. Spurred on by the economic advantages that accrued in the years following the Union of 1707, merchants and manufacturers quickly took advantage of the benefits of being a partner in one of the most extensive trading zones in the world. Clydeside tobacco merchants rivaled their English competitors in Bristol and Whitehaven by the 1730s, and by 1770 Glasgow had overtaken London as Britain's premier tobacco port. In the same period, the volume of Scottish linen exports to America rose by two to three times. The growing contribution of Scotland to the metropolitan economy affected all parts of the country but was particularly noticeable in the Lowlands, where the concentration of towns, population, mineral resources, prime farming land, and capital accentuated age-old cultural differences with the Highlands. During the half century after 1750, Lowland society, like parts of England, experienced rapid population growth, urbanization, and industrialization, encouraging the flow of commerce and technology between the two countries and overseas. "The westward reach of the Scots to America," writes Eric Richards, "was a variant of their penetration of England.... Lowland Scotland had overcome its provinciality and had become an autonomous source of technological, intellectual, and political ideas, all of which were broadcast across the Atlantic world and within Scotland itself" ("Scotland and the Uses of the Atlantic Empire," p. 91).

Highland society, characterized by a largely Gaelic-speaking population, few churches and large parishes, an eclectic form of worship which embraced Protestantism, Catholicism, and older pre-Christian traditions, poverty, lawlessness, and, above all, the persistence of the clan as the most important social unit above the family, was by no means immune to the changes taking place elsewhere in Britain. The destruction of the military and political power of the clans after the Jacobite rising of 1745 combined with a continuing increase in demand for black cattle and sheep encouraged more progressive landlords to adopt farming methods practiced in the Lowlands. They envisaged Highland society developing along the same lines as Lowland rural society: large capitalist farmers running their estates wholly as commercial enterprises supported by a pool of dispensable landless laborers. This happened to various degrees in some areas, but in others population growth, the reluctance of crofters (tenants who worked small farms) and cotters (cottage-dwelling farm laborers) to leave the land, and the adoption of the potato as a field crop led to the steady subdivision of already small plots of land, a development that, although at first sight appearing to be a successful compromise between Lowland and Highland patterns of agriculture, ultimately led to disaster.

The bifurcation of Scottish society in the eighteenth century had a profound influence on emigration. Poverty was not new to the Highlands. After the battle of Culloden (1746), the region had long been synonymous with primitive living conditions and backwardness, but population growth and pressure on the land gave added impetus to emigration that had begun in the 1740s, generally on the initiative of substantial tenants ("tacksmen") who had seen the writing on the wall. As in eighteenth-century Ireland, the determination of profiteering landlords to improve their lands, consolidate holdings, and raise rents had a profound impact on the well-being of the peasantry. Much of the movement from both countries can be explained by the commercialization of agriculture and the resultant dislocation of traditional agrarian society. Commenting on the Highlands, Samuel Johnson and Henry Dundas were convinced that the breakdown of social unity that followed the destruction of the clan system was the main contributor to emigration. Social prestige and military power, associated with numerous inhabitants, was no longer the major consideration for chieftains anxious to maintain their "influence in the country." Ties of reciprocal obligations—the chiefs to support and protect their people, the clansmen to serve and, if necessary, take up arms for their leader—were fatally undermined by the punitive legislation which followed the '45 (the abortive invasion in support of the Stuart pretender in 1745) and the penetration of an ethos ("civilizing the Highlands") which placed a higher value on the market economy than on social cohesion. Increasingly in the second half of the century, the size of a chieftain's rent roll or profits, not the number of his retainers, indicated his status. Highland emigration cannot be attributed solely to economic factors however. The breakdown of the "quasi-feudal" relationships of the clan system involved for thousands of smallholders the end of a way of life. Social, as much as economic, change encouraged migration, and was reflected in the transplanting of entire communities to America.

Two different types of emigration, an expression of Scotland's social rift, can be identified on the eve of the American Revolution. Lowland emigration included large numbers of artisans, especially from the industrial West Lowlands which included Glasgow, Greenock, Paisley, and other important textile centers. The area suffered a severe depression in the early 1770s that reduced thousands of textile workers "to the utmost distress for want of employ," many of whom were forced to emigrate "to prevent them from starving." Three-quarters of 369 emigrants of known occupations from the area who embarked for America between December 1773 and March 1776 were artisans. Emigrants from the Borders and the East Lowlands were more evenly divided between trades and crafts, agriculture, and laboring, but still artisanal

occupations represented the largest category (35–39 percent). By contrast, half the migrants from the Highlands and Western Isles were recorded as laborers and 30 to 40 percent came from farming backgrounds. Far fewer artisans emigrated than from the Lowlands.

The distinctiveness of the two migration streams is underlined by the pattern of settlement in America. From the Highlands, groups of families organized by local lairds, tacksmen, or ministers tended to emigrate together and settle in particular locales, such as in the Cape Fear Valley of North Carolina, the Mohawk and Upper Hudson valleys in New York, and parts of Georgia. The determination to conserve traditional ways of life, reflected by the emphasis given to pastoral husbandry, the maintenance of their religion, and the persistence of Highland dress and Gaelic over several generations, lent a cohesiveness to their communities and set them apart from other ethnic groups in the backcountry. Like the Scotch-Irish, they were considered ideal settlers for the frontier—"shock troops" thrown at the rough edge of European settlement, according to William Brock—and were much sought after by colonial legislators and land speculators seeking to extend or stabilize their farthest boundaries. Lowlanders, on the other hand, did not keep themselves separate from the general colonial population and were active in all kinds of professions (commerce, law, medicine, the church, and education) as well as farming. Their willingness to integrate into the broader society and their rapid dispersal throughout the colonies resulted in little collective visibility in America.

THE COLONIAL LEGACY

It is obvious that the history of America would have taken a very different course without the massive immigration of British settlers (numbering approximately a million) during the seventeenth and eighteenth centuries. But what were the main consequences of settlement? To what extent was the cultural, economic, and political life of colonial America, and subsequently the United States, shaped by the transfer of elements of British society in this period?

As a sobering corrective to Whiggish eulogies of the success story of European settlement in the New World, the appallingly destructive forces that conquest and colonization unleashed should be kept in mind. From Massachusetts to the Caribbean, the establishment of British colonies was achieved at the expense of dispossessing, reducing, and destroying indigenous peoples. British ethnocentrism and economic imperatives justified (in their eyes) the destruction of Amerindians who inhibited commercial enterprise or who got in the way of white settlement. Despite occasional outcries there was remarkably little opposition to the Indians' removal. For the aboriginal peoples of America the European invasion of their lands was an unmitigated disaster. Similarly, the voracious demand for labor by the plantation colonies, the existence of a complex tangle of European beliefs and customs surrounding slavery, and the development across the early modern period of full-blown racism set in motion the tragedy of the enslavement and transportation to America of millions of Africans. Genocide, slavery, and economic exploitation were the hallmarks of European colonial expansion from the sixteenth century onward.

From the standpoint of the evolution of European society and what might be termed the dominant culture, the most important contribution of the colonial period was the establishment of a permanent British presence in North America, sanctioned and legitimized by the metropolitan state. During the seventeenth century three main population centers emerged: the West Indies, Chesapeake, and New England. On the mainland, much of the settlement was confined to the Atlantic littoral and river valleys, allowing easy access to coastal waters and sea lanes that linked the colonies to the wider world. By 1700, settlement had extended southward into the Carolinas and there had been rapid population increase in the Middle Colonies, particularly New York and Pennsylvania, adding a third major population center in continental America. During the next century, the quickening pace of demographic growth encouraged the large-scale movement of settlers into the piedmont. Scotch-Irish migrants initially settled in the New England backcountry but from the 1720s they moved into the interior of Pennsylvania, pushing westward beyond the Susquehanna into the rich lands of the Cumberland Valley, and in succeeding decades trekking southward to western Maryland, the Shenandoah Valley, the Carolina backcountry, and Georgia. Shortly before the American Revolution, other groups crossed the Alleghenies and settled in the area around Pittsburgh, foreshadowing the major migration of the nineteenth century into the Ohio River valley, Kentucky, Tennessee, and the territories west of the Mississippi. The entire back-

country became a polyglot of different ethnic groups, predominantly Scotch-Irish, German, Highland Scots, and English, organized in discrete and sometimes mutually hostile communities along the frontier.

By the time of the first census in 1790 the United States exhibited an ethnic diversity, not present a hundred years earlier, that presaged the regional concentrations of different ethnic stocks in the first half of the nineteenth century. New England had the greatest proportion of inhabitants of English extraction (between 77 and 87 percent of its population), compared with between 50 and 60 percent in the South, and only 25 percent in Pennsylvania (Table 3). Although German-speaking and Dutch settlers were to be found in large numbers in the Middle States, descendants of immigrants from Britain nevertheless constituted the overwhelming majority (four-fifths) of the new nation's population.

Emphasis given to the manifold differences between the various sections of colonial America have tended to obscure the underlying similarities among them. From the beginning, colonization, even when undertaken by private corporations, was conducted under the political aegis of the English state. There were to be no private fiefdoms in America. All the colonies were closely linked to England, where supreme authority rested with the crown, officers of state, and Parliament. By the eighteenth century, colonial polities, to one degree or another, mirrored in form and function British procedures and political theory in espousing representative forms of government augmented and checked by the executive powers residing with the governor and council; a balance and separation of powers between "democratic," aristocratic, and regal spheres that contemporaries believed to be the genius of the British constitution. It was a model that profoundly influenced the thinking of the Founding Fathers and that was a central issue in the debates leading to the ratification of the federal Constitution of 1789. American Revolutionary ideology was drawn from a rich heritage of English and Scottish political disquisition, including libertarian proposals for radical constitutional reform during the English Revolution, the development of a "country platform" and reform movements in the eighteenth century, and the blossoming political and moral philosophy of the Scottish Enlightenment. In large part, American political culture was an offshoot of British political theory. Local government and the development of the judiciary were

TABLE 3 British National or Linguistic Stocks as Proportion of White U.S. Population in 1790

State	English	Welsh	Scotch-Irish	Scottish	Total
Maine	77.6	2.2	8.4	4.2	92.4
New Hampshire	81.4	2.3	8.0	4.0	95.7
Vermont	81.4	3.5	7.3	3.6	95.8
Massachusetts	84.4	3.5	5.3	2.7	95.9
Rhode Island	79.9	2.3	7.0	3.5	92.7
Connecticut	87.1	3.1	4.5	2.2	96.9
New York	50.3	3.4	8.7	4.3	66.7
New Jersey	50.6	3.6	6.8	3.4	64.4
Pennsylvania	25.8	3.6	15.1	7.6	52.1
Delaware	63.3	5.5	9.2	4.6	82.6
Maryland	52.5	4.6	10.4	5.2	72.7
Virginia	61.3	6.5	11.7	5.9	85.4
North Carolina	53.2	6.2	15.8	7.9	83.1
South Carolina	47.6	6.2	18.9	9.4	82.1
Georgia	58.6	7.9	12.1	6.1	84.8
Kentucky	54.8	3.6	16.5	8.3	83.2
Tennessee	50.6	4.8	17.8	8.9	82.1
United States	59.7	4.3	10.5	5.3	79.8

Source: Adapted from Thomas L. Purvis, "The European Ancestry of the United States Population, 1790," *William and Mary Quarterly,* 3d ser., 41 (1984), table II, p. 98.

also fundamentally influenced by British precedents. Throughout the colonies, English common law, simplified and adapted to suit local conditions, became the basis of colonial law. The premise that everyone had a duty to uphold the peace, had the right to trial by peers, and was innocent unless proven guilty was transferred to America, along with a firm commitment to local government exercised variously through provincial legislatures, county courts, town meetings, and the parish.

Immigration on a large scale would not have occurred without the incentive of material gain. Even those forced by desperation to leave Britain must have believed that they had a better chance of earning a living in America than at home. Depending on where they settled, colonists introduced traditional farming techniques carried over from Britain or adopted new patterns of husbandry such as the extensive cultivation of tobacco, maize, rice, and sugar. The primary unit of production, as of consumption, was the family, and the major organizing principle was capitalist production for the market, not subsistence. Individual pursuit of profit received renewed impetus in America. "The values and motivations of the pioneer settlers before and after the Revolution," writes Robert D. Mitchell,

"remained virtually unchanged and quite possibly intensified. The socially defined goals of landownership, profitable enterprise, and wealth accumulation for immediate consumption and for the next generation, expressed within an emerging national system of liberal democracy, continued to dominate American ways of life" ("The Formation of Early American Cultural Regions," p. 89). Jefferson's "pursuit of happiness" was translated in Virginia's Declaration of Rights to include not only "the enjoyment of life and liberty," but also "the means of acquiring and possessing property." According to Bernard Bailyn, the "sanctity of private property and the benefits of commercial expansion were simply assumed" (*Faces of Revolution,* p. 206) and were perceived to be entirely compatible with the "civic rectitude" that the new republican government claimed to embody. Such values were not unique to America, but it could be argued that the trend toward liberalism, individualism, and materialism was accentuated in the New World. American society developed a preoccupation with the acquisition and protection of private property that proved to be as enduring as it was pervasive.

Individualism and the calculus of profit did not undermine the general significance attached to the social foundations of society, however, notably family, community, and church. In the 1970s and 1980s, historians have devoted considerable attention to the enormously important role played by family and community in helping to create stability in the most adverse conditions and in providing continuity between Old and New World experience. The nuclear family was the fundamental social, political, and economic unit in both societies, and the establishment of a permanent British presence in America would have been impossible without it. Equally unthinkable would have been a society devoid of community and church. Among some immigrants, New England Congregationalists and Scottish or Scotch-Irish Presbyterians, for example, religious conviction and church organization were vital to social cohesion and identity, even though doctrinal controversies frequently led to discord.

Immigrants' religious impulses were an expression of the major religious trends of the day and their own regional and ethnic backgrounds. Scotch-Irish Presbyterianism was frequently at odds with the Scottish and English forms, the growth of radical religious groups in Britain during the seventeenth century and of evangelicalism in the eighteenth was reflected by the rapid spread of Quaker and Baptist congregations and recurrent movements of revivalism in America, and an increasingly latitudinarian Church of England in the mother country after 1690 found its counterpart in American Anglicanism. An inveterate hostility toward Roman Catholicism, a direct legacy of settlers' British origins, was to play a crucial part in nativist movements and the hostility toward Catholic Irish in the nineteenth century. The religious landscape of America was profoundly influenced by the religious character of British immigration. Non-established dissenting denominations in England—Congregationalists, Presbyterians, Quakers, Baptists, and Methodists—constituted the majority of organized churches in America. On the eve of the American Revolution they made up about two-thirds of all congregations, compared with the 15 percent of the Church of England.

During the seventeenth and eighteenth centuries, "the foundations of modern American civilization were laid. In this great transformation," to paraphrase Brock, settlers of British descent, adhering to British traditions, "played the leading role in all fields" (*Scotus Americanus,* p. 1). The British phase of settlement was formative in endowing America with the political, economic, and social institutions that established the parameters of future development. Although the subsequent history of the United States was by no means predetermined, it is clear that the fundamental political, cultural, and socioeconomic principles that would shape society, and the response to change, over the ensuing two centuries had been firmly established.

THE NINETEENTH AND TWENTIETH CENTURIES

The character of British immigration changed significantly during the late eighteenth and early nineteenth centuries. Recent research suggests that the volume of immigration increased markedly and that much of the movement was by free migrants rather than indentured servants and redemptioners. Assuming that between 800,000 and 900,000 people settled in North America and the Caribbean during the colonial period, estimates by Henry Gemery and Robert Fogel indicate that as many, if not more, settlers arrived in the United States from Europe in the period from 1780 to 1820 alone. Over the next hundred and fifty years approximately thirty-eight million immigrants of European descent made their way to the United States, the great majority of whom arrived in the century after 1850. Not all of them stayed and there was a substantial flow of people back to the Old World, but unquestionably the scale of immigration in the nineteenth and twentieth centuries was of a different order than that of the earlier period.

Between 1820 and 1970 about 4.8 million emigrants left England, Scotland, and Wales, and a further 4.7 million left Ireland, representing about a quarter of total European immigration (excluding southern Ireland the figure drops to 17 percent). Table 4 illustrates the sustained high level of emigration and different timing of movement from Great Britain and Ireland. Irish emigration peaked in the 1840s and 1850s compared with a high point from Great Britain between 1860 and 1890, but emigration from both Ireland and Great Britain remained significant until at least 1930. A more detailed picture of the rate of immigration by country of origin can be gained from Tables 5 and 6, which summarize the numbers and proportions of British-born settlers in the United States from 1850 to 1970. The data confirm the heavy influx of English, Scottish, and Welsh immigrants in the last quarter of the nineteenth century and the early decades of the twentieth. Although English immigrants far outnumbered Scots and Welsh settlers,

TABLE 4   Immigration from Great Britain and Ireland, 1821–1970, in Thousands per Decade

	Great Britain (England, Scotland, and Wales)	Ireland (Including Eire)
1821–1830	25	51
1831–1840	76	207
1841–1850	267	781
1851–1860	424	914
1861–1870	607	436
1871–1880	548	437
1881–1890	807	655
1891–1900	272	388
1901–1910	526	339
1911–1920	341	146
1921–1930	330	221
1931–1940	29	13
1941–1950	132	27
1951–1960	192	57
1961–1970	206	40
Total	4,782	4,712

Sources: Richard A. Easterlin, "Immigration: Social Characteristics," in Stephan Thernstrom, ed., *Harvard Encyclopedia of American Ethnic Groups* (1980), table 4, p. 480; U.S. Bureau of the Census, *Historical Statistics of the United States, Colonial Times to 1970* (1975), vol. 1, ser. C 89–119, pp. 105–106.

the highest rates of gross and net emigration were from Scotland. Annual figures are not available for Ulster, but Maldwyn Jones estimates that approximately half a million Scotch-Irish emigrants went to America between 1815 and mid century, and another million left down to 1914, after which immigration to the United States declined in favor of immigration to Canada.

The two major causes of European emigration in this period were a rapidly increasing population and the profound readjustments in regional economies that followed the advance of industrialization and urbanization. Lesser factors (but nonetheless important) include the enormous increase in the volume of transatlantic commerce during the century, itself a reflection of the expansion of the American economy, the development of more efficient and therefore cheaper transportation, a perception of the economic opportunities offered in America, the removal of government restrictions on move-

TABLE 5   British-Born Population of U.S. by Country of Birth, 1850–1970, in Thousands

	England	Scotland	Wales	Ireland	N. Ireland	Eire
1850	279	71	30	962		
1860	433	109	46	1,611		
1870	555	141	75	1,856		
1880	664	170	83	1,855		
1890	909	242	100	1,872		
1900	841	234	94	1,615		
1910	878	261	82	1,352		
1920	814	255	67	1,037		
1930	810	354	60		179	745
1950	—	—	—		—	505
1960	528	213	23		68	339
1970	458	170	17		41	251

Source: U.S. Bureau of the Census, *Historical Statistics of the United States, Colonial Times to 1970* (1975), vol. 1, ser. A 6–8, C 228–295, pp. 8, 117–118.

TABLE 6 British-Born Population by Country of Birth, as Percentages of Total
Foreign-Born and Total Population, 1850–1970

	England		Scotland		Wales		Ireland			
	F-B	Pop	F-B	Pop	F-B	Pop	F-B	Pop	F-B	Pop
1850	12.4	1.2	3.1	0.3	1.3	0.1	42.8	4.1		
1870	10.0	1.4	2.5	0.4	0.4	1.3	33.3	4.7		
1890	9.8	1.4	2.6	0.4	1.1	0.2	20.2	3.0		
1910	6.5	0.9	1.9	0.3	0.6	0.1	10.0	1.5		
							N. Ireland		Eire	
1930	5.7	0.7	2.5	0.3	0.4	0.1	0.5	0.2	5.2	0.6
1950	—	—	—	—	—	—	—	—	4.8	0.3
1970	4.8	0.2	1.8	0.1	0.2	*	0.4	*	2.6	0.1

F-B Percentage of foreign-born population
Pop Percentage of total population
*   Negligible

Source: See Table 5.

ment, and until the late nineteenth century an open door policy on the part of the United States government. In the context of mass immigration, religious and political factors were much less significant than economic imperatives. "Through overseas migration and intra-continental movements," as one historian puts it, "people were redistributed from regions of lower to higher labour productivity, from the countryside and rural occupations to urban and industrial occupations."

Geographical Differences Emigration from England did not occur on a large scale until the 1830s when the combination of a serious agricultural depression, violent swings in trade and manufacturing, population increase, and chronic underemployment sparked off a "mania for emigration" in some regions. From the 1820s to the 1840s the majority of migrants came from the more rural and less developed southern and western areas (Sussex and Cornwall had the highest rates of emigration of English counties in 1841), but midland and northern counties, such as Derbyshire, Cheshire, Lancashire, Yorkshire, and Cumberland, were also represented. Emigrants came from a variety of occupational backgrounds. In 1831, according to Charlotte Erickson, 35 percent of male emigrants aged over nineteen years came from artisanal or trade backgrounds (tailors, shoemakers, millers, butchers, grocers, blacksmiths, coopers, wheelwrights, building workers, and miners), 25 percent were farmers, 10 percent were laborers, and 16 percent from the newer sectors of industry. Three-quarters arrived in family groups. Skilled emigrants attracted to the United States by the prospect of

high wages and regular work included hand- and power-loom weavers, calico printers, factory cotton spinners, carpet weavers from Kidderminster, ironworkers from Staffordshire, colliers from South Wales, and Cornish miners—those whom William Cobbett described as the "industrious people of England," which the country could ill-afford to lose. Although most emigrants were from rural areas, it appears they were not chiefly farmers and agricultural workers, but came from a miscellany of craft, trade, and manufacturing backgrounds, of sufficient means to pay their own passage. While pauper emigration rose significantly in the hard times of the 1830s and 1840s, stimulated by official and private schemes to aid the removal of the poor, it did not constitute a major element of emigration.

Erickson has suggested that English emigration changed significantly during the second half of the century. By the 1880s there was less occupational diversity, a much higher proportion of unskilled emigrants, an overwhelming majority from urban centers, and far less family migration. Doubts have been expressed about these findings, particularly the emphasis given to the proportion of unskilled emigrants. Brinley Thomas's figures (adapted in Table 7) show that laborers and servants made up 44 percent of English emigrants in 1875 compared with 45 percent from professional, entrepreneurial, and skilled backgrounds. Between 1880 and 1888 common laborers and servants accounted for about half of all immigrants (with occupations) but by 1895 the proportion of unskilled had fallen to 29 percent, whereas skilled and professional groups had risen to 60 percent. The evidence indi-

TABLE 7 Occupations of Immigrants from England, Scotland, and Wales, 1875–1925, in Percent

Occupational Categories	1875	1885	1895	1905	1915	1925
England						
Professional	2.1	1.6	3.3	10.1	14.5	10.0
Entrepreneurial	5.1	3.7	4.6	10.0	5.9	4.4
Skilled	38.8	33.0	52.7	50.2	37.7	41.5
Farmers	7.4	5.9	5.1	2.4	5.6	7.8
Farm Laborers	0.5	—	—	1.9	3.2	4.5
Common Laborers	33.7	41.8	12.9	8.8	6.8	8.8
Servants	9.5	10.3	16.0	13.9	15.2	6.8
Miscellaneous	2.5	2.4	5.4	2.7	11.1	16.2
Not Stated	0.4	1.3	—	—	—	—
Scotland						
Professional	3.6	1.5	2.4	4.9	10.5	9.3
Entrepreneurial	8.1	4.1	4.3	5.8	3.5	3.7
Skilled	47.0	41.2	53.2	61.9	41.3	43.8
Farmers	11.8	7.1	4.5	2.1	5.8	7.1
Farm Laborers	0.3	—	—	2.4	3.1	4.1
Common Laborers	15.7	28.6	8.9	6.6	6.8	7.5
Servants	10.1	14.6	21.9	13.8	18.8	8.9
Miscellaneous	3.3	2.1	4.8	2.5	10.2	16.3
Not Stated	0.1	0.8	—	—	—	—
Wales						
Professional	—	1.9	1.8	4.9	10.3	12.6
Entrepreneurial	4.3	1.4	2.5	4.7	2.6	4.9
Skilled	51.7	46.4	58.1	57.7	47.5	39.4
Farmers	6.5	8.5	7.4	2.9	6.1	10.6
Farm Laborers	—	—	—	3.1	4.9	4.6
Common Laborers	20.7	31.8	19.4	7.3	5.3	7.0
Servants	14.2	6.0	7.5	17.6	14.6	7.7
Miscellaneous	2.2	4.0	3.3	1.8	8.7	13.2
Not Stated	0.4	—	—	—	—	—

Source: Adapted from Brinley Thomas, *Migration and Economic Growth: A Study of Great Britain and the Atlantic Economy.* 2d ed. (1973), Appendix 4, tables 81, 83, 84, pp. 383, 385–386.

cates that there was a notable increase in unskilled immigrants in the 1880s which dropped away rapidly after the early 1890s, and that a consistently high level of skilled emigration was maintained between 1875 and 1925. Without more detailed studies of American labor markets and the circumstances that generated emigration from English regions it is impossible to be conclusive about changes in the pattern of emigration during the late nineteenth century. It may be, however, that the increasing independence of American industry from European technology, which has sometimes been viewed as a factor that discouraged skilled emigration from Britain, in fact had little effect. The massive expansion of America's industrial and marketing sectors created a sustained demand for entrepreneurs and skilled men while, at the same time, there was constant demand for all sorts of unskilled workers, especially in the construction and service industries of the burgeoning cities.

Welsh immigration to the United States in the nineteenth and early twentieth centuries was much smaller and of less consequence than migration from other parts of Britain. Rural depopulation was not translated into a mass exodus as, for example, from the Scottish Highlands, depressed agrarian regions of southern England, and Northern Ireland, primarily because long-run economic growth in South Wales followed rapid industrialization and the huge rise in international demand for steam coal absorbed much of the country's surplus labor. For most of the period between 1850 and 1920 Welsh economic growth "was strong enough to retain nearly the whole of the country's natural increase or even to attract an appreciable net inflow from the rest of the United Kingdom" (*Migration and Economic Growth,* p. 295). Workers displaced from the land found jobs in the towns, ports, and pits of South Wales or migrated across the border into England. A vibrant industrial sector in South

Wales attracted migrants who might otherwise have gone to America and was, in a sense, the region's own "New World."

Obvious contrasts can be made with Northern Ireland and Scotland in the nineteenth century. Despite impressive industrial growth in regions such as around Belfast and the Lagan Valley, Ulster's manufacturing sector was unable to expand sufficiently to absorb the rising numbers of poor rural workers put off the land. Population pressure in the countryside (in 1820 Northern Ireland was one of the most densely populated areas in Europe) led to the subdivision of land into minute plots inadequate for profitable farming or even subsistence. In some parts of the province, landlords anxious to recoup losses in the wake of the sharp fall in grain prices after the Napoleonic Wars pursued a policy of consolidation of their lands and conversion of arable to pasture leading to a wave of clearances in the 1820s. In addition, mechanization of the textile industry gradually undermined traditional methods of production based on domestic industry. Unemployed textile workers, mainly independent linen weavers from the south and west, together with Belfast cotton spinners, made up a steady stream of migrants across the Atlantic from the 1820s onward.

Areas that experienced rapid demographic growth and profound changes in the agrarian sector with the spread of capitalist farming techniques, and whose nonagricultural sectors were incapable of absorbing all the surplus labor generated by displacement from the land became the major sources of immigrants to other parts of Britain, and to Europe and America. No better example could be given than the Highlands during the period of the Clearances between the 1780s and 1850s. In some cases, movement occurred directly from the countryside, such as Highland emigration from the ports of the Western Isles and western Scotland, but more commonly emigration was preceded by the migration of the rural poor and others attracted by prospects in towns, cities, and industrial areas. Continued population growth and intermittent recessions in the manufacturing and service sectors periodically put severe pressure on the availability of work, leading to further waves of movement, either to other regions or overseas. Emigration must therefore be set in the context of regional economic development and migration within Britain, as well as the ebb and flow of opportunities in the United States and British dependencies.

Occupational Patterns   To a large extent, the distribution of British-born immigrants in nineteenth-century America was influenced by the oc-

cupations of settlers and location of industry in the United States. Lancashire cotton workers went to New Bedford, Massachusetts (the "Bolton of America"), and other regions where cotton goods were manufactured, such as in Rhode Island, New Hampshire, New York, and Pennsylvania. Woolen manufacture and carpet weaving were also located in New England and the Middle Atlantic states and attracted immigrants from Yorkshire, the English West Country, and Lowland Scotland. Staffordshire potters went to East Liverpool, Ohio, and Trenton, New Jersey; Cornish miners were to be found in the lead regions of Wisconsin and Illinois and the copper and iron mines of Michigan; Welsh miners from the valleys of Glamorgan, Carmarthenshire, and Monmouthshire went to the anthracite coalfields of eastern Pennsylvania or to the bituminous mines of western Pennsylvania, Maryland, West Virginia, the Midwest, and Far West, where they worked alongside English colliers from Staffordshire, Durham, and the Scottish fields; iron, steel, and tin plate workers went to the rapidly growing towns of Pittsburgh, Cleveland, and Chicago among others. By 1850 the great majority of British-born immigrants were therefore to be found in central and southern parts of New England, in the Middle Atlantic states of New York, New Jersey, and Pennsylvania, and scattered throughout the Midwest, particularly Illinois, Ohio, and Wisconsin. During the second half of the century, settlers moved west of the Mississippi to the new mining and farming regions of the West and Far West, as well as continuing to locate themselves in the established industrial areas of the eastern states above the Mason-Dixon line. Neither before or after the Civil War did the southern states attract large numbers of British immigrants.

Through the provision of industrial technology, skilled workers, and raw labor, British immigrants played a key role in the transformation of economy and society in the United States during the nineteenth and early twentieth centuries. In some regions, such as parts of New England, the Middle Atlantic, and the Midwest, they replenished descendants of British populations who had been there since colonial times. In others, alongside newly arrived European, Hispanic, and Asian immigrants, they moved farther into the interior to develop the vast resources of the West and Far West. Along with aspirations for a better life, they brought with them to varying degrees a consciousness of a distinctive identity—not British, but English, Scottish (Highland and Lowland), Welsh, and Scotch-Irish—expressed in the formation of immigrant societies, the erection of churches and schools, the preservation of dialects and languages, traditional dress, and cultural events and celebrations. Though they did not form powerful political blocs, such as the Catholic Irish, they could exert political pressure when they believed their interests were threatened. In all these ways, like other immigrant groups, they contributed to the rich cultural diversity of American society. By the last years of the nineteenth century, however, their influence began to wane. The great surge of immigration from southern and eastern Europe after 1890 introduced a new dimension to American ethnicity in terms of social, economic, and political developments. By 1910 British-born immigrants made up only 19 percent of the total foreign-born population of the United States compared with 47 percent in 1870 (includes immigrants from southern Ireland). By 1970 the figure was less than 10 percent. Nonetheless, the enormous significance of British immigration across the centuries, especially that of the English and Scotch-Irish, can hardly be doubted. British settlers and their descendants established the first substantial European presence in North America, provided the human and material resources for sustained territorial expansion, created the basic political and economic infrastructures by which society was ordered, and left an indelible cultural imprint on the social landscape. It proved an enduring legacy.

BIBLIOGRAPHY

General Works

Jones, Maldwyn Allen. *American Immigration* (1960). Still one of the most useful general surveys.

Kearney, Hugh. *The British Isles: A History of Four Nations* (1989).

Thernstrom, Stephan, ed. *Harvard Encyclopedia of American Ethnic Groups* (1980). A valuable and concise guide. See in particular the entries on the English, Cornish, Welsh, Scots, and Scotch-Irish.

The Colonial Period

Allen, David Grayson. *In English Ways: The Movement of Societies and the Transferal of English Local Law and Custom to Massachusetts Bay in the Seventeenth Century* (1981).

Altman, Ida, and James Horn, eds. *"To Make America": European Emigration in the Early Modern Period* (1991). Considers the general context of European emigration in this period.

Anderson, Virginia DeJohn. "Migrants and Motives: Religion and the Settlement of New England, 1630–1640." *New England Quarterly* 58 (1985). Restates the significance of religious motives.

Archer, Richard. "New England Mosaic: A Demographic Analysis for the Seventeenth Century." *William and Mary Quarterly,* 3d ser., 47 (1990). Questions conventional views of New England immigration.

Bailyn, Bernard. *Voyagers to the West: A Passage in the Peopling of America on the Eve of the Revolution* (1986). Provides an exhaustive analysis of emigration from Britain, 1773–1776.

———. *Faces of Revolution: Personalities and Themes in the Struggle for American Independence* (1990).

Breen, T. H., and Stephen Foster. "Moving to the New World: The Character of Early Massachusetts Immigration." *William and Mary Quarterly,* 3d ser., 30 (1973).

Brock, William R. *Scotus Americanus: A Survey of the Sources for Links Between Scotland and America in the Eighteenth Century* (1982).

Campbell, Mildred. "Social Origins of Some Early Americans." In *Seventeenth-Century America,* edited by James Morton Smith (1959). A seminal study.

Cressy, David. *Coming Over: Migration and Communication Between England and New England in the Seventeenth Century* (1987).

Dickson, R. J. *Ulster Emigration to Colonial America, 1718–1775* (1966). The best study of Ulster emigration in the eighteenth century.

Fischer, David Hackett. *Albion's Seed: Four British Folkways in America* (1989).

Galenson, David W. *White Servitude in Colonial America: An Economic Analysis* (1981). Valuable survey of indentured servitude and the labor market.

Gemery, Henry A. "Emigration from the British Isles to the New World, 1630–1700: Inferences from Colonial Populations." *Research in Economic History* 5 (1980).

———. "Markets for Migrants: English Indentured Servitude and Emigration in the Seventeenth and Eighteenth Centuries." In *Colonialism and Migration: Indentured Labour Before and After Slavery,* edited by P. C. Emmer (1986). Good summary of recent literature.

Graham, Ian C. C. *Colonists from Scotland: Emigration to North America, 1717–1783* (1956).

Greene, Jack P. *Pursuits of Happiness: The Social Development of Early Modern British Colonies and the Formation of American Culture* (1988). Excellent synthesis and a provocative argument.

Horn, James. "Servant Emigration to the Chesapeake in the Seventeenth Century." In *The Chesapeake in the Seventeenth Century: Essay on Anglo-American Society,* edited by Thad W. Tate and David L. Ammerman (1979).

Leyburn, James G. *The Scotch-Irish: A Social History* (1962). Good general account of origins, emigration, and settlement in America.

Mitchell, Robert D. "The Formation of Early American Cultural Regions: An Interpretation." In *European Settlement and Development in North America: Essays on Geographical Change in Honour and Memory of Andrew Hill Clark,* edited by J. R. Gibson (1978).

Purvis, Thomas L. "The European Ancestry of the United States Population, 1790." *William and Mary Quarterly,* 3d ser., 41 (1984).

Richards, Eric. "Scotland and the Uses of the Atlantic Empire." In *Strangers Within the Realm: Cultural Margins of the First British Empire,* edited by Bernard Bailyn and Philip D. Morgan (1991).

Sher, Richard B., and Jeffrey R. Smitten, eds. *Scotland and America in the Age of the Enlightenment* (1990).

Nineteenth and Twentieth Centuries

Berthoff, Rowland T. *British Immigrants in Industrial America, 1790–1850* (1953). A useful general introduction.

Conway, Alan. "Welsh Emigration to the United States." *Perspectives in American History* 7 (1973).

Dinnerstein, Leonard, and David M. Reimers. *Ethnic Americans: A History of Immigration and Assimilation* 3d ed. (1988). A straightforward summary of European immigration.

Erickson, C. J. "Who Were the English and Scots Emigrants to the United States in the Late Nineteenth Century?" In *Population and Social Change,* edited by D. V. Glass and Roger Revelle (1972). An important article questioning the character of immigration.

Fogel, Robert W., et al. "The Economics of Mortality in North America, 1650–1910: A Description of a Research Project." *Historical Methods* 11 (1978).

Gemery, Henry A. "European Emigration to North America, 1700–1820: Numbers and Quasi-Numbers." *Perspectives in American History* 1 (1984).

Johnson, Stanley C. *A History of Emigration from the United Kingdom to North America, 1763–1912* (1913). Now considered a classic.

Jones, Maldwyn A. "The Background to Emigration from Great Britain in the Nineteenth Century." *Perspectives in American History* 7 (1973).

Miller, Kerby A. *Emigrants and Exiles: Ireland and the Irish Exodus to North America* (1985). An excellent study.

Richards, Eric. *A History of the Highland Clearances,* Vol. 2. *Emigration, Protest, Reasons* (1985).

Thomas, Brinley. *Migration and Economic Growth: A Study of Great Britain and the Atlantic Economy* (1954; 2d ed. 1973). Important, if not wholly convincing, argument.

Willcox, Walter F., ed. *International Migrations.* 2 vols. (1929–1931). Valuable statistical data and essays.

SEE ALSO **Immigration**; **Religion**; and various essays in the sections "**Periods of Social Change**" and "**Regionalism and Regional Subcultures.**"

THE SCANDINAVIANS

B. Lindsay Lowell

SCANDINAVIAN EXPLORERS, toward the end of the Viking period, were the first to find the distant shores of America. It was also during this period that the Scandinavians made their greatest impact upon the outside world and that the kingdoms of Norway, Denmark, and Sweden first took shape. Denmark and Norway vied for control of the territories of Greenland and Iceland. An exile from Norway, Eric the Red, explored and colonized Greenland about 985; as these settlers hunted for seals, they were carried near American shores. Eric's son, Leif, found and unsuccessfully attempted to settle the wooded coast of Labrador. Archaeological finds at the ancient settlement of Vinland and other sites suggest that these hardy hunters may have traveled as far south as New England.

The colony of New Sweden was established in the vicinity of the present site of Wilmington, Delaware, during the period of earliest European colonization of the eastern seaboard. Swedish and Dutch stockholders formed the New Sweden Company, which in 1638 sent two small ships with twenty-five soldiers and officials to establish a colony and to trade for furs with the Indians. The venture was successful in making a treaty with the Indians but was otherwise a loss for its investors. This outpost never had much more than a few hundred Swedish and Finnish settlers and soldiers. In 1654 the Dutch brought Swedish control to an end by purchasing from the Indians land that had previously been sold to the Swedes, and by raiding farms and fortifications. Among the greatest legacies of New Sweden were the introduction of the log cabin to America and the establishment of good relations with the Indians. When the Englishman William Penn arrived in 1682, his success in founding Philadelphia built upon the extant Swedish community. Further Scandinavian presence was to wait a century and a half.

IMMIGRANTS AND THE FOREIGN BORN

Scandinavian emigration was greatest in the period of mass European movement to America during the latter half of the nineteenth century. Movement from Scandinavia during the eighteenth century was negligible and during the first half of the nineteenth century was small. Yet it was the nature of international mobility that earlier emigrants pulled family and friends after them. The emigration during the 1830s and 1840s was very important in establishing the interpersonal networks that both stimulated and eased travel to the New World.

The accompanying table shows United States entry and census data for the foreign-born for most of the nineteenth century through the 1980s. Column 1 shows the official count of all persons and column 2 shows the number of Scandinavians entering the United States. Columns 3 and 4 show the total foreign- and Scandinavian-born populations enumerated in the census. The last column shows these first-generation Scandinavians and their children living in the United States at the end of each decade. A better understanding of the ebb and flow of Scandinavian presence in the U.S. can be gained by comparing the data in these columns.

The first notable growth of Scandinavian immigration and settlement took place when some thirty-nine thousand, primarily from Norway and Sweden, crossed the Atlantic to settle in America between 1841 and 1860. These few immigrants comprised no more than 1 percent of the entire inflow into the United States and a far smaller proportion of the American population, yet they established a presence in the new land. Mass emigration from Scandinavia began late in the 1860s, peaked during the 1880s and into the 1890s, and, after a lull surrounding World War I, ended prior to the Great Depression. Between three and eight of every one

Scandinavian Immigrants, Foreign-Born and of Mixed Parentage, Compared with Total Immigration and Foreign-Born Population (Thousands, 1831–1989)

| | Immigration | | Population at Decade End | | |
Decade	Total	Scandinavia	Foreign Born	Scandinavian	Scandinavian and Mixed
Early Emigration and Settlement					
1831/40	515	2	—	—	—
1841/50	1,713	14	2,245	18	—
1851/60	2,598	25	4,139	72	—
Mass Emigration					
1861/70	2,315	126	5,567	242	—
1871/80	2,812	246	6,680	440	—
1881/90	5,247	656	9,250	933	—
1891/00	3,688	372	10,341	1,072	1,208
1901/10	8,795	505	13,516	1,251	1,618
Interwar and Depression					
1911/20	5,736	203	13,921	1,178	1,910
1921/30	4,107	198	14,204	1,125	2,069
1931/40	528	11	—	—	1,825
Modern Period					
1941/50	1,035	27	10,421	636	1,836
1951/60	2,515	57	9,738	455	1,769
1961/70	3,322	43	9,619	289	1,461
1971/80	4,493	15	14,080	141	9,317
1981/89	5,802	18	17,185	—	—
Total	55,221	2,518	—	—	—

Sources: U.S. Immigration and Naturalization Service, *Statistical Yearbook . . . 1990,* Table 2; U.S. Census Bureau, *Historical Statistics . . . ,* Tables C 195–227 and Table C 288–295; U.S. Census Bureau, *Statistical Abstract . . . 1190,* Table 48, based on self-reported "multiple ancestry group" affiliation of any of Norwegian, Swedish, or Danish.

thousand Swedes and Norwegians emigrated from their homes to the United States between the 1860s and the 1880s. During the peak years of emigration somewhere between eight and eleven of every one thousand Scandinavians crossed the Atlantic. By 1910 approximately one of every seven Scandinavian-born persons lived in the United States. Perhaps, in the absence of emigration, Scandinavia's total population would have been 30 to 40 percent larger by 1980. In comparison, only the loss of emigrants from Ireland was greater.

These Scandinavian immigrants made up between 5.4 percent of the flow of immigrants into the United States during the 1860s and 8.7 percent during the 1870s. During the peak years in the 1880s, Scandinavian immigrants comprised fully 12.5 percent of all immigrants. The U.S. Census count of Scandinavians grew during these years and into the twentieth century. By 1900 there were a little over one million Scandinavians born abroad and living in the United States, about 10 percent of all foreign-born persons.

The number of foreign-born, and persons of foreign-born and mixed single-Scandinavian parents, grew to over two million in 1930. Since then, the number of foreign-born Scandinavians has steadily decreased to around one hundred thousand in 1990. The 1980 U.S. Census asked individuals if they had any Scandinavian heritage; over nine million Americans claimed such heritage. Still, the total Scandinavian population, defined as either born abroad or of foreign-born parentage, has never made up more than 2 percent of the total American population.

The tendency to live together means that Scandinavians have always comprised a significant share of the population in specific states, cities, and rural locales. Beginning with the earliest immigrants, Scandinavians went overland to Chicago and Milwaukee from eastern ports like New York and Boston, then further west to the northern reaches of the Mississippi, Missouri, and Illinois rivers, and west of the Great Lakes. The economically depressed southern states after the Civil War were not a destination for most immigrants, and Scandinavians concentrated upon the more familiar climes of the northern states. If the winter was as cold as in much of Scandinavia, the relative flatness and fertility of the land were a great improvement.

At the turn of the twentieth century 70 percent of Scandinavian immigrants lived in the Upper Midwest: fully 80 percent of Norwegians and 60 percent of the Danes and Swedes. The Swedes tended to populate Minnesota, Illinois, Iowa, Michigan, and Nebraska, while the Norwegians settled in Wisconsin, North Dakota, South Dakota, and Minnesota; the Danes were more sparsely spread throughout Iowa, Minnesota, Wisconsin, and Illinois. In 1980 not quite half of persons claiming any Scandinavian origin still lived in the Upper Northwest; 50 percent of Norwegians and 40 percent of Danes and Swedes. Approximately one-third of the balance of Scandinavians now inhabited the American West, with the remainder divided evenly between the East and the South.

Residentially, the Scandinavian immigrant population is further concentrated in urban areas; fewer than 3 percent work in agriculture, and well over 80 percent live in metropolitan areas. Scandinavians joined in the new migration that redistributed the U.S. population from the Northwest to Western cities during the 1970s. As of the 1980 census, Californian cities had become the new destination for many Scandinavian immigrants—one out of every eight Norwegians and Swedes and one out of every four Danes. Otherwise, the Danes remain more spread out than their fellow Scandinavian immigrants; Norwegians and Swedes tend to move to New York, Washington State, and Illinois.

Scandinavian immigrants are highly educated and, more so than natives or other immigrants, they can be found in skilled occupations. Sixteen percent of Scandinavian immigrants are employed as executives, twice the percentage of other immigrants, and they comprise 5 percent of all foreign-born executives. Another 46 percent of Scandinavians find employment either as professionals or in technical occupations. This comparatively high level of occupational achievement is also associated with the fact that most foreign-born Scandinavians have been in the United States far longer than other immigrants. Eight out of every ten foreign-born Scandinavians counted in the 1980 census had im-

migrated prior to 1960, whereas over six-tenths of all immigrants to the United States had arrived since then.

EARLY SETTLEMENT, 1815–1862

A shift from the political philosophy of mercantilism to liberalism took place during the late eighteenth and early nineteenth centuries. The new order encouraged the formation of markets where goods were exchanged for cash and created laws that extended civil rights as well as facilitated commerce. For example, this shift led to the lifting of barriers to international trade and to the lifting of restrictions on emigration.

The development of national and international markets for agricultural products stimulated the modernization of the rural farming system. An expanding demand for agricultural goods went hand in hand with demand for rural labor. Throughout the first half of the nineteenth century the numbers of small farmers who owned land, peasants who had leasehold right to land and cottages, and laborers who worked on large farms continued to grow.

During the second half of the nineteenth century the number of large, independent farmers stabilized, but the numbers of small farmers and non-landowning workers declined. While part of the decline is associated with the mass emigration, the rural proletariat were not the first to emigrate. Rather, it was the better-off families that were the first to move to the New World. These first emigrants established communities that later attracted the proletarian agricultural classes.

The roots of the earliest nineteenth-century emigration to America were manifested in many complex forms of the changing world order. The rise of pietistic religious movements led to conflicts with traditional Lutheranism. While retaining a Lutheran framework, these movements emphasized lay priesthood, simplification of ritual, and a distrust of the formal authority of the Lutheran state church. German Quakers influenced the earliest group of emigrants from Norway. The Quakers had first sought refuge in Stavanger and then greater religious freedom in America. Cleng Peerson led the followers of the religious visionary Hans Nielsen Hauge to America. A group of fifty-two Quakers and Haugeans crowded onto the forty-five-ton sloop *Restauration* and set sail in July 1825 on a three-month voyage across the Atlantic.

The Sloopers, as they were called, settled in Kendall Township in upper New York State, on the shores of Lake Ontario. Peerson soon found better land further west that was close to a proposed canal to be built between Lake Michigan and the Illinois River. The Fox River settlement formed a transit point to the frontier that was used by the Norwegians and Swedes who followed. Letters written to family in Norway described the rich soil and inexpensive farmland, and praised American freedom and equality. These letters, copied by hand and in local presses, were widely circulated in the countryside.

The Latter-day Saints, also known as Mormons, found converts among the Danes. From their base in Copenhagen, missionaries converted several thousand Danes during the 1850s and throughout the remainder of the century. They joined the community of Mormons on their long overland trek to the New Zion in Utah. "Better folk" seeking improved opportunities made up the first regular party of Swedes under the leadership of Gustaf Unonius. About twelve families followed the route of Norwegian settlers and moved to Pine Lake, close to Milwaukee, in 1841. The harsh Wisconsin winters made life in the colony hard and some, including Unonius, soon moved to Chicago (where he became an Episcopalian minister and community leader).

Religion played a part among those immigrants encouraged by the Methodist minister Olof Hedström and his brother Jonas. In New York, Olof met and directed Swedish immigrants westward to Illinois, where Jonas had settled in Knox County. While the Norwegian settlements continued to be centered in Wisconsin, the steady stream of immigrants influenced by the Hedströms established the state of Illinois as a focus of Swedish settlement. In 1846 the self-styled prophet Erik Jansson founded the first large-scale Swedish settlement at Bishop Hill, Illinois. The colony experimented with communal forms of living and ownership. Members shared the purchase of the release of their young men from Swedish military service and the cost of travel overseas and inland, farmland, and the looms to produce linen and carpeting. There was a short period of success, but after the murder of Jansson the colony suffered mismanagement and economic failure of its industries. By 1861 all property was converted to individual ownership.

Scandinavians played a part in the building of Chicago, the gateway for most immigrants to the Northwest. Chicago became the third permanent settlement of Norwegians during the 1830s. They worked in trades as varied as printing, land investment, crewing on sailboats, trading between lake communities, and as laborers on the construction of the Illinois and Michigan Canal. By 1860 the federal census counted 1,313 Norwegians, 816 Swedes, and a small number of Danes, all of whom made up just over 2 percent of the city's populace. All three groups lived in close proximity, but Pan-Scandinavian feelings were second to their national identities. When the famous Norwegian violinist Ole Bull visited in 1854, after a failed attempt to found a colony in Pennsylvania, Swedes and Danes were barred from a banquet in his honor. A fundamental change in the character of Scandinavian migration was to take place in the next decade.

MASS IMMIGRATION, 1862–1914

Of many events that mark the starting point for mass emigration, none is more notable than the Homestead Act of 1862, which ushered in an epoch of agricultural extension of the western United States with an offer of free land to settlers who would live on it for five years. The growth of the smallhold and peasant classes in the preceding period created a population ready to escape the imperfectly matched barter and new-money economies. The growing smallhold and peasant classes did not own their own land, nor did they receive a cash income sufficient to permit them to purchase goods or land. The small leasehold farmer was attracted by the possibility of owning land in America. A growing European demand made the farming of cash grain crops profitable.

Famine in northern Sweden, Norway, and Finland in 1867 fueled a small flight from poverty at the outset of the period of mass emigration. This marked the start of Finnish emigration. Over eighty thousand Swedes left in the following two years, but fewer than one thousand Finns did so. Catastrophic volcanic activity in the northern territories prompted the first Icelandic emigration in the 1880s. Yet, just as the importance of religion in early Scandinavian emigration can be overemphasized, so can parallels with catastrophic events such as the Irish flight from famine.

Where diversified means of making a living were possible in the homeland, there was less motivation to emigrate. For example, Danes were reclaiming the land in Jutland, and the continental demand for dairy and animal products created a demand for labor. In both central and northern Norway and Sweden, extensive forests provided building materials for sizable merchant fleets, as well as for export. Norway at that time possessed the world's third largest sailing fleet. Swedish forges exported bar-iron and steel products from small foundries spread throughout central Sweden. Such alternatives were vulnerable to local and global events, however. The herring fisheries of the North Sea inexplicably failed during the 1880s, causing many to emigrate. The shipping depression of the 1890s led to the start of widespread emigration from the coastal communities of southwestern Norway in the 1890s.

A complex set of causes interacted with apparent overpopulation to drive the mass emigration. Emigration provided a safety valve during periods of instability, but overpopulation was not the primary cause of the mass emigration from Scandinavia. Rather, a change from subsistence farming to market production loosened the bonds between agricultural workers and the land. The consolidation of small farms during the 1880s encouraged emigration from western Sweden and from southern and western Norway. The proletarianization of the agricultural population created the motivation for families to seek opportunities afforded by landholding in America.

Other historical developments and the settlements established during the early emigration multiplied the attraction. The end of the Civil War made travel feasible. The introduction of the passenger steamer lowered the cost and eased the strains of overseas travel. Competition drove the cost of steamer tickets down throughout the rest of the century. Instead of spending months slogging overland in horse-drawn wagons, or sailing on the Great Lakes, or moving inland by barge, immigrants could travel by rail.

Railway companies grew by acquiring land grants, and they sought passengers by actively advertising in the United States and abroad. Agents such as Minnesota's Swedish American secretary of state, Hans Mattson, placed advertisements in Swedish- and Norwegian-language papers encouraging settlers to come to western Michigan. In his work for the Lake Superior Railroad, he traveled in 1871 to Sweden, where he emphasized not the quality of land or the wages paid in sawmills, but the positive experience of earlier Scandinavians in the United States. Returning American cousins with their stories of success had a powerful influence on those considering emigration. Swedish data show that the practice of returning home increased over the period of mass emigration. Only about 6 percent of Swedish emigrants returned home before 1890, but as the stream matured, over 20 percent returned between 1890 and 1910. By the 1920s over 40 percent of emigrants made the trek back.

Strong endorsements by fellow Scandinavians exerted great influence among the families and communities where members were considering the risky move overseas. A flood of "America letters" to those at home provided the most effective encouragement. One immigrant wrote, "We can truthfully call to the burdened cotter, the many hungry and impoverished families of servants, and the poor laborers and craftsmen in the old dear Norway: Come over to us. Here is land for the landless and bread for the breadless, so that you and your children can have a happy future" (Blegen, *Norwegian Migration to America,* p. 461). The practice of sending tickets home increased during this period. For example, nearly half of the emigrants from the communities of Dovre and Balstrand, Norway, traveled on prepaid tickets. The prepaid ticket marked one of many changes as the epoch of mass emigration continued into its saturation phase in the latter 1880s.

Demographically, there was a shift from the emigration of families toward a greater number of young adults in the emigrant stream. By the waning years of emigration, following 1900, two-thirds of all emigrants were between the ages of fifteen and thirty. The share of women increased, except among the Finns, where males continued to dominate. Urban-based emigration also became more important from the Stockholm region and Copenhagen during the late 1880s and 1890s. It coincided with the growth of opportunities in the wage economies of established American cities and their Scandinavian communities. The decline in the availability of American land, the modernization of Scandinavian agriculture and the depletion of the landless classes, signaled the end of the epoch of mass emigration. The greatest losses occurred in districts where the numbers of leasehold crofters and cottagers, who experienced the greatest growth before the mass emigration, "voted with their feet" against the intensification of agriculture.

RELIGIOUS ORGANIZATIONS

The Lutheran church played the single largest role in the religious life of Scandinavians and provided their central social organization in America. Most immigrants were opposed to the state church and the professional clergy in their homelands. In their new homes they remained loyal to pietistic forms of Lutheranism and quickly organized ethnic congregations in which they spoke their native language. Elling Eielsen organized Elling's Synod among the Norwegians in the Fox River, Illinois, settlement in 1846. However, Elling's insistence on low-church, informal ritual caused dissension among many of the members. In response, traditionally inclined Norwegian and Danish settlers formed the Norwegian Evangelical Lutheran Church in America in 1853. In 1860 the Swedes organized the Augustana Synod, which included some Norwegian members who remained active until 1870.

Each group created not one but several organizations to meet their needs. A Scandinavian Laestadian revivalist congregation emphasizing lay priests and the personal confessions of sins, broke apart in 1871 when the Finns created their own organization. More traditionally minded Finns created the Suomi Synod in 1890. By 1872 there were enough Danes to establish the Danish Lutheran Church in America, following the precepts of Bishop Nikolai Grundtvig. In 1884 those Danes remaining in the Norwegian-Danish Lutheran Conference of 1870 withdrew to form the more devout Blair Synod. Competition with Unitarians spurred the creation of the Icelandic Lutheran Synod in 1885. Several more schisms and reorganizations occurred throughout the balance of the century.

Despite the importance of each individual group, membership was small. In 1910 fewer than one-fourth of first- and second-generation immigrant Swedes belonged to the Augustana Synod. The next three leading denominations comprised little more than 3 percent of the Swedish population. Similarly, the membership of the two major Danish organizations made up no more than one-fourth of ethnic Danes. Slowly the distinctiveness of each group lessened and the use of Scandinavian languages in services became problematic because of the American nativism of the time. In 1917 the three major Norwegian groups merged to form the Norwegian Lutheran Church in America, which was the largest Scandinavian organization at that time. The membership rolls continued to decline, however, and in 1960 the American Lutheran church (German) merged with the Norwegian Lutheran church and the United Evangelical Lutheran church (Danish).

One great accomplishment of these organizations was their role in the establishment of schools and colleges during the second part of the nineteenth century that have survived to the present. The Swedes founded Augustana College and Theological Seminary in Rock Island, Illinois (1860); Gustavus Adolphus College in Saint Peter, Minnesota (1862); Bethany College in Lindsborg, Kansas (1881); Upsala College in East Orange, New Jersey (1893); and the Mission Friends' North Park College in Chicago (1891). Norwegians, sometimes with Danes and Swedes, founded Augsburg College in Minneapolis (1869); Luther College in Decorah, Iowa (1861); the Luther Theological Seminary in Madison, Wisconsin; Saint Olaf College in Northfield, Minnesota (1874); Concordia College in Moorhead, Minnesota (1891); and the Pacific Lutheran University in Parkland, Washington (1890). Danes founded Dana College in Blair, Nebraska (1884), and Grand View College in Des Moines, Iowa (1896). Many short-lived folk schools and theological seminaries also served Scandinavians.

Other religious influences included the Methodists, who had taken an active role in Swedish emigration. Methodists were particularly successful at winning Scandinavian membership; they first established separate Norwegian and Danish churches and in 1884 organized the Norwegian-Danish Conference. Baptists, Episcopalians, Seventh-Day Adventists, and Latter-day Saints also achieved successes. The Latter-day Saints, or Mormons, organized very early in the 1840s at the Norwegian Fox River settlement. However, most Mormons settled in the intermountain West. The large numbers of converted Danes joined the trek to Utah and were the majority among the Scandinavian converts.

COMMUNITY LIFE

Many secular organizations grew to serve the needs of Scandinavian communities throughout the nineteenth century. The first such organizations were mutual-benefit or charitable organizations established in the larger cities where the number of Scandinavians was large enough to support such undertakings. Philadelphia was the site of the first major Scandinavian Society in 1768; New York had one in 1844, and San Francisco in 1859. These organizations were founded by middle- and upper-class immigrants who desired clubs where they could speak their languages, share common interests, and plan cultural events. By the 1880s Pan-Scandinavian feelings were on the decline in the United States, and the size of each ethnic group permitted the establishment of separate ethnic organizations.

Large cities remained the focal point for such organizations. Song societies were popular and, especially during the 1870s and 1880s, male choruses and quartets and a cappella choirs gave public concerts, marched in parades, and participated in competitive events. The United Scandinavian Singers of America, formed in 1886, arranged biennial music festivals, with a particularly successful songfest held at Minneapolis in 1891 in which fifty clubs participated. Literary and dramatic societies were common in cities, as well as in smaller towns where the Scandinavian population was large enough to support the endeavor. Song societies exist to this day in Minneapolis, Chicago, Seattle, and Brooklyn, New York.

Excellent education in their home countries stood Scandinavians in good stead in the United States. Literacy was widespread among Scandinavian immigrants. Whereas, overall, three-quarters of immigrants who arrived between 1899 and 1910 declared themselves able to read or write, better than 99 percent of adults from Scandinavia were literate. The Swedish Svea Society, established in 1857 at Chicago, collected Swedish books and newspapers for a library and was involved in politics. Icelandic immigrants organized reading circles in which books were read aloud. Norwegians from the same region formed *bygdelag* organizations that compiled genealogies, published yearbooks, and held summerfests at which participants wore traditional folk costumes and danced to the music of Norwegian fiddles.

Scandinavian newspapers and periodicals emerged and grew in number, only to die as their readership became assimilated into American culture. By the second decade of the twentieth century nearly six hundred Norwegian-language publications had been started. Given the similarity in their languages, Danes and Norwegians regularly wrote for each other's newspapers and journals. Some fifty Danish-only newspapers were brought to print by 1914. The "Danish Newspaper King," Christian Rasmussen, published Danish as well as Norwegian books around the turn of the century. He controlled weekly papers in three states, magazines, printing plants, and an advertising agency. Over three hundred fifty Finnish and Swedish-Finnish publi-

cations were initiated. By 1910 not quite twelve hundred Swedish periodicals had been started in several states. From several hundred periodicals, serving a combined readership of just under one million around the time of World War I, the number of Scandinavian publishing houses had dwindled to a dozen by the 1980s.

A concern for the "common man" has left its mark on the contribution of Scandinavian writers. Finns and Norwegians, in particular, organized workingmen's societies, socialist federations, and farmer and consumer cooperatives, and published their views widely. Although relatively successful before World War II, they weakened under the pressure of McCarthyism's repression of liberal institutions in the 1950s. The Norwegian working-class activist Marcus Thrane immigrated to the United States in the decade before 1900 and edited newspapers in Chicago. Thorstein Veblen made a lasting contribution with *Theory of the Leisure Class* (1899), which was critical of the culture of the privileged elite. The Dane Jacob Riis, a well-known American muckraker during the last half of the century, was critical of the treatment of New York's poor in *How the Other Half Lives* (1890).

A variety of Scandinavian and Scandinavian American authors have chronicled the early years of the immigrant experience. During the 1880s a Norwegian American, Hans A. Foss wrote "Hussmandsgutten," (*The Cotter's Son;* 1884), which appeared in the *Decorah-Posten*. The Norwegian author Bjornstjerne Bjornson wrote for the *Skandianven* and influenced the immigrant Hjalmar Hjorth Boyesen, who wrote in English. Another immigrant, Ole E. Rølvaag, described rural immigrant life in *Giants in the Earth* (1927), *Peder Victorious* (1929), and *Their Father's God* (1931). The harsh experiences of the frontier were written about by the Swedish author Vilhelm Moberg, whose novel *The Emigrants* (1949) was also made into a movie, and a series of four other books were translated in the 1950s and 1960s. The lot of Danish tenant farmers in the Nebraska territories formed a trilogy of novels written by Sophus Keith Winther in the 1930s. In a lighthearted vein, Garrison Keillor has popularized modern small-town Norwegian Americans in Minnesota on the radio program "A Prairie Home Companion" and the novel *Lake Woebegon Days* (1985).

Fraternal organizations were formed along the lines of American orders, complete with initiation ceremonies and rituals. The Danish Brotherhood was founded in 1866 at Omaha to provide insurance for Danish war veterans, and was reorganized along its present lines in 1882 to include maintenance of the Danish culture in America. The Sons of Norway was started as an insurance organization in 1895 at Minneapolis and later evolved into a Norwegian-only fraternal order. Finns founded the Knights of Kaleva in 1898. Among the most successful Swedish institutions was the Vasa Order, founded in 1896 at New Haven, which made the transition from an insurance provider to a broadly based organization for the preservation of Swedish culture.

Many organizations that exist today were formed to promote Scandinavian heritage. The Norwegian-American Historical Association, founded in 1925, regularly publishes books and a journal that chronicle the American experience. It is based at Saint Olaf's College in Northfield, Minnesota. Similarly, the Swedish-American Historical Society, founded at Chicago in 1905, publishes books and a quarterly emphasizing ethnic history. In Oregon the Danish American Heritage Association, founded in 1977, publishes a newsletter, a journal, and books. These organizations play a major role in preserving the cultural heritage of all Scandinavians, and their publications are a primary source of information for persons interested in American history.

BIBLIOGRAPHY

Data Sources

Hutchinson, Edward Prince. *Immigrants and Their Children, 1850–1950* (1956).

U.S. Bureau of the Census. *Historical Statistics of the United States, Colonial Times to 1970* (1975).

———. *Foreign-born Population in the United States: Microfiche* (1985). (Individual countries.)

———. *Statistical Abstract of the United States, 1990* (1990).

U.S. Immigration and Naturalization Service. *Statistical Yearbook of the Immigration and Naturalization Service, 1989* (1990).

Emigration from Scandinavia

Akerman, Sune, Hans Christian Johansen, and David Gaunt, eds., *Chance and Change: Social and Economic Studies in Historical Demography in the Baltic Area* (1978).

Gjerde, Jon. *From Peasants to Farmers: The Migration from Balestrand, Norway, to the Upper Middle West* (1985).

Hvidt, Kristian. *Flight to America: The Social Background of 300,000 Danish Emigrants* (1975).

Kero, Reino. *Migration from Finland to North America in the Years Between the United States Civil War and the First World War* (1974).

Lovoll, Odd S., ed. *Norwegian-American Studies.* Vol. 29 (1983).

Lowell, Briant Lindsay. *Scandinavian Exodus: Demography and Social Development of 19th-Century Rural Communities* (1987).

Norman, Hans, and Harald Runblom. *Transatlantic Connections: Nordic Migration to the New World After 1800* (1988).

Semmingsen, Ingrid. *Norway to America: A History of the Migration.* Translated by Einar Haugen (1978).

Scandinavian History

Derry, Thomas Kingston. *A History of Scandinavia: Norway, Sweden, Denmark, Finland, and Iceland* (1979).

Hagen, Rolf M., et al. *Norsk historisk atlas* (1980).

Mead, William Richard. *An Historical Geography of Scandinavia* (1981).

Scandinavians in the United States

Babcock, Kendric Charles. *The Scandinavian Element in the United States* (1914).

Barton, Hildor Arnold. *Letters from the Promised Land: Swedes in America, 1840–1914* (1975).

Beijbom, Ulf. *Swedes in Chicago: A Demographic and Social Study of the 1846–1880 Immigration.* Translated by Donald Brown (1971).

Blegen, Theodore C. *Norwegian Migration to America.* 2 vols. (1931–1940).

Hasselmo, Nils. *Perspectives on Swedish Immigration* (1978).

Kastrup, Allan. *The Swedish Heritage in America* (1975).

Kolehmainen, John I. *The Finns in America: A Bibliographical Guide to Their History* (1947).

Ljungmark, Lars. *For Sale: Minnesota. Organized Promotion of Scandinavian Immigration, 1866–1873* (1971).

Lovoll, Odd S. *The Promise of America: A History of the Norwegian-American People* (1984).

——. *Scandinavians and Other Immigrants in Urban America* (1985).

——. *A Century of Urban Life: The Norwegians in Chicago Before 1930* (1988).

Ostergren, Robert C. *A Community Transplanted: The Trans-Atlantic Experience of a Swedish Immigrant Settlement in the Upper Middle West, 1835–1915* (1988).

Runbolm, Harald, and Dag Blanck. *Scandinavia Overseas: Patterns of Cultural Transformation in North America and Australia* (1986).

SEE ALSO **The Great Lakes Industrial Region; Immigration;** and **The Upper Midwest.**

THE DUTCH

Herbert J. Brinks

NETHERLANDIC INVOLVEMENT in America began with Henry Hudson's 1609 explorations on the eastern seaboard. His investigations of New York's harbor and river system led to the establishment of inland trading posts such as Fort Orange (now Albany) in 1615 and the port community of New Amsterdam (now New York City) in 1625. Since then the Dutch have participated in nearly every phase of American immigration. They numbered fewer than 8,000 when the British seized New Amsterdam in 1664, but typically high colonial-era birthrates increased their number to 100,000 by 1790. Additional Dutch immigration was negligible until after 1815, when, in line with general European migration patterns, Hollanders participated in the dramatically increased wave of emigration that characterized the post-Napoleonic era. Approximately 380,000 Dutch immigrants arrived between 1820 and 1920, and in the aftermath of World War II another 89,000 joined the Dutch American populace. Currently the descendants of these immigrants number about four million.

Each of the three migrations—colonial, nineteenth-century, and late-twentieth-century—was unique. The first, to the colony of New Netherland (present-day New York and New Jersey), was a commercial venture that, like those of the English and Spanish, aimed to extend the paths and products of commerce. The second, between 1820 and 1920, was a free migration of a generally poor but not destitute agricultural populace in search of economic improvements. The post–World War II immigration consisted of largely urban people seeking to escape the problems of an overpopulated, war-ravaged nation that was offering incentives for emigration. Yet, despite their distinguishing features, the three movements exhibited common characteristics. For example, over the centuries a large majority of Dutch Protestants shared identical creeds that were connected with national heroes like William of Orange (1533–1584) and Maurice of Nassau (1567–

1625). In addition, Dutch settlements, both colonial villages like Poughkeepsie (1687) and twentieth-century towns like Lynden, Washington (where the Dutch enclave developed after 1900), were inclined to ethnic exclusivity. Thus, despite many intra-ethnic differences, Dutch American settlements appeared to be monolithic to outside observers.

COLONIAL DUTCH

Bearing testimony to its commercial purposes, the original populace of New Netherland (1624–1664) consisted of traders, a military garrison, and a few farmers and craftsmen. These settlers, together with peasants and day laborers drawn from Amsterdam's underclass, were joined by Belgian Walloons and French Huguenots, both groups refugees from religious persecution. The Dutch West India Company, which acquired a charter to the colony in 1621, attempted to gain residents by providing large land grants under the patroon system, which gave feudal rights to landholders who could attract settlers. This and other efforts failed, but after 1638 trade restrictions were relaxed to encourage private enterprise, which tended to stabilize the population. When the Dutch West India Company lost its Brazilian colony (1654), a portion of that region's large Jewish community migrated to New Amsterdam, and after 1652 African slaves were brought into the colony. Thus, by 1664, when Peter Stuyvesant capitulated to a small British fleet, New Amsterdam contained a diverse and polyglot population, which proved to be a continuing characteristic of New York City.

Lenient terms of surrender, allowing the Dutch to retain their property and religious observances, prevented a mass exodus. Instead, over the next fifty years, when the English and French populace combined to dominate the city's economy and political affairs, many Dutch residents moved to

711

nearby regions, where they organized and maintained communities such as Kingston, Catskill, and Poughkeepsie on the Hudson, and Niskayuna, Schenectady, and Herkimer on the Mohawk that remained primarily Dutch American until well into the nineteenth century.

Along the Hudson River and its tributaries (the Mohawk in particular), dozens of Dutch settlements were established between 1660 and 1750. In these frontier communities the migrants carved farms from the wilderness that surrounded their village churches and schools. Until at least 1800 the Dutch language prevailed in their shops, classrooms, and churches. A similarly structured Dutch contingent occupied major river valleys in New Jersey. The Bergen County community on the Hackensack River, dating from the 1660s, became a starting point for additional settlements along the Passaic River (1693–1740) and in the Raritan Valley (1699–1766). From New Jersey the Dutch migrated into Bucks County, Pennsylvania, and also joined the westward movement across New York, Kentucky, and Ohio. Not only did the enclaved residents retain their attachments to the Dutch Reformed church and their native language, but the French, German, and English who settled among them usually acculturated into the dominant Netherlandic patterns. At the same time some Dutch families and individuals left the enclaves to join more typically frontier settlements with varied ethnic composition, like Rochester, Detroit, and Chicago.

Because Amsterdam's religious authorities continued to govern the colonial Dutch Reformed church until 1772, the New World's leading clergymen were trained in the Netherlands, assuring the continued use of the Dutch language. A number of pastors were also trained in local parsonages, but throughout the colonial period the Dutch Reformed church was insufficiently staffed. For example, in 1776 just forty ordained clergymen were available for the one hundred Dutch American congregations. Despite a growing insistence during mid century (1720–1760) that pastors be trained in North America, the Dutch Reformed church did not establish a functionally effective educational program until 1784, when John Henry Livingston became professor of theology to the General Synod.

The first English-language sermon was preached in New York City by A. Laidlie, who entered the North Church pulpit in 1763. His hand-picked successor, Livingston, arrived in 1770. But by then Dutch influence in the city had been vastly diminished. English dominance was already evident in the 1703 tax lists, which indicated that the English and French had become the city's wealthiest inhabitants. That same ethnic coalition gained political prominence early in the eighteenth century.

The Dutch descendants of colonial immigrants maintained close ties with the nineteenth-century immigrants, particularly in ecclesiastical matters, but the two groups had been moved to emigrate for vastly different reasons. The founding residents of New Netherland had occupied the fringes of the growing and prosperous Dutch empire. During the sixteenth century Holland's commercial expansion, sea power, and artistic achievements made the Dutch Republic a leading European power. Dutch banks financed much of the Western world's commercial and military efforts, and Dutch ships, textiles, foodstuffs, and munitions were marketed throughout Europe. In the context of the republic's commercial sphere of influence, which ranged from the Baltic and Mediterranean seas to the Dutch East India Company's Indonesian colonies, the New Amsterdam settlement was minimally significant. Even in the New World the Dutch West India Company devoted most of its attention and capital to the slave and sugar trade between Africa and the Caribbean. New Amsterdam was little more than a port of call with a somewhat profitable fur trade. By contrast, when the first mass emigration from the Netherlands occurred in the 1840s, that country had become a minor European power with a generally backward economy.

NINETEENTH-CENTURY DUTCH

During the eighteenth century Great Britain largely supplanted Holland in commercial prominence. And from 1795, when the French occupied the Netherlands, until 1813, when Napoleon was defeated and the Dutch regained independence at the Congress of Vienna (1814) the French exploited the Dutch economy. With the establishment of a constitutional monarchy in 1815, William I (1815–1840) attempted to modernize the Dutch state, but his attention was diverted by international and colonial objectives that required crippling tax rates. These taxes, combined with the monarch's autocratic management of the economy and a doubling of the poverty rolls, created social unrest. Consequently a sporadic migration to the United States, which began in the 1830s, increased by the mid 1840s to become Holland's first mass emigration.

The dramatic increase occurred in 1846, when over two thousand émigrés sailed to America. This migration stemmed partly from the fractured and isolated character of Holland's economy. The agricultural provinces functioned almost independently of each other, and collectively they had few sustained links with the urban mercantile provinces. Growth in manufactured goods was restricted by the limited number of roads and canals leading primarily to local markets; and apart from butter and cheese, little agricultural surplus was produced for export. These conditions prevailed until the 1880s, when the pace of agricultural modernization quickened. Prior to mechanized farming, agriculture in Holland depended largely on seasonal day laborers or hired hands, and the economic prospects for such folk, along with small farmers and skilled workmen, were decidedly bleak. Thus, beginning in 1846 and throughout the following seventy-five years, America attracted a much larger number of Dutch immigrants than during the preceding two centuries.

Although Holland's internal economy grew little prior to the 1880s, its port cities, Amsterdam and Rotterdam, provided regular employment because of an increasing flow of goods in and out of central Europe. Thus, the worst economic prospects were concentrated in the agricultural provinces. The emigrant flow, which grew from 979 in 1846 to 2,631 the following year, experienced that rapid gain as a consequence of two direct causes. The more dramatic of these, a potato famine (1845–1847), followed the blighting of just over 80 percent of the total crop in 1845. One province, Drenthe, suffered a total loss. But by itself, the crop failure cannot explain the increased emigration of 1847. A large portion (35 percent) of the immigrants left Holland because they had suffered from official and social discrimination on account of their deviant religious behavior.

These ecclesiastical dissidents had objected to rationalist influences in the policies of the Netherlands Reformed (state) church and to the loss of local autonomy in church appointments. King William I, whose policies reflected the centralizing tendencies of the Napoleonic era in the Netherlands (1806–1814), attempted to regulate the administration of the Netherlands Reformed church by assembling a synod (1815) that appointed a standing committee to govern the church. In the process he denied regional bodies their traditional autonomy and appointed key officials to the synod and executive committee himself. In reaction six pastors joined several thousand discontented church members and seceded from the national church in 1834. Then, amid the economic disasters of the 1840s, two of the dissident pastors organized and joined the 1846–1847 migration to North America. Albertus Christiaan Van Raalte settled his followers in and around Holland, Michigan, in 1847; Hendrik Pieter Scholte organized the Pella, Iowa, colony that same year.

The founders of these settlements maximized the likelihood of ethnic solidarity by selecting thinly populated areas that were nearly devoid of institutions. Before departing Holland the planners had contacted officials of the Dutch Reformed church in New York to gain assistance, and by 1850 a majority of the immigrant churches merged with those established on the East Coast. The villages and towns the newcomers established in the Midwest were similar to the Dutch American towns colonial Netherlanders had founded in New York and New Jersey. Each community featured farms adjacent to a village center with Dutch Reformed churches and ethnically dominated a chosen landscape. Once established, these ethnically cohesive midwestern sites attracted the majority of new immigrants who arrived between 1847 and 1920.

Dutch immigration, while following the typical patterns of northern European migrations, was distinguished by its predominantly rural character. Throughout the era, immigrants came largely (up to 80 percent) from the agricultural sector. The first wave, which began in 1820 and lasted until the Civil War, came from the sandy provinces of Drenthe, Gelderland, and Overijssel, whose economies consisted of small, marginal farms, locally marketed handcrafts, and some cottage industry. Until these economies changed in the second half of the century, emigration persisted. The original settlers in Holland, Michigan (1847–1860), for example, came primarily from these provinces; thereafter chain migrations from this area amounted to about one-third of the total emigration.

The clay-soil regions, concentrated in Friesland and Groningen on the North Sea and in Zeeland on the southern border, provided over half (55 percent) of all Dutch emigrants to the United States between 1821 and 1920, but that movement did not accelerate rapidly until the 1870s. The Netherlandic agricultural crisis (1875–1895) and available homestead land in America were the principal inducements for immigration between 1880 and 1900. Nearly 75 percent of the period's eighty thousand immigrants were reacting to agricultural disruptions in traditional wheat- and grain-producing regions. The introduction of new crops and mechanization combined to create a labor surplus. Although other employment was available in new agricultural processing plants and in the industrial sectors, a general preference for farming, together with encouraging reports from earlier emigrants, drew many from the clay-soil region to America. As Hille de Vries concluded, "Emigration to America took advantage of the resistance of Groningers, Frisians and Zeelanders to the industrial way of life" (quoted in Swierenga, *The Dutch in America,* p. 93).

Most of these rural immigrants were from middling social strata with sufficient means to transport themselves and to acquire basic farm tools and some livestock. Those of lesser means, usually single men, worked as farmhands to save enough money to become sharecroppers or homesteaders. The wealthiest immigrants acquired well-developed farms on the best land available. Farming prospects led Dutch immigrants to the Midwest and the far West until about 1900, after which the availability of attractive homestead land diminished. Thereafter Dutch immigrants began to join clusters of their compatriots in urban areas.

The ties between Dutch American population centers and their sending communities were strong and persistent because chain migrations flowed regularly from specific regions in Holland to ethnic concentrations in the United States. Nearly 75 percent of 1820–1880 immigrants came from 12 percent of the 1,156 local governmental districts (*Gemeenten*) in the Netherlands. In 1870, 56 percent of Dutch immigrants resided in only eighteen (less than 1 percent) of the 2,295 counties in the United States. Doubtless a clear if not an overwhelming majority of Dutch immigrants were drawn to ethnic strongholds in America. About 40 percent of these ethnic enclaves disappeared when their residents, for various reasons, moved to more attractive Dutch communities or to ethnically mixed communities. Only about 10 percent of the Dutch moved to locations without links to the ethnic subculture.

By the 1920s Dutch Americans were concentrated in three regions: the Great Lakes area, both

sides of New York Harbor, and an agricultural belt stretching from northwest Iowa to Lynden, Washington. The greatest number settled along the semicircular southern border of Lake Michigan, from Sheboygan, Wisconsin, to Muskegon, Michigan. This region included the urban enclaves of Grand Rapids, Michigan, and three areas of greater Chicago. The only significant community of Dutch Catholics, clustered in Wisconsin's Fox River valley, was also on the Lake Michigan belt. On the East Coast most of Amsterdam's Jewish emigrants (about 6,500 by 1880) resettled in New York City or Philadelphia; Paterson, New Jersey, and its surrounding towns attracted several thousand Reformed Protestants. Searching for homestead land in Iowa, a cluster of Pella residents migrated to Sioux County in 1870; by 1900 the Hollanders dominated the county and were spilling over the borders into South Dakota and Minnesota. Dutch farmers from northwest Iowa and elsewhere joined with new immigrants to settle in Montana, Washington, and California. By 1920, five thousand Hollanders were living in Lynden, Washington, and three additional communities were established in California at Ripon, Los Angeles, and Hanford. Thus, when Dutch immigration diminished and virtually stopped during the late 1920s, the ethnic network stretched from coast to coast with urban concentrations on the East Coast and in the Midwest.

Despite their largely rural origins, Dutch immigrants adapted readily to industrialization. They were employed by the thousands in Paterson's silk mills and in the Chicago area's factories and building trades. In Grand Rapids they were both owners and employees in the furniture-making and baking industries. Ethnic concentrations increased in each of these areas until the 1950s, when Hollanders, like many Americans, moved to the suburbs or to outlying villages.

The Dutch were never exclusively rural because Chicago, Paterson, and Grand Rapids had each attracted a Dutch urban core by 1870. At the same time Dutch garden farmers on the fringes of cities sold their vegetables door-to-door or to wholesale brokers. As the cities expanded and engulfed adjacent agricultural hinterlands, real estate values rose rapidly. Some garden farmers sold out and relocated to areas where urban marketing was still possible. Others remained in the developing urban neighborhoods to open shops and set up small businesses. Most of these were family oriented with employees drawn from the ethnic community. Until the 1950s both Dutch suburban towns and Dutch urban neighborhoods grew more populous.

The general Dutch migration to suburbia in the 1950s and 1960s did not destroy the ethnic community. In cases like Paterson and Chicago's West Side, members of urban enclaves regrouped in the suburbs to reestablish their churches and schools. Both the South Side of Chicago and Grand Rapids were ringed by rural Dutch towns founded in the previous century; urban migrants were able to re-settle among their rural compatriots, where traditional ethnic structures were already in place.

The persistence of Dutch ethnic cohesion stems largely from the community's attachment to the Reformed faith. That thread of loyalty extends back to creeds and doctrines formulated in the sixteenth century. Since then the varied interpretations of these foundational documents have engendered tension and divisions within the faith, and significantly the nature of these debates has been of little interest to those outside the ethnic community. Thus, until the 1950s, if not later, the most divisive religious concerns remained intra-ethnic and tended to reinforce the group's cohesion.

Throughout the nineteenth century, ecclesiastical developments in the Netherlands crucially influenced the Dutch American community. Although religion cannot fully explain the mass immigration of 1846–1847, it did, with the establishment of churches and schools and with socioreligious patterns, shape the first settlements. And these social contours also influenced successive waves of immigrants. In 1857, however, the Reformed Church in America separated. In the early 1850s, two separate strains of Dutch Americans had joined under the auspices of the Reformed church: East Coast descendants of the original New Netherlanders and those in the Midwest who had recently arrived from Holland. Dissatisfied with this union, some of these new midwestern immigrants broke off in 1857 to found a new denomination, the Christian Reformed church. This group sought to remain affiliated with parent institutions in the Netherlands and judged that a link with the Reformed Church in America would dilute an orthodoxy symbolized by the Netherlandic religious Secession of 1834. These diverging patterns of ecclesiastical affiliation inherently affected cultural adaptation.

The immigrants who joined the Reformed Church in America were exposed to that denomination's English-language preaching and teaching. The Reformed church had founded a theological school at New Brunswick, New Jersey, in 1810 that was well embarked on adopting ecclesiastical practices selected from American church life. By contrast, the Christian Reformed church looked to the Netherlands for its credentials and did not adopt indigenous ecclesiastical practices until after World War I. In language, liturgical patterns, and theological directions, Netherlandic models remained strong if not dominant until the 1920s. All of this, combined with high rates of intermarriage, assured ethnoreligious cohesion in the Christian Reformed church.

Meanwhile, the congregations of both denominations assembled in nearly every Dutch American village and neighborhood, and because neither could recruit members from the common ethnic pool without demonstrating a measure of loyalty to the Dutch Reformed tradition, both groups remained ethnically cohesive. As immigration continued and expanded between 1880 and 1930, a large majority of the religiously conservative newcomers joined the more traditionally Netherlandic Christian Reformed church. Furthermore, when the Reformed Church in America's leading immigrant pastors died in the 1880s, they were replaced by graduates of the denomination's seminary in New Brunswick, New Jersey, an institution with an American rather than a Netherlandic ecclesiastical focus. Consequently, newly arriving immigrants found the Dutch-oriented Christian Reformed church more compatible with their immigrant status.

True to its origins, the Christian Reformed church nurtured its Old World ties, staffed its seminary with theologians trained in Holland, and therewith gained fresh theological and philosophical influences from Europe. The most significant of these stemmed from a Calvinist revival in the Netherlands (1880–1930) associated with Abraham Kuyper (1837–1920). This movement emphasized social engagement rather than pious isolation, and its "world and life view" asserted that every aspect of human endeavor—familial, educational, political, and economic—should be structured by Calvinist principles. These, in turn, were expressed in the organization of Calvinist schools, labor unions, publications, and a political party. In the Netherlands, where Kuyper became prime minister in 1892, these goals were largely achieved, but his American followers had similar success only within their ethnic strongholds. And although the movement's schools, periodicals, hospitals, and other institutions acquired support throughout the ethnic community, efforts to attract adherents from the general society faltered, and thus, despite its universal claims, Kuyperianism in the United States served mainly to intensify ethnic solidarity.

The combined imperatives—to train professional clergymen and to provide Christian education at all levels—engendered the formation of private schools from kindergarten through high school and at the college level. The institutional coordinator of these primary and secondary schools, Christian Schools International, currently incorporates 302 schools with some 69,000 students in the United States. The earliest colleges, Hope College in Holland, Michigan (1866), and Calvin College in Grand Rapids, Michigan (1876), offered preparatory school training for prospective pastors until each became a liberal arts college with adjacent theological school. The nineteenth-century Dutch and their descendants have founded seven surviving colleges. (The other five are Northwestern College [founded 1926], Central College [1916], and Dordt College [1956] in Iowa; Reformed Bible College [1939] in Grand Rapids, Michigan; and Trinity Christian College [1959] in Chicago.) However, none of these schools have remained ethnically exclusive. The Kuyperian predisposition for creating institutions was most obviously realized in educational efforts, but it also influenced the establishment of the Pine Rest Psychiatric Hospital; the Christian Labor Association (founded 1938), which flourished in the 1950s; child adoption agencies; and a variety of journals of opinion. Consequently, the wave of immigrants who came to America after World War II encountered an institutionally complex Dutch American community that mirrored a considerable portion of the Netherlandic social structure.

POSTWAR DUTCH

The massive ruin that World War II heaped on the Netherlands prompted nearly a third of the populace to consider emigration. And with a doubling of the Dutch population between 1900 and 1950, the government encouraged emigration to reduce unemployment and relieve a severe housing shortage. By offering financial assistance, vocational training, and language instruction, the Dutch government altered its traditionally neutral emigration policies. But because these aids were provided primarily to the destitute, emigration from other socioeconomic groups lagged. After 1951 this policy was modified, but by then the emigration fever had peaked. Still the total emigration from 1945 to 1965 surpassed that of the nineteenth century.

American immigration laws, which allotted the Dutch a quota of 3,136 entrants after 1929, restricted the postwar flow; out of nearly a half million emigrants, only 89,000 came to the United States. A large majority (275,000) immigrated to Canada and Australia. For the 89,000 who came to the United States, the traditional Dutch American regions were the most attractive destinations. The 1970 census lists the highest concentrations of foreign-born Dutch in California (28,000), Michigan (15,000), New York (11,500), New Jersey (8,500), and Illinois (6,000).

California's prominence as the favored location followed general population trends in America. The Pacific Southwest was especially attractive to those Dutch Indonesians who, after fighting on the losing side of the war for Indonesian independence (1949), migrated to the Netherlands and thereafter, under the provisions of the Walter-Pastore Refugee Relief Acts (1958, 1960) came to the United States. A large number of these 35,000 immigrants settled in southern California, where they have rapidly assimilated.

Unlike their nineteenth-century predecessors, the postwar immigrants were largely urbanites, skilled industrial workers, technicians, and professionals. But the orthodox Calvinist contingent among them continued to be overrepresented and, by joining Dutch American population centers, reinvigorated the Netherlandic cultural tradition in America. The postwar immigrants enlivened philosophic and theological discussions in the Christian Reformed community and spurred the creative energies of philosophers like Alvin C. Plantinga and Nicholas P. Wolterstorff. Theologians such as Lewis B. Smedes and John Timmer have gained impetus from their Netherlandic connections. Dutch theological perspectives have likewise invigorated discussions within the Reformed Church in America, but its characteristically ecumenical and American ecclesiastical posture has given birth to nationally prominent preachers like Norman Vincent Peale and Robert Schuller.

Since the 1960s the tightly woven fabric of many Dutch American communities and institutions has begun to stretch and unravel. In both the Christian Reformed church and the Reformed church membership expansion programs are directed at multi-ethnic and mainstream society. The parent-owned Christian schools are similarly concerned to acquire students from across ethnic and denominational lines. At the same time the nearly universal in-group marriage pattern, which persisted in the Dutch Reformed communities until the 1950s, has diminished. The group's colleges and hospitals, which were once directed, staffed, and populated almost exclusively by the ethnic community, have altered traditional policies to incorporate and serve a wider spectrum of religious groups. Other factors, such as suburbanization, gentrification, and diminution of rural populations, and an increasing level of education, have dispersed individuals, families, and whole segments of the Dutch ethnic community. Thus, a traditional ethnic identity bolstered by rural isolation and tightly knit, working-class urban neighborhoods no longer prevails.

After 1960 Dutch immigration and its attendant cultural infusions diminished precipitously. The postwar immigrant generation is dying out, and their children and grandchildren have assimilated into American culture more rapidly than previous generations. It is significant, in this context, that the two most successful immigrant travel organizations, the Dutch Immigrant Society and the Dutch Club

AVIO, have lost over 50 percent of their 55,000 members.

Currently the Dutch ethnic community is rapidly drawing closer to the nation's mainstream sociocultural patterns. Overwhelmingly Republican and business oriented, more than half of the Dutch are service professionals (physicians and teachers), self-employed, small-business owners, and technicians. Less than 10 percent remain full-time farmers. At least 50 percent are educated beyond high school and claim annual incomes between $30,000 and $100,000. Great wealth, though clearly evident among the owners and stockholders of the Grand Rapids–based Amway Corporation and the Chicago-based Waste Management Corporation, is exceptional.

However pressed by changing conditions, Dutch ethnic identity will probably survive for several generations. Dutch settlements like Albany and New Brunswick, which date from the colonial era, became ethnically diverse before the Civil War, and many of the rural settlements organized by the nineteenth-century immigrants are well on the road to ethnic pluralism. Yet within all these places an ethnic contingent is visible when they gather for worship. And, no doubt, these sanctuaries will preserve the final remnants of Dutch ethnicity in America.

BIBLIOGRAPHY

General Surveys

Brinks, Herbert J. *Write Back Soon: Letters from Immigrants in America, 1847–1920* (1986). Narrative including extensive excerpts from immigrant letters.

De Jong, Gerald F. *The Dutch in America, 1609–1974* (1975). Especially useful for the colonial period.

Lucas, Henry S. *Netherlanders in America* (1955). Best general survey.

Van Hinte, Jacob. *Netherlanders in America.* Edited by Robert P. Swierenga and translated by Adriaan de Wit (1985).

Topical Studies

Archdeacon, Thomas J. *Becoming American: An Ethnic History* (1983).

Balmer, Randall H. *A Perfect Babel of Confusion: Dutch Religion and English Culture in the Middle Colonies* (1989).

Boxer, Charles R. *The Dutch Seaborne Empire, 1600–1800* (1965).

Bratt, James H. *Dutch Calvinism in Modern America: A History of a Conservative Subculture* (1984). Best intellectual history of Dutch Americans.

Brouwer, Arie R. *Reformed Dutch Roots: Thirty-five Formative Events* (1977). Denominational history.

De Jong, Gerald F. *The Dutch Reformed Church in the American Colonies* (1978).

De Vries, Hille. "The Labor Market in Dutch Agriculture and Emigration to the United States." In *The Dutch in America: Immigration, Settlement, and Cultural Change,* edited by Robert Swierenga (1985).

Israel, Jonathan I. *Dutch Primacy in World Trade, 1585–1740* (1989).

Jameson, John Franklin, ed. *Narratives of New Netherland, 1609–1664* (1909).

Kroes, Rob. *Dutch Pioneers of the American West* (1991).

Lucas, Henry S., comp. *Dutch Immigrant Memoirs and Related Writings,* 2 vols. (1955).

Swierenga, Robert P. "Dutch International Labor Migration to North America in the Nineteenth Century." In *Dutch Immigration to North America,* edited by Herman Ganzevoort and Mark Boekelman (1983). Twelve papers presented at the Multicultural History Society of Ontario meetings in Toronto.

———, ed. *The Dutch in America: Immigration, Settlement, and Cultural Change* (1985). Survey of recent research by thirteen authors.

Taylor, Lawrence J. *Dutchmen on the Bay: The Ethnohistory of a Contractual Community* (1983).

Van Hoeven, James W., ed. *Piety and Patriotism: Bicentennial Studies of the Reformed Church in America, 1776–1976* (1976).

Zwaanstra, Henry. *Reformed Thought and Experience in a New World: A Study of the Christian Reformed Church and Its American Environment, 1890–1918* (1973).

Research Archives

Calvin College Library Archives, Grand Rapids, Michigan.

Central College, The Henry P. Scholte Collection, Pella, Iowa.

Dordt College Library Archives, Sioux Center, Iowa.

The Joint Archives of Holland, Hope College Library, Holland, Michigan.

Northwestern College Library Archives, Orange City, Iowa.

Trinity Christian College Archives, Palos Heights, Illinois.

SEE ALSO **Ethnicity; Immigration; Religion.**

GERMAN SPEAKERS

A. G. Roeber

TO TALK OF GERMAN SPEAKERS in late-twentieth-century America appears to indulge an oxymoron. No other language group in North America proves that mere numbers are insignificant compared with the persistence or disappearance of a language. As late as the 1980s, fifty-three million Americans considered themselves, in some degree, to be of "German" descent. But outside of Pennsylvania, New York City and its environs, a few pockets of the southern backcountry, and the American Midwest, the language has disappeared as a daily means of communication. German-language newspapers and radio or television programming have dwindled to relative insignificance. Yet, between 1683 and 1783 and after 1860 to 1890, enough German speakers arrived in the British colonies to comprise the largest group of non-English-speaking voluntary immigrants. After interruption by war in America and Europe, in 1804, in 1817, and again in the late 1830s and for another half-century, they resumed this status in the United States. Conventionally, the effects of the two world wars are cited as causes of the decline and rapid assimilation of German speakers after 1914. For Swiss German speakers, German Russians, Lichtensteiners, and German speakers from within the Austro-Hungarian Empire, such nationalist and political dates never adequately explained their changing relationships with North America. Nevertheless, these groups often had to struggle to avoid being tarred by the dominant anglophone culture with the brush of anti-German sentiment that periodically rose among nativists, or was provoked by imperial and National Socialist politics and policies. Still, social historians of those German speakers from within the boundaries of the empire established in 1870 are no longer much inclined to accept terms like decline or assimilation as adequate descriptions of the ways these groups evolved.

The dominant interpretive schema for looking at language groups in North America has operated under the rubrics of "ethnicity" and "assimilation." In the 1980s, these terms were supplemented by the interpretative framework constructed around the concept of cultural transfer and adaptation. Local culture guarded by family, religious denomination, artisanal competence, and deep suspicion of public authority beyond the local sphere survived transit. These characteristics of German speakers, culture historians increasingly emphasize, had long been true in Europe. That pattern of behavior successfully absorbed North American conditions and opportunities, in both rural and urban settings for German speakers from areas as diverse as Alsace, Memel, the Volga, the *Siebenbürgen* (Romania), German-speaking settlements in Transylvania and the Swiss canton of Schaffhausen, as well as Palatines, Hessians, Viennese, and Saxons. For lack of a better term, this pattern is referred to here as "transferred local osmosis." Such adaptations were themselves transferred habits that had been successfully applied to diverse European-Asian settlements before the first German speakers arrived on the American continent. Two theoretical outcomes of this pattern were possible: separatist enclaves defined against the more dominant culture, or redefinition by German speakers of that dominant culture according to both the transferred and selectively absorbed local traits.

Three general topics guide understanding of the people called "German speakers." First, migration, its causes, and its consequences over the course of three centuries have to be seen in the context of the much larger migration within Europe and European Russia. Second, initial settlement and subsequent migration in North America suggest certain social and cultural values of remarkable durability summed up under "transferred local osmosis." Finally, the image of German speakers, their "reception and response," as one scholar has termed the process, has varied because of the vast differences within the linguistically related groups

719

called German speakers. The dominant stereotypes around which images were grouped by both German speakers and others fell early on under the supposed characteristics of Prussia versus Bavaria or Austria: efficient, intellectual, managerial, and militarily ambitious versus musical, easygoing, religious, and good-natured. Ironically, though, the territories invoked as symbols never contributed large numbers to the migrations.

THE COLONIAL PERIOD

Immigration from German-speaking Europe to North America, beginning with colonial Virginia, should be seen in the context of migration within Europe. The first German arrivals (in very small numbers) included the artisans recruited by the London Company of Virginia and those who rensided in the Dutch colony of New Netherland. The northern Hanseatic cities, from Königsberg in the east to villages at the mouth of the Rhine in the west, contributed most of these settlers. Both Lutherans and later Reformed and free church members comprised these first unorganized migrations to the New World. The outbreak of the Thirty Years' War in 1618 devastated territories of the old Reich near the border with France and Switzerland, effectively preventing emigration from there. Instead, between 1648 and 1700 immigration, largely from Switzerland, repopulated principalities like Baden, the Palatinate, the Kraichgau, Württemberg, and smaller locales.

By 1683, with the removal of the Turkish threat to Vienna, Habsburg policies encouraged Catholic migration southeastward into the Banat (at the Croatian-Hungarian frontier) at the same time that Protestant Prussia began actively bidding for recruits to populate both its towns and its rural districts east of the Elbe. North America remained an unknown and insignificant realm for German speakers not connected via the Baltic and North Sea trade with England and Holland. As late as the mid eighteenth century, fanciful artistic representations of America, such as those in the castle at Würzburg, reflected the lack of deep awareness among much of German-speaking Europe about North America.

Between 1683 and 1783, however, these early patterns changed decisively. Some 120,000 German-speaking immigrants poured into the English-speaking colonies, and others sprinkled the Caribbean and the Louisiana coast in the French colonial territories. A deceptive quality of this migration has misled many observers to believe that free church German speakers who joined with Dutch and Swiss emigrants to found Germantown, Pennsylvania (1684), typified the early migration. In reality, mostly Lutheran and Reformed church members came to North America, and the motivation for migration of these family-dominated groups was overwhelmingly economic. The partible inheritance customs of their villages of origin doomed succeeding generations to a marginal existence by the 1730s.

The sources of this migration had shifted. The northern towns and territories remained modest sources, but the vast majority of those traveling to North America came from the German southwest, essentially from along the Rhine, Main, Neckar, Ahr, Mosel, and smaller tributary routes of trade and communication. One important fact favored migration out of this area: prior Swiss migration into the German southwest territories touched off successive further migrations among both free church dissenters and economically ambitious and venturesome residents, many of whom had Swiss family antecedents, especially in the Kraichgau area southeast of Heidelberg.

Had the migration been left to happenstance, both the numbers and the final destinations of this eighteenth-century migration would have been quite different. Instead, when Queen Anne responded to the plight of the Palatine Protestants driven out of their war-ravaged homeland by a combination of bad weather and warfare, the migration took a novel turn. The preferred area of settlement for the 1709–1710 migration was royal New York. This migration, one that eventually brought 2,344 persons to that royal colony, paralleled that of one hundred Bernese adventurers at New Bern, North Carolina (which also attracted some 550 Palatines), which was conceived and executed by Christoph von Graffenried. Troubles with Native Americans in the Carolinas, the failure of a Swiss and Nassau-Siegen mining adventure in royal Virginia, and disputes with a royal governor and his friends in New York drove later migration toward proprietary Pennsylvania, where settlement in the Delaware River valley, and eventually some 150 miles (1,400 kilometers) to the north and west, created the most concentrated German-speaking culture in British North America. William Penn actively recruited in the Rhineland for his colony in 1679, producing the 1683 migration of Krefelder organized at Frankfurt that created "Germantown" in Pennsylvania despite its mixed population from the Netherlands, Switzerland, and the Holy Roman Empire.

By 1728, when migration began in earnest, Dutch shippers and English captains had developed the method of carrying hopefuls from the Reich or Switzerland to North America that came to be known as "redemption." By promising to redeem the costs of their passage by being bound to a prospective buyer, emigrants risked being imprisoned in an American port until someone to pay their passage could be found. But for the first ten years or so, the system operated well. Only as migration reached its peak in 1739–1740 and again between 1749 and 1753 did abuses give rise to the horrendous tales of starvation, thirst, disease, and death immortalized in Gottlieb Mittelberger's pamphlet "Eine Reise nach Pennsylvanien" ("A Journey to Pennsylvania"), almost certainly ghostwritten by, or at least for, the duke of Württemberg as a deterrent to prospective emigrants. In fact, perhaps 10 percent of the German speakers perished in crossing or seasoning, although death rates approaching 50 percent were not uncommon for young children, especially from Baltimore south to Savannah. Reformed Swiss settlements in South Carolina from Charleston to Orangeburg and along the Savannah River at Purrysburg were supplemented by those of French speakers. In the 1730s, exiled Salzburger Lutherans settled across the river in Georgia, at Ebenezer.

Until 1783 settlement patterns of the migration tended to reflect the Protestant southwest German village culture of the migrants. Although the Palatine speech dominated in most of the settlements, no transfers of intact villages occurred. Rather, the mix of skilled and semiskilled artisans, day laborers, and former marginal landholders tended to group together on a religious basis, and in the marketplaces that began at Germantown in 1701. Earliest arrivals occupied the best farmland and made their mark in trade and skilled handiwork; later groups fanned out westward, especially to Lancaster County and, later still, using Lancaster as a subsidiary hub of Philadelphia, moved down the Shenandoah Valley into Virginia and as far south as northwestern South Carolina. Philadelphia remained the real center of immigration, while Baltimore and Charleston fed smaller streams into upland settlements in the South. Moravian decisions to cultivate North Carolina and Pennsylvania as missionary fields also contributed to this pattern of settlement in the middle and southern colonies. New York, Boston, and smaller settlements as far north

as Waldoboro, Maine, remained distant third points of distribution.

The domestic arts cultivated among these German speakers suggest both the centrality of hearth and religious faith, and the crucial role German-speaking women played in perpetuating language, cooking, and adaptation of folk art traditions to North American conditions. The earliest form of domestic folk art was the iron stove plates that replicated the decorations of tile stoves in Europe. Domestic life remained solidly traditional; women's roles were defined by marriage and family except for occasional experiments such as Ephrata Cloisters (ca. 1728–1880s), the only radical Protestant semimonastic experiment in early America. Traditions of witchcraft and hexing also survived, and a host of cures, preventive incantations, and religious rituals guarded households, barns, and persons against curses. Although German women were sometimes accused of witchcraft, no evidence survives of organized violence against them, nor was property taken from them in reprisal. The insistence of German women should be credited as the central reason for the explosion in the numbers of German-language schools and congregations among Reformed, Lutheran, and Moravian groups between 1728 and 1783. German speakers adapted relatively quickly to dominant patterns of inheritance and succession, although early arrivals who had the option preferred to bestow property, including realty, upon children; sometimes they included daughters, with an eye toward keeping children in the vicinity of parents (at least in rural settlements). The English language quickly dominated trade and business; German was retained at home and in religious services.

Imperial prohibition of emigration in 1768, the effects of the Seven Years' War (1756–1763), and, even more significantly, the American Revolution, broke contacts between German speakers and their homelands. With the disappearance of imperial ties with London, support and communication with religious centers like Halle, Herrnhut, and Herborn declined. In post-Revolutionary North Carolina, Lutheran missionaries were sustained for a time by German supporters; increasingly, though, localization and fragmentation into subcultures characterized post-Revolutionary, German-speaking enclaves. The approximately one-ninth of all inhabitants of the United States who were German-speaking in 1790 exhibited both a successful transfer of linguistic, religious, consumption, and artisanal traditions from Switzerland and the southwestern regions of the empire and an adjustment to English-language culture, especially in the realms of trade and commerce, law, and politics—in the latter two areas, however, most German speakers tended to avoid careers beyond the local level. Home and church remained German speaking for another generation, and into the early 1800s marriage patterns still tended to be confined to other German speakers, although not strictly to coreligionists. Lutheran-Reformed marriages, in particular, were common. Urban German Jewish traders from Savannah to New York City remained far smaller in number than Sephardic Portuguese and Spanish groups, but kept alive both language and culture.

THE NINETEENTH CENTURY

Cultural transfer and adaptation began in earnest in the 1830s. The confrontation between radical liberals and conservative church members that persisted for much of the period until the outbreak of World War I, took shape with the arrival of both Catholic and Lutheran émigrés in 1839, followed by the fleeing liberal revolutionaries of 1848. The small 1804 migration of the Rappites, radical Württemberg pietists from the area of Fellbach, and of those spurred by crop failure to leave in 1817, eventually totaled about twenty thousand persons who chose the Midwest as their destination. Catholic Swiss and Austrians who settled in Ohio, Indiana, and Missouri, and "Old Lutherans" from Saxony who migrated through New Orleans and settled in Missouri (they organized the Missouri Synod at Chicago in 1847), helped to shape the contours of mainstream German-speaking cultures. The Lutherans grew prodigiously, so that they remained the largest religious denomination among German speakers in the United States, as they had been in the British colonies. By 1882, when some 250,000 arrived, the "German triangle" within lines connecting Cincinnati, Milwaukee, and Saint Louis was populated by German-speaking Lutherans, Catholics, Jews, and freethinkers. Older states like Virginia and the Carolinas continued to advertise for German workers to enlarge extant communities dating from colonial days, but German-speaking settlers largely streamed westward from New York City and north from New Orleans. Isolated pockets of political and religious idealists in Texas and on the West Coast, whose settlements were populated by poorer rural laborers and artisans, remained

smaller, as did migration of Volga Germans to the Dakotas in the 1880s.

No precise figures can be reconstructed for German-speakers from the Austro-Hungarian Empire for the nineteenth century, but the perhaps two thousand arrivals before 1850 were certainly dwarfed by the more than two hundred thousand who had migrated by 1900; they settled among Germans, and disproportionately in urban areas. Vienna, Burgenland, the Banat, and Transylvania contributed most of the German-speaking Austrians—almost none came from Upper Austria—which may explain the younger, male, working-class and urban artisanal character of Catholic "Austrian" migration and settlement in New York, New Jersey, Pennsylvania, Ohio, Illinois, and Wisconsin.

Much of the migration remained familial, although in the "Hungry Forties" it was characterized by chain migration that brought male members first, and wives, daughters, sisters, and mothers later. The German southwest and Switzerland provided much but not all of the migration before 1861, peaking at 215,009 in 1854. Some Catholic migration from Hannover and other north German states occurred in the antebellum period. Possibly the marginalized moor and fen residents there migrated again, as southwestern German speakers had left eighteenth-century villages for the British colonies. By the 1870s, however, the depopulation of central rural German states like Brandenburg, Mecklenburg, Pomerania, and Thuringia both created the new industrial centers in Saxony and the Ruhr, and contributed young male migrants to North American cities. In the decade 1880–1890, the record decennial rate of over 1.4 million migrants had been reached; it was never repeated because the new German industrial centers absorbed displaced rural workers.

The proportions of urban versus rural settlement in the United States varied over time; pre–Civil War migrants created mostly rural settlements, though there were substantial groups in New York, Philadelphia, and Baltimore. The antebellum migration had already begun to turn cities into German-speaking havens that the later migration completed; Cincinnati, Milwaukee, Chicago, Saint Louis, and Hammond, Indiana, counted German as their second language by 1890. Over time, German speakers were more urban in proportion to their total numbers than native-born Americans; by 1900 half of all German-born Americans lived in towns or cities of over one thousand residents. Nevertheless, rural

Swiss settlements such as New Glarus, Wisconsin; Catholic German transplantations like those at Saint Nanzianz, Wisconsin, and in Stearns County, Minnesota; and Lutheran Volga German farmsteads in Kansas, Nebraska, northeastern Colorado, and the Dakotas were founded at mid century or later.

The local religious traditions and quarrels of Europe shaped settlements that shared the same religion. The Benedictine monastery at Collegeville, Minnesota, an offshoot of the ancient Bavarian house near Regensburg, spread distinctive liturgical and sacramental pieties among its neighbors, as did its sister house at Latrobe, Pennsylvania. Both were different in derivation from the monastery and practices at Saint Meinrad, Indiana, a foundation of the Swiss Benedictines of Einsiedeln. Hutterites and Mennonites spread farm settlements westward and northward, perpetuating the pattern of communal settlements and religious customs that ignore national boundaries in the search for fruitful farmland on which to establish family life and the community of faith. Except within the free church groups, intermarriage quickly tended to include those from different points of origin, although European-born German speakers, regardless of country of origin, did not marry English speakers regularly, and almost not at all in rural settlements, until the second decade of the twentieth century. In Wisconsin, at least, where some marriage patterns have been studied, Swiss-born German speakers were almost four times as likely to marry a German-born person as a German-speaking person from the Austro-Hungarian empire; only in the twentieth century did English-speaking spouses become common.

The language that both bound together a highly disparate group and reflected its complexity had assumed printed form in North America by the 1730s. Christopher Sauer's publication of a High German newspaper and almanac concealed the everyday use of regional "dialect" that eventually was different both from printed High German and from the German used in the churches. Divisions among Palatines, Württembergers, Bernese, Sankt Gallener, Saxons, Hessians, and Prussians in the 1700s grew more intense among larger numbers of even more diverse new arrivals in the nineteenth century. Catholic areas south of the Main in Germany shared certain usage patterns and accents with Swiss, Bohemian, and Austrian regions, and Swiss and Palatine-Rhenish patterns were distinctly different from Bavarian-Austrian endings and usage;

north German Protestant areas developed usages influenced by Dutch, Danish, and even English.

In North America the press bound together highly disparate groups perhaps longer than daily usage warranted. As German-Catholic migration peaked in the Midwest in the Cincinnati-Saint Louis-Milwaukee triangle, conflict with the English-speaking Irish hierarchy ensued. The debate over which language would be used in German schools and German speakers' demands for German bishops, priests, and parishes exercised American Catholicism during the early 1890s. Yet, despite the fervor of a group led by Peter Paul Cahensly and the provocative Lucerne Memorial (1891), which demanded foreign prelates to care for German speakers, adjustment to the English language, a point on which the Irish hierarchy would not compromise, won Rome's support. By 1900 both Roman Catholic and Missouri Synod German-language schools existed, but the language of the playground was English, not German, and purely German-language parishes were the exception, not the rule. German Jewish settlement, especially notable in New York City's flourishing German-speaking culture, protected and cultivated the use of German, not least because it set this Jewish elite apart from the eastern European migration of the 1890s, which was regarded as scandalously uncultured by German-speaking Jews. German Reform Jews in Cincinnati repeated this pattern. Exactly the same distinction was used by the Swiss to look down their noses at Austrians, and by both Austrians and Germans to distance themselves from the Volga Germans, whose daily speech, steppe-originated habits, and pieties isolated them in places like Oshkosh and Sheboygan, Wisconsin, and Lincoln, Nebraska, from other German speakers.

The reception given German speakers and their response varied according to religious affiliation, place of origin and settlement, and language use. Colonial Protestant judgments of German speakers had been favorable, whether of the Swiss, the Prussians, or the Palatines and Württembergers. Grudging tolerance of the few Catholic German speakers in Pennsylvania and of German-speaking Jews tended to characterize these groups' reception through the first half of the nineteenth century, regardless of origin or place of settlement. The some twenty-five thousand to thirty thousand German Swiss of the colonial period continued to enjoy an enviably positive response through the nineteenth century, even as their numbers coincided with Austrian and German arrivals, peaking at 82,000 in the 1880s and from 1850 to 1921 contributing perhaps 250,000 persons to the total of German speakers in the United States.

THE TWENTIETH CENTURY

Americans commented favorably upon German speakers' fondness for Swiss and German folk music and dance and upon the symphonic music tradition created by giants like Leopold Damrosch, the founder of the New York Symphony Society in 1878, and the Bohemian-born Gustav Mahler, who directed at both the Metropolitan Opera and the New York Philharmonic between 1908 and 1911. The same public opinion was less positive about alcohol consumption on the Sabbath. Traditions of picnics, beer gardens, and a too-easygoing attitude toward Sunday blue laws plagued both Germans and Austrians. By the 1880s, German-speaking Catholics, Lutherans, and sometimes Jews found themselves cast into uneasy alliances to defend cultural practices under fire from statutes aimed at eradicating the teaching of the German language or enforcing prohibition at the local or state level. Politically, confessionally oriented German speakers voted the Democratic ticket and liberal Forty-eighters were ardent Republicans. German-speaking Catholics remained loyal to the Democratic party; the alliance of German speakers in the northern states—Jewish, secular, and Protestant—with the Grand Army of the Republic, however, disintegrated in the 1890s as nativist sentiments revived within the Republican party. The outbreak of World War I in 1914, which initially witnessed wild Austrian and German support for the Central Powers, later turned against all German speakers, both the circumspect and those who had indulged in sneering at Hungarians, Czechs, Poles, and Russians. Rural Volga Germans retained their Republican loyalties and a low profile. Swiss Germans were spared, perhaps because 1915 was the fiftieth anniversary of the founding of the North American Swiss Grütli-Bund that successfully drew upon William Tell's struggle for liberty. The Tell legend's supposed links with American values was a theme developed in the 1770s by the colonial printer Peter Miller. Yet even this group, wary of being thought "German," destroyed its German-language records.

A key distinction regarding "reception and response" must be made between governmental policy and popular impressions. Neither Austria nor Germany was particularly significant to American policy in the nineteenth century, and the suppression of the 1848 Revolution did nothing to enhance the reputation of the later German-speaking empires with American administrations. The popular images of Austrians, Germans, and Swiss, however, were largely positive. The brief hysteria of 1917–1918 was overcome with remarkable speed in the 1920s, although real damage had been done to the reputations of local German-speaking cultural institutions. Moreover, the older positive attitudes lingered in the postwar immigration laws that were tightened in 1924 and 1929. Even the continued stubborn insistence of German speakers in Milwaukee, Wisconsin, on sending a socialist to Congress in the person of Victor Berger did not prolong the relatively quick rejection of anti-German hysteria.

Between 1919 and 1932 some five hundred thousand German speakers immigrated to the United States, reflecting the new laws' preference for northern Europeans. It was out of these numbers that the Friends of the New Germany arose in 1932. From its membership the pro-Nazi Bund arose in 1936; it contained almost no older German, Swiss, or Austrian Americans. The flight of both Jewish and Gentile victims of the Nazis further complicated the reception and image of German speakers between 1919 and 1945. Austrian and Swiss sympathies for Nazi policies were effectively obscured in the United States by popular images of the Trapp family saga and the general American goodwill that had always been bestowed on the Swiss. Tourists from the United States in the 1840s discovered in Switzerland the chalet-style architecture they enthused over, creating a popular rage in America that Mark Twain reflected a generation later. This enthusiasm influenced Americans far more than the later German elite accomplishments of the Bauhaus under Laszlo Moholy-Nagy and Mies van der Rohe. The Swiss reputation for neutrality in war and religious tolerance, and the founding of the International Red Cross of Geneva in 1864 also contributed to their positive reception. Ironically, while the reception of Germans per se probably improved by the 1980s, when the tricentennial of German immigration was celebrated, the fiftieth anniversary of the *Anschluss* against Austria in 1988 and the accusations that Austrian Chancellor Kurt Waldheim had been a Nazi raised American doubts about the traditionally positive image of Austrians.

The absence of a unified linguistic, confessional, or political history of Europe and European

Russia accounts for much of the social history of German speakers in North America. The tradition of adapting local patterns of behavior or culturally inherited traits to new settlement areas was well established before North America emerged as a potential goal of German-speaking migrants. Even the gradual shift from familial, rural, or village migration to younger, male, urban migrants paralleled contemporary developments in Europe. Reinforcement of local custom and adaptation by successive arrivals sheared these later German speakers of whatever old country traditions they possessed that did not fit with the already dominant traits of the neighborhood where they finally settled. But their numbers in turn reinforced the prevailing self-definition of a locale. Thus, for example, German speakers around Belleville, Illinois, retained and perpetuated the cultivation of white asparagus. Despite prevailing evidence that most were nineteenth-century north German emigrants, many link their local self-image to the Pennsylvania Dutch, from whom none but a handful of early arrivals derive. Among the Swiss viticulture projects that flourished in North America at places like Nouvelle Vevey (now Vevay), Indiana, and New Switzerland, Ohio, many involved agricultural practices remarkably similar to those at Chabag in Bessarabia, as well as absorption of local agricultural techniques and marketing patterns.

More important, such a process of osmosis tended to redefine for the majority of outward-looking German speakers in a given area what America itself meant. Thus, in the colonial period, the need to draw up legal charters of incorporation to protect schools and churches against potential intrusion by English speakers helped to define America as a place of minimal government where private solutions to what might have been narrowly seen as group interest was broadly understood to be the American way to guard privileges and freedoms by keeping governmental intrusion minimal. In the nineteenth and twentieth centuries, perceptions of what America meant for a group of German speakers depended upon both transferred home country habits and values grouped around religious denomination, family, and occupation, as well as what advantages the local American context afforded. Where the two intersected, the definition was born; the osmosis process had already filtered out what was unusable or inconvenient.

The implications of this process were considerable. First, the perpetuation of transferred tradition among German speakers tended to take the form of a society or club. The *Verein,* organized around singing, gymnastics, religion, or craft and guild practices, tended to adopt a regional linguistic tradition (Swabian, Palatine, Hessian, Bernese). Where this was not possible, a dominant group (e.g., Palatines or New Glarus) became the catchall designation for all German speakers in the area. Second, these societies reinforced the accepted definitions not only of what was "German," "Austrian," or "Swiss" in America, but what was "American" as well. The values dictated by religious denomination, family, and occupation preserved remembered bits and pieces of old rights and privileges despite migration and resettlement.

As a consequence, with the exception of the self-consciously separatist minority, German speakers were able selectively to retain values and judgments even after the disappearance of language and more obvious ethnic habits. Among both Catholic and Lutheran groups—taken together, the largest component of German-speaking migrations—liberal views on economic and employment concerns could easily coexist with conservative, traditional, patriarchal, and hierarchical family and confessional values. Transferred Old World values made it possible for German speakers to become enthusiastic exemplars of American voluntarism, which they identified as "American" because the supposed characteristic of the new land replicated a pattern from their own cultural pasts. In its turn, the success of this process eventually obscured from later generations within and outside the German-speaking groups the perpetuated values that now simply look "American."

Finally, the national experience of the United States with the various German-speaking parts of Europe has reinforced certain of these tendencies while stigmatizing others. The policy of the United States in 1945 of defining Austria as a "victim" of Nazi aggression, coupled with an established sympathy for Switzerland and American military occupation of the German southwest, reinforced a three-centuries-old North American pattern. The proliferation of "Bavarian" folk dress, beer gardens, and music ratified and affirmed Austrian, Swiss, and southwest German cultural identities in popular culture, albeit in a way both amusing and frustrating to German speakers. By contrast, the customs, identities, and images of middle Germany, and even more so the eastern territories and the German areas of Russia, were lost or forgotten, often even among German-speaking descendants of people from those regions.

Nevertheless, by the 1990s, social historians seem to have begun to probe behind these habitual images, not least because of the tearing down of the Berlin Wall and the disappearance of the East German state in 1990. Renewed interest in the general problem of cultural transfer suggests that despite the wide variations among German speakers, social historians currently researching rural Minnesotans, urban working-class groups from New York to Chicago, and town residents have begun to emphasize the process of migration, cultural transfer, and resettlement in remarkably similar fashion. And the varieties of German-speaking settlements in America have properly begun to be seen as a transfer of the same adaptations that had long characterized the European-Asian experiences.

BIBLIOGRAPHY

The starting point for investigating the literature on the various German-speaking groups through the 1970s is *Harvard Encyclopedia of American Ethnic Groups,* Stephan Thernstrom, ed. (1980). See there Frederick C. Luebke, "Austrians," pp. 164–171; Kathleen Neils Conzen, "Germans," pp. 405–425; La Vern J. Rippley, "Germans from Russia," pp. 425–430; Arthur A. Goren, "Jews," pp. 571–598, esp. 576–579; Don Yoder, "Pennsylvania Germans," pp. 770–772; Leo Schelbert, "Swiss," pp. 981–987; and the literature cited in each. The following is a highly selective update drawn from a vast literature published in Europe and America since 1980. Students should consult the comprehensive bibliographies included in the *Yearbook of German-American Studies* and the *Austrian Studies Yearbook.*

Adams, Willi Paul, ed. *Die deutschsprachige Auswanderung in die Vereinigten Staaten: Berichte über Forschungsstand und Quellenbestände* (1980).

———. "A Dubious Host." *Wilson Quarterly* 7, no. 1 (1983).

Conzen, Kathleen Neils. "Peasant Pioneers: Generational Succession Among German Farmers in Frontier Minnesota." In *The Countryside in the Age of Capitalist Transformations: Essays in the Social History of Rural America,* edited by Steven Hahn and Jonathan Prude (1985).

———. *Making Their Own America: Assimilation Theory and the German Peasant Pioneer.* German Historical Institute Annual Lecture Series, no. 3 (1990).

Daniels, Roger. *Coming to America: A History of Immigration and Ethnicity in American Life* (1990).

Gatzke, Hans W. *Germany and the United States: A "Special Relationship"?* (1980).

Grabbe, Hans-Jürgen. "Das Ende des Redemptioner-Systems in den Vereinigten Staaten." *Amerikastudien/American Studies* 29 (1984).

Hacker, Werner. *Auswanderungen aus Baden und dem Breisgau: Obere und mittlere rechtsseitige Oberrheinlande im 18. Jahrhundert archivalisch dokumentiert* (1980).

———. *Auswanderung aus Rheinpfalz und Saarland im 18. Jahrhundert* (1987).

Hobbie, Margaret, comp. *Museums, Sites, and Collections of Germanic Culture in North America* (1980).

Keil, Hartmuth, and John B. Jentz, eds. *German Workers in Industrial Chicago, 1850–1910: A Comparative Perspective* (1983).

Lowenstein, Steven M. *Frankfurt on the Hudson: The German-Jewish Community of Washington Heights, 1933–1983* (1989).

Luebke, Frederick C. *Germans in the New World: Essays in the History of Immigration* (1990).

McMaster, Richard K. *Land, Piety, Peoplehood: The Establishment of Mennonite Communities in America, 1683–1790* (1985).

Moltmann, Günter. "Auswanderung als Revolutionsersatz?" In *Die Deutschen und die Revolution,* edited by Michael Salewski (1984).

Roeber, A. G. "In German Ways? Problems and Potentials of Eighteenth-Century German Social and Emigration History." *William and Mary Quarterly* 3d ser., 44, no. 4 (1987).

———. " 'The Origin of Whatever Is Not English Among Us': The Dutch-speaking and the German-speaking Peoples of Colonial British America." In *Strangers Within the Realm: Cultural Margins of the First British Empire,* edited by Bernard Bailyn and Philip D. Morgan (1991).

Schelbert, Leo. *The Swiss Migration to America: The Swiss Mennonites* (1966).

———, ed. *Yearbook of German American Studies: The Septicentennial of Swiss Independence.* Vol. 25 (1990).

———. "Schweizer Auswanderung in das Gebiet der Vereinigten Staaten von Nordamerika." In *Handbuch der schweizerischen Volkskunde,* edited by Paul Hugger (1991).

Schelbert, Leo, and Urspeter Schelbert. "Portrait of an Immigrant Society: The North American *Grütli-Bund, 1865–1915." Yearbook of German-American Studies.* Vol. 18 (1983).

Trefousse, Hans L., ed. *Germany and America: Essays on Problems of International Relations and Immigration* (1980).

Trommler, Frank, and Joseph McVeigh, eds. *America and the Germans: An Assessment of a Three-Hundred-Year History.* 2 vols. (1985).

von Hippel, Wolfgang. *Auswanderung aus Südwestdeutschland: Studien zur württembergischen Auswanderung und Auswanderungspolitik im 18. und 19. Jahrhundert* (1984).

Wokeck, Marianne S. "Promoters and Passengers: The German Immigrant Trade, 1683–1775." In *The World of William Penn,* edited by Richard S. Dunn and Mary Maples Dunn (1986).

———. "Harnessing the Lure of the 'Best Poor Man's Country': The Dynamics of German-speaking Immigration to British North America, 1683–1783." In *To Make America: European Emigration in the Early Modern Period,* edited by Ida Altman and James Horn (1991).

SEE ALSO **Alternative Forms of Education; American Social and Cultural Geography; Ethnicity; The Great Lakes Industrial Region; Immigration; Jews; Language; Political Culture; Religion.**

IBERIAN PEOPLES

José Ramón Remacha

IMMIGRATION FROM THE Iberian Peninsula to what is now the United States started in the sixteenth century and has been a constant element in the population movements from Europe to America. It can be considered in two periods: from its origins to the late 1800s and since then to the present. The turning point was the events which led to the Spanish-American War (1898), the aftermath of which had negative effects on direct immigration from Spain. Nevertheless, many Iberians went to South America and then made their way to the United States; others were Andalusians who left Spain through Gibraltar, went to work the sugar plantations in Hawaii and from there slowly moved to the San Francisco area in California between 1900 and 1910.

Immigration from Iberia was diminished in the 1920s by American immigration quotas, introduced in 1921 and revised in 1924 and 1927. The quota system remained in place until 1965, when national-origins quotas were abolished. However, the new system has not encouraged Iberian immigration. Consequently, the number of Iberians, compared with other nationalities, is quite low in the twentieth century.

Between 1820 and 1977, more than 250,000 Spaniards entered the United States. During the same period Portuguese immigrants numbered 450,000, almost 40 percent of them arriving after 1958. Settlers from the Canary Islands came to Louisiana and Texas. Minorcans arrived in Florida in the eighteenth century. Portuguese immigrants settled mainly in New England and California. Many Iberians reside in the areas first settled by Spain in the sixteenth to nineteenth centuries; more recent Spanish immigrants are found in Florida and New York. Miners from Asturias work in the West Virginia coalfields. Basques are in Nevada, Idaho, Wyoming, and California.

The motives for immigration have been diverse. Economic reasons have predominated since the sixteenth century. Religious motives were of consequence for Iberian Jews and Catholic missionaries in the sixteenth and seventeenth centuries; political reasons came to the forefront as a result of the political and social upheavals during and after the Spanish Civil War (1936–1939); and in the late twentieth century there has been immigration of professionals seeking to benefit from the advanced technology and science in the United States.

In 1980 the U.S. Census registered 177,437 people born in Portugal and 73,735 born in Spain. In 1990, taking into account official immigration data, the figures were about 89,000 Spaniards and 250,000 Portuguese.

COLONIAL PERIOD

During the sixteenth through eighteenth centuries, Spanish immigrants settled in what are now Florida, Louisiana, Missouri, California, Colorado, New Mexico, Texas, and Arizona. Many existing cities and towns were founded in the Spanish colonial era: Saint Augustine (1565), Santa Fe (1609), Albuquerque (1706), San Antonio (1718), San Diego (1769), San Francisco (1776), Los Angeles (1781), Santa Barbara (1786). Although the total number of immigrants was small, the presence and influence of the Spanish through language, customs, law, religion, architecture, folklore, and way of life left a decisive imprint on the societies emerging in the 1800s, when Manifest Destiny claimed the West for the United States.

Florida Florida has the oldest extant European settlement in the United States: on 8 September 1565, Saint Augustine was founded by members of an expedition, led by Pedro Menéndez de Áviles, which had left Cadiz, Spain, about two months earlier. Its nineteen ships had 1,504 persons on board; they included silversmiths, locksmiths, millers, farmers, and tanners, some of whom were accompanied by wives and children. By 1585 this outpost had a council house, a church, and several stores. In 1598 there were more than 150 houses and a population of 625.

From Saint Augustine the missionaries established a number of settlements for the Indians: by 1674 there were eight on the east coast and twenty-seven in the interior, thirteen of which were in Apalachee, near present-day Tallahassee. In 1571 Spanish Jesuits from Saint Augustine established a mission near what is now Jamestown, Virginia. A census in 1674 counted 13,152 Christian Indians.

The social structure of these communities embraced three groups: soldiers and public officials, missionaries, and laypersons. The *encomienda* system was not followed in Florida; rather, all three groups depended on the annual subsidy (*situado*) drawn from the royal treasury and distributed by the governor. This system gave rise to frequent tensions among the civil, military, and religious establishments. Further roots of tensions among the clergy in the eighteenth century arose from the fact that most of the Franciscans who remained in Florida were not continental Spaniards but Creoles.

Louisiana The population of Louisiana increased by more than 300 percent during the Spanish administration (1762–1803). Two groups of immigrants accounted for the increase: one from Spain, the other from Nova Scotia (Acadia). The former was a group of 2,500 immigrants who came from Spain between 1778 and 1781. A contingent of one hundred, recruited in Granada for the purpose of introducing flax and hemp, brought the seeds with them. The project failed, and most of those farmers returned to Spain by 1784. A contingent of sixty from Málaga obtained the same result, reportedly due to the soil conditions and climate of Louisiana; they decided to stay, however, and founded the town of New Iberia. The third and largest contingent came from the Canary Islands and settled in Galveztown, Valenzuela, Barataria, New Orleans, and Saint Bernard Parish as fishers and hunters.

Spanish Louisiana influenced the legislation of the future state through the Civil Code of 1808, inspired by Spanish law. In the American Revolution Governor Bernardo de Gálvez played a decisive role in defeating the British at Mobile (1780) and Pensacola (1781), and in ousting them from several outposts in Mississippi.

The Acadian immigration consisted of more than three thousand French Canadians desperately looking for a place to settle since leaving North America in 1763. The expedition, financed by King Charles III of Spain, sailed from St. Malo, France, to New Orleans in 1785.

Texas Two Spanish missions were established in eastern Texas in 1690. San Francisco de los Tejas and Santa María de los Tejas did not last long, however, being abandoned by 1693. Five more were founded in 1716 in the same area, near the Neches River, and three more in 1717 near present-day Natchitoches, Louisiana. A presidio (fort) to protect them from French incursions was established in 1721 at Los Adaes, on the Sabine River. The settlers were soldiers, clergy, and farmers; many of the latter were natives. Another group of missions was founded in western and central Texas: five in the second half of the seventeenth century and twenty-one in the eighteenth century.

San Antonio offers a prototype of a Spanish colonial city. There were four social groups: the military, civilians, missionaries, and natives. The first three were organized in three interindependent structures: the presidio, the cabildo (municipal council), and the missions. At the founding of the city in 1718 each chose a different name: San Antonio de Béjar (presidio), San Fernando de Béjar (cabildo), and San Antonio de Valero (mission), respectively. The core of the civilian group was sixteen families who had come from the Canary Islands in 1731. They played a prominent role in municipal affairs, especially in the eighteenth century.

In 1772 the population of San Antonio increased as the result of an official decision to transfer the eastern establishments to the west. In the 1730s there were five missions in the area of San Antonio, each with a considerable number of Indians from tribes of the surrounding area. They were self-governed under the supervision of the Spanish missionaries (one or two per mission). Each mission had a ranch on which cattle were raised, and crops were cultivated; there also were craft workshops and a school.

The census of 1 July 1795 shows a total of 120 military men; the officers were Spanish-born citizens, often of noble origin; the soldiers were 20 percent Indians, 30 percent Creoles, and the rest of mixed origin. The civilian population was 870 in 1770 and 1,200 in 1792.

New Mexico The first settlements in the Rio Grande Valley, San Gabriel and San Juan de los Caballeros, north of Sante Fe, were established by the expedition of Juan de Oñate in 1598. Those settlements were abandoned because of Pueblo Indian claims to that land; in compliance with Spanish colonial law prohibiting encroachment upon Indian lands, the Spanish settlers moved south and founded the city of Santa Fe in 1609. But the permanent settlement of New Mexico took place in 1692 as the result of the expedition led by Don Diego de Vargas, composed of one hundred soldiers, seventy families, eighteen missionaries, and three thousand nine hundred head of cattle. By the end of the eighteenth century, thirty-five missions had been built. The relations between Spaniards and the Pueblo Indians were peaceful and friendly between 1697 and 1821. During the 1700s the quartermaster of Santa Fe purchased grain from the Pueblos, and in times of crop failure the civilians obtained food supplies from the Indians as well. Spanish customs and methods of agriculture can be found among the farm communities in the northern part of the state, and about three hundred families have genealogies linking them directly with the original settlers. Spanish has been maintained as a language in some Indian communities and is officially upheld by the constitution of New Mexico.

California The settlement of California took place late in the eighteenth century. San Diego (1769), Monterey (1770), San Francisco (1776), Los Angeles (1781), and Santa Barbara (1786) were founded as the result of the expeditions led by the Franciscan Junípero Serra and Governor Gaspar de Portolá. Both were Spaniards, from Mallorca and Lérida, respectively, who brought with them a small number of their countrymen. The settlement was accomplished by establishing a chain of twenty-one missions and attracting the Indian population of the surrounding areas to them. The civilian population was few and mainly from New Spain. In 1800 there were forty friars, 1,800 Spanish and Creoles, and more than 10,000 Indians. The Spanish origin of the missionaries accounts for the architectural style of the California missions, which takes after the style of country houses in Catalonia and the Balearic Islands and is quite different from the style of the missions in Arizona and New Mexico.

CONTEMPORARY IMMIGRATION

The Spanish Immigration In the nineteenth century the number of Spaniards who came to the United States was small. Between 1820 and 1900 the figure recorded by the *Annual Report of the Secretary of Labor* (1923) was almost forty-two thousand. Louisiana, New York, California, and Florida were the states with the most Spanish workers in the nineteenth century. The census of 1900 shows only 7,050 Spaniards out of a total of 10.3 million foreign-born residents. However, direct immigration recovered again between 1903 and 1921, reaching a total of 175,000. This trend was halted by the Immigration Laws of 1921, which had a Spanish quota of 912 per year, reduced by the Act of 1924 to 131 and adjusted in 1929 to 252. Three groups of immigrants in this period had similar patterns of immigration, motivation, and degree of assimilation: the Andalusians, the Basques, and the Asturians.

In the first decade of the twentieth century, about eight thousand Andalusians sailed from Gibraltar to Hawaii as workers for the Hawaiian Sugar Planters Association. They were offered free transportation, free housing, and fixed wages. Shortly after their arrival on the plantations, they became interested in moving to San Francisco. By 1920 most of them had settled in the city or its vicinity (San Leandro, Hayward, and Crockett). This immigration flow was large enough that in the census of 1910 California outranked New York in Spanish population.

The Basques started to arrive in the 1850s and, contrary to common belief, the majority of them were not shepherds before their immigration. They simply met a need for herders registered by the American sheep-raising industry in the late 1800s. Since they had been farmers, were used to hard work, and were willing to endure hardships, herding was a logical choice of occupation. Besides, the new job did not require a knowledge of English. The enterprising herder worked his way up to camp tender, took good care of the herd, and since he was often paid in sheep, acquired animals of his own and went into business for himself. Basque shepherds had few competitors in the American West, and people assumed that any Basque was a reliable shepherd.

But during the first years of the twentieth century, stock raisers had access to less and less open land, and the Taylor Grazing Act of 1934 virtually eliminated the open range. Consequently, many Basques returned home; and when they arrived they spread the word that there was no work available in the United States. That made the situation critical again. By the 1940s the ranchers of Nevada, Idaho, and other states petitioned the government for help with an acute shortage of shepherds by increasing the immigration quotas. Consequently, in the 1950s more than one thousand Basques came with three-year contracts as shepherds, under the supervision of the Western Range Association (the California Range Association until 1960). Boise, Idaho, and San Francisco are the main cities where the earliest Basque sheepherders settled.

In the 1890s the Asturians established prosperous communities based on cigar manufacturing, first in Key West and then in Tampa, Florida. Their business has developed into an important industry with thousands of employees. Ybor City, a district of Tampa, is the center for the Spanish community, and its Centro Asturiano is noted for its cultural and social activities. By 1930 the Spanish community in Tampa was about nine thousand. In the late twentieth century Florida ranks second, after New York, in terms of Spanish population. Another group of Asturians settled in West Virginia between 1920 and 1940. They came as coal miners, and some of them later became steelworkers in Clarksburg, West Virginia, and in Gary, Indiana.

THE PORTUGUESE IMMIGRATION

Some Portuguese (as well as Spanish) came to the United States for religious reasons after non-Christians were outlawed in the Iberian Peninsula. The oldest Jewish congregation in the United States, Shearith Israel, was founded in New York City by Portuguese in 1654; services were conducted there in Portuguese or Spanish until the 1850s. In Newport, Rhode Island, another Sephardic synagogue was founded in 1763 by Isaac Touro and sustained by Aaron Lopez, who owned a large whaling fleet.

The immigration of Portuguese workers was initiated in the eighteenth century by recruitment of seafaring men. The opportunity for neutral trade created by the Napoleonic Wars meant growth for the American fleet and an increased need for crewmen. The Azoreans, located in a strategic point of passage for the American vessels, constituted a source of cheap labor for the merchant and whaling fleets of Massachusetts and Rhode Island. But the Azoreans usually ended their service upon reaching American ports. This was usually accomplished after months and sometimes years. Having reached Newport, Boston, or New Bedford, most Portuguese immigrants became fishermen, factory workers, dairymen, or farmers. They settled in Massachusetts and Rhode Island, and some went to California. In 1850 the census recorded only 109 Portuguese in California, settled mainly in the area of San Francisco. In 1860 the figures increased to 1,580 and by 1880 there were 8,061. Drawn by "gold fever," beginning in 1848, they arrived directly from the Azores, traveled overland from New Bedford, or deserted from clippers or whalers when they reached San Francisco.

Another area of settlement was Louisiana, where between 1840 and the 1870s several contingents of Portuguese men arrived with contracts to work on the sugar plantations. They came directly from the Portuguese mainland and also from the islands, their numbers totaling a few thousand; but by the 1880s, due to the hard contract labor conditions, they slowly dispersed and many went to California. Another settlement was made in 1849 near Springfield, Illinois, where a few hundred Protestants from Madeira established a community under the sponsorship of the American Protestant Society.

The Portuguese were particularly hard hit by legislation enacted in 1917 that required prospective immigrants to pass a literacy test. The only ones allowed to enter without passing such a test were those who had come to join their families. By 1920, there were 106,000 Portuguese in the United States, two-thirds of them living in Massachusetts, Rhode Island, and Connecticut. Nearly all were from the Azores.

Accustomed to coaxing crops from the land of their home islands, the Azoreans farmed New England's soil with great success. But between 1870 and 1920 the majority of Portuguese immigrants who settled in New England found work in the textile mills of New Bedford, Fall River, and Lawrence, Massachusetts. The Portuguese communities of California flourished in the area around Oakland, where an immigrant network was very active. They were dedicated to cattle raising and farming. San Leandro had 12,260 Portuguese residents in 1920, most of them from the western Azores, some from Madeira and Cape Verde, and very few from the Portuguese mainland. By 1939, Portuguese dairymen controlled 75 percent of the cattle business in California.

The Portuguese have become among the largest Iberian immigrant groups in the United States. An estimated 161,000 arrived between 1959 and 1977. In the period between 1866 and 1930, there were 783,695 legal immigrants from the mainland, the Azores, and Madeira.

SOCIOLOGICAL DIMENSIONS

Upon arrival, those who had family or friends waiting for them followed a clear-cut path. Others had their destination printed on a card pinned to their clothing and were directed to trains bound to different areas of the United States. The Basques were generally among the former group. Their primary destination was a hotel or lodge run by a compatriot who would direct them to jobs and provide transportation. Those hotels or lodges served as the Basques' homes when they were not on the range, as places to keep their possessions, and as places to meet other Basques. The owner of the hotel often was a reliable patron (as banker, lawyer, judge, adviser, and intermediary with the English-speaking community) for the new immigrant.

In the New World even the church, an important social factor in the Iberian villages, seemed foreign to the immigrants. This was mainly due to the language barrier. Until very recent times the Catholic hierarchy—mainly Irish—strongly discouraged the use of Spanish. Many immigrant communities paid for the transportation of priests who would say Mass in their own language (Spanish, Basque, or Portuguese) and keep the old customs alive. Sometimes traveling priests rode miles to hold services for Basque congregations.

Nevertheless, the Basques have become assimilated; while keeping their own ways and customs, they are proud of being American. During World War II the Basques formed their own company in the Idaho Volunteer Reserve. Elko, Nevada, is the site of the National Basque Festival, held every 4 July.

In the Portuguese communities, many first-generation newcomers never learned English and assimilation was very difficult. They lived in crowded conditions and had to endure long hours of factory work. In the second generation, faced with the pressure to become more "American" many anglicized their names: Perry from Pereira, Curry from Correa, Weaver from Teixedor, Smith from Ferreira, White from Alba, Wood from Madeira, Cross from Cruz, Rodrick from Rodrigues. The third generation often learned a few words from their grandparents. But all in all, the process of acculturation is complete by the fourth generation. And though they have adopted American ways, they still retain much of their national culture. One of the most popular Portuguese festivals is the Festa do Espírito Santo, celebrated at Pentecost. And the feast of Our Lady of Good Voyage (Nossa Senhora de Boa [f.] Viagem), held in Gloucester, Massachusetts, every June, includes the blessing of the fleet by the archbishop of Boston.

Cultural assimilation or acculturation has frequently been assumed to have beneficial consequences for both economic progress and psychological well-being. Although these assumptions seem plausible, findings by Alejandro Portes and Ruben Rumbaut (1990) cast doubt on them. These authors indicate that social integration becomes easier and faster when the immigrant keeps at least a good share of his or her cultural origin; in this sense, the Cuban and Puerto Rican immigrations offer good examples. Other groups which try drastically to substitute one cultural background for another fail economically and psychologically because a crisis of self-esteem in their behavioral pattern often occurs. And as far as the immigration of Iberian groups is concerned, assimilation takes place while a significant degree of the original culture is retained.

BIBLIOGRAPHY

General

Altman, Ida. *Emigrants and Society: Extremadura and Spanish America in the Sixteenth Century* (1989).

Bannon, John Francis. *The Spanish Borderlands Frontier, 1513–1821* (1970).

Bolton, Herbert Eugene. *The Colonization of North America, 1492–1783* (1932).

Fernández-Shaw, Carlos M. *Hispanic Presence in the United States* (1992).

Hoffman, Paul E. *A New Andalucia and a Way to the Orient: The American Southeast During the Sixteenth Century* (1990).

Lick, Sue Fagalde. *The Iberian Americans* (1990).

Lummis, Charles F. *The Spanish Pioneers* (1893).

Portes, Alejandro, and Ruben G. Rumbaut. *Immigrant America* (1990).

Weber, David J., ed. *New Spain's Far Northern Frontier: Essays on Spain in the American West, 1540–1821* (1979).

ETHNIC AND RACIAL SUBCULTURES

Florida

Gannon, Michael V. *The Cross in the Sand: The Early Catholic Church in Florida, 1513–1870* (1965).

Lyon, Eugene. *The Enterprise of Florida: Pedro Menéndez de Áviles and the Spanish Conquest of 1565–1568* (1976).

Tebeau, Charlton W. *A History of Florida* (1971).

Louisiana

Din, Gilbert C., *The Canary Islanders of Louisiana* (1988).

Gayarré, Charles. *The Spanish Domination. History of Louisiana,* Vol. 3 (1854–1866; repr. 1972).

Montero de Pedro, José. *Españoles en Nueva Orleans y Luisiana* (1979).

Oppenheim, Leonard. *Louisiana's Civil Law Heritage* (1958).

Thompson, Buchanan P. *Spain, Forgotten Ally of the American Revolution* (1976).

New Mexico

Bancroft, Hubert H. *Works,* vol. 17, *History of Arizona and New Mexico, 1530–1888* (1889).

Chávez, Thomas E., ed. *Conflict and Acculturation: Manuel Alvarez's 1842 Memorial* (1989).

González, Nancie L. *The Spanish Americans of New Mexico: A Distinct Heritage* (1967).

Texas

Domínguez, Maria Esther. *San Antonio, Tejas, en la época colonial (1718–1821)* (1989).

Myres, Sandra L. *The Ranch in Spanish Texas, 1691–1800* (1969).

Poyo, Gerald E., and Gilberto M. Hinojosa. *The Tejano Origins in Eighteenth-Century San Antonio* (1991).

California

Bancroft, Hubert H. *Works.* Vol. 19. *History of California.* Vol. 2. *1801–1824* (1886).

Cutter, Donald. *California in 1792: A Spanish Naval Visit* (1990).

Guest, Francis F. *Fermín Francisco de Lasuén (1736–1803): A Biography* (1973).

Portuguese

Baganha, Maria Ioanis Benis. *Portuguese Emigration to the United States, 1820–1930* (1990).

Carvalho Arroteia, Jorge. *A Emigração portuguesa: Suas origens e distribuição* (1983).

Basques

Lane, Richard H., and William A. Douglass. *Basque Sheep Herders of the American West: A Photographic Documentary* (1985).

SEE ALSO **Immigration**; and various essays in "**Periods of Social Change,**" and "**Regionalism and Regional Subcultures.**"

THE FRENCH AND FRENCH-CANADIANS

Gerard J. Brault

LIKE THE ENGLISH, the French were relatively late in establishing permanent colonies in America. By the time Jamestown (1607) and Quebec City (1608) were founded, some two hundred thousand Spaniards had already settled in the New World. The French were slow to populate New France, the vast territory they claimed in the seventeenth and eighteenth centuries, and in the end, they were unable to defend it against their English rivals. When New France reached its apogee at the beginning of the eighteenth century, it encompassed the entire eastern half of Canada and the heartland of the present-day United States. Today, a large number of American place names, from Detroit to New Orleans, give some idea of the extent of this empire.

The fact that the French were part of the older European migration to America explains in part the group's high ranking among the largest ancestry groups in the United States, according to the 1980 census: English, fifty million; German, forty-nine million; Irish, forty million; African Americans, twenty-one million; French, thirteen million; Italian, twelve million; Scottish, ten million; Polish, eight million; Mexican, eight million; American Indian, seven million; Dutch, six million. Actually, the statistics for the French are misleadingly low, as persons claiming French-Canadian ancestry, who constitute one of the major ethnic groups in the Northeast (the Franco-Americans), were listed separately. Data concerning the Cajuns of Louisiana were also entered under two classifications. In both areas, respondents were no doubt inconsistent in identifying themselves as being of either French or French-Canadian ancestry.

The number of United States residents born in France—120,200 in 1980—is a much more reliable figure and has remained fairly constant since 1860, fluctuating between a low of 103,000 (1940) and a high of 153,000 (1920). However, the French natives' share of the total United States population peaked in 1860 (34.9 percent) and has been declining steadily ever since (.053 percent in 1980). Unlike many other nationalities, the French-born are widely distributed throughout the United States. Immigrants from France and their descendants do not generally share the traditions and social life of the Franco-Americans of the Northeast or the Cajuns of Louisiana.

Persons whose primary language is French predominate in Quebec and are very much in evidence in certain other Canadian provinces. In the United States, by comparison, French is infrequently heard and, in traditionally francophone areas, on the wane. However, all things considered, the descendants of the early French settlers on this continent have, against overwhelming odds, maintained their language and culture to a remarkable degree, and their survival as an ethnic group is nothing short of extraordinary.

NEW FRANCE

Early Settlements After a number of abortive attempts to gain a foothold at various sites in North America—such as Charlesbourg-Royal near present-day Quebec City in 1541, Parris Island, South Carolina, in 1562, and Saint Croix Island on the border between New Brunswick and Maine in 1604—the French finally succeeded in 1608. In that year, Samuel de Champlain (1567?–1635) founded Quebec City. The first building was an elaborate *habitation,* a wooden fort complete with storehouse, lodgings, gallery, and dovecote, erected where the church of Notre-Dame-des-Victoires stands today in Place Royale at the base of the Rock of Quebec. Trois-Rivières (1634) and Montreal (1642) extended the line of trading posts south and west along the Saint Lawrence River. The many tributaries feeding New France's principal watercourse provided convenient routes to the Great Lakes and other sources of beaver pelts—prized in Europe as the best material for hat felt—and the fur trade soon came to overshadow fishing, the colony's other main industry during the French régime.

The main Indian tribal groups encountered by the French in the early years of the colony belonged to the Eastern Woodlands culture, which stretched southwest as far as Illinois and south as far as North Carolina. Certain tribes responded quickly and favorably to French efforts to enlist their aid in the fur trade, gaining in return goods such as axes, knives, and clothing. However, contact with the newcomers brought deadly epidemics of influenza, measles, and smallpox. Also, the native peoples' culture was profoundly affected. Like the subarctic tribes to the north, they soon abandoned subsistence hunting, fishing, and gathering and became dependent on the French for their livelihood. In 1609, Champlain initiated a policy of siding with the Huron against their enemies, the Iroquois. The latter were constantly at war with the French, and by mid century had dispersed the Huron and their Indian confederates. Down through the years, the Iroquois seriously disrupted the French fur trade.

Port Royal, Acadia, was first settled in 1605 by Pierre Du Gua de Monts (1558?–1628) but was abandoned the following year. Although revived in 1610 by Jean de Biencourt de Poutrincourt (1557–1615), this tiny outpost, as well as others in the region known today as the Maritime Provinces, remained relatively isolated and never experienced the steady growth of the colony known as Canada along the Saint Lawrence during the French régime. Ravaged by war, Acadia changed hands a number of times before coming under permanent British rule in 1710. During the French and Indian War (1754–1763), some seven thousand of its inhabitants were deported to the American colonies to the south and elsewhere in the tragic episode known as *Le Grand Dérangement* (the Great Uprooting, 1755–1757). Only a minority of Acadians returned to their homeland after the Treaty of Paris; the remainder resettled in French Canada, France, Louisiana, and elsewhere.

The Seigneurial System The early colonization of New France was left to companies such as the Compagnie de Canada (1613), the Compagnie de Caën (1621), and the Hundred Associates (1627). The crown granted charters to associations of merchants who, in exchange for a monopoly on the fish and fur trade, contracted to transport colonists to the New World and maintain them there. The Hundred Associates instituted the seigneurial system of land distribution and settlement. An off-shoot of feudal practices that prevailed in France before the Revolution, this form of economic organization was based on the seigneury, a large tract of land divided into long, rectangular lots, the choicest parcels usually fronting a river. The principal owners—noblemen or religious orders—ceded lots to *habitants,* tenants who farmed the land. The original seigneuries were situated in and around Quebec City, Trois-Rivières, and Montreal; later concessions filled in areas between these cities and along the colony's main rivers. Approximately two hundred seigneuries were granted during the French régime, and the system persisted in Quebec until it was finally abolished in 1854.

The companies failed to live up to their agreements to recruit settlers and provide for them, however, and in 1663 there were only twenty-five hundred inhabitants in all of New France (Acadia had now come under British control). Company agents and merchants employed a large number of voyageurs to transport goods and men to and from the hinterland, where beaver were plentiful and Indians were willing to assist in the trapping. French authorities inveighed to little avail against unlicensed *coureurs de bois* (trappers) who flouted the companies' rules and tended to undermine the monopoly. Meanwhile, the population of the American colonies along the eastern seaboard had grown to about eighty thousand and was busily engaged in varied industries and shipping.

Missionaries From the time of Columbus, conversion of the native peoples was one of the stated motives for establishing settlements in America. The first Roman Catholic missionary active in New France was Jessé Fléché (d. 1611?), a secular priest who came to Acadia with Biencourt de Poutrincourt in 1610. Jesuits arrived there the following year. Four Récollet fathers reached the Saint Lawrence outposts in 1615; Jesuits joined them ten years later. Two female-cloistered communities came to Quebec City in 1639: the Hospitalières, who founded the first hospital in New France, and the Ursulines, who opened a school for French and Indian girls. Conversions were sparse until 1642, when Ville-Marie was founded on the site of present-day Montreal for the express purpose of evangelizing the Indians. However, many natives continued to show hostility to the French missionaries, and in the 1640s they tortured and murdered several of them. The *Jesuit Relations,* vivid firsthand accounts of daily living in the infant colony published annually in Paris between 1632 and 1673, were widely read in France and are regarded today as documents of prime historical and sociological importance.

The Rise and Fall of New France   A new era dawned when Jean-Baptiste Colbert (1619–1683), a man of uncommon energy and vision, was named minister of finance under Louis XIV in 1661, and Jean Talon (1625–1694) was appointed to the newly created post of intendant (administrator) of New France in 1665. The Hundred Associates' seigneurial rights in Canada were revoked by the crown and the fledgling colony became a royal province. In 1665, the Carignan-Salières regiment, eleven hundred strong, was sent from France to put an end to Iroquois raids. After achieving a measure of success, the unit was recalled in 1668. Some four hundred officers and men, offered land and other inducements by the crown, chose to settle on land along the Richelieu River at strategic points bordering on New York and Vermont.

In a concerted effort to stimulate population growth, a large number of seigneuries were granted to French noblemen who pledged to recruit colonists, some nine hundred Frenchwomen of marriageable age (the so-called *filles du roi*) were transported to Canada over an eleven-year period beginning in 1665, and single men were encouraged to wed and have large families. Talon also strove mightily to make New France more self-sufficient. However, the development campaign was short-lived and came to a halt after Talon returned home in 1672 and, not long afterward, Colbert fell out of favor with the king. Meanwhile, French explorers and missionaries ranged far and wide from Hudson Bay to the Gulf of Mexico to stake claims for France throughout the continent. The exploits of Louis Jolliet (1645–1700), René-Robert Cavelier de La Salle (1643–1687), the Jesuit priest Jacques Marquette (1637–1675), and Pierre-Esprit Radisson (1636–1710), who spent part of his life in the employ of the British-owned Hudson's Bay Company, are among the proudest achievements of the French in North America.

France reached the zenith of its power and prestige in Europe following the Treaty of Nijmegen in 1678 and the annexation of Strasbourg in 1681, but soon afterward it fell into decline in the wake of military and diplomatic reverses. These events caused major repercussions throughout America, exacerbating local conflicts over territorial and commercial rights. In the complex settlement at Utrecht (1713–1714) after the War of the Spanish Succession, France managed to keep its frontiers intact at home but was obliged to sacrifice the Hudson Bay Territory, Nova Scotia (except the island of Cape Breton), and Newfoundland. Hemmed in on two sides, New France, whose twenty thousand inhabitants were still largely concentrated along the Saint Lawrence, now faced the growing menace of the thirteen English colonies and their 350,000 inhabitants.

The French mounted an ambitious fortress-building program in their North American possessions, the most important construction being at Louisbourg on Cape Breton, guarding the entrance to the Cabot Strait and the Saint Lawrence. Official efforts to stimulate immigration met with success, and by 1754 the population of New France had risen to about seventy thousand. Although the English colonies experienced relatively less rapid growth, they nevertheless boasted over a million inhabitants by mid century.

The defeat at Quebec City in 1759 of French forces led by Louis-Joseph, marquis de Montcalm (1712–1759), by British troops under the command of James Wolfe (1727–1759) proved decisive. By the Treaty of Paris in 1763, France ceded to Great Britain Cape Breton, Canada, and all territory east of the Mississippi River. Meanwhile, in a secret pact ratified late in 1762, France had yielded all her possessions west of the Mississippi and the city of New Orleans to Spain as compensation for entering the war on the French side earlier the same year. In the war, though, Spain lost Florida to the British.

Louisiana   In 1682 La Salle descended the Mississippi River to its mouth and claimed a vast area—parts of the present states of Arkansas, Colorado, Iowa, Kansas, Louisiana, Minnesota, Mississippi, Missouri, Montana, Nebraska, North Dakota, Oklahoma, South Dakota, and Wyoming—for Louis XIV, in whose honor the territory was named. In 1699 Pierre Le Moyne d'Iberville (1661–1706) began building forts along the river, as well as settlements at what are now Biloxi, Mississippi, and Mobile, Alabama, but by 1717 only about four hundred individuals were residing in the entire colony. In that year, the Company of the West, later known as the Company of the Mississippi, was established under the financier and speculator John Law (1671–1729), and it began actively recruiting French emigrants. To augment the total, hundreds of female hospital and prison inmates, and an even larger number of male convicts, were deported to Louisiana. Many Germans and Alsatians were also persuaded to settle there, and slaves were brought from Africa. In 1718 the city of New Orleans was founded, and four years later it became the territory's capital. Land was freely granted to enterprising individuals (Law gave out 119 major concessions), who were later joined by former French plantation owners from the West Indies. The most successful of these became the local aristocracy.

OTHER FRENCH MIGRANTS

About 1758, some three hundred Acadian exiles residing in the American colonies were permitted to emigrate to Louisiana. Hundreds more reached the colony in two successive waves in the 1760s and 1780s. These immigrants, who settled in present-day southern Louisiana apart from the other French population, were the ancestors of the Cajuns. The term "Creole" is a confusing one, for it is applied not only to descendants of early Spanish or French settlers in the Gulf States but also to persons of mixed French or Spanish and black descent.

Of the approximately quarter-million francophones in Louisiana today, one source estimates that about one-fourth speak one of a variety of creole dialects, the rest Cajun French. At the beginning of the twentieth century, a large number of Cajuns migrated west across the Texas border to the Golden Triangle cities of Beaumont, Orange, and Port Arthur, and neighboring communities. Many Cajuns today can be found in the large urban areas of Texas—Dallas, Fort Worth, Galveston, and Houston.

Like many other ethnic groups, the Cajuns of Louisiana experienced a cultural renaissance and gained more political influence beginning in the 1960s. A high point was the passage of a series of laws in 1968 declaring the state to be officially bilingual and establishing the Council for the Development of French in Louisiana. In 1971, twenty-two parishes were designated as a cultural region called Acadiana. A number of Cajun popular singers and musicians came into national prominence about this time.

The Huguenots After 1627, Huguenots (or French Protestants—the term may be derived from German *Eidgenossen,* "confederates") were officially banned in New France, but a few nevertheless managed to settle there, especially in the eighteenth century. They were never, however, granted religious freedom. Du Gua de Monts played a prominent role in early colonization efforts; others became involved in the fur trade or served in the military.

The situation was quite different in the American colonies. After Louis XIV's revocation of the Edict of Nantes in 1685, hundreds of thousands of Huguenots fled France. Hundreds settled in the American colonies, notably in Massachusetts, New York, and South Carolina, where they generally were given a warm welcome. New Oxford, Massachusetts, and New Rochelle, New York, were founded by French Protestant refugees in 1687 and 1688, respectively. Descendants of the Huguenots (for example, Elias Boudinot, James Bowdoin, Alexander Hamilton, John Jay, Francis Marion, Paul Revere) played a prominent role in the American Revolution, while others distinguished themselves in the business world.

Nineteenth-Century French Immigration to the United States In the aftermath of the French Revolution of 1789 and throughout the following century, small groups of French émigrés settled various areas of the United States. Some communities, such as Asylum, Pennsylvania, Champ d'Asile, Texas, and Demopolis, Alabama, were short-lived; others, like Gallipolis, Ohio, absorbed new arrivals and soon lost their French character. At mid century, thousands of Frenchmen, mostly sailors and expatriates living in other parts of the United States or Latin America, joined in the California gold rush. Some six thousand would-be miners headed for San Francisco, which soon had a French quarter and French-language theater. However, just as many natives of France were living in New York City in 1855, and Saint Louis, Missouri, and other urban areas were also popular destinations.

Utopian Communities In 1840 Étienne Cabet (1788–1856) published a utopian novel entitled *Voyage en Icarie,* inspired by the ideas of the Welsh social reformer Robert Owen (1771–1858). He believed in a communistic society involving compulsory work for everyone and equal distribution of the fruits of the group's labor. In 1848 Cabet attempted to put his theories into practice by founding a collectivist colony near what is now Dallas, Texas. When the experiment failed, the French immigrants moved in 1850 to Nauvoo, Illinois, and took over buildings abandoned by a group of Mormons. After nearly foundering again, due in large measure to Cabet's despotic ways, the community relocated to Corning, Iowa, and prospered. The colony gradually went into decline; in 1858, a splinter group migrated to Cheltenham, Missouri, and in 1881 another migrated to California. Both were short-lived, and the main group dissolved itself in 1895.

Meanwhile, in 1855, Victor Considérant (1808–1893), a disciple of the French reformer Charles Fourier (1772–1837), founded Réunion, another cooperative community near what is now Dallas. One of forty such "phalanxes" established in the United States, Réunion attracted immigrants from Belgium, France, and Switzerland, as well as many Americans. The Réunion colony soon split along national lines and disbanded in 1857. In its heyday, the Association movement, of which these Icarian and Fourierist communities were part, appealed to thousands of individuals. Few inhabitants, however, found the Spartan conditions and the regimentation to their liking, and the turnover was great.

French-born Residents of the United States Today In modern times, the vast majority of French expatriates have opted for destinations other than the United States, notably European countries (Belgium, Germany, and Switzerland) and former French colonies (including French Canada). Of those living in America, one-third live in the Northeast, and another half are almost evenly divided between the South and the West (the South having realized the most significant gains in this respect between 1970 and 1980). In the 1980 census, California and New York reported the greatest number of French-born—23,764 and 20,852, respectively—and nineteen states had between 8,495 (Florida) and 1,065 (Indiana) such persons. Of this group, 88.69 percent were concentrated in urban areas, 64 percent were United States citizens, and females outnumbered males 169 to 100. A fairly large percentage would appear to be white-collar workers. Anecdotal evidence also suggests that many French natives in this country are employed in the hotel and restaurant business, as well as in the fashion, hairstyling, and interior decorating industries.

Although the southward migration of Canadians has been continual since the British conquest, there was no major exodus from French Canada to the United States until after the American Civil War. In the thirty years that followed the war, poor farming conditions and rapid population growth in Quebec, on the one hand, and the attraction of the booming textile industry in the northeastern United States, on the other, produced a sharp increase in the number of French-Canadian immigrants to certain areas of New England and upper New York State. Initially, a few agents were employed to recruit labor; travel to and from these communities by rail—usually an overnight trip—was relatively easy and inexpensive. However, word of mouth soon provided all the operatives the mill owners needed. The first wave of immigrants headed mainly for Vermont and Maine; then, beginning about 1870, new arrivals settled increasingly in central and southern New England communities.

By 1900 the French-Canadian population of New England totaled about 573,000, of which 275,000 resided in Massachusetts. In many cities and towns, immigrants from Quebec constituted a very high percentage of the total local population, among them Biddeford, Maine, 62 percent; Brunswick, Maine, 54 percent; Danielson, Connecticut, 64 percent; Lewiston, Maine, 46 percent; Manchester, New Hampshire, 40 percent; Nashua, New Hampshire, 35 percent; Old Town, Maine, 52 percent; Plainfield, Connecticut, 58 percent; Southbridge, Massachusetts, 60 percent; Spencer, Massachusetts, 52 percent; Suncook, New Hampshire, 60 percent; Waterville, Maine, 45 percent; Woonsocket, Rhode Island, 60 percent.

RECENT FRANCO-AMERICAN HISTORY

The immigration phase of Franco-American history gradually came to an end after World War I, mainly as a consequence of the rapid decline of the textile industry in the Northeast. By then, three distinct regions had emerged. Since that time, despite the major demographic changes in the above-mentioned cities and towns as well as in many other Franco-American communities, the overall geography of *Franco-Américanie* remains the same. The first of these regions is northern Maine, in particular the upper Saint John Valley, an area of French Canada that became part of the United States by virtue of the Webster-Ashburton Treaty of 1842. Second are certain cities, towns, and rural communities in western Vermont and upper New York State; many French-Canadian immigrants settled early in this area just south of Quebec. And last but not least are the former textile centers of central and southwestern New England including southern Maine; by far the greatest number of Franco-Americans reside here.

There are an estimated one million to 1.5 million Franco-Americans in the Northeast today. Communities either near the Canadian border or where the group constitutes more than 20 percent of the total population have tended to remain more "French" than others.

Social and Economic Conditions Franco-American tradition has tended to regard the settling-in process as having been relatively easy, and living and working conditions as difficult but no more so than on the farms of rural Quebec. In recent decades, the grim statistics and somber descriptions of sweatshops and ghetto-like existence provided by social historians have gradually altered that view. The "Little Canadas," particularly in the early phases of the immigration to New England, were generally squalid places with high rates of disease and death. Textile mill operatives worked a six-day, sixty-hour week for low wages.

In 1875, more than half of the French-Canadian immigrants in Lowell, Massachusetts, were living below the poverty line or just barely above it. The large families who pooled their earnings and lived a spartan existence for several years fared best. However, such economic success usually involved sending children to work in the mills rather than to school and keeping a tight rein on all unmarried household members. In many New England communities at the turn of the century, 80 percent or more of the Franco-American textile work force was female. Many photographs taken from 1908 to 1931 by Lewis W. Hine for the National Child Labor Committee of New York depict Franco-American boys and girls fourteen years old or younger at work. Like most recent immigrants, French-Canadians were slow to join labor unions, and it was not until after World War I, when the textile mills began to shut down, that most joined labor organizations.

The Role of the Catholic Church   In the aftermath of the British conquest, Roman Catholic prelates convinced most French-Canadians that they were duty bound to remain true to their religion. In the nineteenth century, nationalistic ideologues developed the notion of *survivance,* survival as a people, whose basic elements, bound together in quasi-mystical fashion, were loyalty to faith, mother tongue, and customs. It was firmly believed that the best way to achieve this was to shun cities and stay close to the land. After the collapse of the Patriote Rebellion of 1837–1838, a Catholic revival greatly increased religious vocations, stimulated the growth of parish organizations, and consolidated the church's position in Quebec. From about the mid nineteenth century until the "Quiet Revolution" of the 1960s, the clergy played a pervasive role in education, politics, and social life.

In the late nineteenth and early twentieth centuries, most French-Canadian immigrants continued to be strongly attached to their religion. Wherever their numbers were sufficiently large,

they petitioned local bishops for their own parishes. Several other ethnic groups in New England and elsewhere did the same. The resulting patchwork of parishes came to be a matter of grave concern to the church hierarchy, which viewed such a development as divisive. The bishops, who were mostly Irish, favored rapid assimilation as a way of combating discrimination and persecution. Ethnic priests countered that members of their group would leave the church in droves rather than remain in parishes where they did not feel welcome. In 1900 there were at least eighty-two Franco-American national parishes in New England; by 1949 that figure had more than tripled. Until World War II, the parish was the focus of Franco-American life, and pastors exerted great influence over their flocks.

Franco-American leaders—notably doctors, lawyers, and priests—adapted French-Canadian survivance ideology to the New England situation, stressing the need to maintain their traditional *foi, langue, et mœurs* (faith, language, and customs). Naturally, one would learn English, become a loyal American citizen, and have dealings with other Americans in the marketplace. However, true Franco-Americans would cherish their French-Canadian heritage and find happiness mainly in their families and among their own.

These and related ideas were promoted in church, in parish and social organizations, and, most effectively and enduringly, in Franco-American parochial schools, whose golden age lasted from 1920 to 1950. Franco-Americans founded and supported scores of bilingual elementary schools in New England, by far the greatest number of which were maintained by female religious orders. Over thirty were established in the first decade of the twentieth century alone, and as many again in the 1920s. By about 1950, more than two hundred were operating. The success Franco-American schools had in attracting pupils varied from locality to locality, in most instances probably ranging between half and three-fourths of the community's Franco-American children. It is reasonable to assume, too, that as with public and parochial schools generally, enrollments rose and fell with the birthrate, which tends to reflect economic conditions.

A large number of parochial schools in this country, including more than half of Franco-American educational institutions, shut down in the 1960s and 1970s as a result of inflation, a shortage of religious teaching personnel, a sudden decline in the birthrate following the baby boom, and changes in the Catholic church in the aftermath of Vatican II. Those which survived underwent dramatic transformations. Many schools consolidated, and practically all abandoned or drastically reduced their ethnocentric programs.

The Sentinelle Crisis   The flare-ups between French-Canadian immigrants and Irish bishops over the right to have pastors of their own nationality or to control parish finances—notably in 1884–1886 at Fall River, Massachusetts, at the turn of the century in Danielson, Connecticut, and North Brookfield, Massachusetts, and in 1909–1913 in Maine—were the prelude to the *Sentinelle* Affair, which rocked the Franco-American community in the mid 1920s.

Elphège Daignault (1879–1937), the militant editor of *La Sentinelle,* a French-language newspaper in Woonsocket, Rhode Island, waged a vituperative campaign against the bishop of Providence, William Hickey, whom he accused of brazen attempts to anglicize and to weaken national parishes in his diocese. The group's leadership throughout the Northeast polarized around the opposition between officers of the two major Franco-American fraternal benefit societies, the Union Saint-Jean-Baptiste d'Amérique and the Association Canado-Américaine. The struggle in Rhode Island involved large protest meetings, pew-rent strikes, and, in the end, a civil suit against the bishop. In 1928 the bishop excommunicated sixty-two Sentinellistes in an action that ended the challenge to his episcopal authority but sent shock waves of disbelief and indignation through the tightly knit Franco-American community. In the final analysis, the controversy boiled down to a simple question: Should Franco-Americans accommodate assimilation or fight it tooth and nail? For this reason most scholars today believe the *Sentinelle* Affair was a defining moment.

Franco-Americans Today   Before World War II, Franco-Americans invested heavily in institutions at the grass roots—parochial schools, parish organizations, lodges of fraternal societies, and the like—and supported French-language newspapers as well as institutions of higher learning, notably Assumption College in Worcester, Massachusetts. In this way, they kept alive a dream of ethnicity that was neither shared nor appreciated by many Americans. As memories of the past receded, the cohesion and vitality that once characterized the group faded. The Great Depression, World War II, urban renewal, the turbulent 1960s, and the many events that have transformed modern American

society profoundly affected the descendants of the French-Canadian immigrants. Despite these changes, Franco-Americans remain a distinct group in the Northeast today.

The civil rights movement of the 1960s and the American Revolution bicentennial in 1976 stimulated ethnic consciousness among Franco-Americans and generated considerable interest in the group's cultural and social activities. On the one hand, the "Quiet Revolution" of the 1960s put French-Canadians in the limelight; on the other, the Parti Québecois, which came to power in 1976, sought to strengthen its ties with francophone groups throughout North America. However, the new ethnicity proved to be short-lived in the United States, and political and socioeconomic factors soon limited Quebec's cultural outreach. Declining fluency in French has been a serious obstacle to those Franco-Americans who desire to participate fully in the group's activities or to relate to Québecois, with whom language is often a touchy subject.

Anecdotal evidence strongly suggests that Franco-Americans today enjoy a markedly higher educational and occupational status than earlier generations, and that they are closing the gap which once set them apart from the population at large and from certain other ethnic groups.

Franco-Americans in New Hampshire and Rhode Island have helped several of their own to become governor, a United States representative, or a United States senator, and they have achieved even greater success at the local level as mayors and state legislators. Among the many Franco-American novelists who have achieved national prominence, the best-known are Jack Kerouac (1922–1969), author of *On the Road* (1957), *Doctor Sax* (1959), and *Visions of Gerard* (1963); Grace Metalious née De Repentigny (1924–1964), whose works include *Peyton Place* (1956), *The Tight White Collar* (1960), and *No Adam in Eden* (1963); and David Plante, author of *The Family* (1978), *The Country* (1981), *The Woods* (1982), and *The Foreigner* (1984). In the areas of sports and entertainment, marathoner Joan Benoit won a gold medal in the Olympic Games held at Los Angeles in 1984, and singer Robert Goulet has starred in the musical *Camelot* (1960).

Long neglected as a field of study, Franco-American history and culture has in recent years been the subject of a spate of scholarly books. The French Institute at Assumption College sponsors annual conferences whose proceedings are published, and a variety of related activities.

BIBLIOGRAPHY

New France

Clark, Andrew H. *Acadia: The Geography of Early Nova Scotia to 1760* (1968).

Dictionary of Canadian Biography, 12 vols. to date (1966–).

Harris, Richard C. *The Seigneurial System in Early Canada: A Geographical History* (1966).

Trudel, Marcel. *Introduction to New France* (1938). An excellent synthesis.

———. *The Beginnings of New France, 1524–1633.* Translated by Patricia Claxton (1973).

French-speaking Areas of North America Today

Dufresne, Charles, Jacques Grimard, André Lapierre, Pierre Savard, and Gaetan Vallières, eds. *Dictionarie de l'Amérique française* (1988).

Louder, Dean R. and Eric Waddell, eds. *Du Continent perdu à l'archipel retrouvé: Le Québec et l'Amérique française* (1983). An outstanding collection of essays by leading cultural anthropologists, geographers, and sociologists.

The French in the United States

Creagh, Ronald. *Nos Cousins d'Amérique: Histoire des française aux États-Unis* (1988). First-rate overview, although it omits consideration of the Franco-Americans.

The Franco-Americans

Barkan, Elliott R. "French Canadians." In *Harvard Encyclopedia of American Ethnic Groups,* edited by Stephan Thernstrom (1980).

Brault, Gerard J. *The French-Canadian Heritage in New England* (1986).

Chartier, Armand. *Histoire des franco-américains de la Nouvelle-Angleterre, 1775–1990* (1991). Especially useful for ideological background.

Doty, C. Stewart. *The First Franco-Americans: New England Life-Histories from the Federal Writers' Project, 1938–1939* (1985).

Roby, Yves. *Les Franco-Américains de la Nouvelle-Angleterre, 1776–1930* (1990).

Weil, François. *Les Franco-Américains, 1860–1980* (1989).

SEE ALSO **The Deep South; New England;** and **Religion.**

IRISH CATHOLICS

Paula M. Kane

THE RELATIONSHIP OF the words "Irish" and "Catholic" is complex. In the history of American Catholicism, the Irish, along with the Italians and the Poles, have been widely studied. Yet instead of examining Irish Catholics from the perspective of their combined ethnic and religious identity, historians have tended to assume that the Catholic faith is an inherent part of Irishness, and have concentrated on describing the path of Irish assimilation in America or upon explaining long-term economic deprivation of the Irish. A new direction in the historiography has been signaled by Kerby Miller's effective treatment of the transatlantic emigration as an exile experience (1985) and his careful attention to the role of the Roman Catholic church in identity formation, as well as to the role of relatives remaining in Ireland in keeping nationalism alive. His extensive use of immigrant letters provides a model of scholarship and fresh information about Irish self-perceptions and reactions to America.

Beginning in the 1840s, Irish Catholics provided the first major challenge to the perceived Anglo-Protestant dominance of America, even though they had already constituted the largest group of non-English immigrants to colonial America. Today's Irish Catholic Americans are in many ways indistinguishable as an ethnoreligious group. Rather than being distinctive, they can point to diverse representatives of assimilation and social mobility: talk-show host Phil Donahue; professional football quarterbacks Steve Walsh, Jim Kelly, and Jim McMahon; baseball player Tom Seaver; and politicians Thomas P. ("Tip") O'Neill, Daniel Patrick Moynihan, and John, Robert, and Edward Kennedy. Other twentieth-century notables include journalist Mary McGrory; novelist Mary McCarthy; labor agitators Patrick Ford, Mary Harris ("Mother") Jones, and Mary K. O'Sullivan; suffragists Margaret O'Donovan Rossa and Lucy Burns; mayors John ("Honey Fitz") Fitzgerald and James Michael Curley ("the Purple Shamrock") of Boston and Ed Kelly and Richard Daley of Chicago. Irish Catholics are represented in twentieth-century nonmainstream culture as well: Dr. Tom Dooley, the activist priests Daniel and Philip Berrigan (of Irish-German parentage), and the antiwar politician Eugene McCarthy.

However, twentieth-century mass culture has had a homogenizing impact on all ethnic groups, creating such "Irish" spectacles on Saint Patrick's Day as the dyed-green river flowing through San Antonio, Texas, and the proliferation of "genuine" Irish pubs serving green beer, and corned beef and cabbage, testaments to the Americanization of this Irish holiday and of other Irish customs for capitalist consumption. Irish Catholic culture, it seems, has been reduced to a form of symbolic ethnicity in contemporary America, equated with pub life, storytelling, music making, and an annual parade.

IMMIGRATION AND DEMOGRAPHIC PATTERNS

According to sociologist Andrew Greeley, 12 percent of Americans currently state their principal ethnic background as Irish, and 37 percent of them are also Roman Catholics. Irish Catholics, therefore, represent about twelve million persons, or 4.5 percent of all Americans. Because most of the Irish immigrated during or shortly following the great potato famine of 1845–1849, 71 percent of today's Irish Americans are third generation (grandchildren of immigrants), or higher.

Aside from the first wave of colonial Irish immigrants, who were largely farm laborers settling in the American South, and who generally were Protestants, the two subsequent waves of Irish—the famine immigrants and post-famine groups—were primarily Catholic. The Protestant Irish, or Scotch-Irish, had formed networks of institutions in the coastal cities and on the frontier prior to 1840. In 1845, and for several years after, a blight fungus attacked potato crops not only in Ireland but also throughout central Europe, resulting in severe food shortages, malnutrition, and starvation. Because the Irish diet was so heavily dependent upon potato cultivation, the famine was a decisive event in modern Irish history, causing the death of a million persons between 1845 and the early 1850s, and migration of about 1.6 million survivors to Great Britain and North America between 1845 and 1855. The Irish were primarily the victims of "push" factors in migration (migrate or die), rather than "pull" elements (migrate for wealth or freedom). In addition, the Irish saw themselves as victims of a fated process of exile and exploitation at the hands of the British.

On the eve of the famine, almost 75 percent of employed Irish men were in farming, compared with less than 25 percent in England. The percentage of Irish involved in any kind of manufacturing had actually fallen in the 1820s and 1830s. In 1841, 40 percent, or 500,000, of Irish houses were single-room mud cabins. Thus, the Irish came to America as subsistence-level serf-farmers with no industrial or artisanal skills, a history of low-quality housing, and colonization in their own country by English landlords for three centuries. Further, most Irish landholders fell into the category of "petty cultivators" who occupied, often without owning, between two and ten acres of land, which made them vulnerable to the events of the 1840s when there was no food to eat and no land to subdivide among the next generation. Traveling to the United States, the Irish suffered from poor health due to the ravages of famine and the outbreaks of disease en route, which led to quarantine for many passengers of the "coffin ships" and contributed to the low life-expectancy of the first generation in America.

Sea passage to North America cost approximately twelve to fifteen dollars for a journey which lasted from six to eight weeks. Although some American Catholic bishops tried to discourage the Irish from settling in cities because of the association of cities with vice, the Irish did cluster in urban areas, even in the South, creating ghettos and tenements which were described by horrified observers in language similar to more recent portraits of black slum life. Following a pattern of chain migration, Irish Catholic immigrants were initially concentrated in the maritime regions of Canada and in American cities of the Northeast and Upper Midwest. But by 1870, even in California the Irish constituted the largest foreign-born group. The concentration of the Irish in separate urban neighborhoods throughout the country had mostly disappeared by 1970, except in Boston, New York, Philadelphia, and Chicago.

Irish immigration to the United States declined sharply following the restrictionist legislation of the 1920s, the blunting effect of the Great Depression, and the better economic opportunities seemingly available in Great Britain. After a brief upturn in the 1950s, it nearly stopped after the new quotas established by the 1965 immigration reform law. More recently, the estimated numbers of illegal immigrants in eastern cities may justifiably constitute a fourth wave, further contributing to a steady depopulation of Ireland since the 1840s.

THE COLONIAL PERIOD

In the early decades of immigration to the American colonies, Catholics were not welcome, although small numbers had been sent as virtual slaves of the English Protestants. Priests, especially Jesuits, were excluded by the English Protestant settlers; nevertheless, the Jesuits became the largest order of priests in North America. The execution of Charles I in England in 1640 led to fear of popish plots in the American colonies. As a result of combined religious and political fears among Protestants, Catholics often suffered legal discrimination, and poor economic status as indentured servants. During the reigns of James I and Charles I, English and Irish Protestant officials had shipped small numbers of dispossessed Catholics to Virginia as virtual slaves, where they were received as subversives. Colonial Catholics, mostly English, exerted strong lay leadership which characterized the colonial church. Most Irish Catholics of this era were small farmers or artisans scattered throughout Maryland and Pennsylvania, the two colonies with traditions, frequently interrupted, of Catholic toleration.

By 1800, Catholics numbered only about 1 percent of the total population, but there is evidence that during the Jeffersonian era, Irish Catholics conformed to as yet fluid American ideals of mobility and self-sufficiency. Any landownership, after all, was improvement over their lot in Ireland. In 1800 Philadelphia was the most Irish city in America; a full six generations of Irish immigrants had settled there before the seventh, famine, generation arrived looking for work as sailors, day laborers, dockworkers, and excavators. The city also became a center for Irish journalism, reading rooms, and book clubs. By 1860, however, New York City had the largest percentage of Irish, nearly a quarter of its inhabitants.

THE ANTEBELLUM ERA

Between 1820 and 1900, only the Germans had more immigrants to America than the Irish. By 1850, Roman Catholics constituted the largest religious denomination in the United States. In this period of rapid Catholic growth, the Irish were important contributors to the expansion of the church and its many social, educational, and charitable institutions.

On the most divisive issue of the antebellum decades, the slavery question, Irish Catholics represented the full range of opinions from abolitionist to pro-slavery, usually conforming to their regional surroundings. Bishops were significant molders of public opinion. For example, the bishop of Charleston, Patrick Lynch (1817–1882), campaigned in Europe for political support for the Confederacy, while John Hughes of New York (1779–1864) tried to forestall European support for Southerners. Bishop John Quinlan of Mobile, Alabama, a loyal southern sectionalist, gave his blessing to the Emerald Guards, the Irish units of the Confederate army. When the Civil War began, nearly forty Union regiments were entirely Irish volunteers, and eight southern states had Irish units. The northern Irish, however, were not free of racism. In protest against the Union draft, instituted in 1863, New York City Irish Catholics rioted against being forced to fight to defend the freedom of blacks, who had become their major economic competitors in certain cities and regions. Nonetheless, many of the American abolitionists, black and white, acknowledged their debt to the inspiring speeches for Catholic emancipation in Ireland of the nationalist Daniel O'Connell. In the South, Irish Catholics were already in direct competition for jobs with both slaves and free blacks. The urban presence of the southern Irish was strongest in the border areas, including Louisville, Kentucky, and Nashville, Tennessee.

THE CLASH OF CULTURES

Whatever their different experiences of social and economic progress, and their views on controversial questions, Irish Catholics shared the experience of being attacked by Anglo-Protestant Americans for being Catholics, anti-republican, anti-democratic, and, ultimately, unassimilable. Thus, even prior to the arrivals of the famine immigrants in the 1840s, there were numerous anti-Catholic incidents of both verbal and physical hostility which document the prejudices and often irrational fears of evangelical Protestants who believed that they alone were America's "native" founders. In several states, the 1830s were characterized by nativist mob behavior and conspiracy theories directed against Catholic "foreigners." For example, a convent near Boston inhabited by Ursuline nuns was burned down in 1834 and the arsonists acquitted; two years later, a group of Protestant ministers devised and published a novel under the pseudonym of Maria Monk, *The Awful Disclosures of the Hotel Dieu Nunnery in Montreal,* which was presented to the public as a true account of the life of a Protestant convert to Catholicism who confessed the brutality and sadistic abuses in convent life. Though false, the novel and numerous imitations caused a sensation, and are still used by Protestant fundamentalists who desire to discredit Roman Catholicism.

In 1837 the Massachusetts militia had to be called out to stop a riot between a volunteer fire company and an Irish funeral procession in the streets of Boston, numerous anti-Catholic newspapers were published, and missionaries organized to stop the threat from the "papists," who were seen as aliens not only to America but also to democratic politics. Protestant propagandizers, from the well-respected Rev. Lyman Beecher to inventor and painter Samuel F. B. Morse, warned patriots to save the Louisiana Purchase territory from colonization by "Infidelity and Popery." Underlying these scare tactics were the sexual fears and definitions of deviance of the nativists, who projected them onto the Catholic population as a way of reasserting their own sense of identity. While books like *Awful Disclosures* were not directed specifically at the Irish, they were intended to show that Catholics, of whatever national background, were alien and subhuman. The violent street riots of Philadelphia in 1844, which pitted Protestants against Irish Catholics and led to thirty or more deaths, were but one more example of the high level of social and economic tensions of the 1830s and 1840s which polarized around religious backgrounds.

OCCUPATIONS AND SOCIAL MOBILITY

In the troubled years of pre–Civil War nativism, assimilation and upward mobility of Irish Catholics were slow. Unable to earn the capital or learn the

745

skills needed for cash-crop agriculture, Irish men had few choices but to begin in unskilled labor (canal diggers and ditchdiggers, longshoremen, railroad builders, construction workers), and many never advanced beyond it. Irish labor largely built the Erie Canal and drained the swamps of Louisiana (there is a song describing the death from cholera of "Ten Thousand Micks" who swung their picks to dig the New Basin Canal). Irish miners worked in the coal regions of western Pennsylvania, prospected for gold in California, and mined copper veins in Montana. Although they met the need for a cheap labor pool in the urban Northeast and on the western American frontier, and fulfilled the function of black slave labor in the South, the Irish did not advance easily or evenly into the business and professional classes. The want ads in many city newspapers included the letters "N.I.N.A." (No Irish Need Apply), symbolizing the powerlessness of the immigrants against the economic elites of America. Generally, the Irish found horizontal rather than vertical mobility in the United States.

Irish Catholics did get ahead in the military and the civil service. By 1900 many cities had police and fire departments dominated by Irish-born employees. Soon, Irish Americans also worked in transportation, maintenance, and city engineering. About the same percentages of Irish males were dispersed across white-collar (35 percent), skilled (50 percent), and unskilled (15 percent) labor by 1900 as white Americans of native American-born parents. Wars, too, helped Irish Catholics to assimilate. During the Civil War, Irish regiments proved their loyalty to the Union, constituting one-quarter of all foreign-born Union volunteers, as well as the highest percentage of foreign-born Confederates. During World War I, the loyal service of Irish Catholics helped defuse nativism. In the private sector, some Irish became successful small businessmen as grocers, saloon keepers, and morticians. The priesthood was esteemed as a career choice for young men, and a large percentage of Catholic college graduates in the early twentieth century entered the ranks of the clergy. Irish American and Irish-born Catholics in fact dominated the American priesthood and episcopacy, leading to complaints from other ethnic Catholics of a "Hibernarchy." In secular careers, many Irish Catholics aligned legal careers with successful political ambitions. Politics, especially within the Democratic party, offered Irish Catholics opportunities not open to them in the business world. The alignments of various Irish politicians in American cities formed a microcosm of clan loyalties and squabbles, which reinforced ethnic consciousness and divisions.

After World War II, Irish Catholics experienced their largest economic jump forward and integration into the middle class, assisted by the G.I. Bill, which financed college and graduate degrees for war veterans. About 43 percent of Irish Americans sent their children to college in the 1950s, second only to Jews (59 percent). From the 1950s on, large numbers of graduates of Catholic colleges enlisted in agencies of the federal government, notably the foreign service, the Central Intelligence Agency, and the Federal Bureau of Investigation, as well as being represented in liberal humanitarian projects such as the Peace Corps. At the same time, the power of Irish urban political machines was waning, undermined by the social services initiated by Franklin Roosevelt's New Deal as well as by demographic changes and the dispersal of Irish families to the suburbs. Why, then, has an image of Irish economic inferiority persisted? Perhaps some of this can be explained in reference to regional opportunities available to Irish Catholics.

REGIONAL DIFFERENCES

The histories of Boston and New York Irish Catholics have been overemphasized. Although New England provides the most enduring example of Yankee Protestant nativism and anti-Catholicism, the case of the Massachusetts Irish is somewhat atypical. Accurately referred to as "fossils" in comparison with the rest of Irish Americans, the New England Irish fared worse in terms of assimilation and job mobility over a longer period than their counterparts in other regions, and have remained disproportionately stuck in blue-collar and unskilled occupations. More recent studies have regarded other regions of the country, particularly the role of the Irish in westward settlement, from Detroit to Butte, Montana, to California. San Francisco, in many ways, became a duplicate of Boston. In general, however, western Irish Catholics are more likely to have higher-income professions and to attain higher levels of education.

For the initial generations of immigrants, urban living conditions were desperately poor. Housing in cities was wretched, sanitation was nonexistent, and the popular association of the Irish with urban criminality is suggested by the evolution of the police "paddy wagon" to haul "Paddys" off to jail. In New York State in 1850, 55 percent of those arrested were Irish; in 1855 a Massachusetts report on insanity blamed the high percentages of Irish in lunatic asylums upon their physical and mental weakness. American political cartoons of the era represented the Irish as paupers, apelike drunks, and brawlers. Perhaps it is significant that in athletic competition, the Irish excelled as boxers who emerged from a street-fighting tradition. John Morrissey became heavyweight champion of America in 1853. Paddy Ryan, born in Tipperary, won the title in 1880, but lost to challenger, John L. Sullivan, the "Boston Strong Boy," in a grueling bout in 1882, the last championship prizefight held under bare-knuckle rules. Sullivan, popular for his sayings ("The bigger they are, the harder they fall.") and his bragging, endured until 1892, when he was deposed by another Irish American, "Gentleman" Jim Corbett, under the new padded glove regulations. Corbett lost his title in 1897. Other pugilists, like Jack Dempsey (born Jack Kelly in Ireland) dominated the sport through the 1920s.

By 1900 a small percentage of Irish Catholics had become wealthy. The affluence of this "Irish-tocracy" aligned them with the Roman Catholic church's leaders and power structure, and with the conservative forces of skilled labor unionism. Wealthy Catholic families, including the Cudahys, the McDonnells, the Murrays, the Fitzgeralds, and the Kennedys, imitated the life-style of their WASP counterparts, hoping to secure their own places in the Social Register. Catholic elites gathered at their own summer spots, especially Southampton, Long Island, in response to being cold-shouldered by the blueblood Protestants at Newport, Rhode Island.

Situated between the extremes of rich and poor, the Irish Catholic middle class led an existence divided between its own assimilated goals and the needs of the lower class. Kerby Miller has suggested that the Irish Catholic bourgeoisie disapproved of the survival of peasant and superstitious behaviors, and was itself despised by native-born Irish for being neither good Irishmen nor loyal Americans. The Irish lower class mobilized its resentments through residual peasant behaviors like secret societies and the labor violence of the Molly Maguires in Pennsylvania's coal mining region. The middle class tried to sustain its own hegemony, ironically becoming, over time, the leader of the Americanization process and the cheerleader of American capitalism for new immigrants. The Irish Catholic middle class thus pursued two separate but related projects simultaneously: it tried to ally itself with Anglo-American power and to achieve power over the Irish lower classes.

EDUCATION

Debates over control of American public education in the nineteenth century often pitted Irish Catholics against Protestant Americans involving issues such as the use of the Protestant King James Bible in public schools and the obviously Protestant bias of children's textbooks and moral training. John Hughes, the Irish-born bishop of New York City, led a campaign there in the 1840s to obtain tax money to establish a separate school system. While unsuccessful, the debates at least opened the question of the Protestant prejudices which had long dominated the common schools. Though American public education had not begun to flourish until the late 1830s under the guidance of reformers like Horace Mann, American Catholics did not develop a widespread parochial school system until after 1884, when the American bishops issued a statement at the Third Plenary Council of Baltimore encouraging them. Parish schools were funded by parishioners for their children, but the strength of diocesan systems varied widely. In 1884, only four of every ten parishes had elementary schools. In Irish Catholic strongholds like Boston, more Catholic students attended the public schools, which over time came to be dominated by Irish Catholic schoolteachers. In at least ten other large cities, Irish American women made up 20 percent or more of the public school teaching staffs.

Catholic high schools appeared as well, mostly serving to prepare boys for college and seminary. Many colleges remained tied to their affiliated prep schools for financial reasons. Since there was no Catholic coeducation, girls attended convent day and boarding academies. Daughters of affluent "lace curtain" Irish families frequented the convent schools, often run by the Sacred Heart nuns, which also catered to wealthy Protestants. Otherwise, Catholic girls attended parochial schools, usually in greater numbers than boys. Catholic elementary and secondary schools were staffed by religious orders of priests and brothers, such as the Franciscans and Christian Brothers, and by orders of nuns and sisters such as the Sisters of Charity of Saint Joseph and the Sisters of Mercy, which originated in Ireland. Since most Irish spoke English upon arrival in the United States, they were not overly concerned with the use of schools to preserve use and understanding of the mother tongue, as were the Germans, Poles, and Italians.

Many Catholic leaders regarded public higher education as a threat to their religious belief. Large numbers of Catholics did not attend high school or college until after World War I. The oldest Jesuit institutions—Georgetown (1789), Fordham (1841), Holy Cross (1843), and Boston College (1863)—served primarily Irish Catholic student bodies and were staffed by Irish Jesuits. The Jesuit order still directs the largest number of American Catholic colleges and universities, and a high percentage of Jesuits are of Irish descent. Notre Dame (whose athletic teams' appellation, "the Fighting Irish," gives a symbolic rather than an accurate picture of its players) was founded in 1842 by the Brothers of the Holy Cross, the first such community to settle permanently in America. Irish Benedictines, Dominicans, Franciscans, and Vincentians also founded American colleges.

Catholics were divided on the question of higher education for women. The first Catholic women's college, St. Mary's of Notre Dame, was opened in 1895; in 1900 there were only three; then, 14 by 1910 and 120 by 1967. Outside of marriage, motherhood, and religious vocations, there were few options for women acceptable to the church's leaders; thus the hierarchy was slow to approve higher education and professional training for women, making the presence of a large sector of Irish Catholic single working women something of an anomaly.

The only university belonging to the American Catholic hierarchy is Catholic University of America in Washington, D.C. It was founded in 1889, the product of the agitation of American bishops for a pontifical university in America to help engage the church with the modern world. Bishop John Keane (1839–1918) of Richmond, Virginia, born in Ballyshannon, Ireland, became its first rector, and recruited an international faculty. He was dismissed, however, in 1896, when the Vatican disapproved of his "liberal" Americanizing tendencies.

Catholic institutions of higher learning were dominated by Irish clerical faculty and Irish student bodies well into the 1950s. The laicization of Catholic college faculties did not occur to a significant degree until after World War II, and by the 1980s, over 85 percent of Catholic faculty members were nonclergy. Student patterns followed the national trend of massive increases after 1945. By the late 1960s, 59 percent of Irish Catholics of college age attended institutions of higher learning.

POLITICS AND ELECTORAL PATTERNS

Yet politics, more than education, has been associated with Irish Americans. Daniel Patrick Moynihan observed that Irish Americans excelled at organizational tactics in politics and religion, rather than in business or in intellectual pursuits. Except in New England, Irish Catholic political power in America almost always resulted in improved socioeconomic status. The Irish found that politics could help protect them from discrimination. They formed political machines—networks headed by local bosses who delivered favors, jobs, and patronage in exchange for blocs of votes. The machines helped to offset the effects of job discrimination against the Irish in the public sector and served as a form of ethnic welfarism. Political bosses gave the Irish a reputation for clannishness and for organizing to take care of their own, yet in practice, bosses were obliged to secure the favor of non-Irish as well. One of the best-known Irish machine politicians was George Washington Plunkitt of New York's Tammany Hall, who reported that on an average day in 1905, between 2 A.M. and midnight he had bailed a saloon keeper out of jail; helped fire victims get clothing and shelter; attended an Italian funeral, a church fair, and a Jewish wedding; found jobs for several unemployed men; and heard complaints from various groups seeking relief or jobs.

Irish political machines flourished from the 1870s until the 1970s, weathering charges of graft, nepotism, and anachronism. Some, like the Pendergast machine in Kansas City, were notoriously corrupt. In Chicago in the 1920s, ties between political machines and organized crime were pervasive. Irish Catholics made up much of that city's legendary gangster culture, from Big Jim O'Leary and "Bathhouse John" Coughlin to Bugsy Moran. Some Irish entrepreneurs ran both legal and illegal activities by combining family stores with loan shark operations that preyed upon immigrants who could not get credit from banks or other legal sources. The long-term usefulness of political machines, which generated low-paying blue-collar jobs to reward as many working-class voters as possible, has been challenged by some historians who claim that they may have retarded economic integration. Now largely supplanted by lobbyists and bureaucratized government, the machine has become obsolete, although the Irish are still dominant in the urban politics of Boston, Chicago, and San Diego.

Since their arrival in the 1840s, Irish Catholics have tended to vote Democratic, since that party was originally less nativist in its orientation than other nineteenth-century alternatives. Irish affiliation with the Democratic party was cemented in the decades following the famine immigration. By the 1880s, as Irish Catholics were able to elect their first mayors in major cities, the Democratic party was stigmatized by Samuel D. Burchard, a Protestant minister, as the party of "Rum, Romanism and Rebellion," but its platforms served the interests of Irish America. Although three-fifths of Irish Americans are still Democrats, there have been signs of an increasing conservatism among Irish Catholics in both the upper-middle and the lower-middle class. In 1980, Republican Ronald Reagan received approximately 53 percent of the Irish vote. Today, enduring racial prejudice in Irish Catholic neighborhoods like Boston's "Southie" (South End), which have opposed integration, busing, and civil rights, are perhaps more expressive of white lower-middle-class hostilities than of Irish ethnicity. Nevertheless, Irish Americans remain vulnerable to being manipulated by politicians who play to fears of falling behind blacks and other nonwhite groups.

Religious issues have long been a part of presidential politics. The first Catholic to run for president was Governor Alfred E. Smith of New York, in 1928; he lost to Herbert Hoover. An Irish Catholic, John Kennedy, was victorious in 1960 but was criticized for being more Harvard than Irish. However, anti-Kennedy forces revived much nineteenth-century nativist literature, such as Maria Monk's *Awful Disclosures* and its imitations, demonstrating the enduring quality of political nativism from its first appearance in the 1850s with the Know-Nothings, to the American Protective Association of the 1880s and the Ku Klux Klan of the 1920s.

On social issues like prohibition and temperance, Irish Catholics opposed efforts to close saloons and regulate the sale of liquor. The neighborhood pub remained an important institution for male social bonding, and Catholics saw nothing sinful in drinking. Some Irish gangs ran illegal liquor distilling and distribution rings during Prohibition (1919–1933). Catholics largely opposed the Eighteenth Amendment, against the Protestant "drys." Alcoholism was a health problem for many Irish, however, which led the church hierarchy and many women to support Irish priest Theobald Mathew's temperance crusade in America. In 1869 the Catholic Total Abstinence Union was formed, supported by liberal bishops and the Catholic middle class, who were embarrassed by the Irish reputation for overindulgence.

WORKERS AND LABOR

Irish Catholics have a mixed record on labor issues in America, characterized by a preference for craft unionism, a conservative distaste for strikes, and loyalty to the Catholic church authorities, offset by an equally enduring underground tradition of organized secret societies, labor protest, and radicalism, sometimes led by priests as well as laypeople. Some traditional values of the Irish community were incorporated into labor protest, as in the adoption of the term "boycott" by the Land League to name a tactic they had used against landlords and other hostile parties in rural Ireland.

In America, Irish workers felt that they were being exploited by industrial capitalists in the same way that their peasant counterparts in Ireland were being crushed by English landlords. This shared fear of oligarchy led Irish American laborers and domestics to provide most of the money that supported the Land League in Ireland, and to become ardent supporters of democratic ideology in the United States. Unfortunately, the prospects for working-class solidarity were hampered by divisions between Irish Catholics and Protestants, and by divisions between the Irish and other ethnic factions. In labor disputes, Catholic workers were often at odds with their own church hierarchy, as in the case of their support for Father Edward McGlynn's program based on Henry George's single-tax movement in the 1880s. A small minority in America continues to support Irish nationalist politics and contributes to controversial groups such as NORAID (Irish Northern Aid), which raises money for the dependents of Irish Republican Army men in Ulster. Sociologist Andrew Greeley claims, while admitting the lack of adequate data, that most Irish Americans have scant concern for Irish nationalism.

By the turn of the twentieth century, Irish Catholics led many trade unions of the American Federation of Labor (AFL); in the 1880s, as skilled laborers, they had supported the pro-bourgeois, anti-class-conflict approach of the Knights of Labor, headed by the Irish Catholic Terence V. Powderly. The intervention of Irish American bishops John Keane and James Gibbons in the late nineteenth century prevented a papal ban on the Knights of Labor, nearly condemned by the Vatican as a secret society. However, Irish conservatives in the Knights rejected plans for an inclusive working-class movement, a position which carried over into the AFL. Despite the presence of a small, radical, pro-union minority among Irish Catholics, the Catholic clergy condemned all forms of labor violence, and opposed any militancy inspired by Marxian materialism or socialism.

CULTURAL HISTORY

In the traditional culture of Ireland there seems to have been a reverence for those persons who enhanced community life, including the priest, the craftsman, the hero, the smithy, the poet, and the musician. In a sense, it is a tragedy of Irish history that during the first half of the nineteenth century, the Catholic church strove to wipe out many Celtic, pagan, pre-Christian traditions as a threat to itself. Its decision to impose a Roman model of doctrine and organization stemmed partly from Vatican pressure and partly from the need to modernize in order to stand firm against English conquest. From that point on, Irish culture lost much of its past—the Gaelic language, music, and artisanal production, which various ephemeral movements have attempted to revive from time to time. At the same time, the Catholic church became the agent of modernization and the protector of nationalist patriotism in Ireland. In America, an Irish episcopacy strove likewise to wipe out certain folk elements, such as the custom of rowdy Irish wakes and funerals, which competed with the church's sacramental authority. Evidence of the premigration literacy rates among the Irish in the nineteenth century are conflicting. Some scholars claim that the percentage of literacy was high, compared with the American population and with other European immigrants. Others claim that more than half of the Irish in 1841 were illiterate, still speaking Gaelic rather than English.

In the arts, Irish Americans achieved recognition in literature, acting, and musical entertainment. Their work as performers or creators in the plastic and performing arts was limited by their lack of access to the patronage networks and the world of high culture which dominated cultural production in the United States. Still, the Irish have been tagged by the myth that they excel naturally in literary fields because they are born storytellers, blessed with the gift of "blarney" (skillful flattery). Whether or not this is true, oral tradition has figured large as a basis for Irish literature. As a subcategory, Irish Catholic writing has often served as religious apologetic and as a mirror of the social integration and aspirations of that community. Colonial and early-nineteenth-century Irish American writing was necessarily defensive, against the Calvinist tracts and works of Maria Monk and "her" imitators, which attacked the Irish and their religion. Some exceptions to this rule included novelists Mary Anne Sadlier (1820–1903) and Father John Boyce (1810–1864). From the late Gilded Age to the turn of the century, Irish writers like John Boyle O'Reilly of Boston and Finley Peter Dunne in Chicago tried appealing to a broad American audience while treating issues of social importance. O'Reilly was well known as an abolitionist and an anti-suffragist. Dunne created Mr. Martin Dooley, a fictional mouthpiece of Irish dialect, wit, and wisdom, whose barroom conversations with his friend "Hennessy" covered the range of contemporary issues: firemen, football, muckrakers, bachelorhood, drinking, women's rights, and war.

By 1900 a Catholic subculture or "ghetto" of essayists, novelists, and minor poets flourished, including many women, such as Louise Imogen Guiney, Mary Anne Sadlier, and Katherine Eleanor Conway. However, Catholic fiction also began to address a less explicitly "Irish" audience. It is possible that the resurgence of Anglo-Saxonism from the 1890s through World War I caused a national backlash against all ethnic fiction. Another possible reason for the seeming decline of a distinctively Irish voice is that as an Irish bourgeoisie emerged, Catholicism became a stronger focal point of identity, encouraging writers to address Catholic themes and to serve the expanding network of Catholic publishers, journals, and newspapers. But gradually, Catholic writers became critical of their provincialism. Some turned against the sexual prudery and smug moralism associated with the Catholic subculture.

Consequently, of the generation of the 1920s and 1930s, Irish American writers who gained national acclaim were often Catholic apostates, such as F. Scott Fitzgerald, John O'Hara, and Eugene O'Neill. O'Neill won the Pulitzer Prize in 1919 and 1920, at the beginning of his playwrighting career. His bleak dramas of Irish American life, as in *A Long Day's Journey into Night,* play upon semi-autobiographical themes of addiction, self-destruction, and the dysfunctional family. The demoralizing effect of the Great Depression upon Irish Catholics was depicted in James T. Farrell's "Studs Lonigan" trilogy (1932–1935), which portrayed a generation that was tough, streetwise, and incapable of intimacy. In the 1950s came something of a Catholic literary revival, led by the southerner Flannery O'Connor, a product of the Iowa writing program; Edwin O'Connor, who wrote *The Last Hurrah*

(1956), a fictionalized picture of life in Curley's Boston; and J. F. Powers, who treated midwestern priestly culture satirically. Irish Catholic novelists reflect the regional differences of American fiction in general: from the Chicago of James Farrell and John R. Powers, to Finley Dunne's Bridgeport to O'Connor's Georgia, to Paul Horgan's Southwest, to William Kennedy's Albany, and to the New York City of Mary Gordon, Jimmy Breslin, Joe Flaherty, and Elizabeth Cullinan. Some critics have noted that bleakness and uncertainty now dominate the new breed of contemporary Irish Catholic fiction, as in Mary Gordon's novels.

Irish Americans also made a mark in the theater. The best-known nineteenth-century playwright was Dion Boucicault (1820–1890), who wrote scores of comedies and melodramas. The Irish team of Edward Harrigan and Tony Hart (Anthony Cannon) wrote musicals, and Victor Herbert, born in Ireland, wrote operettas in the late 1800s and early 1900s. Whole families of Irish Americans, like the (George M.) Cohans, began on the vaudeville circuits, and later dominated Broadway and Hollywood. In film directing, Irish Americans John Ford and John Huston, whose final film, *The Dead* (1989), was a James Joyce short story, had productive careers. Irish American movie stars included James Cagney, Bing Crosby, Spencer Tracy, Brian Donlevy, Irene Dunne, Helen Hayes, Maureen O'Sullivan, and Maureen O'Hara, to list but a few.

KINSHIP NETWORKS AND GENDER ROLES

Although huge sums of money were sent back to Ireland by Irish immigrants, few Irish Americans remigrated. Over generations, Irish Catholic society began to stratify into classes. Two different styles of Irish life were noted by the 1880s: the unmannered poor, referred to as the "bog Irish" or "shanty Irish," contrasted with the "lace curtain" or "cut glass" Irish, who, in the puckish definition of Fred Allen, "have fruit in the house when no one's sick." Concern for Victorian norms of propriety and appearances came with the arrival of the Irish bourgeoisie.

Irish Catholic women hold an unusual place in American immigration history because they made up more than half of the total Irish immigrant population (52.9 percent), outnumbering the percentages of women arriving among every other ethnic group. Furthermore, they were more likely than men to become the wage earners for their families

in the first several generations. Between 1852 and 1921, the average female immigrant was young and unmarried, with a median age of 21.2. Single working women supported relatives still in Ireland, as well as parents and siblings in America. Upon marriage, they were expected to abandon their jobs and to serve primarily domestic roles. Nonetheless, Irish women's socialization emphasized preparing them for the job market and for economic functions rather than for marriage; while few continued to work after marriage, they experienced considerable economic freedom as single wage-workers.

Immigrant women gained employment primarily as domestic servants, nannies, seamstresses, and laundresses. Irish domestics worked in the homes of the rich seven days a week, with time off only to attend Sunday Mass. In the second generation, they moved up the occupational ladder as public school teachers, nuns, clerks, secretaries, and telephone operators. Despite the Catholic church's emphasis upon motherhood and married life, over 25 percent of Irish-born women over twenty remained spinsters, a rate higher than in any other immigrant group in the last quarter of the nineteenth century.

The practice of remaining single, or of deferring marriage, extended patterns set in motion by the famine. The Irish learned from the shattering experiences of the 1840s to treat marriage as a fundamentally economic enterprise. Irish families and the Catholic clergy enforced sex segregation among young men and women, and the famine encouraged later marriages and smaller families. Single and married men, consequently, spent much time socializing with other men.

Men were supposed to be good providers, but were criticized within the Irish community for their unstable, argumentative natures and excessive drinking. The church gradually attempted to transform male social life and all-male bonding habits into those of a Christian family man, devoted to his wife and the moral nurturing of his children. In America, Irish Catholics often sustained their premigration propensity toward late marriage or remaining single, and held repressive attitudes toward sexuality and divorce.

THE ROLE OF THE CATHOLIC CHURCH

The Irish arrived in largest numbers at a crucial moment in American history and at a time of transition within American Catholicism. The number of priests in the United States jumped from 480 to more than 1,500 between 1840 and 1850, most of them coming from the same Dublin college and seminary background. In half a century, about 50 percent of the American bishops and the majority of American cardinals were Irish. Orders of sisters, especially the Sisters of Mercy, who arrived in 1843 from Ireland, flourished as teaching orders. Sisters, not bound by the cloistered existence governing nuns, established and directed parochial and convent schools, asylums, orphanages, and hospitals across the nation, and served as nurses during the Civil War.

In Ireland, famine mortality and subsequent emigration increased the ratio of priests to the general population from 1:2,773 in 1845 to 1:1,126 in 1901; the number of Irish nuns increased from 1,500 in 1850 to 8,000 in 1900. In America, as in Ireland, priests often served as financial advisers and counselors, in addition to performing sacramental duties and administrative functions. There evolved a recognizable style of an Irish "Romanized" hierarchy and clergy, loyal to the aims of the papacy to standardize and universalize Catholic belief and practice. An episcopal style of the early 1900s, the "builder bishops" typified by William O'Connell of Boston and Dennis Doherty of Philadelphia, epitomized paternalistic, authoritarian leadership and large-scale diocesan expansion.

For average Irish Catholics, their main point of contact with their religion was the parish, which served as the basic unit of social cohesion and provider of social services. It organized educational, athletic, entertainment, and devotional clubs and societies for the laity. It stood as a mediator between Irish culture and American society. Because of the dominance of the Irish in parish life, non-Irish Catholics were often resentful of their lack of representation. In struggles born of an Irish-German conflict, Irish prelates prevented the German faction from establishing separate German bishops and a separate church structure which would have divided the Catholic church in America.

American Catholics evolved their own system of social services. After the settlement of the famine arrivals and the Civil War came a great increase in the number of extra-parish institutions catering first to survival and, later, to middle-class needs. Among these were reading clubs, sodalities, spiritual retreat groups, and insurance societies. Irish Catholic men provided most of the membership and leadership for these groups, which had fraternal, mutual benefit, social, educational, and devotional functions. Each of these, especially fraternal groups

like the Knights of Columbus, Irish Catholic Benevolent Union, and Catholic Total Abstinence Union, provided economic self-help to the Irish Catholic community. Gradually, however, women's organizations gained huge memberships which often surpassed the men's groups in size. In many American cities, the elected officers and governing boards of Catholic women's groups reflected Irish ancestry into the mid twentieth century.

In the 1920s and 1930s, Irish Catholics were accused of distorting Catholic moral teachings to impose prudish standards. Laymen such as Joseph Breen served key roles in the growing Hollywood entertainment industry as censors. Breen, head of the Production Code Administration (1934–1954), implemented the 1930 production code, which reflected the drive by Roman Catholics to tighten moral standards in movies. For decades, the Breen "purity seal" was essential for the release of a film. Bishops and clergy also put their mark on the social changes of the "Roaring Twenties" by condemning popular entertainments like the tango and radio "crooners," as well as women's shortened hemlines, lipstick, and the right to vote.

The self-image of Irish Catholics as superpatriotic supporters of American toleration and freedom was tarnished somewhat by the emergence of Father Charles Coughlin (1891–1979) in the 1930s as an anti-Semitic demagogue with an extensive radio audience throughout the Midwest. In addition, several American Catholic groups with Irish membership flirted with fascism and evinced anti-Semitic views, but were countered by the expressions of Irish Catholic anti-Nazi activism, anti-Coughlin organizations, and the Catholic episcopacy's statements supporting Jews. The basis of Coughlin's appeal was to lower- and lower-middle-class Irish Catholics who fastened upon his economic conspiracy theories and his contempt for Franklin Roosevelt's New Deal. He was finally silenced by the church in 1939 and returned to serving as a parish priest in Royal Oak, Michigan, until his death.

By the 1950s, Irish Americans were assimilating into American life at a faster rate than ever before due to educational opportunities made available by the G.I. Bill. At that time, some Irish Catholics viewed Senator Joseph McCarthy's anti-Communist witch-hunts as a rallying point for Catholic patriotism; but just as many, notably Irish Catholics associated with the Catholic lay journal of opinion, *Commonweal,* opposed McCarthy. During the 1950s, John Kennedy, whose family had supported McCarthy, rose to power in Massachusetts politics by virtue of his family connections, Harvard education, and considerable personal charisma. Elected president in 1960, Kennedy's short term, dubbed "Camelot" for the mythical associations and utopian optimism it generated, was ended by his assassination in November 1963. No longer the property of an Irish Catholic subculture, Kennedy became a symbol of a national tragedy.

Just as John Kennedy was assimilated to American mythology, so Irish American life has lost much of its distinctiveness to the larger national culture. In contrast with their recent social and economic achievements, which have blurred ethnic differences and have pushed them into the mainstream since 1945, Irish Catholics once insisted proudly upon their difference and their superiority. According to the writer Louise Imogen Guiney, "One of the oddest of Irish qualities is this almost universal grabbism: they claim anything and everything which they think in the least creditable!" (*Letters of Louise Imogen Guiney,* ed. Grace Guiney [1926], vol. 2, p. 234). Guiney's comment was verified by her contemporaries' attempts in the early 1900s to credit Irish Catholics with everything "American," from democratic traditions of governance to the tune of "Yankee Doodle." At the close of the twentieth century, it seems that in many ways the social mobility of Irish Catholics has lessened ethnic identification, reducing it to varieties of romantic nationalism and occasional attempts to trace family genealogies, conserve traditions of Celtic ballads, and the annual "wearin' of the green" on 17 March. Having become quintessentially "American," Irish Catholics have absorbed the individualist values of late-twentieth-century capitalism.

BIBLIOGRAPHY

Articles

Biddle, Ellen H. "The American Catholic Irish Family." In *Ethnic Families in America: Patterns and Variations,* edited by Charles H. Mindel and Robert W. Habenstein (1976).

Blessing, Patrick J. "Irish." In *Harvard Encyclopedia of American Ethnic Groups,* edited by Stephan Thernstrom et al. (1980).

Clark, Dennis. "The Irish Catholics: A Postponed Perspective." In *Immigrants and Religion in Urban America,* edited by Randall M. Miller and Thomas D. Marzik (1977).

Connell, K. H. "Catholicism and Marriage in the Century After the Famine." In his *Irish Peasant Society* (1968).

Larkin, Emmet. "Devotional Revolution." *American Historical Review* 77 (June 1972): 625–652.

———. "Church, State, and Nation in Ireland." *American Historical Review* 80 (December 1975): 1244–1276.

Moore, R. Laurence. "Managing Catholic Success in a Protestant Empire." In *Religious Outsiders and the Making of Americans* (1986).

Background

Brown, Terence. *Ireland: A Social and Cultural History 1922–79* (1981).

Connolly, Sean J. *Religion and Society in Nineteenth-Century Ireland* (1985).

Evans, E. Estyn. *Irish Folkways* (1967).

Hoppen, K. Theodore. *Ireland Since 1800: Conflict and Conformity* (1989).

Miller, David W. *Church, State, and Nation in Ireland, 1898–1921* (1973).

General Works

Bennett, David H. *The Party of Fear: From Nativist Movements to the New Right in American History* (1988). Excellent study of American nativist groups.

Funchion, Michael F., ed. *Irish-American Voluntary Associations* (1983).

Hennesey, James. *American Catholics* (1981). A valuable and readable guide.

Metress, Seamus P., ed. *The Irish-American Experience: A Guide to the Literature* (1981).

Weaver, Jack W., and DeeGee Lester, comps. *Immigrants from Great Britain and Ireland: A Guide to Archival and Manuscript Sources in North America* (1986).

Antebellum Era

Dolan, Jay P. *The Immigrant Church: New York's Irish and German Catholics, 1815–1865* (1975).

Knobel, Dale T. *Paddy and the Republic: Ethnicity and Nationality in Antebellum America* (1986).

Mitchell, Brian C. *The Paddy Camps: The Irish of Lowell, 1821–1861* (1988).

Niehaus, Earl F. *The Irish in New Orleans, 1800–1860* (1965).

O'Connor, Thomas H. *Fitzpatrick's Boston, 1846–1866: John Bernard Fitzpatrick, Third Bishop of Boston* (1984).

Gender, Politics, and Culture

Birmingham, Stephen. *Real Lace: America's Irish Rich* (1973).

Brown, Thomas N. *Irish-American Nationalism, 1870–1890* (1966).

Burchell, R. A. *The San Francisco Irish, 1848–1880* (1980).

Carroll, Francis M. *American Opinion and the Irish Question, 1910–1923* (1978).

Clark, Dennis. *The Irish in Philadelphia: Ten Generations of Urban Experience* (1973).

———. *Hibernia America: The Irish and Regional Cultures* (1986).

———. *Erin's Heirs: Irish Bonds of Community* (1991).

Diner, Hasia. *Erin's Daughters in America: Irish Immigrant Women in the Nineteenth Century* (1983).

Doyle, David N. *Irish Americans, Native Rights and National Empires* (1976).

Emmons, David M. *The Butte Irish: Class and Ethnicity in an American Mining Town, 1875–1925* (1989).

Erie, Stephen P. *Rainbow's End: Irish-Americans and the Dilemmas of Urban Machine Politics, 1840–1985* (1988).

Fallows, Marjorie R. *Irish-Americans: Identity and Assimilation* (1978).

Greeley, Andrew M. *That Most Distressful Nation: The Taming of the American Irish* (1972).

———. *The Irish Americans: The Rise to Money and Power* (1981).

Griffin, William D. *A Portrait of the Irish in America* (1981).

Halsey, William M. *The Survival of American Innocence: Catholicism in an Era of Disillusionment, 1920–1940* (1980).

Handlin, Oscar. *Boston's Immigrants, 1790–1880: A Study in Acculturation*. rev. and enl. ed. (1979).

Leahy, William P. *Adapting to America: Catholics, Jesuits, and Higher Education in the Twentieth Century* (1991).

McCaffrey, Lawrence. *The Irish Diaspora in America* (1976).

Meagher, Timothy, ed. *From Paddy to Studs: Irish-American Communities in the Turn of the Century Era, 1880 to 1920* (1986).

Messbarger, Paul R. *Fiction with a Parochial Purpose: Social Uses of American Catholic Literature, 1884–1900* (1971).

Miller, Kerby A. *Emigrants and Exiles: Ireland and the Irish Exodus to North America* (1985).

Nolan, Janet. *Ourselves Alone: Women's Emigration from Ireland, 1885–1920* (1989).

O'Brien, David J. *The Renewal of American Catholicism* (1972).

O'Grady, Joseph P. *How the Irish Became Americans* (1973).

O'Toole, James. *Militant and Triumphant: William Henry O'Connell and the Catholic Church in Boston, 1859–1944* (1992).

Ryan, Dennis P. *Beyond the Ballot Box: A Social History of the Boston Irish, 1845–1917* (1983). Informative about daily life and habits.

Shanabruch, Charles. *Chicago's Catholics: Evolution of an American Identity* (1981). A superb study.

Shannon, William V. *The American Irish* (1964). Still the liveliest and most interesting survey, by a former ambassador to Ireland.

Steinberg, Stephen. *The Ethnic Myth: Race, Ethnicity, and Class in America* (1981). Essays on the myth of Catholic anti-intellectualism.

Sullivan, Robert E., and James M. O'Toole, eds. *Catholic Boston: Studies in Religion and Community, 1870–1970* (1985). Excellent essays on religious identity and institutions.

Thernstrom, Stephan. *The Other Bostonians* (1973). Compares social mobility of various ethnic groups.

Vinyard, Jo Ellen. *The Irish on the Urban Frontier: Nineteenth-Century Detroit, 1850–1880* (1976).

Walsh, James P. *The San Francisco Irish, 1850–1976* (1978).

SEE ALSO **Immigration**; **New England**; **The New York Metropolitan Region**; and various essays in the section "**Periods of Social Change**."

CENTRAL AND EASTERN EUROPEANS

Victor R. Greene

CERTAINLY MOST AMERICANS know far more about the peoples of western Europe than they do about those of eastern Europe. Part of that lack of information is due to the large number of non–English-speaking groups who live in east central Europe. To better understand the area geographically, one should remember that it lies roughly between the Baltic and the Black seas and is bounded by German-speaking masses to the west and millions of Russian speakers to the east.

The area consists of three sectors: the one in the north along the Baltic, peopled by Latvians, Estonians, and (the largest of the three groups) Lithuanians; the central sector, where Poles, Czechs, Slovaks, Carpatho-Rusyns, and Ukrainians reside; and the southern, home of the Hungarians and Romanians. This essay will mention ethnic Russians who migrated and settled in America from the seventeenth century to the present.

Perhaps the most prominent characteristic of these groups is their wide cultural diversity. In language, for example, only those from the central section are Slavic. Their religious pluralism is surprisingly diverse. There are many Czech, Hungarian, and Slovak Protestants, and sizable groups of Polish, Lithuanian, Slovak, and Hungarian Roman Catholics; Ukrainian and Romanian Greek Catholics; and Ukrainian, Russian, and Romanian Orthodox. They all vary, of course, in social customs.

Despite their differences, these peoples have much in common, especially those who immigrated to the United States. One is that fact itself; all did emigrate, leaving their ancestral homes for the same destination, and with the same hope of living in America and building a new life. American society itself, with its laws, traditions, and economy, forced them to respond somewhat uniformly.

A necessary beginning to understanding why these east central Europeans came to America requires a look at the political situation in the area just after the turn of the nineteenth century. This political setting helps to explain why some early emigrants had to leave their homelands as refugees.

EUROPEAN BACKGROUND

The Congress of Vienna (1815) shaped Europe politically for the next century. East central Europe then consisted of four major monarchies: the German-Prussian in the west, Austria-Hungary and the Ottoman Empire in the south, and Russia in the east. Russia held the Baltic peoples, many of the Poles in an area later called the Congress Kingdom, and the bulk of the Ukrainian land. Prussia, which in 1871 dominated the German Empire, retained the western segment of the Polish-speaking territory, and the Austrian Empire held Bohemia, the Czech land, and the province of Galicia, where Poles, Carpatho-Rusyns, and western Ukrainians called Ruthenians resided. Most Slovaks and some Romanians lived under Hungarian control; other Romanians were under the rule of the Ottoman Turks until 1878, when a segment of them established their own kingdom.

Liberals of the time opposed the restoration of imperial rule after the Napoleonic Wars, and some east central Europeans filled with the ideas of liberal democracy tried (and failed) to establish their own independent states. Their abortive efforts produced refugees forced out of their homelands. Insurrections in Russian Poland in 1830 and 1863 brought a handful of Poles to the United States, which welcomed them as democratic reformers. The more general uprisings of 1848 in central Europe sent overseas not only the famous German "Forty-eighters" but also Czech and Hungarian liberals. The American government received Lajos (Louis) Kossuth and some of his Hungarian followers in 1851.

Other political pressures sent more east central Europeans to America. Through the century

some imperial policies forced assimilation on many of the smaller nationalities. After the *Ausgleich,* the 1867 compromise that established the Hungarian kingdom within the Austro-Hungarian empire, that kingdom embarked on a Magyarization campaign. Thus Slovaks, Romanians, and others found it difficult and even illegal to maintain their own cultural life. Bismarck and the German empire launched a Kulturkampf in the 1870s which did much to suppress Polish Catholicism, and after the insurrection of Russian Poles and Lithuanians in 1863, the tsar instituted a Russification policy.

While this political suppression was the cause of some east central European emigration, the greater influence was economic change. The industrial revolution in the West forced countless agrarian peasants from their homes. Industrialization and the attendant rise of factories and unskilled wage labor took place first and almost exclusively in western Europe beginning in the eighteenth century. Eastern Europe responded far more slowly to the new economic development; in fact, it remained predominantly agricultural into the twentieth century. The only pockets of industrial change were the western tip of Austria, in Bohemia among the Czechs, and in a few cities elsewhere, such as Łódż in Russian Poland and at Saint Petersburg and Moscow. This lag in economic development was largely due to the tight control of the landed aristocracy, who did not want to yield any power to middle-class capitalists.

The regimes at the same time made some superficial changes to ease the lot of the peasants by freeing the serfs. Such emancipation occurred in Prussia in 1807, in Austria in 1848, and in Russia in 1861. The masses were now free to move about as they wished, and some even obtained land of their own. But overall the changes made life no easier for them.

Generally, little redistribution of land took place, and in fact living conditions often worsened, for several reasons: the high population growth in many areas, a constant subdivision of land in other areas, competition with cheaper agricultural goods from mechanized farms in the West, and little industrialization in east central Europe. The rural masses found that whatever land they did own was inadequate to support their families. Thus, for added income many had to move great distances and work where employment was available. That meant transferring to the more highly developed areas of western Europe and America.

To get a better idea of the devastating impact of the new economic conditions on the peasants, a few specific examples will suffice. In the 1850s, for instance, some Prussian landholders amassed huge estates to take advantage of the mechanization of agricultural production. They bought smaller peasant holdings and created huge agricultural factories. These vast farms employed the dispossessed peasants and attracted others from farther east, especially Poles. The result was the formation of a huge agricultural proletariat of east central Europeans.

The high rate of population growth throughout the area intensified the peasants' need for income. The population in the province of Austrian Galicia, for example, the home of Poles, Ruthenians, and others, more than doubled to over 7 million in the 1800s; that in lands controlled by Russia exploded in numbers from 98 million in 1880 to almost 161 million by 1910—despite the vast numbers who emigrated. Romanians doubled their population in the last third of the nineteenth century. In Hungary in the late 1800s, although peasant numbers increased sizably, half the land remained in the hands of a few.

Under these circumstances, the only alternative for many peasants was to look elsewhere for work. Some found seasonal employment in western Europe. Others continued on to the United States. Both agriculture and industry there were expanding during most of the 1800s. At the time of the passage of the Homestead Act (1862) which lowered the cost of land, vast agricultural areas were still available in the American Midwest for those who had sufficient resources to travel there and purchase it. Also, the wages of both agricultural and industrial labor in the New World were far higher than in the Old. In 1891, for example, the Galician farmhand in Austria was receiving about twelve cents a day, one-eighth as much as an American agricultural worker and one-tenth as much as an American industrial laborer.

Hence, as early as 1850, following the departure of many Germans, east central Europeans also decided to leave. This new source of arrivals in America continued until World War I and was massive, probably around 4 million, half of whom were Poles. The rest consisted of about 500,000 Slovaks, 450,000 Hungarians, 350,000 Czechs, 300,000 Lithuanians, 250,000 Ukrainians, 90,000 ethnic Russians, and 85,000 Romanians, with much smaller numbers of Latvians, Estonians, and Carpatho-Rusyns.

Despite the great variety of cultures among the millions in the groups who entered the United States during the period of mass migration, their arrival and adjustment followed a general pattern similar to that of other contemporary European immigrants. One of the more significant features of these east European waves is that their countries of origin shifted over time from west to east. The earliest group to enter America in large numbers was the most western—the Bohemians or Czechs, along with some Poles, a smattering of whom arrived in the 1840s and 1850s. Slovaks and Ukrainians started coming in the 1870s, then massive numbers of Hungarians and Romanians started arriving in the 1890s. This succession suggests that one departing group may have learned about America in part from their neighbors to the west who had left earlier. The pioneer role of Czechs and Poles supports this pattern, for these two groups usually sought proximity in America with previous German arrivals. Among these early immigrants Poles and Czechs often chose German marriage partners and joined German settlements, which suggests close communication between German and Slavic Old World villages.

Other patterns are evident. For example, the early Czechs and Poles who arrived in America from the 1850s to the 1870s had far greater personal resources, were much more literate and more skilled, and also were more likely to have a rural destination than later members of the same groups. This first east central European elite usually settled as families in permanent residences. The post-1870s immigrants were generally unskilled urban workers who were more likely to be single individuals intending to stay for a short while, make money, and then return to Europe.

Most east central Europeans came to America as a part of a chain migration, that is, following kin and neighbors. Thus, departure from the Czech, Polish, Slovak, Lithuanian, and other regions was not indiscriminate. Certain areas in eastern Europe produced many more emigrants than others. This suggests that people left an area as a result of the encouragement of prior departees. That encouragement took two forms: letters written to those who had remained behind, and the efforts of recruiters in America. The latter were highly resourceful people who, being among the first of their group to come, saw the advantage of stimulating others from their home region to move. They understood the needs of later-arriving countrymen and profited from that knowledge. Often they moved into their group's small middle class.

One can best see these facts of departure, travel, and destination in the two earliest east central European groups in America: the Czechs and Poles who came before 1870.

The larger group of early arrivals was the Czechs. Their greater financial resources were revealed in part by their destination; although some remained on the Atlantic coast, where they had landed, many more proceeded inland to the Midwest. A few settled in New York City, but as early as the 1850s Czechs largely went on to the major German settlements inland: eastern Missouri around Saint Louis and southeastern Wisconsin around Milwaukee. Others settled in and near such Great Lakes cities as Chicago and Cleveland. One estimate is that five hundred Czechs had arrived by 1850 and twenty-three thousand by the end of the decade. A few of these Czechs were refugees from the abortive 1848 revolution in central Europe, but many more came for more purely economic reasons. Surprisingly, these agrarians possessed a high level of personal resources. The overall literacy rate, for example, was 97 percent.

This elite maintained close connections with older German settlements. The first Czech newspaper in America, *Flugblätter* (*Leaflets*), was published (1852–1855), by Voyta Náprstek at Milwaukee in German. During the Civil War, Czechs continued to settle in rural areas near Germans. In 1860, for example, the heavily German state of Wisconsin had one-third of all the Czech immigrants. During the 1860s Czechs also were settling in the more rural areas of Minnesota, Iowa, Nebraska, and Texas, which had a considerable number of Moravians. The cheap land and great economic opportunity attracted them, and they had the resources to make the long trip.

Contemporary Polish arrivals moved in a similar manner. Until 1870 a large proportion of their settlements were agrarian, located near German colonies. For instance, the first permanent Polish Roman Catholic parish consisted of immigrants from German Poland, Silesian farmers who came directly as a group from Europe and settled at Panna Maria, Texas, in 1854. Their leader was a Polish priest who had joined the Franciscan order in Germany. Later Polish agrarian settlements were at Parisville, Michigan, and Polonia, Wisconsin. Around this time some German Poles settled in cities, and a few became recruiters for their ethnic countrymen from the Russian and Austrian empires seeking industrial employment in the later 1800s.

The major local example of a Polish founder was Anton Schermann, who settled at what would be his group's largest colony, Chicago. Born in the Poznán district of Prussia in 1818, he presented a notable American success story of social mobility by getting many of his countrymen to follow him to Chicago. He started as a laborer and in time accumulated enough capital to open a grocery store. His establishment soon became the social center for the city's growing Polish colony and was the birthplace of the city's first Polish Roman Catholic parish, St. Stanislaus (1864). Schermann's friend Peter Kiolbassa, a cobuilder of that largest Polonia or Polish settlement outside Poland, was another man of Prussian Polish background who early had come to the Windy City from Panna Maria, Texas. Other German-speaking Polish businessmen organized Polonias: the Detroiters Stanislaus Merlin and John Lemke from West Prussia, and the Milwaukeeans Anthony Kochanek and August Rudzinski, who had come from German Poland in the late 1850s.

These recruiters helped bring in a new type of immigrant by the last quarter of the nineteenth century. The American economy then was industrializing rapidly and the land available for farming was decreasing. A huge demand arose for unskilled industrial labor. The new immigrants were not yet industrial workers. American mines, mills, and factories acted as magnets for eastern Europeans. The Poles, who were most numerous of that group, made up the bulk of the unskilled work force heading for America, but also appearing in the 1870s were the Slovaks, Lithuanians, and Ukrainians.

THE AGE OF MASS IMMIGRATION

The appearance of the new wave of immigrants became something of a public issue as some Americans felt that a new indentured servant system had begun through contracting for the labor of those unskilled Slavs. But despite the passage of laws barring such arrangements, the east European stream of unskilled laborers continued, for it was fueled by both letters home and by assurances of group leaders already here. The supposed villains of recruitment as seen by late nineteenth-century American labor leaders and reformers, the steamship companies and labor agents, were not the basic stimulants for the new arrivals. They provided the facility, the transportation, but not the cause. The largest carrier of east European immigrants around the turn of the century was the North German Lloyd Line, which with its competitor, the Hamburg-America Line, provided most of the ships that carried east central Europeans to the New World. Lloyd's major agent in Bremen, Friedrich Missler, was said to have been responsible for millions of departees. In a sense he and the steamship lines did stimulate the coming of the masses as competition with other steamship lines kept the cost of steerage passage well within the reach of newcomers; around the 1890s it cost about forty dollars at a time when a typical month's wages in America was thirty dollars.

The major basis for the departure of east Europeans was letters of friends and relatives. A steel-mill owner or a mining company superintendent might encourage a worker to write home to get more hands. From the 1870s until World War I, the overwhelming bulk of east central Europeans—Poles, Lithuanians, and Slovaks especially—came to America to fill industrial jobs.

In many ways the Slovak example typifies the chain migration process which worked to bring over the immigrants. Settling with people from the same region or town was of the utmost importance for that group as they decided on their American destination. Their leading emigrant-producing districts in Hungary were Spiš, Šariš, and Zemplín

counties, places from which the early Slovak migrants entered the United States in the late 1870s. In particular their destinations were the coalfields of Pennsylvania and Illinois. John Lesniansky, for example, of western Pennsylvania, formerly from southern Zemplín, was initially responsible for getting the Pennsylvania Railroad to hire his countrymen.

Regional ties were even more important than religious ones. A Lutheran Slovak, for example, would prefer to live near a Catholic countryman than a non-Slovak coreligionist. In a 1907 survey, over 98 percent of all Slovak immigrants stated that they were going to join relatives or friends. One can assume that a similarly high percentage was true for most other east central Europeans.

Regional ties were strong, too, among the Poles, especially for those from its subcultures, such as the Kashubes living near the Baltic, the Gorali from the south, and those from Masuria (near the center of Russian Poland). Other major emigrant-producing provinces in Russian Poland were Łomża, Płock, and Suwałki, from which some Lithuanians also left. The earliest Ukrainians—Ruthenians who arrived here in the early 1880s—were from the eastern part of Austrian Galicia. Their desire to leave was so intense that some villages lost half their population. Their major recruiting pioneer was the Reverend John Wolansky, a Greek Catholic cleric who personally led many to work in the anthracite mines around Hazleton, Pennsylvania.

Among the numerous unskilled immigrants from eastern Europe from the 1880s to World War I, the basic motive that pushed many of them to America was to earn an income in the expanding New World industries, in some of which they may have worked in Europe. Thus the type of job they obtained here was similar to what they had done in eastern Europe: unskilled labor in heavy industry. Until the early 1900s they came for the most part without dependents and joined mining, meat-packing, steel, foundry, and similar firms. Some of these plants were located in the Northeast, especially in the factory towns of Massachusetts and Connecticut, and the New York City area, but they were more likely to be in the larger industrialized centers of the Midwest: Pennsylvania near the Great Lakes, Ohio, Michigan, Indiana, Illinois, Wisconsin, Minnesota, and south to Omaha and Saint Louis. Upton Sinclair's novel *The Jungle* (1906) is an accurate account of the work done by Lithuanian slaughterhouse workers Jurgis Rutkus and his friends in

Chicago's Back-of-the-Yards in the early twentieth century, although as a story of a typical east central European immigrant's conversion to socialism it is more questionable.

Besides obtaining a similar kind of employment as unskilled laborers in mines and mills, these varied newcomers fashioned a similar type of housing arrangement, which was widespread until at least the early 1900s, in the heavily industrialized centers. That accommodation was an important social institution known as the boardinghouse. This type of domicile, of course not exclusively east European, furnished the owner of the establishment with an income and the boarder, usually a kinsman or countryman, with inexpensive housing.

Under this institution a store owner or saloon keeper, or anyone with available rooms, would make sleeping space available to arriving countrymen. One authority, for example, describing the arrangement among Lithuanians in the Pennsylvania anthracite districts, asserted that around 1900 nearly every family in a given ethnic group had boarders. These were single men whose average wages were under four hundred dollars per year, out of which they paid twelve dollars per month for room and board, less if they purchased the food themselves. Some necessary purchases were made cooperatively, and housekeeping was done by the owner's wife.

The boardinghouse was not the only housing for unskilled labor; the companies themselves offered shelter, especially in isolated areas. But the boardinghouse was widespread among immigrant groups, for it met both their economic and their social needs. It constituted an important element in the future growth of ethnic communities.

The boardinghouse lasted much longer and was particularly common among Romanians, a group among the last of the east central Europeans to arrive, beginning in the 1890s. Since their dependents came much later than among earlier-arriving east central Europeans, their boardinghouses disappeared much more slowly. One source states that the typical Romanian house was rather crowded, holding twenty-five or more men who paid somewhat less than the Lithuanians, about eight dollars per month for room and board. Without doubt the arrangement was popular, for as late as 1908 over three-quarters of all Romanian immigrants had lodgers.

Boardinghouses were not permanent living accommodations for east Europeans, for as the workers accumulated savings, they were eager to obtain their own property, return home, or bring their dependents from Europe. Still, these makeshift accommodations were of crucial importance to the growth of the immigrant community because they were the immigrants' first social center. In them were conceived many other social institutions: mutual aid societies, religious societies and parish churches, and other cultural bodies. Clearly, more than any other immigrant gathering place, boardinghouses were the nuclei of east central European life in America.

The widespread availability of boardinghouses indicates that many of the earlier arrivals did not consider themselves to be permanent immigrants. Almost uniformly the idea of many men living together fit in with the initial intention of most east central Europeans to remain only a few years, as temporary workers. The available information suggests that the initial plan of most former peasants was to earn a little nest egg, then return to their native province, purchase land, and live out their days in their traditional home. Obviously this initial idea was discarded; with some exceptions there was no return rush to the Old World in the early 1900s. Many lodgers changed their minds after spending a few years in America and stayed. But a significant minority decided to go back.

It is difficult to determine the significance of reemigration among the east central Europeans. Statistics were not compiled until 1908, and the percentages may have been distorted in that year by the business cycle. Among the Poles, for example, the normal rate of return ran about 30 percent; in the peak year, 1908, just after the Panic of 1907, the figure went as high as 60 percent. The percentage of Romanian returnees was consistently high, about 60 percent from about 1905 until World War I. With the low cost of ship passage, it was relatively easy for a significant number of the east central Europeans to return home until 1914.

Nevertheless, in most cases immigrants preferred to send for their families once they had sufficient funds. Besides the great social attraction of living again with their kin, another advantage was economic. The women and children could work and contribute to the family income, thus making possible the quicker achievement of their desired economic goal, in many cases a home of their own.

Certainly the women did work. Polish women, for example, experienced fewer restrictions on taking jobs in the industrial areas where men worked than did, say, Italian women. A typical job for a Polish female was as a domestic, frequently as a servant in a middle-class home. Another was light factory work. A number of textile and candy plants were built in the Pennsylvania coalfields, probably to draw on the labor the immigrant women could provide. A 1909 study of immigrant women in Chicago substantiated the willingness of Polish and Lithuanian women to take service as well as light industrial employment.

The children were considered chiefly as economic contributors to the family. Their schooling was minimal; extensive education was considered necessary solely for the priesthood. The Anglo-American value of education for individual achievement did gain acceptance in east central European society, but it did so with the development of the many ethnic voluntary associations.

After reviewing east central Europeans' housing arrangements and their usual unskilled work in burgeoning American industry, it is important to examine how well they got along with both their fellow workers and their employers. The matter became a hotly debated national issue at the end of Theodore Roosevelt's administration when the president set up the Dillingham Commission in 1907 to investigate the impact of all the "new immigrants" from southern and eastern Europe who had been flooding the country during the previous twenty years. A distinction was made between them and those who had come earlier—the "old immigrants" from northern and western Europe.

The commission took several years to complete its examination, then concluded broadly that these newcomers with strange religions and languages were lowering the traditional American standard of living. More specifically, one conclusion was that with their lack of assimilation the new immigrants, docile and willing to work for the lowest wages, were weakening labor organization and worsening working conditions of the ordinary American.

It is difficult to give a complete picture of how the millions of east central European workers affected the working conditions of their English-speaking co-workers. Certainly the relationship with American workers and contact with the American labor movement were problematical and not generally harmonious, judging from the labor disputes in which the immigrants were involved.

The Knights of Labor made occasional half-hearted attempts to include east Europeans in their local assemblies in the 1880s. Although the recently arrived Ruthenian Greek Catholic priest, the Reverend John Wolansky, led a local Knights body in the anthracite town of Shenandoah, Pennsylvania, the image of imported "Hungarian" strikebreakers was a common one in the coalfields at that time because they were brought in by employers during labor unrest.

After the founding of the American Federation of Labor (AFL) in 1886, organized labor continued to be ambivalent about including east central European workers in its ranks. Part of the hesitation had to do with the movement's recruitment philosophy: to emphasize the organization of crafts and defer that of industry, the area of the economy which employed most of the immigrants. With one major exception, the United Mine Workers (UMW), the AFL unions hesitated to recruit Poles, Lithuanians, and others. Within the UMW, eastern Europeans were quite assertive, disproving the image of "Hunkies" as timid and naive operatives. And incidents in other industries substantiated the foreigners' willingness to demand their rights.

The most dramatic involvement of east central Europeans in American industrial disputes was an event in the Pennsylvania anthracite industry, the Lattimer Massacre of 1897. By the late 1800s the Pennsylvania anthracite industry was one of the largest heavy industries in the country, employing about one hundred thousand workers, the majority of whom were eastern European laborers. Dissatisfaction among these "new" immigrants arose in 1897 when mine owners began to cut wages for foreign workers and alter work rules so as to reduce the immigrants' incomes even further. The response of what were referred to as "Hungarians and Italians" that fall was to march on the open mines and pressure other workers to close them. The strikers were further upset because representatives of the UMW who were recruiting immigrants were also trying to pass legislation inhibiting the advancement of immigrants to a higher job level, that of certified miner.

Sheriffs of several counties tried to stop the organizing efforts of the east Europeans. One group met a posse at Lattimer, and in an altercation the latter fired upon the unarmed demonstrators, resulting in some fifty casualties—all mine workers—including nineteen deaths. Now the "Hunkies" had labor martyrs. Ultimately, however, some of the companies met certain of the strikers' demands.

The anthracite workers' unrest resurfaced in 1900 and in a larger, industrywide struggle in 1902. In these disputes the east Europeans made up the most militant and cohesive element of the striking work force. The struggle ended in 1903 when the mine owners agreed that the UMW would be the informal representative of their employees.

In other disputes of the period—at the Chicago stockyards in 1904; the McKees Rocks, Pennsylvania, steel strike of 1909; the Lawrence, Massachusetts, and Paterson, New Jersey, disputes of 1912 and 1913; at the national steel strike of 1919—the east central Europeans clearly proved their capacity to support the workers' cause during severe adversity. Such events certainly disproved the conclusion of the Dillingham Commission that having immigrants in them weakened unions. Yet despite all this evidence of their labor militancy, the American labor movement took little interest in recruiting foreign workers until the Great Depression of the 1930s and the formation of the AFL's rival, the Congress of Industrial Organizations (CIO).

One reason for the immigrants' militancy and strong resistance against employer discrimination was the sense of self-confidence they drew from the ethnic communities they constructed. The boardinghouses and other housing arrangements involved people who knew each other, and from those social units emerged an enormous array of religious and mutual self-help societies, parishes, and small insurance institutions.

Newspapers helped to forge strong group ties that became important bonds between labor organizers and workers. Whatever the literacy level of group members, high for the Czechs or low for the Romanians, immigrant journals were an important agency for information exchange, providing both homeland and local news almost from the beginning of ethnic settlements. Listing a few of these journals and their starting dates suggests their significance—some were sent back to Europe—as sources of information and contributors to ethnic community identity. We have already noted the German-Czech *Flugblätter* in Milwaukee. The first Czech-language paper, *Slowán Amerikansky,* appeared at Racine, Wisconsin, in 1860. Another freethinking journal was begun in Racine in the 1870s, and the first Czech daily, *Svornost (Harmony),* started at Chicago in 1875. The first Polish paper, *Echo z Polski (Echo from Poland)* appeared at New York in 1863; a second, *Orzeł Polski (Polish Eagle),* at Washington, Missouri, in 1870, the nationalist *Zgoda* at Milwaukee in 1881, a daily, *Dziennek Chicagoski (Chicago Daily News),* in 1890. The earliest Lithuanian paper, *Lietuwiszka Gazeta (Lithuanian Gazette),* was printed in 1879, and a Lithuanian Catholic one (*Vienybe Lietuoniku, Lithuanian Harmony*) in 1886, the year of the first Ukrainian jour-

nal. The first Slovak Catholic paper, *Slovak in America,* came out in 1889, and the Romanians produced their first regular publication in 1905. Though these papers were often partisan along religious or national lines, they provided information to help newcomers adjust to their new surroundings.

Local self-help associations produced a large number of national religious and fraternal institutions by the 1920s. Czech and Polish Catholic parishes were numerous by that time: over 250 of the former and more than 700 of the latter. These churches encouraged other diverse organizations. The Polish list offers some idea of the nature and scope of national societies: the Polish Roman Catholic Union (1873), the Polish National Alliance (1880), the Polish Singers Alliance (1889), the athletic Polish Falcons (begun 1886 as part of the Polish National Alliance and similar to the German Turners), the Polish Women's Alliance (1898), and the Alliance of Polish Socialists (1896). In 1912 Polish Americans had seven thousand different societies; three-quarters of all Polish immigrants in Chicago belonged to at least one of them.

Membership in ethnic associations was similarly common among all east central Europeans. The Hungarians, centered in Cleveland, New York, and western Pennsylvania, had one thousand of them by 1910. Such ubiquitous voluntary associations had a paradoxical role. They were cooperative self-help bodies, but at the same time they were American societies as well, subject to the laws and regulations of the host society. Thus, having to be run democratically, they inculcated some majority values among the members. East central European immigrants thus were acculturating at the same time they were building self-help agencies.

While the proliferation of ethnic voluntary associations among east central Europeans was common around the turn of the century, that growth was not always harmonious, as philosophical divisions arose. The earliest was the bitter disagreement between the Czech freethinking majority of liberal anti-Catholics and the Roman Catholic minority. The longest and most extensive battle took place between east central European Roman Catholics and ethnic nationalists. The burning issue was whether the ethnic community should be primarily religious or nationalist. The debate festered from about 1850 to World War I. It especially exercised Czechs, Slovaks, Lithuanians, and above all Poles. The outcome left the latter group very much divided around the turn of the century and was in part the cause of the excommunication of certain "independent" parishes. Some of these later grouped to form the Polish National Catholic Church in 1907.

The divisions, however, moderated as World War I approached; Catholics began to work more with ethnic nationalists who, as the conflict neared, saw the real possibility of freeing their homelands. The Slovak League (1907), for example, included both religious and nationalist camps whose goal was to fight the Hungarian oppression of their countrymen. A few Polish Roman Catholic officials joined with nationalists at the unveiling of the Kościuszko and Pulaski statues at Washington, D.C., in 1910. And Polish nationalists and clericalists joined formally in 1914 on the Central Polish Relief Committee. From 1915 to 1918 the Czech National Alliance worked with the Slovak League in arranging for a new state to include those groups along with Carpatho-Rusyns.

IMMIGRATION AFTER 1920

The 1920s began a third era of east central European immigration. Following the various peace treaties creating autonomous or independent homelands in Poland, Lithuania, and Czechoslovakia, the expected rush of American returnees never materialized, although some political leaders did return. The major change experienced by immigrants who remained was a near-hysterical nativism directed against them, in part for fear of the spread of radicalism after the 1917 Bolshevik Revolution. The United States passed new immigration laws during the 1920s that sharply reduced the numbers admitted from eastern Europe. For example, in some years before World War I, Polish immigration had run at 100,000 or more; by the end of the 1920s the allowable figure was about 6,500; for Czechoslovaks, 2,800; for Lithuanians, 386; and for Romanians, 377.

Oddly enough, while the 1920s and 1930s saw a sharp decline in immigrants from eastern Europe, and heightened anti-Catholicism and nativism made being foreign born uncomfortable, in other ways the eastern Europeans did find some advantages in their daily lives. In fact, in some ways their communities flowered. For one thing, the many ethnic fraternal and voluntary associations acquired leadership that increasingly consisted of American-born offspring of immigrants who lacked their parents' ties to the homeland. Thus they began to devote more of their funds and energies to their own communities. The leader of a major Polish American society announced at Warsaw in 1930 that with the homeland independent, the American Polonia was now part of America. This shift in emphasis was true for other east European institutions as well.

This greater rootedness in the New World became apparent throughout the 1920s as east central Europeans experienced a rise in their standard of living. The decade of the 1920s was a fairly prosperous one for those basically working-class groups; some began to move out of their multiple-unit dwellings and purchase their own residences, and perhaps an automobile. For example, the Polish cooperative building and loan societies, which had started in 1881, were reaching their peak by the mid 1920s. Nationally there were 550 such societies with 400,000 members holding $330 million in assets. The Czechs in Chicago also had a significant group of wealthy savings institutions. Statistically, by 1924 Czech building-and-loan associations held over half of all Chicago's assets in such associations.

Besides definite material advancement, in this decade of assimilation Polish and east central European cultural life remained active and occasionally flowered. The number of Polish newspapers was at its height in 1923, with over one hundred in circulation. The larger cities had community centers, called Dom Polskis, which offered a wide array of cultural activities. These normally included a library, an auditorium for lectures and theatrical productions, a gymnasium, and a bar for socializing.

Ethnic music and dancing also experienced a revival in the interwar period. Two dynamic instructors came to America in the 1920s to organize schools of dance especially for the younger members of their communities. One was the Ukrainian Vasile Avramenko, who created a sensation among his people as he traveled around the country in the late 1920s and early 1930s. The other was the Lithuanian Vytautas Beliajus, who started a number of Lithuanian dance groups. In fact, ethnic music and dancing became a national movement after they were featured at the world expositions of the 1930s, especially in Chicago and New York. American record companies in the 1920s helped to maintain both group and nongroup interest in ethnic music by issuing songs, skits, and other musical selections by east central Europeans. By far the most popular single record was "The Ukrainian Wedding," which sold probably one hundred thousand copies in the late 1920s and was available in a Polish version as well.

As one might expect, the depression of the 1930s had a devastating effect on east central European workers; they were an integral part of the work force which suffered severe unemployment. Family living standards declined, and many had to revert to the stringent economies of the immigrant era, reviving the practice of taking in boarders and making other cutbacks. However, the Depression also brought with it a vigorous working-class solidarity among east central European families, who responded enthusiastically to labor unions and to the efforts of recruiters to organize plants. It has been estimated that in the several drives of the CIO to organize heavy industry in the period from 1935 to 1937, perhaps one-quarter who joined were of east European descent. A new, more profound class consciousness, a process of proletarianization, had taken place among the Polish Americans in automobile plants and the Romanian Americans in steel mills.

A final movement affected east central Europeans in America: World War II and the refugees who came to America. These were of the same ethnic background but very different in social class from the older, peasant immigrants. The newcomers were chiefly middle-class professionals and intellectuals. In any event, with the huge population dislocation which occurred after the conflict, America felt obliged to accept a few, chiefly through the passage of the Displaced Persons acts of 1948 and 1953.

Upper-class ethnic Russians had come to the United States earlier, about thirty thousand in the period 1920–1940, and others entered as refugees during the cold war of the 1950s and 1960s. In all, down to 1970 refugees included 152,000 Poles, 90,000 Ukrainians, 60,000 Hungarians, 28,000 Lithuanians, and 10,000 Romanians. The 40,000 Latvians who came as refugees outnumbered the 35,000 who lived in America in 1940.

With the exception of the Latvians, although these new arrivals have constituted only a fraction of their total ethnic communities, a fair number have taken leadership positions in existing associations. However, they have been more eager to form or join their own professional or academic bodies, such as the Polish Institute of Arts and Sciences in America (1942) and the Czechoslovak Society of Arts and Sciences (1958).

With the revolutionary changes now occurring in eastern Europe and the disappearance of the Communist regimes, the future of east central European institutions and ethnic life in this country remains an enigma. Much depends on the success of the independent nations outside the former Soviet Union and what will happen to those nationalities within its crumbling frontiers.

BIBLIOGRAPHY

General Works

Archdeacon, Thomas. *Becoming American: An Ethnic History* (1983).

Bodnar, John. *The Transplanted: A History of Immigrants in Urban America* (1985). The major immigration history synthesis.

Thernstrom, Stephan, et al. *Harvard Encyclopedia of American Ethnic Groups* (1980). A monumental reference work covering 106 ethnic groups.

Group Histories

Alexander, June G. *The Immigrant Church and Community: Pittsburgh's Slovak Catholics and Lutherans, 1880–1915* (1987).

Baker, T. Lindsay. *The First Polish Americans: Silesian Settlements in Texas* (1979).

Balch, Emily Greene. *Our Slavic Fellow Citizens* (1910; repr. 1969). An early classic.

Bicha, Karel D. "The Czechs in Wisconsin History." *Wisconsin Magazine of History* 53, no. 3 (1970).

Bobińska, Celina, and Andrzej Pilch, eds. *Employment-seeking Emigrations of the Poles World-wide, XIX and XX Centuries.* Translated by Danuta E. Zukowska (1975).

Brozek, Andrzej. *Polish Americans, 1854–1939.* Translated by Wojciech Worsztynowicz (1977).

Budreckis, Algirdas M., comp. and ed. *The Lithuanians in America, 1651–1975: A Chronology and Fact Book* (1976).

Bukowczyk, John. *And My Children Did Not Know Me: A History of Polish-Americans* (1987). A distinctive interpretation.

Chmelar, Johann. "The Austrian Emigration, 1900–1914." Translated by Thomas C. Childers. *Perspectives in American History* 7 (1973).

Galitzi, Christine Avghi. *A Study of Assimilation Among the Roumanians in the United States* (1929). Still relevant and important.

Golab, Caroline. *Immigrant Destinations* (1977). Especially good on conditions of Polish immigration to Philadelphia.

Greene, Victor. *The Slavic Community on Strike: Immigrant Labor in Pennsylvania Anthracite* (1968).

———. *For God and Country: The Rise of Polish and Lithuanian Ethnic Consciousness in America, 1860–1910* (1975).

———. *American Immigrant Leaders: Marginality and Identity* (1987).

Halich, Wasyl. *Ukrainians in the United States* (1937; repr. 1970). An early work that still has relevant information on early Ruthenian Greek Catholics.

Kantowicz, Edward. *Polish-American Politics in Chicago, 1888–1940* (1975).

Kučas, Antanas. *Lithuanians in America.* Translated by Joseph Boley (1975). The most complete published account of the group thus far.

Kuzniewski, Anthony J. *Faith and the Fatherland: The Polish Church Wars in Wisconsin, 1896–1918* (1980).

Morawska, Ewa. *For Bread with Butter: The Life-Worlds of East Central Europeans in Johnstown, Pennsylvania, 1890–1940* (1985). An extraordinarily rich account of immigrant lives in a small community.

Parot, John Joseph. *Polish Catholics in Chicago, 1850–1920: A Religious History* (1981). A full account of the rise of Polish independent Catholic churches.

Puskas, Julianna. *From Hungary to the United States, 1880–1914.* Translated by Maria Bales, trans. rev. Eva Palmai (1982).

Stolárik, Marian Mark. "Slovak Migration from Europe to North America, 1870–1918." *Slovak Studies* 20 (1980).

Wolkovich-Valkavičius, William. *Lithuanian Religious Life in America.* 3 vols. [forthcoming]. A huge compendium covering every major group settlement in the United States.

SEE ALSO **Ethnicity; German Speakers; Immigration; The Jews; Minorities and Work; Native Peoples and Early European Contacts; Nativism, Anti-Catholicism, and Anti-Semitism; Social History in Great Britain and Continental Europe; Socialist and Communist Movements; The Upper Midwest.**

THE JEWS

Shelly Tenenbaum

THE COLONIAL AND REVOLUTIONARY PERIOD

As EARLY AS 1585, Joachim Gaunse, a Jewish chemist from Prague who had transformed England's copper smelting industry, settled in Roanoke Island, Virginia, to work as a metallurgist. But Gaunse's sojourn in the new world was brief. After less than a year, he returned to England. Although other individual Jews may have passed through the American colonies, the American Jewish experience did not truly begin until early September 1654, when a group of twenty-three Jews arrived in New Amsterdam from Recife, Brazil. Fleeing from the Portuguese who had recaptured Brazil from Holland and were extending their brutal Inquisition to their South American territories, this small band of Jews emigrated to Dutch-controlled New Amsterdam, where they established America's first Jewish community.

Shortly after this group arrived, Peter Stuyvesant, director of the Dutch West India Company in New Amsterdam, petitioned his superiors in Holland for permission to deport the newcomers because Jews, in his words, were "such hateful enemies and blasphemers of the name of Christ" and were engaged in "deceitful trading with the Christians." Although sympathetic to Stuyvesant's concerns, the Amsterdam Chamber of the company denied his request, in part due to pressure exerted by Amsterdam's Jews, some of whom were principal shareholders within the organization. Stuyvesant then had no choice but to allow the Jews to remain under his jurisdiction. When he persisted in placing barriers in their way—for example, in 1655 he prohibited Jewish participation in the fur trade—members of the fledgling Jewish community continued to seek redress from the Amsterdam directors. And more often than not, they succeeded in overturning Stuyvesant's discriminatory decrees. Stuyvesant's control ended in 1664, when the English asserted their hegemony and transformed Dutch New Amsterdam into British New York.

By the time of the War of Independence, the colonial Jewish community had grown to number almost twenty-five hundred and had formed congregations that sustained an active religious life. Weddings and circumcisions were performed, kosher meat was procured, charity was distributed, and schools, ritual baths, and cemeteries were maintained. Although the majority of colonial Jews were Ashkenazi (descendants of Jews from Central and Eastern Europe), synagogue ritual was conducted according to Sephardic (Spanish and Portuguese) tradition, the tradition of the original settlers. It was not until the turn of the nineteenth century that the first group of Ashkenazi Jews rebelled against Sephardic dominance by breaking away from the Philadelphia synagogue Mikveh Israel and founding their own congregation Rodeph Shalom. This act of ethnic secession, one that was based on cultural difference, marked the beginning of a trend in American synagogue history.

Despite religious tensions between Sephardim and Ashkenazim, their concentration in commercially oriented pursuits engendered close intergroup ties (for example, intermarriage). Although most of the American population was agrarian, the Jewish community was overwhelmingly engaged in urban business enterprises. Having been excluded from European agriculture, Jewish immigrants were particularly well suited to develop America's commercial sector. In 1760, the approximately one thousand Jews residing in Newport, Rhode Island, and its surrounding area owned a host of factories that produced candles, rope yarn, soap, furniture, and potash as well as several distilleries and sugar refineries. Due to their business and family connections in the West Indies and Europe, colonial Jews made their biggest mark in the shipping and whaling industry. With a fleet of about thirty ships, Newport resident Aaron Lopez made his fortune by trading goods between New England, the West Indies, England, and the west coast of Africa. Like many other shipping merchants of his day, Lopez also participated in the slave trade. The port locations of their earliest synagogues reflect Jewish involvement in ocean commerce: New York, Newport, Richmond, Savannah, Philadelphia, and Charleston. By 1820, two-thirds of the nation's Jews resided in Charleston, New York, Philadelphia, and Richmond.

Spurred by the hope of greater freedom, most Jews within the thirteen colonies supported the struggle for American independence. Gershom Seixas (1745–1816), spiritual leader of synagogue Shearith Israel, chose to move his congregation out of New York rather than be subjected to British rule. Many Jews, such as Francis Salvador (who was one of the first to fall in battle), and Major Benjamin Nones, fought against England during the Revolutionary War. To symbolize Jewish support for independence, Philadelphia Jews arranged for kosher food to be served among the offered refreshments at a 1789 parade in honor of the newly ratified Constitution, and Newport's Jewish community presented George Washington with a letter that praised the new government because it gave "to bigotry no sanction, to persecution no assistance."

FROM THE EARLY NATIONAL TO THE POSTBELLUM PERIOD

Emigration from Europe slowed down during the late eighteenth and very early nineteenth centuries. In 1820 it increased again when Jews, along with other Germans, were pushed out of their homelands by severe economic crisis and attracted to the New World by the growing American economy. Repressive legislation, such as restrictions and taxes aimed specifically at Jewish communities, combined with a new wave of anti-Jewish reprisals that emerged as part of a backlash to Napoleon's reforms, provided German Jews—often poor, single men from the rural areas of Bavaria, Baden, Württemberg, and Posen—with a special incentive to leave the Germanic states. As a result of the new influx, the American Jewish population rose from 6,000 in 1825 to 150,000 in 1860. While New York City's total population nearly quintupled between 1825 and 1860, from 166,000 to 805,000, its Jewish population increased eighty fold, from 500 to 40,000 in the same period. Cincinnati's Jewish community of 3,300 in 1850 had more than tripled a decade later, while San Francisco's Jewish population of about 4,000 members during the mid 1850s gained a third more by 1860.

During an era of rapid economic growth, German Jewish men played an important role in American business life. By 1880, most were employed in trade and manufacturing. Around 1870, a disproportionate number of German Jews in Detroit and Columbus were employed as either peddlers or merchants: 70 percent and 82 percent, respectively. Between 1845 and 1861, Boston Jews were four times as likely as other urban workers to be employed as petty merchants. Meanwhile on the West Coast, more than half of San Francisco's Jews were engaged in mercantile trade, often as representatives of their families' eastern firms. With the emergence of the sewing machine and its subsequent revolution of the apparel industry, German Jews became heavily represented among manufacturers of ready-made clothing, almost to the point of achieving a monopoly in the field. By the late nineteenth century, two German Jewish firms—Hart, Schaffner, and Marx, and Kuppenheimer and Sonneborn—controlled ninety percent of the wholesale and eighty percent of the retail clothing market.

As the country expanded westward, the distribution of goods to new frontier communities became a key economic niche for German Jewish immigrants. Julius Rosenwald (1862–1932), for example, transformed Sears, Roebuck into the world's largest mail-order firm, allowing his company to reach consumers in rural areas. Peddling became a very important strategy employed by German Jewish immigrants to meet the nation's new material needs. While peddling was hard and lonely work—it entailed carrying heavy loads and spending days on the road going from door to door—the work had certain advantages. Peddling required little initial capital, since goods were usually obtained on credit; and by enabling many new immigrants to make the transition from carrying a pack to driving a wagon then to owning a small store, this branch of petty trade provided an economic stepping stone.

An ethnic network whereby eastern Jewish manufacturers provided credit to western Jewish wholesalers who in turn supplied credit to local Jewish retailers and peddlers was crucial to nineteenth-century Jewish business development. In at least some cities, Jews were forced to rely on other Jews because borrowing from gentile merchants was not a viable option. In Cincinnati and Buffalo, for example, investigators for the credit information agency R.G. and Dun Company made it difficult for Jewish businessmen by routinely portraying them as dishonest: According to David Gerber (1987, p. 219), their reports included statements such as "a Jew of the hardest mold; don't trust him," and "he is a Jew and although in point of fact he may now be perfectly responsible, yet Jews have a wonderful faculty of becoming at almost any moment they choose entirely irresponsible."

Many German Jews served the commercial needs of plantation owners as merchants and cotton jobbers in the South. Some earned their living as slave traders. In Charleston, for example, four of the city's forty-four slave traders were Jews. While Southern Jews tended to support slavery through their allegiance to the Democratic party, the nation's other Jews leaned toward the politics of the Republican party. In general, however, there was no Jewish consensus on the issue of slavery. The division was reflected by the positions taken by two American rabbis: Morris J. Raphall (1798–1868), rabbi of New York's Congregation B'nai Jeshurun and David Einhorn (1809–1879) rabbi of Baltimore's Temple Har Sinai. When Raphall asserted in an 1861 speech that the Bible sanctions slavery (which was interpreted by many as a Jewish defense of slavery), Einhorn responded by publishing a series of four articles condemning institutionalized slavery based on his understanding of Jewish teachings. Later that year, Einhorn was forced to flee Baltimore because of his outspoken support of the abolitionist cause.

Although the slavery issue failed to unite American Jewry during the Civil War, a collective cry of protest rang out when General Ulysses S. Grant accused Jews for speculating in the cotton trade and subsequently decreed in 1862 that all Jews evacuate the Tennessee Department (consisting of northern Mississippi and parts of Tennessee and Kentucky) within a twenty-four-hour period. Two months after receiving an appeal from a group of Jewish citizens, President Lincoln rescinded the order. By that point, however, Jews in three communities—Holly Springs and Oxford in Mississippi, and Paducah, Kentucky—had already been forced to vacate their homes.

Grant's order stunned the Jewish community. While such government-instigated acts of anti-Semitism were frequent in Europe, they were an anomaly in the United States. In the U.S., a postemancipation society, where the question of whether Jews should have full rights had never been on the national agenda, anti-Semitism had always been on the fringe of the political system. In Europe

though, "the Jewish Question" had been the subject of fierce public debates, and anti-Semitism had emerged on the forefront of politics. Grant's order raised fears among American Jews because it replicated the European experience. That they successfully obtained recourse from the country's highest government authority, however, reflects a crucial difference between the European and American contexts.

Until the middle decades of the nineteenth century there was only one form of Judaism in the United States: traditional Judaism. But the nation's liberal spirit, which led many Jews to want to Americanize their synagogues, shaped the development of Reform Judaism. Innovations such as prayers in the vernacular (English), liturgical alterations, sermons, confirmation ceremonies for boys and girls, mixed seating of women and men, organs, and choirs characterized the Reform synagogues that spread across the land. The rapid growth of the movement led Reform leader Isaac Mayer Wise to establish in 1873 the Union of American Hebrew Congregations, an organization uniting Reform synagogues. Two years later, it was followed by Cincinnati's Hebrew Union College, a seminary to train Reform rabbis, with Wise as president. Through its accommodation to American religious norms, Reform Judaism became a movement that transformed the nature of Jewish religious life.

The Reform movement did not originate in the United States; rather, it began in Germany in the first decades of the nineteenth century. While Reform Judaism in America benefited from the experience of German émigré rabbis such as Isaac Leeser (1806–1868) and David Einhorn, it would be a mistake to view American Reform simply as an import or extension of German Reform. The earliest Reform synagogues in the United States—Baltimore's Har Sinai (1842), New York's Emanuel (1845), Albany's Anshe Emeth (1850), Cincinnati's Bene Yeshurun (1841) and Bene Israel (1855), Philadelphia's Keneseth Israel (1856), and Chicago's Sinai (1861)—did not deliberately set out with a Reform agenda. Rather, they began as traditional synagogues and only gradually introduced changes in their liturgy.

The classical ideals of American Reform Judaism were embodied in the Pittsburgh Platform adopted by Reform rabbis in 1885. It proclaimed that only those laws and rituals that sanctified the lives of American Jews were acceptable, while those discordant with modern civilization should be rejected. Furthermore, the concept of Jewish nationhood and the goal of returning to Palestine were discarded while the notion of religious community was emphasized. Only some fifty years later, after a mass influx of eastern European Jews and a growing commitment to Zionism, would the Reform rabbinate formally embrace a more traditional view of Judaism in the Columbus Platform of 1937. The document highlighted the importance of Sabbath and festival observances, encouraged the use of Hebrew in synagogue services, and affirmed an obligation to make Palestine a Jewish homeland.

During the colonial period, synagogues had been the social welfare arm of the Jewish community. They had provided members with services such as religious education, sick care, burial benefits, and loan funds. In the course of the nineteenth century, however, philanthropy shifted away from the synagogue, and benevolent societies became the primary distributors of charity. At first these mutual aid associations were connected to congregations, but by the late 1840s and the 1850s many had completely severed ties with their parent organizations. These withdrawals were facilitated by frequent synagogue secessions and a growing number of Jews who were unaffiliated with a synagogue but wanted the privileges an association offered. By the 1860s and 1870s, the number of Jewish philanthropic agencies grew so large that a need to coordinate their activities emerged. As a result, umbrella organizations often known as United Hebrew Charities came into existence. This plethora of charitable facilities testifies to the existence of a class of impoverished Jews.

By forming their own separate institutions, nineteenth-century Jewish women contributed to the proliferation of philanthropic associations. In 1819, a group of New York women affiliated with Shearith Israel founded the Female Hebrew Benevolent Society to provide aid to indigent women and their families. At least eight Jewish women's associations existed in New York City by the late 1850s. Ladies' Hebrew sewing societies, organizations that specialized in making and distributing clothing for the needy, were formed in many Jewish communities. Other women's groups, often initiated by men, performed such tasks as arranging flowers and food at synagogue functions. Although women's volunteer work was not very different from their domestic chores, these philanthropic activities provided middle-class German Jewish women with opportunities to gain leadership and organizational skills, which enabled them to take first steps out of the private sphere and into the communal realm.

THE MASS IMMIGRANT INFLUX

Although some eastern European Jews had immigrated to the United States with their German counterparts, their numbers had been relatively small. Between 1881 and 1924, however, the migration from eastern Europe soared: approximately 2.5 million eastern European Jews (mainly from Russia) moved to the United States, altering the face of the entire American Jewish community. The approximately quarter million Jews of German origin became a numerical minority even as the country's percentage of Jews increased significantly. In 1877, Jews comprised .54 percent of the nation's population, and by 1917 they were 3.28 percent. The new Jewish immigrants left their homes to escape intense poverty, overcrowding, and repression, and along with millions of other Europeans, were pulled across the Atlantic by America's industrial opportunities. Furthermore, new forms of transportation, such as the steamship and railroads, made the long journey both affordable and more attractive than it had been previously.

All but a privileged few of the Jews in Russia were restricted to the Pale of Settlement, a 386,000 square mile area that spread from the Baltic Sea to the Black Sea, comprising provinces in Western Russia and Congress (Russian-held) Poland. During the course of the nineteenth century, a high birthrate and low death rate precipitated a population explosion among Jews, making life untenable in the confined Pale. Where eight hundred thousand Jews lived in 1800, by 1900 the figure had climbed to five and a half million. The discriminatory May Laws of 1882, which prohibited Jews from living in rural areas, forced them to live in the already overcrowded cities. This situation was exacerbated by Russia's transition from a preindustrial to an industrial state: Jews, who were overwhelmingly artisans and petty merchants, were severely displaced by the forces of industrialization.

Instigated by the tsarist regime, a wave of pogroms terrorized Russian Jews and further encouraged their mass exodus. After the assassination of Alexander II in 1881, mobs attacked over two hundred Jewish communities killing and wounding people as well as destroying property. However, the very high proportion of Jews who emigrated from Galicia—an area now straddling the Polish-Ukrainian border—suggests that the deteriorating economic status of eastern European Jewry is more salient than the pogroms for understanding the large-scale emigration. Although there were no pogroms in Galicia (Jews had been emancipated in 1867), the poverty rates were very high.

Pogroms may not have been the central factor pushing masses of Jews to uproot themselves, but they did shape a distinguishing characteristic of this immigrant group: their very low repatriation rates. The yearning nostalgia for the native country common to many immigrants was virtually absent among Jews because they had been victims of an intense anti-Semitic climate. Between 1908 and 1912, only 7 percent of East European Jews returned to their countries of origin, compared to 42 percent of all other immigrants. The high percentages of women and children among the eastern European Jewish immigrants further attests to this permanency: women comprised 44 percent and children under fourteen 24 percent. This permanent settler orientation worked to their advantage by encouraging them to lay down roots and to invest time and capital in educational and business pursuits that would yield future financial payoffs.

In general, neither the indigent nor the rich left their homes in Russia. Those on the very bottom rungs of the economic ladder could not afford the price of a ticket, and those at the top had little motivation to uproot themselves. Furthermore, very religious Jews tended not to immigrate: the pious had no intention of moving to a country with a reputation for seducing its inhabitants away from religion. According to Marshall Sklare (1971), when Jacob David Wilowsky, the rabbi of Slutsk, Lithuania, visited New York in 1900, he told an audience that they should never have left Europe: "It was not only home that the Jews left behind in Europe. It was their Torah, their Talmud, their *yeshivot* [schools of Jewish learning]—in a word, their *Yiddishkeit,* their entire Jewish way of life" (quoted in *America's Jews,* p. 17).

Many acculturated and established German Jews saw the hundreds of thousands of eastern European Jews flooding the United States as a threat. They were sensitive to the nation's heightened atmosphere of xenophobia and feared a rise in anti-Semitism. As a result, some German Jews actually fought to halt the tide of immigration. The more common response, however, was to offer the Jewish newcomers a wide range of services—vocational training, civic lessons, homemaking advice, and English classes—in order to ease their transition into American economic life and to socialize them into the cultural fabric as quickly as possible. While ethnic loyalty inspired German Jews to help the eastern Europeans, self-interest guided their ac-

tions as well: were the immigrants to become an economic burden and fail to shed their alien ways, the status of all American Jews might be harmed.

The immigrants' tendency to concentrate in just a few urban centers alarmed America's Jewish leadership. New York proved to be the strongest magnet for the Jewish newcomers: of the nearly one and a half million Jews who disembarked in New York between 1881 and 1911, about 70 percent stayed, and most found their way to the congested Lower East Side. As a result, German Jewish philanthropists such as Jacob Schiff (1847–1920), Jesse Seligman (1827–1894), Leonard Lewisohn (1847–1902), and Oscar Straus (1850–1926) funded projects to divert the eastern Europeans to other regions. Their schemes included colonizing immigrants in agricultural colonies located in sparsely populated areas of Louisiana, Oregon, Arkansas, Colorado, the Dakotas, and New Jersey, or sending eastern European Jews straight from Europe to the port city of Galveston, Texas, in order to avoid their landing (and remaining) in New York. In its seven years of existence (1907–1914), the Galveston Plan succeeded in settling about ten thousand Jews throughout the Southwest. For the most part, however, these dispersal attempts made no more than a small dent in the distribution of Jewish communities across America. The Industrial Removal Office, created by the Jewish Agricultural and Industrial Aid Society to coordinate resettlement efforts, only succeeded in relocating 6 percent of the immigrants between 1900, when it first opened, and 1922, when it closed. In 1925, over 40 percent of American Jews still resided in New York, and more than 80 percent lived in just six states: New York, Pennsylvania, Illinois, Massachusetts, New Jersey, and Ohio.

German Jewish attempts to help the new immigrants were not always welcome. The eastern Europeans often perceived their predecessors as patronizing and condescending, and some strongly resented these Americanization efforts. In order to establish their independence, the immigrants quickly created an impressive institutional network: they organized social welfare institutions (for example, the Hebrew Immigrant Aid Society) and hospitals that met their religious dietary prescriptions. To address their community's social problems, they established reformatories for delinquent youth, homes for unwed mothers, and a national service to locate husbands who deserted their families. Not long after they stepped off the boat, newcomers joined *landmanschaften* (mutual aid organizations based on community of origin) that provided members with important benefits such as burial rights, interest-free loans, insurance, and sick pay. Furthermore, through their Yiddish theaters and newspapers, eastern European Jews created a vital cultural life. At the turn of the century, about two million viewers enjoyed over a thousand Yiddish shows each year; and by the early 1920s Chicago, Cleveland, New York, and Philadelphia each had their own Yiddish dailies.

Immigrant Employment and Economics Contrary to the fears of many German Jews, the eastern Europeans overcame poverty relatively quickly. As with earlier German Jews, trade and manufacturing became the new immigrants' most important vehicles for moving up the economic ladder. In 1900, one-fifth (23 percent of men and 10 percent of women) of all gainfully employed Jewish immigrants living in major cities earned their livelihood in trade, and three-fifths (57 percent of men and 69 percent of women) were engaged in manufacturing. Compared with other groups, Jews were much more likely to own their own businesses. In turn-of-the-century Los Angeles, Jews were three times more likely than other city inhabitants to own their own enterprises. By 1940, 41 percent of Jewish male immigrants in Providence, Rhode Island, ran their own businesses, as compared to 11.5 percent of Italians. Even in predominantly blue-collar Johnstown, Pennsylvania, 75 percent of immigrant Jews were self-employed in trade throughout the four decades preceding the Second World War.

In order to supplement the earnings of their immigrant fathers, Jewish sons and daughters often worked as industrial wage laborers. A 1911 government-sponsored report on immigration found that 36 percent of Jewish families relied on their children's earnings, and that nearly three-quarters of American-born daughters of immigrant Jews worked for wages. In contrast, Jewish immigrant wives rarely sought factory work. According to an 1880 study, only 2 percent of married Jewish women worked outside of the home, and this figure declined to 1 percent twenty-five years later. These statistics, however, underestimate women's actual economic roles because they omit wives who took in boarders as well as wives who contributed to family businesses. Rather than view women's entrepreneurial participation as work, both women and men described it with terms such as "helping out" or "minding the store." While wage labor was viewed as socially unacceptable for married Jewish women, working in a family business was consid-

ered a legitimate means of contributing to the family economy.

Within the field of manufacturing, eastern European Jews specialized in the production of clothing. In 1900, more than one-third of all gainfully employed Jewish immigrants residing in large urban centers were engaged in some branch of the garment trades. Two related factors account for this high level of ethnic concentration. First, at the time the Jewish immigrants arrived in the United States, the apparel industry was growing two to three times faster than the average rate for all industries (and over two-thirds of its production was situated in New York City, the entry port for the vast majority of immigrants). Second, the skills of the eastern Europeans corresponded well with this expanding industry: nearly one out of every three working Jewish immigrants arrived in the United States as tailors and seamstresses, and a full two-thirds possessed some urban industrial skills that they had acquired in their countries of origin. This match between Jewish occupational skills and the needs of the American economy was crucial for the emerging concentration of Jews in the garment industry.

The particular nature of the apparel industry offered the Jewish newcomers possibilities for starting their own enterprises. Its high degree of specialization prompted manufacturers to distribute work to contractors and subcontractors, who then employed a small number of immigrant workers in small firms, often housed in tenement apartments, known as "sweatshops." Roughly sixteen thousand sweatshops existed in New York City in 1913, for example, providing many immigrants with the opportunity to make the transition from worker to entrepreneur. The industry that had once been controlled by German Jews had shifted into the hands of the newer eastern Europeans.

In order to take advantage of available entrepreneurial opportunities in trade and manufacturing, the new immigrants needed access to capital. The informal credit ties that had once served the relatively small German Jewish community did not fulfill the eastern Europeans' monetary needs. Therefore, late nineteenth- and early twentieth-century Jewish immigrants established Hebrew free loan societies—philanthropic organizations based on biblical and Talmudic injunctions to provide the Jewish poor with interest-free loans—which had been common in Europe. By 1927, more than five hundred existed in large urban centers such as New York, Chicago, Boston, and San Francisco as well as in much smaller communities such as Altoona, Pennsylvania, Lafayette, Indiana, Shreveport, Louisiana, and Elmira, New York.

Ethnic culture and religious tradition, however, did not limit the types of immigrant loan activity. In addition to traditional Hebrew free loan associations, eastern European Jews created modern credit unions, organizations that charged interest on loans and therefore had no basis within Jewish law. In 1916, Jews operated half of all urban credit unions in New York State, and by the early years of the Depression, 85 of the state's 117 credit unions had a predominantly Jewish membership. In neighboring Massachusetts, 172 of the state's 311 credit unions existing in 1930 had a majority of Jewish members.

Although the garment industry served as an avenue for economic mobility, it was plagued by harsh working conditions: laboring long hours for low wages, charged for the needles and electricity they used, and women were frequently subjected to unwanted sexual attention from their bosses. In 1911, the death of 146 Triangle Shirtwaist Company employees, mainly young single Jewish or Italian women, came to symbolize the severe reality of factory life: when fire broke out on the upper floors of the large New York factory on a spring afternoon, workers were trapped behind locked doors with no escape but by leaping from windows. In his poem "The Sweatshop," Yiddish writer Morris Rosenfeld (1862–1923) described a worker's feelings of alienation:

> *The machines in the shop whir so wildly.*
> *That often in the rush I forget what I am;*
> *I become lost in the terrible din,*
> *My being becomes void there, I become a*
> *machine:*
> *I work and work, and work without*
> *account,*
> *Pieces are created, and created, and created*
> *without limit:*
> *For what? And for whom? I don't know, I*
> *don't ask—*
> *How can a machine even begin to think?*

A discontented Jewish labor force responded to appalling work conditions by developing a dynamic trade union movement. When members of the shirtwaist makers' union, Local 25 of the International Ladies' Garment Workers Union voted in favor of a general strike in November 1909, twenty thousand workers walked off their jobs. With the support of prominent New Yorkers such as Lillian Wald and Anne Morgan, the strikers won some

concessions from their employers. Although young Jewish women made up the majority of the shirtwaist strikers during the "uprising of the twenty thousand," it was Jewish men who filled the ranks of the sixty thousand cloakmakers who took part in the bitter and often violent 1910 "great revolt." At the behest of a group of wealthy New York German Jews who wanted to end this public spectacle of class warfare, Boston attorney Louis D. Brandeis (1856–1941) agreed to negotiate a settlement between the workers and manufacturers. A "Protocol of Peace" was signed in September, which reduced the work week to fifty hours, established the precedent of the preferential union shop, increased wages, abolished the subcontracting system, and introduced a permanent mechanism for mediating labor grievances.

Social and Religious Ideologies With their vision of a just and equal society, socialists played an influential role in shaping the activities and agendas of Jewish labor unions. Under their guidance, predominately-Jewish trade unions, such as the Amalgamated Clothing Workers of America, were involved not only in a quest for improved working conditions, but also in the building of cooperative housing projects and vacation resorts for their members. Socialism's appeal among eastern European Jewish immigrants was reflected by the popular *Jewish Daily Forward,* a socialist newspaper that attained a circulation of over 130,000 by 1918, as well as by the growth of the Workmen's Circle, a socialist fraternal order. Between 1910 and 1930, the membership of the Workmen's Circle increased from nearly thirty-nine thousand to almost eighty thousand. In addition to providing insurance, sick benefits, and cemetery plots, the national organization sponsored an impressive network of approximately one hundred secular Yiddish schools and a sanatorium for members who suffered from tuberculosis. When Jewish immigrants from the Lower East Side elected Meyer London (1871–1926) to Congress in 1914, their's was the only district in the nation to be represented by a socialist candidate.

Compared with socialism, Zionism was much slower to take root within the immigrant Jewish community. After making the long voyage from Europe to America and acclimating to a foreign setting, few immigrants were attracted to an ideology that espoused a Jewish responsibility to move yet again, to Palestine. It was not until 1914, when Louis Brandeis took over the leadership of the Zionist Organization of America, that the movement began to grow. Rather than pressure Jews to settle in Palestine, Brandeis focused on the compatibility between American patriotism and loyalty to a Jewish state, asserting that "there is no inconsistency between loyalty to America and loyalty to Jewry... The Jewish spirit, the product of our religion... is essentially American" (Feingold, 1974, p. 207). Under Brandeis's direction, influential American Jews such as Felix Frankfurter (1882–1965) and Judge Julian Mack (1866–1943) joined the Zionist ranks, and the overall membership of the movement increased significantly.

German Jewish leaders, ranging from rabbis to the wealthy elite, were particularly resistant to the Zionist cause. Support for a Jewish state, in their view, was dangerous because it augmented Jewish vulnerability to charges of dual loyalty. "To my mind," argued David Philipson (1862–1949), a Reform rabbi and an ardent anti-Zionist, "political Zionism and true Americanism have always seemed mutually exclusive. No man can be a member of two nationalities, Jewish and American" (Feingold, p. 204). It was not until the end of World War II, when most survivors of the Nazi Holocaust languished in Europe's Displaced Persons Camps, that a near-universal American Jewish consensus in favor of a Jewish homeland in Palestine emerged.

Because it had deviated so far from Jewish tradition, Reform Judaism was unable to meet the religious needs of most eastern European Jews. Instead they turned to a new movement—Conservative Judaism—that emphasized both tradition and change. With the financial support of German Jewish philanthropists such as Jacob Schiff and Louis Marshall (1856–1929), New York City's Jewish Theological Seminary was restored in 1902 to train a cadre of Conservative rabbis, and the renowned scholar Solomon Schechter (1847–1915) was brought over from England to be its first president. This endeavor found favor among the German Jewish elite because they saw Conservative Judaism's potential to wean the new immigrants away from Orthodoxy, the most traditional form of Judaism, toward a more American, and hence more acceptable, form of religious worship. The movement grew so rapidly that by the end of World War II it was the largest branch of Judaism.

Orthodoxy provided the immigrants with a second alternative to Reform Judaism. A group of eastern Europeans who had settled in New York attempted to unite their Orthodox synagogues under the leadership of a chief rabbi, Jacob Joseph, who they imported from Vilna (Vilnius), Lithuania, in 1888; their efforts, however, ultimately failed. While Rabbi Joseph's arrival was met with much enthusiasm, his popularity quickly plummeted when he attempted to bring order to the kosher meat industry. Housewives resented the meat tax that was levied to finance the chief rabbi's salary, Orthodox rabbis were threatened by his monopoly over the supervision of kosher products, and butchers formed an association to counteract his control. From the start, socialists rallied against him because they believed that Orthodoxy deterred political and social action. In 1902, at the age of fifty-nine, Rabbi Joseph died a poor man whose paralysis had left him bedridden for five years.

Although Orthodox Judaism was the strictest branch of Judaism, it was also more internally diverse than either Reform or Conservative Judaism. On one end of the Orthodox continuum were those, such as Hasidim, who resisted acculturation and insisted on separation from the larger community; on the other were those more accepting of American influences and more amenable to cooperating with nontraditional Jews. The 1928 founding in New York City of Yeshiva College, an institution that combined secular and Judaic studies, reflected the left-wing or accommodationist strain within American Orthodoxy. Yeshiva College, which later expanded to include a graduate program, was closely allied with the Rabbi Issac Eichanan Theological Seminary (also in New York City), Orthodoxy's largest rabbinical school.

Discrimination and Anti-Semitism World War I curtailed the flow of East European Jewish immigrants, but it was the Immigration Restriction Act of 1924 that virtually shut the gates. Led by the Immigration Restriction League, nativist forces launched a successful campaign, frequently based on racial and "biological" grounds, against the "undesirable" new immigrants who came from Italy and Russia, for example. As a result of their efforts, immigrants who were identified as Anglo-Saxon and Nordic were favored, while the number of immigrants from southern and eastern Europe dropped dramatically. Between the years 1924 and 1925, total annual immigration figures decreased from over seven hundred thousand to less than three hundred thousand, and Jewish immigration declined from fifty thousand to ten thousand.

The 1920s was also an era of heightened social discrimination. As second-generation Jews moved out of their parents' neighborhoods and applied for white collar work, they often encountered barriers. Under the guise of rectifying geographical imbalances, many private Eastern universities institution- alized quota systems limiting the number of Jewish students. Princeton almost halved its number of Jewish students, and Yale implemented a restrictive strategy that would keep its Jewish enrollment at around 10–12 percent of the total student body. Meanwhile Jewish enrollment at Columbia University fell from 40 to 22 percent over a two-year period. When Harvard University's president, Lawrence Lowell, publicly defended his institution's plan to restrict Jewish enrollment in 1922, Louis Marshall and Judge Julian Mack, a member of Harvard's Board of Overseers, led a vigorous campaign to keep Harvard's doors open to Jewish students. They managed to block Lowell's quota policy, but only temporarily. By 1926, Harvard's Admissions Committee began to reduce the Jewish student percentage from 25 to 15 percent of the student body "by simply rejecting without detailed explanation" (Marcia Synnott, *The Half-Opened Door,* 1979, pp. 93–110).

WORLD WAR II AND AFTER

Economic frustration and distress provided fertile ground for continued anti-Semitism throughout the Great Depression years. Father Charles E. Coughlin gained immense popularity with his regular anti-Semitic radio diatribes, in which he repeatedly attacked Jews as communists and international financiers. This hostile climate pervaded the American populace as well as the chambers of Congress, ensuring that the United States would remain closed to European Jews fleeing Nazi oppression. In response to a 1938 poll, two-thirds of Americans said that they wanted to bar all refugees from entering their country. Congress repeatedly voted down legislation to allow European Jews to enter the United States outside of the assigned quota, including the 1939 Wagner-Rogers Bill, which made provision for the rescue of twenty thousand German children over a two-year period.

Anti-Semitism and Responses Despite ideological rifts within the Jewish community (particularly between Zionists and non-Zionists) and a hesitancy among Jewish leaders to promote Jewish issues during wartime, American Jewry did act on behalf of Hitler's victims. Between 1933 and 1941, the Joint Distribution Committee spent over $20 million on aid and assisted the worldwide settlement of over one quarter of a million Jewish refugees. The Jewish community organized a mass boycott of German products, issued proclamations, held memorial services in synagogues and churches, and petitioned the government to persuade the British to modify its 1939 White Paper that severely curtailed Jewish entry into Palestine. After news of the extermination camps reached the United States in 1942, Jewish institutions coordinated symbolic periods of silence to be observed by Americans across the country. In New York City, for example, a half million workers stopped their activities for ten minutes to show their solidarity with Jewish victims of Nazi atrocities. Mass meetings were held at New York's Madison Square Garden, and Jewish leaders met with President Roosevelt as well as with other high-ranking officials. The government, however, was generally unreceptive to proposed rescue plans and missed opportunities to save at least some Jewish lives. Administration officials justified their inaction by arguing that the means for transporting refugees were unavailable; Axis spies would enter the United States posing as refugees; concentrating rescue efforts on Jews would be discriminatory because others were suffering under the Nazi regime; and diverting resources away from the military effort would only prolong the war. It was not until January 1944 when President Roosevelt authorized the formation of the War Refugee Board that serious rescue efforts began. Because government funding was limited, the American Jewish community subsidized most of the War Refugee Board's projects.

Immigration and Diversity Approximately a quarter million European Jews immigrated to the United States either as refugees from Nazi Germany or survivors of the Holocaust. A group of very prominent intellectuals—among them physicist Albert Einstein (1879–1955), psychoanalyst Bruno Bettelheim (1903–1990), and social philosopher Hannah Arendt (1906–1975)—were part of this immigrant wave. With the arrival of many religious Jews during and after the war, American Orthodoxy was infused with renewed vigor by several Hasidic groups, distinguished rabbis, and heads of *yeshivot.* While there had been relatively few Jewish day schools in the early 1930s, by the early 1960s Torah Umesorah, the National Society for Hebrew Day Schools, reported the existence of 306 Orthodox day schools with a total enrollment of sixty-five thousand students in the United States and Canada. Within America's large urban centers the refugees and survivors formed new ethnic enclaves. In New York City, for example, a large percentage of German Jews settled in Washington Heights and the

Hasidim moved almost exclusively to the Williamsburg and Crown Heights sections of Brooklyn.

Jewish immigrants have continued to flock from the Middle East, South Africa, South America, and the Soviet Union to the United States, where they have formed new ethnic subcommunities. After the fall of Iran's Shah Riza Pahlevi in 1979, many Sephardic Iranian Jews settled in the New York area: those from Teheran congregated in Great Neck, Long Island, while their cohorts from Meshed tended to move to Kew Gardens and Forest Hills in New York City's Queens Borough. The approximately 350,000 Israeli Jews who immigrated to the United States since the founding of the Jewish state have ventured into many businesses—among the most conspicuous are their own coffeehouses, falafel shops, and newsstands that carry Israeli papers. In New York, they started a weekly newspaper, *Yisrael Shelanu* ("Our Israel") as well as hosting a variety of radio programs. On the streets of the Brighton Beach section of Brooklyn, known as "Odessa by the sea," Russian is heard frequently, and a variety of shops cater to the needs of its twenty thousand Soviet Jewish inhabitants. When the Hebrew Immigrant Aid Society of Baltimore founded *The News Exchange,* the Russian-English monthly supplemented the roster of weekly Russian newspapers published by the immigrants themselves.

Since Ashkenazim comprise the vast majority of American Jews, Sephardic Jews have found it difficult to maintain their distinctive culture. Ladino, the Judeo-Spanish language spoken by Levantine Sephardim (much as Yiddish was the traditional Ashkenazic language), barely exists in the United States. Their status as a minority within a minority has led to high intermarriage rates with Ashkenazim, and to the younger generation's ignorance of Sephardic folklore, history, and religious rituals. In contrast, Israeli Jews (some Sephardim, others Ashkenazim) have remained on the margins of American Jewish life: many American Jews share the common Israeli perception that Jews who leave Israel, known pejoratively as *yordim* ("those who descend"), have deserted the Zionist cause. Therefore, out of fear of encouraging more to leave the homeland, American Jewish organizations have virtually shunned Israeli immigrants.

Since 1973, when Jews were granted permission to leave the Soviet Union, Israeli politicians have insisted that these Jews immigrate to Israel. American Jewish leaders, however, did not agree with the official Israeli perspective and resisted Israeli pressure to cease helping Soviet Jews. For a variety of reasons, many Israelis have been highly critical of American Jewish efforts to facilitate Soviet Jewish settlement in the United States. Between the mid 1970s and late 1980s, most Soviet Jews opted to move to the United States rather than to Israel; since then, though, the United States government has enacted immigration policies that limit the entry of Soviet citizens, leading to an increased Soviet migration to Israel as well as to the end of the conflict between Israeli and American Jewish leaders.

Geography and Economics During the last half of the twentieth century, the American Jewish community has experienced significant changes. During the 1950s, second-generation Jews tended to move from the old urban Jewish neighborhoods to the newly developing suburbs. Although they dispersed much more widely than their parents, these young Jews moved in clusters to create new Jewish neighborhoods. Not only did they spread out within the boundaries of particular cities, but also across the country. By 1955, Los Angeles housed America's second-largest Jewish population (the first being New York), pushing Chicago into third place. And as Jews, particularly the elderly, moved to Miami in increasing numbers, this southern city has also eclipsed Chicago: according to the 1970 National Jewish Population Survey, one-third of all Jewish household heads in Miami are over the age of sixty-five compared with 21 percent nationally, and in one Miami neighborhood where Jews comprise about 70 percent of the total population, over half of all household heads were over the age of sixty-five.

Although Jews are no longer typically garment workers and peddlers, they remain concentrated in different fields, namely, professional and managerial occupations. In Boston during the mid 1970s, for example, two-thirds of Jewish males were employed as either professionals or managers, compared to less than one-third of Catholics and less than half of white Protestants. Close to 50 percent of working Jewish women were either professionals or managers, compared to slightly over one-fifth of non-Jewish women. Correlated to this predominance in white-collar jobs are high income and educational levels: during the mid 1980s, 41 percent of the nation's Jewish households had incomes of $50,000 or more, which was four times the proportion for non-Hispanic whites. Jewish men were three times as likely as non-Hispanic white men and Jewish women were twice as likely as non-Jewish women to be college graduates. This concentration in particular educational and occupational levels leads to shared lifestyles, leisure activities, neighborhoods, political interests, and family patterns, reinforcing ethnic cohesion.

Although the vast majority of American Jews can be categorized as middle-class, many can be found at the extremes of the economic hierarchy. Jews comprise about 4 percent of directors who sit on the boards of Fortune 500 companies. These upper-class Jews, however, are not evenly distributed throughout the corporate sector, but are congregated in retail businesses. On the other hand, although Jews cannot be said to figure prominently in stereotypes of the American poor, during the 1980s between one hundred thousand and two hundred thousand New York Jews were living in poverty, and an equal number were classified as living on its margins. Similarly, 12 percent of Milwaukee's Jewish population had incomes below $10,000, as did 10 percent of Phoenix's Jews; 7 percent of Philadelphia Jewish households had incomes under $5,000. The ranks of the Jewish poor are largely made up of the elderly and single-parent families. That Jewish women are more likely than men to be poor, suggests that poverty is being feminized in the Jewish community just as it is in the larger society.

Recent Social Currents Evidence from the 1980s points to a rise in the number of Jewish single-parent families. In Denver and Los Angeles, about 14 percent of Jewish households with children younger than eighteen years of age were headed by a single parent; the figure was 12 percent in New York and Pittsburgh, 18 percent in Miami, and 10 percent in Milwaukee. However, it is rising divorce rates rather than extramarital births that accounts for most Jewish single-parent families. Although Jewish divorce rates have increased—even among Orthodox Jews—they still remain half those of Protestants. Following the trend of middle-class families, Jews are marrying later and having fewer children than average Americans, leading to fears that the American Jewish population will shrink. Whether or not the Jewish community is experiencing negative population growth is still open to debate; what is clear, however, is that American Jewry's percentage of the total American population is dwindling: between 1937 and 1980, the Jewish population percentage fell from 3.7 to 2.54.

The high number of professional Jewish dual-career families correlates strongly with depressed Jewish birthrates. As Jewish women increasingly enter the ranks of the educated and professional labor force, they are demanding equality in the sphere of religious life. Feminist Orthodox women have organized separate women's religious services and study groups; mainstream Jewish feminists have fought for the right of women to become rabbis, to be counted as members of *minyanim* (prayer quorums), to be called to the reading of the Torah, and to initiate divorce proceedings; and radical Jewish feminists have been writing new texts that reflect women's experiences and do not assume that God is male. Although Reform Judaism's Central Conference of American Rabbis had ruled in favor of women rabbis as far back as 1922, Hebrew Union College did not ordain its first female rabbi until 1972. Only after a protracted battle did the Rabbinical Assembly of the Conservative movement vote in 1983 to ordain women rabbis.

When the Reconstructionist Rabbinical College opened in 1968, it was the first Jewish seminary to accept women and men on an equal basis. Founded by Mordechai Kaplan during the 1930s, the Reconstructionist movement was an offshoot of Conservative Judaism. Kaplan, a graduate of the Jewish Theological Seminary, taught homiletics at the Conservative movement's rabbinical school for several decades. For Kaplan, Judaism was more than a religion. It was a civilization that included language, art, music, literature, and spiritual ideals. By defining God as "the power that endorses what we believe ought to be, and that guarantees that it will be" (Rapahel, 1984: p. 182), he challenged the notion of God as Being. As a result of his theological beliefs, Kaplan was excommunicated by the Union of Orthodox Rabbis and denounced by some Conservative rabbis.

Before World War II, roughly 3 percent of American Jews married outside of their faith, but during the 1960s the figure jumped to 17 percent, and two decades later to 32 percent. Intermarriage rates vary, however, by geographic location; they are far higher in the West than in either the East or the Midwest. A 1981 Denver study found that more than half of Jews under the age of thirty had married non-Jews; Phoenix had a similar rate, and in Los Angeles it was 39 percent. In contrast, only 14 percent of New York City Jewish men and 12 percent of Jewish women were married to non-Jews in 1981. (These intermarriage statistics include Jews whose non-Jewish spouses, usually women, converted to Judaism.)

Approximately 40 percent of contemporary American Jews identify themselves as Conservative, 30 percent as Reform, and 10 percent as Orthodox.

Of the remaining Jews, most have no denominational affiliation, and a small minority belong to the Reconstructionist movement. While younger Jews tend to be less religiously active than their elders, once they marry and have school-age children, they tend to join synagogues and become more observant. Some holidays such as Hannukah and Passover are practiced nearly universally by American Jews, while others have been virtually discarded by all but the most religious of American Jews. In order to make sense of Jewish religious preferences, sociologist Marshall Sklare has set forth five criteria for what he calls "ritual retention." The ritual must be capable of redefinition in modern terms; it must not demand social isolation; it must accord with the religious culture of the larger community while providing a Jewish alternative; it must focus on children; and it must be performed annually or infrequently (*America's Jews,* pp. 114–117).

CONCLUSION

In terms of residence, occupations, family patterns, and religious behavior, American Jewry has changed dramatically during the course of the twentieth century. What these changes tell us about the viability of the American Jewish community is the subject of sociological debate. Do they weaken the community and threaten its survival? Or do they simply imply the existence of new forms of Jewish cohesion and expression? Increasing intermarriage and decreasing birthrates are central to the arguments of observers who predict assimilation, while those who analyze American Jewish life through a transformationist lens credit modernity with creating new spheres of Jewish identity. Whether or not assimilation is the collective price that Jews must pay for their integration into American society, however, is still a matter of speculation.

BIBLIOGRAPHY

General Works

Feingold, Henry L. *Zion in America: The Jewish Experience from Colonial Times to the Present.* rev. ed. (1981).

Karp, Abraham. *Haven and Home: A History of the Jews in America* (1985).

Marcus, Jacob Rader. *The American Jewish Woman: A Documentary History* (1981).

———. *Early American Jewry.* 2 vols. (1953).

Sarna, Jonathan D. "American Jewish History." *Modern Judaism* 10, no. 3 (1990).

Social and Religious Histories

Cohen, Naomi W. *Encounter with Emancipation: The German Jews in the United States, 1830–1914* (1984).

Gerber, David A., ed. *Anti-Semitism in American History* (1986).

Glazer, Nathan. *American Judaism.* 2d ed. (1989).

Glenn, Susan A. *Daughters of the Shtetl: Life and Labor in the Immigrant Generation* (1990).

Howe, Irving. *World of Our Fathers* (1976).

Jick, Leon A. *The Americanization of the Synagogue, 1820–1870* (1976).

Kuznets, Simon. "Immigration of Russian Jews to the United States: Background and Structure." *Perspectives in American History* 9 (1975).

Marcus, Jacob Rader. *The Colonial American Jew, 1492–1776.* 3 vols. (1970).

Meyer, Michael A. *Response to Modernity: A History of the Reform Movement in Judaism* (1988).

Moore, Deborah Dash. *At Home in America: Second-Generation New York Jews* (1981).

Raphael, Marc Lee. *Profiles in American Judaism: The Reform, Conservative, Orthodox, and Reconstructionist Traditions in Historical Perspective* (1984).

Rischin, Moses. *The Promised City: New York's Jews, 1870–1914* (repr. 1977).

Sociological Studies

Cohen, Steven M. *American Modernity and Jewish Identity* (1983).

———. *American Assimilation or Jewish Revival?* (1988).

Goldberg, Nathan. *Occupational Patterns of American Jewry* (1947).

Goldscheider, Calvin. *Jewish Continuity and Change: Emerging Patterns in America* (1986).

Goldstein, Sidney, and Calvin Goldscheider. *Jewish Americans: Three Generations in a Jewish Community* (1968).

Heilman, Samuel C. *Synagogue Life: A Study in Symbolic Interaction* (repr. 1976).

Sklare, Marshall. *America's Jews* (1971).

———. *Conservative Judaism* (repr. 1972).

Sklare, Marshall, and Joseph Greenblum. *Jewish Identity on the Suburban Frontier: A Study of Group Survival in the Open Society.* 2d ed. (1979).

Steinberg, Stephen. *The Ethnic Myth: Race, Ethnicity, and Class in America* (rev. ed. 1989).

Waxman, Chaim I. *America's Jews in Transition* (1983).

SEE ALSO **Immigration; The New York Metropolitan Region; Nativism, Anti-Catholicism, and Anti-Semitism**; and various essays in the sections "**Education, Literacy, and the Fine Arts**" and "**Popular Culture and Recreation**."

SOUTHERN EUROPEANS

Donna R. Gabaccia

OVER THIRTEEN MILLION Americans in 1980 reported to the U.S. census an ethnic identification that originated in whole or in part with the migrations of their ancestors from southern Europe. The largest numbers called themselves Italians (over twelve million, about 5 percent of the U.S. population) and Greeks (just under one million). Smaller groups included the South Slavs—250,000 Croatians, 125,000 Slovenes, and 100,000 Serbians as well as smaller numbers of Bulgarians and Macedonians—and 39,000 Albanians. As these ethnic identifications indicate, southern Europeans are not a single ethnic group; they do not share a common culture or a sense of ancestry. Still, the many peoples of southern Europe are sensibly treated together because their migrations, reception by native-born Americans, and patterns of adjustment in the United States shared many features.

The ethnic identities of the Balkans and the eastern Mediterranean are tenaciously local and particularistic. Religious and linguistic loyalties do not neatly coincide. The South Slavs, for example, share a mutually intelligible language, but differ in religion. Croatians, Italians, and Slovenes are mainly Roman Catholic; Greeks, Serbians, Bulgarians, and Macedonians are mainly Eastern Orthodox (although with loyalties to differing ecclesiastical authorities). Albanians may be of either faith, but most are Muslims.

Ethnic identity and national origin rarely coincided, especially in the Balkans and the eastern Mediterranean, to the confusion of U.S. immigration record keepers. Both Italy and Greece became independent nations during the nineteenth century, but some Italian speakers and many more Greeks lived outside these nations. The rising ethnic nationalism of Greeks, Albanians, and various South Slav peoples under the rule of the Austro-Hungarian and Turkish empires made the region one of persistent political unrest.

Most migrants from southern Europe entered the United States during the peak years of mass migration—1880 to 1924—and this guaranteed that they shared some broad generational patterns of adjustment to American life, regardless of ethnicity. Virtually all were rural peoples, drawn by the insatiable demand of American industry for unskilled labor. Family building proceeded slowly at first, since most early migrants were male, yet southern Europeans came to be known for their family-centered lives. The exact mix of ethnic community institutions differed from group to group, but the range of institutions was roughly similar for all. The second generation of southern Europeans came of age in the years bracketed by the two world wars, years of economic crisis and political turmoil in the European homelands. Today—despite small recent migrations from southern Europe—a majority of those claiming a southern European ethnic identity are of the third or a later generation, and many are the products of ethnically mixed marriages. These Americans have increasingly moved into the educational, occupational, and residential mainstream of American life, and the meaning of ethnicity for them now seems to have changed significantly as a result.

Southern Europeans shared the experience of being initially stigmatized by native-born and nativist Americans as undesirable and unassimilable. These "new immigrants" (along with those from the Iberian Peninsula, Asia, and eastern Europe) were believed to be inferior to earlier immigrants originating in northern and western Europe; it was even sometimes debated whether Italians, Greeks, and Slavs should be considered "white." The outcry against new immigrants altered America's traditionally liberal migration policy, first with the exclusion of Chinese immigrants (1882), later with the imposition of literacy tests (1917), and national origin quotas (1921, 1924), both of the latter intended

783

mainly to stem the migration of "undesirables" from Europe. Legislation thus diminished migration from southern Europe to a trickle just as the second generation of these ethnic groups was coming to maturity. As race replaced ethnic difference as the focus of public-policy debates in the United States, the descendants of southern Europeans moved into the mainstream of American life as "white ethnics."

MIGRATION, OCCUPATION, AND SETTLEMENT

Although small numbers of Italians, Croatians, and Greeks traveled to the new world during the age of discovery, their numbers in the United States remained negligible until quite late in the nineteenth century. Missionaries and sailors preceded limited migrations of pioneering small businessmen and adventurers to the United States in the nineteenth century. Before 1880 many Italians, Greeks, and South Slavs settled in California and around New Orleans and the Mississippi Delta, where they worked as miners, fishermen, food importers and marketers, and saloon keepers and restaurant keepers. The contributions of Italians, Greeks, and Croatians to the development of local food industries—the cultivation of apples, vines, and figs in California, and oyster cultivation in the Gulf of Mexico—represented a logical fusion of European expertise with entrepreneurial ambitions among the pioneer migrants. For Italians, New York was another early magnet; ten thousand Italians lived in New York by the time of the Civil War. These pioneers were the first to experiment with the creation of an institutionalized ethnic community—Greek merchants in New Orleans founded an Orthodox church in 1864; a fraternal organization for Serbians and Croatians had been founded in 1857 in San Francisco. In other respects, however, pioneer migrants from southern European blended quickly into the American mainstream, especially in the South and the West, where they married Creole, Irish, and Mexican women in considerable numbers.

Beginning around 1880, migration from southern Europe began to assume mass proportions. The precise impetus for migration varied from region to region, and sometimes from town to town. Crop failures (the infestation of vines by phylloxera in Italy and coastal Croatia; poor wheat harvests in Sic-

ily); changes in world markets for export crops (especially the collapse of demand for Greek currants); rapid population growth and the subsequent reorganization of peasant farming (especially the disbanding of joint peasant households in Croatia and Serbia); the collapse of local industry in the face of consolidating national markets; new taxes—all encouraged rural peasants to seek opportunities elsewhere. Many who left southern Europe intended to earn enough in the U. S. to underwrite a more successful life in the homeland; at first they usually did not mean to settle permanently, and return rates were high (see Table 1).

Although official immigration figures must be suspect, they suggest that over 5 million southern Europeans entered the U. S. from 1899 to 1924 (see Table 2). Migrant rates grew as enthusiasm for migration spread outward from one or more pioneering districts: from coastal Croatia and Slovenia southward and inland to Serbia, Montenegro, and Macedonia; from northern Italy south to Sicily; and from Sparta in Greece to the rest of the nation, especially the Peloponnesus, and to Greeks living in the Turkish empire. Migration climbed rapidly after the depression of the 1890s, peaking in 1905–1914. Rates fell sharply in response to World War I and, after rebounding, to the restrictive immigration legislation of 1924. By 1930 fewer southern Europeans had entered the U.S. than had entered in the 1880s (see Fig. 1).

Of course, not all those leaving southern Europe headed for the United States, though it was overwhelmingly the preferred destination, most notably for the South Slavs. Greeks migrated around the Mediterranean basin and, in small numbers, to New World nations other than the United States. But the worldwide migrants without rival during this period were the Italians: fewer than half headed for the United States; large numbers sought work in Switzerland, France, and Germany, as well as in Argentina and Brazil; smaller numbers trav-

TABLE 1   Male Immigrants and Rate of Return, by Ethnicity (percent)

	Male	Rate of Return
Italian	74.5	45.6
Greek	87.8	53.7
Croatian/Slovenian	79.7	36.3
Bulgarian/Montenegrin/ Serbian	90.2	87.4

Source: Thomas Archdeacon, *Becoming American. An Ethnic History* (New York: Free Press, 1983), table V–3.

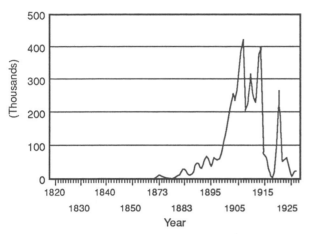

Fig. 1.   Immigrants from Southern Europe.
Source: Imre Ferenczi, comp. *International Migration*, vol. 1 (New York: National Bureau of Economic Research, 1929), tables 13, 19.

eled to northern and southern Africa and to Australia.

The strong pull exerted on southern Europeans by the United States can be explained in a number of ways. By the late nineteenth century the United States was undergoing a second industrial revolution. Investment in capitalist infrastructure (transportation, bridges, cities), exploitation of new mineral resources, and the spread of large-scale factory production created an almost endless demand for unskilled male laborers. Many unskilled jobs, however, were temporary and seasonal. The overwhelmingly male and temporary nature of migration from southern Europe must be traced, then, not only to migrants' hopes to sustain homeland lives with cash earned abroad but also to the peculiarities of American demand.

For both the Greeks and the Italians, and to a lesser extent for the South Slavs, this primarily male and temporary migration was initially channeled to the United States by labor bosses and steamship agents, sometimes called *padroni.* These were intelligent but controversial businessmen—early migrants who sought their fortunes as merchants in flesh, connecting particular American employers to the economically hard-pressed men of dozens of small rural towns throughout southern Europe. As more men gained expertise as temporary migrants ("birds of passage"), dependence on the labor recruiter declined. Chain migrations of friends, kinsmen, and fellow villagers replaced the recruiter-directed migrations. These chain migrations continued to direct new groups of laborers toward American workplaces, and eventually facilitated the migration of wives and families of men choosing to remain in the United States.

The fact that so many women remained behind in southern Europe while men migrated temporarily indicates that American demand for female labor grew less spectacularly than the demand for unskilled men during these years; immigrant women could not compete for the female clerical jobs that were increasing rapidly in number. It also reminds us that peasant women already worked at home: as subsistence cultivators, they ensured group survival and reproduction during long male absences. The representation of women among migrants did increase over time. Unlike some other European groups, however, most women migrants from southern Europe migrated to form or complete families, rather than traveling independently while unmarried, solely for the purpose of working in the United States. By the 1920s, with the severe restriction of immigration and the introduction of exemptions for family members joining naturalized citizens, female immigrants from Greece and the Balkans actually outnumbered male immigrants.

The jobs that southern European men took in the United States heavily influenced the initial settlement patterns of each particular ethnic group. Italian men concentrated heavily in railroad and other forms of outdoor construction, which scattered them widely during the summer construction season. Most, however, returned to cities during periods of seasonal unemployment. Shoe and garment industries also employed large numbers of Italian men. For those able to escape unskilled gang labor and the factory, fruit and vegetable marketing, shoe repair, and a wide range of small service-oriented businesses were typical urban employments. Greek men, too, initially found employment in railroad construction and mills; they moved quickly into a variety of small businesses—the selling of candy and confections; florist shops; produce marketing; shoeshine parlors; restaurants and

TABLE 2   Immigration from Southern Europe, by Ethnicity, 1899–1924

Italian	3,820,986
Greeks	500,463
South Slavs*	702,600
TOTAL	5,024,049

Source: Thomas Archdeacon, *Becoming American: An Ethnic History* (New York: Free Press, 1983), table V–3.

*Includes U.S. categories "Croatian/Slovenian," "Dalmatian/Bosnian/Herzogovinian," and "Bulgarian/Serbian/Montenegrin."

lunchrooms catering to native-born customers—which they soon dominated throughout the country. South Slav migrants were far more likely than the Italians and Greeks to work in mining and steel production; Albanians were found in lighter industries. With their greater occupational diversity, rudimentary divisions between the ethnic working and middle classes were apparent among Italians and Greeks from the turn of the century onward.

Although they came to the United States with family members, daughters of all southern European groups nevertheless worked—in textile mills, garment factories, and family businesses. Wives were less likely to work for wages, and when they did so, it was usually piecework at home. Compared with other groups of immigrant women, relatively few southern European women became domestic servants, for reasons that are unclear. In fact, it is still not possible to distinguish cultural preferences and structural factors in explaining the differing occupational patterns of Italians, Greeks, and South Slavs of either sex.

Closely linked to ethnic occupational variations were patterns of geographic concentration. Like most new immigrants, southern Europeans settled mainly in American cities in the Northeast and upper Midwest. Almost a quarter of all Italian migrants lived in New York, and well over half lived in the Middle Atlantic states and New England. Greeks also concentrated in New York and New England cities; Chicago eventually attracted the largest population of Greeks, and this group subsequently scattered more broadly through the Midwest than did Italians. Undoubtedly because of their work in mines, foundries, and steel mills, South Slavs settled disproportionately in Pennsylvania and in the upper Midwest cities west of Pittsburgh, from Cleveland to Chicago.

FAMILY, NEIGHBORHOOD, COMMUNITY

Because the early migrations of southern Europeans were heavily male dominated, their ethnic communities developed in two overlapping stages. The lives of male laborers, who had migrated without their families, revolved around their communal households, boardinghouses, and centers of commercial sociability. The search for work and that for housing were often intimately connected for these men. In the case of labor gangs, especially those working at rural construction sites, labor agents provided both food and housing for the men they supervised; the opportunities for exploitation in this arrangement were obvious and violent conflict was not unusual. The owners of Greek shoeshine parlors also attracted negative attention for the complete control they exercised over the work and personal lives of their households of "boy" employees; however, most of their boys, when interviewed, emphasized the essential aid their boss had offered during their migration and settlement.

In urban areas South Slavs, Albanians, and some Italian men formed communal households, often headed by a boarding boss—a man of greater experience in America who helped the others find jobs and organized the domestic functions of the household, including preparation of meals. More commonly, men without families fed and housed themselves by becoming boarders, either in a large commercial establishment (run by a fellow countryman) or in the household of a married friend, kinsman, or fellow villager. The small numbers of immigrant wives ran these smaller-scale boardinghouses, since it was essentially their labor that provided the services (meals, laundry, bed making) purchased by boarders. Slavic households generally included larger numbers of men than Italian households; but the inclusion of boarders and relatives in the household was common in both groups. Coffee houses, restaurants, and saloons were additional important gathering places in early male-dominated communities; many of the businessmen of ethnic communities got their start providing food, drink, entertainment, and sociability for the many "men without women" in the early years of settlement.

The arrival of women and the formation of families marked the beginnings of permanent settlement and the second phase of ethnic community formation in the United States. Most southern European communities had an obviously territorial basis during their formative years. Native-born Americans emphasized the degree to which southern Europeans crowded together in segregated neighborhoods, and they feared that permanent ghettos would result. The desire to live among those of one's own background was both broadly shared and understandable. Still, segregation was rarely as extreme as it was in New York, with its dense tenement housing; there, nine out of ten residents of some Little Italies were Italians and their children. In most American cities, by contrast, neighborhoods of multiple- and single-family housing were the rule, and several ethnic communities typically shared any neighborhood. It was the concentration of ethnic businesses, clustered along a single block or street, that gave a neighborhood an outwardly homogeneous ethnic appearance. Of course, self-segregation was possible in such neighborhoods: a resident of an ethnically mixed community might choose to socialize exclusively with and buy from neighbors of her own background. Many southern European immigrants did precisely that.

Southern European immigrants glorified family solidarity, both economically and socially. Parents expected to exercise control over their children, and their children's wages, until they married, making decisions for them regarding school and work, and even choosing their marriage partners. Italian families have sometimes been characterized as father-dominated but mother-centered; the glorification of the father's power and authority was usually tempered by his frequent absence, because of migration or long hours of work. The wife and mother was in practical control of most matters of everyday concern to the household (including, often, the common family purse). Most native-born Americans, however, viewed southern European families as particularly extreme examples of abusive patriarchal power, which included the husband's right to discipline both children and wife physically and to restrict women to domestic activities. Natives noted the misogyny of southern European cultures without seeing the limits that female-centered kin and neighborhood networks placed on men's apparently unbounded power over their families.

Southern Europeans viewed kinship as an important means for cementing each family's relations to a wider group of relatives; they used some forms of fictive kinship to turn friends into relatives. At least for Italians, maintaining the exchanges of mutual aid and support that cemented the kin group together was largely women's work. Almost all southern European immigrants, regardless of background, remember the importance of this aid during the financially difficult years of early settlement; informal socializing, especially for women and children, revolved around a close circle of kin and neighbors—often the mother's relatives and friends. Kin tended to migrate, settle, and move on together; the influence of kinship extended even into the workplace, where kin looked out for each other, especially when their employers were hiring new workers.

Immigrant men took the initiative in creating community institutions beyond the informal but essential ties of family, kinship, and neighborliness. It seems, however, that they began to create institutions only as the informal community, based on family life, gradually replaced male gatherings of sojourners in boardinghouses and coffee houses: birds of passage were not institution builders. Some scholars believe that Italian immigrants were less likely than other southern European immigrants to concern themselves with building community organizations, perhaps because of their particularly strong family ties. The fraternal or mutual aid society, the church or parish, and the press were, however, universal and central institutions for Italians, Greeks, Albanians, and South Slavs alike; there was greater variation in the sorts of cultural organizations that the different groups preferred (for Slavs, singing societies; for Italians, theatrical groups).

Fraternalism had complex European roots and was not completely new to most southern European men; in the United States fraternalism functioned primarily as a form of economic self-help. Large numbers of quite small societies named after European hometowns or provinces, after shared ideals (such as harmony or brotherhood), or after political or religious patrons emerged in the 1890s and early years of the twentieth century. Most fraternal societies provided insurance to members, usually to pay funeral or sick benefits. The more successful and larger societies might use members' contributions to contract with a doctor for medical services. Most fraternal societies also functioned as social clubs—providing meeting rooms, subscribing to newspapers, creating small libraries, or sponsoring yearly banquets, dances, and picnics. Many contributed money to village initiatives in the homeland as well.

For Greek and South Slav immigrants, religion and ethnic or national identity were closely intertwined; thus the financing and staffing of a church or ethnic parish was usually an important early goal—and one that transcended village or provincial loyalties. Among Italians, by contrast, nationalism and anticlericalism more often went hand in hand, especially among men; furthermore, the Roman Catholic Church in America, and its many Irish, French, and German priests, viewed elements of Italian folk religion—especially its religious festivals—with disdain. Although Italians developed their own churches—and fashioned their festivals into events that eventually attracted large numbers of outsiders—churches were never so exclusively the focus of community life as for other southern European groups. Greek immigrants, for example, legally incorporated as religious communities and levied membership fees that enabled the community to recruit priests loyal to either the metropolitan of Athens or the ecumenical patriarchate. In cities where many Roman Catholics lived, Slovenes, Croatians, and Italians followed the precedent of earlier Catholic immigrants in demanding first services, then priests, and finally ethnic parishes of their own.

Although illiteracy rates were substantial among southern European immigrants, those who came to the United States were more literate than those who remained behind; and newspapers in the native language soon appeared in all ethnic communities. By 1884 there were seven Italian-language newspapers in the United States. Heavily dependent on a small group of émigré intellectuals and perpetually cash-starved, many immigrant newspapers were short-lived ventures. For Slavs, whose languages were sometimes officially repressed in the homelands, newspapers published in the United States were often the first of their kind, and some even circulated illicitly in Europe. The character and quality of Italian, Greek, and Slavic newspapers varied considerably with their editors, but among Italians and Slavs an early division between a larger mainstream or middle-class press and a smaller radical and working-class press was evident from the early years of the twentieth century.

As the diversity of the immigrant press suggests, the community institutions founded by southern Europeans were rarely free from internal divisions. Factionalism among Italians and among Greeks seems to have been particularly sharp, and to have been based on personal and political loyalties (especially those originating in the homeland). It was not uncommon to find Italians from one town or province divided between two competing fraternal societies; in Greek communities, splits more often developed over support for competing priests or matters concerning church policy and church building. Other conflicts can be traced directly to class differences within the community and to competition among businessmen or between church-oriented and radical intellectuals for leadership of their communities.

ADAPTATION

Adjustment to life in the United States began with the decision to migrate, and it continued during the period of ethnic community formation—even though the function of the ethnic community in facilitating immigrants' integration was not widely appreciated by native-born Americans at the turn of the century. For the first and second generations, however, the major years of adjustment were those bracketed by the two world wars. Inevitably the special character of events in both southern Europe and the United States during these years made their adjustment somewhat different from that of earlier or later immigrant groups.

In the years around World War I, native-born Americans' concern with the formation of ethnic ghettos and the assimilation of recent immigrants reached a peak. Organized, conscious efforts to stem the flow of migration while speeding the process of Americanization through special educational programs at work, school, or settlement house put many immigrants on the defensive. This was especially true during World War I, when the loyalties of the foreign-born were regularly questioned, despite their disproportionate service in the armed forces. As the numbers of new arrivals from Europe declined after immigration restriction, fundamental changes in both ethnic communities and individual lives quickly became evident.

Xenophobia had reached panic levels with World War I, and native-born Americans' doubts about immigrants' loyalty subsided only very slowly during the 1920s. During most of that decade, it was the contempt of southern Europeans toward prohibition that attracted the most negative attention from native-born Americans, who saw this as further proof of their unassimilability. Although small-scale Italian extortionists had already been misunderstood as threatening "Black Hand Societies" prior to World War I, it was during the 1920s that the persistent public association of Italian Americans and prohibition-related organized crime (stereotyped hysterically as Mafia conspiracies) became entrenched. It is worth noting, however, that prohibition was as unpopular with Greek and Slavic immigrants as it was with Italians; many southern European immigrants regularly ignored the law by making and consuming wine and spirits at home. Still, relatively few actually became involved in the traffic in illegal alcohol that prohibition also spawned.

For many immigrants, regardless of their loyalties and citizenship, homeland politics remained of great concern through the 1920s. Rapid changes occurred throughout southern Europe as a result of the war, and it would have been surprising had immigrants in the United States ignored them. In

Italian communities the rise of Mussolini and fascism in Italy sparked debate and divisions. Many Greeks were initially enthusiastic about their homeland's intention to expand at the expense of the Turkish Empire, even after the cessation of conflict in Europe. Later, Greek churches split as they became embroiled in the conflicts between monarchists and republicans at home. South Slav republicans in the United States also were not pleased with monarchist agitations in the new nation of Yugoslavia, and Croatian fears of Serbian domination of the country persisted as an additional source of tension.

Still, the growing American orientation of southern Europeans by the 1920s was unmistakable, and the Great Depression of the 1930s made the transition especially clear. The insurance programs of many immigrant fraternal and mutual aid societies collapsed during the economic crisis, encouraging southern Europeans to become supporters of the New Deal programs that replaced them nationally. By World War II, in strong contrast with World War I, the loyalties and patriotism of southern European immigrants and their children were rarely questioned. For many the military service of large numbers of second-generation men confirmed the significant reorientation that had occurred since settlement.

With the flow of new arrivals cut off, southern European ethnic urban communities no longer functioned so exclusively as acclimators for the newly arrived, and both their internal life and their connections to the larger American society changed as a result. The linkage of ethnic community to American society proceeded along several fronts. By the 1920s a new generation of ambitious first- and second-generation businessmen and professionals (as well as an occasional radical) competed to represent their neighborhood communities through the American electoral system. Obviously participation in American politics was possible only as the foreign-born acquired citizenship, a little-studied process. Existing evidence suggests that Italian and Greek naturalization increased especially rapidly during the 1920s. The reasons are complex. Sometimes politically ambitious ethnic leaders encouraged naturalization to build a political base. The new and restrictive immigration legislation of the 1920s also encouraged naturalization, since citizens were allowed to sponsor close relatives outside the strict quota system.

Whatever the reasons for rising rates of naturalization, one result was the election of Italians and Greeks, usually to city office but eventually also to state and even national positions. Southern and eastern Europeans often became effective voting blocs within urban Democratic machines. Italians, however, gained a reputation for voting Republican, especially in the East. New York City's Italian voters supported Republicans like the liberal Fiorello La Guardia and the radical Vito Marcantonio. It is also worth emphasizing that the Italians' naturalization rates remained lower than those of earlier immigrant groups or, for example, those of their Jewish immigrant contemporaries from eastern Europe. Some scholars see this as the legacy of southern Italians' political apathy and familism.

Viewed from another perspective, the linkage between ethnic community and wider American society was more effectively accomplished through the workplace and through labor and radical movements for change than through electioneering. Leaders of American unions in the early twentieth century had often viewed southern European birds of passage as strikebreakers resistant to their organizational appeals; just as frequently, however, they simply excluded the foreign-born. Strikes of early male migrants were frequent, spontaneous, and violent; among Italians particularly these actions had roots in their homeland's long history of rural and peasant rebellions. Some Italian and South Slav fraternal societies functioned initially as ethnic trade unions. By World War I, however, Italians had become active in the organization and operation of building laborers' unions and in New York and Chicago garment unions, usually within ethnic locals. South Slavs participated in large numbers in both packinghouse strikes and postwar steel strikes. Their work in heavy industry also made them, and their American-born children, particularly visible in the organizing drives of the CIO unions during the Great Depression. The strikes of southern European immigrant workers often reached beyond the workplace to the community; whole communities, in effect, participated in strike activities.

For other immigrant workers, however, radical movements with ideological roots in Europe were initially as appealing as American-style bread-and-butter unionism, especially in the years before World War I. The influence of anarchists exiled from Italy in communities like Paterson, New Jersey, and Barre, Vermont, is especially well documented; these anarchist exiles were more interested in connecting the immigrant community to worldwide networks of other radicals and to the international working class than to American society. Italians also gained a reputation as tenacious strikers as a result of Industrial Workers of the

World strikes in Lawrence, Massachusetts, and in Paterson; many Italian political exiles found an ideologically comfortable home in this syndicalist union, with its strong emphasis on cross-ethnic solidarity.

Socialists were not without influence in some immigrant communities, especially those with significant numbers of miners; Italians and South Slavs both organized small but vocal Socialist Federations in the early twentieth century, whereas Greek support for leftist movements became visible only after World War I. This is surprising, since the red scare that followed World War I had special significance for most immigrant radicals. Foreign-born radicals came under surveillance, and small numbers were deported. The execution of the immigrant Italian anarchists Nicola Sacco and Bartolomeo Vanzetti in 1927 demonstrated the extent to which xenophobia originating in fear of immigrant radicalism persisted into the 1920s.

As ties between ethnic community and the wider American society proliferated, ethnic community institutions formed in the early twentieth century underwent years of crisis and transformation. Locally based fraternal societies eventually amalgamated or gave way to national organizations like the Sons of Italy, the National Croatian Union, and the Panhellenic Union: these usually promoted pride in the homeland as the foundation for American patriotism. Women's auxiliaries and female "fraternals" also were founded, apparently in response to American models. Just as financial crisis hit the fraternal societies, second-generation sons and daughters withdrew to form their own societies, often for the purpose of supporting education (such as fund-raising for scholarships) or for a more youth-oriented and "American" social life. These, like the fraternal societies of the early twentieth century, were basically local organizations.

In fraternal societies, press, and church alike, language became an increasingly troubling issue. Many Italian, Greek, and Croatian newspapers were publishing English pages or columns by the 1920s; all increased their coverage of American events with each decade, apparently in the hopes of holding their increasingly bilingual readership. At the same time the foreign-language press found itself competing with foreign-language radio broadcasts that offered more music, entertainment, and advertising than news. In Greek churches in particular, debates about the use of English in worship and church life became a source of considerable disagreement, persisting beyond the postwar years.

GENERATIONAL CHANGE

Cultural and structural changes like these can, of course, be traced not only in the ethnic community and its institutions but also in the lives of individuals of the first and second generations in the years since first settlement. Southern European immigrants and their children rapidly came to resemble native-born Americans culturally in many—although by no means all—respects while remaining structurally segregated from them for a much longer period.

Although important, the mobility of individuals of both the first and the second generation failed to bring them unambiguously into the American mainstream. Many central-city ethnic neighborhoods quickly declined in population, especially during the prosperous 1920s. Many leaving these neighborhoods, however, simply reconcentrated in newer relatively homogeneous ethnic neighborhoods in newer areas of the city. For many southern Europeans the move away from the old neighborhood was a new chain migration, sparked by the younger generation's desire for better housing or the older generation's investment in a house. Some southern European groups actually had higher rates of home ownership by the 1930s than did the native-born. Residential segregation, while declining somewhat, did not disappear.

Occupationally and educationally, too, the immigrant and the second generations remained distinctive. Attitudes toward education varied considerably from group to group, and even from family to family, but universally the education of daughters lagged behind the education of sons; and even sons were far less likely to graduate from high school or to attend college than were their native-born counterparts. The fact that many of the second generation reached maturity during the economic crisis of the 1930s inevitably affected both their educational achievements and their occupational futures. Still, mobility was not uncommon, especially in families that emphasized work in a small business as the route upward; perhaps for this reason the upward mobility of Greek sons of immigrants was particularly impressive. For Italians occupational mobility more commonly meant that sons became skilled blue-collar workers; daughters of the second generation gradually made the transition from garment factory to office work as more finished high school during the Great Depression. For many sons of South Slavic workers, the goal was stable work in the same heavy industries that had employed their fathers. In all groups, however, a small and well-educated middle class of professionals emerged in the second generation.

One of the most sensitive measures of individual integration into American society is intermarriage. And here, too, the segregation of the immigrant and second generations persisted, reinforced by religious sentiments in some cases. Although the proportions of Italians and Greeks who married within their own ethnic group declined from the first to the second generation, half to three-quarters of second-generation men and women nevertheless chose partners of their own ethnic group, especially in cities and regions with large communities of their own kind.

While remaining socially segregated in important respects, the immigrant generation and its children experienced significant cultural change as both adapted to life in the United States. Language is usually seen as the most important marker of cultural change among immigrants. The typical pattern of language usage among all southern European groups was for the immigrant generation to become gradually bilingual while maintaining the native language in their families, homes, ethnic businesses, organizations, and churches. Some groups, especially congregations of the Greek churches, worked hard to provide special language schools to reinforce the teaching of the homeland language to the second generation. Most children of immigrants learned the native language at home but preferred English once they began school: indeed, it was the second generation's faltering knowledge of the native tongue that had provoked crisis and change in ethnic newspapers, fraternal societies, and churches. (Worried by the second generation's rejection of its native tongue, Italian educator Leonard Covello mounted a campaign to encourage the teaching of the Italian language in New York schools.) The second generation's preference for English became obvious when these children of immigrants married and had children of their own; rarely was the homeland language passed on to the third generation, except as isolated words and phrases.

Fertility, too, is often viewed as an important measure of cultural change among immigrants. Southern European immigrant women typically bore considerably larger numbers of children than their native-born counterparts at the turn of the century, especially in the urban Northeast, where so many of them settled. Their fertility sparked native fears of "race suicide"—which was in turn used as an argument for the restriction of immigration.

With the second generation, however, fertility declined rapidly. Whether this reflected cultural changes in the value and nurture of children or the sobering effects of the Depression on the large numbers of second-generation men and women seeking to marry at that time is not clear.

One of the greatest challenges of adaptation to life in the United States was posed by America's emphasis on individualism, which stood in such clear contrast with the family-centered cultures of southern European immigrants. Immigrant parents from Italy often viewed American schools, recreational programs, and settlement house or other social programs as undermining their authority over their children. Generally, however, the modification of immigrant familism originated not with outsiders but with immigrants' children. The second generation expressed its fascination with American individualism in many ways—by becoming interested in sports, higher education, or American popular culture; by demanding control over their own wages when they worked; by seeking to date or dress American-style; by insisting on choosing their own spouses.

There is some evidence that southern European immigrant women and their daughters navigated cultural change at a pace and in ways that differed from their male counterparts. Census data show that foreign-born wives were less likely to speak English than their husbands, probably because relatively fewer worked outside the home, where they would meet speakers of other languages. The cultural themes of honor and shame—which placed high emphasis on the proper and sexually modest conduct of daughters and wives—may have rendered changes in women's lives culturally more problematic for Greeks and Italians than for other groups. Some Slavic and Italian men seem to have believed that in the United States "women ruled"; the prevalence of unmarried schoolteachers and social workers, the influence of Protestant women in moral and civic reform movements, and the flowering of the woman suffrage movement during the peak years of migration all seemed to encourage this view. The immigrant press often disparaged American women as poor role models for Italian or Greek girls, yet some immigrant women were eager to grasp the greater individualism that the American concept of womanhood seemed to offer them.

Questions of cultural change and social integration were particularly central for immigrants' children, the second generation. There is little doubt that family conflicts peaked as the second generation matured, and that this generation faced difficult choices in forging satisfying lives and identities for themselves. Some clearly rebelled, denouncing their ethnic identities and moving unambiguously away from their ethnic communities. But these were the minority. Studies of the Greek second generation reveal the many successful ways in which immigrants' children combined individual occupational mobility, American-style romantic love, and even intermarriage with a sense of cultural continuity and ethnic identification. Religious loyalties provided one source of important continuity for the second generation. In almost all southern European groups, too, family sentiments became the focus of ethnic life and identification. Compared with native-born Protestants, the second generation of southern European origin seemed quite concerned with familial deference and respect; most interacted frequently with kin, especially when they lived nearby. The new ethnic neighborhood remained an important focus of social relations for the second generation. But the expression of ethnicity now revolved more around religious and private familial rituals than around the institutions of a neighborhood community that included the recently arrived.

MIGRATION SINCE 1945

The cultural adaptation of first- and second-generation southern Europeans was well under way, and the social integration of the third generation was about to begin, when war and changing laws again opened the door to new migrations from Europe. As one might expect, the arrival of immigrants from Italy, Greece, Yugoslavia, Bulgaria, and Albania both revived declining ethnic institutions and communities and created new tensions within them.

World War II left much of southern Europe in political and economic chaos. Communist revolution in Yugoslavia and civil war in Greece led Yugoslavs and Greeks in the United States to demand abolition of discriminatory quotas, which had helped keep migration from the region low for twenty years. Congress resisted such appeals but did pass special legislation that opened the door to political exiles fleeing communism and to other "displaced persons." Almost thirty-five thousand South Slavs from Yugoslavia entered the United States under the special legislation of 1948 and

TABLE 3 Immigrants from Southern Europe, 1965–1977, by Place of Birth

	Greece	Italy	Yugoslavia
1965	3,002	10,821	2,818
1966	8,265	25,154	3,728
1967	14,905	26,565	5,879
1968	13,047	23,593	6,783
1969	17,724	23,617	8,868
1970	16,464	24,973	8,575
1971	15,939	22,137	6,063
1972	11,021	21,427	5,922
1973	10,751	22,151	7,582
1974	10,824	15,884	5,817
1975	9,984	11,552	3,524
1976	8,417	8,380	2,820
1977	7,838	7,510	2,791

Source: U.S. Immigration and Naturalization Service, *Annual Reports* (Washington, D.C., 1966–1978).

1953. Discriminatory national-origins quotas remained in effect, however, until 1965.

The complete revision of immigration policy in that year again opened the door to migration from southern Europe, as well as from other parts of the world. The numbers of immigrants from southern Europe rose rapidly immediately after passage of the 1965 law but began to drop again during the 1970s (see Table 3). Most new arrivals settled in the same cities and regions where southern European migrants of the turn of the century had made their permanent homes.

Immigration law after 1965 favored the migration of skilled and professional workers and of close relatives of earlier migrants. The former provision guaranteed that new arrivals from Italy, Greece, and the Balkans brought more human capital with them to the United States than had migrants at the turn of the century. Like the political exiles and displaced persons of the immediate postwar period, they were better educated, more highly trained, and more likely to be of middle-class and urban background than the earlier migrants. Aging immigrants from the pre-1924 migration could sometimes use the 1965 law's provisions for family reunification to sponsor relatives who had remained behind in Europe. Generally, however, it was the most recent arrivals who benefited from these provisions, and new chain migrations of kin again connected southern Europe and American cities.

The differential impact of new immigration laws on older and newer arrivals foreshadowed other conflicts that emerged in ethnic communities as the newcomers moved in. In New York City, a small Greek neighborhood in Astoria expanded into a flourishing ethnic community. In many cities the new arrivals replaced and eventually outnumbered the second- and third-generation southern Europeans who took part in the general American rush to the suburbs of the 1950s and 1960s. Of course, not all new arrivals from Greece or Italy gravitated toward ethnic neighborhoods or even ethnic community life. The well-educated and the professional, in particular, often prided themselves on their immediate and, some insisted, unproblematic integration into the American mainstream.

Where older and newer migrants shared neighborhoods and community organizations, disagreements over language could become particularly sharp. Many Greek Orthodox churches faced this issue head-on as a third generation relatively unfamiliar with Greek confronted the new arrivals who insisted that only the homeland language gave a church its Greek character. Recent arrivals from Italy, meanwhile, often disparaged the Americanized Neapolitan and Sicilian dialects spoken by older immigrants and their children. Or they complained about Italian American ignorance of the vast changes occurring in their homeland. Those who had lived for years in the United States and become loyal American Republicans or Democrats were sometimes shocked to confront young Communists among the recent arrivals; having lived through the Depression, they might be puzzled and resentful when new immigrants, arriving during a period of economic expansion, prospered so quickly. In response, recent arrivals liked to contrast their own frugal habits against the Americanized consumer expectations of Italians and Greeks of the third or fourth generation. While real enough, divisions and resentments like these should not be exaggerated; they did not lead to institutional splits and factionalism—which had been common in immigrant community institutions during the early years of the century.

SOUTHERN EUROPEANS AND THEIR DESCENDANTS IN THE 1980s

Most of the Americans who told census takers in 1980 that their ethnicity was Italian, South Slav, or Albanian were the grandchildren or even later descendants of the huge migration from southern Europe during the late nineteenth and early twentieth centuries; only among Greeks were the first and second generations still a (bare) majority. Sociological studies of third- or later-generation "white ethnics" (as the descendants of the new immigrants, including southern Europeans, are now sometimes called) repeatedly confirm that educational, class, income, and occupational differences between them and other Americans have faded to the point where they are almost imperceptible.

Some differences are still worth noting. The geographic concentrations of southern European descendants still reflect original settlement patterns: the strong family ties of southern Europeans may have been responsible for holding each successive generation close to their families' original homes. Educational mobility has been marked among men of southern European descent, but Italian American women, although attending college in increasing numbers in the third generation, still lag behind the women of other ethnic groups in college attendance. Remnants of the family-centered cultures of southern Europeans persist in kinship visiting patterns and in attitudes toward parental authority, at least among Italians, the best-studied group. Some scholars believe that further research on psychological traits of southern Europeans might reveal sharper differences.

More interesting, perhaps, is the persistence of ethnic identity among people whose lives are no longer influenced by the culturally distinctive and socially segregated ethnic communities of the turn of the century. There is some evidence that ethnic identification may actually have increased during the 1960s and 1970s, leading some observers to talk of the "new ethnicity" of the third generation or of the rise of "unmeltable" ethnics. Many of the southern European third generation, and most of the fourth generation, are of mixed ancestry, yet a majority continue to choose an ethnic identity when asked, and a significant proportion, especially of women, argue that their ethnic identity is important to them.

Scholars disagree about why this is so. Is a voluntarily chosen ethnicity of mere symbolic importance—a new way of emphasizing one's individualism and uniqueness, adding spice to an otherwise homogeneous middle-class American culture? Does learning the language of the homeland, traveling there, or reviving the meals or family rituals of earlier generations provide a sense of connection to a vanished community, giving otherwise rootless Americans a communal orientation that will never impinge on their individual freedom? Or is the persistence of ethnic identification among southern Europeans one sign of the emergence of a new ethnic group in the United States—European Americans or "unhyphenated" whites—who differentiate themselves sharply, and racially, from the racial minorities and recent immigrants from Asia, the Caribbean, and Latin America? Although there are no clear answers to questions like these, the ethnic identity of southern Europeans and other descendants of the "new" immigrants promise to persist at least into the twenty-first century.

BIBLIOGRAPHY

Alba, Richard D. *Italian Americans: Into the Twilight of Ethnicity* (1985).

Caroli, Betty Boyd, Robert F. Harney, and Lydio F. Tomasi. *The Italian Immigrant Woman in North America* (1978).

Cinel, Dino. *From Italy to San Francisco: The Immigrant Experience* (1982).

Čizmič, Ivan. "Yugoslav Immigrants in the U.S. Labor Movement, 1880–1920." In *American Labor and Immigration History, 1877–1920s: Recent European Research,* edited by Dick Hoerder (1983).

Gabaccia, Donna. *Militants and Migrants: Rural Sicilians Become American Workers* (1988).

Harney, Robert F., and J. Vincenza Scarpaci, eds. *Little Italies in North America* (1981).

Lieberson, Stanley, and Mary C. Waters. *From Many Strands: Ethnic and Racial Groups in Contemporary America* (1988).

Moskos, Charles C., Jr. *Greek Americans: Struggle and Success* (1980).

Nelli, Humbert. *Italians in Chicago, 1880–1930: A Study in Ethnic Mobility* (1970).

———. *From Immigrants to Ethnics: the Italian Americans* (1983).

Prpic, George. *The Croatian Immigrants in America* (1971).

———. *South Slavic Immigration in America* (1978).

Saloutos, Theodore. *The Greeks in the United States* (1964).

Scourby, Alice. *The Greek Americans* (1984).

Vecoli, Rudolph. "Italian American Workers, 1880–1920: Padrone Slaves or Primitive Rebels." In *Perspectives in Italian Immigration and Ethnicity,* edited by Silvano M. Tomasi (1977).

Yans-McLaughlin, Virginia. *Family and Community: Italian Immigrants in Buffalo, 1880–1930* (1977).

SEE ALSO **The City; Community Studies; Crime and Punishment; Ethnicity; Family Structures; Immigration; Labor: The Great Depression Through the 1980s; Minorities and Work.**

AFRICAN MIGRATION

Philip D. Morgan

FROM THE SIXTEENTH to the nineteenth centuries the roughly 11.5 million Africans shipped to the New World as slaves constituted the largest intercontinental migration then known to man. Although African migration to North America was always on a small scale—only about half a million black Africans reached North America before the United States banned the slave trade in 1808—more North Americans trace their ancestors to Africa than to any continent except Europe. In terms of migration of all peoples to eighteenth-century North America, three slaves arrived for every four free immigrants, whereas in such other regions of the New World as the British West Indies, slaves outnumbered free immigrants by as much as ten to one.

Africans aboard slave ships occasionally mutinied, and some slaves, newly landed, boarded small boats in vain attempts to reach Africa, but in general return migration, which was a common tendency of modern European immigration to the New World, was virtually insignificant for Africans. During the revolutionary war, however, some black Americans secured their freedom and eventually returned to Africa. In 1792 more than a thousand black Loyalists settled what came to be called Freetown in the colony of Sierra Leone.

In the nineteenth century, when the Atlantic slave trade had diminished, voluntary migration by Africans to North America was minuscule. Efforts by black Americans to return to Africa, on the other hand, became more organized during this period. In 1816 Paul Cuffee, perhaps the wealthiest free black in the early republic, used his own ship and largely his own funds to transport seven black families from the United States to Sierra Leone. This individual effort helped lay the groundwork for later colonization efforts in Liberia. Between 1820, when the first blacks were shipped to Liberia, and 1861, when the Civil War curtailed emigration, about twelve thousand blacks, half of them former slaves, reached Liberia under the auspices of the American Colonization Society and its affiliates.

Although the number of African immigrants to America rose in the twentieth century—reaching a few thousand annually in some decades—most African immigrants were white, not black. The majority of black Africans who came to the United States after World War II were students, few of whom settled permanently, and they did not form a cohesive ethnic group. Rather, the overwhelming majority of the roughly thirty million American blacks in 1991 were descendants of those Africans transported against their will two or more centuries earlier.

A return to Africa continued to entice some slave descendants—from Martin Robison Delany and Edward Wilmont Blyden in the mid nineteenth century, through Bishop Henry McNeal Turner around the turn of the century, to Marcus Garvey, who in the 1910s and early 1920s built the first mass movement of African Americans in United States under the banner of "Back to Africa," to W. E. B. Du Bois, who died in Ghana in 1963, and Stokely Carmichael, who left for Guinea in 1971—but most black Americans, whose ties to the New World antedate those of most other ethnic groups, have considered America their home, no matter how desperate their plight.

SLAVERY IN AFRICA

Centuries before the transatlantic slave trade arose in a tidal wave, the Islamic world had incorporated African slaves into societies north of the Sahara where Islamic influence was strong, most notably along the shores of the Indian Ocean, on the northern savanna, in Ethiopia, and along the east coast. In fact, this well-entrenched trans-Saharan slave-trading system, which began in the seventh century and continued into the early part of the twentieth, may have involved even more Africans than the transatlantic trade. Islam sanctioned slavery on the ground that pagans could legitimately be converted through enslavement. Slaves were generally used in military, administrative, and domestic service, although some were employed in productive activities.

Islamic slavery was one of Africa's two main forms of slavery; the other was practiced in West and Central Africa with many local variations. In sub-Saharan Africa slavery was a marginal feature of kinship-based societies. Perhaps the dominant feature of Africa south of the Sahara was its chronic underpopulation. Land was widely available, labor scarce, and agricultural technology simple. Tropical conditions made agriculture difficult and life expectancy short; land was of little value without people to work it. The possession of men and women became both the source and the symbol of wealth and power. Africans, as A. G. Hopkins (1973) observed, measured wealth in men rather than in acres; power resided in man owners rather than land owners. In such a setting, West and Central Africans developed elaborate rights in persons. To have dependents was a central goal, and slavery became part of a continuum of social relationships involving various rights in persons, including kin, pawn, client, and subject ties. Because the structure of society was based on the kinship group, slaves emerged almost as incidental products of the interaction between groups of kin.

Slavery in Africa rarely involved the single-minded exploitation of labor for profit, although economic motives were usually present. For instance, women were more often slaves and consistently fetched higher prices than men: they were valued for their reproductive functions—that is, they could augment a lineage—and because they performed most of the agricultural work in Africa. Additionally, in a few coastal areas some groups like the Akan strove to use slaves for gold mining, head porterage (the carrying of goods atop the head in human caravans), and agricultural production long before the boom in slave exports in the seventeenth and eighteenth centuries. Such endeavors made slavery a central institution rather than a system that functioned on the edge of society, but these were exceptional in a continent where the degree of economic rationalization of slavery never reached New World levels.

Although African slavery emphasized the slave's low status and personal dependence on the master, it was not identified solely with menial labor. African slaves were as often soldiers, administrators, and concubines as they were laborers. African master and slave often were of different ethnic and religious groups, but the master did not develop racial ideologies as a means of controlling the slave. A key characteristic of lineage slavery was its assimilative tendency. A master usually wanted to incorporate the slave into his kinship unit. In many African societies the slave's subordination to the kinship unit was transitional: in time the slave would be assimilated into the group.

Even though slaves in kinship units were in some sense family members, able to incorporate themselves as part of lineages, they suffered devastating cultural subordination as a result of their assimilation. As Frederick Cooper in 1979 has pointed out, African slaves' destruction as individual members of one ethnic group was a consequence of their absorption into another ethnic group. Most slaves became so through acts of violence: they were ripped from the society of their birth and stripped of their ancestry. They had to deny their past before they could be assimilated.

IMPACT OF THE TRANSATLANTIC SLAVE TRADE

The impact of the transatlantic slave trade on Africa is extremely difficult to calculate for a variety of reasons. Attaching sterile numbers to "removals" from Africa may appear an exercise in callousness, an attempt to minimize the dimensions of a colossal human tragedy. Furthermore, the tenuousness of the data on which estimates are based has led at least one historian to argue that attempting to compile global statistics for the slave trade is futile. Estimates range from no fewer than a hundred million to about one million for the number of West Africans killed in wars fought to capture slaves for export between the sixteenth and nineteenth centuries. David Henige concludes, "The unpalatable truth is that we have not the slightest idea (nor any hope of gaining it) of the population of any part of tropical Africa in the sixteenth or the seventeenth or the eighteenth centuries" ("Measuring the Immeasurable," p. 307).

And yet historians, through simulation models, estimates of carrying capacity, backward extrapolations, and the retrieval of censuses and quasicensuses, are continually drawn to the problem. In broad terms, it seems fair to say that the strict demographic impact of the New World slave trade appears not to have been catastrophic. Although West and Central African populations showed little evidence of long-term growth, they may well have suffered little long-term loss. The export slave trade may have kept the population of West Africa relatively static during the years of trade—at about twenty-two to twenty-five million—although depopulation in specific areas over certain periods of time undoubtedly occurred. Some historians have even argued that the trade helped relieve pressures caused by high rates of reproduction in Africa. Furthermore, others have maintained that the introduction into Africa of high-yield New World crops such as manioc and maize generated previously unattainable crop yields, thereby permitting slave exports to increase without diminishing the necessary manpower for agricultural production. Moreover, insofar as depopulation occurred, it may have owed less to the slave trade than to periodic droughts, famines, and epidemics. It has been argued that a cycle of drought, disease, and famine did more to limit population growth than did slave exports.

If this is the general picture—and that is by no means clear—there were undoubtedly significant local variations. On the Bight of Benin, for example, slaves came almost entirely from Aja-speaking peoples. Their losses to the transatlantic slave trade were sufficient to reduce their population substantially. Some small societies in other regions were completely destroyed. Patrick Manning emphasizes that "significant areas of the African continent experienced population decline and social disruption during precisely the century [the eighteenth] when most other continents were beginning to undergo demographic and economic growth" (*Slavery and African Life,* p. 58). Rarely, however, did the trade impose excessive demands on a specific area for a long period of time. Even in regions where the number of slaves exported remained high for many decades, as was the case in West-Central Africa in the eighteenth century, the slaves came from many different and changing groups in the interior. Generally there were not disastrous losses to any one society, although reproductive capacity was often severely diminished. Furthermore, the ethnographic map of West Africa displays impressive continuities, indicating that the disappearance of ethnic groups was rare.

But if populations were not drastically reduced, they were structurally altered. Men of working age were most in demand in the Americas, whereas African slave purchasers valued the social and economic productivity of women (as wives, do-

mestics, and laborers) more highly. Consequently, the ratio of working to dependent populations, of male to female labor, clearly fell with the burgeoning Atlantic trade. The burden of work on the productive members of society increased. Furthermore, the general surplus of women in Africa encouraged the spread of polygyny, driving down the brideprice that women's families could demand and weakening the stability of existing marriages. Monarchs and merchants often established large harems. As Patrick Manning puts it, "The expansion of slaveholding did more to corrupt, subvert, and otherwise transform kinship systems than it did to reinforce them" (*Slavery and African Life,* p. 119). Finally, the number of slaves within African societies increased considerably. Of those seized as slaves, about as many were kept within Africa as were exported. The procurement of slaves for the Americas led to an enlargement of slavery within Africa. Slaves became common in some African regions where they had been rare.

Slaves obviously were likely to be acquired by force or theft. Some have attributed the proliferation of slave capturing to the introduction of firearms in Africa, a view which has become a matter of some debate. In the late seventeenth century Africa imported about twenty thousand muskets a year; a century later this figure had increased to about two hundred thousand a year. Although this is an impressive growth, it represents a low guns-per-capita ratio compared with other parts of the world. Furthermore, we cannot be certain that the weapons operated effectively in humid sub-Saharan Africa, and we do know that guns were put to such practical uses as hunting and protecting crops. Nevertheless, the supply of arms obviously facilitated slave raids, and even if the impact of guns was small over large geographic areas, their effect on localities in which they were highly concentrated could be considerable. The availability of guns buttressed the power of warrior aristocracies whose class interests lay in perpetuating wars and slave raids.

The Atlantic slave trade has been seen as the exploitation and corruption of an Edenic Africa by a greedy, industrializing Europe. Although Europe was the most obvious beneficiary of the trade, Africa was not a passive victim. First, prices for slaves rose rapidly in Africa, faster than in the Americas. Europeans were forced to pay more and more goods and cash for the slaves they bought. The terms of trade shifted in favor of Africa. Second, Europeans adapted to established West African patterns of trade rather than imposed new ones. Africans retained sovereignty over forts and factories, collected customs dues and business fees, and organized systems of delivery and marketing. Europeans possessed certain advantages in their dealings with Africans, but they could not easily dictate to native suppliers; instead, they entered into partnerships or alliances with them. Third, an estimate of the overall impact of the Atlantic trade on Africa concludes that its scale and value were marginal. David Eltis and Lawrence C. Jennings emphasize that the "majority of Africans ... would have been about as well off, and would have been performing the same tasks in much the same socioeconomic environment, if there had been no trading contact" ("Trade Between Western Africa and the Atlantic World," p. 958) with Europe. Finally, the old saw that Africans were content with beads and baubles has been conclusively demolished. African preferences and demands—for certain types of textiles or alcohol, for example—controlled the market. Imports had elite and mass characteristics. The slave-trading elite took the best cloths, the most prestigious luxury items, and most of the firearms; plainer textiles and much of the tobacco and alcoholic beverages reached commoners. Textiles were the cornerstone of trade and were largely for mass consumption. The Atlantic trade led to little wealth creation; it failed to stimulate indigenous manufacturing, but it did not stifle it to a great degree. Rather, its primary effect was a redistribution of existing wealth.

Walter Rodney has argued that the export trade in slaves seems to have led to a marked increase in social stratification. Power in Africa was increasingly concentrated in the hands of an upper class of rulers, officials, and entrepreneurs. Societies organized around kinship, with social and familial authority resting on consensus and tradition, gave way to societies dominated by individuals who had wealth and power through their possession of followers, whether clients, servants, or slaves. This process is well illustrated among the people of the Niger Delta, where a kinship-based social organization was replaced by what came to be known as the "house" system. Based on common economic interests and necessities, the house came to incorporate the master, his family, and his slaves, with each person assigned a rank in the hierarchy that entailed appropriate duties, responsibilities, and privileges. Furthermore, the Atlantic slave trade reduced the assimilative tendencies of African lineage slavery. As slavery became a central institution, the status of slaves became depersonalized, and the status, power, and wealth of the slave owners rose. The rich became richer and the poor, poorer.

The Atlantic slave trade also affected political systems in Africa, although by no means in simple ways. Take the case of Dahomey. The stereotypical view is that this state was largely generated by the Atlantic slave trade. It became a militaristic state, trapped in a vicious cycle of buying guns to capture slaves and capturing slaves to get more guns. Recent research has modified this view, however. It has been estimated that the Atlantic slave trade accounted for a small fraction of the national production of Dahomey. Furthermore, Dahomey rulers relied not on guns to maintain their power but on traditional structures and a system of surveillance and espionage. Annual wars were influenced not by trade but by the ideological, political, and economic strength of the state. Finally, the expansion and centralization of power and authority in Dahomey preceded the gun-slave-gun cycle and was not dependent on a slave-trade economy dominated by a royal monopoly. Nevertheless, there is no question that some states—like the kingdom of Asante—benefited from the imperial expansion associated with slaving wars, while other states—most notably Kongo—were devastated by their slave-trading experiences.

AFRICANS IN TRANSIT

Regional differences are clearly important in understanding the impact of the Atlantic slave trade on Africa, and no less so in understanding the nature of enslavement itself. In general, it has been suggested that about one-third of the slaves who passed into the Atlantic trade were war captives, another third were kidnapped either at home or abroad, and the remainder became slaves in other, rather less violent, ways—perhaps through indebtedness or judicial condemnation, or because they had been sold by their relatives or superiors. Most came from the hinterland and had been brought to the coast by the agents of politically and commercially—and sometimes militarily—aggressive and expansive organizations, whether kingdoms or societies of traders. If this is the general picture, there were considerable variations. War was the general mechanism of enslavement in most of West Africa, but kidnapping predominated on the Bight of Biafra, and judicial procedures played a leading role in Central Africa. These different mechanisms

798

had contrasting effects: where wars predominated, the dead were several times the number captured and exported; where people were enslaved through the judicial process or kidnapping, there was little violence and loss of life. The catchment area for slaves varied considerably from one region to the next and over time. The march to the coast was the shortest on the Bight of Biafra, averaging about 100 kilometers (about 63 miles). On the upper Guinea coast and on the Bight of Benin it was less than 200 kilometers (about 125 miles). In the eighteenth-century Gold Coast and Senegambia it was more than 300 kilometers (about 190 miles), and it reached over 600 kilometers (about 380 miles) in late-eighteenth-century Loango and Angola.

Regional variations in the sexes and ages of African migrants were significant, although in general males and adults were dominant. Slave shipments were usually about 60 to 70 percent males and about 75 to 85 percent adults. But the Bight of Biafra, to take the most extreme case, exported relatively few males—sometimes as few as half of the shiploads. Far more children were purchased in Sierra Leone, on the Bight of Biafra, and in West-Central Africa (in the late eighteenth century, about a third of the cargoes) than in other exporting regions. The reasons for the variations were numerous. Women and children tended to form a greater proportion of exports where the catchment area was close to the coast. The further afield slavers went, the greater the number of men. The most obvious explanation is that the hardships and cost of the journey from the interior put a premium on adult males, but perhaps the influence of the trans-Saharan slave trade and its high demand for women made men more available in the interior.

There also seems to be a correlation between a low ratio of men to women among slave exports and a high population density. Perhaps where the population put strong pressure on resources, there was a greater willingness to part with women and children. On the other hand, women tended to be less available in matrilineal societies, where slave wives were especially valued, and in societies where females were central to agricultural production. Conversely, states that employed numerous slaves as soldiers or bureaucrats, or in commercial or state-run agriculture, retained more male captives. In addition, states engaged in formal warfare were most likely to gain male captives, while kidnapping, pawning, and raiding probably yielded more women and children. This evidence of marked regional variations determining the ages and sexes of exported Africans strongly suggests that supply rather than demand dictated the trade's character. Clearly there was some complementarity of preferences, with women more highly valued in Africa and men in the Americas, but the marked interregional differentials demonstrate African priorities in the composition of the exported slaves.

In general, mortality owed more to preembarkation experiences in Africa than to shipboard mistreatment. Despite the horrific image of sketches like that of the slave ship *Brookes,* showing slaves packed together like sardines, there was little connection between the overcrowding of slaves and mortality rates. Rather, mortality varied markedly according to African port of origin, suggesting that malnutrition, intestinal disorders stemming from changes in diet, and diseases contracted by slaves moving into new epidemiological conditions were critical in determining death rates. Average deaths in transit on British ships in the 1790s ranged from about 3 percent for Gold Coast slaves to about 11 percent for those from the Bight of Biafra. Passage times to the New World also varied from different parts of the African coast, and the length of a voyage was closely linked to mortality rates. Death rates were especially high on ships that were becalmed or for other reasons took much longer than anticipated to reach their destinations. The primary reason for the decline in deaths in transit over the course of the eighteenth century—from about 20 percent in the early years to between 5 and 10 percent by the late years—was a decline in the length of voyages. The reduction in the time slavers spent on the African coast—primarily through "balking," the collection of shipload lots by entrepreneurs and their sale to captains as single units—and improvements in ship design that reduced sailing times were probably the key factors in shorter voyages. At any rate, more slaves were being shipped more quickly by the end of the eighteenth century.

Although some slave voyages had shockingly high numbers of deaths in transit—sometimes more than half of those aboard—slave mortality was on average not markedly higher than that for any travelers on long ocean voyages in the days before steamships. During the seventeenth century about one in ten British migrants to the New World died during the Atlantic crossing, whereas the figure for African slaves was about one out of every seven or eight. Further evidence that tight packing was not the primary cause of slave deaths is that the crews of slave-trading vessels suffered comparable losses. Slaves almost certainly had the worst accommodations of any humans transported across the Atlantic, but shippers had strong economic incentives to minimize mortality. Outbreaks of smallpox and measles were exceptional on voyages; more common were dysentery, vomiting, and sweating, all of which in themselves were not deadly but caused dehydration, which was. About 80 to 90 percent of Africans who embarked on slave ships reached the Americas alive.

If the transatlantic crossing no longer seems the killer it once did to abolitionists, there is no question that the enslavement process was highly threatening to life. Joseph Calder Miller (1988) studied the situation in Angola. He suggests that of every hundred people seized in the interior, about sixty-four arrived six months later at the coast. After a month in the barracoons, only about fifty-seven embarked. An average Middle Passage delivered about fifty-one on New World soil. Deaths during full "seasoning" in Brazil—about four years—left only about thirty alive. After these horrifying statistics, it is hardly surprising that Miller entitles his account of the Angolan slave trade *Way of Death*. The Angolan trade may have been an extreme case, in part because of the long march (more than 600 kilometers, or about 380 miles) from interior to coast, the longest of any African region; estimates from other regions put the losses on the march at about 10 percent. In addition, Brazil had an extremely high rate of seasoning deaths, much greater than those of North America, where, by contrast, about a quarter of new arrivals in Virginia and perhaps a third in South Carolina died in the first few years. But whatever the African or New World region, slaves were at greater risk of death on the march to the coast, in the coastal barracoons, in their loading, and during the first few years in the New World than during an average Atlantic crossing.

Even if the Middle Passage was not the killing experience once depicted, it was unquestionably a traumatic event. Loading was often a protracted affair: in short trade a vessel might pick up slaves at a number of forts and factories; in ship trade the captain would more likely drop anchor at various points along the coast and either send boats ashore or invite canoes to visit the ship in order to put together a full cargo. The typical duration of trading by slave vessels ranged from four to six months in Sierra Leone, six to ten months on the Gold Coast. In many places slaves were more likely to be purchased singly or in pairs, rather than by the dozen or the score. A few days before embarkation, the slaves usually had their heads shaved. They were often branded with their owner's initials, and were inspected to ensure physical suitability. Olaudah Equiano, an enslaved Ibo transported to Virginia and eventually freed, recalled how, when he was first carried on board ship, he "was immediately handled, and tossed up, to see if I were sound" (Curtin, *Africa Remembered,* p. 92). Equiano vividly recalled his terror:

When I looked round the ship too, and saw a large furnace or copper boiling, and a multitude of black people of every description chained together, every one of their countenances expressing dejection and sorrow, I no longer doubted of my fate; and, quite overpowered with horror and anguish, I fell motionless on the deck and fainted. (Curtin, *Africa Remembered,* p. 92)

The slaves were usually stripped naked, apparently to facilitate cleanliness, were chained in pairs, and separated by sex in holds. The space between the decks averaged four to five feet. The effects of this close confinement, the stench, and the general despair and grief led many slaves to avoid food and wish for death.

In general, no separate slave fleets existed. Slave vessels were drawn from the regular merchant marine and transported a varied cargo. As a result, vessels clearing for Africa often had temporary platforms to accommodate slaves that could be removed on the next passage. During the eighteenth century British slaving vessels averaged about a hundred tons, although the size increased later in the century. Most ships were between 50 and 150 tons, and as late as the 1760s, few were more than 200 tons. Brigs and snows, two-masted, middling-sized craft, were the most popular slaving vessels. American slavers tended to use smaller craft, often sloops and schooners. Most Africans brought to North America arrived in British-owned ships, although over time North Americans, particularly Rhode Islanders, gradually infiltrated the trade. But from 1700 to 1808, for every hundred slaves carried by North Americans, the British shipped fifteen hundred. Of the British and American vessels sailing from the Gold Coast between 1755 and 1775, the British ships averaged 273 slaves and the American 124. Over time, ships tended to become larger and more specialized, as merchants responded to the need for speed and capacity. In the 1770s slave merchants were the first to introduce copper sheathing on the hulls of their vessels. This innovation reduced the costs of maintenance and increased the speed of ships.

Slavers tended to be well armed, and their crews were larger than on regular merchant ships.

Feeding, supervising, nursing, and, most important, guarding slaves required many hands: a rule of thumb was one sailor for every ten to fifteen slaves. The presence of a large crew was certainly merited, for there was one on-board slave rebellion every four and a half years (or every fifty-five voyages) in the Rhode Island trade; the British trade saw a slave rebellion every two years.

NUMBERS, ORIGINS, AND DESTINATIONS OF AFRICANS

The most authoritative estimates of the number of slaves brought to North America range from more than four hundred thousand to more than six hundred thousand. Whatever the figure, North America was the destination of only about one in twenty of the approximately nine and a half million Africans who were brought to the New World during the slave trade. Although a few Africans accompanied Spanish explorers in the sixteenth century, the first permanent settlement of Africans occurred in 1619 when a Dutch ship brought twenty or more slaves to Jamestown, Virginia. The colonies of Virginia and South Carolina received the vast majority of all the slaves imported to the continent.

The flow of Africans into North America was just a trickle until the last two decades of the seventeenth century, when annual arrivals began to average by at least one thousand. By the 1710s about two thousand Africans arrived each year, in the 1730s and 1740s about five thousand a year, and in the 1760s about seven thousand a year. The revo-

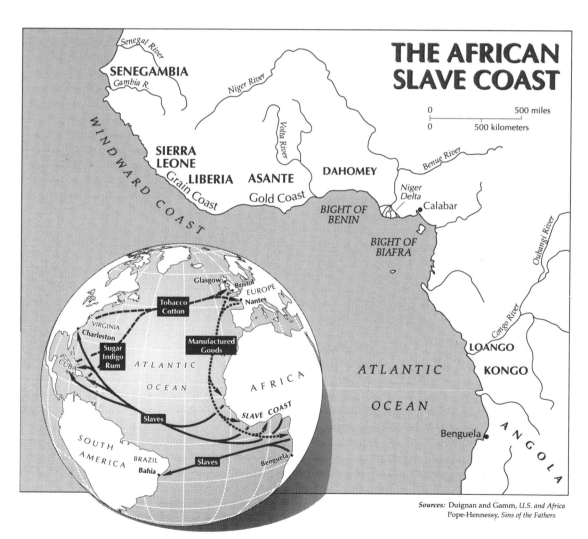

THE AFRICAN SLAVE COAST

Sources: Duignan and Gamm, *U.S. and Africa*
Pope-Hennessy, *Sins of the Fathers*

The Triangular Trade
17th to 19th centuries

801

lutionary war ended slave imports for almost a decade, but from the early 1780s to the end of the century annual arrivals once again averaged about seven thousand a year. In the first decade of the nineteenth century, about 140,000 Africans arrived, twice the number of any previous decade. According to Robert Fogel (1989), almost as many Africans were brought into the United States during the first three decades of the republic as during the previous one hundred and sixty years.

As early as the third decade of the eighteenth century, however, immigration was not the primary means of growth of the North American slave population. Rather, by 1720 the natural increase of the slave population was greater than the increase owing to immigration. This pattern was not true everywhere, for in South Carolina natural increase did not become the primary means of population growth until at least the middle of the eighteenth century. Although absolute numbers of slave imports to the United States were high after the Revolution, immigration contributed only half as much to the growth of the black population as did natural increase. By 1810, there were about 1,400,000 blacks in the United States, a number more than twice the number of Africans imported into the country. Fogel notes that the United States became the continent's leading user of slave labor not because it participated heavily in the slave trade but because of unusually high rates of natural increase.

During the eighteenth and early nineteenth centuries, the British and North American slave trades drew Africans from a variety of regions. By the beginning of the eighteenth century, the Bight of Biafra was a major supplier to British slavers. From at least the 1740s the British were also heavily involved along the Loango coast in West-Central Africa, particularly the area north of the Congo River. These two regions provided over half the slaves taken by the British in the eighteenth century. The Gold Coast and Sierra Leone each accounted for about one-sixth of the British trade; the Bight of Benin and Senegambia supplied even smaller fractions. North American shippers obtained many of their slaves in Sierra Leone, with secondary concentrations in Senegambia and the Gold Coast.

The stream of slaves from the Caribbean to North America was small but steady. The first blacks introduced into many colonies came from the West Indies. The northern colonies, whose markets were not significant enough to merit a large African trade, often relied heavily on slaves brought from the Caribbean. The colonies of New York and Pennsylvania imported a sizable share of their slaves directly from Africa, however, particularly late in the colonial period. Southern colonies quickly turned to Africa as their principal source of slaves. Moreover, many slaves imported from the West Indies had been there only briefly, as a stopover en route from Africa. North Americans did not want "seasoned" West Indian slaves, because they considered them unruly or unfit.

The coastal regions of origin of Africans arriving in North America varied markedly over time and by importing colony. Central Africa was an important supplier to the South throughout the eighteenth century. It was the primary supplier to South Carolina in the 1730s, 1740s, and 1800s and to Virginia in the 1730s and 1760s (see Tables 1 and 2). The Bight of Biafra was a major supplier to the Chesapeake region in the early eighteenth century but not thereafter; it was never an important slave source for South Carolina. Perhaps the most noticeable trend in the coastal origins of African immigrants to both the upper and lower southern colonies was growing heterogeneity. In the upper South, Senegambia, Angola, the Gold Coast, and the upper Guinea coast came to rival, and indeed surpass, the Bight of Biafra as supplying regions. In the lower South, Senegambia, the upper Guinea coast, and the Gold Coast (the last most notably in the 1780s) overtook Angola as chief suppliers, at least until the early 1800s.

This heterogeneity suggests that supply rather than demand considerations were crucial in shaping the composition of any colony's African population. Nevertheless, planter preferences were not completely ignored. Lower South merchants and planters were virtually unanimous in their detestation of "Callabars and Bites"—that is, slaves from the Bight of Biafra. One of the complaints was that Ibos too readily committed suicide. This local chorus of opposition presumably had some effect on the British merchants who supplied the South Carolina market and helps to explain the Bight of Biafra's insignificant share of the lower South market. Chesapeake traders also were not enamored of slaves from the Bight of Biafra, but because their region demanded relatively few Africans, they may well have had less influence than their Carolina counterparts. A further indication that New World demand was only of secondary concern is that Carolina merchants reserved their highest praise for slaves from the Bight of Benin and the Gold Coast but were unable to secure many from either region.

It is difficult to say whether these preferences had any basis in fact or were merely uninformed prejudices. North Americans were generally un-

TABLE 1 Origins of African Immigrants in the Upper South, 1712–1772

| | Percent of Identifiable Origin | | | | |
| | Virginia | | | | Maryland |
Region of Origin	1712–1728	1730–1739	1740–1752	1760–1772	1751–1772
Senegambia	8	27	41	13	52
Sierra Leone	4	—	—	6	—
Windward Coast	4	—	—	9	8
Gold Coast	10	4	8	22	22
Bight of Benin	—	—	—	—	—
Bight of Biafra	57	33	30	—	—
Angola	6	37	21	50	18
Madagascar	11	—	—	—	—
Total	100	101	100	100	100
Number known	11,211	7,644	2,876	3,557	3,606
Percent unknown	35	47	81	67	43

Sources: Walter E. Minchinton et al., eds., *Virginia Slave-Trade Statistics, 1698–1773* (1984); Darold D. Wax, "Black Immigrants: The Slave Trade in Colonial Maryland." *Maryland Historical Magazine* 73, no. 1 (1978): 30–45.

aware of ethnic differences among Africans and labeled immigrants by place of embarkation. Nevertheless, one possible factual support for their preferences is suggested by observations on the different physiques of African groups. South Carolinians were unenthusiastic about "Angolans" because they considered them "short." Almost all slave purchasers were looking for "strong" people like the Gambians. Perhaps even more compelling was the differential healthiness of African newcomers. For slave vessels originating in England, the overall journey to Senegambia and then to the New World was the shortest, on average about seventy to more than a hundred days less than for vessels going to and from Angola or the Bight of Biafra. Thomas Ringold, a Maryland merchant, placed considerable value on the difference, because a Gambian slave generally came in the best health since the journey was short. Conversely, a London firm that sent slaves to Maryland noted that those from Calabar experienced high mortality in their passage. As important as this difference was, it could not have been determinative: a long passage time was characteristic of vessels from the Gold Coast, primarily because of the long stay required to assemble a full cargo, yet few complaints were heard of this region's slaves. Finally, the age and gender composition of different regional shipments may also

TABLE 2 Origins of African Immigrants in the Lower South, 1730–1807

| | Percent of Identifiable Origin | | | | | | | | |
| | South Carolina | | | | | | | Georgia | |
Region of Origin	1730s	1740s	1750s	1760s	1770s	1780s	1800s	1765–1775	1784–1799
Senegambia	12	15	43	22	30	15	6	44	15
Sierra Leone	—	—	4	8	18	3	2	23	43
Windward Coast	—	11	15	28	14	13	23	17	3
Gold Coast	2	—	8	14	18	46	13	5	31
Bight of Benin	—	—	4	3	4	—	1	—	—
Bight of Biafra	8	33	13	—	2	4	3	—	—
Angola	77	41	12	25	14	19	49	10	7
Total	99	100	99	100	100	100	99	99	99
Number known	11,973	1,229	13,106	18,736	16,882	5,777	35,321	3,991	4,658
Percent unknown	40	42	24	20	20	43	11	27	25

Sources: The South Carolina data are drawn from newspaper advertisements for African cargoes; the South Carolina Treasury General Duty Books in the South Carolina Archives, Columbia; the South Carolina Naval Office Shipping Lists in the Public Record Office, London; and Elizabeth Donnan, ed., *Documents Illustrative of the History of the Slave Trade to America.* Vol. 4 (1935; repr. 1969): 235–471. The Georgia data are from Darold D. Wax, "'New Negroes Are Always in Demand': The Slave Trade in Eighteenth-Century Georgia." *Georgia Historical Quarterly* 68, no. 2 (1984): 193–220.

explain planter preferences. Slave shipments from the Gold Coast, Senegambia, and the Bight of Benin generally consisted of fewer children and more men than those from Angola, Sierra Leone, the Windward Coast, and the Bight of Biafra. A buyers' preference for adults made slaves from the former regions particularly attractive.

Not only the coastal regions of African slavers but also their arrival times differed significantly from one colony to another. While the South Carolina slaving season was said by contemporaries to extend from March to October, well over 10 percent of all slaves direct from Africa and a further 20 percent of those brought via the Caribbean arrived outside those months. In Virginia, on the other hand, the slave trade was concentrated into far fewer months. Less than 1 percent of all slaves direct from Africa and only 6 percent of those brought via the Caribbean arrived between October and March. Most of Virginia's Africans arrived during June, July, and August.

The speed at which Africans were dispatched to plantations varied significantly among colonies. Most slaves landed in South Carolina seem to have been sold within two weeks of their arrival. A period of about twelve days (somewhat shorter earlier in the century, when quarantine restrictions were less lengthy) generally separated date of arrival from date of sale, and once sales began, they were generally concluded quickly. Almost a whole shipload of 240 Africans was sold in just 36 hours in 1755. There were, of course, many variations depending on the length of quarantine, the buoyancy of the economy, the number and health of the slaves, and the timing of the arrival of the slave vessel. Still, most Africans probably were resident on their destined plantations within a month of arrival on Sullivan's Island in Charleston Harbor.

The rapid transfer from ship to field owed much to the dominating presence of South Carolina's central port, Charleston. Most of the colony's African immigrants were funneled through this town. Sullivan's Island, where incoming Africans were briefly quarantined, was the Ellis Island of black Americans, as Peter N. Wood (1974) has observed. The central location facilitated quick sales and usually meant that cargoes were sold in one lot. Planters traveled long distances to buy Africans in the city. The Revolutionary statesman and merchant Henry Laurens noted that on one occasion forty or fifty purchasers traveled more than 70 miles (about 112 kilometers) to attend one of his Charleston sales. They went away disappointed because the slaves were in such poor condition, but Laurens maintained that those who traveled the farthest were the keys to a good sale, for they often were willing to pay premium prices in order not to go home empty-handed. The demand for slaves in Charleston could become so intense that, on more than one occasion, the buyers almost came to blows.

In the Chesapeake region, sales took much longer. In the first half of the eighteenth century Virginia slavers generally undertook an initial sale at Yorktown or a similar site on the lower Chesapeake Bay peninsula and then moved upriver to West Point or to other ports. After mid century, however, sites even farther upriver were the initial places of sale, most commonly Bermuda Hundred but also Osborne's Warehouse or Petersburg, which were well inland. Rather than being channeled through one central port, therefore, Africans brought to Virginia were transported to numerous riverside wharves for sale. As the century proceeded, it became common for merchants to buy parcels of Africans whom they tramped from one piedmont courthouse to another until all were sold. For these reasons slave ships to the Chesapeake region took two months or more to complete selling their cargoes. Bristol-based slavers stayed an average of seventy-six days in Virginia but took a third less time to discharge their cargoes and set off for home when in South Carolina.

Carolina Africans were sold not only more quickly and more centrally than their Chesapeake counterparts but also in larger groups. By mid century Henry Laurens began to receive offers from individual planters to take twenty, thirty, even forty Africans at a time. Laurens himself accumulated a labor force of about 230 slaves in less than a decade. On two occasions he specified the precise size of his purchases—in June 1764 he dispatched eleven Africans to his Mepkin plantation, and in June 1765 he sent twenty-seven "new Negroes" to his Wambaw plantation—but, presumably, he regularly bought similar or even larger contingents. In 1771 Peter Manigault purchased fifty-five Africans on behalf of Ralph Izard; and in the following year John Graham went to Charleston to purchase thirty Africans for James Wright. Only about one-sixth of Africans arriving in South Carolina in the 1750s and one-twentieth in the 1780s were bought individually, whereas more than a third of those arriving in the Chesapeake area in the late seventeenth and early eighteenth centuries were purchased singly.

AFRICAN MIGRATION

IDENTITY

After purchase, Africans went through a period of painful adjustment. Some plainly did not wish to adjust, perhaps returning to the site of their sale in a forlorn hope of finding a return passage. Indeed, some Africans explicitly spoke of attempting to return home. In Virginia a thirty-year-old African, "very much marked on his face, arms, and breast, his country fashion, speaks very broken, and can hardly tell his master's name," made at least "three attempts, as he said, to get to his country." Two recent immigrants joined up with several other slaves near Petersburg, "being persuaded that they could find the Way back to their own Country." In South Carolina five slaves from Angola were "supposed to have gone an East course as long as they could, thinking to return to their own country that way." Another group of five—four men and a woman, recently arrived from Africa—commandeered a small canoe on the Ogeechee River in what is now Georgia. The men soon put the woman ashore, however, telling her "they intended to go to look for their own country, and that the boat was not big enough to carry her with them."

Africans, then, commonly absconded, often within a few months of arrival. More often than not, they cooperated when they ran away. Over half the African fugitives in Virginia and South Carolina ran away in groups of two or more, with the groups tending to be larger in South Carolina. Ethnic collaborations were more likely in South Carolina. Quite exceptional in Virginia were the two Senegambians who ran away from a Hanover County master in 1745 or the two Ibos who quit the service of a King William County master in 1773. A quarter of the runaway groups advertised in colonial South Carolina newspapers consisted of Africans who shared the same regional origins.

Shipmates were more likely to maintain or renew acquaintances in South Carolina than in Virginia. In the former, two young men from the Grain Coast ran off with five or six women belonging to a neighboring plantation who had been on the same ship with them. Two shipmates brought to the Charleston workhouse in 1759 identified their master and then declared that he possessed "a negro wench named Betty and that she came out of the same ship with them."

A few African family groups ran away together in South Carolina. Three slaves from Angola who ran away in 1734, taking axes, hoes, and a canoe with them, included two brothers. Thirty years later

two captured Africans explained that they were father and son: the father, aged forty-five, spoke broken English; while his young son spoke better English.

Some Africans fled in the hopes of establishing the kind of autonomous settlements that the Maroons, or fugitive slaves, had formed in Jamaica or Surinam. In fact, wherever Africans congregated in any numbers in the New World, this kind of settlement often flourished. In the upper South, however, the number of Africans was never substantial, and the topography was not particularly conducive to Maroon-type settlements. In the early eighteenth century Africans attempted to establish a few settlements on the frontier, but they were short-lived and never involved more than a score of Africans. In the lower South, on the other hand, Maroon bands of perhaps fifty individuals were far more common. Some low-country groups established organized camps. In 1765 a band of Savannah River Maroons lived in a quasi-permanent settlement. They erected a scaffold as a lookout and, when intruders approached, banged drums and hoisted flags as warnings. The settlement was in the form of a square consisting of four houses, seventeen by fourteen feet in size. The military organization of this village, together with the regularity of its layout and the signs of residential stability, made this one of the more notable examples of Maroon communities in early mainland British America. Nevertheless, all North American Maroon settlements appear insignificant when compared to the size and staying power of their counterparts in Brazil, Surinam, or Jamaica.

The vast majority of Africans neither fled with compatriots nor attempted to set up independent communities; rather, they remained on their plantations, increasingly surrounded by an African American majority. As early as the second decade of the eighteenth century African-born slaves were a minority of all slaves in most parts of North America, and their proportion declined markedly thereafter. Moreover, because slaveholdings were generally small and only large plantations had significant numbers of Africans, members of any given group of immigrants would be fortunate to end up sharing the same residence. Even on a large estate, such as that belonging to Robert "King" Carter in early-eighteenth-century Virginia, the overwhelming majority of immigrant slaves lived in quarters with numerous American-born slaves. Under these circumstances, African names disappeared quickly. In Middlesex County, Virginia, in the late seventeenth and early eighteenth centuries, less than 5 percent of the slaves possessed African names. Ethnic designations also became uncommon among Virginia slaves.

African identity was still a significant presence in the lower South as late as the early nineteenth century. In 1810 Colonel Stapleton's plantation on Saint Helena Island off the South Carolina Coast was worked by 112 slaves. Two old Africans—seventy-nine-year-old Sambo, a superannuated gardener, and eighty-year-old Dorinda, a cripple who crawled on her hands and knees—had undoubtedly immigrated from Africa in the eighteenth century, as may have a third, fifty-year-old Dido, who was from "Morocco." Another twenty-seven Africans—a quarter of the total and fully half of the prime slaves, aged twenty to fifty—had recently arrived in the last great flourish of the African slave trade into Carolina. Of these newcomers almost all were in their twenties; two were brothers; a remarkable number (twenty in all) had paired off in marriage; four of these couples had produced at least one child; one African man had found a Creole wife; five men and one woman were single. These Africans, perhaps in large part because of the demographic structure of this plantation, seemed to look inward for their most important social ties.

African names and designations were far more widespread in the lower South than in other parts of the country. On some plantations in South Carolina at mid century, about one slave in five had an African name. Moreover, not just the number but the range of African names was impressive. In Virginia the standard African names—Cudjo, Cuffee, Quamina, Quash, and Sambo—tended to predominate, whereas in South Carolina they were joined by more unusual names such as Balipho, Bendar, Dabau, Fulladi, Moosa, Noko, Okree, Sogo, Yanki, and Yarrow. Many Africans in South Carolina continued to use a "country name" *after* their masters had christened them. In some cases, as Peter N. Wood (1974) has pointed out, African and Anglo-American names coexisted because they sounded alike. Alexander Wood reported that his slave went "by the Name of Cooper Joe or Cudjoe"; a recent African immigrant brought to the Charleston workhouse gave his name as "Tom or Tomboe." Because most African and Anglo-American names were not readily convertible, however, a newcomer often had to struggle to retain a homeland name. A surprising number were successful. Two Angolan slaves named by their master for the biblical heroes Moses and Sampson continued to be known as Monvigo and Goma.

Isolated Africans could be found everywhere in North America. The sense of bewilderment and frustration at not being able to communicate with fellow slaves or whites is conveyed by an African "of the Horobania country" who, when asked to report his own or his master's name, could only mouth "a word like Fisher, which cannot be understood, whether he means that for his own or his master's name" (South Carolina and American General Gazette, 22 July 1774); consequently, he languished in a South Carolina jail for well over a year. The typical experience for the eighteenth-century African in Virginia must have been rather like that recounted by Olaudah Equiano, who spoke eloquently of his sense of isolation on arrival in the colony:

We were landed up a river a good way from the sea, about Virginia county [country?], where we saw few or none of our native Africans, and not one soul who could talk to me. I was a few weeks weeding grass, and gathering stones in a plantation; and at last all my companions were distributed different ways, and only myself was left. I was now exceedingly miserable, and thought myself worse off than any of the rest of my companions; for they could talk to each other, but I had no person to speak to that I could understand. (Quoted in *Life of Olaudah*, p. 90)

This account rings true, and it may be misleading only in Equiano's assumption that his fellow Africans had companions with whom to talk. More than likely, they did not.

Nevertheless, almost all eighteenth-century North American slaves were aware of at least some homeland associations, whether the survival of a name, distinctive hair braiding, jewelry, cicatrizations, or filed teeth. Homeland memories never evaporated completely. This might amount to nothing more than the recollection of an important personal event. Thus a number of Africans—such as Malinke Ben, who had a large scar on his left arm produced by a knife; or Toby, who had a blotch on his right cheek from a dog bite; or Anthony, who had a hole near his eye from a bullet; or a "Jalunka" (Dyalonke) slave who had a great bump in the small of his back, the result of a fall—remembered receiving these wounds in their "own country." Insignificant as these connections to a homeland might seem in themselves, they were reminders of a valued past. These and many other memories were a resource on which many slaves drew. Africans bequeathed these memories and much else to their descendants.

AFRICAN MIGRATION

BIBLIOGRAPHY

General Works

Duignan, Peter, and L. H. Gann, eds. *The United States and Africa: A History* (1984).

Gemery, Henry A., and Jan S. Hogendorn, eds. *The Uncommon Market: Essays in the Economic History of the Atlantic Slave Trade* (1979).

Rawley, James A. *The Transatlantic Slave Trade: A History* (1981).

Reynolds, Edward. *Stand the Storm: A History of the Atlantic Slave Trade* (1985).

Africa

Cooper, Frederick. "The Problem of Slavery in African Studies." *Journal of African History* 20, no. 1 (1979).

Curtin, Philip D., ed. *Africa Remembered: Narratives by West Africans from the Era of the Slave Trade* (1967).

Edwards, Paul, ed. *The Life of Olaudah Equiano or Gustavus Vassa, the African.* 2 vols. (1789; 1969).

Eltis, David, and Lawrence C. Jennings. "Trade Between Western Africa and the Atlantic World in the Pre-Colonial Era." *American Historical Review* 93, no. 4 (1988).

Fage, John. "African Societies and the Atlantic Slave Trade." *Past and Present,* no. 125 (1989).

Hopkins, A. G. *An Economic History of West Africa* (1973).

Lovejoy, Paul E. *Transformations in Slavery: A History of Slavery in Africa* (1983).

————. "The Impact of the Atlantic Slave Trade on Africa: A Review of the Literature." *Journal of African History* 30, no. 3 (1989).

Manning, Patrick. *Slavery and African Life: Occidental, Oriental, and African Slave Trades* (1990).

Metcalf, George. "A Microcosm of Why Africans Sold Slaves: Akan Consumption Patterns in the 1770s." *Journal of African History,* 28, no. 3 (1987).

Miers, Suzanne, and Igor Kopytoff, eds. *Slavery in Africa: Historical and Anthropological Perspectives* (1977).

Miller, Joseph Calder. *Way of Death: Merchant Capitalism and the Angolan Slave Trade, 1730–1830* (1988).

Northrup, David. *Trade Without Rulers: Pre-Colonial Economic Development in South-eastern Nigeria* (1978).

Rodney, Walter. "African Slavery and Other Forms of Social Oppression on the Upper Guinea Coast in the Context of the Atlantic Slave Trade." *Journal of African History* 7, no. 3 (1966).

The Middle Passage

Cohn, Raymond L., and Richard A. Jensen. "Comment and Controversy: Mortality in the Atlantic Slave Trade." *Journal of Interdisciplinary History* 13, no. 2 (1982).

Garland, Charles, and Herbert S. Klein. "The Allotment of Space for Slaves Aboard Eighteenth-Century British Slave Ships." *William and Mary Quarterly* 3rd ser., 42, no. 2 (1985).

Geggus, David. "Sex Ratio, Age, and Ethnicity in the Atlantic Slave Trade: Data from French Shipping and Plantation Records." *Journal of African History* 30, no. 1 (1989).

Kiple, Kenneth F., and Brian T. Higgins. "Mortality Caused by Dehydration During the Middle Passage." *Social Science History* 13, no. 4 (1989).

Klein, Herbert S., and Stanley L. Engerman. "Slave Mortality and British Ships 1791–1797." In *Liverpool, the African Slave Trade, and Abolition,* edited by Roger Anstey and Paul E. H. Hair. Historic Society of Lancashire and Cheshire, Occasional Series, 2 (1976).

Miller, Joseph C. "Mortality in the Atlantic Slave Trade: Statistical Evidence on Causality." *Journal of Interdisciplinary History* 11, no. 3 (1981).

Minchinton, Walter E. "Characteristics of British Slaving Vessels, 1698–1775." *Journal of Interdisciplinary History* 20, no. 1 (1989).

Steckel, Richard H., and Richard A. Jensen. "New Evidence on the Causes of Slave and Crew Mortality in the Atlantic Slave Trade." *Journal of Economic History* 46, no. 1 (1986).

Return Migration

Staudenraus, P. J. *The African Colonization Movement, 1816–1865* (1961).

Walker, James W. St. G. *The Black Loyalists: The Search for a Promised Land in Nova Scotia and Sierra Leone, 1783–1870* (1976).

Wiley, Bell Irvin. *Slaves No More: Letters from Liberia, 1833–1869* (1980).

The Numbers Game

Curtin, Philip D. *The Atlantic Slave Trade: A Census* (1969).

Henige, David. "Measuring the Immeasurable: The Atlantic Slave Trade, West African Population and the Pyrrhonian Critic." *Journal of African History* 27, no. 2 (1986).

Richardson, David. "The Eighteenth-Century British Slave Trade: Estimates of Its Volume and Coastal Distribution in Africa." *Research in Economic History* 12 (1989).

———. "Slave Exports from West and West-Central Africa, 1700–1810: New Estimates of Volume and Distribution." *Journal of African History* 30, no. 1 (1989).

North America

Coughtrey, Jay. *The Notorious Triangle: Rhode Island and the African Slave Trade, 1700–1807* (1981).

Donnan, Elizabeth, ed. *Documents Illustrative of the History of the Slave Trade to America.* 4 vols. (1930–1935; repr. 1969).

Fogel, Robert W. *Without Consent or Contract: The Rise and Fall of American Slavery* (1989).

———, Ralph A. Galantine, Richard L. Manning, et al. *Without Consent or Contract: The Rise and Fall of American Slavery—Evidence and Methods* (1990).

Klein, Herbert S. "Slaves and Shipping in Eighteenth-Century Virginia." *Journal of Interdisciplinary History* 5, no. 3 (1975).

———. "New Evidence on the Virginia Slave Trade." *Journal of Interdisciplinary History* 17, no. 4 (1987).

Littlefield, Daniel C. *Rice and Slaves: Ethnicity and the Slave Trade in Colonial South Carolina* (1981).

Lydon, James G. "New York and the Slave Trade, 1700 to 1774." *William and Mary Quarterly,* 3d ser., 35, no. 2 (1978).

Minchinton, Walter E., Celia King, and Peter Waite, eds. *Virginia Slave-Trade Statistics, 1698–1773* (1984).

Wax, Darold D. "Black Immigrants: The Slave Trade in Colonial Maryland." *Maryland Historical Magazine* 73, no. 1 (1978).

———. "Africans on the Delaware: The Pennsylvania Slave Trade, 1759–1765." *Pennsylvania History* 50, no. 1 (1983).

———. "'New Negroes Are Always in Demand': The Slave Trade in Eighteenth-Century Georgia." *Georgia Historical Quarterly* 68, no. 2 (1984).

Westbury, Susan. "Slaves of Colonial Virginia: Where They Came From." *William and Mary Quarterly,* 3rd ser., 32, no. 2 (1985).

Wood, Peter N. *Black Majority: Negroes in Colonial South Carolina from 1670 Through the Stono Rebellion* (1974).

SEE ALSO **The Deep South; The Plantation; Slavery**; and various essays in the sections "**The Construction of Social Identity**" and "**Periods of Social Change.**"

ANTEBELLUM AFRICAN AMERICAN CULTURE

Daniel Curtis Littlefield

AFRICA AND THE SLAVE TRADE

THE FORCED MIGRATION of African peoples to the New World and their consequent enslavement differentiates their experience from that of other immigrant groups. Force of circumstances encouraged other peoples to leave their homelands, usually in search of a better life. Force of arms brought over Africans and obliged them to work for the well-being of others. They were part of an economic enterprise based upon the production of exotic tropical staples in overseas colonial possessions for European consumption. This so-called South Atlantic system or, subsequently, "plantation complex," united western Europe, the western coast of Africa, and southern regions of the Americas stretching from Maryland in British North America to Brazil in Portuguese America and including French, Spanish, Dutch, and English islands in the Caribbean. Within this core area, Europeans managed African labor in intensive units of tropical agriculture. Beyond this area, the system had ramifications that included practically all of the Americas. On the fringes, labor was less intensive—in many cases it was not even plantation labor—but the system's effects were to establish an African presence nearly everywhere in the New World that Europeans settled, and to impart a significant African component to the developing cultures, uniting Europeans, Africans, and American Indians.

While the circumstances of African immigration were unique, neither slavery, the plantation, nor overseas units of intensive cultivation have been singularly associated with blacks. The ancient heritage of slavery maintained a continuous existence in southern Europe and qualified the attitudes and outlooks of southern Europeans when it was reinvigorated in the New World. During the Middle Ages, Italian city-states administered a commercial empire in the Mediterranean including sugar estates on Cyprus that were based on a mixed labor force of free peasants, local serfs, and slaves. These slaves derived from several sources: various eastern Europeans from the Black Sea area (Armenians, Circassians, Georgians, Bulgarians, Tartars) as well as black Africans from the sub-Sahara. Nor were blacks confined to the plantation. They served many functions in the Mediterranean world, having prominence in Iberia in particular as domestics, porters, craftsmen, entertainers, and objects of conspicuous consumption, and contributed to the culture of the peninsula, particularly in music and dance.

But the shift in sugar cultivation from the eastern to the western Mediterranean made blacks a growing part of the labor stream flowing through the region, and its requirements made the black slave increasingly a plantation slave. Blacks accompanied sugar culture into the Atlantic when Madeira and the Canary Islands adopted the crop, and the prototype of the New World plantation was created when the Portuguese settled the islands of São Tomé and Principe in the Gulf of Guinea. They created there the first system to depend entirely on African labor, essential features of this society, including a tolerance for miscegenation and social and cultural interpenetration, being replicated in Brazil. The Atlantic slave trade was therefore in some sense merely a redirection southward and westward of African labor from its northward flow into the Mediterranean and southern Europe, and it carried with it social and cultural implications. As it became more capitalistic in the seventeenth century, when adopted by northern Europeans, some of its features changed.

Among the newcomers to the developing slave system were the English. The story is legendary of how one of the first English voyagers to Africa once rejected the proffer of blacks as merchandise saying that "we were a people, who did not deale in any such commodities, neither did wee buy or sell one another, or any that had our owne shapes" (quoted in Jordan, *White over Black,* p. 61). Even at the time this statement was not entirely accurate. Englishmen had already bought and sold black (and white) people, and such scruples as this voyager expressed did not long prevent them from adopting the practice wholesale and from becoming the greatest of slave traders and purveyors of slave-produced crops. In concert with the French and the Dutch, the English displaced the Spanish in the Caribbean and established small farming units worked largely by white indentured servants. In the middle of the seventeenth century, they seized with alacrity the Dutch-sponsored sugar industry taken from Brazil, a concomitant of which was African labor.

The English settled Barbados in 1627, working small tobacco farms with white indentured servants, and began the switch to sugar and slaves in the 1640s. In 1643 European laborers greatly outnumbered African laborers there; in 1655 the number of blacks and whites were nearly equal; by 1680 there was a two to one disproportion, in favor of blacks. In places where white men had labored, it now became fashionable to argue that only black men could work. Africans did indeed have advantages over Europeans when they labored in tropical regions, though not for the reasons their captors alleged. The reasons were epidemiological, however, not climatic. Scholars point out that some midwestern U.S. summers, where the descendants of northern Europeans have labored for years, are hotter than West Indian islands at any season or, for that matter, tropical Africa. Africans came from a wider environment of diseases and had greater tolerance for such maladies as malaria or yellow fever, which decimated Europeans in the tropics. A more important consideration was the fact that undesirable labor conditions were not attractive to men and women of volition, and recourse was thus made to slave labor—a ready precedent.

Although their background provided Africans some advantages in tropical labor, by no means had every imported bondman come fresh from a tropical rain forest. Africa straddles the equator, and three-fourths of its surface area is within the tropics, but differences in altitude have much influence on climate. A true equatorial climate, characterized by high daily temperatures of around 80 degrees Fahrenheit (27 degrees C), is limited to areas within ten degrees of the equator. Rainfall is heavy throughout the year in this zone, sometimes exceeding 80 inches. These hot, humid, rainy conditions give rise to dense tropical rain forests, which stretch in a checkered arc 600 miles wide for 1,400 miles from eastern Zaire to the Gabon and Cameroon coasts and continue along the West African seaboard, 150 to 200 miles wide in places, from the Niger Delta to Sierra Leone. This was the land called "Guinea" by the Europeans (possibly a corruption of "Ghana," an ancient African kingdom, but also derived from the Berber phrase *akal n'iguinawen,* referring to the land of dark-skinned peoples). Fringing the rain forests are tropical savannas or grasslands, with a wider range in temperatures. In West Africa a dry season dominated by the *harmattan,* a dry wind off the Sahara, from November to March, is followed by a generally cooler rainy period brought by southwest monsoons. Moving northward from the equator, this savanna region was known by the Arabs as the Sudan, from *bilad es sudan,* which like the Berber phrase referred to the land of the blacks. The break between savanna and desert is not abrupt but gradual. The land becomes more dry, vegetation less frequent, a transition called by the name "sahel," from the Arabic word for "fringe" or "shore" of the desert. Then comes the Sahara, a dry, desertlike area that was once savanna country supporting pastoral and other peoples but gradually dried up to become the largest desert in the world. Southward from the equator a similar pattern forms.

The great African rivers are navigable for long distances on interior plateaus (and African expertise in negotiating these inland highways was of great use in the Americas), but they plunge over impassable rapids or cataracts as they approach the coastal plain. African rivers typically enter the ocean through deltas, often obstructed by sandbars, rather than through navigable estuaries. There are few natural harbors. These features help explain Africa's isolation for long after Europeans appeared on the coast. It was not easy to move inland, or even to harbor ships. Moreover, the presence of an equatorial climate made the coastline largely undesirable to Europeans. The life expectancy of a European stationed on the coast when they began to locate there in the fifteenth century was scarcely more than a year. Slave ships generally lost about a quarter of their crews. These features also facilitated African control of the coastline. Although many Africans utilized the sea, Africa's smoother coastline meant that fewer Africans than Asians or Europeans did so. Indeed, in some parts of Africa the sight of the sea was forbidden to the monarch or local ruler. The orientation was inland rather than outward. This was especially true in West Africa where, before the age of discovery, trade from the outside world was mediated through North Africa and came across the Sahara. Until the nineteenth century, then, African development was relatively self-contained.

Most imported Africans came from the western coast, in an area stretching from Senegambia to Angola. There is a plethora of ethnic groups, languages, customs, and outlooks complicating the generalizations that must of necessity be made. Savanna regions north and south of the equator supported sedentary populations of agriculturalists, interspersed in the western Sudan with nomadic pastoralists. They cultivated what was called the Sudanic crop complex—millet, sorghum, watermelon, tamarind, kola, and sesame. After the sixteenth century, they added the so-called American complex of maize, manioc, groundnuts (peanuts), and sweet potatoes. The forest zone supports dense populations of agriculturalists raising maize, manioc, yams, and bananas. There are breaks in the forest where savanna reaches the sea and crops and agricultural practices change accordingly. Rice is grown in various northern and southern savanna regions, particularly in the western Sudan and along the Upper Guinea coast, Africans often employing dry rice or rice using natural ponds or flooding. But in coastal Senegal and Sierra Leone the Bagas use intensive irrigation to reclaim mangrove swamps for sophisticated methods of rice cultivation. Domesticated chickens, goats, and dogs exist throughout the region, with sheep in some places and cattle, normally without the milking complex, in the savanna, and horses in the western Sudan. Throughout the region, agriculturalists practice shifting hoe cultivation and, in some places, crop rotation and fallowing.

Iron-age technology and the development of trade facilitated the rise of complex African state systems: in the western Sudan among Mande-speaking peoples (Soninke, Malinke, Bambara) and Kanuri-speaking peoples farther east; along the Guinea coast among Akan-speaking peoples (Asante, Fante), and among the Gã, Ewe, Fon, Yoruba, and Edo peoples; and in southern coastal and savanna regions among Bantu-speaking peoples (Vili, Matamba, Kongo, Mbundu). In general, however, with or without a state system, the local lineage to which people belonged was most important, with villages governed by a clan head or village chief who exercised local authority. State systems consisted of a second level of lineage relationships, the leaders of one group establishing hegemony over others but exacting feudal-like obeisance and obligations rather than a structural reorganization of society. Local authority remained much the same. With trade and state systems went artisanal specialization, including bronze and iron working, pottery-making, and other crafts, knowledge of which Africans brought to the Americas. Artisanal activities spurred artistic expression, and African societies did not segregate the two. In western Africa descent tended to be patrilineal (tracing kinship through the father); in south-central Africa, matrilineal (tracing kinship through the mother); significant exceptions include the Asante in the first instance and the Luba in the second. Few African societies are bilateral (tracing kinship through both mother and father). Most practiced polygyny.

While the northern reaches of the savanna were influenced by Islam, most Africans practiced traditional religions, which had close association with a particular locale. The land, material objects related to it, and ancestors buried beneath it all had essential religious aspects. A person was not autonomous but merely one element in a clan composing the living and the dead, and religion was not personal but communal. While alive, people dwelled beside the ancestors and communed with them for support. At death they entered a family burial ground that held the sources from which they had originally been embodied. Africans believed that objects of the natural world had spirits which were mediums of communication with, or in fact may once have been, their ancestors and therefore commanded veneration. Because of the connection between creed and place, one's removal from a region had acute religious implications. "A person cannot detach himself from the religion of his group," argues John S. Mbiti (*African Religions and Philosophy,* p. 2), "for to do so is to be severed from his roots, his foundation, his context of security, his kinships and the entire group of those who make him aware of his own existence." This helps explain why some Africans in America, and the Ibo in particular, developed a reputation for self-destruction: they hoped to return to the land of their forebears.

African institutions of slavery are related to the issue of kinship. African lineage-based societies and state systems increased their wealth and strength by adding members to the group. This accretion could occur in a number of ways, perhaps most often by marriage—women and children being particular assets. But it could also occur in the involuntary service of war captives or other unfortunates who worked for or were adopted by the state or individual families in patron-client relationships, which accorded them social existence. As members of an extended family they might in many ways be treated like other family members yet not achieve absolute equality, based on their positions as historical outsiders. The longer they were part of a community, the closer they came to absorption, even though their origins might never be forgotten. They could obtain many rights and privileges, secure land of their own for cultivation, and be free from the threat of sale. They might achieve great wealth and political power exceeding even that of free people, and might even acquire slaves of their own.

Trade slaves, those sold to Europeans, were often older war captives perceived as threats to their host communities. They might never adjust and always posed the risk that they might run away. They could best serve the community by their salability. Their position was closest to that of chattel slaves in the Americas, though they often had more privileges, were not distinguished permanently from their masters by skin color as an unquestioned mark of degradation, and did not perform chores that separated them from free men. Younger people, especially women and children, had value beyond the simply pecuniary and were more often kept—adopted, to become part of the local society. Indigenous African servitude therefore had similarities as well as significant differences from institutions of bondage in other parts of the world.

A trade in slaves across the Sahara had existed from the second century A.D. However, the Atlantic slave trade was of much greater extent in numbers if not duration, and its development offered African societies more opportunities to decide how to use captives. It doubtless spurred additional warfare and social disruption. It is possible, too, that the crimes for which one might be condemned to slavery (as opposed to death) increased. But because slaves had a value in African society beyond their sale price, they were seldom viewed as simple commodities or work units, which is the character they attained under capitalist influence in seventeenth-century America. For the prisoner sold overseas such a distinction might not have been meaningful, but not everyone was sold. The disposition of bondsmen was determined by the needs of the state within an African context, and because money was not the sole or even the prime consideration, women and children were not equally available over all the coast. African needs rather than European demands had a decisive influence on availability.

By the end of the eighteenth century, British merchants accounted for more than half of the slave trade, followed by the French, Portuguese, Dutch, and Danes. The bulk of these laborers went to sugar-producing regions in tropical America, with lesser amounts reaching the North American fringe of the South Atlantic system. It is estimated that, over the whole period of the slave trade, about twelve million Africans reached the New World. Averaging less than two thousand annually before the seventeenth century, imports rose to nearly sixty thousand per year by the eighteenth century. Only around five percent of total imports reached the shores of what became the United States. Brazil received almost forty percent of the total. But the single island of Jamaica received eight percent and little Barbados four percent, the one to exceed, the other to almost equal, the number imported to the mainland. Yet by the third decade of the nineteenth century the United States had the largest slave population in the Americas. These facts are essential to understanding the black experience in North America, with important consequences for black life and culture.

EARLY PATTERNS OF BLACK LIFE IN AMERICA

Not having envisioned slavery in the Chesapeake, the Englishmen there had made no plans for it, and there is some uncertainty about the status of the first blacks brought in. Whether they were regarded as servants or as slaves or something else is unclear. They were considered alien, were not legally protected by indentures, and may commonly have been worked for longer periods of time than English people. Some probably were held for life, but there appears to have been no invariable pattern. One John Phillip, a black man christened in England, arrived in the colony sometime before 1624 perhaps not even encumbered by indenture. Anthony Johnson, a black, was a servant in 1625 but free by the middle of the century and claimed head rights for Africans he himself imported. Blacks did suffer from prejudice, but the extent to which these attitudes were acted upon in daily life is unclear. Because they came most often from other European settlements in the Americas, especially from the West Indies, occasionally from Europe, in the early years these blacks had had at least a passing acquaintance with Western culture, in contrast to those imported directly from Africa. Nevertheless, in the 1660s the governments of Virginia and Maryland began to enact slave laws, so by that period clearly the institution of slavery in the Chesapeake had begun to form.

In 1662 Virginia facilitated the shackling of mixed bloods by reversing traditional English practice in making children follow the condition of their mother. Simultaneously, the colony indicated a distaste for miscegenation by doubling its fines in bastardy cases that involved black and white people. Laws in Virginia (1667) and Maryland (1671) declared that Christianization did not alter the person's condition as to his servitude or freedom. These laws facilitated both the development of slavery and of Christianization among blacks, though, in terms of the latter, more in theory than in fact. Virginia's 1667 law was apparently spurred by the fact that several slaves had used their Christian conversion as a basis for successful suits for freedom in Virginia courts, and the law had the possible support of Anglican clergymen in an effort to dilute planter opposition to slave proselytization. Christianity was to become an important element of African American culture, containing less obvious African influences among North American blacks than was evident among African descendants in Brazil or Cuba or Jamaica, yet significantly modified by African cultural attitudes and the needs of the enslaved. Planter opposition, inconsistent Anglican activity, and the survival of African religious practices inhibited the spread of Christianity among slaves newly imported from Africa in the early years. The suspicion of a connection between conversion and emancipation lingered among slaves into the eighteenth century and occasionally caused unrest when expectations in this regard were not vindicated. Not until the evangelical movements of the 1730s and 1740s developed an emotional appeal that touched an ecstatic religious chord from the African background were significant numbers of slaves moved toward Christianity, and even then perhaps the majority remained unaffected.

The legal expression of antipathy toward blacks in the 1660s, however, was not necessarily determinative of social relations. Timothy Breen and Stephen Innes indicate (*"Myne Owne Ground,"* 1980) that the hardening of attitudes expressed in the Virginia Assembly apparently did not affect the thriving black community that existed on the Eastern Shore at the same time. In Northampton County between 1664 and 1677, nineteen percent of black males (ten out of fifty-three) were householders, a significant figure in view of the difficulty of securing freedom. All the blacks there had arrived as slaves.

There were two ways one might become free: manumission as a result of some kind of meritorious service, or self-purchase. Nearly all masters allowed servants or slaves access to vacant land on which to cultivate tobacco for themselves in their free time, and Northampton's blacks normally got their freedom by making agreements to purchase themselves from their masters. Though this was not easy, they were fairly successful. Once freed, they managed to acquire land, raise tobacco and livestock, and interact quite well with their neighbors. There was a close-to-equal sex ratio between black men and women so that a stable black community developed, though at least one of the black men married a white woman. The black population was not a segregated community; scattered around the Eastern Shore, it apparently associated with white counterparts more or less as other black Englishmen did, with the same responsibilities and problems. Largely acculturated to European norms, the African background was nevertheless an essential ingredient of its social makeup and success. Many in the community had come via the New Netherlands from the Congo-Angola region and brought an agricultural heritage that facilitated their individual efforts to free themselves and to maintain themselves in freedom. Indeed, some of them were better suited to that task than some of their English compatriots. Their apparent acceptance by their white neighbors did not prevent significant efforts to sustain connections among themselves.

There is not much evidence of discrimination. Even in the sensitive area of miscegenation, court records reveal little proof of harsher punishment for interracial fornication than for any other, whether the combination was a white man/black woman or black man/white woman. But by the end of the century this situation had changed. Free blacks had either disappeared from the records or been reduced to marginal status.

This transition is explained partly by increased importation of blacks in the 1680s, and by the fact that these were blacks lacking in prior acculturation. There were only about twenty-five hundred blacks in Virginia in 1676, but the growing black presence, coming now directly from Africa rather than from the New Netherlands, the West Indies, or England, brought latent racism to the surface. Ideas about black inferiority began to be expressed. This shift in racial attitudes eroded the position of free blacks. Although it is not clear how many there were in late seventeenth-century Virginia, free blacks were thought to comprise a larger percentage of the total black population than they would at any subsequent period during the era of slavery. From the 1680s on, however, both the numbers and the status of free blacks declined, and with the latter went the hope that blacks, like other immigrants, might be accepted as Englishmen whose skin just happened to be black.

The increase in the number of blacks there heralded a change in the economic and social structure of the Chesapeake. The seventeenth century was characterized by relatively small farms or plantations that could be worked either by a man and his family, by indentured servants, by Indian slaves or servants, or by blacks. This variegated pattern gave way in the eighteenth century to larger plantations usually worked by black slaves. In 1715, Virginia had 23,000 blacks compared with 72,500 whites, making blacks one-third of the population. At mid century the ratio had drastically increased. Maryland in 1750 had 100,000 whites and 40,000 blacks; Virginia in 1756 had 173,316 whites and 120,156 blacks. In some counties blacks outnumbered whites; almost nowhere were they entirely absent. This situation colonials viewed with alarm. A large servile population obviously could pose a threat to the peace, and some thought was given to limiting their importation. Attempts to curb the slave trade, usually in the form of prohibitive duties, were, however, more often than not disallowed by Parliament.

By the middle of the eighteenth century the institution of slavery was firmly established in law and custom, and the words "black" and "slave" were being increasingly and commonly used in a synonymous fashion. Stringent laws were enacted to control the slave population, laws that were often extended to free blacks as well. While the seventeenth century had been characterized by relatively small units of production with master and slave living in close proximity (sometimes even in the same house, and joined perhaps by white indentured servants), the eighteenth century saw larger holdings and greater physical separation between masters and slaves and black and white bondsmen. Despite the consolidation of production units, the slave population was still scattered about the countryside, even large holdings being worked as small farms or quarters, where ten or twenty slaves lived and produced tobacco, grain, or garden crops and cared for cattle, sheep, pigs, and chickens. The home plantation would hold the major barns, stables, storehouses, an impressive mansion, and a larger staff. The large planter considered himself a patriarch with all those under his authority as part of his extended family. Thus, one ended a letter with the statement that "my familey [sic] are all well now some few Negroes excepted." An indentured servant took the same attitude when he wrote home to say that "our Family consists of the Col[onel], his Lady and four Children, a housekeeper, an overseer and myself, all white. But how many blacks young and old, the Lord only knows" (Mullin, *Flight and Rebellion*, p. 23).

In this patriarchal role, planters were concerned not merely with keeping slaves well and at their duties but also took an intense interest in their personal lives. Some of this interest was beneficial in that it led to the forming and keeping of families together, although the master had practical considerations for doing so. When one Virginia planter hired a worker from a neighboring plantation, he soon decided, regardless of cost, to hire the worker's wife and family too, as it became clear that the worker would create problems if he did not. Stable families meant a more stable and dependable work force. For this reason planters sought a more or less equal sex ratio on their plantations so that stable families would be created.

Stable families also meant a situation where the black population could reproduce itself—a striking contrast to plantation systems in South America and the Caribbean. There was a general tendency to ask for slaves in the proportion of two men for every woman. Since both could be worked in the fields easily in North America and women cost less, there may well have been a predisposition to accept more women on the continent, one reinforced by the desire for a more equal sex ratio on plantations.

Paternalistic concern was fueled partly by economic considerations. The harsh treatment common in the West Indies, where slaves were quite literally worked to death in a few years, would make for an unprofitable plantation in the Chesapeake, because there one could not afford to replace the slave force every few years. A combination of factors including paternalism, a large slave population, a more equitable sex ratio than normal in plantation colonies, and a better-developed physical environment which permitted more contact among blacks, eventuating in community and conjugal relations, all contributed to a natural increase in Virginia's black population beginning in the 1730s. Cultural change was also a factor. For example, a shift away from traditional African child-rearing practices, in particular the adoption of early weaning, permitted more frequent conception.

Whereas slavery in the Chesapeake was a gradual development, in the Carolina region the institution was provided for upon the inception of the colony in 1663. And while the black population grew slowly in the Chesapeake, the reverse was true in Carolina. Blacks were imported in significant numbers from about the 1690s, but by 1715 the black population outnumbered the white by about forty percent (10,500 to 6,250), the only colony in English North America where this disproportion existed.

As in Virginia, most seventeenth-century South Carolina slaves came from the West Indies, some accompanying the original English settlers from Barbados. Although the colder winters created some disadvantages for them, they continued to be better equipped than their masters, physically and pharmacologically, to cope with South Carolina's semitropical environment. These slaves' familiarity with tropical herbs, ability to move along inland waterways using canoes or pirogues, skill in fishing utilizing not only nets, harpoons, or other implements but also the drugging of fish with poisons, enabled them to live off the land much more easily than their masters could. Their expertise as well as the rough pioneer conditions of the new settlements facilitated a degree of "frontier" equality that did not obliterate their servile status but doubtless enhanced their self-esteem and their negotiating position because they did have places to run to and the wherewithal to survive after escape. The South Carolina slave code of 1696, based on the Barbadian code of 1688, announced an end to this relatively benign period.

The colony increasingly embraced rice as a staple, the most remunerative such crop on the continent at the time, whose reach extended to low-country Georgia after the middle of the eighteenth century. At the beginning of that century, rice production was developing in the lowlands. Englishmen benefited from the knowledge of their African bondmen, many of whom came from rice-growing regions in Africa and knew more about cultivating the crop than their owners. Indeed, Carolinians adopted a preference for people from the rice-producing Senegambia region that lasted through most of the colonial period (although the vagaries of trade prevented that region's ethnic groups from having a statistical predominance).

Various Senegambian peoples were associated with the African cattle complex and brought expertise in the endeavor, accentuating the planters' regional preference. For while the colonists searched for a staple, South Carolina became "the colony of a colony," providing beef, hides, and other foodstuffs to Barbados and deerskins and naval supplies to England. The practices of free grazing, nighttime penning for cattle protection, and seasonal burning to freshen pastures had West African antecedents. The word "cowboy," predominently connected with the nineteenth-century American western cattle industry, may well have found its first usage here.

By 1700, chattel slavery and staple agriculture had fastened themselves upon North America in both the Chesapeake and the Carolina regions, and the black population of the Carolina low country continued to grow. By 1765 blacks outnumbered whites by more than two to one (ninety thousand to forty thousand) and Charleston was the largest North American slave port.

Slavery was a milder institution in the Chesapeake region than in the Carolina area (including Georgia), at least physically. This situation was related to the prevailing type of crop, the local demography, and the length of settlement. Because tobacco required delicate attention, tobacco plantations were smaller, using small slave crews that worked in close relationship with the master if the farm was small. Tobacco can, however, be raised without slave labor, so a person could start out slowly and build up, a situation which contributed to there being a large number of people with few slaves. The close contact between master and slave typical of tobacco culture helped make slavery in that crop area somewhat more humane in that there was less impersonal cruelty. In many cases the material existence of master and slave was practically the same. Finally, there was a larger percentage of what were called "country born" slaves, those born in the region, which meant that the cultural distance between master and slave was not so great.

Rice and indigo required larger slave crews than tobacco (thirty was the optimum for beginning a rice plantation), so the master and slave were not very close physically. Moreover, in the Carolina region a large number of slaves came over in a relatively short period of time, constituting a greater percentage of "salt water" (African-born) slaves, which meant that the cultural distance between master and slave was greater too. They had different languages and ways of thought. Finally, the mechanical aspects of rice cultivation were physically more taxing than those for tobacco. All these things meant that the external attributes of slavery were harsher in South Carolina than in the Chesapeake.

Psychologically, though, the slave in the Carolinas may have had an easier time because he was much more likely to come into and remain in contact with people from his own ethnic group. Thus, slaves could provide each other moral, spiritual, and sometimes cultural support. The greatest number of Africanisms surviving in formerly British North America are found in the Carolina region. The Gullah language in the sea islands off the coast of South Carolina (Geechee in the sea islands off Georgia), which blends a mostly English vocabulary with an African grammatical structure, is an obvious example. Also, African heritage is exhibited in the practice of decorating graves with objects of the deceased, seashells, or artistic carved or sculptured grave markers; the maintenance of a basket-weaving tradition that has disappeared in other areas; the nurturing of a vibrant African-based folklore which has lost some of its vitality elewhere; and in religion an important locus of the ring shout, an African-influenced dance style used in worship.

The seventeenth-century circumstance of a widely dispersed settlement pattern in the Chesapeake meant that relatively small numbers of blacks were distributed among the white population, encouraging them to acculturate to English norms. A small population and frontier conditions in Carolina encouraged similar development there. However, African importation at the end of the century disrupted these areas' demographic and cultural stability. The effects of "seasoning," or adverse epidemiological conditions on new immigrants, and an unbalanced sex ratio meant an unstable or nonexistent family life for many, and negative population growth. But as the population recovered, it had the wherewithal for greater family and community formation. Furthermore, the increasing importation during the eighteenth century changed the direction of the developing African American culture by imparting to it a greater African component. On large plantations slaves could live in nuclear family units; on small estates families built across plantation lines, an arrangement in which children stayed with the mother and the father was allowed to visit.

Natural increase of the black population began in the decades between 1710 and 1730, earlier in South Carolina than Virginia, though interrupted by increasing imports into the low country after 1720. The growth of a creole, or native-born, population also signaled the formation of a creole culture that was neither African nor European but contained elements of both, modified by the attributes of a new environment and the contributions of native peoples. The African use of gourds, for example, could be related to the Native American use of calabashes. Both peoples had basket-weaving traditions and were both skilled in the use of small watercraft on inland rivers. These similarities facilitated Africans' adjustment to and appropriation of local skills. Perhaps frequently, Africans were the mediators of this knowledge between Native Americans and Europeans.

Pidgin English—concocted as a means of communication between and among masters and various African ethnic groups—evolved into a variant black English found among the native born and assumed the status of a separate creole language among Gullah and Geechee speakers in coastal South Carolina and Georgia. Few African material artifacts survived the middle passage intact, but African artistic and functional values found material expression in the workbaskets and other implements that accompanied rice cultivation in South Carolina; in the "colono-ware" pottery found there and elsewhere; in an Akan-like drum discovered in mid eighteenth-century Virginia; and in the banjo, an African instrument used frequently to accompany black music and dance in the colonial Chesapeake (later appropriated and modified by white musicians, becoming a common companion today of American country rather than black music).

Africanisms more often abided in underlying assumptions about life—outlooks, folkways, folktales, and beliefs—and a cosmology that placed great emphasis on kin and extended family relationships, no doubt strengthened by the fragility of family life under slavery. Having extended kin, fictive or otherwise, helped to ease the burden of children separated from parents, of wives removed from husbands. Naming practices, particularly for son after father (less often daughter after mother) served to memorialize connections that might by physically sundered by forces over which slaves had no control.

While creating their own culture slaves had a significant influence on that of their masters. Black musicians often played at planters' balls and imparted their own interpretation to the music and dance, thus affecting the planters' taste. They also proffered their own dance and music. A visitor commenting on Virginia entertainment at mid century related that "towards the close of an evening, when the company are pretty well tired with country dances, it is usual to dance jiggs; a practice originally borrowed, I am informed, from the Negroes"; another observer noted that these dances were normally performed "(to some Negro tune)" (quoted in *The Transformation of Virginia,* p. 84). At the other end of the scale, a white South Carolinian reported that blacks at their own gatherings sometimes entertained themselves by "the men copying (or *taking off*) the manners of their masters, and the women those of their mistresses, to the inexpressible diversion of that company" (quoted in *Colonial South Carolina: A History,* p. 190)—the kind of activity that led to such dances as the Cake Walk, which became the rage in gilded age America. In other, sometimes subtle, ways slaves modified the language and cosmology of their masters. This was especially the case in coastal South Carolina and Georgia, where blacks were in a majority and plantation children on large estates might spend their formative years surrounded by blacks.

SLAVERY IN THE NORTHERN COLONIES

Although four hundred thousand blacks lived south of Pennsylvania, fifty thousand lived north of Maryland, connected in an auxiliary way to the South Atlantic system. New York had the largest slave population of the middle colonies. The institution of slavery was established soon after the Dutch settled the region in 1626. In 1650 the Dutch New Netherlands had perhaps a larger black population than any other colony on the continent, brought in by the Dutch West India Company for construction, land clearing, and agricultural tasks. Most slaves were company owned prior to 1654, when a change in policy facilitated widespread individual slave use. Slaves became particularly important in the Hudson Valley, where agricultural expansion created labor demand. Slavery under the Dutch was relatively mild, however, little distinction being made between slaves and indentured servants in daily life. In fact, the Dutch established a policy of "half-freedom," which enabled slaves to live on their own in return for a specified amount of labor and an annual payment. Early New Netherland resisted efforts to make the status of "half-freedom" hereditary. There was no slave code, and free blacks were given equal rights with white people.

This situation was to change when the English took over the region in 1664 and renamed it New York. They gave legal recognition to an already existing economic institution and greatly stimulated the slave trade. At the end of the seventeenth century blacks made up ten percent of the population.

Seventy years later (in 1771) the relative proportions of the population had scarcely changed. Despite its comparatively small black population, New York had the harshest slave code outside the South. Blacks comprised about one-sixth of New York City's population in 1740 (2,000 out of 12,000), and although officials did not enforce all the existing regulations against blacks, these laws were nevertheless a source of fear. There were frightening outbreaks of slave unrest in 1708, 1712, and 1741. In the latter instance, slaves were accused of conspiring with poor whites to destroy the city of New York. There was actually very little evidence of such a plot, but the fears of New Yorkers were such that more than 200 people, black and white, were brought to trial. Of the blacks, 101 were convicted, 18 hanged, 13 burned alive, and 70 banished; four white people, including two women, were also hanged. (By contrast, when the largest slave rebellion of the colonial period, the Stono Rebellion, took place in South Carolina in 1739, the reaction of South Carolinians was much more restrained.)

New Jersey, Delaware, and Pennsylvania also had slaves, brought into the region by the Dutch West India Company. They were present in the Philadelphia area in the mid 1680s. William Penn himself preferred black slaves to white servants as the most economical investment. Although the Quakers eventually took a stand against the institution, slaves were a regular part of their mercantile businesses at the turn of the century, when one of every fifteen Philadelphia families owned black bondsmen. There was some opposition to their use, however, and in 1712 the Assembly passed a ban on importation that was later disallowed by Parliament. Slaves' numbers increased after the middle of the century, reaching a high of nine percent in Philadelphia, falling off thereafter. New Jersey joined New York in the severity of its slave codes, with Pennsylvania not far behind. All three states had special slave courts, which in New Jersey lasted until 1768 and in New York and Pennsylvania until after the Revolution.

New England was more interested in carrying slaves to other regions than in bringing them there, but as a result of the region's involvement in the slave trade, slaves were present there. By 1700 there were fewer than 1,000 blacks in New England out of a total population 90,000, and there were only 4,150 blacks to 158,000 whites in 1715, representing less than three percent of the population. The slaves brought there were generally rejects who could not be sold easily in the plantation colonies.

The topography of the New England region did not give rise to the large plantation systems found in other slavery areas, and most of this area's slave-holders owned only one or two slaves. Exceptions were to be found, however, in eastern Connecticut and the Narragansett country of Rhode Island, particularly the latter where a few farmers owned as many as fifty slaves working in mixed farming to raise corn, wheat, dairy cows, and sheep. Others worked as skilled craftsmen. Dairying and related pursuits in South County, Rhode Island, provided that colony with the largest percentage of blacks in New England. In 1755, for example, about one-third of the population in South Kingstown and over half that of Charlestown, at either end of the region, were black. Despite the dearth of blacks in the region as a whole, therefore, some New Englanders had intense, extended relationships with them, and others had frequent contact.

As in the plantation colonies, the seventeenth-century northern black population was largely transshipped by way of the West Indies, giving them some introduction to western—or at least plantation—culture. Still, insofar as they were African born and not long in the islands, these imports may have been no less African in outlook than the direct imports. The most important consideration for the development of African American culture in this period was the fact that these blacks were submerged in a European American sea and thus became rapidly acculturated. In addition, because of their adjustment period in the islands, they had a low death rate. Since they were not brought to plantation colonies, nor came indeed to answer a large demand, the sex ratio in this period was more nearly equal, which permitted these slaves to establish stable family life quickly and increase their population early.

Most blacks worked in agricultural pursuits in support of monocultures in West Indian islands dependent on the mainland for foodstuffs. Cereal farming was seasonal, however, with demands that vitiated slavery's usefulness. Northern farmers supplemented their few slaves with hired hands or indentured servants. As in fifteenth-century Spain, so in eighteenth-century northern colonies in British North America slaves often were regarded as status symbols. Northern slaveholders listed slaves in their wills and inventories along with high-status objects like clocks and carriages rather than with land and agricultural implements.

Most northern blacks worked in rural areas, but significant numbers also congregated in urban locales—Newport, Boston, Philadelphia, New York City. There they performed a variety of tasks, working not only as domestics but with merchants and shopkeepers, innkeepers and tavern owners, as handymen and craftsmen of various sorts. In the countryside, access to horses allowed mobility and opportunity for contact, but in the cities, where blacks were disproportionately located, socializing was easier and this enabled the development of a black subculture. It was not as autonomous as in some areas: by living and working with white families, blacks' own lives were constricted—not only by constant supervision but also by the fact that owners objected to servants having children. Some sold their domestics at the first sign of pregnancy. Others sold or let out young slave children, a practice which perhaps did not appear cruel in a contemporary context, since at that time white youths, particularly in New England, were commonly apprenticed or otherwise brought up by people other than their parents. Slaveholders' objections, together with the absence of coresidential housing among mates and a high sex ratio contributed to a low black birthrate by the second half of the eighteenth century. In some but not all places, blacks also had a high death rate. On the other hand, bondsmen occasionally were permitted to live and hire out, as teamsters, warehousemen, stockmen, sailors, or dockworkers, allowing them a more independent life-style and subculture.

Over the eighteenth century, northern urban slavery shifted steadily away from the home to the shipyard. A concomitant of this shift was an increasing proportion of men. This was partly a result of importation directly from Africa in the century's second half, which imparted a significant African component to the highly Europeanized African American culture that existed. It also made the northern black sex ratio look more like that of the plantation colonies. For example, in Massachusetts after 1750 males outnumbered females two to one, the ratio typical of African slave-trade cargoes. This development altered the earlier situation of relatively stable family life, encouraged interracial marriages between black men and Indian women (thus exciting tensions between black and Indian men), and led to occasional marriages between black men and white women, despite proscriptions (Massachusetts outlawed race mixture in 1705 and Pennsylvania in 1726, the only northern colonies to do so). It also led to a reemphasis on African culture, most apparent on Negro Election Day. This was a ritualistic festival rooted in West African traditions of role reversal that blacks celebrated in New England and various middle colonies. Negro Election

Day attracted blacks from around the countryside for food, music, and good cheer. On the occasion they elected black kings or governors, who exercised symbolic but sometimes real authority among blacks. Whites also participated, and the owners of slaves honored by election were expected to render moral and financial support of their bondsmen in performance of the bondsmen's duties. Such displays, common elsewhere in the Americas, were too threatening to be entertained in North America's plantation colonies and were permissible in the nonplantation regions only because they did not vitiate the hegemony of the ruling classes. Indeed, they reaffirmed it. The elections, infused with African meaning, were modeled on European American practices. The festivities combined amusements from European and African heritages, including such games as quoits (similar to horseshoes) and pitching pennies common among whites, and African styles of dancing, wrestling, stick fighting, and pawpaw (an African shell game). They embraced foot races and other forms of competition shared by both cultures. Yet the nature of the activities struck some whites as travesty: The exuberant shouts greeting election results, where "every voice [rang out] upon it highest key, in all the various languages of Africa" (quoted in *Slave Culture,* p. 75); the elaborate and exotic dress of celebrants and elected officials, consisting more often than not of old clothes dispensed from the master's closet but cleaned and arranged with a flair for color and African notions of attractiveness; the loud and (to white ears) discordant music accompanying costumed bondsmen on parade; the air of studied dignity projected by the transitory kings of governors. The exhibition of African traits on this occasion confirmed in white minds their own superiority and simultaneously helped to undermine black claims to acculturation and equal treatment.

BLACK SLAVERY IN THE AGE OF WHITE INDEPENDENCE

Blacks, like other Americans, were affected by the Revolution. Its appeal to natural law had a particular resonance. When blacks responded to its rhetoric, however, they evoked acute unease among their white compatriots and oppressors. In South Carolina former slave trader and revolutionary patriot Henry Laurens related "a peculiar incident" during the Stamp Act crisis which revealed "in what dread the citizens lived among the black savages with whom they were surrounding themselves .... [I]n January ... some negroes who, apparently in thoughtless imitation, began to cry 'Liberty'" threw Charleston into alarm for two weeks (from *The Southern Experience in the American Revolution,* p. 277). Ten years later another South Carolinian issued a blanket authorization for anyone who found his slave away from the plantation without permission to administer a severe flogging, because the noble-spirited bondsman, whether under revolutionary influence or not, had had "the audacity to tell me, he will be free, that he will serve no Man, and that he will be conquered or governed by no Man."

Since the slaves' prime concern was liberty and the planters who fought to secure their own did not intend to grant it to blacks, the interests of masters and slaves did not necessarily coincide. Indeed, the slaves' interest lay with their masters' enemies, as some perceived it. One of the first offers to support the British came from slaves in Massachusetts who proposed their services in return for freedom. Even before November 1775 when the royal governor, John Murray, Lord Dunmore, proclaimed freedom for slaves and indentured servants who deserted the rebels in Virginia, blacks flocked to his standard. Large numbers of blacks served with the British throughout the war, though their treatment was not always the most honorable. More often than not, they performed fatigue duty or served in labor battalions to relieve white troops. When food was short, their rations were the first to be cut. They did not get the best clothes or care, and unsubstantiated rumors had it that some blacks were sold in the West Indies. For those who cast their lot with the British, there was plenty to give them pause. Yet thousands did so—and thousands left with them at the war's conclusion.

At the same time, other blacks served with the rebels, attempting to force action in line with their revolutionary protestations. In New England in particular, blacks took advantage of the new atmosphere to ask that what their masters were demanding of the British be given to them as well. One group, in Boston, did not ask for freedom as a gift outright even though they felt they deserved it; rather they asked for one free day a week to work for themselves, to accumulate the money to purchase their freedom. Free blacks, taking to heart the cry of "no taxation without representation," asked that they be given the right to vote. Lord Dunmore's Virginia proclamation convinced George Washington to modify an earlier decision to purge blacks from the Continental army and, except for South

Carolina and Georgia, nearly every state made provision for blacks to serve, with their freedom promised or implied. Rhode Island formed a black regiment, and John Laurens, son of South Carolina patriot Henry Laurens, proposed one for that state, but his idea was not favorably received. Even as they fought, however, blacks were reminded of their difference. When blacks joined a crowd of Boston whites in an attack upon British soldiers in 1769, a Boston newspaper commented: "To behold Britons scourged by Negro drummers was a new and very disagreeable spectacle" (quoted in *Before the Mayflower,* p. 52). And when in 1770 a black man aided British soldiers against a Boston crowd, a townsman shouted, "You black rascal, what have you to do with white people's quarrels?" To which the black man replied, "I suppose I may look on" (p. 53).

They did more than look on. Thomas Jefferson estimated that Virginia lost thirty thousand slaves in one year as a result of the war, an estimate that may not be far from the truth. South Carolina lost perhaps twenty-five thousand. As they absconded to the British, to the back country, to the cities, or to the army, their flight eloquently bespoke rejection of servitude.

In the aftermath of revolution, many states moved to live up to revolutionary ideals. Spurred by a black lawsuit in 1783, Massachusetts declared slavery inconsistent with its new constitution. Vermont, where slavery was of little moment anyway, had begun the process of emancipation in 1777, and other northern states, ending with New Jersey in 1804, provided for immediate or gradual abolition. The Chesapeake, with revolutionary fervor aided by an earlier move away from tobacco toward cereal crops that made slavery less useful, joined the trend imperfectly. Slavery there was not abolished but personal emancipations increased, facilitated by a 1782 Virginia law which repealed existing legislation making such acts illegal. Moreover, Virginia freed the slaves who had fought to the rebels' side, though she had not authorized their participation. Between 1790 and 1810, Virginia's free black population increased from 12,000 to 20,000. In Maryland and Delaware the number of free blacks more than tripled. By 1810, Maryland's 34,000 free blacks were almost a quarter of the state's black population, while Delaware's 13,000 freedmen overshadowed its slaves by three to one. Both states were well on the way toward a free economy though slavery, moribund, struggled on until the Civil War. In the North, also, free blacks tripled in

number in the generation after 1790, but to different effect: by 1810 slavery was virtually extinct in New England, and New Jersey remained the only northern state in which slaves outnumbered free blacks. Gradual emancipation meant, however, that in places steadily decreasing numbers of northern blacks remained enslaved until well into the nineteenth century. Only the lower South was resistant to the prevailing sentiment. There the number of free blacks doubled in the decade after 1790, primarily as a result of emigration from Santo Domingo, and more than tripled in the subsequent decade, largely as a function of Louisiana's acquisition.

The principle that all men are created equal was sufficient to confine slavery to the region south of Pennsylvania, but not strong enough to guarantee blacks equal treatment in freedom. Most northern states denied blacks the right to vote, to intermarry with or testify in court against white people, and to serve on juries or in local militias. Moreover, these strictures tightened in the period between the Revolution and the Civil War. From 1819 to 1861 every new state entering the Union limited the franchise to white males. By contrast, free blacks could vote in North Carolina and Tennessee until the 1830s, and even later in Louisiana. By 1840, ninety-three percent of all blacks lived where they could not vote. Where preexisting laws granting blacks the franchise did not change, public opinion made them inoperable. The federal government limited naturalization to whites, had no consistent policy about issuing blacks passports, and restricted their access to public lands. White workers and businessmen often prevented black artisans from exercising skills they had practiced as bondspeople, thus limiting their means of making a living. Black housing was restricted and normally substandard.

The majority of the free black population (55 percent in 1850) was to be found in the South, mostly in rural areas. There they enjoyed fewer social and political rights, but greater economic opportunity. Most legal restrictions affecting slaves extended to free blacks, yet they were not prohibited from owning land, nor from pursuing business or professional callings to the extent of their northern counterparts. Even restrictions against their selling liquor or operating taverns were occasionally overlooked. Rural blacks worked at tenant farming or in the lumber or mining industries. Some owned slaves, normally relatives held in fictitious servitude, but a few (particularly in the lower South) worked significant numbers of slaves and sought planter status.

These Lower South slavemasters were usually mixed bloods related to white planters by aspirations and consanguinity. They were a small group, separated from the mass of black folk, slave and free, by their color, wealth, and outlook. In 1790s Charleston they founded the Brown Fellowship Society, limited to those with light skin. New Orleans, with its French and Spanish heritage, had similar organizations. These people were distinct from both the free black class of the upper South and the North, which was generally darker and, where mixed, had working-class antecedents who were not infrequently white women. These blacks and mulattoes lacked the interest shown by wealthy Lower South planters in what was often their offspring. This concern is reflected in statistics: More than a quarter of all the nineteenth-century's free black professionals inhabited New Orleans; as another example, Charleston joined the Crescent City in offering blacks or (perhaps more properly) free coloreds more opportunity than other places. Southern cities were also more integrated residentially than northern ones—Boston was the most residentially segregated city in antebellum America. Therefore, although some southern blacks did move north, there was certainly no mass exodus of free blacks before the crises of the 1850s, and perhaps not even then.

While free coloreds in the lower South often tried to remain aloof from the black community, free blacks elsewhere worked in association with it. Most white people, beyond those in Charleston and southern Louisiana, made few significant distinctions among blacks. The social hierarchies that blacks developed based on education, wealth, skin color, and professional or artisanal accomplishment meant little to Negrophobes, and blacks' abolitionist allies found them objectionable. But the blacks' social structure did not entirely mirror the whites'. Ministers in particular had a more important position and higher status in the black community, and while blacks certainly did make color distinctions, what John Blassingame said about slaves is doubtless equally applicable to all: there was so much talk about "'yellow bitches' and the sons thereof that it is difficult to accept the proposition that simply being nearly white was any guarantee of status" ("Status and Social Structure," p. 138). Ironically, the small northern black professional class of doctors, ministers, and lawyers was made possible largely by white prejudice and ex-

isted solely to serve the black community. Northern proscription had other effects, equally ironic. Enslaved southern blacks continued to exercise skills denied northern black freemen, and blacks performed a higher percentage of urban southern skilled labor than did northern blacks in their cities, until the turn of the twentieth century.

In the face of this bleak picture of discrimination, blacks built a society apart. Indeed, some considered leaving the country altogether and returning to the lands of their forefathers. Accordingly, slaves in Boston, Massachusetts, ended a request for freedom in 1773 with an expression of their determination "to transport ourselves to some part of the coast of *Africa* where we propose a settlement," at their own expense (quoted in *Race and Revolution,* p. 174). These sentiments, verbalized before the Declaration of Independence, were to surface among African Americans throughout the nineteenth and well into the twentieth century whenever despair reached its nadir. Emigrationist ideology among blacks (frequently characterized as colonizationist when the impetus came from whites) had elements of chauvinism as well as nationalism. It proposed not merely to build a black nation in Africa but also to take there the blessings of Christianity and civilization. Such ideas forcefully highlighted the extent of cultural transformation black people had undergone and divided black community opinion about where blacks' responsibilities lay: overseas in Africa or elsewhere, or in America with their enslaved and slandered brethren. Most blacks, born and bred in this country, were attached to it and accepted lesser degrees of separation as pride and proscription determined.

In fact, there was a strong association between antiemigrationist or anticolonizationist feeling in those cities which had a black community built around churches. Opposition to emigration was based partly on practical considerations of feasibility, partly on the suspicion that emigration by free blacks would strengthen slavery by removing its most implacable opponents, and partly upon the reflection that the departure of the most industrious blacks would weaken a black community already under siege. In Philadelphia, New York, Baltimore, Boston, and other places where the growing free black population suffered increasing discrimination, the tendency was to form separate churches for self-preservation. The move toward separation was precipitated usually by a feeling of unease when, attending services with white congregations, the numbers of blacks grew so large they

823

were made to feel unwelcome. Sometimes the whites aided the blacks in forming a distinct congregation, often associated with and subject to the parent church: blacks remained a part of the original church's organization while exercising a degree of congregational autonomy. At other times blacks had to fight to get recognition of their right to a separate organization, resulting occasionally in formation of an entirely new denomination altogether. Such was the case with Richard Allen and Philadelphia's Bethel African Methodist Episcopal Church (established 1794), which was the nucleus of the first independent black church organization, consolidated in 1816. Disagreements with white Methodists in New York led blacks to found the African Methodist Episcopal Zion Church, initiated in 1796.

Although enslaved blacks normally attended the church of their masters, they had a particular affinity for the evangelical messages of the Baptists and Methodists. In the revolutionary and early national periods, indeed, these denominations possessed an extraordinary degree of egalitarianism in their church services and organizations. In them master and slave were considered equal in the sight of God, and each could bring charges of un-Christianlike conduct, one against the other, before the church for adjudication. Common worship meant mutual interchange, and while blacks adopted some precepts of whites, they contributed in return the African call-and-response musical pattern and ecstatic spirit possession. Strategic as well as religious reasons prompted white observers to attend black services when they worshiped apart, but within the religious community—especially before 1830, and in North as well as South—skin color frequently was irrelevant. Whites as well as blacks flocked to hear Richard Allen in Philadelphia. The white, slaveholding congregation of Hardshell Baptist Church in Giles County, Tennessee, had a black minister as late as 1859, a slave whom the church wanted to buy and presumably free but who refused to leave his master and was reputedly pro-slavery.

Yet there were tensions between blacks and whites, subtle and sometimes not so subtle discrimination which may have been greater in the North than in the South. There were also differences in gospel emphases. Blacks had more use for the story of Moses and the Exodus. Southern whites had more attraction to admonitions of slave obedience. Therefore, independent black church activity was much less acceptable in the South than in the North. African churches were considered seditious and suffered particular repression in times of threatened insurrection—as after Gabriel's Conspiracy in Virginia in 1800, or Denmark Vesey's Conspiracy in South Carolina in 1822. Still, blacks in Baltimore were part of the group that met in 1816 to form the African Methodist Episcopal church and, despite sometimes violent persecution, individual blacks continued their independent church activity in the South, and slaves often found time to "steal away" for their own, sometimes secret, religious meetings.

The eighteenth-century British North American colonies, with their crops of rice, indigo, and tobacco, were on the periphery of a New World plantation economy based most remuneratively on sugar. They moved toward the center of that system in the nineteenth century with their production of cotton by the world's largest slave population. The mechanics of cotton production were much closer to those of tobacco than to rice or sugar. Cotton was not labor intensive and could be produced by a man and his family, factors which facilitated the spread of slavery: the farmer could start off slowly, then gradually acquire bondspeople to expand cultivation. This process can be seen clearly in upland South Carolina, where people settled who did not have the wherewithal to compete in the coastal rice economy. In 1790 these upland counties operated in essentially a free labor society, with fifteen thousand slaves, amounting to no more than one-fifth of the population. The onset of cotton production contributed to a seventy percent increase in the slave population ten years later, when slaves became one-quarter of the population. Then a ninety percent increase by 1810 made slaves one-third of the population. A fifty percent increase in slaves by 1820 made them two-fifths of the population, and another forty percent increase by 1830 brought the slave population to almost equal that of the white. This was in contrast to lowland South Carolina, where blacks had outnumbered whites since the beginning of the eighteenth century. By 1860 cotton accounted for two-thirds of the gross value of all exports from the United States and engaged three-fourths of the country's plantation labor. By contrast, tobacco represented about one-tenth the value and the labor, with sugar and rice even less.

In 1860, fifteen slave states contained four million slaves out of a total population of 12.3 million. More than half the population of South Carolina and Mississippi were slaves. The four Gulf Coast states of Florida, Georgia, Alabama, and Louisiana were over two-fifths slaves. In other states, slaves were less than a third of the population. The majority of slaveholders practiced small-scale farming, but a minority of large planters determined that most slaves lived on estates with twenty or more of their fellows. Most raised cotton, but a significant minority produced sugar and rice, which required distinctive skills and their own modes of production. For one thing, rice was raised using the task system, a method under which a slave, having completed an assigned amount of labor varying from one-quarter to half an acre, depending on the job, was free to work for himself. This system permitted a few slaves to accumulate unusual amounts of personal property and reinforced the family unit by allowing the servitor a role as breadwinner.

Sugar and cotton utilized gang labor in a traditional "sunup to sundown" routine. Sugar production demanded unique skills connected with turning cane juice into a marketable commodity, thus increasing the number of skilled workmen in the population. Artisanal capability on any type of plantation of course gave a laborer status and relieved him from much of the drudgery of field work. Tobacco was less amenable to gang labor and was in any case most often produced on small plots with fifteen slaves or less, a size not conducive to gang labor in any crop.

These considerations are important in establishing the parameters of slave culture. A bondsperson's life on a small farm varied radically from one on a grand plantation. On a small farm, he or she worked side by side in the fields with the master, ate the same food, if not from the same table, and slept in the same house (perhaps in the same room) with the master or mistress. On a grand plantation, the servitor was part of an elaborate slave hierarchy from driver to field hand, artisans and domestics, separate slave quarters and a large, supportive slave community. Small holdings were likely to be tobacco or cotton farms, while big estates most likely produced rice or sugar, though there were large cotton plantations too. Each situation had its advantages and disadvantages. Life on the small farm lacked some of the regimentation of the larger unit; the master perhaps supervised, but there was no labor specialization and each performed every task required as need be. Subject to the master's whim, the slave and master might develop a close personal relationship. If the owner was honest, industrious, and exercised equanimity, the slave's lot might be tolerable. If the owner was dishonest, lazy, and ill tempered, no worse hell could be imagined. In either case, the slave was deprived of the support of a community of slaves unless he had access to an urban center or other plantations. Development of denser settlement patterns meant that relationships could cross plantation boundaries despite difficulties. Frederick Douglass's mother regularly walked twenty miles to see him, and visitors often remarked about slaves traveling great distances at night though they had to be at work early the next morning.

On a large estate, the disposition of the overseer might be of greater moment than that of the owner with whom the slaves might seldom have much contact. Many slaves and masters had fond memories of each other, because the overseer made all the hard decisions about work and punishment, leaving the owner to play the role of benevolent despot. In a few cases the overseer was black. In most, however, he was white and might have one or more black drivers (foremen), depending on the size of the plantation. Drivers were men chosen for their bulk, strength, dependability, intelligence, and ability to command respect among the other slaves. Drivers were responsible for setting the pace of work and making sure that everything ran smoothly.

Although much has been made about the division between field hands and house servants, except on the largest of plantations the distinction was not clear-cut, nearly all hands being required for field work during the harvest season. Even when favored as a valet or wet nurse and spending an inordinate amount of time in the planter's household, domestics still needed ties to the community in the quarters, for socializing and relaxing away from authoritarian scrutiny. They had wives, husbands, and relatives there. The driver had the most delicate position. He was a man in the middle: responsible to the planter or overseer for production efficiency yet answerable to his own community for its well-being, knowing fully well how its members could sabotage his efforts and ruin his reputation.

MARRIAGE AND FAMILY LIFE

The nineteenth-century U.S. slave population was overwhelmingly native born, which affected the dynamics of the master/slave relationship. Both were Americans, although they saw the world from different vantage points. Unlike in the Caribbean, where European planters came close to being submerged in a black sea and slaves could create a divergent, more Africa-based culture, blacks in the

United States experienced a wider, more intense, form of contact with the dominant whites, and thereby appropriated a larger European component for their shared and variant culture. By the 1780s, only about twenty percent of the black population of the new nation was African born. There was massive importation of Africans between 1790 and 1810—almost as many, indeed, as in the previous one hundred sixty years—but the major source of black population growth was natural increase. Rather than reflecting the male-dominated model of immigrant-based slave societies, the nineteenth-century national population exhibited a more naturally occurring model in which there was an excess of women, but not significantly; moreover, it progressed toward par. In 1820 the sex ratio among slaves was 95.1 (i.e., 95 men for every 100 females, as population statistics are expressed). In 1830 it was 98.3, in 1840, 99.5; in 1850, 99.9. Thus was laid the physical foundation for the two-parent family unit that formed the basis of North American slave culture.

Although the family unit suffered great stress, had no legal existence, was subject to outside interference, and was frequently broken up, most slave children were born into two-parent households. This was true even on small units of fifteen slaves or fewer, where the difficulty of contracting and maintaining family relationships was greatest. Single-parent families prevailed in these instances, and divided-residence families were common, but most slave children lived with both parents. Of course, on larger plantations this situation obtained more easily, and was encouraged because it benefited planters by creating a more stable work force.

Still, African American attitudes toward sex and marriage were not simple mirror images of white society, fractured now and then by the exigencies of slavery. They were a mixture of African and European attitudes compounded to form a distinctive view. For example, slaves came out of an African background where the production of children was considered essential to a family's well-being. This was true not only in practical terms under which children were a source of wealth, but also and more importantly in the spiritual sense: children were crucial links in the continuum connecting ancestors with generations of the unborn. Procreation was therefore a religious duty and sex an essential aspect of procreation. Consequently, Africans were not inclined to connect sin with sex the way nineteenth-century Europeans were wont to. This does not mean that African societies were scenes of unbridled promiscuity. Some permitted or accepted premarital sex, and some did not. They all severely punished adultery. But they shared the attitude that sex was a natural function unconnected with shame or sin.

As slaves became Americanized, they lost their understanding of the African religious significance of sex but maintained the outlook that it was a natural function, not dirty or shameful. As they became Christianized they adopted Christian morality and absorbed the connection between sex and sin. Still, this outlook was not nearly as common among slaves as within the master class. Therefore, sexual experimentation among slaves was much more acceptable. This does not mean that it was indiscriminate, that mothers did not worry about their unmarried daughters, or even that it was as commonplace as once thought. Based on data about the black family from large estates, Herbert Gutman argued that young girls typically had intercourse early, conceived a child, then settled into a monogamous relationship, not necessarily with the child's biological father. Another scholar, Richard Steckel, using a larger and more representative sample, found slave women to be much more abstemious. They frequently delayed intercourse and marriage for much longer than suggested by Gutman's findings, and the sequence of sex and marriage was reversed. Their first sexual experience occurred after marriage. Both scholars suggest that premarital sex was often the first step to the establishment of a permanent relationship.

Once marriages had been contracted, unless they were broken up from outside they tended to be long lasting. Partners were expected to be faithful. Christianity was an element of social control among those who accepted it. Those who misbehaved could suffer social ostracism. Even when families were broken up, ties were strong enough that family members often tried to keep in touch. One of the most poignant aspects of the immediate postemancipation period was the movement among slaves attempting to reestablish contact with loved ones. Despite some disagreements about the frequency with which families were forceably separated, John Blassingame's estimate (*Slave Community,* p. 177) that about one-third suffered that fate has received recent confirmation in Michael Tadman's *Speculators and Slaves.* In the slave's view, the dissolution of families was one of the worst crimes and severest punishments they had to endure under slavery and was cause for bitter dissatisfaction and unrest. Some planters tried conscientiously to keep families together, because they saw their interest therein; the family oriented nature of North American slavery is one explanation for its less rebellious character compared to that of other New World plantation systems. But planter paternalism could not withstand the lure of profit, an outlook succinctly expressed in one of Tadman's examples about one man's decision to sell: "The owner says that George has a wife and that he would not disturb him without he was getting more than he was worth" (p. 144).

Black and white were alike in their devotion to family and in their cultivating of kin relationships but, the African background aside, the omnipresent threat of adversity dictated that these ties should be more extensive among blacks. Attachments also tended to be stronger, slaves used the word "parents" for all their relatives. The dispersal of members of ruptured families throughout the vicinity and slave marriages between plantations led to the development of extensive social links in southern localities and the evolution of marriage norms in the slave community. The rules for exogamy were stricter among slaves, who forbade first-cousin marriages, than among planters, where such nuptials were common. Here as in other instances, the culture of master and servant diverged.

"Jumping the broom" was a wedding ritual widespread throughout the South. On some large plantations slaveholders recognized the event with a feast and other signal activities, prominent among them an admonition to be fruitful. Other planters were less celebratory, mindful only of the admonition, which ofttimes amounted to a threat. Additions to its slave family represented an accretion in the value of an estate. While the fabled "stud" farms may not have existed, planters' inducements to procreation amounted to practically the same thing. Moreover, it was a dangerous enterprise, for within the context of nineteenth-century health conditions childbirth carried risk. Infant mortality among blacks was considerably higher than among whites, even on plantations where the owners tried to prevent it. James Henry Hammond, for example, who professed paternal concern and did what he could, had an infant death rate more than twice the already high norm among the slave populace, and suffered a net decrease among his slaves. The diet of slaves was possibly adequate by the standards of the time, but not by modern nutritional criteria nor relative to the requirements of their labor. It was more varied than what the planters supplied, though, because the slaves consumed game and vegetables

won of their own initiative. But the slave diet was inadequate for pregnant mothers who worked too long before confinement and put to work too soon after birth, were denied the wherewithal and time to care for their newborn. If slaves could survive childhood, they had a reasonable chance to be relatively healthy—due partly to their own efforts—but getting to that stage was difficult.

The obligation to bear and care for children was an added burden on slave women, who had to labor in the fields with the men (indeed, in nineteenth-century America there were more women in the fields than men; males were more often trained as craftsmen), prepare meals, do sewing in their cabins (depending on plantation organization) after the workday was completed, and defend their sexual integrity as they could against assault. More than one southern apologist defended the white man's sexual appropriation of black women by reference to protecting the moral integrity of the white woman. And more than one slave man died trying to protect his wife or daughter. Many slave men preferred to marry off the plantation in order to avoid witnessing the physical misuse of the women to whom they were committed, abuse that commonly included rape along with the general bad treatment that was the lot of the enslaved. One of the first actions of postbellum freedmen was to withdraw their women from the fields. This was not a patriarchal decision mandated by men and meekly followed by women but rather a common resolve to create and maintain a traditional male-headed household of the sort denied black men and women in slavery. Consequently, the decision did have patriarchal implications. As Lerone Bennett, Jr. expresses it (quoted in *Before the Mayflower,* p. 188), "Negro women, who were not accustomed to taking orders, submitted to male authority with a great deal of self-consciousness." Exigencies of economic survival did not often permit black women to remain at home or even out of the fields, nor indeed was every black woman willing to accept any form of male authority. Yet the traditional male-headed household was, for most, doubtless the ideal.

URBAN SLAVE CULTURES

At the edges of the agricultural economy, serving as commercial centers, was what historian Richard Wade has called the "urban perimeter." Skirting the seacoast, touching the Mississippi, or resting near the border between free and slave territory stood the ten most populous southern cities: Baltimore; Washington, D.C.; Richmond; Charleston; Savannah; Mobile; New Orleans; Memphis; Louisville, and Saint Louis. Only three of these cities had more than one hundred thousand people, and two of those were in border states. Half had fewer than fifty thousand inhabitants. In 1860 southern cities contained no more than ten percent of the white population and five percent of the black. Clearly, southern society was overwhelmingly rural, and southern slavery was primarily agricultural. Urban slavery, indeed the urban setting, played marginal roles.

Historians, contemporary observers, visitors and planters alike—even former slaves like Frederick Douglass—have all considered the urban environment to be inimical to slavery. A weakening of ties there between master and slave was caused by the servant's too-often unsupervised independent activity, too-frequent fraternization with white and black people not bound to service, and his partaking of attitudes inconducive to subjugation. Civil officials were charged with enforcing restrictions that even responsible owners could not impose on errant servitors absent about town, thus the dilution of the master's authority. These strictures were particularly relevant if slaves were hired out, a practice governments tried consistently but unsuccessfully to curb. Slaves' situation was variable if the owners undertook to hire slaves out themselves, depending on the requirements and disposition of the employer. Slaves performed services that were valuable enough to help them avoid mistreatment yet they might still suffer under stringent regulation, though that too was subject to at least tacit negotiation.

If a slave were allowed to hire himself out, he was then in a position to build a totally separate and virtually independent life, choosing his own work, developing his own family and social life, but obligated to pay his owner so much per week, month, or year or else a percentage of his earnings, according to the specific agreement. A resourceful person might readily perceive that he had little use for his master and set out for another location to set up on his own. Whether he ran away or not, he ceased to be chattel in everything but name. The relationship with the owner became a contractual one, which for a planting oligarchy concerned with maintaining perfect labor subjection was a prospect far from ideal. In fact, though the reasons for it have been contested, slavery in southern cities was in decline by 1860. In Charleston, for example, the black exceeded the white population by fifty-eight percent in 1820; in 1860 the city was a little less than half black, slightly over one-third being slaves. New Orleans was more than half black (mostly slaves) in 1805, but by 1860 the black population (slave and free) had declined precipitously, with no more than one in seven black. Richard Wade (*Slavery in the Cities*, pp. 243–266) has argued that urban slavery decreased because bondsmen could not be effectively controlled and isolated—the city and the peculiar institution were incompatible. Econometrist Claudia Goldin (*Urban Slavery*, pp. 51–128) has responded that a continuing demand for urban slaves disproves Wade's presumption and, while a decline did occur, it resulted from a shifting of slaves from the city to the countryside, the result of a cotton boom in the 1850s. Immigrant labor presented an urban alternative to slave labor, but no such competition existed on the plantation. Rational choices made the shift logical.

It is apparent, however, that in a society based on the assumption (reiterated with particular force after 1830) that blacks were inferior, dependent, childlike creatures in need of firm guidance, an environment corrosive of the desired restraints ran counter to the prevailing creed. Strong, capable, self-directed bondsmen served as a rebuke to the racialist philosophy and as a beacon to similarly inclined rural workers. Probably more slaves absconded to black communities in the urban South than ever ran away to the North, particularly in view of northern prejudices. Barbara Jeanne Fields says it best: "All Southern cities occupied an anomalous place in slave society. All had features that set them aside from their rural surroundings. And all experienced, to some extent, the tension that led rural slaveholders in Maryland to regard Baltimore with suspicion and disquiet" (*Slavery*, p. 50). Urban slavery, therefore, could be tolerated only so long as it was limited. Still, the urban environment performed a more useful function than planters realized. John Boles makes the interesting observation that cities "served as a safety valve for plantation slaves who otherwise might have either committed suicide or killed their master" (*Black Southerners*, p. 131).

Within cities, slave distribution was more widespread than in the countryside. Many families owned one or two slaves, serving mostly as domestics. Living in close proximity to their masters, often confined in housing compounds designed to restrict their movement, they were at the families' constant beck and call. Doubtless they gloried in the opportunity to run errands that removed them from constant supervision and brought them into contact with the outside world. But the urban slave's work experience was not confined to household service. In a succinct summary Goldin comments:

"If one were to have visited the Border State cities of Baltimore and Washington toward the end of the antebellum era, one would have thought of urban slavery as synonymous with the employment of black female domestics. But traveling a little further [sic] south to Richmond and Lynchburg, one would have gotten the impression that slave labor supported all the industry of the South. A trip even further to Charleston, Mobile, and Savannah would have led one to believe that the entire commercial traffic of the South was managed to slaves. (*Urban Slavery*, p. 27)

Traditional family life for slaves was not always a possibility because of a great disproportion of women over men, which increased in the period of 1820 to 1860. If one did not live or work out, a man was normally obliged to visit, or if lucky to live with, his wife or consort at her owner's abode. Children of course stayed with the mother. The unbalanced sex ratio also obtained among free blacks, a quarter of whom inhabited cities. Charleston, for example, contained almost twice as many free black women as free black men. In Petersburg, Virginia, the disproportion was not so great, yet free black women headed over half the free black households—frequently women of property as well as autonomy. Indeed, since the state did not deny them legal ownership, an advantage that marriage would have marred, they sometimes had more than one reason to remain single. It is not wise, therefore, to equate female-headed with unstable. In the white population the imbalance was reversed, with white men outnumbering white women, an obvious encouragement of miscegenation. About half the urban black population was the product of race mixing in 1860, with twelve percent the southern figure overall. Yet only in the cities did free blacks possess sufficient critical mass to form their own communities. Elsewhere they socialized primarily with slaves.

Vestiges of Africa, stronger in some places than in others, still remained among the largely native-born nineteenth-century slave population. A divergent slave culture flourished in Louisiana, for example, because that state was one of the few in North America that permitted slaves to dance on a regular basis, on into the nineteenth century. These dances usually occurred on Sunday afternoons. According to one observer, Dena Epstein in *Sinful Tunes and Spirituals* (p. 52),

They [the slaves] have their own national music, consisting for the most part of a long kind of narrow drum of various sizes, from two to eight feet in length, three or four of which make a band. The principal dancers or leaders are dressed in a variety of wild and savage fashions, always ornamented with a number of tails of the smaller animals.... These amusements continue until sunset.

Because of these practices, African influences survived in the music, dance, and other aspects of slave life for a longer period in Louisiana than anywhere else save the South Carolina–Georgia low country.

Voodoo and conjuring, facets of slave life prominent in Louisiana and the low country, had widespread significance. These beliefs were crucial elements of social control in areas where Christianity might not have been fully accepted and even, perhaps, where it had been. They served to create a sense of unity, to instill values, and to minimize community disputes. For example, one aspect of differential slave morality was the definition of theft. Defined as one slave taking something from another, theft did not refer to stealing from the master. After theft occurred, often slaves depended upon the remedies of conjurers or other folk beliefs to discover the culprit. Such remedies of course had no basis in either established law or science, but derived their effect from an accepted folk wisdom instilled in childhood. One former slave recalled that his great-grandfather had been in charge of taking care of the young children. "We sure had to mind him," the slave said, "because if we didn't we were sure to have bad luck. He always had a pocket full of things to conjure with." Perhaps more often than not, slave precepts were a mixture of Christian, African, and other folk beliefs. Although slaves had much in common with their masters, they also had a world and a culture of their own.

One aspect of slave culture represented both an African cultural derivation and a pragmatic adaptation to a new environment. In New World and Old, African laborers frequently sang while they worked. These songs served to set the rhythm of labor and express community values. They were also the means by which sentiments that might not otherwise be articulated could be vented safely. Attitudes revealed under these circumstances could not be punished, just as in some African societies special days were set aside for the people to express in song, tale, and dance their true feelings about each other and their leaders. If one found the chief objectionable, he might say so without fear of retribution.

Slaves followed the same habit in America, though there was no formal provision for this and their compositions often had to be kept secret. Occasionally, however, a scene developed in such a way as to recall a similar African practice. As one slave related,

One day Charlie saw ol' massa comin' home with a keg of whiskey on his mule. Cuttin' across the plowed field, the ol' mule slipped and massa come tumblin' off. Massa didn't know Charlie saw him and Charlie didn't say nothin'. But soon after a visitor come and massa called Charlie to the house to show off what he knew. Massa say, "Come here, Charlie, and sing some rhymes for Mr. Henson." "Don't know no new ones, Massa," Charlie answered. "Come on, you black rascal, give me a rhyme for my company, one he ain't heard." So Charlie say, "All right, Massa I give you a new one if you promise not to whup me." Massa promised, and then Charlie sung the rhyme he done made up in his head 'bout massa.

> *Jackass rared*
> *Jackass pitched*
> *Throwed ol' massa in the ditch.*

Well, massa got mad as a hornet, but he didn't whup Charlie not that time anyway. And don't you know us used to set the flo' with that song? Mind you, never would sing it when massa was round, but when he wasn't we'd swing all around the cabin singing about how ol' massa fell off the mule's back. (Julius Lester, *To Be a Slave,* pp. 114–115)

These and other facets of slave culture operated then as a protective device and operate now as evidence of the vitality of African traditions. They expressed a sense of personal worth and encouraged the concept of community solidarity. Antebellum African American culture—both those aspects shared with Europeans and those facets held aside—permitted the human being held in bondage or subject to discrimination in freedom to develop and maintain a sense of individual and collective integrity in a trying situation.

BIBLIOGRAPHY

General Works

Bennett, Lerone, Jr. *Before the Mayflower: A History of the Negro in America, 1619–1964* (1962; rev. ed. 1970).

Boles, John B. *Black Southerners, 1619–1869* (1983).

Campbell, Edward D.C., Jr., and Kym S. Rice, eds. *Before Freedom Came: African-American Life in the Antebellum South* (1991).

Davis, David B. *The Problem of Slavery in Western Culture* (1966).

Epstein, Dena J. *Sinful Tunes and Spirituals: Black Folk Music to the Civil War* (1977).

Franklin, John Hope, and Alfred A. Moss, Jr. *From Slavery to Freedom: A History of Negro Americans* (1947; 6th ed. 1988).

Gutman, Herbert. *The Black Family in Slavery and Freedom, 1750–1925* (1976).

Parish, Peter J. *Slavery: History and Historians* (1989).

Rose, Willie Lee. *Slavery and Freedom.* Edited by William W. Freehling (1982).

Stuckey, Sterling. *Slave Culture: Nationalist Theory and the Foundations of Black America* (1987).

Vlach, John M. *The Afro-American Tradition in Decorative Arts* (1978; 2d ed. 1990).

ANTEBELLUM AFRICAN AMERICAN CULTURE

Africa and the Atlantic Slave Trade

Curtin, Philip. *The Atlantic Slave Trade: A Census* (1969).

Fage, John D. *A History of West Africa: An Introductory Survey* (1969).

Littlefield, Daniel C. *Rice and Slaves: Ethnicity and the Slave Trade in Colonial South Carolina* (1981; repr. 1991).

Mbiti, John S. *African Religions and Philosophy* (1969; 2d ed. 1970).

Miers, Suzanne, and Igor Kopytoff, eds. *Slavery in Africa: Historical and Anthropological Perspectives* (1977).

Vansina, Jan. *Kingdoms of the Savanna* (1968).

Seventeenth and Eighteenth Centuries

Breen, Timothy, and Stephen Innes. *"Myne Owne Ground": Race and Freedom on Virginia's Eastern Shore, 1640–1676* (1980).

Dunn, Richard D. *Sugar and Slaves: The Rise of the Planter Class in the English West Indies, 1624–1713* (1972).

Frey, Sylvia R. "Between Slavery and Freedom: Virginia Blacks in the American Revolution." *Journal of Southern History* 49, no. 3 (1983).

Greene, Lorenzo. *The Negro in Colonial New England, 1620–1776* (1942; 2d ed. 1968).

Isaac, Rhys. *The Transformation of Virginia, 1740–1790* (1982).

Jones, Rhett S. "Plantation Slavery in the Narragansett Country of Rhode Island, 1640–1790: A Preliminary Study." *Plantation Society* II (1986).

Jordan, Winthrop D. *White over Black: American Attitudes Toward the Negro, 1550–1812* (1968; 2d ed. 1977).

Kaplan, Sidney, and Emma N. Kaplan. *The Black Presence in the Era of the American Revolution* (1989).

Kulikoff, Allan. *Tobacco and Slaves: The Development of Southern Cultures in the Chesapeake, 1680–1800* (1986).

Littlefield, Daniel C. "Continuity and Change in Slave Culture: South Carolina and the West Indies." *Southern Studies* 26, nos. 3 and 4 (1987).

———. "'Abundance of Negroes of that Nation': The Significance of African Ethnicity in Colonial South Carolina." In *The Meaning of South Carolina History: Essays in Honor of George C. Rogers, Jr.,* edited by David R. Chesnutt and Clyde N. Wilson (1991).

Morgan, Edmund S. *American Slavery, American Freedom: The Ordeal of Colonial Virginia* (1975).

Mullin, Gerald W. *Flight and Rebellion: Slave Resistance in Eighteenth-Century Virginia* (1972).

Nash, Gary B. "Forging Freedom: The Emancipation Experience in the Northern Seaport Cities, 1775–1820." In *Slavery and Freedom in the Age of the American Revolution,* edited by Ira Berlin and Ronald Hoffman (1983).

———. "Slaves and Slaveowners in Colonial Philadelphia." In *Race, Class, and Politics: Essays on American Colonial and Revolutionary Society,* edited by Gary B. Nash (1986).

———. *Race and Revolution* (1990).

Piersen, William D. *Black Yankees: The Development of an Afro-American Subculture in Eighteenth-Century New England* (1988).

Scherer, Lester B. *Slavery and the Churches in Early America, 1619–1819* (1975).

Sobel, Mechal. *The World They Made Together: Black and White Values in Eighteenth-Century Virginia* (1987).

———. *Trabelin' On: The Slave Journey to an Afro-Baptist Faith* (1972; 2d ed. 1988).

Weir, Robert W. *Colonial South Carolina—A History* (1983).

The Nineteenth Century

Berlin, Ira. *Slaves Without Masters: The Free Negro in the Antebellum South* (1974; 2d ed. 1975).

———. "Time, Space, and the Evolution of Afro-American Society on British Mainland North America." *American Historical Review* 85, no. 1 (1980).

Blassingame, John W. "Status and Social Structure in the Slave Community: Evidence from New Sources." In *Perspectives and Irony in American Slavery*, edited by Harry P. Owens (1976).

———. *The Slave Community: Plantation Life in the Antebellum South* (1972; 2d ed., rev. and enl. 1979).

Burton, O. Vernon. *In My Father's House Are Many Mansions: Family and Community in Edgefield, South Carolina* (1985).

Curry, Leonard P. *The Free Black in Urban America, 1800–1850: The Shadow of the Dream* (1981).

Faust, Drew G. *James Henry Hammond and the Old South: A Design for Mastery* (1982).

Fields, Barbara J. *Slavery and Freedom on the Middle Ground: Maryland During the Nineteenth Century* (1985).

Fogel, Robert W. *Without Consent or Contract: The Rise and Fall of American Slavery* (1989).

Fogel, Robert W., and Stanley L. Engerman. *Time on the Cross: The Economics of American Negro Slavery.* 2 vols. (1974).

Genovese, Eugene D. *Roll, Jordan, Roll: The World the Slaves Made* (1974).

Goldin, Claudia Dale. *Urban Slavery in the American South, 1820–1860: A Quantitative History* (1976).

Herman, Janet S. *The Pursuit of a Dream* (1981).

Joyner, Charles. *Down by the Riverside: A South Carolina Slave Community* (1984).

Lebsock, Suzanne. *The Free Women of Petersburg: Status and Culture in a Southern Town, 1784–1860* (1984).

Lester, Julius. *To Be a Slave* (1968).

Levine, Lawrence W. *Black Culture and Black Consciousness: Afro-American Folk Thought from Slavery to Freedom* (1977).

Litwack, Leon. *North of Slavery: The Negro in the Free States, 1790–1860* (1961).

Raboteau, Albert J. *Slave Religion: The "Invisible Institution" in the Antebellum South* (1978).

Singleton, Theresa A., ed. *The Archeaology of Slavery and Plantation Life* (1985).

Stampp, Kenneth M. *The Peculiar Institution: Slavery in the Ante-Bellum South* (1956).

Steckel, Richard. *The Economics of U.S. Slave and Southern White Fertility* (1985).

Sutch, Richard. "The Breeding of Slaves for Sale and Westward Expansion of Slavery 1830–1860." In *Race and Slavery in the Western Hemisphere: Quantitative Studies,* edited by Stanley L. Engerman and Eugene D. Genovese (1975).

Tadman, Michael. *Speculators and Slaves: Masters, Traders, and Slaves in the Old South* (1989).

Wade, Richard C. *Slavery in the Cities: The South, 1820–1860* (1965).

White, Deborah G. *Ar'n't I a Woman?: Female Slaves in the Plantation South* (1985).

Wood, Peter H. *Black Majority: Negroes in Colonial South Carolina from 1670 Through the Stono Rebellion* (1974).

Zilversmit, Arthur. *The First Emancipation: The Abolition of Slavery in the North* (1967).

SEE ALSO **African American Music**; **Family Structures**; **Racial Ideology**; **Racism**; and various essays in the sections "**The Construction of Social Identity**," "**Ethnic and Racial Subcultures**," "**Periods of Social Change**," "**Regionalism and Regional Subcultures**," "**Space and Place**," and "**Work and Labor**."

POSTBELLUM AFRICAN AMERICAN SOCIETY AND CULTURE

Quintard Taylor, Jr.

IN 1871 DANIEL CORBIN, a white South Carolina Republican, summarized the astounding changes affecting the four million recently liberated African American slaves, and the nation as a whole, in the early years of Reconstruction after the Civil War when he declared that "we have lived over a century in the last ten years." The new order began with the fall of Richmond, Virginia, on the night of 2 April 1865. As Confederate troops abandoned the city, President Jefferson Davis and the Confederate Congress went with them. Their evacuation was prompted by black as well as white Union troops converging on the city from three sides. With the next day came a sight few Richmonders would ever forget—a column of black soldiers, many of them former Virginia slaves—marching down the streets of the former Confederate capital. Later that day in the Virginia Hall of Delegates, where only a week earlier the Confederate Congress had been meeting, black soldiers took turns swiveling in the speaker's chair.

Many planters could not imagine a labor system other than slavery. As one young South Carolinian said: "We are discouraged: we have nothing left to begin new with. I never did a day's work in my life and I don't know how to begin." Other planters remained defiant. Once the Freedmen's Bureau officer had read the Emancipation Proclamation on a Louisiana plantation and then departed, the mistress gathered the blacks around her and declared, "That piece of paper don't mean nothing. Ten years from today I'll have you all back 'gain" (Litwack, p. 178).

However, if some planters were determined to retain the old order, blacks were equally determined that it be destroyed. African Americans recognized how the power relationships between northerners and southerners had dramatically changed. The differences could be seen in the poverty of many former plantation owners, in the physical destruction in every Confederate state, and in the new humble tone and demeanor planters took in the presence of "Yankees," which reminded many slaves of the way they had had to respond to their former owners.

With the Freedmen's Bureau behind them, African Americans worked to change the conditions of their labor. Many black ex-slaves now demanded contracts setting out the terms of employment. Black workers also insisted upon the end of the old slave gang labor system. Now, instead of dozens or even hundreds of blacks working on a single large plot, liberated but landless black families became sharecroppers. Despite the abuses of this system that would soon become apparent, most black workers initially saw both sharecropping and the family farming it encouraged as progressive steps away from the old slave labor system.

Additionally, black parents decided that the women and daughters under the age of sixteen should now no longer work in the fields. It is inaccurate to see this step as removing these women from the southern work force, however. Even though black women no longer labored under the direction of an overseer, they still continued to pick cotton and cut sugarcane and tobacco, according to the needs of their own families. For the slaves nothing had so much symbolized their low status as the fact that the men, women, and children had all labored collectively in the fields. Both black women and black men welcomed this change: the women, to whom it meant they would now have time to devote to the nurturing and raising of children; and the men, to whom it at last meant responsibility for their families.

THE BLACK FAMILY

By the time of the 1870 national census, the outlines of the freed families were beginning to emerge. Some 91 percent of the freed persons lived in the rural South. Largely illiterate and poor, they nonetheless shared among themselves, their kin, and neighbors the joys and pains of work. In 1870 the average African American woman had six children, most of whom were destined to a life in the fields rather than regular attendance at school. In 1870 approximately 80 percent of the black households had a male head, a proportion identical to that in the white population. However, black women and children were more likely to work outside the home. By 1870 more than four out of ten black married women listed having jobs outside the house, almost always as field laborers, whereas 98 percent of southern white wives listed their occupation as "keeping house." Moreover, 24 percent of black households had one working child under sixteen years of age, with only 14 percent of white families having working children.

The African American family changed little between 1870 and 1900, although by 1880 it had become increasingly a two-parent household; that is, by that date 90 percent of all black families had both a husband and a wife. By 1900 the average black household had five children. Between 1880 and 1900, however, extended families, meaning those that include a relative in addition to the parents and children, increased from 14 percent to 23 percent. Moreover, the prevalence of local kinship networks suggests that at least one-third of all black families lived near at least some of their relatives.

The nuclear family that was the usual late-nineteenth-century family form began evolving within the context of a larger flexible family network that included neighbors who were often kin and for periods of time lived within relatives' households. Many African Americans in fact lived in kinship clusters consisting of circles of relatives inhabiting a given locality. Thus, few rural, late-nineteenth-century African Americans stood outside the web of family.

Between 1870 and 1900, women headed about 11 percent of all rural black southern households. Some were single or widowed, others sharecropping women whose husbands had hired themselves out to neighboring planters or women who sought work in sawmills, coal mines, turpentine camps, or the cities. Still others included elderly widows supported by their children or forced to live on charity and odd jobs. And a small number of young single women raised children, usually with the assistance of relatives.

SHARECROPPING

By the 1880s, sharecropping and peonage had replaced slavery and ensured poverty for the majority of blacks until well into the twentieth century. Sharecropping arose because few blacks could gain access to land in the postwar South. White southerners, recognizing both the desire of blacks to own land and the relationship of landowning to political power, were determined that the freed people should remain landless. They therefore opposed federal schemes for land confiscation and redistribution and refused to sell land to the few blacks willing and able to pay for it.

The denial of land ownership forced blacks to become sharecroppers, tenants (renters), and contract laborers, under a system called peonage. Under the sharecropping system a family committed itself to producing a crop on land it did not own. Under normal circumstances the two parties agreed upon sharing the harvest for the year of the contract: usually one-third for the cropper family and two-thirds for the landowner, who provided seeds, fertilizer, draft animals, and food and clothing for the cropping family. However, the illiteracy of most former slaves and the caprice of many planters ensured abuse and exploitation. When the books were totaled at the end of the year, a cropping family often found that the cost of the materials advanced to it during the year exceeded the value of the crop, thus the cropping family began the next year with a debt, if it was allowed to remain on the plantation. Planters rationalized this process as being in the best interests of both themselves and the landless blacks and whites, but their desire to control black labor in the post–Civil War South ensured the region's poverty long after it should have recovered from the disruption of agriculture caused by the war.

The poverty created by sharecropping might best be illustrated by imagining the meager surroundings of the croppers. The typical sharecropper's cabin, a crude one- or two-room dwelling, usually measured only some twenty square feet. It was often without glass windows, running water, artificial light, insulation, and ventilation. Virtually all of the family's activities—eating, sleeping, and bathing—took place in one room dominated by a fireplace or, by the early twentieth century, a potbellied stove. The children slept in the main room, warmed by what remained of the fire that had cooked the family's meal, while their parents shared another part of the same room. A prosperous sharecropper might have an extra bedroom or, more likely, a small kitchen, and perhaps a wooden floor or a sleeping loft for the children.

The usual sharecropping family's diet consisted of greens, okra, hogs' feet, and chitlins, which with creativity could be made into palatable dishes. Although most cotton sharecroppers were surrounded by the fiber that was the source for most of the cloth for the nation, the people who produced this crop could afford only the simplest of clothing and usually went barefoot throughout most of the year.

Sharecropping families accumulated few material and domestic possessions, partly because of their poverty, but also because having more furnishings made it difficult to pack and move when the family had to relocate. Instead, black men placed their extra earnings in a mule, plow, or wagon, while black women relied on few household utensils, often just a large tub to bathe the children and scrub clothes, and a cooking kettle and water pail.

Given the poverty of most southern sharecroppers, the pattern of group work that had existed on the larger plantations before the Civil War, and the extensive networks of kin that predominated throughout much of the rural South until 1900, it is not surprising that an ethic of mutual cooperation emerged among rural blacks. The sharecropping family was primarily responsible for the crop; for other needs rural communities pooled their resources, thus developing a strong commitment to cooperation and a certain resistance to the individualism that characterized late-nineteenth-century American life.

The same spirit of cooperation extended from the rural workplace into the social arena. Rural blacks held community celebrations upon the marriage of a young couple, the opening of a school, the arrival of a new minister, or the playing of a cornfield baseball game. Young women took turns visiting different homes on Sunday afternoons to meet together and clean up a yard, iron clothes, or prepare their hair in functions that had as much social as utilitarian value.

A few postwar southern blacks managed to escape the sharecropping system, although not all of them escaped poverty. A small black landowning class emerged, composed of free black farmers who predated the Civil War, augmented largely by former slaves residing on or near lands confiscated by the federal government and allocated to freed people. The two best examples of such land redistribution schemes were along the Union-occupied South Carolina coast and the Davis Bend plantation on the Mississippi River, previously owned by Jefferson Davis. Other blacks took advantage of the Southern Homestead Act of 1867, which made available public land in Alabama, Arkansas, Florida, Louisiana, and Mississippi, while still others acquired land through private purchases, despite the opposition of local whites. By 1900, black farmer owners had, through persistent effort, gained a foothold in the South. In that year the nineteen thousand black farm owners in South Carolina, the state with the largest percentage of them, comprised 25 percent of the black farmers. Fourteen percent of the black farmers in Georgia owned their own farms, with 11 percent of the black Mississippians in that category. By 1910 black farm ownership peaked at 220,000, after which it declined continuously. By 1970 only 53,000 black farm owners remained in the nation.

A minority of southern black men escaped the agricultural life by embracing urban or quasi-urban occupations such as coal mining, lumbering, or railroad work. Others found jobs in turpentine camps, as stevedores or cotton-gin workers, as skilled craftsmen like carpenters, painters, brick masons, and electricians or, in Texas and the Mountain West, as cattle herders. Many of these men migrated seasonally between these nonfarm occupations and their own sharecropping plots or small farms.

THE BLACK CHURCH

If the end of the Confederacy signaled freedom for millions of southern black slaves, it also prompted the emancipation of the black church. The African Methodist Episcopal Church founded in Philadelphia by Richard Allen in 1787 represented the antebellum expression of blacks' religious independence, but the emergence of the black church as a separate institution had to await the end of slavery, since white southerners sought to maintain control over African Americans' worship, for both religious and social reasons. Such services typically emphasized the responsibility of the slave to be obedient and provided biblical justification for black bondage. Slaves had no voice in church affairs and were relegated to the rear of the church or the gallery, as spectators rather than full members of the congregation.

A typical postwar church separation petition was filed by thirty-eight black members of the predominantly white Fairfield Baptist Church in Northumberland County, Virginia, in 1867. Referring to the new political and social status of African Americans, the petitioners said they wanted to "place ourselves [where] we could best promote our mutual good" and suggested "a separate church organization as the best possible way . . ." (A. Taylor, p. 142). A month later the white members of the church unanimously acceded to the petitioners' request, setting the stage for the creation of the all-black Shiloh Baptist Church. In fact, few white southern churches agonized over the departure of their black parishioners. Unwilling to change their policies regarding segregation or to give former slaves significant authority within largely white churches, most southern religious leaders welcomed and encouraged blacks' withdrawal from the original congregation as the only feasible alternative. Thus, both whites and blacks agreed, for different reasons, to racially separate churches.

Once established, black churches spread rapidly throughout the South. Because of their decentralized structure, the Baptist churches led in this proliferation. Frequently, Baptist congregations divided after a faction unsuccessfully challenged the existing leadership. For example, in Aberdeen, Mississippi, the Pine Grove Baptist Church was by 1898 the parent church of seven other Baptist churches, all stemming from internal conflicts and successions. But new churches also emerged because of the missionary activities of black ministers. The Reverend Alexander Bettis, a former South Carolina slave, alone organized more than forty Baptist churches between 1865 and his death in 1895. Through these years he served as pastor for no fewer than four churches at once and was at one point simultaneously minister for ten churches.

As the number of Baptist churches grew, they met regularly in regional conventions that then evolved into statewide and national organizations. By 1866 enough independent black Baptist churches existed in North Carolina to form a state convention, and by 1870 all the former Confederate states had similar organizations. By 1895 the various Baptist associations had formed the National Baptist Convention of America, representing 3 million African American Baptists, primarily in the South.

The African Methodist Episcopal (AME) Church emerged as the second-largest, post–Civil War black denomination. Because of its independence, the AME Church had always been viewed with suspicion in the antebellum South, having been forced out of South Carolina following the Denmark Vesey conspiracy of 1822. The church was reorganized in South Carolina in 1865 by Bishop Daniel Payne and grew to forty-four thousand members by 1877. Similar growth in other southern states gave the AME Church by 1880 a national membership of four hundred thousand—its followers were for the first time concentrated in the South.

Other denominations completed the spectrum of black church organization in the South. The Colored Methodist Episcopal (now Christian Methodist Episcopal) Church, which grew from the black parishioners who withdrew in 1866 from the predominantly white Methodist Episcopal Church, and the African Methodist Episcopal Zion Church each claimed two hundred thousand members by 1880. The Presbyterians and Episcopalians also saw the postwar division of their memberships into white and black denominations, with each of the two black churches having some one hundred thousand members by 1900.

With the division of congregations came the development of a distinct religious observance combining elements of African ritual, slave emotionalism, southern pathos, and individual eloquence. Working-class Baptist and Methodist church services fused African and European forms of religious expression to produce a unique version of worship that reflected the anguish, pain, and occasional elation of nineteenth-century black life in the United States. Such services usually involved three elements: a devotional prayer provided by a leading member of the church, singing by the congregation and choir, and the minister's sermon. The prayer would be made relevant to the daily experiences of its offerer and the listeners as it requested a powerful God to ease the earthly burden of the congregation. The prayer would be enhanced by the congregation's response, an expression of agreement, and an identification with the concerns of the individual advancing the prayer with the words "Yes, Lord," "Have mercy, Lord," and "Amen."

After the prayer the congregation typically showed their devotion through song. Even if a formal choir existed, all the members of the congregation would be expected to participate. Occasionally an individual member outside the choir would stand up and lead the house in song, improvising as she went by interjecting new phrases or verses. By the turn of the century, most southern black church choirs had assumed the responsibility for presenting the hymns, but the "call and response" technique, whereby a minister or prominent choir member led a hymn and was answered by the congregation, continued until well into the twentieth century.

The final element in a typical black service was the minister's sermon. Building on the long tradition of slave preachers and "exhorters," many ministers employed all the drama and poetry at their command, injecting vivid imagery and analogy into their biblical accounts and pressing the congregation to understand the rewards of righteousness and the wages of sin. The congregation participated in the sermon by adding such responses as "amen" and "Speak the truth!" to confirm agreement. Not every minister was capable of eliciting such a response, and a few resorted to emotion-producing techniques for their own sake, thus often leaving their congregations with little of substance. But those ministers who did avoid "emotion without substance" and stirred their congregations to strive for a more profound faith and more righteous way of living in a world of adversity provided spiritual guidance for a people whose faith and capacity for forgiveness was tested daily. For these people the black church was indeed "a rock in a weary land."

While nineteenth-century black churches ministered to the needs of the soul, they also served a host of secular functions, which placed them squarely in the center of black social life. Their church buildings doubled as community meeting centers and as schools until permanent structures could be built, and during Reconstruction they served as political halls. The churches also provided shelter for visitors as well as temporary community theaters and concert halls where religious and secular plays and programs could be presented. In a blurring of spiritual and social functions church members provided care for the sick or incapacitated and financial assistance to students bound for college. They also sponsored virtually all the many fraternal lodges that emerged in the nineteenth-century South.

EDUCATION

For former slaves their inability to read and write was not only tangible evidence of their previous servile condition but also, as they recognized,

a major impediment not only to their prosperity but their very survival as free people. Booker T. Washington has poignantly described the desperate desire of the newly emancipated slaves to acquire the rudiments of education:

> Grown men studied their alphabets in the fields, holding the "bluebook speller" with one hand while they guided the plow with the other. Mothers tramped scores of miles to towns where they could place their children in school. Pine torches illuminated the dirt-floored cabins where men, women and children studied far into the night. (Quoted in Bond, p. 23)

Despite laws prohibiting slaves from acquiring even the most rudimentary learning, a tentative foundation for black education was laid prior to the Civil War. Some slaveowners then provided education for a favored house servant, or religious and philanthropic organizations surreptitiously taught slaves. White children on plantations occasionally taught slave playmates to read, while others learned by spying on the instruction given to white children. Free antebellum blacks had greater access to education, both in the North and in the cities of the South where schools for them existed, as in a Raleigh, North Carolina, institution run by John Chavis, a free-born Presbyterian minister. Thus, despite the laws regarding black education, by 1860 probably 5 percent of the blacks in the South were literate.

The Civil War encouraged a dramatic expansion in black education as the Union army accepted black men into its ranks and then became for many of them a vast, mobile school. Brigade commanders instituted training programs for black noncommissioned officers, with black privates being taught by their officers, by civilian volunteers, or by northern teachers paid by the soldiers themselves.

Wherever the Union army went, in its wake came northern teachers, both white and black. As early as February 1862, northern teachers arrived in the sea islands along the coast of South Carolina to instruct former slaves. As the northern-occupied areas grew and provided access to blacks previously under Confederate control, the Union army intensified its efforts at education. By 1865 that army or its agents operated more than two hundred schools enrolling twenty-one thousand children and adults.

Most schools were staffed by whites, particularly New Englanders, whom Union officers seemed to prefer, but in Union-occupied areas many of the early efforts at black education were initiated by African Americans. In September 1861, Mary Peake, a free black woman working for the American Missionary Association, opened a school at Fortress Monroe, Virginia, for black war refugees. Other black teachers, including northern-born Charlotte Forten in the sea islands and southern-born Susie King Taylor in Savannah, contributed their skills to the considerable challenge of black education.

Black denominations such as those of the African Methodist Episcopal Church and such secular organizations as the African Civilization Society supported schools, as did white religious bodies, foremost among them the American Missionary Association (AMA), a branch of the Congregational church. During Reconstruction, 467 black women and men served as AMA teachers and religious workers. Black and white organizations alike worked with the Freedmen's Bureau, a federal agency begun in early 1865 to establish black schools by appropriating money for the construction of buildings, with secular societies and religious bodies providing the teachers. The Bureau's various "day," "night," "industrial," and "Sunday" schools, the latter so called because people attended them only on Sunday, all proved exceedingly popular. By 1870 the 4,239 schools supported by the Bureau employed more than 9,000 teachers and served 247,000 students.

When African American legislators took their place in the state capitals during Reconstruction, they always put education at the top of the political agenda—higher even than land. They had two related goals: first to establish publicly funded primary schools to teach basic skills, and second to create colleges to educate teachers to serve in these schools. The second goal proved easier. Prior to the Civil War, only two black colleges—Wilberforce in Ohio and Lincoln in Pennsylvania—had existed. Between 1865 and 1870, however, nearly thirty black colleges were created, including Howard University (1867) and Hampton Institute (1868).

With the demise of Reconstruction, state-supported black schools began to suffer disproportionate funding reductions. For lack of funding, black schools were closed in Georgia in 1872 and Arkansas in 1874. Ironically, the Reconstruction-era promise of education to all, including poor whites, meant that the new Democratic administrations were required to meet a rising demand for schools for white children, thus reducing even further the already limited funding for black schools. These reductions reached their lowest level with the formalization of segregated schools in the 1890s. Between 1880 and 1895 the per capita expenditures for white pupils rose from $2.75 to $3.11, whereas outlays for black students declined from $2.51 to $1.05, and in some areas the disparities were far greater. For example, in 1900 Adams County, Mississippi, spent $22.25 for each white pupil while providing only $2.00 for each black student.

With the decline of black political power following Reconstruction, education took on even greater importance, as many blacks and whites came to believe that blacks' rights would be restored only after the former slaves had been properly schooled. Thus, various white philanthropic groups like the Julius Rosenwald Fund supported thousands of black public schools, often taking over ones inadequately funded by conservative regimes in the South or, in many instances, creating entirely new institutions. White philanthropy was also directed toward black colleges. For instance, John D. Rockefeller gave millions to Fisk, Hampton, Tuskegee, and other institutions, and with a single contribution founded Spelman College—named after his wife, Laura Spelman—in Atlanta.

Black colleges also sprang from African American efforts as well. The church donations that created Lane College in Jackson, Tennessee, came from the Colored Methodist Episcopal Church, while Livingstone College in North Carolina was founded by black Episcopalians and Wiley College in Texas evolved from the efforts of black Baptists. The most famous of all the black schools, Tuskegee, was founded by black farmers in Alabama. As conservative governments strengthened their political dominance, destroying any hope that the southern school systems might become truly "separate but equal," black leaders turned to the staffing of such schools by their own teachers. This movement came in response to a period in the 1880s when Democratic officials in the South quickly replaced both white and black northern teachers in the black schools with local whites, thus guaranteeing that the black students would be taught to maintain proper deference in interracial matters.

Unable to challenge segregation and funding inequality directly, black political leaders requested that African American teachers at least be allowed to teach their own race's children. "Give us a High and Normal School where our young people may be instructed by those who have our interests at heart," demanded the *Virginia Star* in 1882. Declaring that "we are tired of having . . . all the machines run by whites," this newspaper urged the "Noble descendants of Ham [to] stand up for pride of race" (A. Taylor, p. 122).

A confluence of developments worked in favor of those demanding black teachers for black schools. The growing call for new schools for white students reduced the necessity for white instructors to seek work in black institutions. And by the 1890s a growing body of graduates from the black colleges in the South stood ready to assume roles as teachers in the public schools. Government officials anxious to save money eagerly hired black instructors for considerably less than the salaries requested by white teachers until by 1900 the majority of the black public schools were staffed by African American teachers.

Typical of such teachers was Anna Julia Cooper, born near Raleigh, North Carolina, in 1839 to a slave mother and her mother's owner. Cooper was educated at predominantly black Saint Augustine's College in North Carolina and Oberlin College in Ohio, then returned to North Carolina, where she worked most of her life in elementary schools. In 1890 she was selected to be the first female principal of the M Street public school in Washington, D.C., where she became known for channeling black students into the most prestigious colleges in the country. In 1906, after retiring from the Washington school system at the age of sixty-seven, Cooper took a Ph.D. in Latin at the Sorbonne in Paris. She then returned to Washington to become one of the founding members of its NAACP chapter.

Cooper and thousands of other dedicated teachers, despite inferior facilities and salaries and the oppressive atmosphere of the segregated South, attempted to instill in generations of their young charges both personal dignity and the "pride of race" that had been suggested by the *Virginia Star.* Moreover, the black communities of the South did gain a small measure of autonomy over their public school systems, which, after the church, became the most important institution in the black rural South.

BLACK MIGRATION

After the decline of Reconstruction, some African American leaders organized various migrations from the South—to Kansas, Colorado, California, Montana, and Oklahoma. These movements were often political in nature, because their goal was more than to homestead the land: the aim was to locate someplace where blacks could develop their lands and resources unmolested.

One of the largest of these migrations was an 1870s exodus led by Benjamin "Pap" Singleton of Tennessee. In 1874 Singleton, a former slave carpenter, distributed a circular titled "The Advantage of Living in a Free State," which extolled the political freedom as well as economic opportunities in

Kansas. Singleton's efforts inspired at least twenty-five thousand African Americans to migrate to Kansas between 1874 and 1880. Many settled in Topeka, with some locating in frontier towns like Dodge City and one group even founding an all-black town in western Kansas called Nicodemus.

One of Nicodemus's settlers, Edward McCabe, was in the early 1880s elected auditor of the state of Kansas, then turned his attention to the Oklahoma Territory. McCabe was convinced that Oklahoma would be a more suitable place for African Americans than Kansas, because of its more southern climate and its Indian population, which included a number of former slaves of Indians. Armed with these ideas, McCabe began writing articles carried in the leading black newspapers to promote settlement in Oklahoma, then followed these up with lecture tours and by organizing immigration societies. By 1886 nearly forty thousand blacks had responded to his appeals and migrated to Oklahoma.

The migration to Oklahoma was the largest political migration of blacks to the West, but every western state and territory received some African Americans. By 1900 more than 145,000 blacks had settled in the sixteen western states and territories excluding Texas. According to Kenneth Hamilton, in the late nineteenth century sixty-six all-black towns or settlements were established in thirteen primarily western states. Virtually all these towns represented a quest for individual opportunity. As Booker T. Washington noted in describing Boley, Oklahoma, one of the more famous such towns, it represented "a dawning race consciousness, a wholesome desire to do something . . . which shall demonstrate the right of the negro, not merely as an individual, but as a race, to have a permanent place in the civilization that the American people are creating" (Washington, p. 31).

Some African Americans such as the Reverend Henry McNeal Turner, a bishop in the AME church, instead gave up on the United States. Turner had an illustrious career as the first black officer appointed in the Union army and as a Congressman from Georgia during Reconstruction. But by the 1880s Turner had lost faith in the capacity of the United States to treat African Americans fairly, and he subsequently publicly advocated their emigrating. Turner and his followers assumed control over the then-defunct American Colonization Society, which before the Civil War had been a predominantly white organization fostering the return of free blacks to Liberia, and made it a vehicle for post-Reconstruction emigration to that African nation.

Between 1890 and 1900 some thirty thousand American-born blacks arrived in Liberia, about three times the number who had migrated there before the Civil War. From his headquarters in Atlanta, Turner continued to work for black emigration until his death in 1906.

If some African Americans looked to the American West and others turned "back to Africa," the largest group became part of the migration evolving from the South to the North. Unlike the other migrations, in which the participants hoped to become landowning farmers, the migration northward was a rural-to-urban hegira, whose origins can be found in the changes initiated by the Civil War.

The first urban migration was entirely southern and came during the Civil War as blacks fled the war-torn countryside to seek safety in the urban centers of Norfolk, Hampton, New Orleans, Nashville, and Memphis, all cities occupied at various times by Union forces. By 1867 many of these refugees had returned to rural areas, but their brief introduction to urban life persuaded some to remain permanently in the cities. For example, between 1860 and 1870 the southern black urban population grew by 75 percent. By 1870, Atlanta, Montgomery, Richmond, and Raleigh were all about 50 percent black. The experience of these southern city dwellers first exposed the enduring dilemma that arose in northern urban life of blacks migrating to the cities and sacrificing family stability and kinship support in pursuit of greater remuneration and respect.

Black women comprised the majority of the rural to urban migrants. In New Orleans in 1870, for example, black women between the ages of fifteen and forty-five exceeded the population of black men of the same age by 50 percent. Single mothers found themselves pushed off the plantations because of their difficulty in renting land and sharecropping. However, single women without children and some married women participated in the rural exodus, either alone or with their husbands, in search of greater opportunity. They found it in steady, if underpaid, work as maids, laundrywomen, cooks, nurses, or seamstresses. As the New South's industrialization proceeded, some black women found work in tobacco plants, textile mills, or seafood-processing plants.

The southern city offered greater opportunities for men, although at only slightly more pay, including work in railroad yards or as railroad porters, or as longshoremen, domestic servants, teamsters, and occasionally as skilled artisans. By 1900, African American males held most of the unskilled jobs in the iron and steel industry in Alabama and in shipbuilding in Virginia.

Southern urban life posed a number of challenges for both male and female African Americans, who were often unable to find steady work, a situation usually exacerbated when they competed with white workers. Their health was threatened by crises such as the yellow fever epidemic that swept through Memphis in 1878 and by less spectacular but more threatening diseases like tuberculosis. But urbanites had a number of advantages over the people who remained in the countryside. City life afforded rich cultural, educational, and religious opportunities not available to blacks scattered across the rural South. And the social structure of the black urban communities was more complex, as some skilled artisans and professionals achieved relatively comfortable standards of living and exerted leadership that had no counterpart in rural areas. In the cities larger churches offered both religious and social services, and educational institutions from elementary schools to colleges provided more opportunity for instruction. Thus, city children were much more likely to stay in school, graduate, and possibly go on to college than were their rural counterparts.

With each passing year, more African Americans made the trek to southern cities, some staying only until harvest season or long enough to earn the money necessary to buy a farm or help their family retire a debt. Others came to the city permanently, merging in a small stream that by 1900 also turned northward and became a huge river of black humanity moving in search of a better life.

THE FIRST NORTHERN MIGRATION: THE 1890s

By 1900 significant urban black populations had emerged in a number of cities, including New York, Chicago, Philadelphia, and Washington, four of the twelve cities whose total populations exceeded forty thousand by that date. The northern black urban communities that emerged at the turn of the century varied in their economic structure, their pattern of racial relations, the size of their pre-1900 African American community, and the origins of their populations. Yet for all their differences there existed great commonality, the most obvious of which was residential segregation. Except for some western cities such as Seattle and San Francisco, segregation swept across urban America in the first few decades of this century, channeling blacks into distinct sections of cities that were almost always characterized by deteriorating buildings and severe overcrowding. As Jacob Riis wrote in 1890, "The Czar of all the Russias is not more absolute upon his own soil than the New York landlord in his dealings with colored tenants. . . . Where he permits them to live, they go; where he shuts the door, [they] stay out" (Riis, p. 110).

Chicago, with its "black belt" across the South Side, perhaps best represented the rise of almost complete residential segregation. Although the belt had begun slowly evolving as early as the Civil War, by 1906 Chicago had become the most segregated city in the North, with 90 percent of its African American population in a racially restricted ghetto.

Despite the evolving concentration of blacks that made that community appear monolithic to outside observers, a socioeconomic hierarchy based on occupation and aspiration generated distinct differences among the new black urbanites. At the top of this hierarchy was a small elite of professionals and service workers: teachers, doctors, lawyers, barbers, and servants for the wealthiest families and private clubs. Their status derived from their concern for manners, "good breeding," and from their antecedents in the city, as in the case of the "O.P.'s," or Old Philadelphians. As David Nielson reminds us, the status of this elite rested not just on proper but on exemplary conduct and superior manners. "If their respectability only had been equal to that of their white neighbors," Nielson has argued, "they knew they would not have been considered respectable."

Below the elites, and constituting the vast majority of black northern urban inhabitants before 1920, was the working class W. E. B. Du Bois called "the respectables" in his 1899 study *The Philadelphia Negro*. These people, including the majority of southern-born migrants, were employed in such steady if poorly remunerated occupations as laborers, midwives, laundresses, housemaids, nurses, butlers, and coachmen for middle-class whites. As this list suggests, and as was true in southern cities, black women often found greater opportunity than men. These people, though poor, appropriated a life-style and mode of public conduct they hoped would generate respect for them within their own community if not the larger society. This respectability was a critical determinant of their sense of self-esteem, since their race, poverty, and location

in segregated slums made them indistinguishable from what would now be termed the underclass.

At the bottom of the black urban social order was a small group of people for whom such social strictures were meaningless. They were, according to one social observer, "undisciplined, unchurched and uneducated," people far more concerned with their survival in the complex, hostile environment of the city than with their image in either the white or the black worlds. These men and women, often involved in "hustling," included gamblers, petty thieves, confidence artists, prostitutes, and procurers, and were the group most inclined to try to manipulate that environment as best they could to their own advantage. As James Weldon Johnson once recalled, they were quite willing to strike back quickly and violently when the white man's discrimination penetrated their customary indifference. Many of these people lived just on the edge of the law, with a flamboyant minority clearly outside its strictures.

THE GREAT MIGRATION: 1915–1920

During World War I half a million black people moved from the rural South to the urban North. This migration ended the overwhelming concentration of black people in the eleven former Confederate states and made the question of black civil rights a national concern for the first time since the 1860s. This migration accelerated the urbanization of African Americans that continued until well into the 1980s. Although its effects were not immediately apparent, this migration also led to the rise of the modern ghetto.

The years between 1915 and 1920 which saw this migration also witnessed a dramatic reorientation of the northern African American community as a rapid urbanization and proletarianization of the black work force arising from the employment of African Americans in the factories, mills, and foundries of the North permanently reshaped the politics, social structure, and culture of the black community. By 1930 a national black community had evolved, possessed equally of a distinct sense of its inferior place in American society and of the desire to marshal all its collective energies to challenge that place. Alain Locke captured this new consciousness when he declared in 1925 that "all classes of people" who are "under social pressure [have] a common experience; they are emotionally welded as others cannot be. With them, even ordinary living has epic depth and lyric intensity, and this, their material handicap, is their spiritual advantage" (Locke, p. 47).

Although as late as 1910 more than 85 percent of the black population still lived in the rural South, this figure was about to undergo abrupt change. In 1915 nearly sixty thousand blacks moved north; in 1916 one hundred thousand more came, and in 1917, the peak year, over one hundred fifty thousand moved north, with another two hundred thousand migrating by 1920. The pattern of migration was selective, with most African Americans being destined for the large northeastern and midwestern cities. The smaller northern cities and the cities of the West were hardly affected. Between 1915 and 1920, Chicago's black population rose from 44,000 to 109,000, New York's from 91,000 to 152,000, and Detroit's from 3,400 to 36,000. In 1920 James Weldon Johnson recalled the migrants he saw in his hometown of Jacksonville, Florida, bound for the north:

I sat one day and watched the stream of migrants passing to take the train. For hours they passed steadily, carrying flimsy suit cases, new and shiny, rusty old ones, bursting at the seams, boxes and bundles and impedimenta of all sorts, including banjos, guitars, birds in cages and what not. The great exodus of Negroes from the South was on. (Locke, p. 305.)

The black migration north of 1915–1920 was generated by four basic push-pull factors: a labor surplus in the South, prompted both by poor crops and the forcing of sharecroppers off plantations; a combination of natural catastrophes, including floods, droughts, and a boll weevil infestation that disrupted cotton production; southern antiblack violence, which though not significantly greater than before was nevertheless a reminder to African Americans of their precarious existence in the region; and a shortage of labor in northern factories brought on by the war-reduced European immigration to the United States. That immigration fell from 1.2 million in 1914 to 110,000 by 1918, just at the moment labor was most needed in northern factories.

As Louise V. Kennedy has noted, the wages paid in the North seemed "fabulous sums promising speedy wealth and success" (p. 44). Being "paid in cold cash by the week or month instead of in store credit once a year" guaranteed the attractiveness of the North to blacks. In Pittsburgh migrants earned $3.60 per day in the steel mills, and in Detroit black autoworkers, the highest-paid group in the North, averaged five dollars a day, compared with the fifty-cents per day paid to southern labor-

ers. Even domestic servants in New York City received $2.50 per day, as opposed to the relatively high sixty-five cents per day they could earn in Virginia or North Carolina. According to a U.S. Labor Bureau survey of 1919, even including the higher expenses in the North, the average migrant made 300 percent more there than in the South.

Rural unskilled black males from the South found a number of occupations in the North. They became steelworkers, automobile assemblers, textile workers, and meatpackers, all being industrial jobs blacks had rarely held in the South before 1915. And the directly war-related jobs like munitions manufacturing and shipbuilding and maintenance produced a range of new industrial skills that could profitably be utilized after the war. Some of the southern blacks brought their skills north: railroad repair and maintenance workers, longshoremen, and freight haulers often found similar occupations after migrating. Moreover, the increase in the North's black population provided more opportunities for a growing black business middle class of bankers, insurance agents, merchants, barbers, undertakers, and newspaper owners.

There was, however, one major exception to this pattern of upward occupational mobility. Most black females, regardless of their demonstrable skills in the South, could only become cooks, nurses, and maids in the North. They found it almost impossible there to get the factory work many of them had had in Richmond and other southern cities and as their white female counterparts had in the North. The southern black professional women, particularly teachers, were not allowed to continue their occupations in northern cities.

High wages were indeed the primary reason for the migration, but as mentioned, many African Americans abandoned the South because of its oppressive conditions and violence. The northern black newspaper the *Chicago Defender,* which unabashedly promoted the migration, urging southern blacks to come to "the Promised Land," regularly published letters from prospective migrants seeking its assistance. These missives, in their simplicity and urgency, suggest the anguish of many southern blacks. From Alabama one person wrote: "I am a poor woman and have a husband and five children living. . . . This is my native home but it is not fit to live in. . . . Will you please let me know when the [railroad] cars is going to stop. . . . Your needed and worried friend" (Scott, p. 332).

The migrants soon discovered that the North was neither the Promised Land of their dreams nor of the *Defender's* description. The growing black population in the North generated a violent reaction from whites resentful of sharing jobs, housing, and political power. Chicago, the *Defender*'s home city, illustrates the best example of the tension and its resulting violence. Between 1915 and 1920, when Chicago's black community grew by 148 percent, African Americans crowded into the existing housing and eventually began spilling over into Polish and Irish neighborhoods on the edges of the black belt. Typically, one intrepid black family would move into a previously all-white block and meet resistance, frequently including bombing of the property. If the blacks then moved away, the block was considered "saved," but if they managed to stay the whites would rapidly move out. In 1918 Chicago recorded sixty-eight bombing incidents involving the integrating of neighborhoods.

Moreover, the labor shortage prompted by World War I ended soon after November 1918, as industries converting to postwar production began laying people off. To make matters worse, returning white servicemen tended to expect to get back their old jobs or receive preferential hiring. This rivalry, in Chicago and other cities, led to what became known as the red summer of 1919, a term which had a dual meaning. There was for one an attack on perceived leftists by the federal government and patriotic organizations such as the newly formed American Legion, and on the other hand the greatest outburst of racial violence in the history of the nation. The Chicago race riot of 1919, which lasted nearly three weeks and caused the death of thirty-eight people, was the single-worst outbreak, but there were similar conflagrations in thirty-six cities, from Washington to Omaha, which took the lives of more than six hundred people.

Despite the violence and growing economic difficulties prompted by the postwar recession, the consensus among the migrants was that life in the North remained better than "going back home," according to an Associated Negro Press survey in mid 1923. This consensus was supported by numerous developments that mitigated the harshest realities of northern urban living. For example, the migration brought a resurgence of political activity. There was no denial of voting rights in the North, and soon African American politicians were being increasingly elected to office. As early as 1915, blacks served on the city council in Chicago, as they did in 1919 in New York. By 1928, Oscar DePriest of Chicago had become the first northern black congressman and the first black man to sit in Congress since 1901, beginning a pattern of continuous northern representation that has held until now. In

key industrial states like Ohio, New York, Illinois, and Pennsylvania black voters often swayed the balance of power between the Republican and Democratic parties, which gave them state and national influence far out of proportion to their numbers. To serve them a new urban black middle class emerged, out of the growth of black community services. Unlike their counterparts prior to 1910, this entrepreneurial class in the larger cities served an exclusively black clientele. Many in this new class were self-made men and women like Sarah Breedlove, who migrated from Louisiana to Indianapolis and finally to New York selling beauty products. She eventually developed a hair-straightening cream that made her the first black female millionaire, after which she adopted the name Madame C. J. Walker.

The migration north created a physically compact black community where individuals with diverse political, educational, and social backgrounds could exchange ideas, especially in New York, where African American migration from the South took place alongside smaller migrations from Cuba, Haiti, Jamaica, and Africa. Out of this intellectual crucible was forged the artistic creativity that generated the Harlem Renaissance. Comparable developments in music led to jazz and the blues becoming widely accepted both within and, for the first time, beyond the boundaries of black America.

The northward migration generated similar sweeping changes in black religion, though along radically differing paths. The first was the growth of the huge urban black churches such as the Abyssinian Baptist Church founded in 1910 by Adam Clayton Powell, Sr., in Harlem. By 1930 this church had become the largest in the nation, black or white, with over twenty thousand members. The Mount Olivet Baptist Church in Chicago had ten thousand members by 1930, and the Bethel AME Church (Mother Bethel) of Philadelphia, with its eight thousand members by the same date, became centers of political as well as religious activity. For instance, Adam Clayton Powell, Jr., the successor to his father as pastor of the Abyssinia Church, became New York's first black congressman in 1944.

The migration north also inspired the growth of so-called storefront churches, usually of the Holiness or Pentecostal denominations. These churches, which sprang up by the hundreds across urban black America, frequently had fewer than fifty members, yet they had strong appeal for the thousands of African Americans alienated by the size and formality of the larger churches. Harking back to the emotionalism of southern black services, these churches saw their members unabashedly illustrating their faith through singing, shouting, and speaking in tongues. Yet another approach was that of messianic religious leaders such as Father Divine and Daddy Grace, who attracted thousands of followers both black and white during the Great Depression, with their particular combinations of religious fervor and social service. Finally, various non-Christian groups such as the Nation of Islam and the Moorish Temple all found a place in the urban religious milieu generated by the northward migration.

THE UNIA AND BLACK CULTURE

The great migration to the northern cities helped generate new black organizations that rejected their assimilation into American society and sought instead to marshal the economic and political resources of the black enclaves to generate some degree of autonomy over the black condition. The most successful of these organizations was the Universal Negro Improvement Association, founded in 1914 by Marcus Garvey.

The UNIA was by far the largest popularly based political and economic organization of its time run by blacks. At the height of its power, in 1924, it included more than 2 million members and had 4 million sympathizers in the United States, Latin America, the West Indies, and Africa. Indeed, the UNIA was the first mass black organization whose every tenet reflected a racial consciousness. Its black-owned enterprises, including the Negro Factories Corporation and its steamship company, the Black Star Line, recalled the earlier emphasis on black capitalism by Booker T. Washington's Negro Business League and the black self-help efforts of the 1840s and 1850s. Its paramilitary arm, the African Legion, and its companion group of white-clad Black Cross nurses exuded a sense of strength and collective purpose rarely exhibited in the black community since the Civil War. Even its African Orthodox church suggested the racial purposes to which religion could be put. Although the UNIA's leaders did not use the term, they were in fact the first advocates of "black power."

By 1924 there were more than four hundred divisions or branches of the UNIA throughout the world, the largest being in New York, Philadelphia, Chicago, Cleveland, Cincinnati, Pittsburgh, and Detroit. These seven cities alone had over 250,000 members and were each financially strong enough to purchase Liberty Halls to house their Garveyite activities. Although the UNIA was primarily an urban organization, its appeal reached out well into the rural areas and small towns of black America. Louisiana, for example, had thirty-three divisions, mainly in small towns rather than major cities, and California's divisions in Monrovia, Fresno, Wasco, and San Bernardino became active before those in Oakland and San Francisco.

The ideals of the UNIA struck a responsive chord among millions of African Americans. The historian J. Saunders Redding has provided a vivid recollection of a UNIA rally in his hometown of Wilmington, Delaware, in the 1920s.

They came with much shouting and blare of bugles and a forest of flags—a black star centered in a red field. . . . They made speeches in the vacant lot where carnivals used to spread their tents. . . . [Y]oung women . . . in their uniforms distributed millions of streamers bearing the slogan "Back to Africa." [The UNIA members] were not people of the slums, they were men with small struggling shops and restaurants, and personal servants. . . . They had been dependable attendants at meetings promising Negro uplift, and loyal though perhaps somewhat awed members of the NAACP. (p. 39)

Like many middle-class African Americans who dismissed the UNIA, Redding as a historian focused primarily on Garvey's blunt exhortations to "look up, you mighty race" without understanding the deep roots of the "new" black consciousness. This new awareness was in part a response to a growing white racial consciousness, as reflected in the South in the emergence of a corpus of segregationist legislation and in the North by a corresponding concern with race. Although black nationalism clearly predates 1900, it was nonetheless accelerated by changes occurring on both sides of the color line. By the turn of the century many urban blacks had given up the dream of Reconstruction that black Americans would eventually be pulled into the economic, social, and political mainstream of the nation. All the solutions suggested to the race problem—education, property accumulation, industrial training, and religion—seemed useless in the quest for acceptance. Even the conservative Alabama educator W. H. Councill was forced to assert in 1899 that "whether North, South, East or West, [the black's] ambition, his aspirations are chained to a stake, are circumscribed by Anglo-Saxon prejudice and might" (p. 576). Only when black Americans "become a people," he said, will they be able to attack this chain.

Becoming a people required the development of a group consciousness promoting racial solidarity, a consciousness that had both its conservative and its radical antecedents. Conservatives such as the supporters of Booker T. Washington's Negro Business League saw the development of black business as the foundation for African American economic autonomy if not independence. Radicals like W. E. B. Du Bois emphasized a variety of reforms, from the promotion of black culture through studying black history to the use of economic boycotts and racially uplifting organizations such as the NAACP to shape an up-to-date African American. Indeed, the turn-of-the-century debate over the proper name to use for themselves—Negroes, Colored Americans, People of Color, African Americans, Afro-Americans—was emblematic of a growing racial consciousness. For many African Americans, "culture" was no longer simply the sum of the characteristics shared by the descendants of African slaves but was now a weapon in the struggle for equality.

Thus, Marcus Garvey's 1916 transferring of the international headquarters of the UNIA from Kingston, Jamaica, to Harlem and the rapid success of the organization by 1920 can be explained only partly by the travail of black America during World War I and its aftermath in the summer of 1919. Black America had in fact been poised for the UNIA's message long before Garvey ever arrived on the mainland. "The UNIA," wrote William Pickens of the NAACP in 1921 in a comparison with the leading white consciousness organization, the Ku Klux Klan, "was neither secret nor sinister," yet it "imbued ordinary black Americans with a massive dose of self-esteem" (p. 751).

THE GREAT DEPRESSION

By the Depression, for the first time in the nation's history two distinct types of African American societies had evolved—an urban culture, best represented by Harlem or Chicago's South Side but which was also inclusive of a number of smaller northern, western, and southern cities from Seattle to Miami, and a rural culture, formed in the aftermath of slavery. These two cultures had in common such features as poverty, segregation and, most importantly, a shared worldview. By the 1930s, as a consequence of the continuing migration to the north, these cultures were inexorably linked. Indeed, after the migration no southern black community, however small, was ever as isolated in the 1930s as it had been in the 1890s.

Yet the two cultures were also on vastly different trajectories. The rural South, which was home to 68 percent of black America in 1930, was giving way to the city in a contest played out virtually every day in thousands of households as individual family members made the fateful decision to move away. Those decisions collectively changed the South as much as they did the North, for the African Americans who remained behind confronted a white South that was often torn between a desire to participate in the industrialization and modernization now common in the rest of the nation and its insistence on maintaining its racial and social patterns held over from an earlier century.

Both of these forces and their challenges could be viewed in the growing militancy of black southern sharecroppers in the 1930s. In 1931, Alabama sharecroppers organized the Sharecroppers Union, whose members demanded the right to raise gardens for their own use, sell their own crops, have a three-hour rest period during the middle of the day, and receive cash wages for picking cotton. The union's non-economic demands included extending the school year to nine months for black children. Despite harassment from local authorities, and the murder of several sharecroppers during a confrontation at Camp Hill, Alabama, the union continued until 1939.

In Arkansas, black sharecroppers and tenant farmers joined the interracial Southern Tenant Farmers Union (STFU) formed there in 1934. This union spread throughout several states until by 1937 it claimed thirty-one thousand members. Under the leadership of Britt McKinney, a black Baptist minister and vice-president of the STFU, this union organized strikes of cotton choppers and pickers and exposed to the public various abuses in the sharecropping system, including forced labor and the denial of civil liberties, while also calling attention to the poverty, illiteracy, and disease common among the croppers.

Southern black urban workers in places as diverse as Gastonia and Greensboro in North Carolina and Birmingham, Alabama, challenged both anti-union and anti-integration sentiments by joining such groups as the National Miner's Union, the Steelworkers of America, and the National Textile Worker's Union. Their efforts and bravery illustrated that the militancy already associated with the New Negro of the urban North had also penetrated to well below the Mason-Dixon line.

The immediate impetus for these movements was not only the continuing poverty of the black South but also, despite the most fervent hopes of migrants, that of the black North. In 1928 the average annual income for black sharecropping families was $135 in Georgia, $108 in Alabama, and $98 in Mississippi. In the peak years of national prosperity in 1927 and 1928, black unemployment rates of 20 percent to 30 percent were common in Baltimore, Pittsburgh, and Chicago. By the time of the Depression, when the national unemployment average for African Americans stood at 48 percent, in Chicago it was 58 percent, in Baltimore 65 percent, and in Pittsburgh 70 percent.

Such economic dislocation took a horrendous toll on black family life in both the North and the South, which led indirectly to significant structural changes in the black family. One consequence was a growing number of single-parent households headed by women. In 1900 the percentage of white and black families headed by women was roughly equal, at 11 percent. By 1940, however, 31 percent of the black families in the United States were headed by women. Numerous reasons account for this rapid rise, including the process of migration itself, which separated families, the severe economic conditions of the time, which prompted abandonment by male breadwinners; and, an often overlooked factor, an excess of females over males, particularly in the cities. As early as 1910, in all the U.S. cities with a black population above twenty thousand, except Chicago, the number of black females per every hundred males ranged from 103 in Memphis to 143 in Atlanta, thus limiting the opportunities black women had to marry and remarry. Perhaps most influential, however, was an emerging welfare system with a contradictory policy of assisting women and children while also discouraging "able-bodied men" from remaining in homes where government support was being provided.

The Social Security Act of 1935 granted the first systematic relief for single mothers, with its Aid to Dependent Children (ADC) program. This program, which provided federal support payments on a matching fund basis with the states, initially affected 20 percent of all black families having a female head and children under sixteen. Yet there were wide discrepancies. In 1939–1940, for example, the average monthly payment per black child in New York was $24.15, whereas in South Carolina it was $3.52.

In the urban North, ADC programs initially improved the quality of family life, as reflected in a 1938 study showing the greatest decline in infant mortality rates to be in black neighborhoods where the number of relief cases was the highest. This study also indicated that nonworking mothers on ADC took greater precautions regarding their own health during pregnancy and also devoted more care to their children after birth than did the women who remained in the work force.

But if the support of relief payments enhanced the black woman's role as mother, they also changed her relationship with her husband. By the end of the Depression decade unemployed men were indirectly assisting their families by deserting them, to enable the mother and children to qualify for relief. These desertions cost fathers their functions as providers as well as the status that went with the role.

WORLD WAR II

World War II initiated yet another transformation in African American life as thousands of black men and women donned the uniforms of the U.S. armed forces to defend the nation and the world while millions of others sought employment in defense plants throughout the country, prompting a second great migration, which this time reached the Pacific Coast. However, the war also accelerated certain paradoxical trends that were already evident in black America, including the desultory impact to date that the rural-to-urban migration had made on impoverished black families, and an expanded sense of racial consciousness expressed in amplified demands for political and economic justice during the war years. Those demands and the campaigns that sprang from them ultimately provided a foundation for the civil rights and black power movements of the 1950s and 1960s.

The demands began in the summer of 1941, months before the U.S. declaration of war against the Axis powers, and were sparked largely by the efforts of then black labor leader and now social activist A. Philip Randolph. By 1940 the United States was already committed to becoming "the arsenal of democracy," which meant that America's factories, being increasingly geared up to provide war production for Great Britain, were generating large-scale employment opportunities. While millions of white Americans were obtaining jobs in defense plants throughout the country in 1940 and 1941, blacks were being excluded, or relegated to menial positions. Then, in January 1941, Randolph toured the country and heard firsthand persistent complaints about defense industry discrimination. His subsequent survey of 120 plants employing over 100,000 people indicated that only 237 African Americans worked in them, all of them janitors. Randolph called for a Fourth of July March on Washington by fifty thousand blacks to protest employment discrimination. Such a march, which would have been the largest demonstration in the history of Washington, D.C., would have embarrassed the federal government in its undeclared propaganda war with Nazi Germany. President Franklin Roosevelt met with Randolph on 25 June 1941, and immediately thereafter issued Executive Order 8802, which prohibited discrimination in the defense industries.

Executive Order 8802 coupled with the general manpower shortage led to tremendous black employment gains during World War II. Nearly 4 million African Americans would work in the defense industries during the war in a variety of capacities. Moreover, the war-prompted job opportunities caused a resurgence of the south-to-north migration that had slowed during the Depression. As a result, African Americans moved to Chicago, Detroit, and Pittsburgh, but also went to work for aircraft companies in Atlanta and Nashville, and for shipyards in Mobile, Norfolk, and Galveston.

However, by far the largest proportionate growth occurred on the West Coast. Between 1941 and 1945 some four hundred thousand blacks migrated to Washington, Oregon, and California, a number almost as large as the entire migration to the north had been during World War I. Between 1940 and 1944, Seattle's black population grew from 3,000 to 15,000, Portland's from 1,300 to 22,000, the San Francisco–Oakland area's jumped from 19,000 to 147,000, and that of Los Angeles, the city registering the smallest percentage increase, nontheless grew from 75,000 to 218,000. Two small Bay Area communities, Richmond and Vallejo, saw their African American populations rise from 800 to 23,000 and from zero to 16,000, respectively.

Black wartime migrants experienced problems throughout the nation, but those on the West Coast felt theirs exacerbated by the absence of black community-based institutions to absorb and assimilate newcomers. For example, many West Coast arrivals were confronted with an absence of adequate housing and subsequent severe overcrowding. In Richmond, in the Bay Area, nearly five thousand people lived in a housing project built for five hundred. In San Francisco black migrants slept in the railroad station and bus depot, and in all the Pacific Coast cities beds rather than rooms were rented out, in eight-hour shifts. As had occurred during the migration in World War I, a lack of housing coupled with a concentration of African Americans in certain areas led to the first West Coast ghettoes.

Despite these problems, World War II generated significant new opportunities for African Americans. The discriminatory practices of labor unions such as the International Brotherhood of Boilermakers did not prevent blacks from working in high-paying jobs in such defense-related industries as shipbuilding and aircraft production. Even though West Coast blacks earned only 95 percent of what their white counterparts made, this was still almost twice as much as the average black wage in the nation, and in Seattle and Los Angeles in particular many migrants retained their jobs after the war ended.

World War II sparked even greater militancy in blacks nationwide, as indicated by the threatened 1941 March on Washington, which had proved that black's demands could be met at the highest levels of government. One consequence of the new militancy was the creation of the Fair Employment Practices Committee to watch for discriminatory practices among both employers and unions. By its very existence as the first federal agency designated to assist blacks in their campaign to establish equal opportunity, the FEPC dramatically raised their expectations.

Finally, World War II made overt racism untenable for most Americans. Because the war had been waged against the most racist regime in the world, Nazi Germany, few people publicly espoused racist doctrines. Moreover, as the tragedy of the Holocaust became generally known, many people began to reassess the horrific consequences of racism. As Roy Wilkins of the NAACP argued with simple and compelling logic, "You can't be against park benches marked 'Jude' in Berlin and be for benches marked 'colored' in Jacksonville." This militancy would intensify after the war and ultimately produce the first cracks in the wall of segregation.

THE CIVIL RIGHTS MOVEMENT

The dramatic transformation of both black America and the nation during World War II inevitably generated the civil rights movement of the

1950s and 1960s, the most sustained campaign against inequality in the history of the United States. Although that movement was replete with examples of individual courage by Rosa Parks, Fannie Lou Hamer, and Martin Luther King, Jr., among many, it grew ultimately out of the collective efforts of the black church, the NAACP, and the black colleges. As Aldon Morris has shown, the black church was the centerpiece of the civil rights movement, providing its leadership, sustaining its development, supplying it with a communications network, and offering it organizational and financial support. Such participation suggests that the civil rights movement was, while obviously responding to immediate political and social changes nationally and globally, also at its heart the culmination of an evolving consciousness and an institutional development that had begun during the years immediately following the Civil War.

Although the movement received powerful encouragement from the U.S. Supreme Court in its *Brown* v. *Board of Education* decision in 1954, its direct-action phase did not begin until a year later with the Montgomery, Alabama, bus boycott. At that time African Americans began a thirteen-month boycott of city-owned local bus lines, prompted by Mrs. Rosa Parks's refusal to accept a seat in the black section. This boycott was the first major victory against segregation in a Deep South city.

The Montgomery boycott's success stemmed from efforts by a number of groups, including middle-class organizations like the local chapter of the Brotherhood of Sleeping Car Porters, headed by Ed D. Nixon, and the Women's Political Council, a group for college-educated black women whose president, Jo Ann Robinson, was an instructor at Montgomery State College. The boycott's success also sprang from the efforts of the members of the Dexter Avenue Baptist Church, served by the Reverend Martin Luther King, Jr., and the Montgomery First Baptist Church, Mrs. Parks's church, where the Reverend Ralph D. Abernathy was pastor. The boycott demonstrated a remarkable unity among the African American community, where at the height of the action some forty-five thousand people stayed off the buses and "walked for freedom."

By 1960 black college students were involved in the civil rights movement. Most were the sons and daughters of the post–World War II black middle class who, unlike earlier student populations, did not come from a background of dire poverty. Their optimism concerning their own upward mobility made unacceptable to them a racial system that limited their futures. These students were im-

patient with the legalistic approach of the NAACP and wanted to "do something" quickly and dramatically to destroy segregation forever. Their strategy was a direct action adaptation of the technique used in the Montgomery bus boycott.

The students' sit-in campaign started inconspicuously enough. On 1 February 1960, Ezell Blair, Jr.; Joseph McNeill; David Richmond; and Franklin McCain, all students at North Carolina Agricultural and Technical College, in Greensboro, were refused service at a lunch counter in a Woolworth's and decided to sit there in protest until they were served. The store closed an hour later, but they returned with fellow student supporters the following day. The "movement" had begun.

In a matter of weeks "sit-ins" had spread across the South, beginning a spontaneous effort that surprised both the sit-ins' supporters and their opponents. By June, sit-ins and other such demonstrations had occurred in 112 cities in the South, from Virginia to Oklahoma. Consequently, Ella Baker, a member of the Southern Christian Leadership Conference who was respected by student leaders, called a conference at Shaw University in Raleigh, North Carolina, out of which evolved the Student Nonviolent Coordinating Committee (SNCC).

By late 1962 a number of civil rights activists had begun to consider holding a national demonstration in support of a comprehensive national civil rights bill then stalled in Congress. The result was the March on Washington of August 1963, a demonstration involving 250,000 marchers, the largest to that point in the nation's history. Finally, in June 1964, nearly a year later, Congress passed the Civil Rights Act. The most comprehensive civil rights measure to date, it outlawed discrimination on the basis of race, color, religion, and sex in public accommodations and created the Equal Employment Opportunity Commission (EEOC) to monitor discrimination.

At the moment the civil rights movement was at its apex, other voices were emerging in black America to challenge its integrationist vision and nonviolent tactics. The most powerful of these voices was that of Malcolm X, born Malcolm Little in the black community of Omaha. Malcolm X joined the Nation of Islam in 1952 after a period of criminal activity and subsequent time in prison. By the early 1960s he had emerged as the chief spokesman for the Nation and as the primary critic of the civil rights movement.

Malcolm X articulated the views of many northern black ghetto dwellers for whom the southern civil rights issues about voting rights and putting an end to segregated schools and public accommodations seemed superfluous. He argued, as had the UNIA in the 1920s, for black unity, the development of an independent black economy, armed self-defense, and both political and cultural identification with Africa—in effect for a merging of black politics and black culture. To pursue these goals, which extended far beyond the vision of the Nation of Islam's leadership, Malcolm in 1964 created the Organization of Afro-American Unity. Malcolm X was assassinated in 1965 before he could develop a coherent political philosophy centered around the OAAU. However, his critiquing of integration when few others were challenging the dominant civil rights leadership, and his advocacy of a new black self-definition inspired virtually all post-1965 black nationalists.

Within a year after the death of Malcolm X, the civil rights movement was eclipsed by the black power movement. It replaced the traditional goal of the civil rights movement to integrate blacks into the American mainstream with demands for black control over the major institutions affecting African American life. If black nationalism did not become then the dominant philosophy in the black community, it was certainly more widely admired than it had ever been before in the history of the black community. Black frustration with racial discrimination expressed itself in a series of urban rebellions beginning with the Watts riot of 1965. LeRoi Jones, who later adopted the name Imamu Amiri Baraka, captured this anger and despair in 1966 when he wrote: "Sometimes, walking along, among ruined shacks and lives of the worst Harlem slum, there is a feeling that just around the corner you'll find yourself in South Chicago or South Philadelphia, maybe Newark's Third Ward. In these places, life and its possibilities have been distorted almost identically. And the distortion is as old as its sources: the fear, frustration, and hatred that Negroes have always been heir to in America. . . ." (L. Jones, pp. 94–95). Much of that fear, frustration, and hatred would soon be channeled into a new thrust—black power.

Stokely Carmichael, the newly elected chairman of SNCC, gave a speech in Hinds County, Mississippi, in June 1966, on the occasion of the end of the March Against Fear undertaken by civil rights leaders following the attempted assassination of James Meredith a month earlier. From that point on, according to Carmichael, SNCC would reject both the tactics and the philosophy of nonviolence and would devote itself solely to establishing economic and political power bases in the predominantly black areas of the South and ghettoes of the North. A SNCC staffer punctuated the end of Carmichael's speech with a call of "Black Power!" and this term, however imprecisely defined, was quickly added to the political lexicon of America.

The new call for black power, despite its appeal to a broad section of political activists opposed to integration, nevertheless proved divisive as various groups sought to adopt its banner for their own goals and objectives. However, by 1967 two groups emerged as the major proponents of the new concept.

The first group, the Cultural Nationalists, believed that a coming black revolution would eliminate the oppression of black people. But they argued that such a revolution must necessarily be preceded by the adoption of a new "African" value system encompassing language, dress, music, and social relationships. If this transformation of values did not occur first, any revolution would destroy itself or be "co-opted" by white radicals. To the Cultural Nationalists black power represented not only political power but also the power to define, guide, preserve, and revere black culture. Maulana (teacher) Ron Karenga's US Organization in Los Angeles and Imamu Amiri Baraka's Kawaida House in Newark, New Jersey, became the primary proponents of cultural nationalism.

Revolutionary Nationalists also believed in the inevitability of black revolution. However, they called for raising black consciousness by exposing the contradictions in American society. They felt that heightened political consciousness, and thus revolutionary action, would come through confrontations with what they saw as the most oppressive elements in American society—the police and the armed forces—and that the Revolutionary Nationalists should encourage such confrontations. The Revolutionary Nationalists called for creating a socialistic economy and strategic alliances with like-minded Third World revolutionary forces and similar groups in the United States. The Black Panther Party, founded in Oakland, California, in 1967 by Huey Newton and Bobby Seale, became the leading Revolutionary Nationalist organization.

By 1975 many of the leading exponents of both Cultural Nationalism and Revolutionary Nationalism were either incarcerated, in exile, or had met violent deaths. But the legacy of culture and politics they had begun expounding in the late 1960s continued to influence black America through the 1990s. Indeed, the 1960s had introduced a stunning sense of black cultural consciousness: the legitimacy of black values and life-styles, the common foods, the routine lives of ordinary black men and women came to be celebrated by artists, writers, painters, and poets and, for the first time, seriously examined—and often admired—by those outside the African American community. For the first time, a black perspective was being called for in all aspects of life—education, social science, the arts, and communication—and black culture was acclaimed to be a major element within a pluralistic American society. Moreover, African Americans themselves eagerly elevated certain aspects of their culture to esteem, often searching the black worlds of Africa, Brazil, and the Caribbean, as well as black America, for cultural artifacts. African names, art, and clothing reflecting African motifs became not simply signs of fashion but badges of honor and, for some, shields against a hostile world.

This new consciousness affected virtually every facet of black life. The black church, for example, reflected these changes through the emergence of such socially conscious preachers as the Reverend Jesse Jackson of Operation PUSH in Chicago, the poet-minister the Rev. Cecil Williams of Glide Memorial Church in San Francisco, and the black nationalist theologian the Rev. Albert B. Cleage of Detroit. This consciousness could also be seen outside Christianity with the continued growth of the Nation of Islam, the development of Yoruba temples in South Carolina, and the rise of the Ahmadiyya movement in New York.

Contemporary black cultural artists have since the 1970s given voice to the masses of working-class African Americans by tapping rich themes of folklore, migration, male-female relationships, and rage and alienation. These artists have included poets such as Haki R. Madhubuti (Don L. Lee), dance troupes such as those of Alvin Ailey, theatrical groups such as the Negro Ensemble Company and, of course, the writers, most notably Alice Walker, Toni Morrison, Ishmael Reed, Paule Marshall, and Maya Angelou, who have collectively produced a literature much larger than that of the Harlem Renaissance and of more lasting significance.

The new black cultural style has carried over into periodicals such as *Ebony, Essence, Black Scholar, Black Enterprise,* and a wide array of more specialized publications that have articulated this resurgent black consciousness. It was seen in the emergence of black studies programs on university campuses in the early 1970s as well as in their later manifestation, the promotion of multiculturalism, where a new generation of black students called for a restructuring of curricula to reflect the diversity of both the population and of America's history and culture. Yet for all their currency, these modern cultural manifestations have their antecedents in the century-old social and economic struggles of African America after the Civil War finally broke the chains of slavery.

BIBLIOGRAPHY

Blair, Thomas L. *Retreat to the Ghetto: The End of a Dream?* (1977).

Blassingame, John. *Black New Orleans, 1860–1880* (1973).

Bloom, Jack M. *Class, Race and the Civil Rights Movement* (1987).

Bond, Horace Mann. *The Education of the Negro in the American Social Order* (1934).

Borchert, James. *Alley Life in Washington: Family, Community, Religion, and Folklife in the City, 1850–1970* (1980).

Branch, Taylor. *Parting the Waters: America in the King Years, 1954–1963* (1989).

Brown, Richard Maxwell. *Strain of Violence: Historical Studies of American Violence and Vigilantism* (1975).

Carson, Clayborne. *In Struggle: SNCC and the Black Awakening of the 1960s* (1981).

Chicago Commission on Race Relations. *The Negro in Chicago: A Study of Race Relations and a Race Riot* (1922).

Cornish, Dudley Taylor. *The Sable Arm: Black Troops in the Union Army, 1861–1865* (1987).

Councill, W. H. "The Future of the Negro." *Forum,* July 1899.

Cox, Thomas C. *Blacks in Topeka, Kansas, 1865–1915: A Social History* (1982).

Du Bois, W. E. B. *The Philadelphia Negro: A Social Study* (1899; repr. 1971).

Dvorak, Katharine L. *An African-American Exodus: The Segregation of the Southern Churches* (1991).

Engs, Robert Francis. *Freedom's First Generation: Black Hampton, Virginia, 1861–1890* (1979).

Franklin, Jimmie Lewis. *Journey Toward Hope: A History of Blacks in Oklahoma* (1982).

Franklin, John Hope, and Alfred A. Moss, Jr. *From Slavery to Freedom: A History of Negro Americans* (1988).

Gatewood, Willard B. *Aristocrats of Color: The Black Elite, 1880–1920* (1990).

Gerber, David A. *Black Ohio and the Color Line, 1860–1915* (1976).

Giddings, Paula. *When and Where I Enter: The Impact of Black Women on Race and Sex in America* (1984).

Grossman, James R. *Land of Hope: Chicago, Black Southerners, and the Great Migration* (1990).

Gutman, Herbert G. *The Black Family in Slavery and Freedom, 1750–1925* (1976).

Hall, Charles E., ed. *Negroes in the United States, 1920–1932* (1969).

Hamilton, Kenneth Marvin. *Black Towns and Profit: Promotion and Development in the Trans-Appalachian West, 1877–1915* (1991).

Henri, Florette. *Black Migration: Movement North, 1900–1920* (1976).

Henry, Charles P. *Culture and African American Politics* (1990).

Hermann, Janet Sharp. *The Pursuit of a Dream* (1981).

Hughes, Langston. *The Big Sea* (1940).

Hutchinson, Louise Daniel. *Anna J. Cooper: A Voice from the South* (1981).

Jones, Jacqueline. *Labor of Love, Labor of Sorrow: Black Women, Work, and the Family from Slavery to the Present* (1985).

Jones, LeRoi. *Home: Social Essays* (1966).

Katzman, David M. *Before the Ghetto: Black Detroit in the Nineteenth Century* (1973).

Kennedy, Louise V. *The Negro Peasant Turns Cityward: Effects of Recent Migrations to Northern Centers* (1930).

Kusmer, Kenneth L. *A Ghetto Takes Shape: Black Cleveland, 1870–1930* (1976).

Levine, Lawrence W. *Black Culture and Black Consciousness: Afro-American Folk Thought from Slavery to Feedom* (1977).

Lewis, David L. *When Harlem Was in Vogue* (1981).

Lincoln, C. Eric, and Lawrence H. Mamiya. *The Black Church in the African American Experience* (1990).

Littlefield, Daniel F., Jr. *The Cherokee Freedmen: From Emancipation to American Citizenship* (1978).

Litwack, Leon F. *Been in the Storm So Long: The Aftermath of Slavery* (1979).

Locke, Alain, ed. *The New Negro: An Interpretation* (1925; repr. 1968).

Martin, Tony. *Race First: The Ideological and Organizational Struggles of Marcus Garvey and the Universal Negro Improvement Association* (1975).

Morris, Aldon D. *The Origins of the Civil Rights Movement: Black Communities Organizing for Change* (1984).

Nielson, David Gordon. *Black Ethos: Northern Urban Negro Life and Thought, 1890–1930* (1977).

Norrell, Robert J. *Reaping the Whirlwind: The Civil Rights Movement in Tuskegee* (1985).

Painter, Nell Irvin. *Exodusters: Black Migration to Kansas After Reconstruction* (1976).

Pickens, William. "Africa for the Africans—The Garvey Movement." *The Nation* 113 (28 December 1921).

Rabinowitz, Howard N. *Race Relations in the Urban South, 1865–1890* (1978).

Redding, Jay Saunders. *On Being Negro in America* (1951).

Redkey, Edwin S. *Black Exodus: Black Nationalist and Back-to-Africa Movements, 1890–1910* (1969).

Riis, Jacob A. *How the Other Half Lives: Studies Among the Tenements of New York* (1902; repr., 1957).

Savage, W. Sherman. *Blacks in the West* (1976).

Scott, Emmett J., ed. "Letters of Negro Migrants of 1916–1918." *Journal of Negro History* 4 (July 1919).

Spear, Allan H. *Black Chicago: The Making of a Negro Ghetto, 1890–1920* (1967).

Stein, Judith. *The World of Marcus Garvey: Race and Class in Modern Society* (1985).

Taylor, Arnold H. *Travail and Triumph: Black Life and Culture in the South Since the Civil War* (1976).

Taylor, Quintard. "The Great Migration: The Afro-American Communities of Seattle and Portland During the 1940s." *Arizona and the West* 23, no. 2 (Summer 1981).

———. "Black Urban Development: Another View, Seattle's Central District, 1910–1940." In *Black Communities and Urban Race Relations in American History,* edited by Kenneth L. Kusmer (1991).

———. "The Emergence of Afro-American Communities in the Pacific Northwest: 1865–1910." In *Black Communities and Urban Race Relations in American History,* edited by Kenneth L. Kusmer (1991).

Toll, William. *The Resurgence of Race: Black Social Theory from Reconstruction to the Pan-African Conferences* (1979).

Trotter, Joe William, Jr. *Black Milwaukee: The Making of an Industrial Proletariat, 1915–45* (1985).

———. *Coal, Class and Color: Blacks in Southern West Virginia, 1915–32* (1990).

———, ed. *The Great Migration in Historical Perspective: New Dimensions of Race, Class, and Gender* (1991).

Walker, Clarence E. *A Rock in a Weary Land: The African Methodist Episcopal Church During the Civil War and Reconstruction* (1982).

Washington, Booker T. "Boley: A Negro Town in the West." *Outlook* (4 January 1908).

Williamson, Joel. *The Crucible of Race: Black-White Relations in the American South Since Emancipation* (1984).

SEE ALSO **African American Music; Racism; Religion; Slavery;** and various essays in the sections **"Ethnic and Racial Subcultures"** and **"Periods of Social Change."**

LATIN AMERICANS: MEXICAN AMERICANS AND CENTRAL AMERICANS

Albert Camarillo

MEXICAN AMERICANS, the nation's second largest minority population, numbered more than 13.5 million in 1990. They are both immigrants who may have crossed the United States-Mexico border yesterday and people who are descended from pioneers who settled ten or twelve generations ago. They are still concentrated primarily in the states which border Mexico—a geographical and regional legacy measured more accurately in centuries than in decades. Yet over time internal migrations within the Southwest, as well as changing patterns of foreign immigration, have shuffled the demographic distribution of the group.

The Mexicans are a native people absorbed into the American nation via war, conquest, and diplomatic negotiation. This does not suggest, however, that Mexican Americans do not share many of the group experiences of European or Asian immigrants who struggled to adjust to life in the United States; it merely indicates a different point of departure for comprehending the group's status in American society. Mexican immigrants, like Asians, have been forced to contend with racial and ethnic barriers.

Mexican Americans' status as a racial or ethnic minority set them apart from their European counterparts and placed them with nonwhites. Yet skin color, one of the variables affecting how African Americans, Native Americans, and Asian Americans were perceived by white European Americans, varied among Mexican Americans. While the majority of Mexican Americans may not have escaped recognition as being racially different because of their appearance, those with lighter complexions could avoid overt discrimination based on skin color if they did not speak English with a Spanish accent or were not perceived as culturally different. The historical experiences of Mexican Americans cannot be told, however, by reference to racial, ethnic, or cultural factors alone. For nearly a century and a half, the history of Mexican Americans as a class of workers in local and regional economies has greatly influenced their status in United States society.

MEXICAN AMERICAN SOCIETY AT A CROSSROADS

During the last decade of the nineteenth century and the first decade of the twentieth, the Mexican-origin population underwent many significant transitions. The end of this period of change coincided with the start of the Mexican Revolution, a series of civil wars which proved disastrous to Mexico's society and economy. The revolution in Mexico with its attendant domestic chaos precipitated the first large-scale immigration of Mexicans to the United States. For some twenty years prior to the revolution, however, a trickle of immigration had occurred across the Texas border, but after 1910 it became a human torrent. Over one million (661,000 legal immigrants were counted by U.S. immigration authorities and tens of thousands entered illegally) Mexicans—a tenth or more of the entire population—entered the United States in the two decades following the start of the revolution, changing forever the composition of most Mexican American communities in the Southwest. As transplanted citizens of Mexico in America they contrasted sharply in some ways with native-born Mexicans of the American Southwest. Although, like the immigrants, these native Texans, native Californians, native New Mexicans, and others spoke Spanish, practiced Roman Catholicism as their religion, and shared common folkways and traditions, they did not perceive themselves as foreigners. Indeed, though they themselves or their parents had been

Mexican citizens at one time, since 1849 the approximately one hundred thousand Mexicans who had come to reside in the northernmost borderlands in the wake of the war between the United States and Mexico had become American citizens by virtue of the diplomatic treaty which settled the war. The Treaty of Guadalupe, Father Hidalgo provided for, among other things, the American citizenship of those former Mexican citizens who chose to remain on their land with all rights under the U.S. Constitution. Under the provisions of the treaty, those who wished to retain Mexican citizenship could do so.

By the time massive numbers of Mexican immigrants arrived in the Southwest after 1910, the native-born Mexicans in the region had witnessed profound changes in their communities. In the growing towns and cities scattered across the landscape from Texas to California, the old Mexican pueblos were overshadowed by, and in some cases obliterated by, development spurred by American capitalism. Such changes were not as perceptible in the rural hinterlands stretching from the Rio Grande Valley of Texas to the villages of northern New Mexico and to the rich agricultural lands of California, but here, too, changes in land tenure and the local economies ushered in a society unfamiliar to Mexican residents.

Americans took control of a vast territory in the period that began with the Texas Revolution of 1836, saw the Bear Flag Revolt a decade later in California, and culminated in the cession of nearly half of Mexico's national domain to the United States in the wake of the Mexican war. Into this land they carried their social and cultural institutions, their political and judicial systems, and a commercial capitalism. The ramifications of this societal change—which was uneven in its effects, depending on locality, on the growth of the American population, and on one's social class—were, in the end, catastrophic for the former Mexican citizens who became the first "Mexican Americans." The borderland societies of the Republic of Mexico (before 1821 the Spanish colonial borderlands, concentrated in New Mexico but with settlements from Texas to California) were largely self-sufficient communities only tenuously connected to the core of Mexico by the time Americans began to travel and settle in the region. By the 1820s and 1830s, especially in Texas, large numbers of American settlers—some welcomed and authorized to establish colonies on Mexican soil but a larger number considered to be "illegal aliens"—were not content to live under the flag of Mexico. Though certainly cultural differences between Mexicans and American settlers were partly to blame for increasing tension, even more important were the institutional and economic considerations which eventually led the white Texans—and some Mexicans—to rebel against the authority of Mexico and proclaim the independent Republic of Texas. Texas represented the vanguard of American interests in the region, and the Texas Revolution portended the fate of the Mexican settlements throughout the borderlands in the 1840s.

The acquisition of northern Mexico after the war of 1846–1848 unleashed development in the region which followed many of the patterns that had changed Texas in the previous decade. The growth of commercial capitalism and the corresponding expansion of the agricultural, cattle-raising, and mining frontiers in the Southwest overturned the pastoral local economies of most Mexicans. In the process, Mexican landholders throughout the region lost their lands. Large landowners in California's ranching economy lost most of their land grants within a generation after the American takeover, because of factors that included squatters, taxes, lengthy and costly legal cases to test the validity of their Mexican land grants before American land claims commissions and courts of law, flood and drought, and glutted markets for beef cattle. Though many Mexican landholders resisted the changes taking place around them for many years, they were generally unable to negotiate the new American legal and judicial institutions. By the late 1880s, almost everywhere in the Southwest, most Mexicans had come to realize the inexorable forces of institutional, economic, and social change that Americanization had brought to the region and to their communities.

Not all Mexican Americans experienced the effects of these changes in the same ways. As in Mexican society in general, class distinctions characterized society in the borderlands before and after American annexation, although some Mexicans and Americans deviated from the norm of intergroup relations to establish mutual political and economic ties. In particular, a small number of elite members within Mexican communities from Texas to California cooperated with American entrepreneurs and political movers to protect their mutual interests, in some cases profiting handsomely from such alliances. Those of the Mexican elite saw themselves as distinct from the majority of working-class *mestizos* (persons of mixed Spanish and Indian blood), superior in class status as well as their cultural and racial background. Intermarriage between the daughters of the elite and prominent American settlers was not uncommon. However, even among those who considered themselves more Spanish than Mexican or as occupying a higher status, not all cooperated with the Americans. Some resisted a political takeover of their communities by organizing their countrymen within the new political system established by Americans or by revolting against the authority of Americans by recruiting others to fight the gringos.

Yet most Mexicans, be they members of the elite or of the working class, chose neither co-optation nor violent resistance but instead managed to accommodate themselves to different circumstances resulting from Americanization. Beneath the glamour and romanticization of the escapades of the legendary Joaquín Murieta in California, or the 1859 revolt led by Juan Cortinas in South Texas, or the night-riding, fence-cutting, resistance activities of the hooded Gorras Blancas (White Caps) of New Mexico (1889–1891), the social and cultural changes among the great majority of Mexican Americans took place largely unnoticed. By the end of the nineteenth century Mexican Americans had developed a bicultural and biracial accommodation which for most resulted in separation from the majority of whites. With the exception of contact between European Americans and Mexican Americans in the arena of employment, the social lives of most Mexican Americans occurred within their rural *colonias* (colonies or small settlements) and urban *barrios* (neighborhoods).

CHANGING RACIAL IDEOLOGIES

The new immigrants from Mexico entered San Antonio's large West Side barrios, the growing barrios of East Los Angeles, the South Side neighborhoods of Tucson, and dozens of smaller Mexican American communities. They entered a society very different from their homeland, they found jobs which often had no relationship to those in the motherland, and they encountered problems in adapting to a new life-style in a new land with different customs, traditions, institutions, and national language. Although their decision to move to the United States encompassed the difficult decision to travel north in search of work and to distance themselves from the ravages of the revolution, Mexican immigrants could take some comfort in the reali-

zation that most of the localities in the Southwest in which they settled had long-standing Mexican communities. In these areas Spanish was the primary language, culture shock was less severe, and Mexican traditions and customs had persisted for generations.

Though Mexican immigrants found much in the existing Mexican communities which made their cultural transition in the United States less abrupt, they also acquired the racial and cultural status of their native-born cousins, which boxed them into prescribed roles as a racial minority and class of workers. For example, during the nineteenth century commentator after commentator condemned Mexicans for their "obvious" laziness, lack of ingenuity, and wasteful neglect of natural resources (e.g., raising cattle on land suited for farming), in contrast with Americans. Furthermore, Mexicans were perceived to be as much heathen as they were Christian. Their Catholicism pitted them against Protestants. Moreover, their Catholicism was infused with Native American and European folkways and beliefs. To make matters worse, in the eyes of Americans, Mexicans were "half-breeds," a dirty "mongrel" race descended from plundering Spanish conquistadors and Indians: mestizos were considered to be only a notch above Indians in the racial hierarchy.

Not all Mexicans were tagged with such labels. Variations of attitudes did exist and were often mediated by class and gender considerations. For example, Americans were quick to make distinctions between the Mexican elite, whom they considered to be more European and white, and the dark-skinned mestizos. They were even quicker to place women of the elite in categories more readily accepted, particularly as many American pioneers viewed these women as potential wives. These views contrasted dramatically with attitudes about mestizas, who were often portrayed as prostitutes and seen as morally suspect women who dressed far too scantily, especially in the opinion of middle-class American women who recorded their travels in published journals. To many American men, Mexican women were seductive sexual objects who were attracted to white men because they were superior to Mexican men.

Manifest Destiny, the notion that it was America's special mission to expand across the continent, had dire repercussions for Mexican Americans, not only as justification for war and annexation but also as a rationale for their ostracism after the war of 1846–1848. Mexican Americans almost everywhere, with the exception of New Mexico, were largely excluded from participation in local and state politics; the majority of their lands fell into white hands by the turn of the century; and increasing poverty, associated with the decline of the pastoral economy, coincided with the rise of commercial capitalism in the Southwest. Mexicans were perceived by many enterprising Americans settling in the region as impediments to progress, as a backward people to be moved aside as a new society took root, and as an inferior race that could not realistically be incorporated into the body politic on an equal footing with white Americans.

As large numbers of immigrants from Mexico arrived in the Southwest in the early twentieth century, it became quite obvious that Mexicans and Mexican Americans were being treated differently than European Americans. And though the immigrants were less concerned about being included in society, they were keenly aware of how differential treatment affected them as workers. During the early twentieth century the idea of Mexicans as a principal source of cheap labor for a growing agricultural economy and an expanding urban commercial economy became wedded to the existing racial ideology to help justify why Mexicans worked in nonskilled jobs that were generally not attractive to white labor and why they should be paid less than white workers. The occupations that came to be associated with immigrants from Mexico during the first third of the century—railroad labor, migratory farm work, mining and construction work, and other manual labor—were often referred to as "Mexican jobs." As the Southwest's labor market grew increasingly dependent on Mexican immigrant labor for particular types of work, a pattern of segmenting a racial minority in the work force developed.

The great majority of Mexican immigrants worked in particular types of jobs which were prescribed for them, at least in part because most had no skills beyond those required by manual occupations. Most immigrants were from rural Mexico, which during the Porfiriato (the dictatorship of Porfirio Díaz) witnessed the erosion of the subsistence economies of small farmers as the land tenure system was increasingly controlled by *hacendados* (hacienda owners). Unable to eke out a living as sharecroppers or as workers tied to the landed elite through a debt-peonage system, Mexicans looked north to escape the ravages of civil war and to survive economically. The revolution propelled more than peasants from the countryside to the United States. Joining the ever-increasing numbers of working-class Mexicans who came to America during the 1910s and 1920s were thousands of political and many religious refugees, members from the middle class and elite sectors of Mexican society.

THE FIRST MASS IMMIGRATION

The number of immigrants from Mexico who settled in America prior to the 1930s overwhelmed and obscured the existing Mexican American population in the Southwest except in New Mexico, a state that attracted relatively few immigrants in comparison with the other border states. The hundreds of thousands of people who ventured north came as individuals—usually single young men—and as members of nuclear and extended families. Often a family member or two migrated north, earned dollars, then sent for the remaining family members. They typically came by rail from the south-central and northern states of Mexico. The border separating Mexico and the United States during this early period was in most respects an imaginary line indicated by a shallow river or a wide expanse of desert. Not until 1924 did America establish the Border Patrol, but a few hundred patrolmen could hardly oversee the two thousand-mile border between the two countries. Even at the primary entry point—El Paso/Ciudad Juárez—through which the majority of Mexican immigrants passed, getting through official immigration checkpoints was pro forma. In fact, private and corporate labor contractors worked both sides of the border, signing up prospective workers with promises of jobs. Many immigrants remained in border towns such as El Paso, Laredo, and Brownsville, Texas, or moved to towns and cities where prospects for work were plentiful: Los Angeles, San Antonio, Tucson, San Diego. Others followed the major rail lines to cities with better job opportunities or to agricultural areas, where entire family units could participate in harvests. Both the railroad and farm work carried Mexicans across the Southwest, from the fertile valleys of south Texas to the fields of California, north to Utah and Idaho, and back east across the Great Plains and eventually to the Great Lakes region. Some were drawn to midwestern cities where they found work in steel foundries, in the auto industry, in meat-packing plants, and in other manufacturing employment in Chicago; Omaha; Detroit; Gary, Indiana; and as far east as Bethlehem,

Pennsylvania. Though only a small fraction of all Mexican immigrants settled outside the Southwest, they initiated patterns of urban development which laid the foundation for subsequent expansion of Mexican American urban society in the Midwest.

Those who decided to remain in the Southwest also established major demographic patterns. Although exact population figures are unavailable, a majority of immigrants settled in areas where Mexicans had resided for generations, either the small towns that dotted the countryside and which served as nuclei for the agricultural economy or the emerging cities where industrial and commercial development were creating many new jobs. As immigrants gravitated to these towns and cities for employment, they settled within a growing community of fellow Mexicans where the social, cultural, recreational, and organizational life provided a cushion against the dislocation experienced in leaving Mexico. They also established new Mexican American enclaves throughout the Southwest and in other regions. Attracted by the prospect of jobs and low-cost housing, immigrants traveled to newer urban areas such as Houston, Dallas, and Phoenix. They also settled in satellite neighborhoods within expanding metropolitan areas.

Just as numerous were immigrants who had followed the harvests and settled in small farming communities. The communities of Mexican farm worker families in the Imperial and San Joaquin valleys of California reflected the tendency to settle in small towns along the pathways of migratory farm labor stretching from Texas and California northward through the Midwest, along the Pacific Coast, through the Rocky Mountain states. By the end of the 1920s the basic demography of "Mexi-America" had been established: the vast majority of Mexican-origin people resided in the Southwest, and by 1930 the majority of Mexican Americans were urban dwellers.

SOCIAL, CULTURAL, AND POLITICAL ORGANIZATION

Regardless of where they settled, Mexican immigrants and their children established networks of social, cultural, religious, and political organizations which helped them negotiate life in America. In virtually every community of Mexican immigrants dozens, if not hundreds, of such social and recreational organizations were formed as mutual aid societies. Sometimes they had been established by native-born Mexican Americans in the 1870s or 1880s. In most cases, however, the immigrants developed these groups for mutual aid and services (insurance benefits, death benefits, credit associations, and the like), for sponsorship of national and cultural festivities and recreational activities, and as a base for political action and self-defense.

Equally ubiquitous in the Mexican community was the Catholic church, which may have served Spanish-speaking parishioners for generations or may have been recently constructed to serve new immigrants. From cradle to grave, the Roman Catholic church was an enormously influential institution in the lives of most Mexican Americans. Even if one were not overly religious and were only nominally Catholic in the eyes of the church, the customs and traditions linked to Catholicism in Mexican life and culture were obvious to all: the baptism of an infant, the feast day of a patron saint, the wedding of a relative, the burial of a friend.

Both Roman Catholicism and the community's organizations were premised on the sanctity and cohesiveness of the family unit. To Mexicans, *familia* was the center of community and society. The relationships which radiated from the nuclear and the extended family were further interwoven into religion and culture through *compadrazgo,* the network of godparent relationships in which trusted friends and relatives became the *padrinos* (godfathers) and *madrinas* (godmothers) to newborn children of neighbors, friends, and relatives. Among both native-born Mexican Americans and Mexican immigrants, family ties at several levels provided a system of shared responsibilities and reciprocal relationships which added another dimension to the meaning of community. Within this context of family and community, however, there were prescribed roles and tensions which were characterized by gender and social class.

Immigrant and native-born Mexicans alike were products of a society in which gender-differentiated roles and expectations operated at many levels. Men were supposed to be the dominant actors in family and community life; women were expected to be submissive and subordinate to males. Women were expected to be chaste, tied to home and children, whereas men were not expected to be sexually faithful. Women were perceived to be more devout, whereas men were allowed more leeway in their religious observances. Men were expected to provide for home and family, while housework and child rearing fell to women. Young men pursued an education or, as was more often the case because of economic necessities, left school to work. Young women were not expected to continue their education because of household duties and were discouraged from working outside the home before marriage.

These expectations of gender relationships and behavior cut across social class lines. Other behaviors and expectations also ignored social class differentiations. For example, celebration of Mexican national holidays—such as the Diesiséis de Septiembre (16 September), Mexican Independence Day, and Cinco de Mayo (5 May), which commemorates the victory of Mexican troops over the French army of occupation in the Battle of Puebla in 1862—or fiestas (community festivities or parties) included immigrants and native-born alike. Differences between and among Mexican Americans tended to blur at these community functions.

But social class, political, and other differences did in fact characterize Mexican immigrants and Mexican Americans during the early twentieth century. These differences were in many ways not unlike those which had existed in earlier times. Social class differences, for instance, had long been evident among settlers during the Spanish colonial period, on the frontier as well as in the center of New Spain. These differences may have diminished somewhat during the Mexican republican period, but they certainly did not vanish. The immigrants who came to America during the early twentieth century brought with them many of the historical divisions which characterized Mexican society. Political refugees from the middle class or the elite who had fled the revolution continued to interact primarily with members of their own class after resettling. These immigrants never viewed America as their home; they believed they would return home once the revolutionary turmoil subsided. Regardless of whether they returned—most did not, at least before the 1930s—the focus of their attention was on the politics, culture, and society south of the Rio Grande. Though very small in numbers, the immigrant middle class and elite had a disproportionate influence on the entire immigrant community; they typically were the editors of the Spanish-language newspapers, the small business proprietors, and the professionals.

The objectives and agendas of middle-class organizations and associations did not focus only on class interests. Some were concerned about their working-class compatriots and tried to eradicate the poverty and discrimination that all Mexicans faced. Some organizations included middle-class and working-class members who cooperated in furthering the interests of Mexicans as a group. In other cases, native-born Mexican Americans collaborated with recent arrivals from Mexico to achieve their aims. For example, in 1894 the Alianza Hispano Americana (Hispanic American Alliance), established by leading Mexican Americans in Tucson, Arizona, was a response to the efforts of some whites to exclude them from local politics. Though political in origin, the Alianza became a mutual-aid type of organization providing benefits for its members in dozens of chapters across the Southwest during the first half of the twentieth century

In Texas, the beginning of large-scale immigration resulted in more severe discrimination and racism directed against Mexicans, regardless of national origin. In 1911 a group of organizations banded together to combat discrimination and form a statewide association to protect the civil rights of Mexican immigrants and Mexican Americans. The Primer Congreso Mexicanista (First Mexican Congress) sought, in particular, to curb the increasing racial segregation of Mexican American children in Texas public schools and to protest the exclusion of Mexican Americans from the political system. The Liga Protectora Latina (Latino Protectorive League), founded at Phoenix in 1914, developed in response to violations of civil rights when mine operators attempted to establish a state law placing a cap on the percentage of Mexican workers employed at any given mine in Arizona.

The Liga's concern for the protection of the rights of workers was repeated many times over during the first half of the twentieth century. Often, in response to discriminatory labor practices, low pay, dangerous working conditions, and other forms of exploitation and disregard, Mexican workers united to challenge management and employers. During the last quarter of the nineteenth century and the first quarter of the twentieth, they banded together in labor unions, typically to press for better wages. In industries as varied as mining, agriculture, urban transportation, sheep raising, and services such as laundries, Mexican men and women in the border states organized unions, all of which failed to endure very long or beyond the local, immediate issues at hand. However, by the 1930s Mexican farm laborers and agriculture-related workers engaged in unionization efforts across the Southwest, sometimes organizing unions exclusively for Mexicans, at other times joining with workers organized by Communist unions or by the more progressive unions under the Congress of Industrial Organizations (CIO) umbrella.

For the most part, the major American labor unions had openly avoided organizing Mexican unskilled workers, but by the late 1930s at least the CIO had changed its policies regarding the unionization of Mexican noncraft workers. The 1930s witnessed some spectacular and violent strikes involving Mexicans: garment workers in Los Angeles in 1933; pecan shellers in San Antonio in 1938 (both of these strikes involved Mexican women almost exclusively); thousands of cotton pickers in the San Joaquin Valley in 1933; packing shed workers in California during the late 1930s and early 1940s.

THE GREAT DEPRESSION

The years of the Great Depression laid bare just how precarious life was for most Mexican-origin people in America. Prior to the 1930s, the majority of Mexican immigrants (who numbered 531,000, 41 percent of all Mexican-origin people in 1930, according to that U.S. census) and Mexican Americans (about 752,000) lived on or below the poverty line. The Depression resulted in high rates of unemployment and underemployment; job loss among Mexican Americans was compounded further when they were identified by federal and local agencies as foreigners who allegedly exacerbated the economic downturn because they supposedly took jobs away from American citizens and overburdened public and private relief programs.

The "crisis" associated with Mexicans on relief during the early 1930s was actually an extension and an intensification of what had been labeled the "Mexican problem" during the 1920s. Mexican immigrants' children, it was argued, made public education more difficult because they required special language instruction, they slowed down the progress of white children in mixed classrooms, and they added higher costs to districts which opted to establish separate "Mexican schools." Mexicans also constituted health problems, in the eyes of public health officials, because they were more likely to harbor contagious diseases as a result of their lack of adequate hygiene and their preference for living in overcrowded housing. And, finally, Mexicans had great difficulty assimilating into American society because of their cultural tenacity and tendency toward clannishness.

During the early 1930s the Department of Labor, first in Los Angeles and later in most urban areas where Mexicans resided, initiated in collaboration with local relief agencies a program of forced deportation and voluntary repatriation. At first, officials conspired with local newspapers to scare Mexicans back to Mexico by threats of impending immigration sweeps, some of which did in fact occur. Eventually, forced deportation programs gave way to offers by local and federal agencies of free transportation to Mexico for any individual or family willing to leave America. Between 1929 and 1934 some four hundred thousand Mexicans and U.S. citizens born to immigrant parents were deported or repatriated. The numbers would probably be much higher if one were to take into account those who left America without government transportation and those who were repatriated throughout the 1930s after the mass deportations.

ORGANIZATIONAL MOBILIZATION

Perhaps most Mexican Americans endured the hardships of the 1930s in silence and without effective means to organize themselves. But others mobilized to confront a worsening situation, though the objectives and means varied. In some cases, Mexican consulates and nongovernmental organizations attempted to aid deportees and repatriates by providing information about conditions in Mexico, a meal en route, or a few dollars for the most destitute families. Other organizations, such as the League of United Latin American Citizens (LULAC), founded in 1929, tended to distance themselves from identification as Mexicans by calling themselves Latin Americans. They publicly declared their status as American citizens—only U.S. citizens were admitted as members—wishing to become full-fledged members of society; they permitted only English to be spoken at meetings and were willing to discard Mexican cultural and national trappings. LULAC was chiefly concerned with the social advancement of Mexican Americans, which, in their view, was achievable only through assimilation. Consequently, it led the Mexican American organizations advocating desegregated schools in Texas, the state where the organization was established.

LULAC reflected a particular organizational means to an end which other groups shared but which they attempted to achieve in different ways. One umbrella organization stands out during the late 1930s—Congreso de Pueblos de Habla Español

(Congress of Spanish Speaking People, 1939)—because it banded dozens of existing Mexican American organizations into a loosely structured confederation. The confederation was spearheaded by Luisa Moreno, a Guatemalan-born labor union organizer with the CIO's United Cannery, Agricultural, Packing and Allied Workers of America. The Congress established a broad agenda including, but not limited to, civil rights advocacy, condemnation of racial discrimination, protection of the rights of immigrants, and support for the unionization of Mexican American workers. Established at a national meeting in Los Angeles, it gathered representatives from over 130 local, state, and national organizations with a combined membership of 840,000 people. The action agenda was to be implemented through local chapters (the great majority of local organizations represented were Mexican American groups from Texas, California, Arizona, and New Mexico, but Puerto Ricans from New York and Cuban Americans from Florida were also represented). The Congress was frustrated in its efforts to develop as a national civil rights association for Mexican American and other Latinos because it was red-baited by the FBI and by local and state agencies and committees. It was also deprived of some of its best young leaders, who were killed in action during World War II. Nonetheless, it was an important model for Mexican American organizations established after World War II.

THE SEARCH FOR INCLUSION

Gone by 1940 were many of the Mexican immigrants who had returned to Mexico or been forcibly deported during the 1930s. Those who remained through the Great Depression were committed to staying in America and to raising families. During the 1930s and 1940s the children of these families came of age and, unlike their parents or grandparents, perceived themselves first and foremost as Americans. They were bilingual and bicultural in many respects, operating in both the larger society and their own communities. These young men and women were profoundly influenced by World War II as they entered the military and served abroad or entered war-related industries, working in industrial jobs for the first time in large numbers. Overseas, Mexican American men distinguished themselves on the battlefields and returned home as decorated war heroes. On the home front, Mexican American women assumed new roles as workers and heads of households.

The return of Mexican American veterans and the laying off of most women from the jobs they had held during the war brought to an abrupt end any hopes for long-term gains. Many saw no visible improvement in the status of their communities and, in fact, were rudely reminded of the subordinate condition of Mexican Americans. For some, especially those living in the Los Angeles area—by 1930 the largest concentration of Mexican Americans in the nation, numbering somewhere near 150,000—evidence of continuing discrimination and racial bias was fresh in their minds in the wake of the Zoot Suit Riots of 1943. For several years, local police departments and the media had identified Mexican American youth as a threat to an orderly society. The stereotype of the "deviant," marijuana-smoking, criminally inclined young street hoodlum—the *pachuco*—was associated by the beginning of World War II with teenagers who wore the baggy outfits called zoot suits. Apparently, an incident involving zoot-suited Mexican American youths and white military personnel ignited five days of mayhem in downtown and East Los Angeles, resulting in mass beatings, arrests, and chaos. Mexican American youths were attacked by club-wielding mobs of sailors and marines in movie theaters, on streetcars, and in other public places.

Mexican American veterans returning from combat soon understood that risking one's life in war did not guarantee better treatment as a civilian. For example, after the war in the southern Texas town of Three Rivers the body of a Mexican American war hero, returned from overseas for burial in his native community, was barred from the local mortuary, operated only for whites. The outraged Mexican American community eventually attracted the attention and support of a young congressman, Lyndon B. Johnson, who saw to it that the body of Felix Longoria was buried with full military honors in Arlington National Cemetery. The group responsible for galvanizing the community in support of the rights of Mexican Americans was formally founded in 1949 in Corpus Christi, Texas, and called the American G.I. Forum. Within a decade the Forum had over one hundred chapters, and later expanded its agenda to include advocacy of educational and economic opportunities.

At the same time that veterans were organizing themselves in Texas, their comrades elsewhere in the Southwest were doing likewise. A group organized in East Los Angeles in an effort to elect one of their own to the Los Angeles City Council, a political body that had been without a representative from the Mexican American community since the

1880s. Though they failed in their first bid to elect Edward Roybal to the council, they were successful in 1949. Calling themselves the Community Service Organization (CSO), the original group expanded to include broader participation of East Los Angeles Mexican Americans and eventually became one of the leading local organizations in California during the 1950s. In addition to political representation, CSO was involved in local police brutality cases, protection of civil rights, lobbying for state legislation beneficial to Mexican Americans, and sponsorship of local improvement programs for East Los Angeles barrio neighborhoods. CSO became a mutual-aid organization by the late 1950s.

Returning war veterans were catalysts in developing community and political organizations in the postwar era, but they were not the only Mexican Americans to establish vehicles to promote the general welfare of their communities. Older organizations such as LULAC continued to advocate for Mexican Americans, especially in the area of enhancing educational opportunities. In Los Angeles, a group of professionals, many of whom were leaders of their respective organizations, worked under the banner of the Council of Mexican American Affairs for a few years during the mid 1950s to develop leadership in their communities while addressing issues of importance to their fellow Mexican Americans.

Other groups formed during the 1950s were products of grass-roots community efforts organized as a response to problems. Such a group, the Asociación Nacional México Americana (ANMA; Mexican American National Association), established many chapters throughout the Southwest and Midwest after its founding in 1949 in Albuquerque, New Mexico. Influenced strongly by its labor union leadership and affiliated during the 1950s with the Independent Progressive Party, ANMA defended Mexican Americans against human rights violations while encouraging people to join unions. During the McCarthy era of the early to mid 1950s, ANMA and many other community organizations were labeled as Communist-subversive groups.

CONTINUING IMMIGRATION FROM MEXICO

There were two different but related aspects to the issue of immigration from Mexico during the 1950s and early 1960s. The first concerned the Bracero Program (named for those who work with their arms, or *brazos*), a binational agreement be-

gun during the early 1940s as a war-related emergency measure to ensure an ample supply of farm labor. However, this program of recruiting workers from Mexico through a cooperative international agreement extended far beyond the war years. Agribusiness interests benefited so much from a program that provided a large supply of low-cost, seasonal labor that growers were able to influence Congress to extend the Bracero Program for some twenty years. Only after concerted efforts by organized labor and Mexican American advocacy organizations, and disclosure of human rights violations and recurrent mistreatment and exploitation of contracted braceros was Congress persuaded to terminate the program, in 1964.

During the height of the Bracero Program in the 1950s, on average more than three hundred thousand Mexican men worked annually on farms from California to Texas and beyond. Thousands of them left their contracts illegally or gained entrance to the United States as documented temporary ("green card") workers. Untold thousands of others married Mexican American women while in America, thereby gaining the right to remain legally. Braceros who opted to stay were joined by legions of compatriots who could gain admittance neither as braceros nor as "green card" immigrants. *Mojados* ("wetbacks," as they were pejoratively called) numbered in the hundreds of thousands during the late 1940s and especially the early 1950s, when growers encouraged illegal immigration in efforts to expand their labor pools during the Korean War. The "invasion" of undocumented Mexican immigrants drew notice from Congress and other public officials, especially during the postwar economic recession. Though the actual number of illegal immigrants is impossible to determine, the figures recorded in the annual reports of the Immigration and Naturalization Service (INS) clearly reveal the extent of immigration: in 1947, 183,000 undocumented immigrants were apprehended and returned to Mexico; the number increased to 865,000 by 1953.

Reminiscent of the 1930s, commentators argued that illegals were taking jobs away from Americans, exacerbating a troubled economy and creating problems for the border patrol. Sentiment against the "wetbacks" became translated into direct policy by 1954, when the newly appointed director of the INS, a retired general, initiated what was called Operation Wetback, a military-style search-and-seizure campaign aimed at catching illegal immigrants where they worked and lived. It was declared a success with the arrest and deportation of over one million immigrants. Apparently, thousands of Mexican immigrants were convinced not to risk seizure by INS agents in the years after 1954, as evidenced by a dramatic drop in the number of reported INS apprehensions (only seventy-two thousand in 1957).

If those who arrived in the United States during the first three decades of the twentieth century constituted the first great wave of Mexican immigrants, the *braceros* of the 1940s and the undocumented workers of the 1950s made up the second and third waves. First- and second-generation Americans of Mexican immigrant parents, adjusting and acculturating as Mexican Americans, were now joined by a massive number of immigrants. This cycle of generational change and immigration had many effects: it meant that Mexican American communities continued to be composed of both native-born and foreign-born; it meant that the Spanish language was reinforced almost everywhere Mexican Americans lived; it meant that aspects of the culture of Mexico were infused into the bicultural society of Mexican Americans; it also meant that negative images, which cast immigrants from Mexico as uneducated, illiterate, dirty peasants who could only perform menial and back-breaking labor, were projected onto the majority of Mexican Americans. It was not uncommon for these views to be internalized within Mexican communities, which resulted in tensions and distance between immigrants and the native-born, especially those attempting to achieve upward social mobility.

Understandably, some Mexican Americans had little sympathy for the plight of the new immigrants. Mexican Americans who saw education as the principal means to achieve progress could rejoice because important court cases during this period struck down de jure segregation of Mexican children on the basis of special educational and language needs. Yet the great majority of Mexican American schoolchildren continued to attend de facto segregated schools where for most education was likely to end during or before junior high school (the median years of schooling completed for Mexican Americans in the Southwest in 1960 was 8.1, versus 12.0 years for whites and 9.7 for nonwhites).

During the 1950s Mexican Americans encountered fewer overt manifestations of racism and discrimination. Gone were many of the signs in store windows barring Mexicans from entering or being served. Nevertheless, Mexicans reported that custom and tradition often prevailed in rules about swimming pools being reserved for Mexicans or blacks on certain days; theater operators who ushered Mexicans into the balconies or toward the backs of the movie houses, away from white customers; restaurants or other public places giving verbal or nonverbal signs to Mexican Americans that their business was not wanted. Mexican Americans who had worked diligently to elect the first of their group to local political office were disappointed by the inability to overcome the effects of gerrymandering of their disticts or other political devices which nullified meaningful participation and representation in local politics.

Those who had achieved modest levels of upward social mobility through better jobs and education became models for others but entrance into skilled trades, high-level white-collar jobs, and the professions seemed to be virtually impossible. According to census data for gainfully employed Mexican Americans in the Southwest in 1950 and 1960, the proportion of men who were professionals, white-collar managers, and proprietors increased from 6.6 percent to 8.7 percent, whereas for women it declined from 8.5 percent to 8.0 percent. Though the percentage of men in skilled trades increased from 13.1 percent in 1950 to 16.7 percent in 1960, the bulk of Mexican workers could not rise out of the ranks of the unskilled and semi-skilled (69 percent of all male workers in 1950 and 64 percent in 1960, and 64 percent of women workers in 1950 and 60 percent in 1960).

During the 1940s and 1950s, all of the major socioeconomic and educational indexes revealed that Mexican Americans had achieved some progress, but integration into mainstream society was still far out of reach for most. Many of the achievements of Mexican Americans as a group after 1960 cannot be separated from their search for inclusion in American society.

"MEXI-AMERICA" FROM THE 1960s TO THE 1990s

Outside the southwestern states prior to the 1960s, Mexican Americans were a "forgotten" people, a "sleeping brown giant." They were relegated to obscurity and neglected by federal policymakers, whose concern for racial minorities was focused primarily on African Americans. Though the early civil rights movement had riveted national attention on the black freedom struggle in the South, nothing comparable had captured the imagination and moral conscience of Americans in the same way for Mexican Americans—at least not until the mid 1960s. Although the census has always undercounted the Mexican American population (variably defined by the Census Bureau after 1930 as Spanish mother tongue, Spanish-surname, or Spanish-origin), the spectacular growth and redistribution of the Mexican-origin population was plainly reflected in the figures from 1950 on. In the five southwestern states of California, Arizona, New Mexico, Colorado, and Texas, where approximately 90 percent of all Mexican Americans were concentrated in 1950, Spanish-surnamed people then numbered 2,290,000, according to the census. By 1960 their numbers in the region had increased to 3,465,000 (96 percent of whom were estimated to be of Mexican origin). A decade later the population of all Spanish-surnamed persons of Mexican origin (87 percent of whom resided in the Southwest) had increased to 4,532,000.

After World War II, Mexican Americans were one of the fastest-growing populations in the nation, a dramatic increase that was characterized by a more and more uneven distribution in certain states of the Southwest. During the first half of the twentieth century, for example, Texas was home to about half of all the Mexican Americans in the region (56 percent of the total Mexican immigrant population in 1910 and 42 percent in 1930), principally because immigrants from Mexico typically entered through and settled within this state. The other important demographic trend of these decades was the steady attraction of California as a destination for both Mexican immigrants and relocating Mexican Americans. By 1940, consequently, California contained 27 percent of all Mexican Americans in the Southwest, while 47 percent resided in Texas. By 1960, California's Mexican American population had reached parity with that of Texas; together the two states claimed 81 percent of all Spanish-origin people in the five southwestern states (the percentages were 6 percent in Arizona, 5 percent in Colorado, and 8 percent in New Mexico).

Another important development was the rapid urbanization of the Mexican American group. In 1930 and 1940 slightly over half of all Mexican Americans lived in cities. They were the most rapidly urbanizing group in the Southwest after World War II, a trend that continued unabated through the 1980s. In 1950, for instance, 66 percent of all Mexican Americans in the Southwest were urban dwellers; by 1960 the percentage had increased to 79 percent; and by 1970, 85 percent of the population was concentrated in cities, especially in the large metropolitan areas.

The changing demography of "Mexi-America" in the post-war decades is one of several factors that helps to explain why an unprecedented social reform movement came to fruition during the 1960s and 1970s. The Chicano movement was partly fueled by the growing numbers of Mexican Americans in urban areas and an increasingly large proportion of second- and third-generation persons—in 1960, for example, only 15 percent of the Spanish-surnamed people in the Southwest were foreign born, compared with 41 percent in 1930—who were critical of the lack of opportunities available to them and who openly scrutinized American institutions. But changing population and place-of-birth figures do not reveal other important developments of the period. For one, the term "Chicano" represented a change in orientation, especially among younger generational cohorts. Although the term had been used within many Mexican immigrant communities since the late nineteenth and early twentieth centuries, "Chicano" took on a new meaning among those who identified with and adopted the term. At one level, *chicanismo* (being Chicano) connoted a cultural identity, one which rejected assimilation as a goal and hyphenated terms such as "Mexican-American," "Latin-American," or "Spanish-surnamed American."

The cultural renaissance and ethnic and racial pride associated with the Chicano movement sprang from a nationalistic sense of group origins that emphasized native cultures and deemphasized American and European origins. The idea of *Aztlán,* the mythological homeland of the Aztec empire, which was believed to have originated in the region of the present-day Southwest, inspired many young people to conceive of themselves as having a historical claim to the region. This emphasis on Indian roots was clearly an influence of the Mexican Revolution and the popular cultural reorientation in Mexico during the 1920s and 1930s which exalted the achievements of pre-Conquest civilizations. Chicanos in the 1960s took great pride in their own revolutionary roots in Mexico and saw themselves as the inheritors of a revolutionary spirit. Perhaps most important, those who identified themselves as Chicanos in the 1960s were critical of American society for the discrimination, inequality, and lack of opportunities they saw in their communities.

In particular, Chicanos were adamant about the educational inequities of the public school education they received. De facto school segregation was indeed a persistent problem, and the realization that a larger percentage of Mexican American children attended segregated schools in 1970 than in 1940 encouraged activists to call for school reform. The lack of political representation at virtually every level of government was painfully obvious to those who sought support for their causes in city halls, statehouses, or Congress. Just as obvious to many observers was the fact that Chicanos had great difficulty breaking out of blue-collar work—in 1960 only about 8 percent of all gainfully employed Mexican Americans held professional or managerial occupations, a figure that increased in 1970 to about 11 percent.

Any explanation of the rise of the Chicano movement would be incomplete without reference to the civil rights movement and other organizations which influenced both the form and the substance of Mexican American efforts toward self-determination. Two currents from these movements were important parts of the Chicano movement: to make existing institutions more receptive and inclusive, and to establish a base from which these groups could help themselves. And, as many black leaders and organizations tied the contemporary efforts at reform to historical foundations, so did Chicanos.

The Chicano movement was, therefore, born of historical legacies and contemporary realities. It was, at the same time, a movement for cultural reorientation and socioeconomic and political reform. But what sparked this movement? Though cities were the hotbeds of Chicano activism, it was events in rural settings that ignited the flames of Chicano revolt. To Chicanos in the 1960s two developments in particular symbolized how historical problems manifested themselves in current issues. In the central California town of Delano, a group of Mexican American farm workers headed by César Chávez led a strike against local grape growers in 1965. Practicing nonviolent resistance, evoking Christian principles of brotherhood and compassion for the poor, rallying around a flag emblazoned with Mexican nationalist (the Aztec eagle, serpent, and cactus) and religious symbols (the Virgin of Guadalupe, the most revered religious figure in Mexican Catholicism), Chávez and his United Farm Workers (UFW) captured the imagination of urban Chicanos. The farm workers' movement attracted much media attention and support for its national and worldwide boycott of nonunion table grapes. Though modestly successful in its efforts to unionize farm workers and to negotiate contracts with major growers in California, the UFW was also partly responsible for inspiring Mexican Americans to organize and to struggle for opportunities in the face of seemingly overwhelming opposition. Finally, it seemed, Mexican agricultural workers had established a viable union after decades of futile effort.

At about the same time the UFW was in the process of formation, another historic struggle was unfolding. The issue of land loss among Spanish-speaking New Mexicans had roots extending back to the nineteenth century, but in 1963 Reies López Tijerina organized a group of New Mexicans who claimed that their ancestral land grants had been illegally acquired by white owners or by the federal government (the National Park Service and extensive national forest lands had enveloped many original Spanish and Mexican land grants). The Alianza Federal de Mercedes (Federal Alliance of Land Grants) galvanized New Mexicans who wanted action taken on their claims of rights to ownership of lands granted to their ancestors. Tension between local authorities and Alianza members resulted in a daring raid in 1967 by Tijerina and his followers on the courthouse in Tierra Amarilla to make a citizen's arrest of the district attorney responsible for jailing several of his compatriots. The ensuing manhunt for Tijerina foused national attention on the rural villages of New Mexico and the plight of the "Hispanos," a term many preferred. Though Tijerina was eventually tried and convicted of trespassing and destruction of federal property on national forestlands and served a prison term for his activities, the lasting significance of the Alianza was its boldness and confrontational tactics, which brought important issues to the attention of the public.

If movements of rural Mexican Americans served as the impetus for the emergence of the Chicano movement, it was in the urban areas that this phenomenon had its most effective cultural, artistic, and political organizational outcomes. Perhaps its most avid supporters were students. As a critical mass of Mexican American students collected on college campuses throughout the Southwest, groups were formed which became the hub of campus and sometimes community organizing. In 1967 many of these student organizations banded together in a loose confederation calling itself Movimiento Estudiantil Chicano de Aztlán (MEChA; Chicano Student Movement of Aztlán). Members of many of these student organizations later moved into leadership positions in other movement groups. For example, José Angel Gutiérrez, cofounder of the Mexican American Youth Organization (MAYO) at St. Mary's College in San Antonio, Texas, in 1967 went on to lead an important third political party for Chicanos, the Partido Raza Unida (Party of United People). Willie Velásquez, another MAYO leader, subsequently helped found the Southwest Voter Registration Education Project (1974).

Perhaps the most visible developments of the Chicano movement were the hundreds of local organizations serving barrio residents. Funded by the federal War on Poverty, by local or state agencies, and sometimes by private foundations, an expanding cadre of organizations ranging from legal aid and medical clinics, to educational support programs, to community development corporations focusing on the economic infrastructure of Mexican American communities was founded. As more Mexican Americans entered the ranks of professionals, one of the offshoots was the establishment of professional associations in education, law, mental health, health care, and other fields. These Chicano professionals and veteran Mexican American organizers in the 1960s helped to establish national advocacy and civil rights groups such as the Mexican American Legal Defense and Education Fund and the National Council of La Raza (formerly the Southwest Council). These groups, concerned directly with policy issues of political and economic opportunity, were built on the foundation of organizations which had emerged earlier in the 1960s, such as the Mexican American Political Association in California and the Political Association of Spanish-Speaking Organizations in Texas.

The Chicano movement was an important catalyst for cultural reorientation and organizational reform initiatives, yet it does not convey the full picture of Mexican American society. Many Mexican Americans oppose those Chicano movement activities they consider to be too radical. Even within the movement's groups and leaders, there are competing ideological views and objectives. No one leader has emerged to speak for Mexican Americans nationwide, and no one organization has claimed to represent all Mexican Americans.

RECENT DEMOGRAPHIC TRENDS

The phenomenal growth of the Mexican-origin population since 1970 was revealed in the 1980 and 1990 U.S. censuses. Even though sizable undercounts were acknowledged by the Census Bureau for both enumerations, the aggregate figures clearly tell the story. Between 1970 and 1980 the Mexican-origin population nearly doubled, from 4.5 million to 8.7 million persons. The historical regional concentration of these people continues through the late twentieth century: 83 percent of all Mexican-origin people lived in the five southwestern states in 1980 (California contained 42 percent of the total and Texas 31.5 percent). The Mexican-origin population increased by 54 percent between 1980 and 1990, to 13.5 million persons. Between 1970 and 1980 natural increase—the excess of births over deaths—probably accounted for about two-thirds of the growth. More than one-third of the growth was attributable to immigration, both legal and illegal, the latter figure being perhaps twice as large (undocumented immigrants from Mexico in 1980 probably numbered somewhere near 1.5 million). High rates of natural growth continue, with no end in sight, because of the relatively youthful Mexican American population and the higher fertility rates among Mexican American and Mexican immigrant women of childbearing age. Likewise, there is no end in sight to undocumented immigration from Mexico as long as severe problems in its economy drive hundreds of thousands to cross the border to work in America. Obviously, a very large number who participate in the cyclical and chain migrations (the social and institutional relationships that link migrants to sending and receiving communities) from their communities of origin stay in America indefinitely. Regardless of immigration legislation passed by Congress or tightening of controls along the border, Mexican and Central American immigrants will take the risks necessary to enter America in search of work and a better life.

The ongoing process of immigration from Mexico to the United States during the twentieth century is unique in American history. Perhaps more so than any single factor, recurrent immigration has had the most dramatic effects on the size and character of the Mexican American population. Immigration from Mexico, however, is only one of many historical forces that have shaped this large, diverse ethnic group. The interplay of circumstances which established Mexican Americans as a national minority in the nineteenth-century Southwest, combined with the consequences of four successive waves of immigration from Mexico, has marked a history that cannot be explained simply as the saga of another immigrant group's cultural adjustment to American society. On the other hand, Mexican American history cannot be properly understood only in terms of race or class relations. The history of Mexican Americans contains elements of both of these and other perspectives. Indeed, as a group constantly subject to both domestic and international influences, Mexican Americans in the late twentieth century—one of the largest ethnic groups in American society—are still very much a part of a dynamic historical process of social change.

CENTRAL AMERICANS IN THE UNITED STATES

Anyone visiting the immediate west side of downtown Los Angeles, San Francisco's Mission District, or the Mt. Pleasant/Adams Morgan areas of Washington, D.C., cannot help but notice the growth of relatively new neighborhoods composed of immigrants from Central American nations. Salvadoran restaurants, discos catering to Nicaraguans, or small stores which rely on their Guatemalan customers dot these and other urban landscapes where Central American immigrants have settled. But it is only within the past fifteen years that these and other communities of Spanish-speaking immigrants from the small neighboring nations of the middle Americas have formed (there are a few exceptions, however, such as the Guatemalan-origin community in New Orleans which has deeper historical roots). Prior to 1970 the number of Central Americans in the United States was very small, but since 1975 a variety of factors combined to increase dramatically the size and visibility of emerging barrios and smaller residential clusters of immigrants and their children in cities scattered across the United States.

The central theme in understanding the history of recent immigration from Central American countries is one that is familiar to most immigrants—the search for jobs and economic opportunity across international boundaries. Economic instability and insecurity in most Central American nations is as much at the heart of contemporary immigration to the U.S. as it is for immigrants who come to the U.S. from Mexico. The lure of job prospects and higher wages is a strong magnet attracting immigrants north. Yet, for a large number of immigrants, especially those from El Salvador, Nicaragua, and Guatemala, other critical factors are at play. Explanations of why thousands of Central Americans continue to flee their countries cannot be separated from other important historical dimensions of U.S. immigration history. One cannot deny that economic imperatives draw immigrants from Central America, but political and institutional imperatives are just as important. In war-torn nations such as El Salvador, Nicaragua, and Guatemala, years of civil war and internecine violence have so disrupted city and countryside alike that tens of thousands have left out of desperation. In addition, political repression and human rights violations have compelled others to escape their countries or face political repercussions and possible death. Dislocation, both economic and political, is thus the twin-push factor accounting for the immigration of most immigrants from Central American nations.

Though more and more immigrants from Central American countries were granted legal resident alien status after 1970 when immigration quotas were liberalized (6,510 were granted legal status in 1960 as compared to 19,848 in 1980, for example), far greater numbers arrived as undocumented, or illegal, aliens. After the passage of the Refugee Act of 1980, signed into law by President Jimmy Carter, hundreds of Salvadorans and Guatemalans applied for refugee status though few were able to qualify for asylum under the new provisions. Consequently, as the domestic situation in many Central American nations deteriorated further during the 1970s and 1980s, tens of thousands entered the United States clandestinely.

The relatively recent formation of communities of immigrants from Central American countries was aptly reflected in the 1980 U.S. census. In that year, the census enumerated 331,219 persons born in Central American countries, 38 percent of whom entered the United States between 1975 and 1980, and another 23 percent who immigrated between 1970 and 1974. Only 14 percent of all Central Americans in the United States in 1980 had arrived prior to 1960. Among the largest national-origin groups identified in the 1980 census were Salvadoran immigrants who numbered over 94,000 (half of whom entered between 1975 and 1980), Guatemalans totaled some 63,000 (46 percent of whom arrived during the second half of the 1970s), with Nicaraguan, Honduran, and Costa Rican immigrant populations ranging roughly between about 50,000 and 30,000.

During the 1980s, the total population of Central Americans—both immigrant and native born—increased dramatically (the Census Bureau's Current Population Studies reports combined figures for South Americans and Central Americans). For example, in 1979 Central and South Americans totaled 840,000; they comprised 7 percent of the Hispanic-origin population. By 1982 their numbers increased to over 1.5 million (9.9 percent of all Hispanics) and by 1989 their total population had reached 2.5 million (12.7 percent of the Hispanic-origin group).

The geographical areas of the United States in which Central American immigrants and their children continue to settle in many ways resemble the patterns long established by Mexican immigrants throughout the twentieth century with some notable exceptions. Not surprisingly, California cities attract the largest numbers of Central Americans, with Los Angeles and San Francisco serving as the poles of population concentration. Salvadorans, the most numerous national-origin group among Central Americans, constituted, for example, the third largest group of legal immigrants in San Francisco and the fourth largest in Los Angeles, comprising between 5 percent and 6 percent of all legal immigrants in these cities in 1987. In California as a whole, the number of Hispanics recorded in the census counts of 1980 and 1990 graphically illustrate the rapid growth of both the Mexican-origin and Central American–origin populations. In 1980, for example, California Hispanics numbered 4.5 million (19.3 percent of the total population in the state), 80 percent of whom were of Mexican origin and 18 percent of whom were Central American or South American in origin. The 1990 census counted 8.1 million Hispanics (26.3 percent of the state population), and assuming the ratio of Central/South Americans to Mexican-origin people was fairly constant over the decade, the population of Central Americans increased probably by as many as 600,000. The number of Central Americans in California in 1990 was about 1.5 million.

Outside of the more traditional areas of settlement in California and the West, however, a large number of Central Americans—primarily Salvadoran immigrants—have gravitated to the nation's capital over the past fifteen years. Here, too, they comprised about 6 percent of all documented immigrants who had settled in Washington, D.C., in 1987. Some preliminary studies suggest that many undocumented Central Americans came to Washington temporarily while waiting for decisions to be rendered on their applications for asylum as refugees, while others settled in the capital because they believed the Immigration and Naturalization Service (INS) was less likely to identify and apprehend them if they did not live in Los Angeles or San Francisco. Whatever the initial reasons which drew Salvadorans and other Central American immigrants to Washington, D.C., the inertia of immigration and settlement, there as in other locales, adds to the growth of Spanish-speaking enclaves. In this sense, the process of community building among Central American immigrants resembles greatly the patterns exhibited by most immigrant peoples coming to America.

The expansion of the Hispanic-origin community in Washington, D.C., between 1980 and 1990 provides a good example of the effects of immigration and net population growth among Central Americans in certain cities. In 1980, 17,679 Hispanic-origin persons were enumerated in the federal census; they constituted 2.8 percent of the total population in the capital. In 1990, the census count indicated that the number of Hispanics in the District, at 32,710, had nearly doubled. According to official census figures, the Hispanic-origin population increased by 85 percent between 1980 and 1990; they accounted for 5.4 percent of the total population in Washington, D.C., in 1990. In 1991, however, the Mayor's Office on Latino Affairs estimated the total number of Hispanics (both illegal and legal) to be at least 65,000, or about 10 percent of the city's population. An even higher percentage was recently suggested by Latino community-based organizations in Washington who estimated that Hispanics constitute about 12 percent of the total population, or about 85,000 people. The actual figures are, of course, somewhere between the official Bureau of Census count and the higher estimates.

The increase in the size of the Hispanic population between 1980 and 1990 was due to both international migration and natural increase (net growth due to the larger number of births over deaths). The official census figures for Hispanics in general in 1980 and 1990, and for Central American–origin persons with no exception, included both undocumented and legal immigrants. There is little doubt that more Central Americans were enumerated in the 1990 census as legal alien residents than in 1980 simply because of the number who applied for legal permanent status under the "amnesty" provisions of the 1986 Immigration Reform and Control Act. In addition, the Immigration Act of 1990 included provisions, under the "Temporary Protected Status" (TPS) sections of the law, which allowed tens of thousands of Central Americans and other refugees to apply for work permits and temporary legal status for a limited amount of time without being subject to deportation. This act specifically granted refugees from El Salvador the right to apply for temporary status for an eighteen-month period beginning in 1991. By April 1991 approximately 130,000 Salvadorans had registered under the TPS provisions. The largest number of registrants were reported in the eastern region (the Washington, D.C., metropolitan area reported the highest number of registrants in the nation) and in the western region.

Regardless of the increase in the number of legal immigrants counted in the 1990 census, the fact remains that the census obviously undercounted thousands of Central American immigrants, especially those without papers. For fear of contact with federal authorities—that might possibly result in apprehension and deportation by the INS—unknown numbers of immigrants were not counted in 1980 and in 1990. Though the numbers are impossible to estimate in any accurate way, the official census figures are generally considered to be quite conservative.

Whether Central Americans are enumerated accurately or not, it is obvious to even the casual observer that their communities continue to grow and, at the same time, to face great difficulties adjusting to life in urban America. They are largely a poor, working-class population overly concentrated in low-paid, service-sector jobs or low-skill manufacturing jobs. Central American women in cities such as Los Angeles and Washington, D.C., commonly work as domestics, both in the hotel industry and in private households, while others may be employed in the garment industry or other minimum-wage jobs. Central American men, too, are typically employed in such low-wage jobs as construction laborers, restaurant workers, or in other service-oriented employment. Low wages and limited resources for a majority of Central Americans in the United States often results in overcrowded and substandard housing. These conditions are painfully visible in many communities of Central Americans and in at least one case—the Mt. Pleasant area of Washington, D.C.—dissatisfaction and pent-up frustrations among Spanish-speaking residents were unleashed in demonstrations of civil disobedience. In a scenario reminiscent of the so-called race riots in African American ghettos and Mexican American barrios during the 1960s and early 1970s, violence erupted for three nights in May 1991 in the Mt. Pleasant area. Sparked by residents' protests against alleged police brutality of a Central American who had been arrested in the neighborhood, angry crowds battled police and in the process a considerable amount of private property was damaged or destroyed. In the wake of the disturbance, a Latino Civil Rights Task Force was formed in the District and later issued a report to the mayor calling for a fair share of jobs, social services, and educational and recreational opportunities for the Latino community.

The political mobilization of Hispanics in Washington, D.C., is dramatic evidence of the growth and proliferation of communities composed of Central American immigrants and their native-born children. Though they are among the most recent of Hispanic-origin groups to settle in the United States, Central Americans are likely to increase in number as a result of unsettled economic and political conditions in their countries. Though small in overall numbers relative to Mexican Americans, there is every indication the various national-origin groups which comprise the Central American population in the U.S. will continue to grow much larger in the years and decades ahead. Like other Hispanic immigrant groups before them, Central Americans will struggle to gain an economic foothold in American society while they attempt to maintain the most important aspects of their unique national and ethnic cultures.

BIBLIOGRAPHY

General Works and Bibliographic Sources
Acuña, Rodolfo F. *Occupied America: A History of Chicanos.* 3d ed. (1988).
Barrera, Mario. *Race and Class in the Southwest: A Theory of Racial Inequality* (1979).
Camarillo, Albert. *Mexican Americans in Urban Society: A Selected Bibliography* (1986).

————, ed. *Latinos in the United States: A Historical Bibliography* (1986).

Grebler, Leo, Joan W. Moore, and Ralph C. Guzmán. *The Mexican American People: The Nation's Second Largest Minority* (1970).

McWilliams, Carey. *North from Mexico: The Spanish Speaking People of the United States* (1948; new ed., rev. by Matt S. Meier, 1990).

Meier, Matt S. *Mexican American Biographies: A Historical Dictionary, 1836–1987* (1988).

————, comp. *Bibliography of Mexican American History* (1984).

Meier, Matt S., and Feliciano Rivera. *The Chicanos: A History of Mexican Americans* (1972).

Topical and Thematic Studies

Acuña, Rodolfo F. *A Community Under Siege: A Chronicle of Chicanos East of the Los Angeles River, 1945–1975* (1984).

Allsup, Carl. *The American G.I. Forum: Origins and Evolution,* Mexican American Monographs no. 6 (1982).

Balderrama, Francisco E. *In Defense of La Raza: The Los Angeles Mexican Consulate and the Mexican Community, 1929 to 1936* (1982).

Camarillo, Albert. *Chicanos in a Changing Society: From Mexican Pueblos to American Barrios in Santa Barbara and Southern California, 1848–1930* (1979).

————. *Chicanos in California: A History of Mexican Americans in California* (1984).

Chávez, John. *The Lost Land: The Chicano Image of the Southwest* (1984).

De Léon, Arnoldo. *The Tejano Community, 1836–1900* (1982).

————. *They Called Them Greasers: Anglo Attitudes Toward Mexicans in Texas, 1821–1900* (1983).

Deutsch, Sarah. *No Separate Refuge: Culture, Class, and Gender on an Anglo-Hispanic Frontier in the American Southwest, 1880–1940* (1987).

Galarza, Ernesto. *Merchants of Labor: The Mexican Bracero Story* (1964).

Gamio, Manuel. *The Mexican Immigrant: His Life Story* (1931; repr. 1971 as *The Life Story of the Mexican Immigrant*).

García, Mario T. *Desert Immigrants: The Mexicans of El Paso, 1880–1920* (1981).

————. *Mexican-Americans: Leadership, Ideology, and Identity, 1930–1960* (1989).

Gómez-Quiñones, Juan. *Chicano Politics: Reality and Promise, 1940–1990* (1990).

Griswold del Castillo, Richard Allan. *The Los Angeles Barrio, 1850–1890: A Social History* (1979).

————. *La Familia: Chicano Families in the Urban Southwest, 1848 to the Present* (1984).

Gutiérrez, Ramón A. *When Jesus Came, the Corn Mothers Went Away: Marriage, Sexuality, and Power in New Mexico, 1500–1846* (1991).

Hoffman, Abraham. *Unwanted Mexican Americans in the Great Depression: Repatriation Pressures, 1929–1939* (1974).

Lane, James B., and Edward J. Escobar, eds. *Forging a Community: The Latino Experience in Northwest Indiana, 1917–1975* (1987).

Massey, Douglas, Rafael Alarcón, Jorge Durand, and Humberto González. *Return to Aztlan: The Social Process of International Migration from Western Mexico* (1987).

Mazón, Mauricio. *The Zoot-Suit Riots: The Psychology of Symbolic Annihilation* (1984).

Montejano, David. *Anglos and Mexicans in the Making of Texas, 1836–1986* (1987).

Muñoz, Carlos. *Youth, Identity, Power: The Chicano Generation* (1989).

Pitt, Leonard. *The Decline of the Californios: A Social History of the Spanish-speaking Californians, 1846–1890* (1966).

Portes, Alejandro, and Robert L. Bach. *Latin Journey: Cuban and Mexican Immigrants in the United States* (1985).

Robinson, Cecil. *Mexico and the Hispanic Southwest in American Literature* (1977).

Romo, Ricardo. *East Los Angeles: History of a Barrio* (1983).

Rosenbaum, Robert J. *Mexicano Resistance in the Southwest: "The Sacred Right of Self-Preservation"* (1981).

Ruiz, Vicki L. *Cannery Women, Cannery Lives: Mexican Women, Unionization, and the California Food Processing Industry, 1930–1950* (1987).

Samora, Julian. *Los Mojados: The Wetback Story* (1971).

Sánchez, George I. *Forgotten People: A Study of New Mexicans* (1940; repr. 1967).

Sheridan, Thomas E. *Los Tucsonenses: The Mexican Community in Tucson, 1854–1941* (1986).

Valdés, Dennis N. *Al Norte: Agricultural Workers in the Great Lakes Region, 1917–1970* (1990).

Weber, David J. *The Mexican Frontier, 1821–1846: The American Southwest Under Mexico* (1982).

Central Americans

Bean, Frank D. et al., eds. *Mexican and Central American Population and U.S. Immigration Policy* (1989).

Bean, Frank D., Barry Edmonston, and Jeffrey S. Passel, eds. *Undocumented Migration to the United States: IRCA and the Experiences of the 1980s* (1990).

Bouvier, Leon F. *Fifty Million Californians?* (1991).

Camarillo, Albert. *Latinos in the United States: A Historical Bibliography* (1986).

Peterson, Linda S. *Central American Migration: Past and Present* (1986).

Public Law 101-469, 101st U.S. Congress. *Immigration Act of 1990* (29 November 1990).

Rodriguez, Nestor P. "Undocumented Central Americans in Houston: Diverse Populations." *International Migration Review* (Spring 1987).

Wallace, Steven P. "Central American and Mexican Immigrant Characteristics and Economic Incorporation in California." *International Migration Review* (Fall 1986).

Washington, D.C., Latino Civil Rights Task Force, *The Latino Blueprint for Action* (October 1991).

SEE ALSO **California; Ethnicity; Immigration; Minorities and Work; The Southwest.**

ASIAN AMERICANS

Roger Daniels

ASIAN AMERICANS, a conglomerate term first used in the late 1960s and early 1970s, refers to immigrants from East and South Asia and their descendants, and, increasingly, to some Pacific islanders as well. It is not used for Caucasians born in Soviet Asia—of whom there are very few in the United States—nor for Iranians and other Asians from the region west of Pakistan generally known as the Middle East. Although there are historical reasons for treating Asian Americans as "a minority," they are, in fact, very distinct minorities. One need only think of how peculiar it would be to make generalizations about "European Americans"—a term that hardly exists in the literature—to understand how inappropriate, in some ways, the category Asian American is.

Before 1980 the Bureau of the Census enumerated only a few Asian groups separately. In that year for the first time it took special notice of a large number of Asian groups and created a new category, "Asian and Pacific Islander," which did not include natives of Australia and New Zealand. It is clearly intended to describe racial categories. Table 1, from the 1980 census, shows the variety of peoples involved.

The more specific enumeration reflects two contradictory phenomena: the great increase in the number of Asian Americans, both immigrant and native born, and the essentially racist nature of even supposedly neutral statistical categories. Almost no one uses the term "Euro-American" because, after a generation or two, all "white people" are simply seen as "Americans," although some residual ethnic identifications remain, especially for those who are not descended from northern European Protestants. The Protestant Ronald Reagan, for example, could be "Irish" when he wanted to; the Catholic John Kennedy had no real choice in the matter; and George Bush is not regarded as having any particular ethnic ties. Asian Americans, along with blacks and Hispanics, are so categorized even if their ancestors have been in America for generations, as are American Indians, who preceded the rest of us by millennia.

CHINESE AMERICANS TO 1943

Although a handful of Chinese came to the eastern United States in the early national period as seamen and supercargoes in the China trade and a few Filipinos had come, via Mexico, to Louisiana in the eighteenth century, numerically significant immigration from Asia to the American West was roughly contemporary with the California gold rush of 1849. Between that time and 1882 perhaps 250,000 Chinese emigrated to the United States, a small fraction of the Chinese diaspora that took large numbers of Chinese laborers and merchants to the four corners of the earth in the nineteenth century. Many in that diaspora, including most of the tens of thousands of Chinese who went to Cuba and Peru, were indentured laborers, or coolies. Despite the claims of some historians, the Chinese who came to North America were free immigrants.

The Chinese who came to the American West were overwhelmingly (more than 90 percent) male and almost exclusively from the Pearl River delta of Guangdong Province. Although the immigration was predominantly of laborers, some students, merchants, and political exiles also came. Many, probably most, of the immigrants intended to work for a time in the "Golden Mountain," as the Chinese characters for California may be translated, and then return, rich men, to China. Some actually did so, but most of those who survived remained poor and became settlers rather than sojourners, as did large numbers of nineteenth-century male immigrants from Europe who came with the same intention.

Three factors set these Chinese immigrants apart from other immigrants: their race, the region

TABLE 1   Asian and Pacific Islander Groups,
1980 Census

Asian	Pacific Islander
Chinese*	Polynesian
Japanese*	Hawaiian*
Asian Indian*	Samoan*
Korean*	Tahitian
Vietnamese*	Tongan
Bangladeshi	Other Polynesian
Burmese	Tokelauan
Cambodian	Polynesian
(Kampuchea)	Micronesian
Hmong	Guamanian*
Indonesian	Other Mariana Islander
Laotian	Saipanese
Malayan	Tinian Islander
Okinawan	Mariana Islander
Pakistani	Marshallese
Sri Lankan (Ceylonese)	Marshall Islander
Thai	Eniwetok Islander
Asian not specified[1]	Bikini Islander
All other Asians	Kwajalein Islander
Bhutanese	Palawan
Borneo	Other Micronesian
Celebesian	Micronesian
Cernan	Ponapean
Indochinese	Trukese
Iwo Jiman	Yapese
Javanese	Carolinian
Maldivian	Tarawa Islander
Nepali	Melanesian
Sikkim	Fijian
Singaporean	Other Melanesian
	Melanesian
	Papua New Guinean
	Solomon Islander
	New Hebrides Islander
	Other Pacific Islander[2]

*Listed separately on the 1980 census questionnaire.

[1]Includes entries such as "Asian American," "Asian," and "Asiatic."

[2]Includes persons who did not provide a specific answer but reported "Pacific Islander."

Source: U.S. Bureau of the Census, *Asian and Pacific Islander Population . . .* , PC 80-S1-12 (1983).

to which they came, and the unique discrimination they encountered. The Radical Republican senator from Indiana, Oliver P. Morton (1823–1877), after chairing an investigation of Chinese immigration, concluded correctly that "if the Chinese in California were white people, being in all other respects what they are, I do not believe that the complaints and warfare made against them would have existed to any considerable extent."

Throughout the nineteenth century more than 90 percent of the American Chinese lived in the ten westernmost states, and more than two-thirds were in California. As was the case with most other immigrant groups, the Chinese were significantly more urban than the nation at large. One city, San Francisco, the undisputed capital of Chinese America, was home to nearly a quarter of the nation's 107,000 Chinese in 1890.

A virulent anti-Chinese movement developed in California in the late 1860s and quickly spread to other parts of the nation. Based on the economic opposition of organized workingmen to "cheap Chinese labor," it had, from its inception, a thoroughly racist character, as did the "pro-Chinese" arguments of employers and their spokesmen. Although the agitator Denis Kearney insisted that "the Chinese must GO!," the movement's real goal was to halt Chinese immigration. Since control of immigration was federal, the legal and extralegal harassment of Chinese by state laws and local ordinances, as well as by persistent mob violence, was ineffective.

Although no significant impediment to Chinese immigration was effected until 1882, the Naturalization Act of 1870 would blight the lives of Asian Americans for more than eighty years. The adoption of the Fourteenth Amendment in 1868 made most black Americans citizens. Logic necessitated a change in the naturalization statute that had, since 1790, restricted naturalization to "free white persons." Although Republican Senator Charles Sumner of Massachusetts and a few others wanted to make naturalization color-blind, explicit anti-Chinese sentiment in Congress caused the legislators to limit the right of naturalization to "white persons and persons of African descent." Thus Asian immigrants were placed in a unique category: they were, as the phrase went, "aliens ineligible to citizenship." However, the Fourteenth Amendment, drafted at a time when few outside of California were concerned with Chinese, had categorically stated that "all persons born or naturalized" in the United States were citizens of both nation and state, so that second-generation Asians had, on paper at least, the same rights as others.

Twelve years later, after several false starts, the anti-Chinese movement won its great victory: the Chinese Exclusion Act of 1882. The 1882 law had a ten-year limitation; it was renewed in 1892 and made "permanent" in 1902. This act was the hinge on which all American immigration policy turned. Prior to 1882 there were no significant legal impediments to the entry of healthy immigrants of any nationality to the United States. But once Chinese had been restricted, other restrictions followed—restrictions that barred not only other ethnic groups but also the very poor (persons "likely to become a public charge"), certain radicals, polygamists (aimed against Mormons, not Muslims), illiterates, and the mentally disturbed.

Despite its name, the act did not exclude all Chinese. Merchants, their families, students, and elite travelers could enter the country, and certain former residents could return, but Chinese laborers were barred. Between its enactment and its repeal in 1943, American immigration records show nearly ninety-five thousand Chinese entered legally, an annual average of about fifteen hundred. Very few of these were female. Between 1906 and 1924 an annual average of 150 alien Chinese wives of "treaty merchants" were admitted. This immigration was ended by the Immigration Act of 1924. A 1930 law relaxed the ban somewhat, allowing the resumption of immigration by merchants' wives if the marriage predated the 1924 law. About sixty women a year entered under this provision between 1930 and December 1941. The effect of these laws on Chinese American population and demography was severe, as Table 2 shows.

The steady decline of the Chinese American population from the 1880s (there was an intercensal population peak of perhaps 125,000 in 1882) to the 1920s and the persistence of a sex-ratio characteristic of the early stages of migration are unique in the history of American ethnic groups. Thus the Chinese American community was an aging one. In 1920, for example, more than a third (35.6 percent) of Chinese males were over fifty years of age, and the median age was forty-two years. Chinese females, on the other hand, predominantly native born, were a young population. Nearly 70 percent were under thirty years of age, and their median age was nineteen years. Such a population, in which there were few women and families and always more older men than younger ones, was not likely to be as receptive to acculturation as were most other immigrant communities. The largely bachelor society that dominated Chinese America until after World War II was highly conservative. Although Chinese still lived predominantly in the western states, their tendency was to disperse slowly. By 1940 a bare majority (51 percent) lived in California and just over three-fifths (60.4 percent) lived in the ten westernmost states. New York City was home to twelve thousand Chinese, more than in all the western states other than California combined, and another three thousand lived in Chicago and Boston. There were few cities of any size that did not have at least one or two Chinese businesses, typically laundries and restaurants.

Chinese labor played an important and little-appreciated part in the economic development of the American West. Chinese built railroads, were miners, cleared land, and were pioneers in market gardening and other forms of agriculture in California and elsewhere in the West. After 1880 more and more Chinese lived in large cities and engaged in urban pursuits. Chinese-owned laundries and restaurants—labor-intensive businesses requiring little capital—employed more and more of them. While some laundries were family-owned and -operated businesses, like the one described in Maxine Hong Kingston's marvelous book *The Woman Warrior*, others employed large numbers of single men at minimal wages and under abominable working conditions. From the very first there were successful Chinese entrepreneurs, and the wealthiest merchants in cities such as San Francisco, New York, and Seattle were as well off as all but the richest Gilded Age magnates.

TABLE 2   Chinese American Population: Sex, Citizenship, and Sex Ratio, 1860–1940

Year	Male	Female	Total	Ratio	Citizen	Alien
1860	33,149	1,784	34,933	18.6:1	n/a	n/a
1870	58,663	4,556	63,199	12.8:1	n/a	n/a
1880	100,686	4,779	105,465	21.1:1	n/a	n/a
1890	103,620	3,868	107,488	26.8:1	n/a	n/a
1900	85,341	4,522	89,863	18.9:1	9,010	80,853
1910	66,858	4,675	71,531	14.3:1	14,935	56,596
1920	53,891	7,748	61,639	7.0:1	18,532	43,107
1930	59,802	15,152	74,954	3.9:1	30,868	44,086
1940	57,389	20,115	77,505	2.9:1	40,262	37,242

Source: U.S. Census data.

After the passage of the exclusion act many Chinese became the first illegal immigrants in American history. Chinese not only crossed the borders illegally and jumped ship but they also took advantage of a natural disaster and American law to perpetrate an elaborate immigration fraud: the "paper sons" scam. The great San Francisco earthquake and fire of 1906 destroyed the Bay City's vital statistics records. Under American law native-born Chinese who returned to China and fathered children there could bring the children—but not their alien mothers—to the United States. Those who had successfully established American citizenship often sold the "slots" that their trips to China created or brought in cousins or other kinsmen rather than sons. It is clear that large numbers of the male citizens recorded in the census were paper sons. In 1930, for example, the census recorded 20,693 male Chinese American citizens and only 10,175 females in that category. Under normal conditions the numbers should have been roughly equal. Community members were now willing to talk about the fraud. One paper son told Victor and Brett de Bary Nee:

In the beginning my father came in as a laborer. But the 1906 earthquake came along and destroyed all those immigration things. So that was a big chance for a lot of Chinese. They forged themselves certificates saying that they were born in this country, and when the time came, they could go back to China and bring back four or five sons, just like that! They might make a little money off it, not much, but the main thing was to bring a son or a nephew or a cousin in. (*Longtime Californ'*, p. 63)

The onset of the Great Depression ended that kind of immigration, and the war years brought major changes to both Chinese immigration and Chinese American life.

JAPANESE AMERICANS TO 1941

Numerically significant immigration of Japanese to the American mainland began in the 1890s, although it had been preceded by a scattering of exiles, students, merchants, and a few laborers since the late 1860s, and by a sizable labor immigration to Hawaii. Table 3 shows the mainland population up to the eve of World War II.

The pattern of Japanese migration and settlement was both similar to and different from that of the Chinese. Like the Chinese, the Japanese migrants were predominantly single men who worked in the American Far West. But, unlike the Chinese, the Japanese migration stream became dominated by females after 1908 and the geographical concentration in the American West and California increased with every census in the period under consideration. In 1900, 75.1 percent of the mainland Japanese lived on the West Coast and 41.7 percent were in California; by 1940 the figures had grown to 89 percent and 73.8 percent, respectively. Occupational patterns also were different: while the Chinese had become highly urban, the Japanese population remained more rural than the nation as a whole; as late as 1940, 54.9 percent of all Japanese lived in rural areas, reflecting their continued concentration in agriculture.

There are complex reasons for these dissimilarities, but the different limitations placed upon them by American law and society are clearly major factors. Chinese American society, as we have seen, was frozen by the Chinese Exclusion Act of 1882 and its successors in an essentially bachelor-society mode. There was agitation, as early as the 1890s, for a "Japanese Exclusion Act," and there can be little doubt that, had Japan not been a rising Pacific power, such a legislative restriction would have been effected in the first decade of this century. The agitation eventually outraged President Theodore Roosevelt, who condemned the "idiots" of the California legislature and noted that "the mob of a single city may at any time perform acts of lawless violence which would plunge us into war." He first settled the San Francisco School Board affair and then negotiated the Gentlemen's Agreement with Japan in 1907–1908.

The School Board affair arose in 1906 when San Francisco's school authorities ordered all Japanese pupils to attend the long-established segregated school for Chinese. When public and governmental protests emanated from Tokyo, Roosevelt verbally attacked the "unjust" order. In actuality there was little the president could do because the "separate but equal" doctrine made segregation the law of the land. He and Secretary of State Elihu Root were prepared to file suit, but only on behalf of alien Japanese children whose rights, the government intended to claim, were protected by treaty. In the event, no suit ever came to trial. The San Franciscans backed down, Japanese children continued to go to regular schools (as did the few black children in San Francisco), and Chinese continued to be segregated. In a few rural California school districts Japanese pupils were segregated, but since no public fuss was made about it,

TABLE 3   Japanese American Population: Sex, Sex Ratio, and Citizenship
1890–1940

Year	Male	Female	Total	Ratio	Citizen	Alien
1890	1,780	259	2,090	6.9:1	n/a	n/a
1900	23,341	985	24,326	24.3:1	n/a	n/a
1910	63,070	9,087	72,157	6.9:1	n/a	n/a
1920	72,707	38,308	111,010	1.9:1	29,672	81,339
1930	81,771	57,063	138,834	1.4:1	68,357	70,477
1940	71,967	54,980	126,947	1.3:1	79,642	47,305

Source: U.S. Census data.

Tokyo never complained. In the rest of California and the nation, Japanese students went to unsegregated schools. Chinese were segregated in a few California cities and in Mississippi, but not elsewhere.

Once the school question was settled, Roosevelt turned his attention to the immigration issue, as he had promised the Californians he would do as part of the bargain that settled the school controversy. The Gentlemen's Agreement allowed Japan to save face by forbidding laborers to obtain passports valid for the United States. (Many Japanese who would have emigrated to North America went instead to Brazil.) But Japanese who were resident in the United States were able to bring over wives and children. Some already had families; others either returned to Japan to get married or had marriages arranged for them with "picture brides."

The result was, as Table 3 shows, an extremely rapid drop in the sex ratio. The existence of growing Japanese family units provided the cheap and controllable labor force on which Japanese success in agriculture was based. As early as 1920, although Japanese controlled only about 1 percent of California's agricultural acreage, Japanese farmers reaped some 10 percent of the cash value of California's crop.

Conversely, the increased strength of western labor unions, a strength that had been nurtured by labor's anti-Chinese struggle, kept Japanese out of industrial pursuits they might otherwise have entered. Japanese American success in agriculture prompted California and other western states to pass so-called alien land acts. These acts, beginning in California in 1913, were directed only against landownership by "aliens ineligible to citizenship," which meant Asians. Although the laws also discriminated against Chinese, Asian Indians, Filipinos, and Koreans, they were aimed at Japanese. When these laws proved ineffective, subsequent ones, such as the California alien land law of 1920, banned land-leasing and sharecropping contracts involving "aliens ineligible to citizenship."

These statutes, too, proved largely nugatory. Legal avoidance was possible in two ways: those Japanese agriculturalists who were particularly well-off, such as the issei entrepreneur George Shima (1863–1926), who pioneered and dominated the growing of potatoes in California and controlled many thousands of acres of prime cropland, simply had Caucasian lawyers form American corporations for them. More common was the legal expedient of putting land or contracts in the names of native-born citizen children. Those who had no native-born children often adopted one. When California attempted to make such guardianship by an "alien ineligible to citizenship" illegal, the federal courts intervened, holding that the citizen children had a natural right to have their parents as guardians. Perhaps the sorriest application of the alien land laws came during and just after World War II. When, as sometimes happened, a nisei "landowner" was killed serving in the United States military, the state of California instituted successful escheat proceedings against the surviving alien guardian.

Thus, for a time, Japanese immigrants had a double protection. Some of their rights were protected by the Constitution; others, such as the right to reunify families, were protected because Japan was a growing military power that the executive branch, at least, did not wish to offend. But this latter protection could last only so long in a democratic society. In the years before and during World War I, powerful presidents restrained some of the excesses of a racist democracy. Although Congress passed a "barred zone" act in 1917, which kept out most Asian groups, Japanese were not included. The weak presidential leadership of the 1920s could not withstand those pressures. In the 1924 immigration act, against the wishes of the executive branch, Congress bowed to the popular will and abrogated the Gentlemen's Agreement by barring all "aliens ineligible to citizenship."

Although that restriction blocked further Japanese immigration—without it Japan would have received an annual quota of one hundred, but it is likely that ten or twenty thousand more wives would have come—a firm demographic basis had already been established for sustained community growth. The slight drop in total Japanese American population between 1930 and 1940 was only temporary, since the second (nisei) generation was just beginning to reach childbearing age.

Despite much bitterness in the Japanese American community about the denial of what it regarded as its rights, the 1930s, a time of troubles for most Americans, in some respects marks the apogee of what I have called Japanese America, the segregated ethnic enclaves created by the first-generation immigrants.

By the end of the 1930s large numbers of immigrant Japanese families, despite the barriers raised against them, had claimed their piece of the American dream, if we define that dream as hard work, modest aspirations, upward social mobility, and the expectation that children would be better off than their parents. Although many issei bachelors and some families still remained agricultural laborers, most families were at least mildly prosperous members of the lower middle class. These families, according to the census data for the Pacific Coast states, where nearly nine of ten Japanese Americans lived, owned real property—farms and businesses—to a much greater degree than did the general population. The 113,000 Japanese there owned more than 6,000 farms aggregating more than 250,000 acres and valued at $72.6 million. The average value of these farms was slightly higher than the value of all farms in those three states ($11,867 and $11,717); most were small, family-run enterprises concentrating on intertilled vegetables, fruit, and specialty crops.

Most Japanese American businesses were of the same scale. A 1935 survey of Seattle, which had some seven thousand Japanese in 1940, listed over seven hundred Japanese-owned businesses, about one for every ten residents. Many of these, such as hotels and dry cleaners, catered to the general population. The largest Japanese American business complex was in Los Angeles, where a highly organized group of Japanese producers, wholesalers, and retailers of vegetables dominated the City Market. Daily market sheets published in Japanese were supplemented by regular Japanese-language radio broadcasts of wholesale prices. Most Japanese businesses in the market were small, one-stall operations, although some of the larger produce houses grossed more than one million dollars annually. The annual wholesale volume for all Japanese businesses there has been estimated at twenty-five million dollars.

It is fascinating to speculate about how the essentially middle-class dreams of the issei would have evolved had they and their children been left to their own devices. There was already much evidence of intergenerational conflict, and the Japanese American society that the first generation had so painfully constructed probably would not have survived that generation. But, of course, the community was not left to its own devices: the mass incarceration of the West Coast Japanese prematurely destroyed Japanese America.

OTHER GROUPS BEFORE WORLD WAR II: FILIPINOS, ASIAN INDIANS, AND KOREANS

There were roughly 250,000 Asian Americans in 1940: 127,000 Japanese, 78,000 Chinese, 46,000 Filipinos, perhaps 5,000 Asian Indians, and an even smaller number of Koreans. They represented less than two-tenths of 1 percent (.0019) of the American population. Their different histories illustrate how meaningless in some ways the category "Asian American" is.

Filipinos Filipinos came to the United States in distinct increments. Apart from the few in Spanish Louisiana noted earlier, almost all came after the American conquest of the Philippines. The earliest, who began to arrive in the first decade of the twentieth century, were students sponsored by the administration of the Philippines. These *pensianados* were chiefly sons—and a few daughters—of the colony's elite. Many returned to the Philippines and had significant careers there. The next echelon of students, almost exclusively male, was self-financed. Although they aspired to higher education, few obtained degrees and many were never even able to matriculate. One of them told an interviewer:

When I finished high school [in the Philippines], I was going to Oregon State University. I went and looked at the campus. Then the Depression came. It was hard for me to find a job. I found a job in the fraternity house, waiting tables for room and board. I was not able to continue my studies. (Tricia Knoll, *Becoming Americans* [1982], p. 100)

Many of these young men, inspired with American ideals as taught in the Philippine schools, became disillusioned after meeting economic hardship and acute discrimination here. The most important Filipino American writer, Carlos Bulosan (1911–1956), spoke for a generation:

Do you know what a Filipino feels in America? . . . He is the loneliest thing on earth. There is much to be appreciated . . . beauty, wealth, power, grandeur. But is he a part of these luxuries? He looks, poor man, through the fingers of his eyes. He is enchained, damnably to his race, his heritage. He is betrayed. . . . (Carlos Bulosan, "Selected Letters of Carlos Bulosan: 1937–1955," *Amerasia Journal* 6, no. 1 [1979]: 143)

But the majority of the young Filipinos who came to the United States in the 1920s came for economic reasons. Most were from Luzon. Many were Ilocanos, a major Filipino ethnic group, whose home provinces had become overpopulated. In America, whatever their aspirations and motivations, most Filipinos worked as migrant laborers in the factories in the fields that had become characteristic of the American West; about two-thirds worked in California. There, in 1930, males outnumbered females by more than fifteen to one. Because of their status as "American nationals" they could not be barred from entering the country, but neither were they eligible for citizenship; and the restrictions that applied to other Asians applied to them. The onset of the Great Depression all but stopped Filipino immigration: the census of 1940 recorded 45,876, only 668 more than had been reported in 1930. A small but violent anti-Filipino movement developed in California; ironically, some of the most blatant racists became supporters of Philippine independence. As part of the Philippines Independence Act of 1934, which contained legislative arrangements providing for eventual independence, the new Commonwealth of the Philippines was given an annual quota of fifty, half of the smallest existing quota. And, as an added incentive to get Filipino Americans to leave, Congress passed special legislation enabling them to have free passage "home" on Army transports.

Indians Small numbers of Asian Indians and Koreans came to the United States in the years before the Immigration Act of 1917 ended their eligibility to enter. The communities that were created were strikingly different from each other and from those of other Asian Americans.

The Indians began to arrive on the West Coast in the first decade of the twentieth century, although an occasional seaman had been reported in eastern ports before 1800. There were also tiny groups of Indian merchants in New York City and one or two other eastern ports from the mid nineteenth century on. As was true of so many other immigrant groups, the Indians came largely from one area, the rich land of the five rivers called the Punjab. And, although polite Americans almost always called them "Hindus" or "Hindoos" (impolite Americans called them "ragheads" for the turbans that they wore as part of their religion), the overwhelming majority were members of the Sikh faith. Sikhism was founded about A.D. 1500 and its adherents are an important ethnic group in north India.

Whereas some members of other Asian groups had migrated to the West Coast via Hawaii, most Indians came through western Canada. From British Columbia they moved first to work in lumber mills of the Pacific Northwest—the only "anti-Hindu" riot in American history occurred in Bellingham, Washington, in 1907—but most of the perhaps ten thousand Asian Indians in the United States before World War I soon were in California. There they worked as migrant laborers, but many became agricultural proprietors, particularly in the newly irrigated Imperial Valley near the Mexican border and in the northern Sacramento Valley. Their frugality was proverbial. One American newspaper justified violence against them by arguing:

It is not a question of race, but of wages; not a question of men, but of modes of life. . . . When men who require meat to eat and real beds to sleep in are ousted from their employment to make room for vegetarians who can find the bliss of sleep in some filthy corner, it is rather difficult to say at what limit indignation ceases to be righteous. (Gerald N. Hallberg, "Bellingham, Washington's Anti-Hindu Riot," *Journal of the West,* 12 [1973]: 173)

A more perceptive American observer noted that most of the Sikh immigrants wanted to buy land in the Punjab and had as their goal saving two thousand dollars. Agricultural workers could expect to save no more than twenty-five dollars a month. Even assuming that optimum amount and continuous employment, it would take almost seven years to amass such a sum. It is clear that many Sikhs did save. The Marysville, California, post office reported that in one eight-month period in 1908, thirty-four thousand dollars in remittances was sent to India. We have no clear notion about how many Indians sent money home or how much they sent. One rare piece of quantified evidence, from a 1909 survey of millhands—somewhat better paid than agricultural workers—reports that thirty-one of the seventy-nine Indian workers claimed to have sent money back in the previous year. The average sum was about $140 for each worker who remitted, but only about $55 apiece for the whole group.

While it is clear that some returned to the Punjab to buy land—a goal of many peasant emigrants of any ethnicity—most did not do so, although most did return. The 1940 census could find only 1,476 "East Indians" in California. Only a handful of Asian Indian women immigrated at this time. Many of the farmers married women of other ethnicities. Bruce LaBrack and Karen Leonard have reconstituted nearly four hundred Asian Indian families in California before 1946. In only nine—2.4 percent— was there an Asian Indian wife; some 80 percent of the marriages were with Mexican American women. Not surprisingly, these marriages were conflict ridden; in Imperial County at least 20 percent ended in divorce. Of the Asian groups in the United States in this era, only Asian Indians and Filipinos married outside of their own ethnic group to any extent.

Early in the century there were several dozen Asian Indian students in at least nine American universities, most significantly at the University of California at Berkeley, where many of them lived in a hostel financed by the American Sikh community. The most famous of these was Dalip Singh Saund, who received an M.S. in food preservation and an M.A. and Ph.D. in mathematics. Saund became a farmer in the Imperial Valley and, after the naturalization of Indians was permitted, was elected in 1956 as the first Asian American member of Congress, and the only one so far to have been born in Asia.

Berkeley was also the center of the Asian Indian freedom movement in America. It was there that the Gadar movement planned the "Hindu Conspiracy" (most of those involved were Sikhs), a quixotic attempt during World War I to overthrow the British Raj by shipping guns (purchased in part with funds supplied by the German government) and a few revolutionaries to India. Gadar (the word means "revolution" or "mutiny") was riddled with spies and agents provocateurs and ended tragically. It is only one of many examples of exile politics conducted by immigrants and their descendants in the United States, that is, political action focused on the mother country rather than on the adopted one.

Asian Indians in the United States suffered from the same restrictions as did other Asians. Most of the California farmers either leased their land or put it in the name of their wives or children. A special irritant was the denial of naturalization, although prior to 1922 a number of Indians and other Asians had been naturalized by various courts. In 1922, in *Ozawa* v. *United States,* the Supreme Court ruled that the words "white person" in the 1870 naturalization statute meant "Caucasian" and thus the Japanese litigant, who was otherwise well qualified, was not eligible. Shortly thereafter the court had before it the case of Bhagat Singh Thind, an Indian-born Sikh who, although his skin was quite dark, was in ethnological terms a Caucasian. Without even blushing, the same Supreme Court justice who wrote the *Ozawa* opinion, British-born George Sutherland, held in *Thind* v. *United States* that what the words *white person* really meant was what they meant "in the understanding of the common man," and thus denied Thind his citizenship. Whatever one may think of the result, it is clear that the court in this instance was adhering to the intent of Congress. In the next three years (1923–1926) the Justice Department succeeded in revoking some fifty naturalization certificates of Indians. In 1926 Sakharam Ganesh Pandit, a California attorney who had been naturalized in 1914, won his suit to retain his citizenship. He argued successfully that it had been procured in a proper court without fraud, and that an established rule of law held that a decision not appealed in three years should stand.

Koreans Korean Americans were the smallest Asian community to settle in the United States in the years before World War II. Immigration records show that some seven thousand Koreans migrated to Hawaii in the years 1903–1905, after which Korea's Japanese overlords all but stopped sizable Korean emigration from Asia. Tens of thousands were allowed to go to Japan or were brought there, where their descendants are still not granted citizenship and other human rights. A fraction of the Koreans in Hawaii came to the mainland; the 1930 census found fewer than two thousand of them in California. Most worked in agriculture; a few became proprietors; and a handful, such as the Kim brothers, Charles and Harry, of Reedley, California, became well-to-do agricultural entrepreneurs.

The social characteristics of the early Korean American community were different from those of other contemporary Asian American groups in three ways. It was largely a community of families; perhaps a majority of those families had converted to Christianity before they came; and political exiles were quite prominent in the leadership of the ethnic community. These differences were largely due to Korea's colonial status. Plantation laborers who in other circumstances might have sent home remittances, instead concentrated on bringing out their families. The appeal of Christianity was heightened by the obvious impotence of the traditional Korean culture and by the fact that becoming the follower of an Occidental missionary could be seen both as an anti-Japanese act and as a way of getting a modicum of protection from an increasingly brutal colonial regime. And although there were some active political exiles among almost every American immigrant group, only the Koreans established and maintained a government-in-exile on American soil, a government that would be installed in Seoul after World War II by the American occupation authorities.

The best-known of these exiles was Syngman Rhee (1875–1965), a Christian who had spent some seven years (1897–1904) in prison in Korea for subversive political activities. He came to the United States in 1904 in a vain attempt to get Theodore Roosevelt's administration to protect Korea, as the United States had promised to do in the Treaty of Chempulpo (1882). (Roosevelt simply wrote off that commitment. He explained to his secretary of state, John Hay: "We could not possibly interfere for the Koreans against Japan. They couldn't strike a blow in their own defense.") Rhee, who received a Ph.D. from Princeton in 1910, remained in the United States, with one brief interruption (1910–1912), until 1945. In 1919 he became the first president of what the exiles called the provisional government of Korea.

The bitter feelings that most Koreans held about Japan were exemplified by a terrorist act committed on American soil in 1908. Durham W. Stephens, a European American who was paid by the Japanese government to advise its Foreign Affairs Department, made public statements in San Francisco that praised the Japanese colonial administration of Korea and demeaned the Korean people. A Korean exile, Chang In-hwan (1875–1930), assassinated Stevens in San Francisco. Sentenced to twenty-five years in prison, he was released in 1919 and committed suicide in 1930. In 1975 his remains were disinterred and taken to Korea, where they were buried with full honors in the national cemetery.

ASIAN AMERICANS AND WORLD WAR II

An analyst who looked at the 1940 census data on Asian Americans would have to assume that their communities—denied the opportunity to grow by American immigration laws that seemed immutable—would eventually wither and die. The Filipinos, Indians, and Koreans constituted groups that were almost too small to notice, and although the Japanese and Chinese communities had clearly reached the stage where natural increase would provide modest growth, both communities together barely topped 200,000 in a nation of 131 million, not even 0.2 percent of the total. It is true that vigorous and thriving Asian American communities existed in Hawaii, where fewer than a quarter of the population of 423,000 was listed as Caucasian. (The major groups there were 158,000 Japanese, 64,000 Hawaiians, 53,000 Filipinos and 27,000 Chinese.) But, although its native-born residents were American citizens, Hawaii was a territory and seemed likely to remain one. Democratic Representative John E. Rankin of Mississippi had noted during the unsuccessful statehood hearings of 1937 that statehood might result in "a senator called Moto."

World War II and the changed world that it created made prewar assumptions invalid. The once nearly closed golden door of immigration began to swing open. But, before that happened, Japanese Americans endured the torment and shame of what one scholar called "our worst wartime mistake," but which was, rather, an almost logical extension of previous anti-Asian policies. The combination of the shock of Pearl Harbor and the stunning string of defeats dealt out to the United States and its Pacific allies provided the special circumstances under which the incarceration of the Japanese took place. The entire ethnic Japanese population of the West Coast—citizen and alien, male and female, adult and child—was shipped off to ten godforsaken inland concentration camps.

The racist nature of wartime antagonism is clear: some German American and Italian American aliens were interned, but citizens of German and Italian descent or birth were immune unless they committed indictable offenses. Similarly, in popular culture the atrocities of Nazi Germany were seen, properly, as the deeds of evil men and women; the atrocities of imperial Japan were seen as the deeds of an evil, subhuman race. About 120,000 Japanese Americans were incarcerated—some for more than four years—without indictment or probable cause, except for the fact that either they or their ancestors had come from the Land of the Rising Sun. The process was instituted by a presidential directive, ratified and made punitive by a unanimous Congress, and given the color of law in three horrendous decisions by the Supreme Court of the United States. Even so, not all Japanese Americans were incarcerated; the few thousand who lived east of the Sierra Nevada and its extensions were left in nervous liberty throughout the war; and in Hawaii, where every third person was Japanese, only a few thousand were deprived of their liberty.

Eventually large numbers of Japanese Americans were allowed to leave the concentration camps for the Midwest and the East; beginning in January 1945, citizens and some aliens were permitted to return to the West Coast, as most eventually did. During the war the United States Army accepted Japanese Americans for military service. In 1948 Congress was willing to pass the very limited Japanese American Claims Act, which provided some compensation for demonstrable losses of real property. At the same time the postwar occupation of Japan and Korea, and later the Korean War, meant that large numbers of Americans would have daily encounters with Asian culture and that some of them would bring home Asian wives.

On the American home front in World War II, while Japanese were abased, other Asian Americans were raised up, if only a little. Chinese and Filipinos became, in comic strips and movies, assistant heroes. Koreans, despite their legal status as Japanese nationals, managed, thanks to the efforts of Syngman Rhee, to get themselves removed from the "enemy alien" category. And, it must be noted, Chinese, Filipino, and Korean Americans participated in anti-Japanese rhetoric and activities like other Americans. West Coast Chinese Americans, for example, often wore buttons to distinguish themselves from Japanese Americans. Some simply read "I'm Chinese"; others read "I'm Chinese and I hate Japs worse than you do."

An even more important change came in December 1943. Congress, at the request of President Roosevelt, repealed the Chinese Exclusion Act, made Chinese (but no other Asians) eligible for naturalization, and gave the Chinese people an annual quota of 105 entries. The language of Roosevelt's special message to Congress is instructive. The commander in chief pointed out that China was our ally and her resistance depended, in part, on "the spirit of her people and her faith in her allies." He insisted:

We owe it to the Chinese to strengthen that faith. One step in this direction is to wipe from the statute books those anachronisms in our laws which forbid the immigration of Chinese people into this country and which bar Chinese residents from American citizenship. (Samuel I. Rosenman, comp., *The Public Papers . . . of Franklin D. Roosevelt . . . 1943,* pp. 429–430)

Probably neither Roosevelt nor any of his advisers realized what the short-term demographic consequences of repeal would be. The tiny quota of 105—for persons of Chinese ethnicity regardless of nationality—applied *only* to quota immigrants. The wives of American citizens were nonquota immigrants, and alien Chinese wives of American citizens, no longer "aliens ineligible to citizenship," were therefore admissible without regard to numerical limitation. Thus, between 1945 and 1952, 11,058 Chinese legally immigrated to the United States, almost 1,400 per year; 90 percent of these were women. The migration of almost 10,000 Chinese women had a tremendous impact on the structure of Chinese America, which, as late as 1950, contained only 28,000 women fourteen years of age and older. Culturally the new immigrants had a dual impact. On the one hand they reinforced Chinese rather than Chinese American values; on the other the increased number of families with children would become a major force for acculturation.

The process of fighting a war against racism— and of an ideological rather than a racial struggle in the postwar world—were major forces for an increased ethnic egalitarianism. Government propaganda, while it often disseminated racist stereotypes about Japanese, actively combated racism. Millions of schoolchildren, for example, viewed the Ruth Benedict–Gene Weltfish filmstrip *Races of Mankind,* which set forth Franz Boas's anthropological notions about racial equality. Thus, as a few historians have pointed out, the World War II era must be seen as the seedbed of the civil rights revolution of the 1950s and 1960s.

POSTWAR CHANGES IN LAW: 1946–1965

Once Congress had made an exception for Chinese, it was difficult to continue to bar other Asians. In separate statutes passed in 1946, Congress used the Chinese exclusion repeal formula to allow Filipinos and "natives of India" both admission and citizenship, with quotas of one hundred each. The special exception for Filipinos was logical: it was to reward their good wartime behavior and to celebrate the Philippines' new status as an independent nation. That for "natives of India" was the result of admiration for India on the part of certain Americans and was triggered by the persuasive efforts of an exceptional Asian Indian lobbyist, the New York merchant J. J. Singh. Neither statute had much immediate demographic impact.

Although President Harry S. Truman persistently called for major immigration reform, Congress was unwilling to scrap the discriminatory ethnic quotas that had begun in 1921. The McCarran-Walter Immigration and Naturalization Act of 1952, which Truman unsuccessfully vetoed because it was largely illiberal, dropped all ethnic bars to immigration and naturalization. The act, a prototypical piece of cold war legislation, retained the quota system and added many other objectionable features, including applying an ideological litmus test to all visitors, even scholars and artistic personalities coming for one lecture or performance.

Although not immigration legislation per se, one other congressional action in this period greatly affected Asian Americans: the admission of Hawaii to statehood in 1959. From then on, there were Asian Americans in Congress who could speak for all Asian Americans. That, and the fact that the jet age made Hawaii much more accessible to other Americans—and the mainland to Hawaiians—was a subtle but significant influence on legislation affecting Asian Americans.

In 1965, that annus mirabilis of American social legislation, a thorough revamping of American immigration law occurred. When he signed the bill into law on Liberty Island in New York Harbor, Lyndon B. Johnson for once understated the impact of one of "his" pieces of legislation, claiming: "This bill that we will sign today is not a revolutionary bill. It does not affect the lives of millions. It will not reshape the structure of our daily lives, or really add importantly to our wealth and power."

Although few realized it at the time, the Immigration Act of 1965 would facilitate an utter reversal of traditional American immigration patterns. It scrapped the quota system completely and seemed to set numerical limitations of 170,000 annually on the Eastern Hemisphere and 120,000 annually on the Western, with no more than 20,000 immigrants coming from any one nation. But superimposed upon these limitations was a complex system of preferences, based largely upon the principle of family reunification and without numerical limitation, under which many immigrants have entered since that time. In 1980, for example, 289,479 immigrants were admitted subject to numerical limitation; another 165,325 were exempt from numerical limitation; an even larger number—341,552—were refugees.

Meaningful refugee admission programs did not begin until the so-called Displaced Persons acts of 1948 and 1950, statutes strictly limited to Europeans. Refugee programs for Asians began with the Refugee Relief Act of 1953, which, while authorizing the issuance of 205,000 refugee visas, earmarked 2,000 of them for refugees "of Chinese ethnic origin" as long as they were vouched for by Chiang Kai-shek's government on Taiwan. These numbers were later dwarfed by the massive refugee programs that stemmed from the misbegotten war in Vietnam.

The immediate postwar liberalizations in both law and practice had increased immigration from Asia significantly; nevertheless, for the period 1931–1960 only 5 percent of all legal immigration came from Asia. In the 1970s that figure leaped to 34 percent, and in the early 1980s it rose to 48 percent.

TABLE 4a Asian American Population, 1960–1990

Year	Number
1950	599,091
1960	877,934
1970	1,429,562
1980	3,466,421
1990 (preliminary)	7,272,662

TABLE 4b Asian Americans, by Major Ethnic Group, 1990

Group	Number
Chinese	1,643,621
Filipinos	1,403,624
Japanese	850,901
Asian Indians	814,538
Koreans	799,993
Vietnamese	610,904
Laotian*	239,000
Cambodian	210,724

Source: New York Times, 12 June 1991, citing preliminary Census Bureau data. *Listed separately on the 1980 census questionnaire.

Conversely, immigration from Europe and Canada, which had constituted 69 percent of all immigration in the earlier period, had shrunk to 14 percent by the early 1980s. During this period, total legal immigration swelled steadily, from half a million in the 1930s to some six million in the 1980s. Tables 4a and 4b show the growth of the Asian American population.

ASIAN AMERICAN ETHNIC GROUPS: 1965–1990

It is not possible, in an essay of this length, to do justice to the increasing variety of the Asian American experience. Even if space were not a problem, we simply do not yet know very much about the history and dynamics of some of the newer groups. Very little, for example, has been written about Thais, whose settlement and acculturation patterns seem quite different from those of most other Asians. All that can be done here is to give a comparative statistical profile and provide a thumbnail and often impressionistic sketch of the six largest communities and try to say something about the changing image of Asian Americans.

Since they are largely immigrant communities, Asian Americans are predominantly younger than white Americans, whose median age in 1980 was 31.3 years. Only the overwhelmingly native-born Japanese Americans, median age 33.5 years, were older. The median for Asian Indians was 30.1 years, for Chinese 29.6 years, for Filipinos 28.5 years, for Koreans 26.0 years, and for Vietnamese 21.5 years. Blacks and Hispanics had median ages of 24.9 and 23.3 years, respectively.

Although one of the standard negative stereotypes about Asian immigrants has been that they "breed so fast," the census data indicate that, except for Vietnamese, Asian American fertility is below that of whites. Data standardized for age distribution of each group for 1980 show that for every 1,000 white women, 1,358 children had already been born. The numbers for blacks and Hispanics were 1,806 and 1,817, quite similar to the Vietnamese figure of 1,785. Other Asian groups had produced children in the following ratios: Japanese, 912; Chinese, 1,020; Korean, 1,139; Filipino, 1,217; and Asian Indian, 1,224. For Japanese, Chinese, and Koreans the data indicated much higher fertility for immigrant women than for native-born: looking at a narrower age spectrum of women, those twenty-

five to thirty-four, the data showed that while all Chinese women in this group had given birth to 939 children per 1,000 women, native-born Chinese women had only 669 children, as opposed to 1,024 for the immigrant Chinese women. There were so few native-born Asian Indian and Vietnamese women in this age group that the recorded differences are meaningless, and among Filipinos native-born women were more fertile—1,520 versus 1,227, probably reflecting the greater number of middle-class professionals among the immigrants.

Asian American families tended to be more traditionally structured than those of most other Americans. In 1980, in five of the major Asian American groups, more than 84 percent of children under eighteen lived in households with two parents, ranging from 84.5 percent for Filipinos to 92.7 percent for Asian Indians. Only Vietnamese were below these high levels at 74.1 percent. Rates for other groups in the population were 82.9 percent for whites, 70.9 percent for Hispanics, and 45.4 percent for blacks. As would be expected for groups that were composed of a high percentage of immigrants, Asian American households were significantly larger than the average American household. Five of the major Asian American groups had household sizes larger than the average white household of 2.7 persons, which was also the average size for Japanese American households. The others ranged from 2.9 persons for Asian Indians to 4.4 persons for Vietnamese. Black households averaged 3.1 persons and Hispanic households 3.5 persons. If one considers only households of those who had come to the United States since 1975, the sizes ranged from 2.9 persons for Japanese to 5.4 persons for Filipinos.

These larger households tend to inflate Asian American income data when calculated at the household or family level, but even individual income data show many Asian Americans earning at levels above those of whites, as Table 5 indicates.

When we compare income and educational achievement data, it becomes clear that although three Asian American groups have incomes at or above the level of whites, there is significant income disadvantage for Asian Americans. These same three groups, plus Koreans and Filipinos, have educational attainments significantly higher than those of whites, so their incomes should be even higher, all things considered. Some writers speak of an invisible or "glass" ceiling, above which many qualified Asian Americans are not able to rise.

TABLE 5   Median Income, Full-Time Workers, 1979

Ethnic Group	Income
White	$15,572
Hispanic	$11,650
Black	$11,327
Asian Indian	$18,707
Japanese	$16,829
Chinese	$15,753
Korean	$14,224
Filipino	$13,690
Vietnamese	$11,650

Source: Robert W. Gardner, Bryant Robey, and Peter C. Smith, *Asian Americans: Growth, Change and Diversity* (1985), p. 34.

The data on poverty show that even relative prosperity is unevenly distributed in many Asian American communities. As Table 5 shows, the median income for Chinese was virtually identical with that of whites in 1979. Medians, however, can conceal great disparities. In the same year 50 percent more Chinese families than white families were below the poverty level: the census data showed 7 percent of all white families and 10.5 percent of all Chinese families in poverty. For other Asian American groups the poverty percentages were Japanese, 4.2 percent; Filipino, 6.2 percent; Asian Indian, 7.4 percent; Korean, 13.1 percent; and Vietnamese, 35 percent. For Hispanics and blacks the figures were 21.3 percent and 26.5 percent, respectively.

THE CHANGING ASIAN AMERICAN IMAGE: THE MODEL MINORITY AND AFTER

These and other data call into serious question the "model minority" label that has been pasted, willy-nilly, on all Asian American groups. The term has a precise history. It was coined in 1964 by a distinguished demographer, William Petersen, then on the faculty at the University of California, Berkeley, who published the most influential single article ever written about Asian Americans in the *New York Times Magazine* in 1966. In an early example of what has been styled the "neoconservative revolt," Petersen used his flattering image of Japanese Americans—and Japanese Americans only—as a point of departure not only to denigrate what he called "problem" minority groups but also to attack what he felt was the lowering of standards in American life as well as the social programs of Lyndon Johnson's Great Society. The crux of Petersen's argument, reminiscent of William Graham Sumner's notion that "stateways cannot change folkways," was that for "problem minorities" and particularly for blacks, there was little hope. "For all the well-meaning programs and countless scholarly studies," he wrote, "we hardly know how to repair the damage that the slave traders started." Conversely, he argued, Japanese Americans had shown that the arguments of liberals about the need for government programs to upgrade the status of minorities were false.

Barely more than 20 years after the end of the wartime camps, this is a minority that has risen above even prejudiced criticism. By any criterion of good citizenship that we choose, the Japanese Americans are better than any other group in our society, including native-born whites. They have established this remarkable record, moreover, by their own almost totally unaided effort. Every attempt to hamper their progress resulted only in enhancing their determination to succeed. Even in a country whose patron saint is Horatio Alger, there is no parallel to this success story. ("Success Story, Japanese American Style," *New York Times Magazine*, 6 January 1966, pp. 20ff.)

Petersen was thus using the word "model" in two ways: to describe what seemed to him exemplary behavior by most members of one relatively small ethnic minority group and, more important, to suggest that other minority groups model their behavior on that of Japanese Americans, a theme that other neoconservatives such as Thomas Sowell have rung changes on.

An expanded notion of model minorities soon became general among social scientists, and in 1982 *Newsweek* magazine ran a feature story, "Asian-Americans: A 'Model Minority,'" which extended the concept to all Asian Americans. Yet, as has been shown, this notion of an essentially middle-class "colored" minority did real violence to the social reality that saw great disparities among the various ethnic groups lumped as Asian Americans.

ASIAN AMERICANS: 1990

According to the preliminary data from the 1990 census, there were almost 7.3 million Asian Americans who represented just under 3 percent of the American population of about 250 million. Group profiles for 1990 would look something like this. Japanese Americans had come a long way from the degradation of the wartime concentration camps. Their socioeconomic profile was solidly middle class: unlike other Asian American groups, their population was overwhelmingly native-born; few Japanese immigrated after a flurry of family re-unification in the 1960s. The year 1990 saw the beginnings of the "redress" payments of twenty thousand dollars to each survivor of the wartime incarceration, authorized by Congress in 1988, along with an apology. Once the most numerous Asian American group, the slow growth of the Japanese American population and minimal immigration made it the third most numerous group in 1990 and a projected sixth in 2000. In 1980 four-fifths of them still lived in the Far West, with 37.5 percent in California and 33.5 percent in Hawaii. Yet even members of this acculturated, assimilating group (some studies showed an exogamous marriage rate of over 50 percent) still felt the stings of subtler forms of economic discrimination: for example, the "glass ceiling" in employment, which did not keep them out of the corporate hierarchy but severely limited their upward mobility within it. Recent economic competition between the United States and Japan, first in the automobile industry and then throughout the economy, produced fits of "Japan bashing," some of which rubbed off on Japanese Americans.

The Chinese American community went through a series of rapid changes both in its image and in its reality. Although the Chinese had been promoted to the status of "assistant heroes" during World War II, the rise of the People's Republic of China and its intervention in the Korean War caused some Chinese Americans to fear that they, too, might be placed in camps, but happily that did not occur. The Chinese population grew substantially through immigration and was further boosted during the aftermath of the war in Vietnam, when large numbers of the refugees admitted were ethnic Chinese. The largest Asian American ethnic group in 1980, a bare majority of Chinese lived in the Far West (50.3 percent) and more than a quarter (26.8 percent) lived in the Northeast. The Chinese community benefited from the "model minority" stereotype, but it also suffered from the gangster image produced by increasingly violent crime in America's overcrowded Chinatowns. Sensational press and film treatment of the semimythical Triad Societies likened them to the Mafia as ethnic villains, but the media's Chinese crime bosses never achieved the humanity attributed to the Corleone family. Perhaps a majority of Chinese, both native-born and immigrant, had achieved middle-class status.

Chinese Americans and some other Asian Americans, but not Filipinos and Vietnamese, were "overrepresented" in America's elite educational institutions. At least seventeen of the forty finalists in the 1991 Westinghouse Science Talent Search for high school students were Asian Americans. Many immigrant Chinese, especially those from Hong Kong, were highly educated professionals who represented a distinct brain-and-capital drain from Asia to North America. (This phenomenon is nowhere more apparent than in Vancouver, British Columbia.) At the same time large numbers of Chinese Americans lived in substandard housing and worked in sweatshop-like conditions in garment factories and other manufacturing enterprises requiring semiskilled labor. Chinese American households were more likely than those of white Americans to need public assistance, but less likely to do so than many other ethnic groups as Table 6 indicates.

The immigration of Filipino Americans since 1965 has been in large part a movement of lower middle-class professionals and paraprofessionals, and highly female. Only they and Koreans have a female majority. Filipino nurses and other Asian-trained medical professionals have become the mainstays of American urban public hospitals. As is the case with other foreign-trained professionals, they are often employed at levels below those for which they have been trained. More than two-thirds of all Filipinos live in the Far West, 45.8 percent in California, and 16.9 percent in Hawaii. There are still significant numbers of aging "pinoys," as they call themselves, among Californian and Hawaiian farm laborers, and they help account for the intermediate position of Filipinos among welfare recipients. During the long rule of Ferdinand Marcos

TABLE 6 Percentage of Households Receiving Public Assistance, 1979

Ethnic Group	Percentage
Japanese	4.2
Asian Indians	4.5
Whites	5.9
Koreans	6.2
Chinese	6.6
Filipinos	10.0
Hispanics	15.9
Blacks	22.3
Vietnamese	28.1

Source: Robert W. Gardner, Bryant Robey, and Peter C. Smith, *Asian Americans: Growth, Change and Diversity* (1985), p. 35.

(1972–1976) many Filipino political exiles came to the United States, the most prominent of whom were Benigno and Corazon Aquino. The latter succeeded Marcos as president.

Two separate streams of Korean Americans have come to the United States since the Korean War. The first and smaller stream consisted of the wives of military personnel and of small children adopted chiefly by middle-class Caucasians. The larger stream, a post-1965 phenomenon, is family migration, although the families often come in stages, or chains, facilitated by the family reunification provisions that have dominated American immigration law. Only a minority of Koreans (42.9 percent) live in the Far West; Hawaii, the focal point of the earliest Korean American community, now has less than 5 percent of the total. Los Angeles's Koreatown, stretching for miles along Olympic Boulevard just west of the downtown business district, is the single largest concentration. Small Korean businesses, often greengrocers, became a fixture in eastern cities. Usually small family enterprises, these stores were often in or on the edge of black and Hispanic neighborhoods, and often the flash points for friction between the owners and their black and Hispanic customers. The most celebrated such incident took place in Brooklyn in 1991, and was exacerbated by a controversial boycott led by the Reverend Al Sharpton. Understandable black resentment of immigrant achievement—what is usually called nativism—is a too-little studied phenomenon of American race relations at the end of the twentieth century. (At the same time it was fashionable to study the largely rhetorical phenomenon of black anti-Semitism.) The overwhelming majority of Koreans—as well as Filipinos, Asian Indians, and Vietnamese—have come to this country so recently that it is difficult to make generalizations about them, but all indications are that they will come to resemble the Japanese Americans without that groups' concentration in agriculture and the Far West.

In purely economic terms Asian Indians stood at the top of the recent Asian immigrant groups, as the very high median income figure in Table 5 suggests. Asian Indians alone of the larger Asian groups were underrepresented in the Far West: only 19.2 percent lived there, as opposed to 34.2 percent in the Northeast, 23.4 percent in the South, and 23.1 percent in the North Central states. While in the Northeast many are professionals and business executives—and thus part of the brain-and-capital drain from Asia—large numbers of other Asian Indians operate small businesses. Asian Indians have moved into one seemingly curious economic niche: owning motels. Asian Indians constitute some 40 percent of the members of the motel owners' association along Interstate 75, which runs between Detroit and Atlanta. Many motels are owned by members of a numerous Gujarati clan named Patel; a community ethnic joke speaks about "hotel, motel, Patel." Motels require relatively small amounts of capital and large amounts of unskilled labor, the latter often supplied by extended family or clan members.

Unlike most of the other middle-class Asian Americans, few Asian Indians have adopted Christianity. Hindu temples have sprung up throughout America. Asian Indian family structure has remained highly traditional: in 1980 92.7 percent of all Asian Indian children under eighteen lived in two-parent families. And despite their middle-class status, increasing instances of anti-Asian racial violence have struck the Asian Indian community. The worst examples were in Jersey City, where a group of working-class white youths, calling themselves "dot busters" (for the *bindi*, the small cosmetic dot that married Hindu women traditionally wear on their foreheads), assaulted a number of Indians on the streets; they killed one young man, a junior executive with CitiCorp.

The most recent large group has been Vietnamese and other Southeast Asian refugees and their children, of whom there were more than a million in 1990. As is often true with refugee populations, the socioeconomic range was tremendous. Many of the elite of the Republic of Vietnam eventually fled to the West. Former Air Marshal Nguyen Cao Ky, for example, was the proprietor of a liquor store near Washington, D.C. At the other end of the spectrum were Vietnamese fisherfolk and Hmong, whose social and economic organization was essentially premodern.

They were, as a group, the least successful of the Asian American communities when measured by standard socioeconomic indices. For example, as Table 6 shows, more than a quarter (28.1 percent) of all Vietnamese households received public assistance in 1979. While the media delight in reporting the success story—"Vietnamese Girl Wins Spelling Bee"—the reality is that a very large proportion of the Vietnamese American population belongs to the underclass. Despite determined attempts by refugee resettlement groups to distribute

Vietnamese refugees throughout the country, by 1980 significant clustering had already occurred in California, where a third of them then lived. That percentage is undoubtedly much higher now. Within California the major concentration point was Orange County, south of Los Angeles. Outside of California the major concentration point was Texas, where a tenth lived. Vietnamese were one of the few contemporary immigrant groups with no sizable concentration in New York, which in 1980 had only 2.5 percent of them. Wherever most of them have gone in America, they have faced a double disadvantage: not only are they Asian foreigners but most of them are also quite poor and lack most of the skills necessary to "make it" in late-twentieth-century America.

CONCLUSION

The conglomerate image of "Asian Americans" is a chimera. Hmong and Japanese are no more alike than Albanians and Scots. Yet because they are not Caucasians, the media, the Census Bureau, and almost everyone else will continue to speak of them as if they were one people. Asian groups will continue to grow, by immigration and by natural increase, both absolutely and relatively. An estimate made in 1985 predicted almost ten million Asian Americans by 2000. If this prediction is correct—to hazard a guess, it would be that it will prove to be too low—Asian Americans will be about 4 percent of the American population, or one person in twenty-five. As recently as 1980 they represented 1.5 percent of the total population, or roughly one person in seventy-five, and in 1940 they had represented slightly less than 0.2 percent, or one person in five hundred. Whatever the numbers are, Asian Americans will surely play an increasingly important role in American life, but a varied one. Large numbers of the latest immigrants and their children will enter the middle or upper middle class, as their current presence in our elite educational institutions predicts. Others will remain mired in poverty. No one appellation or set of attributes can possibly describe them all.

BIBLIOGRAPHY

General Works
Chan, Sucheng. *Asian Americans: An Interpretive History* (1991).

Fawcett, James T., and Benjamin V. Cariño. *Pacific Bridges: The New Immigration from Asia and the Pacific Islands* (1987).

Kitano, Harry H. L., and Roger Daniels. *Asian Americans: Emerging Minorities* (1988).

Reimers, David M. *Still the Golden Door: The Third World Comes to America* (1985).

Takaki, Ronald. *Strangers from a Different Shore: A History of Asian Americans* (1989).

Chinese Americans
Barth, Gunther. *Bitter Strength: A History of the Chinese in the United States, 1850–1870* (1964).

Chan, Sucheng. *This Bittersweet Soil: The Chinese in California Agriculture* (1986).

Daniels, Roger. *Asian America: Chinese and Japanese in the United States Since 1850* (1988).

Glick, Clarence E. *Sojourners and Settlers: Chinese Migrants in Hawaii* (1980).

Kingston, Maxine Hong. *The Woman Warrior: Memoirs of a Girlhood Among Ghosts* (1976).

————. *China Men* (1980).

Lyman, Stanford M. *Chinese Americans* (1974).

Miller, Stuart Creighton. *The Unwelcome Immigrant: The American Image of the Chinese, 1785–1882* (1969).

Nee, Victor, and Brett de Bary Nee. *Longtime Californ': A Documentary History of an American Chinatown* (1973).

Sandmeyer, Elmer C. *The Anti-Chinese Movement in California.* 3rd ed. (1991).

Saxton, Alexander. *The Indispensable Enemy: Labor and the Anti-Chinese Movement in California* (1971).

Tsai, Shih-shan Henry. *The Chinese Experience in America* (1986).

Wang, Yi Chu. *Chinese Intellectuals and the West, 1872–1949* (1966).

Japanese Americans

Conroy, Hilary. *The Japanese Frontier in Hawaii, 1868–1898* (1953).

Conroy, Hilary, and T. Scott Miyakawa, eds. *East Across the Pacific: Historical and Sociological Studies of Japanese Immigration and Assimilation* (1972).

Daniels, Roger. *The Politics of Prejudice: The Anti-Japanese Movement in California and the Struggle for Japanese Exclusion* (1962).

————. *Concentration Camps, North America: Japanese in the United States and Canada During World War II* (1981).

————. *Asian America: Chinese and Japanese in the United States Since 1850* (1988).

Daniels, Roger, Sandra C. Taylor, and Harry H. L. Kitano, eds. *Japanese Americans: From Relocation to Redress.* 2nd ed. (1991).

Glenn, Evelyn Nakano. *Issei, Nisei, War Bride: Three Generations of Japanese American Women in Domestic Service* (1986).

Hata, Donald T., Jr. *"Undesirables": Early Immigrants and the Anti-Japanese Movement in San Francisco, 1892–1893* (1970; repr. 1978).

Ichihashi, Yamato. *Japanese in the United States: A Critical Study of the Problems of Japanese Immigrants and Their Children* (1932).

Ichioka, Yuji. *The Issei: The World of the First Generation Japanese Immigrants, 1885–1924* (1988).

James, Thomas. *Exile Within: The Schooling of Japanese Americans, 1942–1945* (1987).

Kashima, Tetsuden. *Buddhism in America: The Social Organization of an Ethnic Religious Institution* (1977).

Kitano, Harry H. L. *Japanese Americans: The Evolution of a Subculture* (1969).

Miyamoto, S. Frank. *Social Solidarity Among the Japanese in Seattle.* 3rd ed. (1984).

Modell, John. *The Economics and Politics of Racial Accommodation: The Japanese of Los Angeles, 1900–1942* (1977).

Moriyama, Alan Takeo. *Imingaisha: Japanese Emigration Companies and Hawaii, 1894–1908* (1985).

Petersen, William. *Japanese Americans: Oppression and Success* (1971).

Wilson, Robert A., and Bill Hosokawa. *East to America: A History of the Japanese in the United States* (1980).

Yanagisako, Sylvia Junko. *Transforming the Past: Tradition and Kinship Among Japanese Americans* (1985).

Filipino Americans

Bulosan, Carlos. *America Is in the Heart: A Personal History* (1973).

———. "Selected Letters of Carlos Bulosan: 1937–1955." *Amerasia Journal* 6, no. 1 (1979).

Lasker, Bruno. *Filipino Immigration to Continental United States and Hawaii* (1931).

Knoll, Tricia. *Becoming Americans* (1982).

Melendy, Howard Brett. *Asians in America: Filipinos, Koreans, and East Indians* (1977).

Quinsaat, Jesse, ed. *Letters in Exile: An Introductory Reader in the History of Filipinos in America* (1976).

Asian Indian Americans

Chandrasekhar, S., ed. *From India to America* (1982).

Daniels, Roger. *History of Indian Immigration to the United States* (1989).

Jensen, Joan M. *Passage from India: Asian Indian Immigrants in North America* (1988).

LaBrack, Bruce, and Karen Leonard. "Conflict and Compatibility in Punjabi-Mexican Immigrant Families in Rural California, 1915–1916." *Journal of Marriage and the Family* 46 (August 1984).

Melendy, Howard Brett. *Asians in America: Filipinos, Koreans, and East Indians* (1977).

Saran, Parmatma. *The Asian Indian Experience in the United States* (1985).

Korean Americans

Choy, Bong-youn. *Koreans in America* (1979).

Kim, Hyung-chan, ed. *The Korean Diaspora* (1977).

Patterson, Wayne. *The Korean Frontier in America: Immigration to Hawaii, 1896–1910* (1988).

Vietnamese Americans

Freeman, James M. *Hearts of Sorrow: Vietnamese-American Lives* (1989).

Haines, David W., ed. *Refugees as Immigrants: Cambodians, Laotians, and Vietnamese in America* (1989).

Hendricks, Glenn L., Bruce T. Downing, and Amos S. Deinard, eds. *The Hmong in Transition* (1986).

Kelly, Gail P. *From Vietnam to America: A Chronicle of the Vietnamese Immigration to the United States* (1977).

Liu, William T. *Transition to Nowhere: Vietnamese Refugees in America* (1979).

Montero, Darrel. *Vietnamese Americans* (1979).

Strand, Paul J., and Woodrow Jones, Jr. *Indochinese Refugees in America* (1985).

SEE ALSO **Ethnicity; Immigration; Race; Racial Ideology and Social History; Racism.**

MIDDLE EASTERN PEOPLES

Barbara C. Aswad

MIGRATIONS ARE PART of the histories of Middle Eastern peoples. Those who migrated to America represented six distinct language groups, further divided into various ethnic groups within each language family. Each group had its own history, and each settled and organized separately. In addition, most were non-Sunni Muslims or were members of other minorities in the Middle East.

The lengthy migration from the Middle East to America began in the late nineteenth and early twentieth centuries. The most numerous of the early emigrants were Arabic-speaking Syrians and Lebanese, most of whom were Christian, and Christian Armenians from what is now Turkey. Other language communities had fewer representatives, but after World War II increased numbers of Iranians, Turks, Kurds, and Chaldeans, as well as a steady flow of Arabic speakers from Lebanon, Palestine, Jordan, Yemen, and Egypt, immigrated to America. Because of their early arrival, the Syrians, Lebanese, and Armenians have larger populations, some of whose members are highly assimilated, and more cultural and social institutions in America.

The immigrants arriving from the Middle East after World War II were more diverse—from urban and rural areas and from various geographical regions and economic and educational classes—and many had ties to groups or individuals involved in the continuing political turmoil in the Middle East as well as in the increased American economic and political penetration into the area. Some expressed political aspirations that were based on language; others stressed national identities. Later, the unifying effect of Islam increased the influence of that religion in both the Middle Eastern and the American communities. During the second period of migration, many came for a higher education and then stayed on, others came for economic advantage, and still others came to escape the numerous conflicts in their homelands.

The roots of today's Middle Eastern communities in America go back to the empires that controlled the Middle East and that had an impact on the ethnolinguistic and religious identities of local populations. During the thirteen hundred years of primarily Sunni Islamic empires, from the seventh century to World War I, the major distinction among people was religion, and religion persists today as the primary criterion for determining the suitability of a marriage. For example, in Detroit, marriage between a Lebanese Muslim and a Turkish Muslim is less stigmatized than marriage between a Lebanese Christian and a Lebanese Muslim from the same village.

The majority of the peoples in the Middle East are Muslims, and most belong to the dominant Sunni sect; the exception is Iran, in which the majority are Shiites.

Islam originated under Muhammad in Arabia in the seventh century. At that time, religion, politics, and society were strongly linked. Many of Islam's tenets resemble those of Christianity and Judaism, but Islam has its own holy book, the Koran, which is considered to be the word of God revealed to the prophet Muhammad; the Hadith, or the sayings of Muhammad; and its unique historical development.

The religious schism between the Muslim sects began after Muhammad's death when the struggle over his succession resulted in a split between Sunnis, who favored a nonkinship-based leadership, and the Shiites, who favored relatives of Muhammad as rulers of the new Islamic state in Medina in the seventh century. The sunni prevailed, and the Shīʿa became marginalized geographically and politically, except in the eleventh and twelfth centuries. During the Arab and Islamic empires of the seventh to twelfth centuries, Arabic speakers contributed significantly to the studies of medicine, physics, literature, mathematics, and geography.

Christian communities are small in the Middle East, representing approximately 10 percent of the population. Originally all Christians in the area belonged to one of the indigenous Eastern rite churches. The schisms that arose concerned dogma, primarily the nature of Christ, but they also reflected political movements that resisted Byzantine rule (as represented by the Greek Orthodox church).

The large agrarian-based Islamic Turkish Ottoman empire affected minorities. It ruled from 1300 to 1922 over three continents with Istanbul as its capital. Ottoman administrators were Sunni Muslim but religious minorities were given some legal autonomy from Islamic law.

European colonialism greatly affected the status of minorities, supporting them in order to undermine the six-hundred-year-old Ottoman empire in the nineteenth and early twentieth centuries. Initially interested in controlling the region to secure transportation routes to the Far East, Britain and France later began to exploit its resources for their benefit. Agriculture in certain regions was converted from subsistence crops to cash crops, resulting in increased economic dependency among peasants and landlords on European markets and credit. Minorities increasingly became merchants allied with Western capital and trade networks. The divide-and-rule policies and the subdivision of land instituted by the colonial powers further politicized religious and ethnic groups by supporting minorities over majorities. Minorities supported by Western powers were affected by Western ideas and education earlier than the majority population, some of whose members became jealous of the new economic and political power enjoyed by some members of the minority Christian communities.

Western political control was institutionalized at the end of World War I, when the majority of the Arab world was divided into mandates and protectorates ruled primarily by Britain and France and kings and sheiks were created and supported by outside powers. Indigenous nationalisms, often based on language, arose because many twentieth-century country boundaries were drawn by these outside powers to reflect their interests, not those of the local populations. The discovery of oil in the region drew Western powers increasingly into the area.

Migration to America increased as the United States and the Soviet Union replaced Britain and France as controlling powers after World War II. Countries in the Middle East were aligned politically according to their economic policies; those with socialist leanings were supported by the Soviet Union, and those dependent on market capitalism were supported by the United States. The industrial expansion of the United States, which depended on oil, the need of the Soviet Union for ports, and the competition between these superpowers made the Middle East a volatile region, a situation that led to increased migration. During World War I, Great Britain and later the United States supported Zionism and the creation of a Jewish state in Palestine in 1948. Conflicts resulted as European Jews, usually backed by the Western powers, moved onto Palestinian lands and many Palestinians became stateless refugees. This began the major period of Palestinian migration to the United States, and the period in which American Arab communities began to feel the sting of discrimination as a result of the American–Middle East tensions and wars.

ARABS

The 1980 census records approximately 660,000 Arab Americans, far below the actual number, which approaches two million. Their countries of origin range geographically from Morocco in the west to Iraq in the east. The earliest arrivals came primarily from the Lebanese Syrian region, however after World War II other significant communities were also established from Palestine, Yemen, Iraq, Jordan, and Egypt. Whereas the early immigrants were mostly villagers, later arrivals varied more in their occupations, education, and class, as many students and professionals migrated to the United States.

Who Came, and Why? The early Arab immigrants were Christians and minority Muslim groups from the Lebanese mountain region of the Syrian province of the Ottoman empire. They called themselves Syrians and most identified with their region or village and their religion. The geography, which contained high mountains, fertile valleys, and coastal areas led to autonomous regions and separate identities. They include Maronite and Melkite Catholics, Greek Orthodox, Shiite Muslims, and the Druze, an offshoot of Shiite Islam.

Economics played a major part in early migration. Alixa Naff reports that the majority came in response to "enthusiastic reports, the activities of steamship agents recruiting labor from all over the world for American industry, and the efforts of native brokers and moneylenders" ("Arabs," p. 130). In the early twentieth century, some came to escape Ottoman conscription. The economy of Lebanon, made dependent on the world silk market by its French rulers, suffered a decline due to mulberry tree diseases and foreign competition; the Christian Maronites who had been patronized the most by France and deeply involved in cash cropping, experienced economic distress and began to migrate.

Most of the immigrants were middle-income peasants who owned land and worked it as a family. Rich peasants stayed, and the poor could not afford to leave. After their arrival in America, early immigrants often became peddlers, which required no training or skills but did require meeting people and learning the language. Naff believes that immigrant peddlers quickly achieved a relatively high degree of assimilation. Later many immigrants set up stores, which also required contact with the public. There are also reports of Lebanese working as laborers in Massachusetts textile mills and in Pennsylvania coal mines. In the Detroit area, they worked in the auto industry and established what would become one of the largest Arab communities in the United States.

The Role of the Family and Economic Position Arabic speakers settled by religious group and village. In Detroit, for example, the Lebanese Catholic Maronites and the Lebanese Muslims worked in different auto plants and lived in communities adjacent to them. Other large communities of Arabic speakers settled in New York City along Atlantic Avenue in Brooklyn, in Boston, and later in Los Angeles, Texas, South Dakota, and other areas. These early communities resembled home villages, featuring coffeehouses, ethnic restaurants, mosques or churches, and kin clusterings. Many of the later generations went into businesses and professions and moved to the suburbs.

Among Arab immigrants, the extended family is a source of security for the immigrant, as well as an economic entity. The patrilineal descent structure of the majority of Middle Eastern cultures leads to formation of a semicorporate unit that protects and controls its members. The importance of family honor and status is dominant; the individual must think of the family first and of himself or herself second. In return the family gives protection, emotional and economic support, and identity. Families are usually large and may include several hundred people. Cousins, uncles, and aunts who live nearby are a major part of the individual's circle of friends. The extensive loyalty to family is often not under-

stood by Americans who come from a tradition of nuclear families and strong friendships with people who are not kin. Patrilineal descent and patriarchal authority gives older generations power over younger, and men power over women. Yet women have more power than Westerners imagine, especially in the running of the household, and particularly as they become old enough to gain control over sons and daughters-in-law.

As with other ethnic groups, when children and women become employed, positions of traditional authority may be challenged. Second generation children come face to face with the conflict between the new culture of their peers and the "old" culture of their parents. The more the divergence, the harder the problems. For example, today's Arab girls who try to date in the American fashion find themselves enmired in difficulties with their parents and their subculture. Such negotiating between parents and children of immigrant communities absorbs much time and often causes conflicts.

John Zogby has found a high rate of self-employment among Arab Americans, with nearly one in four involved in retail trade. And while Arab American household incomes are higher than the national average, a greater percentage of Arab American households than of other ethnic groups are below the poverty level.

Customs have affected Arab women's employment patterns in America. For example, women seldom worked in the auto industry but often were employed in family businesses under the protection and supervision of male relatives. Some women worked in textile factories, where the majority of workers were female. More recently, women have become more educated and have entered more diverse occupations; many recent immigrants have skills and educations similar to those of Asian groups. Some women open businesses, such as dressmaking and catering, in their homes.

Religious Institutions The first Arab Christian churches, one Melkite, one Maronite, and one Eastern Orthodox, were built in New York City between 1890 and 1895. Muslim immigration occurred a bit later; but a community had been established at Ross, North Dakota, by about 1900. There were no mosques in America, and at first Muslims met in homes. One of the earliest mosques was established in Detroit in 1919, although it was not sustained. Muslims met more discrimination than Christians and were more fearful of losing their faith.

Politics and Organizations Political alliances among Arab Americans, often are based on regional and ethnic groups. Arab Americans joined in the spirit of ethnic revivalism that occurred in the United States in the 1960s. Other factors increased their identification as well. One was increased migration. The intellectuals and disaffected upper class often found themselves or their causes silenced in the United States. In addition, victims of the Middle East conflicts were highly politicized by their experiences. Particularly after the 1967 Israeli-Arab war, in which Israel occupied parts of the neighboring Arab countries including the remaining Palestinian areas of the West Bank and Gaza, numerous organizations emerged that cut across communal identities and that aimed to increase American knowledge of the Middle East and to counter the support for Israel in the government and the media. The small size and limited resources of the Arab community limited its effectiveness, as did the attitudes of some of the ethnic communities that did not favor Arab causes and that distanced themselves from them. Such behavior was shown, for example, by Lebanese Catholic Maronites, many of whom identified as Lebanese but not as Arabs.

Four significant Arab American cross-sectarian groups have emerged in the years since the 1967 Israeli-Arab war. The first was the Association of Arab-American University Graduates. Initiated in 1967 by scholars and political activists to provide information about Arab history, culture, and politics, it established a press and published scholarly articles and books for members who felt discriminated against and who could not get their work published. In 1973 the National Association of Arab Americans was organized as a research and lobbying group concerned with American relations with Arab states. In 1980, the American-Arab Anti-Discrimination Committee was founded to combat negative stereotyping of Arabs, to provide advocacy and legal services for Americans of Arab descent, and to protect their civil rights. In 1985, the Arab American Institute was founded to serve as a clearinghouse and training organization for Arab Americans interested in entering the political arena and to provide information on national and regional elections.

There are many other groups organized to serve Arab Americans, some of them relief organizations to aid various groups in the Middle East, others local, national, or religious groups such as the Syrian Club, the Jordanian Club, and the Cedars of Lebanon. Some of the most active are student organizations at universities.

During the 1991 war against Iraq, some Arabs in America feared that harsh measures would be taken by Americans against Arabs, including placing individuals in detention camps. There were some violent acts, but perhaps because of the brevity of the war and few American casualties most of the feared actions did not materialize. It was, however, a period of great stress for Arabs, especially those from Iraq.

ARMENIANS

The Armenians were one of the first Middle Eastern groups to emigrate in the nineteenth century, at about the same time as the Lebanese and Syrians. Most came from areas that are in present-day Turkey and in the former Soviet Union. Robert Mirak estimates that by 1924, there were nearly one hundred thousand Armenians in the United States. The 1980 census lists 213,000, but other sources estimate that by the mid 1970s the Armenian community in the United States numbered between 350,000 and 450,000; and Amal Rassam estimates that in 1990 close to one million Armenians lived in the United States and Canada. About 45 percent live in the Northeast, 25 percent in California, and 25 percent in the Midwest.

Armenians trace their roots in Asia Minor to the first millennium before Christ. They adopted Christianity as a state religion about A.D. 301, and their language belongs to the Indo-European family. The early kingdoms were destroyed but one remained in what is southern Turkey from A.D. 1080–1375. Armenia was ultimately divided between the Ottoman Turks, Persians, and Russians.

During the Ottoman empire, Armenians were an important and influential minority. In Istanbul, they were in finance and operated as advisers to the Sultan, who gained power as Western capitalism advanced. They were also gold- and silversmiths as well as members of a poor urban class. Most however lived in villages and towns along the Mediterranean and in Central and Eastern Turkey.

Migration to the United States Armenians were influenced by American missionaries who traveled to Turkey to convert Muslims in the nineteenth century. Having little luck with the Muslims, the missionaries turned to helping Armenians and founded schools and universities. Some Armenian students came to the United States for an education as early as the 1830s, and the numbers increased toward the end of the nineteenth century.

As the Ottoman Empire collapsed, the Armenians became caught between the British and Russian rivalry. Burdened by increased taxation, they were open to the influence of revolutionary movements in Europe. Socialist parties were formed, peasants stopped paying taxes and fought the Ottoman military. In their efforts they were supported by rival parties set up in the American Armenian community as early as 1887, which publicized their causes. European powers intervened by supporting the Armenian revolts and ultimately worsened their problems. The first massacres of Armenians by Ottoman government forces and the mountain Kurds began in 1894 and led to major migrations. After the reformist Young Turk Revolt in 1908, which proposed equality for minorities and in which some Armenians participated, there was another year of Ottoman repression and the added fear of conscription, which led to further Armenian emigration. During World War I, systematic deportations, forced movements of population, starvation, and massacres killed up to one million Armenians and left another million homeless. As a result over forty thousand Armenians came to the United States.

Settlement and Economic Patterns Many of the early Armenian immigrants—mostly male—were skilled as well as literate but generally brought few resources. They took jobs in the mills and factories of the eastern cities, lived inexpensively, and sent money home. Later they opened stores, farmed, and began to sell Oriental rugs. Even though there were relatively few women, there was little intermarriage at first. Eventually the immigrants left their primary urban ethnic communities for the suburbs. Others moved to Detroit to build cars or to Fresno County, California, to buy land and establish vineyards; there still are large Armenian communities in these two areas. In Detroit there are close to fifty thousand Armenians.

By 1908, there were three thousand Armenians in Fresno County, and according to Robert Mirak, they owned approximately 60 percent of the land in the San Joaquin Valley. Successful Armenian immigrants generally came from a commercial background and brought capital in contrast with the German, Russian, and Japanese farmers of the region; those without capital worked for fellow Armenians. There were reports of women working in packing houses in Fresno in 1917. The substantial economic success of some in the community often stirred jealousy, and sometimes discrimination, against Armenians. The second generation entered white-collar occupations and the professions. Although most came from what is now Turkey and the newly independent Armenia, some of this early group came by way of Iran and other Middle Eastern countries.

After World War II, Armenian immigrants primarily came from the Soviet Union and the Middle East. Those coming from Iran after the fall of the shah in 1979 often brought considerable wealth and settled mostly in Los Angeles. Their ancestors had gone to Iran in 1600 and had received special privileges that enabled them to monopolize the silk trade and become a merchant elite. Although they are divided from other Armenians by economic class, they have preserved their Armenian language and identity and attend Armenian churches.

Armenians from the Soviet Union tend to be poor but well-educated professionals and artists who experience problems in adjusting to America. Armenian social services have been set up for them in California. Most do not go to church but organize along political lines. Armenians from the Arab countries are frequently multilingual merchants, some of whom lost their businesses prior to emigrating during the conflicts in the Middle East. A good number have settled in California, attracted by the climate and the large Armenian communities there.

Religion, Family, and Organizations The churches became important centers of organization for Armenians. The major ones were the Armenian Apostolic Church, the recognized church in the Ottoman empire (Worcester, Massachusetts, 1891); the smaller Armenian Catholic Church (New York City, ca. 1910); and the Armenian Evangelical Union, started by American missionaries. By 1982 there were an estimated one hundred Armenian churches in North America, with dioceses in New York and Los Angeles.

Early immigrants married other Armenians. Their large families and church activities, as well as Armenian-language classes, kept them so busy that the children sometimes felt left out of American school activities. A strict moral and behavior code kept Armenian children, like other children of Middle Eastern heritage, close to the family. By the 1960s, the third and fourth generations were more assimilated, few knew Armenian, many left home for college, more married out, and some moved away from their families.

As with other ethnic groups, there are conflicts and differences between recent immigrants and earlier ones. Armenians from Russia are less strict about behavior and are generally well educated, and they often feel patronized by the older immigrants with whom they compete for leadership. The older ones feel that because they have been in America longer, they should run the organizations, whereas the newcomers feel the older ones are too Americanized.

The Armenian General Benevolent Union, founded at Cairo in 1906 and established in the United States in 1908, raised endowments and provided day schools in Massachusetts and Michigan, summer camps, counseling, and job assistance. The Armenian Relief Society, founded in 1910 as the Armenian Red Cross, has sixteen thousand members in eighty-five chapters in North America. Many Armenian-American travel agencies began scheduling group tours to Soviet Armenia in 1959, and it is estimated that twelve thousand American Armenians spend several weeks in Armenia annually. Many local political activities have links abroad; within the United States, most Armenians support the Republican party. Assimilation has increased through intermarriage and public education, and the community continues to display both cultural retention and acculturation.

IRANIANS

Migration History and Organization Iran today is a country of forty-five million people, who trace their history from 559 B.C. when Cyrus the Great founded the Persian empire. The major and official language is Persian, an Indo-European language, but significant groups of people speak Turkish, Arabic, Kurdish, and Baluchi. The major religion is Islam which dates back to the seventh century when the Arabs conquered Persia. The government converted from Sunni Islam to Shiite Islam in the fifteenth century in opposition to the expanding Ottoman Sunni empire.

More than 90 percent of Iranians are Muslims, but there are several small non-Muslim populations such as the pre-Islamic Zoroastrians who also speak a special form of Persian. There are Iranian Jews, Armenian Christians, and a few Assyrian Christians who speak a semitic language. Bahais comprise a small but significant religious group that broke from Islam in the nineteenth century. Several of the religious minorities, such as the Armenians, belonged to merchant classes.

In the period 1927–1932, half of the immigrants coming to the United States from Iran were minorities from within the country, primarily Armenians and Assyrians. After World War II, many members of the Muslim majority came to the United States to better their educations, to improve their economic status, or to escape political upheavals. American economic interests in Iranian oil, and the United States' role in replacing Mosadagh after he had nationalized Iranian oil with the shah in the early 1950s, facilitated the migration of students and others. There were few Iranian immigrants in the United States before 1950, but between 1950 and 1977, 34,855 Iranian immigrants entered the country, as did 381,027 nonimmigrants, many of whom were students. From 1960 to 1977 there were 82,233 Iranian students in the United States.

The revolution that forced the shah from power in 1979 prompted religious minorities, leftists, secularists, and students to flee the Islamic fundamentalist regime of the Ayatollah Khomeini, and many who were already in the United States moved to become permanent residents. In 1978 the number of nonimmigrant Iranians in the United States reached an all-time yearly high of 130,545, and in 1980, 51,310 students were enrolled in American colleges. There were an estimated 245,000 to 341,000 Iranians in the United States in 1986.

The majority of Iranian Muslims arrive with a less developed sense of religious cohesiveness and have fewer social organizations than minorities from Iran. Pan-Iranian organizations are often weakened by other, competing allegiances. Iranian student organizations are important political organizations.

General Distribution and Demographics Iranians are concentrated in a few states. According to the 1980 census, 40 percent live in California, primarily in the Los Angeles area. Other major population centers are the New York/New Jersey and the Washington, D.C., areas. Students are more widely distributed.

Iranians are quite distinct from other ethnic groups in that many are younger and many are single, in part due to their student status. They represent a highly educated community, with 44 percent of the nonstudents having college degrees. Many are professionals and have relatively high incomes. In 1979 they had an average per capita income of

$17,900, compared with $11,200 for all Americans. In addition, many brought vast wealth with them.

Those who brought wealth have invested in businesses, while those who left with less often own small stores. Families work together in businesses, though generally the more recent immigrants do not have large kinship groups. Women have been very active in service enterprises in Los Angeles, both as owners/operators of family-run businesses and as employees of small businesses. From the home they work as dressmakers, caterers, hair stylists, teachers of Persian, interior decorators, and baby-sitters. They also work in groceries and other types of small stores.

TURKS

History of Migration   The Turkish population in the United States numbers from one hundred thousand to two hundred thousand. The 1980 census listed 64,691, but that figure is far too low. The term Turk includes people born in the Ottoman empire before 1923 or the Turkish Republic after 1923, a person who is Muslim, speaks Turkish or is from a Turkish-speaking family. The term also embraces Turkish speakers from the regions of Cyprus, Central Asia, China, the Balkans, and other Middle Eastern countries.

Of the early immigrants from the Ottoman Empire, perhaps 10 percent were Turks. After the Ataturk reforms, many educated Turks returned home, leaving a small, unskilled community, primarily of men, in the United States. Many never married, and some married Americans; the community did not expand as the Arab and Armenian communities did.

Beginning in the late 1940s, more professionals began to arrive, many as engineering and medical students. A number of these immigrants married non-Turks; others brought their families. Some had attended the American-run Robert College and had learned English. A number of women professionals had attended the American Girls School adjacent to Robert College. In the 1950s and 1960s, middle-class members of the military attended selected American universities as a result of Turkey's participation in NATO.

Few of the later, more educated immigrants had contact with the early migrants. The new professional communities, more secure economically, were more interested in preserving their culture and language for their children, and their associations differed in content. Members of either the lower or the upper classes who married Americans had fewer marital problems than the lower- and middle-class Turks who rose in status through education and married women who were more educated than they. There are numerous scholars and some artistic professionals, a few owners of large businesses, but many owners of small-scale enterprises such as shops and restaurants. There is little interaction between members of the upper and the lower classes.

Most Turks live in or near urban centers, including New York, Chicago, and Detroit. More recently, professionals, especially physicians, have moved to smaller cities in the Midwest, the South, and the East. The small shopkeepers are primarily in New York City, Rochester, New York, and Los Angeles.

There are many associations, including professional clubs for engineers, physicians, and psychiatrists, as well as soccer clubs and cultural clubs. The Federation of Turkish-American Societies, founded in 1956, includes more than twenty associations and concentrates on political issues. The Assembly of Turkish American Associations, founded in 1979, publishes a bulletin covering history, culture, and politics and holds annual meetings. A political action group, the Turkish American Awareness Group, was formed in 1982.

Many Turks retain their Turkish citizenship, partly because of their high degree of nationalism. The upper-class second generation retains its pride in its Turkish identity, while the middle-class second generation seeks to assimilate. However, in the early 1980s, many Turks became naturalized citizens, thereby strengthening their identification with the United States. Some wives keep their Turkish citizenship, enabling their families to keep a foot in both countries.

Turkish newspapers have had a hard time surviving due to the limited population; television programs have had more success. In terms of their political involvement, virtually no Turks have run for office, nationally or locally. Rather, political activity is limited to letter writing or political advertising in newspapers.

ASSYRIANS

The Assyrians are a Christian minority that originally came from areas of present-day Turkey, Iraq, Iran, Syria, and Lebanon. They number some 150,000 to 200,000 in the United States and live primarily in California, Michigan, Illinois, and the eastern states. They claim descent from the ancient Assyrian empire and speak several dialects of Aramaic, a Semitic language related to Arabic and Hebrew.

There were religious rivalries, based on theology and politics, between the Nestorians, who follow the East Syrian rite, and Jacobites, who follow the Antiochene rite. Most Jacobites are from Syria, whereas Nestorians came from Turkey and Iran. In the sixteenth century, Jesuit missionaries and others made their way to convert the indigenous Christians. Nestorians who united with Rome called themselves Chaldeans. Assyrians had lived under Ottoman and Persian rule, and most were peasants. Like the Armenians, the Assyrians sided with the West against the Turks and were also massacred and expelled. They also had hoped for a homeland. After World War I the League of Nations decided that they were to be settled in northern Iraq around Mosul, but they ended up scattered around the Middle East, and some came to Europe and the Americas. In many ways their history resembles that of the Armenians, with whom they identify, but they retain their own culture, religion, and language.

Settlements and Culture   The first Assyrians came to America in the 1880s, sent by missionaries, and many opened stores. Many Assyrians live around Chicago and in California. Jacobites are found predominantly in New York and Massachusetts, and Chaldeans in metropolitan Detroit. The second major wave of Assyrians came in the 1960s, dislocated by the war between the Kurds and Iraq. The Assyrian American National Federation helps newcomers to find jobs and housing.

The descendants of the early migrations have become professionals and white-collar workers. In 1949 they supported schools that taught their language and culture. More recently, numerous organizations, newspapers, and radio programs have reflected increased interest in their heritage. A political activist group, established in 1976, organized ICAN, the International Confederation of the Assyrian Nation, which seeks a semiautonomous state in the homeland.

There is a Chaldean population of approximately fifty thousand in the Detroit area, and there is a growing community in California. Many speak Arabic, and a few also speak Kurdish. Although they know they are related to the Assyrians, they see themselves as separate. Most come from the town of Telkaif in northern Iraq, but there are also many from Baghdad who speak Arabic, some of whom consider themselves Arabs. In Detroit, they own most of the mom-and-pop stores, which provide the means to further educate their children, who are now becoming professionals and entering white-collar jobs. In Iraq, some were farmers, and some had engaged in hotel management in Baghdad, thus obtaining entrepreneurial experience before entering the United States. In addition, having come to America as a close-knit minority, they assisted each other economically. They are the only Middle Eastern group in the Detroit area that came with refugee status, which carries several advantages such as rapid access to welfare if necessary. This status ended just before the Allied-Iraq War of 1991. The Chaldeans consider themselves distinct from the numerous Arab groups in Detroit and do not live with any of them.

The bilingual law of Michigan allows Chaldean to be taught as a written language for the first time in many years. It had previously been a liturgical written language. Chaldeans have several churches in the Detroit region. Like other Middle Easterners, Chaldeans consider family and kinship extremely important. Most Chaldeans feel they are related to each other, although there are competing clans and headmen. Since some Chaldeans see themselves as Arabs first and Chaldeans second, some have cooperated with Arab groups, but most activities are within their linguistic/cultural group. After the 1991 Persian Gulf War, they were instrumental in organizing a philanthropic charitable organization, Victims of War, which was perhaps the first time that they cooperated with Lebanese Muslim and Palestinian groups in helping victims of the various Middle East wars. Some also joined the American-Arab Anti-Discrimination Committee to protect their civil rights.

The 1991 bombing by the American-led forces during the war against Iraq was a particularly difficult time for the Iraqi Chaldeans, who feared to speak out on American policy. Some supported the Iraqi regime; many did not, fearing the rising Islamic fundamentalism and preferring the secular Baathist socialist regime.

KURDS

The Kurds come from northern Iraq, western Iran, eastern Turkey, the Soviet Union, and eastern Syria. They speak an Indo-European language related to Armenian and Persian. Although there are over twenty million Kurds in the Middle East, they form a small community in the United States. Historically Kurds have inhabited mountainous regions and small towns and, having had a de facto degree of autonomy, have resisted assimilation into the modern states drawn by European powers that divided their population. The Kurds trace their language and culture back thousands of years, before the Turkish and Arabic empires. From their mountain locations, they competed with valley peoples such as Armenians, Turks, and Arabs for control of fertile areas. Often they have been massacred, and they were involved in the Ottoman wars against the Armenians.

During World War I the Kurds were promised a homeland, as were the Armenians and the Jews; however, when the Treaty of Sèvres (1920) was superseded by the Treaty of Lausanne (1923), there was no state for the Kurds. In 1946, because the Soviet Union wanted access to the Middle East, the very small, and short-lived, state of Merhabad was created. Since most Kurds are peasants, nomadic herders, and small-town dwellers, with few living in major cities, their power bases are decentralized. Foreign powers have used them as a fifth column against other states, and the Kurds have usually suffered for it, often losing many lives. In the aftermath of the 1991 American-led war against Iraq, the Kurds rose up against the Iraqi regime, encouraged by the United States. However, the United States did little to help the revolt, and as they took to the hills, many thousands of Kurds died.

Some Kurds came to America from Turkey during World War I. In the 1960s others came as students from Iraq, but most came from Iraq between 1975 and 1977 after a failed revolt that began in 1974, in which the United States, Israel, and the shah of Iran supported the Kurds. In 1975 the shah made a deal with Iraq over the placement of a boundary in the Shatt al 'Arab waterway leading to the Persian Gulf and cut off his support of the Kurdish rebels. The United States had backed a Kurdish faction led by Mustafa al-Barzani, and many members of that faction came to America after the revolt collapsed. It was reported that in the Iran-Iraq war, both sides had used poison gas against Kurdish villagers.

Turkey has not recognized the Kurds, fearing the latter's desire for a separate state, and has often acted to oppress Kurds, not even allowing their language to be used. In fact, Iraq has been the only state where the Kurdish tongue was allowable.

Since many of the Kurds who came to the United States were political refugees and were ed-ucated, the Kurdish population in America is not representative of the Kurdish population as a whole. By 1980, 750 Kurds were counted. Today, they claim several thousand. In San Diego, there are communities from Iran, in Los Angeles from Iraq. There are also communities in Washington, D.C., and in Nashville, Tennessee, where Barzani had gone into exile. They were distributed among various communities by the U.S. government but recongregated in Washington, D.C., and West Coast cities.

Kurds are Sunni Muslims, but many say they do not identify closely with other Muslim groups in the United States. Some of this may have to do with the difficult political relations between the Kurds and other Muslim groups in the Middle East. However, their cultural life is like that of other Middle Easterners.

SUMMARY

Immigrants from the Middle East are extremely varied and see themselves as members of distinct groups. Each group has its own history and seldom interacts with the others, with the possible exception of Islamic groups. The major reasons for migration have included economic benefit and escape from political persecution. Each group must be seen in relation to its region of origin and to the historical period in which migration occurred. They settled and organized by linguistic group and by ethnic group within a linguistic category, often on the basis of religion. The Arabic-speaking Christians and Muslims from Lebanon seldom interact in the United States. Yet religion brings together groups such as Yemeni, Palestinian, and Lebanese Muslims, who would not have known each other in the Middle East. The Armenians from Turkey and Iran have differences depending on their country of origin, when they came, and their economic status. Nevertheless, there are organizations that cross ethnic boundaries to engage in political and cultural activities. These groups did not exist in the Middle East but arose from the needs of the various communities in this country.

In all communities, family and religious institutions are important. The patriarchal family structure, a major source of social cohesion, differs from traditional American family patterns, sometimes leading to conflicts with customs of the host society. Marriage usually occurs within the religious or linguistic community and often involves people from the same town of origin. Religious institutions have flourished. Although a religious minority, Muslims are increasing in numbers, mainly through immigration.

Economic status varies greatly among Middle Eastern immigrants and their descendants and plays a role in their interaction. Politically, the groups do not exert strong influence, but they have made inroads locally into the political process. The strained relations between the United States and various Middle Eastern groups have often made for tensions, fears, and discrimination, and the conflicts in the Middle East have caused tensions between immigrant groups in the United States, for ties to the homeland are often maintained, especially by groups in which refugees continue to migrate and revitalize the existing group. For this reason, Middle East immigrants perhaps have kept their culture alive longer than have other ethnic groups.

BIBLIOGRAPHY

Abraham, Sameer Y., and Nabeel Abraham, eds. *Arabs in the New World: Studies on Arab-American Communities* (1983).

Ansari, Abdolmaboud. *Iranian Immigrants in the United States: A Case Study of Dual Marginality* (1988).

Ashabranner, B. *An Ancient Heritage: The Arab-American Minority* (1991).

Aswad, Barbara C., ed. *Arabic-speaking Communities in American Cities* (1974).

Bates, Daniel, and Amal Rassam. *Peoples and Cultures of the Middle East* (1983).

Bozorgmehr, Mehdi, and Georges Sabagh. "High Status Immigrants: A Statistical Profile of Iranians in the United States." *Iranian Studies* 21, nos. 3–4 (1988).

Chaliand, Gerard. *People Without a Country: The Kurds and Kurdistan* (1980).

Dallafar, A. "Iranian Immigrant Women as Entrepreneurs in Los Angeles." In *American Muslim Families,* edited by Barbara C. Aswad and B. Bilge (forthcoming).

Elkholy, Abdo. *Arab Moslems in the United States: Religion and Assimilation* (1966).

Haddad, Yvonne Y., and Adair T. Lummis. *Islamic Values in the United States: A Comparative Study* (1987).

Halman, Talat. "Turks." In *Harvard Encyclopedia of American Ethnic Groups,* edited by Stephan Thernstrom (1980).

Hitti, Phillip K. *The Syrians in America* (1924).

Hooglund, Eric, ed. *Taking Root: Arab-American Community Studies* (1985).

———. *Crossing the Waters: Arabic-speaking Immigrants to the United States Before 1940* (1987).

Ishaya, Arian, and Eden Naby. *The Role of Minorities in the State: History of Assyrian Experience* (1979).

———. "Assyrians." In *Harvard Encyclopedia of American Ethnic Groups,* edited by Stephan Thernstrom (1980).

Kahn, Margaret. *Children of the Jinn: In Search of the Kurds and Their Country* (1980).

———. "Kurds." In *Harvard Encyclopedia of American Ethnic Groups,* edited by Stephan Thernstrom (1980).

Keddie, Nikki R. *Roots of Revolution: An Interpretive History of Modern Iran* (1981).

Lorentz, John H., and John T. Wertime. "Iranians." In *Harvard Encyclopedia of American Ethnic Groups,* edited by Stephan Thernstrom (1980).

Mirak, Robert. *Torn Between Two Lands: Armenians in America, 1890 to World War I* (1983).

Naff, Alixa. "Arabs." In *Harvard Encyclopedia of American Ethnic Groups,* edited by Stephan Thernstrom (1980).

————. *Becoming American: The Early Arab Immigrant Experience* (1985).

Sabagh, Georges, and Mehdi Bozorgmehr. "Are the Characteristics of Exiles Different from Immigrants? The Case of Iranians in Los Angeles." *Sociology and Social Research* 71, no. 2 (1987): 77–84.

Sawaie, Mohammed, ed. *Arabic Speaking Immigrants in the United States and Canada: A Bibliographical Guide with Annotation* (1985).

Sengstock, Mary C. *Chaldean Americans: Changing Conception of Ethnic Identity* (1982).

Shaw, Stanford, and Ezel Kural Shaw. *History of the Ottoman Empire.* Vol. 2. *Reform, Revolution and Republic: The Rise of Modern Turkey, 1808–1975* (1977).

Suleiman, Michael. *The Arabs in the Mind of America* (1988).

Waldstreicher, David. *The Armenian Americans* (1989).

Zogby, John. *Arab American Today: A Demographic Profile of Arab Americans* (1990).

SEE ALSO various essays in the section **"Processes of Social Change."**

Part VI

REGIONALISM AND REGIONAL SUBCULTURES

NEW ENGLAND

Peter W. Williams

IN OR ABOUT the year 1970, one historian of the American colonies remarked that we now know more about seventeenth-century New England than any sane person would want to know. The study of the six northeasternmost American states is complicated by a superabundance of evidence, which itself is a significant key to the region's distinctive character. Beginning with the Puritans and their notion of the providential meaning of the history they thought themselves helping God to make, New Englanders have been usually preoccupied with their past. In later centuries, this consciousness expressed itself variously in a determination to carry on a deeply rooted tradition of moral reform; in a rather dusty interest in genealogy and family and local history; and in the systematic study of the regional past in the great research universities that had developed "out of smalle beginnings" in its southern tier. The study of New England, then, involves the study of a region with a deeply rooted self-consciousness that has over the centuries profoundly affected interpretations of that region. As the Puritan and Yankee custodians of that heritage have been joined by waves of newcomers, the region's story has taken on greater complexity, but it has never lost a strand of either geographic or cultural and moral distinctiveness.

THE LAND

The boundaries of the area called New England are the Atlantic Ocean on the east, Long Island Sound to the south, the Canadian provinces of New Brunswick and Quebec to the north, and Lake Champlain and New York State to the west. The region is shaped in part by the northeast extension of the Appalachian mountain system, which divides into two distinct ranges: the Green Mountains of Vermont and the White Mountains of New Hampshire. Because of geological differences in the formation of the two ranges, the former is rich in marble and the latter in granite. While modestly important as mineral sources, the rugged beauty of these mountains has itself proven the greater economic asset in the long run.

Southern and central New England constitute a geological peneplain—a rather flat area formed by erosion—punctuated by obdurate bedrock formations known as monadnocks. (Mount Monadnock in New Hampshire is a prime example of such a formation). Except for Cape Cod and the islands off the Massachusetts coast, bedrock is seldom found far below the surface, usually covered with a thin layer of glacial debris known as mantle rock. The resulting soil is not the most hospitable to agriculture.

Major rivers, formed through glacial erosion of bedrock plateaus, interrupt the land in both directions. These rivers provided transportation in the colonial era and invaluable sources of mechanical energy during the early years of industrialization. Prominent among these rivers are the Connecticut, which forms the boundary between Vermont and New Hampshire, and whose broad and fertile valley constitutes a major internal cultural region of New England; the Merrimack of Massachusetts, which powered the early mills of Lowell and Lawrence; and the Penobscot, Kennebec, Saco, and Androscoggin in Maine, which have borne countless logs from inland to the sea. Like many regional toponymies, the names of these rivers all reflect the languages of the pre-European natives.

DEFINITION AND SCOPE

In the simplest terms, "New England" refers to the six northeasternmost of the United States that arose out of the Puritan "holy commonwealths" of colonial times. Four of those states—Connecticut, Massachusetts, New Hampshire, and Rhode Island—were among the original thirteen. Vermont, the fourteenth state, grew out of an independent-minded populace who renounced the claims of neighboring New Hampshire and New York, and who briefly (1777–1791) constituted themselves as an independent republic. Maine, formerly a province of Massachusetts, entered the new republic in 1820 as a free state paired with a slaveholding counterpart as part of the Missouri Compromise.

New England, however, is considerably more complex than its gross political and geographical contours might suggest. It is true enough that its historical and perhaps spiritual core lay in the four Puritan colonies—Plymouth (1621), Massachusetts Bay (1629), New Haven (1638), and Connecticut (1639), which in 1643 banded together to form the United Colonies of New England, or New England Confederation, to provide a common defense against the natives. Further consolidation took place in 1664, when Connecticut absorbed a rather reluctant New Haven under a new royal charter secured by John Winthrop, Jr., and again in 1691, when both Plymouth and the Maine territory were melded into the Massachusetts Bay Colony, also under a new royal charter. A holdout from its first settlement in 1636 was the colony of Rhode Island and Providence Plantations, for which Roger Williams first obtained a land grant in 1644. (After much internal turmoil, a final patent was obtained from Charles II in 1663.) Here, Williams, Anne Hutchinson, and other sectarian exiles from the Bay Colony created what was alternatively seen as a haven of religious freedom or, in the eyes of the disgruntled Puritans, the region's sewer.

Though the early fortunes of the region were firmly entwined with the Puritan movement, not all of the motivation for New England's founding was purely religious (or, as in the case of Rhode Island, purely Puritan). The name New England itself did not come from the Puritans, who were more inclined to regard their colony as a "New Israel"; rather, it was bestowed by Captain John Smith, better known for his secular exploits in Virginia, who helped promote interest in the northern colonies in his *A Description of New England* of 1616. Early exploration and settlement along the Maine coast was primarily commercial, and New Hampshire's emergence as a royal province in 1679 was prompted by similar motives. The economic success of the region as a whole during the later colonial era soon began to erode the theocratic character of the original settlements, and the transition from "Puritan" to "Yankee" was largely complete by the time of independence. ("Yankee," a term of questionable—perhaps Dutch—origin, can mean, with increasing specificity, an American, a northerner, or a New Englander. It is sometimes used to distinguish indigenous, more secularized New Englanders from their Anglo-Puritan forebears, and evokes specifically a rural life-style and its alleged attendant virtues of industry, honesty, and frugality.) Again, though, the moral force of the original religious impulse far outlasted the demise of Calvinist theology; the close alliance of church and state that characterized the "holy commonwealths" persisted into the nineteenth century, and the New England "conscience" has remained a potent part of the regional ethos even into the twentieth century.

The quest for a regional definition becomes more interesting and complex when examined at the margins. Along its northern frontiers, Maine—a name of obscure origin, probably referring to the "main land" as opposed to the offshore islands—borders on Francophone Canada, a source of considerable emigration into northern New England. At the southwestern corner, Connecticut provides commercial centers and bedroom suburbs for metropolitan New York City; conversely, parts of Long Island and northern New Jersey were originally a cultural extension of New England through Puritan settlement. Further north, upstate New York received its first significant settlement of European origin in the wave of Yankees who fled the poor soils of New England and followed the route of the Erie Canal westward early in the nineteenth century. This was the beginning of a still broader movement—the "Yankee Exodus"—that followed lines of latitude originating in New England and passing through Connecticut's Western Reserve and "fire lands" (granted as compensation for losses suffered during the Revolution by British raids) in northeastern Ohio. From Ohio they continued on through Illinois, Wisconsin, and Iowa, terminating in northern California and the Pacific Northwest. The spoor of the Yankee can still be traced through distinctive regional cultural patterns such as the enduring presence of Congregational churches, Greek Revival architecture, and place-names such as Springfield.

Within the area bounded at the ends by Maine's Aroostook and Connecticut's Fairfield counties, further internal variation is abundant. The region's metropolis has always been Boston, the center of the original Bay Colony that so dominated colonial Puritan affairs. Even in Boston, however, an awareness of the economic and cultural influence

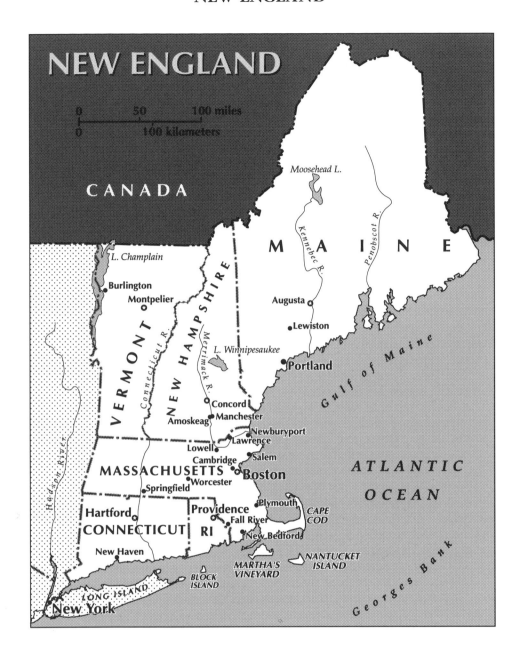

of nearby New York City is powerful. Southeastern New Hampshire has now become part of the Boston metropolitan region, and a significant number of commuters live in the Manchester area. The northern border of Massachusetts—with a few extensions northward—is a useful demarcation line for the grossest division of the region, which can be measured in terms of population density. In 1988 Connecticut, the least densely populated of the three southernmost states, had a ratio of population per square mile of 663.6, while that for New Hampshire, the most densely populated of the northern three, was 120.3. Rhode Island, with the densest population of all the New England states, had a ratio of 940.9; Maine's, at the opposite end, was 38.9. (Interestingly, native peoples prior to the European arrival distributed themselves in roughly the same proportions.)

Another useful geographical distinction is between coastal and inland New England, with the latter subject to still further internal differentiation. The coastline, which stretches some four thousand miles in all its indentations, boasts a number of major harbors—Portland, Newburyport, Boston, Providence, Newport, and New Haven among them. Commercial fishing from ports such as Gloucester on Boston's north shore, for lobsters off the Maine coast as well as for the "sacred cod" whose gilded image adorns the statehouse in Boston, has been a major enterprise since even before the Puritan settlements, especially in the plankton-rich offshore banks.

The varied character of the coastline is an important source of the region's physical attractiveness as a vacation site. The rocky headlands of the Maine coast contrast with the glacial runoff of sand that constitutes Cape Cod and the offshore islands of Nantucket and Martha's Vineyard. Further southwest, the Connecticut shore on the northern side of Long Island Sound abounds in salt marshes and clam flats. Inexorably, the rugged traditional lifestyles of the whalers, fishermen, and clam diggers are yielding to those who seek out the picturesque, and can afford its increasingly steep price tag.

NATIVE PEOPLES

The earliest aboriginal inhabitants of New England may have entered the region as many as ten to twelve thousand years ago, coming in pursuit of big game and staying to establish stable residential patterns. Agriculture and fishing began over the centuries to supplement hunting, and encampments on the shores of lakes, rivers, and bays provided access to fish outside of game seasons. (The Boyston Street fish weir, recently excavated in Boston, dates from ca. 2500 B.C. and contains some sixty-five thousand stakes for trapping fish.) The eventual introduction of the vegetable staples of corn, beans, and squash, which would help sustain the Plymouth "Pilgrim" colonists during their early lean years, fostered agriculture and led to the far denser peopling of the southern parts of the region than would take place in the less hospitable northern reaches. By the time of the arrival of the Europeans, these peoples had separated into a number of individual village bands, each speaking a variety of the broader Algonkian language spoken from the Canadian Maritimes to North Carolina, and that became less intelligible the farther one strayed from a particular locale.

In the northern parts of what would become New England, the eastern Abenaki, Passamaquoddy, and Malecite dominated; further south, the Massachusett, including the Pawtucket and Wampanoag,

lent their name to the Bay Colony, while the Narragansett negotiated with Roger Williams for rights to the lands that became Rhode Island and the Pequot and Mohegan inhabited what would become Connecticut. Although firm numbers are hard to come by, Neal Salisbury estimates that the native peoples experienced close to a ninety percent reduction in numbers during the early years of European arrival, down from a figure variously estimated at from seventy-five thousand to one hundred and fifty thousand. A plaguelike epidemic of uncertain character that raged through southern New England during the years 1616–1617 took an especially high toll, leaving those natives whom the Pilgrims encountered disorganized and nearly decimated.

Though friction often characterized the relations of the natives with the free-floating English adventurers who originally came to exploit the region's wealth, the advent of the more settled Puritans brought about stability and even a measure of harmony in the very early years of first encounter; this was manifest in the invaluable assistance rendered the Pilgrims by the captive Squanto, as well as his presence with the leader Massasoit and some ninety Wampanoag at the Plymouth colonists' first Thanksgiving in 1621. Although the Puritans declared that the evangelization of the natives was a significant goal (an early colonial seal depicted an Indian pleading "Come over and help us"), such efforts were sporadic and only modestly successful; they not only required skilled missionaries but also were predicated on literacy and the Calvinist propensity for propositional theology. The theologically deviant Mayhew family did well in the isolation of Martha's Vineyard, as did John Eliot, the Roxbury "Apostle to the Indians" who translated the entire Bible and other religious works into the Algonkian language. By mid century Eliot had organized over a thousand Massachusetts into several "praying towns," which functioned as sorts of halfway houses between native and European society; at the heyday of the missionary movement on the eve of King Philip's War (1675–1676), perhaps 10 percent, or about twenty-five hundred, of New England Indians had become Christian.

Puritan efforts at providing a European education for the natives were perhaps well-intentioned but usually disastrous; most of those who attended Harvard's short-lived Indian College and similar institutions did not survive long to reflect on the experience. The premature demise of these schools was due not to pedagogical or theological rigor as such but rather a combination of culture shock and exposure to infectious diseases to which native people had no immunity—a familiar legacy of the "Columbian exchange." And, despite Puritan efforts to forbid its sale to natives, alcohol had similarly dire effects on intolerant Indian constitutions.

The coming of the Puritans made the eventual erosion of native life seem, at least retrospectively, inevitable. Intermarriage, though legal, was unusual, and not a major factor in the process. (After the major reversal of King Philip's War, which pitted the Wampanoag against the English, Afro-Indian marriages became reasonably frequent, injecting a new element into the demographic mix.) The fur trade particularly brought the two peoples into regular interaction, and wampum—smoothly polished beads made of shell—supplemented the colonists' meagre supply of specie for several decades, elevating a formerly scarce prestige item to the status of pan-colonial currency and promoting further a shift from a subsistence to a market economy. The growing dependence on European goods acquired through this exchange was a major if subtle corrosive of traditional life patterns, as natives became increasingly specialized in their economic lives in response to European trade demands. Politically, the Puritans came to regard the natives as subjects rather than allies, and the latter were not usually in a good position to object. Finally, as native lands passed through imperfectly understood transactions into Puritan hands, depletion of the soil through ill-advised methods of cultivation led to further, nearly irreparable change as the Indian sense of reciprocity with the land and its issue yielded to a European American notion of land as property and commodity.

The Pequot War of 1636–1637, waged by Puritan and native allies against the Pequot, former Connecticut allies of the Dutch, resulted in the Pequot's decimation and scattering, and marked the introduction of large-scale organized violence into the regional matrix. Natives were also divided later in the even more disruptive King Philip's War in which the Wampanoag sachem Metacomet—King Philip to the English, a son of Massasoit—and his allies suffered losses of some five thousand, while inflicting extremely heavy English casualties. The war, which arose from the Wampanoag leader's frustration with the increasing erosion of native control over the region, drove a sharp wedge through European-Indian relations, consigned the Christianized "praying town" residents to concentration camplike confinement on Deer Island, Massachusetts, and marked the practical end to a significant native presence in New England.

By 1750, the region's native population had dwindled to a few thousand and never recovered, though the isolation of those who survived promoted the retention of tribal identity in the longer run. That population in the later twentieth century remains small—perhaps twenty-five hundred in the region's only reservations, in Maine. Diminution in numbers, however, has not led to docility. In 1980, Maine's Passamaquoddy and Penobscots settled a claim against the state in which they received $81.5 million as compensation for lands they claimed had been wrongly taken from them by the government in earlier years. More recently, in 1991, the Pequot in Connecticut were also successful in securing the right to raise money through legalized gambling operations.

THE PURITANS AND THEIR LEGACY

Although a few scattered fishing settlements dotted the northern New England coast prior to 1620, it was not till the *Mayflower's* arrival in that year that the systematic British colonization of the region began. The "Pilgrims" of Plymouth Rock fame were actually Puritans—English Calvinists—who sought to leave behind them as completely as possible what they saw as an irredeemably corrupt Church of England. These early separatists, who lost half their party the first winter and numbered only some five hundred a decade later, were soon overwhelmed by another and much vaster exodus of co-religionists who differed mainly on the rather moot issue of the English church's salvageability. This "Great Migration" to the Massachusetts Bay Colony in 1630, spearheaded by John Winthrop on the *Arbella,* grew from about a thousand settlers that first year to some nine thousand in 1640 and twenty thousand in 1660. Although population continued to expand steadily thereafter, such growth was due almost entirely to natural increase, with little further immigration after mid century.

With the exception of Rhode Island, the subsequent history of colonial New England was largely that of the expansion and diversification of this original stock. The core of the initial emigration lay in the eastern English counties known as East Anglia—near Cambridge University, the movement's intellectual center—though other Puritans came from widely scattered parts of the nation. The subsequent emergence of the Connecticut and New Haven colonies, as well as the absorption of Plymouth and Maine into dominant Massachusetts Bay, represented variations on a common religious and cultural theme, played out for decades by an ethnically homogeneous populace unified also by the absence of extremes of economic inequality.

The Puritan movement was an English appropriation of John Calvin's drive to subdue the world, through a vanguard of predestined "saints," to obedience to the divine word and law of God. In addition to their manifold religious grievances, Winthrop and his followers were also motivated by fear and loathing of the social changes abounding in early Stuart England. "Masterless men," detached from traditional village society through a population explosion and royally sanctioned enclosures of common grazing lands, now gravitated towards London in alarming numbers, and this seemed to the Puritans an alarming symptom of the destruction of traditional English society.

The American Puritans saw themselves as having been led by God across the sea on an "errand into the wilderness"; once arrived safely in New England, they would create a set of "holy commonwealths" the example of which would ultimately persuade the recalcitrant English of their folly in clinging to the "popish" ways of the Established Church and in breaking up their traditional, organically bonded social order. Every aspect of New England social life—political, ecclesiastical, marital—was thus given theological meaning through the formation of a "covenant," or solemn compact, between the human actors and their God on the model of Israel of old. In its sharp break with the present and its attempt to revive both the English medieval past as well as aspects of both Old and New Testament practices, the New England Puritan movement was simultaneously radical and reactionary—perhaps best described as militantly, though selectively, restorationist.

Virtually every aspect of the collective life of the New England colonists was permeated by this religious ideology; little was relegated to the purely secular realm. Economic life, for example, was controlled in the early decades by the state. Puritan merchants, such as the hapless Robert Keayne, who exceeded colonial dictates as to what constituted an acceptable margin of profit, could be fined and lose considerable face for having let individual self-interest override the common good. Though New England was never a theocracy in the popular sense of rule by the clergy, who were prohibited from holding public office, political governance often was linked with religious status. Qualifications for the franchise varied over times and places, but full church membership was a prerequisite for voting in the Massachusetts Bay and New Haven colonies, especially in colonial elections marked by an "election day" sermon delivered publicly by a prominent cleric.

Education and literacy were also matters of religious import, since an ability to encounter directly God's word in the form of scripture was expected even of the humblest. The result was an extremely high and constantly increasing literacy rate that had reached eighty percent among males by 1760, with female rates straining towards parity in urban areas especially (sixty-five percent in Boston at roughly the same period). By the early nineteenth century, all but perhaps ten or fifteen percent of even the outlying rural population had achieved basic literacy skills in response to practical demands related to earning a living but also reflecting a broader-based culture of reading as well. Widespread public education traced its origins to the Massachusetts Bay Colony's Old Deluder Satan Act of 1647—a reference to His Satanic Majesty, who frowned on an immediate knowledge of Scripture—which mandated that towns with fifty householders maintain a teacher, and those with a hundred, a school. Though this act was spottily enforced, it did underscore the region's commitment to education based on the combination of Scripture and theology exemplified in *The New England Primer* of 1690: "In Adam's fall / We sinned all."

The first institution of higher learning in the English colonies, Harvard College, was founded in Newtown (later Cambridge) in 1636 by Puritans "dreading to leave an illiterate ministry to posterity when our present ministers shall lie in the dust." Harvard's purpose was primarily the training of a learned clergy on the Reformed model, though the preparation of a cadre of civic leaders was a major goal as well. Religious controversy led to the founding of Yale University in Connecticut by more conservative spirits in 1701; the Great Awakening revivals of the 1740s were also a more or less direct spur to the establishment of Brown University by Baptists in 1764 and Dartmouth College as a Congregationalist missionary outreach to the Indians in 1769. Other regional colleges were soon after founded both by Puritan Congregationalists (Amherst, Bowdoin, Williams) and Baptists (Bates, Colby) as well.

Several other early colonial institutions deserve some notice as particularly embodying the ideals of the "New England way." The first was the "meetinghouse," a designation for a place of worship chosen deliberately over the traditional "church," a term that implied that earthly space could somehow be made sacred. The meetinghouse was deliberately of secular design, possibly based on the market halls of late medieval English towns, and resembled a large square house more than an Anglican parish church. Though meetinghouses were designed primarily to provide an austere and functional setting for the proclamation of the word of God (chiefly in the form of lengthy sermons preached each Sabbath), they also could and did function in the early years of settlement as forts, schools, sites for town meetings, or any other purpose that served the commonweal. Though church and state were formally separated, the two realms nonetheless were interwoven inextricably in the pursuit of a common good. In addition, the assignment through sale or rent of box pews in the meetinghouses was generally based on the social standing of particular families, a principle that also affected the allotment of land in newly founded towns and the class rank of scholars at Harvard College.

The Sabbath was another colonial institution in which sacred and secular mixed. Rejecting the traditional term "Sunday" (together with the observance of Easter, Christmas, and other Christian holy days) as pagan, the Puritans adopted the more Hebraic "Sabbath" as their designation for the "Lord's Day," and set it aside on the Jewish model for worship and pious recreation. Attendance at worship by saints and reprobates alike was enforced by the state. Although not all of the minute regulations for conduct attributed to the Puritans by later detractors actually existed, the Holy Commonwealths (the Puritan colonies) did attempt to regulate such matters of everyday life as elaborateness of clothing through "sumptuary laws," reflecting class distinctions as much as religious norms. Order was generally well maintained, sometimes through graphically violent public punishments, in the interest of attaining what David Hackett Fischer has called an ideal of "organic unity" based on collective good rather than individual liberty. Corporal and, for repeaters, capital punishment was inflicted not only on common criminals but also on religious outsiders such as Quaker missionaries who refused to conform to Puritan standards of orthodoxy.

The four colonies that shared "orthodox" principles were subdivided into smaller political and geographical units called towns, which were more like townships or parishes than small cities. Such towns varied considerably according to the origins and character of their settlers, and some were not as deeply imbued with Puritan commitments as others. New England towns, which included the surrounding countryside and its inhabitants as well as dwellers clustered in the center, were usually spin-offs of previously settled communities, and they were founded on a social covenant. A meetinghouse would usually be erected centrally on what often later became the town green or common; land distributed according to a calculus based on wealth, social standing, and family size, with some of it held back for common use or later allocation; and the general economic weal furthered through the building and maintenance of roads and fences, allocation of commonly held pasturelands, encouragement of the settlement of millers and blacksmiths, and other activities that potentially benefited all. Governance was conducted routinely by a small group of elected selectmen; periodically, however, all enfranchised adult males were entitled to assemble for a town meeting, a proto-democratic institution that is still the basis for the polity of many small New England communities.

Though by the mid eighteenth century this communal ideal was becoming secularized through religious diversity and an expanded economy and franchise, the institution of the town served its purpose well in the early years of settlement both as an expression of the covenantal ideology of divinely ordained hierarchical social order as well as a practical way of sharing scarce resources of labor and tools. Timothy Dwight (1752–1817), the latter-day Puritan president of Yale College, expressed the ideal of the New England town in his poem "Greenfield Hill":

> In every village, smil'd
> The heav'n-inviting church, and every town
> A world within itself, with order, peace,
> And harmony, adjusted all its weal.

One sign that the broad ideological consensus on which the original settlements had been based was endangered by inexorable social change was the wave of witchcraft accusations that broke out in Salem in 1692. Although scholars are not in agreement on the causes of this hysteria, Paul Boyer and Stephen Nissenbaum have provocatively argued that the Salem witch trials were simultaneously a manifestation of extra-Christian folk religion with both English and West Indian roots as an occult counterpoint to Puritan monotheism; a last gasp of a long and virulent wave of such persecutions by both Catholic and Protestant Europeans; and a symptom of distinctively local circumstances. The Puritan ethic of hard work and self-reliance was undercutting an older tradition of charity towards the socially marginal, an apt description of most of those accused as witches. Some later scholars have also emphasized the connection of those accused of witchcraft with the Quakers, whose religious views presented a threat to a hierarchically structured society; others have seen the phenomenon as a conflict between pubescent and post-menopausal women represented respectively by accusers and accused, in which the latter posed a symbolic threat to the primacy of the nuclear family. The broader context of these events was the Bay Colony's loss of its original, rather permissive charter, a confusion that abetted the involvement of regional luminaries such as Increase Mather and Cotton Mather. When the dust had settled, the authorities had repented their hasty judgment, but some twenty suspected witches had been killed.

SOCIAL AND ECONOMIC TRANSFORMATIONS

The Puritans came to New England not simply as traditional agriculturalists, but as partakers in a transitional economy and society. Many came from areas of Kent and East Anglia in which farming alone was no longer a viable way of maintaining one's self and family, and many had become skilled craftsmen as well to provide alternative income. Thus, the seeds of a market economy were present in New England from its beginnings, though the needs of subsistence precluded their rapid emergence in the earliest years. Historians differ as to the rate and uniformity of the transition during the colonial period to a primarily commercial economy, but there is little doubt that a steady and profound transformation was occurring—a transformation accelerated by the region's leadership in the national process of industrialization during the early nineteenth century.

The Puritan Ethic Much ink has been spilled over Max Weber's classic thesis that Protestantism,

especially in its Anglo-American Puritan form, exerted an "elective affinity" with what he identified as the "spirit of [nascent] capitalism." The New England Puritans were certainly ambivalent about the changing economic ethic that broke with the medieval prohibition on usury—that is, any lending of money at interest. The 1653 will of the Boston merchant Robert Keayne, for example, was a lengthy exercise in self-justification over his 1639 conviction and fining for having made an excessive profit in his business dealings. This theological pressure to subordinate the individual good to that of the group was rendered memorably in John Winthrop's 1630 sermon, "A Modell for Christian Charity," preached while he and his followers were still on board the *Arbella*. On the other hand, the generic Protestant injunction to labor faithfully in one's secular vocation—what Weber called "this-worldly asceticism"—and the gnawing Puritan desire for assurances of salvation eventually came to focus on interpreting material, worldly success as a sign of divine approbation. At different rates in different places, the ideal of the collective good began to yield inexorably to the pull of individual interest as social cohesion became strained from various quarters and the opportunity for profit in trade increased. Richard Bushman captures the process in the preface of his provocatively titled 1967 study, *From Puritan to Yankee:*

Sometime between 1690 and 1765 Connecticut Puritans became Yankees. The transition had begun earlier and was far advanced in Boston by 1690, but in Connecticut the institutions inspired by the founders' piety persisted to the end of the seventeenth century. . . . My thesis is that law and authority embodied in governing institutions gave under the impact first of economic ambitions and later of the religious impulses of the Great Awakening. (p. ix)

Subsequent historians, one should note, have challenged an overemphasis on the inexorability of this process and have stressed, in Kevin Sweeney's words, "that even in the later 1700s New England remained a section notable for social homogeneity, community orientation, and religiosity." The family, in short, may have been at least as persistent as the market was insistent.

The British Colonial System One major circumstance that affected materially the course of colonial New England's development was the very fact that the region's political units were indeed colonies, and as such part of a broader colonial system. The New England colonies were unusually close-knit, since they shared a common religious raison d'être, and during their first several decades they were allowed to go substantially their own way as the mother country became preoccupied with its own problems with Puritans. Even before the Glorious Revolution of 1688–1689, in which the Stuarts were overthrown and replaced by the House of Orange in the persons of William and Mary, the English proceeded to establish firmer control over the colonies. The Massachusetts Bay Colony's charter had already been revoked in 1684, and it became a royal colony in 1691. Puritan religious hegemony was further eroded by the introduction of Anglican churches, such as Boston's King's Chapel and Christ Church (Old North of Paul Revere fame.)

The imposition of increased royal control had dramatic consequences in the long run, as English attempts to "micromanage" the colonial economy led to parliamentary actions that many colonists eventually came to regard as intolerable infringements on their liberties and grounds for revolution. New England's Puritans were opposed to the sort of tyrannical authority that their ideology did not recognize as legitimate. In the shorter run, the British presence helped undermine Puritan structures of authority through challenges to earlier land allocation, such as those of the Connecticut colony and its towns. The result in this case was a revolution in land ownership, since title to lands was placed now not in the hands of the towns as collectives but rather into that of individual "proprietors." Though in many cases this served simply at first as a loophole, the longer-range result was a shift from collective to individual responsibility for land ownership, distribution, and use.

Continuing New Settlement Wherever and however this transition occurred, the result was a gradual movement towards economic individualism, accompanied by an erosion of the power and prestige of the Puritan social order. In Connecticut, the impact was felt not so much in the older towns but rather in the new areas opened to settlement after 1690. During the period 1690–1720, nearly twice as many new towns were organized as in the three previous decades. Population growth was even more rapid. According to Richard Bushman, from 1670 to 1700, the growth rate was fifty-eight percent; for the next three decades it would rise to three hundred and eighty percent. The new towns, moreover, were qualitatively different from their predecessors in that land became available no longer through communally directed allotment but rather by individual cash purchase. This shift created two new social groupings—absentee proprietors and semitransient renters—neither of whom had a great deal at stake in the social order as such.

The experience of the northern frontier areas, especially in Maine and Vermont, was a variation on the same theme played out several decades later. During the years from 1760 to 1790 this region was first opened to settlement, and drew a tide of in-migration that lasted till the early nineteenth century. Much of the land was grabbed by speculators, who proceeded to sell it to individual would-be farmers. The Puritan notion of the town as an organic unit was thus vitiated: economic individualism played a significant role in this region from its beginnings, and the settlers of new towns came from scattered rather than uniform geographical origins. Although the "New Light Stir" of the revolutionary years swept the region as a latter-day revival similar to the Great Awakening of the 1740s, the dominant ideological conflict acted out in eighteenth-century New England was not Puritan versus dissenter but rather subsistence farmer versus absentee proprietor.

The failure of various protest movements by the former class to attain any significant reforms was compounded by an economic crisis beginning in 1808 that led to an out-migration from all over impoverished rural New England to the literally greener pastures of upstate New York, Ohio, and parts westward. The American Revolution had in fact more broadly served as a catalyst for sharpening emergent class divisions. Earlier populist movements such as Shays's Rebellion in western and central Massachusetts in 1786–1787, fought over issues of taxes, credit, and the availability of paper money, resulted in at best minor amelioration. Participants in this particular uprising seem to have been primarily those with least access to emergent transportation networks linking producers to markets.

Despite attempts to salvage the rural economy through such measures as the introduction of merino sheep in 1802 to supply woolen mills, history was not on the side of upland agriculture. Until its rediscovery as a vacation "paradise" in the twentieth century, northern New England at best served to nurture a culture of backwoods autodidacticism and "Yankee ingenuity." Celibate Shaker communities flourished in sites such as Sabbathday Lake, Maine, and Canterbury, New Hampshire, and lasted there in vestigial form till nearly the twenty-first century. Mormon leader Joseph Smith began his prophetic career in Vermont's Green Mountains, and religious and social critic Orestes Brownson was launched on his spiritual and political odyssey from the town of Stockbridge in the same state. William Gilmore has argued that the massive spread of literacy in this region during the decades following the Revolution produced a new, cosmopolitan rural consciousness that was soon to meet head-on with frustration engendered by the absence of economic opportunity.

Varying Economic Patterns The forces of historical destiny seemed to lie instead with the emergent commerce and industry of urban, southern New England. What economic success did come to outlying northern areas lay in extractive industries such as timbering and fishing, together with allied pursuits such as shipbuilding. Most of the successful agriculture lay in the fertile Connecticut River valley, whose entrepreneurial farmers established a thriving trade of produce and livestock with the West Indies. Fishing, for long a trade handed down in coastal families from father to son, had by the time of the Civil War become an industry based in Gloucester and Boston, staffed by Portuguese islanders and other immigrants rather than Yankees; by the 1890s, fishing for profit had virtually disappeared in other coastal towns. (Lobstering along the Maine coast to this day remains a partial exception.)

One colorful but atypical aspect of coastal economic life was the whaling trade, immortalized in Herman Melville's *Moby-Dick* (1851), a metaphysical novel solidly grounded in the enterprise's social history. The names of Ahab and Ishmael reflect, if quirkily, the New England tradition of biblical onomastics. The name of Ahab's ship, the *Pequod,* is a variant on that of the Pequot tribe. The *Pequod's* owners and Starbuck, the first mate, reflect the Quaker origins of Nantucket and New Bedford, the two great whaling ports of New England's southeastern coast. (Quakers also played a major role in the development of the early Rhode Island society and economy.) The three harpooners—Queequeg, Tashtego, and Daggoo—are respectively American Indian (from Martha's Vineyard), South Sea islander, and African, a reflection of the mixture of peoples drawn into the whaling trade through internal migration, immigration, and stops at exotic harbors in the Pacific.

Life in New Bedford and on its departing whaling ships—Ishmael's "Yale College and my Harvard"—however, was hardly romantic. Local whites tried to keep their distance from this highly unglamorous, dangerous, and low-paying profession, preferring instead to work in auxiliary enterprises such as shipbuilding and outfitting; rural newcomers, criminals, and immigrants provided better pickings for ship's recruiters and "landsharks" looking for easy marks in drunken sailors. (Sailors generally ranked as liminal people near the bottom of the social scale.) Although some fortunes were made by local investors and merchants, the replacement of whale oil by kerosene after the 1859 discovery of oil in Pennsylvania rapidly rendered whaling obsolete, and New Bedford joined the ranks of numerous other New England towns as a site for a new industrial era—that of the textile mill.

Another glamorous but short-lived aspect of New England's coastal development that emerged prior to the heyday of whaling was the fabled "China trade" based in Salem, a few miles north of Boston on the Massachusetts coast. From here entrepreneurs collected various valuables at ports in Europe, the West Indies, and the Americas, and thence sailed around Africa's Cape of Good Hope to acquire exotic nankeen cloth, silk, chinaware, coffee, and ginger to resell at great profit in domestic markets. The stately federal-style homes designed by Samuel McIntire that still grace Salem's Essex Street testify to the spectacular success of the town's elite, who also introduced a taste for ethnology into the region. Though the houses and the exotic artifacts in the Peabody Museum remain, Salem's brief career as a mercantile center came to an end after the War of 1812 as Boston and New York took over most of the enterprise of oceangoing commerce.

Boston also profited from trade with the Far East; ships from that larger port traded cloth and metals for furs with the Chinook of the Oregon coast, and then exchanged the furs for Chinese porcelains, teas, and textiles as well as Russian goods. This round replaced the earlier "triangular trade" of the colonial period in which New England livestock, fish, and timber were exchanged for West Indian sugar and molasses. Molasses was then distilled into rum, which was in turn traded for West African slaves. The cash thus generated could be used to buy manufactured and luxury goods in the mother country, and created many early mercantile fortunes. Much of the impetus for the Revolution came from intensified British attempts to regulate illicit trade with parts of the West Indies controlled by rival European powers. The closing off of these two triangular patterns of exchange, first by the

914

Revolution and the end of the slave trade, then by the coming of peace in post-Napoleonic Europe and the restoration of European dominance in oceanic commerce, forced the region's mercantile princes to look elsewhere for potential investments.

Industrialization Boston's position as an entrepôt with little local industry or natural resources left it in a precarious position, but well poised as a potential center for a new economic pursuit: finance. The Anglo-American world was at the time poised on the dawn of a new industrial era, and experienced Boston capitalists, together with their Providence counterparts, were well positioned to take advantage of a new configuration of circumstances. What was needed for New England to follow its motherland on the trail of the "dark, Satanic mills" of Manchester and Birmingham was capital, technical know-how, mechanical power, and labor. All were to prove available in abundance.

Know-how for the creation of large-scale mass production of cloth was acquired through what amounted to industrial espionage. Samuel Slater, an English artisan, accumulated enough knowledge of Richard Arkwright's system of completely mechanized spinning in England to recreate it from scratch after joining forces with the Quaker capitalist, Moses Brown, in Providence in 1789–1790. Francis Cabot Lowell introduced the English power loom into New England during the War of 1812 era, thus inaugurating the "Waltham system" of manufacturing at the Massachusetts town of that name. After a period of experimentation, parallel though slightly different systems of completely integrated and mechanized cloth manufacturing flourished in Massachusetts and Rhode Island. These early industrialists, together with the "putting-out" system whereby farm families contributed piecework to the nascent industrial process, constituted the beginnings of this nineteenth-century revolution.

The "Boston Brahmins" Another source of capital for the industrialization of New England lay in the fortunes made in part through the China trade. Before long, manufacturing in Massachusetts came to be dominated by the "Boston Associates," an ingrown group of families who also were heavily involved in financial enterprises such as banking and insurance and who dominated the Boston Stock Exchange. Together they formed a local elite who dominated local cultural and civic life until the Civil War era, and whose names are perpetuated in such newly created mill towns as Lawrence and Lowell. As Ronald Story has related, these families were not content simply to constitute a philistine plutocracy. Rather, they donated heavily to cultural and medical institutions such as the Boston Athenaeum, the Massachusetts General Hospital, the Lowell Institute, and Mount Auburn Cemetery, one of the earliest romantic "rural" parklike cemeteries.

The most favored recipient of Brahmin bounty, however, was Harvard College. Harvard, which had earlier been guided primarily by clergy and partly financed by the state, was during the 1820s dramatically transformed through the taking of financial and administrative control by a newly wealthy cadre of local entrepreneurs. These latter, only some of whom were themselves Harvard-educated, helped to socialize future generations into an elite—the so-called Boston Brahmins—bound together by common experience and group loyalties that proved remarkably successful throughout the century and beyond in keeping business and culture allied.

The Emergence of the Mill Town Mechanical power during these early years of the American industrial revolution came entirely from the rivers of New England, though steam would soon provide an alternate source of energy. Where waterfalls were abundant, however, labor was initially scarce. The entire colonial era was marked by a labor shortage, and neither slaves nor indentured servants played a significant role in the New England economy. Independent farmers and artisans abounded, with a handful of great merchant princes arising in Boston, Providence, and the cities along the Connecticut River valley. Unskilled, inexpensive labor to staff the new mills would have to come from other sources.

The first of these new sources was the reservoir of young rural women from a hinterland whose resources were growing strained. The prospect of wage labor in the new mill towns arising along the Merrimack and other rivers of southern New England was initially appealing, as the mill owners promised a virtually utopian life-style under close paternalistic supervision by enlightened and highly moral overseers. Lucy Larcom's account of life at Lowell in the 1820s and 1830s, where the "millgirls" attended church and classes and published a literary magazine in the time left free after a seventy-hour workweek, attracted the attention of many domestic and foreign visitors, and at first seemed like a benign alternative to the awful destructiveness of the English industrial cities. Few if any of these young women envisaged factory work as a lifetime pursuit, and their average tenure on the job was three years. Before long, however, they began to grow restive with working conditions, and by 1834 launched an unsuccessful strike. The seeming idyll of Lowell and its counterparts was approaching an end.

The planned industrial cities of Lowell, Lawrence, Holyoke, Amoskeag, and the rest of the some four hundred New England mill towns that were built during the nineteenth century now had to look elsewhere for appropriate labor, and they found it in the immigration that by the 1840s had begun to transform profoundly the region's population. New Bedford abandoned whaling in favor of manufacturing and drew on Portuguese islanders for a labor supply. The Irish and, following the Civil War, French-Canadians swelled the ranks of mill workers; "new immigration" Poles later gravitated to the factories of Holyoke, Massachusetts, and Greeks to those of Lowell.

In the long run, however, an abundance neither of immigrants nor of waterways could compete with the nonunion labor, easy access to fuel and raw materials, and the aggressively commercial spirit of the "New South" as the nineteenth century drew to a close. New labor laws absent further south promoted union organization and strikes, such as the great walkout at Lawrence of 1912 in which the state militia's brutality prompted a U.S. Senate investigation. Lack of entrepreneurial innovation combined with interregional competition to bring an end to New England's era of industrial dominance, and by 1957 the region's mills had declined to some twelve percent of their onetime production. Today, most of the remainder of what in 1850 had approached nine hundred mills lie abandoned, with some few finding alternative uses in the later twentieth century's drive towards historic preservation and adaptive reuse.

Other Forms of Manufacturing While textile mills dominated much of the industrial landscape of Massachusetts, Rhode Island, and parts of southern Maine and New Hampshire, other forms of manufacturing flourished in Connecticut. Eli Whitney was the Nutmeg State's resident genius, first inventing the cotton gin and then contributing to the development of the manufacture of rifles made with interchangeable parts in his Hamden workshop. Various of the state's cities developed specialized industries, with guns in New Haven (Winchester) and Hartford (Colt), brass in Waterbury, hats in Danbury, and clocks and watches in various towns. Yankee capitalists employing immigrant and, later, black labor became the dominant

pattern, as did industrial decline at varying rates during the twentieth century. The continuing viability of the insurance industry in Hartford, higher education in New Haven, and corporate headquarters in Stamford and other Fairfield County outposts of the New York metropolitan region contrasted selectively with the state's general decline in economic vitality and corresponding rise in social tensions.

New England's social fabric thus became transformed in profound ways from the crucial period of the early nineteenth century until the early twentieth century. Farmers, especially in the northern regions, abandoned their marginal holdings in droves to seek their fortunes in the cities or, more frequently, in the fertile and abundant lands to the west. In the process, much of the rural landscape reverted to forest. Boston, the regional metropolis, consolidated its role as a center for trade, finance, and culture, leaving industry to smaller cities and to the new mill towns that sprang up along the rivers and bore the names of its great capitalist families.

Religious Change Religious life was also affected by these transformations. Puritan Congregationalism had begun to come under fire during the Great Awakening, the religious revival that swept the colonies during the late 1730s and 1740s. The Baptists and "New Lights" it produced went on to challenge the traditional alliance of church and state, though Massachusetts resisted until 1833. By that time, conservatives had realized that they had more to lose than gain from perpetuating the colonial system, and the legislature ended support for the churches. Further, Calvinistic Congregationalism had decisively lost its hold on the Boston elite by 1825, the date of the founding of the American Unitarian Association by William Ellery Channing and other liberal clergy. Harvard College had also fallen to the liberals; in Harriet Beecher Stowe's words,

> All the literary men in Massachusetts were Unitarians. All the trustees and professors of Harvard College were Unitarians. All the elite of wealth and fashion crowded Unitarian churches.

Stowe's father, the ubiquitous Lyman Beecher, found himself similarly besieged in Connecticut, where the standing order of Congregationalist clergy allied with Federalist politicians reluctantly witnessed the disestablishment of their church in 1818 through an alliance of Episcopalians, Jeffersonian Democrats, and what Beecher denounced as "nearly all the minor sects, besides the Sabbath-breakers, rum-selling tippling folk, infidels, and ruff-scuff generally." A hierarchical social order based on deference was clearly yielding to other, more democratic impulses.

Boston's Unitarians, however, did not maintain their position unchallenged as the century progressed. From within, transcendentalists such as Ralph Waldo Emerson mounted a critique of what he dismissed as "corpse-cold" Unitarian rationalism, as well as of the commerce-based social order that had encouraged its development. George and Sophia Ripley's Brook Farm and Bronson Alcott's Fruitlands were two of the better known if short-lived experiments in utopian communal living that presented themselves as an alternative to an increasingly competitive and materialistic society. Irish and subsequent immigration strengthened the influence of the Roman Catholic church, which emerged as a major social force by the turn of the century. Christian Science, established by Mary Baker Eddy in the Boston area in the 1870s, has been interpreted as a protest by alienated urban women against conventional religion and medicine. Finally, the Episcopal church, personified in Trinity Church's charismatic Phillips Brooks, emerged in the same period as a liturgical alternative for the more prosperous classes.

Changing Gender Roles The changes wrought by population increase and diversification as well as economic transformation affected virtually all aspects of the social order. Women, previously integrated into a home- and farm-based economy in a variety of ways, now found themselves pushed in one of two directions. Immigrant women and, at least for a brief period, Yankee farm daughters found themselves part of a work force, partly domestic, partly industrial. As Laurel T. Ulrich has demonstrated, midwifery, once the province of women, began to share its functions with a corps of increasingly professionalized and overwhelmingly male physicians. The clergy, once the bastion of the New England opinion-making, found itself becoming compartmentalized in role, undergoing what Donald Scott has characterized as a transition "from office to profession."

Further differentiation of class and gender roles was promoted by the physical separation of work and residential space especially for the middle classes as public transportation made possible the development of what Sam Bass Warner has called "streetcar suburbs" in the later nineteenth century. As men went off to the city to work, women in families that could afford their voluntary un-employment found themselves isolated from the "dirty" realm of commerce. Though middle-class women were almost universally literate and some few found opportunities for higher education in institutions like South Hadley's Mount Holyoke College (1837), most had to forge a sphere of identity based on family, church, benevolent activity, friendship networks, and other areas outside the realm of the economically remunerative. As Ann Douglas has argued in *The Feminization of American Culture* (1977), Protestant clergy and middle-class women eventually found themselves in a tacit alliance in attempting to shape social values not through their political and economic influence, which was marginal at best, but through an assertion of claims to moral superiority based on their distance from the realm of "filthy lucre."

IMMIGRATION AND ETHNICITY

Following the "Great Migration" of Puritans in the 1630s, few newcomers arrived in New England prior to the Revolution. A small colony of Sephardic Jews was established in Newport, probably in the 1670s, but rapidly dissipated. It was revived by emigration from New York City in the 1740s, and the prosperity of merchants such as Portuguese-born Aaron Lopez (1731–1782) made possible the erection there of the Touro Synagogue—the first in the colonies—in 1763. Later Jewish arrivals generally established communities in Boston, Providence, New Haven, and other large cities. A few Huguenots, Scotch-Irish, and Africans accounted for most of the remainder of the approximately 5 percent of the region's population that was not of English birth or descent at the time of independence.

The transfer of New France and its people to the British Empire by the Treaty of Paris in 1763 had profound consequences for New England's demographics. A consciously traditionalist French-Canadian culture, based on the principle of *survivance* (cultural survival), arose to defend the *habitants* of the region against Anglophone imperialism. However, a combination of population growth and shortage of suitable farmland began in the early nineteenth century to lead to a pattern of emigration southward, sometimes temporary but increasingly permanent. Their numbers reached a high point during the half century following 1845, of whom some two-thirds settled in New England.

The 1950 census, the last to treat them separately, showed nearly a quarter of a million Canadian-born and over a half-million second generation French-Canadians in the United States, with now more than seventy percent in New England.

Patterns of French-Canadian settlement differed in some significant ways from those of other contemporary immigrant groups. The proximity of their land of origin permitted easy communication and transportation, so that maintenance of the old ways received continual reinforcement. Though most shared a common religion with the Irish, who had rapidly come to dominate the American Roman Catholic hierarchy, French-Canadians resisted attempts by the latter to impose the English language on their worship, and fought fiercely though with mixed success for the maintenance of Francophone parishes. (The French language continues to be a major source of ethnic self-assertion in the Canadian province of Quebec, which prohibits the use of English for public purposes.) French-Canadian settlement also clustered in the less-populated northern New England states, and "Little Canadas" developed in towns such as Manchester, New Hampshire, and Lewiston, Maine. After the Civil War, however, economic opportunity lured many to more southerly mill towns such as Woonsocket, Rhode Island, and New Bedford, Massachusetts, where they came to be dominant components of the work force.

Another source of immigration distinctive, though not unique, to New England was the Portuguese, who established other substantial American settlements only in California. Few of these came from the Iberian Peninsula; rather, most came from Madeira, the Azores, and the Cape Verde Islands, beginning to arrive in large numbers after the Civil War and reaching a peak of some ninety thousand in the decade of World War I. These Atlantic islands had for decades been important in the transatlantic trade; their inhabitants began to seek work especially in the whaling industry off the region's southeastern coast and in the fishing ports north of Boston, where they had displaced most of their Yankee predecessors by the late nineteenth century. Later arrivals from the Atlantic islands went to work in the textile and jute mills of southern New England. Cape Verdians, usually mulattoes of Afro-European descent, at times encountered racial discrimination as well as the usual problems facing immigrants.

The era of the new immigration, which began in the 1880s, brought with it representatives of other peoples as well. Poles, though small in number compared with those immigrating to the Great Lakes region, were well represented in the industrial cities of northern Connecticut and western Massachusetts, and local bishops established for them a considerable number of national parishes. Italians followed broader patterns, congregating in distinctive neighborhoods in the larger cities such as Boston's North End, the Federal Hill area of Providence, and New Haven's Wooster Square; by the 1930s the latter city boasted the largest percentage of Italian residents of any in the country. Greeks arrived in small but significant numbers, achieving success especially as restaurateurs.

By far the most significant group of immigrants to New England during the nineteenth century, though, were the Irish; by the end of the age of immigration, "Boston Irish" had probably become as typically regional a descriptive phrase as "Connecticut Yankee." Though both Protestant and Catholic Irish had earlier emigrated to North America, freely or otherwise, in considerable numbers, the potato blight and ensuing famine that culminated in 1845 gave rise to what can only be described as a mass folk migration across the Atlantic in pursuit not so much of prosperity but of sheer survival. Assisted by English landowners eager to be rid of their impoverished tenants, some two and a half million Irish abandoned their native country in the years 1835 to 1865, the poorest of them reaching the Canadian shore as ballast on returning timber ships.

New York, Philadelphia, and, later, Chicago attracted large numbers of Catholic Irish during the middle decades of the century, but their concentration in Boston gave that smaller city the highest percentage of Irish-born of any of the larger metropolitan regions. In 1860, more than a quarter of Boston's residents were Irish-born (45,991); by 1890, the number had increased to 71,441, though the overall percentage had fallen to sixteen. In the twentieth century, the numbers of foreign-born Irish fell substantially, though enhanced in the latter decades by those fleeing their island homeland's dismal economy in search of sometimes illegal residence in the city's strong ethnic neighborhoods.

The arrival of the Irish introduced into New England for the first time since the coming of the Puritans a significant group of newcomers who could not fit readily into the established social order. The one assimilative advantage many Irish possessed was their language; the ancestral Gaelic had by this time yielded in considerable measure to English as their primary language. Religion was a strike against them, though. The fierce allegiance of the Irish to the Roman Catholic church soon dispersed the residual good feeling that had characterized Yankee-Catholic relations in the afterglow of French aid to the revolutionary war cause.

The latent nativism that had in colonial times manifested itself on such occasions as Pope (i.e., Guy Fawkes) Day, erupted in 1834 in the destruction of the Ursuline convent in Charlestown through mob action, and later took the more organized form of the American party, also known as the Know-Nothing party, which captured control of the Massachusetts governorship and legislature from 1854 to 1857. The Know-Nothings, who were by contemporary standards rather progressive-minded reformers in some ways, appealed especially to working-class people of British Protestant background who saw their jobs threatened by the Irish influx. The party soon lost credibility through the indiscretions of the Hiss Nunnery Committee, who submitted as part of their account "expenses incurring from their relationship with a woman 'answering to the name of Mrs. Patterson'" (Ray Allen Billington, *The Protestant Crusade* [1938; 1964], p. 414). The party was soon absorbed by the nascent Republicans, and interethnic tension was temporarily assuaged by the enthusiastic commitment of the Irish, who were allied with rich Yankee mill owners in their opposition to abolitionism, in the defense of the legally established union.

Irish conservatism on the slavery issue arose not so much out of innate racism as from their own economic position, which for decades was at the bottom of the proverbial ladder. The vast majority of the newcomers were unskilled and many were illiterate; what jobs they could command were resented by the poorest of the native-born whites. Young Irish immigrant women, who became known generically as "Bridget," went to work first as domestics—in 1850, 2,227 Irish girls in Boston worked as domestic servants—then as replacements for the rural Yankee mill girls who tired of the regimentation of factory life. Men found work as they could, caring for horses and performing similar menial tasks, then moving into the building trades. High rates of pauperism and minor, alcohol-related criminality, together with the rise of disease-infested tenements created out of partitioned grand homes and former warehouses, accompanied the first generation's economic woes.

Stephan Thernstrom has demonstrated that although economic mobility among the Boston Irish lagged behind that of Jewish and British newcomers, it did in fact slowly come about. By 1884, Hugh O'Brien had been elected Boston's first Irish mayor, and employment in city jobs, especially in the police and fire departments, and political positions rapidly grew for his countrymen and their offspring. By the time of the New Deal in the 1930s, an Irish-American like Joseph P. Kennedy could even be appointed ambassador, ironically enough, to the Court of Saint James; his son was eventually elected president of the United States. Similar political patterns prevailed throughout the cities in the region—and the nation—where the Irish abounded, and various ethnic balances affected politics accordingly.

A major force in the lives of the Irish and several of the other major New England immigrant groups was the Roman Catholic church. The Irish had a particular affinity for the clerical life, which represented organized opposition to the English as well as an attractive vehicle for social mobility. In contrast, for example, to the Italians, who were nominally faithful but residually skeptical of institutionalized religion, the Irish gladly gave their sons to the priesthood and their daughters to the convent. As a result, a vast network of Catholic institutions—churches, rectories, convents, parochial and high schools, hospitals, asylums of various sorts, and eventually colleges and universities—began to cover the urban areas of southern New England under the aggressive leadership of overwhelmingly Irish-descended bishops such as Boston's William Cardinal O'Connell (reigned 1907–1944).

SLAVERY, ABOLITIONISM, AND RACIAL CONFLICT

According to John Hope Franklin, the earliest reliable account of an African American presence in New England dates to 1638, with the arrival of the cargo of the Captain William Peirce's *Desire*. Slaves rapidly became a part of the triangular trade that involved New England with human cargoes making the rounds from Africa to the West Indies and ultimately to North America. The slave trade reached its heyday in the early eighteenth century, with Newport and Bristol in Rhode Island as its New England foci. Though most of the Africans were destined for labor in the southern colonies, in 1700 about one thousand New Englanders, or one out of ninety, were black—a number that increased rapidly during the following century to about fifteen thousand on the eve of the Revolution. The legality of slavery had been recognized in the colonies almost from their beginnings, and numerous laws restricted black liberties. The small-scale character of the "peculiar institution" in the northeast militated against the harshness that accompanied slavery elsewhere, and many slaves acquired skills and literacy to enhance their economic usefulness to their masters; civil marriage was not only permitted but required by law.

The institution of slavery was regionally weak by 1783, and it had been completely abolished by then in Vermont and Massachusetts; in other New England states it was largely phased out. Slavery did not come to a complete end until 1848 in Connecticut—the state with the highest concentration of blacks, employed primarily as household servants. Boston emerged as a center for free black activity, and even prior to the Revolution it had been home to the African-born and later manumitted poet Phillis Wheatley, who had belonged to a local merchant before being freed. The approximately two thousand blacks in Boston at the eve of the Civil War were widely employed in various crafts and professions, and they carried on an associational life through Baptist churches and Masonic and other lodges. Of this number, three-quarters were enrolled in schools, which had been integrated by 1855. On the other hand, in more conservative Connecticut, the Quaker Prudence Crandall's attempt to educate black children in the early 1830s was thwarted by legal action and mob violence.

As antislavery sentiment began to heat up in the 1830s, Boston emerged as a major center, playing host both to William Lloyd Garrison's *Liberator* and to David Walker, whose *Appeal . . . to the Colored Citizens of the World* was published in 1829. Garrison's New England Anti-Slavery Society, organized in 1831, was devoted to the cause of immediate abolition, a cause also sponsored by a number of local black societies. Though prominent New Englanders such as Wendell Phillips, John Greenleaf Whittier, and Lydia Maria Child rallied to the cause, Garrison himself was nearly lynched in 1835 by a Boston mob, indicative of the hostility toward abolition held by elite and working people alike. (Antislavery was considerably stronger in New England's rural areas and small towns than in the metropolis.) In 1851 the case of Shadrach, a slave sought under the Fugitive Slave Act who was rescued and whisked off to Canada, galvanized public opinion more broadly against the institution and its

threats to civil liberties. Connecticut-born Harriet Beecher Stowe, who spent most of her life in New England, used the rural setting of Brunswick, Maine, to fictionalize the observations of slave life in Kentucky she had gathered by living with her father Lyman in Cincinnati; the resultant *Uncle Tom's Cabin* (1852) was even more instrumental in turning the tide of northern sentiment. Finally, when the war came, Robert Gould Shaw led the Fifty-fourth Massachusetts, composed entirely of black soldiers, which performed heroically in the ill-fated assault on Fort Wagner in South Carolina—an event memorialized both in Augustus Saint-Gaudens's relief carving on the Boston Common and in the 1989 film *Glory.*

Boston remained a center for humanitarian and civil rights activities following the Civil War, and freedmen doubled the city's small black population in the decade and a half that followed. During the twentieth century, though, New England's black population experienced concentrated growth primarily in a few metropolitan centers in inner city neighborhoods such as Boston's Roxbury and New Haven's Hill and Newhallville, and it followed closely the region's internal divisions in its distribution as well. In 1970, for example, approximately 382,000 blacks lived in the three southernmost New England states, with only about seven thousand north of the Massachusetts border.

In Boston and other large cities, concentration of blacks in core cities ringed by predominantly white suburbs was the norm; in 1970, for example, one and a half million people, over ninety-eight percent white, lived in Boston's outlying communities while only about one half million—over one hundred thousand black—lived in the city proper, described by Ronald Formisano as "a postindustrial administrative and service center." (This ratio was unusually low in the context of the nation as a whole.) The resulting tensions between blacks and those whites who still remained in the core—mostly Irish-Americans in Dorchester and South Boston—reached a flash point during the period 1974–1975 when federal judge W. Arthur Garrity, Jr. ordered desegregation through busing of a school system that had been informed by patronage politics and traditional ethnic neighborhood boundaries. A protest movement described by Formisano as "reactionary populist" in nature rapidly emerged, resulting in dramatic polarization of the community and occasional violence. New Haven's Black Panther trial in 1970 was another event in which a community similarly divided along racial, class, and geographical lines narrowly avoided serious disruption.

THE PERSISTENCE OF NEW ENGLAND

Henry Adams, the scion of New England's most representative "Brahmin" family, recorded in his autobiographical *The Education of Henry Adams* (1907) an encounter with a Harvard undergraduate:

Their faith in education was so full of pathos that one dared not ask them what they thought they could to with education when they got it. Adams put the question to one of them, and was surprised at the answer: "The degree of Harvard College is worth money to me in Chicago." (Modern Library edition, pp. 304–305)

The students' candidly pragmatic response was in many ways an epitome of New England's situation in the twentieth century, or perhaps even from the time of the Civil War. Its cultural cachet, reflected in such institutions as Harvard and Yale, was still nationally preeminent, though challenged by the rise of other national research universities such as Berkeley, Chicago, and Cornell. On the other hand, New England's political and economic role in the nation was gradually shifting to the margins. As New York and Chicago became the national centers of commerce and finance, and industry gravitated towards the South, the region had to face its new and not entirely welcome position in national life. Boston was no longer the "hub of the solar system" as Oliver Wendell Holmes described it, and Henry Adams's own self-image of being an uneasy exile in Washington, D.C., reflected this shift of power.

Three events in post–World War I America might be taken as vignettes of the changing New England scene. During the 1920s, a cause célèbre that aroused the liberal intelligentsia nationally was the case of Nicola Sacco and Bartolomeo Vanzetti, two Italian-born anarchists who were convicted for their roles in a fatal 1920 robbery near Boston. The presiding judge, Webster Thayer, was an entrenched member of the Boston Brahmin establishment then beleaguered by such perceived threats to the public order as the Boston police strike suppressed in 1919 by then governor Calvin Coolidge. Also Brahmin to the core was A. Lawrence Lowell, the Harvard president appointed by the governor to head a review of the convictions that confirmed the original verdicts and culminated in the anarchists' executions. Lowell, bearing two ancestral names shared with mill towns in which the family fortune had been enhanced, also came under fire from Jewish leaders who took umbrage at Harvard's policy of imposing admissions quotas on minority, and especially Jewish, students, a policy not reversed till after World War II.

New England events were seldom featured in the national news during the ensuing decades of depression and world war. One of the most popular pieces of regional literature during those years was John P. Marquand's Pulitzer Prize–winning *The Late George Apley* (1937), a gentle satire on the wealthy descendent of an eminent Brahmin family who seemed to have no identity apart from the family's, and whose children abandoned New England and its upper-class codes of conduct to seek happiness in more cosmopolitan climes.

It was not till 1960 that a New Englander was again elected president. John F. Kennedy's persona, however, was very different from that of his Vermont-born predecessor, "Silent Cal" Coolidge. Kennedy, who spoke with what many regarded as a charming regional accent, was both a graduate of Harvard College and the grandson of "Honey Fitz" Fitzgerald and another Boston "pol," Patrick J. Kennedy. At his 1961 inauguration, he was flanked by two figures emblematic of the converging regional subcultures he helped bridge. Robert Frost, who delivered his poem "The Gift Outright," had built his work on a strong sense of regional presence, though he himself was California-born. The invocation was delivered by Boston Archbishop Richard Cardinal Cushing, representing a regional Irish Catholic religious establishment that, on the eve of Vatican II, was no longer reluctant to mingle with its traditionally nativist antagonists.

A third glimpse of a changing New England emerged in the 1988 presidential race. George Herbert Walker Bush, the Yale-educated son of Connecticut senator Prescott Bush, soundly defeated Michael Dukakis, a Greek American graduate of Harvard Law School then presiding over a short-lived economic boom, the "Massachusetts miracle," while serving as governor. Dukakis had made his reputation as a progressive-minded technocrat in the Kennedy tradition, nurturing the high-tech electronic industries of Boston's Route 128 beltway. His victorious adversary had downplayed his regional associations, and instead campaigned as a successful businessman from his adopted state of Texas. Though Dukakis lost for many reasons, he derived little benefit from his regional associations.

While gradually losing eminence in the national society, New England was also becoming more integrated into that society in a number of ways. The interstate highway system of the late 1950s linked the region with Interstate-95 in the form of the New England Thruway, just as Interstate-90 became the Massachusetts Turnpike as it crossed the New York border. (The "Mass Pike's" logo still features a Puritan-style hat, but the arrow that once pierced it has been removed.) Urban renewal manifested itself in the same years in mayor Richard Lee's presiding over downtown New Haven's transformation, and in Boston's seedy but colorful Scollay Square's yielding to the controversially modern Government Center. The reflection of Copley Square's Romanesque Trinity Church in the glossy panes of the John Hancock Building provides another glimpse of the regional coexistence of the old and the new.

Though New England could no longer take prosperity and national influence for granted in the twentieth century, and though its economy underwent dramatic vicissitudes, the region nevertheless found ways in which to turn its traditional resources into saleable commodities for the national marketplace. Higher education, a traditional staple, became a mainstay of the regional economy, especially in Boston, which acquired a reputation as a collegiate mecca across the nation and the world. In 1990, 239 colleges and universities were located in the six states, with 120—almost exactly half—in Massachusetts. Undergraduate programs at a myriad of schools attracted tens of thousands of students, while research at Harvard, the Massachusetts Institute of Technology, Boston University, Tufts, and Brandeis helped spawn the Route 128 high-tech complex. Institutions such as Brown University and Boston College, once regionally or religiously restricted in appeal, had by the 1970s acquired reputations as national institutions both in the academic and quality-of-life realms. Harvard, Yale, Amherst, and other academic institutions that for generations had embodied upper-class exclusivity, now vied with one another to recruit and subsidize racially and economically pluralistic student bodies. A seeming cornucopia of colleges, from Vermont's arts-oriented Bennington to Connecticut's Coast Guard Academy, signaled both the continuation of the region's commitment to education as well as its growing diversity.

Geography, which had once worked towards the region's depopulation as arable soil began to vanish, now helped redeem some of the same abandoned stretches of the northern states in particular. Romantic cultural attitudes, urbanization, and an improved transportation infrastructure transformed the region's distinctive combination of shoreline and mountains from stubborn obstacles to civilization into economic drawing cards. For the heirs of Henry David Thoreau and his Transcendentalist comrades, they seemed to be spiritual resources as well.

Since the early nineteenth century, the austere beauty of the New England shoreline had attracted vacationers, especially the wealthy, to locales from Maine's Mount Desert Island to New Haven's Wooster Square—the latter a retreat for southerners escaping their own region's summer rigors. Newport, Rhode Island, emerged by the later nineteenth century as the epitome of conspicuous leisure consumption by the wealthy, as the chateauesque "cottages" on Cliff Walk still reveal. By the 1970s, a combination of new "yuppie" wealth concentrated in the Boston and New York metropolitan areas—now reaching as far as southern New Hampshire and New Haven—and a growing popularity of both skiing and aquatic pastimes among the middle classes enhanced a seasonal recreational boom in Vermont ski locales and at coastal sites. The population of Cape Cod, for instance, now swells to over one half million on peak summer weekends, putting stress both on the environment and on human tempers.

Another New England resource that has been successfully exploited during the twentieth century has been its own history—a lengthy one by American standards, and thus appealing to many seeking a useable, and preferably picturesque, past. Local consciousness of the past was enhanced especially by the Massachusetts Tercentenary in 1930, which resulted in the erection of permanent historical markers still standing at sites of historic interest across the commonwealth. Making the past accessible to tourists continued in the laying out of Boston's Freedom Trail and in the "living history" displays at Mystic Seaport in Connecticut (1929), Plimoth Plantation (1947), and Old Sturbridge Village in central Massachusetts (1946), the latter an amalgam of buildings from a variety of sites. College campuses, such as Harvard Yard in Cambridge, also served as tourist attractions, and the rejuvenation of Boston's Quincy Market into a vibrant urban center provided a magnet for the trade of locals and outlanders alike. In 1991, Salem, long known as Massachusetts's "witch city," was preparing for the tricentennial of those melancholy events in order to lure an enhanced tourist trade.

In addition to the income and employment generated in various ways through recreation and tourism, the New England image of moral high-mindedness and old-fashioned craftsmanship, reliability, and self-reliance has proven marketable in other ways as well. *Yankee Magazine,* the regional counterpart of *Sunset* and *Southern Living,* interprets the region to a variety of audiences, and mixes traditional regional lore and humor with features on recent human interest stories and a good dose of modern ethnic culture, especially recipes. *Down East* performs a similar function for Maine, with a heavy emphasis on real estate advertisements. The craze for catalogue sales that swept the nation in the 1980s had a basis in the remarkable success of the L. L. Bean Company, founded in 1912 in Freeport, Maine, which expanded from a regional supplier of sporting and camping equipment into a national purveyor of clothing and outdoor accessories. When in 1991 Bean's announced a switch from store employees to professionals as its models, an indignant clientele bemoaned its fall from moral grace.

Vermont's image as well has become virtually iconic. As the *New York Times* reported on 4 December 1991,

"Vermont, Inc." . . . is the Vermont of purity, wholesomeness, rural values, tradition, self-reliance, trustworthiness, simplicity, honesty, hard work, environmental awareness and closeness to nature, which residents and visitors described in interviews with the State Agency of Development and Community Affairs for a 1986 survey on Vermont's image. For many, the report concludes, "experiencing Vermont becomes a religious experience: oneness with nature, oneness with self, oneness with the universal life force."

The Vermont Country Store, for example, features a wide range of household goods, such as slow-cooking breakfast cereals, based on an appeal simultaneously to nostalgia and Yankee practicality and durability. Ben and Jerry's ice cream, a "boutique" product based in Waterbury, Vermont, was founded by two young men from Brooklyn attracted to the locale's mystique, who distribute nationally a product appealing to high quality and the firm's support for liberal social causes. Like their southern counterparts, New Englanders, whether native-born or transplanted, have learned to market both traditional and invented culture as export goods.

BIBLIOGRAPHY

Series and Serials

Each of the New England states is treated in a separate volume in the American Guide series, sponsored by the Federal Writers' Project, and also in the bicentennial series "The States and the Nation," published by W. W. Norton in cooperation with the American Association for State and Local History. Both were intended for a general readership, but contain useful information for the scholar as well. Another ongoing series that focuses on material culture is the Annual Proceedings of the Dublin Seminar for New England Folklife (Boston University, 1976–).

Scholarly periodicals of particular interest are the *New England Quarterly* (1928–) and the *William and Mary Quarterly* (1921–). The former focuses on literature but also contains articles and reviews on social history. The latter deals with the entire colonial period, but frequently contains articles and reviews involving New England. More popular journals are *Yankee Magazine* (1935–) and *Down East* (1954–), and the now defunct *Old Time New England* (1910–1981). State historical journals include the *Proceedings of the Massachusetts Historical Society* (1879–), the *Connecticut Historical Society Bulletin* (1934–), *Historical New Hampshire* (1944–), *Rhode Island History* (1941–), and *Vermont History* (1893–). Most of these, along with the Maine Historical Society, have also issued volumes of proceedings periodically. Several of the multitudinous local historical societies in the region also issue journals or bulletins.

See also the sections "Colonial Period to 1775" and "Northeastern or North Atlantic States" in annual volumes of *America: History and Life.*

General Works

Parks, Roger, et al. eds. *New England: A Bibliography of Its History* (1989). One of eight titles in the "Bibliographies of New England History" series, edited by John Borden Armstrong. The other volumes are on the individual New England states.

Geography and Environment

Cronon, William. *Changes in the Land: Indians, Colonists, and the Ecology of New England* (1983).

Jorgensen, Neil. *A Guide to New England's Landscape* (1977).

McManis, Douglas R. *Colonial New England: A Historical Geography* (1975). A digest of monographic literature, including community studies. Valuable as a synthesis and for its bibliography.

Merchant, Carolyn. *Ecological Revolutions: Nature, Gender, and Science in New England* (1989).

Wilkie, Richard W., Jack Tager, and Roy Doyon, eds. *Historical Atlas of Massachusetts* (1991).

Puritanism and the Colonial Era

Boyer, Paul, and Stephen Nissenbaum. *Salem Possessed: The Social Origins of Witchcraft* (1974).

Bremer, Francis J. *The Puritan Experiment: New England Society from Bradford to Edwards* (1976). Good summary of a lengthy heritage of Puritan studies.

Bushman, Richard L. *From Puritan to Yankee: Character and the Social Order in Connecticut, 1690–1765* (1967).

Fairbanks, Jonathan L. *New England Begins* 3 vols. (1982). Catalogue of a Boston Museum of Fine Arts exhibit on Puritan material culture.

Fischer, David Hackett. *Albion's Seed: Four British Folkways in North America* (1989). Emphasis on East Anglian origins of Puritan culture in Massachusetts Bay. See also the symposium on this work with several authors in *William and Mary Quarterly* 3d ser., 48, no. 2 (April 1991): 224–308.

Gross, Robert A. *The Minutemen and Their World* (1976).

Howe, Daniel Walker. "The Impact of Puritanism on American Culture." In *Encyclopedia of the American Religious Experience,* vol. 2, edited by Charles H. Lippy and Peter W. Williams (1988), pp. 1057–1074.

Lockridge, Kenneth A. *Literacy in Colonial New England: An Enquiry into the Social Context of Literacy in the Early Modern West* (1974).

Morgan, Edmund S. *The Puritan Family: Religion and Domestic Relations in Seventeenth-Century New England* (1944; rev. and enl. ed. 1966).

Salisbury, Neal. *Manitou and Providence: Indians, Europeans, and the Making of New England 1500–1643* (1982).

Scott, Donald M. *From Office to Profession: The New England Ministry, 1750–1850* (1978).

Vaughan, Alden T. *New England Frontier: Puritans and Indians, 1620–1675* (1965; rev. ed. 1979). A more traditional study.

Northern, Rural, and Coastal New England

Barron, Hal S. *Those Who Stayed Behind: Rural Society in Nineteenth-Century New England* (1984).

Clark, Charles E., James S. Leamon, and Karen Bowden, eds. *Maine in the Early Republic: From Revolution to Statehood* (1988).

Clark, Christopher. *The Roots of Rural Capitalism: Western Massachusetts, 1780–1860* (1990).

Gilmore, William J. *Reading Becomes a Necessity of Life: Material and Cultural Life in Rural New England, 1780–1835* (1989).

Holbrook, Stewart. *The Yankee Exodus: An Account of Migration from New England* (1950).

Robinson, William F. *Coastal New England: Its Life and Past* (1983; repr. 1989).

———. *Mountain New England: Life Past and Present* (1988). Useful popular narratives with good illustrations but dated bibliographies.

Roth, Randolph A. *The Democratic Dilemma: Religion, Reform, and the Social Order in the Connecticut River Valley of Vermont, 1791–1850* (1987).

Taylor, Alan. *Liberty Men and Great Proprietors: The Revolutionary Settlement on the Maine Frontier, 1760–1820* (1990).

Ulrich, Laurel T. *Good Wives: Image and Reality in the Lives of Women in Northern New England, 1650–1750* (1982).

———. *A Midwife's Tale: The Life of Martha Ballard, Based on Her Diary, 1785–1812* (1990).

Nineteenth-Century Industrialization and Social Change

Brooke, John L. *The Heart of the Commonwealth: Society and Political Culture in Worcester County, Massachusetts, 1713–1861* (1989; repr. 1991).

Cayton, Mary Kupiec, *Emerson's Emergence: Self and Society in the Transformation of New England, 1800–1845* (1989).

Cott, Nancy F. *The Bonds of Womanhood: "Woman's Sphere" in New England, 1780–1835* (1977).

Dublin, Thomas. *Women at Work: The Transformation of Work and Community in Lowell, Massachusetts, 1826–1860* (1979).

Dunwell, Steve. *The Run of the Mill: A Pictorial Narrative of the Expansion, Dominion, Decline and Enduring Impact of the New England Textile Industry* (1978). Well-illustrated, popularly oriented but solid narrative.

Faler, Paul G. *Mechanics and Manufacturers in the Early Industrial Revolution: Lynn, Massachusetts, 1780–1860* (1981).

Gilkeson, John S., Jr. *Middle-Class Providence, 1820–1940* (1986).

Green, Constance M. *Eli Whitney and the Birth of American Technology* (1956).

Hareven, Tamara K., and Randolph Langenbach. *Amoskeag: Life and Work in an American Factory-City* (1978). Oral histories.

Nash, Gary B. *The Urban Crucible: Social Change, Political Consciousness, and the Origins of the American Revolution* (1979).

Story, Ronald. *The Forging of an Aristocracy: Harvard and the Boston Upper Class, 1800–1870* (1980).

Thernstrom, Stephan. *Poverty and Progress: Social Mobility in a Nineteenth Century City* (1964).

———. *The Other Bostonians: Poverty and Progress in the American Metropolis, 1880–1970* (1973).

Thornton, Tamara Plakins. *Cultivating Gentlemen: The Meaning of Country Life Among the Boston Elite, 1785–1860* (1982; 1989).

Warner, Sam Bass, Jr. *Streetcar Suburbs: The Process of Growth in Boston, 1870–1900* (1962).

Race, Ethnicity, and Immigration

Blessing, Patrick J. "Irish." In *Harvard Encyclopedia of American Ethnic Groups,* edited by Stephan Thernstrom (1980), pp. 524–545. See also entries by various authors on other ethnic groups relevant to New England.

Brault, Gerald J. *The French-Canadian Heritage in New England* (1986).

Formisano, Ronald P. *Boston Against Busing: Race, Class, and Ethnicity in the 1960s and 1970s* (1991).

Greene, Lorenzo Johnston. *The Negro in Colonial New England, 1620–1776* (1942).

Handlin, Oscar. *Boston's Immigrants, 1790–1880: A Study in Acculturation* (1941; rev. and enl. ed. 1959; 1991).

Smith, Judith E. *Family Connections: A History of Italian and Jewish Immigrant Lives in Providence, Rhode Island, 1900–1940* (1985).

Sullivan, Robert E., and James M. O'Toole, eds. *Catholic Boston: Studies in Religion and Community, 1870–1970* (1985).

Note: The author would like to thank Profs. Andrew Cayton, Daniel Walker Howe, and Kevin Sweeney for their valuable comments on this essay.

SEE ALSO **The American Colonies Through 1700; The City; The Clergy; Community Studies; English-speaking Protestants; Foodways; The French and French-Canadians; Irish Catholics; Literacy; Labor: Colonial Times Through the Early National Period; The Natural Environment: The North; Rural Life in the North.**

THE NEW YORK METROPOLITAN REGION

David C. Hammack

GEOGRAPHY

THE NEW YORK METROPOLITAN region, which extends roughly from Princeton, New Jersey, to New Haven, Connecticut, has always been shaped by its location around the best Atlantic harbor in North America. Ice-free and protected from ocean storms, New York Harbor lies at a midpoint between the smaller and more exposed ports of New England and Canada to the northeast, and of the Delaware and Chesapeake bays to the south. Through the Hudson River, New York also has easy connections to the interior; through Long Island Sound, easy connections to Connecticut. Human effort has reinforced the region's physical advantages: first by protecting the harbor with batteries, forts, and lighthouses; then by making New York City (and Philadelphia) the center of the most intensively developed road and postal system in the American colonies. Later, New York's central position was reinforced by the Erie Canal and the national telegraph, railroad, and highway systems, and by dredging the harbor and the Hudson River; and in the 1980s by providing Manhattan with one of the most advanced fiber-optic telephone systems in the world.

Waterways gave the New York region its central position in American communications and trade; they also provided the region with many of its distinctive physical characteristics. New York Harbor, Arthur Kill and the Kill Van Kull, the Hudson, Long Island Sound, the East River, and the Long Island and New Jersey shores give the region a remarkably extensive coastline and divide New York City into five far-flung boroughs. The "lordly" Hudson splits the hills that provide a backdrop to the region; its valley provides a distinctive setting for many of the city's northern suburbs in Westchester,

Putnam, Rockland, and Orange counties in New York. The Hudson enters the metropolitan region at the point, above Bear Mountain and Peekskill, where two major south-pointing "prongs" of a geological feature known as the New England Upland divide. Westernmost is the Reading Prong, which emerges in New Jersey as the Ramapo Mountains and in New York as the Hudson Highlands. The Manhattan Prong of the New England Upland runs south from Peekskill and Danbury to Manhattan and Staten Island. To the northeast, in Connecticut, lie the Housatonic Highlands.

The Hudson gives access to the north, but serves as a major barrier to land transportation to the west and south; in the past thirty years much of the region's warehouse and distribution activity has relocated from Brooklyn, Queens, and Manhattan to New Jersey. The Raritan, Passaic, Hackensack, Bronx, Croton, Housatonic, Naugatuck, and other streams flowing down from these various heights further divide the region's landscape. At the fall line and at the coast these streams encouraged early towns: Waterbury, Danbury, New Milford, Paterson, New Brunswick, and others at break-in-transit- and power-producing waterfalls; New Haven, Bridgeport, Norwalk, Stamford, Peekskill, Newark, Elizabeth, and Perth Amboy at small harbors. Between the highlands and the ocean lies the flat Atlantic Coastal Plain, making southern Connecticut, Long Island, and central New Jersey well suited for the mixed farms (and market-towns such as Hempstead, Jamaica, Flatbush, White Plains, Rahway, and Middletown) of the eighteenth and nineteenth centuries, and for suburban subdivisions from the young-family Levittowns of the late 1940s to the retired-adults–only Rossmoors of the 1970s. Altogether, physical geography has encouraged a wide variety of settlement patterns in the New York re-

927

gion, giving the region many early towns and cities and many areas for divergent development at every point in history.

POLITICAL BOUNDARIES

Many of the New York region's major physical boundaries became political boundaries as well. The most important is the division of the region into three separate states, so that a very significant part of the development around New York Harbor is in New Jersey: many suburban and satellite towns are in New Jersey and Connecticut. Another very important boundary isolated the City of New York on Manhattan Island until the end of the nineteenth century, allowing Brooklyn to grow to considerable size as a separate city and leaving the harbor under the disunited jurisdiction of more than forty local governments as well as two states. In general, the early establishment of distinct villages, towns, cities, school districts, counties, and utility districts gave the entire region, and its New Jersey portion in particular, as great a fragmentation of local government as exists anywhere in the United States. In 1960 one analyst wrote of the region's "1400 governments."

The fact that New York State included the entire Hudson and Mohawk valleys, and extended west all the way to Lake Ontario and Lake Erie, was an essential condition for the construction of the Erie Canal as early as 1825. The consolidation of Manhattan and Brooklyn with what became the boroughs of the Bronx, Queens, and Richmond (Staten Island) in 1898 was equally essential for the rapid and—in gross terms—coherent development of Greater New York in the twentieth century. Consolidation made New York by far the largest municipality in the United States, gave it an unusually large and diverse electorate, and placed within its boundaries an unusually large share of the suburban territory that surrounded it. The bistate Port Authority of New York and New Jersey (created as the Port of New York Authority in 1921) has facilitated the coordination and construction of highway, air, and water transportation, though not of rail transport and mass transit.

COLONIAL PATTERNS

Some of the New York metropolitan region's best-known characteristics were established very early. These include the religious and ethnic diversity not only of New York City, but of the entire region; the importance of landlords and tenants; and the tendency toward noisy political factionalism. Colonial New York City was already noted for its close connections with Europe and its cosmopolitan sophistication; the presence, cheek by jowl, of the very rich and the very poor; and its rapid pace of change.

New York's religious and ethnic diversity has been celebrated since the seventeenth century. In 1644 eighteen different languages were spoken in New Netherland. The religious tolerance of the Dutch West India Company (which controlled New York and New Jersey from shortly after Henry Hudson's voyage in 1609 to 1664) exasperated their English successors, but it largely endured. In 1686 Governor Thomas Dongan complained that the Anglicans—favored by British policy—had to compete not only with Dutch Calvinists, French Calvinists, Dutch Lutherans, and Quakers, but also with "Singing Quakers, Ranting Quakers; Sabbatarians; Antisabbatarians; some Anabaptists, some Independents; some Jews; in short all sorts of opinions there are some, and the most part, of none at all" (quoted in *A Factious People,* p. 25). New York City's population grew steadily more English thereafter, but it continued to be, with Philadelphia, the most diverse of any place in the British colonies in North America. All the religious groups that had troubled Dongan remained at the Revolution, and they had by then been joined by many Presbyterians and by Catholic, Methodist, Baptist, and Moravian congregations as well.

Dongan did not attempt to characterize the religious beliefs of the African slaves, but they constituted a significant portion of the region's colonial population. Slaves arrived almost with the first Dutch settlers, and the slave trade continued and indeed grew under the British; it decreased somewhat only after 1733. As elsewhere, the Africans encountered difficult conditions that often seemed to deteriorate; slave revolts in 1712 and 1741 confirmed white fears and were followed by severe punishment and repression (over one hundred African slaves were killed or tortured in 1741; many others were transported to the West Indies), and by calls for the replacement of slaves by white indentured servants. About a fifth of the people of eighteenth-century New York City were slaves; by 1746 they made up nearly a third of the laboring population. There were also significant numbers of slaves in the Long Island, Westchester County, and

928

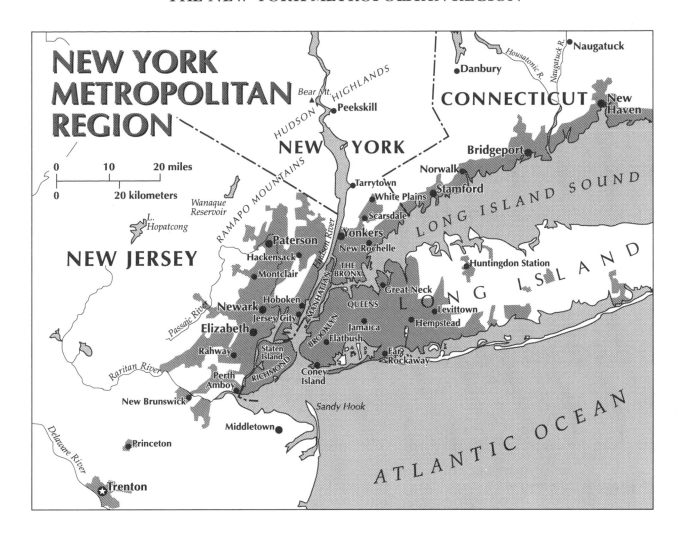

northern New Jersey countryside at the time of the Revolution. New York State law began to emancipate slaves only in 1799; slavery officially continued until 1827. The Native American who first inhabited the region refused to submit to slavery and withdrew into the hills of the backcountry.

The Dutch were concentrated in Manhattan and the Hudson Valley; far up the valley, toward Albany, they still constituted an overwhelming majority in 1776. Dutch settlers were also quite numerous in northern New Jersey; they founded Rutgers University in 1766 as a college for the Dutch Reformed church. Many French Huguenots came to New Rochelle and New Paltz, as well as to Manhattan, after 1685. Germans from the Palatinate came to New York in several large groups, and some of them settled along the Hudson and in New Jersey. Quakers and some Lutherans moved from Pennsylvania into central New Jersey; over the course of the eighteenth century Scotch-Irish Presbyterians also became numerous in New Jersey and

on the western banks of the Hudson. Dutch "patroons" and English "manor lords" hoped to establish neofeudal tenant-farming on large estates in Westchester and the Hudson Valley, but as their land titles were often challenged, and their tenants could always threaten to acquire free hold farmland in the west, the great estates were steadily divided among heirs, broken up, and sold off.

Colonial Connecticut was much more homogeneous. Its "standing order" effectively established the Congregationalist church, granting political advantages to Congregationalists and government support to their churches and to Yale College. Connecticut provided early settlers for Long Island and yielded its claims to parts of Westchester County reluctantly. New England–style townships and Congregationalist churches remained in both places, and when new groups of Yankees sought Westchester farmland in the eighteenth century, Dutch, English, and French settlers resisted them. Conflict between Yankees and Yorkers remained an important theme in the region well into the nineteenth century.

English authorities in New York did what they could to introduce a strong central government backed by an established Anglican church. The highly factionalized politics of the region repeatedly frustrated them. When early-eighteenth-century governors asserted arbitrary powers, the provincial legislature refused to pass essential fiscal laws. When Governor William Cosby sought, in 1735, to silence the harsh criticisms of John Peter Zenger's *New-York Weekly Journal,* clever New York and Philadelphia lawyers persuaded a jury to expand the freedom of the press and accept truth as a defense against the charge of libel. Anglicans secured a large grant of land for the support of Trinity Church, but when they offered part of this land for a new Anglican college to be supported with the proceeds of a public lottery in 1753, they encountered furious opposition from Presbyterians and others. They won a charter and Anglican control but only limited lottery funds for what became King's College (later Columbia University). New York's colonial merchants, landlords, and artisans also found themselves divided by faction and often unable to take concerted action.

The expansive charter that Governor Dongan granted to New York City (1686) also left an enduring legacy in the region. The Dongan Charter gave the city's municipal corporation exclusive control over Manhattan's docks and markets, and over ferries across the East River to Long Island. It gave city artisans and merchants special rights over competitors at other places in the region. And it gave the municipal corporation an extensive grant of land, which it could sell off to finance improvements. The charter reinforced New York City's central location and command of the harbor to make it the dominant economic and political center in the region as a whole.

THE NEW YORK REGION'S NINETEENTH-CENTURY RISE

New York's phenomenal nineteenth-century growth to Walt Whitman's "million-footed city" and then to a cosmopolitan metropolis of over four million by 1900 was due to the rapid expansion of both trade and manufacturing. The region's growth was also due to the extraordinary waves of emigration that moved eastward through Europe after the Napoleonic Wars, and that sent millions of people into

TABLE 1   Population of Greater New York, 1698–1900*

Year	Population
1698	6,954
1746	14,048
1771	25,486
1800	66,255
1820	134,893
1840	360,323
1860	1,080,330
1880	1,843,785
1900	3,437,202

Source: Ira Rosenwaike, *Population History of New York City* (Syracuse: Syracuse University Press, 1972).

*This is the population of the area that became the five boroughs of Greater New York City in 1898.

the Atlantic world in search of new opportunities for employment. By about 1830 New York City had established itself as a central place in American manufacturing, Atlantic trade, and the world's flow of migrants; for about 150 years thereafter, the New York metropolitan region continued to hold exactly twice as many people as its largest competitors—Philadelphia until 1880; Chicago until 1960; Los Angeles until 1980.

At the time of the first United States census in 1790, New York City already stood at the center of communications within the United States and between America and Europe. In the next forty years it established itself firmly at the center of the nation's urban and commercial networks. As early as 1817 competing guidebooks for merchants described the new institutions—regularly scheduled packet service to Britain, auction markets that kept import prices down, hotels and restaurants, and banking, insurance, and shipping services of all kinds—that reinforced the initial advantage provided by the port's central location on the eastern seaboard.

New York's central location and excellent commercial facilities gave the city's investors, merchants, and manufacturers earlier access to more information about markets (and market-relevant political and military events) throughout North America and the Atlantic world than their competitors in any other city in North America. By 1859, R. G. Dun and Company in New York was able to provide up-to-date credit-rating information on almost every business in the United States, from the largest import-export houses down to tiny shops of shoe repairmen and dressmakers. It was in New York that Henry Varnum Poor gathered information about railroad securities; it was on Wall Street that the New York Stock Exchange made the national markets for railroad stocks and bonds and for government securities. New York had become the capital of American capitalism, the central place for American business.

A second major factor in New York City's rise after the Revolution lay within the region itself: the continuing rapid growth of Long Island, the Hudson Valley, and New Jersey. New York City served this entire area as a regional marketing and manufacturing center. New York merchant-investors put many early manufacturing operations into outlying towns, as Alexander Hamilton and his associates in the Society for Useful Manufacturers did when they sought to harness the waterpower in the falls of the Passaic River at Paterson, New Jersey, and as others did when they invested in wrought iron in Trenton, nonferrous metalworking in Naugatuck, or coal mining in Pennsylvania. Other parts of the region prospered with the introduction of specialized farming—a phenomenon whose colonial roots were noted in Benjamin Franklin's remark that New Jersey was a cider barrel tapped at both ends. Manufacturers throughout the region benefited from its growing population, its prosperity, and its rapidly developing division of labor.

Local markets, perhaps even more than national and foreign markets, made mid-nineteenth-century New York City the nation's largest manufacturer of clothing, hats, food and tobacco products, furniture, pianos, and printed materials. Local markets and New York port's strategic place in the import and export of raw materials accounted for the development, around New York Harbor, of some of the nation's largest sugar (and, since the last decades of the nineteenth century, oil) refineries, breweries and distilleries, paint and soap and glue plants. Local and national markets also made New York the center for industries that required the latest information about fashion in Europe and in every part of the New World. After the Civil War, New York City housed the nation's most important markets for printing and publishing, women's fashions, and interior decoration. It housed booking agents for lyceum lecturers, music's Tin Pan Alley, and the theater's Rialto, where producers hired actors for Broadway openings and road shows alike. It was in New York that deals were struck in these fields, and it was in New York that many of the products were contrived, tried out, and made.

Labor in Nineteenth-Century New York
Manufacturing provided large numbers of jobs in New York, but with the exception of the highly skilled jobs in construction, cabinet- and musical-instrument making, and the production and maintenance of complex machinery (engines for steamships, and later, elevators for office buildings), few of these jobs paid well. The rapid growth of New York (and of Newark and other towns in the region as well) accompanied equally rapid changes in the organization of work, changes that reduced the prospects of many workers even as they allowed a few to become rich. Economic inequality increased significantly over the course of the nineteenth century.

Artisans, in trades organized along traditional lines with apprentices and journeymen working in (and often living above) small shops or work groups headed by master craftsmen, still constituted the largest single group of workers in New York as late as the 1820s. By the mid 1850s, fewer than one-eighth of the city's workers were traditional artisans. More than twice as many worked in occupations that had once been organized along artisanal lines, but that had been so transformed that "apprentice" meant "child worker" and "journeymen" had simply become wage workers who enjoyed neither security, control of a craft, nor much prospect of becoming master craftsmen. In these increasingly "sweated" trades, masters who provided tools, workrooms, and even housing were replaced by contractors who provided raw materials but expected workers to rent rooms for working as well as living, and to labor with their own tools. In the 1820s, the 1840s, and the late 1860s, sweated workers saw their incomes drop or stagnate, even as their food and housing costs increased. Over the entire century, however, most workers did see a substantial rise in their standard of living.

Throughout the region, tailors, boot and shoemakers, weavers, furniture makers, and printers increasingly found their work subdivided, controlled by contractors and jobbers who acted for great merchants, and dominated by the production of cheap goods for markets in the south, the west, rural backwaters, and urban low-rent neighborhoods. A few workers in these occupations, like printer James Harper and his brothers, made fortunes by taking advantage of these changes; a larger number did better than their fellows as contractors. The new organization of labor increased production and lowered prices, but it provided many laborers with fewer positions of independence and autonomy.

By the 1850s the greatest proportion of New York's workers were engaged in occupations that had never been organized as crafts. Their work required attention and often real skill, but had always been organized either as service within a household (domestic work, laundry work, hotel and restaurant work, security) or as casual labor, often related to transportation (porters, grooms, teamsters, boatmen, dockworkers). Employment in these fields increased rapidly with New York's development as a national and regional center of transportation.

Many tradesmen fought valiantly, during the first three or four decades of the nineteenth century, to maintain traditional control over their crafts. Many worked with great inventiveness to develop a working-class culture capable of holding a common line against employers and landlords. They articulated an "artisan republican" outlook that celebrated their independence and voting rights as Americans and asserted the virtue of craft traditions. And they organized a Workingmen's party in the late 1820s, the New York General Trades Union in 1834, and the Mechanics' Mutual Protection—a "Christian" secret society—in 1841. These efforts to resist the development of the wage and piecework systems had limited success. Employers in the sweated trades responded with their own organizations, and their workers found it impossible to control access to their rapidly growing trades.

Nineteenth-century New York was distinctive for the many jobs it made available to women. Nationally, only one of ten women worked for pay, but in New York City it was one of three. Still more earned money within their own homes by taking in boarders; in New York the title "widow" became a synonym for "boardinghouse keeper." The segmented labor market concentrated women in domestic and sweated occupations: household service, laundries, and sewing trades, including the making of clothing, millinery, and bookbinding. The more fortunate worked as retail clerks, boardinghouse keepers, and teachers. Women, like men, made efforts to organize, with a Female Industry Association of needle workers as early as 1845, and much later with significant success through the International Ladies Garment Workers Union.

But nineteenth-century New York was as notable for its lack of effective labor unrest as for the cleverness of its labor spokesmen. Several factors help account for this. Many of the industries that thrived in New York lacked the strong tradition of craft organization on which the advocates of artisan republicanism relied. Through most of the nineteenth century these industries recruited young workers, usually new immigrants, who lacked the resources, the social support, or the experience required to organize effectively. When newcomers did enter trades that had had strong craft traditions, older workers often scorned them for their lack of skill and their willingness to accept low wages. And New York's workers were disproportionately female, in an era when women could not vote and carried the heavy burden of household work that had to be performed without the aid of indoor plumbing, central heating, or electricity.

Immigration and Cultural Diversity The New York region's central location brought it a distinctive mixture of immigrants. Between 1840 and the 1880s it received almost as many Irish as the Boston and Providence areas, and as many Germans as Philadelphia and midwestern cities like Cincinnati. Succeeding waves of immigration further complicated the task of those who sought to make a unified working-class consciousness in nineteenth-century New York, or to mobilize workers for concerted political or labor union action on their own behalf. In the 1820s and 1830s labor organizers and political organizers alike confronted a largely native-born, Protestant population, and it was among craftsmen in this population that the ideas of artisan republicanism flourished. But the potato famines of the 1840s swelled the flow of Irish immigrants to a flood, and economic hardship (much more than the famous political upheavals of 1848) soon uprooted thousands of people in the German states as well. By 1865 about three-fifths of New York's voters were immigrants; many more were the American-born children of immigrants.

The immigrants brought their own ideas with them. Essentially all the Irish and about a third of the Germans were Catholic. They immediately faced both strong anti-Catholic sentiment (expressed in riots as well as less violent ways during the 1840s and 1850s) and the need to develop adequate Catholic institutions. They also confronted the fact that Irish and German Catholics sometimes found it difficult to cooperate. All Catholics used the Latin mass, but the Irish and the Germans used different languages for preaching, for confession, and in the parish house and the school. They had also developed somewhat distinct religious traditions and practices: plain religious services, exuberant wakes, vehement temperance campaigns among the Irish; elaborate music and processions, ceremonial first communions and weddings, cheerful after-church gatherings at beer gardens for the Germans. These differences prompted Irish and

TABLE 2   New York City Population by Ethnic Group, 1840–1980 (Percent)

	Native-Born/ Native Parents	German	Irish	Russian/ Polish	Austro-Hungarian	Italian	Other European	Black	Puerto Rican	Asian
1845	64	6	26	—	—	—	2	4	—	—
1860	55	13	24	—	—	—	7	2	—	—
1880	NA	23	27	—	—	—	6	2	—	—
1900	21	23	21	9	6	6	5	2	—	—
1920	21	10	11	18	11	14	5	3	—	—
1940	29	7	7	18	8	15	7	6	1	—
1960	39	2	3	7	3	11	5	14	8	1
1980								24	20	4

Source: Ira Rosenwaike, *Population History of New York City* (Syracuse: Syracuse University Press, 1972).

Percentages may add to more than 100 because of rounding.

German Catholics to develop separate parishes, mutual-benefit organizations, newspapers, hospitals, and orphanages.

Many of the Irish considered themselves to be political exiles from an unjustly occupied homeland; their great objective was to drive out the hated English and return home. Lacking any resource except numbers and determination, they had developed extraordinary techniques for enforcing group solidarity, including the "boycott" or silent treatment as a punishment of those who violated group norms. Some of these techniques clashed with notions of individual autonomy that were much prized by American artisans.

The Germans brought with them a diverse array of political, ethical, and religious ideals. They included Protestants and freethinkers as well as Catholics, socialists and liberals, advocates of "little Germany" and "great Germany" within Europe, liberal idealists and opportunists, and single-minded merchants. A significant fraction of the Germans were Ashkenazic Jews, and they also faced a considerable institution-building task in a city where most of the earliest Jews traced their origins to Spain and the Sephardic tradition.

Few of the Irish immigrants arrived with education, capital, or a skilled trade; in the 1850s over eighty percent of them, and in the 1890s about half, could find work only in unskilled, poorly paid, insecure occupations. In the 1850s about a sixth of the Germans, and by the 1890s about one-fourth, worked as skilled artisans. A seventh of the Germans were sufficiently literate, skilled, and well-off to open small shops in the 1850s; nearly a third had become shopkeepers forty years later. Economic differences thus cut across religious lines among the Germans, as they did among the American-born

of British and Dutch ancestry: but economic differences reinforced the religious identity of the Irish.

Ethnic and class issues combined to produce New York City's three most famous nineteenth-century riots. The Astor Place Riot of 1849 protested the appearance of William Macready, the most famous English actor of his day, at a fashionable theater. The Draft Riots of 1863 reflected Irish frustration with the competition offered by black laborers as well as anger at the class bias of a draft law that allowed conscripts to buy their way out of military service with a payment of three hundred dollars—a sum equal to the entire annual earnings of an unskilled laborer. And the Orange Riots of 1870 and 1871 pitted Irish Catholics against Ulster Protestants and their native-born defenders.

The Orange Riot of 1871 was, however, both a final instance of the tensions and bloody-mindedness provoked by the Civil War, and the last great ethnic conflict involving the Irish. Protestants pulled back from confrontation, and new state legislation provided for equitable treatment of Catholic orphanages and other institutions. Irish political leaders were already rising to eminence as brokers among New York City's diverse peoples. The year 1871 saw the attack on the Tweed Ring, and the man who then put Tammany Hall, the city's most famous Democratic party organization, back together was an Irish New Yorker, "Honest John" Kelly, renowned for his tact and reliability. Like politics, show business also encouraged tolerant, cosmopolitan attitudes: jokes about Irish Catholics might play well enough in Protestant neighborhoods, but they wouldn't do on stages that sought to draw paying customers from the metropolitan region as a whole. In the 1880s and 1890s the city's most famous vaudeville house, Tony Pastor's, was appropriately located next to Tammany Hall on Union Square. It was also in Union Square that the Henry George mayoral campaign of 1886 held its great rally celebrating the unity of organized labor, whether native-born, Irish, or German, Catholic or Protestant.

Throughout most of the nineteenth century, the wealthiest New Yorkers were merchants. The great merchants came from many places, including England, France, Holland, and Germany, and from the metropolitan region itself. So many came from Connecticut that the New England Society's annual dinners became major social events. Early in the century great merchants like John Jacob Astor engaged in all kinds of business, serving as importers, exporters, wholesalers, retailers, bankers, and even as managers of manufacturing through direct orders they provided to craftsmen and to people who worked in their homes. Banking, importing, retailing, and manufacturing gradually became distinct specialties, and by the 1880s Wall Street bankers like J. P. Morgan and Company and Kuhn, Loeb and Company had made a very successful speciality of investment banking. Investment bankers and railroad magnates joined merchants in the region's leading business organization of the late nineteenth century, the Chamber of Commerce of the State of New York.

The members of these elites distinguished themselves socially through their sponsorship of private charitable, medical, and educational societies. Building on the colonial precedent of efforts to establish the Anglican church with grants of land, New York's city and state governments often provided these societies with significant resources. The Humane Society (founded 1787) used municipal appropriations as well as private gifts to move debtors from jail to work and to provide food and medicine to the poor. The Free School Society (a private organization established in 1805, that provided much of the services of a public-school system as were available in New York City until the mid 1840s), the African Free School, the New York Hospital, the Bloomingdale Asylum for the Insane, and the New York Institution for the Instruction of the Deaf and Dumb similarly relied largely on public funds, though they were governed—subject to state law and city funding decisions—by private boards.

The presence of so many wealthy merchants who traced their cultural heritage to Calvinist Connecticut no doubt goes far to explain why New York City became, in the Protestant revivals of the Second Great Awakening after 1816, home to the pros-

elytizing agencies of the "Benevolent Empire," including the American Bible Society and the American Sunday School Union. These agencies took the United States as a whole, especially the newly settled and still raw areas of the South and the West, for their territory. This tradition continued into the twentieth century, with New York serving as headquarters town for the Society for the Suppression of Vice, through which Anthony Comstock carried out his crusade against pornography, abortion, and birth control for forty years after 1872. Other Protestant agencies, such as the Five Points House of Industry and the Association for Improving the Condition of the Poor of New York City, focused on New York City. By the 1860s evangelical philanthropy in New York City, Brooklyn, northern New Jersey, and southern Connecticut had built a complete range of Protestant denominational homes for unwed mothers, foundlings, orphans, the handicapped, the blind, the sick, old men and old women. Many of these were really mutual-benefit organizations, intended for the use of people who belonged to the particular ethnic or religious group that sponsored them.

Jacksonian opposition to government spending limited government subsidies to charitable and cultural societies in the 1830s and 1840s, but Republicans and Democrats alike returned to the policy after the Civil War. Thus the Metropolitan Museum of Art, the American Museum of Natural History, the New York Zoological Society, the Brooklyn Museum, and the Brooklyn Botanic Garden are private societies that operate in government-subsidized buildings on city land. And by 1899 the City of New York was providing a total of $3.25 million to over 280 orphanages and related charitable institutions. New York City developed City College slowly from the 1840s, and Hunter College from 1870; New York and other cities in the region aided private colleges, including Columbia, Cooper Union, Manhattanville College of the Sacred Heart, Pratt Institute, Fordham University, Saint John's University, and Wagner Memorial Lutheran College in New York City; Presbyterian Princeton, Dutch Reformed Rutgers (which received state land-grant funds after 1864), Catholic Seton Hall, Methodist Drew, Swedish Lutheran Upsala, and Stevens Institute of Technology in New Jersey; and Yale and Wesleyan in Connecticut.

These private institutions provided the region's economic elites with many ways to demonstrate their leadership and their values; they also provided important leadership roles to women.

Nineteenth-century New York and New Jersey law discouraged the creation of endowments, so private institutions relied heavily on annual fundraising efforts; by the 1880s society balls for this purpose defined the social season. The overlapping purposes of many institutions raised fears that intended beneficiaries could make overlapping claims; Josephine Shaw Lowell's Charity Organization Society sought to prevent abuses and encourage coordination. And Louisa Lee Schuyler's State Charities Aid Association sought, with state authority, to supervise both state institutions and private institutions that received state funds.

The New York region's wealthiest people were by no means unified in their support of private charitable, educational, and cultural institutions. The upper levels of Greater New York's late-nineteenth-century social geography were worthy of Lewis Carroll, with each of as many as five social elites confidently looking down to the others. Among the Anglo-Dutch population there were distinct elites of ancestor worshipers and celebrators of wealth as well as people devoted to culture—and the latter were further divided according to religious enthusiasm. The wealthiest German Protestants and the wealthiest German Jews had their own, mutually exclusive, elites.

THE METROPOLITAN REGION IN THE TWENTIETH CENTURY

Economic Development, 1880–1960 Between 1880 and the 1960s economic change largely intensified the defining characteristics of Greater New York. The region became more and more the international capital of capitalism. In the late 1890s the New York Stock Exchange began to deal in the stocks and bonds of industrial corporations, confirming the city's status as headquarters for many manufacturing operations that were located outside the region but served national or international markets. Wall Street lawyers, Wall Street investment bankers, and the owners of lower Manhattan real estate were among the chief beneficiaries of the great corporate merger movement of the years after 1900 and then of the European conflicts that badly damaged Frankfurt, Paris, and even London as centers of international finance after 1914. The Federal Reserve System, created by Congress in 1913, was intended to preserve the autonomy of banks in

other regions of the nation, but in fact New York banks continued to manage the nation's interregional and international trade, and through the 1920s the Federal Reserve Bank of New York was usually more than first among equals within the Federal Reserve system as a whole.

The concentration of financial institutions and corporate headquarters in Manhattan attracted other business and professional firms. Financial intermediaries, including trust companies, insurance companies, mutual funds, and retail brokers of stocks and bonds, expanded rapidly near Wall Street's money market institutions, and in nearby Newark and Hartford. Advertising agencies, industrial designers, consulting engineers, accountants, and corporate lawyers clustered near the corporate headquarters.

From the 1880s to the 1960s manufacturing also kept pace in the New York metropolitan region. Some of the manufacturing involved very large firms in such port-related industries as sugar refining, oil refining, paint, soap, and chemical making, the production of cookies, crackers, and pasta, and manufacturing industries such as those dominated by Steinway pianos and Otis elevators. But while New York held the headquarters of very large corporations, it did not house their employees. Many port services were provided by small firms. And small firms dominated most of the region's manufacturing, which concentrated in industries that required the latest possible information about European innovations and American markets: women's clothing, hats, and furs; printing, publishing, and entertainment; artificial flowers and costume jewelry. Small firms also dominated manufacturing with brass works in the Naugatuck Valley, men's hatmakers in Danbury, textiles and lace in Paterson, Passaic, and Hoboken, machine makers in Paterson and Newark, and potteries in Trenton.

And small firms also dominated the region's service and retail industries. Mass tourism expanded rapidly after the turn of the century, benefiting large railroads and many small hotels, restaurants, nightclubs, taxis, tourist homes at the New Jersey beaches, and amusement stands at Coney Island. Despite the region's famous large department stores (Macy's, Gimbels, S. Klein, Abraham and Strauss, Bamberger's), New York City in particular was also distinctive for its very large number of specialty stores of all kinds, and for its many small retail businesses.

The combination of big finance, big publishing, and big corporations with small manufacturers, shops, and service businesses gave the New York region an unusual business mix. Unlike most regions, in New York many very wealthy people had few local employees. Wall Street bankers, lawyers, and corporate executives increasingly lived in the suburbs, outside New York City and Newark. They had little in common with the small proprietors who worried daily about the ups and downs of the region's economy and the demands of its workers.

A Changing and Cosmopolitan Population
The New York metropolitan region's population changed steadily through the nineteenth century; until 1880 it was heavily concentrated in the territory that would become the five boroughs of New York City and was composed of three broad elements: the largely British and Dutch "native stock," the Irish, and the Germans. It became more diverse and changed more rapidly thereafter. It also began to move out from the central city. In 1900 the five boroughs still held eighty percent of the region's 4.3 million people, and while the Irish- and German-born and their children still constituted about forty percent of the region's population, significant numbers of new immigrants from central and eastern Europe had already arrived. By 1940 the five boroughs held only seventy-five percent of the region's ten million people, and Italians and eastern European Jews made up two of the region's largest ethnic groups. African Americans became a smaller and smaller portion of the region's population through the nineteenth century, until they were only two percent at the turn of the century. As late as 1940, African Americans were only about five percent of the region's population, and Hispanics and Asians together were less than one percent.

The changing population brought new religious and political ideas. Greater New York and Newark were perhaps one-third (Irish and German) Catholic in 1880, and at most one-twentieth Jewish. The Catholic proportion remained somewhat over one-third, but only through the addition of very large numbers of Catholics from Italy and significant numbers from Bohemia, Hungary, and Poland—all of whom differed from one another and from the Irish and Germans in their languages, religious customs, and attitudes toward the church as an institution. They fostered another round of Catholic institution-building, with new parishes, new convents, and new colleges to accommodate the new groups of Catholics.

By 1900 the region was more than one-sixth Jewish; by 1910, more than one-fourth. The Jewish population formed many distinct social worlds, from the assimilated, prosperous Reform congregations of German Jews on Manhattan's Upper East and Upper West sides, to the Orthodox congregations and landsmanschaft (village of origin) mutual benefit societies among the Polish, Russian, Lithuanian, Hungarian, and Romanian Jews of the Lower East Side and Newark, to the Orthodox and Hasidic communities in Williamsburg and Borough Park in Brooklyn—and of Yeshiva University in Manhattan. From the 1920s on, increasing numbers of Jews expressed their faith through Conservative congregations that became more and more numerous in Brooklyn, Queens, and the suburbs in Long Island and New Jersey, and that were served by the Jewish Theological Seminary on Morningside Heights, near Columbia University and the Protestant Union Theological Seminary. Many Jewish immigrants were not actively religious; some debated socialist politics on the Lower East Side and in the Bronx, many others sought to create ordinary American lives in apartment homes in Flatbush, Washington Heights, and the Grand Concourse in the Bronx, in Jersey City and Newark—and after World War II in the growing suburbs of New Jersey and Long Island. Jewish refugees from the Holocaust, and later from the Soviet Union, added new facets to Jewish New York.

The outline of the suburban trend was already evident in the 1920s. Commuter trains and auto-

TABLE 3 Population of Greater New York, 1900–1980

	New York City	Metropolitan Region	Percent Black (Metro. Region)
1900	3,437,202	81% of 4,257,196	2
1920	5,620,048	79% of 7,086,255	3
1940	7,454,995	75% of 9,998,000	6
1960	7,781,984	51% of 15,405,000	11
1980	7,072,000	40% of 17,539,000	16

Source: Ira Rosenwaike, *Population History of New York City* (Syracuse: Syracuse University Press, 1972).

mobiles, with highways, bridges, and tunnels, connected Westport, Scarsdale, Montclair, the Oranges, and central Long Island to Manhattan, adding again to the region's interconnections and to the diversity of the population in its outer areas. These early suburbs were for the affluent, and many of them were secular-Protestant in tone; it was Great Neck and Manhasset on Long Island that F. Scott Fitzgerald immortalized in *The Great Gatsby* as "West Egg" and "East Egg." Suburban and business leaders, however, already foresaw much of the mass movement to the suburbs that did indeed follow World War II; through the Regional Plan Association of New York and New Jersey they sought to guide that movement and help utilities and real estate interests cope with it.

Black ghettos had also emerged by the 1920s. The New York region's black population had declined to under two percent by 1900, but the Great Migration from the South and a steady influx of black immigrants from the West Indies produced steady growth thereafter. After 1910 newcomers joined blacks displaced from traditional residential areas in lower and midtown Manhattan in moving to newly built housing in Harlem. Formerly a heterogeneous, white, middle- and upper-income residential area, Harlem quickly became the most famous black residential and entertainment district in the United States. In the 1920s black writers, poets, and musicians, eager to gain access to New York's publishers, came to Harlem from all over the country and created the extraordinary outburst of artistic creativity known as the Harlem Renaissance. Black entrepreneurs created nightclubs and after-hours places, providing venues for black musicians, dancers, and comedians, and catering to whites who sought exotic entertainment. Like the black districts of Brooklyn and Newark, however, Harlem was also the product of racist restrictions that severely limited the availability of housing to blacks: thus its residents were forced to accept high rents, crowding, and, often, inadequate services.

The Rise of Urban Liberalism The changing diversity of the New York region's population posed severe difficulties to political leaders who sought to put substantial electoral coalitions together. Through the last third of the nineteenth century, most Irish voters opposed the idea that government should play an active role in society: they associated strong government with British rule in Ireland and, in New York, with Protestant control of schools, welfare institutions, and saloon licenses. The Irish found it reasonable to work with merchants whose preference for low tariffs led them to prefer weak government as well. But other Irish workers, some British-stock workers who hearkened back to the tradition of artisan republicanism, and many Germans favored a more active government.

By the early 1890s socialists found themselves divided along national lines, with separate English-, German-, and Yiddish-speaking labor federations and with Irish workers debating the merits of the Clan-na-Gael, Germans disputing (in German) the merits of Ferdinand Lassalle, Jews arguing (in Yiddish, Russian, and other languages) over syndicalism and anarchism. In the face of these exciting but acrimonious debates, it was no wonder that Samuel Gompers of New York's cigar-makers union and the American Federation of Labor decided, by the early 1890s, that labor should avoid partisan politics and emphasize only bread-and-butter matters that might yield tangible results. Nor was it surprising that few of the region's political leaders, Republican or Democrat, seemed to stand for concrete principles.

Early in the twentieth century, however, New York City did develop a new consensus that favored a more active government. Republican-led "fusion" campaigns for mayor, around the turn of the century, called for increased public expenditure on public schools, public health, and recreation, and for greatly expanded government regulation of low-income housing, thereby courting immigrants from central and eastern Europe, who came "from European cities that are as progressive as we are backward" (quoted in D. Harmach, *Power and Society* (New York: Russell Sage Foundation, 1982), p. 155). Tammany Democrats in turn protested against Republican interference with workers' rights to live and drink as they pleased, and moved to support labor's right to organize and government regulation of the price of gas. Using his newspapers and a dramatic and often successful series of mayoral and other campaigns between 1902 and 1920, William Randolph Hearst then raised the ante by calling for government regulation of the great corporations and municipal ownership of the rapid transit and gas utilities.

Tammany Hall's Charles F. Murphy, Alfred E. Smith, and Robert F. Wagner responded again, and by the early 1920s had created twentieth-century New York's most significant political contribution, "urban liberalism." They pressed for state regulation of the hours and working conditions in factories, special protections for working women and children, and expansion of public education. They cultivated good working relationships with organized labor, the Catholic church, and Jewish groups, adding the demand that government protect the rights of all citizens regardless of religion or national origin, to their earlier demand for the right of labor to organize. They responded to the requests of Jewish labor unions and other mutual benefit associations for state aid to housing and retirement-home projects. In the 1930s, Wagner played a leading role in the creation of the New Deal's social security and public housing programs.

Liberalism shaped the mayoral administrations of Fiorello LaGuardia (1934–1945), a Fusion-Republican who appealed very effectively to Jewish and Italian voters and who worked effectively with Franklin D. Roosevelt, as well as with mayors nominated by the Democrats—from Jimmy Walker in the late 1920s through Robert Wagner, Jr., in the 1960s. Part of the price of liberal consensus was a narrowing of the range of acceptable politics. As liberalism advanced, leaders who might discredit it found themselves pushed aside: political radicals as well as those associated with corrupt labor, with the criminal underworld, with anti-Semitism or anti-Catholicism or xenophobia. For although liberalism came to dominate New York City, it did not dominate the State of New York—still less the states of New Jersey and Connecticut. Through most of the twentieth century the region's political landscape was sharply divided between the liberal city and the more traditional, conservative, Republican suburbs. To secure tax money and new business regulations, the city's liberals had to win over at least some of the suburban members of the New York State legislature. They also had to pay some attention to state policy in New Jersey and Connecticut, which stood ready to attract both residents and businesses from New York City.

THE DUAL CITY OF THE LATE TWENTIETH CENTURY

Since 1960 the New York metropolitan region has been transformed by the rise of the "Dual City," with great wealth in the headquarters and service businesses of Manhattan and many of the suburbs, and appalling poverty in large parts of Manhattan and the outerboroughs and in the ring of older port and industrial cities that surround them, in New Jersey and Connecticut as well as up the Hudson and on Long Island. Manhattan has remained, with Tokyo and the City of London, one of the three great international capitals of capitalism. It has retained much of its constellation of corporate headquarters, banks and financial companies, corporate lawyers, and the entire array of business services. It has also retained its luxury hotels, its extraordinary array of restaurants, its art galleries, museums, and theaters, with their endless seasons of dance and music.

During the 1970s and 1980s many corporate headquarters did move out of Manhattan, but only because so many other people wished to locate there that rents became very high. Many corporate headquarters simply moved to the region's suburbs—Tarrytown in New York; Stamford and Danbury in Connecticut; Montclair, New Brunswick, and Princeton in New Jersey. These moves encouraged business services to remain in Manhattan, at the center of the region's transportation and communication networks. Some corporate jobs, especially the "back-office" paper-shuffling jobs of the insurance and banking industries, did move—not only to the outerboroughs and Newark but also to North Dakota, Iowa, and even Jamaica and Ireland, where educated workers were cheaper and where electronic communications provided instant communication with Wall Street.

Port-related and manufacturing activity simply collapsed after 1960, especially in the five boroughs of New York City and in the New Jersey towns along the Hudson. Modern ships carrying containers or very large quantities of bulk commodities no longer used the nineteenth-century docks of Brooklyn, Manhattan, or Hoboken. The newer facilities of Port Newark and Port Elizabeth, like the new warehouse distribution centers in the Jersey meadows, employed far fewer people. The region's long-established manufacturing industries also declined sharply as lower and lower transport prices allowed entrepreneurs to move much of the garment and related industries to low-wage workers in Asia and Latin America, and as automation sharply reduced employment in printing. In their effort to drive labor costs down, some garment-industry entrepreneurs re-created the sweatshop and homework conditions of the 1890s in the South Bronx and on Manhattan's Lower East Side. In 1950, thirty percent of New York City's 3.5 million jobs were in manufacturing; by 1985, there were still 3.5 million jobs, but only twelve percent were in manufacturing. Service jobs did increase rapidly, from under 15 percent in 1950 to nearly 30 percent in 1985.

Government jobs also increased, from under 11 percent to 16 percent. But the new jobs that required little education paid less well than had the manufacturing jobs of the 1940s and 1950s, and better-paying jobs often required more education than many job applicants could offer.

Jobs moved to the suburbs because new highways, bridges, and tunnels made it possible for goods and people to move there too, and for industry to take advantage of spacious new factories and warehouses oriented to truck, rail, and air transport rather than to ships. After 1940 most of the region's population growth occurred outside the five boroughs of New York City—and outside Hoboken, Jersey City, and Newark as well. In 1940 the city still held 75 percent of the region's people, but by 1980 its share had fallen to 40 percent.

As in every metropolitan region in the United States, the New York region's people were increasingly segregated by income, life-style, and race. In many public discussions, the Dual City distinction between rich and poor, white and colored, displaced all other distinctions. Anti-Semitism and anti-Catholic attitudes certainly did decline, as Catholics and Jews moved into leadership posts in many institutions, from Princeton to Wall Street to New York Hospital to New Haven, which had actively discriminated against them before World War II. Cultural debates among Catholics, Jews, and Protestants did not, however, disappear. Nor was it true that all blacks were poor.

Blacks and Hispanics (Puerto Ricans, but also significant numbers of Dominicans, Cubans, and others from the Caribbean) greatly increased in numbers. Spreading out from Harlem, the South Bronx, Brooklyn's Bedford-Stuyvesant area, Jamaica in Queens, and from Newark as well as other New Jersey towns along the Hudson, they frequently encountered resistance and conflict. A new wave of Asians, many from Hong Kong and other Chinese communities (including some communities in South America), others from Korea, Japan, and India, further increased the region's diversity. The civil rights movement opened the way for small but significant numbers of blacks to move into managerial and professional jobs—fourteen percent of black men, sixteen percent of black women in 1980. The civil rights movement also opened the way for affluent blacks to move into middle- and upper-middle income neighborhoods throughout the city and the suburbs that had formerly been closed to nonwhites. The poorest were left behind in areas of concentrated, almost hopeless poverty.

By 1980 New York City was about half non-Hispanic white, one-quarter African American, and about one-fifth Hispanic, with about 300,000 mostly very recent Asian immigrants (this number would double by 1990). The region as a whole, however, was only 16 percent black and Hispanic. Overall, as white immigrants and their children and grandchildren left blue-collar jobs for managerial, professional, and better-paying service positions during the 1970s and 1980s, they left the region's older cities as well.

Gender differences had always structured economic and social relationships in Greater New York, but they became an increasingly public source of difference and debate after 1960s. In the region as in the nation as a whole, female-headed households became far more common (one of eight in New York City in 1970, one of six in 1980), and in general, women became almost as likely as men to work for pay. About half of the jobs of white women were in "pink-collar" clerical and office work, but nearly a third were managerial or professional. About half of the black working women also did clerical and office work, while about one-sixth were managers and professionals (both black and white women are teachers and nurses far more often than doctors or lawyers). Although they often expressed anxiety about the potential impact of affirmative action programs designed to increase opportunities for minorities, white men as a group were very well placed to benefit from the region's economy. Through the 1980s, women and minorities became increasingly impatient with their unequal opportunities.

In the 1950s and 1960s, New York City's political leaders responded to the challenges posed by economic and population change by drawing on the liberal tradition. The city had a long tradition of active government investment in public works and government support for private charitable and cultural agencies; it had built a very substantial public health and hospital system. During the Great Depression its leaders had also agreed that it would pay one-fourth of the cost of welfare for its residents. The state administration of Governor Nelson Rockefeller and the national administrations of John F. Kennedy and Lyndon Johnson encouraged the city to build on this tradition. Blacks and others demanded, more and more insistently, that New York and other cities do more to equalize access to adequate housing, medical care, education, and economic opportunity. Their demands reached a crescendo in the late 1960s, with school boycotts, marches on City Hall, and "long hot summers" of threatened riots.

Mayors Robert F. Wagner, Jr., and John V. Lindsay, their administrations, the City Council, and the state legislature responded to these various encouragements and demands by greatly expanding the City University of New York, adding new junior colleges, subsidizing Lincoln Center for the Performing Arts, funding many antipoverty job-training and advocacy agencies, and raising the level of welfare payments. To carry out these actions they secured increased aid from the state and federal governments and increased taxes; by the mid 1970s New York City had the highest sales tax and the highest local income tax in the United States, although it also protected its homeowners with a relatively low tax on residential property.

New York City also financed these activities with borrowed money, especially under Lindsay, and when interest rates rose and federal subsidies dropped in 1974, it ran into a serious fiscal crisis. The era of urban liberalism appeared at an end. Federal funds continued to flow to the people of the region, but under Carter, Reagan, and Bush they flowed less to government and nonprofit agencies and more to individuals in the form of social security checks, Medicare and Medicaid payments to doctors and hospitals, food stamps, and rent vouchers. State and federal action reduced the value of welfare payments by refusing to increase payments to keep up with inflation. Many of the region's voters, in New York City and Newark as well as in the suburbs, new immigrants as well as Connecticut Yankees, insisted that government should do less, that taxes and government regulations should be cut back in order to free individual initiative. Suburban voters throughout the region insisted that more state aid flow to their communities—and they significantly outnumbered big-city voters in the calculations of governors and state legislators. These new views did not, understandably, appeal to most

of the poorest blacks and Hispanics in the central cities, but many of the Hispanics were not citizens and many of the blacks and Hispanics did not register to vote, or did not vote if they were registered. The region had become a Dual City in attitudes toward government as well as in wealth and living conditions.

In New York City, Edward I. Koch, who was twice reelected mayor with the support of white voters who felt more and more embattled, sought to put the best face on the situation, emphasizing his efforts to maintain order, introduce professional and competent management of government affairs, and uphold the city's commitment to fairness and opportunity. Koch did *not* promise to expand the activities of municipal government or to increase government aid to the poor. Many public works projects, including a new subway to serve the East Side, were stopped, and others, including a major new water supply tunnel, were delayed. Government funds for nonprofit antipoverty and advocacy groups were also cut sharply. With the relative decline in its economy, New York City had lost some of its ability to pay for urban liberalism. The region's smaller manufacturing and port towns, including Newark, Jersey City, Yonkers, and Norwalk, suffered even more from the economic and population changes of the 1970s and 1980s; and the cities of New Jersey and Connecticut had to get by with much less state aid than New York provided.

David Dinkins, elected New York City's first black mayor in 1989, sought to revive the traditions of urban liberalism, but faced stiff resistance from the federal government and a state government unable to increase its assistance and significant resistance to increased taxes. In 1991 New York and other large cities in the region lacked the resources to implement liberal programs. It remained to be seen whether in the future they could find the resources, or whether they would develop new ideological traditions.

BIBLIOGRAPHY

Works and Historiography

Bender, Thomas. *New York Intellect: A History of Intellectual Life in New York City, from 1750 to the Beginnings of Our Own Time* (1987).

Federal Writers' Project. *New York Panorama* (1938). The Federal Writers' Project volumes are unusually comprehensive; the "panorama" is in fact a general history, topically arranged.

————. *New York City Guide* (1939).

Kovenhoven, John A. *The Columbia Historical Portrait of New York: An Essay in Graphic History* (1953; repr. 1972).

Lampard, Eric E. "The New York Metropolis in Transformation: History and Prospect: A Study in Historical Particularity." In *The Future of the Metropolis,* edited by H.-J. Ewers, John B. Goddard, and Horst Matzerath (1986).

Mollenkopf, John Hull, ed. *Power, Culture, and Place: Essays on New York City* (1988). Essays on a variety of topics for a variety of periods by Diane Lindstrom, Martin Shefter, and several others.

Pratt, John Webb. *Religion, Politics, and Diversity: The Church-State Theme in New York History* (1967).

Rosenwaike, Ira. *Population History of New York City* (1972). A useful though incomplete compilation.

Still, Bayrd. *Mirror for Gotham: New York as Seen by Contemporaries from Dutch Days to the Present* (1956).

Willensky, Elliot, and Norval White, eds. *AIA Guide to New York City* (1988). A guide to history as well as architecture.

Colonial Period

Archdeacon, Thomas J. *New York City, 1664–1710: Conquest and Change* (1976).

Bonomi, Patricia U. *A Factious People: Politics and Society in Colonial New York* (1971).

Bridenbaugh, Carl. *Cities in the Wilderness: The First Century of Urban Life in America, 1625–1742* (1938).

————. *Cities in Revolt: Urban Life in America, 1743–1776* (1955). Both of Bridenbaugh's books contain extensive general remarks on the people and institutions of colonial New York City.

Condon, Thomas J. *New York Beginnings: The Commercial Origins of New Netherland* (1968).

Davis, Thomas J. *A Rumor of Revolt: The "Great Negro Plot" in Colonial New York* (1985).

Klein, Milton M. *The Politics of Diversity: Essays in the History of Colonial New York* (1974).

Nash, Gary B. *The Urban Crucible: Social Change, Political Consciousness, and the Origins of the American Revolution* (1979). Stimulating though brief discussions of New York City.

Price, Jacob. "Economic Function and the Growth of American Port Towns in the Eighteenth Century." In *Perspectives in American History,* 8, edited by Donald Fleming and Bernard Bailyn (1974).

Nineteenth Century

Albion, Robert G. *The Rise of the New York Port, 1815–1860* (1939; repr. 1961).

Asbury, Herbert. *The Gangs of New York: An Informal History of the Underworld* (1928).

Blackmar, Elizabeth. *Manhattan for Rent, 1785–1850* (1989).

Bridges, Amy. *A City in the Republic: Antebellum New York and the Origins of Machine Politics* (1984).

Cook, A. *The Armies of the Street: The New York City Draft Riots of 1863* (1974).

Dolan, Jay P. *The Immigrant Church: New York's Irish and German Catholics, 1815–1865* (1975).

Dubofsky, Melvin. *When Workers Organize: New York City in the Progressive Era* (1968).

Ernst, Robert. *Immigrant Life in New York City, 1825–1863* (1949; repr. 1979).

Gilje, Paul. *The Road to Mobocracy: Popular Disorder in New York City, 1763–1834* (1987).

Hammack, David C. *Power and Society: Greater New York at the Turn of the Century* (1982).

Mohl, Raymond A. *Poverty in New York, 1783–1825* (1971).

Mohr, James C. *The Radical Republicans and Reform in New York During Reconstruction* (1973).

Pomerantz, Sidney. *New York: An American City, 1783–1803: A Study of Urban Life* (1938; repr. 1965).

——. *Urban Growth and the Circulation of Information: The United States System of Cities, 1790–1840* (1973).

Richardson, James F. *The New York Police, Colonial Times to 1901* (1970).

Riis, Jacob A. *How the Other Half Lives: Studies Among the Tenements of New York* (1890; repr. 1971).

Rischin, Moses. *The Promised City: New York's Jews, 1870–1914* (1962).

Rosenberg, Carroll Smith. *Religion and the Rise of the American City: The New York City Mission Movement, 1812–1870* (1971).

Spann, Edward K. *The New Metropolis: New York City, 1840–1857* (1981).

Stansell, Christine. *City of Women: Sex and Class in New York, 1789–1860* (1986).

Syrett, Harold C. *The City of Brooklyn, 1865–1898* (1944).

Wilentz, Sean. *Chants Democratic: New York City and the Rise of the American Working Class, 1788–1850* (1984).

Twentieth Century

Bayor, Ronald H. *Neighbors in Conflict: The Irish, Germans, Jews, and Italians of New York City, 1929–1941* (1978).

Connolly, Harold X. *A Ghetto Grows in Brooklyn* (1977).

Erenberg, Lewis. *Steppin' Out: New York Nightlife and the Transformation of American Culture, 1890–1930* (1981; repr. 1984).

Glazer, Nathan, and Daniel Patrick Moynihan. *Beyond the Melting Pot: The Negroes, Puerto Ricans, Jews, Italians, and Irish of New York City* (1963).

Goren, Arthur A. *New York Jews and the Quest for Community: The Kehillah Experiment, 1908–1922* (1970).

Gottmann, Jean. *Megalopolis: The Urbanized Northeastern Seaboard of the United States* (1961).

Hoover, Edgar M., and Raymond Vernon. *Anatomy of a Metropolis: The Changing Distribution of People and Jobs Within the New York Metropolitan Region* (1959; repr. 1962). Summary of a multivolume survey of the New York region's economy, society, and politics commissioned by the Regional Plan Association of New York and New Jersey.

Howe, Irving. *World of Our Fathers.* (1976).

Huggins, Nathan I. *Harlem Renaissance* (1971).

Huthmacher, J. Joseph. *Senator Robert F. Wagner and the Rise of Urban Liberalism* (1968; 2d ed. 1971).

Jackson, Kenneth T. "The Capital of Capitalism: The New York Metropolitan Region, 1890–1940." In *Metropolis, 1890–1940* edited by A. Sutcliffe (1984).

Kessner, Thomas. *The Golden Door: Italian and Jewish Immigrant Mobility in New York City, 1880–1915* (1977).

Logan, Andy. *Against the Evidence: The Becker-Rosenthal Affair* (1970).

Lowi, Theodore J. *At the Pleasure of the Mayor: Patronage and Power in New York City, 1898–1958* (1964).

Lubove, Roy. *The Progressives and the Slums: Tenement House Reform in New York City, 1890–1917* (1962; repr. 1974).

Mann, Arthur. *LaGuardia Comes to Power, 1933* (1965; repr. 1969).

Moore, Deborah Dash. *At Home in America: Second-Generation New York Jews* (1981).

Osofsky, Gilbert. *Harlem: The Making of a Ghetto: Negro New York, 1890–1930* (1968; 2d ed. 1971).

Peiss, Kathy. *Cheap Amusements: Working Women and Leisure in Turn-of-the-Century New York* (1986).

Perry, Elisabeth Israels. *Belle Moskowitz: Feminine Politics and the Exercise of Power in the Age of Alfred E. Smith* (1987).

Sayre, Wallace S., and Herbert Kaufman. *Governing New York City: Politics in the Metropolis* (1960; repr. 1965).

Snyder, Robert W. *The Voice of the City: Vaudeville and Popular Culture in New York* (1989).

Taylor, William L. *Inventing Times Square* (1991). Essays on the history of commercial culture in all its forms.

Wakefield, Dan. *Island in the City: The World of Spanish Harlem* (1959; repr. 1975).

Ware, Caroline F. *Greenwich Village, 1920–1930* (1935).

Wood, Robert C., with Vladimir V. Almendinger. *1400 Governments: The Political Economy of the New York Metropolitan Region* (1961).

Late Twentieth Century

Cary, G. *New York, New Jersey: A Vignette of the Metropolitan Region* (1976).

Cuomo, Mario. *Forest Hills Diary: The Crisis of Low-Income Housing* (1974).

Danielson, Michael N., and Jameson W. Doig. *New York: The Politics of Urban Regional Development* (1982).

Horton, Raymond, and Charles Brecher. *Setting Municipal Priorities, 1980* (1979). One of a six-year series of similarly-titled collections of essays on New York City's economy and government, commissioned in response to the fiscal crisis of 1975 and edited by the same two scholars.

Kantrowitz, Nathan. *Ethnic and Racial Segregation in the New York Metropolis: Residential Patterns Among White Ethnic Groups, Blacks, and Puerto Ricans* (1973).

Katznelson, Ira. *City Trenches: Urban Politics and the Patterning of Class in the United States* (1981).

Koch, Edward I., with William Rauch. *Mayor* (1984).

Morris, Charles. *The Cost of Good Intentions: New York City and the Liberal Experiment, 1960–1975* (1980).

Rieder, Jonathan. *Canarsie: The Jews and Italians of Brooklyn Against Liberalism* (1985).

Shefter, Martin. *Political Crisis/Fiscal Crisis: The Collapse and Revival of New York City* (1985).

SEE ALSO **American Social and Cultural Geography; Commercial Architecture; New England; Print and Publishing; The Social History of Culture; Social Work and Philanthropy; Technology and Social Change; Transportation and Mobility; Urban Cultural Institutions; Women and Work;** and various essays in the sections **"The Construction of Social Identity," "Ethnic and Racial Subcultures," "Space and Place,"** and **"Work and Labor."**

THE MIDDLE ATLANTIC REGION

Don Yoder

THE MIDDLE ATLANTIC REGION—Pennsylvania, New Jersey, and Delaware—occupies a key area in America's political, intellectual, and social history, an area where cultural pluralism existed from the very beginning of settlement and where many cultural innovations originated that later spread to other parts of the country. With the addition of New York, the mixture of ethnic and social and religious groups in the region offered a model for a pluralistic America. Although Pennsylvania provided the majority of the innovations, all three states contributed through their close similarity in political structure and social makeup.

DEFINING THE REGION

Until the last decades of the twentieth century, however, American historiography and cultural analysis showed a comparative neglect of the Middle States. According to the results of an influential conference on Middle States historiography at the American Philosophical Society in Philadelphia in 1963, this neglect resulted in part from a weaker regional self-consciousness (or in the language of a later time, a weaker regional identity) than that developed by New England and the South. It was pointed out that, unlike New England and the Old South, the Middle States historically had supported national rather than regional interests. Frederick Jackson Turner, the proponent of the frontier theory of American history, saw the Middle States as "the typically American region" and even asserted that the West was "after a fashion, an expansion of the Middle Region." And Jared Ingersoll, a Philadelphia congressman and historian, in 1832 called the area "that solid, silent center," without which both East and South would be "no more than wings without a body."

What unity the region possesses is the result of common geographical factors and a shared political and settlement history. Several natural features unite the three states. The Delaware River, which forms the border between Pennsylvania and New Jersey and which with Delaware Bay forms much of the eastern boundary of Delaware, served the area as a channel for trade, communication, and settlement. The Appalachian (Allegheny) chain of mountains, extending in a broad band from southwestern and south-central Pennsylvania to northwestern Pennsylvania, continues into northern New Jersey. This chain consists of wooded mountains and long, fertile valleys suitable for agriculture, dairying, and milling. The mountains themselves provided almost inexhaustible amounts of timber for the lumbering industry that developed in the nineteenth century and two large coal deposits that made Pennsylvania a mining center in the nineteenth and twentieth centuries, the anthracite region in northeastern Pennsylvania and the bituminous region in central and western Pennsylvania.

In the colonial period, the location of the Middle States, with their rivers, harbors, and ports, gave them advantages in trade with the other American colonies, the West Indies, and Europe. Philadelphia, with its splendid river facilities for seagoing vessels and its three-state ring of agricultural and industrial areas, was the second-largest city in the British Empire in the colonial period after London. It was not until the nineteenth century that New York overtook it in population and trade. Philadelphia was also the major port of entry for European immigrants in the eighteenth and nineteenth centuries, until New York supplanted it after the War of 1812.

Pennsylvania has three of what geographers call regional gate (or gateway) cities, although only two of them are in the state. Eastern Pennsylvania faces and centers on Philadelphia, which is the state's major gateway—its eye, in a sense—to the world, including Europe. Pittsburgh, at the confluence of the Allegheny and Monongahela rivers, where they form the Ohio River, is western Pennsylvania's gateway to the Midwest and South. Central Pennsylvania, however, has always faced south, because of its great central river, the Susquehanna, which begins in New York State and in west-central Pennsylvania and flows through the state and Maryland into Chesapeake Bay. Hence (with no slur intended to Harrisburg, the state's capital), central Pennsylvania's gateway city is Baltimore. Before the Civil War and especially before the railroad age, it was easier for central Pennsylvanians to transport their goods by water or wagon southward to Baltimore than eastward to Philadelphia. What was true of trade was also true of culture. Central Pennsylvania's early religious organizations were often outposts of Baltimore, as was the case for the Catholics, the Quakers, and the Methodists.

New Jersey, with an area of 7,787 square miles (20,169 square kilometers) is the fourth-smallest state in the nation. It abuts on New York State, with whose population and culture it has been connected from the days of the earliest Dutch settlements. A long maritime coastline on the Atlantic Ocean defines New Jersey to the east and Delaware Bay to the southwest. Northern New Jersey, bordering New York and Pennsylvania, is rolling and partially mountainous; southern New Jersey is relatively flat, sandy, and suitable for the truck gardening and market farming that supply the New York and Philadelphia markets. The fishing industry on the Atlantic and Delaware Bay coast is also one of New Jersey's prime industries. Over part of South Jersey extends a huge area called the Pine Barrens, with a distinctive population and culture.

Tiny Delaware, often called the First State because it was the first to ratify the U.S. Constitution in 1787, or the Diamond State because of its small size and immense worth, is only 95 miles (150 kilometers) long and 40 miles (65 kilometers) wide. With a total area of 2,045 square miles (5,295 square kilometers) and only three counties—New Castle, Kent, and Sussex—it shares the so-called Delmarva Peninsula with the eastern shore of Maryland and the eastern shore of Virginia, with which it is closely related economically. Known at first as "Penn's three lower counties on Delaware," the area remained under the government of Pennsylvania until 1776, when it became separate. Before the Civil War it was a slave state, but northern Delaware, centered on the industrial city of Wilmington, had closer connections with the North. It was in fact a center of the antislavery movement through the influence of the Quakers and others who aided fugitive slaves to escape to freedom via the Underground Railroad. With its northern connections, Delaware took the northern side in the Civil War.

Its three excellent ports—Wilmington, New Castle, and Lewes—early made Delaware an important center for mid-Atlantic trade. Its farms and plantations on the Atlantic plain, in central and southern Delaware, formed a choice agricultural section supplying the Wilmington market. The water connections in the Brandywine Valley with Pennsylvania's wheat-growing areas led to the establishment of the great industrial complex known as the Brandywine Mills at Wilmington, the product of Quaker upper-class economic interests. Shipbuilding and other industries flourished in the nineteenth century, and after 1900 Wilmington developed into a major American industrial center, with carriage and car building, papermaking, canning and food products, textiles, tanning, iron, and other industries. Included in this development, as well as a stimulus for it, has been since 1802 the firm of E. I. du Pont de Nemours & Company, the largest chemical company in the world, with its many subsidiaries.

THE NATIVE AMERICANS
AND THEIR CULTURAL INFLUENCE

The first occupants of the Delaware Valley were the Indians, whose influence is still subtly with us. The major group with whom Europeans came into contact in Pennsylvania and New Jersey were the Lenni Lenape or Delawares, an Algonquian tribe. Farther west, in the Susquehanna Valley, were the Susquehannocks or Minquas (Mingoes), an Iroquoian group related to the tribes in New York. In western Pennsylvania were other tribes in the upper reaches of the tributaries of the Ohio, and in the northwest corner of the state were the Eries.

It is estimated that Indians inhabited the Middle States region for twelve to thirteen thousand years. At the arrival of William Penn the Indians were agriculturalists, organized in tribal governments, making pottery, weaving textiles, and having a minimal knowledge of metals. Penn's attitude toward them was paternal yet brotherly. Like some of his predecessors on the Delaware, he purchased land from them for settlement and attempted to treat them with justice and mercy. Like Cotton Mather and many other colonial Americans, he believed them to be descendants of the lost tribes of

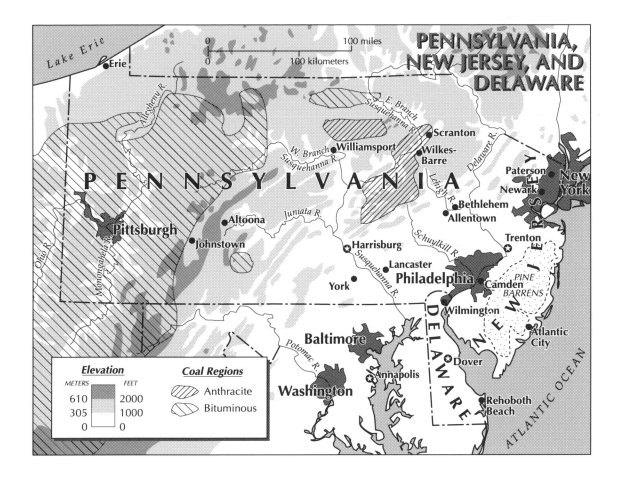

Israel. This fact, and his Quakerism, led him to accent the similarities between European religion and Indian belief in the Great Spirit. The brotherly relation between Quakers and Indians has lasted to the present time.

In many ways the Indian presence affected settlement and pioneer life. Native foods such as Indian corn became staples and remained so. On the Allegheny and western frontiers, the white settlers adopted Indian dress, especially the fringed hunting shirt and moccasins. Indian trails became highways and Indian clearings white towns, as for example Shamokin (Sunbury), Standing Stone (Huntington), and Chinclacamoose (Clearfield). Hundreds of Indian place names still designate mountains, valleys, rivers, creeks, and even towns.

The Indian population was eventually displaced. Most of the tribes moved to the Midwest and the Indian Territory (Oklahoma), where remnants of the Delawares still live, with a handful of native speakers of the Delaware language being studied by anthropologists and linguists. The Corn-

planters, a Seneca offshoot, were displaced from their lands in the Allegheny River valley by the building of the Kinzua Dam in the 1950s. Several partially Indian groups of mixed race have continued in the Middle States, as for example, the Jackson Whites of the Ramapo Mountains of New Jersey and the Nanticokes in Delaware. A Native American Federation of the Delaware Valley was established in the twentieth century to unite the descendants of the remaining ethnic Indian groups.

THE DUTCH AND SWEDES ON THE DELAWARE

It is to Holland and Sweden, European allies in the religious wars of the seventeenth century, that America owes the discovery, early European settlement, and pioneer development of the Delaware Valley and the Middle Atlantic states. Following the exploration of the Hudson River and

Delaware Bay by Henry Hudson, an Englishman working for the Dutch East India Company, the Dutch West India Company, chartered in 1621, established the colony of New Netherland in 1624. The weight of settlement was in the Hudson Valley, with smaller numbers settling in the Delaware Valley. The Dutch authorities also apparently neglected New Netherland in favor of Brazil and other projects, and appeared to rate the fur trade with the Indians more highly than active Dutch colonization.

Dutch neglect led to Swedish opportunity. Sweden under Gustavus Adolphus (r. 1611–1632) was expanding, and the king was leader of the Protestant alliance in the Thirty Years War. Through the help of disgruntled Dutch entrepreneurs like Willem Usselincx, the Swedish South Company was chartered in 1626–1627. In 1638 the first Swedish-Finnish settlers arrived in the Delaware Valley under Peter Minuit, another renegade Dutchman who had earlier been governor of New Netherland. The new settlers built Fort Christina, on the site of Wilmington.

Ignoring the polite Dutch protests that arrived from New Amsterdam, the Swedes began colonization in earnest. Their policy, carried out by Minuit, was to purchase land from the Indians, despite European claims based on discovery, and to grant religious toleration to the Dutch who remained, the Swedes being Lutherans and the Dutch Reformed (Calvinist). Under Governor Johan Printz (governed 1643–1663) the Swedish capital was removed from Fort Christina to Tinicum Island, near what is now Essington, Pennsylvania, thus founding the first permanent white settlement in what became Pennsylvania. When in 1655 the Dutch reconquered New Sweden, there were about four hundred Swedes on both sides of the Delaware who peacefully accepted Dutch rule and, after 1664, English sovereignty.

In 1664 Charles II (r. 1660–1685) transferred the entire area to his brother the duke of York, who on Charles's death became James II (r. 1685–1688). James granted the territory between the Hudson and the Delaware, an area that became New Jersey, to John, Lord Berkeley, and Sir George Carteret. This was later divided into East Jersey and West Jersey. A consortium of Quakers, including Penn, took over West Jersey and in 1675 sent several hundred settlers to plant America's first Quaker colony, at Salem. In 1702 East and West Jersey were united into a royal province.

The cultural influence of the Dutch and Swedish settlements on the Middle Atlantic states has been considerable. The largest area of Dutch settle-ment in the colonial period was New York, including Long Island, Manhattan, Staten Island, and large parts of the Hudson Valley as far north as Albany. From this New York base of Dutch culture, and in part from the New Jersey settlements, the Dutch spilled over into Pennsylvania, where settlements were planted in northeastern Pennsylvania, in Philadelphia, and in Bucks and Adams counties.

Cultural influences of the New World Dutch include distinctive regional house and barn types and foods and the words for them, like "cruller" and "coleslaw." The Dutch festival year gave America New Year's cakes and Christmas customs, including the central figure of the American popular Christmas, Santa Claus (from the Dutch, Sinterklaas). In the political and economic spheres, the Dutch patroon families like the Schuylers and Van Rensselaers, the Vanderbilts and Roosevelts, Van Cortlands, Livingstons, Frelinghuysens and others, have continued, as part of the American elite, to contribute to American life.

The most significant influence of the colonial Dutch was in religion. There was a large pietistic element in the Dutch Reformed church, and according to scholars of the history of religion in America, the Middle Colony phase of the religious revival known as the Great Awakening began in the Raritan Valley of New Jersey in the 1720s, under the preaching of Theodorus Jacobus Frelinghuysen (1691–1748). From his work the revival spread to the Scotch-Irish Presbyterians, whose "log college" for the training of ministers to spread the revival led eventually to the establishment of the College of New Jersey, now Princeton University, in 1746. The Dutch church founded its own college, Queen's College, now Rutgers University, at New Brunswick in 1766, and at the same place its theological seminary in 1784.

The cultural deposit of New Sweden is less extensive, since the number of Swedes in the area was very small compared with the population of New Netherland. But the Swedes built towns and planted Swedish Lutheran churches on both sides of the Delaware. The flagships of Swedish Lutheranism were Holy Trinity in Wilmington and Gloria Dei in Philadelphia, although these as well as all the other Swedish Lutheran churches in the three states eventually became Anglican (Episcopalian). The Swedes also soon intermarried with other ethnic groups, Americanized their names, and very early lost their Swedish sense of identity.

One of the principal Swedish influences on early America was the use of log construction in building. Swedish-Finnish patterns, some scholars

THE MIDDLE ATLANTIC REGION

insist, were the model for the log cabin and log house of the American frontier, although the question is not completely settled, since central European immigrants also used log construction in housing.

In 1938 with the three hundredth anniversary of New Sweden, and in 1988, at the time of the three hundred fiftieth anniversary, various scholarly projects were initiated, such as translations of Swedish Americana and plans for an open-air museum, sponsored jointly by Swedish and American agencies. Through it all the American-Swedish Historical Foundation and Museum, in Philadelphia, has played a leading role of interpreting the history, culture, and contributions of New Sweden.

WILLIAM PENN AND THE ATLANTIC MIGRATION

More important numerically and for their continuing influence on the culture of the Middle States were the English, who began in the 1670s to settle much of the Delaware Valley. The major stimulus to this permanent settlement was William Penn (1644–1718), Quaker preacher and missionary, political theorist, proponent of religious liberty, and colonizer.

Penn, one of the most influential Englishmen of the seventeenth and eighteenth centuries, was able to move in the highest circles of English officialdom, but his conversion to Quakerism in Ireland in 1667 directed him to his life's task, the provision of an American homeland for the persecuted Quakers and other dissenters from the state churches in the British Isles and on the Continent. As a university-educated Quaker and a close disciple of Quakerism's founder, George Fox (1624–1691), Penn became an able propagandist and missionary for the new faith and through his political writings and lawmaking helped to incorporate Quaker principles of simplicity, equality, and peace into the basic laws of the three Middle States.

Penn's knowledge of England and Ireland north and south, his education among the Huguenots in France, and his missionary travels in the Rhineland in the 1670s introduced him to the problems of persecution and migration. His own lengthy periods of imprisonment for his religion in Ireland and England created the practical basis for his theory of religious liberty, which he inscribed into the basic legal systems of the area. The Quaker doctrine of the Inner Light, shared by all mankind,

led him and the Quakers after him to attempt to treat American Indians and African Americans as equals of the white colonists.

Through the influence of Penn, three great streams of emigration headed for the Delaware Valley—the English and Welsh (partly but not exclusively Quaker), the Scotch-Irish from Ulster, and the German-speaking elements from the Rhineland.

The English element spread widely through the three states, centering in Philadelphia but with important auxiliary towns such as Salem, Burlington, Gloucester City, and Trenton in New Jersey, and Bristol in Pennsylvania, and Wilmington in Delaware. With the Quakers came Catholics, Baptists, and other dissenters, as well as Anglicans, all of whom were given freedom of worship and political rights in Penn's laws. (In 1705 Parliament overruled Penn by restricting the civil liberties of Catholics in Pennsylvania, allowing them freedom of worship but disallowing their participation in government.)

Colonial Pennsylvania was a polyglot ethnic mixture, with English, Welsh, Irish, Scotch-Irish, Scots, Germans, Swiss, various Indian tribes, and black slaves and freemen. For the most part they lived together in peace and harmony in Penn's "Holy Experiment," apart from occasional riots between the Scotch-Irish and the Pennsylvania Dutch at colonial elections and Indian incursions during the eighteenth-century wars. The map of Pennsylvania reflects this ethnic mixture in place-names from England, Scotland, Wales, Ireland, Germany, and Switzerland.

The second major colonial group that settled the Middle States was the Scotch-Irish or Ulster Scots of northern Ireland, who migrated to America throughout most of the eighteenth century, continuing into the nineteenth. They were descendants of the Lowland Scots who had been transplanted to the counties of northern Ireland beginning in 1609 to swing the balance from Catholicism to Protestantism in the north and hence to curb and control the native Catholic Irish population. Most of the transplanted Scots were Presbyterians, with democratic institutions of church government: no bishops, lay elders participating in the local church government, and representative synods and general assemblies.

Pennsylvania's Scotch-Irish settlements were spread over a broad but not continuous band in eastern, central, and western Pennsylvania, where they overlapped with the Pennsylvania Germans, who often took over Scotch-Irish areas in the nineteenth century, when many of the Scotch-Irish moved to other frontiers. In their original Pennsylvania settlements the Scotch-Irish planted Presbyterian churches and gave the state some of its earliest colleges, among them Dickinson (1773) and Allegheny (1815). With their interest in public education and their concern for politics, the Scotch-Irish became a major factor in the political history of early Pennsylvania throughout the nineteenth and twentieth centuries. Many of the early lawyers and physicians, and the judges and the assemblymen in many Pennsylvania counties were Scotch-Irish. The Scotch-Irish antipathy to the British government placed most of them on the American side in the Revolution.

The religious impact of the Scotch-Irish on American life and culture has been strong. By 1850 Presbyterianism was one of the three most widespread American religious patterns (the others being the Methodists and Baptists), distributed throughout the north and south. By 1850 Pittsburgh and western Pennsylvania had the largest concentration of Presbyterians in the country. By 1861 the Presbyterians had founded more colleges in America than had any other denomination.

In everyday life the Scotch-Irish had a determinative influence on the vernacular English of central and western Pennsylvania and their Appalachian daughter colonies of the upland South. They gave colonial America much of its dance and fiddle tune traditions, and they were among the principal distillers in early America. After all,

"whisky" is a Celtic word and the word as well as the product came to America with the Ulster migration.

The Pennsylvania Germans, also known as Pennsylvania Dutch, were the third major element in colonial Pennsylvania. The background of their migration lies in developments in Protestant Europe in the seventeenth century, when the Thirty Years War and later wars devastated vast areas of southern Germany, with resettlement by Protestant refugees in many parts of the Rhineland. The Pennsylvania Germans developed a unified culture in America but were themselves an ethnic mixture with several subcultures based on differences in religion. Apart from the Rhineland Germans they included French Protestants (Huguenots and Waldensians), Belgian Protestants (Walloons), Austrian Lutheran refugees, and the Swiss. The Swiss element among the Pennsylvania Germans is particularly strong. Probably over one-third of the entire Pennsylvania German population had roots in Switzerland and immigrated to the New World either directly from there or indirectly from secondary settlements in the Rhineland. The Swiss immigrants were divided in religion between the Reformed, who were adherents of the state churches of the cantons of Bern, Zurich, Basel, and elsewhere, and the sectarian dissenters, Mennonites and Amish, most of whom still bear Swiss surnames.

The influence of the Pennsylvania German

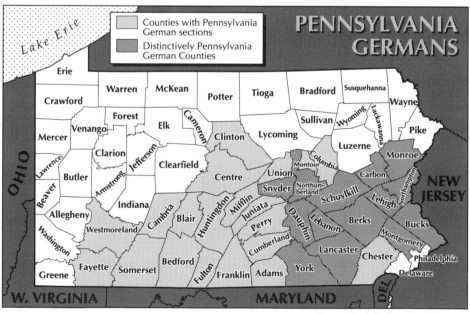

Source: Wood, *The Pennsylvania Germans*

culture on Pennsylvania—and through migration, upon the Midwest, Ontario, and parts of the South—has been profound. Their innovations in material culture in the colonial period include the Pennsylvania bank barn or forebay barn, the Conestoga wagon, and the Lancaster rifle (also called the Kentucky rifle), carried by migrating Pennsylvanians to many American frontiers. Additional Pennsylvania German gifts to America's culture include numerous words and expressions, foods and foodways, and annual customs, among them the Christmas tree and the Easter rabbit. The religious map of the eastern United States and the Midwest also bears the marks of Pennsylvania Germans, who planted Lutheran, Reformed, Moravian, United Brethren, Evangelical, Mennonite, Brethren, and Amish congregations wherever they settled. So pervasive was this Pennsylvania German influence on American life in the preindustrial era that Thomas Jefferson on a journey in 1788 to the Rhineland described it as "the American's second fatherland," after the British Isles.

SOCIAL CHANGE: NINETEENTH AND TWENTIETH CENTURIES

The nineteenth and twentieth centuries brought for the Middle States, as for many parts of the nation, massive urban growth owing to industrialization and continuing immigration. The expansion of the iron, steel, coal, oil, and other industries, for which the area was already famous, attracted migration from rural areas, from other states, and from Europe as well as from many parts of the world not represented in the colonial migration.

The massive nineteenth-century immigration that peopled so many parts of the United States affected the Middle States profoundly. Western European sources of immigration in the colonial era—the British Isles, Germany, Switzerland, and Scandinavia—continued to send large numbers of migrants. The 1880 census of Pennsylvania reported that in that year Germans made up 30 percent of the foreign-born population, Irish 40 percent, and English (including Scots) 17 percent. After 1880 new sources of immigrants were represented—Mediterranean and eastern Europe, Asia, and the Caribbean.

Most of the later immigrants settled in the cities, where they originally formed ethnic enclaves, although today their descendants are found in city and suburb alike, with a scattering in rural areas. The Poles, for example, settled in metropolitan areas, and in Pennsylvania's coal regions, where America's largest Roman Catholic schismatic group, the Polish National Catholic church, is still centered. (This schism, the only significant one in U.S. Roman Catholicism's history, is nearly defunct today.) In Bucks County, the Poles have built a national shrine to Our Lady of Czestochowa, modeled on the original sanctuary in the old country.

After World War II new waves of immigration from other areas rapidly changed the social makeup of the area. In the 1990s the cities of the Middle States showed significant numbers of very recent Southeast Asian refugees—Vietnamese, Cambodians, Thais, and Laotians—who were particularly involved in the world of street foods and ethnic restaurants. Finally, the Caribbean migration included Cubans, Haitians, Jamaicans, and above all, Puerto Ricans. Some of these, particularly the Puerto Ricans, maintain both urban and rural/small-town bases, the latter populated by migrant workers, as for example in the mushroom industry of the Brandywine Valley.

The Jewish migrations to the Middle States began in the eighteenth century with the Sephardic families who founded Philadelphia's first synagogue, Mikveh Israel (1747), and German Jews who founded Rodeph Shalom (1802). The great majority of the Jewish population of the Middle States in the 1990s descended from eastern European Jews from Poland, Russia, Lithuania, and elsewhere who emigrated after 1880. The most recent contingent arrived from the Soviet Union. Jews of the Middle States represent all the major branches of American Judaism—Orthodox, Conservative, and Reform—as well as the Hasidic and Reconstructionist movements.

The growth of the cities of the Middle States has created numerous metropolitan areas. For Pennsylvania, these are Philadelphia, Pittsburgh, Harrisburg, Wilkes-Barre–Scranton, Allentown-Bethlehem, and elsewhere; for New Jersey, the Camden and Trenton areas suburban to Philadelphia and the Elizabeth-Newark-Jersey City and Paterson areas suburban to New York, and Atlantic City as the center of the Jersey Shore resort zone; and for Delaware, Wilmington with most of the rest of the state given over to rural and small-town culture.

Certain areas around Philadelphia suburbanized rapidly in the twentieth century. Delaware County, which before 1900 was known for its well-kept Quaker dairy farms, is now the paradise of the suburban duplex and split-level designers. Chester County still boasts many excellent farms, although an increasing number of these are becoming horse farms, an influence spreading northward from Delaware and its DuPont industrial and residential country. Smaller towns like Kennett Square and Unionville are being gentrified and becoming choice addresses for well-to-do commuters to Wilmington and Philadelphia.

Downtown Philadelphia and Pittsburgh are examples, with Trenton and Wilmington, of what can be done to rejuvenate and rehumanize the downtown space in an American city. The restaurant and theater renaissance movements have made these cities more livable, and the use of "streets for people," in Bernard Rudofsky's phrase, with walking areas and tree plantings, provides here, as in Europe, for a new type of outdoor culture, including street theater.

There is also a strong and healthy small-town and small-city culture in all three of the Middle States. Only the minority of residents live in apartments; the majority own houses, many still with front porches and backyard gardens. Some of these smaller urban environments offer excellent town libraries, orchestras and chamber groups, theater companies, athletic clubs, senior citizen centers, and the usual range of church activities. Some of the region's towns originally based on railroading and the steel industry have, after the decline of these larger industries in the twentieth century, reshaped their economic bases by attracting new, smaller industries. College and university towns include Princeton and New Brunswick in New Jersey, State College and West Chester in Pennsylvania, and Newark in Delaware.

AGRICULTURE AND FOODWAYS IN THE TWENTIETH CENTURY

Despite urbanization, suburbanization, and metropolitanization, all three Middle States had large and productive agricultural areas at the end of the twentieth century. But while at the beginning of the century the region's agriculture was centered in family farms operated by large families with horse-drawn implements, by the end farming had become agribusiness, with tractors and wheeled-tools for every field operation, state regulations of milk production, increasing taxes, and shifting markets.

As farm families grew smaller in the twentieth century some farmers, especially in marginal areas, took part-time or full-time jobs in nearby towns; hence farming deteriorated or dwindled. The huge amounts of capital necessary for agribusiness drove many farmers' sons from the family farm. And the development of farm specialties—dairying, orchardry, animal husbandry, poultry raising, market gardening—all changed the face of the farming country. Most significant, however, was the encroachment of urban space on rural space, particularly around the region's metropolitan areas. In many areas what was farmland in the 1960s became tract houses, shopping malls, and industrial parks by the 1990s. Government figures indicate that from 1964 to 1982 over 27,000 farms were lost to Pennsylvania agriculture, leaving a total of 55,535 in all. Less than one-third of Pennsylvania is still in farms, and only two-thirds of that is cropland.

Among the major farm-related industries of the Middle States are food production and food processing, including canning, smoking, drying, and preserving. Local food marketing is also a major industry. According to the U.S. Department of Commerce, Pennsylvania leads the nation in the number of operating farmer's markets. These preserve the old relationship between the farming class and the nearby towns, a heritage from the European market system. The Philadelphia-area farmer's markets are known by the now-magic name of Lancaster County Farmer's Markets, with token Amish girls trucked in from Lancaster County to sell shoofly pie and cinnamon buns to suburban shoppers. Actually, while the markets are owned and managed by a Lancaster County firm, many of the stands are now manned by others and supplied with products from other counties.

As with all American regions, the Middle States have developed certain food specialties that serve as flags for ethnic and regional preferences. Philadelphia scrapple—a Westphalian–North German meat pudding fried for Pennsylvania breakfasts, brought over as a concept by the earliest Pennsylvania German immigrants, in 1683—provides a culinary symbol for the whole state. Another regional specialty, Philadelphia pepper pot soup, was originally a street food brought by the first wave of Caribbean refugees in the 1790s. Like scrapple, it is now made and sold commercially.

America's pretzel industry began in Pennsylvania in the colonial era, and in the 1990s the majority of this country's pretzel manufacturing firms were located in the state, accounting for 65 percent of national production. Pennsylvania also produced more buckwheat than any other state, about one-third of the nation's crop. And for its buckwheat cakes at breakfast Pennsylvania produced more sausage than any other state, immense amounts of honey, and a large part of the nation's maple syrup supply. Pennsylvania also manufactured traditional candies of various sorts, like clear toys of barley sugar for the Christmas trade, and about half the nation's chocolate production, including products of the Hershey Chocolate Corporation at the industrial town of Hershey, the largest national producer.

New Jersey has developed a few specialty foods identified with it—Trenton crackers, which are served with Delaware Valley oyster stew in many restaurants, and saltwater taffy made at Atlantic City and other seaside resorts. There is also Jersey applejack, a powerful apple brandy, affectionately known in the state as "Jersey lightning."

By the 1990s the older regional foods had invaded supermarket shelves, where they sat shoulder-to-shoulder with "gourmet" foods from the later ethnic groups—matzos and gefilte fish, pasta and olive oil, knäckebröd and feta cheese. Southeast Asian foods—Vietnamese, Thai, Laotian, and Cambodian—also made their appearance in the cities of the area, adding additional ethnic markets and restaurants, variety and spice to the Middle States cuisine.

EXPANSION OF THE "PLAIN" SECTS

During the twentieth century, the "plain" groups (Mennonites, Amish, Brethren) expanded from their traditional bases in Bucks, Montgomery, Lancaster, Lebanon, Cumberland, Franklin, Mifflin, and Somerset counties and other eighteenth-century settlements to new areas in search of cheaper farmland. This is especially true of the "Old Order" groups with their larger families and need for farms for their sons.

All this sectarian migration was part of the larger migration picture of the Mennonite-Amish-Brethren world, the more conservative of which live in tension with the surrounding world of modernity. The twentieth-century migration pattern of these groups has involved both interstate and international migration. Some Pennsylvania Amish and Mennonites, for example, moved to depleted agricultural areas in Delaware, Maryland, Missouri, and to Ontario, Honduras, and Paraguay.

Despite this significant migration, the fastest-growing tourist attraction in the Middle States is Lancaster County, Pennsylvania. The Amish attract tourists because of their semi-archaic culture, which gets along without automobiles, electricity, radio, and television, and in effect shows present-day urban Americans how many of their own ancestors must have lived at the turn of the century.

These dissenters from modernity have other attractions as well. Their distinctive costumes, like those of European peasants, and the gardenlike farming areas of their settlements fascinate Americans and Europeans just as Amish traditional values have led sociologists, anthropologists, and other scholars to study Amish culture. Added to all this is the recent discovery that Amish farm wives produce a unique type of American quilt, using big blocks of dissonant colors like purples, greens, dark blues, and pinks in striking abstract designs that have been compared to some modern abstract painting. Hence, to the tourist the Amishman has become perhaps the only Pennsylvania Dutchman, and what used to be the Quaker State has in fact come to be viewed through the lens of tourism by the nation as a whole as the Amish State.

DISTINCTIVE SUBCULTURES OF PENNSYLVANIA

Pennsylvania, the most populous of the Middle States, has, in addition to the Amish, many distinctive subsocieties and subcultures.

The Philadelphia Elite Until the ethnic awakening of the twentieth century the Philadelphia elite—an interlocking directorate of wealthy families, often Quakers turned Episcopalian—ruled Philadelphia politics, and controlled many metropolitan Philadelphia economic institutions in the 1990s. Examples are the J. B. Lippincott Publishing House, founded in 1792, and the Strawbridge and Clothier Department Store, founded by two Quakers in 1869.

In the nineteenth century this elite developed the coal regions—anthracite in northeastern and bituminous in southwestern Pennsylvania—and the canals and railroads that transported the coal. They developed the glass industry in New Jersey (at Glassboro and Millville, for example), but preserved their Quaker base in Philadelphia. They developed the resort hotels in the Poconos, like the Buck Hill Falls Inn, and Eaglesmere north of Williamsport. They also developed Atlantic City as a Philadelphia resort (it once had a much more staid personality than it acquired as "Babylon by the Sea" after the legalization of gambling in 1978).

This immense influence of these interlocking Philadelphia clans, many of whose ancestors had come to America with William Penn, and their profound impact on industry, culture, literature, and economic life, has come down to the present generation. The Quaker aristocracy founded three centers of higher education that rank with the best in America—Haverford College (1833), Swarthmore College (1864), and Bryn Mawr College (1885)—although many of the old Philadelphia families split their loyalties and their financial support between Princeton and the University of Pennsylvania. At the latter institution, in 1891, the Quaker industrialist Joseph Wharton founded the Wharton School, now the oldest business school in the country.

The Anthracite Region   After the discovery of the properties of anthracite (hard) coal in 1802 by a Pennsylvania Dutchman named Philip Ginder, the coal industry developed in northeastern Pennsylvania, with centers in Carbon, Lackawanna, Luzerne, Schuylkill, and Northumberland counties, a region of mine patches, company coal towns, and industrial cities. The underlying population was in large parts of the area Pennsylvania German and Protestant, but nineteenth-century immigration brought workers from eastern, central, and southern Europe, so that in the twentieth century the coal region became a glorious ethnic, religious, and cultural mixture.

Many of the immigrants, including the Irish—who contributed the accent called with some indelicacy the "coalcracker accent"—were Catholic, but a considerable Ukrainian Orthodox migration brought great wooden churches with onion domes (actually stylized flames symbolizing the Holy Spirit that descended on the church at Pentecost), the unique church music tradition of Eastern Christendom, and icons and icon painters like Nicholas Bervinchak of Minersville, whose altars and icons adorn many Schuylkill County churches. These eastern European miners also brought their ethnic foods, and distinctive Easter and Christmas customs.

The Pennsylvania Dutch Protestant population that moved to the coal towns from the surrounding farm areas to find work maintained its Protestant churches and customs as well. The Welsh of the coal region, with their Welsh singing and preaching in their Congregational, Presbyterian, and Methodist churches, added to the polyglot nature of the region in the early twentieth century.

This was the area too where the Molly Maguires, an Irish terrorist group, operated against the coal company management after the Civil War and where significant roots of the American labor movement developed, uniting many of the competing ethnic groups under the banner of organized labor. As John Mitchell (1870–1919), the leading organizer of the United Mine Workers, put it in his pitch for unionizing the miners, "The coal you dig isn't Slavish or Polish or Irish coal, it's coal."

African Americans   Slavery existed in all three Middle States in the colonial period. Through the antislavery evangelism of John Woolman (1720–1772), a New Jersey Quaker, Anthony Benezet (1713–1784), and other Quaker leaders, the Philadelphia Yearly Meeting of Friends urged its members to manumit their slaves. In 1755 the yearly meeting forbade the further purchase of slaves, and in 1776 it decided to disown (excommunicate) members who refused to give slaves their freedom. The new states of Pennsylvania and New Jersey outlawed slavery in 1780. Delaware remained a slave state until the slaves were freed by the Thirteenth Amendment (1865).

Many early free black settlements in the three states contributed diverse cultural elements to the regional blend. In religion, for example, the first American free black denomination, the African Methodist Episcopal Church, was founded after the Revolution by Bishop Richard Allen (1760–1831), a native of Philadelphia who had bought his freedom in Delaware. Philadelphia also served as a center for black contributions to the economy. For example, black families like the Augustins, originally from the West Indies, founded catering dynasties that survived into the twentieth century. To the popular culture the blacks contributed musical patterns, helping to shape the camp-meeting spirituals and providing fiddle music at country dances.

The great migration of southern blacks to the North after the Civil War accounts for the majority of the present black population in Pennsylvania. By 1900 two-thirds of black Pennsylvanians had been born in the nearby states of Maryland and Virginia. By 1960 there were over half a million blacks in Philadelphia, making up 26 percent of its population. In certain areas of Philadelphia black ghettos now exist, as parts of South and West Philadelphia. Germantown, once an upper-class retreat from the city's bustle and heat (George Washington made it his summer capital in 1793), is now over 75 percent black.

This immense migration has had wide effects on the economic, social, and religious life of the area. According to Arthur Fauset's *Black Gods of the Metropolis* (1944), Philadelphia was one of the leading creative centers for the development of the new urban black religious cults of the twentieth century. Among those he treats, all with Philadelphia connections, are the black Jews (Prophet Cherry's group), the Moorish Science Temple of America (founded in Newark in 1913, it was a forerunner of the present black Muslims), the Sweet Daddy Grace movement (United House of Prayer for All People), and the Father Divine Peace Mission (founded in Georgia, developed in New York, and moved to Philadelphia in 1941). The latter is still based in the Philadelphia area, but now has a worldwide mission. Finally, W. E. B. Du Bois (1868–1963), one of the earliest black interpreters of American black culture, taught at the University of Pennsylvania and produced a pioneer sociological study of American blacks in an urban setting, *The Philadelphia Negro* (1899). He is also remembered, among other things, for helping to found the NAACP in 1909.

SUBCULTURES OF NEW JERSEY

The Pine Barrens The Pine Barrens (also called the Jersey Pinelands) form a huge ecosystem of over one million acres (400,000 hectares), or 20 percent of the state's total area, with many interrelated woodland and water systems, including the largest underground body of fresh water in the eastern United States. In the eighteenth and nineteenth centuries Philadelphia and New York capital promoted the lumber, iron, and glassmaking industries in the area, and in the nineteenth century European immigrants established small towns and ethnic farming colonies, while the automobile age brought commuters to live there.

Given its forests, isolation, and distinctive regional occupations, the Pinelands developed a culture of its own. Its woodland industries include charcoal burning, basket making, decoy carving, cedar-shingle production, moss gathering (for floral arrangements and surgical dressings), cutting of salt hay on the area's salt marshes or salt prairies (used for animal feed, papermaking, and mulching), and boat building (including garveys and sneakboxes used in duck hunting). In addition there is cranberry harvesting from natural and artificial bogs,

blueberry gathering, and a range of berries and fruits, which adds to New Jersey's considerable food production.

The social makeup of this large area is mixed. The earlier inhabitants were Dutch and English as in other parts of the state, while the nineteenth-century immigrants established ethnic enclaves. For example, Egg Harbor City, established by German immigrants in the 1850s, into the twentieth century preserved its Rhineland festivals and German customs. Hammonton was an early Italian settlement, bringing south Italian customs including the festival of Our Lady of Mount Carmel on 16 July, an event that attracts thousands each year. And at Cassville, Russian Orthodox groups established an Orthodox haven with a huge gold-domed church in the Russian style.

It is difficult to lump all this varied human spectrum together under the frequently heard term "Pineys," a stereotype akin to "Cajun," "Ozarker," or "Appalachian mountaineer." The distinctive culture of the area, however, has been treated in all its human aspects by scholars from the American Folklife Center of the Library of Congress, which in 1983 commissioned the Pinelands Folklife Project for fieldwork in the traditional activities of the area.

Growing concern of ecologists for the preservation of the area's sensitive ecosystem followed John McPhee's pioneering book *The Pine Barrens* (1968). Ten years later the federal government designated the Pine Barrens as the first national reserve in the United States, a protected area where land use by private owners is restricted. And in 1979 the New Jersey Legislature passed the Pinelands Protection Act, creating the Pinelands Commission to regulate land use in the area. Thus New Jersey became a pioneer and model for other states in preserving and enhancing natural resources.

Jewish Agricultural Colonies The first Jewish agricultural settlement in South Jersey was Alliance, in Salem County, founded in 1882 by the Jewish Emigrant Aid Society of New York. This settlement was an experiment by Jewish philanthropists to provide European Jewish immigrants with a rural alternative to urban ghetto life. Other colonies followed, bearing the names Rosenhayn, Norma, Carmel, Mizpah, and Woodbine. Woodbine, established in 1891, became the largest and the seat of an agricultural school. By 1901 there were some thirty-three hundred Jewish farmers in these colonies, some of whom raised the same crops as their Italian neighbors while others started cigar and

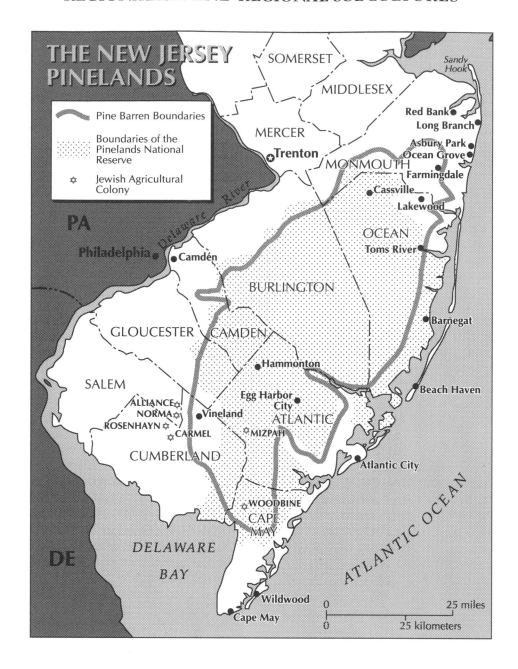

THE NEW JERSEY PINELANDS

Pine Barren Boundaries

Boundaries of the Pinelands National Reserve

✡ Jewish Agricultural Colony

shirt factories. Many of the immigrants had never farmed before; hence the skills had to be learned there.

After 1945 about a thousand Holocaust survivors settled at Farmingdale, Toms River, Lakewood, and Vineland. The colonies turned to poultry raising, founding in 1951 the Jewish Poultry Farmers' Association, and Vineland became known as the "Egg Basket of the East." By the 1970s the colonies dwindled through competition from the southern poultry raisers and the desertion of the younger generation, who entered the professions and left for the cities.

The Jersey Shore A chain of resort towns stretches from Red Bank and Long Branch in the north to Cape May in the south. The largest is Atlantic City, originally a family resort for Philadelphians, later with its boardwalks, gambling casinos, carnival atmosphere, and convention centers serving multiple purposes. Some of the towns on the Jersey Shore, like Asbury Park and Ocean Grove, grew up around Methodist camp meetings catering to evangelical vacationers in the nineteenth century and in a sense formed part of a Methodist Riviera along the Atlantic, of which Martha's Vineyard was a New England counterpart.

Other towns are blue-collar resorts like Wildwood, and upper-class resorts such as Beach Haven and Cape May, which are centers of summer activity for wealthy Main Liners and others. Cape May, renowned for its well-preserved Victorian architecture, was for a time a center of American fundamentalism as the operating base for many of Carl McIntire's institutions.

The Jersey Shore towns also have permanent populations, although the summer visitors, mostly from the New York and Philadelphia areas, number in the millions. The splendid sand beaches and dunes provide swimmers and sun worshipers plenty of space, while the boating, fishing, and seafood restaurants accent the maritime note for urban vacationers. As an economy based on seasonal tourism, the Jersey Shore ranks with Pennsylvania's history-oriented tourist resorts (Philadelphia, Valley Forge, Gettysburg) and Lancaster County's Amishland.

New Jersey's position as corridor between New York and Philadelphia has affected its political, economic, social, and intellectual history from the very beginning. The Newark-Paterson urban complex is part of metropolitan New York, while the western urban complex from Trenton to Camden is part of metropolitan Philadelphia. Economically, New Jersey is what economists refer to as a "supply state," furnishing agricultural and manufactured products, people, and services for its two larger neighbors. It can with justification be called the "Commuter State," since a significant proportion of its residents commute to work either in the New York or Philadelphia areas. New Jersey forms a convenient residence for apartment commuters, who prefer the space, air, better schools, and lower rents across the Hudson from Manhattan and across the Delaware from Philadelphia.

THE RELIGIOUS SITUATION IN THE TWENTIETH CENTURY

While in the nineteenth century the Delaware Valley was a center of liberal and intellectual religion, in the twentieth century the Philadelphia metropolitan area, including the adjoining sections of New Jersey and Delaware, increasingly became a center of fundamentalist and conservative religion in both Protestantism and Catholicism. This conservatizing of organized religion follows national trends, but the local evidence is striking. Both the Methodists and the Presbyterians suffered fundamentalist schisms in the area, and the Baptists for a time maintained two seminaries, one conservative, the other liberal.

The Philadelphia archdiocese of the Roman Catholic church has always had a reputation for conservatism, but in the twentieth century, under John Cardinal Krol and Anthony Cardinal Bevilacqua, the reins on the institution have been tightened, with the church strengthening its parochial-school system and engaging in activist political campaigns to oppose abortion rights, which are favored by the liberal denominations. The liberalizing promoted by Vatican II in liturgy, interdenominational, and interfaith relations, however, continued.

Apart from these larger movements, there was a significant growth over the three states of fundamentalist Bible churches, which were often independent of each other. In an age of uncertainty, of world tension, and of American social disintegration, these churches attracted larger memberships. It would seem that at the end of the century, in contradistinction to the situation in the first quarter of the century, the liberal churches (Quakers, United Church of Christ, Unitarian-Universalist, and others) were growing very slowly or not at all, while the fundamentalist, scripture-based churches, with their emphasis on the letter of the Bible and a strict pietistic morality, were growing.

Despite this generalized conservatism, the area's liberal traditions were not without their witness. Under Penn and the early Quakers, the three Middle Colonies were shaped by the liberal-radical wing of the Protestant Reformation. The strong intellectual, moral, and spiritual leadership of Quakerism continued into the twentieth century, strengthened and channeled to other groups through the writings and thought of such leaders as Rufus M. Jones (1863–1948), Howard H. Brinton (1884–1973), and Henry Cadbury (1883–1974). The Quakers, with their tradition of English dissent, and the continental Mennonites, Amish, and Brethren, with their insistence on the right to be different from the culture around them, continued to insist on equality and individual rights of conscience.

While the American peace movement had many roots, in New England and elsewhere, Philadelphia and its rural hinterlands on both sides of the Delaware have always been a vital center of the American peace movement. Here the concentration of Quakers and Pennsylvania German peace churches has made it possible for these dissenters to make a statement to other Americans that war is the wrong way to settle international disputes.

The Delaware Valley's pacifist denominations have provided significant proportions of conscientious objectors to war, from the Revolution to the two world wars, Korea, Vietnam, and the Persian Gulf. In 1940, with the Selective Training and Service Act, Congress for the first time allowed COs to perform alternative service, in hospitals and other institutions, housing them in Civilian Public Service camps. The CPS camp experience, the fiftieth anniversary of which was celebrated all over the United States in 1990 by former sojourners, led to deeper cooperation between the Quakers and the Pennsylvania German peace churches, and increased their cooperation in relief, peacemaking, and other common tasks. Out of World War I came vital new institutions for peace education and relief such as the American Friends Service Committee (1917) and the Mennonite Central Committee (1918); the Brethren Service Committee followed in (1939).

One additional influence of this liberal contingent of the Delaware Valley is an emphasis on women's rights. Here too it was the Quakers who provided leadership, basing their political activism on their doctrine of the Inner Light, a corollary of which is the absolute equality not only of the races but also of the sexes. The Quakers were in fact the first Protestant group to give women equal access to the ministry, a radical step forward that not all denominations have dared to follow. In the political movement for women's rights, Philadelphia Quakerism provided a long line of leaders, from Lucretia Mott (1793–1880) to Alice Paul (1885–1977), the New Jersey Friend who wrote the Equal Rights Amendment.

To the American nation as a whole the Middle Atlantic region has been since the colonial period a central, creative culture hearth for new ideas, and a central, balancing social area between New England, the Old South, and the Midwest. Whether or not the three states see themselves as a unified region, in a very real sense it can be said that "America began here." The fact that ethnic and cultural pluralism has characterized the three states from the very beginning made them a seedbed and trial arena for the democratic, pluralistic America of today.

American cultural geography demonstrates graphically the region's decisive influence upon the material culture, language, foodways, architecture, town planning, and religious patterns of the Midwest and other North American areas settled by migration from the Middle States.

And just as decisive has been the impact of the area's culture upon American political, moral, and spiritual direction. The democratic institutions forged here in the colonial period, the principles of religious liberty lifted here from theory to practice, the peace movement, the women's rights movement, and the ideal of a simplified, directed, concerned life as exemplified by William Penn, the Quakers, and their plain sister churches continue to be lasting ideals for all Americans, providing hope for America's future.

BIBLIOGRAPHY

Ahlstrom, Sydney E. *A Religious History of the American People* (1972).

Baltzell, E. Digby. *Philadelphia Gentlemen: The Making of a National Upper Class* (1958).

———. *Puritan Boston and Quaker Philadelphia: Two Protestant Ethics and the Spirit of Class Authority and Leadership* (1979).

Barber, John W., and Henry Howe. *Historical Collections of the State of New Jersey* (1844).

Benjamin, Philip S. *The Philadelphia Quakers in the Industrial Age, 1865–1920* (1976).

Berthoff, Roland. "The Social Order of the Anthracite Region, 1825–1902." *Pennsylvania Magazine of History and Biography* 89 (July 1965): 261–291.

Bodnar, John E., ed. *The Ethnic Experience in Pennsylvania* (1973).

Bowen, Ezra, et al. *The Middle Atlantic States: Delaware, Maryland, Pennsylvania* (1968).

Brandes, Joseph. *Immigrants to Freedom: Jewish Communities in Rural New Jersey Since 1882* (1971).

Buck, Elizabeth Hawthorn, and J. Solon. *The Planting of Civilization in Western Pennsylvania* (1939).

Carroll, Jackson W., et al. *Religion in America: 1950 to the Present* (1979).

Cochran, Thomas C. "The Middle Atlantic Area in the Economic History of the United States." *Proceedings of the American Philosophical Society* 108 (April 1964): 156–157.

Cohen, David Steven. *The Folklore and Folklife of New Jersey* (1983).

Cuff, David J., et al., eds. *The Atlas of Pennsylvania* (1989).

Cunningham, Barbara, ed. *The New Jersey Ethnic Experience* (1977).

Davis, Allen F., and Mark H. Haller, eds. *The Peoples of Philadelphia: A History of Ethnic Groups and Lower-Class Life, 1790–1940* (1973).

Delaware: A Guide to the First State. (1938). American Guide Series.

Fletcher, Stevenson W. *Pennsylvania Agriculture and Farm Life, 1640–1840* (1950).

———. *Pennsylvania Agriculture and Farm Life, 1840–1940* (1955).

Hostetller, John A. *Amish Society* 3d ed (1980).

Illick, Joseph E. *Colonial Pennsylvania: A History* (1976).

Jamison, Wallace N. *Religion in New Jersey: A Brief History* (1964).

Johnson, Amandus. *The Swedish Settlements on the Delaware: Their History and Relation to the Indians, Dutch, and English, 1638–1664.* 2 vols. (1911).

Klees, Fredric. *The Pennsylvania Dutch* (1950).

Lemon, James T. *The Best Poor Man's Country: A Geographical Study of Early Southeastern Pennsylvania* (1972).

Leyburn, James G. *The Scotch-Irish: A Social History* (1962).

Lorant, Stefan, ed. *Pittsburgh: The Story of an American City* (1964).

McPhee, John. *The Pine Barrens* (1968).

Miller, Donald L., and Richard E. Sharpless. *The Kingdom of Coal: Enterprise and Ethnic Communities in the Mine Fields* (1985).

Moonsammy, Rita Zorn, David Steven Cohen, and Lorraine E. Williams, eds. *Pinelands Folklife* (1987).

Moore, John M. *Friends in the Delaware Valley: Philadelphia Yearly Meeting 1681–1981* (1981).

Munroe, John A. *History of Delaware* (1979).

New Jersey: A Guide to Its Present and Past (1939). American Guide Series.

Pennsylvania: A Guide to the Keystone State (1940).

Pomfret, John Edwin. *Colonial New Jersey: A History* (1973).

Porter, Glenn. *Regional Economic History: The Mid-Atlantic Area Since 1700* (1976).

Rudofsky, Bernard. *Streets for People: A Primer for Americans* (1969).

Shryock, Richard H. "The Middle Atlantic Area in American History." *Proceedings of the American Philosophical Society* 108 (1964): 147–155.

Stevens, Sylvester K. *Pennsylvania: Birthplace of a Nation* (1964).

Swank, Scott T., et al. *Arts of the Pennsylvania Germans* (1983).

Tolles, Frederick B. "The Culture of Early Pennsylvania." *Pennsylvania Magazine of History and Biography* 81, no. 2 (April 1957): 119–137.

Wacker, Peter O. *Land and People: A Cultural Geography of Preindustrial New Jersey: Origins and Settlement Patterns* (1975).

Wallace, Paul A. W. *Indians in Pennsylvania* rev. ed. (1981).

Ward, Christopher. *The Dutch and Swedes on the Delaware, 1609–1664* (1930).

Weigley, Russell, ed. *Philadelphia: A Three-Hundred Year History* (1982).

Wertenbaker, Thomas Jefferson. *The Founding of American Civilization: The Middle Colonies* (1938).

Weslager, C. A. *The English on the Delaware, 1610–1682* (1967).

Wilson, Robert H. *Philadelphia, U.S.A.* (1975).

———. *Philadelphia Quakers, 1681–1981: A Tercentenary Family Album* (1981).

Wolf, Edwin, and Maxwell Whiteman. *The History of the Jews of Philadelphia from Colonial Times to the Age of Jackson* (1957).

Yoder, Don. "The Pennsylvania Germans: A Preliminary Reading List." *Pennsylvania Folklife* 21, no. 2 (Winter 1971–1972): 2–17.

———. "Pennsylvania Germans." In *Harvard Encyclopedia of American Ethnic Groups,* edited by Stephan Thernstrom (1980), pp. 770–772.

SEE ALSO **Agriculture; The American Colonies Through 1700; The American Colonies from 1700 to the Seven Years' War; Central and East Europeans; Collegiate Education; Ethnicity; The Federal and Early National Periods; Feminist Approaches to Social History; German Speakers; Jews; The New York Metropolitan Region; Peace Movements; Religion; The Seven Years' War Through the Revolution; Village and Town.**

THE OHIO VALLEY

Andrew R. L. Cayton

THE OHIO RIVER is an interior waterway. Despite its almost one-thousand-mile length and the size of its drainage area it empties into another river, not the sea. Like the Missouri River, the Ohio traverses a huge expanse of the North American continent, only to be swallowed whole into the Mississippi. Unlike the great rivers of the world—the Nile, the Ganges, the Amazon, the Saint Lawrence—the Ohio never meets the ocean on its own terms. There is no great delta or city at its terminus to mark its disappearance, although the founders of Cairo, Illinois, clearly saw the parallel. As a tributary the Ohio is the orphan of the Mississippi: the power of its current, the treacherousness of its shoals and eddies, the significance of its commerce, the attractions of its lore all pale in comparison with those of the larger river.

The Ohio is, nonetheless, an integral part of the system of waterways that makes up one of the foundations of the economic success of the United States. Few countries in the world are as blessed as it is with as extensive a network of navigable streams. Together the Mississippi and its tributaries facilitated the remarkably rapid settlement of the North American interior by European and African Americans in the nineteenth century. Not only did these streams carry people to new homes; they carried their crops and products to markets throughout the Caribbean and Atlantic.

It is precisely as part of this extensive transportation network that the Ohio has figured so prominently in North American history. For centuries, human beings approached the river in a utilitarian fashion. Rarely awed by it, frequently bored by it, most people saw the river primarily as the best means to get cheaply and quickly from one place to another. Today we tend to view the Ohio as a majestic, predictable natural phenomenon, a focus for recreation and reflection, but this is a decidedly twentieth-century attitude. Before the 1900s the Ohio seemed fickle and dangerous. More im-

portantly, it exerted extraordinary influence over the development of the economic and social structures of the peoples who lived along its banks and those of its tributaries.

THE VALLEY OF THE OHIO

If its drainage area is one definition of a region, the Ohio Valley is huge. It extends westward from the eastern continental divide, where springs and snows in western Pennsylvania, Maryland, and West Virginia give birth to creeks that grow into rivers with names such as the Clarion, the Cheat, and the Youghiogheny, which in turn create the Monongahela and the Allegheny. Together they form the Ohio at what is now Pittsburgh. There the river begins its west–southwesterly course, cutting through the mountains of western Appalachia to the more rolling countryside of southern Indiana, Illinois, and northwestern Kentucky. The Ohio continues to grow, adding the force of a multitude of creeks and small streams. Eventually, larger rivers contribute to its current. The Muskingum, Hocking, Scioto, and Miami rivers tie the soil and people of central and southern Ohio to the valley; the Kanawha flows north out of West Virginia; the Licking runs over 300 miles through the humpback of Kentucky; the Wabash brings together several streams that flow west to east through Indiana before joining the Ohio; and the Kentucky flows north from central Tennessee through western Kentucky to give the Ohio a final jolt as it plunges headfirst into the Mississippi.

Before the construction of a series of locks in the early twentieth century, the Ohio was an unpredictable but critical force in the lives of those who resided along it and used it. In the early 1800s annual and seasonal variations in snow and rainfall meant that the river's depth varied greatly, depending on the time of year. After a wet winter and spring the Ohio was sometimes as deep as sixty feet (18 meters). Overflowing its banks, the river toyed with both natural and human creations, rearranging the landscape for thousands of feet on either side with a current of astonishing breadth and power. At such times the Ohio became a muddy maelstrom of uprooted trees and possessions.

By late summer, however, the river often shrank to virtually nothing. In 1819 surveyors reported the width of the Ohio at Louisville to be only twenty-four feet (7.2 meters). Above that city traffic all but stopped for weeks at a time, as boats were unable to draw enough water to float. People claimed to be able to ford the river on foot between late August and October. Although this made communication across the stream easier, it severely disrupted the main flow of commerce.

Nor was the Ohio without its share of natural impediments. The most famous was the falls of the Ohio at Louisville, where the river drops some twenty-five feet in the space of two miles. A trip over this stretch of fast water may seem thrilling to some, but it was not so to those who had all of their worldly possessions on flatboats. Other impediments—limestone ledges, islands, shifting banks, occasional bursts of currents—made the navigation of the Ohio difficult, if not as challenging as that of the lower Mississippi. Nineteenth-century Americans never felt completely in control of the river, never certain of its power or boundaries. They could not even agree on exactly how long it was.

THE OHIO RIVER AS TERRITORIAL BORDER

Since the eighteenth century, travelers and writers have emphasized the notion that the Ohio is a dividing line between two different kinds of society. The foundation of this argument was obviously geographic. The river flows between two regions well defined by water: the Great Lakes area, which drains toward the Saint Lawrence and the Atlantic, and the Deep South, which empties into the Gulf of Mexico. However, the idea of the Ohio River as a border also originated in the struggles of different peoples and governments for control of the Ohio Valley.

By the second half of the eighteenth century there had developed a general sense in the trans-Appalachian West that to cross the Ohio was to enter dangerous territory. After the Battle of Point Pleasant, at the juncture of the Ohio and the Kana-

wha, in 1774, most of the Indians living north of the Ohio, particularly the Shawnees, Miamis, and Delawares, tacitly accepted the Ohio as the northern boundary of Anglo-American expansion. To be sure, raids between settlers in Kentucky and Indians in the Old Northwest continued for several more decades. Still, there was a sense that the river was truly a barrier. Indians traveled south of the Ohio and Anglo-Americans north of it only at their own risk.

In the 1780s political developments in the new United States legally designated the Ohio River as a territorial and jurisdictional border. In 1784 the state of Virginia officially ceded its claim to the region north of the Ohio to the United States while retaining its claim to Kentucky. The national government moved quickly to secure its title to this vast and valuable terrain by passing a series of ordinances designed to initiate surveying and bring American government to the region. Politically, the Ohio River divided federal from state land. Virginia retained control of the river by having its authority extend to the northern bank. From that point on, however, the government of the United States was in charge.

Article VI of the Northwest Ordinance of 1787, forbidding the introduction of slavery north of the Ohio, not only reinforced the role of the river as a territorial border but also appeared to make it a cultural frontier. By the early nineteenth century one of the favorite conceits of travelers such as Alexis de Tocqueville was to compare the free soil and society of those on the northern bank of the river with those embracing chattel slavery to the south. Most believed that there was industry, order, and respect for human rights and dignity to the north but degradation, sloth, and social anarchy to the south.

In important ways these observers were right. Slavery did make a difference, as did topography and the kinds of crops people grew. But travelers' obsessions with the impact of slavery obscure the essential cultural unity of the Ohio Valley. White and black people from what some historians have called the upland South or Appalachia have dominated southern Ohio, Indiana, and Illinois as much as West Virginia and Kentucky since the arrival of Americans in the region in the late eighteenth century. Indeed, there was strong support for the legalization of slavery among southerners living north of the Ohio in the nineteenth century. And, from the beginnings of settlement, the hinterlands of cities and towns in the Ohio Valley extended well into the countryside north and south of the river.

To a great extent, however, arbitrary territorial boundaries made southern Ohio, Indiana, and Illinois different from Kentucky and West Virginia in that their residents share a political world of regions settled by immigrants from the northeastern United States and Europe. As states, Ohio, Indiana, and Illinois developed differently from Kentucky and West Virginia because they are part of more than one geographic region. However, with the exception of important concentrations of New Englanders, Germans, and Irish in Cincinnati and a few other urban areas, the people of southern Ohio, Indiana, and Illinois have had more in common with the people across the Ohio than with their fellow citizens in Cleveland, northern Indiana, or Chicago. No one can deny the power of laws and governments to shape people's lives. It is nevertheless the interaction between the Ohio River and its tributaries and the kinds of people who have lived along them, particularly in the nineteenth century, that has given the region as a whole its cultural cohesion.

THE AGE OF COMMERCE

Indians had lived in the Ohio Valley for centuries before the Anglo-American conquest of the region. Evidence of their impress upon the landscape still exists in hundreds of burial and ceremonial mounds. Before the 1700s they lived primarily by hunting and gathering food and by relying on the Ohio and other streams for water, fish, and transportation. At the end of the seventeenth century the powerful Iroquois Confederacy, centered in western New York, drove the Indians of the Ohio and Wabash countries to the western shores of the Great Lakes. There they became extensively involved in trade with French Canadians. By the time the Miami and other Indians migrated back toward the Ohio in the early eighteenth century, they had become full partners in a vast commercial and diplomatic alliance with the French.

Since the French were interested in a waterway that would link their provinces in Canada and Louisiana directly, they initially believed the Wabash River to be more important than the Ohio. But the Ohio's significance became obvious as Anglo-American traders and settlers began to push over the Appalachians in the middle of the eighteenth century. In the 1750s and 1780s the French and the British affirmed the centrality of the Ohio to control of the trans-Appalachian West by fighting a series of battles over the forks of the river at present-day Pittsburgh.

In the aftermath of the French surrender of Canada to the British in 1763 the Ohio River became the most important highway to the west of the Appalachians. Such Indians as the Shawnees and Delawares migrated to the Ohio country on it and used it in their trade with British colonists. Starting in the 1770s, hundreds of Virginians and Pennsylvanians, now freed from the restrictions of the British government, annually traveled down the Ohio, surveying and claiming land along its banks or migrating to new settlements in central Kentucky.

Eighteenth-century people found both the speed and the size of the migration down the river truly astonishing. The fact that 146 boats carried an estimated 3,196 people past them in the fall of 1787 startled soldiers at Fort Harmar, an outpost of the United States Army at the mouth of the Muskingum River. It was in fact a number that dozens of congressmen, speculators, and travelers found remarkable. Even more startling, however, was the fact that it happened again and again. In the spring of 1789 these soldiers watched 3,151 people in 185 boats float by them.

By the early 1800s migration down the river was on a scale unimaginable only a few decades earlier. The defeat of the Indians living north of the Ohio, a series of land cessions to the United States government, and the Harrison Land Law of 1800, which made federal lands available in small quantities (a 320-acre minimum) at a relatively low price of two dollars per acre and on credit (one-fourth down and four years to pay), brought tens of thousands of people to the Ohio Valley. Almost overnight, the region became part of the United States. Kentucky's population rose from 73,677 in 1790 to 406,511 in 1810. Ohio, which had only a few thousand Americans in 1790, had more than 200,000 by 1810. By 1820 Congress had admitted all the territory along the banks of the Ohio River and its tributaries into the United States. And even before then the destinations of many travelers were well beyond the Ohio Valley. By the 1820s many were simply passing by what appeared to them to be a settled country.

These migrants were a heterogeneous lot including such Europeans as the French settlers of Gallipolis, Ohio, and an Irish gentleman named Harmon Blennerhassett, who bought an island south of Marietta, Ohio. There were also emigrants from the northeastern United States. New Englanders established settlements in the Muskingum Valley, with people from New Jersey and New York tending to congregate in Cincinnati and the Miami Valley. However, the vast majority of the travelers were from Virginia, Maryland, and Pennsylvania. Their ancestors were often Scots-Irish, German, or English, although many had been African. Some white Virginians and North Carolinians, mainly Quakers and Methodists, brought their freed slaves with them to homes in Ohio and Indiana. Others carried them along as slaves to work in the bluegrass region of central Kentucky. Even though slavery was not widely practiced in northwestern Virginia and northern Kentucky, African Americans made up a significant number of the immigrants on the Ohio.

Generally, travelers went downriver on what were called family boats. Made cheaply and quickly, these were oblong flatboats, some thirty to forty feet long, which carried entire households. On their decks rested small shacklike buildings furnished with the possessions of the owners. Domestic and farm animals milled about among all kinds of furniture and equipment. These boats carried everything the family needed to succeed as agricultural producers in the early nineteenth century: plows, looms, spinning wheels. Together, women and men, children and servants (or slaves), chickens and horses floated as a household unit down the Ohio on boats they could barely navigate.

A few people were able to afford to travel on the larger and sturdier so-called Kentucky and New Orleans boats. From fifty to one hundred feet long, these had the advantages of drawing very little water and being more easily controlled. Clearly, the most impressive of the riverboats was the keelboat. Its long keel gave it stability, and it could be powered by the current, by oars, or by a rope tied to the shore. All these larger boats primarily carried freight and were generally manned not by the immigrants themselves but by young men who worked along the river for a living.

None of these craft moved downriver very quickly. Since the Ohio's current was only about two or three miles per hour, travel before the arrival of the steamboat was at about the same rate as walking. People crammed into small quarters craved release from the slow pace of river travel. In order to take advantage of the great demand they created for goods and services, many of the small towns that speculators and families had established on both sides of the river oriented themselves toward the river trade. They would typically have an inn or tavern where people could get hot food and perhaps a soft bed. They would also sport some

kind of general store where people could buy odds and ends to repair broken tools or amuse themselves. Most people wanted merely to get downriver as quickly as possible, but more leisurely or wealthier travelers preferred to stop at places boasting interesting features such as Indian mounds, some pretense to higher culture, or perhaps a resident of some reputation.

The larger towns appeared at particularly appealing locations. Usually such a site was elevated, offering some protection from floods. More importantly, the promising urban centers were usually near an intersection of a north-south transportation route with the river. Only occasionally, however, were they to be found at the precise conjunction of the Ohio and a tributary. Marietta, Ohio, forfeited a promising future in large part because floods regularly covered its location between the Muskingum and the Ohio, but Cincinnati thrived. Not only did it offer an elevated plain on which the town could grow to the north, but it was opposite the mouth of the Licking River (and thus exposed to the trade of north-central Kentucky) and between the mouths of the Little and Great Miami rivers, which made it a key to southwestern Ohio. The fact that Cincinnati was the military headquarters of the Ohio Valley for over half a decade also boosted its chances. The city had from the beginning a commercial economy geared to the production and sale of foodstuffs and consumer items.

Still, the Ohio largely dictated the locations of towns and determined their success or failure. Louisville prospered not only because it was a central entrepôt for western Kentucky but because people stopped above the falls to rest, to prepare to run the rapids with the help of local pilots, or to journey around them altogether. And Maysville, Kentucky, did well in the early nineteenth century because it was the embarkation point for people traveling to the bluegrass region of central Kentucky.

The arrival of the steamboat in the decade after 1810 altered the structure of river travel. These new contraptions, which could travel against the current as well as faster than it, were more easily navigated than their predecessors. As important, however, is that they combined the business of carrying passengers and goods. Before 1818 nearly forty steamboats were built on the Ohio. Then, after a brief respite in the wake of the financial depression brought on by the panic of 1819, production took off. In 1826 fifty-six new boats appeared on the Ohio. Within a few years Cincinnati's builders were constructing that many just on their own.

These steamboats were impressive sights. Usually at least 250 feet long, they normally had a wheel on the side and a smokestack near the bow. The biggest of them, the *United States*, had a keel more than 165 feet in length and was powered by eight boilers. Their size allowed them to have better accommodations for travelers. With cabins and salons on two or three decks most steamboats could handle one hundred to two hundred passengers in relative comfort, in addition to carrying several tons of goods.

The dominance of the steamboat in the second quarter of the nineteenth century helped reinforce the hierarchy growing among the river's towns and cities. The well-established cities like Cincinnati and Louisville became regular stops for travelers, many of them now headed upriver. These cities' hotels became larger and fancier and provided more elaborate services. Yet not everyone traveled by steamboat. Throughout the nineteenth century, people floated down the Ohio on all kinds of jerry-rigged craft.

Despite the trappings of the steamboats and the courtesies extended to travelers, the process of exchanging goods and services along the Ohio was exceedingly impersonal. There was a bustle of activity on the waterfronts, with boats arriving and departing. Strangers stopped by for a few hours or a couple of days, bought supplies, rented a hotel room, and perhaps spent some money on diverting themselves. Businesses catered to the demands of these consumers. Along the riverfront would be plenty of places to buy alcohol or a woman. Everything in this world was a commodity.

The rougher environs of Pittsburgh, Cincinnati, Louisville, and dozens of smaller places were also familiar to the thousands of men who worked as rivermen and what amounted to longshoremen. Many of these were young white men working for a few years before returning to family farms away from the river. Others were black. In 1840 Cincinnati was home to 2,258 African Americans (4.9 percent of a total population of 46,338). Of 493 with identifiable occupations, 229 (46.5 percent) worked as boatmen, fourteen (2.8 percent) in commerce, eleven (2.2 percent) in navigation, and four (.8 percent) with steamboats. In Louisville, where nearly every boat stopped because of the falls, free blacks and slaves both worked along the waterfront.

Most of these men, white and black, lived in inexpensive housing along the waterfront. They also sought cheap entertainment and relief from the rigors of tedious, demanding labor, which they found in the taverns and brothels of the riverfront areas. By the 1820s people who thought of themselves as being more respectable were complaining regularly about drunkenness, violence, and prostitution in the areas near the landings in Pittsburgh, Louisville, and Cincinnati. Particularly notorious was the Levee on Front Street in Cincinnati, where, complained one white person, there were "nightwalkers, lewd persons, those who lounge about without any visible means of support, and especially the *negro house gamblers*" (Koehler, *Cincinnati's Black Peoples,* p. 6). In 1820 the Western Navigation and Bible Tract Society dedicated itself to reforming the character of the estimated twenty thousand "thoughtless, profligate, and degenerate" rivermen working on the Ohio (Koehler, p. 121).

Not far from the landings, laboring men and women found jobs in warehouses and processing centers. The river trade had from the beginning encouraged the production of crops and goods for distant markets and had whetted the appetites of people for foreign goods. For instance, in the eighteenth century the French residents of Vincennes on the Wabash and Kaskaskia on the Mississippi had traded furs and skins acquired from the Indians for French wine, fine china, silk curtains, elaborate hats, and books.

The Americans who came west in large numbers in the early nineteenth century replicated such transactions of the French and the Indians, but they operated on a larger scale and traded with different kinds of products. These Americans specialized in farming, particularly in producing corn and grain and hogs and cattle. These were all goods difficult to store and transfer in bulk. Many farmers thus put their corn and grain into their animals or milled them into meal or flour. Once fattened, the animals were then taken to slaughterhouses, where their meat could be sold in sections, as hams or bacon or sides of beef. In 1822 a reported $3,198,800 worth of goods passed the falls of the Ohio on their way to market, amounting to 11,200 tons of tobacco, 10,000 tons of hams and bacon and another 7,500 tons of pork, 2,000 tons of cornmeal, 750 of beef, 11,250 of (corn) whiskey, and 30,000 tons of flour. By 1829 Louisville's share of commerce had risen to an estimated $13 million, the city was serving more than 1,000 steamboats annually, and the warehouse had become its architectural symbol.

Given the nature of this economy, even the small towns along the Ohio and its tributaries had to have mills and slaughterhouses. Cincinnati specialized in both, earning it the nickname of

Porkopolis. Characteristically, farmers in northern Kentucky and southern Ohio and Indiana grew corn, fed it to hogs, then drove them to Cincinnati to be slaughtered and processed into more easily transportable products. One difference of these farmers from Kentuckians was that the latter tended to produce most of the tobacco and hemp grown, crops that required less processing and thus created less of an urban concentration.

In short, the towns of the Ohio Valley, particularly the large metropolitan areas, had the feel of inland ports. The populations of these nineteenth-century towns were constantly fluctuating: full of visitors during the early summer and humming then with activity, they could fall into the doldrums in the heat and humidity of late summer when the river was low. By now the urban renewal projects of the late twentieth century have sanitized and streamlined the Ohio's riverfront areas in ways that would make them unrecognizable to nineteenth-century travelers.

THE AGE OF INDUSTRY

As the entrepôt of the Ohio Valley, Cincinnati had an increasingly complex economic structure. Thousands of its citizens worked in commerce or transportation, and even more were involved in industrial production. In addition to steamboat construction and the providing of amenities for travelers, the town had a host of other businesses indirectly tied to the river trade—pork processing, textile mills, ironworks. Cincinnati's imports and exports for 1826 reflected the nature of the local economy. The city's citizens sold some $740,020 worth of flour, pork, lard, ham, bacon, and whiskey and produced a growing number of hats, clothes, and furniture. In return they imported almost $2 million worth of goods, mostly dry goods and beverages such as tea, coffee, and European liquor.

Social stratification accompanied economic diversification. At the bottom of the society in terms of both wealth and status were African American laborers. Males generally found employment working in the river trade or related industries, females as domestic servants. South of the Ohio most blacks were slaves, but there were thousands of free blacks in the major river ports. Only 10 percent of the population of Louisville in 1860 was black and a significant proportion (1,917 out of a total of 6,820, or some 28 percent) was free. The river was central to black life. In fact, when railroads replaced the Ohio as the central transportation hub this made it more difficult for African American males to find work.

Like blacks, white working people hauled freight, cleaned homes, slaughtered hogs, and assisted in hotels and taverns, but many whites had occupational opportunities unavailable to blacks. The more-skilled workers were attracted to jobs as printers, coopers, blacksmiths, and carpenters. The better-educated people turned to clerkships in stores, law offices, and banks. Still others worked as doctors, lawyers, and bankers.

By mid century the spatial arrangement of cities and small towns had come to reflect an increasingly stark economic stratification. In 1860 the top 10 percent of Cincinnati's population held 67 percent of the city's wealth, the bottom half only 2 percent. Working people continued to live as close to their place of employment as possible. Meanwhile, in an effort to escape the noise, smells, and dangers of commerce and industry, the families of merchants, industrialists, and professionals moved away from the rivers. Plowing their money into visible symbols of wealth and authority, these people began to construct houses around square blocks a mile or more from the Ohio. Interspersed with their homes of red brick and wrought iron were imposing churches and architectural monuments to the supposedly more refined and orderly tastes of these bourgeois citizens. The wives of leading citizens spent much of their time in local improvement and historical projects, attempting to refine the image and origins of the place in which they lived. By the end of the nineteenth century, population growth and improved transportation had led the wealthier citizens to live on small estates on distant bluffs even farther away from the bustle and confusion of the riverfront.

The increasing division between the working and the middle classes was not limited to the major cities. It also appeared in smaller places such as Marietta and Dayton in Ohio and Madison, Indiana. Middle-class citizens attempted to distance themselves both physically and culturally from the world of the river. Even in the villages there was a small core of persistent families, people who had lived in the same place for generations and served as its leading citizens while acquiring a fair amount of property. Large farmers, bankers, and store owners dominated their areas. Others—laborers and transients—moved in and out of localities, following the rhythms and labor requirements of the seasons.

966

South of the river there were also urban centers with professional and business people. West Virginia and Kentucky nevertheless remained more rural, harder to reach from the Ohio, and had slave labor until the 1860s. Because in those states the production of tobacco and hemp predominated, there was less need in them for urban concentration and economic specialization. Still, even south of the Ohio the river remained the primary factor in peoples' lives in the first half of the nineteenth century. Planters such as Henry Clay and Andrew Jackson, who traveled between their homes in Lexington and Nashville and Washington, D.C., normally used the Ohio River.

The economic success of the Ohio Valley also contributed to its greater ethnic diversity by attracting thousands of European immigrants. Most important were the Irish and German Catholics and German Jews, who began to arrive in Cincinnati and other urban areas in large numbers in the 1840s. By 1860 half of Cincinnati's 161,044 residents were foreign born. The immigrants worked on canals and the river, got jobs as skilled artisans and tradesmen, and labored as seamstresses. Others arrived with professional training or capital and quickly did well. In particular, German-born Jews, who swelled in numbers from one thousand in 1840 to ten thousand in 1860, became leading figures in the cultural and social life of Cincinnati. The city became a center of Reform Judaism, the home of the only rabbinical seminary in the United States at the time, Hebrew Union College (1875).

When the nation fought the Civil War in the 1860s the Ohio Valley split as much along class and ethnocultural lines as along the axis of the Ohio River. There was strong support for the Confederacy in southern Ohio, Indiana, and Illinois. Thousands of working-class people joined with Southern sympathizers to vote for the Democratic party. Meanwhile, the core supporters of the Republican party and the Union were the middle-class businessmen and professionals in urban areas. Slavery was only one of the issues dividing these people, who were also at odds over such issues as temperance and public education, both of which middle-class Republicans tended to support.

There was a similar division of opinion over the river itself and, more specifically, over the economic future of the valley. Many, particularly the small farmers and working people, had learned to live with the Ohio and to accommodate themselves to its whims. They took what it would give. Everyone of course feared the onset of deadly diseases

such as the cholera outbreaks of the 1830s. However, middle- and upper-class professionals generally resented the power of the Ohio over their lives and fought it when they could. They disliked its fickle currents and depths, deprecated its plodding speed and meandering course. In an era of progress and improvement it made no sense to businessmen for the region's economy to be so dependent on whimsical rivers.

Land speculators and entrepreneurs had tried since the late eighteenth century to master the river, to make its power more predictable and efficient. Occasionally they worked through governments, at other times turned to private companies. Generally they envisioned improving the river. They fought its current, developed steamboats that could move upriver without a tremendous exertion of human labor, and dredged sandbars. They built canals in Ohio and Indiana in the 1820s and 1830s to link the Ohio with the Great Lakes and to turn some of its traffic toward the northeastern part of the United States. They constructed a canal around the falls of the Ohio between 1826 and 1830 at a cost of some $750,000. They talked about bridges to connect the two banks of the Ohio, and succeeded in building some. For example, in 1849 a bridge was finished at Wheeling, then in Virginia, where the National or Cumberland Road met the Ohio, and in the late 1860s a Roebling suspension bridge traversed the river at Cincinnati.

Other businessmen sought to bypass the river altogether by turning to the railroad, although not without resistance from those dependent on the river trade. In the 1840s and 1850s private companies laid thousands of miles of track throughout the region, especially north of the Ohio. Here was transportation that could be controlled, that they could count on. Trains could be made to run on time, unlike boats. Tracks went where they were supposed to go, not rising and falling with the vagaries of the weather. By the middle of the nineteenth century the railroad had supplanted the river as the primary transportation network in the valley and now dictated the course of commerce.

The railroads ultimately enticed economic development away from the Ohio. In the beginning they were intended only to intersect with and supplement the river trade. Their very names—the Madison and Indianapolis, the Louisville and Nashville, the Baltimore and Ohio, and Chesapeake and Ohio—reflected the continuing importance of the Ohio River. During the Civil War, however, and especially just after it, the railroads replaced the rivers altogether. Small cities that had once survived as stops on the National Road (constructed in the 1820s and 1830s from Cumberland, Maryland, west through Wheeling, Virginia, and central Ohio and Indiana) or as government centers like Columbus, Ohio, and Indianapolis, Indiana, began to grow and prosper. The railroads became the wide, deep rivers these towns had never had. In the second half of the nineteenth century Chicago emerged as the most important railway center in the region. Cincinnati and Louisville did not disappear, but they no longer grew as rapidly, either demographically or economically.

The railroads rearranged the landscape, tempering the power of the Ohio. The river could still flood, could still bring waves of humidity north from the Gulf in the dog days of summer, but it no longer controlled the economic and social structures of the region. By the turn of the twentieth century, railroads had long supplanted steamboats as the major passenger and freight carrier operations in the Ohio Valley. By 1886 steamboats were carrying only 5 percent of the commodities traded in and out of Louisville and Cincinnati. The total tonnage in the valley fell by 75 percent between 1870 and 1910.

In the upper Ohio Valley the conjunction of railroads and the demand for coal created an economic boom. Suddenly the difficult terrain of West Virginia, southeastern Ohio, and western Pennsylvania became valuable. Pittsburgh had lagged behind Cincinnati in population growth, rising from 46,601 in 1850 to only 49,217 in 1860 because of competition from the National Road and its distance from the markets of the Mississippi and Gulf of Mexico. Then, spurred by a sense of stagnation, in the 1850s Pittsburgh's leading citizens aggressively pursued railroads. The city had long had a strong manufacturing base, which allowed it to prosper in the iron and steel business of the second half of the nineteenth century. With the demand for tracks and weapons during the Civil War Pittsburgh consolidated its economic growth. If the first half of the nineteenth century had belonged to the lower half of the Ohio Valley with its centers at Cincinnati and Louisville, the second half was the heyday of the upper valley.

In this period mines and factories began to appear along the banks of the Ohio and its tributaries in southeastern Ohio and West Virginia. Wheeling, which had been a major rival of Pittsburgh because of its location at the intersection of the National Road and the Ohio River, now sat in the middle of a long line of industrializing communities. Pittsburgh and its environs attracted tens of thousands of migrants in its economic take-off. In 1920 over half of the city's population was either foreign born or the children of immigrants. Many of the rest were blacks and whites from the rural South.

The largest city in the state of West Virginia, Huntington, is a particularly good example of the impact that railroads and mining had on the Ohio Valley. Chartered in 1871 and named for Collis P. Huntington, the owner of the Chesapeake and Ohio Railroad, this city flourished with the capital pumped into railroad yards and ancillary businesses. Other railheads, where major lines intersected the Ohio—such as Parkersburg, West Virginia, and Evansville, Indiana—had similar stories. In tandem with the expansion of the railroads and of the coal and mineral industries, the development of a tugboat and barge system helped rekindle business along the Ohio in the early twentieth century.

The consolidation of industries and railroads in the hands of the owners of a few large corporations such as the Carnegie steel company was not without its social costs, however. Pittsburgh and other towns along the Ohio became notorious for their black skies, polluted waters, and general filth. Miserable working conditions, low wages, and a lack of benefits encouraged resistance among laborers and built support for such union movements as the Knights of Labor and the American Federation of Labor. There were serious strikes and confrontations between labor and management in Cincinnati in the 1880s and in Pittsburgh in the early 1890s. In the first third of the twentieth century miners in the upper valley, many of whom were members of the Industrial Workers of the World, led the fight for occupational safety, respectable wages, and social justice.

For good or ill, the impact of railroads and industrialization on the Ohio Valley was enormous. Not only had they together undermined the trade and status of the rivers, creating instead new roads and encouraging the growth of different cities, but industry had surpassed agriculture and commerce as the most important business in the valley. By the early twentieth century the coal mines, steel mills, and chemical factories that lined the Ohio River had replaced the riverfront communities of the nineteenth century as both the centers and symbols of economic life.

THE OHIO RIVER AS HISTORICAL ARTIFACT

In the last half of the twentieth century, yet another economic transformation occurred in the Ohio Valley. Like most other citizens of the United States, the largely urban and suburban residents of the region became increasingly involved in consumer and service occupations. The leading employers shifted from being auto factories and steel corporations to hospitals, universities, governments, and marketing firms.

The most spectacular growth occurred in the political and educational centers. Not coincidentally, Columbus, home both to a large state government and one of the biggest state universities in the country, prospered. Indianapolis too benefited from the growth of government and a demand for sporting events to fill increasing amounts of leisure time.

Again, as in other parts of North America, consumerism seemed to blur ethnic and class lines. Racial divisions nevertheless remained close to the surface in the Ohio Valley. Tensions were especially high between African Americans and the huge numbers of white as well as black migrants from Appalachia who traveled to Cincinnati, Dayton, Pittsburgh, and elsewhere seeking blue-collar jobs in the automotive and related industries. In 1980 there were 130,587 blacks living in Cincinnati, almost 34 percent of the city's total population. At the same time, the Urban Appalachian Council estimated that more than 100,000 Appalachians had migrated to the city since 1940. Perhaps 20 percent of Cincinnati's metropolitan population of 150,000 to 200,000 in the late 1970s had Appalachian ancestry. Both whites and blacks found adjusting to the transition from an industrial to a service economy to be difficult. Each group experienced discrimination while seeking housing and jobs, although the hostility toward blacks was far more widespread and virulent; they in particular had difficulty finding jobs. The legitimate frustrations of these groups found expression less in society's organization for change, however, than in racial hostility and mutual suspicion.

The Ohio River also changed in the twentieth century. The U.S. government became an active participant in a renaissance of river traffic. Since the 1840s the U.S. Army Corps of Engineers has worked to improve river navigation and control water levels and travel speed with a series of projects. In this century they have constructed dozens of locks and dams that have made the Ohio's depth and current more predictable and have ensured year-round traffic. Today from its headquarters in Cincinnati the Ohio River Division of the Corps of Engineers monitors and plans the future of the Ohio, perhaps the most controlled river in the United States.

The rebirth of river traffic has yet to produce a rebirth of life along the Ohio. Recent riverfront renaissances in Pittsburgh, Cincinnati, Louisville, and elsewhere owe far more to basic changes in the social and economic structures of the region than to the river itself. More than anything else, the truck and the automobile broke the stranglehold of the Ohio over the residents of its valley. The speed with which people can now traverse the dozens of bridges along its course reflects the relatively insubstantial role the river plays in their lives. They worry about it during chemical spills, fearing that they will lose a beautiful natural resource, but they do not need it. The very fact that we compare its nineteenth-century role to that of an interstate highway demonstrates how different the Ohio Valley is today.

Ironically, however, cars and consumerism are behind the rebirth of the riverfronts along the Ohio. New restaurants resting on barges or modeled on steamboats now line the banks of the river in urban areas. Townhouses have been restored and condominiums built along it. But despite this renewal of interest and business, the Ohio River is no longer the economic hub of the valley. Rather it is where many go when they want to relax or to reflect on the loss of some pristine past. They boat, ski, and fish on the Ohio, run beside it, listen to concerts there, and watch fireworks displays over it. In the lives of most valley residents the river is today a symbol of leisure. In the 1960s Pittsburgh and Cincinnati attested to this change by clearing away warehouses and taverns to build huge recreational complexes in their stead. Cincinnati's Riverfront Stadium brings people to the Ohio River again. But now the river is there as a backdrop, as a setting, for the real reason people come to the waterfront.

The Ohio Valley is still a world of river towns and cities, but today the Ohio intrudes upon the people of the valley only in their imaginations and their spare time. Its impact is indirect. Indeed, when most people look at the Ohio River, visit one of the exhibits devoted to its nineteenth-century history, or watch the *Delta Queen* travel by with its calliope playing, they think not of the Ohio Valley as it is but of what they imagine it used to be. Unlike their nineteenth-century predecessors, they see an idealized past in the tamed waters of the Ohio River, rather than the possibilities of a limitless future.

BIBLIOGRAPHY

Abbott, Carl. *Boosters and Businessmen: Popular Economic Thought and Urban Growth in the Antebellum Middle West* (1981).

Allen, Michael. *Western Rivermen, 1763–1861: Ohio and Mississippi Boatmen and the Myth of the Alligator Horse* (1990).

Bigham, Darrel E. *We Ask Only a Fair Trial: A History of the Black Community of Evansville, Indiana* (1987).

Brown, Ralph H. *Historical Geography of the United States* (1948).

Buley, R. Carlyle. *The Old Northwest Pioneer Period, 1815–1840* (1950).

Cayton, Andrew R. L., and Peter S. Onuf. *The Midwest and the Nation: Rethinking the History of an American Region* (1990).

Dannenbaum, Jed. *Drink and Disorder: Temperance Reform in Cincinnati from the Washingtonian Revival to the WCTU* (1984).

Dowd, Gregory Evans. *A Spirited Resistance: The North American Indian Struggle for Unity, 1745–1815* (1991).

Holt, Michael Fitzgibbon. *Forging a Majority: The Formation of the Republican Party in Pittsburgh, 1848–1860* (1969).

Hulbert, Archer Butler. *The Ohio River: A Course of Empire* (1906).

Jakle, John A. *Images of the Ohio Valley: A Historical Geography of Travel, 1740 to 1860* (1977).

Koehler, Lyle. *Cincinnati's Black Peoples: A Chronology and Bibliography, 1782–1982* (1986).

Madison, James H. *The Indiana Way: A State History* (1986).

Miller, James M. *The Genesis of Western Culture: The Upper Ohio Valley, 1800–1825* (1938; repr. 1969).

Philliber, William W. *Appalachian Migrants in Urban America: Cultural Conflict or Ethnic Group Formation?* (1981).

Reid, Robert L., ed. *Always a River: The Ohio River and the American Experience* (1991).

Ross, Steven J. *Workers on the Edge: Work, Leisure, and Politics in Industrializing Cincinnati, 1788–1890* (1985).

Sarna, Jonathan D., and Nancy H. Klein. *The Jews of Cincinnati* (1989).

Scheiber, Harry N. *Ohio Canal Era: A Case Study of Government and the Economy, 1820–1861* (1987).

Share, Allen J. *Cities in the Commonwealth: Two Centuries of Urban Life in Kentucky* (1982).

Wade, Richard C. *The Urban Frontier: The Rise of Western Cities* (1971).

White, Richard. *The Middle Ground: Indians, Empires, and Republics in the Great Lakes Region, 1650–1815* (1991).

Wright, George C. *Life Beyond a Veil: Blacks in Louisville, Kentucky, 1865–1930* (1985).

SEE ALSO **Agriculture**; and various essays in the sections "**Processes of Social Change**" and "**Space and Place**."

THE GREAT LAKES INDUSTRIAL REGION

Jeremy W. Kilar

A GREAT LAKES ore-carrying ship, the *Edmund Fitzgerald,* sank in 1975 during one of Lake Superior's treacherous November storms. It went down quickly, with little trace and no survivors among its twenty-nine-member crew. The sinking, often remembered in song and legend, could be a timely metaphor. The industrial heartland of America, today's "Rustbelt," stretching from Buffalo to Milwaukee, likewise began to sink in the mid 1970s amid yet another of the economic storms that frequent the Great Lakes industrial region. While recent economic disaster was not as precipitous as the sinking of the *Edmund Fitzgerald,* the havoc wrought by industrial collapse affected the lives of millions. The survivors, who are struggling to stay afloat in the heartland, are again relying on a regional history of resourcefulness and buoyancy to retain their share of the nation's industrial and agricultural wealth.

In the last years of the twentieth century successful regional efforts were made to ameliorate some of the worst aspects of the area's economic decline, yet the dynamic growth and expansion of the past century remained slow. The area's automobile industry—its lifeblood—continued to shrink. In the major metropolitan centers—Buffalo, Cleveland, Cincinnati, Detroit, Chicago, and Milwaukee, and also in smaller cities like Erie, Dayton, Toledo, Flint, Saginaw, and Gary—economic distress was exacerbated by crime and racial tensions.

Beginning in the 1970s the movement of manufacturing away from the old industrial cities caused population loss and economic and social dislocation. In the 1980s the attrition continued. In Michigan, for example, a bellwether state, residents fled in the early 1980s; the exodus slowed in mid decade, but picked up again into the early 1990s. The state lost 530,000 people between 1980 and 1990 (more than any other state), mostly to Florida and western Sunbelt states. Although the overall population rose slightly—because of births and foreign immigration—the people who left the rustbelt were the educated and older people with money, whom the region could ill-afford to lose.

A fault line of population loss ran through the metropolitan regions. Buffalo lost nearly one half of its population between 1970 and 1990. Cleveland lost 68,206 people in the 1980s and barely lays claim to half a million residents. Detroit, which once stood near two million, is struggling to be a city of one million in 1990. Flint and Saginaw lost more than 10 percent of their people in the 1980s. Likewise, Chicago, though somewhat more diversified and resilient, saw nearly a quarter million residents leave in the 1980s and is no longer the nation's second city. Milwaukee has also continued to feel the effects of the struggling manufacturing industries, although its population loss in the 1980s (down 8,209 people) is not as drastic as other midwestern cities.

Population fluctuations, though, reflect the historic resilience of the nation's heartland. Constant change has sometimes seemed to be the order of things in the Midwest. Many remain confident that they can shed the political and economic baggage of the 1980s and reaffirm the social and cultural instincts that have historically made the Midwest the "builder of the nation, the breadbasket of the world."

GEOGRAPHY AND EARLY SETTLEMENT

Settlers were attracted to the Great Lakes by the region's geographical features. Rivers and broad, expansive lakes were the main routes of communication before the transportation revolution. The rivers and lakes of the Old Northwest defined and isolated the region, the Mississippi River to the west, the Ohio River to the south, and the five Great Lakes to the north. Along a wide band through the center of this area populations grew and urbanization occurred on a grand scale as set-

tlers traveled along the shores of lakes Erie, Huron, and Michigan. The completion of the Erie Canal in 1825 was perhaps the most important transportation link contributing to the rise of the industrial belt. Millions of eastern pioneers came to Buffalo along the canal and departed daily on steamships for Great Lakes port cities. Nothing defined the Great Lakes industrial region more than the transportation network that emanated from upper New York and radiated westward along the lakes and rivers. Today, more than half of the region's forty million people are concentrated in this 200-mile-wide band of industrial cities.

The Native Peoples The waterways that transported native peoples and fur traders, and shaped the lives and culture of early inhabitants of the Great Lakes region, were the product of four glacial movements. These icecaps began over a million years ago and periodically advanced and retreated as the climate cooled and warmed. About thirty-five hundred years ago the remnants of the last glacier receded and left the Great Lakes in their present forms as well as gouging, scraping, and scooping

out the areas that became inland lakes and rivers. The weight of the glacier also cut gorges and moved ancient rocks, bringing to the surface copper and iron deposits that would be so central to the region's later extractive industries.

Several native cultures were located in the central Great Lakes region previous to contact with settlers of European descent, but the "original" or "first people" (*aniŝŝina·pe·*), as they saw themselves at the time of contact, were the Anishnabeg people of the "three fires"—Ojibwa, Ottawa, and Potawatomi. These natives, who were members of the Algonkian linguistic group, along with the Iroquois, formed two separate and distinct cultures. While all migrated from the northeast, the Anishnabeg occupied the western and upper Great Lakes, and the Five Nations of the Iroquois confederation settled in western New York but reached into southern Ohio and even into Canada along Lake Superior. Both cultures were bound together by the network of rivers and lakes and the aquatic environment that sustained them with abundant resources. The Anishnabeg lived together as clans, and

974

affiliation and allegiance were determined by the father's lineage. In contrast, the Iroquois evolved a form of representative government among the Five Nations in which authority descended through women and their daughters. Eventually these two peoples became bitter enemies. When the French fur traders arrived, the allure of trade goods, whiskey, and guns exacerbated animosities and engendered bitter and endemic warfare.

The Iroquois in the eastern Great Lakes left a legacy of "democracy" within their confederation system to which Benjamin Franklin paid tribute as he sought to organize the English colonies. The Anishnabeg as well as the Iroquois left a lasting impact on the region's language, ecology, agriculture, fishing, and transportation. Perhaps the most obvious legacy is the modern road network that binds and crisscrosses the Great Lakes states; the roadways nearly always run parallel to the ancient pathways of the natives. Despite efforts by European settlers to manipulate the native cultures and environmental resources, to a remarkable degree historic native traditions continued to exist among these peoples.

The French Regime The French were the first Europeans to settle the Great Lakes region, and they not only left a major cultural imprint of their own, but they began the process of changing the culture of the Native Americans. Geography determined the extent of French incursions inland. While the English on the Atlantic seaboard were barred from the interior by the eastern mountain ranges and treacherous waterways, the French discovered the Saint Lawrence River and, in quest of a route to the Far East, ventured inland.

French Recollect and Jesuit missionaries also carried Catholicism into the wilderness in search of natives to convert. By the end of the seventeenth century, French priests had built mission churches from one end of the lakes to the other—from Montreal to Detroit to Green Bay, and from Sault Sainte Marie to Chicago and Kaskaskia. In the struggle to bring Christianity to the Indians the French priests undermined traditional cultures. French settlement and expansion, though, was largely determined by the extent to which the French were able to get along with the Indians. The Indians' skill at trapping made them a necessity in the fur trade, which quickly supplanted exploration and missionary efforts as the main purpose of French expansion. North America's thick and shiny beaver pelts found ready buyers in Europe. It was only a short time before the French found they could rely on the re-

gional contacts of the Anishnabeg tribes to operate and develop the fur industry.

French contact with the Indians was encouraged because of the small male population. It never took many Frenchmen to buy, sell, and transport furs. Frenchmen, in a predominantly male population, often married Indian women, giving rise to a sizeable population of métis—individuals who represented a combination of French and Indian cultures. These marriage alliances were important, for they strengthened trading bonds, opened tribal networks to French voyageurs, and enabled the trader to travel the interior with a knowledgeable and hardworking native wife.

The fur trade left the greatest imprint upon the Native Americans. Metal products—guns, kettles, and silver jewelry—raised their living standards. Cloth goods and imported foodstuffs made life easier. In time farming came to be neglected as the tribes turned more to trade and dependency upon the French. Alcohol, inexpensive and easily transportable, did the most harm. Whiskey made the Indians easier to exploit, markedly changed cultural patterns, and created an image of desultory native peoples, which persisted for centuries.

Few permanent French settlers actually came into the Great Lakes area. Less than seventy thousand people populated all of New France by the mid eighteenth century. Frenchmen did not want to take on the harsh environment, and non-Catholics were forbidden to settle the region. Those who did settle permanently, the French habitants, in several small forts along the lower Great Lakes—notably Detroit—left an early cultural pattern. Hardworking and conservative, they were primarily French peasant-immigrants. Most of the habitants were illiterate—schools were infrequent—and democratic institutions were unknown. Political involvement was nonexistent; all governmental decisions were made by the governor at Montreal.

Despite their isolation and conservatism, the French habitants evidenced a sense of order. Their long, narrow "ribbon" farms stretched back from the rivers and lakes, establishing a street pattern in some cities that can still be seen from the air today. French Catholicism guaranteed order and was an early force that helped give the Great Lakes its present character. Outside of Louisiana, there is no region in the country that has been as thoroughly marked by French-Catholic heritage. Because early accounts of French settlement were often written by New England Puritans, the French Catholics are often represented as irresponsible backwoodsmen who were essentially lazy and carefree. French settlers, though, worked hard in a difficult environment; their efforts at farming were never very successful, though, because there were no local markets. The French authorities were never able to change economic interests away from the transient fur trade. When French religious and political control gave way to British rule, most of the French people and their cultural patterns remained.

Under British Rule   Even though the Union Jack was to fly over the Great Lakes for thirty-six years (1760–1796), British control was never firmly established in the region. Because of Indian uprisings in the West, England's Proclamation of 1763 prohibited white settlement beyond the Alleghenies. Government policy and the rarity of settlers prevented Britain from exploiting the region as a source of revenue. In general, British culture evidenced a superior attitude toward the Indians and French habitants. Post commanders were haughty, aggressive, and tightfisted in trading with the Indians. British fur brokers often cheated the Indians, stole their furs, or gave inferior trade goods. This treatment was far different from the more amicable relationships that had characterized the French period.

British military rule in the West was administered from Quebec and only partially altered the traditional French feudal system. Catholicism was protected and, while a legislative council was established to govern the western lands, it was an appointed body. The English legal system prevailed, but French civil law was permitted in local areas. The Indians eventually accepted English rule, and the French habitants were satisfied with it as well. Their heritage was not markedly changed. In fact, once hostilities with the French ended, new traders began to operate in the Great Lakes region. Dutch from Albany, Scots and Irish from the mountain regions, and some Puritan New Englanders began to settle along the lake shores and in the Ohio Valley. Some, like the French, intermarried with the Indians and became permanent settlers.

British policy, by denying colonists the right to settle west of the Alleghenies, earned the resentment of expansionist-minded settlers, adventuresome frontiersmen, and aggressive speculators. Taxes in the colonies were raised by decree largely to pay for the French and Indian War and to maintain garrisons along the Great Lakes. The British outposts protected the fur trade, which profited London merchants and placated the Indians, whom colonists wanted off western lands. Britain's efforts to administer western lands interfered with well-developed colonial individualism and self-governance. These circumstances encouraged the American Revolution and contributed to the eventual victory of the colonists.

American Expansion   Despite the American victory over the English in 1783, the Great Lakes region remained in the hands of the British for some time. Until 1796 Great Britain occupied several military outposts, including Fort Niagara, Detroit, and Michilimackinac. During these years traditional British law was introduced and elective assemblies were created. English-speaking settlers came down through lower Canada to build farms and establish businesses in the region.

In the Ohio Valley, Americans began to exert control. Geography largely determined that the southern part of the Great Lakes states would be settled first. Pioneers crossed through at Cumberland, followed the Monongahela River north to the Ohio and headed westward along its course. Others came overland from Philadelphia to Pittsburgh and down the Ohio. In the north, a somewhat more difficult route ran up the Hudson to Albany, west along the Mohawk River valley to Lake Erie and from there through the Great Lakes westward. However, British control, the lack of roads, and large swamps—like the Great Black Swamp in northwest Ohio—discouraged settlement inland from the lakes themselves.

The mania for land along the Ohio River and in western New York set the stage for the frenzied movement westward that was eventually to characterize much of the Great Lakes' early settlement. The 1785 land ordinance of the Continental Congress provided for sale of land in the northwest. Land was acquired by Congress from the Indians and then surveyed into townships. In 1787, the Northwest Ordinance defined the Northwest Territory and established a plan of government that guaranteed freedom of religion and trial by jury, encouraged education, and outlawed slavery. Taken together these laws further defined the rather contradictory character of the settlers who were soon to pour into the Great Lakes region.

The land ordinance reinforced the rigid patterns of life that had been long characteristic of New England. The entire West would be planned out in rigid north-south lines. Orderly planning also encouraged land speculation. As land became easier to acquire, speculation in farms and town lots—much of it fraudulent—often determined settlement patterns. Even as speculators promoted their settlements and defrauded pioneers, they planned public squares in these "paper cities" to house government buildings, schools, and churches. In these institutions the individualistic democracy of the Northwest Ordinance would come to be guaranteed. In the years of settlement of the Great Lakes, democracy often amounted to giving everyone an equal right to make money.

No sooner had the West opened than the hardy New England pioneers began to move down the Ohio River and Great Lakes shores. Marietta, Ohio, was settled in 1788 at the confluence of the Muskingham and Ohio rivers and became the territorial capital. New England land companies began the wholesale development of the area. Moses Cleaveland set out along the shores of Lake Erie in 1796. He stopped at the mouth of the Cuyahoga River, found an ideal site, and laid out a plan for the city of Cleveland. Absentee ownership, though, often characterized settlement and investment patterns in the Northwest. Cleaveland himself left a small group of fifty settlers and returned east.

The Holland Land Company and its agent Joseph Ellicott laid out the town of New Amsterdam (Buffalo) in 1803. Augustus Woodward redesigned the street plan for Detroit in 1805 after fire destroyed the French settlement. New England settlers along the Great Lakes tried to recreate the community patterns they knew best. Their motives, moreover, were to secure private profit, and the movement west was often directed by individuals or land corporations that sought to guarantee lucrative financial returns as quickly as possible. Public control and government institutions to protect the common interest were often seen as obstacles to profit. These beliefs in profit, individualism, and minimal regulation soon came to be regarded as a midwestern tradition—a tradition that became, in the nineteenth century, synonymous with the conservative, independent, and isolated nature of the heartland.

Despite the efforts of land speculators, for much of the Great Lakes area the scene changed little in the first quarter of the nineteenth century. Some new towns grew slowly and some disappeared. French voyageurs continued to bring pelts to frontier outposts along the upper Great Lakes. After the War of 1812, the British presence was finally removed and various tribes began to cede vast tracts of land to the United States. Surveyors moved into Michigan and Wisconsin; Lewis Cass, Michigan's territorial governor, launched an expedition through the Great Lakes in 1820 in order to explore and promote settlement.

New means of transportation after 1815 laid the foundations for Great Lakes industry. Roads built by the army ran to Toledo, Detroit, Saginaw, Chicago, Milwaukee, and Green Bay, as well as connecting the interior with the historic waterways. The first steamboat, launched at Buffalo in 1818, inaugurated regular trips to Detroit. Still, roads were often poorly constructed and offered slow, unattractive passage. Steamboats remained scarce; there were only three on the lakes in 1825.

The most important route of transport west—which was to drastically change the population makeup and, more than anything else, give the industrial belt a regional identification and overcome commercial limitations—was the opening of the Erie Canal in 1825. The canal connected Lake Erie at Buffalo with Albany on the Hudson River. New England families by the thousands, anxious to leave poor soil and crowded agricultural areas, now had an inexpensive, if not especially fast, means to go west. Irish and German immigrants also followed the canal westward. Cheap goods and manufactured items moved west, and for the first time Great Lakes farmers had easy and reasonable access to eastern markets.

Money also moved west. The pattern of speculation on farmlands and haphazardly established city lots would soon create a phenomenal urban growth rate unrivaled in the nation. More important, the Erie Canal established a regional commercial and entrepreneurial network that reached from the Great Lakes states eastward. Capital and technology followed a rather narrow lateral migration route westward. The fur-trading posts and later the lumber-shipping centers at Albany, Buffalo, Tonawanda, Toledo, Detroit, Saginaw, Green Bay, and Milwaukee were all bound together by traders, entrepreneurs, and lumbermen who invested and profited along this Great Lakes highway. The transfer of both labor and capital from the eastern regions ensured that the towns developing along the Great Lakes would share a common culture and background.

THE INDUSTRIAL BELT EMERGES

The new immigrants, with their culture, skills, and money, began the transformation of the Great Lakes from an isolated trading and agricultural paradise to a dynamic, modern, industrialized society. The men and women who came between 1830 and the Gilded Age brought with them values and ideals that changed the region into one of the most progressive industrialized areas in the world: an aggressive optimism and an entrepreneurial drive that envisioned a prosperous future. Enterprising men began to ship lumber eastward; others processed the age-old copper-and-iron deposits of the northern Great Lakes. Frontier outposts were transformed into industrial boomtowns.

Still, original settlers as well as some newcomers tried to maintain traditional patterns. Inevitably, though, conflict arose, particularly in politics and religion, and later in labor and race. Distinct viewpoints developed that created a truly heterogeneous Great Lakes industrial region.

Initially, the new wave of people who settled the midwestern states' industrial areas were not unlike frontiersmen found everywhere. Neither poor nor rich, they were adventuresome and possessed a vitality and an energy needed to work hard in order to get ahead in life. Most were young and not overly ambitious; they simply sought better opportunity for themselves and their children.

Youthfulness gave the Midwest a stamp, an identity, that it possessed well into the mid twentieth century. Because the settlers were young, they brought little sense of the past with them. They looked to the present and quickly identified with a region that rewarded their disciplined vigor and hard work. Young people wed themselves to the land, exploited its natural resources, and soon achieved one of the highest standards of living in the nation. The geographical isolation of the Great Lakes region separated the people from other sections of the country. They were suspicious of Eastern institutions, felt superior to the South, believed they physically built the undeveloped West, and were extremely sensitive about government intrusions. Isolation and a certain insularity encouraged a self-satisfied well-being among midwesterners.

Yankee Settlement The Erie Canal, other canals, and eventually the east-west railroad link brought most of the early settlers from New England and New York. The region's values and lifestyle were shaped by New Englanders. Yankees brought with them a familiarity with self-government and a progressive outlook developed in a more advanced society back east. Religiously they brought Congregationalism and the Protestant revivalism that swept western New York State in the second quarter of the century. Politically they were egalitarian and dedicated to preserving well-organized party politics. They also were humanitarians: the Yankee zeal for abolition of slavery and the building of schools and asylums propelled a surge of reformism westward.

New Englanders and New Yorkers also brought with them the "Yankee dollar" and an economic outlook that was based on frugality, driving ambition, hard work, and shrewd bargaining. These migrants settled in older cities, founded new cities at the mouths of rivers and along waterfalls where they could establish manufacturing centers, and sought out good farmland. They populated the southern half of Michigan, northern Ohio and Illinois, and the rivers and shores of south-central Wisconsin. By 1860 fully one-quarter of Michigan's population consisted of transplanted "York staters." Similar percentages represented the number of New Englanders settling Wisconsin and Illinois. Their financial acumen and ability to attract investment dollars from the East along the regional trade networks established earlier enabled New Englanders to dominate the Great Lakes economically.

In 1870 Yankee farmers in Illinois were worth approximately 50 percent more numerous than native-born or immigrant farmers. In Michigan 80 percent of the lumbermen who owned sawmills in Saginaw, Bay City, and Muskegon—the state's leading lumber towns—had ties back East. Nearly all the prominent financial and industrial leaders of the nineteenth century were New Englanders. Commonality of cultural background and social characteristics created and sustained the upper classes in the Great Lakes and made it difficult, but not impossible, for newcomers to climb to the very top rungs of the economic ladder.

The Irish and the Germans Besides New Englanders, settlers from nearby states, and native-born residents, immigrants from Ireland and Germany made up a significant part of the Great Lakes states' population by the time of the Civil War. Irish Catholics initially followed the canal routes west. Poor and unskilled gangs of laborers came from Ireland, often via Canada and New York, and found work on the midwestern canals and railroads. Many remained behind to work in the industries of Cleveland, Detroit, Milwaukee, and especially Chicago. Some became farmers, as in the Irish Hills of southern Michigan or rural settlements like Saint Croix County, Wisconsin. Irish Catholics often insulated themselves from the cultural and economic influences of the New England Protestants who dominated the public schools and business world. They made sacrifices to support Catholic churches and schools and lived in isolated shanty towns. Insulation and low-paying jobs slowed their rate of upward mobility and sometimes contributed to poverty, drunkenness, and broken homes. However, the sense of oppression and group loyalty also paved the way for success in American electoral politics.

German immigrants poured into Illinois, Michigan, and especially Wisconsin at a rate unrivaled by any other immigrant peoples. They were often financially comfortable, educated, and hardworking people who fled Germany for a variety of reasons, including political, economic, and religious discrimination. Most in mid century came as farmers and settled in rural, sometimes extremely isolated, agricultural settlements.

Because of their numbers, their origins in many different provinces in Germany, and their varied reasons for leaving, it is difficult to generalize about German immigrants. Many were Catholic, but there were almost as many Lutherans, some Evangelicals, Methodist, and other sects. While some lived in tight-knit, rural communities—like Frankenmuth and Westphalia in Michigan or Watertown and Sauk City in Wisconsin—other Germans dispersed into large industrial cities and often assimilated quickly into the urban culture. Politically they may have favored the Democratic party, but after the Civil War some espoused the party of Lincoln. Others, like the Forty-eighters—revolutionaries who fled Germany after the failure of the 1848 liberal uprising—were freethinking, socialist, and antireligious.

While diversity and fragmentation make generalization difficult, and although Germans assimilated into the region's ethnocultural mix, aspects of the German character—rural conservatism, a strong work ethic, and dogged persistence—became an integral part of Great Lakes society, influencing behavior patterns, culture, and attitudes in rural areas and in some towns throughout the region to the present.

By 1880, when industrialization brought a second wave of immigrants, the Irish, German, and Scandinavian immigrants had established cultural influences on the industrial Midwest. Least affected was Indiana, an agricultural state that in 1880 had the highest proportion of native-born whites of any state in the country; only 7.3 percent of its population was foreign-born, while Ohio reported 14 percent. Most of the European newcomers settled in Michigan (24 percent foreign-born), Illinois (23 percent), and especially Wisconsin (44 percent). Wisconsin had almost the nation's highest proportion of immigrants to native-born (except California), while Indiana possessed the lowest. One-third of Buffalo's population, in the eastern end of the region, was foreign-born. The industrial cities, chain migration, and official state recruitment efforts of Germans by Michigan, Wisconsin, and Illinois invited large numbers of Europeans into these states.

Two Cultures   Through the second half of the nineteenth century, the Great Lakes settlements were troubled by ethnic, religious, and political tensions, which persisted in varying degrees well into the twentieth century. The values and life-styles of the new immigrants were especially offensive to the men and women from New England. Straitlaced Calvinists, Presbyterians, Methodists, and Baptists reacted strongly against immigrant revelry on Sundays, public drinking, and parochial schools. Much of this antagonism was directed at Catholics, whether Irish or German. Native-born Protestants also looked with suspicion upon the German Lutherans, who were inwardly directed and isolated in rural parishes.

In all the Great Lakes states older settlers tried to enact legislation that would stop immigrant celebrations on Sunday, shut saloons, and close non-public schools. Originally the Whig and later the Know-Nothing parties tried to mobilize nativists. The politicians of these groups resented immigrants because they remained isolated and often formed monolithic voting blocs that supported the Democrats. Nativist parties were successful in extending naturalization periods, banning Sabbath activities, and in some cases, mandating the English language and Bible reading in schools. In 1854, when the Republic party was first organized at Ripon, Wisconsin, and met as a state organization for the first time at Jackson, Michigan, nativists joined the fledgling, antislavery expansion party.

By the time of the Civil War, the Irish and German Catholics had rallied to the Democratic party. In Chicago, as early as 1860, one-fifth of the elected officials in the city were Irish-Democrats. The Republican party came to be identified with nativism. Many German Catholics and Lutherans, as well as the Irish, voted against Lincoln in 1860. During the Civil War the passage of conscription laws further antagonized immigrants, many of whom had come to America to avoid military service. Draft riots broke out across Wisconsin's Catholic areas and in cities in several other states. In time, however, many Irish and Germans joined or were drafted into the army. They soon came to support Lincoln. The Republican party, which downplayed nativism and focused on patriotism, industrial growth, and the evils of slavery, eventually secured the loyalty of some German Lutherans, second-generation Americans, veterans, and enterprising businessmen. Although the Irish and German Catholics, and some Lutherans, remained Democrats, by the gilded age the Republican party had captured control of midwestern politics.

The success of the Republican party was not based on its support for emancipation or black suffrage. In Michigan and Wisconsin black voting rights were voted down after the Civil War. As long as they could avoid agitation over race, temperance, Sabbatarianism, and religion, the Republicans remained in the majority. When these issues were revived in the late nineteenth century, though, they alienated immigrant voters and often plunged electoral politics into fierce and sometimes violent clashes between Republicans, Democrats, Fusionists, and Populists.

Religion and politics contributed to two very different cultures that struggled to dominate Great Lakes social and political life. New Englanders, northern Europeans, and some Germans saw modernization occurring in their homelands. Denied the benefits of economic progress, they fled, yearning for the freedom of opportunity available in the West. They prized individualism, hard work, and ambition. These ideals, often voiced by Republican spokesmen, sometimes left little room for countervailing viewpoints.

Irish Catholics and other Catholic immigrants from southern Europe, in contrast, often came to escape oppression or simply to avert starvation. Their goals were more realistic and less ambitious: they sought solidarity in their churches and neighborhoods and distrusted strangers. Later political involvement, especially in the Democratic party, gave them outlets and the semblance of success within the democratic-capitalist system. Unfortunately, as industrialism, commerce, manufacturing, and large-scale farming rapidly restructured society and the economy in the last quarter of the century, those who already had established themselves through regional and family ties more easily achieved dominance in the highest ranks of business, industry, and the professions. Later immigrants, blacks, and rural southern whites migrating northward, often were cut off from the social and economic opportunities that could have mitigated conflict in an emerging industrial society.

THE INDUSTRIAL HEARTLAND

New England traditionalists' emphasis upon education set the stage for modern industrial growth in the Great Lakes region. Public schools inculcated traditional values and aspirations. Discipline and hard work in school held out the promise of success, happiness, and comfort. Ever since the Northwest Ordinance set aside land to fund public schooling, midwesterners believed that education was the key to progress. Normal schools were built in mid century to train teachers, and private sectarian colleges flourished. Education encouraged ambition and inventiveness and paved the way for the tinkerers who, like Henry Ford, Thomas Edison, Orville and Wilbur Wright, Harvey Firestone, and Dr. John H. Kellogg, came to exemplify the practical and mechanical mind of the Great Lakes peoples.

The Exploitation of Natural Resources New England capitalists also spurred the exploitation of the natural resources of the Great Lakes region. Lumbering and mining provided the financial and technical resources necessary for industrial growth. Boston dollars poured into northern Michigan in search of copper and iron ore. By 1886 Michigan produced more copper than any other state (a claim that lasted until 1900, when it was surpassed by Minnesota); it was also the nation's leading iron-ore producer. The lumber industry after the Civil War likewise shifted from New York to Ohio, Michigan, and Wisconsin. Lumbermen and laborers followed the Erie Canal network westward and cut pine along the lakes' interior tributary streams. Between 1868 and 1900 the nation's lumber supply came from the Lakes States.

It was Michigan pine that rebuilt Chicago after the devastating fire in 1871. The new Chicago became the hub of the Midwest because of the rail network that bound the Great Lakes to the West. Pine boards, railroad ties, and fence posts went west; wheat, corn, cattle, and hogs went east. Transportation linkage encouraged large-scale manufacturing and production not only in Chicago but all along the rail and water routes of the Great Lakes. Lumber towns like Saginaw, Bay City, Muskegon, Eau Claire, and Oshkosh boomed overnight. Mining towns flourished in the northern regions and populations burgeoned. The demand for raw materials and efficient transport encouraged technological innovations in machinery and processing tools. Inventors came up with new methods to saw pine and to extract copper and iron, as well as to produce steel, meat products, cereals, and furniture. By the turn of the century this transformation in infrastructure and manufacturing made cities from Chicago to Green Bay, Battle Creek to Bay City, Detroit to Toledo, Cleveland to Buffalo household names across the country.

THE GREAT LAKES INDUSTRIAL REGION

Great Lakes regional identification at first may have been slowed somewhat by absentee investment in the extractive industries. When New Englanders invested in mining and New Yorkers in lumbering, they maintained economic allegiance to their hometowns in the East and not to the region where they exploited the natural resource. In lumber towns and especially mining settlements, profits were seldom used to build the community. Employees in these industries often were torn between loyalty to town and loyalty to transient company. Consequently some nineteenth-century boomtowns—like Bay City and Calumet, Michigan, or Marinette, Wisconsin—never regained the prosperity they once enjoyed.

Lumbering, though, often prepared the way for other industries that replaced those in decline. Great Lakes lumbering and logging operations were never controlled by a region-wide monopoly. The newcomer—often the small operator—frequently prospered, and enough of these pioneers who did succeed remained committed to their newly developed hometowns. Individuals like Charles Hackley in Muskegon and Arthur Hill in Saginaw built and financed new industries often unrelated to wood manufacturing. They took risks in building foundries and machinery-fabricating shops and thereby laid the basis for the automobile industry. In doing so these entrepreneurs helped to maintain community and retain capital in the Great Lakes region.

Chicago, as a transportation hub, attracted ambitious entrepreneurs who built fortunes in meat packing, steel, wholesaling, and finance. They kept their money in town, supported cultural and educational amenities, and also relied on the Great Lakes for new markets and investment opportunities. By 1920 Chicago and the emerging auto and steel industries had reestablished the regional economic identity of the Great Lakes.

Chicago depended on agricultural products as much as it did on manufacturing and merchandising. Much of the city's success evolved from mechanical innovations that improved life on the farm. Indeed, the Great Lakes region maintained a flourishing agricultural economy in addition to its burgeoning reliance upon heavy industry. The family farm run by traditional New Englanders, Germans, and increasingly by some Polish settlers, provided stability and continuity to the Great Lakes economy. Although pressures of new technology, fluctuating farm prices, and rural-to-urban migration took their toll, larger and more efficient farm operations developed and maintained agriculture communities.

Midwest farm life and small-town existence often caught the attention of the visitor to the heartland. Tight-knit communities—religiously and ethnically monolithic—symbolized the old Midwest. Residents felt a deep sense of communal interdependence. Neighbors helped each other and showed a gregariousness that welcomed the newcomer. Of course, critics often believed that these communities harbored ignorance and intolerance, and that they lacked vision for the future. Living in the Midwest was like being reborn in Victorian England, remarked Graham Hutton, a British Information Services officer stationed in Chicago. But small-town life, when compared to aggressive capitalism of the big cities, seemed far less reprehensible to most who thought about life in the farm belt.

Industrialization and Labor Industrial and agricultural transformation between 1890 and 1930 meant that the Great Lakes region had to make room for millions of additional European workers. The cultural and social mosaic would expand once again as more foreign-born moved into the region than during any other period of economic prosperity in the country's history. Southern and eastern Europeans—Poles, Russians, Italians, Jews, Slovaks, Hungarians, and Greeks—dominated. Different languages and economic backgrounds led these newcomers to gravitate into ethnic ghettos and to isolate themselves religiously and culturally. This insulation hampered communications and made for slower assimilation into the regional culture group.

Every city in the industrial belt received the new immigrants. Cities from Buffalo to Milwaukee, once primarily German and secondarily Irish, became ethnically diverse. In all these industrial cities between 35 and 45 percent of the populations were foreign-born at the turn of the century (Milwaukee, 39 percent; Detroit, 39 percent; Saginaw and Muskegon, 40 percent; Bay City, 44 percent). Until the Great Depression, the cities of the Great Lakes retained large immigrant populations proportionately well above the average for the nation's cities as a whole.

Though the population makeup of the industrial towns changed, the traditional attitudes toward the newcomers remained. New Englanders, and even some second- and third-generation Germans and Irish, imbued with the new tenets of social Darwinism, continued to view working-class immigrants as "thick-headed" and "ignorant foreign rabble." Yet, because new immigrants worked for poor wages and demanded little of their employer, manufacturers and industrialists continued until World War I to recruit foreign help for their mines, mills, and machine shops. Indeed the clash among traditional ideologies, modern industry, and old-world values and work habits led to a large number of strikes.

Labor unrest began in the railroads of Chicago, spread to the lumberyards of Michigan, and then to the coal and copper mines of the region's outlying districts. Workers demanded better wages and shorter workdays. Owners, brought up with traditional, individualistic, austere values, strenuously fought labor unions. Employers used the legal powers of the state against the workers, and employee frustration often led to violent confrontations. The Haymarket riot of 1886, the Pullman strike of 1894, and the Calumet copper strikes of 1913–1914 led to a number of deaths and injuries. Emotions over labor-capital conflicts flared frequently in the Great Lakes industrial cities and often exacerbated ethnic and religious tensions. For a time before World War I, two societies existed within the industrial heartland, the upper and middle classes and the immigrant laborers—poor, Catholic, Eastern Orthodox, or Jewish, who experienced social ostracism at the bottom rung of the economic ladder. Segregation into social and economic groups did little to create effective regional consciousness.

In addition to immigrant and labor antagonisms, racial conflicts arose. The Great Lakes industrial cities received significant numbers of black and Mexican American migrants in the years before and after World War I. The availability of jobs, recruitment efforts, easy transportation northward, and an eagerness to escape rural poverty in the South pulled and pushed these people northward. The poorest of the poor crowded into ghetto neighborhoods. They found employment, but for men it was often hard, unskilled work and for women domestic or service jobs. Often blacks were brought in as union-busters or scab laborers. Because they competed for jobs with white immigrants or lived in nearby, rapidly expanding ghettos, urban blacks came into conflict with one or another newer European group. Racial segregation added to the polarization that obstructed regional identification in the years of industrial growth.

Women also experienced important changes in their social and economic status in these transition years. By World War I thousands of women had migrated from the farms, from the South, and from Europe into the Great Lakes industrial cities. Some followed their husbands, but màny came alone. In the industrial city they could find work in clothing factories or as servants and domestics. Others who received some education or training became nurses, teachers, clerks, and secretaries. Equally important, industrialization and modernization contributed to the emergence of the middle-class homemaker. Sewing machines, stoves, vacuum cleaners, refrigerators, and indoor plumbing made life easier. It was to this developing market that merchandisers such as Potter Palmer, Marshall Field, and J. L. Hudson appealed with the department stores they innovated.

Middle-class women were also involved in voluntary societies. They began in the temperance crusade, spread into the settlement-house movement of Jane Addams in Chicago, and then initiated campaigns across the region for voting rights and political equality, helping to spread progressive reform across the region.

Progressive Reform   Of all the Great Lakes states' responses to the social dislocation brought on by urbanization and industrialization, reformism may be the most important. Often called the "Wisconsin idea," progressive reform was an effort at government and economic change led by trained experts. Adherents of the movement believed that better government would evolve if an educated electorate chose leaders based on informed choice. Beginning with the term of Governor Robert La Follette in Wisconsin (1900–1906), the progressive ideal expanded to include social-welfare legislation and government regulation of private corporations.

In the Great Lakes industrial cities, torn by rapid industrial and population growth, progressive politicians led the nation. In addition to La Follette, Detroit's mayor Hazen Pingree in 1894 pushed public work projects and direct relief programs for the city's poor. In Toledo, Mayor Samuel "Golden Rule" Jones (1897–1904) instituted the eight-hour workday for city employees and reformed urban politics. At the same time, Mayor Tom C. Johnson in Cleveland (1901–1909) created civil-service reform, brought municipal services under city control, and developed a humane program of social welfare. Although a disillusioned Lincoln Steffens believed the progressivism of these reformers "would take a thousand years" to accomplish real change, their ideas nevertheless took hold. The efforts of Midwest progressives to recapture politics from special-interest groups and offer renewed hope to workers was a regional action that spread eventually to the nation's capital.

THE GREAT LAKES INDUSTRIAL REGION

Although widespread progressive reform may have revitalized a sense of regional identity in the Great Lakes states, it came during a period of prosperity and sustained economic growth. Political amelioration was accompanied by the end of immigration after World War I. Migrants and immigrants adjusted to urban life, experienced high wartime wages, and slowly rose in status to blue-collar, semi-skilled, or skilled workers. After a generation, they developed stable neighborhoods and strong church and family ties and maybe even accumulated some savings. The urban homeowner could pass his life in contentment and exhibit a neighborliness that resembled the sense of community found in the Midwest farm belt.

In the cities one-fourth of the children of immigrants achieved higher-status jobs as white-collar workers. A tenth became skilled craftsmen. Still, the majority remained laborers struggling to avoid the calamities, the uncertainties, and the daily toll of industrial working life. Yet, like those who had preceded them, immigrants moved along the Great Lakes transportation corridor. Kinship lines extended for Poles, Slovaks, Irish, and Italians from Buffalo to Cleveland to Detroit to Chicago. The railroads and the automobile linked these people together. These transportation improvements and the prosperity of the postwar years brought a reemergence of regionalism by the time of the Great Depression.

The automobile industry, especially in the Great Lakes states, dominated the region economically; in the 1920s the automobile affected the lives of more Americans than any other new mechanical invention. The Great Lakes region had the advantage of local sources of iron and wood, experienced workers in foundries and machine shops, the widespread use of the new gasoline engine, and capital from lumbering, agriculture, and mining. Detroit had all of these ingredients, plus entrepreneurs like Ransom E. Olds, Henry Ford, and William C. Durant; and although automobiles and parts were built in all of the Great Lakes' industrial cities, Detroit dominated in part through luck, but more because of Ford's assembly line, five-dollars-a-day wages, and Model T. The Model T made auto transportation affordable to a vastly larger market and ensured the creation of an urban Midwest. By 1930 Detroit's "Big Three" (Ford, General Motors, and Chrysler) were producing 75 percent of the nation's cars.

The automobile industry and heavy manufacturing brought thousands of people into industrial cities. Detroit grew from a city of a quarter million in 1900 to over one and a half million by 1930; Chicago from 1,600,000 in 1890 to 3,400,000; and Flint from an almost nonexistent lumber town in 1900 to 156,495. By the time of the Depression most of the people of the Great Lakes states resided in the industrial cities. Growth was facilitated by state legislatures' and the federal government's promotion and financing of road construction. Road improvements together with the general prosperity of the 1920s linked cities together, broke down rural isolation, and transformed life.

The Heartland The Depression years, the 1940s, and the post–World War II period are the years of nostalgia, the years when attachments to neighborhood, the town, the community, and the land created the memory many still possess of the Great Lakes heartland. Verlyn Klinkenborg remembers these years in post–World War II Buffalo as "the last fine time." An urban immigrant society flourished that was optimistic, upwardly mobile, and confident that capitalism offered rewards and that government served a useful purpose. It was the rural heartland that John Steinbeck remembered in his *Travels with Charley* (1962), where "people were more open and more outgoing," where "strangers talked freely to one another without caution." In 1946 Graham Hutton wrote of his travels in *Midwest at Noon:* "The Midwest is where the most likeable American characteristics are at their most likeable. . . . Certainly midwesterners are the kindest, most generous, and most hospitable people in a country famed for these great virtues."

These sorts of observations create a distinctive image—indeed a mythology—of the Great Lakes region. During the first half of the century a flood of literature gave an additional identity to the contradictions and struggles for success within both the rural and industrial Midwest. Much of the early literature was social criticism. Exposure of the squalor of industrial towns in books like Upton Sinclair's *The Jungle* (1906), the decay of contemporary morality as seen in the works of Theodore Dreiser, and the attack on life in small-town America was characterized in the regional novels of Sinclair Lewis and Sherwood Anderson. Between the wars literature reflected urban street life and attracted journalists and would-be adventurers like Carl Sandburg, James T. Farrell, Ring Lardner, and Ernest Hemingway, who often used the Midwest as a backdrop.

A mature regional identity took palpable form in architecture. The Midwest achieved a reputation and sustained leadership for its grandiose skyscrapers, public buildings, and industrial centers. The edifices became the symbol of the culture and economics that powered the industrial region. Louis Sullivan's nineteenth- and early-twentieth-century skyscrapers combined ornamentation with function and influenced the Prairie School of Frank Lloyd Wright and the International Style of Ludwig Mies van der Rohe. Until his death in 1969, Mies, a stonemason's son from Germany, represented the Chicago school of steel skeletons and glass houses. However, if Sullivan and Mies built up, Albert Kahn, a Detroit architect, built out, designing the vast, well-lighted, modern factory. Henry Ford and others made Kahn the leading designer of factories in the world.

The Great Lakes Region in the Late Twentieth Century After World War II, in much of the industrial belt, the middle and upper classes abdicated political responsibility. The vacuum was often filled by the working class and it representatives. In Chicago the dominance of the Democratic party machine persisted well into the last quarter of the twentieth century. In other industrial cities the decision by organized labor to continue its support of New Deal Democrats provided financial support and voter enthusiasm that revived the party and frequently elected Democratic governors and mayors. However, the rural heartland between the industrial centers remained conservative and largely Republican. As small industry in pursuit of lower wages and cheap land moved in the 1960s and 1970s to rural areas and urbanites sometimes moved back to the land, Democratic party affiliation followed. Ticket splitting became common in the 1980s. Republicans often were supported for national office, but Democrats retained state offices. More recently taxes and racial issues have turned traditional Democrats, especially in suburban and rural areas, into Republican voters.

Racial unrest at the end of the twentieth century, while often depicted as an anomaly that upset the prosperous working-class neighborhoods of the 1950s and 1960s, was actually a continuation of earlier clashes that involved society's exploited. Civil rights disturbances in Detroit, Buffalo, Chicago, and Milwaukee, inflamed by blockbusting realtors, highway construction, and urban renewal, displaced millions of whites and blacks. Ethnic Americans fled to the suburbs and often continued to harbor racist attitudes and provincial outlooks. As industries often followed the urban and regional flight blacks and the poor remained in the inner city. Two decades after the civil rights unrest of

1967, blacks in the Great Lakes industrial cities progressed little. They may have captured political power, but inner-city blacks remain economically depressed, and deep-seated antagonisms have emerged between the declining industrial city and its suburbs. Lawmakers in state capitals far beyond the industrial cities did little to salvage the inner cities. Race served as a stumbling block and divisive factor that prevented intraregional cooperation. Socially, regionalism remained a contradiction since there were important segments of the population that found it difficult to identify with one another, let alone with the region.

There is still a regional economic identity, though, and the area has its heavy industry, its steel, its automobiles, its machines, and its merchants and traders. It also has an agricultural base, which continues to provide prosperity for thousands who survived the farm crisis of the mid 1980s.

While agriculture persisted, the exodus of industrial jobs and workers continued through the 1980s. In the 1990 census, the Great Lakes states population gain was well below the national average. Michigan gained 0.7 percent; Ohio 0.9; Indiana, 1.3; Illinois, 0.4; and Wisconsin, 4.3 (*New York Times,* 28 December 1990). The recession of the early 1990s and continued foreign competition caused auto sales to plummet to their lowest level since the 1970s energy crisis. Cities like Detroit, Flint, and Kenosha lost one-half of their automobile-related employment in the decade. Manufacturing operations continued to move to the South, the West, and Mexico in search of cheaper labor and open-shop environments. After fifteen years of economic ups and downs in the auto industry, the region remained narrowly focused on transportation-related manufacturing. It seemed—judging by new resistance to fuel-efficiency standards and the exorbitant wages paid to auto executives despite widespread layoffs—that in the Great Lakes industries old habits die hard.

Despite industrial malaise, the resources that surround the Great Lakes states and their people remain geographically interrelated. The Great Lakes themselves make it clear that the region will retain an impressive share of the nation's industry and agriculture. In the 1960s the lower lakes, especially Lake Erie, were being turned into polluted swamps and serving as a refuse point for industrial runoff. Fortunately, local and federal officials, governors, and members of Congress responded quickly enough to stem the tide of industrial waste and to revitalize the lakes ecologically. Industry itself, often prodded by government pollution standards, spent billions of dollars to clean up discharges and dumping sites. By the last decade of the century, Lake Erie—once a "dead sea"—had recovered to a remarkable degree. Milwaukee had spent millions rebuilding its sewage disposal and Cleveland's Cuyahoga River was no longer the fire hazard it was in 1960 when its industrial runoff was consumed in an historic conflagration.

The Great Lakes cleanup created cooperation between states and businesses, industries and local governments. It exemplified the ideal of regional action to preserve the key natural resource that provides the area's lifeblood. If environmental and economic cooperation can be maintained, the Great Lakes states still may envision a worthwhile future. There was vision and leadership to redirect the region when environmental calamities threatened. The question remains, though, whether this vitality can be sustained and redirected to resurrect the inner cities, overcome racial antagonisms, and rebuild a diversified industrial base. Economic regionalism persists in the Great Lakes, but the endless diversity of cultures, ethnicity, and society often limits commonality to subregions, communities, and neighborhoods. Age-old beliefs in private profit and minimal government involvement restrain farsighted, ambitious rehabilitation programs. There indeed has always been a limit to what people can or are willing to comprehend about one another. These limits are fortunately not static, and if history shows us anything, coherence and cooperation can be extended regionally in the Great Lakes area to solve common problems.

BIBLIOGRAPHY

General Regional Studies

Ashworth, William. *The Late, Great Lakes: An Environmental History* (1986).

Buley, R. Carlyle. *The Old Northwest: Pioneer Period, 1815–1840* (1950).

Carter, William. *Middle West Country* (1975).

Caruso, John Anthony. *The Great Lakes Frontier: An Epic of the Old Northwest* (1961).

Cayton, Andrew, and Peter Onuf. *The Middle West and the Nation* (1991).

Chauncey, A. E. *America's Greatest Subdivision: The Northwest Territory* (1957).

Fenton, John H. *Midwest Politics* (1966).

Flader, Susan L., ed. *The Great Lakes Forest: An Environmental and Social History* (1983).

Hatcher, Harlan. *The Western Reserve: The Story of New Connecticut in Ohio* (1949; rev. ed. 1966).

Holli, Melvin G., and Peter d'A. Jones, eds. *The Ethnic Frontier: Essays in the History of Group Survival in Chicago and the Midwest* (1977).

Jensen, Merrill, ed. *Regionalism in America* (1951).

Jensen, Richard J. *The Winning of the Midwest: Social and Political Conflict, 1888–1896* (1971).

Kilar, Jeremy W. *Michigan's Lumbertowns: Lumbermen and Laborers in Saginaw, Bay City, and Muskegon, 1870–1905* (1990).

Klinkenborg, Verlyn. *The Last Fine Time* (1991).

McLaughlin, Robert. *The Heartland: Illinois, Indiana, Michigan, Ohio, Wisconsin* (1967).

Malkus, Alida. *Blue-Water Boundary: Epic Highway of the Great Lakes and the Saint Lawrence* (1960).

Mason, Ronald J. *Great Lakes Archaeology* (1981).

Odum, Howard W., and Harry Estill Moore. *American Regionalism: A Cultural-Historical Approach to National Integration* (1938).

———. *Folk, Region, and Society* (1964).

Peirce, Neal R., and John Keefe. *The Great Lakes States of America: People, Politics, and Power in the Five Great Lakes States* (1980).

Turner, Frederick Jackson. *The Significance of Sections in American History* (1932).

State Histories

Bliven, Bruce, Jr. *New York: A Bicentennial History* (1981).

Catton, Bruce. *Michigan: A Bicentennial History* (1976).

Current, Richard Nelson. *Wisconsin: A Bicentennial History* (1977).

Davis, Charles M., ed. *Readings in the Geography of Michigan* (1964).

Dunbar, Willis F., and George S. May. *Michigan: A History of the Wolverine State* (1980).

Havighurst, Walter. *Ohio: A Bicentennial History* (1976).

Howard, Robert P. *Illinois: A History of the Prairie State* (1972).

Jensen, Richard J. *Illinois: A Bicentennial History* (1978).

Nesbit, Robert C. *Wisconsin: A History* (1973).

Peckham, Howard H. *Indiana: A Bicentennial History* (1978).

Roseboom, Eugene H., and Francis P. Weisenberger. *A History of Ohio* (1953).

Wilson, William E. *Indiana: A History* (1966).

Urban Histories

Babson, Steve. *Working Detroit: The Making of a Union Town* (1984).

Cronon, William. *Nature's Metropolis: Chicago and the Great West* (1991).

Fine, Sidney. *Violence in the Motor City: The Cavanaugh Administration, Race Relations and the Detroit Riot of 1967* (1989).

Still, Bayard. *Milwaukee: The History of a City* (1948).

Van Tassel, David D., and John Grabowski, eds. *Cleveland: A Tradition of Reform* (1987).

Wheeler, A. C. *Chronicle of Milwaukee: Being a Narrative History of the Town From Its Earliest Years to the Present* (1990).

Woodford, Arthur. *All Our Yesterdays: A Brief History of Detroit* (1969).

SEE ALSO **Central and Eastern Europeans; The French and French-Canadians; German Speakers; Immigration; Industrialization; Labor: The Great Depression Through the 1980s; Scandinavians; The Upper Midwest; Urbanization.**

THE UPPER MIDWEST

Susan E. Gray

THE LOCATION OF the Upper Midwest depends upon the location of the Midwest, a peculiarly complex geographical referent. Most commonly defined by where and what it is not—the East, the West, the South, or Canada—"the Midwest" usually refers to some or all of a twelve-state area in the middle of the United States: the five states carved from the Northwest Territory between 1803 and 1848—Ohio, Indiana, Illinois, Michigan, and Wisconsin—and known as the Old Northwest; the three subsequently settled states of Minnesota and the Dakotas, known as the Northwest until the Pacific states acquired the term; and Iowa, Nebraska, Kansas, and sometimes Montana.

THE VARIOUS MIDWESTS

As James R. Shortridge has shown, the term "Midwest," or "Middle West," was first applied by the antebellum travel writer Timothy Flint to Kentucky and Tennessee, and it meant literally the middle of the trans-Appalachian West. It reappeared in newspaper editorials in Kansas and Nebraska in the 1880s, and again meant the middle of the West, the high plains then being settled. In the 1890s, however, in the midst of severe economic depression, the Middle West became associated with pastoralism: it evoked a youthful, virtuous, agrarian world of small producers, the true America that the aged, corrupt, industrial East had ceased to be. The Midwest then moved, so that by World War I, it and the Old Northwest were one and indivisible.

The relocation of the Midwest to the Old Northwest was not accidental. As Andrew R. L. Cayton and Peter Onuf have argued, the Old Northwest had been seen since the 1850s as "the very model of a highly developed commercial society fully integrated into national economic and political structures." Such had been the vision of the framers of the Northwest Ordinance of 1787; by the decade before the Civil War it had become the ideology of a hegemonic, white middle class that found its fullest expression in the organization and long reign of the Republican party in the region. By the late nineteenth century, however, the revolutionary values of the 1850s had become traditional ones; as the middle-class Midwesterners struggled to come to terms with industrial capitalism and political pluralism, their embeddedness in national economic structures and inability to dictate their values to ethnic and working-class interests. They sought the origins or "frontier" of midwestern, and by extension American, culture in the triumph half a century earlier of bourgeois values and commercial capitalism in the Old Northwest. A chief proponent of this powerful ideology of nostalgia was the historian Frederick Jackson Turner.

One consequence of the identification of the Midwest with the Old Northwest as true America was that the Midwest acquired a second, darker connotation without losing its earlier pastoral characterization. The pastoral denotation of the Midwest as Kansas and Nebraska had referred to conditions at that time; in the Old Northwest, the concept of Midwest conjured a glorious past to ease a problematic present and future. But the Midwest has also been used since the 1920s, in Frederick J. Hoffman's phrase, as a "metaphor of abuse," standing for a dull land of middle-class Babbitts. These Janus images of the Midwest have remained locked in competition. To the extent that the pastoral characterization has prevailed, it is because the region has been associated with the agricultural states of Minnesota, Iowa, Nebraska, and Kansas, and not the Rustbelt of the Old Northwest along the southern shores of the Great Lakes.

THE UPPER MIDWEST

The shifting ideological dimensions of the Midwest have resulted in equally fluid boundaries for the Upper Midwest. When coined in the 1950s, the term "Upper Midwest" referred to three states—Michigan, Wisconsin, and Minnesota—whose historical experience both confirmed and deviated from the pastoral image of the Midwest. One key to this anomaly is topography. Northern Michigan, Wisconsin, and Minnesota are extensions of the Canadian Shield, the southern edge of which divides these states into northern and southern zones—the latter composed of prairie and deciduous forest ecotones, and the former of mixed deciduous-coniferous and coniferous ecotones. The line separating the northern and southern zones of the Upper Midwest begins at Bay City, Michigan, on Saginaw Bay, and extends west to a point north of the mouth of the Grand River on Lake Michigan between Muskegon, Michigan, and Manitowoc, Wisconsin. In Wisconsin, the line follows the Fox River south to Portage. To some observers, it then runs west along the Wisconsin River to the Mississippi; others trace the line northwest to a series of waterfalls along the edge of the Canadian Shield. In Minnesota, the line separates timber from agricultural land near the Minnesota River valley.

The northern and southern zones had powerful consequences for the development of the Upper Midwest. First, the line separating them delimited the possibilities of agriculture in the region for both native peoples and white settlers. South of the line, Indian peoples pursued a migratory economy based on seasonal hunting, fishing, and agriculture—primarily corn and squash. The short growing season and thin soils in the north limited agriculture to the harvesting of wild rice. Similarly, in "the Cutover"—the name given to portions of the northern zone ruthlessly deforested by nineteenth-century lumber companies—the efforts of white settlers to practice mixed agriculture foundered.

The true lure of the northern zone for European Americans has been a series of extractive industries. The fur trade was pursued successively by French, British, and American companies from the late seventeenth to the mid nineteenth century. Logging began in the 1830s in the northern half of Michigan's Lower Peninsula and spread across the Upper Peninsula and northern Wisconsin to end in northern Minnesota in the 1910s. Copper mining boomed on Michigan's Keeweenaw Peninsula from the late 1840s through the first quarter of the twentieth century; so did iron mining, first in Michigan's Upper Peninsula and northern Wisconsin, and by the turn of the century on Minnesota's Mesabi Range. In the twentieth century the economy of the northern zone has increasingly depended on tourism.

The designation of Michigan, Wisconsin, and Minnesota as the Upper Midwest, therefore, derived primarily from their economically diverse development, agriculture combined with extractive industry. Before the appearance of the term "Upper Midwest," some writers had avoided any regional characterization of the states, while others had considered the line separating the northern and southern zones as the northern border of the Midwest. Thus, the Upper Midwest referred to states of, and yet not of the Midwest, for the development of Michigan, Wisconsin, and Minnesota both confirmed and challenged the pastoral conception of the region. Commercial agriculture predominated in the southern zone of the Upper Midwest, while in the northern zone extractable resources were heavily exploited in the second half of the nineteenth century, a period in which the social and economic structures of commercial capitalism were giving way to those of industrial capitalism. The ideological terms for the development of the Old Northwest were largely set before Michigan, Wisconsin, and Minnesota emerged as distinct economic entities.

Michigan became a state in 1837 and Wisconsin in 1848. Minnesota Territory was separated from Wisconsin the following year, and was admitted to the union in 1858. In all three cases, such development as had occurred before statehood was agricultural and confined to a portion of the southern zone. Between 1847 and 1887, however, Michigan was the leading copper-producing state, and by 1880 was the leading producer of iron. Between 1869 and 1889, the state also ranked first in the production of board-feet of lumber. Wisconsin was the leading lumber state in 1899, followed by Michigan and Minnesota. In 1919, Minnesota ranked first in iron production, Michigan was second, and Wisconsin was fifth.

The combination of agriculture with extractive industry thus persisted in Michigan, Wisconsin, and Minnesota well into the twentieth century, giving rise to their label as the Upper Midwest. Economic change in recent decades, however, particularly in Michigan, has led to a remapping of the region. By the 1950s, Michigan had ceased to be a leading agricultural state, and in the next decade, iron mining ended in the Upper Peninsula. In the meantime, the triumph and the crisis of the auto industry first gained for the state an image of national industrial preeminence, and then associated it with the decaying urban East. Powerful or impoverished, Detroit dramatically underscored the divergence of Michigan's economic path from that of Wisconsin and Minnesota, whose economies have never lost their agricultural sectors, have never acquired substantial heavy industry, and have remained economically diversified.

In *America's Northern Heartland* (1987), the geographer John R. Bochert designates the Upper Midwest as the hinterland of Minneapolis-Saint Paul, formed when the Twin Cities emerged in the second half of the nineteenth century as a wheat milling and transport center. In more recent decades, Minneapolis-Saint Paul has consolidated its position as the central place for the north central United States through its dominance in banking and high-tech industry. This new map of the Upper Midwest considers the "primary region" as that part of the United States which is closer to the Twin Cities than it is to any other "high-order metropolis"—an area extending from the Bear Paw Mountains in north central Montana to the Porcupine Mountains on Lake Superior, from the Rainy River on the Canadian border to the Skunk River in central Iowa to South Dakota. The periphery of the Upper Midwest, delineated by the banking region of the Twin Cities, consists of Michigan's Upper Peninsula, western Montana, and southwestern South Dakota.

Another recent rendition of the Upper Midwest is a geographic, although by no means an analytical, compromise between the Michigan–Wisconsin–Minnesota and Minneapolis–Saint Paul–hinterland formulations. This Upper Midwest comprises Wisconsin, Minnesota, Nebraska, and the Dakotas on the grounds that the region was opened to settlement before the Civil War and fully occupied by the 1890s, and that foreign immigrants, although arriving after the American-born settlers, shaped its character. By the end of the nineteenth century, no commonly recognized region could claim such a high proportion of immigrants settled on the land as the Upper Midwest. This version of the Upper Midwest is explicitly intended to turn on its head Frederick Jackson Turner's notion of the Midwest as an "assimilated commonwealth" in which foreign immigrants acquired the values of native-born Americans.

None of these definitions of the Upper Midwest is wrong, but they are analytically limited in that they do not relate the ideological connotations of the term "Midwest," and its variant "Upper Midwest," to the historical development of the region. In one sense, this is a quixotic task. Since "Midwest" and "Upper Midwest" have been applied to a vast portion of the interior of the United States, any use of the terms in relation to some part of the area is legitimate. Nevertheless, there is a historical rationale for reverting to the original designation of the Upper Midwest as Michigan, Wisconsin, Minnesota, of which diversified economic development is only one aspect. However they are labeled, these states share striking similarities in the culture of their native peoples and the dimensions of Indian-white contact; in the distinctive migration streams and settlement patterns of native- and foreign-born settlers; and in the ethnic politics of a supposedly "assimilated commonwealth."

THE SEVENTEENTH AND EIGHTEENTH CENTURIES

White contact with the native peoples of the Upper Midwest began with the penetrations of the northern Great Lakes by French explorers and missionaries in the early seventeenth century. The subsequent history of relations between European Americans and Indians belongs to that of a larger, triangle-shaped region extending from Montreal to Lake of the Woods on the Ontario-Manitoba boundary, and having the Mississippi and Ohio rivers as western and southeastern borders. White-Indian contact in this region was the product of first French, then British, and finally American imperial design. Within the Upper Midwest, roughly the western half of the larger region, the principal Indian peoples were the Ottawa of lower Michigan, concentrated near the Straits of Mackinac; the Ojibwa, located around Lake Superior; the Potawatomi of Wisconsin and southwestern Michigan; the Menominee, who lived west of Green Bay; the Mesquakie (Fox) and Winnebago, also of Wisconsin; and the Dakota, of western Minnesota. All of these peoples belonged to the Algonkian language group, except the Dakota and Winnebago, who were Siouan speakers.

Long before white contact, the trade and communications nexus for the entire Great Lakes region was the Straits of Mackinac, from which water

routes stretched east to Montreal; north and west to Lake Superior and the headwaters of the Mississippi; and south and west to the Mississippi at Prairie du Chien, Wisconsin. Other trade and communication lines extended south from the Straits of Mackinac along the western shore of Lake Michigan to the Chicago River, the portage to the Illinois River, and from there to the Mississippi; south along the eastern shore of Lake Michigan to South Bend, Indiana, the portage to the Kankakee River, and on across Indiana and Illinois; and south along the western shore of Lake Huron, through Lake Saint Clair and the Detroit River, and on to Lake Erie and the Ohio Country.

By the early eighteenth century, officials of New France had established a commercial system along these routes that remained largely in place until, in the first half of the nineteenth century, the fur-bearing animals that were its raison d'être were trapped out, and the Indians were forced to yield their lands to the advance of white settlement. French authorities attempted to regulate the market

for furs and white-Indian contacts by licensing traders. Recognizing their dependence on the Indians to harvest the pelts, they also strove to maintain ties with various tribes through scrupulous dealings and gift giving. The trade in furs was conducted at posts and military forts located where tribal heads had places of established residence. After fall harvest or fishing, most Great Lakes peoples broke into small groups at winter hunting camps, moving in the spring to maple groves for sugar making and to fishing sites, and then returning to their home bases for planting. The work of traveling to the encampments to collect the Indians' furs was performed by voyageurs, who commonly took Indian women as wives, further cementing French-Indian relations.

Except at Detroit, and at Kaskaskia and Cahokia in Illinois, the French regime made little attempt to establish white agricultural settlements in its commercial empire. Both the French and the British, who acquired all French possessions in North America in 1763, were far more interested in main-

990

taining peace among the tribes and reaping the rich harvest of furs. Thus, before 1815, when the Americans finally secured control of the Northwest Territory after a generation of bloodshed, there were few non-Indians in the Upper Midwest. In the meantime, the fur trade, the matrix of white-Indian relations, spawned a distinct kind of settlement inhabited by a people neither white nor Indian. Wholly devoted to the business of fur, the Great Lakes trading settlements were communities predominantly populated by métis—the children of Canadiens and their Indian wives. Foodstuffs, clothing, tools, utensils, and building materials were either imported Indian trade goods or adopted from the Indians.

For much of the eighteenth century, the most important trading community was the fort, founded between 1715 and 1717, at Michilimackinac on the south shore of the Straits of Mackinac. Besides military personnel and other officials, Michilimackinac was home the year round to petty merchants and their families, and home in summer months to voyageurs who wintered at distant trading posts or with hunting bands. Most residents lived within the fort; few gained title to lands outside. Except for family gardens, they made little attempt to farm, acquiring their foodstuffs from the nearby Ottawa and the Potawatomi and Menominee at Green Bay, and some staples and luxury goods, such as tea and coffee, from Montreal.

The disinclination of the métis traders to farm, and the reluctance of the French and later the British to grant land titles, controlled the growth of the Michilimackinac community. Those who could not afford to stay were forced to seek new settlements. Even after 1779, when the British relocated the fort to Mackinac Island, on which several American and British traders established farms, most island residents continued to eschew agriculture for trade, to practice intermarriage, and to live in semi-Indian fashion. Indeed, the practice of agriculture and the rate of *métissage* apparently were inversely related. Such was the case at Detroit, where the French government encouraged agricultural settlement and where, consequently, many residents were not directly involved with the fur trade and intermarriage was less common than at Michilimackinac.

When British and American traders inundated Detroit after 1765, however, the Canadien population began to disperse, to shift from farming to trade, and to take Indian wives. In the 1780s, some moved to the nearby Raisin River, where they acquired land from the Potawatomis, although not title to it from the British. Rivière Raisin or Frenchtown, like Green Bay, Prairie du Chien, Saint Ignace, and Sault Sainte Marie, represented a second type of Great Lakes métis settlement. These corporate trading towns were the result of British conquest and population pressure and reduced economic opportunities in the older settlements. The towns were located along rivers, bays, and lakeshores, near trade junctions or portages and Indian agricultural lands, often at the site of former French forts and missions. The towns were corporate in that they laid out land, prosecuted local offenses, and transferred real property. They were not, however, economically complex. Neither commercial nor military centers, the towns were wholly devoted to the fur trade. The inhabitants made little attempt to raise livestock, and they produced only what they could not acquire from local Indians or from Michilimackinac or Detroit.

Late in the eighteenth century, a third type of Great Lakes settlement appeared—the American-named "jack-knife post." Posts such as LaPointe, Wisconsin, Milwaukee, and Chicago proliferated throughout the Upper Midwest, reaching far into Minnesota. Small villages of a few traders, their native wives, children, voyageurs, *engagés* (hired laborers of the fur trade), and Indian and occasionally black slaves, they were often located near the wintering ground of a tribal band containing relatives of the traders' wives. Again, the inhabitants of the tiny settlements did little farming, relying for supplies on their Indian neighbors and on imports from the commercial centers. Unimpeded by any effective civil government in the Upper Midwest before 1815, the trading families settled where they pleased, attempting always to monopolize dealings with the local Indian band.

THE NINETEENTH CENTURY

By 1815, a network of métis towns and villages covered the Upper Midwest. By the end of the 1820s, métis communities contained an estimated ten thousand to fifteen thousand inhabitants, a population at least as great as that of the largest tribe in the Upper Midwest. The métis were related by blood to over half a dozen tribes, and the dominant métis trading families were linked by marriage. The métis had established a distinct culture, neither white nor Indian, in relative isolation from interference by French or British authorities who were little interested in promoting white settlement. The Americans, however, had a different agenda.

Effective American presence in the Upper Midwest after 1815 coincided with a shift in federal Indian policy from acculturation to removal. Grounded in republican ideology and self-interest, the older policy had maintained that Indian peoples should be compensated for their land cessions, and taught the rudiments of civilization, especially farming. The policy was drastically undermined by Tecumseh's confederation of tribes against further white advance into the Northwest Territory, the culturally revivalist preachings of his brother, Tenskwata (the Prophet), and the War of 1812. In the view of white policymakers after 1815, "civilization" had failed. Although they had acquired a taste for some emblems of white technology, notably firearms and alcohol, Indian peoples showed little interest in becoming small farmers. In the emergence of this view as it affected federal efforts to organize territories for white settlement in the Upper Midwest, the métis played a key role.

Not only were the frontier settlements of the Upper Midwest dominated by the métis, but the tribes themselves contained large biracial populations. As their Canadien forebears had done for them, the métis offered the Indians a model of acculturation. That model was the world of trade that the métis had always known. They hired tribesmen as agents in Indian communities, as seasonal laborers at trading posts, and as *engagés*. The métis's eschewal of settled agriculture conflicted directly with the federal program for Indian civilization and American views of how the West should be developed.

For the Americans, the métis failed on every count as models of acculturation: they did not speak English; "lazy" and unable to understand the principles of republican government, they were judged to be an amalgamation of the worst racial traits of both the French and the Indians; indeed, in many ways they lived no better than the Indians. Worst, the métis wasted the land, for they did not farm to accumulate a marketable surplus as the Americans did. If such people were an example to the Indians, of what use was a federal program to teach farming to native peoples? Thus, particularly after it became official policy under Andrew Jackson in the 1830s, the Americans pursued an aggressive program to remove métis and tribal bands alike from the Upper Midwest. These peoples were relocated to new lands in the trans-Mississippi West or confined to northern reservations. Some fled to Canada. Indian land cessions were completed in Michigan in 1842, in Wisconsin in 1848, and in Minnesota in 1863.

IMMIGRATION

White settlement in the Upper Midwest coincided with the process of Indian land cessions and removal. For reasons not yet well understood, native-born migrants to the nineteenth-century midwestern frontier, writes the geographer John Hudson, "almost exactly reproduced the latitudinal zonation of their birth places." The common nineteenth-century belief that climate followed lines of latitude may have influenced the migration streams, but they were more likely the result of family-based chain migration and the state of transportation technology. Contemporary observers, well aware of the phenomenon, were inclined to attribute moral character and potential for economic growth of the new settlements to the regional origins of the settlers.

In any event, two migration streams, one channeled between 42° and 43° north latitude and the other above 43° north latitude, brought native-born Americans to the southern and northern zones of the Upper Midwest. The first stream created a subregion called "Greater New England" in the late nineteenth and early twentieth centuries, and more recently called "Yankeeland." Upstate New York, settled from southern New England, was the source region for Yankeeland. The water route west via the Erie Canal and steam-powered vessels on the Great Lakes brought Yankees to southern Michigan in the 1830s, southern Wisconsin in the 1840s, and southeastern Minnesota in the 1850s. Each settled area in Yankeeland became a staging ground for the next frontier. Yankees settled the best lands first in the prairie-forest ecotone, particularly seeking the small prairies that were the extensions of the great prairie triangle in western Illinois and eastern Iowa. They were reluctant to settle in the less agriculturally desirable mixed deciduous and coniferous forest ecotones.

In the 1870s and 1880s, Yankees, along with first-generation German- and Norwegian-Americans from southern Wisconsin and Minnesota, moved into western Minnesota and the eastern Dakotas. Although southern Wisconsin birthplaces were most typical of this generation of migrants, their origins were far more dispersed than formerly, and included New York, New England, and Canada.

Thus, the highly origin-specific migration of Yankees faded at roughly the western border of the Upper Midwest. A similar phenomenon characterized native-born migration to the northern zone. Just as the Erie Canal and passage through the lower Great Lakes served as the conduit for the peopling of Yankeeland, so the Saint Lawrence and the upper Great Lakes provided the northern route to the Upper Midwest. Canadians of New England descent from the Saint Lawrence Valley; New Englanders from New Hampshire, Vermont, and Maine; and New Yorkers from the extreme north of the state whose parents had been born in Vermont, as well as Swedes, Norwegians, Germans, and Finns, found their way to the northern Upper Midwest by that route.

Native-born migration to Michigan, Wisconsin, and Minnesota was thus far more homogeneous than it was in the older states of Ohio, Indiana, and Illinois, through which streams from several eastern settlement hearths had run parallel or had commingled. But the opening of the Upper Midwest to settlement also coincided with the beginning of substantial foreign immigration to the United States, thereby guaranteeing the continued cultural heterogeneity of the region. Latitudinal migration streams, chain migration, and the clustered settlements of both native- and foreign-born arrivals created settlement patterns of the Upper Midwest that have been rightly termed a "mosaic," a "patchwork quilt," and a "polyglot of transplanted communities." Spatial segregation can be broadly described. The locus of Yankee settlement in Wisconsin, for example, extended west from Lake Michigan to Madison, but it was often expressed in highly localistic, particularistic ways. The major Dutch colony in the Upper Midwest, centered in Holland, Michigan, and extending into adjacent counties, was in reality a conglomeration of settlements, each with its Dutch place-name designating the inhabitants' local origins in the Netherlands. In these communities, settlers spoke local dialects, established their own churches and schools, and maintained distinctive customs in dress and foods.

Such patterns of settlement assured that cultural conflict in the Upper Midwest occurred less among native-born Americans than between a particular kind of American, the regionalized Yankee, and foreign groups whose ways ran counter to his values. The native-born, white middle class of the Upper Midwest at mid century did not define its values in terms of perceived morally freighted differences between Northerners and Southerners, as it did in the earlier settled states of the Old Northwest. What mattered for such self-definition was a substantial, diverse foreign presence. In 1850, the foreign-born comprised 13.8 percent and 34.9 percent of the populations of Michigan and Wisconsin, and 33.7 percent of the population of Minnesota Territory. By 1880, they made up 23.7 percent of the population in Michigan, 30.8 percent in Wisconsin, and 34.4 percent in Minnesota. In the same year, British Canadians, Germans, English, Irish, and Dutch comprised much of Michigan's foreign-born population. Germans accounted for nearly half of Wisconsin's foreign-born and Scandinavians for a sixth. Scandinavians and Germans together made up nearly two-thirds of Minnesota's foreign-born.

Because native-born Americans initiated commercial farming in the Upper Midwest and controlled economic and political institutions, scholars have devoted much attention to the assimilation of immigrants as measured by their adoption of American farming practices. There is now substantial evidence that although immigrant groups readily adopted American crops and techniques, they invested farming with values that distinguished them both from the Americans and from one another. In his study of Norwegian farming communities, for example, Jon Gjerde explores the complex, evolutionary relationship between Old World values and New World environment. Norwegian immigrants retained the custom of postponing marriage until they had secured livelihoods, yet they married younger, had more children, and tended to move away from their parents. Scarce, expensive farm labor encouraged greater reliance on large families. At the same time, adoption of American agricultural practices expanded traditional male roles and shrank those of women. As a result, women directed more of their attention toward childrearing. Their acceptance of bourgeois values was also reflected in household consumption patterns and enforcement of premarital chastity. Clergymen had promoted such values in Norway; New World circumstances had encouraged their adoption. Thus, while Norwegians over time became increasingly American in outlook and behavior, their acculturation occurred within a Norwegian context.

Immigrant groups varied enormously in their efforts to promote intergenerational continuity, and thereby to preserve familial and communal identity in the new settlements. Although there is not yet a systematic explanation for the range in inheritance strategies, Kathleen Conzen has suggested some of the likely variables. First, Old World value systems shaped attitudes toward children's education that were reflected in inheritance practices. Scandinavian farmers, for example, placed greater weight on education for sons, thus prompting their departure from agriculture, than did German Catholic farmers, who restricted their children's access to education. Such conservatism was at least in part a function of cultural beleaguerment, as German Catholics isolated themselves from both their American Protestant and their Irish Catholic neighbors.

Second, clustered settlements varied in their ability to promote ethnic distinctiveness. Geographic isolation, size, and degree of homogeneity—as measured by intensity of religious affiliation and localness of homeland origins—all played a role. A small community bound by strong religious belief and Old World familial and communal ties could as effectively promote the persistence of its members and its cultural distinctiveness as a much larger, more geographically isolated, but less internally cohesive community. The "generation" of a settlement—whether it was a major or a daughter colony—also affected persistence and cultural distinctiveness. As migration streams became better established, immigrants had less need to form tight communities for mutual support. The key seems to be both the ability of a migration chain to direct and concentrate settlement and the permanence of the original clustered settlements. This variable may be as applicable to Yankee as to foreign migration and settlement patterns in the Upper Midwest, for it would account for the dispersion of the settlers' origins with distance and over time from the New York-New England settlement hearth.

Third, the more closely the values of an immigrant group resembled American values, the more likely that members would be drawn away from ethnic farming communities. The general conclusion is that the degree of persistent ethnic difference ranged from highly retentive Germanic immigrants to Slavs and Scandinavians, to Irish and British along a "spectrum of ethnic intensity." The issue is not only the similarity of immigrant and American values, and the sharpness of immigrant perception of difference, but also how well a group's Old World values and institutions supported familial and communal persistence in the New World environment.

POLITICS AND ETHNICITY

The role of immigrants in state and local politics, particularly in rural areas, in the Upper Midwest after the Civil War is not as well understood as it might be. The reigning Republicans had risen to power in the 1850s by promoting a social and economic vision that wedded bourgeois values to commercial capitalism, and by attacking those who did not share it: Southerners and foreigners. After the Civil War, however, the Republican party lost its moral urgency as large-scale foreign immigration and a nationalizing, industrializing, and increasingly corporate economy undermined its vision. The party became primarily concerned with maintaining its political power and with defending corporate freedom as it had once advocated individual enterprise.

Political response to these changes was complex. The attempt of the Granger Movement, which climaxed in the 1870s, to lower and regulate railroad and grain elevator rates in Wisconsin and Minnesota, as well as Iowa and Illinois, demonstrated that many did not embrace the new world of industrial capitalism, as did the rise in the 1880s of the Knights of Labor, founded in 1869. The new social and economic structures, moreover, transformed formerly homogeneous, hegemonic middle-class values. In rapidly growing cities such as Detroit and Milwaukee, immigrant groups were segregated from one another and from the native-born middle class by neighborhood, work experience, religion, language, and customs. To some observers, the immigrants either could not or would not acquire "right" values and behavior. As for the immigrants themselves, when they acted politically, they did so less from a shared sense of working-class consciousness than from a desire to defend their communal cultures.

In such circumstances, political partisanship in the late nineteenth century had several layers of meaning. Although elections were closely fought and voter turnouts were very high, little distinguished the parties' platforms. Republicans, defenders of the new corporate order, advocated the economic stimulus of a protective tariff, while Democrats upheld laissez-faire economic principles for the good of the common man as consumer. Such policies do not explain the huge numbers of people who voted. Richard Jensen and Paul Kleppner have shown that the Republican party drew its support from native- and foreign-born evangelical Protestants. The chief appeal of the Democratic party to Catholics and non-evangelical Protestants was its defense of local control in moral matters in the face of Republican-sponsored efforts by middle-class reformers to impose temperance and public school education on immigrant groups.

It was precisely these reform efforts that finally cracked Republican-party power in the last decade of the nineteenth century. In Wisconsin, for example, immigrant opposition to the Republican-sponsored Bennett Law, requiring all children to attend a public or private school where teaching was in English, enabled the Democrats to sweep the state elections in 1890. Throughout the Midwest in the early 1890s, Republicans lost elections for the same reason that they had won them nearly half a century earlier: they attacked immigrants and Southerners for their failure to conform to middle-class values. The turning point came with the presidential election of 1896, in which the Republican party turned its back on issues of cultural control and embraced a platform emphasizing economic prosperity across ethnic and class lines that enabled it to remain in control of politics in Michigan, Wisconsin, and Minnesota until the Great Depression.

Thereafter, a realignment occurred that resorted the old variables of class, ethnicity, and reform to create a new, intensely competitive "issue-oriented" politics. In the nineteenth century, the Republican party had championed the vision of social and economic development of a hegemonic middle class against the localism and particularism of Democratic voters. By contrast, the politics that emerged in the Upper Midwest by the middle of the twentieth century presumed the protection and promotion by state government of widely shared social and economic values. Issue-oriented voting reflected differences in the interpretation of these values as shaped by persistent ethnic loyalties in the context of class allegiances forged during the Depression. In general, the more industrial the state, the greater the role played by class, as opposed to ethnicity, in the realignment. It may also be that the "spectrum of ethnic intensity" helps to explain the greater resonance of ethnicity in Wisconsin and Minnesota politics than in Michigan. In Michigan, there was no equivalent to the rural, German Catholic vote so critical to the Wisconsin and Minnesota realignments. In all three states, the New Deal helped to energize the Democratic party and to create a new consensus of social and economic values. Since the realignment a coalition of labor

and liberal or reform-oriented interests has continued to dominate the Democratic party in Michigan, Wisconsin, and Minnesota and to shape politics in the states.

Depression and the New Deal ended Republican rule in Michigan in 1932. The legitimation of collective bargaining under the National Labor Relations Act (1935) helped to bring the United Auto Workers (UAW), which under the leadership of Walter Reuther dominated the Michigan labor movement, into the Democratic party. In the short run, however, the party could not sustain its gains. After a Republican-controlled state legislature passed a merit system for the selection of state employees in 1941, the Democratic party, deprived of its ability to make patronage appointments, weakened. The vacuum was filled in 1948 by a liberal-labor coalition sponsored by Americans for Democratic Action, a public interest group of businessmen and professionals, and the UAW.

By the late 1940s and early 1950s, Michigan voters had achieved a broad consensus based on their acceptance of such New Deal programs as higher pensions for the elderly, public works projects to avoid unemployment, corporation taxes, and a federal health program. The appeal of the parties turned on their approach to such issues. Republicans advocated programs to improve the status quo—better administration and the use of tax and service incentives to attract industry. Democrats, as promoters of the unions and the working class, were more willing to reallocate resources to promote a more egalitarian society. They relied on heavy support in the Detroit area and on increasing their percentage of the vote in rural and urban areas throughout the state. Significant for the composition of the Democratic constituency, if not from the number of voters attracted, the party received strong support from the heavily ethnic mining districts in the Upper Peninsula. Republicans fared best in urban counties with rapidly growing small cities where the working class allied itself with business instead of labor interests.

Between 1857 and 1940, the Democratic party in Wisconsin won a gubernatorial election only once. Before the 1930s, disagreements over economic issues occurred among Republicans, not between the two parties. Under the leadership of Robert M. LaFollette, Sr., Progressive Republicans seized control of the party and Wisconsin state government between 1900 and 1914, enacting, among other measures, a civil service law and regulations governing railroads, public utilities, insurance companies, and women's and children's labor. Unable to sustain their reform movement within the Republican party, the Progressives split with the Republicans in 1934; and although they subsequently won several gubernatorial elections, they went into decline. After Joseph McCarthy beat Robert M. LaFollette, Jr., in a senatorial primary in 1946, the Progressives disbanded and moved into the Democratic party.

The Republican party in Wisconsin had traditionally drawn its strength from native- and foreign-born—particularly Scandinavian—evangelical Protestants. The Democrats had polled well among relatively prosperous rural German Catholics and poorer, urban Irish and eastern European Catholics. This long-standing political configuration changed in 1946. If Progressives could no longer use the Republican party as a vehicle for their reforms, neither could the Democratic party rely on the support of anti-New Deal, conservative German Catholics. In the new realignment, the Republican party lost the Scandinavian vote in the northwestern portion of the state, gained the German Catholic vote in the Fox River valley, and retained some of its native-born Protestant vote. The rest of the Catholic vote stayed with the Democratic party, to which was added the support of the Progressive Republicans. Thus, in Wisconsin, even more sharply than in Michigan, the new party divisions occurred along ideological, political, economic, and ethnic lines.

For much of the period 1860–1930, a coalition of Lutheran Scandinavians and native-born evangelical Protestants enabled the Republican party in Minnesota to best the Democratic party, which was supported by Catholic Germans, Irish, and, after 1890, eastern Europeans. Politics in the state, however, was hardly tranquil; it was rocked by successive waves of farm and labor reform movements: the Grangers and People's Anti-Monopoly Party in the 1870s, the Farmers' Alliance in the 1880s and 1890s, the Progressive movement of the early 1900s, and the Nonpartisan League after 1915. By responding to these calls for economic reform, the Republican party retained its constituency, regulating, for example, railroad, freight, and elevator charges between 1871 and 1885; enacting a child labor law in 1895; and prosecuting the National Securities Company, a scheme to monopolize railroads, between 1901 and 1905.

In 1918, however, the Republican party indicted the antiwar Nonpartisan League as the "party of treason." Scandinavian and German supporters of the League countered by organizing the Farmer-Labor party, which ran second to the Republicans in the general elections. Thereafter, the Democratic party became the third party in Minnesota. The Republicans became primarily a party of the native-born; the Democrats, a party of Catholics; and the Farmer-Laborites, a party of reform across ethnic lines. Advocating a union of farmers and workers to promote the welfare of producers, a platform that would fit nicely with New Deal programs, the Farmer-Laborites captured the state government in 1930. With the death of Governor Floyd B. Olson in 1936, and the Republican party's subsequent adoption of a more reform-minded program, however, the Farmer-Labor party declined. The critical realignment occurred in the early 1950s, when a leadership vacuum in the Republican party encouraged Democrats and Farmer-Laborites to merge and to bid successfully for power. The support of the Olson administrations for the New Deal helped to make the Democratic party palatable to Farmer-Laborites. Urban Irish and Polish Catholics stayed within the Democratic party. As in Wisconsin, rural German Catholics moved into the Republican party.

CONCLUSION

It cannot be said that inhabitants of the Upper Midwest have ever identified themselves as upper midwesterners, although at times in the long history of the region some have identified themselves as midwesterners. This essay has sought only to establish the utility of the Upper Midwest as a historical construct. It has emphasized the topographical bifurcation of the region into northern and southern zones, the former blessed with an abundance of extractable resources and the latter highly suitable for agriculture.

Cultural heterogeneity, conflict, and accommodation have also been a constant theme in the history of the Upper Midwest. Indian-white contact resulted in the literal creation of a new people. Although the native-born migration to the region in the middle decades of the nineteenth century was relatively homogeneous, the Upper Midwest became home to immigrant groups who varied greatly in their predisposition to accept American ways and values. Native-born Americans serve as the fulcrum for linking the historical experience of the métis and the immigrant groups in the Upper

Midwest. The status of both métis and immigrants in the region was evaluated in the light of a vision for the social and economic development of the region first articulated in the Northwest Ordinance of 1787. The métis were found wanting and displaced; in the second half of the nineteenth century, some immigrant groups were deemed to be in need of reformation, and they resisted it.

The similarity between métis and immigrant experiences ends here. Métis and native peoples were removed to prepare the way for a glorious civilization. The reformation of immigrants was undertaken by those who saw their culturally homogeneous world of small producers threatened by the social and economic structures of industrial capitalism. Ethnic differences continued to play a role in the twentieth-century politics of the Upper Midwest, yet out of the New Deal rose a new consensus about the role of government in social and economic affairs, the partisan response to which was increasingly along class and ideological, rather than ethnic, lines.

BIBLIOGRAPHY

General Works

Berkhofer, Robert F., Jr. "Space, Time, Culture and the New Frontier." *Agricultural History* 38, no. 1 (1964): 21–30. Still presents a useful comparative, theoretical perspective.

Borchert, John R. *America's Northern Heartland: An Economic and Historical Geography of the Upper Midwest* (1987). The most recent economic geography of the Upper Midwest.

Cayton, Andrew R. L., and Peter S. Onuf. *The Midwest and the Nation: Rethinking the History of an American Region* (1990). The best account of political ideology and regional identity.

Hoffman, Frederick J. *The Twenties: American Writing in the Postwar Decade* (1965). Useful account of the emergence of midwestern regional literature.

Shortridge, James R. *The Middle West: Its Meaning in American Culture* (1989).

Smith, Henry Nash. *Virgin Land: The American West as Symbol and Myth* (1970). The classic work on American pastoralism.

Turner, Frederick Jackson. *The Frontier in American History* (1920; repr. 1986). Still essential reading for midwestern historiography.

———. *The Significance of Sections in American History* (1932; repr. 1950).

White, Richard. *The Middle Ground: Indians, Empires, and Republics in the Great Lakes Region, 1650–1815* (1991).

Native Peoples

Clifton, James A. *The Prairie People: Continuity and Potawatomi Indian Culture, 1665–1965* (1977).

Edmunds, Russell David. *The Potawatomis, Keepers of the Fire* (1978).

———. "'Unacquainted with the Laws of the Civilized World': American Attitudes Toward Métis Communities in the Old Northwest." In *The New Peoples: Being and Becoming Métis in North America,* edited by Jacqueline Peterson and Jennifer S. H. Brown (1985).

Peterson, Jacqueline. "Many Roads to Red River: Métis Genesis in the Great Lakes Region, 1680–1815." In *The New Peoples: Being and Becoming Métis in North America,* edited by Jacqueline Peterson and Jennifer S. H. Brown (1985).

Ritzenthaler, Robert E. "Southwestern Chippewa." In *Handbook of North American Indians,* vol. 15, *Northeast,* edited by Bruce G. Trigger (1978).

Roger, E. S. "Southeastern Ojibwa." In *Handbook of North American Indians,* vol. 15, *Northeast,* edited by Bruce G. Trigger (1978).

Tanner, Helen Hornbeck, ed. *Atlas of Great Lakes Indian History* (1987). The single best source.

Social and Economic History

Atack, Jeremy, and Fred Bateman. *To Their Own Soil: Agriculture in the Antebellum North* (1987).

Clayton, James L. "The Growth and Economic Significance of the American Fur Trade, 1740–1890." In *Aspects of the Fur Trade: Selected Papers of the 1965 North American Fur Trade Conference,* edited by Russell W. Fridley and June Drenning Holmquist (1967).

Cox, Thomas R., et al. *This Well-Wooded Land: Americans and Their Forests from Colonial Times to the Present* (1985).

Cronon, William L. *Nature's Metropolis: Chicago and the Great West* (1991). Excellent on the marketing of midwestern grain and lumber.

Johnson, Hildegard Binder. *Order upon the Land: The U.S. Rectangular Survey and the Upper Mississippi Country* (1976).

Landis, Paul Henry. *Three Iron Mining Towns: A Study in Cultural Change* (1938; repr. 1970).

Lankton, Larry. *Cradle to Grave: Life, Work, and Death at the Lake Superior Copper Mines* (1991).

Murdoch, Angus. *Boom Copper: The Story of the First United States Mining Boom* (1943).

Oberly, James W. *Sixty Million Acres: American Veterans and the Public Lands Before the Civil War* (1990).

Rohrbough, Malcolm J. *The Land Office Business: The Settlement and Administration of American Public Lands, 1789–1837* (1968).

Walker, David Allen. *Iron Frontier: The Discovery and Early Development of Minnesota's Three Ranges* (1979).

Williams, Michael. *Americans and Their Forests: A Historical Geography* (1989).

Winters, Donald L. "The Economics of Midwestern Agriculture, 1865–1900." In *Agriculture and National Development: Views on the Nineteenth Century,* edited by Lou Ferleger (1990).

Immigration and Ethnic Communities

Conzen, Kathleen Neils. "Peasant Pioneers: Generational Succession Among German Farmers in Frontier Minnesota." In *The Countryside in the Age of Capitalist Transformation: Essays in the Social History of Rural America,* edited by Steven Hahn and Jonathan Prude (1985).

———. "Immigrants in Nineteenth-Century Agricultural History." In *Agriculture and National Development: Views on the Nineteenth Century,* edited by Lou Ferleger (1990). The best single source on foreign immigration.

Curti, Merle E. *The Making of an American Community: A Case Study of Democracy in a Frontier Country* (1959). A Turnerian perspective; one of the few accounts of rural immigrant political participation.

Gjerde, Jon. *From Peasants to Farmers: The Migration from Balestrand, Norway, to the Upper Middle West* (1985).

Hudson, John C. "Cultural Geography and the Upper Great Lakes Region." *Journal of Cultural Geography* 5, no. 1 (1984): 19–32.

———. "Yankeeland in the Middle West." *Journal of Geography* 85, no. 5 (1986): 195–200.

———. "North American Origins of Middlewestern Frontier Populations." *Annals of the Association of American Geographers* 78, no. 3 (1988): 395–413. The best source on native-born American migration streams.

Ostergren, Robert C. *A Community Transplanted: The Trans-Atlantic Experience of a Swedish Immigrant Settlement in the Upper Middle West, 1835–1915* (1988).

Swierenga, Robert P., ed. *The Dutch in America: Immigration, Settlement, and Cultural Change* (1985).

Politics

Elazar, Daniel J. *American Federalism: A View from the States,* 3rd ed. (1984).

Fenton, John H. *Midwest Politics* (1966).

Jensen, Richard J. *The Winning of the Midwest: Social and Political Conflict, 1888–1896* (1971).

Kleppner, Paul. *The Cross of Culture: A Social Analysis of Midwestern Politics, 1850–1900* (1970).

Nye, Russel B. *Midwestern Progressive Politics: A Historical Study of Its Origins and Development, 1870–1958* (1959).

SEE ALSO **Agriculture; The Frontier; Immigration.**

THE GREAT PLAINS

James R. Shortridge

ALTHOUGH THE TERM "Great Plains" implies a physical region, it has been increasingly used to describe a distinctive set of cultural traits and values. In 1931 Walter Prescott Webb argued that attitudes and land uses brought to the plains from humid lands would fail. Aridity, he said, was the central fact of existence in this place; it demanded a new approach to life.

The Webb theory lies at the core of most studies of the region. Scholars agree on many of its aspects. Certainly agricultural practices and other sectors of the plains economy are different from the eastern Middle West. Wheat replaces corn, ranching and irrigation become important, and individual land holdings increase vastly in scale. The open question is the extent to which aridity, space, highly variable weather, the ranching and wheat economies, and other physical and economic realities have modified the psyches of plains people. The evidence is often subjective and thus necessarily obscure, but nearly all interpreters of the region have sensed a considerable degree of cultural distinctiveness.

This essay attempts to sketch major aspects of plains culture as seen by geographers and a variety of other observers and to discern distinctive cultural regions within the plains. It will raise several paradoxes and, especially, try to classify traits within a time-space framework. A series of six maps, arranged in chronological order, constitutes the focus. Initially the article considers questions of settler origins and traditional cultures. Modifications to these largely old-stock American cultures began with the influx of various European ethnic groups and the settlement of native Indian peoples on reservations. Indian Territory, with its transposed hybrid culture from the American South, and the Spanish southwest Plains are special cases. Additional, ongoing modifications to plains culture accompany mining, urbanization, and tourism. The situation of the plains in the 1990s reflects the cumulative effect of history, economy, and physical environment. This article concludes by describing regions within the plains, identifying a core region, where values and attitudes are most distinctive and homogeneous, plus transition areas and anomalies.

Although objective data are presented where available, readers should be forwarned that much of any culture study resists objectification. The ideas that follow have been voiced by many observers, but the emphasis given to each is personal, a reflection of my own encounter with plains literature and life. Another warning concerns the delimitation of the area being studied. The only obvious boundary is on the west, where county boundaries are used to approximate the Rocky Mountain front. To the east, the region includes the area influenced by cattle culture and, to the south, it includes the transition zone between northern and southern cultural influences in Oklahoma and the Texas Panhandle. The southern plains have been excluded.

SETTLEMENT

Initial American conceptions of the plains grew out of exploring and trading missions. The central theme of these conceptions was that the region was a transit zone between east and west, an expanse that had to be crossed to reach good fur waters, the Mexican trade, or mines. Passageways were needed, but the land itself was largely ignored. There are negative and positive assessments of its value, but the presence of open lands to the east meant that few people were overly concerned one way or the other. The naming of eastern Kansas and Nebraska as Indian Territory for displaced eastern tribes in 1834, for example, drew little attention as did the determination in 1818 that the British outpost of Pembina in the Red River valley was actually on American soil.

REGIONALISM AND REGIONAL SUBCULTURES

Important as the concept of the east-west passageway remains as a theme in regional identity, it was joined in the mid nineteenth century by other views. The best known of these is the "garden in the grasslands" idea, a typically optimistic American view of the plains as a new agricultural frontier. It was promoted by faith in the general notions of Manifest Destiny and Jeffersonian democracy as implemented through specific policies of railroads and the General Land Office. The federal government dispatched the Indians to a more southern territory and, by 1855, had surveyed large acreages in Kansas and Nebraska.

Lands across the Missouri River from Council Bluffs, Iowa, and Kansas City and Saint Joseph, Missouri, were initial foci for migrants and, when the Civil War ended the first wave of settlement expansion, Kansas was a state and Nebraska Territory was on the brink of statehood (Map 1). Their general forms, rectangles elongated from east to west, reflected the transportation routes they controlled. Their cultural characters also were similar, mixtures of settlers and speculators, Lincoln Republicans in politics, generally drawn from Illinois, Indiana, and Ohio stock.

Pro-Southern settlers from Missouri and elsewhere were common in territorial Kansas but withdrew once the free-state cause there was ascendant. Many moved back into Missouri, while others followed the Texas Trail into Indian Territory and beyond. The result was a sharp political, religious, and general culture fault line running from Saint Joseph southward along Kansas's eastern border and from there southwestward along the frontier of settlement in the Cherokee lands of Indian Territory. This line, coinciding as it did with several traditional jumping-off points for the trek West and with the old Indian border, soon came to be acknowl-

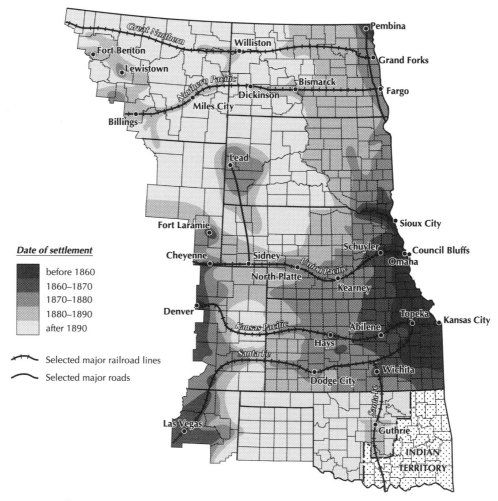

Map 1. Settlement

edged as the eastern border of the "plains," a term already carrying significant and complex cultural associations.

Incremental westward advance from Missouri and Iowa was the dominant mode of plains settlement, but not the only one. In the western part of Minnesota Territory, a north-south flow of people and goods along the Red River valley had existed since early in the century. This flow connected Winnipeg, an important settlement of five thousand by the mid 1850s, with Ontario via the Red and Minnesota River valleys and old Fort Snelling (Saint Paul). Furs moved south and manufactured goods moved north, first in carts and, after 1858, in steamboats. By 1860 numerous permanent settlers occupied the American part of the Red. Dakota Territory, created in 1861, extended farther north and south than it did east and west, reflecting that region's dominant orientation of settlement.

Territorial shapes and boundaries are also useful indicators of the settlement forces at work in the western plains. Kansas and Nebraska stretched from the Missouri River completely across the plains to the crest of the Rockies in 1854, yet when the two territories were admitted as states, their western borders followed the 102d and 104th meridians. These meridional lines, far from being a natural division of the plains, symbolize instead the concept of the western plains as wasteland. The lines were drawn arbitrarily across the most isolated, least desirable section of the region to separate the westward-advancing farmers from another frontier zone along the base of the Rocky Mountains.

Settlers in the western strip had several origins. Hispanic peoples had begun to advance northeastward along the Santa Fe Trail early in the century. Fort Laramie was a major post on the North Platte transportation artery. These groups were augmented by a series of mining towns, first in Colorado in 1857, and in Montana by 1862. Between this scattered settlement band and the farming frontier to the east was 600 miles (960 kilometers) of land having, at best, somewhat suspect value.

The mining bonanzas of the Rockies and beyond heightened the traditional role of the plains as transit region. Five major railroads pushed westward beyond the farming frontier to make connections with the Rockies, drawing settlers with them. Flow along the Northern Pacific, for example, overwhelmed the traditional north-south movement in Dakota Territory. The railroads were also partially responsible for introducing the cattle industry to the region, an important new source of people and ideas.

Texas ranchers saw markets in supplying meat to railroad workers, miners, and even Indian peoples. Shipments to eastern cities was another, and potentially even bigger, market. Ideal business and weather conditions in the 1870s and early 1880s led to an almost immediate realization of this potential. Railroads undercut one another to secure the trade and new rails across Dakota and Montana opened additional territory. Wyoming Territory, created in 1868 after the construction of the Union Pacific tracks, had mild weather during its first three winters, and Montana miners had also been successful in wintering stock without shelters or supplemental feed. The boom perhaps reached a peak in 1881 when the Northern Pacific line reached Miles City, Montana, and sold its land grant in huge blocks.

The realities of overproduction, encroachment by farmers, and climate—most notably a combination of drought and blizzard in 1885 to 1887—abruptly ended the cattle boom, but the western plains maintains an important cultural legacy from it. This legacy is strongest in Wyoming, eastern Montana, western North Dakota, Nebraska's Sand Hills, and Southwestern Oklahoma, where Texans were the initial European American settlers and where ranching traditions have been maintained. It also survives to some extent in eastern Oklahoma, where the Five Civilized Tribes traditionally practiced herding economies, and as far eastward in the other plains states as the Flint Hills of Kansas, a traditional cattle-fattening area, and old cow towns such as Abilene, Kansas, and Schuyler, Nebraska.

As the western plains core was being encroached upon simultaneously from the east, west, and south during the early 1870s, it seemed possible that the Black Hills region of southwestern Dakota Territory and adjacent portions of Nebraska, Montana, and Wyoming might avoid European American culture in any of its forms. This was the heart of Sioux and Crow country. Main transportation routes (the Northern Pacific, the Union Pacific, and the Missouri River) all skirted the region, and Wyoming had no mines to lure an additional railroad. The federal government's agreement to close the Bozeman Trail linking the Union Pacific route with the Montana mines across northeastern Wyoming also seemed to promise a permanent land allocation for those Indian nations. A major gold strike destroyed this promise in 1874. Miners rushed in and transportation links were built. The

Sioux justifiably revolted, most notably at the Little Big Horn River in 1876, but the ultimate result of smaller reservations and lasting embitterment was predictable. Instead of being the focus of plains isolation, southwestern Dakota became still another center for population expansion.

The 1890 isoline in Map 1 generally represents the limit of the continuous advance of settlement into the plains that began in the aftermath of the Civil War. Frontier stagnation had actually set in a few years earlier. Expansion of ranching ceased after the severe winters of 1885–1886 and 1886–1887, whereas a long series of droughty years beginning in 1885 taught farmers about the reality of plains climate. Enough stubborn ranchers and farmers remained to prevent wholesale abandonment of the land, but there was no major settlement advance in the northern plains until 1898. Favorable weather and markets, together with a belief in a new cropping technique called "dry farming," then produced a "second Dakota boom" and related movements, which together swept wheat farming across the remaining frontier.

A major exception to the frontier stagnation of the late 1880s occurred in Indian Territory. Lands west of those occupied by the Five Civilized Tribes were only sparsely settled by various Indian peoples. As farmers progressively spread across Kansas and Nebraska, many cattlemen found that grazing leases obtained from these Indian groups provided the best way to continue their livelihood. The region gradually became prominent as a cowman's country, occupied more by whites than by Indians. Other white Americans soon wanted a place in the game. Land speculators and farmers mounted pressure to open the land to "a higher level" of civilization than that attained by either the "nomadic" Indians or the "monopolistic cattle barons." The first capitulation of the government came in 1889, when land previously unassigned to any tribe was opened. Twelve other tracts followed between 1891 and 1906, producing a series of spectacular land runs and instant cities. When all was over, the cowmen had been largely replaced by farmers. North of the Canadian River, Kansans predominated; Texans were the major group to the south.

TRADITIONAL CULTURES

Extensions of traditional culture complexes from the east, west, and south created four major regions (shown in Map 2) on the central and north-ern plains by the end of the frontier era. All were essentially rural, though each contained "islands" where mining and other industrial activity produced a somewhat aberrant cultural picture.

A Hispanic area was the most distinctive of the four, a nineteenth-century expansion of peoples from the Rio Grande basin. The area depicted on the map is where Hispanics constituted 50 percent or more of the local population in 1900. Here traditional, self-sufficient villages were the rule, sheep raising a dominant activity, and Spanish the everyday language. Some Hispanic people lived outside this region, but in such places they usually were landless and segregated, laborers in an Anglo world.

Indian Territory was another culturally distinctive part of the plains. Late-nineteenth century observers saw it as a hybrid, more Southern than Native American in origin. The process of hybridization began with acculturation and interracial marriage by the Five Civilized Tribes in their homelands prior to removal. This acculturation continued in Indian Territory. Resident whites and slaves constituted 18 percent of the total population in 1860, and such aliens represented an amazing 72 percent in 1890. More than a third of the white population in 1860 had come from the South Midland (Upper South) states of Arkansas, Missouri, Tennessee, and Kentucky, and nearly a quarter from the Lower South. Each group had distinctive patterns of settlement and culture. Lower Southerners clustered on Creek and Choctaw holdings in the rich lowlands of the Red and Arkansas rivers. There they established a plantation economy including major slave holdings, cotton, tobacco, and some dry-field rice. South Midland people dominated elsewhere. They kept slaves, too, but only in moderate numbers. Corn, wheat, and cattle were their major agricultural endeavors.

Indian Territory's Southern identity was solidified by the Civil War and its aftermath. Although only the Choctaw Nation was firmly committed to the Confederate cause, the territory had to choose sides and opted for the South. The Nations were raided repeatedly and, in the end, lost their slaves, were forced to cede western lands, and suffered the trials of Reconstruction. This suffering intensified their Southern mindset. Additional cultural reinforcement occurred when economic recovery began and the tribes hired Confederate veterans as laborers to replace the slaves.

North of Indian Territory and the Spanish Southwest, cultural distinctions on the plains around

1900 were blurred considerably. Kansas and Nebraska were usually regarded as similar places and different somehow from the Dakotas, but observers sometimes found it difficult to put the perceived differences into words. Similarly, the plains portions of Montana, Wyoming, and Colorado were allied with their eastern neighbors, yet somehow apart. Much of this blurring can be attributed to the multiple origins of early settlers. Missouri River traders and Texas cattlemen, bringing with them elements of Southern culture, were the initial Anglo occupants of many parts of the northern plains. Montana's Chouteau County and Fort Benton took their names from prominent Saint Louis families, for example, and many of that territory's legal statutes were copied from Missouri examples. Words associated with Southwestern ranching traditions such as "corral" and "range" are still in use throughout most of the northern and central plains (Map 2)

The east-to-west expansion of people across the plains transcended early Southern influences in most places, but the new settlers themselves were of varied origins. Even ignoring the foreign-born for the moment, considerable mixing had occurred in a broad band across the northern parts of Ohio, Indiana, and Illinois, and in central Iowa between peoples from New England and the Northern states and those from Pennsylvania and other North Midland states. These "mixed" areas, in turn, supplied large numbers of plains settlers. Cultural mixing reached a pinnacle in the Black Hills and other mining sites along the Rocky Mountain fringe.

Contemporary observers of the plains, although recognizing that cultural mixing was common, nevertheless still saw three primary divisions of the region in 1900. Each was based largely on extensions of culture complexes from the east, and their names were straightforward: Southwest, Middle West, and Northwest. The Southwest (Texas and Indian Territory) was defined almost wholly in cultural terms. Differences between Yankee and Midlander were also acknowledged as a factor in the Northwest–Middle West distinction, but stages of economic development were of equal importance. Kansas and Nebraska—the Middle West—were seen as reasonably mature rural states by the late 1890s. Most parts had been settled for more than a decade; their farmers had survived both a boom and a prolonged depression and had emerged with a well-adjusted perspective on life. Observers saw youthful enthusiasm tempered with maturity, producing something close to a pastoral ideal. In con-

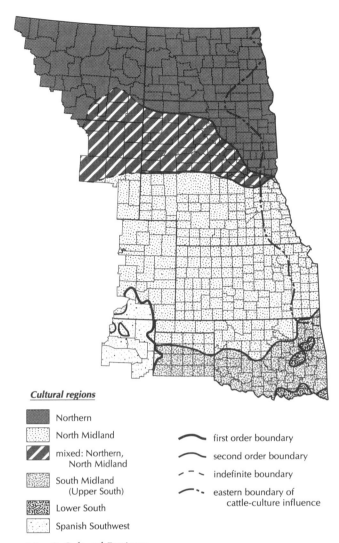

Cultural regions

- Northern
- North Midland
- mixed: Northern, North Midland
- South Midland (Upper South)
- Lower South
- Spanish Southwest

- ⌒ first order boundary
- ⌒ second order boundary
- - - ⁓ indefinite boundary
- ⌒⁓ eastern boundary of cattle-culture influence

Map 2. Cultural Regions

trast, the Northwest was still a frontier in 1900. Expectations ran high in the trans-Missouri plains of the Dakotas and Montana, but so did speculation about everything from crop choice to city location. It was classic, capricious "next-year country."

The coalescence of Northern cultural inheritance and frontier status was strongest in the flatlands of western North Dakota and eastern Montana, although eastern Dakota's widely publicized bonanza farms helped to maintain a frontier-like atmosphere there throughout the 1890s. South Dakota, eastern Wyoming, and Nebraska's Sand Hills are best seen as a transition zone. Eastern South Dakota was Northern in culture but no longer a frontier, the Sand Hills still frontier but more Midland in settler origin. Pioneers in the Black Hills and Wyoming were from widely varied places. A secondary cultural division complicated matters further, a meridional one separating Southern, ranching traditions from those of eastern farmers. The position of this "line" had varied through time and was still in flux as of 1900. The boundary shown on Map 2 represents the extreme eastern limit of ranching ideas as measured by regional vocabulary.

ETHNIC GROUPS

Just as an initial veneer of Southern culture in the northern plains had given way to Yankee immigration, Yankee settlers themselves soon were outnumbered in many counties by European immigrants. Norwegians and ethnic Germans from Russia were the most numerous of this highly varied group of settlers. Their pattern of distribution, with a heavy concentration in North Dakota, greatly influenced regional culture (Map 3). What had been

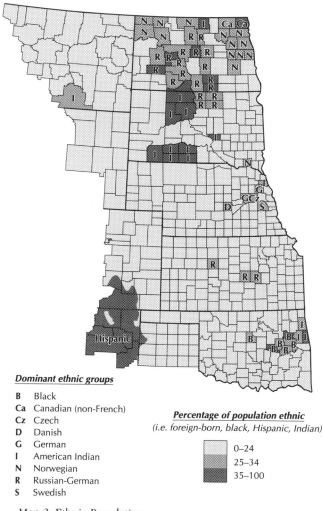

Dominant ethnic groups

B   Black
Ca Canadian (non-French)
Cz Czech
D   Danish
G   German
I   American Indian
N   Norwegian
R   Russian-German
S   Swedish

Percentage of population ethnic
(i.e. foreign-born, black, Hispanic, Indian)

  0–24
  25–34
  35–100

Map 3. Ethnic Population

"New England extended" became a rich, and sometimes confusing, mosaic.

The reasons underlying the concentration of European migrants in North Dakota are not completely clear. Timing accounts for it in part. A major flow of people began about 1870 because of a combination of conditions in Europe, liberal American land policies, and the end of the Civil War. Eastern Kansas and southeastern Nebraska were largely settled before that time and the central parts of these states were beginning to fill rapidly without elaborate promotional efforts. Promoters were more active in soliciting European settlers on the harsher, more open frontier to the north. Here, too, groups of settlers were more likely to find land in large blocks. Another advantage, especially for Scandinavians, was the area's proximity to ethnic (Scandinavian, German, and Slavic) communities in Minnesota and Wisconsin.

Studies in North Dakota show that, although Norwegians and German-Russians occasionally were pioneers in the areas they now occupy, the more common pattern was to expand outward from core communities, buying farms from Anglo frontiersmen. Spring Grove, Minnesota, was a major hearth for Norwegians coming to eastern North Dakota, and the Yankton, South Dakota, area played a similar role for German-Russians bound for Eureka and other settlements in the north-central part of South Dakota. North Dakota by 1910 was dominated by these two ethnic groups. Foreign-born people and those born in the United States of foreign parentage constituted an astonishing 71 percent of its total population. An older Yankee culture had named all the towns but no longer controlled the society.

Indians were a second major component of the ethnic mosaic on the northern plains. The once extensive holdings of the Sioux and Crow peoples had gradually been diminished during the settlement period, and by 1910 even the remaining reservations sometimes contained more white than Indian occupants. Still, Indians dominated in several counties, particularly in west-central South Dakota where the Oglala and other Teton Sioux groups constituted about 90 percent of the population. Other significant Indian clusters included Chippewa-Métis in Rolette County, North Dakota; Crows in Big Horn County, Montana; Yankton Sioux in Buffalo County, South Dakota, and Omahas and Winnebagos in Thurston County, Nebraska.

The percentage of the foreign-born population dropped as one moved south on the plains at the end of the frontier period. Occasional clusters existed, but usually ethnic populations were intermixed with Anglo settlers. Besides the strong Hispanic contingent in the Southwest, only two major ethnic concentrations stood out. Blacks constituted 40 percent of the population in both Okfuskee and Wagoner counties, Oklahoma, in 1910 and were important also in three adjacent counties. All five were part of the old Creek Nation with its slave history. Langston University created an outlier in Logan County. Oklahoma's Indian population, although large, was diffuse. Its percentages were high only in the heart of the Cherokee Nation, especially in the hills of Adair County, where tradition-minded tribesmen tended to isolate themselves.

The dominance of various plains counties by European ethnic groups at the close of the frontier actually was greater than suggested by the percentages shown in Map 3, for the map numbers do not include the American-born children of immigrants. Sheer numbers alone indicate that such groups would greatly modify the regional culture in North Dakota and elsewhere, and local influence might be increased further if a group maintained a sense of exclusivity over time. German-Russians and Norwegians have done this to a high degree in North Dakota. Pioneer German-Russian men married within their ethnic group 97 percent of the time, for example, as did 93 percent of Norwegian men. The figures for Swedes and immigrants from Ontario were 62 and 55 percent, respectively.

Another measure of exclusivity and culture strength is language retention. Figures for 1980 reveal two major centers in this regard: the Hispanic area and the German-Russian heartland in central Dakota, with outliers in Kansas and Montana (Map 4). A comparison of the distribution of these groups in Maps 3 and 4 also indicates an expansion of their influence during the twentieth century. Spanish American culture traits are well enough known not to require elaboration here, but the continuing German-Russian influence in North Dakota, especially in conjunction with Norwegian ethnicity, deserves some discussion.

The North Dakota population in the 1990s was composed of about equal proportions of German-Russians, Norwegians, and all others (including old-stock Americans, Ukrainians, Métis, Sioux, and Canadians). The groups cooperated in economic matters but remained socially discrete. The German-Russians, perhaps because they came directly from Europe to Dakota and because of the cohesion they had acquired during their residency in Russia, remained the most apart. Their loyalty is to land, church, and family; they avoided state politics, higher education, urban places, and even the En-

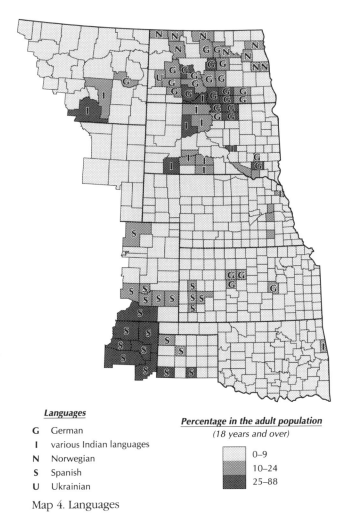

Languages

G   German
I   various Indian languages
N   Norwegian
S   Spanish
U   Ukrainian

Percentage in the adult population
(18 years and over)

0–9
10–24
25–88

Map 4. Languages

glish language almost completely until World War II. William C. Sherman says in his *Prairie Mosaic* that these people "wanted to be Germans in America," not simply Americans (p. 50). The tight-knit character of German-Russian communities naturally aroused suspicion from outsiders. Neighbors branded them as greedy, dirty, aloof, and even (for their insistence on retention of the German language) traitorous. Teetotalling Norwegians also looked askance on the Germans' love for wine. Some of these feelings linger.

Norwegian ethnic identity was more subtle than the German-Russian. In addition to their prohibitionist tendency, Norwegians always placed high value on education and somehow managed to assimilate easily into the American cultural mainstream while still maintaining ethnic loyalty. The most significant Norwegian traits, however, at least in terms of influencing regional culture, were ones they share with the German-Russians: religious devotion, a strong work ethic, a preference for farm (but not ranch) life, and a progressive, frequently radical political attitude. Devotion by the two groups to various Lutheran, Catholic, and Mennonite churches created a northern Bible Belt. Rural radicalism, expressed through the Nonpartisan League and other vehicles, made North Dakota a leader in the long-standing plains protest against control by railroads, grain monopolies, and other agencies presumably owned by urban, Eastern businessmen. The strong work ethic, in combination with what some observers have called a stubborn, stolid, even unimaginative mindset, probably also served these peoples well in the harsh northern plains environment. After all, this was and still is a place where "sheer grit and cussedness alone frequently meant the difference between success and failure—or even life and death" (*North Dakota: A Bicentennial History,* p. 74).

URBANIZATION AND OTHER CHANGES

The Great Plains counties are often seen by outsiders as rural America. This perception can be justified in a relative sense, but by the late twentieth century the region had become more urban than rural, and urbanization was responsible for important modifications to and variations in regional cultures. Urban counties are usually the richer ones, for example, and the centers of economic and political power. Such concentration produces rivalries between the haves and the have nots. A map of median family income provides a good basis for assessing the present status of these and related developments (Map 5).

Several traditional rural cultures are characterized by relative poverty. For one of these cases, however, the map may exaggerate the true situa-

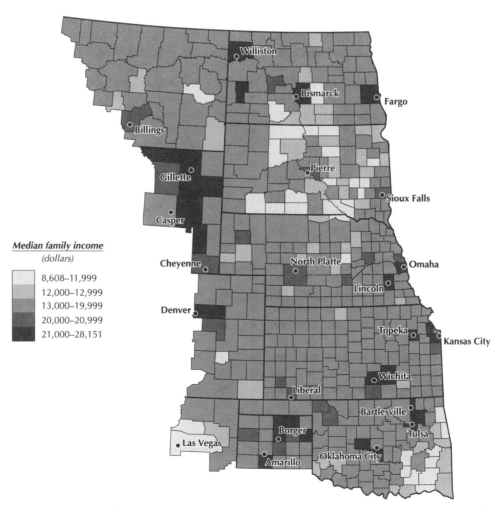

Median family income
(dollars)

8,608–11,999
12,000–12,999
13,000–19,999
20,000–20,999
21,000–28,151

Map 5. Median Family Income

tion. Because German-Russian communities revere the ideal of self-sufficiency, not all aspects of their economy are on a cash basis that can be officially recorded by a census. The same is true of Hispanic communities to some degree, although not so much as in the past. Hispanic people are becoming a minority in their own heartland, frequently facing an undesirable choice of staying in the old villages and foregoing modern conveniences or entering the Anglo world and being restricted to menial jobs by barriers of language and formal education. Poverty results in either case; the median family income for Mora County, New Mexico, is the lowest in the plains.

Most Indian reservations, especially those of the Sioux in South Dakota, form another zone of low incomes. Interpretations of this situation differ. Some Anglo neighbors blame the Sioux themselves, charging lack of motivation and overdependence on government aid. Others note language and education problems, decades of cultural deprivation, and overpopulation. The quality of land on the reservations is certainly not first-rate, and the better sections are frequently owned by whites. Most Indian counties saw their populations increase in the 1980s while their industrial and agricultural bases remained static. Rolette County, North Dakota, is an extreme case. Here fifteen thousand Métis overflow the two townships of Turtle Mountain Reservation.

Parts of southern Oklahoma constitute a discontinuous fourth area of low incomes. The regional names that have evolved, "Greer County" in the west and "Little Dixie" in the east, are defined in part by a rural poverty brought about by generations of tenant cotton farming. The situation in the west is exacerbated by sandy soils and precarious rainfall; declining coal mining has contributed in Little Dixie. Little Dixie's poverty is legendary in Oklahoma. It spawned a strong Socialist movement in the 1910s, intensified racism, and eventually prompted some one hundred thousand residents to emigrate during the Great Depression. Little Dixie, not the Dust Bowl counties of northwestern Oklahoma, was the source of the "Okies" of John Steinbeck's *The Grapes of Wrath* (1939).

Whereas the poverty zones in the plains reinforce and help to define certain traditional, rural cultures, the richer areas are frequently growing, often urban, places that diverge sharply in many ways from the counties that surround them. By 1990 urban areas were so influential that they affected income levels even in certain rural counties, perhaps most notably through highway linkages.

Places away from the main interstate system, counties such as Baca in Colorado, Elk, and Smith in Kansas, Carter in Montana, and Hayes and Pawnee in Nebraska, tend to have low incomes. They are the plains "yonland," isolated, with declining economies and aging populations (Kraenzel, "Sutland and Yonland Settling").

Prosperity in several counties is tied to the exploitation of oil, natural gas, and coal. Income from such minerals can be ephemeral, but three major areas of the plains have enjoyed minerals-borne prosperity in the late twentieth century: central and northeastern Oklahoma (oil); southwestern Kansas and the Oklahoma-Texas panhandles (natural gas); and Wyoming, southeastern Montana, and western North Dakota (coal).

Oil, which had been discovered in Kansas and Oklahoma in the late nineteenth century, began to boom in the 1920s. Kansas reserves were exploited first and that state thus had refineries established when the bigger Oklahoma fields were tapped. Tulsa, ironically a place with no fields of its own, emerged as the focus of development when city businessmen bridged the Arkansas River to form a link between the Kansas refineries and oil fields to the south. New refineries soon chose to locate in Tulsa as did many of the new oil millionaires. Today the city, together with nearby Bartlesville, is a somewhat self-conscious center of high culture on the plains. It has passed the stage of parvenu in some ways, but still is insecure; in 1985 it threatened to sue over a poor showing in one of the numerous national quality-of-life surveys.

People with only a passing acquaintance with the plains are surprised to learn of prosperity in the Dust Bowl counties in and around the Texas Panhandle. Some of this wealth comes from the utilization of ground water for irrigation, but huge natural gas reserves are the major factor. Natural-gas money enabled many residents to endure the dry climatic cycle of the 1930s and since then it has brought real prosperity. Wealth here seems to be more understated and more evenly distributed than in eastern Oklahoma. Money from the gas is frequently used to supplement farm incomes. Perhaps the gamble of farming in this region keeps even the wealthy humble.

Coal is responsible for the newest boom on the plains. The Fort Union Formation, extending from the Powder River basin of Wyoming into North Dakota, is thick, low in sulphur, and easily mined by stripping. Isolation kept exploitation low until the Arab oil embargo of 1973. Suddenly, everything changed. New power plants and railroad spurs sprang up, as did several boomtowns. Williston, North Dakota, and Billings, Montana, grew tremendously, but Gillette, Wyoming, best symbolizes the activity. By 1990, Gillette had doubled and redoubled its 1960 population. It thrives but is garish. Like the gold-rush towns of the nineteenth century, its vitality is accompanied by vice, rampant speculation, and similar problems. Major beneficiaries of the new coal money include the Crow and Northern Cheyenne Indians, whose reservations contain about 30 percent of the reserves in Montana. Gateway cities to the plains account for most of the remaining high-income counties on Map 5. A string of these places follows the eastern border: Fargo-Moorhead, Sioux Falls, Sioux City, Omaha–Council Bluffs, Kansas City, and Fort Smith. Each has prospered since the early settlement period and still serves as a transportation focus, an exchange point between East and West. Billings, Cheyenne, and Denver serve a similar function on the western plains border.

Each gateway city, by definition, belongs to the plains only in part. It may host such traditional regional events as rodeos and livestock shows, but plainsmen distrust the financial, transportation, and agribusiness operations there. The suspicion that such businesses benefit outside investors more than people of the region has always been a part of plains culture, and the mistrust has increased through time as business centralization has concentrated power in fewer and more distant hands. Modern studies of metropolitan influence measured through banking linkages, migration fields, and the like reveal that most of the plains falls within the sphere of somewhat remote Minneapolis–Saint Paul, Chicago, and Dallas–Fort Worth. Denver and Kansas City control smaller pieces. At another scale, Chicago dominates nearly the entire region. As the novelist Wright Morris remembered from his youth in Nebraska, "all of the railroad lines converged on Chicago, the home of Montgomery Ward and Sears and Roebuck" (*Will's Boy: A Memoir* [1981], p. 14).

PLAINS CULTURE

The preceding discussion highlights the considerable complexity that underlies modern plains culture. Before attempting to depict this complexity on a map, it is necessary to concentrate on the unifying forces for the culture. The central idea is the concept known as Middle West.

The plains was the birthplace of the term "Middle West." As noted earlier, it originated in the 1880s to describe the maturing yeoman society living in Kansas and Nebraska. By 1912 or so the description and label were being applied to an expanded area, including the northern plains and a portion of Oklahoma west of the old Indian Territory border and north of the Canadian River. This expansion signified a cultural fusion. Differences in stage of development, which formerly had distinguished the northern from the central plains, had gradually begun to diminish. Accompanying this process, the parallel but always weak distinctions between Northern and Midland culture also disappeared from the popular literature of the time. Yeoman imagery became the controlling symbol for the region. Commentators saw the people as clear-eyed, pragmatic folk who had confidence in their own abilities and respect for the land. This portrait of the plainsman remains remarkably intact in modern literature.

A financial crisis in the 1890s was a major factor in fostering the cultural fusion of the central and northern plains and the concurrent break between these places and the East. Eastern capital had financed much early development on the plains, and defaults on loans created hard feelings on both sides: Easterners saw plainsmen as irresponsible; plainsmen viewed Easterners as heartless exploiters. Populists, who gave political expression to this plains feeling, regularly damned the East for railroad monopolies, unfavorable tariff policies, and, generally, for treating the plains as if it were a colony. The validity of such charges can be (and has been) debated, but clearly the Populists were critical in creating a common purpose and identity for the plains.

Although largely unnoticed at the time, forces similar to those splitting the East from the plains were also creating a new division within the plains in the 1890s. Populism and related ideas were expressed most intensely in two locations: central Kansas and Nebraska, and North Dakota. Coincidently, these areas possessed the most severe climates of the plains areas then settled. Farmers trying to install a corn-hog economy in central Nebraska, for example, experienced greater financial stress than did their neighbors to the east. North Dakota radicalism ultimately may have been environmentally inspired, too, although Norwegian and German-Russian predilections toward radical behavior are well documented. The important point is that even in the late 1890s a discerning observer might have detected a core emerging for the new plains culture. Areas around cities such as Sioux City and Omaha, with their longer settlement histories and traditional corn-belt economies, were seen as almost "Eastern" by frustrated and increasing radical settlers to the north and west.

Historical relationships between the plains and the Eastern states, especially regional stereotypes, underlie a great deal of the modern personality of the plains. In particular, these relationships help to explain two major paradoxes: the plainsman as pawn of the East yet somehow still self-reliant and independent, and the plainsman as heroic yeoman yet also backwoods hick. Residents of the plains wore the yeoman label proudly until the 1920s, reveling in the long list of complimentary traits associated with it; they were living the American dream. However, the role of myth bearer soon became a mixed blessing. When dependency on business and government decisions made in the East became painfully clear during the agricultural depression of the 1920s, what were plainsmen to do? They could complain, but thereby they exposed the falseness of the cherished yeoman values; they could be silent, but they thereby suffered still greater economic hardship. A parallel dilemma has arisen with the rapid urbanization of America: Should plainsmen continue to extol their rural virtue or stress that they too are part of the new urban scene?

A reading of the literature generated in and about the region shows that both dilemmas continue to exist. In fact, the mixed feelings inherent in them lie close to the core of the composite personality of the region. Both situations have been cyclic to a degree. The victim idea, what some have called the "conspiracy theory of history," is expressed most frequently during times of economic depression, when the plains, as a producer of agricultural and other primary materials, is naturally affected most severely. Other examples include anger over deleterious strip-mining policies made in the East and the 1985 crisis over farm credit. Challenges to the heroic view of rural life reached a peak during the 1930s. As symbolized by the Okies, plains farmers acquired an image of failure. Pictures of gaunt faces suggested negative associations of all sorts: poor education, dependency, even laziness. Surveys suggest that college-aged people, at least, continued to view the plains negatively in the 1990s. The tendency existed even among residents of the region.

Despite all the challenges, the yeoman ideal remains the most important single component of plains culture. In a 1989 national survey, agricultural characteristics were used as regional descriptors twelve times more frequently than were industrial ones (*The Middle West,* pp. 74–82). More to the point, pastoral traits continued to dominate the cultural characteristics volunteered by respondents, who used terms such as "friendly," "easygoing," "natural," "honest," "thoughtful," "moral," and "modest." Residents of the plains states listed such terms at rates even higher than the national average. The wave of urban disillusionment and rural nostalgia sweeping the nation in the 1990s may be producing a revival of yeoman values.

Observers of plains life in the early twentieth century frequently augmented their pastoral imagery with an analogy of the region as a young adult. This view, contrasted with Eastern old age and Western youth, heightened regional distinctiveness and produced progressive ideas of all sorts. Examples included the initiative, the referendum, state-owned banks, and many improvements in social justice. The Republican party dominated throughout the region but the entire political spectrum shared in the idealist concern.

The progressive spirit of young adulthood continued as a strong cultural force on the plains into the 1920s, but then faded. The Depression again seems to have been a watershed, "aging" the plains rapidly. Kansas soon was called "the eclipsed state," for example, and conservative thought became dominant throughout the region (*The Great Plains States,* p. 221). Plains residents now even see themselves in this light. On a 1989 survey they volunteered conservative traits as descriptive of their region more frequently than liberal ones, materialistic terms more than idealistic ones, and even "narrow-minded" more frequently than "broadminded" (*The Middle West,* pp. 74–82). The composite regional image is that of a yeoman farmer, but one who has aged and become set in his ways.

The paragraphs above have argued that historical forces and national myths have shaped much of the value system found on the plains. Another powerful shaping agent, the plains environment itself, with its vast distances, sparse population, and harsh, unpredictable weather, has often lurked between the lines. Linkages between environmental phenomena and such human characteristics as self-reliance and a vigorous, outgoing personality are nearly impossible to establish conclusively, but most writers on the region agree that such linkages are of fundamental importance. Humanists, who perhaps are more able than others to see truths beyond those easily quantified, make the boldest statements.

The traits quoted here correspond closely to the yeoman ones previously discussed. Good land was necessary for the origination of yeoman-farmer ideals, and it seems likely that low population, harsh weather, and the like have acted to keep them strong in the region. Friendliness, for example, might be expected to flourish when people are spread thin, humbleness where nature is powerful and capricious, and independence where one is isolated. Coping with life in a severe climate even can produce regional pride. A bumper sticker popular in North Dakota proclaims that "−43° Keeps Out the Riff-Raff."

Space itself, the vastness of the plains, has been said to influence behavior in many ways. Certainly when combined with a low population density, it makes life expensive. Per capita costs for power, roadway maintenance, and other services, along with those for distributing manufactured goods, are high. To enjoy a movie, residents of Jordan, Montana, must add the cost of driving 170 miles (270 kilometers) to their ticket prices. Space also necessarily isolates plains towns from one another and, on a different scale, the region from the nation. Insular attitudes develop and lead to the half-truths of stereotyping. Tourists, who annually cross the plains in large numbers, might provide a counter to this isolation, but do not. They speed along the interstate highways to pass over the frightening miles as quickly as possible, seeing nearly nothing of the world beyond the guardrails.

Space may engender positive human qualities. Writers from the pioneer era frequently stressed how the new land made people ponder life on a grand and utopian scale. Willa Cather in her novel, *My Ántonia* (1918), said of early Nebraska, for example, that it was "not a country at all, but the material out of which countries are made." Some of this hoped-for grandeur necessarily faded over time, but the vast scale of things on the plains remains. Where land holdings and sky both are large, it seems logical for human aspirations to expand as well. Many writers hold that this enlarged viewpoint is still one of the greatest assets of the region. Residents see themselves in proper perspective, and thus possess a certain inner calm and a lessened sense of parochialism. "In the dry places," as Wright Morris put it, "men begin to dream" (*The Works of Love* [1952], p. 3).

CULTURAL REGIONALIZATION

As one contemplates the evolution of plains culture, it is natural to think also about its localization. Where are the distinctive values found in purest form? What is core and what periphery for the place? Figure 6 shows the results of speculations on these questions. The approach was essentially one of elimination. Extensions of Spanish and Southern peoples into the southwestern and southeastern parts of the area, respectively, have created cultures clearly different from the one sketched here. The

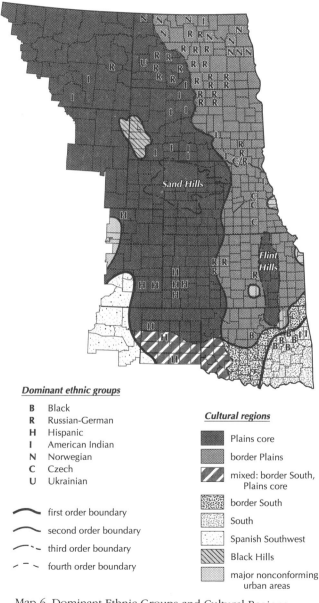

Dominant ethnic groups

B Black
R Russian-German
H Hispanic
I American Indian
N Norwegian
C Czech
U Ukrainian

first order boundary
second order boundary
third order boundary
fourth order boundary

Cultural regions

Plains core
border Plains
mixed: border South, Plains core
border South
South
Spanish Southwest
Black Hills
major nonconforming urban areas

Map 6. Dominant Ethnic Groups and Cultural Regions

Denver, Kansas City, and Tulsa-Bartlesville urban areas are equally separate. Omaha and Wichita, smaller places also set apart, are admittedly more questionable choices. Finally, tourism and mining traditions isolate the Black Hills culturally.

The remainder of the plains north of Texas, although sharing a common cultural heritage, can be subdivided based on the intensity with which the values of the culture are held. The boundary between the subdivision runs north and south. Dakotans, for example, recognize "East River–West River"—the river being the Missouri—to be the fundamental split in the northern plains, not the state boundary tracing the forty-sixth parallel. West River people have lived since the 1890s in a harsher, more demanding environment than the one east of the Missouri River. This has led to differences in choice of livelihood, in population density, and, ultimately, in values. The yeoman ideals fit reality better in the West; there, too, the real and perceived effects of space and sky are maximized. The West River country, as the location for recent drilling and strip-mining activity, also has become a focus for dialogue on regional exploitation and, by extension, on the meaning of plains culture. People have begun to state, examine, and affirm traditional values whose existence and importance heretofore were grasped only vaguely.

The East River–West River division is clearly defined in South Dakota by massive Lake Oahe and the north-south alignment of Indian reservations. North of Standing Rock Reservation the line is less obvious. German Russian colonies occupy both sides of the river and the river itself changes direction. The boundary shown was drawn to group the mining area around Williston with the other coal centers. The terms "East River" and "West River" necessarily disappear south of the Dakotas, but the cultural boundary persists. The phrase "Sand Hills" in Nebraska refers to a cultural world as much as to a physical environment. Kansans use "High Plains" and "Western Kansas" in a similar way, and, for Oklahomans, the analogous terms are "Panhandle" and "Greer County."

It is interesting to speculate on possible focal points for plains culture within the core region. Again, one can begin with an elimination procedure. The Texas Panhandle certainly is not a candidate, with its anamolous Democratic politics and Southern Baptist churches. Much of the Colorado plains can be excluded through its proximity to cosmopolitan Denver. Gillette, Wyoming, and Willis-

ton, North Dakota, although providing forums for debate on plains values, are nonetheless themselves hybrid places not truly representative of these values.

A good case for a cultural focus on the state level can be made for Montana and, especially, for Wyoming. Montana, after all, declares itself to be "big sky" country and Wyoming is "the cowboy state." Contrast these terms with the "cornhusker" and "jayhawk" symbols for Nebraska and Kansas, words referring to ideas from the eastern borderlands of these two states. A noted regional scholar, Clark C. Spence, has put the argument well: "Montanans, probably more than any other people in the West, are convinced that unspoiled space and those who survived the tough process of conquering it handed down a special something of abstract but inestimable value" (*Montana,* pp. 192–193). Continuing talk about the Nebraska panhandle switching allegiances to Wyoming provides another illustration. The people would still live in a panhandle, but they would feel that their ideas would match those in Cheyenne better than those in Lincoln. If specific cities must be named as cultural foci, Cheyenne, Wyoming, would be a good choice, along with Miles City in Montana, an old cattle and railroad town, isolated enough to be forced to think for itself yet near the new mining activity.

Most of the other plains states also have candidates for focal cities. Often these are college towns, places with people more likely than most to give voice to the still largely unstated local belief system. Dickinson, North Dakota, Hays, Kansas, and Guymon-Goodwell, Oklahoma, all serve this function. The most serious rival to Miles City and Cheyenne for regional "capital," though, is North Platte, Nebraska. North Platte, on Interstate 80 in the rich Platte Valley, is connected with mainstream America yet apart from it. It services a large trade area that contains traditional and modern expressions of plains economies and values. To its south lies big wheat country, in the valley proper are major irrigation agriculture and cattle feedlots, and to its north lie the ranches of the Sand Hills. The Sand Hills are the key. Cattlemen have controlled most of this vast area from the period of initial settlement. The holdings are large, the grass is good, and the people are secure and self-confident. In this pristine realm one can still sense the wonder, awe, and hope so well expressed in Willa Cather's early novels and so central still to the ultimate human meaning of the plains.

BIBLIOGRAPHY

Overviews of Plains Settlement and Culture

Allen, John L. "The Garden-Desert Continuum: Competing Views of the Great Plains in the Nineteenth Century." *Great Plains Quarterly* 5, no. 4 (1985).

Blouet, Brian W., and Frederick C. Luebke, eds. *The Great Plains: Environment and Culture* (1979).

Borchert, John R. *America's Northern Heartland: An Economic and Historical Geography of the Upper Midwest* (1987).

Emmons, David M. *Garden in the Grasslands: Boomer Literature of the Central Great Plains* (1971).

Fiedler, Leslie. "Montana; or, The End of Jean-Jacques Rousseau." In *The Collected Essays of Leslie Fiedler,* vol. 1 (1971).

Hudson, John C. "North American Origins of Middlewestern Frontier Populations." *Annals of the Association of American Geographers* 78 (1988).

Kollmorgen, Walter M. "The Woodsman's Assaults on the Domain of the Cattleman." *Annals of the Association of American Geographers* 59 (1969).

Kraenzel, Carl F. "Sutland and Yonland Settling for Community Organization in the Great Plains." *Rural Sociology* 18 (1953).

Mather, E. Cotton. "The American Great Plains." *Annals of the Association of American Geographers* 62 (1972).

Peirce, Neal R. *The Great Plains States of America* (1973).

Shortridge, James R. *The Middle West: Its Meaning in American Culture* (1989).

Webb, Walter P. *The Great Plains* (1931).

State and Local Studies

Alwin, John A. "Jordan Country: A Golden Anniversary Look." *Annals of the Association of American Geographers* 71 (1981).

Doran, Michael F. "Population Statistics of Nineteenth Century Indian Territory." *Chronicles of Oklahoma* 53, no. 4 (1975–1976).

Hudson, John C. "Migration to an American Frontier." *Annals of the Association of American Geographers* 66 (1976).

Kloberdanz, Timothy J. "Symbols of German-Russian Ethnic Identity on the Northern Plains." *Great Plains Quarterly* 8, no. 1 (1988).

Morlan, Robert L. *Political Prairie Fire: The Nonpartisan League, 1915–1922* (1985).

Nostrand, Richard L. "The Hispano Homeland in 1900." *Annals of the Association of American Geographers* 70 (1980).

Roark, Michael O. "Oklahoma Territory: Frontier Development, Migration, and Culture Areas." Ph.D. diss., Syracuse University (1979).

Sherman, William C. *Prairie Mosaic: An Ethnic Atlas of Rural North Dakota* (1983).

Spence, Clark C. *Montana: A Bicentennial History* (1978).

Wilkins, Robert P., and Wynona Huchette Wilkins. *North Dakota: A Bicentennial History* (1977).

Wilkins, Wynona H. "The Idea of North Dakota." *North Dakota Quarterly* 39, no. 1 (1971).

THE GREAT PLAINS

SEE ALSO Agriculture: American Indians of the West; The Frontier; German Speakers; Immigration; Labor: The Great Depression Through the 1980s; Native Peoples and Early European Contacts; The Natural Environment: The West; Regionalism; Rural Life in the West; Scandinavians; Village and Town.

THE SOUTHERN TIDEWATER AND PIEDMONT

Allan Kulikoff

ENVIRONMENT, MIGRATION, AND SOUTHERN CULTURES

THE TIDEWATER SOUTH, or the Atlantic coastal plain, stretches from Maryland south through Georgia. The piedmont South, located west of the tidewater area in the same states, comprises the hill country just east of the Appalachian mountain chain. The warm climate, generally long growing season from late winter to late fall, fertile soils, rainfall of forty or more inches a year, and flat to hilly topography of these regions made them ideal places for Europeans to establish market-oriented family farms and slave- or servant-based plantations. For three centuries after the initial colonization of these areas, in the early seventeenth century, an international market demand for such commodities as tobacco, rice, and cotton structured the tidewater and piedmont cultures.

The English first conquered the coastal plain from Maryland to Georgia, then slowly penetrated into the hillier piedmont areas. As soon as the Indians had been dispossessed, white planters and their black slaves rushed to "improve" the rich lands the Indians had vacated. While most early white settlers of the tidewater were English, a substantial minority of the first white colonizers of the piedmont were Scots, Irish, or Germans, who formed separate and often culturally distinct communities. By the early nineteenth century, nearly the entire tidewater and piedmont regions were fully settled, and white families began leaving for the more fertile and sometimes cheaper frontier lands west of the Appalachian Mountains in the Mississippi River valley and the Old Southwest. Between 1790 and 1860 some 660,000 whites over the age of ten left the states surrounding the Chesapeake and the Carolinas for Kentucky, Tennessee, and the Deep South.

In order to produce cash crops, or "staples," for the English and European markets, the tidewater and piedmont farmers and planters needed numerous field hands. The more laborers farmers put into crops like rice and cotton, the more the output per person could climb. To gain these economies of scale, planters searched for a permanent, productive labor force. Because free white men wanted and could usually procure their own farms, the growers turned to unfree labor—especially slaves—to produce tobacco, rice, cotton, and sugar. The need for slavery thus originated in the economic development of the region, which was made possible by its climate and soils. Even after the demise of slavery, the continued production of staples still required massive numbers of subservient workers, a need filled by sharecroppers (semiproletarian workers) and wage laborers in southern cotton fields. Only with the invention of mechanical harvesting equipment did the ongoing need for labor decline.

The labor needs of planters, predicated upon an international demand for southern staples, structured the forced migration of Africans and their African American descendants. Between 1700 and 1775, tidewater and piedmont planters brought over some two hundred thousand Africans and set them to work in their tobacco and rice fields. As the black population began to grow through its own natural increase, the demand for African slaves in the tidewater area diminished. At the same time, however, planters living in the newer, piedmont frontiers of South Carolina and Georgia, who owned fewer slaves, demanded continued access to "new Negroes" from Africa to raise production. These planters imported one hundred thousand slaves from Africa between 1790 and 1808, when the African slave trade was ended. After its abolition, southern planters procured slaves through natural increase, inheritance, and a vigorous intraregional slave trade. Between 1790 and 1860, as many as one million African American slaves, most of whom were born in the Chesapeake states and

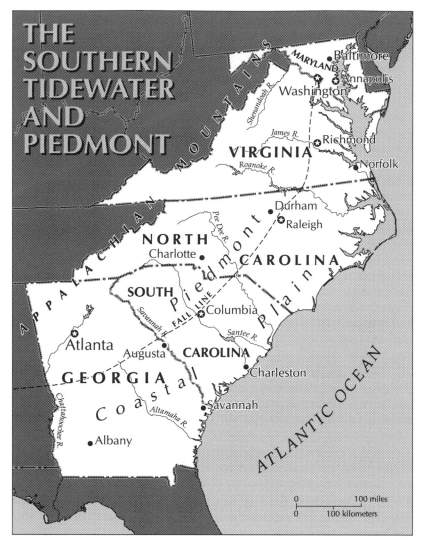

THE SOUTHERN TIDEWATER AND PIEDMONT

Map 1

North Carolina, were forced to move from their original homes to plantations in Georgia, Kentucky, Tennessee, the Deep South, and Texas.

The labor needs of tidewater and piedmont planters created and sustained a biracial society. As early as 1750, two-fifths of the population of the tidewater and piedmont regions was black, nearly all of whom were enslaved. Despite heavy migration out of the region by slaves, this proportion of blacks grew slightly over the next century. The part of the population enslaved varied from one-third in the general farming communities of piedmont North Carolina to between two-fifths and one-half of the populace of tobacco counties and fully nine-tenths of the people along the rice-growing coast of

South Carolina and Georgia (see Map 2). After the emancipation of slaves in 1865, some black families moved to the region's growing cities, but few migrated north, and in 1900 two-fifths of the population of the region was still African American. The two great migrations to northern cities, between 1914 and 1929 and 1940 and 1960, profoundly changed the composition of the tidewater and piedmont populations. By as early as 1950, only a quarter of the region's people—less than a fifth of the populace in Maryland and Virginia—remained black.

It is within the context of these economic and environmental constraints that the origins and development of the white and black southern cultures should be seen. Southern gentlemen and large planters became accustomed to having absolute rule over their slaves and expected to govern poorer whites as well. Gentlemen came to dominate government, the church, and the economy. The small farmers or yeomen acquiesced to this rule as long as the gentlemen protected their property and considered racial superiority to be more important than class differences. Slavery and the later sharecropping and debt peonage notwithstanding, blacks sustained a vibrant African American culture based upon family ties and Afro-Protestant faith.

Staple production and slavery distinguished the South from the North, especially after the northern states had freed their slaves. Whereas cities grew rapidly in the Northeast, city populations stagnated in the Chesapeake states and the Carolinas, which had been settled at roughly the same time as the Northeast. Industry, canals, and railroads proliferated in the Northeast during the antebellum era but appeared only slowly in the South. In the tidewater and piedmont regions the great surge in industrialization and railroad construction took place

after the Civil War, when northern and indigenous entrepreneurs strove to create there a modern, capitalist economy.

The changing impact of staple production and black labor on the history of the southern tidewater and piedmont areas can be seen in an overview from colonization to the post–World War II era. After the initial colonization of the region, which took place from the early seventeenth to the late eighteenth centuries, whites and blacks formed their own communities and created discrete subcultures. Then as cotton and slavery spread together during the first half of the nineteenth century, white planters built a precapitalist society that ultimately struggled against the North for dominance. Once the slaves were emancipated, new labor systems consistent with the adoption of capitalist wage labor developed, which made it possible for a new belt of southern industry to emerge in the piedmont Carolinas and Georgia. The era from World War I to the 1960s saw greater change in tidewater and piedmont society than had occurred there since the initial white occupation of the land. Not only did outmigration to northern cities reduce the proportion of blacks in the area's population, but the mechanization of agriculture and the growth of southern cities sustained a new civil rights movement that transformed racial relations.

COLONIZATION AND ECONOMIC DEVELOPMENT: 1607–1770

The first English settlers came to Virginia to make an easy fortune by sending goods that were in great demand—gold, plants to make dyes, iron, furs, pitch or tar—back to England. These overwhelmingly male, young, unskilled, and adventurous settlers were hardly the kind to found agricultural settlements. They discovered no riches but faced instead starvation, epidemics, and hostile Indians. Lacking both the skills and the desire to grow their own food, they relied on getting it from the Indians.

The Indians fed and clothed themselves by having the women grow corn and the men hunt. They were able to subsist and even produced small surpluses, but they grew insufficient corn to feed the hungry English settlers, who numbered just over a thousand in 1622. By 1617 the English settlers had discovered that tobacco, grown in small quantities by the Indians, was Virginia's gold. The

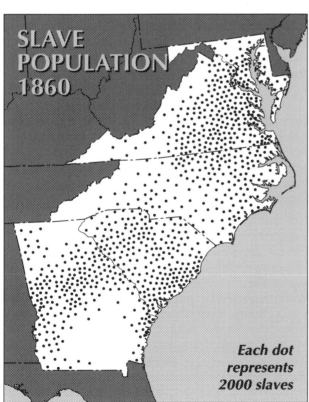

SLAVE POPULATION 1860

Each dot represents 2000 slaves

Source: Hilliard, *Atlas of Antebellum Southern Agriculture*

Map 2

English wanted the profits tobacco would bring so much that they forced Indians to grow corn for them so that they could concentrate on growing tobacco, which set the Indians on the warpath in 1622. The Indians killed about a quarter of the settler population before ultimately suffering defeat.

The colonists learned how to grow tobacco from the Indians, but they put this knowledge to vastly different uses. Whereas the Indians consumed tobacco locally, using it in their religious ceremonies, the English exported tobacco to England and Europe, hoping to make great fortunes. With the colonists' knowledge of tobacco cultivation so low and demand abroad so high, tobacco prices boomed in the 1620s. But as the settlers came to learn the best tobacco-growing techniques, their productivity rose and as a result prices fell, ending the boom. Nonetheless, planters continued to grow tobacco readily with only family labor, and small landowners produced substantial quantities of tobacco throughout the colonial era. Because each person could cultivate only a certain number of plants, however, each additional laborer meant more income, an incentive for planters to buy indentured servants or slaves.

Thus, from the 1630s to the 1670s planters bought thousands of servants. To repay their passage to the Chesapeake region, indentured servants worked five to seven years for their master, clearing land, building houses, and cultivating corn and tobacco. Labor discipline was often harsh; masters sought to gain the maximum amount of labor from their often sickly servants before giving them their freedom. Most servants were male, but nearly all the white women who immigrated were under an indenture agreement. Like the male servants, the women also cultivated tobacco. Every servant hoped eventually to become a planter or a planter's wife, but many died before completing their term of indenture. At the end of the term, a servant received what was known as "freedom dues"—an ax and a hoe for tobacco cultivation, and three barrels of corn, which was not enough to rent a farm with. A former servant who lived would eventually acquire sufficient capital to buy land. Every planter wanted servants, but the English supply of labor declined after 1670 just as the number of planters was increasing.

Once the supply of servants declined, the tobacco planters turned to African slaves. At first they imported slaves from the West Indies, but by the 1690s African slave traders began to call at ports on the Chesapeake. By 1710 the vast majority of unfree laborers in the region were of African origin. Owners found great advantages in using slaves rather than servants. They not only gained lifetime labor from their slaves but owned the children their slave women bore and could buy or sell them as they saw fit. However, the Africans rebelled at their new status, often running away or refusing to cultivate tobacco.

The first settlers in the Carolina low country, like those who went to the Chesapeake region, expected to produce staple crops for distant markets. During the 1670s they arrived from Barbados, where the scarcity of land made farming difficult. Many of them owned slaves, who they brought with them to farm their Carolina lands. At first, in lieu of a profitable cash crop, these white settlers turned to herding. In the open range of the early Carolina country the hogs and cattle that the settlers brought with them multiplied rapidly, producing an abundant supply of meat to export to the West Indies. Although the white settlers had little experience at herding on open ranges, some of their African slaves had participated in similar activities at home. Whites generally thought herding beneath them and gave their slave cowboys a great deal of independence, letting them operate on the range with only minimal interference.

The slaves living on the South Carolina frontier in fact performed a wide variety of tasks. The early South Carolina blacks were indeed enslaved, but their labor was so necessary to the survival of the colony that they achieved substantial autonomy, sometimes living separately or carrying weapons. Because white artisans were scarce, some blacks worked as craftsmen making barrels, laying bricks, painting houses, cobbling shoes, or building houses. Others labored in forest crafts, felling trees or producing pitch or tar. Blacks transported goods to market in canoes and even on occasion traded with the Indians or sold liquor at the Charles Town market.

Throughout the late seventeenth and early eighteenth centuries, South Carolina planters searched for a marketable staple product that was in demand in Europe to increase their wealth. Planters experimented with rice, but they had no experience with that crop. Many of the slaves, however, had grown rice in Africa and understood the crop. Whether willingly or under duress, they taught their masters the proper way to produce rice, thus ensuring the prosperity of the colony. Rice exports skyrocketed from 1.5 million pounds in 1710 to 20 million in 1730. Heavy demand in Europe made rice planters the richest men in early America.

Rice cultivation was both capital- and labor-intensive. Planters required hundreds of pounds sterling to establish a plantation and many enslaved workers to operate it—but these high investments yielded great profits. Planters not only plowed their profits into building magnificent plantations but also into importing slaves to increase their wealth even more. Between 1700 and 1740, South Carolina planters brought over thirty-two thousand Africans (in 1740 only twenty thousand whites lived in the colony) and imported another sixty thousand by 1775.

The growth of rice cultivation strengthened the slave system and reduced the precarious privileges slaves had enjoyed. With rice the most valuable commodity produced in the colony, black cowboys and artisans found themselves having to work in the rice fields, ending their autonomy. The diminished opportunities for native-born South Carolina slaves, combined with the importing of thousands of Angolans hostile to enslavement, led plantation slaves to greater resistance, which culminated in the 1740 Stono Rebellion. This uprising, one of the most serious slave rebellions in American history, saw some twenty-five whites and thirty-five slaves killed.

The demands of rice cultivation, the expertise that slaves had in it, and the difficulty of finding whites to supervise slaves combined to create a "task" system of slave management. Each slave was expected to complete a daily series of tasks like hoeing or ditching on a quarter to three-quarters of an acre. The task system reduced management costs by letting each slave either work independently or cooperate with other slaves. Slaves gained more labor autonomy with this system than they had in tobacco or cotton cultivation. Often these tasks took an entire day, but if the slaves finished their tasks early, the rest of the time was theirs. They could relax or, more likely, raise crops for their own subsistence or for trade. Naturally, they resisted any attempt to impose more stringent oversight. Once the task system was in place, by the mid eighteenth century, it remained relatively unchanged until 1865.

THE ORIGINS OF
SOUTHERN CULTURES

Distinctive class cultures emerged during the eighteenth century from the interaction of master and slave, African and Anglo, husband and wife, yeoman and planter. Social classes agreed with or struggled against each other within interrelated social institutions. Tidewater and piedmont residents, free and enslaved alike, lived in households headed by a white master and husband. These income-pooling production units not only sold staple goods on the international commodity markets but also grew most of the food needed by the white family and its slaves. Hierarchical patterns of authority quickly developed: white women who were subservient to their husbands in turn gained authority over their children and the slave women their husbands owned. Beyond the household, the county government, with its local justices, court days, and militia muster days, along with the parish of the local Anglican church, established the relations between white yeomen and gentlemen. Planters large and small took their disputes over debts and credits, roads, and enclosures to the local court; parish vestries ran the parishes and in Virginia even allocated poor relief. The Regulator riots of the 1760s show the importance of county institutions. In the North Carolina riots rebels attacked unfair justice; in South Carolina they demanded more efficient county government to repel Indians and control marauding white gangs.

In the early tidewater strong households developed slowly. Not only were there far more men than women in these societies, making marriage and household formation difficult, but malaria weakened immigrant whites, ensuring that epidemic diseases like influenza became more virulent. In the Chesapeake area a third of the infants died before their first birthday, and those who reached adulthood usually lived only another twenty-five years or so. With adults dying so young, most children lost one or both parents, making orphanages and complex families—made up of stepparents, half-siblings, stepsiblings, and siblings in the same household—quite common. Native-born whites had somewhat greater resistance to malaria, and after immigration declined in the late seventeenth century life expectancy rose and the proportion of simple nuclear families increased. More patriarchal households, with authoritarian husbands, emerged among the landholding families once life expectancy improved.

Gentlemen, who built their wealth on the labor of blacks and the sale of rice or tobacco, came to rule over increasingly large numbers of slaves, especially in the South Carolina low country. Their wives ran large households by directing the labor of slave women in the kitchen, dairy, and garden.

Gentlemen sustained their rule over white society by serving as justices of the peace and colonial legislators and by lending money to white yeomen. With the increased income and leisure that slave labor provided, they built large mansions, bought luxury goods like silverware, watches, or fine china from England, sent their children to private schools and colonial colleges, and formed literary and social clubs.

In staple-producing areas the yeomanry were the majority of the white populace. Like gentlemen, they sent tobacco or, less often, rice to international markets. They grew corn and reared cattle and hogs for their own subsistence and sometimes took up crafts to supplement their farm income. They were often wealthy enough to buy land and a slave or two, but they acquiesced to the rule of gentlemen, hoping to find in them patrons to expand their operations. On occasion the children of the wealthier yeomen even married into the gentry. As best they could, yeomen emulated the culture of the aristocracy, as can be seen most clearly in the patriarchal households they tried to maintain. Despite the greater production that might come from deploying their wives in the tobacco, corn, or rice fields, they generally left the production of staples to white men and slaves.

In contrast, in the farming districts of piedmont Carolina and northern Maryland yeomen—the vast majority of the population in those areas—could not compete with the slave-owners in growing staple crops, for they lacked access to credit and sometimes transportation to markets. Yeomen there lived as subsistence farmers, producing most of the family's food, typically corn, pork, wheat, and sweet potatoes. But they did sell some wheat and drove large herds of pigs and cows to distant markets. Families performed all the farm labor, because few of them owned slaves. While the fathers and sons cultivated the field crops, the mothers and daughters carried water, cooked, cultivated the vegetable garden, and tended the cows. These farmers were not entirely self-sufficient in food, nor did they have enough labor at planting and harvest time. Neighbors therefore cooperated at such times, exchanged labor and produce, and joined together in such activities as logrolling, corn shucking, or barn and house raisings. Farmers insisted that their neighbors fence in their crops but leave unrestricted access to the rest of their lands. They could then graze their cattle and let their hogs run wild, gathering them only as needed for food or for the long drive to market.

By the 1770s, slaves everywhere had created their own African American culture, which was based upon slave families and their own form of Afro-Protestantism, but the character of that culture varied greatly from the tobacco-growing to the rice-growing areas. On tobacco plantations slaves were divided among the main farm and various outlying quarters. Roughly six slaves worked on a given quarter. The masters generally avoided the cabins and quarters, which allowed slaves to create their own family networks and devise their own quarter communities somewhat freed from white control. Such slave communities were even more important where rice grew on the Carolina coast, nine-tenths of the people there being black by 1790. Half the slaves on tobacco plantations lived on units with twenty or more slaves, mostly in units of twenty to fifty. In contrast, half the slaves in the low country resided on massive plantations with a hundred or more slaves.

From the outset of settlement to the 1760s, the established Anglican church dominated white religious life in the tidewater and piedmont areas. The parish church was a center of social life for both the gentry and the yeoman families. Church gatherings became the place for the gentry to plan social activities and talk politics and for the yeoman to show proper respect to their social superiors. The Anglican church failed, however, to reach slaves and many white yeomen families. Thus a series of revivals by Presbyterians (1750–1760) and Baptists (1760–1770) incorporated many from these groups into their more egalitarian churches, which took the spiritual equality of women and even slaves seriously and challenged such social aspects of the gentry as drinking and dancing. The Baptists gained adherents especially in piedmont Virginia, but the Baptist and Methodist denominations spread throughout the tidewater and piedmont regions in the 1780s and 1790s. Thereafter the Anglicans never regained their predominance; in 1850 three-quarters of the church seats in the tidewater and piedmont could be found in Baptist and Methodist churches.

THE DIFFUSION OF SLAVE ECONOMIES AND SOUTHERN CULTURES

The social matrix that had developed in the tidewater and piedmont areas by the mid eighteenth century persisted through the antebellum era, often in strengthened form. The emigration of potentially surplus white farmers and the poorer white families allowed those who remained in the tidewater and the older parts of the piedmont to perpetuate established eighteenth-century social relations. When they came, changes were often involuntary, and social relations become even more intensely patriarchal, hierarchical, and race conscious than before the Revolution. A majority of farmers still grew staple crops, including cotton now, often with slave labor. Gentlemen, now called planters in this more republican age, retained their power over slaves, yeomen, and poor whites.

The reception of the northern bourgeois cult of domesticity among southern white women illustrates the strength of conservative social relations. Southern white women read domestic tracts and sentimental novels as did their northern sisters; southern clergymen likewise preached temperance and urged companionate marriages much in the spirit of their northern counterparts. Yet midlevel southern white women, unlike those in the north, gained neither an enhanced position in the household nor greater moral authority. They lacked the power northern women had achieved in their evangelical churches and voluntary associations. And however much they complained about having large families, they failed to join northern women in trying to limit fertility.

The white yeomanry, who had fought in the Revolution, afterward demanded greater democratic rights for themselves, petitioning government on social and economic issues, standing for office themselves, and insisting upon the right of election as local officials. After 1800, political parties based upon platforms rather than the personalities of gentlemen restructured politics. Nearly all white men gained the right to vote. The emergence of political parties and the widening of the franchise to vote bent but did not break the control of the large planters over local and state politics. Local justices retained great power in their counties. The state did its part by continuing to protect the slave property of the largest planters against attack either internally within the region or, with increasing frequency, from the north.

For a brief moment in the 1780s and 1790s the slave society of the Chesapeake states threatened to unravel. Influenced by revolutionary ideology and religious egalitarianism, thousands of slaveowners in those states manumitted their slaves. Soon a small class of free black people appeared all over the region. Planters horrified at the bad example

free blacks set for those still enslaved soon restricted manumission, encouraged free blacks to move north, and strictly controlled the few who stayed. As a result, by 1850 a large class of free blacks could be found only in northern Maryland. In Virginia just one in ten blacks was free, and in the Carolinas and Georgia fewer than one in twenty-five had gained freedom.

The strong commitment of both planters and yeomen to slavery permitted Chesapeake-area whites to preserve the institution despite major changes in agriculture. For one, the demand for tobacco failed to keep pace with the number of laborers capable of growing it, especially after the French Revolution, when the market for snuff disappeared. The production of tobacco slowly vanished from most of the tidewater area, and by 1800 Chesapeake-region tobacco was grown only in southern Maryland and one part of the Virginia piedmont. Tobacco cultivation then moved west with settlers to Kentucky and Missouri. Unable now to market tobacco, its former growers improvised, using the slaves they needed but hiring out the rest to neighbors who had no slave labor of their own. Such a pattern of course distributed the labor among a greater number of white families but separated more black families.

Soon after the Revolution, the eighteenth-century small-farming districts of piedmont South Carolina and Georgia took up cotton production with slave labor, influenced by the growing demand for the fiber from English textile mills. During the late eighteenth and early nineteenth centuries, new inventions mechanized both spinning and weaving. English factories thus needed vast quantities of cotton fiber to operate efficiently, and factory owners turned to cotton producers in the southeastern states to supply this need.

The results of this demand can easily be seen. Before 1780, only small quantities of cotton were grown along the Carolina coast, which were used to spin and weave homespun cloth. Then a number of men, aware of English developments, searched for an efficient system to gin seed out of short-staple cotton fibers. Eli Whitney's 1793 invention of the cotton gin made possible commercial production of cotton for foreign markets. On the one hand, cotton planters and their slaves produced ever-increasing quantities of cotton, on the other, the demands of the textile mills required more and more workers in the cotton fields. Because cotton was more profitable than any other crop, cotton planters could easily buy slaves or take their own with them when they moved to piedmont cotton plantations.

The large antebellum cotton plantation households in the piedmont were complex, including the master and mistress, their children, a white overseer, and at least twenty slaves, of all ages. The planters served multiple roles: as plantation manager, directing slave labor and deciding when and how to plant crops; as master of discipline, in charge both of incentives like small sums of cash and of whipping slaves; and as legal head of the household, owner of all the family's property, even that brought into the marriage by his wife. Most planters did no agricultural labor themselves. If some treated their slaves well, others were violent, but even good masters sold or bequeathed slaves, thereby breaking up families. The mistress managed her house servants and directed the cooking, cleaning, child care, and gardening. However, she did not actually carry out any of these functions, leaving them to her slaves. The relationship between mistress and female servants could be a close one, but the mistress often whipped her slaves.

At any given time about half the slaves in piedmont Georgia and South Carolina lived on large plantations, and many more had lived on one at some time in their lives. Nearly all slaves—men, women, and children as young as nine or ten—worked as field hands growing cotton, corn, and vegetables and tending livestock. On the large cotton plantations field hands were divided into plowing, planting, weeding, or chopping gangs. Young adult men, who were the strongest laborers, worked on the plow gang, the most difficult task, while the women and children weeded the crop. Everyone joined the harvest gang. The masters divided up the pickers by age and sex, separating the most productive men from the women and children, who came along in the "trash" gangs that followed the initial pickers. They sometimes set different harvest gangs one against another, offering the most productive group such incentives as extra cash or consumer goods but punishing those who failed to pick a daily quota set by the master or overseer.

Most large planters hired a white overseer, who was usually a young man trying to accumulate capital to afford his own farm. The overseer directed the daily activities of slaves in the cotton fields, trying to carry out the master's orders for high production and a stable labor force. Meanwhile, the slaves sought to slow the pace of labor and resisted the overseer, despite his power to whip them.

Slaves on cotton plantations worked from sunup to sundown except on Sundays, but in the remaining hours they could make a life for themselves: family, kinship, and religion became intertwined elements of slave culture. Even though the interstate slave trade broke up slave families, in the cotton South not only did nuclear families live together on large plantations but after a few years extended family networks of grandparents, cousins, uncles, and aunts reappeared. These kinfolk cooked and prayed together and celebrated holidays as family events. On Sundays they listened to their black preacher, whose message likely concealed ideas of equality and hope.

Fewer than half of all slaveholders in the cotton-producing piedmont owned as many as ten slaves. Other farmers owned just a few, or none at all, and grew far less cotton. The poorer whites either remained subservient to the large planters or emigrated, often in family and community groups, from the tidewater or piedmont regions to upcountry and mountain areas. Small general farmers or tobacco farmers did, however, gain a foothold in much of tidewater Virginia and in North Carolina. These farmers survived by practicing only the most tried-and-true forms of agriculture, much as had their colonial antecedents. They not only grew corn and raised hogs but produced their own cloth at home. The spinning of yarn and weaving of homespun cloth persisted far longer among the poorer southern farmers than anywhere else in the country.

Because the tidewater and piedmont areas remained committed to slavery, many fewer cities developed there than in parts of the Northeast and Old Northwest that were settled about the same time. The only large city in the region was Baltimore, which was located on the edge of a northern free-farming area. Charleston, one of the major cities in the colonial era, lost ground to newer northern cities after the Revolution. Southern towns remained small commercial centers rather than growing manufacturing cities. Although planters and farmers did employ artisans, they resisted the development of a wage-labor force. The planters refused to permit their slaves to work in factories, fearing they would thus gain too much economic autonomy. And they distrusted white labor, wishing to avoid the creation of a class of white dependents who might even make common cause with the slaves.

Moreover, the home market for manufactured goods remained small in the tidewater and piedmont. The vast majority of the inhabitants there were either slaves or whites too poor to have much disposable income. The wealthy planters often imported their manufactured goods from New York or London. Nor were southern manufacturers willing to solicit business from outside the South. Thus, without either a home market or markets outside the South, manufacturing atrophied in the tidewater and remained small in the piedmont, despite vigorous campaigns in both the 1830s and 1850s to establish factories. The piedmont's cotton planters sent their cotton to be manufactured in New England or England, not Augusta or Charleston.

EMANCIPATION AND THE GROWTH OF WAGE LABOR

The Civil War brought revolutionary social change to the southern tidewater and piedmont. The emancipation of slaves destroyed the old social order but was replaced by a new, equally oppressive regime based upon the wage labor of blacks and poor whites and the rise of an indigenous class of rural and urban capitalists, though this system developed only after long conflict. By the late nineteenth century, nearly all blacks in the tidewater and piedmont region were either working land for a share of the crop or laboring for wages. At the same time, the destruction caused by the war and the eventual decline of cotton prices impoverished many white yeomen and poorer farmers, who turned to the growing industries in the piedmont for subsistence.

Emancipation brought freedmen "nothing but freedom." They gained the right to a secure family life, the privilege of educating their children if they could find the money to do so, and the freedom to contract for wages, but little else. Everywhere, however, freed blacks wanted to become independent farmers able to regulate their own labor. They argued that their uncompensated work under slavery entitled them to "forty acres and a mule." The blacks could not fulfill these aspirations. The former slave-owners wanted to reestablish plantation discipline, a goal the freed slaves adamantly opposed. The Freedmen's Bureau, set up by the federal government in 1865 to guarantee black rights, agreed, but its officials usually wanted blacks to work as wage laborers in much the fashion as poor northern men.

The level of independence that blacks could achieve in the late nineteenth century depended upon the crop in question. Many former slaves in the Chesapeake states procured small quantities of land, but it served only to supplement their pro-

ceeds from leased or sharecropped land or wage labor. In the cotton piedmont the freed slaves reached an uneasy accommodation with their former masters. They moved off the old plantations onto their own farms, but they worked the land as sharecroppers, receiving a half share of the cotton they raised. These neoplantations, prevalent in the cotton South from 1870 to about 1935, permitted a planter to maintain control over the crop while giving blacks familial and some economic autonomy. In the rice country of tidewater South Carolina and Georgia, former slaves succeeded with regularity in gaining land for themselves. With land of their own they often refused to work in the rice fields or, if they did, engaged in strikes for better working conditions. The rice planters, who lacked capital to hire wage laborers and keep up their operations, let their plantations atrophy. After 1890 little rice was produced in the low country.

Whites, whatever their class, viewed the blacks' aspirations with great alarm. In a society where the economic differences between poor white and poor black families could be small, the white ruling class insisted that the social distinctions be strengthened. Until the end of the century, blacks retained some political rights and the support of northern whites, so southern white men of substance turned to violence to control blacks they considered unruly. In May 1866 whites organized the first Ku Klux Klan to terrorize successful black farmers, and lynched black men thought to be too friendly toward white women or unwilling to appear subservient to whites. Then once the white redeemers had deprived blacks of the right to vote, they imposed a new racial etiquette that lasted until the 1950s. Public accommodations and schools became formally segregated, and blacks had to be deferential toward all whites, especially women.

Most blacks found few opportunities for advancement in either the tidewater or the piedmont. Once Reconstruction governments had been replaced, the education of their children diminished: where in the late 1860s and early 1870s taxes of whites had supported black schools, by 1900 the taxes of blacks were supporting white schools. To avoid the poverty that sharecropping ensured blacks often moved to towns and cities, constituting, for instance, two-fifths of the population of both Richmond and Atlanta by 1900. There they quickly fell into the lowest-paid working-class types of urban jobs. Some 360,000 blacks left the region between 1870 and 1900, most moving to the newer southwestern states of Texas, Oklahoma, and Arkansas, where their opportunities proved only marginally better than at home. Lacking knowledge about opportunities in the North, they rarely left the South.

The destruction of slavery had a substantial impact upon the security of white yeoman families. In the South Carolina and Georgia piedmont numerous yeomen took up cotton cultivation after the Civil War to take advantage of high prices, but when prices dropped they were so heavily in debt that they could not return to the proven forms of agriculture they had practiced before the war. The planters, who were now transformed into renters and capitalists, no longer required the support of poorer whites to sustain the racial system. Therefore they increasingly challenged yeomen's prerogatives and successfully lobbied to enclose the open range, which further reduced the yeomen's security. Many small landowners thus found themselves forced into tenancy or sharecropping. A political alliance with blacks might have mitigated this decline, but the racist attitudes of most yeomen and poor whites precluded such interclass solidarity.

The dispossession of white farmers from the late-nineteenth-century Carolina and Georgia piedmont created a surplus army of white families available for urban or industrial employment. At the same time, the descendants of piedmont planters, who were sometimes aided by northern capitalists, began to invest in manufacturing by building cotton textile mills in the region and tobacco-processing factories in piedmont Virginia. White migrant men, women, and children flocked to work in the newly built mills, thus encouraging the construction of further mills and turning textile villages into mill towns.

The white urban migrants brought their yeoman culture with them. Valuing their independence, at first many of them viewed factory work as only a supplement to agriculture and returned periodically to the farm. Not surprisingly, they attempted to resist the imposition of a time-oriented labor discipline so alien to their traditional way of life. Sustained by their belief in the sinfulness of humankind, they remained members of increasingly conservative Baptist and Methodist churches. These churches, transported to mill villages, not only provided an alternative society away from the mill but also promised redemption in another life.

THE TWENTIETH CENTURY

Although the emancipation of the slaves set into motion profound changes in the tidewater and piedmont South, many factors linked the region to its past. Like the rest of the South, it remained a biracial, agrarian society lagging behind the rest of the nation in development and income—in 1900 the per capita income in the region was less than half that of the country as a whole. Three-fifths of its people lived on farms in that year, whereas fewer than one-third of the populace did so outside the South. Most of the rest resided in small villages: one-sixth of the tidewater and piedmont population lived in towns of more than twenty-five hundred people, but outside the South half lived in places as large. With the region's wages and opportunities for industrial employment still relatively low, immigrants, who arrived in America in large numbers between 1880 and 1914, avoided the area. Immigrant households constituted only one in twenty people in the region, although they represented one in three for the country as a whole.

During the middle half of the twentieth century, tidewater and piedmont society became thoroughly transformed. Three interrelated and sequential changes that were behind this shift deserve particular attention. The first is the agricultural mechanization and changes in national farm policy that reduced the labor requirements for staple agriculture. These reduced demands for labor combined with the development of a national labor market to impel rapid rural to urban migration, which ultimately depopulated tidewater and piedmont farms and villages. Especially in the growing cities and towns, blacks were sustained by these structural changes and their own abiding egalitarian, evangelical religion to challenge white hegemony, ending the oppressive racial system that had characterized the entire South since the seventeenth century.

New Deal agricultural policies, along with the mechanization of staple production, led to rapid reductions in the farm population and the relocation of staple production out of the region. To reduce existing surpluses of agricultural commodities and raise their prices, New Deal legislation mandated payments to landowners for acreage they kept out of production. Especially in the cotton areas, landlords responded by evicting black sharecroppers and working their remaining land with wage laborers instead.

Mechanized production of staple crops completed the process. Highly mechanized rice production in Louisiana and Arkansas replaced plantations in tidewater Carolina and Georgia; by 1980 more than a third of all American rice was being grown in Arkansas, with most of the rest cultivated in Louisiana and California. The decline of both sharecropping and cotton cultivation in the southeastern piedmont can be traced to the invention of machinery for picking cotton. Once cotton-harvesting machines were perfected in the 1940s, the remaining sharecroppers were forced off the land, almost disappearing by 1960. Harvesting machines can be used most efficiently on flat, irrigated lands, so cotton cultivation disappeared from the Southeast. By the 1970s, most domestic cotton was being grown in arid, flat West Texas, New Mexico, Arizona, and California.

Changes in agriculture and new demands for labor in northern and midwestern cities led to massive movement from the rural tidewater and piedmont to northeastern and southern towns and cities by both whites and blacks, particularly during the 1914–1929 and 1940–1960 periods. Motivated by opportunities for unskilled and semi-skilled jobs in wartime industries and by the cutoff of foreign immigration, 161,000 tidewater and piedmont blacks moved to northeastern cities between October 1916 and May 1917 alone. The flood of migration within black and white families alike continued, especially after Congress restricted overseas immigration in 1924. In all, 1.4 million people left the region betwen 1910 and 1930. The growth of war industries also impelled migration in the 1940s, but the mechanization of cotton supported even greater movement, despite the decline of opportunities in the urban North. In all, between 1940 and 1960 more than a million people left the Carolinas and Georgia for other regions.

Migration and the urban development of the tidewater and piedmont areas changed the face of the region, transforming its social structure. Some rural areas, especially those near the coast, suffered depopulation. By 1960 half the region's people were living in towns and cities of more than twenty-five hundred, compared with one-sixth in 1900. A third were in metropolitan areas of one hundred thousand or more. Only one-sixth remained on farms. Emigration gave blacks an alternative to the hierarchical, racially segregated society of the South. Not only were blacks in tidewater and piedmont cities more isolated from daily contact with and subservience to whites than those in rural areas, but all knew about the greater freedom those who moved north enjoyed.

As agrarian change and emigration weakened whites' control, southern blacks began to demand the abolition of segregation and greater citizenship rights. The tidewater and piedmont blacks, like those who lived in the Deep South, supported the civil rights movement. The sit-in strategy, for instance, aimed at desegregating restaurants and other public facilities, began in 1960 at Greensboro, in the North Carolina piedmont, before spreading to other parts of the South. White middle-class business and political leaders typically responded with an "all reasonable speed" evasion, claiming that their communities were not yet ready for black equality, or with massive resistance. When the federal courts ordered desegregation, local authorities in Prince Edward and Norfolk counties in Virginia closed schools rather than desegregate them. By the late 1970s, after more than two decades of legal action, federal civil rights laws, and nonviolent resistance by blacks, most public institutions in tidewater and piedmont cities and suburbs had peaceably desegregated, even to the extent of supporting the busing of schoolchildren to ensure school integration.

The civil rights movement brought into being a truly New South, with a new and vigorous bourgeoisie, both white and black. Northern industrialists, who had long avoided the South while its racial turmoil continued, now rushed to the region to take advantage of its mild climate, made livable in summer by air conditioning, and prevalent low wages. Then as economic conditions improved, managers and professionals moved from the Northeast to the urban South. Numerous blacks whose parents and grandparents had earlier migrated to northern cities were among them. Prosperous enclaves began to appear all over the piedmont, notably in the Virginia suburbs outside Washington, the Raleigh-Durham and Charlotte metropolitan areas of North Carolina, and around Atlanta. The social structure of these places, with their prosperous wealthy and middle classes and depressed ghettoes filled with black underclass families, now resembled northern cities more than any earlier South.

However new late-twentieth-century urban society in the tidewater and piedmont region might appear to be, links between the contemporary region and its historical past abound. The gradual disappearance of black farmers notwithstanding, today the rural tidewater and piedmont area remains biracial, with significant minorities of black people. Outside the metropolitan South, and particularly in still-rural tidewater regions of the Carolinas and the rural piedmont, subsistence and staple agriculture, older forms of racial etiquette, and evangelical and fundamentalist religion flourish among both whites and blacks.

REGIONALISM AND REGIONAL SUBCULTURES

BIBLIOGRAPHY

General Works

Boles, John B., and Evelyn Thomas Nolen, eds. *Interpreting Southern History: Historiographical Essays in Honor of Sanford W. Higginbotham* (1987).

Fox-Genovese, Elizabeth, and Eugene D. Genovese. *Fruits of Merchant Capital: Slavery and Bourgeois Property in the Rise and Expansion of Capitalism* (1983).

Gray, Lewis Cecil. *History of Agriculture in the Southern United States to 1860* (1941).

Wilson, Charles Reagan, and William Ferris, eds. *Encyclopedia of Southern Culture* (1989).

Colonial Tidewater and Piedmont

Kulikoff, Allan. *Tobacco and Slaves: The Development of Southern Cultures in the Chesapeake, 1680–1800* (1986).

Merrens, Harry Roy. *Colonial North Carolina in the Eighteenth Century: A Study in Historical Geography* (1964).

Morgan, Edmund S. *American Slavery, American Freedom: The Ordeal of Colonial Virginia* (1975).

Sobel, Mechal. *The World They Made Together: Black and White Values in Eighteenth-Century Virginia* (1987).

Tate, Thad W., and David L. Ammerman, eds. *The Chesapeake in the Seventeenth Century: Essays on Anglo-American Society* (1979).

Wood, Peter H. *Black Majority: Negroes in Colonial South Carolina from 1670 Through the Stono Rebellion* (1974).

Antebellum Tidewater and Piedmont

Ayers, Edward L., and John C. Willis, eds. *The Edge of the South: Life in Nineteenth-Century Virginia* (1991).

Ford, Lacy K., Jr. *Origins of Southern Radicalism: The South Carolina Upcountry, 1800–1860* (1988).

Fox-Genovese, Elizabeth. *Within the Plantation Household: Black and White Women of the Old South* (1988).

Genovese, Eugene D. *The Political Economy of Slavery: Studies in the Economy and Society of the Slave South* (1965; rev. ed. 1989).

———. *Roll, Jordan, Roll: The World the Slaves Made* (1974).

Hahn, Steven. *The Roots of Southern Populism: Yeomen Farmers and the Transformation of the Georgia Upcountry, 1850–1890* (1983).

Hilliard, Sam Bowers. *Atlas of Antebellum Southern Agriculture* (1984).

Postbellum Tidewater and Piedmont

Foner, Eric. *Reconstruction: America's Unfinished Revolution, 1863–1877* (1988).

Goodwyn, Lawrence. *Democratic Promise: The Populist Moment in America* (1976).

Hall, Jacqueline Dowd, James Leloudis, Robert Korstad, Mary Murphy, Lu Ann Jones, and Christopher B. Daly. *Like a Family: The Making of a Southern Cotton Mill World* (1987).

Jones, Jacqueline. *Labor of Love, Labor of Sorrow: Black Women, Work, and the Family from Slavery to the Present* (1985).

Kousser, J. Morgan. *The Shaping of Southern Politics: Suffrage Restriction and the Establishment of the One-Party South, 1880–1910* (1974).

Twentieth-Century Tidewater and Piedmont

Chafe, William H. *Civilities and Civil Rights: Greensboro, North Carolina, and the Black Struggle for Equality* (1980).

Kirby, Jack Temple. *Rural Worlds Lost: The American South, 1920–1960* (1987).

Mann, Susan Archer. *Agrarian Capitalism in Theory and Practice* (1990).

Piven, Frances Fox, and Richard A. Cloward. *Regulating the Poor: The Functions of Public Welfare* (1971).

SEE ALSO **Slavery**; and various essays in the section "**Ethnic and Racial Subcultures.**"

APPALACHIA

John Alexander Williams

A CENTURY AND a quarter ago Will Wallace Harney wrote of Appalachia as "a strange land and a peculiar people" ("A Strange Land and a Peculiar People," in W. K. McNeil, ed., *Appalachian Images,* pp. 45–58). The adjectives in this statement have been debated ever since, but the nouns remain constant: throughout the twentieth century, the term "Appalachia," originally a specialized term limited to geology, has referred both to a place and to a people. The problem of defining the region thus turns on finding a principle of definition that applies to both. This has been difficult. In fact, definitions have been so elusive that some experts have denied the existence of either place or people as definable entities. This viewpoint sees "Appalachia" as existing purely in the realm of ideas, signifying no more than a reflection of what is "other" within a configuration of values that the definer assigns to American society as a whole.

Partly this problem of definition stems from the fact that Appalachia, unlike the South, the West, New England, or other regions, cannot be defined in terms of boundaries drawn along existing state lines or studied by means of aggregate data or archives gathered on a state-by-state basis. Social scientists usually take historic political boundaries as givens, not worrying much about variations near the state lines that form a region's periphery. Appalachia, on the other hand, has only one political boundary—the jurisdictional bounds of the Appalachian Regional Commission (1964)—and this was clearly the product of congressional logrolling, taking in 397 counties in thirteen states extending from southern New York to northeastern Mississippi. Consequently, the boundaries of the region shift from one study to another, depending upon the interests and perspectives of the scholars involved. In addition, difficulties exist in data collection and comparability among studies, since the boundaries of census divisions and other data collection units slice across Appalachia along the state lines (see Map 1).

INTERPRETATIONS OF APPALACHIA

No matter how it is defined, Appalachia consists of all or most of West Virginia and parts of six to twelve additional states. Within each of those states, inhabitants of Appalachia complain of being their state's "backyard" or "lost provinces," of being in effect some other region's periphery. With the partial exception again of West Virginia, there are no state institutions in Appalachia whose territorial and service mandates are drawn in such a way as to define the region. This means there are no library stacks full of old-fashioned institutional and political histories or biographical compendiums or tomes of census data pertaining solely to Appalachia. It also means that Appalachia benefited little from the process by which historians "enclosed" state and local historical resources such as journals and archives and harnessed them to regional studies in the early twentieth century. Thus, although "Appalachian" is one of the oldest geographical names on present-day North American maps (dating from the de Soto expedition of 1539–1541) and although the environmental, cultural, and social patterns observable within the region during the late nineteenth and early twentieth centuries inspired influential regional studies in the disciplines of geology and geography, folklife, and sociology, historians' participation in the study of Appalachia lagged a full generation behind the maturation of southern, southwestern, New England, and "borderlands" studies. The absence of the traditional framework of regional historiography may account for the persistent feeling among some historians that Appalachia as a place is "unreal" (see Map 2).

Geologists and geographers, folklorists, and sociologists have had no such problem, however. Appalachian scholarship in these disciplines goes back a century or more and provides theoretical frameworks for historical research that regional historiography fails to provide. Geologists and geographers have tended to define the region in environmental terms, emphasizing physical and cultural features associated with mountainous terrain: limited availability of land suited to commercial agriculture, relatively short growing seasons, a lack of railroads and wagon roads, and related impediments to the development of the region's abundant timber, mineral, and agricultural resources. "A glance at the topographical map of the region shows the country to be devoted by nature to isolation and poverty," wrote geographer Ellen Churchill Semple in an influential essay of 1901. The region's people, she added, were prime examples "of the influence of physical environment, for nowhere else in modern times has that progressive Anglo-Saxon race been so long and so completely subjected to retarding conditions" ("The Anglo-Saxons of the Kentucky Mountains," in W. K. McNeil, ed., *Appalachian Images,* pp. 147, 174).

Yet despite their elaborate descriptions of these features and the underlying physiography, it was difficult for scholars in the earth sciences to attribute all the contrasts that separated Appalachia from the surrounding lowlands simply to the mountains themselves. For one thing, as their own studies showed, the Appalachian mountain system is not a unitary range like the Alps or the Rockies, with a central dividing ridge. Rather it is a series of adjacent physiographic provinces, running parallel in a roughly uniform direction from southwest to northeast, that are the product of distinct eras of geological history. Its central feature is not a ridge but a trough, the Great Appalachian Valley, which separates the peaks of the Blue Ridge, Black, and Great Smoky mountains on the east from those of the Allegheny and Cumberland mountains on the west. The valley is a great natural thoroughfare through the center of the Appalachian system but is itself crossed at right angles by the region's major rivers—the Susquehanna, Potomac, New-Kanawha, and Tennessee—whose rapid flow and rocky gorges offered poor transportation connections to the surrounding coastal and interior lowlands. Moreover, the two sets of mountain ranges flanking the central valley are themselves flanked by two plateaus, the Piedmont on the east and south and the Appalachian Plateau (locally more familiar as the Allegheny and Cumberland plateaus) on the west and north. The two plateaus share some features of the mountain and valley provinces—poor water transportation, for example—but they also offer striking and complex contrasts in other environmental features with neighboring provinces and with each other—for example, in the relative accessibility and productivity of agricultural land. Finally, none of the four physiographic provinces that make up the system is confined to southern Appalachia, where most of the contrasts that distinguished Appalachia from the rest of the country were observed and mapped in the late nineteenth century. The system as a whole embraces much of Pennsylvania and parts of Ohio, New York, and New Jersey. Thus, implicit in the analysis of the region by environmental determinists was a question that was difficult for their theories to answer: which environment? Isolation, poverty, poor transportation, and limited agriculture could be observed at some point nearly everywhere in the region at some time in its past, but there were few places where these attributes could both be observed completely and consistently over a sustained period of time and at the same time be explained by the broad physiographic features that the geologists and geographers mapped.

In spite of their formal commitments to "scientific" principles of environmental determinism, writers such as Semple relied heavily on a portrayal of Appalachian people and culture that in 1901 was primarily the product of a generation of impressionistic local color and travel writers, journalists, and educational and religious missionaries. While geologists and geographers constructed the place Appalachia, this latter group defined its people, cataloguing an inventory of behaviors and customs that set the people apart from what was then considered to be the American mainstream. The inventory inevitably began with speech patterns and personal comportment and included both expressive culture (notably vernacular log architecture, folk music and dance, handicrafts, woodcraft, superstitions, and religious practices) and social behavior, with emphasis on deviance such as illiteracy and an alleged propensity for feuding and brawling. To a significant extent, the image of Appalachian people so constructed was a Manichean one: a positive set of attributes associated with the quaint but stalwart mountaineer and a negative set identified with the ignorant and impoverished hillbilly.

Appalachia's image as a territory of cultural deviance was reiterated in dozens of popular magazine articles in the early twentieth century and by numerous two-reel "mountain melodramas," some filmed on location in the Blue Ridge Mountains and shown in movie theaters all over the country. The first book-length studies of the region both codified and challenged cultural stereotypes. Emma Bell Miles, Horace Kephart, and John C. Campbell were each of them outsiders who settled in the mountains and became intimately involved with their neighbors and informants. Their books offered many correctives to the distortions and oversimplifications of earlier writers, but essentially they confirmed at least the positive aspects of mountaineer culture and reiterated the preservationist concern that the attractive features of the culture would be overwhelmed and destroyed by the advance of urban-industrial society into the mountains. The folklorists and musicologists who succeeded these amateur scholars in the documentation of Appalachian culture amplified this concern and pursued their work with an urgent interest in authenticity and purity, certain that the expressive forms they were documenting were on the verge of degradation and destruction.

Environmental and cultural factors explained Appalachia's deviance to the satisfaction of geographers and folklorists during the 1920s and 1930s and also to missionaries and educators who worked in areas such as western North Carolina or north Georgia, where farming, logging, and the resort industry remained the chief features of the local economy. But the study of social relations was unavoidable to anyone who wanted to understand what was happening at this time in the Appalachian coalfields. The West Virginia Mine Wars (1912–1913 and 1920–1927), outbreaks of labor violence caused by coal operators' resistance to union organizing drives, along with other violent labor-capital confrontations in the Kentucky coalfields and in Tennessee, Georgia, and Carolina textile mill towns located in or near the mountains, drew further attention to the peculiarities of Appalachia and inspired a search among social scientists for the causes of the region's difficult and incomplete incorporation into the nation's economic system. To a large extent, this search took the form of community studies, both of communities passed over by industrialism and of those created by coal or other extractive industries. The result was an infusion of social realism into the study of Appalachia, realism echoed in the novels and poetry that appeared in the region after 1930, such as James Still's *River of Earth* (1940) and Harriette Arnow's *The Dollmaker* (1954).

A favorite genre of sociologists and anthropologists, community studies extended to every corner of Appalachia and dominated the region's scholarly literature from the 1930s well into the 1980s. Such studies focused on the problems of "adjustment" as Appalachian communities became enmeshed in the wage work and consumer spending of advanced industrial capitalism and as they underwent demographic change induced by migration. Sociologist James S. Brown, for example, studied the inhabitants of "Beech Creek," Kentucky, in 1940 and then followed his informants north to Ohio after World War II and studied their adjustment there as well as the fate of the diminished community back home. Anthropologist Patricia D. Beaver studied how a North Carolina mountain community coped with the decline of rural institutions such as country churches, schoolhouses, and stores, along with its first encounters with two new types of outsiders— the voluntarily poor idealistic and romantic young exurbanites who came into the mountains in order to come "back to the land" during the 1960s and 1970s and the rising tide of seasonal visitors drawn by the mushrooming tourist industry in the Blue Ridge districts nearest to big Sunbelt cities. The most controversial community study, Jack E. Weller's *Yesterday's People. Life in Contemporary Appalachia* (1965), analyzed a West Virginia community from the standpoint of a frustrated Presbyterian missionary from the Midwest. While acknowledging the reality of outside control of the region's resources and economy, Weller decided that the community's failure to acquire its fair share of the American dream was due ultimately to the culture of the people themselves—their fatalistic religion, their inward-looking orientation, and their resistance to change. Thus, for Weller, as for the romance writers and folklorists, Appalachia's economic peculiarities were grounded in its cultural peculiarities.

Collectively, the community studies portrayed a region of much greater complexity than that described by earlier writers. These Appalachian places featured immigrants as well as migrants; a class structure headed by absentee resource owners, with a small middle class composed of the owners' agents and clients as well as of prosperous farmers and a much larger working class of miners and millworkers, part-time and hardscrabble farmers, and dependents living on transfer payments or remittances from family members who had migrated to the urban Midwest and Sunbelt. Social scientists turned the region's characteristic forms of religious expression into symptoms of alienation, testimony more of social dysfunction than of doctrine or tradition. Reflecting the community studies authors' concern for social realism, folklorists such as Archie Green and Michael Owen Jones published influential studies which linked the analysis of social context to the study of folklife genres. Instead of the isolation portrayed by geographers a generation earlier, this Appalachia enjoyed a form of integration into the larger American society and

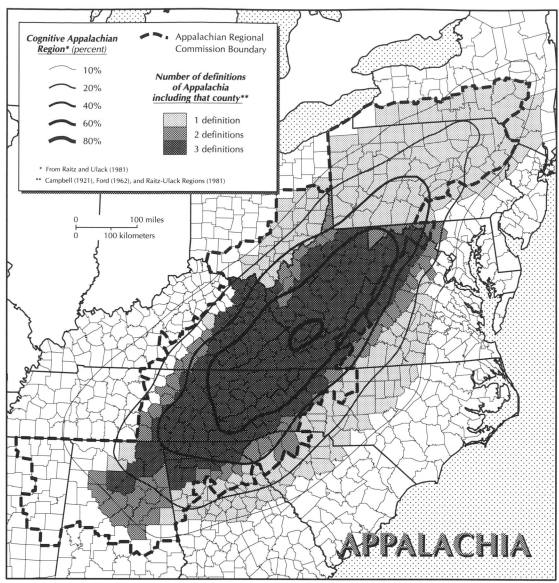

Cognitive Appalachian Region* *(percent)*

10%
20%
40%
60%
80%

- - - Appalachian Regional Commission Boundary

Number of definitions of Appalachia including that county*

1 definition
2 definitions
3 definitions

* From Raitz and Ulack (1981)

** Campbell (1921), Ford (1962), and Raitz-Ulack Regions (1981)

0   100 miles
0   100 kilometers

APPALACHIA

Source: K. Raitz and R. Ulack, *Appalachia: A Regional Geography*

Map 1

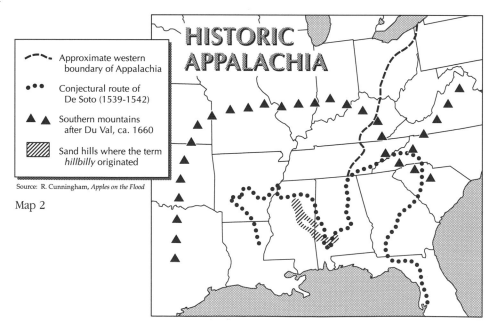

HISTORIC APPALACHIA

- ·- Approximate western boundary of Appalachia

••• Conjectural route of De Soto (1539-1542)

▲ ▲ Southern mountains after Du Val, ca. 1660

▨ Sand hills where the term *hillbilly* originated

Source: R. Cunningham, *Apples on the Flood*

Map 2

economy, but in ways that reinforced the region's deviance from national norms. The Ford Survey (Thomas R. Ford, 1962), a foundation-funded compilation of social and economic statistics, provided a reliable set of parameters that clearly demarcated the region's deviation from the nation at large. The creation of the Appalachian Regional Commission, though its boundaries enclosed nearly twice the area covered by the Ford Survey, provided for the first time an institutional framework for regionwide planning. A regional elite of businessmen and politicians maneuvered to take advantage of ARC largesse, over half of which went to building highways and the rest to vocational education, health care, and other infrastructure programs. Liberal economists called the pattern that inspired this intervention "underdevelopment." Radical younger scholars, some of them drawn from the ranks of dissident relief workers and other veterans of the federal "War on Poverty," proposed in 1964, discoursed about a "colonial economy" and wrote about analogies between Appalachia and the neocolonial Third World.

As the centennial of Harney's essay approached in 1973, the formal study of Appalachia had extended over five decades and had embraced several disciplines. Despite the fragmentary nature of the literature, a liberal synthesis had emerged that could be adequately summed up in two sentences by the authors of the second Beech Creek community study:

The Beech Creek way of life as it was [consisted of] an economy based upon subsistence agriculture, a kinship-dominated social organization differentiated along class lines, and a traditionalist value system that emphasized familism, puritanism, and individualism. These very characteristics, which enabled Beech Creekers to cope with the problems of existence under unfavorable external circumstances, eventually gave rise to conditions that resulted in a mass exodus from the mountains. (*Mountain Families*, p. 214)

In other words, the successful adaptation of Appalachian people to the rigors of mountain life in preindustrial times created a culture that was ill suited to industrialism and modernity. A radical critique of this synthesis challenged the latter premise, turning the failures of modernization into a critique of capitalism, not of mountaineers, but accepted the liberal notion that preindustrial Appalachia had enjoyed a golden age of homespun prosperity and equality.

The fragmentary view of Appalachian history available prior to the 1970s thus emphasized discontinuity, with unconnected glimpses of Appalachia's connection with great national events, such as the American Revolution and the Civil War, and with a particularly sharp break between the industrial and preindustrial periods of regional history. It has been the achievement of social historians to restore continuity to the region's history and in particular to illuminate pathways from the preindustrial eras of settlement and sectionalism to the eras of industrialization and social unrest. The emphasis of most work to date has been on social structure and class conflict in politics and work relations, but a foundation has been laid for further research in male-female relations and family and environmental history. It is now possible to trace the history of both the place and the people from the eighteenth to the twentieth century and to evaluate the social validity of many elements of the mountaineer/hillbilly cultural stereotypes popularized among readers and scholars at the turn of the century (see Map 2).

THE SETTLEMENT PERIOD AND ECONOMIC CHANGE

The occupation by European Americans of the territory now known as Appalachia began in the middle third of the eighteenth century and continued for roughly a century thereafter, with the most decisive stages being the early ones. Large numbers of Scotch-Irish and German immigrants from Europe arrived in the port of Philadelphia beginning in 1717 and moved quickly into the fertile farmlands of the Great Appalachian Valley in south-central Pennsylvania. From this point the migrant stream turned south, following the natural thoroughfare of the Great Valley, where it encountered smaller streams of migrants moving west from the plantation districts of the Chesapeake colonies, Maryland and Virginia. By 1760 the central section of the Great Valley in Virginia, Maryland, and southern Pennsylvania had been occupied and widely separated outposts had been established in the New River and upper Tennessee watersheds in southwest Virginia, in the upper Potomac and upper Ohio watersheds on either side of the Allegheny Front in western Virginia and western Pennsylvania, and in the Yadkin and Catawba valleys of the Carolina piedmont, which lay directly south of a gap in the Virginia Blue Ridge where the Great Valley thoroughfare divided into southwestern and southeastern forks. In the Carolinas, the southward-moving migrants encountered another westward-moving stream of settlers from the coastal settlements centered on Charleston. Like the stream originating in the tidewater Chesapeake, this one included African Americans as well as whites, and the whites included small numbers of European Americans of French Huguenot and Caribbean origin as well as Anglo-Americans. It seems likely also that refugees from the coastal regions' forced labor systems had preceded the migrants into these backcountry districts. Certain place names (such as the "Negro Mountains" found on the maps of western Maryland and western North Carolina) attest to this, as does the survival in West Virginia and east Tennessee of "tri-racial isolate" communities of mixed African American, Native American, and European ancestry.

Thus, Appalachia was characterized from the beginning by significant ethnic diversity, and questions about the ethnic origins of features later associated with the culture of the region (such as log architecture, stringed musical instruments, folk religious practices, and whiskey making) have been subjects of lively debate among scholars. It should be noted in this context that terms like "Appalachia," "piedmont," "Scotch-Irish," "Native American," and "African American" are terms of art invented long after the settlement period. During the eighteenth century, the scattered Appalachian districts were known simply as "the backwoods" or collectively as "the backcountry." During the nineteenth century, sparsely settled mountain districts of a given Appalachian state were often referred to as that state's "interior." Polite discourse embraced a variety of ethnic tags, including "Irish" (comprising those of Scots origin as well as Irish Catholics), "Dutch" (i.e., Deutsch or German), "French," "Negro" or "black," and of course "Indian," all of which are abundantly represented by settlement-era place names.

The occupation of the Great Valley's central reaches and of the North Carolina piedmont encountered little resistance from indigenous peoples, but north, south, and west of these areas resistance was fierce and recurrent throughout the latter half of the eighteenth century. The two most powerful native societies of eastern North America, the Iroquois confederation and the Cherokees, claimed the northern and southern halves of Appalachia, respectively, and though colonial authorities quieted these claims by treaties, violent conflicts occurred between whites and both of these societies and also between whites and the Shawnees of southeastern Ohio, who contested the white ad-

vance into western Virginia and Kentucky. Rival European imperial powers based in Canada and Louisiana (initially French, later British and Spanish, respectively) encouraged and abetted this resistance. The result was a generation of "border" or frontier warfare extending from 1755 to 1795. Even after the Iroquois and Shawnees gave up on their claims, the Cherokees survived in significant numbers in the Carolina and Georgia Blue Ridge into the 1830s, when President Andrew Jackson ordered their expulsion by federal troops. While the majority of Cherokees either resettled in Oklahoma or perished en route on the notorious "Trail of Tears" (1838–1839), a refugee remnant survived in the Great Smoky Mountains of North Carolina, where they were recognized by state and federal authorities and allocated the 63,000-acre (25,200-hectare) Qualla reservation after the Civil War.

The exploits of Indian fighters such as Jackson, Daniel Boone, and Lewis Wetzel provided material for the construction of origin myths by early state historians in Tennessee, Kentucky, and West Virginia, but from the standpoint of social history the more enduring impact of border warfare was its disruption of an orderly land allocation process in the backcountry. Due to the mountainous character of the region, its most desirable sections for agricultural development were scattered through the upland valleys of the Blue Ridge and Valley physiographic provinces and in narrow ribbons of "bottomland," or land adjacent to the streams of the neighboring piedmont and Allegheny/Cumberland plateaus. Such land did not lend itself to precise description and survey, which fact, combined with the recurrent shifting back and forth of the frontier due to Indian and international warfare, led to successive occupations of the same land by different claimants. The task of unraveling this situation after the end of Indian warfare in 1795 was greatly complicated by the numerous encouragements to land speculation that were built into colonial land policies and carried forward by successor state governments.

The politics of land speculation explains the prominence in the annals of frontier Appalachia of such corporate land enterprises as the Ohio Company of Virginia or North Carolina's Transylvania Company. It also explains the recurrent efforts to create new political jurisdictions or a "fourteenth colony" in the Ohio and Tennessee valleys, such as "Vandalia" and "Westsylvania" in western Virginia and Pennsylvania, "Transylvania" in Kentucky, and the "State of Franklin" in southwest Virginia/northeast Tennessee. Regionalist historians, following

Frederick Jackson Turner, have tended to tout these efforts as evidence of frontier democracy and to justify the separation of Kentucky and West Virginia from Virginia and of Tennessee from North Carolina. In fact, they are more accurately understood as the attempts of groups of speculators to bypass the influence of rival claimants in the colonial or state capitals. Since entities such as the Ohio and Transylvania companies and Franklin actually issued land titles based on some pretense of legality, these efforts also contributed to the multiplication of overlapping land claims.

The social impact of these circumstances was considerable. First, it discouraged settlement in Appalachia south of the Ohio River when the settlement process resumed when the fiercest of the Indian resistance had been subdued, and encouraged thousands of migrants from the Appalachian states to move north of the river where land was better and titles more secure. Second, it stimulated the growth of a farm-and-forest economy in the mountain districts in which "squatting" on unoccupied land claimed by nonresidents was common and the free use of such land for hunting, foraging livestock, cutting timber, and harvesting forest products was even more so. Third, it created a situation in which nearly every owner or claimant needed the services of surveyors and "distinguished land attorneys" and so constituted these individuals—who were almost always the agents of nonresident claimants as well as accumulators of claims in their own right—as the prototypical links between the political economy of the mountain districts and the centers of commerce and politics in the surrounding lowlands. Fourth, it created the possibility—later realized with depressing regularity—of dividing ownership or occupation of mountain agricultural land from ownership of the same land's timber and mineral resources, since mountaineers could be persuaded by rival claimants' threats of reviving dormant claims to surrender timber and mineral rights in return for a supposedly secure title to the surface ("supposedly" because the notorious broad-form deed could later be used to expel surface owners in the interests of the owners of mineral rights). Finally, the dependence of the poorer participants in the farm-and-forest economy on unimpeded access to vacant land rendered them vulnerable to dispossession as deforestation, the quieting of land titles, and the adoption of fence, stock, and game laws increasingly restricted access to the forest and its resources.

The legacy of the settlement period was a resident Appalachian social and political elite whose primary asset was privileged access to the region's premier economic resource, its undeveloped land. This elite's interests were by no means confined to land speculation and lawyering, however. Its assets included gristmills and sawmills, town lots and buildings in the emerging courthouse towns of the region, salt-manufacturing and coal-mining enterprises along the Kanawha River in western (now West) Virginia, textile and iron manufacturing in the towns of the Great Valley, and hotel and tavern facilities associated with the region's emerging resort industries centered in the (West) Virginia springs country and the Asheville and Flat Rock districts of North Carolina.

The acknowledgment of the Appalachian elite's existence helps also to explain much about antebellum politics and the Civil War. The sectional programs advanced by Appalachian leaders in antebellum state politics consistently supported the democratization of electoral and representational practices and had the effect of enlarging the influence of their districts at the expense of each state's plantation or "black belt"; they also promoted state-financed transportation improvements that would enhance the value of their landholdings. Success in each of these enterprises entailed commitments to the defense of plantation slavery, which explains why the leaders of western Virginia and western North Carolina both opposed secession and supported the Confederacy and why Unionist separatism in West Virginia and east Tennessee flourished during the Civil War under substantially different leadership than that which had spoken for those districts in antebellum politics. After the Civil War, the Appalachian elite turned to private investors in its search for development capital, and though it surrendered control of the largest tracts of land to outside investors, its members tended to flourish as lawyers and land agents, town developers, and political leaders who provided pliant law enforcement and low taxes to both local and nonresident capitalists.

Analysis of social relations also discloses some connections among the sporadic outbreaks of violence that both attracted and appalled the late-nineteenth-century "discoverers" of the region. Thomas P. Slaughter's analysis of the Whiskey Rebellion (1794), for example, had portrayed it in terms both of interregional and class conflict, with smallholders and squatters of the Allegheny frontier pitted against nonresident landowners (President George Washington prominently among them) and their local agents and allies. While the rebellion ended in the suppression of insurrection in western Pennsylvania and northwestern (West) Virginia, it also ended federal attempts to collect excise taxes from whiskey makers in the Appalachian region until after the Civil War. Then federal authorities embarked on sustained and coordinated drives to stamp out moonshining, an effort that both enjoyed the enthusiastic support of middle-class town-dwelling residents of the region and established the supremacy of federal courts at a time when these courts were the principal arenas for the adjudication of land disputes involving nonresident owners. Phillip Paludan's examination of the Civil War in the mountains, focused on the 1863 murder of thirteen Unionist mountaineers by Confederate troops in Shelton Laurel, North Carolina, portrays a conflict between town-dwelling, development-oriented mountain leaders and subsistence farming mountaineers who had declined to follow the local elite into the Confederacy and who harbored Confederate deserters as well as pro-Union sentiments. Altina Waller's reexamination of the Hatfield-McCoy feud also finds social conflict between locally based and outside developers of the Tug Fork valley of West Virginia and Kentucky to have been a driving force in violence that was sensationally interpreted by metropolitan journalists as evidence of the mountaineers' backwardness and depravity. It is likely that similar forces were at work in the so-called "Allen outrage" in Carroll County, Virginia, in 1912, where violence broke out between development-oriented officials in the courthouse town of Hillsville and members of a prominent family from a remote district along the North Carolina border. This was the incident that led the Baltimore *Sun* to propose a choice of two cures for Appalachia's peculiarities: education or extermination.

The creation of modern Appalachia's "underdeveloped" or "colonial" economy was therefore not something imposed on the region from the outside but instead was created with the enthusiastic and profitable support of the region's elite. Similar internal forces shaped the creation of an industrial working class from portions of the region's population of smallholders and squatters. However, this process has not received as much attention from scholars as have the roles of the elite and of formal working-class institutions such as labor unions.

While much of what was written about mountaineers during the era of "discovery" can be dismissed as sensational or romantic nonsense, there is enough agreement on some points to merit their acceptance as serious social observation. Local-color writers, missionaries, and journalists alike depicted the features of a subsistence economy: limited cash incomes and still more limited access to commercial markets for agricultural products, a notable degree of self-sufficiency in mountaineer households, an intimate acquaintance with the surrounding forest environment (which manifested itself variously as skill in hunting and woodcraft and harvesting of products such as herbs, honey, pelts, and timber for consumption or sale). Although most historians agree generally with this portrayal, some argue that mountain farms were more prosperous than casual observers realized. Mountain farmers aimed at subsistence, but their strategy of combining crops and herds with the harvest of forest products often produced marketable surpluses. This viewpoint attributes the subsequent poverty of Appalachia's farm families to several causes: to the general impoverishment of the South after the Civil War (which restricted the most readily accessible markets for mountain products), to population growth that limited the ability of mountain farmers to provide nearby arable land for their offspring, and to natural disasters such as the chestnut blight of the 1920s, which swiftly destroyed a tree whose wood, bark, and nuts had played a vital role in the farm-and-forest economy.

Victorian observers also commented disapprovingly upon a division of labor by sexes in which women seemed to be confined to the household and overworked while men ranged free in the forest or lounged lazily around their cabin doors. The cabins themselves, though often praised for their sturdiness and prized as a link between "pioneer" ways and contemporary life, elicited negative comments about their small size and the consequent lack of privacy between the sexes and between young and old. Other frequent observations emphasized the importance of kinship networks within the mountain settlements and the persistence over time in certain families of specializations in one or another of the genres—such as music or whiskey making—associated with Appalachian folk culture.

How did such attributes fare in the transition to an industrial economy? For one thing, the division of labor by sexes had the dual effects of smoothing the transition from subsistence farming to wage work and of sustaining a household's relative autonomy even after it had become dependent on wage work as its primary source of income. The male role in the farm-and-forest economy, for example, was performed largely beyond the gaze of observers who confined their attention to brief and infrequent visits to mountaineers' cabins. This role included not only hunting and gathering in the forest but also such tasks as plowing and clearing, cutting brush and timber, maintaining buildings and fences, trading and marketing livestock, whiskey, and forest products, and in general handling all transactions between the household and the outside world. There was considerable seasonal variation in men's work, whereas women worked mostly to diurnal rhythms. Men were afforded numerous opportunities to range abroad to places distant from the household; women and girls were confined to the household and to nearby neighborhood homes and gathering places. The timber industry, whose appearance was the first step toward industrialization in almost all mountain districts, provided part-time wage work that fitted into slack periods for farm work (such as winter and early spring), and even workplaces in which seasonality was less desirable (such as sawmills and tanneries) seem to have tolerated a lot of coming and going among their employees. Long after logging had given place to mining and textiles as the principal industries employing mountaineers, the opportunity to cut timber seasonally or to sell an occasional load of pulpwood or tanbark provided mountain men and boys with the means of earning cash without abandoning the subsistence farming homestead.

The farm-and-forest economy provided men with variable tasks as well as seasonal variation, along with considerable personal autonomy for the fathers who organized the work and mobilized the labor of their sons and other male relatives and neighbors. The same was true of coal-mining work during the early industrial era. Under the conditions of "hand loading," which prevailed in Appalachian mines until the introduction of hourly wages, strip mining, and mechanical loading during and after World War II, a miner engaged in multiple tasks and enjoyed a considerable degree of freedom in regulating the pace of work and in choosing helpers from among less experienced males. To judge by the complaints of employers, miners also imposed their own forms of seasonality, disappearing during planting, harvest, and hunting seasons. This practice in turn helped the miners to sustain their families during the industry's own seasons of un- or underemployment, which recurred both annually and in tune with the ups and downs of the business cycle.

It is clear from employers' complaints and from the recollections of mountain families' descendants that their initial migrations to coal camps or mill towns were usually regarded as temporary;

even after their moves became permanent, habits brought from the family farm could sustain the migrants in hard times and difficult circumstances. In particular, a kitchen garden attended by women and children, along with a milk cow or chickens and pigs, cushioned dependence on wages (but only in coal camps and mill towns that allotted land for this purpose), while relocation enabled women to form friendships and mutual support networks outside of their own households and families and to acquire some control of that portion of household budgets spent on store-bought goods. They also found employment in coal camps as boarding-house keepers and store and office clerks and occasionally even as miners, especially during the two world wars. In the mill towns, of course, women and girls worked at the same factory jobs as men and boys and eventually came to predominate in the textile industry work force. David Corbin's study of southern West Virginia coal camps shows that the support of miners' wivers and union auxiliaries was critical in sustaining militancy during United Mine Workers' Association (UMWA) organizing drives. Mountain women provided labor heroines in the textile industry as well, notably the martyred Ella May Wiggins, whose murder in 1929 attracted national attention to an abortive effort to organize a Gastonia, North Carolina, mill.

Two questions that remain to be dealt with in the social history of Appalachian industrial labor are the extent to which the culture and outlooks of native mountaineer workers were adopted or modified by the other ethnic groups that came to work in the region and the explanation for contrasts in the labor histories of the region's two major industries: textiles and coal mining. Well over 40 percent of Appalachia's coalfield work force in 1910 consisted of immigrants from southern or eastern Europe or African American migrants from the former plantation districts of the lowland South. It seems likely that, until demand for coal ceased to rise after World War I, life in the coal towns was an improvement for both groups over what they had known and that, like the native mountaineers, the miners' backgrounds as European peasants or southern sharecroppers had prepared them to value the relative autonomy and variability of mine work during the hand-loading era. While the owners of coal camps regularly housed such workers in clusters that segregated black, foreign-born, and native-born miners, the UMWA managed to achieve an interracial and multiethnic solidarity that was rare among American labor unions before the civil rights era, notwithstanding the persistence of legal segregation and job discrimination against blacks throughout the region.

The emergence of the Appalachian string band is a favorite emblem among liberals of this multicultural Appalachia, with its fiddle (of British origins), banjo (African), guitar (Hispanic), mandolin (Italian), and occasional dulcimer (of disputed origin, either British or Central European) and dobro (southeastern Europe). The string band appeared just south of the coalfields, however, in the upper New River valley and adjacent districts in southwest Virginia and eastern Kentucky. While its instrumental assemblage may have owed something to multiethnic logging or railroad work crews, a more likely explanation is the widespread availability by mail order from the 1890s on of inexpensive factory-made musical instruments. The descendants of foreign-born mine workers, while retaining some ethnic foodways and religious practices, have generally adopted the culture and outlooks of native-born miners, but blacks migrated from the coalfields in much larger proportions as employment in the industry turned downward after World War II.

Within the coal industry, Appalachian workers achieved an unparalleled degree of interracial solidarity and of union militancy. Almost the exact opposite is true in the textile industry. How are we to account for this? Coal camps and mill towns were variant forms of captive communities, and both drew workers from the same ethnic and cultural backgrounds. Both industries were labor-intensive and plagued with inelastic demand curves that exerted downward pressure on wages; both were decentralized rather than oligopolistic, a form of organization that might have generated more stability, and both were dominated by outside capitalists and nonresident owners (although both industries included paternalistic mine or mill owners and model company towns). Both were the scenes of celebrated strikes during the first third of the twentieth century. Yet the differences persisted, even in fabric mills and garment factories that employed the wives of militant UMWA unionists from coalfield or nearby districts after World War II. Does the explanation lie in environmental or cultural differences between the piedmont and the Cumberland/Allegheny plateaus, or in the feminization of the textile work force, or in the contrasting nature of the work in the two industries which, at least until recently, has accommodated gang labor and close supervision of workers much more readily in textiles than in coal? These are some of the questions that must be answered before a regionwide social history of the Appalachian work force can be written.

APPALACHIA TODAY

It has been said that all mountain regions must import capital or export people. During the latter two-thirds of the twentieth century, Appalachia has done both. The most consistent source of outside capital during this period has been the federal government, and the region's elite, having secured a minority shareholding of the private investment that came into Appalachia during the period of industrialization, has worked with considerable success to ensure that federal intervention, whether in the form of transfer payments or direct investment, has taken place on terms not threatening to the social status quo. Frequently, this has meant collaborating in federal policies the effects of which are to encourage working-class migration, though it is by no means clear that this has always been an intended effect or the only cause of Appalachian migration. The region as a whole sustained a net migration loss as early as 1910, but this loss was disguised before the 1950 census by a relatively high birth rate and by the seemingly temporary nature of war-related migration during the two world wars. It seems likely that the migration loss would have occurred earlier and cut deeper into the region's total population had it not been for industrialization, for mountain families were already confronting a demographic crisis as smaller and less productive mountain farms were subdivided repeatedly among the members of large families.

Still the paradox remains that, while many federal programs have been justified by a desire to stem the flow of Appalachian people from the region, the overall impact has been to stimulate migration. Partly this results from lack of coordination among federal agencies, some of which have given little or no thought to the social consequences of their policies. The creation of the Shenandoah and Great Smoky Mountain national parks, for example, resulted in the direct expulsion of thousands of people from mountain homes through the collaboration of park planners, who derived their models from the unpopulated expanses of western parklands, with local promoters who wanted the tourism-related development that the parks were expected to bring. The creation of the Tennessee Valley Authority and its dam-building program—accelerated in the name of national emergency during World War II—led to further confiscation and forced moves, in these cases from productive bottomlands rather than remote mountain coves. The military draft and forced-march industrialization associated with World War II acted as further stimuli, drawing workers from the mountains to defense installations in the coastal South and industrial Midwest and giving thousands of Appalachian soldiers and sailors their first acquaintance with the possibilities of life and work in distant parts of the nation. After the war, the cold war stimulated the growth of military-industrial complexes around Oak Ridge, Tennessee, and Huntsville, Alabama, both based on abundant supplies of subsidized TVA power. None of these programs was intended to stimulate migration from the rural farm-and-forest districts of Appalachia, but that is exactly what they did.

War-stimulated prosperity shielded the Appalachian coalfields from these effects during the 1940s, but with the collapse of this boom and an accelerated pace of mechanization in the coal industry, migration reached unprecedented heights, with some 3.3 million people leaving the region between 1950 and 1970. The appearance of Appalachian "ghettoes" in Cincinnati, Chicago, Detroit, Columbus, and other cities made the stemming of migration a national concern and a primary mission of the Appalachian Regional Commission after its creation in 1964. Following the advice of post-Keynesian economists who regarded this phenomenon as a natural "resource flow" of human capital, the commission's planners did not attempt to stem migration but rather to contain it within the region by building a multibillion-dollar network of superhighways (called "Appalachian Development Corridors") converging on "growth centers" such as Charleston or Beckley, West Virginia; Asheville, North Carolina; Pikeville, Kentucky; or the Tri-Cities region of southwest Virginia and northeast Tennessee. The theory was that an improved infrastructure would stimulate industrial expansion in such districts, enabling them to absorb the migrant flow from the coalfield and rural areas, thus stanching the flow of productive workers and tax dollars from the Appalachian states, though doing little for the smaller communities from whence the migrants came. Further infrastructure improvements were expected from heavy investments in vocational education or "vo-tech" schools intended to offset the fatalism, traditionalism, and poor work ethic diagnosed by Jack Weller and others who attributed Appalachia's underdevelopment partly or wholly to the people and their culture. Other frequent recipients of ARC funds were the resort and recreational facilities—conference centers, private resorts, state parks, and the like—that were intended to supplement and update the tourism potential of the national parks developed during the interwar period.

Judged by the goals of the ARC's promoters and framers, these tactics must be judged a failure. While the new highways did indeed stimulate development, the so-called growth centers barely held their own. Rather the new roads stimulated the growth of metropolitan centers near but not in the mountains, places like Atlanta, Charlotte, Columbus, Lexington, Nashville, and urban agglomerations such as Greensboro/High Point/Winston-Salem and Washington/Baltimore. The development corridors turned out to be fingers reaching out from the big cities, enabling them to expand the scope and value of their hinterlands and encouraging capitalists and consumers alike to bypass the smaller centers. The hinterlands turned out to include the mountains' recreational and scenic amenities, which became more accessible to urban consumers via the new roads. But development for recreation and tourism emerged as a limited achievement in terms of social and economic impact. In his critical study of the ARC program David E. Whisnant noted that Pipestem, a "Resort State Park" developed in southern West Virginia with $13 million in federal funds, employed only a third of its workers on a year-round basis, at an average annual wage well below the poverty line. Most of the new resort and recreational facilities were located far from the suffering coalfields, and even for the localities which attracted them they turned out to be a mixed blessing. A study of Sevier County, Tennessee, between 1970 and 1984 found that recreation and tourism development created mostly low-paying service jobs in restaurants and hotels, promoted further feminization of the wage work force, and created heavy demands on public social services because of the limited or nonexistent fringe benefits received by employed service workers and high levels of unemployment during off-seasons. Professional jobs in recreation and tourism industries tend to go to persons from outside the region, according to the study. Men find employment in related construction and maintenance jobs, but the continued vitality of construction in tourism-impacted areas carries with it an implied future threat through overdevelopment to the recreational and scenic amenities that attract tourists to the region in the first place.

From the perspective of the early 1990s, one cannot be optimistic about the survival of Appalachia as a distinctive environment, for postindustrial society now has the tools to reshape the land in ways that would have been unimaginable a century or even a few decades ago. Giant 100-ton (90 megagrams) "drag lines" now make possible the strip mining method known as "mountaintop removal." Thus, in the coalfields of Ohio, Kentucky, and the Virginias, the familiar razorback ridges of the Appalachian Plateau are giving way to sere tablelands resembling the mesas of the intermountain West. In underground mining, increased reliance on the long-wall method of coal extraction makes possible dramatic increases in coal output without disturbing the long-term decline in employment but it also increases dramatically the danger of surface subsidence in the coalfields, since long-wall mining requires none of the underground supports that older methods left behind. In eastern Kentucky and southern West Virginia, the U.S. Army Corps of Engineers has built dams and flooded valleys on a scale paralleling the achievement of the TVA farther south. The now-submerged cliffs of the Gauley River's gorges have turned out to be a mecca for scuba divers, while water-skiers skim across other river valleys whose riders were once confined to the adventurous loggers who rode the spring ties down to the Ohio. Highway engineers have built bridges that soar to treetop heights across West Virginia's New River Gorge or around the flanks of North Carolina's Grandfather Mountain, while superhighways slice across the parallel ridges of the Great Valley through breadknife cuts several hundred feet deep. Bulldozers and blasting powder have made possible the building of shopping malls and airports in coalfield towns once confined to narrow floodplains; in Pikeville, Kentucky, the ARC and other federal agencies actually financed the relocation of a river from one side of a mountain to the other. Other machines have scraped ski runs on the higher slopes of Blue Ridge and Allegheny peaks and have carved out golf courses on the gentler hillsides below. Landscape designers have rendered the North Carolina resort town of Cashiers, near the Georgia border, all but indistinguishable in appearance from a prosperous Atlanta suburb.

Appalachia is thus no longer a strange place for visitors who find comfort in the familiar landscapes of metropolitan America, but the region's "peculiar" people still interest scholars.

Of special note is the recent emergence of a new form of religious studies. In contrast to other aspects of Appalachian folklife, mountain religion did not lend itself to commercialization or to revival movements among urban and exurban enthusiasts. The highly emotional character and chiliastic beliefs of the region's numerous small, sectarian Protestant churches tended to generate at best indifference but more commonly horrified fascination among cosmopolitan observers, while missionaries and philanthropists associated with mainstream Protestant churches have seen Appalachia as prime mission territory, its people candidates for conversion to more optimistic doctrines and more sedate forms of worship. Scholars who interpret religion from the perspective of economic relations and social structure have identified traditional religion as a symptom of Appalachia's alienation and economic dislocation. During the 1980s, scholars such as Howard Dorgan and Jeff Todd Titon published important studies of Appalachian religion *as religion,* approaching the topic through the examination of doctrinal tradition, church organization, worship styles, music and other aspects of expressive religious behavior. Appalachian churches, according to Titon, "are better understood as adapting inherited traditions, not creating pathetic delusions" (*Powerhouse for God,* p. 7).

This new understanding extends to religious history, including the doctrinal controversies which led to the creation of numerous Baptist subdenominations during the mid-nineteenth and again in the early twentieth centuries, and to organizational forms and worship practices which continue to set these churches apart both from mainstream Protestantism and from the modern evangelical movements associated with television ministries and large suburban "temples." Appalachian churches tend to eschew the many worldly activities of their mainstream or evangelical counterparts (such as schools and social service or other outreach activities) and to focus on matters which conserve and strengthen a congregation's effectiveness as a community. Organized as small, functionally independent churches within loose subdenominational associations, the congregations overlap with communities of families and neighbors. The intense expressive styles of their worship services, according to sympathetic scholars, function both as links with the past and as markers which serve to distinguish in their variations the different subdenominations from one another. The churches function as conservators of traditions, including patriarchal traditions of male dominance in both congregational and family life, even though the homes of family members no longer cluster around a patriarch's rural "home place" and women church members usually work outside the home. Through their practices of formal visits and association with other congregations of similar size and persuasion, contemporary Appalachian churches have retained a regional scope comparable to the "circuits" established by the Methodist and Baptist preachers who planted this type of religion in Appalachia during the early nineteenth century. They have even extended into areas of late twentieth-century Appalachian migration such as the industrial Midwest and the Sunbelt, as well as to the Appalachian towns and cities where most of the worshipers now live and work.

Cultural historians have also been offering new variants of Appalachian studies in the form of a "neoregionalist" interpretation which makes the region not a periphery of the lowland South or of urban-industrial America but the core of a much broader region whose domain extends across the entire upper South and adjacent regions of the Midwest and Southwest. The cultural forms that give shape to such definitions include not only the traditional expressive forms which folklorists have pursued through much of the last century but contemporary cultural constructions such as country music, stock car racing, mobile homes, and "plain folk" religion (including modern evangelical churches that religious studies specialists do not regard as traditional). These interpretations are intensely controversial among Appalachian studies scholars and have yet to be tested thoroughly by social history research. It is likely that such testing will absorb the attention of the coming generation of scholars and provide new definitions of Appalachia, both the place and its people, for many years to come.

BIBLIOGRAPHY

General Works

Appalachian Journal (1972–).

Journal of the Appalachian Studies Association (1989–).

Campbell, John C. *The Southern Highlander and His Homeland* (1921).

Caudill, Harry M. *Night Comes to the Cumberlands. A Biography of a Depressed Area* (1963).

Eller, Ronald D. *Miners, Millhands, and Mountaineers: Industrialization of the Appalachian South, 1880–1930* (1982).

Ford, Thomas R. *The Southern Appalachian Region: A Survey* (1962).

Kephart, Horace. *Our Southern Highlanders* (1913; repr. 1984).

King, Duane H. *The Cherokee Indian Nation: A Troubled History* (1979).

Lewis, Helen, et al., eds. *Colonialism in Modern America: The Appalachian Case* (1978).

McNeil, W. K., ed. *Appalachian Images in Folk and Popular Culture* (1989).

Miles, Emma Bell. *The Spirit of the Mountains* (1905; repr. 1975).

Raitz, Karl B., and Richard Ulack. *Appalachia, A Regional Geography: Land, People, and Development* (1984).

Shapiro, Henry D. *Appalachia on Our Mind: the Southern Mountains and Mountaineers in the American Consciousness, 1870–1920* (1977).

Turner, William H., and Edward J. Cabbell, eds. *Blacks in Appalachia* (1985).

Community Studies

Beaver, Patricia D. *Rural Community in the Appalachian South* (1986).

Gaventa, John. *Power and Powerlessness: Quiescence and Rebellion in an Appalachian Valley* (1980).

Schwarzweller, Harry K., James S. Brown, and J. J. Mangalam. *Mountain Families in Transition; A Case Study of Appalachian Migration* (1971).

Weller, Jack E. *Yesterday's People. Life in Contemporary Appalachia* (1965).

Religion and Folklife

Dorgan, Howard. *Giving Glory to God in Appalachia: Worship Practices of Six Baptist Subdenominations* (1987).

————. *The Old Regular Baptists of Central Appalachia: Brothers and Sisters in Hope* (1989).

Green, Archie. *Only a Miner. Studies in Recorded Coal-mining Songs* (1972).

Jones, Michael Owen. *Craftsman of the Cumberlands: Tradition and Creativity* (1989).

Titon, Jeff Todd. *Powerhouse for God: Speech, Chant, and Song in an Appalachian Baptist Church* (1988).

Social History Case Studies

Corbin, David. *Life, Work, and Rebellion in the Coal Fields: The Southern West Virginia Miners, 1880–1922* (1981).

Dunn, Durwood. *Cades Cove: The Life and Death of a Southern Appalachian Community, 1818–1937* (1988).

Inscoe, John C. *Mountain Masters, Slavery, and the Sectional Crisis in Western North Carolina* (1989).

Mitchell, Robert D., ed. *Appalachian Frontiers: Settlement, Society, and Development Before the Industrial Era* (1991).

Paludan, Phillip. *Victims: A True Story of the Civil War* (1981).

Slaughter, Thomas P. *The Whiskey Rebellion. Frontier Epilogue to the American Revolution* (1986).

Trotter, Joe William, Jr. *Coal, Class, and Color: Blacks in Southern West Virginia, 1915–32* (1990).

Waller, Altina L. *Feud: Hatfields, McCoys, and Social Change in Appalachia, 1860–1990* (1988).

Whisnant, David E. *Modernizing the Mountaineer: People, Power, and Planning in Appalachia* (1980).

————. *All That Is Native and Fine: The Politics of Culture in an American Region* (1983).

Williams, John Alexander. *West Virginia and the Captains of Industry* (1976).

Cultural History

Cunningham, Rodger. *Apples on the Flood: The Southern Mountain Experience* (1987).

Fischer, David Hackett. *Albion's Seed: Four British Folkways in America* (1989).

Jordan, Terry D., and Matti Kaups. *The American Backwoods Frontier: An Ethnic and Ecological Interpretation* (1989).

SEE ALSO **Anthropological Approaches and Studies of Folk Cultures; Community Studies; Folk Music; Geographical Mobility; The Great Depression and World War II; Housing; The Middle Atlantic Region; Oral History; Regionalism; Religion; The Southern Tidewater and Piedmont.**

THE DEEP SOUTH

Henry M. McKiven, Jr.

THE DEEP SOUTH, consisting of the states of Alabama, Mississippi, and the panhandle of Florida, has often been defined by reference to distinctive social relations, values, and political practices. While certain characteristics of the region have distinguished it from other regions in the United States, it has been neither as homogeneous nor as distinctive as has often been argued. Geographical differences within the region supported diverse patterns of economic development, social interaction, and cultural practice. These patterns, in turn, both shaped and were shaped by state and national politics.

During the period from about 850 to the early 1540s the Deep South was the domain of a number of native tribes archaeologists classify as "Mississippian." Mississippian societies built permanent towns, ceremonial centers, and villages linked to each other and to neighboring societies by extensive trade networks. Social, political, and religious structures were hierarchical.

European exploration and settlement of the Southeast undermined and eventually destroyed Mississippian societies. The first European contact came with the explorations of Hernando de Soto and other Spaniards. Military assaults on tribes, destruction and consumption of tribal food supplies, and disease reduced native populations between 1540 and 1640. Concerned about this depopulation, the Spanish government altered its settlement strategy, opting for a policy of coexistence. Nevertheless, the decline of native societies continued under Spanish, French, and British dominance of the region.

This process of displacement continued with large-scale American migration into the region in the late eighteenth and early nineteenth centuries. Eli Whitney's invention of a cotton gin that could efficiently separate the fiber from the many seeds found in short-staple cotton made possible abandonment of long-staple cotton, which could be grown only in a limited region along the Atlantic coast. Planters from the southern piedmont and tidewater made their way into the Alabama and Mississippi territories to take advantage of fertile soils and weather—200 to 210 frostless days and 20 to 25 inches of rain—that were ideal for cotton cultivation. Many of them were members of established households seeking to expand the family enterprise. Many others were upwardly mobile young men hoping to build their fortunes on the new frontier.

As settlers moved into the Deep South, they carried with them the economic institutions that had evolved in the tidewater and piedmont. Foremost among those was the slave labor system and the plantation form of agricultural organization. As economic historian Gavin Wright has convincingly argued, large agricultural units were not necessarily more efficient than family farms. The difference between the two was that labor on the family farm was limited to household members. Slavery overcame this limitation, making possible the virtually indefinite expansion of the extended household and of production. Desiring to produce as much cotton as they could, migrants into the "black belts" of the region took slaves with them and, after the closing of the slave trade in 1808, augmented their labor force through purchases on the interregional slave jarket. Between 1790 and 1860 over 800,000 slaves were transported from the eastern seaboard states to the western cotton-producing states.

Organized in labor gangs, slaves worked from sunup to sundown. Each phase of the production process—planting, cultivating, and harvesting—was divided into a number of smaller tasks that a driver (a slave foreman) could closely supervise. Most planters considered rigid discipline and constant, hard labor to be the keys to profitable operation. They were, however, frequently frustrated in their efforts to instill in slaves their ideas about time and work discipline. Through a variety of creative tac-

THE DEEP SOUTH

tics, slave laborers managed to define a work pace somewhat slower than their owners desired. Still, they produced enough cotton to make the Deep South the world's leading supplier by 1840.

With slave labor, plantations could produce for the world market and remain largely self-sufficient. Planters developed an elaborate division of labor in order to make most efficient use of their slave work force. Slave artisans produced needed iron products and built and repaired plantation structures. On some plantations, slaves produced clothing and ran cotton gins. On larger plantations a number of slaves were assigned to the main house, where they cooked, provided child care, and served the planter's household in a number of other ways. This division of labor was the basis for a labor hierarchy among the slaves. Planters allowed artisans and other specialists privileges not extended to field hands. They held out to field hands the op-

portunity for advancement up the occupational ladder as a reward for hard work.

While slave-owners carved out their estates and farms, a second stream of migrants filled in the less desirable hill country and pine barrens of the region. This migration was, in part, a response to the expansion of slavery into the piedmont of Georgia and the Carolinas. As large-scale agriculture spread inland, those who could not afford slaves, or who desired neither to enter the ranks of slaveholders nor to live among them, moved west, where relatively cheap lands were available. Some crossed the Appalachians into Tennessee, Kentucky, and the Old Northwest; others followed the valleys of the Appalachians south into northern Alabama and Mississippi; still others settled in the wiregrass and pine barrens of southern Alabama, northern Florida, and southern Mississippi.

What all of these settlers had in common was

that they occupied lands on which large-scale staple crop production was difficult or impossible. Not only was the soil less fertile than in the "black belt," but transportation networks outside of cotton-producing regions were poorly developed before the 1850s. Farmers in the hill country and pine barrens who did produce staple crops incurred transportation and marketing costs, which sharply limited their profits. Other important factors in the farmer's choice of crops were the uncertainty of the world market and the inability to maintain self-sufficiency while producing cotton. Unless small farmers could purchase slaves, and the majority in the antebellum period could not, they could not produce for the world market without abandoning self-sufficiency and placing their households at the mercy of forces beyond their control. Few were willing to take such a risk.

The distinctive economic orientations of sub-regions within the Deep South generated a much-remarked maldistribution of wealth. Slave ownership and large-scale production of cotton were the sources of enormous wealth for a small proportion of the region's population. Only about one-third of all southerners entered the ranks of slave-owners between 1830 and 1850. By 1860 this minority held between 90 percent and 95 percent of agricultural wealth. Differences in wealth holding did not, however, necessarily reflect the dispossession of the yeoman farmer. Economic historians agree that small-scale producers generally increased their share of landholdings during the antebellum period; much of the difference in total wealth was due to the value of slaves. Still, a minority of slave-owners reaped the benefits of southern economic prosperity.

The profits to be made from cotton growing, combined with an inadequate supply of industrial workers, hindered the growth of southern manu-facturing. Slaves could have been profitably em-ployed as industrial laborers; owners of coal mines and iron foundries in Alabama made extensive use of slave labor. But southern investors could do bet-ter if they employed their slaves in the production of more cotton, especially during the boom of the 1850s. Industrialists, therefore, had to compete with agriculture for labor and investment capital.

Those manufacturing concerns which were es-tablished found it difficult to secure enough labor. Industrialists such as Daniel Pratt tried to recruit native whites to work in textile plants but found a deeply felt hostility toward non-agricultural labor.

Some industrialists tried to solve the labor problem by encouraging foreign immigration, but they met with limited success. Immigrants tended to stay away from the South, where, they feared, they would have to compete with slave or free black la-bor. Those who moved to southern cities did en-counter bosses who used black labor to control recalcitrant white workers. In Alabama white labor-ers attempted to secure legislation to prohibit this practice but were unsuccessful.

Social and cultural development in the Deep South reflected the diversity of its economy. Here again the presence or absence of slaves was the decisive influence. Relations within slaveholding households and communities in the plantation belt were strikingly different from relations within non-slaveholding households and communities.

Relations within non-slaveholding households were shaped by the labor demands of the farm and individuals' beliefs concerning the proper roles of husbands, wives, and children. On the farm there was a gender-based division of labor. The head of the household was responsible for clearing and cul-tivating the fields in order to provide at least a mod-icum of security for his wife and children. Around the age of ten, sons joined their fathers in the fields and began to learn the responsibilities of their gen-der. How much a non-slaveholding farm produced depended largely upon the number of sons in the household. This need for labor was one reason for relatively high birthrates in non-slaveholding households. Around the homestead, wives and daughters performed a range of critical chores. They processed crops, prepared meals, cultivated gardens, produced clothing, and tended dairy cat-tle. It has been estimated that women were respon-sible for the production of between one-third and one-half of households' subsistence needs.

Authority within these households rested with the household head. Wives were obligated by cus-tom to obey their husbands. Ministers and the authors of advice manuals repeatedly reminded women that harmony within the household de-pended upon their submission to their husbands' will. The law affirmed and reinforced the domi-nance of men. Women's property rights in marriage were severely restricted. It was more difficult for a woman to obtain a divorce than it was for a man, even if the woman could prove that she had been a victim of physical abuse. If a woman was granted a divorce, the court was likely to deprive her of her children.

Children, as dependents, were expected to be submissive to their fathers. A father's power over his children was rooted in his control of productive resources the children needed to get a start in life. His sons might remain under his control until their mid twenties or later, when they would receive their portions of the paternal estate. A suitable marriage partner for a daughter might depend upon the dowry her father could provide. Out of necessity, settlers in non-slaveholding regions created more tightly knit communities than did settlers in the plantation belts. Without slaves to augment production, households had to depend upon neighbors, many of whom were relatives, for some necessities of life. Self-sufficiency became a communal endeavor.

Cooperation in the maintenance of local roads and fences, in the processing of some crops, and in the construction of homes and other farm structures reinforced communal bonds. Such occasions combined work and recreation. For men recreation meant some form of competition through which they could demonstrate their physical prowess before the community and win the esteem of their peers. In this way they affirmed their standing in the community, their equality with other men of honor. Participants in corn shuckings, for example, often divided the corn into two piles, chose teams for a "race," and went to work. The losers sometimes started fights with the winners in an effort to redeem their honor. Such violence, which was common among non-slaveholding males, reflected a cultural emphasis on male toughness that was, at least in part, a product of the uncertain, hard life on the frontier.

While the men worked, drank plenty of corn liquor, and reinforced their masculinity, women engaged in their own social activities. Cooperative work activities provided opportunities for women to gather and talk among themselves. Frequently at social gatherings women held quilting bees and sewing parties. If the men were sober enough when all the work was done, they might join the women for a dance to end the day's activities.

Religious institutions brought communities together as well. Methodist, Baptist, and Cumberland Presbyterian ministers attracted large followings as they made their circuits through the more remote regions of the Deep South, holding meetings in the homes of church members. The work of the itinerant ministers received reinforcement in revivals and prolonged camp meetings. At these meetings, people listened to ministers deliver intense, emo-

tional, and lengthy sermons. Some participants, claiming to be possessed of the spirit, screamed, danced, and, in some cases, threw themselves on dirt floors in paroxysms of joy. Congregants became so active at times that the minister could not be heard above the din.

Slaveholders shared with non-slaveholders certain fundamental beliefs about the roles of men, women, children, and blacks in households and in the larger society. But the presence of slaves in a household dramatically altered the everyday lives of household members. Slavery also generated a distinctive relationship between the slaveholding household and the larger community.

The husband, father, master was, of course, the dominant member of the slaveholding household. His responsibilities within the household varied with the number of slaves owned. The owner of only a few slaves was in the fields each day, working. A prosperous slaveowner spent much of his time managing the plantation or supervising the overseers and drivers who were responsible for day to day management. Regardless of the size of the plantation, the household head's primary responsibility was to provide for the care and security of his dependents—wife, children, and slaves.

In return, the patriarch expected dependents to be deferential and obedient. Women learned to be submissive to their fathers as preparation for their roles as wives. Southern ladies were to be the embodiment of all that was best in the society. They were to be models of morality and, as mothers, the link between the traditions of the past and future generations. One of the most important roles of the wives of slave owners was, then, the early education of children. In addition to child rearing, wives in households with only a few slaves performed many of the duties described above for wives of non-slaveholding farmers. On larger plantations, domestic slaves took over the cooking, sewing, and cleaning responsibilities.

Children began to learn their roles at an early age. When their sons were about the age of ten, fathers began to teach them habits of command. Sons learned to be assertive, aggressive, self-reliant, and physically courageous. Such lessons were combined with instruction in deference to those in authority, thus creating confusion among children, who were not always sure whom to obey. Planters' sons commonly defied authority figures, especially nonfamilial authority. Parents, in such cases, were likely to support their child's spirit and defense of family pride. When daughters were very young, there was not much difference between their up-bringing and that of their brothers. They learned to ride horses and in some cases to fire a gun. But by the time they reached the age of eight to ten years, they started to learn the lessons of domesticity that, it was hoped, would win them a husband of appropriate standing in the community.

Slave-owners, particularly the wealthier ones, were more likely than non-slave-owners to provide formal education for their children. The labor of sons was not as essential on a slave plantation as it was on a yeoman farm. Thus, planters' sons received tutoring or attended academies in preparation for matriculation at colleges or universities where they acquired the polish, if not the knowledge, they needed before they assumed their places as leaders of society. Even daughters received some formal training in female academies. The purpose of education for women was to enhance their roles as wives and mothers by introducing them to classical and religious literature. It was certainly not to encourage women to question their place in the social order, though in some cases that may have been the result.

The bonds that held yeoman communities to each other were not as powerful within the plantation belts of the Deep South. Plantations could achieve self-sufficiency with little or no assistance from neighbors, so the cooperative work central to community life among non-slaveholders was unnecessary. Other forms of dependency did link plantation households to each other and to the operators of small farms in the black belt. For instance, small farmers in the plantation belts often looked to planters, who might be relatives, for assistance in ginning and marketing their cotton crops.

There were a number of occasions during which people in the plantation districts affirmed their places in the social order and reinforced the values they shared. Formal religious observances and other gatherings provided opportunities for the planter elite to display its power and authority before the public. Slave owners, like non-slave owners, indulged in demonstrations of their courage, physical ability, and other attributes that made them men of honor. But the contests of the planter class reflected the erosion of "primal honor" by the values of the market economy. They were more formal, more disciplined, and more decorous than the contests of backwoodsmen. Violence, while certainly an integral part of male subculture among planters, tended to be more controlled. Gentlemen

settled disputes with ritualistic duels rather than the rough-and-tumble of the backwoods brawl.

In the slave quarters, African Americans created a community and culture of their own. The basic unit of the slave community was the family. Although slaves formed their own households within the plantation household, slave families were always subject to the intervention of masters, who provided basic necessities for slaves, disciplined household members, and could, if they chose, sell family members.

Most masters recognized the stability that family life could bring to the quarters, not to mention the economic gains to be had from slave reproduction, and encouraged their slaves' desire to marry and have children. Approximately two-thirds of all slaves grew up in two-parent households. Within those households, paternal authority was the rule, though the power of masters deprived slave fathers of traditional sources of authority. Given that reality, slave fathers went to great lengths to establish their responsibility for family survival in other ways. Some slave men placed their lives at risk by defending wives and children from beatings. Many hunted and fished in order augment the diets of their families.

Slaves' jobs on the plantation were not always defined by gender; both men and women worked in the fields. This merging of gender roles did not, however, generate equality between black men and women within the slave household. African Americans brought with them with a cultural tradition of male dominance within the immediate and extended household, a tradition reinforced in male-dominated America. Though they may have had more power than did wives in white households, slave women were subordinate to their husbands. Within slave households, there was at least a limited gender-based division of labor. When wives returned from work in the fields or elsewhere on the plantation, they performed a range of household duties, such as mending clothing, preparing food, and cleaning.

Slave households were linked through kinship networks, which extended beyond individual plantations, and a number of communal institutions and traditional practices. The most important social institution within the slave community was the church. Plantation owners tried to impose a theology on their slaves that justified and reinforced white supremacy. But even where masters forbade independent religious services, slaves held their own in secret. A combination of African belief and American Protestantism, African American religious practice was emotionally charged. A call-and-response–style of preaching kept congregations actively involved in sermons. Those sermons were likely to emphasize the biblical promise of deliverance from bondage in this world. Slaves likened themselves to the children of Israel, and they awaited a Moses to lead them to a promised land of freedom. The centrality to slave theology of liberation from bondage mocked masters' use of biblical text to defend their domination.

Politics in the Deep South reflected widespread white support for the institution of slavery and deep division on most other issues. Regardless of socioeconomic status, whites linked their freedom and social status to the enslavement of blacks. White devotion to slavery did not, however, bridge differences over the best way to defend the liberty of the citizenry. Non-slaveholders and small farmers with a few slaves did not do the bidding of slaveholders. In the Deep South socioeconomic distinctions extended into the political arena and shaped the political party system until the late 1850s. The Democrats, with their advocacy of limited government intervention in economic and social affairs, tended to attract hill country farmers and other citizens on the margins of the market economy. Whigs, with their program of aggressive government action to extend the market, tended to attract large planters and others immersed in the market economy. Though this political alignment was only a tendency, it remained fairly consistent throughout the period.

Southern Democrats and Whigs, like Democrats and Whigs across the nation, struggled over a number of economic issues before the 1850s. Debates over government responsibility for banks, internal improvements, and a variety of other services raged in political campaigns and in state legislatures. The Democratic constituency most wanted to be left alone and supported candidates who promised to restrict any expansion of government power. Whigs attempted to counter the Democratic appeal with images of the prosperity and opportunity that would result from economic development. More often than not, Democratic candidates had the better of the argument, but the Whigs remained competitive.

This competitive two-party system generated solutions to socioeconomic conflict and defenses of slavery when that institution was threatened. Politicians in the Deep South served the people by attacking designs against liberties that the people identified. The role of the politician began to change in the 1850s as the region confronted perceived threats to slavery as well as internal crises that accompanied expansion of the market economy into subsistence farming areas. Large numbers of people were vulnerable to the fluctuations of the market for the first time, and many of them suffered for their decisions to abandon safety-first agriculture. At the same time, governments were extending their power in a number of ways, including the active promotion of economic expansion.

All of this produced a generalized fear of the future that politicians sought to exploit. They did not, as in the past, try to identify what the people saw as the source of their troubles. Younger politicians believed that it was not enough to follow the lead of the citizenry. It was the duty of politicians to lead the people, to reveal to them the true sources of their anxiety. This is what southern secessionists ("fire-eaters") did in the 1850s. They managed to persuade white southerners that the real threat to their freedom came from northern Free-Soilers and abolitionists who created the Republican party. Among other things, fire-eaters told their listeners, the Republicans wanted to deprive southerners of the right to move to the West, where they might find prosperity and advance into the class of slaveholders. With this message, the fire-eaters were able to sweep away any opponents who might offer alternative solutions to the sectional and social crisis. They led the people of the Deep South down the road to secession and Civil War.

Although large areas of the Deep South were spared the physical destruction of war, the region faced, along with the rest of the former Confederacy, the daunting task of rebuilding a socioeconomic order based upon free labor. Three visions of the free labor South emerged in the immediate postwar years. Some southern leaders renewed their pleas for the creation of an economically diverse "New South." This New South would, its advocates argued, create non-agricultural opportunities to achieve personal autonomy. Others called for a return to the ways of the Old South with new forms of labor coercion. Still others took the middle ground, calling for the creation of an economy evenly divided between manufacturing and agriculture.

Regardless of the vision one embraced, the problem of labor had to be solved before the economy of the Deep South could begin to recover. Emancipation thrust labor markets in the old plantation belt into chaos. Freedmen left their plantations to search for family members, to move to town, or to test their freedom. Plantation owners, few of whom believed blacks would work in the absence of close supervision, attempted through coercive measures to return the freedmen to the land in a condition little different from slavery. Labor contracts and, for a brief time, Black Codes restricted black mobility and, in some cases, defined for black laborers the proper use of their free time.

Hoping to secure their own land with the assistance of the radical Republicans, freedmen resisted these efforts to return them to a gang labor system. When it became clear that there would be no general redistribution of land and that southern whites would not voluntarily facilitate black land-ownership, freedmen across the region accepted an alternative arrangement called sharecropping. This system satisfied neither planters nor freedmen, but it did offer some benefits to both parties. It was a way for planters to secure needed labor and for freedmen to achieve a measure of freedom from constant white supervision.

Some historians have argued that sharecropping was a repressive system of labor little different from slavery. Sharecropping agreements and the laws governing them could, in theory at least, restrict black mobility. But "labor-tying" contracts and legislation had a limited impact in practice. Turnover among sharecroppers was high; in 1910 only 28 percent of black sharecroppers in the region including the Deep South states had been on their farms for two to four years.

This is not to suggest that sharecropping in the Deep South was a benign institution. Merchants and planters who provided croppers with supplies collected exorbitant rates of interest through double pricing of goods bought on credit and other practices. A crop lien, held by the creditor, secured the sharecroppers' debts. If commodity prices were high, croppers might be able to pay back creditors and break even at the end of the year or even have a little surplus income. If prices declined, as they regularly did during the postbellum period, croppers could descend into a cycle of indebtedness from which they might never escape. Herein lay the roots of southern rural poverty.

Sharecropping was not limited to blacks. From 1866 through the end of the nineteenth century, large numbers of white farmers descended the agricultural ladder into some form of tenancy. This phenomenon was a direct consequence of white farmers' continued shift from subsistence agriculture to production for the market. A combination of high prices in the years immediately following the Civil War and more accessible transportation facilities lured self-sufficient farmers into the market economy. Statistics on crop mix suggest the extent of the change. In Alabama, Mississippi, and Florida, per capita corn and hog production fell sharply between 1860 and 1880. At the same time, cotton production in the hill country and other subsistence farming areas increased significantly. As production surpassed demand, white farmers found it difficult to pay the debts they had incurred for the purchase of supplies and of necessities they no longer produced themselves. Many fell into the same cycle of indebtedness that trapped black sharecroppers. Since merchants insisted upon production of cash crops in return for credit, it was difficult for farmers to return to subsistence agriculture once they fell into debt. Eventually many farmers lost their land to the men who held their crop liens.

While the reconstruction of southern agriculture proceeded, advocates of the New South (or "new departure") pursued their dreams of an industrial South that would rival the industrial North. Expansion of the South's railroad network was an essential first step in the process of industrialization. Completion of a rail line through Alabama's mineral belt made it possible for entrepreneurs to fully exploit rich deposits of coal and iron ore. Beginning in the 1870s, owners of land in Jefferson County, Alabama, began aggressively pursuing potential investors in blast furnaces, rolling mills, and other metal-producing establishments. With offers of cheap land, unlimited mineral rights, and tax breaks, promoters attracted investors to the town they named Birmingham. Although Birmingham would never realize its full potential as an iron- and steel-producing center, it would, by 1920, be the largest industrial center in the Deep South.

Railroads were also critical to the growth of the textile industry. Easy access to transportation was one of the factors promoters could cite as they sought investments in the mills they believed essential to the prosperity of their towns. Mill building became a community project. Residents of towns bought small amounts of stock in mills; many of them paid for the stock on the installment plan. By the early twentieth century, textile mills dotted the region from the Chattahoochee River valley on the east to the Mississippi on the west.

Accompanying the rise of southern industry was a dramatic expansion of the non-agricultural working class. For the first time, thousands of white and black southerners earned their livings in factories or mines rather than on the land. Tired of a seemingly endless cycle of indebtedness and poverty, southerners made their ways to industrial cities and towns, looking for opportunity and, at the very least, a modicum of economic security.

The growth of the working class forced a redefinition of race and class relations. Before the Civil War, class tensions had been contained not only by white devotion to the ideology of white supremacy but also by widespread white ownership of productive resources. Community leaders feared that as the white working class expanded, the supposed racial unity of the antebellum years would give way to the economic class warfare they associated with older industrial societies. What would hold white society together when a large proportion of white men no longer owned the productive resources that set them apart from slaves? Builders of the New South had to find a way to create a biracial industrial society that preserved white privilege and unity.

The solution to the problem was a modification of the antebellum conflation of class and race. In the New South, the best jobs would be reserved for "virtuous" whites. These white workers would be served by a subordinate class of black unskilled laborers. They would unite with white capital on the basis of a common pursuit of prosperity and a shared commitment to the doctrine of white supremacy. Industrial segregation would reinforce the supposed natural harmony between capital and labor.

The effects of this industrial caste system could be seen in all areas of life. White skilled workers in cities like Birmingham lived in middle-class neighborhoods and maintained domestic lives that closely approximated the Victorian ideal. They formed labor organizations to defend their prerogatives at work, including the white monopoly of skilled work. Blacks held the worst jobs and lived in inferior housing, but the rigid system of segregation did not prevent many blacks from improving their condition. In a variety of ways they managed to achieve a measure of control over their working lives, though relatively few were permitted to enter white-controlled unions. Black migrants also created thriving subcommunities bound by kinship ties and associational networks that provided stability and support in times of crisis.

The independent subcommunities that workers built in some cities were in stark contrast with employer-controlled communities. Through a management philosophy known as corporate welfar-

ism, employers, particularly operators of textile mills, sought to attract workers, to educate them in the ways of the industrial world, and to secure their loyalty to the company. Managers and owners, as self-styled heads of the company family, attempted to extend their influence into all areas of their workers' lives. They provided housing and enforced rules of conduct in company quarters. Companies established schools, churches, and recreational facilities where workers received lessons in the time and work discipline essential to the operation of the modern factory. If corporate welfarism worked as its practitioners hoped, workers would work hard and remain loyal out of a sense of "reciprocal obligation."

Corporate welfarism never quite achieved what its practitioners hoped it would. Southern workers never became the docile men and women of promotional literature. When employers violated workers' sense of what was fair, the latter responded with strikes and other forms of resistance. A system designed to promote harmony between capital and labor frequently became a source of class tension and conflict.

Divisions generated by the social and economic reconstruction of the Deep South shaped political life. In the immediate aftermath of the Civil War, during two years of "self-reconstruction," the contours of the new political system began to appear. When constitutional conventions met to establish state governments under the presidential plan of reconstruction, the factional alignment reflected differing ideas about the economic destiny of the South. New South men in Alabama and elsewhere managed to secure constitutions that would allow them to implement their plans for economic development.

White yeoman farmers often clashed with the modernizers in the political arena. They demanded greater equity of representation in state legislatures, where they hoped to secure stay laws (which extended the deadline for meeting a debt), repudiation of debts, and other legislation to relieve their financial distress. Advocates of the New South opposed this legislative agenda because, in their view, it would hinder their efforts to attract northern capital.

A third political faction consisted mainly of planters who wanted to ensure the continued political dominance of the black belt. The planter class did, in fact, maintain considerable political clout during the immediate postwar years and thereafter. They used their political power to secure a series of laws, known collectively as the Black Codes, designed to return freedmen to a status little different from slavery. Planters did not, however, enjoy unquestioned political authority. Modernizers, for instance, saw that the immobilization of black labor would deprive manufacturers of a source of cheap labor and thereby undermine their plans for economic development. Thus governors in Mississippi and Alabama who were supportive of the modernizers vetoed portions of the Black Codes. By the end of 1866 Alabama and Mississippi joined other southern states in repealing those laws which applied only to blacks. Nevertheless, discrimination in enforcement of vagrancy, breach of contract, and apprenticeship laws continued. In addition, state legislatures approved tax and property laws, acceptable to all white factions, designed to force freedmen to work for wages.

Without the right to vote, there was little freedmen could do to prevent the passage of discriminatory legislation or racially biased law enforcement. They did engage in extralegal acts of resistance to repressive laws. In addition, black leaders demanded extension of voting rights to black males. Radical Republicans in the U.S. Congress not only encouraged black demands for voting rights but also proposed a thorough social and political reconstruction of the South under close federal supervision. Citing the Black Codes as evidence of a southern plan to reverse the results of the Civil War, the radicals swept aside President Andrew Johnson and imposed their own plan of reconstruction.

Under the congressional plan of Reconstruction, the southern states were required to hold new constitutional conventions. These conventions included representatives of the three white factions discussed above in addition to representatives of the freedmen. In the conventions, a Republican coalition of blacks, white modernizers, disaffected yeomen, and urban and small-town artisans dominated the proceedings. Each faction within the southern Republican party wanted to write a constitution that would protect its distinct social and economic interests. Thus constitutions ensured blacks the right to vote (a federal requirement) and established the public schools that blacks and modernizers wanted, allowed state governments to underwrite the New South program, and increased the representation of white counties. Generally all of the interest groups got a little of what they wanted.

But the Republican coalition remained shaky as different groups vied for dominance in state leg-

islatures. Representatives of white counties often objected to policies that blacks and modernizers supported, especially when they involved increases in taxation to fund programs that benefited blacks or corporations. Democrats took advantage of tensions within the Republican coalition. They played on white resentment over increased taxation and a resurgence of white fears of government power. They also exploited racial hostility by linking the growth of state power to an alleged plan to destroy white supremacy. The Democrats did not limit their offensive to political campaigns. Terrorist organizations throughout the region used violence and threats of violence to intimidate black and white Republicans. The Democratic assault, combined with inept Republican leadership and the withdrawal of federal support for Republican governments, brought Reconstruction to an end in all the Deep South states by 1877.

Democratic "redeemers" assumed the reins of government, promising tax reductions, smaller government, and unquestioned white supremacy. Alabama's "redeemer" constitution, reflecting agrarian ascendancy in the Democratic party, eliminated important components of the New South program for economic development. It prohibited state aid for internal improvements and sharply reduced government expenditures for schools and other public institutions. The Democrats did not, however, completely abandon the vision of a New South. With the collapse of the southern Republican party, modernizers entered the Democratic party and exercised considerable influence. They were able to secure tax breaks for corporations. Moreover, the laissez-faire philosophy of the Democrats ensured a relaxed regulatory climate that was appealing to potential investors.

As promised, the redeemers moved to reverse the gains that blacks had made under Republican governments. They did not deprive blacks of the right to vote, but they did reduce their representation through imaginative drawing of legislative districts and other devices. Having eliminated effective black political opposition, legislatures passed laws intended to limit the mobility of black laborers. Although such laws never provided the framework for a thoroughly repressive system of labor, many planters did use them effectively as the number of cases of debt peonage in the late nineteenth and early twentieth centuries attests.

White small farmers were not necessarily beneficiaries of redeemer policies. Political conflict between plantation and small-farm districts raged in the 1880s as farmers struggled to survive economically. Small farmers demanded positive government action to relieve their economic distress but often found themselves fighting legislation, such as the closing of the open range, that threatened to worsen their economic plight. The successful closing of the range forced many farmers even further from self-sufficiency, speeding their descent into tenancy.

Neither whites nor blacks meekly submitted to redeemer rule. Throughout the 1880s and especially in the 1890s, they jointly and separately challenged the self-styled saviors of the South. Blacks frequently united with dissenting whites on the basis of their common opposition to redeemer Democrats and voted for Republican candidates. Before 1900, Republican presidential candidates continued to win from 25 percent to 40 percent of votes in Mississippi, Alabama, and Florida. But the legacy of reconstruction and the ever-present tensions of a biracial coalition undermined Republican efforts to cut into Democratic strength. Many political rebels therefore formed independent third parties that were free of the taint of "black reconstruction."

The most decisive challenge to Democratic hegemony had its roots in the Southern Farmers' Alliance, an organization created in the mid 1870s to find ways to relieve farmers' economic distress. Alliance platforms called for government regulation of railroads, government sponsorship of a cooperative marketing plan, and a variety of other reforms. Unable to achieve their goals through the established party system, leaders of the Alliance formed the People's, or Populist, party. Populist candidates, and Democrats allied with them, challenged the Democrats in state and local elections. A combination of fraud, white loyalty to the Democrats, and racial and class divisions within the movement worked against Populist candidates, though some did win elections. Still, by 1896 the Democrats remained in firm control in all of the states of the Deep South.

The political turmoil of these years fueled movements to "purify" southern politics. Whites—Democrats as well as their opponents—began to push for disfranchisement of blacks and other groups deemed unworthy of the vote. Advocates of voting restrictions had various reasons for their position. Many Democrats seem to have feared that a coalition of blacks and lower-class whites might disrupt the mythical "solid South." Former Populists were enraged over alleged Democratic manipulation of the black vote. Many of them had long demanded disfranchisement of blacks because they thought the result would be increased power for white counties. Beginning in 1890, with the adoption of a new constitution in Mississippi, the states of the Deep South employed literacy tests, poll taxes, and other voting restrictions to disfranchise blacks and, much to the dismay of representatives of predominantly white counties, a significant proportion of lower-class whites.

After purging blacks from the electorate, Democrats congratulated themselves for having finally produced a solid Democratic South. As always, however, white unity was more apparent than real. Continuing economic change generated tensions that undermined the order that disfranchisers thought they had created. As cities grew, citizens of the Deep South and the nation had to come to terms with problems of race relations, labor relations, poverty, crime, housing, and inadequate city services.

The urban middle class, its power enhanced by the purification of the electorate, sought to impose its own version of order. Organizations and movements appeared throughout the Deep South to promote a wide array of "reforms." Women were particularly active in humanitarian reform efforts, such as the movements to restrict child labor and to enact compulsory education laws. Within cities, women often played leading roles in the creation of settlement houses and in the building of playgrounds and kindergartens where the children of the working classes could engage in "wholesome" and "productive" activities. The Women's Christian Temperance Union led the fight against the alcohol abuse by males that its members believed threatened to destroy the family and, ultimately, society.

Other reformers addressed the problem of race relations in cities and towns. They were the architects of a system of legalized segregation that extended into almost all areas of life. Laws and city ordinances prohibited racial mixing in theaters, hospitals, cemeteries, and residential neighborhoods. This "Jim Crow" system, reformers thought, would reduce contact between whites and blacks, and thereby lessen the potential for racial violence. Moreover, by defining social privileges only whites could enjoy, proponents of Jim Crowism hoped to reinforce white racial solidarity.

But caste privilege was never enough to bridge class divisions. Most reform movements were middle-class efforts to alter some behavior that reformers associated with working-class life. The objects of uplift recognized the poorly concealed class biases of reformers and resisted imposition of their ideas about appropriate behavior. Many workers fought child labor and compulsory education laws because they could not afford the loss of a child's earnings. Government, they insisted, had no right to interfere with a household head's control of his or her children. Even workers who supported child labor legislation did so for reasons that set them at odds with the middle-class leaders of the movement.

This class resentment found expression in the campaigns of demagogues such as Theodore Bilbo of Mississippi, James Thomas ("Tom-Tom") Heflin of Alabama, and Sidney J. Catts of Florida. With a combination of racist appeals and populist attacks on corporations and the well-to-do, these politicians and others successfully harnessed popular antagonism toward the "gentry." They did not reverse the Progressive program. Rather, they placed more emphasis on the "people's" continuing struggle against "alien" corporations. Thus, state regulation of corporations in the name of the people tended to be a focus of the demagogues once they won office.

The Progressive era brought a few indirect benefits to blacks but was generally a time of deteriorating social and economic conditions. Rural blacks suffered from the destruction of cotton crops by the boll weevil and, in the 1920s, falling commodity prices. Those who fled to southern cities were relegated to the most demeaning, low-paying jobs available. When they left work, they faced stark reminders of their status in a thoroughly segregated world where to be black meant living in the poorest neighborhoods and attending barely adequate schools.

Black southerners did not, however, become helpless victims. They formed organizations that worked to alleviate the worst abuses of the Jim Crow system. But the most effective and historically important black protest was migration out of the region. This movement began during World War I, when sharply reduced European immigration and war-induced economic growth in northern cities created a demand for black labor. The "Great Migration" continued into the 1920s. Black populations in the Deep South fell through the 1920s as men and women left the region looking for opportunity in the "promised land."

A steady stream of black and white migrants flowed into northern and southern cities between the 1930s and the 1960s. In the 1930s, the Roosevelt administration unintentionally contributed to the uprooting of rural southerners with the crop reduction programs of the Agricultural Adjustment Administration. Displaced sharecroppers first turned to wage labor and then, when mobilization for World War II began, moved to cities and towns where there were jobs in war industries. As cities such as Mobile, Alabama, and Pascagoula, Mississippi, filled with men and women seeking war-related jobs, planters lost their laborers. This reduction in the rural labor supply provided the incentive for mechanization of the cotton harvest, a development that pushed even more whites and blacks out of the rural South in the 1950s, 1960s, and 1970s.

The collapse of economic institutions such as sharecropping and the subsequent mass movement of rural southerners to northern and southern cities were essential preconditions for a revolution in southern race relations. In northern cities blacks could vote, and by the 1930s the black vote had become a significant factor in urban and national politics. Moreover, blacks in northern cities formed organizations such as the National Association for the Advancement of Colored People (NAACP) to work through the legal system to secure blacks' civil and political rights. The efforts of the NAACP and other organizations, combined with black political pressure, brought about increased attention to the southern situation by the federal government. In the 1930s and 1940s the U.S. Supreme Court handed down a number of decisions striking down parts of the South's caste system. At the same time, national political parties, particularly the Democratic party, began moving toward support for federal action to end discrimination against blacks.

Encouraged by these developments, southern blacks took matters into their own hands. Urban residents, who experienced the oppression of the racial caste system most directly, led the assault on racial barriers. After Supreme Court decisions that eased some voting restrictions, black organizations sponsored voter registration drives in hopes of building enough political power to begin to chip away at the Jim Crow system. While the number of blacks who were able to register remained small, in some cities there were enough black voters to have an impact on close elections. Blacks in Montgomery, Alabama, led by E. D. Nixon and Jo Ann Robinson, began to apply pressure to a city administration that owed its election in part to black votes. Although they wanted only a modification of harsh Jim Crow practices on city buses, the city commission refused to act. It took Rosa Parks's refusal in December 1955 to give up her seat on a city bus to a white man and a yearlong boycott led by Dr. Martin Luther King, Jr., to end segregation on city buses.

The Montgomery experience transformed the emerging civil rights movement. King and his followers learned that there could be no compromise with segregation. Between 1955 and 1965, blacks in the Deep South attacked Jim Crow through more boycotts, sit-ins, and protest marches. White southerners resisted mightily; few wanted to lose the privileges they had enjoyed for close to a hundred years. The determination of southern blacks, combined with the intervention of the federal government and national support for black civil equality, overcame intense, frequently violent white resistance.

Blacks' successful struggle for civil and political equality wiped out the most glaring remaining distinction between the Deep South and the rest of the nation. Occupational integration has become a reality, and progress toward ending de facto segregation in other areas of life continues. One indicator of the improved racial climate is a growing migration of northern blacks to the homeland of their ancestors. While these modern migrants do not find a model of racial cooperation, they do find a society more at ease with its ethnic and racial differences than many of the northern cities they left behind.

The states of the Deep South have been much less successful in addressing a problem of poverty that is colorblind. Blacks and whites suffer from inadequate health care, poor educational facilities, and stagnant economies. Efforts to solve these problems are ongoing, but racial and class divisions impede progress. Most whites, regardless of economic status, tend to support political candidates who cling to the politics of the past. They do so because they, like their ancestors, see government activism as primarily a benefit for blacks. But, as always, whites are divided. A significant minority of mainly urban middle- and working-class whites tend to join blacks in support of positive government action to raise the region out of its economic malaise. If the majority of voters remain content with the politics of stasis, however, the Deep South is destined to remain distinctive as the most impoverished, poorly educated region in the nation.

BIBLIOGRAPHY

Black, Earl, and Merle Black. *Politics and Society in the South* (1987).

Daniel, Pete. *Standing at the Crossroads: Southern Life Since 1900* (1986).

Flynt, Wayne. *Cracker Messiah: Governor Sidney J. Catts of Florida* (1977).

———. *Poor but Proud: Alabama's Poor Whites* (1989).

Fox-Genovese, Elizabeth. *Within the Plantation Household: Black and White Women of the Old South* (1988).

Genovese, Eugene. *Roll, Jordan, Roll: The World the Slaves Made* (1972).

Goldfield, David. *Promised Land: The South Since 1945* (1987).

Gorn, Elliott J. "'Gouge and Bite, Pull Hair and Scratch': The Social Significance of Fighting in the Southern Backcountry." *American Historical Review* 90 (February 1985): 18–43.

Grantham, Dewey. *Southern Progressivism: The Reconciliation of Progress and Tradition* (1983).

———. *The Life and Death of the Solid South: A Political History* (1988).

Hyman, Michael R. *The Anti-Redeemers: Hill-Country Political Dissenters in the Lower South from Redemption to Populism* (1990).

Kirwan, Albert D. *Revolt of the Rednecks: Mississippi Politics, 1876–1925* (1951).

Newby, Idus A. *Plain Folk in the New South: Social Change and Cultural Persistence, 1880–1915* (1989).

Norrell, Robert J. *Reaping the Whirlwind: The Civil Rights Movement in Tuskegee* (1985).

Oakes, James. *The Ruling Race: A History of American Slaveholders* (1982).

———. *Slavery and Freedom: An Interpretation of the Old South* (1990).

Perman, Michael. *The Road to Redemption: Southern Politics, 1869–1879* (1984).

Thornton, J. Mills. *Politics and Power in a Slave Society: Alabama, 1800–1860* (1978).

Woodward, C. Vann. *Origins of the New South, 1877–1913* (1951).

Wright, Gavin. *The Political Economy of the Cotton South: Households, Markets, and Wealth in the Nineteenth Century* (1978).

Wyatt-Brown, Bertram. *Southern Honor: Ethics and Behavior in the Old South* (1982).

SEE ALSO various essays in the sections "**Ethnic and Racial Subcultures,**" "**Family History,**" "**Popular Culture and Recreation,**" "**Space and Place,**" and "**Work and Labor.**"

PENINSULAR FLORIDA

Gary R. Mormino

IMAGINE A MAP of the continental United States without the Florida peninsula. The mainland assumes the shape of a rough-edged box. But imagine again a map of the Caribbean basin and the southeastern United States. It becomes inconceivable without the obstrusive flying foot of peninsular Florida.

The changing map illustrates a problem that has confounded historians. Just where does Florida belong? During the land boom of the 1920s a promoter gushed, "Florida is the finger of Uncle Sam pointing the way to paradise." Congressman John Randolph saw Florida differently. Opposing an appropriations bill supported by Andrew Jackson's administration, the cantankerous Virginian insisted that he "would not give up an eligible position in hell for all Florida."

One's vision of Florida depends largely upon timing and perspective. For much of the region's history the land was too wet, the climate too hot, and the environment too challenging. The twentieth century has witnessed an extraordinary transformation, as developers, politicians, and bureaucrats have attempted to impose a new order upon the land. In 1890 the population of Florida had not yet reached four hundred thousand persons. Only about 20 percent of the state's people inhabited "peninsular" Florida, the vast area south of a west-to-east line roughly stretching from Cedar Key in the Gulf of Mexico to Ocala and across to Daytona Beach. A century later the 1990 census revealed that Florida had become the nation's fourth largest state, with most of its thirteen million residents living in south and central Florida, where metropolises and suburbs have been built on swamp and forest lands.

The largest state east of the Mississippi, Florida is 65,758 square miles (170,970 square kilometers) in area and has about 8,500 miles (9,010 kilometers) of tidal shoreline. Tallahassee, the state capital, lies 20 miles (32 kilometers) from the Georgia border and 500 miles (800 kilometers) from Miami. Key West, the most important island of an intricate archipelago off the Straits of Florida, lies just 90 miles (144 kilometers) from Cuba but about 800 miles (1,280 kilometers) from Pensacola.

Napoleon Bonaparte, ever mindful of the significance of distances, once observed that Italy was too long to be a country. Florida, it can be argued, is too long to be a state: the sheer distance from north to south has certainly influenced the natural history and development of Florida. The panhandle, from the bayous of Pensacola and Apalachicola bays to the red piedmont hills of Tallahassee, is a distinct region that shares a heritage more with southern Georgia and Alabama than with peninsular Florida. Writers for *Florida: A Guide to the Southernmost State* noted this oddity in 1939, observing, "Politically and socially, Florida has its own North and South, but its northern area is strictly southern and its southern area definitely northern."

The vast interior of Florida presents a series of diverse ecosystems. Spanish missionaries established cattle *ranchos* on the savannas of north central Florida. To the south, cattle ranged across a large expanse of piney woods and scrubland. The sandy soil there only grudgingly supported grasses and palmetto scrub—a single steer or cow needed twenty acres to feed on—but the longhorn cattle had few competitors on this open range. (Indeed, cattlemen exercised sufficient political clout to delay the end of the open range until 1949.) The geography of the Florida interior largely determined early settlement. Pioneers quickly discovered the fertility of the high hammock lands along the peninsula's many rivers. Over thirty thousand lakes, rivers, and springs interlace Florida. A wag had the West in mind when he said, "Whiskey's for drinkin'; water's for fightin' over," but his aphorism is equally true of Florida. Much of the state's water is stored below the surface in aquifers, immense porous limestone basins that act like sponges.

The abundant waters of the Kissimmee River arise from the Green Swamp south of Orlando and once meandered 90 miles (145 kilometers) down into Lake Okeechobee. Fed by the river and by the landscape's sheet-flow, the 750-square-mile (1,850-square-kilometer) lake resembles a saucer, a shallow basin that regularly overflows to nurture the vast tract of saw grass marshes and prairie known as the Everglades before it escapes into the Gulf of Mexico 120 miles away. In 1947, President Harry Truman dedicated the Everglades National Park, a 1.4-million-acre (560,000-hectare) preserve. The following year the U.S. Army Corps of Engineers began a $94-million project to build a matrix of canals, pumping stations, and levees designed to reclaim a thousand square miles (twenty-six hundred square kilometers) of virgin lands for agricultural purposes. In 1970 the Corps finished "C-38" (Canal 38), a euphemism for a dubious project that straightened the Kissimmee by diverting its water through a concrete-lined ditch, thus shortening the distance to Lake Okeechobee from 90 miles to 52 miles (157 to 83 kilometers). The result is more a sewer than a river.

Anyone who looks at a topographical map of the Florida peninsula will quickly grasp what has been the vision of countless promoters, colonists, and politicians: to build a canal across the flat terrain, thus creating jobs while shortening the passage around the Florida cape. Pedro Menéndez de Avilés and John Quincy Adams dreamed of the idea, but it took the public works largess of the New Deal to authorize the project in 1935. Congress refused to appropriate any money for the canal, however, and little work was done. The idea won favor again during World War II—the canal would serve as a sanctuary for U.S. ships—but even though Congress authorized the project, again it refused to appropriate funds. What the Great Depression and the war failed to do, Lyndon Johnson's Great Society was determined to accomplish. Engineers diverted the Oklawaha River and built reservoirs, but the harebrained Cross-Florida Barge Canal still was not completed. President Nixon, heeding the advice of conservationists and trimming the sails of the Great Society, halted the controversial project in 1971. No further work has been done.

FLORIDA INDIANS

When Juan Ponce de León first touched land in 1513, the aboriginal inhabitants had lived on the Florida peninsula for at least ten thousand years. Indeed, some of the earliest evidence of Indian life in North America is found along the Gulf Coast at Little Salt Springs and Warm Mineral Springs. Never dependent upon agriculture, native Floridians enjoyed a protein-rich diet from the abundant supply of marine life and forest game.

Contact with Europeans in the sixteenth and seventeenth centuries proved fatal to native Floridians. Most scholars now believe that at least several hundred thousand, perhaps three-quarters of a million Apalachee, Timucua, Calusa, Tequesta, and Ais lived along the peninsula on the eve of the encounter. By the late eighteenth century the original inhabitants of Florida had vanished, victims of disease, Spanish depredations, the slave trade, and forced relocation.

Early in the eighteenth century a new, relatively small tribe, the Seminoles, formed in Florida from various groups, including Creek refugees from Georgia, remnants of the native Apalachees, and runaway slaves. The tribe fought many battles with the United States military in the early nineteenth century before being forced to move to Oklahoma in the 1840s. A small group remained, though, withdrawing deep into the Everglades; they finally agreed to settle on a reservation in 1934.

LA FLORIDA

When Spanish sea captains returned from their global voyages, royal cartographers scrutinized the ship logs, hoping to gain information about new lands and bodies of water. They recorded the data on a master chart called *el Padrón Real,* the map of the known world. At some point early in the sixteenth century a spit of land north of Cuba appeared on Spanish maps. As Lucas Vázquez de Ayllón, Hernando de Soto, and others probed the new frontier, the spit of land became a peninsula, in time revealing that *la Florida* was an appendage of a great continent.

This geographic confusion runs to the marrow of Florida history. For much of its Spanish history Florida was only a poor outpost on the fringe of a powerful and vast empire. Spanish colonial policy and local customs dictated the rhythms of Florida history for centuries. A vigorous missionary system, public works, and the settlement of Saint Augustine (1565) marked Spanish life in Florida.

In 1763, as part of the terms of the treaty ending the Seven Years' War, Great Britain returned

PENINSULAR FLORIDA

Cuba to Spain in exchange for Florida. British rule lasted only twenty years, and little of consequence occurred on the peninsula. In 1783, Spain was rewarded for helping the American colonies defeat Great Britain in the revolutionary war, recovering Florida at the peace table. By this time, however, Spain's empire was in decline, and its colonies throughout the Americas began winning their independence. After 1800 the inexorable push of pioneers into southern Georgia and Alabama, and the stirrings of American nationalism, made it a question of when, not whether, the United States would seize Spanish Florida. A series of regional disputes over runaway slaves and clashes with the Seminole Indians, supercharged by the War of 1812 with Britain and hatred of things Spanish and Catholic, provided the excuse for General Andrew Jackson to lead an invasion force into Florida. This was the First Seminole War, and it culminated in Spain ceding Florida to the United States by the Adams-Onís Treaty, ratified in 1821.

FLORIDA'S COLUMBIAN EXCHANGE

Although the Spaniards withdrew from Florida, the consequences of their rule continued to affect the new Florida. The encounters between Europeans and Native Americans that began with the voyages of Christopher Columbus set in motion a series of events that has come to be called the "Columbian Exchange." For three centuries the peninsula served as a meeting ground for Europeans, Africans, and Native Americans. Creoles, mestizos, and mulattos created new groupings and notions of ethnicity and nationality.

Perhaps the most visible reminder of the Columbian Exchange was the plethora of European animals that came to the Americas. The introduction of horses, cattle, donkeys, sheep, goats, swine, and poultry not only changed the diet of native Floridians, but also dramatically altered the environment. In addition, plants were taken back and forth between the Americas, Europe, and Africa, and many non-native species found fertile soil in Florida. Quickly gardens and farms began growing such produce as watermelons, broad beans, sugarcane, tomatoes, potatoes, and peppers. Subtropical trees and plants, including bougainvillea, coconut palms, and Seville oranges, now identified as the quintessence of Florida, all came from elsewhere.

Spanish Florida and English Carolina may not have shared the same passion for piquant peppers, but both cultures embraced slavery, albeit under differing customs and laws. African slaves accompanied *conquistadores* during some of the early *entradas*. Spain fully expected to exploit native Floridians, but epidemics reduced the value of the *encomienda* (forced labor contract). African slavery was one solution to this persistent labor shortage. When the Spanish crown authorized major projects, such as the Castillo de San Marcos (1672–1696), officials recruited Apalachee Indians, convicts, Creole artisans, and Afro-Caribbean slaves to do most of the work. However, slavery in Spanish Florida was never widespread, nor did it mirror the "peculiar institution" that evolved in Anglo America.

Spanish law held that slavery insults the laws of nature. Slaves had rights, such as the chance to hold and transfer property. The Catholic Church protected slaves, too, ensuring them the sacraments. Spain encouraged slaves in the Carolinas and Georgia to seek asylum in Florida, provided that they accepted the "True Faith" and swore obedience to the crown. Maroons—fugitive slaves from the Caribbean—also founded sanctuaries in the peninsula's secluded expanses. In 1738, Governor Manuel de Montiano authorized the establishment of a refugee community for British slaves north of Saint Augustine. This became Fort Mose, the first free black settlement in North America. When England acquired Florida in 1763, the inhabitants of Fort Mose joined thousands of other Floridanos who departed for Cuba. New values and laws again changed the meaning and definition of slavery when Florida became a territory of the United States in 1821.

THE FRONTIER

The lure of prime cotton lands enticed thousands of settlers to Florida during the territorial period, 1821–1845. Cotton and slaves defined power in antebellum Florida. Like sugar, cotton required intensive labor, which in the Americas generally meant reliance upon slaves. The economic dominance by planter interests and the rapid settlement of middle Florida (the stretch between the Apalachicola and Suwannee rivers) had enormous implications for the future. The selection of Tallahassee as capital and the establishment of political, educational, and economic institutions in middle Florida reinforced that region's power, much to the detriment of peninsular Florida. Politically, Florida remained a prisoner of these nineteenth-century patterns well into the following century.

South Florida remained the last great frontier east of the Mississippi, a region largely unsettled prior to the 1880s. When Florida became a state in 1845, its population density was about one person per square mile. On the eve of the Civil War about five thousand persons resided in peninsular Florida. Dade County, which then included the future megacounties of Dade, Broward, and Palm Beach, numbered eighty-three persons. Only a handful of pioneers had settled there, mostly along the Miami River and Biscayne Bay.

Farther south, Key West had become Florida's largest city by 1860, its 2,832 residents hailing from the Bahamas, New England, and the South. Founded in 1823, Key West saw thriving sponge and salt industries begin in the 1850s. The city's economy fluctuated depending upon the size of military appropriations and the success of the infamous wreckers, who claimed salvage on the many ships that foundered going through the Straits of Florida. Key West's slaves—there were 435 in 1860—worked at a variety of artisan trades and construction jobs.

The island architecture, a blend of Caribbean accents, New England carpentry, and shipwreck timber, radiated a distinctive and functional style. Nineteenth-century visitors noted the widow's walks and cisterns, the latter necessitated by Key West's lack of freshwater wells.

The Second Seminole War (1835–1842) and the Third Seminole War (1855–1858) left the Florida peninsula crisscrossed with crudely constructed military roads, blockhouses, and forts. Towns often grew from military cantonments, evidenced by Fort King (Ocala), Fort Meade, Fort Lauderdale, Fort Dallas (Miami), Fort Myers, Fort Brooke (Tampa), and Fort Harrison (Clearwater). These early wars taught a valuable lesson to sutlers, promoters, and developers: during war federal appropriations pour into Florida, but peace drastically reduces the flow.

The Armed Occupation Act of 1842 and other inducements to homesteaders did not result in a land rush to peninsular Florida. Two persistent problems retarded progress. First, the vast expanse of central and south Florida was inaccessible and isolated: only a handful of stagecoaches served the interior, and ships offered irregular service from Cedar Key and Tampa. Second, yellow fever was a persistent scourge, especially in the port cities. As late as the 1880s two epidemics ravaged Florida, killing 430 people in Jacksonville and nearly 100 in Tampa.

The Florida frontier exacted a harsh price from the first settlers. Mosquitoes, snakes, and panthers annoyed and threatened people and livestock. The sandy terrain and swamp muck were not easy to farm. It required decades of experimentation to find the right balance of growing season, crop selection, and soil management. Winter freezes frequently ruined everything. The terrible winter freeze of 1894–1895, which came in the wake of a national depression, ranks as one of Florida's great catastrophes. Periodic hurricanes and storms (1848, 1871, 1878) provided stern lessons in survival.

A Florida folk saying suggests that the frontier was heaven for men and horses, hell for women and oxen. Both the birthrate and infant mortality were very high. Violence was also endemic to central and south Florida, taking a cruel toll on families, workers, and minorities.

Despite the problems, in the 1840s a steady stream of farmers and ranchers filtered into Florida's river valleys. Within two decades pioneers had settled the Indian River interior on the east coast and the Alafia, Manatee, Peace, Withlacoochee, and Caloosahatchee river valleys on the west coast. Drawn principally from the Deep South, the now-celebrated but then much-ridiculed "Crackers" raised corn, sweet potatoes, sugarcane, and small amounts of tobacco and cotton. Farmers rarely cultivated all of their land, instead allowing cattle, hogs, and goats to roam in the timber and open range. Some farmers also worked as fieldhands on the large cattle ranches. Cattle, not land, typically defined power in the antebellum Florida peninsula. On the eve of war Florida ranked second only to Texas in per capita livestock value.

Slavery existed in central and south Florida, but never played a vital role in the region's economy. In 1860 slaves constituted one-sixth of Hillsborough County's population. Robert Gamble spent a fortune attempting to grow sugar along the Manatee River, but in 1858 he lost his 102 slaves when the financial panic hit Florida. Typically, slaveholders consisted of small farmers living in rural hamlets, but there were some slaves in Tampa and other urban areas who worked as day laborers, servants, and artisans.

THE CIVIL WAR

The Civil War did not ravage Florida as it did many Confederate states. Tallahassee, locals proudly point out, was the only Southern capital east of the Mississippi not to be captured. Of course, critics can easily argue that Tallahassee was not worth capturing and that Florida was, in Whitelaw Reid's words, "the smallest tadpole in the dirty pool of secession." Although Florida's fifteen thousand troops (another thirteen hundred joined Union forces) suffered grievous losses, the state contributed relatively little to the Confederate cause. Florida's industrial capability was scant, as was its population—140,424 in 1860, which included only 77,747 whites.

As Southern losses mounted, however, the Confederacy relied on Florida for two critical commodities, salt and cattle. Profiteers and patriots erected hundreds of boilers from Saint Andrews Bay to Charlotte Harbor, in an effort to extract salt from seawater. Florida's cattle became especially vital following the fall of Vicksburg in 1863 and the consequent loss of western beef. The Cow Cavalry, created as a special military unit within the commissary department, drove thousands of cattle north from the Kissimmee and Peace river basins. Guerrilla warfare came to the peninsula as Union Rangers attempted to disrupt civilian morale and the supply of cattle. Widespread damage to homes, livestock, and farms resulted from Florida's inner civil war. Union forces seized major ports and imposed a blockade throughout the war, resulting in severe shortages of medicine and staple goods.

The Civil War's long-term consequences for the South and Florida still invoke debate, but the conflict's impact upon peninsular Florida seems insignificant. In retrospect the 1860s seem far less important than the transportation revolutions (railroads and automobiles), the technological change (DDT and air conditioning), and the conflicts (especially World War II) that came later. When the Confederacy surrendered in 1865, south and central Florida had changed little since the bombardment of Fort Sumter; the region was isolated, desperately poor, and a prisoner of the environment. African Americans exchanged chattel slavery for an uncertain status as wage laborers. Extralegal groups, such as the Ku Klux Klan and the Regulators, inflicted a harsh price upon freedmen but also targeted whites for vigilante violence. Frequently the lynchings and floggings were carried out by leading citizens.

The railroad did not come to Florida until much later. In 1861 the state was last among Confederate states in railroad mileage, its 327 miles of track comparing poorly to Virginia's eighteen hundred miles or even South Carolina's thousand. Florida fared little better during Reconstruction, as bond defaults and shady financiers left the state nearly bankrupt.

COMING OF AGE: THE 1880S

In his novel *From the Earth to the Moon,* Jules Verne imagined a giant cannon that could thrust a rocket into space. He selected the fictional south Florida town of Stones Hill as the launch site. But the real propellant for Florida's takeoff was not gunpowder but rather steel and steam, hard currency and liquid capital. The revolution of the 1880s reshaped peninsular Florida, altering its living spaces, recasting its economy, and increasing its population.

"How the railroad kills time and space!" exclaimed the Ocala *Banner* in 1884. The arrival of the railroad transformed the peninsula, integrating a once-isolated region into the national economy and communications system. Central Florida now rushed crates of oranges to new markets, each bearing labels from groves in towns like Frostproof and Winter Haven. Florida vegetables quickly became synonymous with winter. The state's cities began to specialize to meet the demands of urban America: Fort Myers became the gladiola capital, Sanford touted celery, Plant City marketed strawberries, and Zellwood advertised its coveted corn.

Florida established an Internal Improvement Fund to encourage northern investment in return for state lands. In 1881 desperate Florida officials induced a Philadelphia manufacturer, Hamilton Disston, to purchase a staggering four million acres in south Florida for one million dollars. Disston struggled to dredge canals and rivers and to establish a land company and agricultural empire, but his efforts never matched his dream.

Henry B. Plant and Henry M. Flagler enjoyed considerably more success than Disston. Plant, a Connecticut Yankee and the embodiment of the Gilded Age robber baron, acquired an empire of railroads, steamships, and hotels that he ran under one nameplate, the "Plant System." By Plant's death in 1899, his transportation empire had brought the Gulf coast into an international network of travel, trade, and tourism. By 1884 Plant's railroad connected Tampa with Jacksonville, then plunged southward (followed by grandiose hotels). The arrival of the railroad also coincided with the discovery of prodigious amounts of phosphate in the Bone Valley and along the Peace River. Freight trains hauled the phosphate to another Plant creation, Port Tampa, where it was loaded aboard ships bound for domestic and foreign markets. Eventually, Plant's railroad pushed as far south as Fort Myers.

Wild, exploitative, and reckless, the Gilded Age left Florida pockmarked with phosphate pits and denuded forests, but the era's creative energies also refined the art of tourism and travel. Many Americans, flush with the successes of unbridled capitalism, began to seek therapy for nerve-racked bodies. Recreation, once the antithesis of work, was becoming its restorative tonic. A distinctive travel style evolved as Americans discovered Florida. The 1870s and 1880s marked the golden age of Florida steamboating; a journey down the twisting Oklawaha River became an obligatory rite in the new Eden. Writers such as the Georgia-born poet Sidney Lanier trumpeted the joys of an undiscovered Florida.

But if the 1870s evoked charming sternwheelers and hunting lodges, the 1880s introduced fast trains and hotels fostering conspicuous consumption. The 1870s belonged to Jacksonville and Silver Springs; the new era pointed to Palm Beach and Miami. The link between tourism and the urban development of Florida's east coast is inseparable and owes much to the vision of Henry M. Flagler. A multimillionaire by virtue of his association with Rockefeller's Standard Oil Company, Flagler launched a second spectacular career in the 1880s. Beginning in Saint Augustine with his Ponce de Leon Hotel in 1888 and culminating in 1912 with the completion of the "impossible railroad" to Key West, Flagler defined the future of the east coast. He methodically pushed the Florida East Coast Railroad from Saint Augustine to Daytona Beach to Palm Beach and Miami, building such stunning hotels as Miami's Royal Palm in the process. The birth of modern Miami coincided with the coming of Flagler's railroad.

Florida's population center began to shift perceptibly in the late nineteenth century. In 1880 three-quarters of the state's inhabitants still lived in north Florida; by 1900 that figure had been reduced to two-thirds, and by 1920 it was less than half. In those days Florida, like the Deep South, attracted relatively few immigrants from overseas. In 1880 only 9,909 immigrants resided in the state. Florida's foreign-born exerted influence far out of proportion to their numbers, however. In 1868 a rebellion in Cuba sparked an exodus of refugees to Key West. "Cayo Hueso" quickly became an expatriate Cuban capital, home to a burgeoning cigar industry.

Labor strife and political unrest troubled Key West, causing the Spanish entrepreneur Vincent Martínez Ybor to move his cigar operations to Tampa in 1886. Ybor City quickly became the manufacturing center for hand-rolled cigars, home to two hundred factories and ten thousand Spaniards, Cubans, and Italians (all called "Latins" in the vernacular). A rich institutional life evolved, resulting in progressive mutual aid societies and a fiery labor movement. Latin women played a creative role in Ybor City, working at the factories and rallying support for causes such as Cuba Libre—the movement to free Cuba from Spanish rule—and labor unions. In 1898 Tampa was the port of embarkation for American troops on the way to Cuba.

THE FLORIDA BOOM

Florida became Florida during the 1920s. The decade accelerated changes that had been occurring since the 1880s and were increasing the socio-economic distance between the peninsula and the Deep South. In the 1920 census, when Florida came up just short of one million people, for the first time in the state's history a majority of residents were recorded as living downstate. Peninsular Floridians, in contrast to their counterparts in the Deep South, lived in urban centers. Miami, Fort Lauderdale, Sarasota, and Saint Petersburg were maturing as cities when the real estate boom of the 1920s quickened their pace and heightened their profiles.

Florida trafficked optimism and sunshine to a nation looking for a release from the horrors of World War I. The state held a fascination for Americans drained by the business of business. The Mediterranean Revival architecture fit the subtropical landscape, and architects such as Addison Mizner and George Merrick designed Palm Beach, Boca Raton, and Coral Gables with vision and style. To make the Sunshine State even more attractive, Flo-

ridians amended the state constitution in 1924 to prohibit taxes on inheritance and income, a decision with profound consequences for future lawmakers.

Tourism served as handmaiden to growth, as many visitors bought into the Florida dream. If the steamboat and railroad defined tourism and travel in the late nineteenth century, the Model T and the airplane did so in twentieth-century Florida. The automobile helped to democratize tourism. The "Tin Can Tourists," who traveled with supplies of canned food in the backseat and preferred the auto campground to a hotel, personified this new breed of traveler.

Cities perfected the art of public relations. Saint Petersburg photographed sun-seeking visitors and sent pictures to hometown-snowbound newspapers. By promoting its image as a healthy and wholesome city, Saint Petersburg grew from 4,127 persons in 1910 to 14,237 in 1920, to over 30,000 in 1926. Glittering achievements accompanied this population surge, including construction of the "million-dollar pier," a half-dozen lavish hotels, and the Gandy Bridge spanning Tampa Bay. John Ringling established the winter headquarters of his circus in Sarasota and helped to transform the city and nearby islands. The Tamiami Trail, south Florida's first cross-state highway, opened up Fort Myers, "the City of Palms."

This bubble burst in 1926, victim of overspeculation, shaky financing, bank failures, and negative publicity. A devastating hurricane and the arrival of the Mediterranean fruitfly punctuated the losses. Even so, the 1920s left behind a very different Florida. With the influx of retirees, Florida now had the lowest annual birth rate in the South. While other states in Dixie were losing people, Florida's influx brought about a 52 percent increase in population from 1920 to 1930.

Florida also became the whitest Deep South state. In 1880, African Americans constituted nearly half of Florida's population; by 1930 the percentage of blacks had declined to 29 percent. Most newcomers to the state were white; and many north Florida blacks had been lured to the industrial North. In this same period many displaced farmers moved to the dynamic cities of Miami and Tampa.

The Great Depression added to the state's woes. Florida cities, in particular, suffered throughout the 1930s because neither an urban infrastructure nor a civic commitment had been developed to deal with medical, housing, or educational problems. By 1932 nearly a quarter of the state's population received some kind of government assistance. The average annual wage in Florida sank to $289 in 1933. Sarasota, once a prosperous city, was described in the 1930s as "a ghostly town with its poor empty skyscrapers."

The New Deal forged a new relationship with states, and Florida benefited from the flood of federal monies, despite state officials' vacillation in response to President Franklin Roosevelt's New Deal programs. The Agricultural Adjustment Administration (AAA) brought order to the competitive citrus and vegetable markets, ensuring the survival of the biggest firms. The Public Works Administration (PWA) and the Works Progress Administration (WPA) built over two hundred major projects in Florida, including many new schools, bridges, and airports. Overall, federal expenditures in Florida rose from $13 million in 1930 to $63 million in 1934. Yet, in the end, World War II, not the New Deal, ended the Great Depression.

WORLD WAR II

World War II forms a bridge connecting early-twentieth-century Florida with the 1990s. The war and its aftermath transformed Florida from a developing state into a Sunbelt phenomenon.

The most tangible evidence of war in the state was the exponential growth in the military establishment. Since the Era of Good Feeling in the 1820s, Floridians had linked prosperity with defense funds, but a two-theater war unleashed unprecedented amounts of federal spending. Wings over the Sunshine State became a familiar sight: in 1939 Florida claimed six aviation schools, but on VJ Day there were forty. Overall, 172 military complexes breathed economic life into rural and urban Florida. The military even occupied the Gold Coast, the strip of hotels from Palm Beach to Miami, converting hundreds of tourist hotels into barracks and hospitals.

War diversified Florida's economy, which prior to Pearl Harbor was concentrated in the narrow sectors of tourism, agriculture, and extractive industries. Defense contracts revived the moribund shipbuilding industry along the Gulf coast. Still, the war never transformed Florida into an industrial power; the state remained more campground than arsenal. In heavy industry—chemicals, plastics, oil refining, iron, and steel—Florida continued to fare poorly. Even during war its greatest assets were sunshine and beaches.

World War II also intensified the movement toward large-scale agriculture. Thousands of marginal farmers left the land for well-paying defense jobs. The wartime labor shortage provided an excuse for agricultural interests to import foreign labor to harvest crops, a policy that continued after the war. Two scientific breakthroughs, the development of DDT and the perfecting of frozen juice concentrate, had a dramatic impact upon postwar agriculture and the environment.

The war also swept women into its vortex: agriculture officials estimated that one-quarter of Florida's wartime farm workers were women, and women performed myriad roles during the war, as workers, volunteers, and soldiers.

World War II may have threatened life and liberty but not the pursuit of happiness. Black markets, resort centers, and racetracks thrived, almost uninterrupted by the conflict. The *Miami Herald* observed in 1942, "Come wars, booms or depressions, there will always be a Greater Miami tourist crop." Novelist Philip Wylie, astonished at the wartime carnival of consumption, wrote in 1944, "Midas has moved back to Miami."

Florida emerged from the war unscathed and emboldened for the future. Big business and big agriculture expanded and protected their spheres of interest. Florida's future growth was set by powerful forces in Washington, the Caribbean, and elsewhere. The military-industrial complex ensured a profusion of steady spending. In Washington, Congress expanded or endowed entitlement programs such as the GI Bill, Social Security, and the Interstate Highway Trust Fund, all of which had enormous consequences for residents of the Sunshine State.

SUNBELT FLORIDA

Florida passed from Old South to New South to Sunbelt in an astonishingly brief period, and its experiences in the 1940s and 1950s augured the future. Florida's population grew by 46 percent during the 1940s and a remarkable 79 percent in the following decade. By 1950 almost two-thirds of Floridians resided in urban areas, compared to less than half for the rest of the South. Growth begat growth over subsequent decades. During the 1980s Florida gained nearly 3.5 million persons, an increase of 33 percent. Almost all of the new growth has been on the peninsula. During the 1980s nine of the nation's fastest growing metropolitan areas were in Florida, only two of them (Orlando and Ocala) in the interior. The Naples area, which in 1930 boasted fewer than three thousand persons, grew by 77 percent during the 1980s.

Demographically, the "graying" of Florida represents one of the century's newest phenomena, personified by Claude Pepper, the congressman from Florida's Eighteenth District who became identified with advancing the rights of senior citizens in the 1970s and 1980s. Florida's over-65 population increased 40 percent during the 1970s and again during the 1980s; by 1980 the state's median age (34.7) and percentage of population over age 65 (17.3) led the nation. More concretely, retirement living defined the life-styles and policies of more and more south Florida communities. In 1950, Pasco County's median age stood at 32; by the late 1980s it had risen to 55. In Gulf coast counties such as Hernando, Charlotte, and Citrus, Social Security and pension checks represent *the* major "industry." The aging of Florida has spawned new and vexing problems, such as medical care, generational conflict, and the feminization of poverty—for women, on average, live about seven years longer than do men.

Many of retirees are first- and second-generation white ethnics who have left the Rustbelt for the Sunbelt. The Jewish diaspora to Miami began in the 1930s. By the 1980s a four-square-mile area of high-rise condominiums in North Miami Beach claimed status as the most densely populated Jewish enclave in the world. In recent decades, as Miami has become increasingly Hispanic, Florida's Jewish center has shifted northward to Broward and Palm Beach counties. Today, over half a million Jews reside in this corridor, a figure that rises to over a million during the winter season. In addition, large numbers of Italian and Slavic Americans have retired and moved to central and south Florida. Fort Lauderdale, which had no Italian immigrant community during the early twentieth century, now is home to over one hundred thousand Italian Americans.

Jewish and Italian migrants pale in comparison to the Hispanic presence in the southeastern part of the state. Not since Jewish immigrants chose New York as the promised city has one ethnic group so dynamized and altered the course of a U.S. community as did Cubans in Miami. In 1959 Miami was a medium-sized resort city on the decline—until the government of Fulgencio Batista was overthrown by Fidel Castro, resulting in a series of Cuban exoduses. Each was distinct but each re-

shaped Miami. The first migration, the Golden Exile, 1959–1962, consisted mostly of light-skinned, well-educated Cubans. Many escaped with no assets but their own abilities, and the American government and Miami were tolerant and generous. The early Cubans flourished in Miami. From 1965 to 1976 an "air brigade" regularly brought large numbers of new Cubans, and Miami became increasingly Hispanicized. The center of the Cuban community, Eighth Street, became better known as Calle Ocho. In 1980 the controversial Mariel boatlift brought some 125,000 Cubans, many of whom were poor and dark-skinned; their arrival met with less welcome.

Other revolutions have brought waves of Central American and Caribbean peoples to Miami. The 1990 census revealed that over one million Hispanics reside in Dade County and that over half of Miami's population is Latin. Haitian refugees, too, have became a major presence, and the city's ethnic cauldron has bubbled over on numerous occasions as minor events precipitate ethnic and racial tensions. Miami, quipped a commentator, is the only American city with a foreign policy.

Miami's transition from a tourist city to a hemispheric center of trade and commerce paralleled an equally dramatic shift in the flow of tourists from south Florida to Orlando. Prior to the 1950s tourism was a six-month enterprise. Visitors fleeing the northern cold flocked to Florida beaches and golf courses, frequenting mom-and-pop motels and local attractions. Then air conditioning allowed Floridians to have their sunshine and cool it, too, and Walt Disney changed the way Americans play.

Interstate highways, the American obsession with leisure, a postwar baby boom, and unprecedented affluence allowed developers to market Florida as a winter *and* summer playground. Retirees and tourists found the Sunshine State irresistible all year round. New economic trends and technologies allowed promoters to design new environments, even to give form to fantasies. Beaches and alligator farms had become commonplace; theme parks offered new experiences.

In 1971, Walt Disney World opened. After 1982, when Disney's Epcot Center opened, the complex became the world's greatest tourist attraction, luring twenty million visitors annually. Busch Gardens in Tampa and Sea World in Orlando bring in an additional seven million travelers, part of a forty-million-strong annual tourist crop in 1990. Compare that to 1933, when one million tourists sought solace in Florida, or to 1950, when a then-record five million visitors arrived.

In the iconography of popular culture Florida has become front-page fare. But nothing is forever in Florida. Population estimates have the shelf life of a political coup or new trends. During the 1980s, Miami Beach changed rapidly from a depressed haven for senior citizens into a fashionable enclave for the young and upwardly mobile. Beneath the veneer of caricatures is a complex social reality that reflects the passage from New Spain to Old South to New South to Sunbelt.

BIBLIOGRAPHY

Arsenault, Raymond. "The End of the Long Hot Summer: The Air Conditioner and Southern Culture." *Journal of Southern History* 6 (1984).

Bernard, Richard, and Bradley Rice, eds. *Sunbelt Cities: Politics and Growth Since World War II* (1984).

Blake, Nelson M. *Land into Water—Water into Land: A History of Water Management in Florida* (1980).

Brown, Canter, Jr. *Florida's Peace River Frontier* (1991).

Dietrich, T. Stanton. *The Urbanization of Florida's Population: An Historical Perspective of County Growth, 1830–1970* (1978).

Dillion, Rodney E., Jr. "South Florida in 1860." *Florida Historical Quarterly* 60, no. 4 (1982).

Dobyns, Henry F. *Their Number Become Thinned: Native American Population Dynamics in Eastern North America* (1984).

George, Paul S. "Brokers, Binders, and Builders: Greater Miami's Boom of the 1920s." *Florida Historical Quarterly* 64, no. 1 (1986).

Landers, Jane. "García Real de Santa Teresa de Mose: A Free Black Town in Spanish Colonial Florida." *American Historical Review* 95 (1990).

Mahon, John K. *History of the Second Seminole War, 1835–1842* (1967).

Milanich, Jerald T., and Susan Milbrath, eds. *First Encounters: Spanish Explorations in the Caribbean and the United States, 1492–1570* (1989).

Miller, Randall M., and George E. Pozzetta, eds. *Shades of the Sunbelt: Essays on Ethnicity, Race, and the Urban South* (1988).

Mormino, Gary R., and George E. Pozzetta. *The Immigrant World of Ybor City: Italians and Their Latin Neighbors in Tampa, 1885–1985* (1987).

Otto, John S. *The Southern Frontiers, 1607–1860: The Agricultural Evolution of the Colonial and Antebellum South* (1989).

Poyo, Gerald E. *"With All, and for the Good of All": The Emergence of Popular Nationalism in the Cuban Communities of the United States, 1848–1898* (1989).

Taylor, Robert A. "Rebel Beef: Florida Cattle and the Confederate Army, 1862–1864." *Florida Historical Quarterly* 67, no. 1 (1988).

Tebeau, Charlton W. *A History of Florida* (1971) Especially useful for political and economic overview.

SEE ALSO **The Natural Environment; The Deep South.**

TEXAS

Daniel D. Arreola

TEXAS IS A DISTINCTIVE place in our minds but a fragmented mosaic on the cultural map of America. In a leading assessment of the cultural geography of the United States made in the early 1970s by Wilbur Zelinsky, it was proclaimed that Texas undoubtedly is a special place culturally. Yet unresolved was the larger issue of whether the Lone Star state was simply a piece of the greater South or had evolved so divergent an identity that it could be given first-order status as a major cultural region. The reason for this complex regional picture has been present since the beginnings of European American settlement and in large part is the result of the planting and persistence of several different cultural groups. This essay will reconstruct in necessarily broad strokes the cultural-historical framework of Texas regionalism.

TEXAS CULTURAL AREAS TO 1900

A culture area implies a relative rather than an absolute uniformity, and three types of spatial categories are significant in this connection: points, serving as cultural hearths and centers; lines or avenues of cultural dissemination and penetration; and continuous or interrupted areas of distribution of given culture types or elements. Recent interpretations have asserted that cultural ecology, and in particular the concept of preadaptation, offers an explanatory dimension to the more descriptive assessments of earlier culture-area delimitations.

The earliest European American cultures to settle Texas brought distinctive cultural systems that were, in some instances, preadapted to particular environmental settings. The successful planting of these systems provide evidence of the first European American culture areas to imprint the landscapes of Texas.

Spanish-Mexican Hispanic culture dominated the first three centuries of contact and settlement in what would become Texas. While early-sixteenth-century reconnoiterings along the Gulf Coast ultimately led to overland *entradas* and even some sixteenth- and seventeenth-century settlement nodes like Paso del Norte (present Ciudad Juárez–El Paso) or La Junta (present Ojinaga-Presidio), the implantation of Spanish culture in Texas was a product almost solely of the eighteenth century. This settlement push was launched from Saltillo and Monclova in Coahuila, Mexico. In the first three decades of the century, it extended northeast to the piney woods of east Texas and Louisiana. Significant settlement nodes were established on the Rio Grande at San Juan Bautista (present Guerrero, Coahuila) near Piedras Negras; at Los Adaes across the Red River from the French settlement of Natchitoches (present Robeline, Louisiana); at San Antonio de Bexar on a spring-fed river near the midpoint between San Juan Bautista and Los Adaes; and at La Bahía on the Gaudalupe River, relocated to the southeast of San Antonio (near the present Goliad) (Map 1).

These pivot points formed a lazy T of settlement on the map, stretching from the Rio Grande to the Red River, below the hills and tableland of the Edwards Plateau and fanning across the Gulf coastal plain. This subtropical environment was humid and forested on its eastern extreme and semiarid grassland and scrubland on its western periphery. The Spanish established their missions and *presidios* at strategic riverine locations, but most were abandoned or consolidated to the points and cross of the T by the third quarter of the century.

In 1749 a separate and significant settlement effort was launched to colonize the middle and lower Rio Grande region south of the Nueces River. This zone of present south Texas was jurisdictionally Nuevo Santander during the Spanish colonial era. A private colonization scheme organized by José de Escandón resulted in settlements that strad-

Map 1. Spanish Settlement

dled the Rio Grande, like Camargo and Reynosa, Tamaulipas, by 1749, and Laredo in 1755.

By late in the eighteenth century, the Spanish settlements at Los Adaes were largely retracted to San Antonio, although a small group persisted at Nacogdoches in far east Texas. The Spanish settlement framework was thus perched on the various riverine locations and anchored to the *camino* or road that tied San Juan Bautista to Nacogdoches via San Antonio and from this pivot south to La Bahía. The settlements along the Rio Grande at Laredo, Camargo, and Reynosa were not oriented to Spanish Texas by trade or social interaction.

Populations were scattered in clusters at the respective settlement nodes, with most people residing at San Antonio de Bexar, the political capital, where perhaps two thousand people lived by the close of the century. Outlying posts at La Bahía, Nacogdoches, and the Rio Grande settlements had less than one thousand each. Successful settlement was predicated on the Spanish ability to irrigate bottomlands along the rivers to produce corn, beans, squash, chili, and sugarcane, especially at the San Antonio mission San José, which often traded its surplus to other communities. Open-range herding of sheep and cattle proved the most common economy. The ranching system was especially well suited to the subtropical and semiarid grasslands that bordered the riverine settlements, and wool and leather became staple trade items.

During the brief Mexican period (1821–1836), the political administration of Texas was modified, but effective settlement was still ecologically oriented to riverine habitats and grassland herding economies. As part of the Mexican state of Coahuila y Tejas, Texas was divided into three departments: Bexar centered on San Antonio; Brazos fixed on San Felipe; and Nacogdoches, governed through the town of the same name. The Mexican colonization law of 1824 prompted the influx of Anglo settlers from the United States, so that by 1836 Texas had achieved in nine years what Spain was unable to do in one century: populate the region. However, the some forty thousand Texans were overwhelmingly Anglo, with ethnic Mexicans making up less than 10 percent of the total population, mostly concentrated in the department of Bexar. These numbers do not include the Mexican populations of the middle and lower Rio Grande that were effectively administered by separate states of Mexico—Chihuahua and Tamaulipas, respectively.

Lower and Upper Southern Anglo Texans are chiefly descendant from the Lower and Upper South subcultural regions of the United States. The Lower South refers to the low-elevation portions of the Atlantic and Gulf coastal periphery. This province stretches from the Chesapeake Bay estuary along the eastern Virginia shore to northern Florida and west across the deep South to east-central Texas. The presumed cultural hearths of this subcultural area are Chesapeake Bay, coastal South Carolina and Georgia, and New Orleans and its local hinterland. The Upper South defines the upland mountain and valley portions of Virginia, Tennessee, the Carolinas, Georgia, and Arkansas, and reaches into north-central Texas. Its single cultural hearth is southeastern Pennsylvania.

Southern culture has been characterized ethnically as a British-derived ancestry peppered with intermarriages among Scotch-Irish, Welsh, Pennsylvania Germans, Hudson Valley Dutch, French Huguenots, Delaware Valley Finns and Swedes, and others. While the Lower Southern subculture was distinctive from its Upper Southern complement, especially by dialect and political orientation, its greatest distinction was on the basis of rural economy. Lower Southerners were principally a planter class, based largely on a plantation system dominated by cotton, but also including the production of rice and sugarcane. By 1850, old-stock Southern Anglo Americans comprised 53 percent of the Texas population, and nine years later the state ranked fifth among cotton-producing states.

The Lower Southerners were also a slaveholding subculture. During the Mexican era, Southern Anglo colonists who brought slaves to Texas converted them to indentured servants for life to avoid Mexican antislavery laws. During the period of the Republic and through the Civil War, however, black slaves became an accepted part of the cotton economy. Numbering only five thousand in 1836, by 1850, black slaves were some fifty-nine thousand strong, representing 27 percent of the total state population and owned by some eight thousand slaveholders, chiefly Lower Southerners.

The geography of Lower Southerners and their black slaves in antebellum Texas reveals a decidedly southeastern distribution, principally below a line that extended from San Antonio to Texarkana and east of the Guadalupe River. Concentrated in this region were the greatest cotton-producing counties and the greatest percentage of slaves per county population in 1860 (Map 2).

Environmentally, this was the wettest part of the state with annual rainfall ranging between thirty and sixty inches (750 to 1,500 millimeters), a subtropical climate that was conducive to cotton without the need for irrigation. Rivers that cross this coastal plain flow from northwest to southeast and give access to the interior. These arteries concentrated settlement and became the conduits of

Map 2. Antebellum Texas

movement for the cotton trade in Texas, especially the lower Colorado, Brazos, and Trinity rivers and Buffalo Bayou above Trinity Bay, as well as Big Cypress Bayou that joined to the Red River via Louisiana. Cotton cultivation was therefore regulated before the war by the extent of practical navigation on these streams. At least two important foci emerged. First, the counties of Waller and Brazoria on the lower Brazos proved fertile bottomlands from which cotton was moved south and east toward break-in-bulk points along Buffalo Bayou before reaching its ocean-export destination at Galveston. Second, Marion and Harrison counties along Big Cypress Bayou produced cotton that was exported on watercraft via the Red River and Shreveport, Louisiana, before making its way to the Mississippi and New Orleans for transshipment.

The Upper Southerners were principally slaveless yeoman farmers whose rural economy was fixed on the cultivation of corn and the raising of livestock, especially hogs. Unlike their Lower Southern kin, the Upper Southerners were backwoodsmen, dedicated to small, intensely worked farmsteads. This background proved a moderately successful preadaptation as Upper Southerners invaded Texas north and east of the San Antonio–Texarkana line, a subtropical environment of prairie grasslands, mixed with oak and pine woodlands, wetter on its eastern margins and drier as one moved southwest and west.

Upper Southerners were not quick to embrace the Lower Southern cotton economy. This was not because the prairies were unable to sustain cotton, but rather because it would be difficult to transport cotton to market since the streams across this part of Texas were not readily navigable to the Gulf. The Upper Southerners' disinclination to slaveholding and opposition to the antebellum cotton economy was evident in their rejection of the secession vote in Texas. However, once railroads entered Texas from the north after the Civil War and the antebellum railnet extended north from Houston, many Upper Southern Texans caved in to the lucrative cotton trade that could now be capitalized on with railroad access for export.

European Colonization directly from the continent of Europe was significant in the nineteenth-century settlement of Texas. Although the Republic in 1840 proposed several tracts of land for Franco-Texienne settlement, chiefly in the Edwards Plateau interior along the San Saba and upper Colorado rivers, the threat of Comanche raiding blocked an effective foothold. Alsatians were successful in colonizing Castroville in Medina County west of San Antonio, but most European immigrants were of Germanic and Slavic stock.

Germans entered Texas largely under organized colonization schemes that routed them by sea through two points: Galveston and Indianola. While some Germans remained in these ports, especially Galveston, most headed inland seeking farmland. They were particularly attracted to the Blackland prairies, fertile grasslands bordered by woodland stretching northeast to southwest across the Gulf coastal plain. German colonists who entered from Galveston settled a belt that encompassed land between the Brazos and Guadalupe rivers. Concentrations were pronounced in Washington, Austin, and Fayette counties. By way of Indianola, Germans moved inland to found communities near Cuero and Yoakum in DeWitt and Lavaca counties, to New Braunfels in Comal County, and to San Antonio. A third zone of collection was the scattering of small farming-ranching towns of the Hill Country behind San Antonio running through Kendall, Gillespie, and Mason counties.

Czechs (Moravians and Bohemians) as well as Poles (Silesians) also settled the Blackland prairies and their geographic coincidence with Germans in the nineteenth century was striking, if not surprising. Czech nodes included Fayette, Washington, and Austin counties; Poles favored Karnes County below San Antonio and several outlier locations east of the Brazos River. Other European subcultures that peppered nineteenth-century Texas included Wends, Danes, Swedes, Norwegians, and Irish, but none of these groups approached the central European groups in concentrations or total numbers.

By 1850 Europeans numbered sixteen thousand or 7.5 percent of the Texas population. Continued migration and natural increase raised their numbers to 225,000 in 1887, representing 11 percent of the state population, and ranking third as a collective cultural-ethnic group behind southern Anglo Americans and blacks. By the close of the century, their distribution was conspicuous in nine counties where they formed the largest cultural group: Galveston, Harris, Austin, Fayette, Guadalupe, Comal, Kendall, Gillespie, and Medina (Map 3).

The Hispanic-Anglo Ranching Frontier The post–Civil War era witnessed the expansion of two cultural traditions: a Hispanic ranching subculture and a southern Anglo stockraising subculture. While the hearths of these traditions can be traced to Iberia by way of Mexico and northern Europe by

Map 3. European Distribution

way of the American South, the grasslands of south and central Texas were the first contact zones for the meeting of these subcultures. That they were distinctive yet similar traditions is evident today from the vocabulary used for common terms. In the Hispanic tradition, the activity of herding livestock, especially cattle, was performed on a *rancho,* hence in the English translation, a rancher is one who follows this lifestyle. In the southern Anglo subculture, the same individual was a stockraiser. The enclosure for cattle in the Hispanic tradition was the corral and in the Anglo world a cowpen. Hispanic ranchers worked on horseback and used a rope or lariat and a horned saddle to secure the rope; the southern Anglo stockraiser was similarly mounted except his saddle was hornless and traditionally he used a whip and dog to manage a herd.

The Hispanic herding tradition entered Texas from south and west of the Rio Grande. It encountered the southern Anglo herding complex mainly along the Gulf coastal prairies, the latter having slowly diffused westward from the Carolinas and Louisiana. A second contact zone was the mixed grassland-woodland margin of north-central Texas known as the Cross Timbers. Here the northward-drifting Hispanic ranching complex mixed with the southern stockraising stream that had entered Texas from across the Red River. From these two hearths, a mixed Hispanic-Anglo cattle-ranching complex diffused westward into grassland environ-ments. The south-Texas coastal plain focus spread across the shortgrass drylands of the Edwards Plateau to the high-elevation tallgrass basins of the trans-Pecos. The Cross Timbers complex diffused west to the so-called Rolling Plains grassland below the Caprock Escarpment, and after 1870, onto the high-plains grasslands above this divide.

In both regions, the expansion of cattle culture was facilitated by the slow but deliberate control of the Comanche and Apache by the American military which strung out a chain of forts that not surprisingly became major consumers of beef from cattle ranches, as they universally came to be called. The cattle drives from south Texas to the early railheads in southern Kansas were part of this process, but a short-lived one, from roughly 1867 to 1880, by which time northern railroads drove deep into Texas, dealing a fatal blow to the drives north. The persistence of a mixed Hispanic-Anglo cattle complex in western Texas and much of western America is the true legacy from this time and place.

Urban Nodes Before the Civil War, Texas urban culture was principally southern. Northern Anglo Americans made up only 4.5 percent (ten thousand) of the population in 1850. Natives of New England, New York, Pennsylvania, and New Jersey, however, were largely town dwellers, and thus even in antebellum Texas there was a strain, albeit a small one, of Yankee entrepreneurship especially focused on Galveston, San Antonio, and Houston.

These three cities vied for urban supremacy for almost four decades between 1850 and 1890, with Galveston and San Antonio trading places as the most populous city of the state. Galveston and Houston created a symbiotic relationship fed by the cotton economy (described above), while San Antonio became a supply point for the south and west Texas ranching economies as well as the military garrisons of these frontiers. After the war, as railroad lines entered Texas from the north, Dallas emerged as an inland cotton entrepôt and evolved as the principal urban and service center of the north Texas plains. By 1890, Dallas was the largest city in Texas, counting nearly forty thousand, followed by San Antonio with almost thirty-eight thousand, Galveston at approximately twenty-nine thousand, and Houston close to twenty-eight thousand. By the turn of the century, San Antonio would rise to the top of the urban hierarchy, with Houston and Dallas close behind. Texas as a whole, however, was still a predominantly rural state in 1900 with only 17 percent of its three million plus population

1073

residing in places greater than twenty-five hundred people.

REGIONAL CHANGE, 1900–1990

Texas population jumped from less than one million in 1870, when the state ranked nineteenth in the union, to over three million in 1900 to become the sixth largest state. Almost a century later, Texas counted over seventeen million people, ranking third in the nation after California and New York. The critical demographic shift, however, that would transform Texas from a predominantly rural state to an urban one did not occur until the 1940s. When the census count is tabulated in 2000, the ethnic composition of the Lone Star state may well be chiefly Hispanic. The rapid rise of Texas as a population center, its transformation to an urban way of life, and the resurgence of Hispanic ethnicity are three pivots of Texas's evolving regional identity through the twentieth century.

Demographic Explosion The accompanying table illustrates the steady growth experienced by Texas from 1900 to 1990. Significantly, the state showed a gain each decade, with the two greatest leaps forward measured by the percent increase coming in the 1900s and the 1970s. Like most of America during the Great Depression, Texas slowed down, but still managed to grow 10 percent in the 1930s. The greatest numerical boost occurred between 1970 and 1980, when over three million Texans were added. Both the percentage increase and absolute number of new Texans declined in the last decade, but not by much. The four decades of the post–World War II period witnessed the addition of over nine million Texans, greater than half the present population, averaging nearly one-quarter million per year.

While natural increase (live births minus deaths) was the principal stimulus to Texas population growth during the early 1960s, by late in that decade, net migration (in-migrants less out-migrants) became the basic explanation for the burgeoning population. At the height of this migration into Texas between 1980 and 1983, nearly two-thirds (almost one million) of the state's population growth was attributable to net migration, a larger net increase from migration than any other state, including Florida, and a greater net migration total than all the Pacific states plus Alaska and Hawaii combined. This pull was, in part, the result of a national demographic shift that saw people leave the industrial Midwest as well as the Northeast and California for economic opportunity in Texas and elsewhere in the South and Southwest. By the middle 1980s, however, the migration stream to Texas began to ebb as the state suffered setbacks from a soft oil economy and other fiscal difficulties. In 1987 Texas was still growing, albeit more slowly, and again, natural increase accounted for roughly two-thirds of population growth and net migration only a third.

Rural to Urban At the turn of the century, less than one of every five Texans lived in a city. By 1920, nearly one in three resided in an urban place, and by 1950 the state had become predominantly urban. In 1990, more than eight of every ten Texans were city dwellers, and most of these in one of the twenty-six metropolitan areas of the state. Texas's three largest cities—Houston, Dallas, and San Antonio—ranked as the fourth, eighth, and tenth largest cities in the nation in 1990. The rise of Houston and Dallas to the first and second spots of the Texas

TABLE 1 Texas Population Change, 1900–1990

Year	Population	Percent Change	Absolute Change
1900	3,048,710	—	—
1910	3,896,542	27.8	847,832
1920	4,663,228	19.7	766,686
1930	5,824,715	24.9	1,161,487
1940	6,414,824	10.1	590,109
1950	7,711,194	20.2	1,296,370
1960	9,579,677	24.2	1,868,483
1970	11,198,655	16.9	1,618,978
1980	14,228,383	27.1	3,029,728
1990	17,059,805	20.0	2,831,422

urban hierarchy transpired during the 1920s. Each participated in the booming oil economy of Texas, with Houston the manufacturing and technological center for the industry and Dallas the financial and banking center.

During the 1960s, these cities grew substantially, widening the gap between them and all other urban places in the state. Most of the urban growth, however, was not in the central cities of these metropolitan areas, but on their suburban peripheries. In the 1970s, some of the fastest-growing counties in the state included Montgomery, Liberty, Hardin, Fort Bend, and Brazoria northwest and southwest of Houston, and Denton, Collin, and Rockwell counties north and east of Dallas–Fort Worth. The 1980s witnessed the meteoric rise of Austin, the state capital, from sixth to fourth largest city in the state, spiraling past El Paso and Fort Worth on a wave of electronics manufacturing, research and development, and a local economy buffered from severe economic cycles because of its political orientation.

The Rise of Hispanics   In 1980, Texas's nearly three million Hispanics were 21 percent of the state population. They represented the second largest concentration of Hispanics in the nation after California's 4.5 million. El Paso and San Antonio were predominantly Hispanic places in 1980, and Houston, Corpus Christi, and Dallas each counted between 100,000 and 250,000 Hispanics. In south Texas, long a Hispanic stronghold, thirteen counties stretching along and inland from the Rio Grande between Del Rio, Alice and Brownsville, and Alice were each greater than 50 percent Hispanic in 1980. A second tier of fifty-two counties extending south and east from the Panhandle near Lubbock to the Gulf below Houston counted Hispanics between 25 percent and 50 percent of their respective populations.

Because the Hispanic population in Texas is the youngest by median age among the major ethnic-racial groups—21.9 versus 24.6 for black Texans and 29.5 for white Texans—it is projected to grow faster than any other group in the state. By the year 2035, it is estimated that Texas will be 36 percent Hispanic. This trend may be the most significant population shift to take place in Texas since Anglo Americans overran the Mexican state of Tejas in the nineteenth century.

The growth in the number and distribution of Hispanics across the state will pose serious challenges for Texas employment, education, and politics into the twenty-first century. In 1980 median

family income for Hispanic Texans ($15,670) was significantly below that for non-Hispanic white families ($24,787) in the state. The percentage of all Hispanic households with incomes below the poverty level in 1985 was 29 percent versus 10 percent for non-Hispanic white households. Moreover, employment opportunities in the same year revealed 47 percent of Hispanic males in craft and nonfarm labor categories, with only 15 percent in professional and managerial positions; for non-Hispanic whites the respective percentages by occupation were 25 percent and 38 percent, an index of dissimilarity of 32 percent. Discrepancies are also visible in education, especially in the largest urban areas like Houston and Dallas. In 1980, Hispanics were 18 and 12 percent of these city populations, yet constituted 24 and 14 percent, respectively, of the independent school districts in the same cities. Statewide in 1988, half of the first-grade class was Hispanic. Whereas only 18 percent of the non-Hispanic whites in the state had an eighth-grade level of education or lower, for Hispanics the measure was 51 percent. It should not be surprising, then, that only 6 percent of all students enrolled in four-year colleges in Texas during the 1980s were Hispanic.

While Hispanics have largely been underrepresented in the state in white-collar employment and have generally achieved low levels of education, they are quite visible in the political arena. In 1984, Texas had more Hispanic elected officials (1,427) than any other state, including California. However, political representation has not necessarily translated into improved conditions for the group. Social and economic change for many Hispanics in Texas has largely been the result of victories won by grassroots organizations like Communities Organized for Public Service, the Southwest Voter Registration and Education Project, and Valley Interfaith.

A COMPLEX AND CHANGING REGIONAL IDENTITY

From the early eighteenth century, Texas was part of a northeastern settlement frontier of colonial New Spain, a land ultimately divided among five separate provinces whose boundaries shifted over time: Tejas, Coahuila, Nuevo Santander, Nuevo Vizcaya, and Nuevo México. During the Mexican interregnum (1821–1836), Tejas and Coahuila were one; they became separate politically, yet remained territorially joined provinces that straddled the middle Rio Grande.

In the nine years of the Republic of Texas (1836–1845), territorial sovereignty was extended south to incorporate part of the former Spanish province of Nuevo Santander and the Mexican state of Tamaulipas, the present south Texas. Texan claims to this region were never officially recognized by Mexico. Further, Texas asserted itself westward and northward to encompass half of New Mexico and pieces of present Colorado, Wyoming, Kansas, and Oklahoma, but relinquished these claims when it entered the union in 1845. After Texas became part of the United States, it chose to align itself with the Confederacy at the outbreak of the Civil War despite a significant vote against secession by counties in the north and west-central settled areas of the state. This affiliation was not unreasonable, as the eastern half of Texas was strongly imprinted by Southerners and southern culture. This southern orientation has persisted in the eyes of some regionalists, who see all of Texas, except the far western tip centered on El Paso, as part of the western rim of the South.

By the early twentieth century, the state's regional identity was, however, beginning to shift west. Regionalists included Texas, along with Oklahoma, New Mexico, and Arizona as part of a "southwest." The reasons for this alignment are not altogether clear but perhaps reflect, in part, the strong image of west Texas, a ranching subregion with a decidedly Hispanic flavor. Whatever the basis, this regional link has persisted: Zelinsky ("North America's Vernacular Regions") found Texas still largely identified as a southwestern vernacular region (according to the names of metropolitan enterprises given in telephone directories).

Another twentieth-century regional orientation has Texas affiliated with the semiarid plains of the middle of America. Clearly, this allegiance was given its greatest credibility by Walter Prescott Webb in *The Great Plains* (1931), which identified Texas with its post–Civil War ranching heritage, although the origins of this social and economic system are antebellum. This heartland regional association has been extended and reinforced by more contemporary authors who have included Texas as one of the Great Plains states.

Some of the more recent geographical writings on regional identity have argued for a subcultural interpretation internally as well as outside the present state borders. Donald W. Meinig divided Texas into nine subcultural areas in his now classic cultural geographic interpretation, *Imperial Texas* (1969). Others have placed Texas at the southern intersection of the Old South, the Great Plains, and the southwestern borderland. These changing regional orientations support the recent assertion by Jordan et al. that Texas is, in fact, "a border province where are joined Anglo-America and Latin America; the Bible belt and Roman Catholicism; South, West, and Midwest" (*Texas: A Geography,* p. 5). Texas will likely remain a distinctive place in our collective national consciousness, but its cultural-historical geography is a clear patchwork of varied ethnic and regional traditions sewn onto the map of America.

BIBLIOGRAPHY

Barr, Alwyn. *Black Texans: A History of Negroes in Texas 1528–1971* (1973).

Bolton, Herbert Eugene. *Texas in the Middle Eighteenth Century: Studies in Spanish Colonial History and Administration* (1915).

Castañeda, Carlos E. *Our Catholic Heritage in Texas, 1519–1936,* 7 vols. (1936–1958).

De León, Arnoldo. *The Tejano Community, 1836–1900* (1982).

Gerhard, Peter. *The North Frontier of New Spain* (1982).

Hatcher, Mattie Austin. *The Opening of Texas to Foreign Settlement, 1801–1821* (1927).

Jackson, Jack. *Los Mesteños: Spanish Ranching in Texas, 1721–1821* (1986).

Jackson, John Brinckerhoff. *The Southern Landscape Tradition in Texas* (1980).

John, Elizabeth A. H. *Storms Brewed in Other Men's Worlds: The Confrontation of Indians, Spanish, and French in the Southwest, 1540–1795* (1975).

Jordan, Terry G. "A Century and a Half of Ethnic Change in Texas, 1836–1986." *Southwestern Historical Quarterly* 89, no. 4 (1986).

———. "Preadaptation and European Colonization in Rural North America." *Annals of the Association of American Geographers* 79, no. 4 (1989).

Jordan, Terry G., with John L. Bean, Jr., and William M. Holmes. *Texas: A Geography* (1984).

Lowrie, Samuel Harman. *Culture Conflict in Texas, 1821–1835* (1932).

Meinig, Donald W. *Imperial Texas: An Interpretive Essay in Cultural Geography* (1969).

Montejano, David. *Anglos and Mexicans in the Making of Texas, 1836–1986* (1987).

Scott, Florence Johnson. *Historical Heritage of the Lower Rio Grande* (1937).

Silverthorne, Elizabeth. *Plantation Life in Texas* (1986).

West, Richard. *Richard West's Texas* (1981).

Wheeler, Kenneth W. *To Wear a City's Crown: The Beginnings of Urban Growth in Texas, 1836–1865* (1968).

Zelinsky, Wilbur. *The Cultural Geography of the United States* (1973).

———. "North America's Vernacular Regions." *Annals of the Association of American Geographers* 70, no. 1 (1980).

SEE ALSO **American Indians of the West; American Social and Cultural Geography; The Frontier; Latin Americans; The Natural Environment; Regionalism; Rural Life.**

THE SOUTHWEST

Roger L. Nichols

THE SOCIAL DEVELOPMENT of the Southwest offers a story of cultural change and conflict. Through the centuries since about 1200 markedly different peoples have lived in the region. Until about 1200 the Indians who had settled there in prehistoric times had the area to themselves. Then invading tribes moved in, forcing many of the native villagers to flee or to reconstitute their societies. During the sixteenth century the Spanish entered New Mexico from the south, and for the next two hundred fifty years they fought with and tried to dominate the local Indian societies. With Mexican independence in 1821 the authorities, hoping to stimulate trade and to expand the local population, encouraged numbers of Anglo-Americans to enter what are now the states of New Mexico and Arizona. After the United States seized the area in 1846, more Anglo-

Americans moved in. By the twentieth century, these newcomers had reduced Indians to an outcast minority, and the descendants of earlier Spanish and Indian intermarriage saw their homeland ever more dominated by English-speaking Americans.

While definitions of which states the Southwest includes vary widely, this article will focus on Arizona and New Mexico. Several factors distinguish these two states from the rest of the region. Natural features such as the Mojave and Sonoran deserts, the canyonlands of the Colorado Plateau, and the southern Rocky Mountains and Llano Estacado (Staked Plain) surround them. Until the twentieth century, these geographical features tended to ensure the two states' cultural development in relative isolation. The existence of continuing Indian societies also distinguishes the two states from their

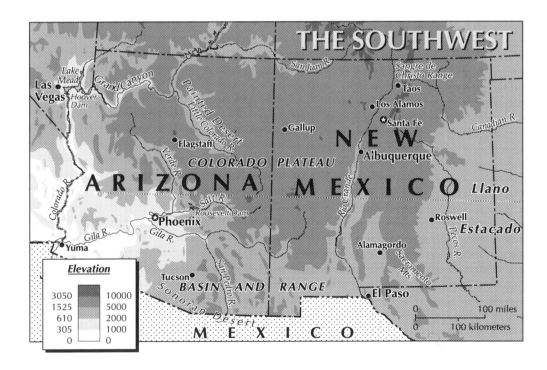

1079

neighbors. While tribal peoples inhabited most of the West in the latter half of the nineteenth century, New Mexico and Arizona contain the largest concentrations of these peoples in the 1990s.

Not only the presence of Indians and the relative isolation of the two states have helped to shape the societies that evolved in the Southwest; space and distance also have been important. These two states are among the ten largest in area in the country. Despite their size, Arizona and New Mexico faced major obstacles to economic development. In particular, the climate makes life difficult for humans. It varies from semihumid at best in the highlands of both states to arid in the Rio Grande Valley of New Mexico and the Sonoran Desert in southern Arizona—areas that rarely receive more than ten inches of rain a year, and often get much less. The Sacramento Mountains and the Sangre de Cristo range in New Mexico get over twenty inches (500 mm) of rain and snow a year, but they lack other essentials for successful settlement.

THE EARLIEST
SOUTHWESTERN PEOPLES

Early peoples entered the Southwest as hunters of large game between ten and fifteen thousand years ago. Following the mammoth, giant sloth, bison, camel, and antelope, these hunters traveled throughout the region, leaving little trace of their wanderings except for a few spearpoints still embedded in the bones of the animals they killed. When the large animals became extinct, the hunters apparently migrated east onto the plains, leaving the Southwest nearly vacant. Gradually during the next five thousand years, new people known as desert dwellers settled the area. While hunting and gathering remained important to these people, they learned to harvest plants, to sow their seeds, and to domesticate dogs and turkeys. Over a period of centuries this pattern of subsistence led to the formation of sedentary villages and a social differentiation and organization not possible before the building of permanent homes.

Three distinct cultures emerged. In south-central and western New Mexico the Mogollon people evolved as a distinct society. Highly skilled basket makers, by 300 B.C. they had begun producing high-quality pottery as well. They raised large crops of corn, beans, and squash. To the north of the Mogollons in New Mexico the Anasazi culture developed some centuries later. By 700 they had become sedentary farmers living in villages of pit houses, often with a religious center in each settlement. To the west, in Central Arizona, the Hohokam people emerged. All three cultures depended on hunting, gathering, and farming for their food supply. By 1000 they built rectangular, aboveground dwellings that their descendants, the Pueblos, would enlarge and make famous.

Despite their apparent economic strength and social cohesion, these prehistoric societies crumbled and then collapsed between 1200 and 1400. Archaeologists offer many opinions on their demise, but all three of these early civilizations experienced similar difficulties. By about 1200, Athapascan raiders, called "Apaches" (enemies) by the sedentary puebloan people, invaded the Southwest. In 1276 a drought lasting more than twenty years struck. In an area perpetually short of water, this brought disaster. Some scholars have suggested that the large-scale farming needed to feed the substantial villages may have depleted the soil and that the irrigation water for the crops eventually brought too many minerals into the village croplands, thus destroying crops or limiting yields. Others think that the villages outgrew their ability to dispose of human refuse and waste safely, and that recurring disease forced people to abandon their established settlements. Because of these factors, by 1400 the Anasazi, Mogollan, and Hohokam societies had disappeared.

By the late sixteenth century, when the Spanish pushed up the Rio Grande Valley into northern New Mexico, nearly forty thousand Indians occupied villages in present-day Arizona and New Mexico. Most of these people lived in the sixty or more pueblos located along the course of the Rio Grande. Other village dwellers lived as far east as the Pecos River, and west to Acoma, Laguna, and Zuni in New Mexico and the Hopi mesas in Arizona. Nomadic hunters and raiders surrounded the pueblo peoples. The Utes lived to the north, the Comanches to the northeast, the Apaches to the southeast and the southwest, and the Navajos to the west and northwest. Farther west, the small Colorado River tribes lived at the fringe of Arizona, while the Pimas (or 'Ó'odham people) dwelt in the southern deserts of Arizona.

Although related by language, shared customs, and similar economies, the Pueblo societies that emerged became intensely local. Each established social and religious practices to explain its origins, cure the sick, and gain success in hunting and farming. Secret societies in every village controlled the seasonal ceremonies to bring rain, good harvests, or successful hunting. Shamans played a significant role in Pueblo society because the villagers' beliefs placed their everyday activities within a closely knit religious context. To the Indians, the spirit world was real, significant, and even central to their lives. After generations of contact, the migratory raiders adopted some practices and ideas that appeared similar to the Pueblo beliefs. But although they continued to trade and to raid, they brought only limited changes to the villagers.

THE SPANISH AND MEXICAN REGIMES

The Spanish invasion of the Southwest forever changed Indian societies and cultures. Throughout the sixteenth century, Spanish explorers led expeditions probing northward into California, New Mexico, and Texas. By the late 1590s, the Spanish felt strong enough to conquer the Rio Grande Pueblos. In mid July 1598 Juan de Oñate led a party of about four hundred soldiers, friars, and settlers, accompanied by some seven thousand animals, into northern New Mexico. Within a decade the invaders established their headquarters in present-day Santa Fe, which has remained the capital of New Mexico.

While their efforts at political control and economic exploitation had some impact on the southwestern peoples, the Spaniards' presence proved crucial in regional social development. The invaders introduced the Indian people to various European diseases such as measles, influenza, and smallpox. Because the villagers had few natural immunities to the new pathogens, sickness and death swept through the Pueblos, and over the next century the native population of New Mexico plunged sharply. In addition, the Spanish demanded that the Indians accept a position as subjects of the crown, adopt Catholic Christianity, and provide labor and foodstuffs. Throughout the seventeenth century, Spanish priests and friars labored at chapels and missions in or next to the Pueblo villages. There they strove to discredit the native shamans, to disrupt the village religious and social ceremonies, and even to destroy the masks, prayer sticks, and other religious items deemed sacred by the Indians.

After more than three-quarters of a century of struggle against the Spanish attacks on their culture, the New Mexico Pueblos exploded in open revolt in the late seventeenth century. Causes of the uprising varied from one community to another, but a general pattern of Spanish avarice, religious persecution, violence, and general incompetence combined to push the long-suffering Indians into rebellion. In 1675, at San Ildefonso pueblo, one of the friars accused the Indians of practicing witchcraft when he learned that they had continued their native religious practices. The Spanish arrested nearly fifty medicine men and soon hanged three of them (a fourth hanged himself). This outraged the Indians. They sent a delegation of leaders from many of the pueblos to demand that the authorities release the shamans still in custody. The governor did this, but anger over the friars' persistent meddling in their religious affairs kept the villagers in a state of turmoil. In August 1680 a San Juan Indian, Popé, led a major rebellion.

The victorious Indians destroyed as much of the evidence of Spanish occupation as they could, burning churches, houses, forts, and even books and government records when they found them. The Spanish tried to reenter the Rio Grande Valley in 1681, but they lacked the strength to face down the still rebellious Pueblos and so left a second time. In 1690 Popé died, and when no other native leader stepped forward to coordinate the Indian resistance, it faded. In 1692 Diego de Vargas led a victorious army north to awe, bluff, and defeat the Indians and to reimpose Spanish domination over the region. Although the returning conquerors had no easy time in retaking the area, by the end of the seventeenth century the Spanish seemed firmly in control.

In Arizona matters took a different turn. There, instead of soldiers, a handful of missionaries ventured north to bring Christianity to the native people. Eusebio Francisco Kino, a Jesuit missionary, led the Spanish thrust northward. In 1687 he had founded a mission in Sonora, and from there he ranged north as far as the Gila River. In 1700 he began work on what became his principal mission base in Arizona, San Xavier del Bac, just south of present-day Tucson. During Kino's several decades of work and travel he founded twenty-nine missions in Arizona and Sonora, and he never reported major difficulties with the Indians of the sort that marked the relations between the races in New Mexico. The clear difference in the two societies that emerged resulted from the lack of settlers from

Spain or Mexico in Arizona. The population remained almost entirely Indian, with few outsiders and only a modest number of mixed-blood people who called themselves Spanish Americans or Hispanos.

Three concurrent trends marked social development in New Mexico during the eighteenth century. The Pueblo population shrank steadily, so that by 1800 no more than eight to ten thousand of the village Indians remained, while the number of pueblos dropped from more than sixty to nineteen. Increasing raids by Apaches, Comanches, Utes, and Navajos, recurrent epidemics of smallpox and other European diseases, and severe droughts and crop failures reduced the Indian population drastically.

While the pueblos' populations dwindled, the number of "Spaniards" grew steadily. The *ricos* who lived in a few of the larger towns, plus some officials who had come directly from Europe or Mexico, a few army officers, and some of the church workers actually were Spanish. Most of the rest had descended from earlier intermarriage between Spaniards and Indians. The resulting mestizo people considered themselves Spanish and not Mexican, and by 1800 nearly ten thousand of them lived in the towns, cities, and farming villages of central and northern New Mexico. Their presence in the region brought about a gradual increase in the hold of Spanish language and customs and of Catholic Christianity.

As these two trends continued, the nomadic raiding tribes that had entered the area between 1200 and 1400 became more important. During the eighteenth century they acquired firearms and horses, which made them formidable as raiders. Their frequent incursions drove back the limits of settlement. Among the raiding peoples, only the Navajos adopted some of the customs brought into the region by the Spanish. They took up sheepherding and became skilled craftsmen, weavers, and potters. The Apaches, Comanches, and Utes remained significant as raiders. In fact, their cultures came to depend heavily on seasonal forays against the settled communities of New Mexico and the struggling missions of southern Arizona.

In Arizona repeated Apache raids nearly drove the Spanish from the region. After the Jesuits left Spanish territory in 1767, Apache raiders sacked and burned San Xavier mission. A Franciscan, Francisco Garcés, and the Pima-Papago people there began to rebuild that same year, and completed the task within a decade. In 1775 a soldier, Juan Bautista de Anza, led an expedition north along the Santa Cruz River from Tubac to present-day Tucson, then turned west across the desert to California. That same year another soldier, Hugh O'Conor, led troops and settlers north and founded Tucson. Despite this flurry of activity, few Europeans or people from Mexico moved into present-day Arizona. As a result, it remained an area primarily characterized by raiding and warfare between the agricultural Indians living along the Gila and Santa Cruz rivers and the roving bands of Apache who attacked them and the few tiny Spanish enclaves.

Prior to the nineteenth century well over 90 percent of the people in the Southwest lived in New Mexico. Spread from Taos south toward El Paso, they resided mostly in the Rio Grande Valley. The descendants of the few hundred Spanish and Mexican people who had migrated north into the region came to number more than ten thousand. Because of their isolation and the preponderance of Indian people living nearby, intermarriage became common. As a result, after several generations the population became mostly Indian in blood but predominantly Spanish in culture. In language, clothing, social behavior, and religion, the mestizos became ever more Europeanized and, because of its distance from the rest of New Spain, the society that evolved had distinct peculiarities.

The Catholicism that developed differed from that practiced elsewhere, at least in its local applications. For example, by 1712 the Santa Fe town council established the town's own saint's day to honor Our Lady of the Rosary, sometimes called La Conquistadora, in commemoration of the 1693 reconquest of the area by Spanish troops. In the late 1700s, when imperial Spain halted its support of church missions in the area, local religious groups replaced the missionaries. The villagers formed groups known as the Penitentes, which used new rituals to satisfy their religious needs. During Holy Week some of the members used whips of yucca and cactus to beat themselves while others hanged people from large wooden crosses, occasionally with fatal results. The Penitentes also met social-welfare needs formerly provided for at least in part by the church, and some of their rites continue today.

In Arizona only a few small villages and two modest presidios stood in an area inhabited by large numbers of Pimas, Papagos, and Apaches. The Indians clearly had the upper hand throughout the centuries of Spanish influence. To the east in New Mexico, a more balanced situation prevailed. Although the Spanish colonists increased their numbers to somewhere between fifteen and twenty thousand, the people living there in 1820 had become far more like the Indians than their ancestors could have believed. The growing numbers and increasing strength of the nomadic and raiding tribes such as the Utes, Navajos, Apaches, and, after 1700, the Comanches became significant. Nevertheless, the Hispano population of the Rio Grande Valley grew steadily. Beginning during the 1790s and continuing for at least seventy-five years, this population expansion determined the ethnic makeup of central New Mexico. Occurring mostly during the era of Mexican control of the region, this gradual population movement led to establishment of small farming villages and modest-sized ranches. Sheep raising became a significant occupation to the northeast as the Hispanos moved gradually onto the attractive grasslands there. During the 1840s several hundred families settled in the Mesilla Valley, about 50 miles (80 kilometers) north of El Paso.

The New Mexican settlements were so far from other developed regions that residents suffered from continuing shortages of necessary items. A chance meeting between William Becknell, a Missouri trader bartering with the Plains Indians for horses and mules, and some Santa Fe residents in 1821 opened business relations between the American frontier settlements and New Mexico. The new trade met the needs of southwesterners for clothing and textiles, household items, and tools. People from both societies made large profits, and the New Mexican elites strengthened their local dominance. At the same time, opening their isolated society to the aggressive pioneer merchants from Missouri marked the beginning of the slow weakening of the solidarity of Hispano communities and of Anglo-Americans achieving positions of social and economic prominence.

THE COMING OF THE ANGLO-AMERICANS

Except for a modest number of trappers, fur traders, and businessmen in New Mexico, few Anglo-Americans impinged on the Hispano population of the Southwest prior to 1848 when the United States acquired the region from Mexico. By the late 1840s the society in New Mexico included some six to eight thousand Pueblo Indians and perhaps sixty thousand Hispanos surrounded by the nomadic Navajos, Apaches, Utes, and Comanches. In Arizona the Apache raids had reduced the sedentary population to between about five hundred to one thousand Hispanos and Christian Indians living at or near Tucson, San Xavier, and Tubac. While the Papagos or Tohono 'Ó'odhams to the west and the Pimas in the Gila Valley to the north lived in established villages, their numbers and distances from the raiders gave them some respite from the continuing attacks. The situation in the Southwest, then, was that the hostile Indians controlled Arizona, while the Hispanos and Pueblos outnumbered the nomadic raiders in New Mexico and had achieved a kind of uneasy balance between themselves and their difficult neighbors.

The imposition of American authority in 1848, following the cession of the region by Mexico, brought long-range changes for many of the Indian groups in the Southwest. Although the Navajos and Apaches continued their raiding practices, army units from the United States entered the region. The Civil War lessened American military activity briefly, but by 1862 volunteers from California marched east to reoccupy both Arizona and New Mexico, which had been proclaimed Confederate territory. General James Henry Carleton, who led those men, soon dispatched Colonel Kit Carson against the Apaches and Navajos. For more than two years beginning in 1863, Carson led his troops through the Navajo country, destroying crops and orchards and driving off livestock. With their economy collapsing and their people starving, tribal leaders surrendered and the army marched its captives to the Bosque Redondo in southeastern New Mexico, where the troops and government agents tried to force the Indians to farm on the nearly waterless and sterile plain. The Navajos suffered greatly on what they called the Long Walk, and they remained at peace after 1868, when they returned to their homeland in the north.

Other tribes had varied experiences with the incoming Anglo-Americans. The established Pueblos had their land grants recognized and suffered little loss of property. No agents tried to disrupt life at the villages and no clerics worked to destroy the remaining religious ideas and practices. The Apache raiders, in contrast, felt the hand of the government as army posts sprang up nearby, and between 1870 and 1886, they found themselves herded onto reservations. This did not occur easily or quickly, and when the last of the Apache wars ended in 1886, settlers throughout the Southwest, particularly in Arizona, breathed a sigh of relief.

During the 1880s the Southern Pacific and the Atchison, Topeka, and Santa Fe railroads laid their tracks across the region, bringing increased employment and attracting miners, ranchers, farmers, and laborers to the Southwest. Organized politically as the New Mexico Territory in 1850 and as separate territories of Arizona and New Mexico after 1863, the area drew growing numbers of newcomers who gradually upset the balance between Indians and Hispanos. Large numbers of Texas ranchers and cattlemen migrated to eastern and southern New Mexico and southern Arizona. At the same time Anglo-American farmers migrated west from Illinois, Missouri, and Kansas into northeastern New Mexico. In some places these homesteaders competed for land with the Hispano sheepherders and farmers or the Texas ranchers. From the north modest numbers of Mormon pioneers drifted down to the Arizona Strip, the part of that territory between the border of Utah and the Colorado River. Some of them established small towns in the mountains of eastern Arizona and western New Mexico. Their presence further altered the racial and ethnic population mix.

GROWTH OF THE TERRITORIES

In 1860 New Mexico recorded some 93,516 non-Indian residents, while the first census in Arizona, in 1864, soon after it became a territory, counted only 4,573 non-Indian inhabitants; by 1900 this number had grown to about 123,000 people. New Mexico continued its social development as the population climbed steadily from the 1860s; the 1900 census recorded more than 195,000 inhabitants. Both territories benefited from the continuing flow of workers and migrants headed west because of the transcontinental railroads that crossed the area. Arizona, more than New Mexico, received a large influx of workers during the mining rushes of the 1870s and 1880s. Earlier gold discoveries proved to be minor, but silver deposits attracted hundreds of fortune seekers. Although both territories had some silver mining, in the long run, copper proved more significant for attracting people to the region. The mountains separating the two territories held rich ore veins and, for Arizona in particular, mining became a mainstay of the economy well into the middle of the twentieth century.

The federal government helped the economic development of the Southwest repeatedly through reclamation and water projects. In 1911 Roosevelt Dam on the Salt River in central Arizona was the first of several water-related undertakings. In New Mexico, projects such as Elephant Butte Dam in 1916 and the attempt to bring water from the San Juan River to Albuquerque via tunnels through the mountains in 1968 continued these efforts. In 1990 work continued on the last stages of the Central Arizona Project to bring water from the Colorado River to the southern part of the state. Clearly these and other federal actions made the Southwest economically attractive. Farmers and ranchers were assured of more water, while the lakes created by the dams offered attractive recreational areas for boating, fishing, and camping. Businesses benefited from the additional electric power generated by such facilities as Hoover Dam on the Colorado River.

While governmental actions encouraged Anglo-Americans to migrate into the Southwest, its policies also affected the local Indians. Gradually after 1900 the Bureau of Indian Affairs reduced its dependence on boarding schools for the children and began to operate day schools on the reservations. After a 1912 Public Health Service investigation disclosed that vast numbers of Indians were suffering from such treatable diseases as trachoma and tuberculosis, the government increased appropriations for medical and nursing care on the reservations. In 1924 the Indians received American citizenship, but that action alone did little to alter their situation. In 1934 the Indian Reorganization Act (Wheeler-Howard Act) authorized the formal organization of tribal governments and the economic development of reservations throughout the country. In the Southwest, this laid the foundation for gradual changes as groups such as the Navajos and the Apaches developed modern governments. These organizations allowed the Indians to function much as local city or county governments in dealing with their Anglo-American neighbors. As a result, by 1990 the Navajo Nation had its own capital (Window Rock, Arizona), police force, economic development office, public schools, and Navajo Community College (at Tsalle, Arizona), one of the most successful tribal colleges in the country.

As the situation of the Indians changed during the first half of the twentieth century, popular perceptions of the Southwest shifted as well. From considering the region as an isolated, barren area with little to commend it, people living elsewhere gradually came to recognize the region's natural beauty. This gradual shift resulted from several simultaneous trends. In New Mexico in particular, an influx

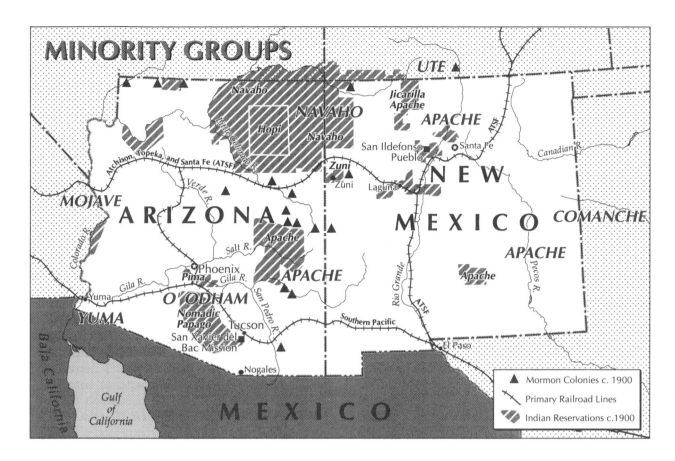

MINORITY GROUPS

Symbol	Legend
▲	Mormon Colonies c. 1900
	Primary Railroad Lines
	Indian Reservations c.1900

of writers and artists brought national attention to the region. Authors such as Alice Corbin Henderson, editor of *The Turquoise Trail;* Erna Fergusson, who wrote *Dancing Gods;* Mary Austin, writer of *The Land of Journey's Ending;* Willa Cather, author of *Death Comes for the Archbishop;* D. H. Lawrence, author of *Mornings in Mexico;* and Oliver La Farge, writer of *Laughing Boy,* all came to the Southwest.

During the same decades artists settled in Santa Fe and Taos and soon drew national attention to the area. In 1915 the Taos Society of Aritists was founded. At first made up chiefly of painters who specialized in New Mexico landscapes, the group soon expanded. Georgia O'Keeffe's work and growing fame attracted more attention to the Southwest. At the same time, Indian crafts production expanded because of skillful marketing and the attention of the Anglo-American writers and artists in the area. Navajo rugs and blankets became popular; Navajo, Zuni, and Hopi silversmiths effectively developed their skills and expanded their markets. Potters such as Maria and Julian Martinez devel-

oped traditional black pots at San Ildefonso Pueblo. Their work brought artistic acclaim and recognition for tribal craftspeople, and their success strengthened tribal cultural pride. During the 1970s and 1980s national interest in southwestern tribal crafts and artwork increased sharply, so that today Indian jewelry, pottery, blankets, and paintings can be found at expensive shops in any major city in the country.

WORLD WAR II AND POSTWAR SHIFTS

World War II brought fundamental shifts in the demographics and economy of the region. Until that time the Southwest had remained thinly populated and isolated from the national industrial network. With few people and vast open spaces, much of the West became a training ground for the armed services as military posts of many varieties sprouted almost overnight, permanently changing the face of both New Mexico and Arizona. In the 1990s army, air force, and marine installations dotted the countryside, bringing into local economies millions of dollars annually.

The decision to proceed with developing atomic weapons during World War II brought significant changes to New Mexico. In 1942 the army acquired an isolated site at Los Alamos, northwest of Santa Fe, and there J. Robert Oppenheimer assembled a group of physicists and engineers who began work on the atomic bomb. By July 1945, when the first atomic bomb was detonated near Alamogordo, the concentration of scientists working on the project represented a new element within the society. The presence of this isolated, highly educated group comprising a virtual national elite had a major impact on Los Alamos, Albuquerque, and Alamogordo in particular. Their success brought an immediate demand for uranium, leading to the discovery that most of the uranium deposits in the nation lay in the rocky formations of the Colorado Plateau, including much of northern New Mexico and Arizona. The area became the source of most uranium production for the nation.

World War II not only increased the military presence and the number of government installations in the Southwest but also offered thousands of GIs a taste of the region's attractions. As a result, beginning in the 1950s, large numbers of Americans from other parts of the country moved into the Southwest as part of a larger migration to the entire Sunbelt, a region stretching south and west from North Carolina to California. This migration had a greater effect on Arizona and New Mexico than on more populous states because the Southwest had so few people when it began. In 1950 each of the two states had about seven hundred thousand people; by 1970 Arizona had at least 1.7 million, and New Mexico had just over 1.3 million, inhabitants. During the 1970s Arizona experienced a vast increase in migration; by 1980 its population stood at 2.7 million, while New Mexico grew to about 1.3 million people. The census count for 1990 stood at 3.6 million for Arizona and 1.5 million for New Mexico.

This flood of newcomers into the two states brought major changes to their societies. Arizona in particular saw thousands of migrants from Mexico, many of them legal immigrants but some not, enter the state during the 1970s and 1980s. Their presence crowded facilities in the Hispanic parts of the cities, and the presence of illegal aliens kept wages low in some job categories. New Mexico was much less industrialized than Arizona in 1990, and so it offered a less attractive situation for the Mexican immigrants. In both states, however, the immigrants' presence stretched social services such as health clinics, bilingual classes, and employment services to their limits. The influx strengthened cultural and family ties to Mexico and slowed the pace of acculturation and assimilation into American society. By 1990 parts of both states resembled areas in Texas and California, in that the Hispanic population was the majority of the population and most of the local inhabitants spoke Spanish rather than English.

The influx of hundreds of thousands of new residents since the 1960s upset more than conservative Anglo-Americans. In New Mexico the Hispanos felt under increasing pressure from the newcomers. Their feelings of being overwhelmed broke into the open during the 1960s when Reies López Tijerina arrived from Texas. By 1963 he had founded the Federal Alliance of Land Grants, an organization dedicated to recovering the land that he claimed Anglo-Americans had stolen from the ancestors of the Hispanos in northern New Mexico. An electrifying speaker, López Tijerina held mass meetings and led demonstrations demanding the return of the lands in question. In 1966 he and several others tried to use citizen's arrest against forest rangers in the Carson National Forest. This brought their arrest and conviction for assaulting federal officers. The following year he led an occupation of the Tierra Amarilla courthouse that resulted in the shooting of one deputy sheriff and the beating of another. López Tijerina was sent to prison, and in 1970 disassociated himself from public affairs, at least temporarily. While his efforts brought mostly noisy news coverage and little help to his followers, they did illustrate the hopelessness and frustration felt by many Hispanos in New Mexico at the time.

Because many of the Anglo-Americans moving into the Southwest since the 1960s tended to be cultural conservatives, they saw Mexican migration as an unwelcome invasion. In addition, the rising number of illegal immigrants from Mexico and Central America raised fears among some Anglo-Americans of being overwhelmed by a foreign horde. The international drug trade also tended to increase ethnic tensions, particularly during the late 1980s in Arizona. The anti-Mexican attitudes resulted in calls for making English the official language in Arizona that bore fruit in 1988, when a ballot proposition to that effect passed.

For Native Americans and blacks, the other noticeable minorities in the Southwest, the situation was unclear at the beginning of the 1990s. Blacks had drifted into both states in small numbers during the late-nineteenth-century cattle-ranching era and as soldiers during the Apache campaigns of the 1880s. In the twentieth century they came to work in the growing factories. In the 1990s Indians outnumbered blacks by about two to one, and together the two groups comprise about 4.5 percent of the population of the Southwest. Although many blacks initially migrated into the Southwest to work as farm laborers, in the 1960s, 1970s, and 1980s most of them were found in the cities of Phoenix, Tucson, and Albuquerque. Into the 1960s blacks faced the remnants of segregation in housing, jobs, and education, but well-established ghettos like those in other major urban centers around the country have not developed. Instead, the approximately one hundred thousand blacks in Arizona and thirty thousand blacks in New Mexico tend to live in mixed-race neighborhoods.

For the tribal peoples in both states, the situation in the 1990s differed from that of the Hispanos and the blacks. The Indian population continued to grow steadily, although most reservation dwellers still suffered from the effects of unemployment or underemployment and poverty. Tourism helped tribal finances at places such as the Hopi mesas and Taos, while the continuing strong interest in Indian arts and crafts meant that potters, weavers, silversmiths, and others received more reasonable prices for their work. These conditions, however, affected only a modest number of Indians. For the rest, their relative isolation made getting well-paying jobs difficult. The Navajo tribe employed large numbers of its own people, while the White Mountain Apaches owned and operated a ski resort and summer recreation area. Education for Native Americans in both states improved gradually, but young Indians still trailed their Anglo-American neighbors in academic achievement.

For much of the period between the 1950s and the 1990s, politicians in the Southwest tended to be conservative. In Arizona, U.S. Senator Barry Goldwater held center stage from 1960 until the late 1980s, speaking out repeatedly on regional and national political and economic issues. He was a controversial presidential candidate in 1964. Governor Bruce Babbitt (1978–1987) provided a moderate voice in national presidential politics. Morris Udall represented liberal Democratic ideas for thirty years, focusing his efforts chiefly on conservation and environmental issues. During those same de-

cades, few New Mexico political leaders received anywhere near the same national attention as the three Arizona politicians. Despite the preponderance of male politicians, in Arizona women actively pursued political careers. Both Carolyn Warner and C. Diane Bishop served as state superintendent of education during the 1980s, and Warner ran for governor as a Democrat in 1986. In 1988 Rose Mofford assumed the governorship after Evan Mecham's impeachment and removal from office.

By 1990 the Southwest appeared to much of the nation to be a calm area where people could get a new start, avoid the bureaucracy found elsewhere, and join with others holding related convictions. This view was erroneous because the region included many groups, each with a variety of needs and desires. The Southwest had not been a wide-open region where would-be entrepreneurs could come to seek their fortunes any more than elsewhere. It was, however, a rapidly growing area, with its resources and governments facing strains because of continuing population growth. As large states with modest-sized populations, both Arizona and New Mexico spent large parts of their annual budgets on highways, bridges, and law enforcement. Yet their tax bases remained modest-sized, although growing. The result was that their annual budgets were stretched and they rarely had enough funds for adequate support of public education and other expensive social services.

Despite such difficulties, the modern Southwest appeals to many in American society. Perhaps some of the fascination with the region dates back to the days of Western motion pictures, many of which were filmed there. Some certainly results from cultural myths about the frontier and western adventure that include famous Indian wars, gunfighters, mineral rushes, and similar colorful events of the nineteenth century. The impact of Western novels by Zane Grey, Max Brand, and Louis L'Amour, as well as the Navajo detective stories of Tony Hillerman, also was great. These and the aura of the Southwest as somehow different from most of America's urban society created a sort of fantasyland identification for the region. While the colorful mountains, rivers, and sunsets are real, ideas about the openness, cleanness, absence of urban crime, and apparent personal freedom available in the modern Southwest represent only myth or, more accurately, wishful thinking. Each decade that passes brings the region more into line with the major trends present in the rest of the nation.

BIBLIOGRAPHY

Bannon, John Francis. *The Spanish Borderlands Frontier: 1513–1821* (1970).

Dutton, Bertha P. *Indian Americans of the Southwest* (1983).

Fergusson, Erna. *New Mexico: A Pageant of Three Peoples* (1964).

Hollon, W. Eugene. *The Southwest: Old and New* (1961).

Lamar, Howard R. *The Far Southwest, 1846–1912: A Territorial History* (1970).

Malone, Michael P., and Richard Eutlain. *The American West: A Twentieth Century History* (1989).

Meinig, Donald W. *Southwest, Three Peoples in Geographical Change, 1600–1970* (1971).

Nash, Gerald D. *The American West in the Twentieth Century: A Short History of an Urban Oasis* (1977).

Perrigo, Lynn I. *The American Southwest: Its Peoples and Cultures* (1971).

Powell, Lawrence Clark. *Arizona: A Bicentennial History* (1976).

Roberts, Calvin A., and Susan A. Roberts. *New Mexico* (1988).

Spicer, Edward H. *Cycles of Conquest: The Impact of Spain, Mexico, and the United States on the Indians of the Southwest* (1962).

Wagoner, Jay J. *Early Arizona: Prehistory to Civil War* (1975).

Weber, David J. *Foreigners in Their Native Land: Historical Roots of the Mexican Americans* (1973).

SEE ALSO **American Indians of the West; The Frontier; Latin Americans: Mexicans and Central Americans; Native Peoples and Early European Contacts; Native Peoples Prior to European Arrival; The Natural Environment: The West; Rural Life in the West.**

THE MORMON REGION

Kenneth H. Winn

THE MORMON REGION of the intermountain West was born in bitter despair over a corrupt American nation. This bitterness arose from the almost perpetual conflict, often violent, between the Mormon church and its neighbors, which dated from the church's founding. Emerging in 1830 from the religious heat of western New York's "burned-over district," the Mormon movement was founded by a young farmer named Joseph Smith, Jr., a self-proclaimed prophet of God, who promised the restoration of "primitive" Christianity. Smith announced that with divine guidance he had recovered golden plates from an Indian mound, which is now known as Hill Cumorah, near Rochester, New York. These plates, the content of which Smith translated as the Book of Mormon, revealed the history of a pre-Columbian Christian America whose religious practices, undefiled by the innovations of the Catholic church, or the "hireling priests" of the Protestant churches, offered instructions to those confused or repulsed by the upheaval of America's Second Great Awakening.

As a radical religious movement, the Mormon church (officially the Church of Jesus Christ of Latter-day Saints) believed all temporal life was within its purview and attracted converts with its promises of economic equality and social cohesion. The totality of its control over its members' lives was enhanced by the Mormon doctrine of "the gathering," that is, bringing the righteous out of doomed "Babylon" into a single geographic area.

The Saints' ensuing political, social, and economic clannishness, enhanced by their demographic concentration, intimidated their non-Mormon ("gentile") neighbors already offended by the Saints' claim of religious superiority and rapidly transformed an initial skepticism toward the church into outright hostility. Extralegal violence against Mormon "despotism" sent the church on a sixteen-year hegira through New York, Ohio, Missouri, and Illinois. In the latter two states conflict was especially

vicious. In 1838, during the Mormon War, the governor of Missouri ordered that all Mormons in the state be either driven beyond its borders or "exterminated." Six years later, at Carthage, Illinois, an angry mob murdered Joseph Smith and his brother.

Smith's death fragmented the Mormon movement. Doctrinal differences, as well as a power struggle, separated various groups as they fought over the definition of the church. In the early 1840s Smith had introduced a number of important doctrinal innovations into the church, including polygamy (although the practice was officially denied), that cut Mormonism adrift from its original primitivist moorings. For a substantial minority of church members these innovations proved too much. Many of these people, attempting to remain faithful to earlier church practice, eventually coalesced around the prophet's eldest son, Joseph Smith III, forming the Reorganized Church of Jesus Christ of Latter-day Saints in 1852 (headquartered today in Independence, Missouri).

Most Mormons, however, willingly embraced the teachings of the 1840s and the leadership of the Quorum of the Twelve Apostles, headed by Brigham Young, who upheld them. Hostility toward the church, however, had not ended with Smith's martyrdom, and a year and a half later the Saints' alienation from American society was complete. In February 1846, after sixteen years of persecution, the Mormons decided to abandon not only their home in Illinois but the United States altogether.

Since 1843 the church leadership had quietly explored the possibility of creating a new Mormon homeland in locations that ranged from the Texas Republic to imperial Russia. After considerable study, however, church leaders decided upon the Rocky Mountain region, in the vaguely defined portion of Mexican territory called Upper California; the specific selection of the Great Basin area came only en route. Accordingly, in February 1846 the "Camp of Israel" began its exodus across the plains.

The migration proved a memorable achievement, notable for its sophisticated organization, discipline, and comparatively low mortality rates—as well as for its numbers. By the time the long series of migratory waves lasting several years had ended, ten thousand to fifteen thousand people had come, with the first pioneers reaching the Salt Lake Valley in July 1847.

Running eighty miles from north to south and thirty-five miles from east to west, the Great Salt Lake lay in an enormous intermountain basin that loosely marked the eventual extent of Mormon settlement. Bounded by the Rocky Mountains on the east, the Colorado River on the south, the Sierra Nevada on the west, and the Columbia River on the north, the Great Basin covers some 210,000 square miles, encompassing almost all of Nevada, western Utah, and portions of Wyoming, Idaho, Oregon, and California.

What made the Great Basin the promised land for the Mormons was that they had few neighbors with whom to contend. Initially, this included the Indians. Although approximately twenty thousand Native Americans lived in what would become Utah, the earliest church settlement on the Great Salt Lake fell on the uncontested border between the Shoshone and Ute tribes, and north and west of the traditionally claimed land of the nearby Hopis, Navajos, Apaches, Gosuites, and Pauites. As Mormon settlement expanded, however, conflict inevitably erupted, leading to a series of wars during the early 1850s and through much of the 1860s, finally culminating in treaties that removed the Indians as a significant presence in the area in 1869.

Despite the familiarity of this pattern, Mormon and Indian relations were highly atypical of Indian-white relations in many ways. According to the Book of Mormon, the Indians are a remnant of an ancient Christian civilization destroyed by apostasy and wickedness. Part of the Saints' eschatological responsibility is to recall the Indians to the faith of their ancestors. Consequently, from the church's founding to the present day, the Mormons have taken a special missionizing interest in the Indians. While in recent years critics have charged that church programs undermine Indian religion and culture, in the context of the nineteenth century the Saints' religious views caused them to treat the Indians with greater respect than did most other whites. Much to the consternation of federal Indian agents, mountain men, and other gentiles in the region, the Indians came to distinguish sharply between Mormons and non-Mormons. In the late 1880s, the long-held fear that the Mormons incited the Indians against other white people seemed verified to some when elements of Mormon religious teachings appeared in an apocalyptic Ghost Dance cult. Spreading from tribe to tribe, the cult eventually created the tension that resulted in the massacre of Sioux Indians by federal troops at Wounded Knee, South Dakota, in December 1890.

Irrespective of the fairness of this charge, the church, already under intense pressure over its practice of polygamy, deemphasized its Indian missionary work. Since resuming it in the 1940s, the church has focused primarily on educational efforts, both religious and secular, which include the highly successful, if controversial, Indian student placement program, under which disadvantaged Indian children are placed in Mormon homes in order to attend public school and participate in Mormon religious life.

The earliest Mormon settlers intended the Indians to be a part of the Kingdom of God that they were determined to build. The creation of a distinctive Mormon region was, in fact, one of the most consciously planned large-scale settlements in American history, and this building of Zion gave the Saints a sense of territoriality that has diminished only slightly in recent decades. Originally, the Mormon empire the Saints envisioned was to be carved out of Mexican territory. Yet, ironically, scarcely had the Mormons escaped the territorial limits of the United States when the land ceded by Mexico to the United States at the conclusion of the Mexican-American War dragged them back in.

The scope of Mormon ambition was revealed in 1849, when the church proposed to Congress the creation of the state of Deseret, a Book of Mormon word for "honeybee" (meant to symbolize productivity). Deseret was to be bounded on the east by the Continental Divide, on the west by the Sierra Nevada, on the north by the watershed of the Columbia River, and on the south by the Gila River, with a southwestern extension that ran all the way to the Pacific Ocean to give the Saints a seaport.

Congress, however, proved indifferent to Mormon aspirations when, as part of the Compromise of 1850, it organized the more modest Utah Territory, named after the local Indians. Although the church attempted to establish a series of outposts along Deseret's proposed borders, most notably at San Bernadino, California in 1853, most of these settlements floundered and were abandoned when all church members were called home to defend Zion against federal troops sent by President James

Buchanan to put down a rumored Mormon upris-ing against the government in 1857.

If the Saints' territorial grasp initially exceeded their reach, the church did grow impressively. This growth was fueled by a remarkably successful mis-sionary effort that brought a rich harvest of converts from the British Isles, Scandinavia, and Germany to the Great Basin. Many of these Europeans paid their way to the United States by drawing upon the Per-petual Emigrating Fund, a revolving fund that gave financial assistance to converts in exchange for re-payment once they had settled in the West. By 1870, over fifty thousand Mormons had received direct assistance from the fund, and European-born adults made up the majority of Utah's population. Once mustered, both natives and European immigrants were "called" to form communities (over five hundred during the nineteenth century) through-out the Great Basin, each of which was carefully organized to encompass the diversity of skill, ex-perience, and talent that would ensure its viability.

After 1857 Mormon settlements were generally contiguous, beginning along the western edge of the Wasatch Mountains. These western Wasatch val-leys eventually made up the core of Mormon settle-ment. Although the region received only ten to twelve inches of rain annually, summer runoff from melting mountain snow made it feasible to irrigate the surrounding available land. The land had little timber, however, and while it did have impressive mineral riches in copper, iron, lead, silver, gold, and coal, the Saints ignored them, believing that they tended to require occupations unsuited to sound religious life.

From the Wasatch range, the Mormons pushed to the southwest to Utah's "Dixie," where the church founded Saint George in 1861, in an effort to take advantage of the warmer climate to produce subtropical crops, especially cotton. Unfortunately, the stark, arid land had only sparse vegetation. Only church-financed projects, most prominently the building of a temple, along with the importation of food, saved the town from early disbandment.

The Mormon drive to the southwest was halted by the Mojave Desert; the drive east, by the lack of an adequate water supply, boulder-strewn canyons, and an Indian reservation; and migration to the west, by the salt flats. Thirty years after the Saints first arrived in the Great Basin, they had settled all of the contiguous available land except that to the north. Ironically, southern Idaho, now second only to Utah in percentage of Mormon population, pos-sessed good land and experienced milder winters

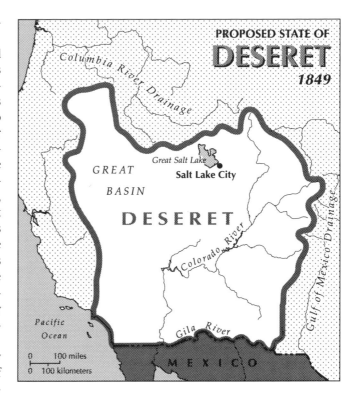

than the Wasatch Valley. Brigham Young, however, insisted that the area was too cold for cultivation and forbade Mormon emigration into the area. This resulted in Idaho's being settled first by gentile miners, ranchers, and traders, most of whom were hostile to the church. In the 1880s, after Young's death, Mormon desire for Idaho land could no longer be contained, and church settlers streamed up the Snake River, founding Rexburg (1883) as their main trading center and then pushing east into Wyoming's Star Valley.

During this same period other church colonies were founded in Colorado, Oregon, and most ex-tensively, Arizona, beginning in the 1870s. During the 1880s the federal government's crusade against Mormon polygamists led to the founding of refugee settlements in Chihuahua, Mexico, and in Alberta, Canada, where the Saints founded Cardston. By the end of the 1890s, however, the organized founding of colonies drew to a close and the Mormon pop-ulation growth shifted toward urbanization.

Geographical expansion, as vividly rendered by the dream of Deseret, represented one of the most obvious expressions of the Saints' quasi-nationalistic drive that emerged out of their disillusionment with U.S. society at mid century. The Mormons had long since come to regard themselves as a "peculiar people," different from other Americans; and in establishing themselves in the West, they had turned inward, shunning contact with outsiders whenever possible. Most Saints, in fact, lived in small, highly structured, homogeneous villages in which everyone belonged to the church. Moreover, as the local bishop and his counselors tightly regulated village life, Brigham Young and his immediate successors tightly regulated Zion as a whole. Indeed, until his death in 1877, Young largely directed the economy, indefatigably striving to free the Saints from dependence on the larger society by fostering self-sufficiency and at the same time fulfilling Joseph Smith's communal teachings. As part of this effort, the church experimented with communitarian living during the 1850s and again in the United Order of Enoch during the 1870s. In between was the cooperative movement of the 1860s, of which the department store ZCMI (Zion's Cooperative Mercantile Institution) remains as a legacy, at least in name.

Left largely to their own devices, the Mormons created many religious customs that separated them from mainstream Protestantism. Many of these were developed from the doctrines that Joseph Smith introduced in the 1840s. These doctrines included baptism for the dead, which offered salvation to those who died before learning the "restored" gospel, and has led to the church's well-known interest in genealogy; the concept of an eternal progression toward godhood; and a new understanding of the marriage bond. Smith taught that married couples were to be "sealed" for time and eternity (non-Mormons were married for time only), and that a man built up his heavenly kingdom in proportion to his righteousness and that of his children. Intimately related to this was "plural marriage," more popularly known as polygamy, the practice of which would lead to one's greater exaltation in the afterlife. Earlier, Smith had revealed the existence of three levels of "glory," or salvation, that one might attain. The highest exaltation was reserved for spiritually advanced males deemed worthy to have plural wives. Sealed women benefited from plural marriage because their status in the afterlife was dependent upon that of their husband.

Once safely ensconced in the Great Basin, the church formally acknowledged the practice of polygamy in 1852. Initially confined to a small elite group, plural marriage gradually became more widespread, especially in the wake of the "Mormon

Reformation" of 1856–1857. It is difficult to determine just how extensive plural marriage actually became. For a long time the number of these marriages was inflated or deflated to serve the political purposes of the church or its enemies. The vast majority of Mormon marriages, however, were monogamous, and it seems likely that at the institution's peak in the late nineteenth century, about 15 to 20 percent of Mormon households were headed by polygamous men. Despite the image of Mormon harems, most polygamous males had only one additional wife, and fewer than 6 percent ever had five or more wives.

Plural marriage varied widely from community to community within the Mormon region, from a town like Rockville, Utah, where in 1880 about 10 percent of the households were polygmous, to Orderville, Utah, in which 67 percent were polygamous. Despite these variations, the pressure to enter into polygamous relationships could be quite intense, especially on successful men, or men who aspired to positions of church leadership. Women who resisted plural marriages were also pressured by Mormon leaders, and sometimes publicly condemned for failing to follow "counsel." Yet if pressure could be intense, it was only occasionally needed. Most men and women participated in polygamy willingly, considering it essential to their salvation.

If, nestled in the Great Basin, the Mormon church was sufficiently removed from the larger American society to develop culturally divergent institutions like plural marriage, it nonetheless never lacked opponents who wished to punish the Saints for their social deviance and their political separatism. Beginning in the 1850s, the Mormons came into constant conflict with the terrritorial judges sent from Washington to rule them. In 1857 President James Buchanan, in response to grossly exaggerated reports from federal officials, sent the "Mormon Expedition" to end alleged systematic Mormon resistance to the national government's authority. Brigham Young, then territorial governor, responded by declaring martial law, evacuating Mormon settlers to southern Utah, and pledging to torch abandoned church settlements before allowing them to fall into the army's hands. Fortunately, a confrontation between the federal troops and the Saints was headed off, but tragically, not before the war hysteria led Mormon militiamen and their Indian allies to brutally massacre a wagon train of California-bound migrants at Mountain Meadows, Utah. Although the attack lacked the church's sanction, it besmirched the Saints' reputation for decades.

Most of these early troubles originated outside of Utah. Mormon isolation, although never complete, was fated to end. Even as church expansion bumped against gentile settlement in Idaho and Arizona, non-Mormons were invading the Saints' Utah stronghold. Some were miners from southern Europe taking up work the church shunned. Some were soldiers who came to man military posts. Still others came as merchants and traders hoping to exploit Salt Lake City's location as a way station for far western travel and commerce. To a great degree, much of this development was made possible by the completion of the transcontinental railroad in 1869, making immigration for Mormons and non-Mormons alike much easier and helping to swell the growth of Salt Lake City and Ogden.

Many of these newcomers quickly developed an intense dislike for the Mormon church, which they viewed as corrupt and despotic. In 1870 they banded together to form the Liberal party, dedicating themselves to ending the church's political and economic domination of the region. When the Mormons countered by creating the People's Party, the battle was joined, and the shape of Utah and Idaho politics was defined for the next quarter of a century. Although Mormon numbers were overwhelmingly superior, gentiles found a powerful ally in the federal government; and as long as Utah remained a territory, non-Mormons exercised a disproportionate influence on its affairs. The Saints, who had attempted to win statehood for Deseret in 1849, became obsessed with gaining statehood for Utah as a means of freeing themselves from their enemies. Their opponents became no less obsessed with preventing it.

The gentiles' strongest hold upon the Saints was the church's practice of polygamy. Victorian America revered the family as the basis of society and saw in plural marriage a threat to its foundation. The sacredness with which the Mormons held the marriage bond was lost on the middle-class critics, who regarded the practice of plural marriage as transparent proof of the church's moral degeneracy. Buchanan's willingness to send troops to Utah in 1857 had arisen in part from a growing national consensus against the church. The previous year the new Republican party presidential platform lumped polygamy with slavery as "twin relics of barbarism," and called for its eradication. In 1862 Congress passed the Morrill Anti-bigamy Act, criminalizing plural marriage. Only the distraction of the Civil War and Reconstruction kept the law from being enforced.

In the mid 1870s the Saints' controversial marriage practices began receiving renewed national attention. In 1874 Congress passed the Poland Act, which strengthened federal authority over Utah by stripping Mormon-controlled probate courts of their irregular jurisdiction in criminal and civil cases, and by reorganizing the territorial government to give greater power to the U.S. marshal and district attorney general. Despite Mormon claims that the Morrill Act unconstitutionally violated their religious rights, the Supreme Court in *Reynolds* v. *United States* (1879) upheld the criminalization of polygamy with only a single dissenting vote.

The *Reynolds* case galvanized national opinion against the Saints and made the 1880s among the very hardest years in the church's history. In 1882 Congress passed the Edmunds Act, which significantly reduced the difficulty of prosecuting polygamists; disqualified them from voting, holding office, or serving on juries; and created a special federal commission to oversee elections. With the passage of the Edmunds Act the anti-Mormon crusade had reached fever pitch. Alleged polygamists were hunted by teams and their homes raided; once caught, they were denied bond and tried by gentile juries, and their wives were made to testify against them; when convicted, they received lengthy prison sentences.

Most polygamists, including the top church leadership, lived in a shadowy underground world, often on Mormondom's periphery in Colorado, Arizona, Nevada, Canada, or Mexico. John Taylor, Brigham Young's successor, died in hiding in 1887. That same year, the Edmunds-Tucker Act dealt the Mormons another harsh blow by disincorporating the church and declaring all of its property valued in excess of $50,000 escheated to the federal government. The act also placed further restrictions on the political process, including ending women's suffrage, which had been granted by the Mormon-controlled territorial legislature in 1870 to increase the Saints' voting power. In 1890 both Salt Lake City and Ogden fell under the control of gentile politicians.

With ever harsher laws pending in Congress (some of which had already been enacted by the gentile majority in Idaho), the pressure on the church became unbearable. In September 1890, after prayerful inquiry, church president Wilford Woodruff announced a revelation officially discountenancing the teaching and further practice of plural marriage. Although the church covertly sanctioned some polygamous marriages for another fourteen years, the Woodruff Manifesto finally brought the worst of the conflict between Mormons and the federal government to an end. The Saints disbanded their People's Party and somewhat artificially separated themselves into Democrats and Republicans. The federal government returned its property to the church, and in September 1894 President Grover Cleveland granted amnesty to all polygamists who had married plural wives before 1890. In 1896 Utah at last obtained statehood, forty-six years after the Saints first sought it.

By 1890 the church had started down a long road of social adjustment that would bring it more into line with the dominant culture. But that road was by no means an easy one to travel. Moreover, if the debate over Mormon polygamy had lost some of its intensity, it had hardly abated. When Utahns elected B. H. Roberts, a prominent church leader and open polygamist, to Congress in 1898, the House of Representatives refused to seat him. Of greater significance, however, was the controversy surrounding Apostle Reed Smoot's election to the U.S. Senate in January 1903. Smoot, unlike Roberts, was monogamous, but he was popularly cast as a representative of a morally corrupt and tyrannical church. His election caused an uproar across the nation. Debate over his seating sparked a three-year Senate investigation into the church that elicited over three thousand pages of testimony and inspired numerous muckraking attacks upon the Saints.

Moreover, in regard to polygamy, there was plenty of sensational material to find. Not only had the church surreptitiously approved new plural marriages, but after Utah's achievement of statehood the number of these unions increased. In the face of renewed national scrutiny, Prophet Joseph Fielding Smith issued the "Second Manifesto" in 1904 ending church-sanctioned polygamy. This and other church efforts, along with the assistance of President Theodore Roosevelt, finally led to Smoot's seating.

Polygamy, however, did not die easily, and is still not extinct. The Saints had long been taught that their exaltation in the afterlife depended upon entering into plural marriage, and some saw that man, rather than God, had commanded its revocation. This view gave rise to the Fundamentalist movement, and there are about thirty thousand practicing polygamists in the Mormon region today. By the 1920s, however, the leadership of the church found its polygamous past an embarrassment and routinely excommunicated any member found entering into plural marriage. Moreover, by the 1930s the church actively encouraged the legal prosecution of polygamists and kept up a surveillance of Fundamentalist homes. Systematic prosecution of polygamists eventually ended in 1960. Despite the dramatics of a few small polygamous cults, most of those currently engaged in plural marriage live quiet and in other ways law-abiding lives.

The abandonment of polygamy was emblematic of a sea change within the church in the period between 1890 and 1940. After the turn of the century, pentecostalism and faith healing within the church were actively discouraged. Reflecting the Progressive era's interest in organization and process, the church's bureaucracy was updated and rationalized. The importance of the gathering was deemphasized as converts were quietly urged to remain at home. By the 1920s the millennium and the coming of the Kingdom of God were pushed deeper into the vague future.

These religious changes were mirrored by a retreat from secular affairs. Prior to 1890 the Mormon church had been a total institution. During the next half-century the church gradually surrendered its claim to absolute control over purely secular matters, most notably in politics and the economy. Abdication of authority in these areas, however, has never been complete. Most church members do not need to be told what their generally politically conservative leadership wishes. (They do not always obey them, however; vast numbers of Mormons voted for Franklin Roosevelt in 1936.)

The church leadership becomes more conspicuously involved in politics, especially when it believes that important moral issues are at stake, as in its strenuous effort to prevent adoption of the Equal Rights Amendment. At the same time, if the leadership's experiments with economic communitarianism had ended, it took a special responsibility for helping the Mormon poor during the Great Depression and continues to help economically disadvantaged Saints. It has also given enthusiastic support to Mormon businessmen, lobbied government on their behalf, encouraged them to keep their investments within the Mormon region, and sometimes has punished those whose business dealings have become too involved with those outside the faith.

The church's cultural adjustment after 1890 had the effect of lessening tension between Mormons and American society, so much so that by

1930 the majority of Americans had come to view the church in a positive light. Still, hostility to the larger culture never ended. Mormons, to a great degree, derived their identity by opposition to what they regarded as the hedonism and the decline of society's moral values, and they continue to do so today. In suspending an active quest for the kingdom, the church refocused its attention on private life, giving renewed emphasis to the marriage covenant and the family, encouraging the genealogical work necessary for the baptism of the dead, and, most notably, obedience to the Word of Wisdom—dietary guidance urging abstinence from alcohol, tobacco, and "hot drinks" (interpreted as coffee and tea). First offered to the Saints by God (through Joseph Smith) in 1833, it was upgraded to a commandment only in the twentieth century and now serves, in part, as a badge distinguishing the Saints from other Americans.

Maintaining a separate identity outside the vast array of Protestant churches has become increasingly difficult for the Mormon church since World War II. This has caused some ambivalence among the Saints. On the other hand, this blurring of identity reflects a general acceptance of the church and the economic success of Mormons as a group. While this integration into American life is generally welcomed, the church continues to stress its claim to religious uniqueness. Although the Saints in the Mormon region will never be marginalized in the same way they were during the nineteenth and early twentieth centuries, they have continued to vacillate between a quest for acceptance in American society and a desire to stand outside it as critics. Yet, in a way that reveals much about change among the Mormons, the Saints now defend some of the more conservative customs and power arrangements in American society. Consequently, the Mormons have found themselves most at ease during periods of social and political conservatism like those of the immediate postwar years, and during the 1960s turned back to their more accustomed role of critics of perceived moral decadence.

Since its founding the church has provided authoritative answers to not only the most fundamental religious questions of life but social, political, and cultural questions as well. Once the church has offered an official answer on any of these topics, Mormons have been reluctant to change their views on it. This has, accordingly, given rise to three basic challenges to the modern church, one of which has been resolved and two others that will continue to pose problems for some time.

The first of these is a part of America's continuing problem with racism. Until recently, no black could be ordained into the Mormon priesthood, a status the church routinely conferred on twelve-year-old white boys. Although consistently racist, the early Mormon church displayed an ambivalence on racial issues. The Book of Mormon repudiated slavery, and while few blacks requested admission into the church, those who did so were denied neither membership nor the priesthood. When Joseph Smith ran for the American presidency in 1844, he did so as an avowed abolitionist. More important, however, Smith produced two theological works, the Book of Moses (1833) and the Book of Abraham (1835), which implied that blacks were the descendants of Cain and Ham, cursed because in the primordial state their spirits had stayed neutral in the struggle between God and Satan.

After the church canonized these two works (1880) as the Pearl of Great Price, they served as the formal justification for denying blacks the priesthood, a practice the church had informally begun by at least 1849. By 1907 anyone having a black ancestor, no matter how remote or distantly related, was prohibited from participation in Temple ordinances. In Utah, blacks were banned by custom from many public places, segregated in others, and discriminated against in housing, education, and employment. When the civil rights movement gained momentum in the 1950s and early 1960s, some church leaders issued warnings about forced racial amalgamation and declared the movement largely inspired by communists. In the mid 1960s civil rights activists began direct attacks on the church. Brigham Young University athletic contests were boycotted by competing teams and sometimes disrupted by spectators. Within the church, at the same time, there were forces at work moving to overthrow the heritage of discrimination. Mormon intellectuals attacked the historical and theological foundation for church policy, while church leadership was sensitive to the attacks on prominent Mormon political leaders, such as presidential contender George Romney, who, like Reed Smoot before him, was politically weighed down by this baggage. Moreover, the success of Mormon missionaries in making sweeping conversions in Latin America, especially Brazil, where heritages of mixed blood were common, brought additional pressure to change church policy. These forces finally crystallized in a revelation to Mormon prophet Spencer Kimball in June 1978, which led to acceptance of black men into the priesthood.

MORMON CULTURE REGION

Source: Meinig, 1965

Although it has yet to become as divisive as the struggle over race became, the status of women in the church will probably prove more intractable in the long run. In Mormondom women are defined by their relationship to men in both the religious and the secular spheres. They are not ordained to the priesthood, and in Mormon theology the quality of their afterlife remains dependent upon mar-

rying godly Mormon men. They are expected to be obedient to men in the home, and the well-ordered management of a large, loving family is held up as their highest ideal. The church's energetic opposition to the adoption of the Equal Rights Amendment created some highly publicized confrontations, but a more telling dissent from official doctrine is the changes Mormon women are making in their lives. While the average Mormon family consists of 4.6 people, fertility among Mormon women has been rapidly declining since 1980: 3.2 to 2.5 births per woman (compared with 1.8 for all American women), and fully half of all Mormon women work at least part-time outside the home (compared with 57 percent of all American women). While the church leadership has found the changes disquieting, it appears that the rate of change is increasing rather than decreasing.

Often more noisy, but probably less menacing to the leadership, are the periodic clashes between church authorities and Mormon intellectuals. From the time of Brigham Young to the present, church leaders have viewed intellectuals with suspicion. As a self-improving group, the Mormons have historically placed a good deal of emphasis on education, but have always felt more comfortable with vocational training than humanistic learning. The professionalization of Brigham Young University following its elevation to university status in 1903 caused a good deal of strain, most notably in 1911, when church leaders removed a number of popular new faculty members whose views they deemed theologically unacceptable. More recently, church leaders have repeatedly censured Mormon historians for failing to write faith-promoting works and for dwelling instead upon the human foibles of early church leaders and diminishing the sacredness of the Mormon story by putting it into historical context. In 1985, when a forger of letters documenting Joseph Smith's interest in folk magic attempted to maintain his deception by using letter bombs to cover his fraud, a deeply embarrassed church leadership had had enough. In recent years pressure to avoid controversial subjects has increased, and permission to use the church archives has become highly restricted, with a good deal of material closed to examination altogether.

While Mormonism is a history-centered faith, historians and other intellectuals appear to pose little threat to its well-being. The church, in fact, is thriving as never before. Nearly insolvent in 1900, it is now wealthy. Just how wealthy is a tightly guarded secret and a subject of frequent speculation. Most of its wealth comes from tithing, but it owns a good deal of commercial real estate as well as church property, numerous agribusiness enterprises, a newspaper, television and radio stations, banks, department stores, insurance companies, and a textile mill. Most of these are located in the traditional Mormon region. Yet the Mormon region has at last burst its old boundaries. While Utah still has the highest concentration of Mormons in the United States (1.3 million, more than 70 percent of its population), only half of the Mormons in America live in the Great Basin; the other half live mostly in neighboring states like California, Washington, and Texas.

The church, however, is at last becoming truly international. Although Mormonism claims 7.3 million adherents, only 4 million of them live in the United States. This trend away from a regionally based religion is rapidly escalating. Although the apostasy rate for new converts is high, over a quarter of a million people become Latter-day Saints every year, and most of them are outside the United States. The design of Deseret, once the symbol of Mormon ambition, has proved unambitious after all.

BIBLIOGRAPHY

General Works

Allen, James B., and Glen M. Leonard. *The Story of the Latter-day Saints* (1976).

Arrington, Leonard J., and Davis Bitton. *The Mormon Experience: A History of the Latter-day Saints* (1979).

Hansen, Klaus J. *Mormonism and the American Experience* (1981).

Limerick, Patricia Nelson. *The Legacy of Conquest: The Unbroken Past of the American West* (1987).

Poll, Richard D., gen. ed. *Utah's History* (1978).

Ruthven, Malise. "The Mormons' Progress." *Wilson Quarterly* 15 (Spring 1991): 23–47.

Shipps, Jan. *Mormonism: The Story of a New Religious Tradition* (1985).

Period Studies

Alexander, Thomas G. *Mormonism in Transition: A History of the Latter-day Saints, 1890–1930* (1986).

Lyman, Edward Leo. *Political Deliverance: The Mormon Quest for Utah Statehood* (1986).

Winn, Kenneth H. *Exiles in a Land of Liberty: Mormons in America, 1830–1846* (1989).

Specialized Studies

Arrington, Leonard J. *Brigham Young: American Moses* (1985).

———. *Great Basin Kingdom: An Economic History of the Latter-day Saints, 1830–1900* (1958).

Arrington, Leonard J., Feramorz Y. Fox, and Dean L. May. *Building the City of God: Community and Cooperation Among the Mormons* (1976).

Bringhurst, Newell G. *Saints, Slaves, and Blacks: The Changing Place of Black People Within Mormonism* (1981).

Foster, Lawrence. *Religion and Sexuality: Three American Communal Experiments of the Nineteenth Century* (1981).

Logue, Larry M. *A Sermon in the Desert: Belief and Behavior in Early St. George, Utah* (1988).

Meinig, D. N. "The Mormon Culture Region: Strategies and Patterns in the Geography of the American West, 1847–1964." *Annals of the Association of American Geographers* 55 (June 1965): 191–220.

Van Wagoner, Richard S. *Mormon Polygamy: A History,* 2d ed. (1989).

SEE ALSO **Religion** and various essays in "**Family History.**"

THE MOUNTAIN WEST

Patricia Nelson Limerick
Aimee Nicole Blagg

THE ROCKY MOUNTAINS are the largest mountain chain in North America, running from Mexico to Canada. Within the borders of the United States, the varied terrain of these mountains has become part of the states of Montana, Wyoming, Idaho, Colorado, Utah, Nevada, New Mexico, and Arizona. In this region one finds towering peaks, but also open valleys, parks, and plains. Higher in altitude than most other parts of the nation, the region's remarkable landscape was well stocked with wildlife, minerals, timber, soil, and grass—natural elements that Euro-Americans were pleased to classify as marketable commodities. Since the nineteenth century, the harvesting of the area's natural resources has been a focus of business and settlement. As a result, the social history of many Rocky Mountain locations provides some of the nation's clearest case studies of the ways in which economic activity can shape community life. This pattern is far from the mystical environmental determinism once offered by Frederick Jackson Turner and traditional frontier historians. As countless examples in the Rocky Mountain region have shown, a community whose fate rests on an extractive economy will find many of its qualities and conditions shaped by that economy. The value and supply of the extracted resource will often determine whether the community continues to exist. In a similar vein, the reality of the landscape and the climate—the difficulty of much of the terrain, the harshness of the climate, the uneven distribution of water—has had a clear impact on human society.

The Rocky Mountain region has become home to a population varying widely in origin, occupation, social organization, and worldview. The diversity of this population makes it impossible to tell the story of the region's colonization in the traditional, nationalistic terms of the American westward movement. Long before Meriwether Lewis and William Clark introduced an official American presence into the northern Rockies, different societies of Indian people had settled the region, and traded, negotiated, and contested with each other. Two centuries before Lewis and Clark, the Spanish colonization of New Mexico and the introduction of the horse had triggered a new configuration of Indian society and group relations. In the context of the prior presence of Indian people, the northward movement of Spanish-speaking colonizers, the southwestward movement of fur traders from French and British Canada, the eastward movement of Asian American immigrants and of Anglo-American prospectors traveling from California to the continental interior, the westward movement of white American pioneers toward the Rockies becomes only one part of a much more complicated story of a convergence from a variety of directions.

In the area now known as the Four Corners, where the states of Colorado, New Mexico, Arizona, and Utah now intersect, Indian people lived in centralized villages, supporting themselves by farming and following complicated ceremonial lives. Around 1300 the Anasazi people left their homes, evidently as a consequence of drought, and resettled in other areas of what would become New Mexico and Arizona. At roughly the same time, Athapascan people from the interior of Canada moved into the area from the north, encountering Pueblo Indian villages located, primarily, along the Rio Grande. In 1540, when Francisco Vásquez de Coronado led a party north from Mexico, the entrance of the Spanish added one more complication to what was already a changing social landscape. With permanent Spanish colonization in 1598, sedentary Pueblo people, Athapascan seminomads, and Spanish fortune hunters, missionaries, and soldiers constructed a complex society of conquest. In large part, economic affairs set the terms of their relations: the Spanish civil agents struggled with the Spanish missionaries for the control of Pueblo labor; the Athapascans both raided and traded with Pueblos and Spanish settlers.

But other variables besides economic ones played their part. Much of the Pueblo encounter with the Spanish centered on the missionaries' effort to restructure relations between men and women within Pueblo society. Traditionally, Pueblo sexuality was both sacralized and freely expressed; sexual intercourse maintained the harmony of the universe. Confronted with this very different religious ordering of daily life, the Franciscan missionaries cringed, and fought to reorganize Pueblo marriage and sexuality. The relations of conquest thus shaped society in every sphere, from the most public to the most private.

Introduced by the Spanish, the horse came into the possession of the Athapascans (Apaches and Navajos), increasing their mobility and their success as raiders. Moving north from New Mexico, the horse was an agent of enormous social change. Some tribes moved away from the mountains and onto the plains in order to pursue buffalo; tribes acquiring horses took up new definitions of status, new reasons for and new techniques of warfare, and new patterns of seasonal migration. Throughout the Rocky Mountain region, the Ute, the Navajo, the Comanche, the Arapaho, the Cheyenne, the Crow, the Shoshone, the Bannock, the Coeur d'Alene, the Kootenai, the Nez Percé, the Sioux, the Assiniboine, the Gros Ventre, and the Blackfeet took up new habits in response to the horse.

In the north, French and British fur traders provided the personnel for another intrusion of European Americans into native peoples' terrain. In the late eighteenth century, the Canadian fur traders made alliances with the northern tribes, including the Blackfeet; intermarriage between fur traders and Indian women had already begun to create a mixed-blood population. Lewis and Clark thus entered a region where changes introduced by European Americans radiated from both the south and the north before American explorers entered from the east.

Encouraged by favorable reports from Lewis and Clark, American fur traders eyed the Rockies. By the 1820s, the abundance of beaver in the Rocky Mountains had inspired several hundred Americans to take up a temporary, shifting residence. Significantly, most American trappers did their trapping themselves, bypassing the traditional fur-trade role of Indians as laborers and commercial partners. The trappers were unofficial agents of empire, using the wildlife as if they had some negotiated property right to it and acquiring the geographical knowledge that later colonizers would put to use.

The Rocky Mountain fur trappers certainly embodied the proposition that economic activity shapes way of life; their hunter-scavenger work habits, their mobility, their relationships with Indian women, and the transitoriness of their extractive industry as their hunting brought on the depletion of the beaver showed the stark relationship between the nature of the extracted resource and the pattern of an individual's way of life.

Just as important, the mountain men demonstrated another pattern of Rocky Mountain social history: in this case, as in many others, the historical significance of a population far exceeded its numbers. Only a few hundred men, the American fur trappers were vastly outnumbered by Indian people, and certainly by Americans in the eastern United States; nonetheless, the trappers had a substantial impact on a vast physical environment, as well as on Indian/white relations. In the general picture of American history, the population of the Rocky Mountain area has always been comparatively sparse. And yet, as in the case of the much romanticized trappers of the Rocky Mountain fur trade, a small population dispersed over vast spaces can still have enormous impact on local affairs and, often enough, on the national imagination and memory.

In the southern part of the region, a wagon trade connecting Missouri to Santa Fe and Chihuahua brought Mexicans and Americans into a commercial exchange. After the Pueblo Revolt of 1680 and a reconquest in the 1690s, Spanish colonists and Pueblo Indians had arrived at a more accommodating relationship, with diminished expectations on the part of the Spanish for either grand fortunes or the dramatic conversion of the natives. By the 1820s, the chain of Mexican villages had developed a distinctive folk culture, with a locally adapted variety of Catholicism and with networks of kinship and of family ordering daily life. Here, too, as in the fur trade, the economic exchange of the Santa Fe trade had ramifications for society in general. Marriage between American men, especially those of Irish Catholic background, and Mexican women incorporated some of the trappers into local society, while an enthusiasm for imported goods made it nearly impossible to retreat or withdraw from the trade. Like the fur trappers, the merchants of the Santa Fe acted as an entering wedge for Anglo-American conquest. In 1846, Stephen Watts Kearny's Army of the West took advantage of the groundwork performed by the merchants to complete the conquest of New Mexico.

THE MOUNTAIN WEST

The Rocky Mountains seemed at first to present an insurmountable barrier to Anglo-American conquest. Crossing the mountains to the north, Lewis and Clark had faced a labyrinth of difficult terrain and precarious paths. To the south, explorers like Zebulon Pike and John C. Frémont encountered a comparable labyrinth in the Colorado Rockies—dangerous terrain for travel, especially in winter. But in the middle, in what is now Wyoming, fur trappers located South Pass, an avenue that was broad and level enough to permit wagon travel. The discovery and utilization of South Pass changed the geopolitical implications of the Rockies. Instead of a barrier to the American nation's expansion, the Rockies now provided an opening for travel to the Pacific. In the 1840s and 1850s, the majority of overland travelers to California and Oregon used South Pass as their route across the continent. To these Americans, the Rocky Mountain region was a strange and interesting landscape glimpsed in passing. A number of the overland travelers admired the scenery, but the tight timing of the trip compelled them to hurry on in order to reach the coast before winter. Many travelers found the crossing of the continental divide to be a powerful symbolic moment. To pause at the point where the continent divided, with one stream flowing to the Pacific and another to the Atlantic, was to feel the full power and range of one's adventure, standing in a place that could only be imagined by most Americans.

To most overland travelers, the altitude, semi-aridity, remoteness, and vast dimensions of the Rocky Mountain region made it a poor candidate for the category "home." To one distinctive group of Americans, however, those very conditions qualified it as a prospective home. Driven from the Midwest, the Latter-day Saints, or Mormons, chose the Salt Lake area as a refuge from friction with "gentiles" (non-Mormons). The fact that the site would not appeal to conventional American settlers was precisely what made it attractive to the Mormon leader, Brigham Young. Arriving in Utah in 1847, the Mormons almost instantly adapted to semiaridity, constructing the ditches and dams that would make irrigated agriculture possible.

Living in a virtual theocracy, the members of the Church of Jesus Christ of Latter-day Saints could work under a kind of central planning and organization of colonization that most Anglo-Americans would have found distressing. With religious belief integrated into virtually every aspect of daily life, the Mormons created a distinctive enclave in the Rocky Mountains. Since they now practiced plural marriage openly, their society seemed very different from eastern American life. And yet in their dedication to hard work, their faith in progress, and their determination to convert natural resources into property and profit, the Mormons seemed very American indeed. Certainly for the Indian people of the area, Mormon colonization meant the appropriation of native land and resources. Although the Mormon leaders did, on some occasions, try to minimize conflict by feeding rather than fighting Indians, the construction of the Latter-day Saints' Jerusalem meant hardship and loss for the natives.

While traders, Mormons, and overland travelers significantly affected local conditions, many areas of the Rockies seemed, at first, to discourage Anglo-American settlement. Evidently quarantined by altitude, difficult terrain, and qualities of soil and water supply ill adapted to conventional American agriculture, large parts of the continental interior seemed to be on their way to status as a permanent Indian homeland. The California gold rush of 1848, and the recruiting of a restless, energetic informal army of prospectors, destroyed that possibility. In 1858, prospectors came upon gold in the mountains near what would become the city of Denver. The Pike's Peak rush inaugurated a series of mineral rushes that would scatter pockets of Anglo-American settlement all over the region.

In what would become the states of Colorado, Montana, Idaho, Wyoming, Utah, Nevada, New Mexico, and Arizona, precious metals inspired Americans to plant mining camps and towns in the most improbable locations. Rocky Mountain mining sites did not necessarily have adequate water, workable routes of transportation, a hospitable climate, or friendly Indians. Initially, mining towns were the most dependent of human communities; with attention and energy devoted to the extraction of the mineral, most residents depended on outside supplies of food and equipment, just as their prosperity rested on transportation that would permit them to move minerals to markets. Under these circumstances, transportation lines focused and polarized community emotion; when Indians, hostile to this uninvited invasion, threatened the security of movement over trails and roads, miners reacted with fury. Predictably, the expansion of mining in the Rocky Mountains led to some of the most volatile encounters between Indians and whites in American history.

In the territory of Colorado, the context of the Civil War increased the explosiveness of the situation. With Union troops withdrawn from the West, whites in Colorado felt dramatically unprotected, their routes of communication to the eastern United States daily at risk from Indian attack. This jumpiness led to the formation of a civilian volunteer force, under the command of a sometime Methodist minister, John Chivington. On 29 November 1864, the troops attacked a group of Cheyenne and Arapaho camped at Sand Creek. A few Indian men fought to defend their people, the majority of whom (and the majority of victims) were women and children. Denounced by regular army officers as well as by official investigations, the savagery of the Sand Creek attack carried one clear lesson: the development of the western mining industry ended any vision of the Rocky Mountain region as a refuge for Indian people.

On the other hand, the growth of the mining business was hardly universal good news for white Americans. The majority of participants in mineral rushes found themselves disappointed, having invested their money, time, energy, and sometimes health in an unrewarded gamble. Mining camps were the most improvised of settlements, with poor housing and even poorer sanitation. They were, moreover, notoriously transitory; many Rocky Mountain mining towns rose and fell within the course of a decade or two, leaving the landscape punctuated with ghost towns. Some miners emigrated in company with their wives and families; cooking, laundry, and the operating of boardinghouses, as well as prostitution, provided women with significant financial opportunity. But many mining town residents were single men or men separated from their families, and a kind of socially "unmoored" behavior marked by violence, alcohol abuse, and loneliness characterized much of life in the mining camps.

Mining, moreover, moved rapidly from placer mining, in which one or two men could sift dirt, to more complicated forms of separating minerals from rock and soil. Hydraulic mining used water to blast banks of soil to pieces; hard-rock mining tunneled into the earth. Many of the ores in the Rocky Mountains posed a challenge; complicated smelting and refining techniques had to be developed to separate the mineral from the rock. The sinking of underground mines and the construction of smelting plants required capital; in this phase of the industry, the majority of miners became wageworkers, often employed by capitalists who ruled over their businesses from San Francisco or New York. By the late nineteenth century, the Rocky Mountain mining industry had become a national center of union activism and of often violent counterattacks from owners.

The expansion of mining presented opportunities for other enterprises. Farmers and livestock raisers responded to the opportunity represented by the mining towns' demand for food. High altitudes, of course, meant short growing seasons. Similarly, relying on rainfall meant precarious farming; dependable water supplies came at the price of considerable labor in the construction of ditches and dams. Conditions in the Rocky Mountain region, in other words, posed a considerable test to the well-established American agrarian ideal. In New Mexico and in southern Colorado, Pueblo farmers and Hispanic villagers had long recognized the difficulty of large-scale agriculture in this environment, as well as the necessity for shared labor in the maintenance of systems of water supply. Confronting the conditions of agriculture in semiarid conditions, the later-arriving European American farmers developed an understandable enthusiasm for outside help. The prospect of federally subsidized irrigation projects would become more and more appealing as the centuries passed, and the 1902 Newlands Reclamation Act made such federal help a genuine possibility.

Cattle raisers also responded to the opportunity presented by miners who had an appetite but no inclination to grow their own food. In the years after the Civil War, cowboys brought cattle, drawn primarily from the great herds of Texas, into Colorado, Wyoming, and Montana. The construction of the transcontinental railroad made bigger national markets accessible to cattle from the Rocky Mountain territories. In the mountains, cattlemen adopted the practice of seasonal migration, driving cattle into the valleys and parks for the winter months, and returning them to summer pasture in the higher altitudes. By the 1880s, cattlemen began to recognize the precariousness of a complete dependence on grass on the public lands; drought, overgrazing, or a particularly severe winter could leave herds vulnerable to starvation. As ranchers adopted the practice of raising forage crops, as a backup for winter feeding, the boundary between farmer and cattleman blurred. Growing hay and alfalfa, the ranchers turned to irrigation and to a more permanent, family-based residence. Rocky Mountain cattle raisers thereby launched themselves on a path of action that would make their ranches into enclaves. Like the Pueblo Indian settlements, the northern New Mexico Hispanic villages, and the Mormon towns and farms, the ranches of the region would become the home base for a rural folk culture, with strong ties to the land and with an unwillingness to take part in the homogenization of national life.

The expansion of ranching, farming, and mining formed the economic basis for the rise of towns and cities. Salt Lake City provided the Mormons with their metropolis; Denver based its growth on the momentum of the region's mining; and a chain of smaller cities and towns connected ranches, mines, and farms to markets. The life of the rural cowboy chasing cattle through the wide-open spaces and the life of the urban merchant chasing profits and expenses through account books might have seemed, on the surface, to be very separate indeed, and yet the two lives were very much related. Just as rural people often resented the seemingly parasitic prosperity of the city, so city people sometimes squirmed under their association with rural enterprise. In the nineteenth as well as the twentieth century, urban boosters struggled to identify their towns and cities with the most advanced, sophisticated, and progressive qualities of American life in fashion, architecture, and high culture. For this sort of booster, the shame of having Denver (or Boise or Cheyenne) appear to be a "cow town" was too much to bear. Dependent on the business of their hinterlands, the residents of Rocky Mountain towns and cities sometimes seem determined to deny their geography, trying for a veneer of eastern sophistication to conceal their western locale.

In the late nineteenth century, both cities and countryside were places of considerable ethnic diversity. After the wars and treaties of conquest, the federal government had assigned Indian people to reservations. Despite the hope invested by some Anglo-Americans in the prospect of the "vanishing Indian," the reservations—nearly eighty of them—would remain permanent features of the region. At the edges of the reservations were "border towns," places like Gallup, New Mexico, and Cortez, Colorado, where descendants of the invaders and descendants of the natives met, sometimes in amicable trade and sometimes in friction.

The mining towns had been magnets for European immigration. Cornish miners found a particular opportunity as skilled workers with considerable experience in the British Isles. As mining shifted to include copper and coal, the Rocky Mountain mining towns drew workers from nearly every European country. Butte, Montana, developed an Irish cast; the mines of Carbon County, Utah, became a center for Greeks; Italians, Czechs, Sloven-ians, Serbs, and Croatians distributed themselves through the Colorado mines.

Chinese immigrants had followed both mining booms and railroad construction jobs into the region; in Idaho in the 1870s, as much as 30 percent of the population was Chinese. In the region's towns and cities, Chinese people took up the economic opportunities represented by restaurants and laundries. Perceived as competition for white people's jobs, the Chinese were periodically subject to harassment, expulsion, and even murder. In Rock Springs, Wyoming, in 1885, white workers attacked Chinese workers, killing twenty-eight in an episode of wild mob violence.

After the Chinese Exclusion Act of 1882, Japanese immigrants found opportunity in the region as railroad workers and as farmers. The Japanese American presence in the Rocky Mountains was much increased in the 1940s, when racism and suspicion inspired the relocation of people of Japanese origin from the Pacific Coast. At Heart Mountain, Wyoming, the Japanese American internees experienced imprisonment in a stark landscape and a harsh winter climate; elsewhere in the region, the War Relocation Authority installed families in hastily constructed barracks at Amache, Colorado; Topaz, Utah; Minidoka, Idaho; and Poston and Gila River, Arizona. A number of these forcibly relocated Japanese American families chose to stay in the area after the end of the war.

African Americans had been a significant presence in the area for years. In his early crossing of the northern Rockies, William Clark had been accompanied by his black slave York; black men participated in the fur trade and played an important role in the western army as members of two black regiments. African American individuals worked in many mining towns and on many cattle ranches; while they were a small percentage of the region's population until the mid twentieth century, numbers and percentages do not tell the whole story. Whites imported antiblack attitudes into these territories, making it no easy matter for blacks to claim a share of local opportunity.

Facing a straitened economic situation in their homes in northern New Mexico, Hispanos pursued jobs in the mines and sugar beet fields of Colorado. For a time, the women in these families remained at home, maintaining gardens and a sense of continuity while their husbands traveled for seasonal labor. At the same time, Mexican immigrants, facing severe job scarcity in their homeland, renewed the northward migration of Spanish-speaking people, traveling as far north as Idaho to take agricultural jobs.

Rather than contracting over time, the human diversity of the region had expanded. This was not only a matter of national origin, language, or imported culture; the increasing diversity of the region was also a matter of the creation and growth of new folk cultures and enclaves. Life on reservations inspired a sense of tribal identity among Indian people whose ancestors had seen themselves more as members of bands or villages than as a tribal whole. After a long and bitter battle over polygamy, the Mormon people of Utah, southern Idaho, and northern Arizona emerged as a distinctive people, patriotic supporters of American values but also loyalists to a distinctive package of family customs, church-based social institutions, and a sense of their own sacred history. By the mid twentieth century, the Hispanic villages of northern New Mexico had a history of ten or more generations, with an understandably strong sense of the difference separating them from recent Mexican immigrants. Celebrated in national and international mythology, the symbolic, independent cowboy bore only a remote resemblance to the families who raised cattle in the region; and ranch women employed many of the same outdoor skills as ranchers. A number of these ranches had long family traditions of ownership behind them; the rancher owners had come to think of themselves as natives of the area and as the true and deserving stewards of the physical environment.

Throughout the region, there were second-, third-, and fourth-generation residents who thought of themselves as natives, people to whom the Rocky Mountain region was home and not an exotic place "out there," on the edge of American imagining. The most eloquent statement of this sentiment appeared in essays and novels. The works of Ivan Doig, descendant of Scottish immigrants to Montana, convey this recognition of the Rockies as *home;* Rudolfo Anaya performs a similar service for Hispanic New Mexicans, as does Levi Peterson for Mormons in Utah. This process of transforming a colonized region into home ties the social history of the region to the history of many other parts of the planet. From Latin America to Australia, from the Rockies to South Africa, the evolution of "settler societies," moving from the status of invaders with questionable legitimacy to the status of self-perceived natives with fully assumed legitimacy, ties the history of the planet together.

In 1982, Richard Lamm, governor of Colorado and coauthor with Michael McCarthy of *The Angry West,* railed against recent invaders of the Rockies. Speaking for Westerners who had lived in the region for some time (at least before the 1970s), Lamm declared, "They—we—are the new Indians. And they—we—will not be herded to the new reservations." The "old" Indians must have found this a fairly extraordinary claim, but it certainly conveyed to them, without ambiguity, the settler society's intention to claim indigenousness. Lamm's remark conveyed, as well, the ways in which legitimacy of residence remained an unsettled and shifting matter in the region. With their centuries of presence, the Indians had the best-established claim to legitimacy, even if their cultures, economies, and identities had been much reshaped by the workings of conquest. Hispanos, too, had an undeniable claim of "prior appropriation" on regional residence.

And then, in the mid twentieth century, just as Mormons and a variety of white rural Westerners began to feel themselves solidly settled in, the onset of World War II unleashed a new demographic transformation. The Rocky Mountain West presented a number of compelling opportunities for military and industrial development. Defense spending kicked off an enormous boom in western military development; while the Pacific Coast got the lion's share of this prosperity, parts of the Rocky Mountain West took their share. Already the administrative center for many federal services, especially for land-management bureaus, Denver became more and more a federal subcapital, and federal wages a central support for the local economy. With the cold war, defense spending continued to inspire industrial development and to provide wages for workers at missile installations and army bases. And in the Four Corners region, the arms race fueled a latter-day mineral rush as prospectors driving jeeps and armed with Geiger counters combed the area for uranium deposits.

All of this activity, as frenetic as any boom of the nineteenth-century "frontier," shook whatever balance the region's society might have reached. By and large, the cities prospered from the post–World War II boom; by and large, despite occasional booms followed by hard-hitting busts, the small towns and countryside lost ground. In the 1970s, the national energy crisis put a premium on the development of the Rocky Mountains' supply of oil and coal; the mining industry seemed to acquire a

THE MOUNTAIN WEST

new lease on life. Following many of the same patterns as their nineteenth-century predecessors, boomtowns rose and—with the end of that particular energy crisis and with a cataclysmic drop in energy prices—then fell, leaving the rural and small-town West with an increased revenue of bitterness.

These urban/rural tensions were heightened by the steady growth of tourism. In the late nineteenth century, the ease of railroad transportation permitted the rise of the Rocky Mountain tourism business as hotels and railroads recruited wealthy vacationers, offering them the chance to contemplate the American equivalent of Europe's Alps. A landscape that had once been a fearful barrier to travel was now becoming an occasion for travel, a spectacle to be contemplated from the window of the railroad car or from the veranda of the hotel. As the first national park, so designated in 1872, Yellowstone with its geysers met the standard for spectacle. The designation of many areas in the Rocky Mountain region as national parks, national forests, and national monuments furthered the region's stake in tourism, especially as these federal classifications reduced, or even prohibited, the possibility of making other economic uses of the public lands.

The marketing of the automobile democratized tourism, putting a visit to the parks of the Rocky Mountains within the reach of many middle-class and working-class families. On the one hand, tourists wanted to see a landscape that looked natural, without the visible blights of mining, overgrazing, or clear-cutting of timber. On the other hand, most tourists wanted roads, parking lots, restaurants, rest rooms, and campgrounds, to give them comfortable access to this "natural" landscape. By the 1970s, an increasingly audible kind of tourist wanted a simpler, starker encounter with nature, an experience shaped by the rhythm of the hiking boot on turf rather than the rhythm of the tire on pavement.

Often urbanites, from both within and outside the Rocky Mountain region, these varieties of nature lovers added tremendously to the volatility of the area's tensions between city and country. To many rural people, long dependent on jobs in extractive industries, environmentalists were imperial meddlers, imposing their standards for a pristine landscape at the expense of the hardworking local people. And yet, at the same time, rural communities resented the power and capital behind the extractive industries on which they relied. Angry at urban environmentalists and at urban capitalists, rural people could harmonize these contradictory resentments with a generalized hostility to the city, home to both preservers and developers.

The cities, meanwhile, faced their own internal tensions. It was no accident that one of the major civil rights lawsuits against school segregation originated in Denver (*Keyes* v. *School District 1* [1973]). Throughout the region, white emigrants had imported familiar racial prejudices, and then been confronted with the complicated social mosaic of blacks, whites, Mexican Americans, Asian Americans, and Indians. Indeed, the cities of the Rocky Mountain states, especially Denver, Albuquerque, Phoenix, and Tucson, faced so many of the familiar problems of urban America—racial friction, tensions between affluent suburbs and impoverished city neighborhoods, traffic congestion, and smog— that it was sometimes difficult to see any regional distinctiveness. And yet their geographical setting remained an important variable, as the cities

reached for water traditionally used by rural areas, and as the contest wore on between city dwellers wanting the Rocky Mountain countryside to provide them with restorative recreation and rural people wanting to make a living.

Tourism embodied the conflict, both in its problems and in its possibilities. Why not embrace tourism as the joint cause of city and country? Why not find the salvation of the rural economy in the provision of tourist services? Why not recognize the market potential of the distinctive folk cultures of the region? Why not, in essence, sell the region's distinctive social history? Because, critics argued, tourist-economy jobs are third world, colonial jobs, underpaid and of low status. Because marketing a culture—a reservation, a ranch, a village—erodes that culture, transforming authenticity into self-conscious spectacle. Tourist curiosity, by this argument, is simply another round in the endlessly repeating regional cycles of invasion and conquest.

Other manifestations of curiosity offered a more hopeful prospect for reciprocal and mutual inquiry. In 1991, Jim Carrier, a reporter for the urban *Denver Post,* went on a prolonged assignment to western Colorado. For weeks, he followed a family of cattle ranchers through spring calving season, the move to summer pasture, and the family's contests with urban environmentalists. He moved on to the Ute Mountain reservation in the southwest corner of Colorado and followed a family of Indian people through tribal elections, ritual dances, and livestock herding. The Ute struggled against alcohol, against diabetes, and against an educational system that repeatedly seemed to force them off the track of success.

While writing this series, Jim Carrier saw himself literally as a carrier of messages, letting white people know about the persistence of Indian people and letting urban people know about the reality of rural life, pressed hard against nature. Published as *West of the Divide,* Carrier's messages embodied the outcome of the social history of the Rocky Mountain region. Separate as the residents might have seemed from each other, a long and complicated history bound them into the same narrative. Divided as their destinies might have seemed in the 1990s, a network of historical relationships tied urbanite to rancher, white to Indian. The extraordinary landscape of the Rocky Mountains provided their battlefield and their common ground. True to the patterns of the region's history, the population of this area still seems sparse in comparison with the density of other American regions. And yet, the people of the Rocky Mountain West offer a poignant and dramatic case study of a national dilemma: the quest of a settler society to reach a lasting peace among its members, with the indigenous people, and with nature.

BIBLIOGRAPHY

Anaya, Rudolfo. *Bless Me, Ultima* (1972).

Arrington, Leonard J., and Davis Bitton. *The Mormon Experience: A History of the Latter-day Saints* (1979).

Brown, Ronald C. *Hard-Rock Miners: The Intermountain West, 1860–1920* (1979).

Carrier, Jim. *West of the Divide* (1992).

DeBuys, William. *Enchantment and Exploitation: The Life and Hard Times of a New Mexico Mountain Range* (1985).

Deutsch, Sarah. *No Separate Refuge: Culture, Class, and Gender on an Anglo-Hispanic Frontier in the American Southwest, 1880–1940* (1987).

Doig, Ivan. *This House of Sky: Landscapes of a Western Mind* (1978).

Embry, Jessie L. *Mormon Polygamous Families: Life in the Principle* (1987).

Emmons, David. *The Butte Irish: Class and Ethnicity in an American Mining Town, 1875–1925* (1989).

Gardner, A. Dudley, and Verla R. Flores. *Forgotten Frontier: A History of Wyoming Coal Mining* (1989).

Gulliford, Andrew. *Boomtown Blues: Colorado Oil Shale, 1885–1985* (1989).

Gutiérrez, Ramón A. *When Jesus Came, the Corn Mothers Went Away: Marriage, Sexuality and Power in New Mexico, 1500–1846* (1991).

Hogan, Richard. *Class and Community in Frontier Colorado* (1990).

Jordan, Teresa. *Cowgirls: Women of the American West* (1982).

Larson, Robert W. *Populism in the Mountain West* (1986).

Lee, Rose Hum. *The Growth and Decline of Chinese Communities in the Rocky Mountain Region* (1978).

Leonard, Stephen J., and Thomas J. Noel. *Denver: Mining Camp to Metropolis* (1990).

Nash, Roderick. *Wilderness and the American Mind,* 3d ed. (1982).

Peterson, Levi. *The Backslider* (1986).

Smith, Duane A. *Rocky Mountain Mining Camps: The Urban Frontier* (1967).

White, Richard. *It's Your Misfortune and None of My Own: A History of the American West* (1991).

Whiteside, James. *Regulating Danger: The Struggle for Mine Safety in the Rocky Mountain Coal Industry* (1990).

SEE ALSO **Asian Americans; Immigration; Industrialization; The Mormon Region; National Parks and Preservation; Transportation and Mobility; Travel and Vacations**; and various essays in the sections "**Periods of Social Change**" and "**Space and Place**."

THE PACIFIC NORTHWEST AND ALASKA

Eckard V. Toy, Jr.

THE PACIFIC NORTHWEST (Washington, Oregon, and Idaho) and Alaska were Asian and European before they were American, and Spanish, Russian, and English place names and Japanese, Taiwanese, and German investments still reflect that heritage. Oregon (1859) is the second oldest state on the Pacific Coast; Alaska (1959), the first of these states to be settled by European Americans, is the newest. Washington (1889) and Idaho (1890) gained statehood after the transcontinental railroads linked the region to the already developed eastern sections of the United States, opening new markets and facilitating migration. Although several time zones and the western provinces of Canada separate Alaska from the other states, grandly diverse landforms, resource-based economies, and a shared history confirm their kinship.

Except for the Columbia River, which separates much of Oregon from Washington, the borders with Canada and the state boundaries seldom conform to geographical features. The western coastline of the Northwest forms part of the eastern shore of the Pacific Rim, and the eastern boundary extends in a great northward arc from the arid Great Basin in the south along the western slope of the Rocky Mountains to the Arctic tundra. Mountain ranges and rivers dissect Alaska into a multitude of maritime and continental climate zones, the Cascade Mountains and the Coast Range divide Oregon and Washington into coastal, central valley, and eastern subregions, and Idaho has three north/south subregions—the Panhandle, the diverse central region, and the Mormon-dominated southeast—whose history has been shaped by social and economic factors.

The dramatic variations in landforms, habitat, and climate in the area are one result of the region's huge size. Massive formations of uplifted mountains, volcanic peaks, and glacier-sculpted valleys contrast with rain forests, wetlands, and deserts, and extremes of rain, snow, and aridity have their counterparts in vegetation and wildlife. The towering spruce, hemlock, fir, and cedar forests of the coastal areas and the fir and pine trees of the Cascades and the Rocky Mountains contrast with the sagebrush, greasewood, and juniper trees of the arid eastern parts of the Northwest and the hardy, stunted vegetation above timberline in the mountains and in the frigid Arctic tundra. There is equally great variety in wildlife, although many related species of mammals, birds, and fish can be found throughout the region.

Few good harbors indent the rugged coastline, but the Columbia River and its tributaries penetrate the interior valleys, Puget Sound forms a great inland waterway, and the Inner Passage of southern Alaska provides many protected inlets. While there are several large rivers in Alaska, none matches the historical and economic significance of the Columbia River and its principal tributaries, the Snake and Willamette rivers. The Columbia River has been a primary transportation route and salmon fishery for thousands of years; since the 1930s a series of massive dams has altered its flow and condition. Today, the fisheries are endangered, but the dams and the lakes behind them provide electricity, irrigation, recreation opportunities, and flood control.

Historically, dependency and distance have been basic factors in the relationship of the Pacific Northwest with the federal government. For much of the nineteenth century, the region was run as a territory of the United States; even today, most of Alaska, nearly two-thirds of Idaho, half of Oregon, and more than one-fourth of Washington are public land. Congress establishes policies and approves budgets for that land, and the National Park Service, the U.S. Forest Service, and the Bureau of Land Management have administrative authority over significant portions of each state. In addition, each state has numerous military facilities and Indian reservations ranging in size from a few acres to several thousand square miles.

The diverse and rich natural environment of the Northwest influenced native cultures and has shaped political and economic activities within the states. Most of the population and manufacturing in Washington, Oregon, and Alaska are concentrated in the western valleys and in the metropolitan centers of Seattle, Portland, and Anchorage. Spokane, Yakima, and the Tri-Cities region of Richland, Kennewick, and Pasco in eastern Washington and Fairbanks in Alaska are the only significant exceptions. Isolated coastal communities, with their typically small populations and economies dependent on fishing, logging, dairying, and tourism, often have little in common with the towns in the agriculturally diverse Willamette and Cowlitz valleys (in Oregon and Washington, respectively) or the huge wheat and cattle ranches of the Palouse Hills in eastern Washington and the Umatilla Plateau in Oregon. The irrigated apple and pear orchards of the Hood River valley in Oregon and the Wenatchee and Yakima valleys in Washington and the sugar beet farms of southern Idaho typically have depended on migrant labor of varying ethnic backgrounds. In Idaho, mining, forestry, and a radical labor tradition in the Panhandle contrast with the more diversified agriculture and politics of the central part of the state near Boise and the conservative political climate of Mormon-dominated southeastern Idaho.

EARLY HISTORY, EXPLORATION, AND SETTLEMENT

The ethnic and racial diversity that has characterized the Northwest since the beginning of its exploration by Europeans had parallels in the languages and cultures of native peoples. Native inhabitants of the frigid Alaskan North Slope, such as the Aleuts, Eskimos, and northern Alaskan Indians, responded to the limited resources of a harsh Arctic environment in different ways, and all lacked the wealth of the coastal Indians. Although the Kwakiutl, Haida, and Tsimshian of British Columbia generally had more material goods and slaves than other coastal tribes, like the Makah of the Olympic Peninsula and the Tlingit of southern Alaska, the different tribes lived in similar plank houses and hunted whales, seals, and sea otter, and fished in sturdy seagoing canoes formed from cedar or fir logs. These coastal tribes and the Indians of the interior valleys sometimes spoke related languages and had similar religious systems. However, their diet and clothing differed markedly. Similarly, the salmon culture of the Indians at the Celilo Falls of the Columbia River differed from the culture of the desert-dwelling Paiutes of the Great Basin, and both differed from the Nez Percé horse culture.

While the Oregon Trail was a primary factor in the westward movement of population and influence after the 1840s, the prehistory of the region and the first exploration, trade, and settlement by whites actually began in the west and moved east. As maritime exploration led to permanent settlement, contact between whites and the native peoples changed the economies and cultures of the latter. Contact had the most immediate effect on the Aleuts, Eskimos, and coastal Indians of Alaska; sexual liaisons and intermarriage altered their genetic makeup, and disease, alcohol, and conflict with the invaders took a deadly toll. Yet Native Americans proved highly adaptable. Metal, firearms, and trade modified their weapons, art, and hunting techniques; nevertheless, they adjusted to capitalism and Christianity without submitting fully to either. For some natives, living at a distance from the ocean provided insulation from the impact of the white settlers. Indians of the Columbia River basin, for example, traded and held joint celebrations with coastal tribes, but they were more or less isolated from the social and economic consequences of contact with European culture until the early 1800s, when the Lewis and Clark expedition of 1804–1806 and the arrival of fur traders breached their isolation.

Only a few daring Spanish explorers and England's Francis Drake in the *Golden Hind* had sailed up the Pacific coast in the sixteenth century, Drake possibly reaching the coast of present-day Oregon in 1579. For nearly the next two hundred years, Native Americans on the Northwest coast had little contact with Europeans and other outsiders. Only some Indian tales about shipwrecked Chinese and Japanese sailors filled this historical vacuum until the 1741 voyage from Siberia to the Aleutian Islands and Alaska led by Vitus Bering, a Danish-born explorer who sailed for imperial Russia. The Russians, whose always tentative hold on the huge peninsula was to last 126 years, gave it the Aleut name *Al-a-aska,* or "mainland." (An alternative derivation is from the Eskimo word for "great land.")

The Russians soon established a monopoly in the trade for the "soft gold" of seal, sea otter, and beaver pelts that lasted nearly half a century after 1743. Initially, dozens of Russian companies competed, and fur traders (*promyshlenniks*) killed, kidnapped, and subdued Aleut men, whose skills with the kayak (*baidarka*) and harpoon were needed in the maritime fur trade, and married Aleut women. But permanent settlements were few and small, and the warlike Tlingits and other Indian tribes of the Alaska mainland were more of an obstacle than the passive Aleuts. Over the generations, Russian Creoles (descendants of mixed marriages) became effective intermediaries in blending the Russian and indigenous economies and cultures. In 1799, after nearly sixty years of periodic plundering and brutality by Russian traders, the tsar granted the Russian-American Company a monopoly over the fur trade and the virtual right to govern.

During the last quarter of the eighteenth century, the maritime fur trade revived the rivalry for empire between Great Britain and Spain and brought the United States into the contest. The voyage of English Captain James Cook in the late 1770s informed Europeans about the Northwest coast and China's passion for sea otter fur. Expeditions led by the English navigator George Vancouver and several Spanish captains mapped the coastal areas and inland waterways in the 1780s, and in 1792 Robert Gray, the captain of an American trading ship, the *Columbia Rediviva,* made the last important discovery of the eighteenth century when he sailed his ship into the river he named for his vessel.

By the 1780s, British ("King George's men") and American ("Boston men") sailors were challenging the Russian-American Company's dominance. Although lacking permanent trading posts and skilled Aleut hunters, the English and American sailors perfected shipside trading and gained agreements with China that barred the Russians from Canton. However, this maritime fur trade barely survived into the nineteenth century, devastated by the depletion of sea otter herds, increased competition from beaver pelts, and expansion of the overland fur trade. After enduring several decades of diminishing returns from the fur trade and ever-increasing administrative costs, the Russian-American Company sold Alaska to the United States in 1867.

Whites knew little about either the inhabitants of the land between the Mississippi River and the Pacific Ocean or the land itself until the late eighteenth century, when competition for the fur trade between the North West Company and the Hudson's Bay Company spurred overland exploration and trade. In 1789 and 1793, the Scottish explorer and fur trader Alexander Mackenzie of the North

West Company explored beyond the Rocky Mountains; American explorers soon followed. After the Louisiana Purchase of 1803, President Thomas Jefferson established the Corps of Discovery to explore the headwaters of the Missouri River and beyond to the Pacific Ocean. From 1804 until 1806, Meriwether Lewis and William Clark led an expedition, including soldiers, French-Canadian hunters, the Shoshone woman Sacagawea, and Clark's slave York, that explored an immense region of disputed territory and consolidated the American claim to the so-called Oregon Country.

The rivalry between the London-based Hudson's Bay Company and the Montreal-based North West Company intensified after the latter forced John Jacob Astor's American fur traders to abandon their post at the mouth of the Columbia River during the War of 1812. Within the next fifteen years, Hudson's Bay absorbed the North West Company and established its headquarters at Fort Vancouver on the Columbia River. Under Chief Factor John McLoughlin, the personnel at Fort Vancouver and at Hudson's Bay's satellite posts on the Columbia, Spokane, and Snake rivers reflected the ethnic and racial diversity of the fur-trapping period. Iroquois and Delaware Indians and even some Hawaiians, or Kanakas, were among the trappers and laborers at Fort Vancouver. Company officials, who were usually English and Scots, sometimes had Indian, or in McLoughlin's case, mixed-blood wives. French-Canadian trappers and their Indian and mixed-blood wives also contributed to the growing métis (mixed blood) population that, with the encouragement of Hudson's Bay officials, established small settlements in the Willamette and Walla Walla valleys during the 1820s.

When Spain and Russia abandoned their claims to the Oregon Country after the Napoleonic Wars, Great Britain and the United States signed treaties of joint occupation in 1818 and 1827. The Hudson's Bay Company maintained its hegemony until the 1840s, when American settlers, who arrived in increasing numbers after 1843, formed a provisional government south of the Columbia River. In 1846, Great Britain and the United States finally agreed to divide the Oregon Country at the forty-ninth parallel. By then, a few American mountain men and their families and several groups of Protestant missionaries, catalysts for American settlement, had been in the region for more than a decade.

As the spirit of Manifest Destiny stirred national pride and the westward movement in the 1840s, the first large groups of Americans followed the Oregon Trail along the North Platte River and through the south Pass of Wyoming before turning northward along the Snake and Columbia rivers to the Willamette Valley. More than 250,000 emigrants caught "Oregon fever" and journeyed overland between 1843 and the 1880s. Those first waves of settlement came primarily from Kansas, Iowa, Illinois, and Missouri. Additional thousands of emigrants from New England and New York went to Oregon by sea, some taking the route around Cape Horn but most crossing the Isthmus of Panama. Initially the majority of emigrants were men, but by the 1850s the typical wagon train included more families; there were few single women and few adults older than fifty. Accidents and disease posed far greater dangers than did Indians, and if the trail experience did not fully liberate women from the constraints of culture, it often gave them new responsibilities and a new awareness of their role.

In the absence of official authority, the early settlers in Oregon approved a provisional government at a meeting in Champoeg in 1843. An elected assembly adopted a law code based on that of Iowa, provided a militia for fighting Indian wars, and settled property disputes. The new government rejected slavery in Oregon but also barred entry to free blacks, setting a precedent for articles that would be included in the state constitution drafted in 1857 (despite the fact that statehood was not granted until 1859).

Congress granted territorial status to Oregon in 1848, separated Washington Territory from it in 1853, and carved Idaho Territory from Washington Territory in 1863. With territorial status came lim-

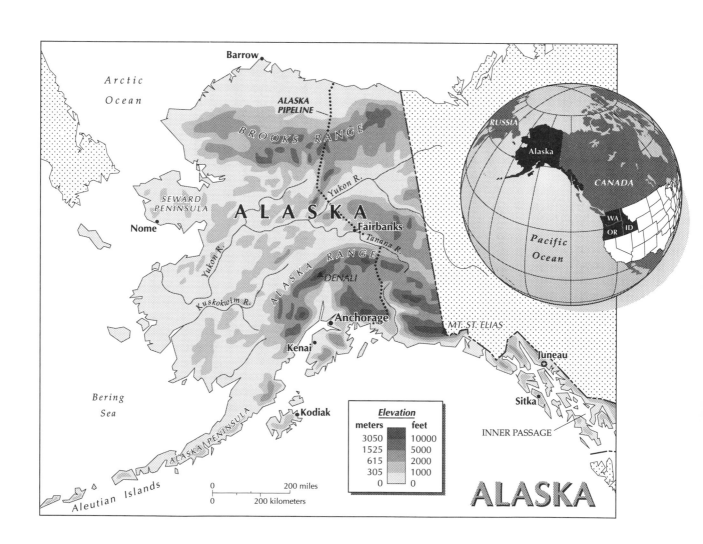

ited military and economic aid, federal Indian policies, and land grants. When Congress passed the Donation Land Act for Oregon in 1850, the law allowed white male settlers to claim 320 acres and set an important precedent by granting their wives the right to claim an equal amount of land.

The Indians of the Pacific Northwest lost their independence and most of their land long before the end of the nineteenth century. A series of treaties in the 1850s confirmed the weaknesses resulting from disease and warfare, and the Nez Percé war of the 1870s was merely an anticlimax to decades of encroachment. Pushed east of the Cascade Mountains or concentrated on a few reservations, Indians had only a short time before the demand for agricultural and forest land in the 1880s reduced their holdings even more.

ALASKA AFTER THE PURCHASE

Cycles of fortune and misfortune characterize Alaskan history after 1867. For nearly seventeen years after purchasing Alaska, Americans generally ignored their newest acquisition, and the United States military was often the only visible government. Finally, on 17 May 1884, Congress designated Alaska a district, with laws modeled on those of Oregon. With a population estimated at 33,426 in 1882 (430 white, 1,756 Creole, 17,617 Eskimo, 11,478 Indian, and 2,145 Aleut), Alaska had only a few widely separated towns, basic ethnic divisions, and little demand for its natural resources. The few whites in Alaska ruled and sometimes mingled with the indigenous people, but most native villages were in isolated locations on the coast or scattered throughout the interior. Liquor and the decline of the fur trade weakened social and economic stability, and great distances between settlements and the lack of roads and trails impeded economic development and political union. With civil government nearly unworkable, a system of authority derived from Indian and Russian custom functioned as a substitute until the 1890s.

By then, the depletion of natural resources had become a concern as easily accessible timber was cut and unregulated catches of whales, fur seal, and salmon threatened these basic resources. But euphoria replaced concern after 1896 when the gold rush transformed Alaska and the Yukon Territory of Canada. Towns grew rapidly as gold seekers pursued fortunes, and some businessmen and

prostitutes made them. Portland, San Francisco, Vancouver, and Seattle sent men, women, and supplies and became partners in a complex transportation and social network.

By 1900, the gold-inspired boom had dissipated, and in the decades that followed, Alaska endured a lengthy period of economic stagnation. Its population of 64,356 in 1910, while double that of the 1880s, had grown by only 764 since 1900. Yet in the aftermath of the gold rush and American expansion into the Pacific after 1898, Congress attached new importance to Alaska and, after a decade of debate, granted it territorial status in 1912. But slow growth and renewed neglect by the federal government delayed statehood for nearly another half a century.

Despite warnings from conservationists, Alaskans seemed compelled simultaneously to exploit their natural resources and to complain about their colonial status. Their economy drifted through the 1920s and slowed even more during the Great Depression. New Deal programs gave some assistance, but World War II was a more significant contributor to Alaska's economic recovery; military spending expanded significantly during and after the war (and remained important into the 1980s).

Alaska's strategic location during World War II and the cold war reinforced its political and military value to the federal government. Further, by the 1960s, Anchorage, the largest and most cosmopolitan city, had become a primary stop for Pacific Rim air travel and seaborne tourists. Alaska's natural resources and beauty enhanced its image in the "lower forty-eight," and its Republican tendencies balanced the Democratic tilt of Hawaii. After nearly a century of neglect, by the 1950s Congress suddenly regarded Alaska as something more than a frigid military outpost. President Dwight D. Eisenhower signed the Alaska statehood proclamation on 3 January 1959, just one month before Oregon celebrated its statehood centennial.

But statehood did not free Alaska from the federal government, which initially owned more than 90 percent of the land, or from continuing dependency on natural resources and outside capital, much of it from Japan. The petroleum crisis of the 1970s stimulated drilling on the North Slope and the construction of the 789-mile Trans-Alaska Pipeline from that region to the port of Valdez on Alaska's southern coast, but as oil prices dropped and resistance to taxes increased in the 1980s, optimistic projections of huge revenue endowments faded.

TABLE 1   Population, 1850–1990

	Alaska	Idaho	Oregon	Washington
1850			13,294	
1860			52,465	11,594
1870		14,909	90,923	23,955
1880	33,426	32,610	174,768	75,116
1890	32,052	84,385	313,767	349,390
1900	63,592	161,772	413,536	518,103
1910	64,356	325,594	672,765	1,141,990
1920	55,036	431,866	783,389	1,356,621
1930	59,278	445,032	953,786	1,563,396
1940	72,524	524,873	1,089,684	1,736,191
1950	128,643	588,637	1,521,341	2,378,963
1960	226,167	667,191	1,768,687	2,853,214
1970	302,583	713,015	2,091,533	3,413,244
1980	401,851	944,038	2,633,105	4,132,156
1990	550,043	1,006,749	2,842,321	4,866,692

Sources: 1850–1980 from *Statistical Abstract of the United States;* for 1990 from *Portland Oregonian,* 21 February 1991.

In the first decades after the Alaska purchase, federal officials encouraged but seldom funded schools. Protestant missionaries responded by establishing many private schools, and a two-tiered educational system survived into the twentieth century. Governments also neglected higher education before the 1950s. Although the territorial government established the University of Alaska in Fairbanks as a land grant institution in 1917, the school had an enrollment of only 847 in 1958. But statehood changed the image and role of the university. Facing only limited competition from Alaska Methodist (now Alaska Pacific) University, which was opened in Anchorage in 1960 by the United Methodist Church, the University of Alaska doubled enrollment within a decade and developed a system of night schools and community colleges. Federal funding aided the establishment of research centers for Arctic research, fisheries, and forestry, and by the 1980s, the university had expanded its Anchorage campus into a full-scale institution and established satellite centers from southern Alaska to Point Barrow.

As oil revenues fluctuated and concerns about the economic viability of native land reserves increased, Alaskans faced critical questions about how to provide education and health care for a small and scattered population. They had faced and survived forest fires, volcanic eruptions, and earthquakes, but man-caused ecological disasters like the massive 1990 oil spill from the tanker *Exxon Valdez* or the potential failure of the Alaska Pipeline made many Alaskans less optimistic about their future.

TABLE 2   Area in Square Miles

Alaska	591,004
Idaho	83,564
Oregon	97,073
Washington	68,139

Sources: Collier's Encyclopedia and *Almanac of the 50 States.*

Note: The statistics are from Schwantes, *The Pacific Northwest* (1989); Johansen and Gates, *Empire of the Columbia* (1967); and *Portland Oregonian,* 21 February, 28 May 1991.

THE PACIFIC NORTHWEST SINCE THE GILDED AGE

Despite some dissenting voices and a tendency to support Democrats, Northwesterners remained loyal to the Union during the Civil War and often voted Republican afterward. With the only state government in the Northwest and with Portland the region's dominant economic and cultural center, Oregon grew more rapidly than its neighbors until the 1880s. The Oregon Steam Navigation Company, owned by Portland bankers and merchants, controlled transportation on the Columbia River with a network of sailboats, steamboats, and short-line railroads from the 1860s until 1883, when the Northern Pacific Railroad built a transcontinental line through Portland on the way to its terminus at Tacoma on Puget Sound.

From its founding in the 1840s, Portland remained the wealthiest and largest city in the Northwest until 1910, when Seattle passed it and never looked back. A small mill town of 3,553 in 1880, Seattle outpaced neighboring Tacoma after it became the terminus for James J. Hill's Great Northern Railway in 1893. Immigrants and businesses followed the rails, and the Alaska gold rush and the growing Pacific trade added impetus. Portland and Seattle both grew rapidly in the early twentieth century, prospered briefly during World War I, and then stagnated until World War II. Each city had a high proportion of foreign-born citizens early in the century, but Seattle had a more cosmopolitan atmosphere. Portland had the conservative character of a New England town, whereas Seattle displayed the rawness and drive of Hong Kong.

Railroads were a catalyst for growth and an indicator of economic change. They brought new residents and contributed to the expansion of salmon canning, lumbering, commercial agriculture, and mining. Many of the new jobs were seasonal and required large numbers of unskilled and semi-skilled migrant laborers. Most of these workers were young, single men; many were immigrants from Scandinavia or southern and eastern Europe. However, there were also some blacks, Chinese, and, after 1890, an increasing number of Japanese, Filipinos,and East Indians. These migrant laborers often lived temporarily in camps or company towns and wintered in the skid rows of Seattle, Portland, Tacoma, and Spokane. With them came saloons, prostitution, gambling, and conflict with townspeople, reformers, and conservative politicians.

Although the percentage of racial minorities in the Northwest was and remains small, diversity has existed since the earliest explorations. The proportion of blacks, Asians, and Hispanics has been similar for Oregon and Washington at each historical stage; in contrast, Idaho, which had thousands of Chinese miners in the 1860s and 1880s, has had few Chinese residents in the twentieth century, and few blacks. How minorities fared in the area has been largely determined by their number, gender, and economic circumstances. The black population in Oregon, which was just over twenty-five hundred in 1940, had increased by almost nine thousand by 1950. Oregon's Chinese population, which was predominantly male, shrank after 1920; in contrast, its Japanese population, most of whom were married, increased after 1920. Resentment at the success of Japanese Americans in agriculture fueled racism, resulting in state laws restricting Japanese ownership of land, a congressional ban on immigration, and the infamous relocation of Japanese Americans during World War II.

From the Knights of Labor onward, organized labor attracted only a small part of the work force; it had its greatest successes in the mills and logging camps of Washington and the mines of Idaho. Labor disputes generally centered on wages and working conditions, but race and ethnicity were also factors because blacks, Chinese, and new immigrants were sometimes recruited for low-paying jobs or as strikebreakers. Anti-Chinese violence erupted in Seattle and Tacoma in the 1880s, but labor militancy and antilabor violence established their regional character in strikes by the Western Federation of Miners in the Idaho silver mines in the 1890s, agitation by the Industrial Workers of the World before and during World War I, and strikes by longshoremen in the 1930s.

The political culture of the Northwest reflects moderate-to-conservative traits, with an occasional bit of radical brashness. Voters have deviated only occasionally from national trends in presidential elections but have voted more idiosyncratically in state contests. The Populist party was strongest in Idaho and Washington in the 1890s, and William S. U'Ren, a spiritualist and former Populist, successfully adapted some of its platform to his "Oregon System" of initiative, referendum, and recall during the Progressive Period. While Washington acquired a reputation for fostering political radicalism in the 1930s, masterful politicians like Democrats Warren G. Magnuson and Henry M. Jackson were more typical after World War II. Idaho and Oregon, generally considered more conservative, nonetheless elected independent-minded U.S. senators like Republican William E. Borah and Democrat Wayne L. Morse.

Regional attitudes toward women have alternated between images of the pioneer mother and of the social activist. Women constituted a minority of the population in the area during most of the nineteenth century, but they had some property rights and were enfranchised before the passage of the Nineteenth Amendment in 1920. The regional campaign for women's suffrage began in 1871, when Abigail Scott Duniway accompanied suffragist Susan B. Anthony on a speaking tour across the Northwest and established a newspaper, *New Northwest* (1871–1887). Idaho gave women the vote in 1896; Washington, after several false starts, followed suit in 1910; and Duniway's home state of Oregon did so in 1912. Winning election to office took women longer; Idaho elected a few women to

TABLE 3   Population Percentage by Race, 1990

	Alaska	Idaho	Oregon	Washington
White	75.5	94.4	92.8	88.5
Black	4.1	0.3	1.6	3.1
American Indian, Eskimo or Aleut	15.6	1.4	1.4	1.7
Asian or Pacific Islander	3.6	0.9	2.4	4.3
Other Race	1.2	3.0	1.8	2.4
Hispanic*	3.2	5.3	4.0	4.4

Source: Portland Oregonian, 21 February 1991.

*Hispanics may be of any race, so the total may exceed 100%.

the state assembly in the 1890s, and in the years since World War I, women in Oregon and Washington have been elected as legislators, mayors of Portland and Seattle, governors, and U.S. representatives and senators.

Northwesterners have often had ambivalent attitudes about requiring and financing public education, but their essentially Protestant sentiments and democratic tendencies typically inhibited their enthusiasm for private and parochial schools. Attitudes toward higher education also reflected the cultural biases of the early settlers. If Oregon resembled New England in its town names, it also resembled the Middle West in the proliferation of denominational colleges. But support for public colleges evolved slowly in the region, with Oregon and Idaho especially lagging behind. The University of Washington grew with Seattle, and its location, state policies, and aggressive grantsmanship after World War II aided its transition into a major regional university. Though less prestigious, the region's land grant colleges played significant roles in the state economies through their scientific research and applied technology, and public community colleges in Oregon and Washington evolved rapidly after the 1960s.

Its formative years finished and its social patterns and cultural institutions in place, the Pacific Northwest echoed national concerns about prohibition, immigration, and urbanization in the 1920s. The Northwest conformed to national trends in other ways as well. The Ku Klux Klan, which entered Oregon in 1921, spread rapidly throughout the region. Klansmen exploited the historical residues of racism, nativism, and anti-Catholicism to make Oregon the home of the most politically successful Klan on the Pacific Slope. The Klan had more members but less political strength in Washington and was weaker still in Idaho and Alaska.

The Great Depression accelerated regional declines in agriculture and the timber industry that had begun in the 1920s. Although economic recovery was slow and there were few local self-help programs, thousands of refugees from the dusty Great Plains were drawn to the Northwest. Some economic aid was provided by New Deal programs that expanded and institutionalized the role of the federal government in public works projects, hydroelectric development, and regional planning.

World War II ended the Depression and had revolutionary consequences for the people and economy of the Northwest. The federal government expanded and added military bases, and Port-land and the Puget Sound area became major supply centers for the war in the Pacific and absorbed thousands of new residents. Workers produced ships, aircraft, aluminum, and plutonium for the war effort. Many women worked in the shipyards of Henry J. Kaiser and in aircraft plants and lumber mills. The most negative development resulting from the war was the relocation of Japanese Americans in 1942, many of them to the internment center at Minidoka, Idaho.

The decline of shipbuilding after the war, the intensification of the cold war, and the growth of commercial aviation combined to strengthen the Boeing Company's position as Washington's largest employer. The Weyerhaeuser Company and the lumber industry grew with suburbia in the postwar years, but economic fluctuations and high unemployment periodically plagued the industry. By the end of the 1980s, the impact of a century of intensive logging, plus a soft domestic housing market, log exporting, automation, and environmental issues challenged the regional myth of perpetual abundance.

IMPACT OF RELIGION ON THE PACIFIC NORTHWEST

Although Alaska and the other Northwest states currently rank among the lowest in percentage of church members in the United States, religion was a significant factor in their early history. Beginning in the eighteenth century, Russian Orthodox priests left a trail of converts and onion-domed churches across the Aleutian Islands and Alaska, and a few Roman Catholic priests, who made little effort to convert Indians, accompanied Spanish expeditions to Nootka Sound on Vancouver Island. The nineteenth century contained new factors. The land-based fur trade brought French-Canadian Catholics and Presbyterian Scots together in more permanent trading posts. Although the posts run by the Hudson's Bay Company were nominally Anglican and company policy required religious and moral guidance for its employees, John McLoughlin, the chief factor, and many employees were Roman Catholic. In response to their requests, Franciscan priests François Norbert Blanchet and Modeste Demers came to the Oregon Country in 1838 to minister to the French-Canadians and Indians. They established the Saint Francis Xavier mission on the Cowlitz River and their headquarters mission, Saint Paul,

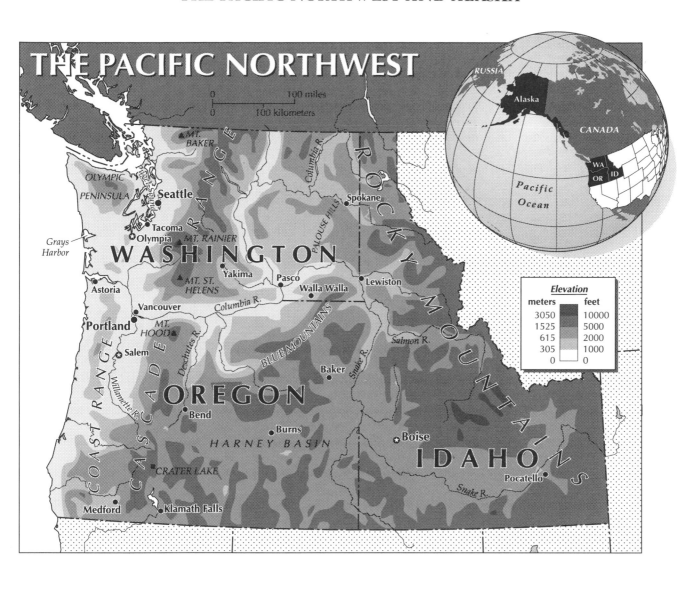

THE PACIFIC NORTHWEST

near the French-Canadian settlements along the Willamette River. Jesuit priest Pierre Jean De Smet, a Belgian, and fellow Jesuits established missions among Flathead and Coeur d'Alene Indians in the interior valleys beginning in 1840.

But it was an aggressive band of Protestant missionaries, mainly New Englanders, who had the greatest impact. Their activities and the first waves of settlement in the Oregon Country coincided with the antislavery and temperance campaigns and the waves of anti-Catholic agitation and nativism that stirred American politics during the 1830s and 1840s. Each of these attitudes would leave a legacy in the Northwest. Methodists Jason Lee and his nephew Daniel established a mission on the Willamette River (near present-day Salem, Oregon) in 1834, with missionaries sponsored by the American Board of Commissioners for Foreign Missions (Congregationalist, Presbyterian, and Dutch Reformed) arriving soon after. Marcus and Narcissa Whitman went to Waiilatpu near Walla Walla to minister to the Cayuse Indians, and Henry and Eliza Spalding settled among the Nez Percé at Lapwai near the Clearwater River in 1836. Elkanah and Mary Walker and Cushing and Myra Eells established a mission among the Spokanes in 1839. After initially attempting to aid and educate local Indians, Jason Lee and some of his fellow Methodists showed more interest and success in farming, business, and promoting settlement. But the Whitman massacre in 1847, in which Marcus and Narcissa Whitman and twelve others were killed and fifty-three women and children were held for ransom by the Cayuse, drew the most attention to the Ore-

TABLE 4   Growth Rate of Metropolitan Areas, 1980–1990

	1980 pop.	1990 pop.	% change
Seattle-Tacoma	2,093,285	2,559,164	22.3
Portland-Vancouver	1,297,977	1,477,895	13.9
Spokane	341,835	361,364	5.7
Eugene-Springfield	275,226	282,912	2.8
Salem	249,895	278,024	11.3
Bremerton, WA	147,152	189,731	28.9
Olympia, WA	124,264	161,238	29.8
Tri-Cities, WA	144,469	150,033	3.9
Medford, OR	132,456	146,389	10.5
Bellingham, WA	106,701	127,780	19.8

Source: Portland Oregonian, February 21, 1991 and May 28, 1991.

gon Country, added Narcissa Whitman's martyrdom to national folklore, and reinforced the Protestant role in the region. This Protestant influence continued into the twentieth century, but, by then, Baptist denominations, reflecting significant shifts in population and religious preference, outnumbered the early missionary faiths. The Baptists, in turn, faced challenges as other evangelical and fundamentalist denominations grew rapidly after the 1970s.

Despite the dominance of mainstream Protestantism, other faiths have long histories in the Northwest. The Mormon exodus to Utah also began in the 1840s, and southeastern Idaho soon became a virtual Mormon enclave, a fact that irrevocably shaped the culture and politics of that part of the state. But Mormons also bore the burden of anti-Mormon sentiments that were a product of the social and religious ferment of the nineteenth century. However, as Mormons prospered and became more socially conventional and more politically conservative, their missionary efforts grew bolder. By the mid twentieth century the Church of Jesus Christ of Latter-day Saints had increased in membership and influence throughout the Northwest; in the 1980s, Mormons built imposing temples in wealthy suburbs of Seattle and Portland and increasingly demonstrated the political vitality of their conservative social values.

Since the end of World War II, internal migration and accelerated immigration have revived the multicultural dimension of the region's early religious history. The massive northward movement of Hispanics and the arrival of thousands of Catholic immigrants from Southeast Asia have reinforced Catholicism. Similarly, the rapid growth of the Asian population since the 1970s has revitalized Buddhism, which was long established among Asians in the Northwest and which attracted converts among hippies and commune dwellers in the 1960s and 1970s.

Though few in number, Jewish congregations have been historically significant in the small gold mining town of Jacksonville, Oregon, and in the larger urban centers. A small number of German Jews, predominantly young, unmarried merchants, arrived in Oregon in the 1850s. After gaining some prosperity and social acceptance, the Jewish community in Portland established Congregation Beth Israel in 1858 and Congregation Ahari Shalom in 1869. Jews in Seattle, who generally arrived later but came from similar backgrounds, established Congregation Bikur Cholia in 1889. Although Jews from eastern Europe and the Middle East, who began arriving in the 1870s, soon outnumbered their predecessors, they found less economic opportunity and faced more discrimination. Nevertheless, members of both groups had some success in politics, especially in Oregon. Rabbi Stephen S. Wise was a prominent social reformer in Portland in the early 1900s, and Jews were elected to local, state, and national offices, beginning with a mayor in Portland in the late 1860s.

Although historically there have been few Muslims in the Pacific Northwest, Muslim congregations had built several mosques in university towns and larger cities by the 1980s. Most of these Muslims were foreign students at universities or recent refugees from strife in the Middle East. Despite latent prejudices and continuing international tensions, these small congregations have found tentative acceptance in their communities.

The Pacific Northwest may lack the esoteric diversity of California, but small religious and spiritual groups have ranged from the late nineteenth-century revitalization movement of Native American prophet Smoholla and the simplicity of the Native

American Shaker church in Oregon and Washington to the exotic importations of Bhagwan Shree Rajneesh in the mid 1980s. The controversial members of Rajneeshpuram, as the Bhagwan's commune was called, introduced a colorful mixture of Eastern philosophies, Western materialism, and New Age ideas into rural central Oregon. Rajneeshpuram initially aroused curiosity and revived memories of both spiritualist and free-love groups that thrived in Oregon and in communes on Puget Sound during the late nineteenth century and in communes in southwestern Oregon in the 1960s. But it also aroused antagonism and fear among local residents. Negative reactions to the Bhagwan's large fleet of Rolls Royces, the sexual freedom of his followers, and the machinations of Ma Anand Sheela, the Bhagwan's chief adviser, and her inner circle dissipated only after the collapse of the Oregon commune in the late 1980s.

CONCLUSION

Myth and history are linked in the Pacific Northwest. Alaska's conservative populism blends past with present, and images of the Old West and the New West coexist in the Columbia River Gorge as Indian fishermen, cowboys, loggers, farmers, and wind surfers meet where earlier generations of Native Americans gathered to trade and fish for salmon. Small towns hold rodeos and timber festivals in the shadow of computer companies in the "silicon forest" near Portland and the Boeing Company's headquarters in Seattle.

Residents of the Northwest struggle to reconcile the ethnocentric and economic assumptions of their historical conceit about a people of plenty in a promised land. Although the region's population was more than 90 percent white in 1990, the number of blacks, Asians, and Hispanics had increased significantly. Demographic projections indicate that trend will continue, so Northwesterners, who generally prize toleration, will have to confront the racial supremacists who have declared their goal of creating a separate nation for whites in the Pacific Northwest.

Economic factors, which are at the center of this concern about racism, also explain why Northwesterners are now confronting their historical identity. While there are many reasons for the loss of jobs in fishing, mining, and lumbering, ecological issues have highlighted the shift from a primarily extractive economy to one increasingly based on tourism, service occupations, and the computer industry. As federal agencies and the courts moved laboriously in the early 1990s toward designating protected habitats for endangered species, timber interests and environmentalists debated the social benefits and the economic costs of each step. Environmental issues also forced Northwesterners to face problems about land use regulations, waste management, and water quality, raising fears that they would have to choose either economic development or the radical premise of Ernest Callenbach's novel *Ecotopia* (1967), which described an environmental utopia in the Pacific Northwest and northern California after these regions had seceded from the United States. As they confront this dilemma, Northwesterners also repeat their history by casting a wary eye eastward while looking hopefully toward the Pacific Rim.

BIBLIOGRAPHY

General Works

Edwards, G. Thomas, and Carlos A. Schwantes, eds. *Experiences in a Promised Land: Essays in Pacific Northwest History* (1986). The most useful essays.

Gruening, Ernest. *The State of Alaska* (1968).

Johansen, Dorothy O., and Charles M. Gates. *Empire of the Columbia: A History of the Pacific Northwest,* 2d ed. (1967). The classic study.

Meinig, Donald W. *The Great Columbia Plain: A Historical Geography, 1805–1910* (1968).

Naske, Claus-M., and Herman E. Slotnick. *Alaska: A History of the 49th State,* 2d ed. (1987).

Pomeroy, Earl S. *The Pacific Slope: A History of California, Oregon, Washington, Idaho, Utah, and Nevada* (1965). A broader regional context and acute analysis.

Schwantes, Carlos A. *The Pacific Northwest: An Interpretive History* (1989). The best brief study.

Exploration and Contact

Cook, Warren L. *Flood Tide of Empire: Spain and the Pacific Northwest, 1543–1819* (1973).

Golovin, Pavel N. *Civil and Savage Encounters: The Worldly Travel Letters of an Imperial Russian Navy Officer, 1860–1861.* Translated and annotated by Basil Dmytryshyn and E. A. P. Crownhart-Vaughan (1983). Perceptive observations.

Moulton, Gary E., ed. *The Journals of the Lewis and Clark Expedition,* 7 vols. to date (1983–). The most complete and accurate version.

Ronda, James P. *Lewis and Clark Among the Indians* (1984).

Sturtevant, William C., ed., *Handbook of North American Indians.* Vol. 2. *The Northwest Coast,* edited by Wayne Suttles (1991).

Economics and Labor

Clark, Norman. *Mill Town: A Social History of Everett, Washington* (1970).

Ficken, Robert E. *The Forested Land: A History of Lumbering in Western Washington* (1987).

McGregor, Alexander Campbell. *Counting Sheep: From Open Range to Agribusiness on the Columbia Plateau* (1982).

Oliphant, J. Orin. *On the Cattle Ranges of the Oregon Country* (1968).

Urban Studies

Abbott, Carl. *Portland: Planning, Politics, and Growth in a Twentieth-Century City* (1983).

Sale, Roger. *Seattle: Past to Present* (1976).

Women and Minorities

Blair, Karen J., ed. *Women in the Pacific Northwest: An Anthology* (1988).

Daniels, Roger. *Asian Americans: Chinese and Japanese in the United States Since 1850* (1988).

Edwards, G. Thomas. *Sowing Good Seeds: The Northwest Suffrage Campaigns of Susan B. Anthony* (1990).

Halseth, James A., and Bruce A. Glasrud, eds. *The Northwest Mosaic: Minority Conflicts in Pacific Northwest History* (1977).

Jeffrey, Julie Roy. *Frontier Women: The Trans-Mississippi West, 1840–1880* (1979). A standard work.

McLagan, Elizabeth. *A Peculiar Paradise: A History of Blacks in Oregon, 1788–1940* (1980).

Moynihan, Ruth Barnes. *Rebel for Rights: Abigail Scott Duniway* (1983).

SEE ALSO **The Frontier; The Natural Environment: The West; Rural Life in the West.**

CALIFORNIA

James N. Gregory

CALIFORNIA IS NOT just another state. Lord James Bryce recognized that truth in 1888 when he devoted a chapter of his two-volume study, *The American Commonwealth,* to California "because it is in many respects the most striking in the whole Union, and has more than any other the character of a great country, capable of standing alone in the world" (vol. 2, repr. 1922 p. 426). In the 1990s that statement no longer evokes surprise. The state population now exceeds thirty million, and there are more Californians than there are Canadians, Australians, or Greeks; more Californians than Czechoslovaks and Hungarians combined; more Californians than Swedes, Norwegians, and Danes. Still more striking is the state's share of global economic activity. California's gross domestic product makes it the seventh largest economy in the world, ranking ahead of Russia and the People's Republic of China and just behind Great Britain and Italy. And if consumption is the measure, the California presence looms still larger. Californians possess more automobiles, VCRs, and personal computers than do residents of any entity except the entire United States and four other countries, each with at least twice California's population. The state holds the same distinction in the consumption of water, petroleum, and chemicals and in the generation of trash.

But Bryce was not talking about size. In 1888 he located the uniqueness of California in its exuberance, its unconventionality, its admixture of populations, and most of all in its location, half a continent removed from the rest of American civilization. An outpost on the Pacific, California was in Bryce's day a staging ground for the settlement by white Americans of the final third of the continent, the mountain region and the Pacific West—a mission that encouraged California's premature expressions of grandeur and spirit of independence.

Today the mission has changed. The state's function within the national community is no longer peripheral. In the regional restructuring in the late twentieth century, California has emerged as the nation's second financial and cultural center, a rival, though still junior, to the East Coast power corridor. Global economic shifts and the massive internal redistribution of population, industry, and public policy priorities since World War II have turned the United States into a bipolar nation. California is the capital of the newer America that faces west and south, toward Asia and Latin America.

The state's growing authority in world and national affairs rests least of all on formal politics. Although southern California's wealth and celebrity play a large role in national politics and while two of the last four Republican presidents have been southern Californians, it is in the realms of business and media that California's influence is chiefly felt. Key industries—electronics, bioscience, and aerospace—are concentrated there. Moreover, California is the chief port of entry for Far Eastern goods and capital; for that reason the Japanese collaborate with us in the development of this West Coast power center, investing in banking, real estate, and in the all-important high-tech sector.

Media strength is the other source of California's preeminence. First with the advent of Hollywood as the international film capital in the 1920s, then with the addition of television studios in the 1950s, southern California has played a major role in the production of popular entertainment and the consequent shaping of consumer values. In the 1970s and 1980s, Los Angeles made a multibillion-dollar effort to become a high-culture capital with the establishment of new museums (the Getty, the Norton Simon, the Armand Hammer, the Museum of Contemporary Art), symphonic and performing arts centers, and dozens of theater groups. As Mike Davis notes in *City of Quartz,* his penetrating study of Los Angeles in the 1980s, southern California's elites have been engaged in recent years in the kind of wholesale art grab that brought "culture" to Gilded Age New York in the late nineteenth century.

Like Texas and one or two other states, California is really a region unto itself. Geography makes it part of the western United States, but history sets it partially outside the regional culture area called the West. To be sure, it shares with the other states of the Pacific and Mountain time zones a number of characteristics that lend coherence to the region. Its topography—mountains, valleys, deserts—is decidedly western, as are its mostly arid climate and the resulting water distribution problems. Its political economy also followed developmental patterns common to the region: cities, mining, and railroads came first, then agriculture; the federal government owned, and still owns, much of the land and played, and still plays, a critical role in economic development. Furthermore, one can speak of the state's politics as western. Turn-of-the-century sectional and developmental conflict yielded a western "progressive" political system, with weak parties, strong executives, and liberal provisions for voter initiative. Also in the western mode, California has remained a stronghold of the Republican party throughout the twentieth century.

But there are other historical features that California does not share with other western states, matters of demography and mythology that advance California's claim to uniqueness. Underpopulation and a system of ethnic relations based on what Patricia Limerick calls the "legacy of conquest" have been, until recently, defining features of the West. Most western states have known minimal diversity, with few African Americans or foreign-born immigrants. What they have had is minority populations of Native Americans or Mexican Americans living in clear subordination to a largely undifferentiated white population. And western regional mythology dwells on that relationship, celebrating the founding dramas of conquest and repopulation with the same callousness that the South shows in its plantation mythology.

California has built its population and its identity quite differently. Rapid growth and escalating ethnic diversity are the keys. Throughout its American history, California has been a population accumulation zone without parallel. For nearly a century and a half the state has sustained a growth rate that doubles its population every two decades. And that has kept the state's demography in motion. Indeed, continuous repopulation is the critical drama of California's history and the source of some of its unique cultural claims. Wave after wave of newcomers from an ever-changing list of places have remade California again and again, each time adding something new while allowing the state to retain its most paradoxical tradition—the tradition of change.

While none of this resembles typical western regional traits, it does accord with population processes that the nation as a whole celebrates but that actually occur only in a few dynamic cities and states. In this and in many other matters, California earns its right to claim a distinction not through difference but through emphasis. As novelist Wallace Stegner put it, California is just like "America only more so . . . the national culture at its most energetic end" ("California Rising," in *Unknown California,* p. 8).

The state's mythology and sense of identity also diverge from the western "conquest" model. Pioneers, cowboys, and other conquest figures do not dominate the symbolic landscape; indeed, California's lore reads like something of an inversion, with pristine nature idealized and a romanticized role reserved for the Franciscan missions of preconquest California. The state's self-concept descends principally from a pair of founding myths that partially obscure California's own very real legacy of conquest. The first is the gold rush, that extraordinary drama of luck and adventure that forever fixed the state's reputation as a land of dreams. The second derives from the invention of southern California in the late nineteenth century and turns on edenic images of the Mediterranean climate, of sun, sand, and citrus, of new and healthful ways of life. All of this, to be sure, is related to the essential western myths of the big land and the fresh start. But California softens and pluralizes the symbolism, moving away from images of tough men in a rugged land and presenting itself instead as gentle and therapeutic.

One thing California does share is the western emphasis on geography. Land, climate, and location are never far from consciousness and more readily than in other regions suggest their powerful impact on human habitation patterns. The incredibly varied topography and the rich array of land-use capacities have made California both comparatively wealthy and sociologically diverse throughout its long history of habitation.

EARLY CALIFORNIA

The state's original inhabitants, its Indian peoples, set the pattern for diversity and perhaps also abundance. Before European settlers arrived, California was the most densely settled part of what is now the United States and home to one of the greatest varieties of discrete cultures of any place on earth. Quilted into the complex of valleys, foothills, deserts, riverbanks, and coastal strips were well over one hundred different tribes speaking nearly eighty discrete languages. Only the Mohave and the Yuma of the Colorado River basin practiced agriculture; the rest lived simply but with remarkable stability on the foodstuffs that their small tribal territories provided—seafood for coastal peoples like the Chumash, salmon for the river tribes of the northern areas, acorns a staple nearly everywhere.

Geography provided for early Californians in another way. Their home was essentially an island, with the sea on one side and barely passable mountains and deserts on the other three. For a thousand years, Californians had been protected by the difficult terrain from the kinds of warfare and invasions that remade tribal boundaries in other parts of the continent. The sea protected them, too. Two centuries after most other coastal portions of the Americas had felt the diseased and devastating presence of Europeans, California still belonged to Native Americans.

In truth it is not geography per se but geography in an ever-changing historical context that has shaped California's patterns of use since that first European contact. The region's history has been closely tied to geopolitical processes of globalization that have transformed distances, boundaries, and civilizations. California has been transformed and repeopled in three broad historical phases, each distinguished by demographic, cultural, and economic changes, each ushered in by revolutionary advances in transportation and global political economy. Along the cultural and demographic axis the first period of transformation can be labeled Hispanic, the second period Anglo-American, and the third period plural American. In spatial terms, California started off being seen as a Pacific island, spent its first American century becoming a region within an Atlantic-centered nation, and during the years since 1940 has reoriented outward, turning west toward Asia and south toward Latin America.

The Spanish visited California once, in 1542, during the first great surge of European exploration and a few more times near the close of the same century, but they found little of interest. From the standpoint of the sixteenth-century explorers, or for that matter that of the explorers who came to the region over the next two centuries, California was one of the remotest spots on earth, reachable only by navigating against the winds and currents of the western Pacific. So little did Europeans know about the place that as late as the early 1700s it appeared on some maps as an island.

For the two centuries from the mid 1500s to the mid 1700s, Spain regarded the western Pacific as its private realm, controlling what little commerce that vast region saw. Then, in the mid eighteenth century, the monopoly ended as English, French, and Russians sailed into the area, mapping the Pacific and looking for trading possibilities. Concerned particularly about the string of fur-trading posts that the Russians were establishing, Spanish authorities decided it was time to solidify the claim to California. In 1769 a small colonizing expedition set out from Baja California, composed of the usual Spanish frontier complement of soldiers, civilians, and priests, the first two to establish presidios and pueblos, the last to convert the Indians. Thus began the first phase of the repeopling of California: an eighty-year period of Mexicanization.

The story is usually told in terms that emphasize the Spanish flag. Mexico had charge of California only from 1821, when Mexico separated from Spain, to 1846. But the soldiers and settlers who colonized the region beginning in the late eighteenth century were Spanish only in the limited way that George Washington and George Rogers Clark were English when they drove the French from the Ohio Valley. Spain guided the settlement of California, but, with only a few exceptions, the settlers themselves were mestizos from Mexico. More important, the civilization that took shape in those eighty years, with its unique racial amalgamation, economic institutions, and cultural forms, belonged exclusively to the New World, to Mexico.

Compared with the Americans who came later, Mexicans trod lightly on the land and peoples of California. Spanish frontier traditions had long emphasized the efficiencies of minimal colonization. Hispanicization of the indigenous population rather than removal and replacement by land-hungry immigrants was the model settlement plan. Franciscan padres were the chief instrument of colonization. Within thirty years of the arrival of the first Mexican settlers, they had established a string of missions from San Diego to San Francisco and had brought the Indians living in the coastal portions of California under their effective control. Mostly it was done without the sword, the cross and corn proving effective enough. Drawn to the missions by the foodstuffs that the padres were soon able to produce, the Indians became the work force for expanded levels of production, giving up in the process not only their hunting and gathering economy but also much of their culture and all of their freedom. It was a poor bargain, especially when the matter of disease is factored in. The missions were death traps. By the early 1800s the Franciscans were burying more Californians than they baptized, and by the end of the Mexican period the native population of coastal California had been reduced by three quarters.

Immigration provided only a few replacements. California's remoteness remained a major impediment to Mexican immigration throughout the period. Nearly impossible to reach overland because of deserts and hostile Indians, California was tied to the Mexican mainland by the occasional visits of ships carrying news, supplies, soldiers' pay, and, far less often, new recruits. Spanish land use and mercantile policies exacerbated the problem of isolation. Trade with foreign vessels was prohibited, and virtually all of the productive land was held by the missions. With nothing more than soldiering or subsistence farming to attract them, immigrants arrived rarely and left almost as frequently. When the United States seized the area in 1846, there were fewer than eight thousand Mexican Californians.

Dating the end of the Mexican period and the start of Americanization is not easy. Formally California became part of the United States in 1848, but the American presence began long before then; well before the flags changed, California had become economically dependent on American ships and American goods.

The whaling ships and trading vessels that began to appear off the California coast in the 1820s represented yet another stage of global reorganization, the start of a great age of transportation improvements that would bring vast new areas into the trading and colonial system of the North Atlantic economies. Over the course of the nineteenth century, the far corners of the Pacific region would gradually lose their remoteness. Still an island in every sense but the literal one at the start of this period, California would by century's end be firmly bound to the American mainland by blood, outlook, and economy.

Paradoxically, Mexico's independence from Spain, gained in 1821, opened California to American economic penetration. Abandoning the restrictive policies set by the Spanish that had strangled economic activity in the province, the new government in Mexico City allowed free access to the ports, began the redistribution of mission lands, and liberalized immigration procedures. This was good news to the shoe and candle manufacturers of New England, who now provided a market for the products made from the great herds of cattle that grazed the California hills. By the mid 1830s the California economy had been completely remade from one based on self-sufficient agriculture controlled by the missions to a privatized ranching economy (still based on Indian labor) geared to the production of hides and tallow for export in Yankee ships.

The trade brought new wealth to the province and also new people, most notably Americans. A steady trickle of merchants and former sailors took advantage of lax immigration rules and settled in the coastal pueblos, sometimes becoming ranchers, more often providing commercial and artisanal services that were in short supply. More ominous from the Mexican point of view was the growing presence of Americans in the inland valleys. Coming overland or drifting down from Oregon, these newcomers stayed clear of the Mexican settlements and Mexican law and built their own base of operations in the Sacramento Valley. Openly talking insurrection, some of them were intent on "playing the Texas game." By 1846 the Yankees in California numbered close to eight hundred, roughly ten percent of the non-Indian population.

AMERICAN CALIFORNIA

American trade and immigration after 1820 hinted at the eventual takeover of California. But the official statements of the American government made that goal quite clear. Even as Mexico was securing its independence from Spain, American ambassadors were offering to buy California, either by itself or with other parts of what eventually became the American Southwest. The port of San Francisco, ideal from both military and mercantile standpoints, was of particular interest, and in 1835 the federal government made an offer solely for it. These negotiations reveal an important aspect of America's geographic ambitions. The purpose was not necessarily transcontinental completion; the nation was seeking a Pacific outpost. For all practical purposes, California remained an island, reachable only by sea, every bit as remote as the Sandwich Islands that lay on the same trade route.

Ultimately, America's first Pacific acquisition came about not through negotiation but through war. California was one of the prizes of America's first full-scale expansionist war, fought on Mexican

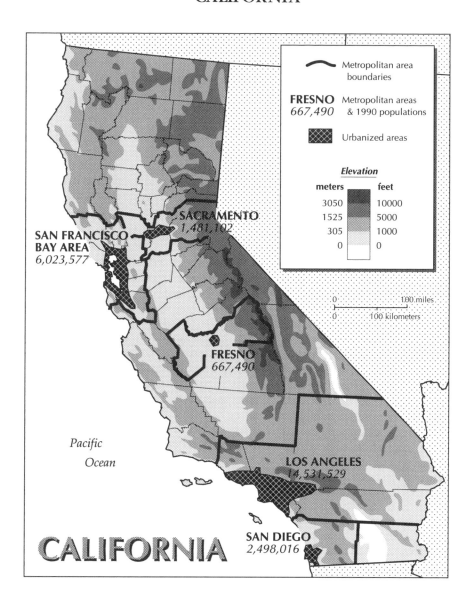

CALIFORNIA

soil in 1846 and 1847. It was in itself not a brutal experience for the residents of California, who resisted valiantly but without great loss of life. But that was merely the prelude. Signatures had not yet been affixed to the Treaty of Guadalupe-Hidalgo when the real act of conquest began. The discovery of gold in early 1848 did for California in five extraordinary years what generations could not do in New Mexico: it completely Americanized it.

The gold rush was, as John Caughey put it in 1948, "the cornerstone," the seminal event in the creation of American California—indeed, in the whole later history of the far West. As an economic event, it transformed the meaning and purpose of the frontier West. The old West, the Mississippi Valley, had been a frontier of trappers and farmers whose slowly developing commerce with the rest of the nation depended on river towns and riverboats. The new West that gold-rush California introduced was not really a frontier at all. It was a ready-made enterprise zone of miners and ranchers, followed almost immediately by cities and railroads. There was nothing gradual about it. As Carey McWilliams put it, for California "the lights went on all at once" (*California: The Great Exception,* p. 25). In 1848 California had been a sleepy port of call in the hide and tallow trade. Two years later, with one hundred thousand new residents and one of the busiest ports in the world, California had become the newest state in the United States—the only one west of Missouri. That was just the beginning. This instant state also claimed a sophisticated

1125

economy based not just on mining but also on a dynamic urban sector that ultimately provided the financial and commercial services to begin the development of the rest of the West. And it started off with political muscle, too: within ten years Congress would be talking about building a transcontinental railroad.

The key to all this was the state's instant population, the real fortune that California earned in the gold-fever years. A quarter of a million newcomers poured into California between 1848 and 1853, all but obliterating the existing inhabitants. The tiny Mexican population was numerically overwhelmed and quickly put at an economic and cultural disadvantage. Outnumbered twenty to one and unaccustomed to the laws, language, and business culture that now governed their lives, the Mexicans struggled to hold on to the land and the way of life that was guaranteed them by treaty. Within a generation, both had been lost as courts, lawyers, bankers, squatters, drought, and recession forced the sale of most of the original ranchos and as the usual manifestations of Yankee racism and religious prejudice undermined their cultural authority. By the 1880s, many of the "Californios," as the Mexican settlers called themselves, were eking out shabby lives in the barrios of southern California. Poor and forgotten, they had become strangers in their own land.

California's remaining Indian populations fared much worse—even worse than the usual horror that attended American westward expansion. With Congress forsaking all efforts to set up reservations, Indian policy fell to the new settlers, who opted for extermination. A twenty-year campaign of slaughter abetted by the spread of disease became a veritable holocaust. Some tribes were completely eliminated, leaving not a single survivor. In 1880 census takers could find only seventeen thousand Indians, just 6 percent of the area's estimated original population of three hundred thousand.

Thus began the American repopulation of California, a process that would steadily change the demographic mix over the years as California adopted new roles in the global political economy. Its first new population reflected its initial role as a place of high adventure, attracting an international assortment of the daring and the enterprising, nearly all young males. They came principally from places reached by the rapidly expanding North Atlantic commerce system and accessible to California by water. Two-thirds were Americans, mostly from the Atlantic seaboard, especially New York and New England. Ireland, England, Germany, and France

supplied most of the rest, but the ports of the Pacific region also contributed: Valparaiso, Sydney, Canton, Honolulu.

This population came to hunt gold but stayed to build California, especially the San Francisco Bay Area, which stood ready to rechannel the acquisitive energies of the immigrants once the placers and mines began to play out. By 1880 the Bay Area housed 40 percent of the state's population, and the city itself had 234,000 residents, including, finally, a substantial number of females. These first decades were California's "Boston" period, a time when the commercial and cultural commitments of New England imprinted decisively on the new state. With merchants, lawyers, and other New England entrepreneurs heavily represented in the gold-rush generation, California was soon blessed with an elaborate business infrastructure and an impressive array of manufactures to supply the local market with everything from shoes to steamboats.

The New England impress had even more to do with culture. In *Americans and the California Dream,* Kevin Starr argues that the creation of a regional culture began with the Yankee preachers and literary lights who set out to civilize gold-rush California. Here was born the state's intellectual infrastructure: the networks of churches and newspapers, then schools, colleges, publishing houses, and literary societies that gave the state its early cosmopolitan aura and flair for self-promotion. And here, too, was born California's transcendentalist engagement with divine nature, the key to later reinventions of the state's identity.

Boston in the 1850s was shared by Yankees and Irish, and so was San Francisco, which goes a long way toward explaining the turbulent pattern of California politics of the late nineteenth century. The Catholic working class and Protestant business class faced off repeatedly in these decades, at times with incendiary results. In 1856 a businessman's group calling itself the Committee of Vigilance seized power, hanged several suspected criminals, and tried and deported a number of Democratic party activists, mostly Irish. Twenty-two years later the revolution came from the opposite quarter. Beaten down by the depression of the mid 1870s and inspired by the great railroad strike of 1877, the city's Irish and laboring population joined Denis Kearney's Workingmen's party and in a climate of violent expectation elected a mayor and various other officials, thereby initiating a long period during which San Francisco's working class would enjoy a measure of political influence unparalleled in any other major American city.

Yet there was a uniquely California aspect to this Yankee/Irish contest. The overlapping tensions of class and religion were mediated by a third factor, race, that worked to the advantage of the white working class. The Chinese were, as Alexander Saxton put it, "the indispensable enemy." Constituting 9 percent of the city's population in 1870 and competing for laboring-class jobs, they became the focal point of late-nineteenth-century working-class politics as well as the targets of riots, lynchings, and arson campaigns. The brutal "Chinese Must Go" campaigns of the 1870s and 1880s left several legacies, one of which was a tradition of anti-Asian politics that lasted through World War II. And the Chinese were only the first victims. Later migrations of Japanese, Filipinos, and East Indians would be curtailed by similar explosions of organized hatred. "Yellow peril" politics was California's "peculiar institution." Just as in the South, the presence of a racial "other" made it possible for whites to transcend their differences. White ethnic and religious tensions were muted, and immigrant groups such as the Irish found greater economic and social opportunities in San Francisco than in Boston, in part because of the political dynamics of race hatred.

If in its first American generation California was a mining and urban frontier, its second incarnation was as a farming economy, an orientation that became practical after the completion of the transcontinental railroad in 1869. The event marked the end of California's "island" status. Travel to eastern population centers now took days instead of weeks or months. More important, for the first time products could be moved easily overland. The vast ocean of plains, mountains, and deserts had finally been bridged.

The railroad turned the state into a second Midwest, encouraging first the production of wheat and then, with the spread of irrigation and the invention of refrigerated cars, a shift to the cultivation of fruits and vegetables. While the state remained more urban than rural, by 1870 the fastest-growing areas were the inland valleys to which the Central Pacific and other promoters were steering immigrants, luring them with a campaign of advertising conducted extensively in heartland states like Iowa and Illinois. By 1890 midwesterners had replaced Northeasterners as California's principal population group and would remain the largest force in the state's population until World War II.

Foreign immigration to California continued, but at a pace that did not match the other sources of population growth. Once 40 percent of the population, the foreign-born accounted for less than 20 percent by 1930. Immigration in this period was almost entirely from Europe and Canada, and mostly from the same European regions that populated the Midwest: Germany, Britain, Ireland, and Scandinavia. After 1880 Italians and Portuguese came to California in substantial numbers, but not many of the eastern Europeans who in the turn-of-the-century decades were pouring into the industrial cities of the East. Meanwhile the proportion of non-Europeans in California was much reduced. Latin Americans and Asians had accounted for 15 percent of the state's population in 1860. By 1900 they were less than 7 percent, and they remained at about that level through the 1930s. Working mostly in agriculture or in the tiny service sectors that their isolated, much harassed communities could support, Chinese, Japanese, Filipinos, Mexicans, and the equally small population of African Americans held on precariously. Like that of the Midwest, California's population was emphatically European American.

Midwesternization entered a second phase around the turn of the century with the invention of southern California. In 1880 the six counties of southern California claimed fewer than fifty thousand residents, only 6 percent of the state's population. By 1930 there were 2.8 million southern Californians, just about half of the state's total. This new population magnet was built out of orange groves, oil, tourism, real estate, and a huge dose of imagination. Railroads again opened the way, pushing competing lines into Los Angeles in 1876 and 1885, thereby setting off an immediate fare war and putting both the Southern Pacific and the Santa Fe into the business of promoting southern California.

Tourism was what the railroads promoted. Southern California was the creation of a maturing industrial society with a growing middle class and new appetites for leisure. The Gilded Age wealthy had discovered Europe and the grand tour. Southern California, with its Mediterranean climate, became the middle-class alternative, especially for midwesterners, a mere five days away by rail. Sun and beaches, the area's natural endowments, were only part of the appeal. As Carey McWilliams and Kevin Starr have pointed out, southern California was an exercise in fantasy, a barnumesque work of promotion and imagination focused initially on the theme of Mediterraneanization.

Italy, Greece, and especially Spain rose anew in turn-of-the-century Los Angeles. Using stucco as the chief building material, developers laid out a revival cityscape of villas, châteaux, temples, and haciendas, creating not only fanciful homes but entire theme communities, the most famous of which was Abbott Kinney's seaside Venice, complete with canals, imported gondoliers, and stucco re-creations of Renaissance buildings. But Spain rather than Italy supplied the most compelling version of southern California's Mediterranean idyll. In the region's heretofore denigrated Hispanic past, especially in the crumbling Franciscan missions, southern California gained, says Starr, "the public myth which conferred romance upon a new American region." Spanish colonial architecture, "Old Spanish Days" parades and fiestas, new streets and towns tagged with Spanish names, new history lessons in the tourist magazines and school texts—after a generation of deliberate Anglicization of form and consciousness, California now reversed course in a carefully constructed campaign to claim a Spanish (but not Mexican) past.

Collaborating with the image makers was the one grounded industry that southern California could claim in its first period of growth. Orange growing became another exercise in Mediterranean romance, a gentlemanly form of agriculture ideally suited to the fantasies of inhabitants of harsher climes, farmers and townsfolk alike. Later there would be a less glamorous blue-collar economy, with oil producing most of the revenues and construction most of the jobs and with a growing branch-plant manufacturing sector. But southern California's image as a leisure frontier had been firmly set. The gold in the second California population rush lay in sun and oranges.

Hollywood completed the fantasy. Chasing the sun like everyone else, the infant film industry drifted into Los Angeles in the early years of the twentieth century just as movies were replacing vaudeville as the dominant popular entertainment medium. The young city and the young industry were a perfect match, each thriving on artifice and invention, both products of an era that was rapidly democratizing the pleasures of consumerism.

Hollywood also gave California its first glimpse of its future influence. By the 1920s the film industry had kicked into high gear. Attracting a growing colony of celebrities, writers, and artists, the studios cranked out miles of celluloid to be seen weekly by tens of millions not just in the United States but around the world. The leading edge of American globalism, Hollywood's films spread enticing images of American opulence and equally refracted representations of California far and wide. To the older imagery of climate, health, and wealth were added new suggestions of experiment and excess.

Replacing Greenwich Village as the symbol of social experimentalism, Los Angeles became synonymous with sex, celebrity, hedonism, architectural and religious oddities, and wacky politics—in short, with nearly everything new and outrageous. Film would make Los Angeles the Peter Pan of American cities, bringing legions of dreamers and doers who would keep the cycles of reinvention going, making sure the city would never slow down, that it would never grow up.

Hollywood aside, California's first American century was about development and integration into the evolving regional structures of industrial America. American regional relations during much of this period have often been characterized as neocolonial, favoring the interests of the industrial Northeast to the detriment of the South and the West. That does not fit the California case. Its role was definitely subordinate, but unlike the single-export economies of the South and the Great Plains and the mining and ranching states of the far West, California supplied the nation with a range of specialized products and services—fruits, vegetables, oil, lumber, tourism, film—for which in most cases it was well paid. And although state leaders decried the discriminatory railroad policies and Wall Street investment patterns that deflected the state's economy from manufacturing, in fact a large internal market left room for a variety of consumer manufacturers. The result was hardly exploitative. Californians enjoyed one of the highest standards of living in the nation and an economy diverse enough to cushion many of the downturns that battered other areas. Nevertheless, despite its 5.6 million people, making it the fifth largest state in 1930, California was definitely on the periphery. "The Coast," as it was called in eastern circles, was an amusing, distant place known for its redwood trees, its orange groves, and its Hollywood luminaries—not a place anyone took very seriously. But this would all change very shortly.

MODERN CALIFORNIA

World War II initiated California's third developmental era. After a century of looking east, California now turned westward, assuming much of the responsibility for America's involvement on the Pacific Rim. No longer peripheral, the state would now become a leading center of both economic and cultural production, home to some of the critical industries and cultural innovations that Americans have developed since the 1940s.

The federal government was almost entirely responsible for California's new role. Federal policy had always to some extent privileged the state, reflecting the nation's interest in maintaining a credible military presence in the Pacific. A naval shipyard alongside San Francisco Bay was the first substantial federal investment in the region in the 1850s, and there would be others. Transportation services were the major nineteenth-century target for federal funds, and California received more than its share for harbor and river improvements and for railroad building. Federal land reclamation and water development projects pumped additional millions into the state in the early decades of the twentieth century, as did the Pacific military buildup that began in earnest in the 1890s. By the end of World War I, California already possessed a substantial military-industrial complex, including shipyards, navy and army bases, and the beginnings of the aircraft industry that was to be so important to its later development.

World War II turned this stream of federal funds into a torrent. Committed to a two-ocean war, Washington poured 10 percent of its entire war budget into California. Some of this went into building and operating the more than one hundred military installations that funneled men and matériel into the Pacific war. Most of the rest went into war production, giving the state a huge new industrial base. The San Francisco Bay Area became the nation's shipbuilding center, while southern California plants turned out more than 200,000 planes. Every bit as important for California in the long run were the federal dollars spent on scientific research, principally for the nuclear program at the University of California and the rocketry research at the California Institute of Technology.

Second only to the gold rush, writes historian Gerald Nash, the war remade California and other western states, giving them the kind of economic structure and population that moved them beyond the regional margins. California emerged from the war with a highly diversified economy, perhaps the most modern in the world. A huge military-industrial complex weighted toward the fast-breaking aerospace and electronics industries now complemented the increasingly efficient agricultural economy. Added to these sectors was an educational/business service sector that developed rapidly in the 1950s and 1960s as forward-looking state officials invested massively in schools and universities, building what

they hoped would be the finest public education system in the country. All this turned California into a job-creating and population-attracting machine unlike any other in the late twentieth century. Numbers tell the story. The 1940 population of 6.9 million jumped to 15.7 million by 1960, hit 23.7 million by 1980, and raced on past 30 million in 1990. Along the way, somewhere about 1962, California became the nation's most populous state.

California's new economy also brought a new demography, one befitting the increasingly global outlook of both state and nation in the second half of the twentieth century. In these years, California broke completely with the midwestern pattern. Ninety percent white in 1940, California had become an ethnic kaleidoscope by 1990, with 43 percent of its population claiming Asian, African, Latin American, or Native American ancestry.

African Americans had been only a slight presence in California before the war, preferring the industrial North to the unknown West during the great diaspora from the South of the 1910s and 1920s. But after 1942, shipyard jobs primed the pump for a massive migration from the western South. By 1950 California had a population of almost half a million blacks, which spiraled to 1.4 million by 1970. Migration slowed after that and even reversed somewhat in the 1980s, bringing the 1990 black population to just over 2 million (7 percent of the state's population).

Latin American population growth followed a different trajectory. Beginning after the turn of the century and especially during the revolution in their native land that began in 1910, Mexican immigrants initially sought mainly farm and construction labor jobs in southern and central California. The Great Depression of the 1930s brought that cycle of immigration to a close, but a new one began in the 1940s, spurred mostly by urban opportunities. Much of this was legal immigration, since Mexicans enjoyed various loopholes and entitlements under the immigration restriction statutes passed in the 1920s. But an increasing percentage of the postwar flow was undocumented. The state's largest ethnic minority, with an estimated four hundred thousand members in 1940, the Chicano/Latino population grew exponentially, passing the three million mark in 1970, then exploding in the next two decades. In the 1990 census Hispanics numbered 7.7 million, more than one-quarter of the state's population. Although most Hispanics were of Mexican heritage, there were also substantial communities from each of the Central American countries.

The Asian story is different still. Although World War II and its immediate aftermath removed some of the restrictions on Asian immigration, it was not until Congress rewrote immigration law in 1965 that the way was cleared for the extraordinary proliferation of peoples that in the 1970s and 1980s gave new meaning to the term "diversity" in California. One out of every two legal immigrants into the United States in this period came from Asia or the Pacific Islands, and more than half of these immigrants went to California. This new wave was entirely different from the earlier immigration from China, Japan, and the Philippines, which consisted mostly of unskilled laborers. Often well educated and equipped with commercial or technical skills, the new Asian immigrants came from all around the Pacific Rim: from Korea, Taiwan, Hong Kong, the Philippines, Vietnam, Cambodia, and Laos, as well as from India and Pakistan, giving the state a combined Asian population of 2.7 million in 1990, 9 percent of California's total.

Perhaps the most intriguing aspect of the new demography has been the repopulation of California by Native Americans, who now number almost two hundred thousand. Some of this can be credited to the original California peoples, whose numbers have grown steadily throughout the twentieth century. But the largest increase has come from outside the state, as Navajo, Lakota, Cherokee and Choctaw, as well as members of other nations of the interior, have followed the trail of postwar opportunity to California.

The trail ends in Los Angeles, which is to the late twentieth century what New York was to the century before: a crossroads of the world, the Pacific half of the globe in microcosm. Here, spread out in the legendary city of sprawl, are the unmelted millions, dozens of ethnicities and nationalities, no one constituting a majority: one million African Americans, over three million Latin Americans, the largest concentration of Japanese outside Japan, of Koreans outside Korea, and of Vietnamese outside Vietnam, and Chinese from several nations, as well as substantial enclaves of Filipinos and South Asians. Then there are the recent Arab, Iranian, Israeli, and Russian immigrants, as well as the older ethnic communities: the Jewish West Side and the South Side Okie suburbs. The story goes on and on.

Demography is only one of the foundations of the new, plural California of the last half century. Cultural and political trends that have opened debate about the priorities of modern society have made an especially powerful impression in California, creating a cornucopia of cultural experiments and social movements while demonstrating that Californians are divided by place, life-style, and ideology as well as by ethnicity.

Having pushed past San Francisco as the industrial, financial, and population capital of the West, and extended its domination of American media with the addition of radio, television, and record industries, Los Angeles might have been expected to play a leading role in the creation of the cultural products and agendas for the new era. And to some extent it did. America's great postwar cult of youth broke first in southern California, in the Anaheim orange groves that became Disneyland, on the white sand beaches that launched the surfing craze, in the music and film now targeting the largest generation ever of young consumers.

But media-drenched Los Angeles was too invested in the ways of consumer society to foster the kinds of oppositional subcultures that were to be the most important social innovations of late 20th century. That role, ironically, would fall to San Francisco, a city that only a few years before had been known for its stodgy old wealth and no-nonsense labor unions. By the late 1960s the San Francisco Bay Area had been reinvented as the capital of alternative America, identified near and far with a succession of new social and political movements: Beat poetry in the late 1950s; the Berkeley Free Speech movement in 1964; Haight-Ashbury, hippies, and acid rock a few years later; then the Black Panther Party in nearby Oakland; and in the 1970s the nation's first politically powerful gay and lesbian community. Meanwhile the Bay Area had played a substantial role in the revitalization of the environmental movement and had nurtured into prominence several New Age religious groups.

If these ideas and movements helped change the nation, they affected California even more profoundly, adding to the welter of voices that increasingly complicated the state's political system. What analysts liked to describe as the state's erratic political behavior was really a matter of escalating diversity. The electorate that could make Ronald Reagan governor one moment and Jerry Brown the next, that could maintain both leftists and reactionaries in Congress, that could send former SDS (Students for a Democratic Society) leader Tom Hayden and former John Birch Society members to the same legislature, was no longer one entity. In the postindustrial age, as in the pre-European one, California had become a mosaic of subregions with very different sociopolitical characteristics. Economic function as well as demography underlay the irreconcilable political differences between the conservative techno-burbs of Orange, San Diego, and Santa Clara counties and the experimental university towns scattered about the state; between the privileged coastal communities with their tourist base and growth-control politics and the mountain/lumber zones that resist environmental regulation; between the core urban areas where multiracial populations and public-sector employment promote Great Society liberalism and the agricultural valleys where the social system is white over brown and the politics follow the needs of agribusiness.

And yet out of this mosaic have come some new public policy priorities. One has to do with population and the environment. Prior to World War II the state had unabashedly pushed population growth except during depression cycles, when Asians, Latin Americans, and occasionally other groups were targeted for exclusion. Since the war both boosterism and xenophobia have diminished greatly, replaced, especially since the 1960s, by a politics of overpopulation anxiety that so far has focused more on infrastructural and environmental regulation than on unpopular social groups.

The result has been some of the toughest environmental legislation in the nation. Ambitious air-pollution programs and water-quality standards, successful campaigns to protect endangered species, stop offshore oil drilling, save wilderness areas and wild rivers, and halt nuclear power plants, special agencies to control development along the coast and in the Lake Tahoe basin, local growth-control initiatives and statewide battles over water supplies, state and local recycling programs, a pioneering law regulating the use and labeling of toxic substances—despite opposition on various fronts the public's concern with issues of environmental quality probably counts as one of the few areas of general consensus. That is not to say that anything of real consequence has been resolved. The problems of resource abuse, air pollution, water scarcity, and waste disposal remain, and will, as long as the culture's chief concern is escalating consumption.

The second new pattern in California politics since World War II involved the readjustment of racial hierarchies. This of course has been the great postwar agenda throughout American society, but the California story has some particular twists. The state's moment of conscience came not in the mid 1950s but a decade earlier, when it began to con-

sider the awful consequences of its last brutal exercise in xenophobia.

Pearl Harbor provided the excuse to carry out the agenda that had many times tempted the state's powerful anti-Asian lobby. Pressured by the West Coast press and members of Congress, President Roosevelt authorized the removal and incarceration of the region's entire Japanese population, some 93,000 persons from California, two-thirds of them citizens. Forced to sell or abandon homes, farms, and businesses, the internees spent most of the war in guarded, barbed-wire-enclosed camps in remote spots in the western interior.

California turned a corner in the years following this last xenophobic exercise. After the war, the state began to dismantle its legal apparatus of caste and exclusion. In 1948 the state's supreme court threw out the long-enforced antimiscegenation statute and four years later invalidated the notorious Alien Land Law that kept first-generation Asian immigrants from owning property. Meanwhile, Congress and the U.S. Supreme Court abolished provisions in immigration law that prevented Asians from becoming naturalized citizens. Two changes were evident in these moves: the liberalizing trend that would soon result in the broad civil rights agendas of the late 1950s and the 1960s and a shift in the axis of racial tension from Asian/white to black/white, a change that brought California into line with the rest of the nation.

The rest of the civil rights era followed conventional northern patterns. White Californians readily abandoned de jure racial restrictions but not so readily de facto segregation. It took a decade of legislative battles before the state passed its first law banning racial discrimination in employment in 1959. When that was followed four years later by "fair housing" legislation, the white majority rebelled, passing a 1964 repeal initiative by a two-to-one margin, only to see the courts overturn the overturners and reinstate the antidiscrimination measure.

The Watts section of Los Angeles exploded in the summer of 1965, leaving thirty-four people dead and initiating a decade and a half of desperate racial conflict in the streets and courts. A rising tide of militancy in the black and later in the Chicano communities was matched by the backlash mood of many whites, particularly when the courts in the 1970s began ordering school boards to initiate desegregation plans. Affirmative action programs raised further resistance. As was the case nearly everywhere, the result was a standoff. The old system of racial caste had been broken, but neither equality nor integration had taken its place. The new system of inequality joined principles of class to the factor of race, privileging middle-class minorities with both occupational and political opportunities but isolating all those who could not make the cut: the working poor, the dependent, the non-English-speaking.

Today, the new social order's ambiguities are heightened by the multiethnic character of California society and by the uneven distribution of problems and opportunities among the different groups. Asians, African Americans, and Latinos occupy different niches in the social order. Blacks face the greatest economic and social difficulties but have developed the greatest political resources, wielding political influence out of proportion to their numbers at both state and community levels. Asians are in the opposite position: more economically successful (in the aggregate) than other minorities but politically almost voiceless. Latinos fall in the middle, gaining economic standing and slowly emerging as a political force.

Where it will all lead is anything but certain. Along with the rest of America, California entered the 1990s poised to move either forward into a new era of pluralist understanding or backward into familiar cycles of conflict. The recent past offers portents of both. There is on the one hand the example of the University of California at Berkeley, where the undergraduate student population has become a showpiece of colors and cultures and where the inevitable tensions are muted by a nearly consensual desire to make it work. On the other hand there are the ominous signs that Mike Davis reads in the changing polity and cityscape of Los Angeles, where white homeowner associations erect gated "fortress" communities, where billions are spent on the fine arts while poverty proliferates, where English-only ordinances and building codes are used to fight immigrant "invasions," where industry and public officials alike retreat from the central city, where the war on drugs turns into a police war against a whole generation of blacks and Latinos,

where a modern metropolis veers toward the grim future foretold in Ridley Scott's film *Blade Runner.*

The events of 29 April–2 May 1992 seem to confirm that nightmarish prediction. After a suburban jury acquitted four white police officers charged with brutality in the videotaped beating of Rodney King, a black motorist, crowds of young blacks, Latinos, and some whites took to the streets in the worst sequence of urban violence that Americans have seen this century.

When it was over, more than 50 people were dead, more than 2,000 were injured, and 12,000 were arrested. South-Central Los Angeles, already the site of escalating poverty and neglect, faced the task of rebuilding some 5,000 stores and structures burned or damaged in the four-day conflagration.

Still many Californians remain optimists, citing the state's transcendent cultural traditions, in particular, its capacity for innovation and change. This notion, itself a feature of the newer, global California, operates more on the plane of myth than of fact. Despite the record of cultural creativity, it would be hard to demonstrate that Californians in the aggregate are any more receptive to change than anyone else; what they have developed is a capacity for social diversity and political schizophrenia, for sustaining a range of discrete, even antagonist, subcultures while moving erratically between public policy agendas. It is all nicely postmodern—the many voices, the invented personas and plastic lifestyles, the short attention span—a microburst cultural system capable of continuous surprise.

Whatever its entertainment value, it is hard to believe that mercurial California has any special gift for solving the complex problems of pluralism, let alone the other pressing issues of a globally interdependent age. In the end, like the nation that it aspires to lead, California will try to get by as it has always gotten by: relying on its geographic gifts and economic good fortune to feed the inflated consumer passions of its growing and changing population, hoping that the regime of abundance will last forever, or at least for another generation.

BIBLIOGRAPHY

General Works

Eisen, Jonathan, and David Fine with Kim Eisen, eds. *Unknown California: Classic and Contemporary Writing on California Culture, Society, History, and Politics* (1985).

McWilliams, Carey. *Southern California Country: An Island on the Land* (1946; repr. 1973).

———. *California: the Great Exception* (1949; repr. 1976).

Nunis, Doyce B., and Gloria Lothrop, eds. *A Guide to the History of California* (1989). The most recent bibliography.

Rice, Richard B., William A. Bullough, and Richard J. Orsi. *The Elusive Eden: A New History of California* (1988).

Before 1848

Bancroft, Hubert Howe. *History of California,* 7 vols. (1884–1890).

Camarillo, Albert. *Chicanos in a Changing Society: From Mexican Pueblos to American Barrios in Santa Barbara and Southern California, 1848–1930* (1979).

Cook, Sherburne F. *The Conflict Between the California Indian and White Civilization* (1976).

Heizer, Robert F., and Albert B. Elsasser. *The Natural World of the California Indians* (1980).

Hurtado, Albert L. *Indian Survival on the California Frontier* (1988).

Monroy, Douglas. *Thrown Among Strangers: The Making of Mexican Culture in Frontier California* (1990).

Weber, David J. *The Mexican Frontier, 1821–1846: The American Southwest Under Mexico* (1982).

1840–1940

Balderrama, Francisco E. *In Defense of La Raza: The Los Angeles Mexican Consulate and the Mexican Community, 1929 to 1936* (1982).

Caughey, John W. *Gold Is the Cornerstone* (1948).

Fogelson, Robert M. *The Fragmented Metropolis: Los Angeles, 1850–1930* (1967).

Gregory, James N. *American Exodus: The Dust Bowl Migration and Okie Culture in California* (1989).

Holliday, James S. *The World Rushed In: The California Gold Rush Experience* (1981).

Issel, William, and Robert W. Cherny. *San Francisco, 1865–1932: Politics, Power, and Urban Development* (1986).

Kingston, Maxine Hong. *The Woman Warrior: Memoirs of a Girlhood Among Ghosts* (1975).

———. *China Men* (1980).

Limerick, Patricia Nelson. *The Legacy of Conquest: The Unbroken Past of the American West* (1987).

Lotchin, Roger. *San Francisco, 1846–1856: From Hamlet to Modern City* (1974).

Pisani, Donald J. *From Family Farm to Agribusiness: The Irrigation Crusade in California and the West, 1850–1931* (1984).

Romo, Ricardo. *East Los Angeles: History of a Barrio* (1983).

Saxton, Alexander. *The Indispensable Enemy: Labor and the Anti-Chinese Movement in California* (1971).

Starr, Kevin. *Americans and the California Dream, 1850–1915* (1973).

———. *Inventing the Dream: California Through the Progressive Era* (1985).

————. *Material Dreams: Southern California Through the 1920s* (1990).

Takaki, Ronald. *Strangers from a Different Shore: A History of Asian Americans* (1989).

Recent History

Davis, Mike. *City of Quartz: Excavating the Future in Los Angeles* (1990).

Kotkin, Joel, and Paul Grabowicz. *California, Inc.* (1982).

Nash, Gerald D. *The American West Transformed: The Impact of the Second World War* (1985).

Walters, Dan. *The New California: Facing the 21st Century* (1986).

Wollenberg, Charles. *All Deliberate Speed: Segregation and Exclusion in California Schools, 1855–1975* (1976).

SEE ALSO **Asian Americans; Immigration; Latin Americans: Mexicans and Central Americans; The Natural Environment: The West; National Parks and Preservation; Rural Life in the West**.

HAWAII

David E. Stannard

HAWAII IS DIFFERENT from most other states in a number of striking ways—demographic, cultural, and political—each of which in turn is traceable to a single primary characteristic: the islands' geographic remoteness. Not only is Hawaii as far removed from the American mainland as London is from Cairo, but the Hawaiian islands as a group are the most isolated archipelago on earth.

Because of its great distance from other bodies of land, lying just south of the Tropic of Cancer, 2,400 miles (3,800 kilometers) to the west of San Francisco, Hawaii was not settled by humans until around the first century A.D. The earliest human residents—Polynesians who had been moving slowly from island to island across the Pacific from ancestral homelands in Southeast Asia beginning at least four thousand years ago—lived in almost total isolation from the outside world for nearly two millennia until they were stumbled upon by the British sea captain, James Cook, in 1778. By that time the indigenous Hawaiian people had grown in numbers to somewhere between 750,000 and 1,000,000 people, according to the most recent estimates.

Traditionally, the islands were divided into numerous political districts and subdistricts, with even the highest ranking individual chief's power rarely extending beyond the confines of a single island. Still, within those autonomous polities, Hawaiians lived in the most steeply hierarchical political culture in the Pacific. That political culture apparently emerged gradually during the centuries prior to Western contact, growing increasingly elaborate as the burgeoning population required the organization and control of large numbers of workers to construct irrigation canals and terraces, aquaculture facilities, religious temples, and other engineering projects for which the Hawaiians are famous in their part of the world. A complicated system of social status and political power guided the transfer of land- and water-use rights from one generation to the next, but private ownership of land did not exist.

Although geographically small compared with most American states (Hawaii's land area of about 6,400 square miles [16,600 square kilometers] ranks forty-seventh among states, midway in size between Connecticut and New Jersey), it is large by most Pacific island standards. For example, its single largest island, the island of Hawai'i, is nearly double the combined size of the dozens of islands that comprise Tonga, the Marquesas, the Society Islands (including Tahiti), and Western and American Samoa. As a result, although its population at the time of Western contact may seem high, its population density was quite conventional compared with other Pacific island groups.

THE EFFECTS OF WESTERN CONTACT

It did not remain at that level for long, however, since introduced European diseases created a catastrophic population collapse among the native people. Epidemics of typhoid fever and various respiratory infections combined with venereal disease and tuberculosis to simultaneously kill large numbers of people and destroy many of the survivors' reproductive potential. Within forty years following Captain Cook's first visit, Hawaii's native population was down to 200,000—approximately a quarter of what it had been in 1778. During that time an ambitious and powerful chief named Kamehameha (ca. 1758–1819), hailing from the island of Hawai'i (known most commonly by the colloquial term, "the Big Island"), conquered or otherwise subdued the governments on the other major islands in the chain—Maui, Lāna'i, Moloka'i, O'ahu, and Kaua'i. Thus, by the time American missionaries established residence in 1820, all the islands of Hawaii had been merged under centralized political rule for the first time in their history. Until the end of the nineteenth century, Hawaii would be governed by a dynastic monarchy deriving from Kamehameha.

For some years prior to the missionaries' arrival American and European traders had established themselves as intermediaries in lucrative exchange arrangements with China involving Hawaiian sandalwood. Soon after, whaling ships began using the Hawaiian port towns of Lahaina on Maui and Honolulu on O'ahu as rest and stopover points. And a bit later still, some American entrepreneurs discovered that sugar flourished in the island soils. The first permanent sugar plantation was established on the island of Kaua'i in 1835, with teams of yoked native men pulling plows in the absence of draft animals.

By mid century the sandalwood trade was finished, the island forests having been stripped of their supplies in fairly short order. But the whaling and sugar industries were enjoying boom times. The number of whaling ships calling at Hawaiian ports each year had increased from 78 in 1825 to 542 in 1845; even with fluctuations in the industry over the next decade and a half, arrivals of whalers averaged well over four hundred ships each year. Meanwhile, sugar exports had grown from an average of only 6,000 pounds (2,700 kilograms) per year in 1836 and 1837 to well over half a million pounds (about 225,000 kilograms) per year in the late 1840s. Other agricultural products were developed in the late 1840s—including Irish potatoes, sweet potatoes, and coffee—with a surge in the export markets for these items and for sugar coinciding with America's acquisition of Oregon and California. Exports to California grew especially strong following the discovery of gold there in 1848.

Major problems were brewing for Hawaii's American settler businessmen by this time, however. First, a high tariff was making it difficult for Hawaii's agricultural products to compete in the West Coast markets. Second, although Hawaii was recognized internationally as a sovereign nation, attempts had been made by both British and French military units to take the islands, and fears persisted among American settlers that they might yet be seized by a European power. Third, under a constitution approved in 1840 the land-tenure system blocked individuals from fee-simple land ownership, a provision that infuriated land-seeking Americans. And fourth, the dwindling native Hawaiian population was unable to supply sufficient labor for the growing agricultural industry.

THE REMAKING OF THE POPULATION

By 1848 the indigenous population was down to fewer than 100,000 when sudden epidemics of measles, whooping cough, and influenza swept the islands, killing more than 10,000 native people. In thirty years the population had fallen by more than half—following the previous four decades in which it had declined by 75 percent. From pulpits and editorial pages white missionaries and merchants were declaring the extinction of the native population to be imminent. Also in 1848, the same year in which those epidemics had literally decimated the population, the king gave in to pressures from missionaries and businessmen (though often they were one and the same) to divide up the land and permit fee-simple ownership. A series of other legislative moves followed and by 1855—after a smallpox epidemic had taken another fearful toll, killing perhaps one out of four native people on the island of O'ahu alone—the property redistribution was complete. While the government still controlled most of the land, foreign purchases and speculation were rampant, and the native people themselves were left with less than 1 percent of the islands' area. In all, only one out of five native Hawaiian adults received any land at all—and much of what they did receive was so small and of such poor quality that it soon was lost as well. The native people were not only dying; they also had effectively been dispossessed.

Plantation owners began looking to Asia for laborers to replace the Hawaiians. By 1860 about eight hundred Chinese immigrants were numbered among the islands' ethnic populations. And now leprosy (Hansen's disease) was loose among the natives. Associating it with the newly arriving Chinese, the Hawaiians referred to leprosy as *ma'i pake* (Chinese sickness); thousands of them succumbed to it, living out their drastically shortened lives in a hastily constructed leper colony in a remote valley on the island of Moloka'i. By 1890 the number of immigrant laborers from China had increased to 15,000—and the Chinese by then had been joined by 12,000 contract workers from Japan, 8,600 from Portugal, and another 15,000 from other parts of Europe, the United States, and elsewhere. The native population was down to 40,000; in little more than a century it had fallen by 95 percent and the natives were now a minority in their ancestral land.

Since the 1850s white businessmen had been calling for American annexation of Hawaii, both for military protection and to maximize their export

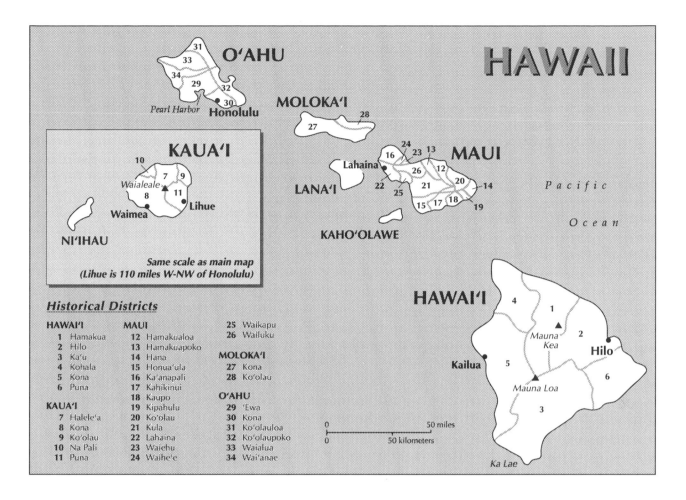

Historical Districts

HAWAI'I	MAUI	25 Waikapu
1 Hamakua	12 Hamakualoa	26 Wailuku
2 Hilo	13 Hamakuapoko	
3 Ka'u	14 Hana	MOLOKA'I
4 Kohala	15 Honua'ula	27 Kona
5 Kona	16 Ka'anapali	28 Ko'olau
6 Puna	17 Kahikinui	
	18 Kaupo	O'AHU
KAUA'I	19 Kipahulu	29 'Ewa
7 Halele'a	20 Ko'olau	30 Kona
8 Kona	21 Kula	31 Ko'olauloa
9 Ko'olau	22 Lahaina	32 Ko'olaupoko
10 Na Pali	23 Waiehu	33 Waialua
11 Puna	24 Waihe'e	34 Wai'anae

profits. Finally, in 1893 a coalition of businessmen and American marines overthrew the Hawaiian monarchy and replaced it with a provisional government under the control of a white settler oligarchy. After imprisoning Queen Lili'uokalini the provisional government implored the United States to annex the islands. For five years the American government hesitated, for reasons both admirable (official investigations had shown that the overthrow was clearly illegal) and lamentable (a strong current of racism in the United States Congress was opposed to the absorption of any large numbers of people of color into the American body politic). But in 1898—a banner year for American imperialism in the Pacific as well as the Caribbean—the Congress voted to annex Hawaii.

The doors to immigration now opened as the islands' plantation owners scoured Asia for field laborers. Between 1896 and 1900 the population of Hawaii increased by more than 40 percent, from 109,000 to 154,000. More than 80 percent of that in-

crease was attributable to in-migration from Japan. Between 1900 and 1920 the population jumped by another 66 percent, two-thirds of which occurred in the local Japanese and Filipino communities. Ten years later the overall population was up another 44 percent—from 256,000 to 368,000—of which, again, almost two-thirds was caused by Japanese and Filipino increases.

A HAOLE-DOMINATED COLONY

Hawaii was now a territory of the United States, and was being run by a white Republican party that was controlled by the Sugar Planters' Association. Sugar was king of the Hawaii economy by this time, and 96 percent of the annual sugar output of more than a million tons (900,000 metric tons) was being produced by just five companies. The labor force was segregated and stratified by race, with Caucasians (known in Hawaii as *haoles,* from the Hawaiian word for "foreigner") holding all the top positions and Hawaiians and Asian immigrants the lower-status jobs, although whites constituted barely 20 percent of the population. Hawaii may have been a territory of the United States in name, but it was a colony of the United States in fact—a colony protected by a standing American military force of 20,000 to 25,000 men.

Although efforts were constantly made to keep racial and class tensions beyond the range of visibility, confrontations kept occurring that belied the myth of tropical tranquility. The most famous such incident, known as the Massie case, burst on the local and national scene in 1931 and 1932 when Thalia Massie, the wife of an American military officer stationed in Honolulu, accused a carload of native Hawaiian and Asian men of raping her. The evidence for the prosecution was slight at best, and the trial of the accused men ended in a hung jury. Before the case could be retried, however, Massie's mother, husband, and two other men from the American military base kidnapped and murdered one of the Hawaiian men Thalia Massie had charged. The legal machinery then turned to the murder trial of the four whites—who promptly hired Clarence Darrow to defend them. Darrow failed, later complaining that he had been unable to read the inscrutable nonwhite faces of the jurors during the trial, and Massie's mother, her husband, and his two associates were convicted of manslaughter and sentenced to ten years of hard labor. Their sentences, however, were commuted by the territory's federally appointed governor—the scion of an old missionary family—and together they served one hour of captivity in the governor's office, which was located in the palace of the Hawaiians' late deposed queen.

A few years later in the town of Hilo, located on the Big Island, violence of another sort broke out when two hundred men and women representing several labor unions attempted to demonstrate against the arrival of a ship in Hilo's harbor. The workers themselves—largely Japanese, Filipino, and native Hawaiian—were not on strike, but were making a show of solidarity with striking Boatman's Union workers in Honolulu. Apparently without provocation, the police guarding the docks turned on the demonstrators with guns, hoses, gas, and bayonets. Although none of the unionists died from the attack, fifty of them were hospitalized with serious injuries, and the event became known as the Hilo massacre—both a tragedy and a rallying cry for the infant trade union movement in the islands.

The Massie case and the Hilo massacre were, of course, only well-publicized symptoms of the less visible, but no less real, racial and social strife that had been festering in Hawaii for years. Those problems did not disappear in the 1940s, but rather were put aside temporarily while World War II was being waged.

The military population of Hawaii increased from 27,000 in 1939 to 407,000 in 1944—an increase from just over 6 percent of the population to more than 47 percent within five years. Hawaii's largely working-class and politically powerless people of color—who represented 75 percent of the islands' resident population—were being inundated by hundreds of thousands of transient people of a type they had hardly seen before: people with white skins and working-class backgrounds. At the same time, large numbers of ethnically Chinese, Japanese, Filipino, native Hawaiian, and other nonwhite residents of Hawaii were fighting as members of the United States armed forces all over the world. It was obvious that once the war was over the white oligarchy that had ruled Hawaii for half a century was going to face a challenge unlike any it had faced before.

During the war years the islands had been placed under martial law, strikes were prohibited, and the union organizing efforts that had begun in the 1930s ground to a standstill. No sooner had the war ended, however, than organizing began again and the first test of union strength occurred. The International Longshoremen's and Warehousemen's Union (ILWU) controlled the dockworkers in Hawaii's ports, as it did those in San Francisco, but in the wake of the war the union expanded its control over sugar and pineapple workers as well. On 1 September 1946, more than 21,000 workers on thirty-three plantations walked off their jobs, demanding wage increases and shorter working hours. The settlement, more than two months later, awarded the workers a higher pay increase than they had asked for in the first place. Harry Bridges, the head of the ILWU, wired congratulations from his office in San Francisco, proclaiming that as a result of the workers' success Hawaii was "no longer a feudal colony." Membership in the ILWU shot up from barely nine hundred at the close of the war to thirty thousand by the end of 1947. More strikes—and more labor successes—followed.

Moving from the economic realm to the political, the ILWU attempted to take over the helm of the traditionally anemic Democratic party. Although it failed to capture the party leadership, the union did seize enormous influence and the takeover effort itself greatly energized the Democrats, who then moved aggressively to recruit membership from the islands' effectively disenfranchised people of color. Non-*haoles* constituted 75 percent of Hawaii's population—and Japanese Americans alone made up half of that potential voting block. In the elections of 1954, for the first time since annexation, the Democratic party took control of the territorial legislature. Five years later, with the achievement of statehood, governors became elected rather than presidentially appointed officials. The governor elected in that year's special election was, like the majority of the state's legislators, a Democrat—the first Democratic governor ever. From that time, Republicans have never held the governorship and have never come close to controlling the legislature. Prior to 1954 Hawaii had been under the almost total control of one political party, the Republican. Since 1954, Hawaii has been under the complete control of the Democrats.

THE NEW ECONOMY OF TOURISM

During the 1950s and early 1960s Hawaii's economy was dependent on two major sources of supply—agriculture and the military. Statehood, however, occurred at the same time that commercial airlines were adding long-range, large-capacity jet aircraft to their fleets. And in the 1960s Hawaii's tourist industry took off. In 1958, the year before statehood, the islands—with a resident population of a little more than 600,000—had received a total of 124,000 tourists. That is, approximately one tourist for every five residents. By 1963, only five years later, the number of tourist arrivals had more than doubled. By 1966 it had more than doubled again. And again by 1970. By the middle of the 1970s more than two million tourists were arriving in Hawaii every year. By the mid 1980s the ratio of tourists to residents was the reverse of what it had been on the eve of statehood: instead of five residents for every tourist, it was five tourists for every resident. And by the early 1990s the numbers were roughly seven million tourists each year and just over one million residents. Export agriculture and military expenditures continued to be important contributors to Hawaii's economy, but even when combined they were dwarfed by the revenues generated by tourism, which now accounted for half the gross state product.

As a relatively low-wage service economy largely controlled by multinational corporations with home bases outside Hawaii—and many of them outside the United States—tourism meant enormous affluence for a relative handful of people, but income stagnation and decline for most. At the same time it has meant skyrocketing prices, especially for land. As a result, since the early 1980s Hawaii's per capita and family incomes have held at just above the national average, but its housing and food costs have been by far the highest of any state in the country. As an illustration, the median price of a single-family home on the island of O'ahu was ten times Hawaii's median family income at the start of the 1990s, a cost-to-income ratio approached by no other state or metropolitan area. And that median family income was 25 percent lower than the federal government's estimated budget requirements (for food, clothing, and housing) to maintain in the islands an "intermediate" standard of living. Despite the fact that Hawaii has a higher proportion of multiple wage-earner families than any other state, it also has the lowest proportion of owner-occupied housing.

Hawaii's unbalanced modern economy and political structure have created other problems as well. The island of O'ahu, for example—which is coextensive with the city and county of Honolulu—has a population density greater than the Detroit metropolitan area. Fresh water on O'ahu is in short supply. On the other hand, the island of Moloka'i has a population density equal to about half that of the state of Iowa, and has no shortage of water—but has an unemployment rate that consistently is at least three to four times higher than O'ahu's. Hawaii is renowned for its rich and colorful flora and fauna, yet it accounts for fully a third of the entire nation's endangered and extinct plant and animal species. And while the state continues to nurture an image of itself as a place of gentility and easy living, as a consequence of the booming market in land prices during decades of single-party control of state politics, major scandals involving political figures and real estate speculation became routine in the 1970s and 1980s. One locally best-selling book on the subject quoted a federal investigator who previously had worked in New Jersey and Louisiana to the effect that he had never before seen anything to compare with the political corruption he had witnessed in Hawaii.

THE QUESTION OF LAND

Meanwhile, since the late 1960s, Hawaii's native people have been organizing politically. After reaching a population nadir of less than 40,000 at the close of the nineteenth century, the numbers of native people began to increase, although intermarriage meant that by the 1930s most Hawaiians were of mixed ethnic ancestry. In an effort to forestall Hawaiian homesteading claims on valuable sugar land (through the exercise of a loophole clause in the congressional act that had facilitated Hawaii's annexation) Congress in 1921 set aside approximately 200,000 acres (80,000 hectares) of what at the time was described as "third-grade agricultural lands and second-grade grazing lands" for leasing exclusively to the native people in order to effect their social and economic "rehabilitation." A gubernatorially appointed Hawaiian Homes Commission was to oversee the operation of these lands, but no funds were provided for the commission's operation or for clearing land or developing infrastructure. As a result, land was leased to non-Hawaiian entities (often at scandalously low "sweetheart" rates) in order to generate income for the commission's affairs, but very few native people received any land.

By the mid 1950s, when most Hawaii residents were pushing for statehood, a public opinion survey revealed that 70 percent of the native people, now numbering more than 100,000, were opposed. Still resentful of America's seizure of their land and government in the 1890s, many Hawaiians continued to hope for a return to at least quasi-independent or semi-sovereign status for the islands—or at least for the native people within the islands—and statehood therefore seemed just one more enormous step in the wrong direction. Partially in response to this concern, with recognition of statehood status, the federal government returned to the new state government 1,400,000 acres (560,000 hectares) of so-called ceded land that had been the property of the Hawaiian crown and government at the time of the monarchy's overthrow. In the statehood act the federal government stipulated that these ceded lands were to be used for the benefit of two groups, the general public and the native people.

Thus, the combination of the Hawaiian homes trust and the ceded lands trust—if legally enforced—would have been of huge benefit to the historically dispossessed and terribly damaged Hawaiian people. But they were not enforced. And so for years, although their numbers continued to increase, the native people—like American Indian residents of other states—remained the poorest of the islands' ethnic groups, the least educated, the most commonly incarcerated, and the group with the worst health profile and by far the lowest life expectancy. But then, apparently inspired by the civil rights and Native American movements on the mainland, in the late 1960s and 1970s a native cultural renaissance and political movement erupted in the islands. As with those other movements it underwent a variety of changes and stages, with some leaders pushing for a form of native sovereignty while others quickly accommodated themselves to newly proffered opportunities in party politics. By the early 1990s these diverse pressures had resulted in the election of the first governor of Hawaiian ancestry (who was strongly opposed to most of the plans of Hawaiian activists and nationalists) and a self-proclaimed sovereign government known as *Ka Lāhui Hawai'i* (the Hawaiian Nation) with about 10,000 active members and a lobbying arm seeking federal recognition.

Two thousand years after its discovery by Polynesians, then, two hundred years after its discovery by Europeans, and a hundred years after its seizure by American troops and businessmen, Hawaii is a study in cultural, political, and environmental contrasts.

Excluding military personnel, 80 percent of its population of just over one million is divided among people of the following ancestries: Japanese (24 percent), Caucasian (23 percent), Hawaiian (21 percent), and Filipino (12 percent). Less than 2 percent of the population is African American. Hawaiian hula festivals, Japanese bon dances, and Chinese New Year celebrations are at least as popularly attended as are the festivities associated with most American holidays. Hawaii has as many Muslims as Jews, but its more than twenty Buddhist congregations have sixty-five times as many members as there are Jews and Muslims combined—and there are five times as many Catholics (by far the largest of all religious groups) as there are Buddhists.

Racial and ethnic relations in the islands that seem paradoxical to outsiders go unnoticed by local residents. Thus, each year almost half of all resident marriages in Hawaii involve partners of different races; yet voting patterns divide sharply along racial and ethnic lines. For years some of Hawaii's most popular entertainers have been humorists whose comedy routines so savagely caricature different ethnic groups that visitors from other states invariably find them racially offensive, while appreciative mixed-race local audiences wait in line for standing-room-only accommodations.

Politically, Hawaii in many ways is the most enlightened of states: it was the first state to ratify the proposed Equal Rights Amendment to the Constitution; it was the first state to institute a taxpayer-supported and very nearly universal health coverage program; for decades its congressional delegation has been almost entirely people of color, while its state legislature possesses the same characteristics, as well as having one of the highest proportions of female legislators in the country. But it also is a political system permeated with corruption and influence peddling that infects and cripples every major institution in the state. Also, with only four municipalities in the entire state (one of which contains 80 percent of the state's population), a legislature that is in session for barely three months of each year, and a governor with more influence relative to the state's size than any other governor in the country, Hawaii's political power base is the narrowest and most centralized of any state in the nation.

And, of course, much of Hawaii remains a dazzlingly beautiful place of white—and black—sand beaches, lush green rain forests, waterfall-dappled mountain ranges, huge and mysterious volcanic craters, sleepy island villages—and commercial development so grotesque and massive and rampant that the entire natural environment seems perpetually on the brink of destruction. In all its splendid isolation—and also largely because of that splendid isolation—Hawaii stands as a dramatic land of contradictions that represent both the best and the worst of the modern world's possibilities.

BIBLIOGRAPHY

Cooper, George, and Gavan Daws. *Land and Power in Hawaii: The Democratic Years* (1985).

Culliney, John L. *Islands in a Far Sea: Nature and Man in Hawaii* (1988).

Fuchs, Lawrence H. *Hawaii Pono: A Social History* (1961).

Hawaii Department of Business and Economic Development. *The State of Hawaii Data Book* (annual).

Joesting, Edward. *Hawaii: An Uncommon History* (1972).

Kameʻeleihiwa, Lilikala. *Native Lands and Foreign Desires* (1991).

Kuykendall, Ralph S. *The Hawaiian Kingdom, 1778–1893.* 3 vols. (1938–1967).

Parker, Linda S. *Native American Estate: The Struggle over Indian and Hawaiian Lands* (1989).

Stannard, David E. *Before the Horror: The Population of Hawaiʻi on the Eve of Western Contact* (1989).

Part VII

SPACE AND PLACE

THE NATURAL ENVIRONMENT: THE NORTH

Donald Worster

OVER THE PAST four centuries no part of the global environment has been changed more dramatically than the northern United States. What once was a vast forest and grassland inhabited by a native farming and hunting folk has been transformed into the world's largest industrial complex, supporting a dense population of more than one hundred million people linked in a network of sprawling megalopolises and satellite farms and towns. Bears once roamed across what is now the island of Manhattan, loons swam on the ponds of Connecticut, and dark, drifting herds of bison and elk grazed from Chicago to Pittsburgh. Now the only glimpse most northerners have of wild animals comes around the backyard birdfeeder or from a two-week vacation into the countryside. Nature is still a powerful force in their lives, but it has become more impersonal and distant to the point of invisibility: drought lowering the water level in a city reservoir, fungus attacking a corn crop, ice glazing a sidewalk. Nature has yielded an enormous wealth to Americans, but the cost of affluence has been a drastic impoverishment of the natural environment and a high degree of abstractness in human ecological relationships.

The region called the North is more a cultural than a natural entity, defined as it was by the Civil War, but there are some environmental unities to be found. Fronting the Atlantic Ocean in a myriad of bays, islands, and sandy beaches, the North stretches west all the way to the 98th meridian (which passes through the states of North and South Dakota, Nebraska, and Kansas), where the rainfall drops below 20 inches (500 millimeters), too low for European-style agriculture. The Ohio River suggests a southern boundary. Separating the North from Canada is that other "seacoast," the Saint Lawrence River–Great Lakes complex, the largest body of fresh water on earth, which once offered a rich fishery and an indispensable doorway into the continental interior.

Over the past million years this region has been repeatedly scoured by glaciers that penetrated as far south as Long Island in the east and the Missouri River in the west. Only a few areas like Pennsylvania escaped those grinding forces. As the glaciers retreated (the last did so about ten thousand years ago), they left behind a landscape of gravelly moraines, denuded mountains, potholes, and lakes, and a vast till sheet that was thin in New England but hundreds of feet thick in the Midwest. On this foundation both the native and immigrant peoples would build their civilizations.

THE IMPACT OF EUROPEAN ARRIVAL

When the Europeans arrived, they found growing over much of this glaciated soil a luxuriant forest, one of the greatest in the world, as extensive as that of Brazil today. Ecologists divide the early forest into two broad provinces, more or less arranged in horizontal bands across the map: the northern or transition forest, comprising coniferous trees—hemlock, balsam fir, white pine—and such deciduous species as the sugar maple, American basswood, and yellow birch; and the mixed deciduous forest, populated by at least thirty major species, ranging from oaks, hickories, and maples to yellow poplar, white ash, chestnut, and black cherry. Accounts differ as to how thick those early forests were; some observers found them dark and gloomy, others open and parklike, a condition they attributed to Indian burning practices. Unquestionably, the natives fired them to encourage new grass growth and draw their prey closer to their habitations and to open up clearings of such cultivars as corn, beans, pumpkins, and tobacco. The northern environment supported hundreds of thousands of these first Americans, and at least one large city, Cahokia, in present-day Illinois, long before the white people came.

But despite these important human presences, the European newcomers were most impressed by the extent and grandeur, the power and richness, of the forest. They called it a "wilderness," meaning a nature beyond human control, inhabited by dangerous creatures; and in the minds of early Puritan clergymen, that howling wilderness became a common metaphor for an ungodly, unruly world needing Christian cultivation. Paradoxically, that same wilderness appealed to poor refugees from a Europe that had cleared away much of its own forest many centuries earlier. They found in the New World an endless supply of the most important natural resource, after soil, that they needed to create a prosperous life for themselves: wood. The forest provided plenty of fuel, and they cut immense woodpiles to keep themselves warm through the long northern winters. The forest also offered building materials for their houses, barns, churches, and fences, as well as for an overflowing cornucopia of the miscellaneous necessities of life—plows, rakes, bowls, ladles, wagons, gristmills, boats and ships, foodstuffs like game, sugar and nuts, pegs, caskets, bridges—even coins. The first promise of American abundance came from the forest, a promise that would take centuries of use to spoil and deplete.

Everywhere they went the European Americans tried to recreate the agricultural environment they had left behind in the Old World. They divided the country into estates of private property, irregularly shaped at first, following the contours of river and hill, but west of the Appalachians more regularized by federal surveyors, who imposed a rigid cadastral (property boundary) grid on the diverse lay of the land. To populate their properties the invading farmers introduced not only familiar crops and weeds but also a horde of domesticated animals, including sheep, cattle, pigs, and horses, all of which would radically alter the indigenous vegetation and fauna. They chopped down trees at a prodigious rate; before 1850 Americans cleared over 100 million acres (40 million hectares), and in the peak decade of clearance, 1850 to 1859, cleared almost 40 million acres (16 million hectares) more. These changes in the landscape, made with so little restraint, so little sense of what was being lost, added up to an ecological revolution. Whole species became extinct, such as the passenger pigeon, which once migrated in flocks as thick as clouds, as noisy as thunder, flocks numbering, by one reckon-

ing, as many as four billion birds. Wild turkeys, beaver, wolves, mountain lions, wolverines, caribou, even deer disappeared. By the mid nineteenth century almost every acre in the state of Massachusetts had been cut over at least once, and men and women began to feel the pinch of scarcity. Wood, land, and game alike were harder and harder to come by cheaply.

Farther west the forest thinned naturally, making axes increasingly unnecessary, until eventually in Illinois, southern Minnesota, Iowa, northern Missouri, Kansas, Nebraska, and the Dakotas the landscape became the tall-grass prairie, almost devoid of trees. Away from the wooded river valleys the vegetation was dominated by big bluestem and Indian grass, both growing up to 8 feet high (2.5 meters), and by switchgrass. This was an environment that their European agricultural heritage did not prepare white farmers to settle or understand. Some wondered whether it offered a fertility equal to forest soils. Others argued that the grassland would have been covered with trees too if the Indians had not burned it, a view that held some truth but underestimated the role of a drier climate. Whatever the origin of the grassland, it posed a challenge to a society used to enjoying and exploiting a wealth of forests. Although the grassland would eventually offer its own kind of natural abundance, soils of far greater depth and humus content than those of the forest, settlers would take a while to discover that fact and turn it to their advantage. Had it not been for a continuing boom in Europe's population, forcing millions to look abroad for their living, that discovery might have been delayed indefinitely.

THE FORCE OF INDUSTRIAL CAPITALISM

But a force beyond demography was pushing the white settlers forward in their relation to the land, the force of a rising and expanding industrial capitalism, which would profoundly alter people's use of nature in America and throughout the world. Its greatest achievement, and yet its most destructive, was to develop new sources of energy that could run factories, run railroads, and run the commodities of the land back and forth to consumers. The first such source was falling water, the second was anthracite coal. Together, they far overshadowed the old energy supply provided by the animal muscle power of humans and their beasts of burden, a form of energy that had always been severely limited by the quantity of food that could be raised in the growing season and stored for winter. That old source of energy remained as confining in North America, notwithstanding the abundance of wood, as it had been in other societies. Not until the nineteenth century did a rising group of engineers and entrepreneurs figure out how to escape the limits of muscle power, and thus remove all constraint on ambition. They did so by exploiting water and the fossil fuels, and as a consequence of that energy breakthrough the North left behind the old local, rural household economy of wood and soil and moved into a vastly more affluent life which drew its resources from the most distant corners of the continent and beyond.

The emergence of an industrial mode of production is conventionally dated to the mid 1830s, when northerners began to see for the first time a significant improvement in their per capita income. But during the preceding forty years they learned how to harness the power of rivers running from the mountains to the sea. Their most impressive achievements came along the Merrimack, which had its headwaters in the White Mountains of New Hampshire, where an abundance of rain and snow fell. In 1822 a group of Boston entrepreneurs came to the river's banks and began to construct the factory town of Lowell; within a few years they had managed to gain control of virtually the entire watershed, setting up on site after site their coordinated system of dams, canals, overshot waterwheels, multistoried factory buildings, and female laborers to manufacture cotton cloth. The system spread throughout the Northeast, and everywhere the outcome was devastating for anyone who depended on rivers in their natural state. The milldams stopped anadromous fish like salmon from migrating upstream to spawn, and they flooded the low-lying meadows used for fodder. With more and more people living and working along their banks, the rivers became increasingly polluted by sewage, forcing towns to look far and wide for fresh, safe water supplies. In order to exploit the kinetic energy of New England's rivers the early industrial capitalists had literally to take them apart and extract their power, a process they could not accomplish, given the technology at hand, without nearly killing them as ecosystems.

There were not many Merrimack Rivers around, however, and the potential of water power was soon exhausted. Every rivulet had its full complement of gristmills, and every large stream its facto-

ries for making cloth, shoes, wooden implements, or whatever. Move beyond the mountainous terrain into the Ohio and Mississippi River valleys, moreover, and the prospects of a new energy abundance become dimmer; the rivers there were too wide and flood-prone, too gradual in their fall, to harness. Fortunately for the advocates of economic growth, another energy breakthrough occurred that would make that flatter, more open country the heartland of modern industry.

THE COMING OF COAL

Americans had before them the model of Great Britain, which, after exhausting its own wood and water-power resources, had turned to burning coal, mined at great depths in the ground. Coal mining, it was said, produces manufacturing, and manufacturing produces railways, and railways produce money. If the equation worked in Britain, it ought to work in the United States too. The new nation had a great deal of coal, both hard anthracite and soft bituminous, formed in peat deposits 250 million years ago, but most of it tended to be found in rugged, inaccessible Appalachian mountain valleys, where the beds lay folded and pitched by geological processes. How to get that coal dug out and carried to markets was the challenge. The markets, moreover, were mainly limited to urban consumers in Philadelphia and Baltimore, who, unable to buy enough wood for home heating, sought coal to burn in their Franklin stoves. Anthracite, though it burns long and hot, is very difficult to ignite, so householders were reluctant to turn to it as long as they could get soft coal from the riverbanks of Virginia. So if Americans wanted to follow the British model, they had to reverse the formula: they had to find capital to establish mines, develop transportation, encourage a market among iron foundries and manufacturers, and only then would the coal bring wealth and power. This was the challenge facing capitalists, and they soon appeared with solutions as they had in New England.

In the late 1820s and early 1830s the critical breakthrough to large-scale anthracite use occurred, and the North started down the road toward a fossil-fuel economy. Three major canals—the Pennsylvania Main Line, the Chesapeake and Ohio, and the Lehigh—were dug in those years, connecting the anthracite coalfields of eastern Pennsylvania with New York and Philadelphia, ports from which it was shipped up and down the seaboard. By 1837 the coal carried on those canals reached nearly 900,000 tons. Almost overnight an incredible source of energy had materialized for both household and industrial consumption, and at prices cheaper than wood, charcoal, or even that inferior Virginia bituminous. Great fortunes were waiting to be made, and coal towns like Scranton, Wilkes-Barre, Hazleton, Pottsville, and Shamokin began to appear on the map, representing an entirely new relationship with nature. From this point on people drew their energy from places they had never been and most likely would never see, and from a living world that had long ago died and been buried. Consumers depended on capitalists and their employees to extract that energy and bring it to them. All of them lived by mining, which is to say, by depleting. By 1859 other entrepreneurs had located a new fossil fuel called petroleum, or "rock oil." Together, these two black smelly substances, coal and oil, both erupting from the bowels of the Pennsylvania earth, would change the American landscape more profoundly than any force since the glaciers.

The fossil fuels helped towns and cities begin to grow at a phenomenal rate, but especially those engaged in manufacturing, which now had the energy to greatly expand their plants and hire more workers. By the early 1850s the factory had become largely an urban institution. Cities grew up around factories. They grew rapidly outward as coal allowed the mass production of iron, which in turn could be worked into railways and locomotives, streetcars and trams, the means of rapid transportation from suburb to downtown. Cities also began to grow upward as coal was used in the manufacture of steel, and inexpensive steel offered a wonderful new structural material for urban buildings, higher and stronger than wood or bricks could ever be. Coal became the very lifeblood of the northern metropolis as it was of the new economy.

By the middle of the nineteenth century, new metropolises were rising on the western side of the Appalachian mountain chain: Pittsburgh (which had its own ample supplies of coal), Cincinnati, Cleveland, and, above all, Chicago, the key city of the inland "coast" and the center (especially after it began to rebuild following the great fire of 1871) of an expanding commercial and industrial empire. Over all of them hung the polluted air of coal-burning chimneys and blast furnaces. Americans generally, from miners toiling deep in the tunnels to the conductors collecting tickets on the railroads, now had to endure smoke and coal dust penetrating their lungs and causing disease, as well as polluted water in their lakes and rivers. This new man-made environment was hardly healthy for the masses of people. By way of compensation they stood at the receiving end of a complex, far-flung system of food and raw-material production, one that seemed to be boundless in capacity. Cheap energy brought them corn and wheat from what had been the tall-grass prairie, meat and hides from as far away as Montana and Texas rangelands, oysters from Long Island Sound, whalebone from the Arctic, wine from France, sugar from Louisiana and Hawaii. The old giddy sense of living in the midst of extraordinary natural abundance began to give way to a fantasy of a technological horn of plenty, much more impressive, some thought, than any forest or prairie could be.

THE FATE OF THE FOREST

The fate of the northern forest in this new era of cheap, abundant fossil-fuel energy deserves particular notice. As coal began to replace wood as the primary source of energy—a point achieved by 1870—and iron began to replace wood in tools, machinery, and bridges, and as people began to live more and more in cities where the only trees they saw were the few that had been planted, the forest was no longer so prominent in the popular imagination. But, remarkably, the old deforestation continued apace, though now it was lumber companies doing much of the cutting, and the lumber was to construct housing for the masses.

Towering above all the other northern trees was the white pine, *Pinus strobus,* whose range extended from New Brunswick to Minnesota and down the Appalachians to Georgia. According to one estimate, there were over 100 billion commercially usable board feet of this tree standing in the primeval forest of Indian America. Over large areas it formed pure or nearly pure stands, and in the most favorable settings could reach over 200 feet (60 meters) tall. Its wood, especially in the more northern zones, was strong, light, durable, and easily worked—a good tree to go after—and here again capitalists were not reluctant. By 1837 there were, so Henry David Thoreau noted in *The Maine Woods* (1864), 250 sawmills on the Penobscot River north of Bangor, Maine, an area that became the cradle of the northern lumber industry. Their equipment was primitive—water-powered saws, human-powered axes, oxen teams, and the rivers themselves as a means of transportation—but it was effective. By 1860 the best stands of Maine pine trees had been cut, and the lumberjacks were forced to turn to spruce. Some simply picked up and went west to find virgin stands in New York State, then in Pennsylvania, and then in the extensive Great Lakes pineries, where they settled down for a few years to reduce the forests to shingles and boards.

The Saginaw Valley of Michigan had some of the best pine forests on the continent, and there were more such growths north of there all the way to the Upper Peninsula. Lumber crews arrived to do the cutting in winter, skidding the logs over the frozen ground to streamside; when spring arrived and the ice went out, they dumped the logs into the rivers and floated them down to saw mills on Lake Huron or Lake Michigan. Ships, and later railroads, carried the sawed lumber to Chicago and other cities and to farmsteads scattered across the land. Inevitably under such market demand, the supply of trees had to run out here too, and by 1900 the fabled North Woods had become the Cutover—a wasteland of stumps, slash and debris, clogged rivers, and ready tinder waiting for fire. A slash fire broke out at Peshtigo, Wisconsin, in 1871 killing fifteen hundred people, and others followed in quick succession, until the Cutover had become in truth the Burntover.

As the forests were depleted, the lumber companies once more packed up to leave, some going to the Pacific Northwest, others to the South. The deforested land they abandoned was unfit for agriculture, unlike the cleared acres of Ohio, and it was left to regenerate itself as best it could. A full century later the primeval grandeur has still not come back to the country. Hardly anyone who had bought Great Lakes pine ever anticipated this lingering consequence; they seldom saw the men who cut the forest down, or the mess they left, or the fires they created. As consumers, they knew pine trees only as a pile of two-by-fours at the lumber yard, just as they knew wheat only as fine white flour purchased in a coarse cloth sack or a range cow as a restaurant steak. Without cheap fossil-fuel energy, that distancing of people from the land would have been impossible to achieve so completely. On the plus side, the new order of ecological relationships meant that daily life was easier in many ways and food and housing less expensive in labor or cash. But on the negative side, the growing distance between people and their natural environment left them more irresponsible and complacent about their impact.

THE AUTOMOBILE AGE

By the 1870s large industrial corporations dominated the natural as they did the human environment. They alone could afford the new technology of production that sprang from the minds of inventors like Thomas Edison and George Westinghouse. As a result, they also came to own most of the country's resources. The corporation called Swift and Company, for example, founded by Gustavus Swift, a New England farm boy who became one of Chicago's greatest meatpackers, bought plains cattle by the millions and put them through a "disassembly line" that took their carcasses apart—and then bought ice-filled refrigerator cars that carried the meat to East Coast butcher shops. By 1900 such vertically integrated corporations were responsible for two-thirds of all the goods manufactured in the United States. As these economic institutions grew larger and larger (U.S. Steel started in 1901 with $1.4 billion of capital), they needed whole armies of workers. Thus began a vast influx of job-seekers, abandoning the rural countryside and swelling the size of the industrial cities. The population of New York City and its environs grew from less than 1 million in 1860 to more than 3 million in 1900. By 1920 a majority of Americans lived in urban areas of two thousand five hundred people or more.

After World War I the region entered the automobile age, both as manufacturer and consumer, and the implications for the natural world were profound. Detroit and its satellites became, after Henry Ford built his immense assembly plant at River Rouge, the mouth of an octopus that stretched its tentacles toward natural resources in every area of the continent and overseas—toward steel, wood, wool, rubber, copper, aluminum, plastic, even soybeans for making auto bodies. Putting society into private automobiles demanded more resources from the earth than any other technology in history. The coming of the automobile also led to the opening up of roads into the most remote areas, then paving and lining them with service stations, billboards, and hot-dog stands; down the roads came a flood of city dwellers looking for homes in the country. The products of the land began to move in the opposite lanes toward urban markets by means of an enormous fleet of trucks, all burning, as did the automobiles, great quantities of gasoline. Even the farms came to run essentially on this volatile fuel; by 1970, raising a single acre of corn in Illinois required the equivalent of 80 gallons (300 liters) of gasoline for plowing, cultivating, drying, harvesting, and shipping to the processor. So dependent were people on their cars, trucks, and tractors, so accustomed were they to expecting an abundance of energy in the form of coal-generated electricity as well as gasoline-driven transportation, that they became the world leaders in consuming fossil fuel. The consequences of that fact could be seen in the explosive growth of shopping malls, power lines, and refineries that spilled out of cities across the landscape.

THE EFFECTS OF POLLUTION

Less obvious for a long time were the slowly accumulating effects of pollution on the atmosphere. Burning coal and gasoline put into the air a number of pollutants, such as sulfur and carbon, that might better have been left in the ground. The rain that fell over northern lakes and mountains became polluted with sulfur, forming sulfuric acid, which killed trees and aquatic life. The carbon in the fossil fuels turned into carbon dioxide, which began to increase significantly as an atmospheric gas, leading many scientists to warn of a "greenhouse effect" in which the sun's radiation would be trapped by the gas, warming the planet by three to five degrees centigrade, and causing a dangerous uncertainty in the climate. Nebraska might become another west Texas, and New York another Alabama, if profligate use of the fossil fuels continued.

By the end of the twentieth century the daily litany of insults to the natural environment reported in the news were overwhelming and amounted to a deadly critique of modern industrial society. Lake Erie was nearly dead from pollution, New York City had no place to dump its garbage, much of Iowa's groundwater was undrinkable because of nitrates from fertilizer, Pennsylvanians were worried about the radioactive effects of a near-meltdown of the nuclear power plant at Three Mile Island, and songbird populations were plummeting along the East Coast due to real estate development. Everywhere there were crowds of people trying to go in the same direction or use the same water: Massachusetts had, by 1985, more people per square mile

than the Netherlands; New Jersey more than Japan or India; even Indiana had a higher population density than several Central American countries. As depressing as those facts might seem, they had to be confronted if the region was to understand fully what its history had been and what it had produced. Suddenly, it seemed to many observers, the very principles and institutions of an industrial capitalist society had to be questioned—notions of unlimited economic growth, liberal immigration, mass advertising to boost consumption, aggressive market freedom, and global trade.

All the news was not bad. Set over against the mounting evidence of environmental decline were a number of hopeful trends, chief among them the growth of an environmental concern that was as old and active as any in the world. The North had been a seedbed of such concern since the days of Henry David Thoreau (1817–1862) and George Perkins Marsh (1801–1882), a Vermont-born leader in conservation and the author of the path-breaking book, *Man and Nature,* published in 1864. What bothered them most at that early date was the heedless deforestation of New England, "breaking up the floor and wainscoting and doors and window frames of our dwelling," as Marsh put it, "for fuel to warm our bodies and seethe our pottage" (1965 ed., p. 52). Their warnings would be followed by those of John Muir (1838–1914), who left a pioneer farm in Wisconsin for California, where he founded the Sierra Club; by Frederick Law Olmsted (1822–1903) the designer of Central Park in New York and a major influence on the national park movement; by Gifford Pinchot (1865–1946) who as chief of the Division of Forestry in the Department of Agriculture from 1898 to 1910 put the national forest system together; by two environmentally active presidents, Theodore Roosevelt and Franklin Roosevelt; and by Aldo Leopold (1886–1948), an Iowan who did more than any other individual to create the new profession of wildlife management and who gave the country the idea of a "land ethic," which called on citizens to expand their moral horizons beyond society to include the preservation of the natural world, the diverse biological heritage that had been delivered into American hands. In 1962 this tradition of environmental reform took a disturbing new direction with the publication of *Silent Spring,* by Rachel Carson (1907–1964), a woman who had grown up in western Pennsylvania and was moved to write by reports of the harm that the pesticide DDT was causing to wildlife and people. Out of Brooklyn came the scientist-activist

Barry Commoner, a critic of the pollution caused by profit-seeking corporations. All these regional voices contributed to a tradition of organized political action to achieve nature preservation and improve public health, and by the 1990s it had millions of supporters, some of them protesting toxic dumping in Buffalo's Love Canal, or sewage floating in Boston's harbor, or strip-mining of coal in West Virginia. Their common theme was that the natural environment is more limited, scarce, and vulnerable than a long history of easy abundance and industrial dependency had prepared Americans to see.

Inevitably, however, their message had to be a lament for what had been lost in the drive for power and prosperity and an urgent, often shrill sermon on ecological responsibility for a people whose very institutions had made freedom from responsibility a way of life.

What was surprising, and often difficult to keep in view, was how much of the original beauty and diversity of the natural environment survived— whether by public action or natural tenacity—the ravages of economic development. Unlike the tropical rainforests, the woods of the North did manage to return over large areas, and a state like Massachusetts, heavily populated though it was, could boast that two-thirds of its area had reverted to forest. One could stand on Fairhaven Cliff in Thoreau's Concord, look in all directions of the compass, and see hardly a rooftop among the sea of trees. With the return of the forest came black bears—over three hundred of them in that state in 1990—along with deer, beaver, even coyotes and a stray moose or two. The major reason for that regeneration was that agriculture had almost completely disappeared from the state; by the last decade of the century, Massachusetts was importing 85 percent of its food,

much of it from what had been the grasslands. Yet, out there where the food was produced, little regeneration of nature was permitted; less than 1 percent of the tall-grass prairie is left today, and almost none of what is left is publicly protected.

Elsewhere, the federal government has used a small part of its gargantuan wealth to preserve remnants of the natural heritage in the form of parks, forests, and seashores. On the coast of Maine, for instance, Acadia National Park can provide a reasonably good sense of the pristine landscape that the French explorer Samuel de Champlain saw in 1604. On Isle Royale National Park in Lake Superior, the gray wolf still can be heard howling at the moon on crusty winter nights. The largest wilderness left in the region is the one set aside by New Yorkers in 1885, the Adirondack State Park, and a hundred years after its founding the state is still seeking to enlarge it for a growing population to experience a nature left to its own rhythms. Even near the dense metropolises of New York and Chicago one can find such natural areas as lakeshore dunes, riverine forests, and quaking bogs complete with frogs and muskrats. And the once-majestic Mississippi, dammed and locked and barge-laden though it is, still offers substantial stretches of quiet water, where eagles soar overhead, catfish rise to the surface, a mink prowls along the bank looking for dinner.

Nature may have moved to the edges of our predominantly urban imagination so that it is no longer the vivid, immediate force that confronted our ancestors; and as self-determining ecosystem or wild landscape, much of it may have disappeared under the heavy wheels of agricultural and industrial progress; but even after four hundred years of radical change it has not altogether vanished from our presence, our memory, or our fate.

BIBLIOGRAPHY

Cayton, Andrew R. L., and Peter S. Onuf. *The Midwest and the Nation* (1990).

Cronon, William. *Changes in the Land: Indians, Colonists, and the Ecology of New England* (1983).

———. *Nature's Metropolis: Chicago and the West, 1848–1893* (1991).

Dunlap, Thomas R. *DDT: Scientists, Citizens, and Public Policy* (1981).

———. *Saving America's Wildlife* (1988).

Flader, Susan L., ed. *The Great Lakes Forest: An Environmental and Social History* (1983).

Hays, Samuel P. *Conservation and the Gospel of Efficiency: The Progressive Conservation Movement, 1890–1920* (1959).

———. *Beauty, Health, and Permanence: Environmental Politics in the United States, 1955–1985* (1987).

Johnson, Hildegard Binder. *Order upon the Land: The U.S. Rectangular Survey and the Upper Mississippi Country* (1976).

Melosi, Martin V. *Coping with Abundance: Energy and Environment in Industrial America* (1985).

Merchant, Carolyn. *Ecological Revolutions: Nature, Gender, and Science in New England* (1989).

Miller, Donald L., and Richard E. Sharpless. *The Kingdom of Coal: Work, Enterprise, and Ethnic Communities in the Mine Fields* (1985).

Nash, Roderick. *Wilderness and the American Mind* 3d ed. (1982).

Pyne, Stephen J. *Fire in America: A Cultural History of Wildland and Rural Fire* (1982).

Scarpino, Philip V. *Great River: An Environmental History of the Upper Mississippi, 1890–1950* (1985).

Steinberg, Theodore. *Nature Incorporated: Industrialization and the Waters of New England* (1991).

Vietor, Richard H. K. *Environmental Politics and the Coal Coalition* (1980).

Williams, Michael. *Americans and Their Forests: A Historical Geography* (1989).

SEE ALSO **The Great Lakes Industrial Region; The Great Plains; Industrialization; Landscape; The Middle Atlantic Region; National Parks and Preservation; New England; The Upper Midwest; Urbanization.**

THE NATURAL ENVIRONMENT: THE SOUTH

Mart A. Stewart

THE DEFINITION OF the South as a region owes much more to culture than to geography. No natural feature or combination of features demarcate or bound the South as a distinctive environmental region. Quite the contrary, two of the distinguishing geographical features of the region, the Mississippi River and the Appalachian Mountains, link the South to other regions and repeat ecosystems found as far away as Canada. The southern climate in general has a distinctive cast, but a visitor can find New England winters in the Great Smoky Mountains and tropical summers in Florida. Though some features and characteristics of the natural environment of the South are unique to the region—the Mississippi Delta and the Okefenokee Swamp, for example, have no counterparts elsewhere in North America—culture, not nature, has determined the region's boundaries and distinctiveness.

People have usually used the land on a much more local than regional scale, and most modifications of the land—previous to the mid twentieth century—were discernible mainly on the local level. Southern society in the long duration has developed within certain broad contours, however, that have remained relatively unchanged. These physiographic traits have given structure and character to the larger history of the mutual development of culture and nature in the region.

Several features dominate the physical character of the South: a long coastline, backed by an extension of the continental shelf—the Coastal Plain—connects land and sea on the edge of the southeastern and lower South. The eastern and southeastern portion of this plain breaks at an ancient coastline—at the "fall line"—into a series of foothills, the Piedmont, where both soil and climate change. The Appalachian mountains create both relief and barrier in the topography of the region, and extend the range of montane conifers into a deciduous woodlands region. The Appalachians consist of three formations with different histories: the

Blue Ridge, which is the backbone of the mountains and has the highest elevations; the "valley and ridge," a series of parallel flat, fertile valleys separated by sharp, folded ridges to the west of the Blue Ridge; and the Appalachian Plateau, the knobby hill country of West Virginia, Kentucky, Tennessee, and northern Alabama.

Mountains, piedmont, and plain are cut through and connected by several major rivers: the Roanoke, Shenandoah, Santee, Savannah, Altamaha, Chattahoochee, Alabama, and Tombigbee. Other important rivers connect the southern hinterland to the Mississippi: the Red, Arkansas, Missouri, Tennessee, Cumberland, and Yazoo. The Mississippi River and the alluvial valley it has created constitute yet another central feature. The Mississippi, because of both size and periodic floods, adds a waterfront and dynamic physical force to the region.

The western reaches of the South merge with the Central Lowlands of North America, which stretch from the Appalachians to the Rockies. The relief of the southern portion of this vast plain is cut through by the Mississippi and raised up by the Ozark and Ouachita mountains. For several cultural reasons, the Balcones Escarpment in central Texas, which marks the eastern boundary of the High Plains, has been regarded as the physiographic boundary between South and West.

The soils of the South vary with topography and locale, but have had several general characteristics. Though the Mason-Dixon line was not drawn to mark the southern advance of the glaciers, the soils south of the line are different from northern soils because they escaped the last glaciation. Southern soils do not have the topsoil of minerals ground mostly to dust by ice nor, like midwestern soils, the deep loess carried by wind from nearby glacial regions. They are old soils, in a region where high rainfall, humidity, and temperatures favor rapid decomposition of organic matter and leaching of soil minerals, and therefore tend to be acidic, low in humus content, and do not store water well. Within this general profile, many variations are prominent. Soils of the Coastal Plain, for example, often have higher proportions of sand—depositions from ancient advances of the sea—and lose organic material by leaching even more rapidly than Piedmont soils with their higher proportion of clay. The soils of the restless Mississippi River valley, by contrast, are constantly new, made up of layerings of sediments carried by water down the enormous watershed of the Mississippi.

The influential historian of the South, U. B. Phillips, claimed that it has been the weather that has made the South distinctive. The Southern climate has, indeed, been conducive to certain adaptations unique to the region. In general, summers are hot, winters are mild, and growing seasons range from an average of two hundred days in all but the higher elevations of the uplands, to two hundred and seventy days along the coast. Most of the South receives more than thirty inches (750 millimeters) of rainfall annually, but quantities vary in time and space.

The heat and humidity of a southern summer often impart the hazy quality to the vegetation of the region that W. J. Cash described in *The Mind of the South*: "blurring every outline and rending every object vague and problematical." The lush vegetation that has covered most of the region has been a changing mosaic with distinct boundaries, however, that can be clearly defined. Most of the South shares a dominant temperate deciduous vegetation with the rest of the eastern woodlands. The most widespread association in the deciduous forest in the South has been the oak-hickory, which dominates the forests along the Piedmont south into the Gulf Coast states, west to central Texas, and north to Minnesota. In the Piedmont the mature stands of oak and hickory have been and are sometimes very dense; in east Texas trees grade into grasslands.

Species of oak and hickory are usually mixed with pine in the Piedmont and Gulf states. In the area that became Georgia, for example, the presettlement Piedmont forest probably consisted of thirty-five to forty percent hardwood stands— mainly oak and hickory—forty-five percent mixed pine-hardwood stands, and fifteen percent pine stands. Pine is particularly suited to the infertile, porous soil throughout the region, especially around and below the "fall line," and was also maintained by fires caused by lightning or people. Much of the Coastal Plain has been covered by a broad band of

pine barrens that separated the maritime forests of the coast and the deciduous forests of the Piedmont. These pine forests have been remarkably uniform in composition, broken only by swampy areas and open savannas. On the other hand, the coastal forests—dominated by cypress, tupelo, and oak on the floodplains, and by magnolia, holly, laurel oak, and bay elsewhere—are unusually varied, because of the variety in moisture and nutrient conditions on the floodplains, in tidewater marshes and swamps, and on elevated hammocks and ridges throughout the coastal area. Other exceptional mixes of vegetation—for example, the subtropical forests of southern Florida and the temperate conifer forests of high altitudes in the Great Smokies— can be found in several parts of the South.

ENVIRONMENT AND SOCIETY IN THE PRECONTACT SOUTH

At the time Europeans came to this part of North America, Native Americans had been living in the river valleys and along the coast of the region for millennia. Most Indians in the region had an economy based firmly on horticulture, with maize, beans, and squash as the main crops, and supplemented by hunting, fishing, and gathering. All these practices shaped the land, sometimes profoundly, and created a unique landscape that reflected the settlement patterns and land use practices of the people of the oldest South.

Village sites and fields for growing crops required open spaces, and Indians created these by girdling trees and burning off underbrush and grasses. The combined effects of clearing and of gathering wood for fuel resulted in some deforestation. When Indians abandoned fields with declining fertility and took up new ones nearby, the old fields—called "tallahasees" by the Creeks—grew up in grasses, shrubs, and sun-loving species of young trees in the early stages of forest succession. Many Indian communities sometimes broadcast-burned the vicinity of the village to destroy vermin and weeds and to open up the landscape. This also favored mixed grasslands and young forests, and the deer, rabbits, turkey, grouse, and quail that live in such habitats. These animals remained wild, but Indians created a local environment that favored their survival within easy hunting distances. When the fields and firewood in a particular area played out, Indians moved their villages, usually not far from the earlier site. When Indians located their vil-

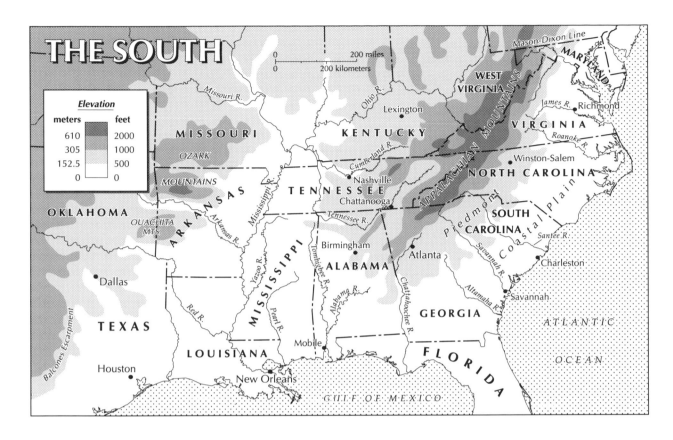

lages on the more fertile terraces along southern rivers they greatly extended the length of occupation, but used the surrounding forest land in the same ways. In the hands of the natives of the region, village locales became a hodgepodge of old fields, open spaces, shrublands, and young forests.

Indian-set fires thinned out some forest beyond recovery and extended the range of grasslands. The anomalous expanse of prairie in western Kentucky that was later colonized by European bluegrass, for example, was probably created by Indian burnings. The creation of prairies in turn created an environment for the bison, which moved from west of the region into the southeast during the late prehistoric period. Fires—many of them set by Indians—changed the vegetation composition of the forests to the extent that in some areas fire-tolerant species, such as longleaf, loblolly, and slash pine, became dominant. The pine forests, and the savannas and prairies that made up the "natural" landscape of the South when Europeans arrived, were largely a consequence of the Indian use of fire.

A parklike forest through which a man on horseback could gallop without impediment, partly created by Indian fires, greeted the first European explorers to the region. When disease microorganisms, packed to North America by explorers and colonists, killed natives who had no immunity to them, the natural environments of the area were opened up even more to the newcomers. They put the land to different uses and soon produced another landscape.

COLONIZATION AND DEVELOPMENT OF A PLANTATION LANDSCAPE

A variety of motives propelled Europeans to the New World, but the most common was the desire for profit. The Spanish in Florida sought to save Indian souls, but also wanted to consolidate a wealth-producing colony. The English who came to the South to trade and settle were even more determined to extract local resources and to produce valuable commodities. The climate made English-

1155

style farming difficult in the region, and colonists had to find new means for subsistence and profit. The market economy that was developing around the Atlantic drove them in this adventure and conditioned their perceptions of the environment they sought to inhabit and to exploit. Timber, furs, deerskins, and ginseng became valuable in whatever quantities they could be procured. Colonists justified by the same rationale the transformation of portions of the natural environment for the production of naval stores, livestock, tobacco, indigo, and rice.

The English also regarded "wild" environments as inferior landscapes, and sought to civilize them with "improvements." Buildings, roads, fences, and cultivated fields established in tangible form English conceptions of property, brought order to the environment, and mirrored the countryside at home. Moreover, the English used the apparent failure of Indians to "improve" the land as a justification for appropriating it from them.

By the mid eighteenth century, the colonists had created a characteristic landscape of plantations, villages, small farms, and cowpens in Virginia, North Carolina, South Carolina, and Georgia. African slaves did most of the clearing and cultivating, girdling and firing trees much as Native Americans had. They herded cattle on the open range in South Carolina and Georgia, erected the hydraulic systems of banks, canals, and drains for tidewater rice plantations in the southeastern Atlantic tidewater, and planted, tended, harvested, and processed plantation crops throughout the colonies.

Staple-crop production expanded in the nineteenth century. Eli Whitney's invention of the cotton gin in 1793, and a market for cotton among British, and later, American textile manufacturers, rapidly made short-strand cotton the most important staple crop in the South, and assured the expansion of the plantation system. The spread of row-crop monoculture etched the plantation landscape into a larger proportion of the region, and the Cotton South took shape. By the 1820s and 1830s, production had become significant west of the Appalachians in the rich prairie lands—the black belt—of central Alabama and Mississippi, on alluvial river bottoms, and on uplands throughout the region, and this area became "southern" in character. Southern rivers—especially the Mississippi—were essential to this growth, linking cotton ports on the rivers to ocean ports. By 1860 three-fourths of the area's cotton was moving on the South's river sys-

tem through Mobile, New Orleans, and the young Texas ports.

Plantation agriculture altered profoundly some parts of the natural environment. On cultivated lands, the removal of ground cover and monoculture made soils vulnerable to erosion. When planters had their slaves plow instead of using the hoe to prepare the ground, soils eroded even more quickly. Within a few short years after planters in the Chesapeake shifted from producing tobacco with hoe culture to growing wheat on plowed lands, for example, some streams were closed to navigation because of silting. Row-crop agriculture that "skimmed" the land also destroyed soil fertility, made floods and droughts more common, and modified the southern landscape by changing the relationships between ecosystems.

Large areas of the South remained uncultivated—nearly eighty percent of the region in 1860—and forests, wetlands, and savannahs were more common on the antebellum landscape than plantations, farms, and cultivated fields. Little of this land was unused, however. Small farmers and hill folk ranged cattle on wiregrass savannahs and in canebrakes, and hogs in mast-bearing deciduous woods. They hunted and gathered food in the untilled environment near their homes, and also burned the woods—in much of the South this was an early spring ritual—to destroy insects and improve forest understory and savannah browse for their cattle. Southerners also selectively used all kinds of woods from the region's forests for an array of purposes—cypress and cedars for shingles; hardwoods for staves and hoops, fences, and shipbuilding; and pine for scantling, tar, pitch, turpentine, and firewood—thereby modifying forest composition and extent.

SOCIETY AND THE ENVIRONMENT AFTER THE CIVIL WAR

Though the Civil War destroyed slavery and blasted much of the plantation landscape, Southerners remained committed to commodity-crop plantation agriculture. They often had little choice. The war and Emancipation left them capital-poor, and crop choice became hitched up to a chain of credit and market relationships that hinged on conditions outside the region. This "colonization" of the South was intensified by the development of extractive industries that were largely capitalized and commanded by northern investors. Southerners had few resources for economic development; like other undeveloped areas in a global capitalist economy, they experienced economic growth only by selling their labor and raw materials to outside investors at bargain prices. The consequence was the growth of an economy that did damage to the natural environment.

Cotton culture remained the dominant force in shaping the region's environment. By 1879, Southerners had returned cotton production to its prewar levels, and by 1900 they were producing three times the 1860 level. A combination of factors made cotton agriculture after the war even harder on the land than antebellum production had been. Since labor could no longer be as easily coerced, control of land and of credit became the means to control labor; landowners seldom developed fresh lands, but forced sharecroppers and tenants into debt and then required them to produce cotton year after year on the same land. Monoculture, as always, provided excellent habitats for population explosions of insects. In the early twentieth century the boll weevil, with devastating consequences, ate its way through cotton fields across the South from its point of entry in Texas. Crop rotation—even with corn, another heavy feeder—was seldom practiced. Cheap, easily available fertilizers created the illusion of fertility on soils that seldom had the structure to develop it, and allowed cotton-growers to continue to use poor soils. Erosion, gullying, and rapid runoff became a larger problem than it had been before the war.

In many places, but especially in the upper Coastal Plain and Piedmont, cotton production was expanded onto lands cleared by another major environment-shaping force of the period, industrial timbering. While other extractive industries, such as strip-mining in Appalachia and the petrochemical industry in Texas also caused massive damage to the environment, industrial logging cleaned off large blocks of the entire region. Northern lumbermen exhausted the timber resources of the Great Lake states then came south to clear another region's forests, spurred on by low acquisition costs, improved rail access, and unrestricted entry (after the repeal of the 1866 Southern Homestead Act, which limited land entries to eighty acres [32 hectares] in 1876). They were also supported enthusiastically by New South boosters who sought the development of industry. Northerners and Europeans bought up huge acreages of southern forests in the 1880s and used new industrial technology to strip them of timber.

The extensive longleaf forests of Georgia were the first to go, followed by the pine forests of Alabama and Mississippi. By the 1890s, Texas was the leading producer of lumber, and in 1900 Louisiana surged to the lead, producing 3.5 billion board feet. In the 1890s, lumbermen using a new pull-boat technology began extracting bald cypress from southern swamps and bayous—the hitherto worthless Yazoo lowlands in the lower Mississippi Valley and the Okefenokee Swamp, for example, now contained valuable resources—until unrelenting exploitation began to deplete the supply of cypress. Trunk rail lines penetrated some of the most rugged areas of the Appalachians and lumbermen there cleared out hardwood coves. By 1909 timbering and milling operations were producing nearly one hundred and forty million board feet per year, nearly half the total production for the United States. This high rate continued until the 1920s when the industry ran out of woods to cut.

MODERNIZATION, THE SUNBELT, AND THE ENVIRONMENT

The 1930s were a watershed for the shaky Southern economy and the eroded, gullied, deforested landscape of the region. The already sagging economy hit bottom during the Great Depression, but New Deal relief programs provided the capital for southern planters to begin to modernize. New Deal capital, then the appearance of cheap petroleum agricultural chemicals, the out-migration of labor, higher cotton prices during World War II, and mechanization—the appearance of a mechanical cotton picker in 1941 was crucial—transformed southern agriculture and the agricultural landscape.

At the same time that yields and efficiency increased, the production of the traditional crops began to decrease. Cotton production declined in the western portion of the cotton South and disappeared from much of the eastern portion. Great areas of the Piedmont had become too eroded and gullied for agriculture and the small, hilly parcels of land there were unsuited for large-scale mechanized production. By the 1980s most of the cotton produced in the region was grown in the Mississippi Valley. Corn acreages also dropped by more than two-thirds between 1929 and 1982 and became concentrated on the South Atlantic coastal plain and parts of Kentucky and Tennessee. Tobacco, still a highly profitable crop, remained essential to the farm economy of North Carolina and Kentucky, but total acreages of this oldest of southern staple crops declined by more than half between 1930 and 1985.

Agriculture continued to be a transforming force in the southern environment, however, as new crops replaced the old and the cropland base shifted. By the 1980s, soybeans had become the leading crop in every southern state except Virginia, with over twenty-five million acres devoted to their production. Increased market demands, reduced labor supplies, and poor agricultural land converged to make soybeans profitable in the post–World War II years. Though rice did not carry the importance of soybeans as a crop, it rose in significance. The modern, heavily capitalized rice agriculture was based on the midwestern wheat technology, developed late in the nineteenth century, that changed the prairies of eastern Arkansas, Louisiana, and parts of east Texas.

The decline of farming and a new silviculture together created new forests. Some practices favored the expansion of hardwood forests. The removal of the highest quality trees by timbermen meant that little old-growth forests remained, but where pines were selectively logged for mixed-species forests, hardwoods extended their cover. Federal and state fire-control programs largely eliminated natural fires and reduced fires set by small farmers to clear land or "green up" the range for cattle, and removed a major force that favored fire-adapted pine species at the expense of the more vulnerable hardwood species. Mixed deciduous hardwood forests still cover the more rugged slopes of the Appalachians and several forces worked toward the slow domination of hardwoods in mixed-species forests.

Other practices favored the expansion of pine forests. Abandoned croplands grew up largely in loblolly and shortleaf pines, often called old-field pine; these varieties also colonized land cut clear of longleaf pine. Modern forest-management practices, which shaped southern forests for commercial purposes, focused on increasing total forest fiber output by planting fast-growing species of pine. In addition, private forest companies created large plantations of pine that they plant and manage like crops—using controlled burning and herbicides. The result has been new pine forests with even less diversity of species than the barrens of the old ones.

Southern watersheds were also modified by large-scale calculated action, especially through the New Deal and other government programs. The most ambitious has been the New Deal's Tennessee Valley Authority, which engaged in the wholesale development of both land and water in an entire river basin. Through the TVA the federal government engaged in the management of nature on a grand scale, and established a model for future resource management programs in the South. By the late twentieth century, the South had more water management projects in place than any other region except California.

Disciplining the region's rivers—and especially the Mississippi—had long been the aim of Southerners who lived on them. On the Mississippi, two hundred years of levee building was completed in the 1890s by the Corps of Engineers and the Mississippi River Commission, and was apparently successful in controlling the often unpredictable pulses of the river. This controlled river abided the discipline of engineers most of the time, but was much more dangerous than the old when it did not. Because overflow areas were closed off and the channel was streamlined, the river moved much more quickly and was more dangerous when it topped or broke through the levees. Flood control also encouraged settlement on the floodplain. In 1927 the Mississippi escaped its embankments with disastrous consequences, flooding millions of acres and creating nearly seven hundred thousand refugees.

Federally sponsored Mississippi flood-control projects applied a new approach to flood control in the wake of the 1927 flood. These programs strengthened levees, deepened and straightened channels, developed floodways and storage reservoirs, and succeeded in establishing control along this largest of American alluvial valleys. Flood control has meant increased settlement along the river, and bottomland hardwood forests have become soybean fields. At the same time, however, flood control projects have channeled the sediments out from the Delta and into deep water, the river has ceased to build land on the Gulf Coast, and the Louisiana coastline is receding.

As the southern economy modernized and was integrated into the larger national economy, the development of Sunbelt cities transformed large portions of the southern landscape and changed profoundly the natural environment. Cities remained small, developing later in the South, and took a different form than in other regions. The usual form of Sunbelt metropolitan development was the planned sprawl: urbanlike settlements stretching from one urban center to another. In 1960 the largest of these stretched from Pensacola to Houston and had a relatively low-density population of 3,400,000.

The appeal of the Sunbelt to migrants from other regions was greatly enhanced by changes in the disease environment. The long warm season of the region had perennially favored pathogens and vectors that seldom appeared in other regions. The South had been a land of fever since malaria became endemic in the early colonial era and yellow fever became a frequent visitor. After World War II the eradication of the vectors for the disease, the *Anopheles quadrimaculatus* and *Aëdes aegypti* mosquitoes, through the use of DDT and large-scale drainage projects, made the South a safer place, especially to newcomers who had no immunities. The progressive decline of hookworm and pellagra also contributed to the success of the new image of the South as a healthy Sunbelt.

The development of air-conditioning made southern summers less enervating and stimulated Sunbelt urban growth. By the late 1960s most public buildings and private homes were air-conditioned and designs for new office buildings, hotels, and enclosed shopping malls took this kind of climate control for granted. By the 1980s automobiles were also air-conditioned, and the average southerner—or migrant from elsewhere—could depend on an artificial climate to buffer the real one.

Rapid growth, changes in agriculture, reforestation, and the large-scale manipulation of watersheds caused dislocations for wildlife. Resilient species thrived: wild turkey, the ubiquitous opossums, and raccoons maintained large populations; white-tailed deer populations expanded enormously in old-field habitats. Some changes played to specific species; mechanical harvesting increased the grain supply in wheat and corn fields, for example, providing winter feed for the brown-headed cowbird and the common grackle. Other species that are adapted only to a specific habitat—wood storks, Florida panthers, the pitcher plant, for example—were put under pressure. Competitive newcomers in some places were much more successful than less adaptable natives. Most prominent of these was

kudzu, an invasive vine introduced for erosion control and cattle food that has swallowed up enough of the southern landscapes—both in the countryside and on empty lots in cities—to have inspired its own folklore.

Sunbelt growth and prosperity did not come without a price. Both agricultural and industrial pollution increased. Because southern states have sought to attract American and foreign industry through reduced environmental standards and because the environmental movement was until recently weak in the South, industry was often free to contaminate air and water without penalty. Effluents from paper mills, toxic discharges from chemical plants, oil spills (especially in the newer oil belt that has developed just off the Gulf Shore), accidental spills of radioactive wastes from nuclear power plants, and less specific fertilizer, pesticide, and herbicide pollution all accompanied the Sunbelt's industrial development. Federal environmental quality standards and less-relaxed state standards later put a lid on many of the more serious pollution problems, but pollution still compromises the Sunbelt South's image as an attractive, healthy place to live and work.

In the last decades of the twentieth century, the relationship between human beings and the natural environment has been more seriously complicated by much larger by-products of an industrial economy and a consumer society. Acid rain, much of it originating in the highly industrialized Ohio Valley, may be reducing growth rates of southern forests at higher elevations. Ozone pollution produced in and around sprawling cities where automobiles are essential—and especially serious in the South's sunny, muggy summer climate—stunts the growth of both cultivated and natural vegetation. In the future, global warming because of the "greenhouse effect" could have several consequences, especially on agriculture in the area, if temperatures rise and precipitation patterns change. In the late twentieth century, environmental problems that are global in magnitude also affect the natural environment of the South and further weaken any claims of geographical distinctiveness. At the same time, the Sunbelt remains unique: a modern incarnation of regional distinctiveness and yet another creation of the changing relationship of culture and nature in the South.

BIBLIOGRAPHY

Arsenault, Raymond. "The End of the Long Hot Summer: The Air Conditioner and Southern Culture." *Journal of Southern History* 50, no. 4 (1984).

Brown, Ralph H. *Historical Geography of the United States* (1948).

Clark, Thomas D. *The Greening of the South: The Recovery of Land and Forest* (1984).

Cobb, James C. *The Selling of the South: The Southern Crusade for Industrial Development, 1936–1980* (1982).

Cowdrey, Albert E. *This Land, This South: An Environmental History* (1983).

Daniel, Pete. *Breaking the Land: The Transformation of Cotton, Tobacco, and Rice Cultures Since 1880* (1985).

Earle, Carville. "Regional Economic Development West of the Appalachians, 1815–1860." In *North America: The Historical Geography of a Changing Continent,* edited by Robert Mitchell and Paul Graves (1987).

———. "The Myth of the Southern Soil Miner: Macrohistory, Agricultural Innovation, and Environmental Change." In *The Ends of the Earth,* edited by Donald Worster (1988).

Fite, Gilbert C. *Cotton Fields No More: Southern Agriculture, 1865–1980* (1984).

Goldfield, David R. *Cotton Fields and Skyscrapers: Southern City and Region, 1607–1980* (1982).

Healy, Robert G. *Competition for Land in the American South: Agriculture, Human Settlement, and the Environment* (1985).

Hilliard, Sam Bowers. *Hog Meat and Hoecake: Food Supply in the Old South, 1840–1860* (1972).

———. *Atlas of Antebellum Southern Agriculture* (1984).

Hunt, Charles B. *Physiography of the United States* (1967).

Kirby, Jack Temple. *Rural Worlds Lost: The American South, 1920–1960* (1987).

Shelford, Victor E. *The Ecology of North America* (1963).

Silver, Timothy. *A New Face on the Countryside: Indians, Colonists, and Slaves in the South Atlantic Forests, 1500–1800* (1990).

Vance, Rupert. *Human Geography of the South* (1932).

Vankat, John L. *The Natural Vegetation of North America: An Introduction* (1979).

Williams, Michael. *Americans and Their Forests: A Historical Geography* (1989).

SEE ALSO **Agriculture; African Migration; The Great Depression and World War II; Landscape; Native Peoples Prior to European Arrival; The Plantation; Regionalism; Rural Life in the South; Sectional Conflict, Civil War, and Reconstruction; Slavery; Technology and Social Change**; and various articles in the section "**Regionalism and Regional Subcultures.**"

THE NATURAL ENVIRONMENT: THE WEST

Patricia Nelson Limerick
W. Clark Whitehorn

THE WESTERN UNITED STATES contains a wide variety of physical environments. From the semi-arid Great Plains to the humid Pacific Northwest, flora and fauna vary as widely as does the topography. For all its diversity, much of the West beyond the hundredth meridian differs from the rest of the nation in its greater altitude and aridity. The deserts of the Great Basin and the Southwest and the peaks of the Rockies, Sierras, and Cascades are the most visible markers of the West's distinctiveness.

Human beings first came into the region over the Bering land bridge between 25,000 and 10,000 B.C. Archaeologists believe that these nomadic people were following large animal herds on which they depended for food and clothing. Climatic changes beginning in 8000 B.C., along with the possible overkill of large mammals, altered the subsistence opportunities for these early hunters.

INDIANS, HISPANICS, EARLY ANGLOS

Small-game hunting and gathering practices intensified with the disappearance of the large herd animals. Ears of corn found in southwestern archaeological digs suggest that agriculture developed around 5000 or 4000 B.C., evidently through contact with MesoAmerican cultures. The possible predecessor to the Pueblo cutures, the Anasazi, began to practice communal agriculture around the time of Christ. By 1300, the Anasazi had developed large population centers at Mesa Verde, Colorado; Chaco Canyon, New Mexico; and Kayenta, Arizona. Their fate is a matter of uncertainty; probably at the end of the thirteenth century a combination of drought and attacks from nomadic raiders induced the Anasazi to leave their villages and settle along the more fertile Rio Grande Valley.

Along the Pacific coast and in the interior regions of the Great Basin and the northern Rockies, people held more closely to the hunter-gatherer tradition. Game was abundant, as were berries, seeds, and tubers. In the Pacific Northwest, salmon provided local people with a reliable source of protein. In villages along the west-to-east-running Plains rivers, farming added corn and beans to the supply of game and wild plants. In the arid Southwest, both floodplain and irrigation agriculture provided a significant portion of the diet, as well as the foundation for the rituals and beliefs of community life.

In many areas of the West, Indians practiced cyclical burning to improve certain areas as habitats for game and to encourage the proliferation of some plant species while reducing the numbers of less useful plants. With fire, hunting, gathering, and farming, Indian people had placed a human imprint on the land; what white Americans would later call pristine wilderness was in part a human creation. Just as important, native people had invested the landscape with social and religious meaning. Indian religions dealt in sacred places, pilgrimages, and codes of conduct for human behavior toward nature.

In 1540, Francisco Vásquez de Coronado led the first organized European expedition into the American West. His tour represented the arrival of behavior directed at transforming the land's resources into individual wealth. Nonetheless, in terms of minerals, New Mexico struck Coronado as a great disappointment. In a pattern common to colonization, his men might well have perished had they not seized Indian resources—food and clothing—for their own use. Spanish officials saw his journey as a failure and concentrated support on the silver mines of Zacatecas and Durango in what is now northern Mexico.

In 1598, Juan de Oñate brought permanent Hispanic settlers to New Mexico. Along with Christianity, missionaries introduced European livestock and crops. The Spanish presence strained the delicate balance that the Pueblos had created through irrigation of a limited amount of land. Spaniards devoured Pueblo corn, and took Pueblo people from their own fields to labor in settlers' fields. In 1680 the Pueblos joined in revolt and drove the Spaniards from New Mexico. Reconquered in the 1690s, New Mexico was a place of diminished economic ambition. Hispanic people settled in villages, relying on livestock and on small-scale agriculture supported by *acequias* (irrigation canals).

New Mexico was soon joined by Spanish colonies in Texas, Arizona, and California. Iberian cattle adapted readily to all these areas. And the horse, introduced by the Spanish, migrated northward and into the cultures of many tribes, turning hunter-gatherers into nomadic horsemen following the massive buffalo herds. Ironically, the horse provided nomadic natives in the Southwest with an unforeseen advantage: they could now raid Hispanic cattle and sheep herds with relative impunity. In many ways, the propagation and distribution of livestock drew the lines of power and conflict in colonization.

Only one European import significantly protected Hispanic settlements from annihilation. Disease, especially smallpox and measles, provided the essential vehicle for conquest. No one will ever know the number of Indians killed by disease, but estimates range between a third and a half of the total population west of the Mississippi River. Moreover, disease did not require continual European presence; Indians fleeing from the horrifying effects of smallpox spread the disease all the way to Canada. Anglo-Americans exploring westward through the Great Plains and Rockies brought disease to the upper Missouri tribes. Smallpox came close to eliminating the once powerful Mandan and Arikara tribes. Before the arrival of white settlers in what they would call "wilderness," disease had brought enormous political, social, and religious changes. Disease wiped out chiefs, shamans, and other tribal leaders. Some tribes, remnants of formerly large cultural entities, were absorbed by other tribes. They had lost the right to determine their own tribal policies. In other areas new people assumed the role of chief or tribal leader.

EXPLOITATION OF THE WEST THROUGH THE GREAT DEPRESSION

Along with disease, westward-moving Anglo-Americans brought a more exploitative environmental ideology. Unlike Indians and Hispanics, Americans took on the project of mastering the resources of the West with strong corporate and political backing. Viewing the West as an endlessly bountiful supplier of resources, individuals and institutions wanted a return on their investments of capital, energy, and faith. For decades to come, the pursuit of profit would dominate American environmental behavior in the West.

Preceded in a number of cases by French-Canadian and British fur traders, American fur trappers followed Meriwether Lewis and William Clark (1804–1806) into the West, hoping to trap the abundant beaver. Unlike the British Hudson's Bay Company, the American fur companies relied on European-American trappers, thereby elbowing Indian people out of their central role in the fur trade as both trappers and middlemen. Though traditionally portrayed as exemplars of rugged individualism, the American trappers of the 1820s and 1830s served as agents for eastern-based corporations. The trappers relied on companies for powder, lead, traps, and markets for their furs. The profitability of the fur trade led to intense competition between companies. Trappers raced each other to the richest beaver streams, reducing the animals to near extinction. From the fur trade on, the policy of exploiting western resources for eastern corporations became a standard practice in the West. A rapid shift from boom to bust characterized the fur trade, as well as the many extractive industries that followed it.

Other wildlife shared the same fate as the beaver. The arrival of steamboats on the Missouri River beginning in 1832 permitted the export of the otherwise difficult-to-transport buffalo hides. After the Civil War, the U.S. Army encouraged the slaughter of the buffalo in order to "pacify" the Plains Indians through the elimination of their food supply. The conquest of the Indians thus rested as heavily on environmental change as it did on military engagements.

With the removal of the buffalo, the grasslands of the Plains became a temporarily unoccupied ecological niche. Livestock drovers responded to that opportunity, replacing the herds of buffalo with herds of cattle and sheep. If not kept constantly moving, these animals ate the native grasses of the Plains to the roots. Once the original ground cover was destroyed, the soil became vulnerable to erosion by the intense winds of the area. With land too densely populated with cattle, the Plains' range cattle industry faced a near collapse in 1887, after a severe winter combined with overgrazing to kill off many of the malnourished animals.

Farmers, too, responded to the apparent opportunity of the Plains. In the years after the Civil War, a spell of abundant rainfall encouraged farmers to move onto the Plains. The return of more characteristic, sparse patterns of rainfall, as well as cycles of grasshopper infestation and periodic fires, broke the hopes of many farmers. For some, the technique of dry farming seemed to provide a solution. With the constant cultivation and packing of topsoil to trap a water reservoir, dry farming made it possible for crops to grow where conventional techniques were only wasted effort. In the long run, however, the plowing of the Plains contributed to one of the most dramatic environmental catastrophes on the continent; taking to the air during the droughts of the 1930s, Plains soil earned the region the grim name of the Dust Bowl.

In a pattern that seemed, superficially, to be very different from farming, the California gold rush of 1849 inaugurated a series of rushes to every territory in the West. Individual placer mining for precious metals quickly gave way to heavily capitalized industrial mining. Most gold and silver veins lay embedded in solid rock. Hydraulic mining washed away the economically useless bedrock and most of the hillsides in which the minerals lay buried. Stamp mills crushed the rock to expose the metals within, and smelters separated marketable metal from useless matter. Sold and transported out of the region, precious metals left behind a landscape dotted by abandoned mines and piles of tailings.

Precious metals were only a part of the mining story. Copper mining boomed in the late nineteenth century with the advent of electricity as a power source. In addition to creating a constant demand for copper wire, electricity provided a cheap source of power to run ore cars, air compressors, and pumps. In the late nineteenth and early twentieth centuries, coal mines proliferated in the Rocky Mountain states. Gold, silver, copper, or coal, the mines were generally industrial operations worked by wage employees hired by absentee owners.

Underground mining created a heavy demand for timber to support tunnels and drifts; viewed from a distance, mines in places like the Comstock Lode in Nevada would have looked like enterprises in which humans cut down local forests in order to bury them underground. Despite demands for mine timbers, for housing, and for fuel, the western timber industry remained a relatively small-scale operation until the end of the nineteenth century, with large-scale cutting instead in the Great Lakes region. At the turn of the century, however, the Weyerhaeuser Timber Company began purchasing large tracts in the Pacific Northwest. Mechanized sawmills and increased railroad connections enabled the western timber industry to boom. Tree removal led to erosion, loss of wildlife, and the silting of rivers.

Mining, farming, livestock grazing, and lumbering may have involved very different techniques and employed different labor forces, but they shared a pattern in common: an intensive extraction of raw materials until the resource became too expensive or too rare to exploit. By the dominant point of view of the nineteenth century, economic development counted as "improvement." But cut-over lands, blasted mining sites, overgrazed ground cover, and eroded soil suggest destruction more than improvement.

THE CONSERVATION AND PRESERVATION MOVEMENTS

The transformation of the forests through lumbering and grazing provided the impetus for both the preservation and the conservation movements of the late nineteenth and early twentieth centuries. John Muir, a Scottish immigrant in California, became the most visible and audible advocate of preservation, as he fought the intrusion of loggers and sheepherders into his beloved Sierra Nevadas. At the same time, the conservation movement, most commonly associated with Gifford Pinchot, appointed chief of the Division of Forestry in 1898, undertook to shift the gears of resource extraction from profligacy to "wise use." Frequently jumbled together under the shared label "conservation," Muir's preservation movement and Pinchot's conservation movement actually had very different motives and very different agendas for the management of western resources.

In 1872, the Yellowstone area became the first national park. Set aside for its distinctive geothermal features, the park came to exist before there was any philosophy, or even any institution, for the management of preserved lands. It was almost fifty years before Congress passed the act creating the National Park Service in 1916.

In California, Yosemite was a state park until 1890, when it became a national park. At Yosemite, the question of definition—both of the status of parks and of the differences between preservationists and conservationists—came into focus. The boundaries of Yosemite National Park included the Hetch Hetchy Valley, a smaller-scale version of

Yosemite Valley's steep walls. Depending on one's point of view, Hetch Hetchy was either a valley of irreplaceable beauty or a naturally designed site for a reservoir. When planners and developers in San Francisco targeted the Hetch Hetchy Valley for a city reservoir, the battle was joined. John Muir and his allies fought for the sanctity of the national park and of the undammed canyon; the city of San Francisco, in company with its ally Gifford Pinchot, fought for the declared necessity of increased urban growth and water use. In 1913, the victory went to the city; Hetch Hetchy Valley has been a lake for most of the twentieth century. Defeated in battle, the preservationists had, however, learned how to fight; and John Muir's Sierra Club would be a power to reckon with in later struggles over western resources.

The arrangement of power on the federal side in these matters was by no means clear and consistent; power over public lands was divided among several agencies. Lodged in the Department of the Interior, the National Park Service was entirely separate from the Forest Service in the Department of Agriculture. The national forests originated in a law passed in 1891 that permitted the president to set aside forest reserves. Theodore Roosevelt especially made vigorous use of this power, finally installing his friend Pinchot as the ruler of this new bureaucratic domain. Forest Service policy required multiple use; lumbering, mining, grazing, and recreation were all to receive their due. Created in 1902 by the Newlands Reclamation Act, the Bureau of Reclamation, located within the Department of the Interior, pushed for the construction of large dams and the provision of water for agriculture and, increasingly, of electrical power for cities. In 1934, responding to the overuse of public lands, the Taylor Grazing Act created the Grazing Service, later named the Bureau of Land Management. Located in the Department of the Interior, the bureau was to supervise and allocate—by no means to eliminate—grazing rights on the remaining public domain.

Each of these agencies—Park Service, Forest Service, Bureau of Reclamation, and Bureau of Land Management—had its own turf to defend, traditions to maintain, and appropriations to secure. Even though they squabbled among themselves for position and privilege, the rise to power of federal land management agencies nevertheless gave Westerners the impression that a monolithic power based in Washington, D.C., had taken over control of their natural resources. From time to time, western businessmen would launch campaigns, as much matters of rhetoric as of substance, to return the public lands to state control; as recently as the late 1970s, the so-called Sagebrush Rebels returned to this familiar demand. In fact, the very idea of "public lands" raised a fundamental issue of property and legitimacy. If the lands belonged permanently to the people of the entire United States, then local Westerners had no particular privileges of use or ownership over the federal lands in their vicinity.

With or without federal restrictions, western resource developers did not slow down in deference to any theoretical "end of the frontier" at the turn of the century. Already developed on a small scale in California (1893–1894), the western oil industry took off in 1901 with the discovery at Spindletop in Texas. Coal mines continued to expand, and experimental extractive industries, like the oil shale business on the Western Slope of Colorado, made tentative beginnings. The timber industry in the Pacific Northwest continued to grow. Often with federal sponsorship and subsidy, irrigation created farms on desert lands that had once seemed to be permanently and resolutely "useless." With water diverted from the Colorado River, California's Imperial Valley produced fruits and vegetables for growers who relied heavily on migrant labor. Homesteading continued on a large scale after 1890; fruit orchards went into production in the Pacific Northwest and in southern California; cotton moved out of the South and into the Southwest. By the mid twentieth century, Plains agriculture and ranching seemed to have gained a new lease on life as gasoline-powered pumps drew water from underground aquifers.

Perhaps most important, western cities expanded their populations and their resource demands. Towns and cities had, of course, been an important part of western expansion in the nineteenth century. Santa Fe governed the territory of New Mexico and served as an entry point for Americans trading in Mexico; San Francisco bankrolled a series of mineral rushes; Salt Lake City provided both a religious and a business center for the Mormons; Denver supplied miners with tools and capital; Los Angeles underwent a dramatic land boom in the 1880s. In the twentieth century, these cities attracted workers, investors, retirees, businessmen, and industrialists. Making the most of the region's wide-open spaces, western cities tended to expand horizontally rather than vertically, creating conditions that seemed to demand heavy use of automobiles. In many towns and cities, homeowners tried to replicate familiar landscapes from the eastern United States, planting lawns and gardens that required constant watering. As users of land, water, fuel, food, and electricity, western towns and cities became major players in the region's environmental history.

EXPLOITATION OF THE WEST SINCE WORLD WAR II

World War II acted as a major accelerator of western population growth. With the demands of the war's Pacific theater, the ports of Washington and California acquired new importance, and West Coast shipbuilding and airplane manufacturing prospered. Western aridity proved to have major value for defense operations; the dryness and remoteness of much western terrain, as well as its status as public land, gave the region the edge when it came to locating everything from air force bases to installations for the development of the atomic bomb. The military had played a vital part in the development of the region in the nineteenth century, and its role in land use in the twentieth century was just as, if not more, important. The opportunities presented by World War II inspired a population rush to the region that dwarfed the westward movement of the nineteenth century.

To the majority of Westerners, growth had long been a synonym for prosperity. Yet growth had always come with costs, even if the beneficiaries habitually dismissed them. Kicked into high gear by World War II, Los Angeles grew with a vengeance in the postwar years. Fumes from manufacturing facilities (especially synthetic rubber plants), carbon monoxide from millions of automobiles, water shortages, and an understandable reluctance to face up to these problems characterized Los Angeles and a number of other western cities. If the West had once promised opportunity, abundance, and a better way of life, it was, by the mid twentieth century, a promise obscured by smog and congestion. In the Southwest, especially Arizona, population boomed with the spread of air-conditioning. Even if it meant an enormous seasonal use of electrical power, technology seemed to have transcended the overwhelming summer heat that had previously limited the area's attractiveness for Anglo settlers.

Looking for refuge from the trials of urban areas, and joined by tourists from the eastern United States—indeed, from the whole planet—Westerners brought congestion to some rural areas as well. Cars jammed Yosemite National Park; parades of huge recreational vehicles lumbered through Yellowstone; backpackers bumped into each other on remote trails; those eager to raft down western rivers waited, for months, for permits and licenses. At the end of the nineteenth century, the aesthetic appreciation of nature and the attractions of outdoor places for recreation seemed to present a new, and entirely different, approach to the physical environment. But in the mid twentieth century, it began to seem possible that outdoors enthusiasts might, in fact, come to "love nature to death." With tourism and recreation emerging as crucial western industries, nature appreciation seemed to be another, temporarily disguised, form of commodity consciousness. Where previous generations of resource developers saw a piece of nature waiting to become a mine or a logging site, by another, only superficially different point of view, another kind of developer saw a site waiting to become a ski resort or a service station with a minimart.

The question of water use brings all these issues of growth and development into focus. Fifteen states now depend upon three major river systems for their water needs: the Colorado, the Columbia, and the Missouri rivers. The rivers have been dammed beyond recognition, yet they still fail to meet the demands of the thirsty West. The Colorado River provides the starkest case study of an overallocated resource. In 1922, an interstate compact divided the estimated annual flow of the river between the upper basin states of Colorado, Wyoming, Utah, and New Mexico, and the lower basin states of Nevada, Arizona, and California. International agreements gave Mexico a share of the water as well.

Basing its estimate of annual flow on several well-watered years, the Colorado River Compact of 1922 turned out to have allocated more water than the river, in some years, contains. Playing water politics with enormous skill, the lower basin states got a head start in river development with the enormous project of Hoover Dam, completed in 1936. For Mexico, United States' use of the Colorado has meant a silty and salinized trickle of water arriving on the other side of the border, and long fights over both water quality and water quantity; for the western states, the development of the Colorado has triggered endless squabbles over who owns the rights to how much water, with the upper basin states striving to develop their claims to water that now benefits Arizona and California. Environmentalists clamor for an end to the disruption of free-flowing rivers by dams and reclamation projects; ranchers and farmers hope for more projects in their areas; urban users continue to water their lawns and depend heavily on electricity produced by waterpower. Through the middle of all these contests runs the legendary, overallocated river that carved the Grand Canyon.

An added variable in western water conflicts stems from the question of Indian water rights. In the *Winters* v. *the United States* decision of 1908, the Supreme Court ruled that the Indians on the Fort Belknap reservation deserved a share of the Milk River, which stockmen and settlers had diverted for irrigation projects. Since the creators and planners of reservations had intended Indians to farm, the justices reasoned, reservations have an assumed, reserved water right. Though the case has not yet significantly altered or improved Indian water projects, it has provided a valuable opportunity for Indian people to assert their rights; at the same time, the *Winters* doctrine sketches an unsettling prospect for non-Indian water-users.

As environmental historians have found in every part of the planet, the history of the physical environment and the history of human groups are not separable. Even if professional specialization has divided the turf, the fact that humans are biological beings makes social history and environmental history interdependent. In the American West, the last two centuries of environmental change have created a tangle of consequences, a direct inheritance from the people of the western past to the people of the western present.

Radioactivity is the most recent addition to that heritage. The development of the atomic bomb during World War II had its center of gravity in the New Mexican town of Los Alamos, chosen for its remoteness. Similarly, looking for a location for the production of plutonium, Leslie Groves and the planners of the Manhattan Project chose a site in eastern Washington with isolation and access to hydropower and cooling water from the Columbia River in its favor. The small town of Hanford, along with thriving orchards, was forced to yield ground to the new, and secret, Hanford Nuclear Reservation. The rush to produce plutonium led to careless handling of radioactive substances; before the war was over, Hanford had an almost casual system of waste disposal. Dumped into trenches in the ground, nuclear waste drained into the Columbia River and headed downstream to the major population centers of western Oregon, while the dominant west-to-east winds carried airborne radioactive material from Hanford to local towns and farms, as well as to the city of Spokane in western Washington.

In the cold war, nuclear development kept its western center of gravity. Within the United States, the major deposits of uranium proved to lie in the Black Hills of South Dakota and in the Colorado Plateau (where the states of Colorado, Utah, Arizona, and New Mexico meet). Uranium rushes had some of the same flair and energy as nineteenth-century mining rushes, even if the prospectors now carried Geiger counters. But mining and processing this resource involved a wholly new set of health risks; in the late twentieth century, the veterans of uranium production reported a high rate of illness and mortality. Seeking a continental site for nuclear testing, government planners made the usual choice in favor of western aridity and remoteness, and developed the Nevada Test Site, with above-ground testing through the 1950s and underground testing since then. In the same vein, when it came to sites for missiles and warheads, the West won most of the contests. Domestic use of nuclear power, as well as military use, made radioactive waste disposal an increasingly urgent question. Congress then had to choose a part of the United States to play permanent host to the nation's store of radioactive material. True to the pattern of previous atomic decision making, the West won again, with a controversial storage site planned near Carlsbad, New Mexico, and a much larger, permanent, and equally controversial, site slated for Yucca Mountain, Nevada.

TOWARD THE FUTURE

For nearly two centuries, when the Anglo-American mind met the enormity of western space, the result was a curious kind of optimism. By this faith, the western plains, mountains, and deserts were, in and of themselves, a solution to the problems of the eastern United States, a cure for the demographic, economic, and psychological congestion of the "older" region. Tested repeatedly, and not always successfully, this faith nonetheless had enormous staying power. The Dust Bowl of the 1930s was surely an enormous challenge, yet the clouds of blowing dirt produced little in the way of changed environmental attitudes. When the rains came back, optimism was their first crop. "The future is just opening up," one Plains resident put it. "Our future is all before us." This resilient faith in a second chance had important consequences in behavior, encouraging a resistance to regulation and restraint, a reluctance to look at the long-term costs and consequences of growth and development, and an unwillingness to face up to the actual limits of resources in the West, especially the finite supply of water. Tempered and moderated by the conservation movement, the commodification of western nature nonetheless remained the name of the game.

In 1893, the frontier historian Frederick Jackson Turner prematurely proclaimed the end of one era of western American history and the arrival of another. The frontier ended in 1890, Turner said, and his followers in the field of western American history stuck by this improbable article of faith, even as full-speed-ahead resource development continued in virtually every part of the West. And yet, in nearly all aspects of the human relationship to the physical environment, the last decades of the twentieth century suggest that a much more significant age of reckoning with environmental limits has come upon the region. On this count, Turner may have been right about a fundamental shift in the momentum of westward expansion; he simply missed the date by a century.

In the 1990s, examples of this reckoning are everywhere in the region. Abandoned mines drain toxic chemicals into western streams, and western states, in a time of strained budgets, struggle with the question of reclaiming and repairing these damaged sites. Environmentalists seek to restore wolves and other predator populations while ranchers oppose the reintroduction of any threat to their livestock. Dams on the Columbia River interfere with the migration and reproduction of salmon, a formerly abundant natural resource valued—and fought over—by Indian tribes, sport fishermen, and commercial fishermen. Irrigation produces not only crops but also increased salinity in the soil; meanwhile, the mounting federal deficit threatens to dry up the flow of federal cash that had underwritten the water empire of the West.

In a system called water ranching, western cities buy up agricultural water rights, a move applauded by some on the premise that irrigated farming had always been an inefficient and expensive use of water, and denounced by others who feel that a rural farm culture has its own legitimacy and rights to preservation. Pumps pull water from the Ogallala aquifer, the enormous deposit of underground water that supported much of Plains farming and ranching, depleting it faster than natural sources can replenish it.

A prolonged crisis of the farm economy also wore away at the underpinnings of rural life. As settlements on the Plains lost population, a courageous team of land-use analysts, Frank and Deborah Popper, argued that the heavy settlement of the area had been a mistake; that rural depopulation was a clear, established trend; and that social planners should aid in and ease the process. The Plains environment, the Poppers suggested, could reverse history and return to the ecological job it did best: supporting roaming herds of untamed herbivores. Restored as Buffalo Commons, the Plains would recover from its century-and-a-half-long interlude of error. Whether or not one embraced a vision of Omaha, Nebraska, as a jumping-off point for Plains safaris, the prospect of a regional future shaped by an awareness of limited water was hard to evade.

The sense of reckoning exemplified in these western crises was by no means unique in the nation or on the planet. But the West had for decades held onto its mythic standing as a place of abundant, even endless, resources, supplying Americans with infinite opportunities for second chances. The recognition of limits hit particularly hard in this region—hard enough, perhaps, to inspire a prudent and beneficial change in well-established habits of western resource use.

BIBLIOGRAPHY

Abbe, Donald R. *Austin and the Reese River Mining District: Nevada's Forgotten Frontier* (1985).
Bartley, Paula. *Plains Women: Women in the American West* (1991).
Bean, Lee, Geraldine P. Mineau, and Douglas L. Anderton. *Fertility Change on the American Frontier: Adaptation and Innovation* (1990).

Beck, Warren A., and Ynez D. Haase. *Historical Atlas of the American West* (1989).

Billington, Ray Allen. *Westward Expansion: A History of the American Frontier.* 5th ed. (1982).

Brown, Dee Alexander. *Bury My Heart at Wounded Knee: An Indian History of the American West* (1970).

Carpenter, Allan. *The Encyclopedia of the Far West* (1991).

Chittenden, Hiram Martin. *The American Fur Trade of the Far West* (1935; repr. 1986).

Cochrane, Willard Wesley. *The Development of American Agriculture: A Historical Analysis* (1979).

Coe, Michael, Dean Snow, and Elizabeth Benson. *Atlas of Ancient America* (1986).

Cox, Thomas R. *Mills and Markets: A History of the Pacific Coast Lumber Industry to 1900* (1974).

Crosby, Alfred W. *The Columbian Exchange: Biological and Cultural Consequences of 1492* (1972).

Davis, James Edward. *Frontier America, 1800–1840: A Comparative Demographic Analysis of the Settlement Process* (1977).

Davis, Mike. *City of Quartz: Excavating the Future in Los Angeles* (1990).

Dawdy, Doris Ostrander. *Congress in Its Wisdom: The Bureau of Reclamation and the Public Interest* (1989)

Ebeling, Walter. *The Fruited Plain: The Story of American Agriculture* (1979).

Goetzmann, William H. *Exploration and Empire: The Explorer and the Scientist in the Winning of the American West* (1966; repr. 1978).

Gregory, James Noble. *American Exodus: The Dust Bowl Migration and Okie Culture in California* (1989).

Hazlett, Thomas W. *The California Coastal Commission and the Economics of Environmentalism* (1980).

Hurt, R. Douglas. *The Dust Bowl: An Agricultural and Social History* (1981).

Hyde, Anne Farrar. *An American Vision: Far Western Landscape and National Culture, 1820–1920* (1990).

Katz, William Loren. *The Black West* (3d rev. ed. 1987).

King, Philip B. *The Evolution of North America* (rev. ed. 1977).

Knoll, Tricia. *Becoming American: Asian Sojourners, Immigrants and Refugees in the Western United States* (1982).

Lamar, Howard R. *The Reader's Encyclopedia of the American West* (1977).

Lange, Dorothea. *An American Exodus: A Record of Human Erosion* (1939).

Lee, Lawrence Bacon. *Reclaiming the American West: An Historiography and Guide* (1980).

Limerick, Patricia Nelson. *The Legacy of Conquest: The Unbroken Past of the American West* (1987).

Lowitt, Richard. *The New Deal and the American West* (1984).

McCabe, James Dabney. *History of the Grange Movement: or, the Farmer's War Against Monopolies* (1874).

Malone, Michael P. *The American West: A Twentieth-Century History* (1989).

Mander, Jerry. *In the Absence of the Sacred: The Failure of Technology and the Survival of the Indian Nations* (1991).

Matson, R. G. *The Origins of Southwestern Agriculture* (1991).

Popper, Frank J., and Deborah E. Popper. "The Reinvention of the American Frontier." *Amicus Journal* (Summer 1991).

Reinhartz, Dennis, and Charles C. Colley, eds. *The Mapping of the American Southwest* (1987).

Robbins, William G. *Lumberjacks and Legislators: Political Economy of the U.S. Lumber Industry, 1890–1941* (1982).

Roosevelt, Theodore. *Good Hunting: In Pursuit of Big Game in the West* (1907).

Rosenberg, Bruce A. *The Code of the West* (1982).

Spence, Clark C. *Mining Engineers and the American West: The Lace-Boot Brigade, 1849–1933* (1970).

Steffen, Jerome O., ed. *The American West: New Perspectives, New Dimensions* (1979).

Turner, Frederick Jackson. *The Frontier in American History* (1962; repr. 1975).

Twain, Mark. *Roughing It* (1913).

White, G. Edward. *The Eastern Establishment and the Western Experience: The West of Frederic Remington, Theodore Roosevelt and Owen Wister* (1989).

White, Richard. *"It's Your Misfortune and None of My Own": A History of the American West* (1991).

Worster, Donald. *Rivers of Empire: Water, Aridity, and the Growth of the American West* (1985).

———. *Under Western Skies: Nature and History in the American West* (1992).

SEE ALSO **Agriculture; The Great Depression and World War II; Landscapes; The Mormon Region; Native Peoples Prior to European Arrival; Rural Life in the West; Technology and Social Change;** and various articles in the section **"Regionalism and Regional Subcultures."**

GEOGRAPHICAL MOBILITY

Robert Howard Freymeyer

AMERICANS HAVE BEEN a highly mobile people. Their geographical mobility has shaped the history and development of the United States. They have moved to the frontier to take advantage of the country's abundant land and natural resources, and they have moved to the cities to work in expanding industries and factories. Both of these migration streams exemplify how available opportunities attract migrants trying to better themselves through their movement.

Theories of geographical mobility have at least implicitly considered conditions thrusting movers away from an area and the opportunities attracting them to a destination: the "push" and "pull" factors. Furthermore, much of past research has suggested that migrants respond primarily to economic conditions. According to this labor mobility model, labor flows from areas with few economic opportunities to areas with surplus opportunities as a means of establishing equilibrium between available jobs and available workers. Yet, just as not all areas have equal resources, so not all workers have equal abilities to take advantage of an opportunity. To understand mobility fully, therefore, it is necessary to consider how the patterns of movement differ for specific groups within the population. For example, mobility patterns differ by age and socioeconomic status, and these differences have varied over time.

Geographical mobility involves a change in an individual's usual place of residence. Measuring this change in residence has been somewhat problematic. Typically, place of residence is compared at two points in time. If the locations differ, the individual is assumed to have moved once. Of course, frequently the individual has moved more than once. The possibility also exists that an individual who has moved more than once may not be counted as mobile at all if the second move is back to the original residence.

An additional issue involved with this measure is how different the location must be before mobility is assumed to have occurred. Movement across the country is different from movement across town. Considering any change of residence, no matter how short the distance involved, as mobility, as is done in the United States, will produce much higher mobility rates than if only those moves crossing some specified boundary are considered. In fact, the Census Bureau does distinguish between mobility (any move) and migration (crossing a county line), and finds many more people who are mobile than who are migrants.

HISTORICAL TRENDS

Colonial Period Much of what is known about geographical mobility during the early history of this country comes from studies of persistence within a community. These studies attempt to follow individuals over time by using records available for a community at two or more points in time. Several types of records have been used for these studies, including tax rolls, militia registers, and city directories. If an individual is recorded at both points in time, he or she is considered not to have moved away from the community. Persistence rates, the percent of the population still in the area at the second time, calculated from these sources are not completely accurate. Some people could have not been enumerated at the second time even if they had not moved. For example, rather than moving, the person could have died. Furthermore, enumeration was probably more complete for higher-status individuals. Given the limitations of record linkage, results from these studies should be viewed with caution.

In spite of their limitations, studies determining persistence rates do provide some information about geographical mobility. They suggest that commercial cities on the East Coast, like Boston, had lower persistence rates than smaller farming towns in the interior, like Andover and Dedham, Massachusetts. Such a difference should not be surprising. The coastal cities frequently served as ports of entry for immigrants who were pulled to the interior by better opportunities. As long as they had land, those living in the interior villages did not need to seek opportunities elsewhere.

Some of the mobility that occurred in the smaller towns was within the town limits, as in Andover, where many of the original settlers moved from the town center to the periphery for better farmland. The original settlers also were able to limit movement of their children through their control of the community's land—movement that has been learned about through the use of record linking as well as of wills and property records. First-generation fathers in Andover restricted the movement of their sons, especially the eldest, by withholding land from them until the sons were older, thus causing the sons to marry relatively late in life. Often along with the inheritance would come an obligation to care for the father's widow, a duty that further restricted the son's mobility. Parents also controlled their daughters' mobility through both inheritances and marriages. If a woman married a man from another town, she typically moved to his town.

Movement into the interior of the continent was restricted by the Appalachians. These mountains served as a formidable physical barrier to migrants and also marked the line beyond which the British attempted to restrict settlement. A royal proclamation of 1763 forbade surveys beyond the Appalachians although this policy was altered over the next several years to open new lands in the Ohio region.

Natural barriers forced those leaving the Middle Atlantic region to move south. This stream was dominated by Scotch-Irish but also included smaller groups with other ethnic backgrounds who settled throughout the Southeast. One such group was the German Lutherans, whose descendants can still be found scattered throughout the predominantly Baptist-Methodist South today.

Pennsylvania, Maryland, and Virginia appear to have been losing young men through out-migration before the American Revolution. They were pushed from older, densely settled coastal regions in search of open spaces for new settlements. Many of these migrants moved to the Carolinas. Another stream flowed northward into upstate New York and parts of New England; it originated mostly north of Pennsylvania and contributed to the high in-migration to New York and New Hampshire.

Advancing the Frontier The first census of the United States, taken in 1790, provided a reasonable count of the nearly four million citizens of the new country. It did not, however, provide any information on previous places of residence from which mobility patterns could be ascertained. Not until the 1850 census was even place of birth asked. After the 1800 census, it was possible to compare records for two time periods, thereby providing an additional source for record linkage to determine migration.

Many studies using record linkage have found higher persistence rates—lower rates of geographical mobility—among higher-status individuals. Again, these results may reflect weaknesses of the method. Higher-status individuals were more likely to be recorded. It is not too surprising that the unskilled, the propertyless, and the poor would find a need to move during the nineteenth century. The costs of mobility were relatively low, and the benefits of settling in a new area could be great.

Almost 95 percent of the population in 1790 lived east of the Appalachians. In fact, most of the 1790 population lived on or near the coast in the Northeast and Middle Atlantic regions. Thus the geographical center of the population was about 23 miles (37 kilometers) east of Baltimore—the farthest east it would ever be.

The barrier of the mountains was soon overcome. Led by frontiersmen like Daniel Boone, whose exploits have become an important part of the frontier culture, settlers followed the Wilderness Road, which Boone had helped to cut in 1775. Many of these pioneers were children of the settlers who had moved into Virginia from Pennsylvania a generation earlier and now were pulled to new frontiers opening farther west.

Some of these settlers and their families continued into Indiana and Illinois (Abraham Lincoln's family was among them). Interestingly, much of the movement was almost directly westward. Some Virginians, as well as newer Kentuckians and Tennesseeans, began to push up into Ohio and other East North Central states. The Middle Atlantic states also sent settlers to the Ohio basin who took with them their beliefs and practices.

Northerners, particularly New Yorkers and southern New Englanders, were attracted to the opportunities in the Midwest at latitudes similar to those of their origins; they settled in upper Ohio, southern Michigan, and Wisconsin before pushing even farther into the middle western plains. The opening of the Erie Canal in 1825 provided a new water route, and many took advantage of improved transportation to move to the interior. This new means of transportation facilitated the movement of goods as well as people. By 1800 over fifty thousand people were living in what are now the states of Ohio, Indiana, Illinois, Wisconsin, and Michigan, the majority of them in Ohio.

New Englanders played a more significant role than their numbers might suggest. In both the first and the second decades of the nineteenth century, the New England region experienced net out-migration: 1 percent in the first decade and 2 percent between 1810 and 1820. New Englanders took with them their educational system as well as their business skills. Regional origins were identifiable when people moved into the Midwest, but a new culture blended the traits of the various regional groups.

Also important in expanding the country were the Louisiana Purchase in 1803 and the reduction of tensions between the United States and Britain at about the same time. Gaining the Louisiana Territory further opened the area west of the Mississippi. Between 1810 and 1820, Louisiana almost doubled its population from about 77,000 to over 153,000. Then Texas declared its independence from Mexico on 2 March 1836. Mexico had consistently tried to limit the number of American settlers in the Southwest. The settlers, over thirty thousand when the fighting began, wanted to Americanize Texas and led the fighting against Mexico. Texas quickly won its independence, thereby increasing its attractiveness to those from the United States. With the granting of statehood at the end of 1845, Texans finally won what they had sought since moving to the region. Five years later the first federal census of the state found that it had almost 213,000 people.

During the 1820s and 1830s a few hundred traders followed the Santa Fe Trail to New Mexico. The Mexican government permitted this movement, probably not overly concerned because of the small number of people involved. As in many areas of the West, the early settlers established a foothold and laid the groundwork for further movement to the Southwest.

A similar foothold was established in the Pacific Northwest. Methodists established a mission in Oregon in the early 1830s, and they spread the word about favorable conditions in the region. By the 1840s, hundreds of pioneers were traveling the Oregon Trail, passing through Missouri and Wyoming, and eventually reaching Oregon. By the middle of the decade about five thousand Americans were settled in the region.

The Gold Rush Traders and other explorers blazed the trails that later were followed by the wagon trains. The discovery of gold created an economic pull for miners seeking a quick fortune. The Forty-niners rapidly increased the population of California from fewer than a thousand Americans in 1846 to 93,000 in 1850. Other important gold strikes included one near Pike's Peak (1858), which attracted perhaps one hundred thousand in search of wealth that many did not find. The last important strike occurred at Cripple Creek, Colorado, in the early 1890s.

Many of these miners did not strike it rich by discovering gold, but some did contribute to the belief that social mobility could result from physical mobility. Yet for every successful gold mining settlement, there is probably at least one ghost town where the gold quickly ran out. Those settlements which survived and prospered frequently had more resources than just gold. They had favorable environments allowing residents to engage in activities other than mining. Perhaps they were at the intersection of transportation lines, as was Sacramento, founded at the junction of the Sacramento and American rivers. Many people who originally went west in search of gold became successful after they switched from mining to other activities. They opened stores, or more likely trading posts, and provided other services to the miners and settlers who followed. Eventually a stable community grew to replace the boisterous mining settlement.

The discovery of gold was a stimulus for movement to California and contributed to the territory's growth. California also attracted migrants because of the importance of its ports. Ships from the East Coast called regularly. In addition, individuals of Spanish descent were settling in California, thereby contributing to its distinctive Spanish flavor. By 1860 the state had grown to a population of almost four hundred thousand, about four times its size in 1850.

The Mormons At about the same time that adventurers were seeking their fortune in the gold rush, others were searching for an area where they could pursue another type of reward: fulfilling the promises of their religion. The Mormon religious movement had begun in the early 1830s in upstate New York. Pushed out of New York because of conflict over their beliefs, the Mormons, in a continued search for a homeland free from religious persecution, moved to Ohio, Missouri, Illinois, and finally Utah.

Following the death of their founder, Joseph Smith, in 1844, Brigham Young took over the leadership of the Mormons. Young left Illinois in 1846 with a small, well-prepared group, much better organized and equipped than most groups moving west at the time. By 1847 these migrants had arrived at the Great Salt Lake, an area that proved to be an ideal home for the Mormons. It was isolated enough for them to practice their religion without interference and was protected from attack by natural features; yet it was close enough to the Oregon Trail for trade with passing settlers. The area was rather barren, but to the Mormons it provided opportunities. Working together under the leadership of church authorities, they survived and prospered.

These towns also had as strong a religious influence as colonial New England towns had often had. Mormons carefully planned their towns in the New England style, in contrast with the isolated homestead patterns characteristic of much of the rest of the region. Mormons established an irrigation system permitting agricultural development. As they became secure and prosperous, they spread throughout what was to become Utah, taking with them their religiously based social system and their form of community organization. The Utah Territory almost quadrupled in size between 1850 and 1860, at which time it had over forty thousand residents, most of whom were Mormon.

Manifest Destiny One of the biggest challenges in settling the frontier came from Native Americans, who did not leave easily or peacefully as they continued to be pushed westward. The conflicts between the settlers and the natives played an important part in the history of the West, a role that has been documented by both the academic community and in popular entertainment media. Certainly these battles played a significant role in shaping the culture that emerged around the old West. Children today play cowhands and Indians, imitating their favorite figures from this earlier time. Furthermore, a large number of books portray the settling of this region. The Western movie may even have helped Ronald Reagan to become president—he became well known through his ap-

pearances in films and television programs about the western experience.

Citizens of the United States came to see it as their manifest destiny to fill the continent—at least the part which they felt Canada could not reasonably claim. In fact, filling the frontier became almost an all-encompassing passion of the country. The land beckoned with opportunities attracting settlers. The people drawn by these opportunities were the restless ones who saw the chance to better themselves. They worked to create a new life for themselves while creating the institutions and organizations of a new community.

Frontier values spread and became incorporated into American culture. The frontier was a place of opportunities for those willing to work hard and to take a chance. With hard work an individual could survive and prosper. The frontier was also a land of plenty contributing to the wasteful overconsumption characteristic of American culture. But perhaps the overriding value emerging from the frontier was optimism. The United States became the land of opportunity both for those already here and for millions of immigrants. Opportunities for geographical mobility were readily available, and geographical mobility was perceived by many to lead to social mobility. All was possible for the individual in a democratic society.

As the Civil War approached, there was increased concern about geographical mobility. In 1850, for the first time, the census asked about place of birth. Almost one-fourth of the native-born population reported living in a state other than the one in which they were born. Further evidence of increased concern about mobility is the fact that a census conducted in New York State asked respondents how long they had lived in their community.

These studies demonstrated a mobile population; in addition, they showed a population moving westward in search of opportunities. By the Civil War almost half of the population lived west of the Appalachians. Americans were already following Horace Greeley's suggestion that they go west. The geographic center had moved west to 20 miles (32 kilometers) southeast of Chillicothe, Ohio. Mountains obviously were no longer a barrier to migration. Trails had been cut through the mountain valleys and passes, and water routes carried migrants westward. Even though a significant proportion of the population was no longer living on the East Coast, the United States had not yet fulfilled its manifest destiny. Most of the West was still wide open, waiting for the coming of the railroad to transport settlers and goods to the region.

After the Civil War The Civil War marks an important turning point in the history of the United States. A number of changes in the mobility patterns of the country began about this time. Many southerners, both black and white, were displaced by the war and its aftermath. Some of these southerners pushed west; others moved to the industrializing cities of the North.

The South also attracted significant migration during Reconstruction. Carpetbaggers, Republican northerners moving to the South, are probably the best-known of these migrants. While the number of Carpetbaggers was not great, their influence on the region and its history is significant. In addition, other northerners who were neither Republican nor politically active settled in the South.

The total number moving into the South was small. In 1870 only about 133,000 of the 6.5 million counted in the census South (a Census Bureau region that includes more states than were in the Confederacy) were born in New England or the Middle Atlantic region. Some of these individuals moved south before the war. Including those born in East-North Central states doubles the number of "northern" born, who still were only a small percent of the total number of southerners.

Many moving to the South saw the region as a land of economic opportunities—an image that many southern states tried to cultivate. This image further demonstrates the historical importance of the labor mobility model for explaining geographical mobility. During this period southern states actively tried to recruit new residents. Many states had agencies to advertise their opportunities. They even sent representatives to Europe to recruit immigrants.

Some in-migrants during Reconstruction were Union soldiers who had fought in the region and had been attracted by the southern environment. Others moved to the South because they felt they could help rebuild the region. Many of this latter group saw the potential for personal profit and advancement, but others had more altruistic motives for their movement, such as helping to educate the freedmen.

Closing the Frontier Southerners who could no longer support themselves in the South left the region. They sought new lands in the West, in the Midwest, and in the border states. They joined others seeking their fortunes in newly opened lands.

Poor farmers and laborers felt they could be more successful by moving. They saw the opportunity to own their land, to be their own boss. Between 1870 and 1900, more new land was settled than had been settled in the history of the country. Over 430 million acres (172 million hectares) were opened, much of which went into agricultural production.

Increased population pressure contributed to the development of new areas, as did increased industrialization and improvements in transportation. In addition, more reliable information coming from the West about the types and amounts of land available provided a better picture of the opportunities. Many Americans, gaining their information from geography texts published during the first half of the nineteenth century, had an image of the great American West as the great American desert. As traders and settlers moved across the region, more accurate information filtered back to the East.

Many of the pioneers moving to the Great Plains were pushed by dissatisfaction with their home or by perceived overcrowding. During the 1870s most of the states bordering the Mississippi, with the exception of Arkansas, experienced net out-migration. Tennessee, for example, is estimated to have had 91,800 more people move out than move in. Texas, Kansas, Nebraska, and the Dakotas were all gaining people. Texas added over 308,500 more than it lost, Kansas 366,800, Nebraska 204,400, and the Dakotas 86,800. These territories attracted both rural and urban dwellers, and new cities grew to provide services. A hierarchy of cities emerged, each higher order serving an increasingly larger hinterland (as principles of central place theory would suggest).

The agriculturalists developing the rural areas faced many problems. The environment often was harsh. In years of favorable weather, settlements increased, only to decline in years with poorer conditions. For example, the grasshopper invasion of the mid 1870s forced many pioneers to reconsider their decisions to settle the prairie and to seek other places of residence.

Those who stayed had to develop new methods of farming and ranching. The wide-open spaces of the Great Plains required fencing to contain cattle in a given area, leading to the invention of barbed wire as an inexpensive means of fencing the prairie. Lack of trees and water led to innovations such as sod houses. Windmills were developed to help pump water, and dry farming techniques were employed to conserve limited water supplies.

Another technological development that made possible the settling of the Great Plains was the railroad. One of the most significant events in the history of the West was the joining of the Union Pacific and the Central Pacific at Promontory Point, Utah, in 1869. In addition to transporting settlers to the West, the railroad provided a means for shipping the goods they produced to the markets in the East.

Railroads contributed to closing the frontier in other ways. They were large property holders, having been granted extensive rights-of-way along the tracks. They went to considerable effort to advertise and to sell this land. Selling their land helped to create settlements, which in turn created demand for the railroads to carry freight that would help the companies meet their expenses. In Wyoming, for example, towns such as Cheyenne and Laramie were laid out along the railroad right-of-way, although they remained sparsely settled for years.

The passing of the homestead acts, one in 1862 and another in 1866, further contributed to settlement of the Great Plains. Many industrialists opposed passing these acts because opening up new lands would decrease the supply of labor for their factories.

The Homestead Act of 1862 had some success. Any citizen could pay a ten-dollar filing fee and claim 160 acres (64 hectares) of public domain in the West. After five years of residence, the claimant would receive title to the land. The 1862 act was not a complete success, however. Much of the best land was claimed by speculators who hoped to sell it at a profit. They prevented many farmers and laborers from being able to move by keeping land prices high. Farmers and laborers could not afford enough land for profitable farms if they also had to cover the cost of moving.

The Homestead Act passed in 1866 was primarily directed toward providing land in the Southwest for the freed slaves. As with many programs to help African Americans, this one was a failure. Some blacks did join the movement west, however. Many followed Henry Adams and Benjamin "Pap" Singleton in the Kansas Exodus of 1879. Pushed by social and economic discrimination in the South, these blacks were attracted to a promised land free from racial intolerance. Estimates of the number of blacks involved vary. Between 1870 and 1880 the Census Bureau reported an increase in the black population of Kansas from 17,000 to 43,000.

Probably the most famous land rush occurred in 1889, when Oklahoma was opened for settlement. The federal government negotiated with Native Americans to free the Oklahoma Territory for white settlement. When the horns were sounded, signaling the opening of the territory, thousands rushed to stake their claims. In many cases they found "sooners" already there. These sooners had entered the territory early to grab the best land. By the time Oklahoma became a state in 1907, more than a half a million inhabitants had been attracted.

When Oklahoma became a state, the frontier was closing, at least in the minds of many. In 1890, about the time that Frederick Jackson Turner was declaring the significance of the frontier in American history, the superintendent of the census was declaring the frontier closed. Over one-fourth of the population of the United States lived west of the Mississippi. There remained open spaces in the West, as well as in the East, but no line could be drawn to mark the frontier. Settlements across the country served as bases for further movement into the remaining open spaces and allowed the country to turn its attention away from the frontier to other types of settlement.

Urbanization Movement to the frontier constituted one major migration stream throughout the history of the United States. A second major stream was the movement to urban areas. In fact, in many ways the city served just as much as a safety valve for a rapidly growing population as did the frontier. Cities began with the colonization of the continent, and they played an important role in American development. The majority of growth throughout the nineteenth century was in cities, not at the frontier. But city growth, and more generally growth in urban areas, increased dramatically during the latter part of the nineteenth century, about the time the frontier began to close. However, rapid urbanization was due to more than the closing of the frontier.

Immigrants made a major contribution to urban growth, and immigration increased during the late nineteenth and early twentieth centuries. Immigrants were most important for cities in the Northeast and Midwest. Rural-to-urban migration increased during this time period, being especially significant for the growth of southern and western cities. Rural migrants were both pushed from the countryside and pulled to the cities. Increasingly mechanized agriculture required larger farms, but fewer people, for greater efficiency. Smaller farmers such as southern sharecroppers could not compete. Southern farmers also were losing the fight against the boll weevil, and were forced to leave their farms for cities. By 1880 less than half of the labor force was employed in agriculture.

The implements being introduced on the farms were produced in urban industries. Northern cities began to industrialize first, but not long after the Civil War, southern cities followed. Birmingham, Alabama, for example, built steel mills, and Greenville, South Carolina, attracted textile mills. As opportunities became limited in rural areas and new opportunities were created in urban areas for unskilled laborers, rural dwellers moved to take advantage of the opportunities.

Young people, both male and female, white and black, left their parents' homes to seek jobs in the new factories, both to improve their life chances and to establish their independence. Men found jobs in factories and in emerging service industries that were developing to meet the needs of an increasingly larger population. Women also worked in factories, particularly textile mills in New England and later in the South. Furthermore, many women found jobs as domestics. For young women, working outside the home usually lasted until they married, at which time they quit their paid job. Not until World War II did a large percentage of married women living in cities work outside the home.

Movement away from home did not break family ties completely. Young people sent money home to help support their families and returned to visit. In addition, they received support from relatives living in the cities, typically the relatives who had provided information about the urban opportunities in the first place. Households in the cities took in both related and unrelated boarders and lodgers, providing a homelike atmosphere for first-generation city dwellers. With marriage, these boarders established their own households.

Young men and women wanted jobs in industrializing cities, but the bright lights and excitement of city living also attracted them. Some of the literature of the day discussed the dullness of rural life and the freshness of the city, though not all scholars presented the city in a positive light. Many of the early American sociologists, particularly those at the University of Chicago, were concerned with the social problems that faced rapidly growing industrial cities such as Chicago. They longed for the idyllic experience, the gemeinschaft, of smaller settlements. Many city dwellers had that same longing and moved back to the rural areas they had left.

Poor southern textile workers were noted for their frequent movement between factories and farms.

Cities continued to grow and to spread their influence. By 1920 only the South, of the four major census regions, had more people living in rural than in urban areas. It is difficult to underestimate the importance of industrialization for movement to urban areas. There were, however, other technological innovations that contributed to movement. Improvement in transportation greatly increased the size of a city's hinterlands, making it possible to move goods over greater distances. The railroad, for example, played a major role in the growth of midwestern cities such as Chicago. More recently, growth in air transportation has contributed to Atlanta's emergence as a regional center. Furthermore, the invention of the elevator allowed for expansion upward and for greater spatial concentration. Only with extensive automobile ownership were cities able to spread out to create the urban sprawl familiar today.

Black Migration Blacks tend to move less than whites, and they tend to move over shorter distances. Before emancipation, blacks had been limited in their ability to move, and their movement was largely forced on them by their owners. Those who gained their freedom before the Civil War often sought refuge through the Underground Railroad in the North. By moving to the North, blacks felt they could escape the racial intolerance of the South and find opportunities for paid employment.

With emancipation, blacks as a whole gained more freedom to choose their place of residence, although their movement was still restricted by economic and social conditions. As noted before, some blacks were attracted to Kansas. Other freed blacks chose cities in both the South and the North. The few who moved to the North during the nineteenth century blazed the trails for later generations of blacks. They established both support networks and information networks to ease the burdens on future migrants. Family members and friends followed these pioneers to the same northern cities.

During the two world wars, large numbers of blacks moved north to cities. The 1920 census found that the North had gained about 695,000 southern-born blacks through domestic migration. Between 1940 and 1950, New York State alone gained almost 244,000 blacks born in another state. Illinois added 180,000 during this period and Michigan 163,000, reflecting the flow of black migration into New York, Chicago, and Detroit. Demand for labor for the wartime industries was high. The traditional sources of labor were low. White males were fighting the war. Immigration was restricted, especially during World War I, leaving positions available for any able-bodied individual, including blacks.

Black movement was influenced by economic conditions, and thus it experienced a significant decline during the Great Depression between the Wars. Social conditions also strongly influenced black movement. Blacks desired to escape the castelike southern system and perceived more equal treatment in the North—which, of course, was not always the case. Still, the desire for greater equality contributed to black movement to northern cities into the 1950s and 1960s.

Okies and Hillbillies　During the Depression, general residential mobility declined. Nevertheless, some of the most enduring images of internal migration come from this period—images of poor, displaced farmers moving from Oklahoma and the surrounding Dust Bowl to the bountiful West. As many as one hundred thousand Oklahomans moved to California during the 1930s, accompanied by another quarter of a million moving from the surrounding states to the West.

The strongest of these images, perhaps, comes from John Steinbeck's *The Grapes of Wrath* (1939). His descriptions brought the Okies to the country's attention. Steinbeck showed that migrants often faced hostile conditions. Their movement did not necessarily produce immediate benefits but frequently led to a period of struggle for basic necessities. As Steinbeck suggested, many of the Okies, who included migrants from Texas, Arkansas, and Missouri in addition to those from Oklahoma, had to live in their cars or in tents or shacks. The term "Okie" was not one of endearment; it was used by natives to denigrate migrants. Internal migrants were seen in a negative light, not as rugged pioneers changing residences for upward social mobility but as poor, homeless families with little hope for the future.

A negative image of migrants also can be seen in the treatment of those who left Appalachia during the 1930s and 1940s, and even among those moving more recently. Poor whites left the hills of Kentucky, Tennessee, and West Virginia to seek a better life in the cities of the Midwest. By 1930 over 390,000 people born in these three states lived in Ohio. These "hillbillies," a term with connotations much like those of "Okies," did not totally leave

their old communities behind. They maintained close family ties and communication links both back to the hills and with their fellow migrants. Like the Okies, this group was not always appreciated or admired in its new residences. In midwestern cities such as Cincinnati, the "hillbilly" neighborhoods can still be seen.

Suburbanization　Recognizing the interdependence between a city and its surrounding counties, the Census Bureau in 1950 created the Standard Metropolitan Area, later replaced by the Standard Metropolitan Statistical Area and still later by the Metropolitan Statistical Area. Metropolitan areas included the central city and the surrounding counties that were socially and economically integrated with the city. The Census Bureau was somewhat late in recognizing the existence of such areas. Growth around cities—suburbanization— had started much earlier.

During the first half of the twentieth century, growth in suburban areas accounted for about half of "metropolitan" growth. As the central cities filled, urban dwellers began to move to the open space surrounding cities. This trend accelerated during the 1950s. Approximately 80 percent of the metropolitan growth during this decade was suburban.

The post–World War II baby boom contributed to suburbanization. Newly formed families with young children sought residences with enough land for a yard in which the children could play, but they wanted to be close enough to the city to take advantage of its social and economic opportunities.

Suburbs provided the ideal compromise, especially since the government was building a system of limited-access highways making movement between the cities and the suburbs easier. The government also began to provide low-interest home loans through the Federal Housing Administration and the Veterans Administration. The 1950s were characterized by economic expansion. Stable jobs meant that people could afford to buy their dream homes in the suburbs. The development of mass home-building techniques made these homes more affordable, but the middle class remained most likely to take advantage of these opportunities.

Up to 1970, suburbs were almost totally white as blacks became increasingly concentrated in central cities. More recently diversity has increased significantly in the suburbs. Suburbs have continued to attract whites trying to escape the buildup of central cities, and since the 1970s more blacks, especially middle-class blacks, have been moving to the suburbs. Suburban neighborhoods remain highly racially segregated, as do central-city neighborhoods; but suburbs in general contain rising numbers of minorities.

RECENT TRENDS

Gentrification   While the twentieth century witnessed large-scale migration from central cities, a small yet significant movement into central cities began in the mid 1960s. Cities throughout the country experienced this gentrification, although only a limited number of people were involved in each city. Middle- and upper-middle-class whites moved into older areas to revitalize dilapidated buildings. These people, most of them young and either single or married with no children, desired a city lifestyle and rejected suburban living. Many moved from apartments in the city to their first house elsewhere in the same city.

Aesthetic and economic benefits, such as an increased inner-city tax base, resulted from gentrification. It had negative consequences as well. Many of the residents of the areas being revitalized were displaced as multifamily dwellings were restored to their original single-family use. Most of the displaced were minorities, frequently elderly, and had no other source of low-cost housing.

Nonmetropolitan Movement   During the 1970s, nonmetropolitan areas grew faster than metropolitan areas, a surprising turnaround in migration patterns. At first, movement to nonmetro areas was thought to be a continuation of suburban growth, with people moving to nonmetro counties adjacent to metropolitan areas. But nonadjacent counties grew as fast as, and in many cases faster than, adjacent ones. Furthermore, this growth was evident in all regions of the country, with about 80 percent of the nonmetropolitan counties gaining population. The average annual growth rate of all nonmetropolitan counties during the 1970s was 1.34 percent. Between 1970 and 1975, the years of most rapid nonmetropolitan growth, 2.3 million more people moved into these counties than left.

Social science surveys have long noted a preference among Americans for living in uncongested, open areas such as those in nonmetropolitan places. During the 1970s movement reflected these preferences. As improvements in transportation had contributed to suburbanization, so further improvements contributed to this movement. In addition, technological innovations in communica-

tions and the infrastructure in general made nonmetropolitan living more attractive.

Nonmetropolitan movement was not a return to the soil. The percentage of the population engaged in agricultural pursuits continued a long-term decline. Industries and services moved out of the cities, taking advantage of better transportation and communications technology. Furthermore, an increased retirement-age population had moved to these areas. In spite of the attention paid to this nonmetropolitan growth by the media, or perhaps because of it, this growth was rather short-lived. By 1975 growth rates had peaked, and by 1980 traditional migration patterns to the metropolitan areas were evident. In fact, during the 1980s most large metropolitan areas experienced substantial growth.

Sunbelt Migration   For the first half of the twentieth century, the South experienced net out-migration of both blacks and whites. These losses were not uniform throughout the region. Rural areas lost more as southern farms mechanized and jobs became available in industrializing cities. During the century's second half, the dominant direction of migration changed. The South's first gains from migration were between 1955 and 1960, when it attracted three hundred thousand more migrants than it lost.

Led by Florida, which had positive net in-migration as early as the 1920s, every state in the census South had more net in-migration than out-migration of both blacks and whites at some point during the 1970s. California, at the western end of the Sunbelt, also had a long history of attracting migrants, as illustrated by the gold rush and the Okies. Virginia, Texas, and Arizona are other Sunbelt states that have experienced substantial in-migration. Growth rates for states between the censuses of 1950 and 1990 were phenomenal: Florida grew by 366 percent, Arizona by 388 percent, California by 181 percent, Texas by 120 percent, and Virginia by 86 percent, as compared with 64 percent growth in the United States as a whole.

Numerous factors have been suggested to account for this turnaround. One of the most important technological innovations was probably central air-conditioning, which greatly improved living conditions. Northerners moved to escape the harsh winters, and now a way had been found to make the hot summers more tolerable. It is somewhat ironic that a means of modifying the climate contributed to movement, since the climate itself had attracted many. For example, the buildup of military establishments throughout the South during World

War II occurred because training could take place year round. In addition to the climate, other environmental conditions contributed to the South's growth. Plentiful supplies of clean water attracted industries, as did timber for lumber and paper manufacturing. Industries also were drawn by the lower cost of doing business. Labor costs were low, and southern opposition to labor unions, it was thought, would help to keep them that way.

The Sunbelt also attracted retirees. Again, Florida, California, and Arizona led the way. In fact, about 20 percent of the migrants to Florida in recent years have been age sixty-five or older. Other elderly migrants wanted a more moderate climate, such as that found in the mountains of Arkansas.

Every migration stream has some impact on its destination. Transplanted northerners are no exception. The South has a long history as a distinct region at least somewhat in opposition to the North; after all, it had fought a war against the North. What impact will all these Yankees have on southern culture? The final answer to this question cannot be determined. Northerners in the South do have views distinct from those of southerners. They tend to be more Republican than natives, and the South has recently experienced the growth of a two-party system. While northerners cannot take all the credit, or blame, for this development, they have assumed leadership roles reflecting the traditionally high rates of political participation characteristic of members of higher social classes. These migrants also have more conservative economic views than do natives. They even tend to be less supportive of labor unions—most likely reflecting their white-collar occupational status. Furthermore, transplants have more liberal views on social issues than do native southerners, suggesting the potential for changes in southern culture. The distinct South should not be written off too quickly, however. It has survived greater threats than that posed by a few million migrants.

FUTURE TRENDS

Americans have spread across the continent, settling the frontier and filling the cities. They have developed technologies and facilities to overcome all the obstacles in their path. Railroads increased accessibility to the West; automobiles made suburbanization possible; and satellite dishes improved communications in remote nonmetropolitan areas. These technologies may indirectly contribute to the next mass movement in this country—movement away from coastal areas that may become necessary if global warming occurs as a result of the predicted greenhouse effect.

In recent years the typical American has moved about once every five years. There are reasons to suspect, however, that mobility may slow down. Young people just starting a career are the most mobile segment of the population. The number and percentage of young people in the American population is decreasing as the baby boom generation ages; thus the number of highly mobile persons in the population is declining.

Another change within American society reducing mobility is the increase in two-career families. With both spouses working, especially where they have similar occupations and incomes, geographical mobility becomes increasingly problematic. Migration rates tend to be lower for these families because two new jobs are necessary in order for the family to relocate. When these families do move, they are more likely to move short distances than are other families.

The presence of two-worker families has increased the number of "commuter marriages" in which each spouse has a job and a residence in a separate place. A growing number of professional couples live in different parts of the country. These couples move frequently between two different residences, creating a new type of mobility.

Historically, migration has played an important role in relieving labor imbalances between areas and in providing a way for individuals and families to improve their standard of living. Today, economic causes of mobility are still important; but as economic conditions become more similar throughout the country, other factors take on more importance. The South, the region that had lagged behind in economic development, is now one of the fastest-growing regions, with new residents attracted by its warm climate and its economic opportunities. Movement by the elderly also exemplifies the decreased importance of economic conditions. Retirees, not being dependent on where a job is located, often base their selection of an area on life-style considerations. With further economic standardization in the twenty-first century, noneconomic opportunities will exert even more influence on migration. It also seems that there will be an increase in movement between similar types of areas. Instead of rural-to-urban or city-to-suburb, for example, there will probably be more urban-to-urban movement—a trend that has already begun.

BIBLIOGRAPHY

Allen, James P. "Changes in the American Propensity to Migrate." *Annals of the Association of American Geographers* 67, no. 4 (1977).

Biggar, Jeanne C. "The Sunning of America: Migration to the Sunbelt." *Population Bulletin* 34, no. 1 (1979).

Frey, William H. "Metropolitan America: Beyond the Transition." *Population Bulletin* 45, no. 2 (1990).

Gerhan, David R., and Robert V. Wells, comps. *A Retrospective Bibliography of American Demographic History from Colonial Times to 1983* (1989).

Hudson, John C. "North American Origins of Middlewestern Frontier Populations." *Annals of the Association of American Geographers* 78, no. 3 (1988).

Johnson, Daniel M., and Rex R. Campbell. *Black Migration in America: A Social Demographic History* (1981).

Kirby, Jack Temple. "The Southern Exodus, 1910–1960: A Primer for Historians." *Journal of Southern History* 49, no. 4 (1983).

———. *Rural Worlds Lost: The American South, 1920–1960* (1987).

Kuznets, Simon Smith, and Dorothy Swaine Thomas, eds. *Population Redistribution and Economic Growth: United States, 1870–1950.* 3 vols. (1957–1964).

Lebergott, Stanley. "Migration Within the U.S., 1800–1960: Some New Estimates." *Journal of Economic History* 30, no. 4 (1970).

Lee, Everett S. "A Theory of Migration." *Demography* 3, no. 1 (1966).

Long, Larry. *Migration and Residential Mobility in the United States* (1988).

Parkerson, Donald H. "How Mobile Were Nineteenth-Century Americans?" *Historical Methods* 15, no. 3 (1982).

Ritchey, P. Neal. "Explanations of Migration." *Annual Review of Sociology* 2 (1976).

Sharpless, John. "Population Redistribution in the American Past: Empirical Generalizations and Theoretical Perspectives." *Social Science Quarterly* 61, nos. 3 and 4 (1980).

Thernstrom, Stephan. *Progress and Poverty: Social Mobility in a Nineteenth-Century City* (1964).

Tindall, George Brown. *America: A Narrative History* (1984).

Turner, Frederick Jackson. *Frontier and Section: Selected Essays of Frederick Jackson Turner* (1961).

United States Bureau of the Census. *Historical Statistics of the United States, Colonial Times to 1970. Bicentennial Edition* (1975). Also published in other years.

Vinovskis, Maris A. "Recent Trends in American Historical Demography: Some Methodological and Conceptual Considerations." *Annual Review of Sociology* 4 (1978).

Wilkie, Jane Riblett. "The United States Population by Race and Urban-Rural Residence 1790–1860: Reference Tables." *Demography* 13, no. 1 (1976).

SEE ALSO **American Social and Cultural Geography; The Frontier; Immigration; Regionalism; Transportation and Mobility.**

THE FRONTIER

Gregory H. Nobles

"THE FRONTIER" is a troublesome term for historians. On the one hand, it evokes one of the most important processes in American history, the movement of European peoples across the American continent. It encompasses exploits of heroic exploration and violent warfare and, though less dramatic but no less significant, the spread of settlements and social relations. Unfortunately, the notion of the frontier has become encumbered with many misleading images based on assumptions of racial and national superiority. Above all, the dislocation and destruction of native tribes in the face of European American advance has often been taken for granted as an inevitable, even necessary, step in American history, the price of "progress." The bias built into the story of the frontier has been regularly reinforced, not just in popular fiction and film but also in the work of professional historians.

The foremost, if not the first, historian to focus scholarly attention on the American frontier was Frederick Jackson Turner. While still a young professor at the University of Wisconsin, he wrote a pathbreaking essay, "The Significance of the Frontier in American History" (1893), that became a classic work in American historical writing. Indeed, over the course of the next half-century, Turner and the disciples of his "frontier thesis" formed one of the most prominent schools of historical thought in the United States. Turner identified the frontier as a "fertile field for investigation," a distinct conceptual category that could "be isolated and studied as a factor in American history of the highest importance." More to the point, he argued that "American history has been in a large degree the history of the colonization of the Great West. The existence of an area of free land, its continuous recession, and the advance of American settlement westward, explain American development" ("Significance of the Frontier," p. 1). The frontier was, in short, the most important element in the evolution of the United States, the critical factor that made the American

people culturally unique. From the earliest days of colonial settlement, westward movement to successive frontiers promoted the "steady movement away from the influence of Europe" and thus helped Americans develop new standards of democracy and equality. As long as people had the prospect of moving west to free lands, they could "escape from the bondage of the past" and "escape to the free conditions of the frontier." Unfortunately, Turner argued, that prospect had dimmed by the end of the nineteenth century: "the frontier has gone, and with its going has closed the first period in American history" ("The Significance of the Frontier," p. 38).

Turner was a remarkably creative and insightful historian, but his "frontier thesis" was seriously flawed. Throughout the first half of the twentieth century, and especially in the 1930s and 1940s, other scholars refined or rejected his argument, challenging both his scholarship and his historical vision. According to Turner's critics, he overstated the effect of the frontier environment on the development of democracy and individualism, and he offered rather loose and imprecise definitions of those terms. He took little or no account of the impact of urbanization and industrialization on American society. Moreover, his emphasis on American exceptionalism overlooked or obscured the continuing significance of European influence on American culture. In general, by the 1950s, Turner's "frontier thesis" had become if not a ruin, then certainly a relic. It still stood as an impressive monument to an important academic achievement, but it no longer formed a stable foundation for future scholarship.

One issue that was not resolved by the scholarly debate over Turner's frontier thesis was the very idea of "the frontier" itself. Both Turner and his critics used the term freely, sometimes arguing about its precise definition but seldom questioning its inherent assumptions. Yet it is important to note that "the frontier" is an ethnocentric notion that has meaning primarily from the standpoint of Europeans or European Americans, but not from that of Native Americans, the people Europeans called Indians. Turner, for instance, described the frontier as "the outer edge of the wave—the meeting point between savagery and civilization" ("Significance of the Frontier," p. 3). Even when stripped of its most obvious cultural bias—the distinction between Indian "savagery" and European "civilization"—the description of the frontier as "the outer edge of the wave" still adopts the point of view of the advancing (or, indeed, invading) culture. For those native inhabitants resisting or retreating before that advance, the idea of the frontier had a very different meaning—or, more accurately, no meaning at all.

For that reason, recent historians have attempted to develop alternative terminology or at least to take a more multicultural approach to the study of the frontier. Rather than describing the frontier as a line or an edge of cultural division, many scholars prefer to talk of "contact zones" of intercultural exchange. In this sense, the emphasis is on the plurality of frontier regions in North America, and not just on the Anglo-American wave of westward expansion. More important, the emphasis is not so much on place as on process, the patterns of interaction between different peoples. Again, plurality is important; there was no single, predictably repeated process of frontier interaction. Historians now seek to understand the varieties of interaction among different groups at different times in different places. Indians and Europeans frequently engaged in warfare and violent conflict, but they also cooperated as allies and trading partners. Whatever the case, neither group remained unchanged by extended contact with the other. The recognition of the two-way relationship helps break down the distinction between "savage" and "civilized," and offers a more complex and ultimately more compelling history of human interaction on the North American continent.

THE COLONIAL FRONTIERS

The early period of intercultural contact makes one point clear: just as one cannot talk of a single frontier, much less a single frontier experience, neither can one talk of "Europeans" and "Indians" as single, monolithic entities. Both groups included people who exhibited significant differences in language, identity, and interest.

On the eve of European colonization, the native population of North America was both large and diverse. Descended from nomadic groups that crossed the Bering Strait from Asia over thirty thousand years before, Indian people had been well established in North America for thousands of years. Thus they, rather than Europeans, were not only the original discoverers of America but also the first settlers. Indeed, some North American Indians, like the Hopewell culture of the Ohio Valley or the Mississippian culture, had developed complex and sophisticated societies and then, long before the advent of Europeans, had begun to decline. Population estimates for the area north of Mexico in the pre-European period vary widely, ranging from a low of around one million to a higher (and more recent) figure of over ten million.

The Indians of North America comprised hundreds of linguistic and societal groups. Some, like the Siouan peoples of the Great Plains, were primarily nomadic hunters, but far more were comparatively settled agriculturists. In the desert Southwest, for instance, the Hopi and Zuni cultures had developed elaborate irrigation systems to facilitate farming in their arid region. Moreover, their villages of substantial, multiroom, apartment-like houses (called *pueblos* by the Spanish) stood as monuments to the people's persistence. To the east, especially along the Atlantic seaboard and in the interior piedmont region, people of the Muskogean, Algonkian, and Iroquoian language groups combined hunting, gathering, fishing, and farming.

Numbering about half a million and divided into dozens of kinship networks, chiefdoms, and confederacies, Indians of the eastern woodlands lived in villages within distinct tribal territories. Unlike Europeans, they did not emphasize individualism or private property but tended to share land and other natural resources communally among members of the village or tribe. Men and women shared a greater degree of equality than was common in European culture. Like Europeans, however, eastern woodland tribes had sometimes cordial but often conflicted relations with groups outside their own. They traded extensively with each other, but they also fought ferociously to avenge violations of tribal territory or honor. Indeed, long-standing antagonisms between some tribal groups mirrored the traditional rivalries of the European powers and contributed to the complex military and diplomatic alliances of the early North American frontier.

The major European colonizers of North America—the Spanish, French, Dutch, and English—shared a common goal of extracting wealth from the New World, and the pursuit of that goal led them into fierce competition. Indeed, they fought against each other as much as against the Indians; their New World settlements became imperial outposts in a broader struggle for economic and military supremacy on both sides of the Atlantic. Even their maps of the New World were designed to reflect not so much geographical accuracy as imperial policy. Cartographers often claimed much more territory than military men could hope to acquire, and the maps of the major European colonizers almost always showed competing claims to vast expanses of the North American interior. Moreover, when Europeans actually settled on the land, their respective modes of colonization revealed strikingly different strategies of social and economic development. Those strategies had long-term implications not only for the continuing competition among the European powers but also for their relationships with the natives of North America.

The Spanish, for instance, did not make a significant attempt to establish large-scale, well-populated settlements inhabited by emigrants from their own country. Rather, they sought to continue along the path of plunder that had taken them through South and Central America, extracting the riches of the New World to send back to Spain. Lured northward by their lust for gold and silver, sixteenth-century Spanish explorers laid claim to large parts of what is now the southern United States, from Florida and the Gulf of Mexico to the coast of California. One conquistador, Francisco Vásquez de Coronado, pushed as far north as present-day Kansas in his search for the fabled Seven Cities of Cibola. He never found the gold he sought, nor did the other Spaniards in North America. Still, by the end of the sixteenth century, they had set up numerous small military garrisons and Catholic missions, from which they managed to impose considerable control over the economic and religious lives of the native peoples. Moreover, they used these outposts as bases of military operations against other European powers. Although their numbers were never very large, the Spanish played an important role in North America well into the nineteenth century.

Similarly, the Dutch and French established a significant presence in North America without sending over large numbers of settlers. Both nations developed an extensive fur trade with native tribes, and during the first half of the seventeenth century they did a lively and lucrative business in beaver pelts. From their main settlement at New Amsterdam (present-day New York City), the Dutch dominated trade in the Hudson, Connecticut, and Delaware river valleys. In the third quarter of the seventeenth century, however, a series of wars between the Dutch and the English resulted in the loss of Dutch territory and trade on the North American mainland.

The French, by comparison, maintained control of an increasingly extensive North American trade network. They established fishing operations along the northern Atlantic coast in the sixteenth century, and beginning in 1534, the explorer Jacques Cartier led expeditions up the Saint Lawrence River. The Saint Lawrence soon became the first major area of French influence in North America. In 1608, Samuel de Champlain established a small settlement at Quebec, and by the 1620s French traders had ventured into the North American interior as far as the Great Lakes. In the 1670s and 1680s other French explorers—most notably Louis Jolliet, Father Jacques Marquette, and René Robert de La Salle—pushed west well beyond the Missouri River and south to the mouth of the Mississippi River. By the end of the seventeenth century, then, the French claimed a huge expanse of territory that reached from southern Canada to the Gulf of Mexico and covered roughly the middle third of what is now the United States. Like the Spanish, they reinforced their claim by creating a network of trading posts, military garrisons, and Catholic missions. Still, the number of French colonists in North America in 1700 totaled little more than ten thousand.

The English adopted a much different strategy for North American colonization. They were comparative latecomers to New World exploration and settlement, and they did not establish a permanent foothold on the North American mainland until 1607, with the creation of Jamestown in Virginia. Like the other European colonizers, the English sought to extract the abundant riches of the New World—fish, furs, and, if they were fortunate, gold and silver—but they did more than set up forts and trading posts. They planted permanent agricultural communities populated by English and other European emigrants. From the staple-producing plantations in the South to the quasi-communal farming villages of New England, these colonists quickly spread over the landscape in their quest for land.

By the 1750s, England's North American colonies reached from present-day Maine to Georgia and as far west as the Appalachian mountain chain.

Although this area was quite small compared with the vast territories claimed by Spain and France, it held a comparatively large population of nearly a million and a half English subjects. This approach to colonization had important implications for the future of the Anglo-American frontier: unlike the Spanish and French, the English sought not only to subdue the native tribes but also to remove them.

This process of removal had begun in the first period of contact. Everywhere they went, Europeans carried with them diseases—especially smallpox, diphtheria, and measles—against which North American natives had no natural or acquired immunity. Long before the main force of European colonizers arrived in North America, imported illnesses had swept the native peoples, devastating tribes in every region and depopulating some by as much as 90 percent. Especially along the eastern seaboard of North America, in the region ultimately dominated by the English, Indians suffered a demographic catastrophe that greatly undermined their ability to resist European invasion. Thus the early colonizers accomplished more through this unwitting germ warfare than they could ever have achieved through force of arms.

FRONTIER WARFARE BEFORE 1800

Force of arms did, of course, play a critical role in the longer history of the North American frontier. Warfare on the frontier was seldom a clear-cut contest between European invaders and Indian resisters. The European colonizing powers fought among themselves, and so did native tribes. Both Europeans and Indians took advantage of the other's animosities, creating complex intercultural alliances out of overlapping layers of long-standing hostility. They used those alliances to further their own diplomatic and military ends, and when making new alliances served their purposes, they did so.

In the seventeenth and eighteenth centuries, the imperial wars of the European powers brought Indian-European diplomacy into play on a broad scale. Although the contest in the colonies was essentially a sideshow to the larger, long-lasting Old World conflict, the American frontier increasingly became both battleground and prize in the struggle among the European powers.

For instance, in the major imperial struggle of the colonial era, the Seven Years' War—or the French and Indian War, as it was called in the British

American colonies—Great Britain established dominance over a huge expanse of territory on the American frontier. This conflict began with a series of clashes on the Pennsylvania frontier in 1754 and spread throughout North America, from Canada to the West Indies. Within a few years, almost thirty thousand British regulars joined colonial militia units to combat a much smaller French force aided by a substantial number of Indian allies.

Both the British and the French attempted to gain Indian support. In the early years of the conflict, a few hundred Mohawk and Cherokee warriors fought briefly for the British as mercenaries, but they were hardly loyal or long-standing allies. The Iroquois confederacy, of which the Mohawk were a part, chose for the most part to adopt a position of neutrality, letting the Europeans fight between themselves while accepting gifts from both. Only when the military situation began to shift in favor of the Anglo-Americans—especially after their victories over the French at Louisbourg in 1758 and at Quebec in 1759—did the Iroquois tilt toward the British side.

In the South, the Cherokee turned toward the French after their limited alliance with the British turned sour, and after 1758 they posed a serious threat to Anglo-American settlers in the southern backcountry. They attempted to bring the powerful Creek into the war against the Anglo-Americans in a multitribal alliance with other southern Indians. But the Creek, like the Iroquois, played one European side against the other for favorable trade concessions. In the end, this position of neutrality proved beneficial. The Iroquois and Creek emerged from the European conflict with their trade relations and tribal lands intact; the Cherokee suffered because of the loss of French trade goods, and they had to accept territorial boundaries imposed by the victorious British.

By 1763, at the end of the war, the British had greatly expanded their North American territories. Above all, the removal of the French presence from the trans-Appalachian interior promised new opportunities for Anglo-American expansion, and thousands of land-hungry settlers looked forward to moving west.

But almost immediately two obstacles rose to stop them, or at least impede them. In 1763, a chief of the Ottawa tribe, Pontiac, led the tribes of the Great Lakes region in a resistance movement to stop Anglo-American encroachment. Pontiac's forces attacked and destroyed several British garrisons, and they threatened to drive the British army out of the area. By 1764, war-weary British regular troops, just returned from fighting the French in the West Indies, managed to break up Pontiac's forces and maintain a presence in the Northwest. Still, the volatile situation in the region led British policymakers to try to prevent further conflict between Indians and Anglo-Americans by keeping white settlers out of Indian territory. While Pontiac's uprising was still in progress, the government in London imposed the Proclamation of 1763, which prohibited settlers from moving west of the Appalachian Mountains. The British army was too sparsely stationed to enforce the policy effectively, and thousands of whites simply ignored the ban and moved west anyway. Nonetheless, the policy seemed oppressive to many potential migrants, and the government's attempt to restrict access to the trans-Appalachian West was one of the many tensions contributing to the antagonism between Britain and its American colonies.

The American War for Independence had important implications for the future of the frontier. It created a new North American nation that took over not only the territory formerly held by the British but also the lands of native tribes. As was the case in the Seven Years' War, Indians were considered valuable allies in frontier fighting, and both the British and their rebellious colonists sought to recruit them. In the North, tribes of the Iroquois confederacy fought on both sides, sometimes attacking each other and often suffering devastating losses. Once the war was over, the Iroquois confederacy was weakened almost beyond repair, and its leaders were forced to concede a large area of western land to the victorious United States in the Treaty of Fort Stanwix (1784). In the South, the Cherokee fought for the British—or, more properly, against American expansion. Like the Iroquois, they suffered greatly from retaliatory expeditions, and at war's end they, too, had to surrender territory to the new American republic.

THE STRUGGLE FOR ORDER ON THE AMERICAN FRONTIER

The acquisition of western land both from the native tribes and from the British fueled expansionist fever among white Americans. Having been legally limited by the Proclamation of 1763, settlers and speculators now eagerly sought to take advantage of the opening of new lands in the Old Northwest. One of the main tasks (and few successes) of the American government under the Articles of Confederation was the organization of orderly settlement in that region. Beginning in 1785, government surveyors divided the territory into a gridwork of townships, each six miles square with thirty-six one-mile-square sections of 640 acres, which could be subdivided into smaller lots and sold. (In fact, this straight-line design became the model for the government's land policy of the west throughout the nineteenth century.) The assumption was that, once populated with productive settlers, these western territories would enter the Union as new states, thereby adding to the size and strength of the new nation.

But the imposition of an orderly plan on the western territories did not guarantee control. Although the British were required by the Treaty of Paris (1783) to relinquish their military garrisons in the Northwest, they did so very slowly. The United States government, with its army demobilized and somewhat demoralized at the war's end, could do nothing to hurry the British on their way. The Spanish likewise caused trouble in the West. They held New Orleans, which they had acquired at the end of the Seven Years' War, and thus controlled the outlet from the Mississippi River to the Gulf of Mexico. In 1784 they closed New Orleans to American shipping, denying frontier farmers access to foreign markets and discouraging the commercial development of the trans-Appalachian interior. To make matters worse, Spanish agents were reported to be encouraging western settlers to break away from the United States and ally themselves with Spain. At the same time, native tribes throughout the trans-Appalachian region, from the Ohio country to Georgia, resisted further white expansion and attacked settlers who encroached on tribal lands.

By the time the first federal government under George Washington took office in 1789, the western frontier of the United States was a vast but extremely vulnerable appendage to the original thirteen states. Foreign intrigues and Indian unrest made the region a source of national insecurity, and the government's claims to control rang hollow. Washington himself—who had had extensive experience in the western country as a military leader and who still held a sizable financial interest there as a land speculator—made securing the frontier one of the main items on his political agenda. There was little he could do militarily to oppose Britain and Spain, but he could take action against North American inhabitants.

Washington committed a large armed force to combat native tribes in the Northwest Territory, and in 1794, at the Battle of Fallen Timbers in northern Ohio, United States troops under Major General Anthony Wayne gained a decisive victory against a combined force of Shawnee, Ottawa, Ojibwa, and Pottawatomi warriors. In the same year, Washington sent (and for a while personally led) a huge military expedition into western Pennsylvania to suppress the Whiskey Rebellion, an uprising of local farmers opposed to the Washington administration's excise tax on whiskey, a marketable commodity crucial to the local economy. The rebellion broke up before Washington's army arrived, so there was no climactic battle like that against the Indians. Still, by dispatching federal troops to assert governmental authority, Washington made clear his resolve to put down frontier unrest, whether it came from Indians or whites.

The Whiskey Rebellion points to a phenomenon that had long been part of Anglo-American frontier relations: intracultural, as well as intercultural, conflict. That is, Anglo-Americans not only fought against Indians and other Europeans for control of the frontier, they also fought among themselves. This conflict manifested itself dramatically in a series of armed insurrections, the most notable of which were Bacon's Rebellion in Virginia (1676), the Land Riots in New York (1766), the Regulator movement in North Carolina (1766–1771), and the Regulator movement, or Shays's Rebellion, in Massachusetts (1786–1787), and then the Whiskey Rebellion. In each case backcountry settlers felt themselves economically and politically oppressed by their fellow countrymen, both the elite in their own frontier regions and the merchants and officials in the more established regions to the east. When their pleas and petitions to the established authorities brought no positive result, they rose up in arms to seek redress of their grievances. Even though these frontier insurrections were usually suppressed by the superior military might of the government, they still represented a recurring threat to the established order of Anglo-American authorities.

On a lower, less dramatic scale, frontier folk frequently lived in tension with those lawmakers and landowners who sought to impose their notions of spatial, social, and economic order on the process of settlement. Elite proprietors of backcountry tracts hoped to populate the frontier with sturdy, stable, hardworking farmers who would improve the land (and land values) and produce a marketable commodity. They also wanted settlers who would pay proper respect to the landowning elite. For this reason proprietors often tried to attract German and Swiss immigrants, ethnic groups that were thought to fit the profile of the productive settler.

Yet large landowners often found that the people who actually settled (and sometimes squatted) on their land were not the people they had planned for. The early American backcountry attracted an ethnically diverse group of settlers, not only sturdy Germans but, more often, Scotch-Irish immigrants who had been driven out of Ireland and were hardly more popular in the American colonies. The Scotch-Irish made up a sizable proportion of the emigrants who swept down the Shenandoah Valley of Virginia in the middle of the eighteenth century. Members of the Virginia gentry found these new inhabitants of the western lands to be hardly the decent and deferential sort they had expected. Instead, these newcomers tended to be independent-minded people who had their own ideas and expectations about making their way in the wilderness. Rather than making the kinds of permanent improvements needed for commercial development, these settlers lived off the natural bounty of the environment. Rather than engaging in such gentlemanly forms of competition as horse racing, dancing, and dueling, they took sport in cockfights and brutal gouging matches. Rather than accepting the orderly religion of the Anglican church, they lived according to the spiritual, almost supernatural, intensity of enthusiastic, evangelical religion.

Bound together by mutual need and mystical belief, people in the Virginia backcountry and elsewhere on the American frontier formed their own communities that existed outside of, and even in defiance of, the control of elite landowners. Accordingly, those landowners increasingly came to scorn these settlers as disorderly, slothful people who, according to the common complaint, lived like Indians. In fact, the term "white Indians" became a common slur cast against these settlers by members of the Anglo-American elite. In their eyes, these "white Indians" represented obstacles to orderly development, and therefore they, no less than "red" Indians, had to be subdued or removed.

NATIONAL EXPANSION AND MILITARY CONQUEST

In the first half of the nineteenth century, the United States government pursued an aggressive policy of territorial expansion, acquiring huge

1188

tracts of land by both peaceful and violent means. The first and most dramatic step came with President Thomas Jefferson's purchase of the Louisiana Territory from France in 1803. Although he acted without proper constitutional authority, Jefferson bought over eight hundred thousand square miles of land that reached from the Gulf of Mexico as far north as the headwaters of the Mississippi River and as far west as the Rocky Mountains—for less than two dollars a square mile. In addition to being a remarkable bargain, the Louisiana Purchase created great opportunities for future frontier farmers. Indeed, the expansion of an agrarian republic was one of the main motivations behind Jefferson's move to acquire the Louisiana Territory.

Expansion would first require exploration, and Jefferson acted quickly to send expeditions into the newly acquired territory. In 1804, a team of explorers led by Meriwether Lewis and William Clark left Saint Louis, on the Mississippi River, to begin a two-year trek northwest across the northern Plains and the Rocky Mountains to the Oregon Territory and the Pacific coast—far beyond the bounds of the Louisiana Purchase. While Lewis and Clark were heading northwest, the government sent Zebulon Pike to explore other regions of the American frontier. In 1805, Pike led an expedition northward from Saint Louis along the Mississippi River to what is now Minnesota. In 1806, Pike set out on a second trip westward to the southern Rocky Mountains and south into Mexico before returning to Louisiana. In the years following these early exploratory expeditions, the United States government established a handful of military outposts west of the Mississippi River. In the first two decades of the nineteenth century, then, the path had clearly been prepared for the massive migration of white settlers into the western frontier.

In the 1820s, several thousand of these settlers moved out of the United States into Texas, a Mexican possession. Mexico, which had gained its independence from Spain in 1821, encouraged settlement of its northern borderlands by offering generous inducements to immigrants. Farmers from the American South, many of whom were slave owners, responded eagerly to this opportunity to acquire new lands for cotton production. By the end of the decade, settlers from the United States far outnumbered Mexicans in the Texas Territory. At that point, the Mexican government attempted to curtail their influence in the region by outlawing slavery and blocking additional immigration from the United States. The resulting tension between the Mexican government and the North

American emigrants developed into armed conflict in 1835–1836, during which rebellious settlers defeated a Mexican army and declared Texas an independent republic. For nine years thereafter, expansionist political leaders in the United States government pushed for the annexation of Texas, and finally, in 1845, Texas entered the Union.

The annexation of Texas accelerated the engines of expansion. Claiming that the nation had a divine mission, or "manifest destiny," to control the whole continent, expansionist politicians and their allies in the press promoted a final push to the Pacific. In 1844 the Democratic party had made acquisition of the Oregon Territory a major plank in its platform, and the Democrats took a very aggressive stance toward Great Britain, which disputed the United States' territorial claims. In 1846 James K. Polk, the Democratic president, negotiated a treaty with Great Britain that compromised American territorial demands but nonetheless gave the United States its first foothold on the Pacific. In the same year, lingering tensions over Texas brought the United States into war with Mexico, and the American victory two years later forced the Mexican government to cede a huge expanse of land stretching from Texas to California.

In less than half a century, the results of expansionist policy proved dramatic. Between 1803 and 1848, the United States had tripled its original territory and, in the minds of many of its citizens, had fulfilled its manifest destiny to reach from the Atlantic to the Pacific. Moreover, warfare and diplomacy had reduced the power and presence of Spain, Britain, and Mexico in North America, and the United States faced no foreign competition for its continued conquest of the continent.

Foreign powers were not, of course, the greatest obstacle to national expansion. Native tribes had occupied much of the North American interior for hundreds, even thousands, of years, and they would not easily accede to the more recent claims of the United States. Indeed, in the earliest years of nationhood, the federal government adopted an official policy of recognizing traditional tribal lands as legitimate territorial possessions that could be acquired only through treaties. At the same time, however, the young agrarian nation's demands for new land increasingly led political and military leaders to exact territorial concessions from Indian tribes through warfare rather than diplomacy.

In the years after the Battle of Fallen Timbers, for instance, the United States government continued to push for land cessions from tribes in the Old Northwest, especially in the Indiana and Michigan territories. In response to this growing pressure from whites, two Shawnee leaders, Tecumseh and his brother Tenskwatawa ("the Prophet"), began to organize widespread resistance among Indian people, and established a sizable confederation of tribes in the region. In response to the Indians' threat to white expansion, the territorial governor of Indiana, William Henry Harrison, sent an armed force against Tecumseh's warriors. In two decisive engagements, the Battle of Tippecanoe (1811) and the Battle of the Thames (1813), Harrison defeated the tribal confederacy and killed Tecumseh. The destruction of the confederacy reduced Indian resistance in the Midwest and opened the Indiana and Michigan territories to rapid white settlement. Harrison's victories also provided him with a claim to military fame as a frontier fighter that proved useful in his campaign for the presidency in 1840.

In the South, a similar pattern of conquest was played out in the first four decades of the nineteenth century. The Creek tribe, which inhabited much of present-day Georgia and Alabama, sought to stop white encroachment onto tribal lands. Beginning in 1813, they carried out a series of devastating raids on recent settlers. Whites reacted with horror and hostility, and another future president, Andrew Jackson, organized a punitive expedition of militiamen from Kentucky and Tennessee and Indian warriors from tribes hostile to the Creek. Over the spring and summer of 1814, Jackson won decisive victories, most notably at the Battle of Horseshoe Bend in Alabama. Then, having subdued the Creek militarily, Jackson demanded land cessions of more than twenty million acres in the Southeast. Like William Henry Harrison, Andrew Jackson built his political career on a foundation of his fame as a frontier Indian fighter—a new kind of American hero.

Even those tribes which chose not to resist forcibly suffered eventual defeat. The Cherokee, who had supplied fighters for Jackson's campaign against the Creek, attempted to maintain friendly relations with the United States. During the first three decades of the nineteenth century, they even developed a society which mirrored that of the whites, with settled farms, African slaves, a written alphabet, and, in 1827, a tribal constitution modeled on the state constitutions of their white neighbors.

But nothing appealed to whites so much as Cherokee land. During the 1820s, several southern states, most notably Georgia, began to push the federal government to remove Indians to lands west of the Mississippi River. Moreover, in response to the framing of the Cherokee constitution, the Georgia legislature declared it invalid and laid claim to all Cherokee land within state boundaries. The Cherokee were to be considered nothing more than "tenants at will," with no legal right to call the land their own. Playing by the white man's rules, the Cherokee challenged Georgia's action in the United States Supreme Court, which ruled in favor of the Cherokee in *Worcester* v. *Georgia* (1832).

But Andrew Jackson, the former Indian fighter who had been elected president in 1828, had little regard for either the Cherokee or the Supreme Court, and he refused to enforce the Court's ruling. Indeed, Jackson had already promoted the Indian Removal Act (1830) in Congress, giving the federal government the power to force the Cherokee and other tribes to exchange their tribal lands for territory in the West. Between 1831 and 1839, thousands of Chickasaw, Choctaw, Creek, Seminole, and Cherokee people were forced to move to reservations in what is now Oklahoma—an area of vast plains that scarcely resembled the eastern woodlands they had known. The Cherokee's forced migration along the "Trail of Tears," which claimed the lives of nearly a fourth of the tribe, underscores one of the most unfortunate features of frontier history: like whites, Indians also moved west, but seldom of their own accord and almost never with the prospects of a better future.

THE EMIGRANTS' EXPERIENCE

The westward migration of white Americans did not result in the same degree of cultural dislocation as that of the native Americans, but it was not without its share of social, familial, and individual crises. There was, in fact, no single pattern of "frontier life" for whites moving west, but a complex and often conflicted interplay of expectation and experience.

Throughout the first half of the nineteenth century, the image of the West took on a decidedly romantic tinge in the minds of many Easterners. Popular writers—most notably James Fenimore Cooper, but also scores of other novelists and journalists—depicted the frontier as a region of danger, drama, and heroic deeds. Similarly, in the era before photography, prominent painters such as George Catlin and Albert Bierstadt offered eastern audiences vivid eyewitness views of the West and its native inhabitants. The result was that people setting out for the West often began their journey with a great sense of anticipation and adventure.

Along the way, however, the trail exacted its toll on settlers' spirits, and the romanticism of the East eventually faded in the face of the realities of the West. The trip west proved a difficult test of endurance, both for individuals and for the social units they formed. Most emigrants traveled in groups, and their caravans became short-term communities of necessity, mobile models of the established social order. At least at the outset, the social organization of migrant trains tended to reinforce the standard gender roles and power relationships of the white American family. Even the decision to move west reflected different perceptions. What might have seemed to men an opportunity for a new life often seemed to women the loss of an old life, a separation from the relationships of kinship and community left behind. Once under way, migrant communities generally replicated the division of labor according to customary notions of "separate spheres." Men took primary responsibility for driving and defending the wagon train, while women cooked, cared for the children and the sick, and generally provided the emotional support that kept the family—and the migrant community—together.

As the trip wore on, internal conflict often threatened to drive the migrant community apart. The arduousness of the journey caused roles to change and relationships to become strained. Men argued among themselves about who should determine the route and pace of migration; sometimes these disagreements boiled over into open power struggles that ultimately resulted in the division of the migrant community into two separate caravans, each going its own way. Within individual families, necessity caused women to assume new roles and take on tasks that had formerly been the exclusive responsibility of men. In the end, the long, difficult trip not only tarnished people's expectations about the adventure of moving west, it also challenged some of their basic assumptions about fundamental human relationships.

Once they reached their destination, migrant groups generally sought to re-create the familiar patterns of community life they had known before. In the early nineteenth century, for instance, towns on the farming frontier of Ohio, Indiana, and Illinois often took the names of the towns from which the majority of the initial inhabitants had come. Especially in new communities settled by New Englanders, government and church reflected the form and even the composition of the town of origin, and leaders in each tended to be a preselected, self-perpetuating local elite. The re-creation of the established social order thus resulted in the reinforcement of social inequality. The more prosperous first settlers had a distinct advantage in being able to acquire land and set down permanent roots. Their poorer counterparts, not to mention those who came later, often stayed only a comparatively short while and then moved on, looking for land and better prospects elsewhere. While the towns on the midwestern frontier included some people in their strong ties of community, they excluded others—as had been the case in the New England towns from which they originated.

In the settlements farther west, the familiar social patterns were more fluid and fragile. For instance, in the wake of the discovery of gold in California in 1848, thousands of migrants swarmed west, most of them young, single, and eager to get rich. Almost overnight, they created dozens of little mining camps inhabited largely by prospectors and prostitutes. With men outnumbering women sometimes by more than ten to one, life in these new communities tended to be volatile and violent, and there were few churches, schools, or other institutions of moral guidance and social control. In time, however, with the growth of commercial centers such as San Francisco and Portland, the cities of the West began to offer at least a pale—or sometimes quite gaudy—reflection of the genteel life of the urban East.

The western replication of eastern society and culture was not simply a matter of popular preference, it was also an important question in national politics. Throughout the second quarter of the nineteenth century, westward expansion heightened the conflict between two competing models of eastern society: the free labor system of the North and the slave labor system of the South. Both northerners and southerners came to believe that the expansion of their particular way of life was crucial to the future of their respective regions, and therefore the future of the frontier became especially crucial to both. From the acceptance of slavery in Missouri in 1820 to its rejection in California in 1850, political leaders had attempted to reach a compromise on the issue in the new states created out of the western territories. Compromise, rather than offering a complete resolution of the controversy, increased tensions over the future of the territories.

That tension turned to open violence in 1854, soon after Congress passed the Kansas-Nebraska Act, which had been sponsored by Senator Stephen A. Douglas of Illinois. Douglas's original intent had been primarily to promote a northern route for a proposed transcontinental railroad, not to add more fuel to the debate over slavery. But to gain southern support, he agreed to open the question of slavery in the Kansas and Nebraska territories to the doctrine of "popular sovereignty," the notion that the inhabitants of the territories, and not Congress, should have the right to decide on slavery for themselves before entering the Union. When the Kansas-Nebraska Act passed, thousands of pro-slavery and anti-slavery settlers rushed into Kansas, each faction intent on shaping this rich farming region according to its particular social system. The conflict quickly turned to armed struggle, and "Bleeding Kansas" became the scene of small-scale but brutal civil war. Indeed, the violence on the farming frontier foreshadowed—and, to some degree, triggered—the larger, bloodier struggle that would engulf the whole nation in 1861.

INTEGRATING THE
WESTERN FRONTIER
INTO INDUSTRIAL SOCIETY

While the North and South were locked in civil war, the United States government adopted two policies that would have a profound effect on the future of the West. First, Congress passed the Homestead Act in May 1862, to encourage settlement and development of the western frontier. Any settler could get 160 acres of land essentially for free, on the condition that he cultivate it and live on it for at least five years. Although unscrupulous speculators succeeded in turning the law to their own advantage, thousands of actual settlers were lured west by the promise of free land.

Two months after Congress passed the Homestead Act, it authorized massive land grants and other benefits to railroad companies to promote the construction of a transcontinental railroad. Two companies started working toward each other, the Union Pacific moving west across the plains from Omaha, Nebraska, and the Central Pacific heading east through the Sierra Nevada. After years of backbreaking and often deadly labor by ethnically distinct work forces—the Irish of the Union Pacific and the Chinese of the Central Pacific—the two lines of

track met at Promontory Point, Utah, in May 1869. Technology and human toil had finally forged an iron link between the Atlantic and the Pacific. Thus, in the post–Civil War era, uniting the rapidly growing West with the industrializing East became as important a process as reuniting the North and the South.

The combination of cheap land and easy transportation spurred a remarkable surge of settlers to the West. A trip that once took up to six or seven months by wagon train now took six or seven days. Those who came west on the railroad, like those who built it, added greatly to the ethnic diversity of the region. Recent immigrants from almost all parts of northern and eastern Europe—England, Ireland, Scandinavia, Germany, Poland, Russia—joined native-born settlers in the search for new farmland. Often they formed distinct ethnic communities, and in some territories, like Minnesota and Wisconsin, the concentration of Scandinavians and Germans created an immigrant culture that shaped the future of the states.

No matter where they settled, or with whom, the new immigrants faced a difficult struggle to secure a living from the soil. Although the land of the Great Plains was generally fertile, it was also quite dry and bare. Such discouraging environmental conditions challenged even the most committed and courageous farm family. Sometimes living in miserable huts made of prairie sod and always contending with violent weather and voracious insects, many families soon gave up in one place and moved on to another. In some midwestern regions, the rate of persistence from one decade to the next was well below 50 percent, and in some cases was even below 30 percent.

Those who stayed, however, eventually managed to make a decent if sometimes precarious living. Building modest yet handsome frame houses, schools, and churches, they made the Midwest the mythical as well as the geographical center of the nation, America's heartland. Moreover, using new agricultural technology developed in the middle of the nineteenth century—more efficient plows and harrows, large, horse-drawn reapers and threshers—grain farmers made the Midwest one of the most productive agricultural regions of the nation, America's breadbasket. The high cost of modern farm equipment encouraged most farmers to specialize in one main crop, usually corn or wheat, that had a high market value. Connected to large milling operations by the railroads, frontier farms in the newly opened parts of the West soon provided a significant part of the foodstuffs needed to feed an increasingly industrialized East.

So, too, did western cattle ranches. Although cattle ranchers and farmers were usually bitter enemies in the competition for access to prairie lands, they played a similar role in the national economy. Cowboys drove huge herds to new stockyards adjoining railroads in Kansas, and from there the cattle were shipped to slaughterhouses, the largest and most technologically advanced of which were in Chicago. After the cattle had been killed and sent through a "disassembly line," the meat could be shipped in refrigerated railroad cars to eastern cities. About half the beef consumed in the United States originated on the western cattle ranches. Here again, the inhabitants of the West—including the cowboy, the highly romanticized but very hardworking and low-paid laborer in the cattle industry—helped feed those who worked in the offices and factories of the East.

Along with cattle and grain, the third critical contribution the West made to the economic development of the industrializing nation was its vast mineral resources. Mining operations extracted gold, silver, copper, lead, zinc, and other valuable minerals from the high plateau west of the Great Plains. Rich discoveries in the Rocky Mountains and the Sierra Nevada created new gold and silver rushes to rival that of the 1848 California boom. As had been the case earlier, some of the rough, rapidly growing, and predominantly male mining camps soon turned into sizable—and surprisingly civilized—towns, complete with elegant hotels, restaurants, and theaters. They did so, in part, because of the increasing concentration of wealth in the hands of a few mine owners. Individual prospectors usually sold their claims to large entrepreneurs, and mining became part of industrial capitalism, with high-priced machinery and low-paid workers.

NATIVE RESISTANCE TO NATIONAL INTEGRATION

Throughout the post–Civil War era, the settlement, development, and national integration of the western frontier may have seemed an inexorable process, but it did not go unopposed. Despite the extensive claims of the United States government, the trans-Mississippi West was still home to more than three hundred thousand Indians, dozens of tribal groups that inhabited the region from the

Great Plains to the desert Southwest to the coastal Northwest. These native inhabitants of the West lived in a variety of ways—some farmed, some fished, some followed the buffalo—but despite their diversity, all eventually faced the common fate of encountering the huge influx of white settlers. As had been the case more than two centuries before, in the first period of Indian-white contact on the eastern coast of North America, new diseases decimated the Indian peoples of the trans-Mississippi regions. Some tribes were repeatedly devastated by the sicknesses brought by white settlers, and they were virtually helpless to resist the steady encroachment of white society. Other tribes resisted forcefully and, for a while, successfully. Eventually, however, even the most warlike tribes were reduced by disease and military defeat, and had to accept being limited to life on government-controlled reservations. The struggle and ultimate subjugation of the western Indians in the second half of the nineteenth century remains one of the most dramatic and tragic chapters in the history of the American frontier.

The majority of these western Indians lived on the Great Plains, and there the buffalo became the source, or certainly the symbol, of the conflict between Indians and whites. For over three centuries—ever since the Spanish had introduced horses to North America—Plains Indians had been skilled, wide-ranging hunters who depended on the buffalo for their survival. They used the meat for food, the hide for clothing and shelter, and virtually all parts of the animal for some purpose, including ceremonial dress and religious symbols. In the post–Civil War era, whites developed an apparent need for the buffalo, but more for show than for survival. Seeking skins for blankets and heads for trophies, whites hunted the buffalo for sport and profit. So extensive was the hunting by the end of the 1870s that the once-vast herds were near extinction, the number of buffalo having dropped from the tens of millions to only a few thousand in the space of less than two decades. The decline of the buffalo spelled the decline of the Indian as well.

The native inhabitants of the Great Plains faced not only a devastating decline in the buffalo population but an equally threatening increase in the white population as well. The United States government's policy of promoting orderly settlement and economic development in the West did not allow Indians their accustomed access to the land. Rather, Indians were to be restricted to reservations, far removed from the railroad routes and new farming communities, where they could be regulated by the government's Bureau of Indian Affairs and reformed by Christian missionaries. Some Indian tribes accepted removal to reservations without open resistance. Others, however, refused to accommodate themselves to the demands of the white man, and they fought back in a bitter warfare. From the Apache in the Southwest to the Nez Percé in the northern Rockies to the Sioux, Cheyenne, Comanche, and other tribes on the Great Plains, Indians' resistance made white expansion a costly and deadly process.

The Sioux played the most dramatic role in this war for the West. Although several western Sioux tribes in the Dakota, Montana, and Wyoming territories of the Upper Midwest and the northern Rocky Mountain region had been assigned to a reservation by the Treaty of Fort Laramie (1868), many Sioux refused to be limited to the reservation. Moreover, the discovery of gold in the Black Hills of South Dakota, which was part of the Sioux reservation, prompted a rush of white prospectors into Indian territory. To push the Sioux onto the reservation and thereby to promote settlement by white miners and farmers, the United States government sent a military expedition to the region in 1875. Government troops led by a flamboyant young general, George Armstrong Custer, suffered a crushing defeat at the hands of the Sioux leader Sitting Bull at the Little Bighorn River in the Montana Territory in June 1876. The massacre of Custer's force frightened white Americans and encouraged Native Americans, but it proved to be the exception rather than the rule in the war between the Sioux and the United States. Over the next five years, the United States Army stalked and eventually subdued the Sioux, forcing them not only to return to their reservation but also to cede about a third of their land to the government.

In 1889, however, the Sioux once again rose up in resistance. Reservation-bound Indians began to practice a new ritual, the Ghost Dance, which reinvigorated their sense of their culture and created a new sense of defiance. Concerned federal officials saw the implications inherent in this ritual of resurgence, and they used armed force to put an end to the Ghost Dance movement. The results were disastrous for the Sioux. The government's attempt to take Sitting Bull into custody ended in his being shot and killed. Two weeks later, on 29 December, a detachment of the Seventh Cavalry—Custer's old regiment—rounded up some 350 Sioux at Wounded Knee, South Dakota; and when someone fired a shot, the soldiers massacred about 300 Indians in a matter of minutes.

The slaughter at Wounded Knee was not the last step in the suppression of Indians—some tribes still engaged in armed struggle against the United States government well into the twentieth century—but it did signal the end to Sioux resistance. Moreover, it symbolized a more widespread defeat for Indian peoples throughout the West. By 1890, the reservation had become virtually their only recourse. The superintendent of the 1890 census declared that the process of white settlement had spread so completely across the continent that "there can hardly be said to be a frontier line." That simple bureaucratic pronouncement inspired the historian Frederick Jackson Turner to see the "closing of a great historic movement" ("Significance of the Frontier," p. 1). Indeed, the "closing" of the American frontier led to the opening of a new area of interest in the writing of American history.

THE ENDURING SIGNIFICANCE OF THE AMERICAN FRONTIER

It is difficult for historians to declare the frontier truly closed. The frontier is, as noted at the outset, an ambiguous, often deceptive, concept. Yet the notion of the frontier has become so deeply embedded in American culture that it cannot be dismissed no matter how inaccurate or anachronistic it may be. From the fiction of James Fenimore Cooper and other popular novelists to nineteenth-century "Wild West" shows and twentieth-century "westerns," the frontier has been a powerful mythic symbol of unfettered individualism, a place where a person could live, perhaps thrive, without the standard constraints of society. In a word, the frontier represented freedom.

For many people, the promise proved to be true, at least to a degree. Not only white men but black men as well rode the ranges as cowboys. African Americans could never fully throw off the burden of prejudice in American society, but in the West they could escape the institutionalized racism that prevailed in the South (and often in the North). Similarly, women could not completely overcome the legal and cultural restrictions imposed on them, but in some western states they gained the right to vote almost fifty years before woman suffrage became the law of the land. Moreover, in an era when it is no longer easy, as Huck Finn put it, to "light out for the territory," many people in twentieth-century America still long to escape "civilized" society by going to the "wilderness," whether in the vast spaces of Alaska, in the relatively confined and well-designed recreational areas of national and state parks, or in the even greater comfort of a motor home.

But as the experience of Indian peoples made clear, the history of the frontier is not a chronicle of openness and opportunity for all. Indeed, whatever freedom most Americans gained as a result of national expansion came at the expense of the freedom, even the very existence, of Native Americans. The remnants of tribes restricted to reservations in the twentieth century now struggle to preserve a culture that once covered the continent.

The fate of Indian peoples mirrors that of the land itself. The ever-expanding resource demands of industrial capitalism have led to the exploitation and near-extinction of the wilderness. Beginning in the nineteenth century, nature writers began to express concern for the future of the American wilderness, and at the turn of the century the naturalist John Muir issued a clear call for the preservation of the natural beauty and grandeur of the western landscape. Accordingly, state and federal governments began setting aside parks and nature preserves in the nineteenth century, and today there are still vast wilderness areas that remain essentially undeveloped. But even these are not safe from the nation's increasing need for timber products, minerals, and water. Alaska, for instance, is now connected to the "Lower Forty-eight" by a lengthy oil pipeline, a controversial project that has brought both economic benefits and environmental disaster to the "last American wilderness."

The debate over the Alaska Pipeline is merely the latest, and certainly not the last, chapter in a history of human and environmental interaction that began on the North American continent thousands of years ago. The experience of the past, with all its promise and pitfalls, is still the best guide to the proper path to whatever frontier may yet exist in America's future.

BIBLIOGRAPHY

General Works
Billington, Ray Allen. *America's Frontier Heritage* (1966; repr. 1974).
Limerick, Patricia Nelson. *The Legacy of Conquest: The Unbroken Past of the American West* (1987).
Turner, Frederick Jackson. "The Significance of the Frontier in American History." In *The Frontier in History* (1920).

Historiographical Works
Hofstadter, Richard, and Seymour Martin Lipset, eds. *Turner and the Sociology of the Frontier* (1968).
Nash, Gerald D. *Creating the West: Historical Interpretations 1890–1990* (1991).
Nobles, Gregory H. "Breaking into the Backcountry: New Approaches to the Early American Frontier, 1750–1800." *William and Mary Quarterly,* 3d Ser., 46, no. 3 (1989).

Native Americans
Hoxie, Frederick E. *A Final Promise: The Campaign to Assimilate the Indians, 1880–1920* (1984).
Jennings, Francis. *The Invasion of America: Indians, Colonialism, and the Cant of Conquest* (1975).
Prucha, Francis Paul. *The Great Father: The United States Government and the American Indian.* 2 vols. (1984).
Utley, Robert M. *The Indian Frontier of the American West, 1846–1890* (1984).

European-American Expansion

Faragher, John Mack. *Women and Men on the Overland Trail* (1979).

Jeffrey, Julie Roy. *Frontier Women: The Trans-Mississippi West, 1840–1880* (1979).

Kolodny, Annette. *The Land Before Her: Fantasy and Experience of the American Frontiers, 1630–1860* (1984).

Nash, Roderick. *Wilderness and the American Mind* (1973; 3d ed. 1982).

Paul, Rodman Wilson. *Mining Frontiers of the Far West, 1848–1880* (1963).

Robinson, Walter Stitt. *The Southern Colonial Frontier, 1607–1763* (1979).

Slotkin, Richard. *Regeneration Through Violence: The Mythology of the American Frontier, 1600–1860* (1973).

———. *The Fatal Environment: The Myth of the Frontier in the Age of Industrialization, 1800–1890* (1985).

SEE ALSO **Agriculture; American Indians of the East; American Indians of the West**; and various essays in the following sections "**Periods of Social Change**," "**Regionalism and Regional Subcultures**," and "**Space and Place**."

THE PLANTATION

James M. Clifton

OF ALL THE CHARACTERISTIC components of the society and civilization of the Old South, by far the most important was the plantation. This institution largely influenced virtually every aspect of southern existence—political, judicial, social, cultural, economic, and religious. Southern planters (those with twenty or more slaves, the number that commonly qualified one as the proprietor of a plantation), while constituting little more than a tenth of the slaveholders in 1860 but owning over half the slaves, held most of the important political offices—local, state, and congressional—as well as the top judicial posts. They also established social and cultural mores for southern society in general and determined the economic posture of the antebellum South, with its commitment to large-scale agriculture and the considerable neglect of other aspects of the economy, such as industry, commerce, and banking. And with the exception of the backcountry, they were the leading members of most of the churches.

Neither small slaveholders (owning fewer than twenty slaves) nor nonslaveholding yeomen felt uncomfortable with the large measure of power and influence in the hands of the planters. They realized that the planter class, by producing the exportable surplus of southern staples, raised the living standard of all southerners. Less than 7 percent of the 1860 cotton crop in Mississippi, for example, was produced by free labor, with the major portion being grown by the big planters with fifty or more slaves. Slaveless farmers in Virginia produced only 5 percent of the tobacco crop. And hemp in Kentucky was characterized as a "nigger crop," with virtually the entire crop produced by slave labor.

The social structure of white southern society was relatively fluid, with small slave owners by dint of thriftiness, hard work, and a little luck very often able to move up to the planter group. Even a slaveless farmer could, by using a surplus bale or two of cotton, move up the economic stairway to first become a small slave owner and then possibly achieve the prized position of planter. By 1860 the number of landholdings qualifying as a plantation (in excess of 500 acres, 200 hectares) varied from only 2 percent in North Carolina to almost 9 percent in Mississippi and to more than 10 percent in South Carolina, which had the largest average-size landholding of any state in the United States.

A number of these plantations were held by self-made men. For example, a propertyless man in eastern North Carolina by great industry and thrift was able to acquire the farms of ten to twelve small owners and thus become the greatest landed proprietor in his area, living in style in an elaborate plantation house. Sometimes even overseers became plantation owners. President James K. Polk's overseer, Ephraim Beanland, accumulated enough land and slaves in Mississippi to elevate his family to a point where one son could become a physician and the others could achieve positions of standing in their communities.

Whether the southern landowner was slaveholder or nonslaveholder, planter or farmer, he achieved a great measure of self-respect and independence from being able to farm land that he could call his own. With the exception of South Carolina, where there was a virtual caste system—especially among the low-country chivalry of rice and the sea island cotton planters, where one's standing was based almost entirely on one's family affiliation and holdings in land and slaves—there was no common discrimination of slaveholders against nonslaveholders or planters against farmers in the antebellum South. Nor did any of these groups consider fieldwork degrading for white men. During emergencies even large slaveholders were sometimes forced to work in the fields, and their sons normally did so during college vacations. And in areas with few slaves, any farmer (slaveholder or not) could be elected to local offices, especially that of county sheriff.

Across the antebellum South planters committed themselves to a paternalistic ethos that was based on the concept of reciprocal responsibilities for master and bondsperson and the implicit recognition of the slave's humanity. Thus, the plantation provided a composite unit, where master and slaves could pool income and resources within the slaveholding household. Such a household always included the plantation house, outbuildings, fields, gardens, and slave quarters. The size, complexity, and comfort of the buildings varied considerably from one plantation to another, as did the size and variety of fields, gardens, pasture, orchard, and forest.

By gender the master assumed principal responsibility for the household, maintaining an appropriate balance between the care and safety of his dependents and the economic efficiency of the plantation. He determined what crops to plant and when, the work cycle on the plantation, the disciplining of field hands (especially male), the marketing of the crop, and any other responsibilities that tied the household to the market or to the outside world. Managing his black dependents—who were to him an extension of his family or in effect his own children—consumed the greater part of his time.

The plantation mistress, normally the planter's wife but sometimes his widow, mother, daughter, or sister, operated within the world of ruling lady, a position assigned to her by gender and class. She was the recognized superior of all other women of the household. The mistress oversaw the running of the plantation house, flower and vegetable gardens, and dairy. She carried, as a symbol of her status as supervisor of feeding and clothing members of the household, keys to the domestic buildings and the various plantation storehouses. She supervised the plantation infirmary and aided in childbirth. And should the master be absent from the plantation for any great length of time, the mistress assumed full control of the operation, although generally with some difficulty. Her training would have included little pertaining to the internal workings of the plantation or to its affiliation with the outside world. The male-dominated plantation hierarchy could never quite accept her as being anyone other than a delegate of the master and male authority.

Pooling of income and resources within the plantation household brought the slaves little opportunity to determine their own lives, relations, and culture. As property of the master, they could not legally hold property themselves. While they had some control over the composition of their subhouseholds, they had no legal rights there. Only in a marginal way could slaves affect the income that they received in way of food, clothing, and shelter. Most of their food came from crops and livestock they produced themselves. Much of the clothing was made by slave seamstresses. And slaves built their own cabins.

The relationship between master and slave was always one of give-and-take. Wise masters would accommodate a measure of slow work, pilfering, faked illness, or even running away. They also allowed the slaves to tend their own gardens and livestock and generally gave them Saturday afternoon and Sunday off to care for these. On the other hand, slaves had little say over the master's use of their labor or in how they should be compensated for it. Slaves justified their stealing from the plantation storehouses in terms of "taking" what should have been theirs already—in short, they were simply providing for a fairer distribution of the plantation's resources. While the slaves could never accept the master's justification for keeping them as permanent dependents, they realized that the success of the plantation determined the basic income and resources for themselves as well as for the planter's household. Thus, if the master were more prosperous, some of the prosperity might trickle down to them.

THE FORMATIVE PERIOD

The earliest antecedent of the southern plantation seems to have been the sugar estate of ancient India, characterized by extensive commercial acreage and a large labor force divided into clustered villages under centralized control. Arab traders introduced the Indian mode of operation to the eastern Mediterranean, especially the Levant, in the seventh century, whence it was carried to the western Mediterranean by the Crusaders of the eleventh and twelfth centuries. The Spanish and Portuguese imported black African slave labor to their plantations in the Iberian Peninsula and the Canary, Madeira, and Cape Verde islands in the 1400s and thence to their great sugar empires in the Caribbean and Central and South America the following century. Great Britain entered the overseas world of sizable sugar estates with massive slave forces in the 1640s in Barbados. By 1680 hundreds of Englishmen had developed virtually all the arable land of Barbados as sugar plantations, averaging 200 acres (80 hectares) of sugar fields with one hundred slaves who cultivated provision crops during the off-season of sugar.

The initial beginnings of the plantation in British North America were in the Chesapeake tobacco country of Virginia and Maryland. John Rolfe developed a sweet-smoking variety of tobacco at Jamestown in about 1612, and within a year or two tobacco was being shipped to England. Production of good-quality tobacco required painstaking care and mature judgment in performing a variety of operations; consequently, tobacco was generally produced on small units with a handful of highly skilled workers.

Indentured servants provided the principal labor force for the small tobacco plantations from the beginning; black Africans, although brought to Jamestown as early as 1619, numbered only about 2,500 as late as 1680. In the 1680s, however, with indentured servants becoming less and less available because of improved economic conditions in England and African slaves readily obtainable at affordable prices as a result of the saturation of the Atlantic slave trade, an increasing number of Chesapeake planters turned to slaves as a more dependable and economical means of labor. Nevertheless, the need for indentured servants who could perform skilled and managerial labor existed in the Chesapeake through the time of the American Revolution.

Out of the West Indian setting, however, a more mature plantation pattern was introduced to the American South. The saturation of sugar production in Barbados by 1680 prompted a number of the planters—at least 10 percent of the 175 wealthiest planters (with sixty or more slaves) and an even larger number of the lesser gentry (with twenty to fifty-nine slaves)—to seek large landholdings in South Carolina. This semitropical locale, it was thought, would provide the advantages of Caribbean agriculture in the more wholesome environment of the North American mainland. Thus, these West Indian planters brought to South Carolina two things of major importance: the most extensively developed plantation system in British America and slavery on a massive scale.

However, it was not sugar that gave rise to the southern plantation but rice, although it proved to be exceptionally difficult to develop as a crop. While the Spanish in Central and South America, the Portuguese in Brazil, and the Dutch in the West Indies had all developed a highly successful rice culture, there is no evidence that any knowledge of rice planting was brought from any of these areas to South Carolina. Thus, rice production there, beginning about 1685, was largely through trial and error, even though 330 tons (2,000 to 2,200 barrels of 350 pounds [29.7 metric tons] each) were exported in 1700, according to Edward Randolph, surveyor of customs for North America from 1691. Recent scholarship has indicated that black African slaves from Madagascar and West Africa (a portion of which was called the Rice Coast) in the 1690s and early 1700s taught the white South Carolinians (whom they outnumbered by 1708) the techniques of rice growing as practiced in their homelands. With the application of irrigation to the rice plants by about 1724, half a century after the colony's founding, the rice industry needed only the successful development of suitable facilities for threshing and polishing the crop to reach full maturity.

Between 1685 and 1720, in conjunction with the rice industry, there had been a blending in coastal South Carolina of three factors essential to a plantation system: the land use system begun in the Levant and transplanted to the western hemisphere, a viable commercial crop suited to the plantation mode of production, and the development of a frontier colonizing project in conformity with the British concept of "plantation" as applied to their colonizing of Ireland in the sixteenth and early seventeenth centuries. In Ireland extensive landholdings had been granted by the British crown to English and Scottish settlers, and were manned by large labor forces (men of arms and their families brought over) committed to agriculture. Each family was assigned a "planting" (field), and a collection of these constituted a "plantation," sometimes as large as 12,000 acres (4,800 hectares).

The first half-century in South Carolina saw considerable use of both free and indentured labor and a limited use of native Indian slave labor, more than in any other English mainland colony. After 1720, however, the rice plantation complex necessitated large importation of black African slaves (especially those with experience in rice culture), to the extent that perhaps as many as 40 percent of the slaves brought to British North America entered through the port of Charleston. In addition, highly sophisticated techniques of plantation management (generally associated with plantations of the antebellum era) were developed; the plantations constituted literal "factories in the field," with few limitations in the way of economies of scale in either acreage or labor force.

The scarcity of shipping during the War of Jenkins's Ear (1739–1743) and King George's War (1744–1748) led to a glut in the Charleston rice market and a precipitous drop in rice prices—by 40 percent in the first conflict and down to 10 shillings per hundredweight by 1746, less than one-seventh of the peak prices of 1738. Among the alternatives open to the rice planters was the development of a second staple, more valuable for its size, to cope with the scarce shipping. Out of this circumstance indigo, grown on a small scale in the early years of the colony, was successfully developed as a crop by Eliza Lucas (Pinckney) in 1744 and produced in considerable quantities (spurred by a British bounty to compensate for loss of access to high-quality French West Indian indigo). It accounted for 10.39 percent of the value of the colony's exports by 1748 (compared with 54.78 for rice).

The period after 1750 (with peace restored and rice prices back up to 63 shillings per hundredweight) was one of exceptional prosperity for the rice planters. They now produced two staples, with each slave able to grow two acres (0.8 hectares) of indigo (produced on the higher areas of the plantation, in a work cycle that dovetailed well with that of rice) along with three acres (1.2 hectares) of rice (grown in the swamplands, which could be periodically flooded). A number of planters amassed enormous holdings of land and slaves. Henry Middleton and Gabriel Manigault accumulated 50,000 acres (20,000 hectares) of land each; Henry Laurens, 20,000 (8,000 hectares); and John Stuart, 15,000 acres (6,000 hectares). Middleton possessed 800 slaves; Laurens, 500; Manigault, 300; and Stuart, 200. Manigault and Laurens, as was common among the South Carolina aristocracy, were heavily involved in merchandising, to the extent that they were the two wealthiest men in the colony. Indeed, these four and a number of others were truly the elite of American plantation society, with their wealth based on the firmest footing anywhere in the British mainland colonies. In fact, these Carolina planters were virtually equal in prosperity and prominence with their Barbadian counterparts.

Rice culture spread from South Carolina northward to the Cape Fear River in North Carolina in the 1730s and southward to Georgia along the Savannah, Ogeechee, and Altamaha rivers in the 1750s. While rice never achieved much status in North Carolina, remaining throughout the colonial period as only an adjunct of the naval stores industry, along with indigo it achieved considerable

proportions in Georgia, once the restrictions on landholding and slavery were removed in 1750. By the time of the American Revolution, a number of Georgia planters rivaled those of South Carolina in holdings of land and slaves.

On the eve of the revolutionary war tobacco plantations in Virginia and Maryland were much smaller than rice and indigo plantations in South Carolina and Georgia. The greatest planters—the Byrds, Carrolls, Carters, and Dulanys—who owned many thousands of acres of land and slaves by the hundreds, divided their operations into numerous "quarters" where the work force seldom exceeded a dozen or so laborers. This was necessitated by the closely supervised and highly regimented labor format used in tobacco culture. Robert Carter of Virginia, for example, dispersed his 500 slaves over eighteen widely scattered plantations, as opposed to Henry Middleton's 800 slaves who were densely congregated along the Ashley River above Charleston.

Perhaps as much as 35 percent of the tobacco in the Chesapeake was produced on small farms employing no slave labor, whereas virtually all of the rice and indigo was produced on large units employing dozens of slaves. Thus, tobacco did not enjoy the economy of scale of rice and indigo in either acreage or work force. And while per capita tobacco exports from the Chesapeake by 1770 averaged about £3 for each free resident, the exports of rice and indigo from South Carolina brought £9 per white. Nine of the ten wealthiest men who died in the English mainland colonies in 1774 made their fortunes in South Carolina.

The post-Revolutionary era saw considerable change in the southern plantation system. Indigo, with the loss of the British bounty (essential to its profitability) and market (England now turned to the East Indies for its supply), and the invasion of the indigo fields by a destructive caterpillar in about 1780, virtually ceased to exist as a commercial crop. But it left behind a social structure and labor routine perfectly adaptable to the production of a new staple, sea island cotton, so called because it thrived best in the Sea Islands along the coastline of Georgia (to which it was introduced in 1786) and South Carolina.

The variety of cotton, with a silky fiber of from 1½ to 2 inches (37.5 to 50 millimeters), was used principally for the fine cambric and laces of the wealthy. Consequently it fetched premium prices, sometimes as much as $1.25 per pound but more commonly from 20 to 40 cents—two to three times the price of upland, short-staple cotton, of which the fiber was only an inch (25 millimeters) or less. The bulk yield of sea island cotton was about half that of the short-fiber, and it was considerably more difficult to produce and process for market. However, the higher prices and the suitability of sea island cotton as a replacement for indigo more than compensated for the difference. Profits were high, sometimes as much as 10 to 12 percent, with virtually the entire crop produced by large-scale slave labor.

Whereas climate confined sea island cotton to the littoral of South Carolina and Georgia and middle Florida (where its production was developed in the 1850s), upland cotton, once Eli Whitney had perfected an inexpensive and workable gin in 1793, could be profitably produced anywhere the growing season was at least two hundred days and the annual rainfall 20 inches (500 millimeters)—on virtually any kind of soil, on flat or hilly land, and on a small scale by one-horse farmers or in massive amounts by large planters with dozens or hundreds of slaves.

THE ANTEBELLUM PLANTATION

By the early 1800s, and especially after the War of 1812, Atlantic seaboard farmers and planters with badly worn soils and declining incomes—especially those of South Carolina and Virginia—moved west and southwest to the Black Belt of Alabama, to central Tennessee, to the lands along the Mississippi River from Arkansas and west Tennessee to the Gulf of Mexico, and eventually to east Texas in search of cheap, fertile lands—by then the price was $1.25 an acre (0.4 hectare) for government-owned land—and a new stake in life. With the insatiable British demand for cotton to fuel their booming textile industry keeping prices high, southern cotton production doubled about every ten years between the War of 1812 and the Civil War—from less than 150,000 bales (averaging about 450 pounds [202.5 kilograms] each) in 1814 to over 4,500,000 by 1860, the value of which amounted to 57 percent of the total exports from the United States.

Indeed, the Cotton Kingdom of the antebellum South stretched for a thousand miles (1,600 kilometers) from South Carolina westward to Texas, with a breadth from north to south of some two hundred miles (320 kilometers) in Carolina and Texas and 600 to 700 miles (960 to 1,120 kilometers) in the Mississippi Valley—a total of about 400,000 square miles (1,040,000 square kilometers). On the periphery the other great staples were produced—tobacco across the upper South (with more production west of the Appalachians by 1860 than east), hemp (used principally for cordage and bale cloth) in Kentucky and Missouri, sugar in Louisiana, and rice along the lower reaches of some seventeen tidal rivers on the South Atlantic coast from the Cape Fear River in southeastern North Carolina to the Saint Johns River in northern Florida.

But it was cotton—more than all the other staples put together—that dominated southern society, economy, and politics. Cotton could be produced with some profit by small independent farmers holding few, if any, slaves (more than half the landowners in the Cotton Kingdom owned no slaves at all); however, the greatest prosperity (especially in the 1850s) was enjoyed by the three thousand to four thousand big planters who owned most of the land and slaves and received as much as three-fourths of the annual cotton income.

Natchez, Mississippi, became the great mecca of cotton wealth, with perhaps a third of the millionaires in America in 1860 clustered there; and they made their great affluence visible in the hundred or so grand mansions that arose in and around the city. Individual landownerships and yields in the Natchez area were amazing. In 1859 (the crop year for the 1860 census) Levin R. Marshall, a Natchez banker who either owned or had a share in more than 25,000 acres (10,000 hectares) in Louisiana, Mississippi, and Arkansas, produced 4,000 bales; Stephen Duncan, with six cotton and two sugar plantations and 1,018 slaves (plus 23 at his residence near Natchez), 4,000 bales; John Routh, once called the "largest cotton planter in the world" but who by this time had settled much of his land on his children, 3,500 bales; and Frederick Stanton, with five large plantations in Louisiana and a small holding in Mississippi comprising 15,000 acres (6,000 hectares) and 444 slaves, 3,000 bales. Cotton sold in 1860 for 11 to 12 cents per pound. An average bale of 450 pounds (202.5 kilograms) would thus be worth about $50.

In Louisiana in 1859, Meredith Calhoun in Rapides Parish produced 3,800 bales on his plantation of 5,000 improved and 10,000 unimproved acres (the largest number of bales produced in the South on a single plantation), along with 531 hogsheads of sugar and 30,000 bushels of corn for the plantation's 700 slaves; Alfred Davis of Concordia Parish, 3,400 bales; and Joseph A. S. Acklen of West Feliciana Parish, 3,100 bales. Nine other Louisiana planters produced between 2,000 and 3,000 bales. In Georgia, Joseph Bond of Macon produced 2,199 bales in 1859, making him the largest producer in that state.

Among the producers of the other staples, only the great rice nabobs of South Carolina and the sugar magnates of Louisiana could rival the cotton lords in ownership and production. The rice princes were Nathaniel Heyward of Colleton District, largest of the rice planters, with 5,000 acres (2,000 hectares) of improved land and 30,000 unimproved acres (12,000 hectares) on seventeen plantations and over 2,000 slaves; Joshua John Ward in Georgetown District, with 3,000 improved and 7,000 unimproved acres (1,200 improved and 2,800 unimproved hectares) on seven plantations and 1,100 slaves; and William Aiken of Colleton District, with 700 slaves on his Jehossee Island plantation of 4,000 acres (1,600 hectares), 2,000 (800) of which were improved (Aiken and Meredith Calhoun of Louisiana were the only planters in the entire South in 1860 with as many as 700 slaves on a single plantation). The value of their crops rivaled or exceeded that of the largest cotton planters. The largest sugar holdings were those of John Burnside of Ascension and St. James parishes, comprising about 7,500 improved and 22,000 unimproved acres (3,000 improved and 8,800 unimproved hectares) on five plantations and 950 slaves. Samuel Hairston, with numerous plantations in both Virginia and North Carolina and 1,600 slaves, was the only tobacco planter of this magnitude.

Not only did these great planters build stately mansions adorned with colonnaded Greek Revival porticoes, finely furnished and surrounded by lush gardens, they also built or purchased expensive town houses in Charleston and New Orleans. Samuel Hairston beautified his plantation house and grounds with such lavish splendor that a neighboring minister described paradise as being "as beautiful as Mr. Hairston's."

As a result of the great holdings of these and lesser planters, the South in 1860 had 83 percent of the farms in the United States with 500 or more acres (200 or more hectares), fifty counties with populations of over 75 percent slaves, and the twelve richest counties in the country; Adams County, Mississippi (of which Natchez was the county seat) was the richest of all and had a slave population of more than 90 percent.

By 1850 the southern plantation system had reached maturity, with cotton plantations (those producing five or more bales) numbering 74,031;

tobacco (raising 3,000 pounds [1,350 kilograms] or over), 15,745; hemp, 8,327; sugar, 2,681; and rice plantations (producing 20,000 pounds [9,000 kilograms] or more), 551. The fact that such a small quantity of production was needed to qualify a unit as a plantation doubtless means that many thousands of small cotton and tobacco farms with but one or two working hands were included in these numbers. One field hand could produce five bales of cotton, the normal yield from ten acres (4 hectares); two slaves could grow 3,000 pounds (1,350 kilograms) of tobacco, the average output of five acres (2 hectares); and two laborers could raise ten acres of rice, which should produce 20,000 pounds. Even including these many small units, there were only 101,335 plantations out of a total of 569,201 farms and plantations, slightly less than 18 percent.

With respect to the kind of staple produced, the number of slaves generally was inversely related to the number of plantations growing that kind of crop. The superintendent of the 1850 census estimated that 2.5 million slaves of all ages were directly engaged in agriculture: 60,000 in the production of hemp, 125,000 in rice, 150,000 in sugar, 350,000 in tobacco, and 1,815,000 in cotton. Thus, the rice plantations in 1850 would have 226 slaves per estate; sugar plantations, 55; hemp, 7; tobacco, 22; and cotton, 24.

What largely determined the physical size of the plantation was the walking distance from the slave quarters to the most distant field. Planters did not want this to exceed an hour or so; consequently, the middle-sized plantation consisted of 1,000 to 1,500 acres (400 to 600 hectares). While most planters used a portion of the improved land to produce provisions for their own use and that of the slave force, the principal function of the plantation was to produce a commercial crop for export. Thus, it was essential that it be located along a suitable transportation route (most often a river) and have fertile soil.

Planters in general were scientific farmers, as evidenced by their subscriptions to agricultural journals and the large number of articles written by planters for these journals. They practiced crop rotation to preserve soil fertility, and where practical and feasible they used fertilizing materials such as marl and guano and planted winter cover crops. Planters adapted agricultural procedures to their slave labor, using the latest techniques of planting and the most advanced machinery, tools, and implements. They were constantly striving to improve the quality of their seeds, draft animals, and livestock. And the planters wrestled with the problems of slave management, avidly reading the advice on such matters in the agricultural magazines and often writing responses.

THE CULTURE OF THE PLANTATION

The antebellum plantation constituted a composite community. The bulk of the slave population consisted of field hands used directly in producing the commercial staple and the provision crops, such as corn (the most widely grown crop in the South), oats, peas, and potatoes. However, each plantation had another group of slaves employed in nonfield pursuits. They included animal raisers, baby keepers, barbers, blacksmiths, bricklayers, butchers, butlers, carpenters, coachmen, cobblers, cooks, coopers, engineers, gardeners, ginners, laundresses, maids, millers, nurses, seamstresses, shoemakers, tailors, tanners, valets, waiters, and weavers. Many of these skilled slaves were trained to perform two or more trades and could also double as field hands during critical labor periods such as the harvest. After accounting for the young, old, and infirm (who could do no more than a quarter to half the work that a prime hand could do), gender differences (women could do three-fourths as much as a prime hand), and days lost to illness (generally from one to two a month), the planter's slave numbers were reduced in prime worker equivalency to little more than half. Thus, a plantation with one hundred slaves of all ages could expect the work of only fifty to sixty prime hands.

The focal figure in administering the plantation was the overseer, who had complete charge of the plantation for the period of his contract (usually a document written in January for the calendar year). He was consequently responsible for the labor and well-being of the workers, the maintenance of the property, and, most important, the success of the crop, on which the renewal of the contract very often depended. Although in 1860 there were 46,274 slaveholders with enough slaves (20 or more) to justify the employment of an overseer, William K. Scarborough (in *The Overseer*) was able to find only about 25,958 overseers in the entire South at that time. Rice plantations, whose owners were away from the plantation during the malaria season (May to November), needed overseers, as did most of the large sugar plantations. Apparently many large cotton and tobacco planters, disgusted at bad experiences with overseers, who generally came from the small farmer or poor white classes, chose to administer their own plantation. Bennet Barrow of West Feliciana Parish in Louisiana, for example, supervised his plantation with two hundred slaves, using a slave foreman, or "driver," as assistant. Overseers were normally paid $500 to $700 annually, but those on large rice and sugar plantations often made $1,000 to $1,500; on his massive Jehossee Island rice plantation in South Carolina, with a slave force of seven hundred, Governor William Aiken paid $2,000. The tenure of an overseer was generally about three and a half years.

Below the overseer in the plantation hierarchy was the driver, who had direct responsibility for the day-to-day performance of the workers. The driver got the slaves to the fields in the mornings, organized the work gangs for the day, and excused them upon the satisfactory completion of the day's labor. He also generally administered plantation discipline. In addition, the driver was responsible for proper decorum in the slave quarters. He had certain perquisites: better food, clothing, and housing than was the lot of slaves in general; freedom from physical toil; and the prestige and authority accompanying the position of supervisor. At the same time the driver operated under a number of handicaps. His workday was longer than that of other slaves; he often experienced considerable difficulty in being fully accepted by the other slaves in the quarters; and he was buffeted by demands from the owner and overseer above and the slaves below. Planters generally selected a driver for each fifty slaves and considered the services of a good driver more important than those of the overseer; consequently the tenure of the driver normally was much longer than that of the overseer.

The slaves on the plantation lived in simple quarters some distance from the plantation house, in single cabins or double houses of wooden boards or shingles with a chimney in the middle and occupied by two families. There was also a "sick house," where the plantation nurse cared for slaves suffering from various maladies and fevers (and occasionally from such deadly diseases as cholera). She administered the medicines prescribed by the doctor who looked after the health of the slaves on a number of plantations at once, normally under contract for $1.25 to $1.50 per year for each slave in his care.

Clothing was issued twice yearly to the slaves—in late April or early May for the summer season and in late November or early December for the winter. In addition, the winter issue included blankets. Rations, given out weekly, generally consisted of three and a half pounds of bacon and a peck (fourteen pounds) of cornmeal for each adult, with lesser amounts for children. The slave family was usually given a piece of land for a garden to supplement its diet and was allowed to raise its own chickens and pigs. The planter also attended to the religious welfare of his slaves by employing local ministers to preach and encouraging the holding of religious classes on the plantation, and by allowing them to attend churches of their faith, usually Baptist or Methodist, in the general neighborhood.

The labor system on most plantations was that of gang labor, with individual squads working under the supervision of the driver or a squad leader from sunup to sundown. The exception was on the rice plantations, where discipline would have been virtually impossible without the task system. Because the planter was gone from early May to the killing frosts of November, leaving only the overseer and slave drivers to control affairs, a labor format was needed in which the slaves could largely direct themselves. The task system provided for an assignment that the poorest worker could complete in eight to nine hours. In practice, however, most slaves finished their tasks by mid afternoon and could devote the rest of the day to working in their gardens, farming small tracts of rice of their own, looking after their livestock, or hunting or fishing. More than anything else, the task system kept lonely slaves on the isolated rice plantations from becoming restless and rebellious.

There was little interchange between rice slaves and those from the other plantations. Tobacco or cotton slaves would have difficulty acclimating to the isolated existence of the rice plantation and adjusting to the rice diet and the task system of labor. Thus, new hands on rice plantations were generally acquired from other rice plantations where sales were necessitated by the planter's overextension, by the breakup of the estates, or by slaves being too refractory to retain. The natural increase of slave numbers on rice plantations was normally about 5 percent. Conversely, rice slaves would not adapt very easily to the gang labor system of the cotton, tobacco, or sugar plantation.

Southern planters, with a considerable amount of fixed capital in their slaves, attempted to use their work force in the most efficient and profitable manner. Thus, they planted a much greater acreage in cash crops than in food crops (mainly cotton versus corn) and committed a larger share of the labor time of slave households to market production than was generally true for free families (mainly women doing fieldwork instead of housework). They could collectivize such household duties as food preparation and child care, thus freeing additional labor for fieldwork. The off-season of the commercial staple left ample time for the slaves to grow sufficient provisions; otherwise, as a fixed labor supply, they would have had little to do during much of the year.

As a result of these factors, slave labor was probably more efficient than free labor. The household economy of the plantation, with the work force able to produce great quantities of the staple, ample provisions, and most of the commodities needed on the plantation, doubtless contributed to the plantation's profitability. While most planters provided little more than bare subsistence in the way of food, clothing, and shelter for the slaves (as compared to what they took from the plantation profits for their households), there is ample evidence to demonstrate that planters well understood the correlation between fair treatment and the willingness of the slaves to work. In short, the masters who treated the slaves the best generally got the most efficient labor from them. Conversely, masters who were cruel to the slave force in the main found the slave labor output declining accordingly. Thus, the measure of treatment was a major factor in slave discipline on the plantation, generally of more effect than the constant threat of punishment. However, even the most generous master occasionally had to punish disobedient slaves to keep order among his work force.

While the plantation system brought high per capita incomes to individual planters (recent studies have demonstrated that plantation profitability was at least as much as the earnings of stocks and bonds in the North—6 to 8 percent—and sometimes considerably more), it ensured that the South, with its commitment to large-scale production of a few agricultural commodities in world demand, was dependent with respect to manufacturing (except for the household production on the plantations), merchandising, and banking. Southern planters showed little interest in internal improvements or in developing urban centers of manufacturing. However, while the South had only about twenty thousand manufacturing establishments in 1860, compared with one hundred thousand in the North, the gap is narrowed considerably when such facilities as cotton gins and rice and sugar mills on the plantations are considered in the South's overall manufacturing.

With respect to cultural matters, the southern planters put great stock in education to prepare their sons for public service and the professions. Accordingly, a large number of excellent academies sprang up throughout the southern states, and the area had the largest number of college students in the United States. At the same time, the planter elite saw little need to educate the masses, thus preventing much in the way of public schools. From the standpoint of religion, they supported the Episcopal church, whose ministers not only preached the gospel of slavocracy but often were slaveholders themselves (Leonidas Polk, the Episcopal bishop of Louisiana, owned four hundred). Some planters were Presbyterian or Roman Catholic (mostly in Louisiana), while the populace in general subscribed mainly to the Baptist and Methodist faiths.

The great planters buttressed their economic domination with political power. They produced great leaders such as John C. Calhoun, Robert Toombs, and Jefferson Davis, and exercised virtually total power at both the county and the state level (every governor in all the southern states in the 1850s was a slaveholding planter) and a large measure of control within national circles, especially in Congress and on the Supreme Court. At the same time, they drew together in support of such issues as the tariff and the westward expansion of slavery, developing the extreme doctrines of nullification and ultimately secession—a measure of how far the ultraconservative political views of South Carolinians had come to influence the section.

In alliance with the Old Northwest, the southern planters controlled the Democratic party from 1830 to 1860 and largely shaped the policies of the national government. They were able to force the lowering of the tariff in the nullification controversy of the 1830s and were in large part responsible for the Mexican War, fought to acquire new lands for the expansion of slavery and the plantation system westward to the Pacific. However, their insistence that all the newly acquired territory be open to slavery, and that Cuba and Central America were possible targets for annexation, alienated their western allies and ended their control of the party. The election of a Republican president committed to containment of slavery in 1860 made the threat of secession a reality, bringing on the Civil War.

THE PLANTATION LEGACY

Although the invading Union forces wreaked massive destruction upon the plantation facilities and the slaves were ultimately freed, the plantation system largely survived intact but with a vastly different labor format. Probably as many as half of the plantations changed hands over the following ten to fifteen turbulent years. The planters, labor lords before the war, were now landlords and thus forced to accommodate the demands of the emancipated blacks for more control of their lives and conditions of work. At first they tried to operate with a cash wage system, with the blacks living in their former slave cabins and subject to plantation discipline under the newly enacted black codes. However, this plan did not work well for either group. The planters could not force the blacks to work as hard as they had when they were slaves, nor could they be certain of how dependable the blacks would be to see the crop through. In addition, little capital was available to the planters, and where it was, the interest rates were prohibitive—2.5 to 3 percent a month. From the blacks' standpoint, the wage system resembled slavery too much and gave them little say in their own working lives.

Cotton and tobacco planters soon came up with a sharecropping system under which the blacks would be rented certain portions of the land (to which they would move, thus getting away from the distasteful slave quarters) and share in decision making with the owners. To the blacks the new system brought a large measure of independence; to the planters it brought a more dependable and cheaper labor supply. Generally, the planter furnished workers with land, seed, fertilizer, draft animals, and tools, and in exchange took half to two-thirds of the harvested crop.

Under this new organization the plantations survived with little change until the 1930s, but not without great difficulties. The cotton crop of 1875 equaled that of 1859 in amount but not in profits. A saturation of the world supply of cotton depressed prices (by the mid 1890s they were little more than a third of the inflated prices of the late 1850s), and the resulting economic hard times created as much havoc for cotton planters as the Civil War had. Indeed, the antebellum cotton planters would have fallen on hard times had there been no war nor emancipation of the slaves.

Other staples fared less well. The sugar crop in Louisiana was back to its prewar level by 1879, but the plantations largely survived through outside capital, with about half of them owned by northerners.

Rice made the poorest recovery of all. The former slaves were not willing to go back into the snake- and mosquito-infested swamps, nor were they willing to do the "mud work" of cleaning out ditches and repairing banks. Outside capital was not available, and competition soon developed on uplands in Louisiana (led by Dr. Seaman A. Knapp, president of Iowa State College, and a group of midwestern grain farmers), with powered irrigation and harvesting machinery too heavy for the soggy swamplands of the Carolinas and Georgia. The new competition, coupled with a series of very destructive hurricanes around the turn of the century, spelled the death knell for the old rice coast. The plantations were converted to residential housing, resorts, and wildlife refuges, or allowed to return to their natural state.

The New Deal of the 1930s dealt a sharp blow to the plantation system. What may be called an "American enclosure movement"—like the English movement of the 1500s that turned fields into sheep pastures, driving out agricultural workers—encouraged the displacement of sharecroppers and tenants (generally whites who had lost their small farms in the 1890s and early 1900s, and by now outnumbered the black sharecroppers), the expansion of home farms cultivated by family members rather than sharecroppers, and more reliance on hired labor. The concomitant development of mammoth farm machinery, including mechanical cotton pickers and tobacco harvesters, and the effective use of chemical herbicides and pesticides led to such a reduced need for labor that blacks and whites were forced to migrate in droves to the cities of the Northeast and Midwest to seek new employment. Thus, by the 1970s the plantation, the focal point in shaping southern life for three centuries, was little more than a memory, shrouded in such nostalgic distortions of the *Gone With the Wind* variety that it very often was difficult to separate the mythical from the real.

BIBLIOGRAPHY

General Works

Clinton, Catherine. *The Plantation Mistress: Woman's World in the Old South* (1982).

Eaton, Clement. *The Growth of Southern Civilization, 1790–1860* (1961).

Foner, Eric. *Reconstruction: America's Unfinished Revolution, 1863–1877* (1988). Excellent coverage of the plantations during the Reconstruction era.

Fox-Genovese, Elizabeth. *Within the Plantation Household: Black and White Women of the Old South* (1988).

Gaines, Francis P. *The Southern Plantation: A Study in the Development and Accuracy of a Tradition* (1924).

Genovese, Eugene D. *The Political Economy of Slavery: Studies in the Economy and Society of the Old South* (1965).

———. *The World the Slaveholders Made* (1969). Marxist interpretations of the old South.

Kirby, Jack T. *Rural Worlds Lost: The American South, 1920–1960* (1987).

Oakes, James. *The Ruling Race: A History of American Slaveholders* (1982).

Phillips, Ulrich B. *Life and Labor in the Old South* (1929). Best introduction to the southern plantation.

Roark, James L. *Masters Without Slaves: Southern Planters in the Civil War and Reconstruction* (1977).

Scarborough, William K. *The Overseer: Plantation Management in the Old South* (1966).

Taylor, Rosser H. *Ante-Bellum South Carolina: A Social and Cultural History* (1942).

Thompson, Edgar T. *Plantation Societies, Race Relations, and the South* (1975). A sociological interpretation of the southern plantation.

Wright, Gavin. *Old South, New South: Revolutions in the Southern Economy Since the Civil War* (1986).

Cotton Plantations

Moore, John Hebron. *The Emergence of the Cotton Kingdom in the Old Southwest: Mississippi, 1770–1860* (1988).

Rosengarten, Theodore. *Tombee: Portrait of a Cotton Planter with the Journal of Thomas Chaplin (1822–1890)* (1986). The account of a sea island cotton planter.

Woodman, Harold D. *King Cotton and His Retainers: Financing and Marketing the Cotton Crop of the South, 1800–1925* (1968).

Hemp Plantations

Hopkins, James F. *History of the Hemp Industry in Kentucky* (1951).

Rice Plantations

Clifton, James M. *Life and Labor on Argyle Island: Letters and Documents of a Savannah River Rice Plantation, 1833–1867* (1978).

Dethloff, Henry C. *A History of the American Rice Industry, 1685–1985* (1988).

Heyward, Duncan C. *Seed from Madagascar* (1937).

Smith, Julia F. *Slavery and Rice Culture in Lowcountry Georgia, 1750–1860* (1985).

Sugar Plantations

Sitterson, Joseph Carlyle. *Sugar Country: The Cane Sugar Industry in the South, 1753–1950* (1953).

Tobacco Plantations

Kulikoff, Allan. *Tobacco and Slaves: The Development of Southern Cultures in the Chesapeake, 1680–1800* (1986).

Robert, Joseph C. *The Tobacco Kingdom: Plantation, Market, and Factory in Virginia and North Carolina, 1800–1860* (1938).

Slavery

Boles, John B. *Black Southerners, 1619–1869* (1984).

Genovese, Eugene D. *Roll, Jordan, Roll: The World the Slaves Made* (1974). A ground-breaking study of slavery from the vantage point of the slave.

Joyner, Charles. *Down by the Riverside: A South Carolina Slave Community* (1984). A superb study of a local slave community (on rice plantations on the Waccamaw River, probably the densest slave population in the South) from the interdisciplinary viewpoint.

Phillips, Ulrich B. *American Negro Slavery: A Survey of the Supply, Employment and Control of Negro Labor as Determined by the Plantation Regime* (1918).

Stampp, Kenneth M. *The Peculiar Institution: Slavery in the Ante-Bellum South* (1956).

Wood, Peter. *Black Majority: Negroes in Colonial South Carolina from 1670 Through the Stono Rebellion* (1974).

Agriculture

Daniel, Pete. *Breaking the Land: The Transformation of Cotton, Tobacco, and Rice Cultures Since 1880* (1985).

Gray, Lewis C. *History of Agriculture in the Southern United States to 1860*. 2 vols. (1933).

SEE ALSO **African Migration; The Deep South; Race; Racial Ideology and Social History;** and in various essays in **"Periods of Social Change"** and **"Work and Labor."**

RURAL LIFE IN THE NORTH

Jack Larkin

NOWHERE IS THE DISTANCE between the agricultural past and the postindustrial present greater than in "the North": the fourteen states of New England, the Middle Atlantic, and the Old Northwest, ranging from Maine to Wisconsin. Now the most urban and industrial part of the United States, this region has great ethnic and social diversity; but its rural history, although complex, can usefully be considered as a whole. It is primarily the history of men and women of European descent, who began to arrive and farm in North America in the early seventeenth century and were completing the agricultural settlement of this area by the time of the Civil War. Here, slavery was comparatively unimportant and later nonexistent, free family labor was the norm, and the ownership of land was widespread. Here too, agricultural society was first transformed and then overshadowed by the market, the city, and the factory.

The vast majority of Americans once lived on scattered farms or in small hamlets, worked according to the cycle of the seasons, and passed their lives within the compass of face-to-face communities. But with the successive transformations that have washed over American society, those ways of life now only survive in a few traditionalist enclaves, or as re-creations in museums of living history.

Completely satisfying definitions of "rural" and "urban" elude historians and social scientists. The census dividing line between places of under and over twenty-five hundred people is arbitrary, but it can be applied continuously over time. It roughly marks off the low-density settlement landscapes of open countryside and small villages from the denser concentrations of town and city life. At least up through the early twentieth century, the census line also consistently demarcated communities whose economies were primarily agricultural, or at least deeply intertwined with farming. This simple measure shows great change. In 1800 the settled area defined as the North was 91 percent rural; in 1850, after an enormous surge of westward expansion and the growth of commercial cities, it was 79 percent rural. By 1900 the rural proportion had dropped below half, to 43 percent. And in 1980 the North's rural population was holding steady at 23 percent; but only a small proportion of these country dwellers still had anything to do with agriculture.

CREATING THE COUNTRYSIDE

It is important to realize that the earliest American rural communities were not literally carved out of a trackless wilderness. Instead they were imposed on landscapes long inhabited by a diverse array of Algonkian-speaking Native American societies, whose tribal economies combined farming, fishing, hunting, and gathering in various ways. Their numbers greatly reduced and their morale weakened by previous visitations of European disease, they were dispossessed through negotiation and economic coercion, the force of arms, and the sheer accumulating numbers of the settlers with a voracious appetite for ownership of the land.

The creation of European agricultural communities in the North began with the landing at Plymouth in 1620, and the subsequent Puritan migration to Massachusetts Bay between 1630 and 1640. In those twenty years a few thousand English farmers and artisans and their families, with a sprinkling of ministers and magistrates, founded New England. Their prolific descendants soon created North America's most populous agricultural society. In the 1620s Dutch and Swedish farming settlements began in the Hudson and Delaware valleys. When in 1664 the British seized the New Netherlands and renamed it New York, they brought under the crown's authority several thousand largely Dutch settlers along the Hudson and on eastern Long Island. Swedish settlement proved impermanent, and British emigration to the Delaware Valley, dominated by Quakers from England and Wales, began with the founding of Pennsylvania in 1681. They were joined by a rapidly growing number of German settlers from the Rhineland, and later in the eighteenth century by emigrants from the north of England, Scotland, and northern Ireland. By 1720 there were over 250,000 people living along an arc from what is now southern Maine to southeastern Pennsylvania. Almost three-fifths of the total lived in New England. The first federal census, in 1790, counted two million people, the vast majority of whom were still in agricultural communities. The growth of New York and Pennsylvania, due to continuing in-migration from the British Isles and Germany, had outpaced that of New England, which now contained just under half of the North's population.

Europeans transformed the landscape of Native American settlement, where ownership was a fluid concept, boundaries were loosely defined, and cultivation was communal, by laying out permanent fields and building fences on land that had never seen either. They further appropriated the soil by reorganizing the land in familiar systems of land measurement, title, and transfer. Settlers also brought with them the cultural baggage of farming: their own local and regional specific ensembles of crops (and weeds), livestock, tools, patterns of building, and practices of cultivation. These forms of material culture and work were diverse in their details, but taken together they constituted a single vast invasion. During the seventeenth century, rye, wheat, oats, barley, garden crops, and English grasses for hay and pasture colonized the New World, along with cattle, horses, pigs, sheep, chickens, geese, and goats. With their houses and barns, their plows and carts, scythes and sickles, winnowing baskets and felling axes, settlers created material worlds that were at first outposts of rural Europe.

Juxtaposed with these agricultural inheritances was the shaping power of a new environment. North America's continental climate, untouched by the Gulf Stream that warmed western Europe, confounded the expectations of the first generations of settlers, who felt the impact of blistering summers, frigid winters, and unpredictable frosts, and painfully adapted their ways of farming. Abundances of wood and land and a scarcity of labor shaped resource-intensive patterns of farming, fencing, and building, ensuring that American farmers would be careless of natural resources and preoccupied with the felling of trees and the clearing of land for many generations.

In the seventeenth century, agricultural settlers moved gradually westward from the coastal edge, exploiting the clearings created by Native American cultivation and searching out land that appeared fertile to European eyes. The early populations were small, and the process of settlement often moved in discontinuous jumps. In New England, for example, the rich and level alluvial terraces of the lower Connecticut Valley, although many miles inland, were settled several decades before farm families moved from the coastal plain into the hilly terrain of central Massachusetts and northeastern Connecticut. Those areas were filled up during the early eighteenth century as subsequent generations reached out for land, creating a landscape of continuous rural settlement.

Northern agriculture became a synthesis of European and native crops and traditions of cultivation. Corn, beans, squash, and pumpkins, plants unknown to Europeans but which thrived in hot North American summers, were swiftly adopted by the settlers. Corn was to become the single most important American crop, and the autumn rituals of the cornhusking emerged as a distinctive harvest celebration in virtually every American rural community. However, in most respects the settlers' diet and ensemble of crops remained heavily dominated by their European inheritances: wheat and rye for breadstuffs, oats and barley, beef and pork, butter and cheese.

The land was abundant beyond anything known in Britain or western Europe for centuries. Settlers may have been in part echoing Native American agricultural practices when they adopted the long fallow as their regime of cultivation. Prodigal of abundant land rather than manure or scarce labor, American farmers would exhaust the fertility of their tillage fields in a few years and then abandon them for new ones. Increasingly scruffy and overgrown, the "old fields" lay fallow for a decade or two and then were cycled back into cultivation. In consequence, American farmsteads appeared wildly wasteful and slovenly to observers from Britain and western Europe, where land was expensive and labor relatively abundant.

THE PATTERNS OF EARLY RURAL SOCIETY

Some of the immense particularity of British and European village life was transplanted to North America, as emigrants struggled to reenact familiar ways on unfamiliar soil. The new settlements, with their rail fences and recently built houses, could not have looked much like their ancestral communities. But dialect, the ways of family and church, the remembered patterns of customary regulation and land use, were at first traditional and wholly familiar. They changed slowly into the distinctive patterns of provincial rural America.

Many of the patterns of rural time and place changed in these emigrant societies. The two most powerfully formative streams in the North's culture, Puritanism and Quakerism, accomplished in America what they could not do in Britain: they radically simplified the traditional church and village calendars of country life. Saint's days and the elaborate observances of Christmas and Easter were abolished in many places, and their very absence became a matter of tradition. Even less radically Protestant communities, because they were new, lacked the long, place-specific histories on which customary observances and village festivals were based. With settlers mingling from many different places, local European traditions transplanted poorly. Thus the public calendars of American agricultural communities were somewhat austere and uneventful by the standards of Europe, and local landscapes had little to hallow them. The weeks were punctuated by the recurrence of the Sabbath; time was otherwise marked by yearly and quarterly civil occasions such as militia trainings, court sessions, and town meetings.

Other seasonal calendars were far more reminiscent of Europe. The rhythms of plowing, planting, cultivation, and harvest shaped intimate behavior as well as work. Most marriages in the northern countryside came in the early spring or the late fall, avoiding both the dead of winter and the months of heavy farm work from May through October. Couples married either in anticipation or in fulfillment of the cycle of planting and harvest. The seasons dictated another, more mysterious rhythm of procreation and sexuality. Births rose and fell with the seasons, peaking in the late winter and early spring, and then falling to a minimum in the later spring and summer, and sometimes rising to a second, smaller peak in the early fall. Rural couples were thus most likely to conceive in the planting season, between April and June, and least likely in the months of haying and harvest, from July through September.

The sociability of rural Northerners was structured by the household, the congregation, and the neighborhood, those little communities whose boundaries and intricate social webs encompassed most daily experience. The patterns of that world are now shrouded in contemporary nostalgia, but they were real enough: visiting and neighborly exchanges of work and goods, cooperative work rituals such as cornhuskings, house and barn raisings, logrollings, quilting parties, and spinning frolics. Ways of gathering and drinking, courting and marrying were distinctive among America's New Englanders and Quakers, Dutch and Germans, Ulster Irish and Welsh. Rooted in the social patterns of their ancestral regions, they were evolving toward a provincial American diversity.

The countryside between Maine and Pennsylvania became one of the healthiest and most prolific areas in the world. Abundant food, relatively low population densities, agricultural opportunity, and a temperate climate (contrasting sharply with the malarial South) meant that by the standards of rural Europe northern farm families produced many children—in some places averaging seven to eight per completed family—and saw more of them survive into adulthood. Natural increase combined with heavy eighteenth-century in-migration south of New England, particularly to Pennsylvania, to create an enormous surge of population. The North's population tripled between 1700 and 1750, fueling rural families' hunger for land.

Patterns of rural settlement for a time echoed and then increasingly diverged from inherited ones. Some of New England's early-seventeenth-century communities were tightly clustered villages surrounded by intricately subdivided tillage fields. They resembled those in many grain-farming regions in England, particularly the Puritan heartland of East Anglia. Village living had the sanction of tradition, made communities more defensible in conflict with the Native Americans, and was encouraged by New England's rulers because it made community life easier to supervise. But in most places it did not endure. Tradition, defense, and communal order yielded to the requirements of a more pastoral, livestock-centered agriculture and the constant pull of available land. By the early eighteenth century, a widespread pattern of dispersed settlement had emerged, with houses scattered along the roads that linked family farmsteads. In Pennsylvania there was an even swifter transition. Settlers in the first generation abandoned or ignored the village plans of the colony's proprietors to create an open rural landscape of dispersed settlement.

New Englanders continued to live more closely together than other rural Americans, and the form of the New England town, with its central meetinghouse and common, the placing of town center, and the radial roads leading to the center, remained distinctive. Most northern agricultural communities were less sharply defined in space. Churches, stores, and taverns were often strung along the roads, and families traded and socialized in country neighborhoods whose existence was clear but whose boundaries were not clearly marked.

Rural landscapes were also powerful statements of economic and social stratification. The distribution of one- and two-story, "mean" and "commodious" houses mapped out the zones of soil fertility and embodied the distribution of wealth and power. The unpainted dwellings and debris-strewn homelots of ordinary farmers contrasted sharply with the painted houses, fenced dooryards, and orderly gardens of the gentry.

Up through the end of the eighteenth century, old limits on the tools and motive powers of agriculture held fast. Virtually all work was accomplished by the muscles of men and women and draft animals, marginally assisted by the power of falling water. Oxen in New England, horses elsewhere, hauled the harvest, pulled plows and harrows, and dragged stones and timber. Waterwheels drove small-scale mills for grinding grain, sawing lumber, and fulling handwoven cloth. Almost all other tasks were performed by human effort, using the heavy, locally made implements of regional tradition.

Men's and women's tasks were intertwined and interdependent, but in space, time, tools, and authority they were generally distinct. Farmyard, garden, house, kitchen, and hearth, in diminishing concentric circles, enclosed and bounded women's daily realm. The world of men's work faced outward, from farmyard to fields and then out to neighborhood, community, and the roads leading elsewhere.

Women's work, although it had some seasonal components, was, for the most part, daily, repetitive, and constantly liable to interruption. Men's work, although it included daily chores, was far more strongly seasonal and varied more from day to day. With their edge tools, heavy implements, and care of large animals, men occupied the realm of major physical force. Cooking pots, crockery, washtubs, churns, spinning wheels, cloth, needles, and thread were counted as distinctively female. Men and boys usually handled the raw materials of farm production and undertook the first steps in processing them, after which they handed them over to women and girls to finish. Families worked

as patriarchal units, governed by their male head. Men's work, and men's decisions about work, were primary.

Gender boundaries, however, were not absolute. The urgency of the harvest traditionally blurred the sexual division of labor. During the wheat harvest in eighteenth-century Pennsylvania, women worked alongside men, reaping, gathering, and binding. Haying season in New England sometimes brought women into the field to help rake and load the region's most important crop. Accepted boundaries also varied according to ethnicity. German-American women often undertook the heavy outdoor labor of preparing flax for spinning, greatly surprising observers from New England, who thought of it as men's and boys' work.

The North's abundance of both land and children meant that gaining control of land, holding on to it, and passing it along to the next generation were the crucial concerns of most rural families. Over the course of each family's span, parents struggled to acquire property and productive resources and then, as their children matured to parcel them out. Land, if possible, went to sons; other and lesser property went to daughters.

After a couple of generations of settlement, most members of the younger generation had to leave their communities to acquire land elsewhere. American farms were divisible only to a limited extent. Most rural places in the North, as they became fully settled agricultural communities, developed remarkably stable structures of landholding and the distribution of productive resources. The number of farms in most communities changed relatively little and remained virtually unchanged for a century or longer.

Contemporary travelers and some rural Northerners themselves, joined by later historians, proclaimed a roughly equal distribution of property as the defining signature of their communities. This was not strictly true; landless men and families, tenancy, and substantial inequality could be found everywhere, although in varying proportions that depended on the nature of initial settlement, the productivity of the land, and the strength of markets. Landholding was most widespread among household heads, although not universal, in New England, where farms were smaller and less productive than farther south. Tenancy was the powerful reality in the early Hudson Valley, where thousands of families lived on the immense proprietary estates of the "patroons." Pennsylvania had both a majority of independent proprietors and a substantial minority of tenants. Everywhere in northern rural America there came to be substantial numbers of families who did not own enough land for a viable, household-sustaining farm; many of them were genuinely poor. In virtually every community there were households supported by day labor; in other households, older children left to work for more prosperous families.

Nevertheless, in the broadest sense these commentators were right. When measured against the landholding systems of rural England, or the burgeoning economic inequality of the plantation South and American seaport cities, the rural North seemed egalitarian indeed. Tenancy itself did not always signal poverty or economic marginality. In areas of highly productive agriculture and expensive land it was a strategy for access to land that could sustain "middling" farm families—although family proprietorship remained the cherished goal.

Market, family, and community all shaped rural economic life. Northern farm families were unfailingly conscious of the need to sustain their lineages, but bought, sold, and mortgaged their property within a free market for land. They sought to produce their own food and raw materials, but almost never practiced household "self-sufficiency." Instead, they participated in intricate networks of neighborhood exchange of goods, labor, and the use of tools and livestock. They reckoned up their accounts with monetary values for prices and wages—but did not charge interest, settled up irregularly, and often carried debit balances for years. Depending on their location and their resources, they pursued markets for surplus grain, hay, livestock, butter, and cheese. Yet their drives to pass land to their children, to maintain linkages of kinship and community, clearly informed their search for such opportunities.

Also enmeshed in the exchange networks of country neighborhoods were the artisans, whose largely British-descended skills created most of the physical fabric of rural life. Blacksmiths, house wrights, cabinetmakers, shoemakers, potters, and coopers combined their crafts with farming and transmitted their skills and tools, as precious resources, to their sons or nephews. Rural American artisans usually practiced a much wider range of skills than their European counterparts, early establishing a distinctive pattern of occupational fluidity and versatility. Northern woodworkers might combine coopering, cabinetmaking, and housewrighting, while other "mechanics" undertook both blacksmithing and pottery, or combined clockmaking

and cabinetwork. Their shaping of houses, furniture, tools, and other everyday objects began with European models but gradually and subtly developed into regional and local traditions.

ECONOMIC AND SOCIAL TRANSITION IN THE NORTHEAST

Beginning late in the eighteenth century two powerful and unsettling processes of change took shape in northern rural society. One was a transformation—the reshaping of society and economy in long-settled communities. The other was an expansion—an immense surge of movement that multiplied farm families and rural communities across a thousand-mile stretch of territory.

Stimulated by a long-term upswing in European population and food consumption, the pattern of northern agricultural production began to intensify. Adopting some of the precepts of England's earlier "agricultural revolution," farmers gave up the long fallow for continuous cropping production on their fields, adopting crop rotation, the intensive use of manures, and the planting of root crops to maintain fertility. They cleared and planted increasingly larger portions of their farms, creating a more open agricultural landscape with unobstructed views.

Between the Revolution and the Civil War, northeastern farm families were drawn deeper into the market economy than before. Small streams of trade became torrents, moving over greatly improved and expanded roads. They increasingly turned toward more specialized and market-driven forms of agriculture, impelled both by competition from western farms and the emergence of city and village markets close at hand. As grain production lost its profitability, sometimes even for domestic use, farmers modified their patterns of diversified farming to concentrate on marketable crops. Zones of production emerged, determined principally by distance and transportation costs. Farms continued to produce goods for the household's use, but specialized in cheese or butter, wool for textile factories, livestock, hay for horse fodder, or, for those closest to city markets, whole milk, vegetables, and fresh meat. By mid century, most New England farm families abandoned the cultivation of bread grains entirely; like city folk, they were eating bread made from New York and Ohio flour.

In those years, too, the rural Northeast became the site of America's first industrial revolution. In the countryside from Pennsylvania to southern New Hampshire, small manufacturing villages grew up along hundreds of small- and medium-sized streams. Adapting British technology and organization, most of these rural factories harnessed water-power to drive machinery for spinning and later weaving cotton and wool; others turned chair legs, gun barrels, or clock parts. Marginal rural families left their meager holdings to cluster around the mills; their children and unmarried daughters became the nation's first factory workers.

Outside the mills, a variety of other forms of rural production for distant markets emerged. Working in small shops or their own houses, rural "mechanics" made shoes, assembled chairs and clocks, forged farm implements, printed books, and built wagons. Women and girls braided straw, made palm-leaf hats, finished shoe uppers, or painted furniture, clock dials, and tinware. As late as 1850, the northeastern countryside accounted for a major share of American industrial production. In terms of total output and employment, rural mill villages kept pace with the great factory cities such as Lowell, Massachusetts, and Manchester, New Hampshire, until the 1840s. Villagers and market-oriented artisans, who did not produce much of their own food, became major consumers of agricultural produce.

Clustered settlements reappeared in the rural Northeast in the early nineteenth century, but as outposts of commerce and industry. Commercial villages emerged at the nodes of a swiftly improving road system. In New England they were called "center villages" and arose at the traditional town centers. All of them were settled primarily by shopkeepers and artisans; they were places where farm families came to trade and find services and where small-shop production became concentrated. In most places they became the focal points of social life, economic organization, and political leadership in the countryside.

A revolution in rural childbearing also began in the same years. The age of marriage rose in many places, and married couples began to limit their fertility—lengthening the interval between children or having their last child earlier. These changes happened first in the earliest settled, most densely populated parts of the countryside. They were places where family limitation would seem economically rational: land was increasingly expensive and the cost of settling children in agricultural security was becoming substantial. They were also communities, with high literacy and widespread schooling, where new attitudes toward procreation would logically take shape. Between the 1760s and the 1840s, average completed family size in some communities dropped from nearly eight children per couple to five and a half.

In the process of industrial and commercial transformation, many traditional ways were altered or abandoned. Cash transactions began to supplant long-term local exchange. Agricultural reformers denounced huskings, frolics, and customary labor exchanges as wasteful and inefficient and persuaded many farmers to give them up. A highly successful temperance movement, coming to power in the 1820s, successfully attacked another rural tradition, heavy drinking in the course of work and sociability.

THE WESTWARD EXPANSION OF RURAL SOCIETY

At the end of the eighteenth century, an enormous number of families responded to what by American standards was crowding on the land as their ancestors had done, by moving dramatically outward in search of new farms. In a great migration far swifter than the generations-long progress inland of the colonial period, hundreds of thousands of northerners filled up the western and northern margins of the established states and went on to settle five more east of the Mississippi. Migrants from southern New England pushed north to take up lands in Vermont, Maine, and northern New Hampshire. Michigan and Wisconsin were settled primarily from the northeastern states. With some exceptions, like the substantial New England presence in southeastern Ohio around Marietta, the northern and central sections of those states were claimed by New Englanders, Pennsylvanians, and New Yorkers. Many of the paths of migration roughly paralleled the lines of latitude. Western New York, northern Ohio, Indiana and Illinois, and southern Michigan and Wisconsin all bore the heavy imprint of New England settlement. In the central and southern sections, Pennsylvanians were joined by large numbers of emigrants from Kentucky, Tennessee, western Virginia and North Carolina, mostly poorer families who were leaving the slave economy behind. Indiana, with the highest proportion of upland southerners and the fewest New Englanders, was the most clearly "southern" state in the North.

Migration was not a single wave but an immense succession of overlapping movements. In

1860 in the westernmost states of Illinois and Wisconsin, the largest proportions of adult residents had been born not on the eastern seaboard but in western New York, Vermont, and Ohio; they were the children and grandchildren of original emigrants.

This expansion of northern rural society in the years between 1780 and 1860 was in many ways deeply destructive; it involved many deaths in battle and massacre and the violent displacement of tens of thousands of Native Americans and the obliteration of their camps and villages, fields and hunting grounds. From the victorious settlers' point of view, their invasion was also enormously creative, leading to the building of hundreds of thousands of new farms and the founding of thousands of new communities. In the process of penetrating to the backcountry, emigrant families gave up much in the way of material comfort and settled society, even risking early death. Adult life expectancy was lower and infant and child mortality were substantially greater in new communities than in the settled Northeast. They undertook the enormous physical challenge of clearing new land and endured often debilitating isolation—expecting not short-term benefits but agricultural opportunity for themselves and their children.

Travel times and the cost of moving goods declined rapidly in the process of America's nineteenth-century revolution in transportation, which had a dramatic impact on the North's rural economy. The expansion and improvement of roads and vehicles, the building of canals, the development of the river steamboat, and the appearance of the railroad meant that the new rural settlements, although much farther away in miles from the eastern seaboard than their colonial counterparts, decade by decade became effectively far closer in time and cost of travel. The completion of the Erie Canal in 1825, providing low-cost transportation between New York City and the farms of western New York, was only the most dramatic of these developments. Connections with wider markets followed the advancing edge of settlement with increased speed.

The rural economies of newly settled areas, like those in the East generations earlier, were sustained by semisubsistence farming, elaborate networks of local exchange, and a trickle of outside trade. But when their communities came within reach of efficient transportation to markets, farm families found themselves responding to a changing structure of prices and opportunities by adapting

and reshaping their patterns of labor, production, and marketing. As the relative costs of production and transportation changed, the geography of wheat cultivation, for example, altered dramatically. In 1800 the area of heaviest wheat production was still centered in eastern Pennsylvania. It then shifted westward across the northern states to western New York, then to northern Ohio, and by 1860 to northern Indiana and Illinois, the center of the wheat belt at the time of the Civil War. Farmers in each successive "old" wheat growing area adjusted by gradually moving away from the crop and shifting to a variety of production patterns depending on soil and location: hay and dairy, cattle, wool, corn, and hogs.

As late as 1860, mechanization played a minor role in increasing agricultural productivity. Northern farmers had widely adopted improved farm implements—cast iron and then steel plows; more effective mass-produced scythes, hoes, axes, and shovels; better farm vehicles. These made work more efficient and, along with changes in land use and cropping, allowed for the Northeast's expansion of production on long-used land. But the burgeoning output of western farms was simply based on the opening of new and highly fertile land to cultivation.

Changes in technology, some advance in productivity, and the expansion of markets allowed for a long-term increase in rural standards of living. After 1830, mass-produced implements, utensils, cloth, and furniture began to fill the households of the countryside as well as those of the city. Country cabinetmakers gave way to chair factories; rural blacksmiths early lost their roles as fabricators of tools and became repairmen. Even carpenter-builders, whose trade necessarily remained part of the local economy, moved away from traditional styles and house-framing systems. The shapes of farmhouses, plows, and chairs became far less distinctive identifiers of locality. In the Northeast this transition was long and complex. Later on and farther west, communities could go from pioneer privation to mass-produced goods, acquired via the railroad, in a couple of decades.

The great surveys of the territory north of the Ohio and east of the Mississippi, carried out under the Land Ordinance of 1785, comprised the most massive project of mapping, recording, and ordering the land undertaken up to that time. From northwestern Ohio onward they created a rectilinear rural landscape of square-cornered fields and gridded roads. For the first decade or two some settlers tried to lay out farms and houses in the more irregular patterns of the East, but all eventually conformed to the logic of the survey. This new landscape of habitation, with its 640-acre (256-hectare) sections and 160-acre (64-hectare) quarter sections, was laid out on terrain far more rolling and open than that of the East. These lines of demarcation differentiated the new rural communities of the North even more from those of rural Europe. The survey system, with its widely separated, right-angled roads, was subsequently blamed for imposing scattered settlement on nineteenth-century rural America and diminishing the cohesion of community life. But the vast majority of arriving emigrants came from places that had had dispersed farmsteads for generations. The grid system simply strengthened their existing ways of settlement. Settling groups could easily have created small hamlets of three or four dwellings where farm boundaries cornered at road intersections, but rarely chose to do so.

The new communities did not develop as the egalitarian frontier societies of American myth. In their economic structure they came to resemble the communities that the settlers had left. Substantial inequalities in wealth emerged; early-arriving families with substantial land claims were often able to gain control of the best land. Tenant farmers and marginal laboring families became as common in settled Illinois communities as in Pennsylvania.

THE NOONTIDE OF RURAL SOCIETY

By 1860, ten million Americans were living in thousands of rural communities from Maine to Wisconsin. This population was still most heavily concentrated in the eastern core—southern New England, the lower Hudson Valley, and eastern Pennsylvania and New Jersey—but aside from the northern reaches of Maine, Wisconsin, and Michigan, rural life everywhere was at least into its second or third generation. The daily texture of community life had in most places become relatively dense. Women and children were much less likely to lead isolated lives on their farmsteads, extensive networks of visiting and organized voluntary societies were appearing, schools and churches were more numerous and closer at hand.

Across this great expanse from the Atlantic shore to the Mississippi there was still considerable variation in material standards and the risks to health. Although considerably less isolated and gradually becoming healthier, many of the newer settlements were still difficult and dangerous environments. Malaria, for example, had not yet been banished from the river valleys of Indiana and Illinois. But overall, no large rural population in history had ever been as healthy, as materially prosperous, and as widely literate and numerate. The expansion of markets for farm production had also brought an increasing array of manufactured goods to farm households.

During the eighteenth century, New England's tax-supported district school systems had been the first to put elementary literacy within the grasp of the great majority. By the mid nineteenth century, schooling was widely accessible, although not everywhere free, across the North. Schoolhouses became focal points of neighborhood life—and neighborhood conflict. In many settlements, the oral ways of upland southerners mingled, and sometimes collided, with the print-oriented culture of New Englanders; Yankee account keeping, for example, often offended migrants from the South, who relied on their memories and took the ledger book as a sign of mistrust. In most places, the arrangements for schooling, and often the teachers themselves, bore the Yankee cultural stamp. On the whole, however, the country people of the mid-nineteenth-century North had become far better connected with the world—through books, newspapers, periodicals, and the expanding postal system—than previous generations had been.

As the revolution in childbearing moved across the North in the nineteenth century, there were sharp east-west variations in family size and marital fertility. Families were largest—echoing the high birthrates of the colonial period—in new communities just behind the edge of settlement. Here land was most available and disincentives to fertility the fewest. Families grew smaller in each successive generation after settlement, as communities approximated the conditions—expensive land, high literacy, and widespread information—that triggered the transformation. Over the decades, the maximum birthrates of new settlements started to decline as well; communities with the highest fertility in 1860 were still substantially lower than their counterparts had been in 1800. The east-west gradient of rural fertility narrowed greatly over the nineteenth century. By 1900 rural families across the North were averaging no more than four or five children; their birthrate continued to decline, moving toward urban levels, but it was always somewhat higher.

Although rarely acknowledged, and pushed to the social margin, African Americans and Native Americans were enduring presences in the settled countryside. Throughout the nineteenth century blacks could be found widely, if thinly, scattered across the rural North: most sparsely settled in northern New England with about 0.5 percent of the population, most densely in New Jersey with 3 percent, and in most other places between 1 and 2 percent. Most northern blacks had lived in the region for generations, the descendants of farm and household slaves, while some had come more recently from the South. Living in a sea of white faces, rural African American families held on to the lowest rungs of the occupational ladder as laborers and marginal tenant farmers, much more rarely as landowners or skilled craftsmen. Usually too scattered to form cohesive black communities but obviously distinct, they lived as hybridized "Afro-Yankees." Everywhere they faced racial hostility; it was most powerful, both in law and practice, in Ohio, Indiana, and Illinois, where southern emigrants were most numerous.

There were long stretches of the countryside in which few Native Americans remained; yet sizeable remnant groups still lived in many eastern communities. Farming on dwindling ancestral lands or leading a semi-itinerant existence, they traded traditional crafts or doctoring skills with their neighbors. They intermarried with African Americans and whites to create a complex, sometimes ambiguous social and cultural identity; it was one they often protected by concealment, taking on many of their white neighbors' most visible ways as a protective social front.

The great tides of foreign immigration in the nineteenth century flowed disproportionately to the cities of the North; the majority of immigrants gave up both agriculture and their ancestral soil at the same time. The northern countryside received relatively small, but visible, numbers of newcomers. By 1880 the agricultural work force had significant numbers (5 percent or more) of the Irish in southern New England, New York, and New Jersey; of French-Canadians in Maine and Vermont; of British Canadians and Dutch in Michigan; and of immigrant Germans, the largest foreign-born group in rural America, more evenly spread from New York westward through Ohio, Indiana, Michigan, and Illinois. But in each of these states, immigrants remained significantly underrepresented in agricultural work; Americans of long-settled British stock continued to dominate farming. Substantial next to

the uniformly African American and Anglo-American complexion of the southern countryside, this sprinkling of ethnic diversity was relatively meager compared to the polyglot complexity of the region's cities. Only in Wisconsin was there a different balance. There Scandinavian and German immigrants were primarily rural, taking up the North's newest lands in equal numbers with the native-born.

During the nineteenth century, many kinds of production once central to the work of northern farm households moved outside its sphere. The most significant and symbolically important was the manufacture of woolen and linen cloth. In early America the vast majority of textiles for domestic use was produced in the household, although not all families spun and wove and there was substantial local exchange of cloth and yarn. Loom and wheel were the preeminent implements of female labor. But when cheap, factory-made cotton and woolen fabric became widely available to rural families, they reduced and finally abandoned household production. In southern New England wheels and looms had vanished almost completely by the 1840s. By 1860 they were disappearing across the North as the railroad penetrated the countryside and the "homespun frontier" receded across the Mississippi. Although seen by some observers as a calamitous abandonment of female industry, the disappearance of textile production created little leisure for rural women. They turned to more intensive dairying and gardening, outwork, or ever-expanding sewing.

The traditional division of work between the sexes—the oppositions of field and household, large animals and small, edge tools and needles, seasonal swings and daily repetitions—altered gradually. Probably fewer northern farm women performed fieldwork than in the eighteenth century. And there were significant changes in dairying. As grain production, primarily men's work, lost its economic importance on northeastern farms, dairying, traditionally women's work, became more widely shared between the sexes. Many farmers started to milk along with the women and some began to manage the dairy, churning butter and making cheese as well. In part, at least, men were moving to take greater control of what was now their farms' most important production process. In prosperous farm households from Massachusetts to Illinois, wives moved toward the "genteel" urban pattern, leaving garden and dairy entirely to husbands and hired help in order to concentrate on cooking, housekeeping, and child-rearing. But by the second half of the nineteenth century, there seemed to be an even wider range of possibilities; in at least a few households wives moved in the opposite direction to share more traditionally male tasks like plowing and haying.

Starting around 1850, rural industrialization in the Northeast began to stagnate and then to reverse itself. A few of the bucolic manufacturing villages—those with major locational advantages—became cities. The others gradually succumbed to the economies of scale offered by urban factories, whose increasingly steam-driven technologies were independent of waterpower sites. The small production shops, once widely distributed in the countryside, and the extensive networks of outwork manufacturing in rural households yielded as well to centralization.

The great seasonal cycles of marriage and conception, so unmistakably the signature of rural society up through the early nineteenth century, began to attenuate. Births and marriages in the countryside, starting with communities closest to the cities, lost their connections with the rhythms of farm work and approximated the far less seasonal urban pattern.

THE OVERSHADOWING OF RURAL SOCIETY

The countryside had grown faster than the cities in colonial America, but after the Revolution this was no longer true. Starting from a very small base, urban centers developed rapidly, outpacing the still high population growth of rural communities. After 1800 rural communities in the Northeast began to lose ground in relative terms. As urbanization and industrialization developed a powerful momentum from the mid nineteenth century onward, rural predominance declined in the newer states of the North as well. In 1860, three of every four northerners lived in rural communities—a proportion that varied from one out of two in southern New England to nearly nine out of ten in Indiana and Illinois. By 1900, fewer than half of the region's people lived in the countryside.

In absolute numbers, rural population continued to grow through the end of the nineteenth century—simply much more slowly than the burgeoning cities. Although their birthrates continued to decline, rural families still produced sizeable numbers of children. As they usually had in the past, most of them left the localities of their birth—

an increasing number moving farther west or to the cities, whose growth had always been fueled by rural out-migration. But their numbers were much less often replaced by in-migrants than in the past. Settled rural communities ceased to grow and their populations became increasingly older. The most marginal places—hill communities with poor soil, hardscrabble settlements isolated by geography—lost population, but most maintained a rough equilibrium. With much justification, local chroniclers and orators began to lament the loss of their best and brightest to out-migration.

Northern agricultural society faced inescapable constraints and powerful forces of transformation. The long-established land and labor patterns of American agriculture and the expectations of rural families—exemplified in the striking stability of the number of farms and the scale of farming—did not allow for the continuing subdivision and ever more intensive cultivation of the land. In the early nineteenth century, New England regional spokesmen and agricultural reformers who wanted to stem emigration and see the rural population increase had already proposed precisely this "English solution" to their countrymen, but in vain.

The enduring structures of northern agricultural society thus put a ceiling on the size of the farming population settled rural society could sustain. Other forces would drive it down. In the years after the Civil War, mechanization began to have a powerful impact on the operation of northern farms. Horse-powered reapers and threshers, mowers and cultivators, binders and hayrakes, were widely adopted by ordinary farmers. They transformed fieldwork and vastly increased the productivity of agricultural labor. Fewer hands could raise and harvest ever larger crops. Agricultural wages, and the rate of return on investment in agriculture, remained lower than those in the urban-industrial sectors of the economy. Farmland remained relatively expensive to acquire. Economic forces pulled sons out of the region to farms farther west, or pushed them out of farming entirely. Daughters found rural marriage and employment opportunities even less promising and left in larger proportions.

Added to this was the continuing cultural marginalization of rural life. In the early nineteenth century, many rural families had begun to shed much of the material slovenliness of the early American agricultural world. With painted houses and more orderly yards they strove for a gentility that beckoned from village centers and more distantly from cities. But it was not enough. They confronted a powerful sense, shaped by the now-dominant standards of the urban middle class, that the ways of the countryside were no longer normative, but painfully ungenteel, rustic, and backward. The persisting images of the "country bumpkin" or the "hick" also did their share to pull more migrants from farm to city.

Between 1880 and 1910, depending on the place, agricultural society in the North began a long and uneven absolute decline. Farm population—families living and working on farms—peaked at about 9,000,000 people in 1900 and then started a precipitous fall, with an accelerating decline in the demand for agricultural labor. The number of farms and the total acreage in cultivation declined as well. The least productive lands were abandoned; other farms were swallowed up by the expansion of cities and towns. As some fields went back to forest, the northern rural landscape reversed a three-hundred-year process of clearing and increasing openness.

THE PROBLEM OF RURAL LIFE

As early as the middle of the nineteenth century some influential northerners had begun to look at the countryside with a mixture of nostalgia, concern, and condescension. They saw agriculture and the rural landscape as a world of the past that was gradually slipping away. Men often no more than a generation removed from the farm cherished rural life—from afar—as a reservoir of physical vitality and moral virtue. But this was coupled with a growing disdain for what else they saw in rural life: narrow horizons, drudgery, and physical coarseness.

By the early twentieth century, these concerns had crystallized in the work of the Country Life movement. Social analysis and engineering emerged as a response to the enormously complex problems faced by the United States as it became a nation of cities, immigrants, and large-scale industry. Most of the Progressive Era's experts concerned themselves with slum housing, immigrant assimilation, industrial labor, or economic regulation; a few turned to the "problem" of rural life. The investigations of the Country Life Commission of 1912, and the broader work of the Country Life movement, assumed that American society was weakened by rural depopulation, social stagnation, and cultural decline. Only the countryside, in their

view, could supply the cities with a sturdy "Anglo-Saxon" stock to revitalize an enervated urban population and counter the threat to native Protestant cultural and racial dominance posed by the immigrants. They feared the depletion of the rural population reservoir, and sought to reverse it by making the countryside a better place to live. But their solutions—revitalized churches, improved schools, programs of recreation and social activity—were not sought by country people themselves. When rural folk were surveyed, they wanted not social reconstruction but higher incomes.

The loss of agricultural population did not mean that the countryside was in desperate economic decline. Northern farm families continued to live well by the standards of other societies, and between 1900 and 1920 real farm incomes were rising. But they probably felt some relative deprivation. The differences between the ways in which farm families and middle-class urban households lived, although quantitatively no greater than they had been fifty years earlier, were increasingly visible and dramatic. Indoor plumbing, gas light, and easy availability of popular entertainment and a wide range of consumer goods, readily available public transportation for shopping and visiting, and even the future prospect of telephone service, electric lighting, and appliances were alluring standards not easily attained.

The Country Life movement could not reverse a half century of technological change or redistribute American incomes. Its aims in fact were rooted in professional and urban needs and realities, not rural ones. Most of its major figures were men born in the rural North who had themselves left the countryside for higher education and professional careers. They aimed at revitalizing a countryside that would be a bulwark of social stability as the United States lurched toward modernity. Their work helped to create both the discipline of rural sociology and the widespread network of Agricultural Extension agents and services rarely familiar in the countryside; but they did not massively alter rural life or put an end to population decline.

THE COUNTRYSIDE EMPTIES
AND FILLS

From 1900 to 1950 the agricultural population of the New England and Middle Atlantic states and the number of farms decreased by half, while farm acreage dropped by one-third. On the more productive lands from Ohio to Wisconsin, change was substantial but less dramatic. The farming population fell by one-third, the number of farms decreased by one-fifth, but total acreage held roughly steady.

The meanings of "agricultural" and "rural" began to diverge in the twentieth century. As measured by the census, rural population actually increased during these years, while the number of farms and farm families fell. An increasing number of rural places lost all or most of their agriculture and became outer suburbs, residential communities of usually well-to-do urban commuters. In other communities people moved within the rural landscape, leaving farms to live and work in villages. High agricultural productivity meant that a declining farm population could sustain a substantial service and transportation infrastructure. Over the long term, the villages and small towns that functioned as centers of trade, service, and sociability for farming neighborhoods would lose customers, prosperity, and finally population. But this happened more gradually than the exodus from the farm.

The technological development of horse-powered equipment continued into the twentieth century, but a different kind of mechanization began to transform the work of farming again, beginning after 1920 and continuing into the 1950s. A proliferation of power equipment of all kinds—gasoline-powered tractors, harvesters, and giant combines; electric milking parlors and refrigerators—continued to reduce the role of agricultural labor. During roughly the same years, rural electrification, the expansion of the telephone system, and the widespread use of the automobile connected the communities of the northern countryside with the emerging national systems of power, communications, and transportation. These changes surely made rural life more attractive, but did not alter the long-term decline of farm population.

The Great Depression years saw the only reversal of these trends in the twentieth century. Between 1930 and 1940, farm population, total acreage, and the number of farms in the North increased slightly. The virtual disappearance of economic opportunity in the cities reduced the flow of population from the countryside and prompted a powerful counterstream of returning rural emigrants seeking security and lower living expenses on the farm.

In the 1940s, however, farm depopulation accelerated again. During World War II, the largest stream of rural emigration in American history left the countryside to serve in the armed forces or to take city jobs in wartime factories. In the climate of postwar prosperity relatively few of them returned. By 1950, only 8 percent of the North's people were living on farms.

Farming today is pursued by a minuscule fraction of the North's population; the immediate postwar figure of 8 percent dropped to less than 3 percent in 1980. There are productive farms in every state, but agriculture is dwindling in the Northeast. A "back to the land" movement among some well-educated urbanites, stressing organic farming and the conservation ethic, began in the 1970s. It has had some cultural impact, but has not been of great economic or demographic significance. Dairy farming is under severe economic stress, and much of the Northeast's best farmland has been converted to other, more profitable uses. So many less valuable fields have gone back to forest that the percentage of wooded land in the New England states is returning to levels below those of the late eighteenth century.

Farms in Illinois, Indiana, Wisconsin, and parts of Michigan and Ohio are still part of America's agricultural heartland. Fertilizers, pesticides, and genetically engineered crop varieties, the products of biological and chemical engineering applied to agriculture, have created immense harvests. Along with them ecological damage has appeared from toxic materials and repetitive monoculture. Although corporate farming, or agribusiness, is expanding in some highly productive areas, the great majority of Northern farms remain family operations. But the successful ones are very different from the farms of earlier times; they are highly mechanized and even computerized. Average farm size has nearly doubled since the early twentieth century, and the capital costs, for land and equipment, of farm operation have become enormous. Beginning in farming is now as expensive as starting up a small factory; even the most costly college education is now far cheaper than settling a child on the land.

Since 1950, changes in transportation, communications, and work have made possible an ex-urban pattern of rural life for an increasing number of American families. Now that rural distances have yielded to high-speed highways and houses can be built or rebuilt with superior domestic technology virtually anywhere, many families have pushed well past the suburbs in their search for affordable housing and open space. In the process, many Americans have accepted long commutes to work. Others can travel to workplaces in the countryside; in many of the new service and knowledge industries, telecommunications and networked computers have nullified the old economic advantages of urban concentration.

The new patterns of rural life in the North have nothing to do with actual agriculture, but they are ironically intertwined with its history. Seeking an uncluttered landscape and low-density settlement, urban and suburban American families are returning to lands that their predecessors once took up—just as hopefully, but with far different purposes in mind.

BIBLIOGRAPHY

Barron, Hal S. *Those Who Stayed Behind: Rural Society in Nineteenth-Century New England* (1984).

Bidwell, Percy Wells, and John I. Falconer. *History of Agriculture in the Northern United States, 1620–1860* (1941).

Bowers, William L. *The Country Life Movement in America, 1900–1920* (1974).

Cronon, William. *Changes in the Land: Indians, Colonists, and the Ecology of New England* (1983).

Danhof, Clarence. *Change in Agriculture: The Northern United States, 1820–1870* (1969).

Faragher, John Mack. *Sugar Creek: Life on the Illinois Prairie* (1986).

Fletcher, Stevenson W. *Pennsylvania Agriculture and Country Life, 1640 to 1940.* 2 vols. (1950–1955).

Garkovich, Lorraine. *Population and Community in Rural America* (1989).

Gates, Paul Wallace. *The Farmer's Age: Agriculture, 1815–1860* (1960).

Gross, Robert A. *The Minutemen and Their World* (1976).

Hahn, Steven, and Jonathan Prude, eds. *The Countryside in the Age of Capitalist Transformation: Essays in the Social History of Rural America* (1985).

Hart, John Fraser. *The Look of the Land* (1975).

Jensen, Joan M. *Loosening the Bonds: Mid-Atlantic Farm Women, 1750–1850* (1986).

Lemon, James T. *The Best Poor Man's Country: A Geographical Study of Early Southeastern Pennsylvania* (1972).

Osterud, Nancy Grey. *Bonds of Community: The Lives of Farm Women in Nineteenth-Century New York* (1991).

Prude, Jonathan. *The Coming of Industrial Order: Town and Factory Life in Rural Massachusetts, 1810–1860* (1983).

Rutman, Darrett B. *Husbandmen of Plymouth: Farms and Villages in the Old Colony, 1629–1692* (1967).

Shannon, Fred A. *The Farmer's Last Frontier: Agriculture, 1860–1897* (1945).

Thornton, Tamara Plakins. *Cultivating Gentlemen: The Meaning of Country Life Among the Boston Elite, 1785–1860* (1989).

Underwood, Francis H. *Quabbin: The Story of a Small Town with Outlooks upon Puritan Life.* New foreword by Robert A. Gross (1893; repr. 1986).

SEE ALSO **Agriculture; American Social and Cultural Geography; Household Labor; Immigration; The Natural Environment: The North; Urbanization;** and various essays in the section "**Regionalism and Regional Subcultures.**"

RURAL LIFE IN THE SOUTH

Carville Earle

THE AMERICAN SOUTH, by my definition, encompasses some 700,000 square miles (1,820,000 square kilometers), nearly one-fourth of the land area of the coterminous United States. It stretches some 900 miles (1,440 kilometers) from the banks of the Ohio River to the Gulf of Mexico and some 1,200 miles (1,900 kilometers) from the Outer Banks of North Carolina to the edge of the semiarid grasslands of Texas and Oklahoma. In these spans, the region cuts across a myriad of environments, ranging from the sandy lowlands of the Gulf-Atlantic coastal plains to the highlands of the Appalachians and the Ozarks, from the cooler continental climates on the north to the steamy subtropics on the south, and from the humid and rainy biomes on the east coast to the margins of the dryland plains on the west. Amid this spacious diversity, however, southerners have forged an abiding and almost unique attachment to region and to place, an attachment that binds them together even as the winds of change transform the social and economic bases of regional consciousness.

Rurality lies at the heart of southern identity. In this most rural of American regions, the overwhelming majority of southerners during the past four centuries have been born and bred in rural communities, on plantations and farms, quarters and tenements, dispersed in open-country neighborhoods. As late as 1860, when the rest of the nation experienced an industrial and urban revolution, the countryside was home for nine out of every ten southerners. A century later, nearly half of all southerners reported a rural residence. Rurality thus has served as a powerful force shaping the South's distinctive regional identity, an identity that has not been lost despite the region's extraordinary environmental, economic, racial, ethnic, and ideological diversity.

To understand the South is to come to grips with the region's rural history and its derivatives: material derivatives such as the plantation and staple crops, slavery, race, and juxtapositions of poverty and concentrated wealth; and nonmaterial derivatives of gentility and violence, of evangelical religion, of an acutely refined sense of history (and of defeat), of bravery and courage, and of provincialism and orthodoxy. What was life like in this vast regional sea of rurality? How did it differ from life elsewhere in the nation? How have southern lives and landscapes changed over the past four centuries? These are questions that in one way or another return us to the origins of the South some four centuries ago.

THE FIRST SOUTH: CHESAPEAKE ORIGINS

The story of the rural South properly begins on the dawn of the seventeenth century, with the death of Queen Elizabeth (1603) and the establishment of an English colony named in her honor. The Chesapeake colony of Virginia, established in 1607 by the Virginia Company of London, would become a model for southern society, economy, and culture. By 1700, that model presented a place that was resoundingly rural, that was animated by planters and bond laborers who scattered widely across the tidewater landscape in pursuit of profits from a plantation staple crop, in this case, tobacco. The society that evolved in the Chesapeake, however, was hardly the one envisioned by the company on the outset of colonization. The directors in London envisioned instead an urban society of highly skilled artisans and craftsmen engaged in producing commodities that were in short supply in England—potash from the forests, grapes and wine, spices, silk from imported worms and native mulberry leaves, citrus fruit, and the like.

The chief flaw in the company's plan was its reliance upon a geographical theory that ascribed

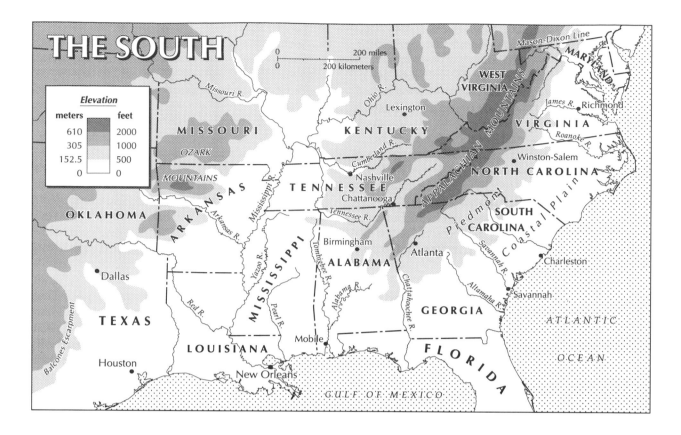

climate to latitudinal position. The directors believed, quite wrongly, that Virginia's location in Mediterranean latitudes would duplicate the environs and the commodities of France, Portugal, and Spain. American realities proved quite different. Dispensing with outlandish theory, colonists on the scene rapidly adapted their economy to this robust land. Within a decade of settlement, Virginians abandoned the quest for exotic Mediterranean commodities and turned instead to the bounty of native crops—to Indian corn and what King James regarded as "the stinking weed," tobacco.

Tobacco changed everything. The "weed's" adoption by Chesapeake colonists was truly ineluctable since prices were outrageously high, a pound (.45 kilograms) of tobacco leaf bringing as much as three shillings before the mid 1620s. Capitalizing on the European demand for pipe tobacco, Virginians of modest means enjoyed huge profits, earning seven times or more what they could have earned as common laborers in England. Wealth and its accoutrements were instantly acquired. Within a decade of initial settlement, Virginians

planted tobacco everywhere, even in the streets of the capital at Jamestown. In time, these Virginians styled themselves as "planters," their settlements "plantations"—terms which meant nothing more than an agrarian commitment to a *planted* row crop such as tobacco—in contradistinction to "farms" and farmers committed to sown or broadcast (farmed) crops such as wheat and other small grains.

Ignoring the company's continuing insistence on the production of Mediterranean crops, Virginians sought to secure the land and labor required for growing tobacco on dispersed plantations. Land was cheap and readily available; labor was neither. To solve the problem of labor scarcity, the planters turned to the bond labor of servants and slaves. Although a score of African slaves came into the colony in 1619, the institution of chattel slavery made little headway until very late in the century. Planters initially preferred the labor of English indentured servants. The indenture or contract obligated the servant's labor for four to seven years in exchange for the planter's provision of transportation and, at term's end, a small amount of land, tools, and clothes. With the gearing up of the servant trade, Virginians secured regular supplies of labor (several thousand bonded servants and slaves each year) and expanded the region of settlement from its initial nucleus in the James River valley across the sandy coastal plain and along the estuarine valleys of the York, the Rappahannock, and the Potomac.

The Chesapeake frontier at first expanded at a modest pace. Following the dissolution of the Virginia Company of London in 1624 and the decline in tobacco prices at the end of that decade and into the 1630s, settlement remained concentrated in the James Valley and the peninsula between the James and York rivers. The establishment of Maryland in 1632 brought a new wave of settlers to the Chesapeake. Following a decade or so of experimentation with feudal systems of land tenure, Marylanders also turned to tobacco and dispersed plantation settlement. The pace of frontier expansion quickened noticeably after 1650 (aided by the productivity-improving innovations of tobacco topping and house curing); indeed the rate of expansion in the next quarter century (over 3 percent per annum) ranks among the largest in the history of the American frontier.

The results, however, dismayed visitors to the Chesapeake in the 1670s and 1680s who lamented the recklessness and disorder of expansion. They were horrified by a landscape of small, slovenly maintained clearings punctuated by hilled rows of tobacco and corn, animals running freely about the landscape, isolated ramshackle dwellings and crude barns (the early tobacco houses), and the utter absence of towns—all of which in their view jeopardized a civilized English way of life. Nor was life entirely agreeable for settlers themselves, faced as they were with a short life (on average, about forty years for those who survived to twenty years of age), high infant mortality, the debilitations of malaria and assorted waterborne diseases, and in consequence, an unusual number of the widowed and orphaned. In all this bleakness, however, there was the beacon of modest opportunities for achieving a rude and egalitarian sufficiency. Not a few servants became free, moved up into the ranks of the small planter, married, and had children. Somehow, this disordered, disheveled, and dispersed way of life seemed to be working. But all of that was about to change.

The rough egalitarianism of Chesapeake life in 1680 gave way by 1730 to a class-structured society, stratified in descending order of wealth and status. Among the freemen, planter elites stood at the top, ordinary planters in the middle, and white tenants at the bottom; slaves were, of course, lower still. This massive transformation of Chesapeake society was set in motion by the wholesale importation of slaves, mostly off-loaded from West Indian sugar plantations strapped with huge debts accumulated during the economic crisis of the 1680s. Chesapeake blacks, who accounted for scarcely 5 percent of the population in 1675, contributed 25 percent by 1710. In the most productive tobacco counties, slave proportions occasionally exceeded 50 or 60 percent by the time of the American Revolution. Simultaneously, the indentured servant virtually disappeared from Chesapeake probate inventories.

Although the reasons for this sudden labor transformation in the Chesapeake are in dispute—was it purely a market response, on the one hand, or planter dissatisfaction with the unruly and rebellious behavior of servants, on the other—scholars do not disagree about slavery's structural effects on Chesapeake society. The mass importation of slaves at once narrowed the ordinary planter's opportunities for economic mobility and concentrated wealth and income in the hands of those with the capital sufficient for slave purchase. Given the tenfold (and often more) differential between a solitary planter's annual income from tobacco and the costs of a slave, slave ownership—and productive power and wealth—soon became concentrated in the hands of half or fewer of the white households. Low tobacco prices in the 1680s and 1690s exacerbated the problems of the poorer planters, such that in some tobacco districts as many as a third of the white households in 1710 owned neither slaves nor land. The revival of tobacco prices offered little solace; tenancy continued to grow, encompassing half or more of all households in some areas by the Revolution. For many in the Chesapeake, tenancy had become a permanent status. Simultaneously, the planter elite solidified its wealth and power. Between 1720 and 1750, the largest planters—those owning thousands of acres and a hundred or more slaves—differentiated themselves from the lesser sorts through the refinements of conspicuous consumption, formal education, Anglicanism, provincial politics, and local patronage and philanthropy.

In this ossifying social system, exit offered the principal option for poor white planters and tenants. Accordingly, the outflow of tidewater migrants to the piedmont and the backcountry became a flood as the century progressed. Frontier expansion lurched forward. (It had previously been slowed to a trickle by the depression of the 1680s and 1690s, increasing at a rate of barely 1 percent per annum.) In the back parts of Maryland and Virginia, the tidewater's refugees mingled with others from Pennsylvania who came in search of land or freedom from religious and political persecution. Out of this curious mélange of tidewater creoles, pietist Germans, Scots, and Scotch-Irish emerged a new rural ethos, one that was disposed toward freedom, egalitarianism, religious enthusiasm, and the appeals of the Great Awakening. Evangelical preachers on the circuit found their most receptive audiences among these isolated, often aggrieved, and oddly cosmopolitan peoples.

THE SECOND SOUTH: CAROLINA

As Chesapeake planters made the turn toward slave labor and poised for expansion into the backcountry, the Carolina proprietors were giving birth to a second South some 500 miles (800 kilometers) away. Having secured a colonial charter following the restoration of the Stuart monarchy in return for their loyalty to royalist causes, the Carolina proprietors envisioned a colonial refuge for nobility, lordly ideals, and feudal baronial tenures. After a series of false starts, settlement was launched at Charleston in 1680 and the town's progress exceeded all expectations. Charleston grew rapidly as it attracted the well-to-do dispossessed—the West Indian sugar planters escaping hard times and the French Huguenots (Protestants) fleeing the Counter-Reformation—as well as English traders seeking profits from the deerskin trade with the dense Indian populations of the interior.

As the town grew and settlement spread into the surrounding lowlands, the feudal dreams of the proprietors quickly slipped by the wayside. Carolinians sought a more enduring and practical economic base for their colony. The Indian trade and provisions exports to the sugar islands in the West Indies proved serviceable for the pioneer economy, but these trades gradually gave way to productions of rice and, at a later date, indigo. Rice—and its corollary, slavery—swiftly assumed hegemony over the Carolina economy. Between the successful introduction of rice in the late 1690s and 1730, wealthy Carolinians and their slaves installed one of the most sophisticated agrarian systems in American rural history. They deployed an irrigation system that relied upon the technology of tidal hydraulics for raising and lowering water levels in the fresh-

water back-swamps where rice was grown. The intricate system of embankments, canals, channels, sluiceways, and subtle gradients required by rice demanded an enormous investment in the preparation and maintenance of irrigation's infrastructure. This system was unthinkable in the absence of massive labor inputs. The minimum cost of entry, by most accounts, was ownership of fifty slaves per rice plantation. With initial investment running at £3,000 (and often more), Carolina's agrarian economy precluded all but the wealthiest men. But for those who could afford it, the investment paid enormous dividends. By the early eighteenth century consumers in southern Europe and in England were more than willing to pay a premium for the moist, full-bodied rice of the Carolina low country.

Carolina's prosperity soon shaped a distinctive social geography unlike any other along the Atlantic seaboard of North America. The wealthiest men in America, and perhaps the world, merely sojourned on their vast rice plantations. Most of them and their families spent only a few months of the year in the humid back-swamps of coastal Carolina and among their slaves (many directly from Africa) who constituted anywhere from 70 to 90 percent of the population, depending on the season. Plantation overseers conducted most of the daily business, especially in the summer and early fall when planters and their families fled the fetid air, malaria, and dysentery in favor of their town houses in Charleston or the healthier climes such as Newport, Rhode Island. As one observer, Johann David Schöpf, remarked about this region, it was in the spring a paradise, in the summer a hell, and in the fall a hospital. Rich planters and their families simply evacuated the region when conditions grew hellish; slaves and overseers meanwhile endured the insects, the muck, the sickness, and the death in anticipation of October's glorious relief.

Although the Carolinas and the Chesapeake by 1730 shared the institution of slavery, the two regions in other respects could not have been more unlike. Only the very elite among the Chesapeake planters could compare in wealth with Carolina rice planters. In the Chesapeake, ownership of fifty or one hundred slaves was exceptional; in Carolina, these were the minimal costs of entry. Consider too the contrasting meaning of rurality in these two regions. In the Chesapeake, except for an occasional trip to the capital or the rare trip to Europe, planters and their families spent their days in the countryside. Middling and small planters were even more isolated, their travels limited to the county court, country stores, local inns, and tobacco inspection stations. Oddly enough, owing to the numerous tidal tributaries of the Chesapeake Bay, news from England was often more readily available than news of one's neighbors several estuaries away. In the Carolina low country, by contrast, rurality for the rich was seasonal. When the planters left the swamps in late spring, the social scene shifted to their town houses in Charleston. Their flight, in turn, enabled the black majority in the rural districts to preserve and to nurture a distinctive way of life that accented African cultural traits and values—a way of life that was denied to slaves in the Chesapeake, divided up as they were into small groups and scattered among the far-flung plantations.

THE UPLAND SOUTH

If coastal Carolina was a world apart, so too was its backcountry. Superficially, South Carolina's backcountry seemed merely an extension of migrant streams that had flowed along the Appalachian flanks in Virginia and North Carolina; but in fact, the differences in these two frontiers were profound. To the South Carolina frontier goes the distinction of having served as the seedbed for a new American, what we have come to know variously as the upland southerner or, less kindly, as the "cracker" and the "redneck." This type traces its origins to the interior's sociogeographic insularity. The upland South was insulated, in the first instance, by its geographical distance from the coastal life of South Carolina—the linear distance of some 100 miles (160 kilometers) or more and the social distance between the arrogance of great wealth and the humility of rude sufficiency—and, in the second instance, by the frontier's unusual ethnocultural homogeneity—mostly migrants originating from the margins of the British Isles, from Scotland, Wales, and northern Ireland—and its reinforcement by the dense distribution of these groups. Unleavened by coastal Anglicanism or the German pietism that was so widespread in the Virginia and North Carolina backcountry, the upland southerners of South Carolina and Georgia adhered to a more austere Presbyterianism that was nonetheless well suited to an economy of subsistence and, as applied by the privileged coastal elite, a provincial polity that neglected the backcountry.

As the American Revolution unfolded, the British military sought to take advantage of the geopolitical tensions that divided South Carolina's upland from its low country. Following their humiliating defeat at Saratoga in 1777, the British shifted the theater of action south from New England to the West Indies, South Carolina, and Georgia. On the mainland, they quickly won control of Charleston. Soon after the city was secure, they thrust units into the interior hoping to capitalize on the upland's disaffection. The British strategy was foiled by the military genius of General Nathanael Greene. Although winning few battles in the upland and the backcountry, Greene succeeded in extending British supply lines, forcing the invading army to commandeer provisions and materials from the residents of the interior, and shifting the upland's allegiance from the British to the American cause. More important for the rural South, there emerged from this maelstrom a new southerner—devout and evangelical, intensely rural, tough, and, when necessary, violent—poised for the headlong expansion that was to come.

THE COTTON SOUTH

The rural South stood at the crossroads in the years immediately following American independence. The path taken led to the region that we know today; the path not taken led in an entirely different direction, into the American mainstream. The latter path for the South, in fact, seemed more probable as late as 1790. At that point, the future of the institution of slavery was clouded; many tobacco planters, faced with unusually soft markets for their crop, abandoned the "weed" in favor of wheat and corn. These crops lent themselves to seasonal wage labor rather than slave labor. Most Americans in the 1780s seem to have envisioned a withering away of slavery to a residual nucleus confined to the coastal swamps of South Carolina and Georgia—all of which may explain the constitutional abolition of slave importation by 1808.

This vision, however, did not allow for the invention of the cotton gin in 1794 nor for the spectacular profitability of short-staple upland cotton, nor even for the concatenation of gin, cotton, slavery, and the evangelistic farmers of the upland South. Wedding themselves to this new and revitalized plantation economy, upland southerners swept southwestward and around the tip of the Appalachians, planting slavery and cotton in the Georgia piedmont, the fertile black belt of central Alabama and Mississippi, and the rich alluvial soils in the valleys of the Alabama, Tombigbee, Pearl, and Mississippi rivers. In the flush times of high cotton prices between 1800 and 1830, the rate of expansion on the southern cotton frontier was astonishing, tripling or quadrupling rates of expansion elsewhere in the nation. Many of these settlers, especially those from the Upper South, brought slaves with them, but most upland southerners, having no prior experience with slavery, brought only their families, acquiring slaves as their ensuing prosperity and the domestic slave trade allowed. Although opportunities for economic advance were vastly improved through slave ownership, the lack of slaves did not preclude small planters from engaging in cotton production; indeed, many white households in the cotton belt relied exclusively on family labor, women included.

The breakneck pace of southern frontier expansion effectively came to an end with the long depression that began in the late 1830s. During the next two decades, frontier expansion gave way to intensification, to the concentration of people and cotton production in regions of fertile soil. Cotton output, aided by the muscular economic recovery of the 1850s, increased to over five million bales per annum by 1860. Cotton was king, commanding the economy of the Lower South and, with 52 percent of the value of all American exports, influencing the economy of the nation at large.

The cotton belt and rurality were synonymous on the eve of the Civil War. The rural economy offered little scope for cities and towns since the marketing of cotton created very modest demands for transportation and handling services. The usual marketing margin (the proportion of the market price allotted to mercantile services and transportation) for cotton of 7 or 8 percent was half to a fifth the margin charged for Northern grains and livestock. Moreover, the exceptionally high level of wages in Southern cities—a reflection of the returns one could make in the countryside—further blunted the urban impetus. Cities and towns accordingly were few in number, and those that did exist served as mere adjuncts to the cotton trade—coastal entrepôts, for example, or the tiny steamboat landings that lined the riverways. Most of the rural population of the South, 90 percent or more, worked cotton plantations; roughly half of their plantations used slave labor, supervised in the case of large plantations by white overseers; those who did not own slaves hoped to do so, by first acquiring land and then a mule or two. Although wealth was highly concentrated among the larger planters, small planters were rarely poor. So long as cotton prices remained high, the economy offered tangible opportunities for social advancement; the dramatic increase in cotton demand and slave prices

during the 1850s was worrisome to their prospects however.

The mentality of cotton planters is much debated among historians. Some historians see a mentality of quasi-feudal paternalism embedded within a two-tiered society of planter elites and poor whites; others describe a rational, market (capitalist) mentality operating within a continuously differentiated social structure. More recently, proponents of the dual-society hypothesis have argued that evidence of high levels of subsistence production (corn and hogs) among the lesser planters at once warrants seeing them as peasant-like yeomen and confirms the more general hypothesis. Conversely, critics of this hypothesis point out that subsistence production was in fact a rationally efficient strategy of crop management in which planters rotated cotton with corn intercropped with soil-renovating cowpeas. That strategy enabled planters to maintain profits while reducing the costs of soil erosion (declining productivity and out-migration expenses). The success of this sophisticated system of crop rotation explains, according to the proponents of a capitalist mentality, the cotton belt's self-sufficiency in food as well as its increasing disregard for frontier expansion. One thing seems clear after the dust has settled around this debate—nonslaveholding planters in the cotton belt were not poor by standards elsewhere in the South or in the nation.

THE OTHER ANTEBELLUM SOUTH

A case in point is the sad fate of the first South and its planters who lived alongside the tidal estuaries of the Chesapeake Bay. Their woes were several: the post-Revolutionary introduction of a series of unwise agrarian reforms, including the substitution of plowing for hoe-hilling (the practices of hoe-tillage and planting crops in tiny mounds or "hills"); the ensuing erosion and exhaustion of once-fertile soils; the migration of tobacco production into the piedmont; and the incessant fluctuations in tobacco markets and prices. Devolution of the coastal economy was manifested in a series of regional pathologies—a dual economy of poor whites and threadbare elite planters; a fiercely competitive labor force mottled by poor whites, recently manumitted blacks, and hired slaves; and a boiling mix of class and racial enmity.

Here in the first South was a hothouse for extremist ideology. And each class found its standard-bearer; for the threadbare elite, the Virginia planter

George Fitzhugh (1806–1881) called for order through the paternalist enslavement of all men, poor whites as well as blacks; for the poor whites, the North Carolinian Hinton Rowan Helper (1829–1909) called (in virulently racist language) for the emancipation of poor whites through the African repatriation of American blacks; and for blacks, the Virginian Nat Turner (1800–1831) called for the emancipation of slaves through his example of violent rebellion. Reactions varied. Northern abolitionists, papering over the extremism of ideologies nurtured in the decay of the Old South, rather too eagerly projected these insensibilities to the South as a whole. In truth, planters in the cotton belt, or for that matter in the tobacco belt of the Virginia and North Carolina piedmont, had little sympathy for any ideology other than the one which justified their continuing pursuit of profit in a slave society.

The South in 1860, then, was not a monolith. More correctly, it consisted of a curious patchwork of disparate rural regions and conflicting ideologies bound together only by slavery's thin strand. Regional ideologies, ranging from the cotton belt's capitalist boosterism trumpeted in *De Bow's Review* to the mid South's pragmatic accommodationism voiced by the legatees of Henry Clay in Kentucky and Tennessee to the tidewater extremism of Fitzhugh, Helper, and Turner, were as varied as the South itself. Secession joined the first and the third of these in an uneasy and sometimes contradictory coalition, which nonetheless fought valiantly and at great cost in behalf of the preservation of slavery and the various meanings that were attached to a "southern way of life."

THE POSTBELLUM SOUTH

The grisly costs of the Civil War were especially high in the rural South. In just four years of war, over a quarter of a million Southerners died; hundreds of thousands of others were injured. Physical destruction decimated parts of the South, especially the war-torn valleys of the Mississippi and the Tennessee rivers, the corridor from Chattanooga to Atlanta to Charleston, and tidewater Virginia. Other parts escaped relatively unscathed. But the outcome of the war reached into every corner of the region. Slavery was abolished once and for all, and Southerners set about reconstructing a new way of life.

Perhaps the hardest adjustment for the postwar South involved piecing together a rural economy that had been smashed apart by emancipation.

The task amounted to a reunification of the property rights in labor which henceforth were vested in black freemen with the property rights in land which remained in the hands of planters—some desultory attempts at land reform notwithstanding. The reunification occurred through a series of private negotiations, later reinforced in law, between the white owners of land and the black owners of labor. Planters assumed the initiative, introducing a bewildering array of contractual agreements for the right to use their lands. These tenancy agreements ranged from straightforward cash rentals of land to highly ornate contracts specifying the freeman's share of the crop in return for the planter's provision of land, implements, seed, and capital.

These agreements achieved their highest refinement in the cotton belt. The share or cropper contracts provided poor blacks and poor whites with an annual lease on land, equipment, mules, seed, fertilizer, and provisions in return for delivering to landowners some negotiated fraction of the crop output at harvest. The share of the crop delivered in these agreements usually ranged from one-third to three-quarters, the amount depending on such factors as labor scarcity and the inputs contributed by the cropper and the landowner. These agreements soon fragmented the orderly geography of the antebellum plantation landscape into a myriad of small tenantries of twenty to forty acres (eight to sixteen hectares) dotted by the frame cabins of the freemen. By 1880, tenant farms constituted over half of all farms in the cotton South; of these, three-fifths were worked on sharecropping agreements.

The restructuring of postbellum land tenure and plantation settlement was accompanied by dramatic changes in crop combinations and land management. Planters and tenants soon abandoned antebellum crop diversification with its rotation of cotton, corn, and cowpeas in favor of cotton monoculture and commercial fertilizers. The availability of cheap fertilizers—using phosphate rock mined from the South Carolina coast after 1868—ignited a "guano craze" in the eastern cotton belt in the 1870s. Persuaded of fertilizer's low costs and high yields by the promotional efforts of the industry and state agricultural experts, planters and their tenants eagerly switched to a system of cotton monoculture. Henceforth, on credit accounts with country stores and local merchants, they purchased corn, pork, and other provisions as well as fertilizers.

Initially, the returns from the new agrarian system were promising, but yields soon declined owing to nitrogen deficiencies in the commercial manures. Seeking to counter declining yields, planters and tenants applied even more fertilizer. Debts for the additional fertilizer and provisions mounted, and crop liens ensued. As debts accumulated, claims on the cotton crop were projected two, three, or more years into the future, all of which has been summarized under the label of "debt peonage." Flight was one of the few ways of escaping out from under this mounting debt burden—and many did just that; state legislatures, in response, attempted to check debt flight by enacting laws that restricted mobility.

As the adversities associated with cotton monoculture, fertilizers, and debt peonage diffused ever westward into the cotton belt between 1870 and 1910, it collided with an equally devastating pathology that was working its way east. The boll weevil came east from Texas in the 1890s, to Louisiana and central Mississippi by 1910 and to South Carolina and Georgia by 1920. In the wake of this destructive insect, cotton acreage and yields fell by 27 and 31 percent, respectively. In Georgia, yields declined by half.

The boll weevil's advance constituted an "economic black death" for the cotton belt; the invader set in motion a sharp reduction in cotton acreage, calls for diversification, and a glut of excess labor. Croppers and tenants, mainly black, left the South in growing numbers. Between 1900 and 1930, 712,000 blacks left the region, a fivefold increase over the 1890s. Although black population in the South continued to grow, out-migrants from the region exceeded net additions by 70 percent. In some parts of the South, black evacuation reached such proportions that labor shortages ensued. Planters in the rich plantation districts along the Mississippi River, for example, looked increasingly toward mechanization as a solution to the heavy losses incurred by the black exodus.

Elsewhere in the South, the Civil War and slave emancipation resulted in similar restructurings of rural life and landscape. In the postbellum tobacco economy of Virginia and North Carolina, plantations were fragmented into scores of small cropper and cash tenements. Two differences were noteworthy, however. First was the spectacular rise in the world demand for tobacco. Unlike southern cotton production which peaked in 1930 at nearly fourteen million bales and then fell to eight million bales, tobacco output increased rapidly between 1890 and 1930 and has maintained that position since. Second was the need for quality control in tobacco production and the advantage that need

conferred upon tenancies based on rentals rather than shares. In the case of sharecropping agreements, responsibility for quality control rested with the landowner; in cash rentals, the incentives for quality were shifted to the tenant. Black as well as white tenants thus acquired increasing responsibility for the wider range of entrepreneurial decisions that are usually associated with a market economy. The market's penetration into the tobacco belts of Virginia, North Carolina, and central Kentucky received an added fillip by the taking off of the cigarette industry after World War I with its even more exacting demands for high-quality leaf and quality differentiation.

Much more might be said about postbellum restructurings in other parts of the South—for example, among the vast and highly capitalized plantations that lingered on in the old coastal rice districts of South Carolina and Georgia and in the riverine sugar plantations in southern Louisiana. The scale of operation in these regions precluded the profusion of tenancy and devolved instead toward a production system reliant principally upon wage labor, bound by various devices to the production units. Least affected by emancipation perhaps were the many small and diversified farms that fringed the great staple regions of cotton, tobacco, sugar, and rice. Corn, hogs, and assorted other crops continued to provide subsistence and small market surpluses for farmers in the Appalachians, the sandy Gulf Coast, and Kentucky and Tennessee distant from the rich alluvial soils or the productive basins around Nashville and Lexington.

THE NEW SOUTH: RESTRUCTURING AGRARIAN ECONOMY AND SOCIETY

The most recent changes in the history of the rural South have been the most sweeping in their scope. An Old South has given gave way to a New South. Originating in the calamities that beset the region earlier in this century—the boll weevil, falling cotton yields and acreages, massive outmigration, and finally the Great Depression—the New South presented by the 1960s a stripped-down, mechanized, and diversified version of the traditional rural economy. In the process, cotton moved from the center to the margin of southern rural life. The core regions of cotton production shifted westward into Texas and, eventually, the irrigated fields of Arizona and California. Southern cotton output fell from fourteen million bales in 1930 to about eight million bales by 1970. Tenants and croppers, white and black, left the countryside en masse; constituting 40 to 50 percent of farm operators as late as 1950, their proportion had fallen to 12 percent by 1974. Black farm population declined from 536,000 in 1950 to 56,000 in 1978. Concurrently, rural population fell from some 70 percent in 1930 to about 40 percent by 1970. The painful human consequences associated with these dislocations is not hard to imagine.

A new way of life filled the void left by the evacuees. Farm machinery, often subsidized by federal crop-support payments, quickly replaced the croppers, tenants, and mules. Over one-fifth of all southern farms in 1950 used tractors for cultivation. Mechanized cotton pickers, developed in the 1940s, harvested a quarter of the cotton in the Delta counties of Mississippi by the early 1950s. The peanut harvest was increasingly mechanized. Tobacco planters introduced the riding primer for harvesting the leaf in the 1950s followed by the bulk curing barn and the tobacco combine. Chemical weed killers were added to this technological arsenal during the 1950s. These technologies set in motion what one historian has called the "great enclosure." Southern landowners reassembled the fragmented southern landscape. Reconstituting the miniholdings of departed or displaced croppers and tenants, farmers and planters created a neoplantation that bore a striking resemblance to its antebellum precursor. Southern farm size increased steadily; abandoned cropper cabins were bulldozed under, monoculture was abandoned in favor of diversified production—livestock (facilitated by pasture improvements and veterinary medicine), fruit, peanuts, soybeans, wheat, poultry, forestry products; machines replaced the labor of men and mules; agrarian decision making was returned into the hands of a relatively small number of landowners. Rural residents declined from 60 to 70 percent of the population in the 1930s to 30 to 40 percent by the 1970s.

The invasions of electrification, industrialization, urbanization, and the state into the countryside contributed also to the transformation of the rural South. Federal and state policies promoted rural economic development; subsidized electrification, mass communications, and agricultural mechanization; and encouraged diversification of the agrarian economy. Rural industrialization, though dating to the 1880s and the rise of textile factories in the Carolina piedmont and steel mills in central Alabama, accelerated dramatically after World War

II. Attracted by cheaper labor, anti-unionism, and state subsidies, industrial firms have flocked into the rural South. In the 1990s automobile assembly plants and parts suppliers have transformed the rural landscape of Tennessee much as petrochemical plants previously reconfigured riverine and coastal Louisiana and Mississippi in the first half of the twentieth century. Mobile, Alabama, once a great cotton entrepôt second only to New Orleans, claimed fame as the world's leading port for the export of pulp and paper manufactured in interior mills. A string of cities, an incipient southern megalopolis, tied together the country from Winston-Salem in North Carolina to Birmingham, Alabama. Many other cites experienced rapid growth, pulling to them non-southerners and rural southerners alike and increasing the religious and ethnic diversity of the region.

The paradox of the rural South is that its values and mentalities endure even as its material substrate evanesces. Consider the continuing impress of rurality in southern culture, in matters of faith, race, honor, and history. The Baptist faith, as any map of American religion plainly shows, remains the rock of southern religious life for blacks and whites. The evangelicalism, the revivals, and the awakenings first nurtured by backcountry settlers in the eighteenth century and later syncretized into slave society during the nineteenth century persist into the present. In the matter of race, the rural South is unique among American regions. Although the nearly four centuries of southern race relations have been unusually difficult for both races, that history has on occasions such as the civil rights movement produced moments of extraordinary heroism and creativity.

The rural South's refined sense of personal honor similarly endures in its tradition of military service, as casualty maps from the Civil War to the Vietnam War readily attest. It endures too, less felicitously perhaps, in the region's historical propensity for extralegal violence and vigilantism—from colonial duels to slave insurrections, from secession to lynching. And last there is the burden of southern history, the reality that the South alone among American regions has suffered the crushing defeat of war. Could it be, paradoxically, that in the troubles that the rural South has seen—in matters of faith, race, honor, and defeat—lie the seeds of the unusual loyalty and allegiance of its diverse peoples.

The continuing vibrance of southern ruralism is no mere cultural lag, as the sociologist John Shelton Reed is at pains to point out. Regional consciousness in the South, he observes, transcends ethnicity, race, gender, class, and the transformations imposed by the New South. Its origins lie in a uniquely rural geography, a distinctively troubled history, and the heightened sensitivity that ensues from relentless external critique. It is one thing for one southerner to call another a "redneck," a "cracker," a racist, or the like; it is quite another for the outlander who tries to follow suit.

BIBLIOGRAPHY

General Works

Cooper, William J., and Thomas E. Terrill. *The American South: A History* (1991).

Gray, Lewis C. *History of Agriculture in the Southern United States to 1860.* 2 vols. (1933).

McCusker, John J., and Russell R. Menard. *The Economy of British America, 1607–1789* (1985).

Reed, John Shelton. *One South: An Ethnic Approach to Regional Culture* (1982).

The First South

Earle, Carville. *The Evolution of a Tidewater Settlement System: All Hallow's Parish, Maryland, 1650–1783* (1975).

Isaac, Rhys. *The Transformation of Virginia, 1740–1790* (1982).

Morgan, Edmund S. *American Slavery, American Freedom: The Ordeal of Colonial Virginia* (1975).

The Second South and the Upland South

Clowse, Converse D. *Economic Beginnings in Colonial South Carolina, 1670–1730* (1971).

Coclanis, Peter A. *The Shadow of a Dream: Economic Life and Death in the South Carolina Low Country, 1670–1920* (1989).

Fischer, David H. *Albion's Seed: Four British Folkways in America* (1989).

The Cotton South and the Other Antebellum South

Fogel, Robert W., and Stanley L. Engerman. *Time on the Cross.* 2 vols. (1974).

Genovese, Eugene D. *The Political Economy of Slavery: Studies in the Economy and Society of the Slave South* (1965).

Moore, John H. *The Emergence of the Cotton Kingdom in the Old Southwest: Mississippi, 1770–1860* (1988).

Woodman, Harold D. *King Cotton and His Retainers: Financing and Marketing the Cotton Crop of the South, 1800–1925* (1968).

Wright, Gavin. *The Political Economy of the Cotton South: Households, Markets, and Wealth in the Nineteenth Century* (1978).

The Postbellum South

DeCanio, Stephen. *Agriculture in the Postbellum South: The Economics of Production and Supply* (1974).

Earle, Carville. "The Myth of the Southern Soil Miner: Macrohistory, Agricultural Innovation, and Environmental History." In *The Ends of the Earth: Perspectives on Modern Environmental History,* edited by Donald Worster (1988), pp. 175–210.

Ransom, Roger L., and Richard Sutch. *One Kind of Freedom: The Economic Consequences of Emancipation* (1977).

The New South

Daniel, Pete. *Breaking the Land: The Transformation of Cotton, Tobacco, and Rice Cultures Since 1880* (1985).

Fite, Gilbert C. *Cotton Fields No More: Southern Agriculture 1865–1980* (1984).

Wright, Gavin. *Old South, New South: Revolutions in the Southern Economy Since the Civil War* (1986).

SEE ALSO **Agriculture; Antebellum African American Culture; The Deep South; English-speaking Protestants; The Natural Environment: The South; The Plantation; Postbellum African American Culture; Racial Ideology; Sectional Conflict, Civil War, and Reconstruction; Slavery; The Southern Tidewater and Piedmont.**

RURAL LIFE IN THE WEST

R. Douglas Hurt

NATIVE AMERICANS

Among the Native Americans, the first farmers in the American West, the women primarily controlled the use of the land and planted, cultivated, and harvested the crops. As early as 1300 B.C., Indian farmers in the Southwest had adopted agricultural practices from Mexico. By about the beginning of the Christian era, the Hohokam, who lived along the Gila and Salt rivers in present-day Arizona, had developed an extensive irrigation system. These canals, built by both men and women, extended across the land in a veinlike fashion for at least 150 miles (240 kilometers), earning these people the sobriquet "Canal Builders." This culture not only established the only true irrigation culture on the North American continent before white settlement, but also made an agricultural life possible where farming would have been nearly impossible without it. At the beginning of the Christian era, the Indian farmers in the Southwest had made the seed selections necessary to develop the plant varieties best suited to the climatic conditions of that region.

On the fringe of the Great Plains the Native Americans began agriculture about 1500 B.C., by farming the river floodplains. Probably they had learned agriculture from the Hopewell and Woodland peoples in the Mississippi Valley. At the time of European contact, the Caddo, who lived on the eastern fringe of the Great Plains in present-day Texas, tilled the soil. They may have created the "hearth" from which Indian agriculture spread onto the Great Plains.

The Mandan and Hidatsa were the most skilled agriculturists on the fringe of the Great Plains at European contact. They occupied permanent villages along the tributaries of the upper Missouri, where the women raised corn, beans, and squash in the rich alluvial soil. The Indian women of the West became skilled plant breeders whose ability to select the best seeds for plant improvement remained unsurpassed until the creation of the agricultural experiment station system during the late nineteenth century. Mandan and Hidatsa villages in present-day North Dakota became important trading centers. The hunting tribes of the High Plains, such as the Sioux and Cheyenne, craved vegetables, particularly corn, and the Mandans and Hidatsas traveled to the High Plains annually to trade for buffalo meat and antelope hides. This trade was beneficial and hazardous. The Sioux, who were good customers of these farming tribes, were temperamentally unpredictable, and any trade with them had to be conducted with extreme caution. When white settlers moved into the trans-Mississippi West, they adopted many of the seed varieties and agricultural methods, including the use of old irrigation canals, of the Native American farmers.

The Indian women not only tilled the soil but also controlled the use of the land. Most tribes or cultural groups adopted two forms of land tenure. Ultimate land tenure depended upon village sovereignty over a particular area, while individual control of a field depended on the actual occupation and use of the land. Usually the individual farmer controlled the use of the land as long as she or he cultivated it. Generally the Indians in the West did not think of private property as an absolute personal right or consider land a commodity that could be bought, sold, or permanently alienated. Among the Native Americans, the community owned the land, while the individual claimed a portion by cultivating it. Moreover, land tenure or control was vested with the lineage or household, not the individual. This control unit could be either patrilineal or matrilineal, depending on the particular culture. Among the Plains tribes, land usually passed from mother to daughter. Among the Yuman-speaking tribes in the Southwest, men inherited the land, whereas a matrilineal land inheritance system prevailed among the Pueblos.

By the mid nineteenth century, white settlement began to encroach on the lands of the Native Americans in the West. White settlers considered the lands of the agricultural and hunting tribes underutilized. Although the federal government removed many tribes to reservations, the rapid settlement of the West created great demand for Indian lands. By 1887, the federal government could no longer resist white pressure for unused tribal lands, and Congress passed the Dawes General Allotment (also called the Severalty) Act to enable the transfer of reservation land to white farmers. This legislation gave each head of a tribal household 160 acres (64 hectares) of reservation land, but Indians who received allotments could not take full title for twenty-five years. After that trust period, they had the same rights to their lands as any white farmer because they could sell, lease, or cultivate it. The federal government intended this act to help force the Indians to become small-scale farmers who would not rely on the government for support. Without experience in landownership as white culture understood it, most Indians who had received allotments lost their lands. By 1932 more than 90 million acres (36 million hectares) had been lost by the Native Americans. Without land, credit, capital, technology, or scientific aid, the Native Americans did not have any chance to become small-scale, independent farmers, as federal Indian policy had intended, to ensure acculturation and assimilation.

Although the Indian New Deal attempted to restore tribal culture and stopped the sale of Indian lands, the Native Americans remained too poverty-stricken and without adequate educational and financial support to develop into small-scale, family farmers in the white tradition. With the exception of the Navajo, most tribal groups did not have the land base or the financial means to support either self-sufficient or commercial agriculture. By the late twentieth century, only several thousand Indian farmers remained on the land. Most Native Americans continued to live in the rural West, but they were not agricultural. Although the Native Americans were once the most skilled farmers in the American West, their considerable agricultural achievements had been relegated to the distant past.

THE COLONIAL PERIOD

When the Spanish began establishing settlements north of Mexico during the late seventeenth century, they adopted the crop varieties of the Native Americans and, in time, taught them to raise wheat and sheep among other Spanish agricultural endeavors. At first, however, the Spanish primarily were interested in cattle ranching. As early as 1690, the Spanish brought cattle to their newly established mission of San Francisco de los Tejos in East Texas. In 1718, they established the presidio and settlement of San Antonio, where cattle raising became the most important economic activity. By 1746, the diamond tip of Texas (an area bounded by San Antonio on the north and the Gulf Coast on the south, with the sides of the diamond formed by lines drawn west from San Antonio to Laredo on the Rio Grande and to the Gulf Coast on the east) had been settled by large-scale ranchers, and thousands of cattle and sheep grazed the land. As the herds grew, the ranchers needed markets for their cattle because they could not make enough money from slaughtering their livestock for tallow and hides. By the mid eighteenth century, Spanish ranchers had developed an important cattle trade with New Orleans.

Farther to the west, in present-day California, the Spanish based their colonial expansion on military power, the Catholic church, and agriculture. In many respects, the agricultural and rural history of the American West began along the Pacific Coast during the late eighteenth century. In 1769, Spanish soldiers established the first presidio at San Diego; and in 1777, Spain established the first pueblo or town in California, San Jose. The Spanish pueblo grants favored private citizens and groups that promised to establish communities. After four years of cultivation, the government provided full title for individual ownership. The Spanish based their colonial policy in California on the philosophy that land should be used to support subsistence agriculture and that farming would strengthen Spanish authority over an increasingly large empire. Spain continued to make other land grants for the creation of presidios, pueblos, and missions until the Mexican Revolution in 1822.

Although Spanish supply columns brought seeds of all kinds to the newly established presidios, missions, and pueblos, cattle raising became the most important economic endeavor in California. The early ranchers in California, like those in Texas, slaughtered their livestock primarily for the hides and tallow because they did not have a market for fresh meat and could not adequately preserve their beef for shipment to foreign markets. By rendering the fat for soap and the tallow for candles, and preparing the hides for leather, these early agriculturists capitalized on distant foreign markets. The export markets, especially the New England trade, became particularly important after 1810. As cattle raising and the ranches expanded, the roundup became the major annual activity.

Despite these agricultural introductions and improvements, profit was not the overriding motive for agricultural development among the Spanish in California and the Southwest. Rather, the Spanish intended subsistence agriculture to enable colonization, religious conversion of the Indians, and military defense of the frontier. With the exception of the large-scale landowners, who grazed cattle, most settlers cultivated small plots of land and lived in poverty. They did not develop a market economy for commercial gain.

THE OPEN-RANGE CATTLE INDUSTRY

Between 1820 and 1840, the Spanish cattle industry merged with the Anglo-American cattle culture on the humid coastal prairies of Texas. The settlers who emigrated from the southern United States brought a different cattle-raising tradition with them that they established in northeastern Texas. The Spanish, however, were responsible for establishing the open-range livestock industry that spread into the central and northern Great Plains after the Civil War.

Although cattlemen had driven herds to Ohio in 1846, to California in the 1850s, and to Chicago in 1856, major expansion of the livestock industry did not occur until the late 1860s. With buyers in Chicago offering ten times the price that ranchers received in Texas, cattlemen began trailing their herds to northern markets. In 1867, Joseph G. McCoy founded Abilene, Kansas, as a railroad shipping point; more cattle from Texas were moved north than ever before, destined primarily for stockyards in Chicago. During the late 1870s, the open-range cattle industry expanded into the northern Great Plains. Eastern and foreign investors often financed large-scale cattle companies that controlled several thousand acres and operated with a multimillion-dollar capitalization. The Swan Land and Cattle Company, for example, controlled more than 500,000 acres (200,000 hectares) in Wyoming and Nebraska, grazed 120,000 head, and operated with a capitalization of 3.7 million dollars. In 1885 the XIT Ranch, controlled by the Capitol Freehold Land and Investment Company in Chicago, exceeded all other ranches in size. Capitalized with $15 million,

it covered more than 3 million acres (1.2 million hectares); its headquarters was at Buffalo Springs, Texas. The cattle companies competed with small-scale ranchers for the use of the public domain, that is, for the free grass on the federal lands.

Few ranchers or cattle companies actually owned their grazing land. Rather, they occupied specific ranges by custom and consent. In time, they viewed their grazing lands as private property. Whenever they purchased land, they usually selected grasslands that bordered streams or surrounded water holes to prevent the use of that rangeland by other cattlemen or farmers. In order to protect themselves from the large-scale cattle companies, small-scale ranchers organized stock growers' associations, such as the Wyoming Stock Growers' Association, the Colorado Stock Growers' Association, and the Montana Stock Growers' Association. These organizations regulated roundups, prevented rustling, registered brands, and aided in the shipping and marketing processes. The stock growers' associations improved breeding practices and promoted better range management with the use of barbed wire fencing and windmills to pump water.

The open-range cattlemen did not provide adequate care for their livestock. Ranchers left their cattle to fend for themselves, and they did not provide feed or shelter. During the mid 1880s, recurring drought and hard winters culminated in disastrous blizzards and bitter temperatures during the winter of 1886–1887 and destroyed the open-range livestock industry. Many cattlemen sold their herds. Those who remained improved their range management practices, pared their herds, and emphasized winter feeding and sheltering.

THE FARMERS' FRONTIER

With the collapse of the open-range cattle industry, farmers claimed the grasslands and moved west of the 100th meridian onto the High Plains. By 1860 many farmers had moved onto the fringe of the Great Plains from the humid prairie lands of Iowa, Missouri, and Minnesota. They did not, however, know about the harsh environmental limitations of the semiarid Great Plains. During the late 1860s and early 1870s, settlers moved onto the Great Plains in a rush. They acquired land from the federal government under the Homestead Act of 1862, or they purchased it from the railroads that had been granted public domain to help finance construction, or from the states that had received land grants from the federal government.

Prior to passage of the Homestead Act in 1862, settlers in the trans-Mississippi West acquired land in two major ways—purchase from the federal government or preemption. Between 1820 and 1862, many people acquired farms under the Land Act of 1820. This statute enabled a settler to purchase a minimum of 80 acres (32 hectares) for $1.25 per acre after the land had been surveyed. Many settlers, however, squatted or claimed public domain prior to survey and sale, and they pressured the federal government for a preemption act that would permit them to purchase the land that they had settled and improved before it could be sold to another settler or a speculator. Although Congress provided a limited preemption act in 1830, it legalized squatting with the Preemption Act of 1841. This act enabled squatters to purchase 160 acres (64 hectares) at $1.25 per acre. Settlers purchased much of the land in Iowa and Missouri under the Land Act of 1820 and the Preemption Act of 1841.

Many settlers could not afford two hundred dollars for 160 acres, and westerners continued to advocate cheap or free land to encourage settlement and the development of a strong agricultural economy that would benefit the nation. Others advocated expensive public lands to help provide operating revenue for the federal government. Both positions received extensive discussion in Congress. Although public land policy became entangled with abolitionism because southerners believed northerners wanted to block the expansion of slavery in the territories, westerners continued to advocate free public land and state legislatures passed resolutions that supported those demands. Finally, after the secession of the South, Congress passed the Homestead Act and President Abraham Lincoln signed it into law on 20 May 1862. This act provided 160 acres of public domain free to settlers who lived on the land and improved it for five years. Or, after six months' residence, a settler could purchase the land for $1.25 per acre. Both men and women twenty-one years of age or older could claim a homestead, provided they were citizens or had filed a declaration to become a citizen. The Homestead Act finally realized the demand of westerners for free public land.

Although the first homestead was claimed near Beatrice, Nebraska, on 1 January 1863, a homesteading boom did not occur until the early 1870s on the Minnesota, Dakota, Nebraska, and Kansas frontiers. By 1900 more than 400,000 settlers had applied for homesteads. Not all western lands were open for homesteading, however, because the transcontinental railroads, state governments, and Indian tribes claimed millions of acres. Still, approximately 605 million acres (242 million hectares) of public domain were available for acquisition under the Homestead Act. Much of this land, however, was in the desert Southwest and the arid intermontane region, where agriculture was impossible without irrigation or because of the mountainous terrain. Moreover, the environmental and geographical limitations of the West, as well as economic depression, insufficient financial reserves, and inadequate agricultural knowledge, caused two-thirds of the homesteaders to fail by 1890.

The Homestead Act remains one of the most important laws in American history because it provided free land and, along with other federal legislation, stimulated the settlement of the West. However, homestead land often was distant from transportation and markets because the railroads controlled the best lands. Those settlers who bought railroad lands paid higher prices, but they had relatively easy access to market. The transcontinental railroads, which controlled 110 million acres (44 million hectares) of land, lured settlers to the West with massive publicity campaigns. Settlers often preferred to purchase railroad land because they could pay over a ten-year period with only one-fourth of the purchase price down. Easy terms such as these were more important than the price, which often reached ten dollars per acre, and the railroads became the most important creditors in the West. Still, the Homestead Act enabled settlers to gain a propertied stake in society and economic independence, provided they had adequate financial reserves and access to a railroad, and withstood the harsh climate of the Great Plains.

The early settlers on the Great Plains first built sod houses because there was little timber for constructing the traditional log cabin of the forested East. Then they turned their attention to breaking the prairie for cropland. This was hard work, because the grassland did not plow easily, and they were lucky to turn 10 to 15 acres (4 to 6 hectares) for corn, wheat, and potatoes during their first year. Those who arrived too late to plant and harvest a crop suffered if they did not have adequate money for supplies to carry them through their first winter. If homesteaders could survive for two or three years, their chances for success improved substantially, although they always had to contend with the possibilities of drought, grasshoppers, and low prices that could bring bankruptcy and failure. Often the homesteaders took outside employment on nearby railroad construction crews or left the farm during the winter for jobs in town, either near or far away. Often wives and children remained on the land, enduring the hardships of isolation and the environment, until the men returned with money to help meet their needs during the next crop year.

The settlers in the West never were completely self-sufficient, and subsistence agriculture was not their primary goal. Rather, they sought economic gain by producing a cash crop. At first this crop was corn because of their cultural heritage—that is, they raised corn because they had been taught to do so by family and friends on farms in the humid East. In time, they learned that the Great Plains had inadequate precipitation for corn, and they converted to wheat production during the mid 1870s.

During the late 1870s, settlers had expanded onto the central plains, and above-normal precipitation enabled them to settle far west of the 100th meridian, where farming based on traditional methods was impossible in times of average or below-normal rainfall. In the 1880s, a boom psychology prevailed among settlers who moved onto the northern Great Plains. When drought came in 1889, the agricultural boom collapsed and a sharp decline occurred in the farm and rural population. Those farmers who remained on the land adjusted by adopting new farming techniques, such as summer fallowing, and by planting wheat, raising drought-resistant grain sorghum, and diversifying with more cattle. But drought, crop failure, and economic hard times kept the farm and rural population from expanding, and also caused the agrarian revolt and the formation of the People's party. With the return of normal precipitation during the late 1890s, agricultural expansion boomed again, particularly after 1900 in South Dakota west of the Missouri River.

THE AGRARIAN REVOLT

By the last quarter of the nineteenth century, most of the farmers in the West no longer were engaged primarily in self-sufficient, subsistence agriculture. They had become commercial farmers who concentrated on the production of wheat and corn. Because of this specialization, their fortunes were closely tied to the banking, railroading, and manufacturing interests. They no longer were masters of their own destiny. They sold their grain on an unprotected international market but bought most of the items needed for daily living at high prices because of the protective tariff. Overproduction at home and abroad drove prices down, while an insufficient currency supply kept farmers in need of cash and credit.

The western farmer was caught in a vicious cycle: by using new farm implements, he could increase production and ease his labors; greater production forced agricultural prices still lower; and he tried to recover lost income by producing still more. Eastern land companies often held western mortgages, and the interest rates reached usurious levels. Monopoly in the form of barbed wire, farm machinery, and fertilizer trusts kept prices high, and the railroads discriminated and overcharged for their services. Grain elevator companies unfairly graded the farmer's crops and offered prices below the fair value.

Confronted with these problems, the western farmer first attempted to gain economic reform through the organization of the Patrons of Husbandry (the Grange) and the National Farmers' Alliance and Industrial Union. Both organizations championed collective action to reduce operating costs and provided a social organization to help eliminate the isolation and monotony of rural life in the American West. The Grange was most active and successful during the mid 1870s, and the Farmers' Alliance spread rapidly during the late 1880s. In addition to supporting cooperative buying and selling, the Farmers' Alliance advocated nonpartisan political activity. Although the organization was not a political party, the Alliance men and women believed it should support any politician who advocated its reform program. Although the Patrons of Husbandry and the Farmers' Alliance failed to improve the economic position of western farmers and miners, both organizations provided the experience farmers needed to organize the People's (Populist) party in 1892. The People's party was a vociferous advocate of major economic change through the political process until its defeat in the presidential election of 1896.

Westerners who supported the People's party advocated government ownership of the railroads to ensure fair competition and rates. The party also demanded reduction of interest rates on mortgages, expansion of the currency supply, and government credit through a subtreasury system that would enable farmers to obtain loans at a low interest rate from the federal government with their crops pledged as security. The party also favored an eight-hour day, woman suffrage, the initiative and referendum, and the direct election of senators.

The Populists advocated paternalism by the federal government and a mild dose of socialism to ensure economic and social equity. Mary Elizabeth Lease, a Populist leader in Kansas, typified the party leadership and gained national attention with her strong party loyalty and her forceful public speaking, the latter trait earning her the nickname "Mary Yellin" from her enemies. To her friends, she clearly described the problems of the western farmer and worker, and she told the public that only the People's party could remedy the ills of American society. These views earned her the sobriquet among her friends of "Patrick Henry in Petticoats."

Ultimately the Populists failed to achieve major economic and social reform through the political process because the Democratic party stole their platform and the Republican party remained too entrenched in certain areas to enable a political victory at the polls. In 1896, William McKinley, the Republican nominee, defeated William Jennings Bryan, the Democratic (and Populist) candidate for the presidency, and the People's party quickly disintegrated. Before it did, however, the party had enabled western farmers, miners, and townspeople to express their dissatisfaction with the economic system through political means. It also had established an agenda for progressive reform that, with the exception of federal ownership of the railroads and telegraph systems, would be achieved by the end of the New Deal.

TECHNOLOGICAL CHANGE

The prairie sod in the trans-Mississippi West was too tough for the wooden moldboard and cast-iron plows that farmers used in the East. These plows bucked out of the ground or became clogged with the sticky prairie soil. In 1837, John Deere developed a "singing plow" with a steel shear and a highly polished wrought-iron moldboard that easily cut through the prairie grasses and scoured the sticky soils of Iowa, Missouri, and Minnesota. Deere's plow and others like it soon became popular on the prairie of the trans-Mississippi West. Western farmers also used seed drills to plant their small-grain crops, such as wheat and oats. They seeded their corn crop with check-row planters, lister seeders, or one-row, horse-drawn planters;

and they weeded their crops with a variety of walking and sulky cultivators.

Farmers used the header in the prairie/plains regions and in California to harvest their small grain crops. During the 1860s, the header became the most important harvesting machine in California, and a decade later it gained popularity in Kansas and Nebraska. In contrast with the reapers which became popular in the Midwest by the 1850s, headers eliminated binding, shocking, and hauling the sheaves to the threshing site and reduced the number of workers required at harvest time.

During the mid 1870s, the self-binder achieved popularity. This implement cut and bound the grain into sheaves ready for shocking. Binders further reduced the manpower required to harvest grain because only one man, the driver, was required to operate it. In 1880, implement companies began manufacturing twine binders to replace the original wire binders. After the grain had been harvested, farmers threshed it with a horse- or steam-powered machine. Although the gasoline tractor replaced the steam tractor during the 1920s, the threshing machine remained a necessary implement for the grain farmer until tractor-powered combines became readily available during the 1930s.

In California, grain farmers began using combines during the early 1880s. These giant machines often required at least thirty horses or mules for draft power, and they were suitable only for flat lands. During the 1890s, steam- and horse-powered combines almost completely replaced the header on the bonanza wheat farms in California. The combines that farmers used east of the Rocky Mountains prior to World War I operated on the Great Plains, where the dry climate made the wheat suitable for machine harvesting.

Technological change during the late nineteenth and early twentieth centuries had an important effect on rural women besides saving the household time and money. As manufacturers developed and improved various grain harvesters and threshing machines, fewer hired hands were needed at harvest and threshing time. As a result, technological change lightened the cooking burden for farm women who had the responsibility of preparing three hearty meals, and frequently an afternoon lunch, at harvest and threshing time.

During the twentieth century, tractors with internal-combustion engines and mechanical cotton pickers became the most important mechanical developments for the agriculture of the American West. The gasoline tractor helped reduce the drudgery of plowing, planting, cultivating, and harvesting cereal grains and other crops, while the cotton picker eliminated the bottleneck at harvest time. Combines also became practical for the small-scale wheat farms of the Great Plains. Center-pivot irrigation systems, which rely on deep wells and powerful pumps to deliver the water to the surface, made arid and submarginal lands agriculturally productive. In West Texas, irrigation technology helped extend the cotton kingdom far onto the semiarid High Plains. Irrigation from deep wells also enabled corn production on the High Plains, where this crop would have been impossible without it, and feedlots and meat packers moved into the region to capitalize on this new form of agriculture. At the same time, however, the water table dropped rapidly and water mining threatened the future of irrigation agriculture on the Great Plains. After the mid twentieth century, biotechnological change influenced agricultural and rural life more than did changes in hardware. Farmers increased production and reduced costs with the adoption of hybrid seeds, commercial fertilizers, herbicides, pesticides, and drugs to prevent and cure animal diseases.

These technological changes increased the farmers' dependence on bankers for capital, necessitated the improvement of their management skills, and encouraged the consolidation of farms. Technological change during the twentieth century had other negative effects. Tractors encouraged the cultivation of submarginal lands subject to erosion, and the cotton, tomato, and sugar beet harvesters replaced thousands of workers in the fields. The tractor also increased operating costs because it is expensive, and it contributed to one-crop agriculture. Farmers increased their application of pesticides and fertilizers to boost production and profit from their lands to pay for their new implements. The result was environmental damage, overproduction, low prices, and depopulation as many farmers fled the land for jobs in the towns and cities. As the agricultural population declined, the farms decreased in number and became larger as more prosperous farmers bought out the less successful agriculturists.

THE TWENTIETH CENTURY

The economy of the West remained agricultural during the early twentieth century. Adequate precipitation, new crop varieties, and international demand helped increase production and boost prices. On the Great Plains farmers expanded west of the 100th meridian to the slopes of the Rocky Mountains and beyond. In 1909, Congress encouraged this settlement process by enacting the Enlarged Homestead Act, which provided land grants of 320 acres (128 hectares) in some semiarid western states, with full title granted after five years of residency. In 1916, Congress passed the Stock Raising Homestead Act, which enabled settlers to receive 640 acres (240 hectares) of land that was unsuitable for crop production but that could support cattle and sheep raising. Between 1902 and 1910, more than ninety-eight thousand homesteaders claimed 18 million acres (7.2 million hectares). The rate of settlement became so great during the first two decades of the twentieth century that farmers homesteaded more land than during the nineteenth century following the Homestead Act.

In the arid West, the federal government entered the irrigation business with the Newlands (or Reclamation) Act of 1902. This legislation enabled the federal government to develop irrigation projects on arid public lands prior to their sale in order to encourage settlement. Congress created the Reclamation Service, which became the Bureau of Reclamation in 1923, to supervise this work. The Reclamation Service constructed many reservoirs for irrigation purposes, such as those formed by Roosevelt Dam on Arizona's Salt River, Arrowrock Dam near Boise, Idaho, and Imperial Dam in California. Much of the impounded water, however, benefited the large-scale, capital-intensive growers rather than small-scale farmers. By the late twentieth century, increasing competition for water between the urban and rural West had generated considerable litigation and bitter debate about who had the legal right to use the water. Despite a policy that favored large-scale growers, the Bureau of Reclamation helped create an oasis environment in the West, where irrigated valleys enabled the production of vegetables, fruits, and grains.

The number of farmers and ranchers in the West peaked during World War I, when high prices encouraged maximum production and investment in new technology. In 1920, European readjustment and surplus production caused agricultural prices to fall precipitously, and the region plunged into an economic depression that lasted until World War II, when wartime demands increased prices and boosted production. In the meantime, many farmers lost their farms in bankruptcy and the rural population diminished. Farmers now had to become better businessmen, use the best technology, reduce unit costs, increase productivity, and manage efficiently in order to survive.

Faced with economic difficulties beyond their control, farmers in the West turned to economic and political associations to resolve their problems. In 1915, the Nonpartisan League organized in North Dakota and remained a strong political force until 1922. It advocated state ownership of banks, mills, and terminal elevators to ensure equitable treatment. The National Farmers Union (1902) and the American Farm Bureau Federation (1920) advocated cooperative marketing, and western congressmen formed an ad hoc "farm bloc" during the 1920s to gain federal aid for agriculture. With declining numbers, however, western agriculturists no longer had significant political power, and the conservative Republican presidential administrations during the 1920s did not favor direct economic aid to farmers. The federal government's unwillingness to aid agriculture helped provide the stimulus for the creation of the radical, violent Farmers' Holiday Association, which was active in Iowa, Nebraska, Minnesota, and Wisconsin from 1932 to 1937. The Farmers' Holiday Association blockaded roads to prevent the sale of agricultural commodities and to force price increases. The penny auction sales—in which friends and neighbors bid only a few cents for the property of bankrupt farmers, frequently returning it to them and leaving the creditor with a pittance—also grew out of this movement.

The rural West did not receive agricultural support until the "First Hundred Days" Congress that followed Franklin Delano Roosevelt's presidential inauguration on 4 March 1933. With Roosevelt's support, the federal government began to provide economic aid to help western farmers remain on the land and regain sound agricultural operations. During the Great Depression, Roosevelt's New Deal policies initiated a revolutionary role for the federal government in western agriculture. Economic depression, combined with drought and dust storms on the Great Plains, brought unprecedented federal intervention in agriculture.

Congress passed the Agricultural Adjustment Act (AAA, 1933), which authorized the federal government to pay farmers to reduce production in order to increase prices, particularly for wheat, cotton, and hogs in the trans-Mississippi West. On the Great Plains the federal government sponsored the Emergency Cattle Purchase Program (1934) to enable the removal of surplus cattle from the open market. Under this program the federal government bought thousands of cattle for slaughter and distribution to needy families. The federal government also created the Soil Conservation Service (1935) to help farmers practice the best soil conservation methods. The Resettlement Administration (1935) and the Farm Security Administration (1937) sponsored a land purchase program that returned submarginal, wind-eroded land to grassland. In 1960 these land utilization projects became national grasslands, twenty-two of which are located in the West. The Soil Conservation and Domestic Allotment Act of 1936, which Congress expanded with the Agricultural Adjustment Act (Pope-McGill Farm Act) of 1938, enabled farmers to reduce surplus production by planting soil-conserving crops while receiving monetary support from the federal government for their cooperation.

In the Far West, the Taylor Grazing Act (1934) opened federal rangelands to stockmen who obtained grazing permits. This act also closed federal lands to public entry—that is, to claim and purchase—and ensured better range management practices. The Rural Electrification Administration (REA, 1935) was the most popular New Deal agency in the West. Although farmers along the Pacific Coast had easier access to electricity because of hydroelectric development, most farmers did not have the advantage of such favorable locations. The REA loaned money to cooperatives to build power plants, string electric lines, and wire homes. With electricity, farm men and women could use labor-saving implements such as stoves, irons, feed mills, and cream separators. Electricity also enabled indoor plumbing, hot water heaters, and leisure activities at night.

The New Deal programs of the federal government played an instrumental role in helping western farmers remain on the land until normal precipitation returned and until World War II increased prices and eliminated agricultural surpluses. But the New Deal did not have a beneficial effect on everyone. The AAA drove many tenant farmers from the land. Landlords in Oklahoma and Texas released their tenants in order to collect AAA checks for reducing cotton production. They often used these funds to purchase tractors and additional equipment for the production of other crops. Forced from the land, many tenants moved west to California. Their plight was portrayed by John Steinbeck in *The Grapes of Wrath* (1939).

ETHNIC DIVERSITY

Many ethnic groups contributed to the agricultural development of the American West, particularly the Mexicans, Chinese, and Japanese. During the late nineteenth century, the bonanza wheat farmers in California employed contract Asian laborers. After completion of the transcontinental railroads, many Chinese sought work on these large-scale farms, but the panic of 1893 caused Anglos to complain that the Chinese deprived white Americans of jobs. After violence drove the Chinese from the farms and into the cities, the landowners sought docile, reliable, and industrious workers in the Japanese community. Racial hostility toward Asians reemerged during the early twentieth century, and the growers increasingly turned to Mexican workers to meet their labor needs.

During the twentieth century, the Hispano-Americans became the most important ethnic group in the West. Millions of Mexicans entered Arizona, California, and Texas to find employment, usually as stoop labor in the fields. The growers exploited them with low wages, abysmal living conditions, and arbitrary authority. The large-scale growers and the federal government particularly exploited migrant workers with the bracero program from 1942 through 1964. Under that program, growers could hire workers temporarily from Mexico to prevent labor shortages. This policy kept labor plentiful and wages low, both of which contributed to the abject poverty of these people.

On several occasions the migrant workers in California attempted to organize and bargain collectively in order to improve their wages and working conditions. They achieved some success with the Cannery and Agricultural Workers' Industrial Union (1931), the National Farm Labor Union (1946), and the Agricultural Workers Organizing Committee (1959). The United Farm Workers Union (1965), led by Cesar Chávez, had the greatest success representing the migrant workers. Most migrant workers, however, are not union members. The large-scale growers responded to the unionization efforts of the migrant workers by adopting labor-saving implements such as the cotton, tomato, and sugar beet harvesters.

Other ethnic groups have played important roles in the development of the rural West. On the Great Plains, the Germans have been the largest non-English-speaking ethnic group. By 1900, approximately one-third of the white population in Texas claimed German heritage. Large groups of Scandinavians settled in the Dakotas, and Czechs became an important ethnic group in Nebraska. In Kansas, Swedish and Volga German communities enriched the cultural milieu. Although the people of west European descent quickly assimilated, the dark-skinned Hispanos suffered racial discrimination and social segregation.

The Mormons, while not an ethnic group, are a religious group whose original support of polygamy made it a distinctive and unwanted sect in established settlements. Fleeing persecution, Brigham Young led the first Mormons to present-day Utah, where they settled near the Great Salt Lake in 1847. The Mormons developed an irrigation agricultural system in which each head of a household received a plot of land to permit subsistence farming and enough water to make it productive. The strong sense of group identity and cohesiveness helped the Mormons establish a successful community based on agriculture which expanded into Arizona, Nevada, Idaho, and Oregon. The Mormons became the most important cultural group to colonize the intermontane West.

WOMEN IN THE WEST

The women in the rural West were closely tied to the soil during the nineteenth century. Although many single young women acquired land under the Homestead Act, particularly in the Dakotas, most did not farm but only established claims for the purpose of selling for high capital gains when land prices increased. Usually the women who migrated to the American West did not have primary responsibility for cultivating the soil. Instead, these women of Euro-American cultural heritage attended to a host of domestic tasks that were determined by gender, because farming with a plow generally was considered "man's work." Frontier women contributed to the survival of the family farm even though they often were not included in the decision-making process. Many women, however, considered their work to be cooperation with their husbands, and they did not believe themselves to be second-class partners. Frontier women adapted to the physical and psychological realities of western rural life with a realistic understanding, particularly in regard to the harsh environment, isolation, and loneliness.

In the frontier West women pursued a host of domestic tasks, such as cooking, cleaning, raising children, tending gardens, and helping with the farm and ranch work. They preserved the family's historical record, often in the Bible, and maintained cultural or ethnic traditions. In the towns, they often occupied gender-determined positions, serving as schoolteachers, shop clerks, milliners, nurses, and domestic servants. These positions were closely linked to the jobs women performed in the home and were, therefore, socially acceptable.

Socially, women participated actively in community life. They organized clubs and church socials and attended dances and picnics, and they sought anti-prostitution, anti-gambling, and temperance reforms. Nevertheless, the primary focus for most women, whether single or married, was their household world. For the most part, gender determined their place and work in the West far more than did ethnicity, social class, marital status, race, education, or religion. When women deviated from societal expectations, they often met with criticism and social rejection. In general, women usually experienced greater similarities than differences in their lives because of gender and generally agreed-upon concepts of women's work, which invariably centered on domestic service. This service was wide-ranging, from hoeing the garden to bearing and caring for children to cooking for the threshing crew. Women were not less important than men; their social roles differed. Homogeneity, not heterogeneity, governed their lives.

Technological change affected the lives of women more slowly and less dramatically than the lives of men in the nineteenth century. Not until the twentieth century, particularly with the increasing availability of electricity after the creation of the Rural Electrification Administration, did women have access to technology in the form of electric irons, refrigerators, washing machines, lights, and water pumps, all of which made their daily tasks easier.

During the twentieth century, the domestic world remained the focus of women in the rural West. Whether they lived and worked in small towns or on farms and ranches, whether they married or lived with family or alone, gender—rather than ability and opportunity to excel or to exhibit independence in the social, economic, and political world relegated to men—governed household and social responsibilities. Still, near the mid twentieth century, western women, compared with northern and southern women, were better educated, held more varied jobs, adhered less to traditional religious beliefs and denominations, maintained optimism, accepted change with greater flexibility, and approved of equality between the sexes. In all of these areas, the values of western women continued to be influenced by the frontier past.

Since the Great Depression of the 1930s, women as well as men have left the rural West. Many of those who remained could not support themselves on their land, and were forced to take jobs in the nearby towns and cities. Others left the farm because of the lure of better-paying jobs, with less drudgery and isolation, in urban America, although there, too, gender both limited and defined the lives of women. Many who can neither leave the land nor earn an adequate living from it are Hispanic women whose lives remain tied to the vegetable fields in California and the Southwest. Bound by both family—that is, domestic responsibilities—and a migratory way of life, they continue to suffer from inadequate education, nutrition, and health care.

Hispanic and other women who worked in the fields and canneries for low wages joined unionization activities; took part in confrontations with growers, strikebreakers, and thugs; and sometimes lost their lives in these struggles. Usually the growers relegated Hispanic women to the lowest-paying jobs. Although most Hispanic women now live in the urban barrios of Los Angeles, Phoenix, and San Antonio, many remain in rural areas. For them, the West is a rural ghetto from which there is no escape. Across the West, poor rural women work in low-paying service, clerical, and light industrial jobs. Although these women do not rely on agriculture for their livelihood, many continue to live in rural areas and commute to their jobs.

In the late twentieth century, gender continued to determine the life of middle-class women who remained on the farm. But rural women had assumed responsibility for many farm-related tasks that previously had been considered the province of men, such as keeping farm accounts, driving trucks and tractors, and providing general farm management, particularly if their husbands held off-the-farm jobs. The most rural of all women in the late-twentieth-century West, however, were the Native Americans. Approximately three of every four Native American women lived in rural areas, where they suffered from poverty, discrimination, and high mortality.

THE LATE TWENTIETH CENTURY

By the last half of the twentieth century, agriculture in the American West was more productive than ever before. The federal government attempted to curb the production levels of farmers through various programs in order to maintain prices. But science and technology, in the form of hybrid seeds, fertilizer, pesticides, herbicides, improved tractors, grain drills, and combines, made farmers more efficient and productive. As productivity increased, however, low prices kept many farm families from earning an adequate income and many left the rural West for better jobs in the towns and cities.

As farmers left the countryside, corporations or more prosperous farmers bought their land. As a result, farms decreased in number but increased in size. With the decline of farms, the social structure of the rural West changed significantly. With a decline in the farm population, merchants in the towns often suffered severe financial hardship. Tax revenues declined and local governments reduced services in both towns and countryside. Until the late twentieth century many people had considered the family farm a symbol of democratic government. The decline in the rural population, however, decreased the political power of the rural West, which shifted to the urban areas of the region. With the economic and political position of the family farm in jeopardy, many westerners began to defend the family farm on moral grounds. For them, farming represented independence, ensured democratic government, and preserved a good life. By the late twentieth century, however, farming had become more than a way of life; it was a business, and little room remained for small-scale, undercapitalized, and inefficient farmers. Government programs favored the large-scale, capital-intensive farmers. With little economic and political power, and a declining social position, many farmers left the land.

Near the end of the twentieth century, western farmers continued to advocate higher commodity prices while the public pressed political leaders to maintain relatively low food prices through tariff adjustments, reduced price support programs, and restrictions on exports. Farmers also confronted a public that increasingly demanded accountability for the use of chemical fertilizers, herbicides, and pesticides to prevent the pollution of drinking water and to ensure safe, healthy foods. Bad weather, inflation, and foreign markets, production and exchange rates, and international events remained beyond the control of farmers and affected the lives of all residents in the rural West. There were no easy solutions to the economic, social, political, moral, or ethical problems of the region. Yet while uncertainty often prevailed, the people of the rural West generally preferred their way of life, because they believed it to be much safer, more peaceful, and more fulfilling than any alternative. Their tenacious, independent spirit enabled many to remain in the rural West even during hard times. Nevertheless, the transformation of the West from a rural to an urban society reflects a major change in American society in general. No one can say what effects that change will have on rural life during the twenty-first century.

CONCLUSION

The harsh arid and semi-arid environment of the American West has shaped the agricultural and rural life of the people from the frontier period to the present. Although environment determines the parameters for life in the region, culture, social relationships, technology, and institutions, particularly legal institutions, enabled westerners to gain increased control over the environmental limitations of the region. Western agriculture remains an extractive industry. The people have little control over markets and prices, and they depend on others for capital and policy, both domestic and foreign. Since the New Deal, however, the federal government has dominated western agriculture and rural life with a host of programs to help cushion the effects of domestic and international economic problems. By the late twentieth century, much of the agricultural income in the West was dependent upon government subsidies.

Since the 1920s, western farmers and ranchers have confronted the problems of surplus production and declining population. Technological and scientific developments have increased efficiency and reduced the need for a large number of farmers. The chemical and biotechnological revolutions enabled farmers to improve production but required improved business expertise for the best management of land and capital. With low prices and high operating costs, urban employment lured many men and women from the land. As residents left the farms for better jobs, more money, and a higher standard of living, many small towns suffered severe economic decline. Stores closed, schools and churches consolidated, and the rural population decreased further.

By the late twentieth century, however, agriculture still dominated the economy of the West; the Dakotas had the highest percentage of residents engaged in agriculture. North and South Dakota remained the most rural states in the West, with more than 50 percent of the population living outside cities of more than 2,500 people. California was the most important agricultural state, primarily because of the high productivity in the Central and Imperial valleys, and the marketing centers of Fresno, Bakersfield, and Sacramento supplied the nation with much of its food and fiber. The Great Plains, including Texas, remained the primary cattle- and wheat-producing region. The corn belt extended west of the Mississippi into Iowa, Minnesota, Missouri, and the Great Plains.

Agriculture remained important in the West during the late twentieth century, and farmers and ranchers continued to be affected by influences beyond their control. As the population of the West continued to grow, urban demands for water affected agricultural activities. The continued use of chemical fertilizers, pesticides, and herbicides threatened to pollute drinking water supplies, and irrigation from the underground supply endangered the water table. The environment influenced the settlement of the West during the nineteenth century; the federal government dominated rural life during most of the twentieth century; and the availability of water increasingly affected agricultural and rural life during the late twentieth century. No one could say what effects these influences and the trends toward consolidation and flight from the land would have on rural life in the West and on American society during the twenty-first century.

BIBLIOGRAPHY

General Works

Briggs, Charles L., and John R. Van Ness. *Land, Water and Culture: New Perspectives on Hispanic Land Grants* (1987).

Fite, Gilbert C. *The Farmers' Frontier, 1865–1900* (1966). An excellent topical introduction to western agricultural history in the late nineteenth century.

Paul, Rodman W. *The Far West and the Great Plains in Transition, 1859–1900* (1988).

Shannon, Fred A. *The Farmer's Last Frontier: Agriculture, 1860–1897* (1945; repr. 1975).

Westphall, Victor. *Mercedes Reales: Hispanic Land Grants of the Upper Rio Grande Region* (1983).

The Great Plains

Blouet, Brian W., and Frederick C. Luebke, eds. *The Great Plains: Environment and Culture* (1979).

Hurt, R. Douglas. *The Dust Bowl: An Agricultural and Social History* (1981).

Kraenzel, Carl Frederick. *The Great Plains in Transition* (1955).

Miner, Craig. *West of Wichita: Settling the High Plains of Kansas, 1865–1890* (1986). A good introduction to agricultural and rural life in a Great Plains state that has application to the general region.

Nelson, Paula M. *After the West Was Won: Homesteaders and Town-builders in Western South Dakota, 1900–1917* (1986). An excellent social history of rural life in western South Dakota during the early twentieth century.

Webb, Walter Prescott. *The Great Plains* (1931). The standard rural history of the Great Plains during the nineteenth century by an environmental determinist. Webb does not discuss political affairs, such as the Farmers' Alliance or the People's party.

The Cattle Industry

Atherton, Lewis. *The Cattle Kings* (1961). An important social history of the cattle industry.

Dale, Edward Everett. *The Range Cattle Industry: Ranching on the Great Plains from 1865 to 1925* (1930; new ed. 1960). A standard introduction to the range-cattle industry.

Osgood, Ernest Staples. *The Day of the Cattleman* (1929).

Schlebecker, John T. *Cattle Raising on the Plains, 1900–1961* (1963). The best history of the cattle industry on the Great Plains during the first half of the twentieth century.

The Far West

Gibson, James R. *Farming the Frontier: The Agricultural Opening of the Oregon Country, 1786–1846* (1985).

Jelinek, Lawrence. *Harvest Empire: A History of California Agriculture.* 2d ed. (1982). A brief but useful survey.

Lowitt, Richard. *The New Deal and the West* (1984). An essential source for an overview of the New Deal in the West.

Malone, Michael P., and Richard W. Etulain. *The American West: A Twentieth-Century History* (1989). The best survey of the twentieth-century West; includes a useful introduction to agriculture and rural life.

Agricultural Labor

Craig, Richard B. *The Bracero Program: Interest Groups and Foreign Policy* (1971).

Daniel, Cletus E. *Bitter Harvest: A History of California Farmworkers, 1870–1941* (1981). A comprehensive study of agricultural organization in California.

Jenkins, J. Craig. *The Politics of Insurgency: The Farm Worker Movement in the 1960s* (1985).

McWilliams, Carey. *Factories in the Field: The Story of Migratory Farm Labor in California* (1935).

Meister, Dick, and Anne Loftis. *A Long Time Coming: The Struggle to Unionize America's Farm Workers* (1977). A good general survey of the efforts to organize California's farm workers.

Ethnicity

Luebke, Frederick C., ed. *Ethnicity on the Great Plains* (1980).

McQuillan, D. Aidan. *Prevailing over Time: Ethnic Adjustment in the Kansas Prairies, 1875–1925* (1990).

Agrarian Revolt

Clanton, Gene. *Populism: The Humane Preference in America, 1890–1900* (1991).

Hicks, John D. *The Populist Revolt* (1931). The standard introductory work on populism in the Great Plains. It is particularly good for economic causation.

Larson, Robert W. *Populism in the Mountain West* (1986).

McMath, Robert C., Jr. *Populist Vanguard: A History of the Southern Farmers' Alliance* (1975).

Morlan, Robert L. *Political Prairie Fire: The Nonpartisan League, 1915–1922* (1985).

Saloutos, Theodore, and John D. Hicks. *Agricultural Discontent in the Middle West, 1900–1939* (1951). A standard overview of the major agricultural organizations, with emphasis on the Great Plains.

Native Americans

Castetter, Edward F., and Willis H. Bell. *Pima and Papago Indian Agriculture* (1942; repr. 1980).

Hurt, R. Douglas. *Indian Agriculture in America: Prehistory to the Present* (1987). A survey of Indian agriculture with emphasis on the trans-Mississippi West.

Parman, Donald L. *The Navajos and the New Deal* (1976).

White, Richard. *The Roots of Dependency: Subsistence, Environment, and Social Change Among the Choctaws, Pawnees and Navajos* (1983).

Technology

Hurt, R. Douglas. *American Farm Tools: From Hand Power to Steam Power* (1982).

Rogin, Leo. *The Introduction of Farm Machinery in Its Relation to the Productivity of Labor in the Agriculture of the United States During the Nineteenth Century* (1931).

Wik, Reynold M. *Steam Power on the American Farm* (1953).

Women in the West

Jeffrey, Julie Roy. *Frontier Women: The Trans-Mississippi West, 1840–1880* (1979).

Myres, Sandra L. *Westering Women and the Frontier Experience, 1800–1915* (1982). An excellent topical introduction to women in the West.

Riley, Glenda. *The Female Frontier: A Comparative View of Women on the Prairie and the Plains* (1988). The standard source on the rural experiences of women on the midwestern prairie and Great Plains.

Schlissel, Lillian, Vicki L. Ruiz, and Janice Monk, eds. *Western Women: Their Land, Their Lives* (1988). A wide-ranging topical study of women in the West, with an emphasis on the rural West.

SEE ALSO **American Indians of the West; Agriculture; California; The Frontier; The Great Plains; Latin Americans: Mexicans and Central Americans; The Mormon Region; The Mountain West; American Indians of the West; The Natural Environment: The West; The Southwest; Technology and Social Change; Texas.**

VILLAGE AND TOWN

Richard Lingeman

THE HISTORY OF America can be traced through its towns and villages and hamlets. These have served as the primary cells of the body politic, outposts of a migrant, westward-moving people, embryos of cities, and repositories of the dream of community. The small town has engraved a durable image upon the American collective unconscious—in social myth, literature, historical memory, ideals. Perhaps in no other national culture do the words "small town" pulsate with such strong positive and negative emotional currents—especially among those who grew up in such places. They elicit a deep ambivalence: attraction and repulsion, affection and repugnance, nostalgia and frustration. In a mobile, individualistic, ever-urbanizing (and suburbanizing) society the small town (a nonmetropolitan place of as few as two or three hundred up to twenty-five to thirty thousand people) has shown a remarkable durability, despite the social and economic forces impinging upon it, and it continues to be a symbol of deeply held American values of roots and community.

THE COLONIAL ERA

European immigrants, mainly from England in the early seventeenth century, planted the precursors of the modern American town. When the tide of transoceanic migration reached these shores, it divided into two streams, one originating on the land of the Massachusetts Bay Colony and the other on the territory of the Virginia Company. These disparate environments further influenced the patterns of early urbanization.

The first settlers of both regions were adjured to form towns. The obvious reason for such instructions was to provide mutual protection against the "hideous howling wilderness." But the principals in England also saw commercial advantages in settling groups of people with complementary skills on a single site, thus providing a division of labor capable, it was hoped, of exploiting the putative riches of the New World. The owners also regarded collective settlement as a means of ensuring social control, to prevent these good English men and women from reverting to savagery.

Virginia The Virginia Company ordered the teams of "planters" it backed to found "handsome towns," later modified to "compact and orderly villages." But the investors' vision of rows of brick houses along cobbled streets quickly shattered on the reefs of reality. The first settlement, Jamestown, founded in 1607, was a collection of huts surrounded by a wooden palisade. It was sited in a marshy area, and malaria wiped out large numbers of its inhabitants; fires and Indian raids finished the job.

Subsequent colonizing efforts similarly failed, until the settlers found their salvation in the profitable cultivation of tobacco (*Nicotiana tabacum*). This single-crop economy favored a plantation system of agriculture rather than one centered in the agricultural villages of Europe that provided the model in Massachusetts. Under the dominance of the landed proprietor, plantations became self-sufficient communities with their own stores and artisans—and a labor force of indentured servants and later slaves. A sprinkling of small farmers and freed bond servants formed a loose society of neighborhoods—networks of people who lived close enough to one another that each might practice some specialized trade useful to the others as well as cultivate a crop for private profit.

The primary governing institution of planter society, aside from the colonial legislature, was the county court; in the courthouse the records of all-important land transactions were kept, property disputes were settled, and justice was dispensed. Those with legal business journeyed many miles and put up at nearby taverns. Court sessions were social as well as civic events; the planters clattered in astride their fine horses and wearing colorful coats and high boots, seeking diversion from isolated plantation life. Churches were similarly situated in open countryside; the parish was the basic unit of religious governance.

The first settlements in Virginia were ports to which planters brought their crops for shipment to England and where they purchased a wide range of supplies. These entrepôts, comprising a few houses and stores, their docks piled with bales of tobacco at harvest time, were located at the heads of the numerous inlets, bays, and estuaries that formed natural harbors along the coastline of tidewater Virginia and neighboring Maryland's Chesapeake Bay.

And so Thomas Jefferson wrote in his *Notes on the State of Virginia* (1781): "We have no townships. Our country being much intersected with navigable waters, and trade brought generally to our doors . . . has probably been one of the causes why we have no towns of any consequence." The result was a scattered society that to visitors from England seemed primitive and anarchic. The writer John Aubrey (1626–1697) described some squatters he happened upon as "mean people who live lawless, nobody to govern them, they care for nobody, having no dependence on anybody."

Another inhibition to urban development in the South was the tendency of new groups of settlers to split up and claim individual tracts of the fertile bottomland rather than to band together to found a town. Periodically, the British authorities complained about the slow pace of urbanization, and they sent detailed plans with each new contingent of emigrants. But nearly one hundred years after the settling of Jamestown, the historian Robert Beverly (1673–1722) wrote that the people of Virginia "have not any place of cohabitation among them that may reasonably bear the name of town."

Massachusetts Bay In contrast, by 1717 the Massachusetts Bay Colony claimed more than one hundred towns. The people in the northern stream of settlement were largely Puritan dissenters organized into homogeneous congregations. The first civic act of these groups was to draw up a covenant, setting forth the rights and obligations of each inhabitant, which all the original grantees (proprietors) had to sign. Town and church were coterminous, and congregations were self-governing. That unique New England institution, the town meeting, evolved from a church body into a political assembly open to all property holders and dealing with secular matters. Town meetings were the first independent political units of colonial America. As Alexis de Tocqueville wrote, "the doctrine of the sovereignty of the people came out of the townships and took possession of the states."

The system of town-founding by congregations was codified in colonial law. A group of people wishing to "plant" a town was required to draw up a covenant and apply to the legislature for a land grant. The proprietors then apportioned their tract among themselves according to need and rank. They laid out their habitats in the immemorial pattern of the English agricultural village—a parallel row of houses along a single street with long, narrow strips of fields extending perpendicularly behind the houses. Common land was set aside for the church and for pastures and meadows—thus the New England village green, site of the square wooden meetinghouse with its cupola and bell (later replaced by a tall-spired church). Initially, plots of land were worked communally, with families living in the village. But gradually communal farming gave way to individual ownership and control, and the more independent souls moved farther out. They were disapprovingly called "outlivers," and it was feared that, deprived of daily surveillance by pious neighbors, their morals would degenerate. They were required to live within a day's travel so they could at least attend church on the Sabbath.

Under the tight lid of religious conformity, enforced by the minister and church elders, the Puritan towns were small theocracies. Beneath a surface harmony, they bubbled with tensions and spites. The religious authorities sought to mediate the resulting disputes, lawyers being anathema to the Puritans. There were also incessant theological arguments, and the bacteria of dissenters might fester and poison the Christian ideals of love, harmony, and cooperation. Eventually the infection came to a head, and the dissenters were excommunicated or won control of the town meeting or seceded in a body—"hiving off," it was called—to found a new church elsewhere.

Collective agriculture was soon abandoned, as the harder-working, more proficient farmers accumulated additional tracts of land. Disparities in landed wealth formed the basis of class divisions between rich and poor. At death, the father's property was divided among all the sons and daughters (as dowries). In an era when families of ten or twelve children were common, the third generation found its portions too small to provide a living. As a result, the young and ambitious looked north and west, where virgin land abounded. Also eyeing this territory were speculators in town plots—a new breed of entrepreneurs who bought up a tract and sold it off in parcels, setting aside church and school lots, to groups or individuals. Thus the covenant gradually gave way to the cash nexus.

THE MIDWEST
IN THE NINETEENTH CENTURY

After the war of 1812, the vast public domain west of the Appalachians, known as the Old Northwest Territory, was opened to settlement. Communal groups from New England founded towns much like the ones they had left, but Puritan-style theocracy did not take hold; there were too many competing sects on the frontier. Nor did the town meeting prosper in the villages founded by New Englanders. The states carved out of the Northwest Territory adopted the township-county system as a compromise between New England and Virginia. If the architectural emblem of the New England town was the church spire, in the Midwest it was the courthouse cupola, symbolizing a society governed by secular, legal norms rather than religious precepts.

Many southern pioneers retained their aversion to town life and cleared small farms in the vast forests. Although some scions of the landed gentry brought slaves with them, the plantation system itself did not take root for a variety of reasons, political, moral, and economic. Instead, wealthy speculators became the largest landholders, buying up huge tracts of the best soil and selling portions to settlers or hiring tenants to farm them.

The pioneer villages of the Midwest sprouted around crossroads taverns, along wilderness trails, at ferry landings, on the sites of forts built during the Indian wars. A few sprang up near deposits of coal and iron ore and carried on elementary manufacturing. Many a town grew up around a gristmill to which farmers brought their corn to be ground, or a general store where they bartered pork and cornmeal for supplies.

Economic rivalry among the embryonic pioneer towns was endemic. Competition for designation as a county seat, which guaranteed an economic base of courthouse business, touched off the fiercest battles. New settlements energetically vied for the prize, using bribery, trickery, and sometimes violence to advance their claims. Communities also competed for the farmers' trade. Inevitably, the economic interests of farmers and town merchants began to diverge as the latter charged what the traffic would bear. Farmers complained that dealers' grain prices were too low, storekeepers' prices too high, and bankers' interest rates too dear.

The typical midwestern country town of the nineteenth century had been founded as a real estate proposition by a speculator. Streets and town lots were laid out in the ubiquitous gridiron or checkerboard pattern, which was best adapted to the sale of individual lots. The boomers' cries of a glorious future were taken to heart by those who settled there, and they became an article of faith of the gospel of growth. Civic pride was perverted into the admonition "Boost, don't knock," and ever-rising property values became the central goal.

Yet in those towns which survived the vicissitudes of pioneer days, people put down roots and acquired a sense of belonging; in the nineteenth century it was said that people were "born into" a town much as they were born into a church. Memories of pioneer days, when people helped each other out of necessity and when birth and status counted for little, were still alive, contributing to a spirit of community. In the postpioneer period, a rudimentary civic spirit veneered the raw acquisitive energy and survival drive that had dominated the early days. Women, in their traditional role as nurturers and promoters of domesticity and culture, became vocal, demanding the introduction of amenities. One of the first gestures to posterity in western towns was to plant trees along the unpaved streets.

Pioneer towns were little more than log cabins strewn helter-skelter along a single street. Gradually they metamorphosed into rows of frame houses with porches and lawns and backyards, along shaded streets down which clopped the spring wagons of merchants. The bell of the trolley car might be heard as it meandered along its appointed route, stopping whenever anyone hailed it. In the business district office blocks of beef-red brick rose two or three stories, a modest but dignified vernacular architecture. New, more elaborate courthouses rose in the central squares—edifices of brick or limestone with an imposing tower, elaborate masonry trim, a statue of a Union or Confederate soldier nearby, and benches for the old men who whiled away their days talking and whittling.

Still, the typical midwestern town was on the whole an ugly place of slatternly false-fronted buildings and unpaved streets that were rutted or muddy in winter and dusty and reeking of garbage and horse dung under the summer sun. Nearly every town had been laid out with a main street, often officially called that, which became the main business and social artery. Through it flowed the lifeblood of the town—its strollers and shoppers, its parades and celebrations, its political rallies.

Every Saturday farmers parked their buggies along it and embarked on their weekly shopping trip. To them the country town was a Rome, a Paris, an urban oasis at which to refresh grim, isolated lives. Country folk chatted in the courthouse square, purchased necessities and a few simple luxuries in dimly lit general stores redolent of harness leather and kerosene, and blinked sleepily at the new electric streetlights before heading home.

Meanwhile, the townspeople created their own recreational and cultural life: band concerts, baseball teams, cotillions and at homes, reading clubs, lectures by itinerant savants, shows by traveling theatrical troupes at the new opera house, circuses, revival meetings. The public schools were a boon to the farmers' sons and daughters who could attend them. High schools encouraged social mobility; they were stepping-stones to college and the cities. Human capital became one of the chief exports of the small towns. Surveys showed a disproportionately high percentage of scientists, business executives, and writers came from small towns. But rural areas battered by the ups and downs of farm prices also shipped their surplus sons and daughters to factories in the cities.

So to many, the hometown became the place you were from, a focal point of nostalgia. To its residents, it provided status, identity, and support. It also encouraged an insular civic pride, partly based on rivalry with other places; people felt *their* town was somehow superior to the next one, though an outsider might see little to choose between them. Small towns also declared their superiority to the cities. Preachers and editorialists promulgated the official gospel of small-town goodness and neighborliness, and inveighed against metropolitan alienation, immorality, and corruption.

After the turn of the twentieth century, rising prosperity on the farms, the economic lifeblood of the country town, contributed to a smug sense that here was the good life. Trains arrived eight or ten times a day, wreathed in smoke, noise, and commotion, bringing news and goods and travelers from the city. The station was a favorite meeting place for locals, who watched the trains whizzing by "with the languid scorn a permanent fixture always has for a transient and the pity an American feels for a fellow-being who does not live in his town," as Booth Tarkington wrote in his novel *The Gentleman from Indiana.*

Blacksmith shops, livery stables, drugstores, and saloons were male bastions of somewhat shady repute. Women's lives centered on their homes; their labors were dawn to dusk, sweating over coal-burning stoves, pumping water, heating water for baths or laundry. The days of their weeks were structured by well-worn ritual: Monday, washing; Tuesday, ironing; and so on through Sunday, reserved for church and the heavy noon meal that followed. Women traditionally held the family together and dominated their homes; outside the home they specialized in religious, charitable, and cultural activities and watched over the morality of their husbands and children. Their husbands pursued their small-business dreams, though many found only a precarious living and sank into a dependent role of "diminished potency and power," in the words of historian Page Smith. A kind of small-town matriarchy prevailed, except in the male preserves of politics and commerce.

Every town had its rich families that dominated civic and economic affairs. They set the social tone and encouraged class distinctions; newcomers aspiring to acceptance found they must undergo a long vetting process. Even small villages had two rudimentary classes: those who worked and saved and went to church, and the rest, who were "no-accounts." The poor were blamed for their plight and formed a separate caste.

Such divisions clashed with the egalitarian ethos small towns still professed. There were invidious racial and ethnic distinctions as well, with blacks and foreigners segregated into "Bucktowns" and "Polish Towns," the poor to their shantytowns. Gossip was a potent weapon of social control, enforcing loosely articulated norms of morality and respectability. Yet the grapevine also carried news of sickness or a death in the family, bringing help from neighbors. Although there was a certain latitude for eccentricity, woe to those who willfully defied public opinion. The tyranny of the majority, which Alexis de Tocqueville identified as the drawback of democracy in America, was most pronounced in small towns, imposing a stifling dullness and provincialism. This, and the lack of economic opportunity for young people, save those who had a family business waiting for them, drove the best and the brightest to seek city lights.

PRAIRIE JUNCTIONS: MINING CAMPS AND COW TOWNS

During the 1870s and 1880s, covered-wagon loads—later trainloads—of immigrants, many of them communal groups from Europe, poured into the Great Plains. The foreign immigrants had been recruited by agents for the railroad companies, which needed to populate the huge land grants along their rights-of-way. Railroads became the leading town promoters in the Far West. They laid out villages along their tracks at regular intervals, and named them in alphabetical order after railroad employees. Existing towns were told that they must pay a subsidy or be bypassed. Impelled by economic imperatives, town officials paid up, raising the money by bond subscriptions. They knew farmers must ship their produce to the cities and would take their trade to the town that had a grain elevator and a depot.

Farmers led lives of unrelieved toil and hardship. Agriculture was a precarious venture on the Great Plains because of the ferocious storms, low rainfall, and plagues of grasshoppers, and this retarded the growth of country towns. Railroads that gained a monopoly in their area added to the struggling farmers' costs by charging exorbitant freight rates, a cause of the Populist revolt of the 1880s and 1890s.

"Precarious" was the word for towns in the gold and silver country of California, Arizona, and the Rocky Mountains. Here, the mining camp was the primary form of settlement; it appeared wherever the precious ore was found. These disposable towns, dubbed "rag cities" because they consisted mainly of tents, plus a store or two and a shack that served as saloon, lasted only as long as the gold or silver held out. Nevertheless, they developed a legal system administered by ad hoc miners' courts which awarded claims, resolved disputes, and held criminal proceedings not far removed from lynch law. Still, the miners kept order, belying the reputation for rowdiness that mining camps acquired in romantic fiction.

Another type of town indigenous to the West with an exaggerated reputation for bumptiousness was the cattle town. Dodge City, Abilene, Wichita, and other Kansas towns served in turn as shipping points for beef on the hoof that had been driven in great herds from Texas to be transported to the abattoirs of Chicago. With the cattle came hordes of dusty, rowdy drovers eager for recreation after months on the trail.

The city officials' way of dealing with the free-spending cowboys was to quarantine them: all the saloons, bordellos, and gambling halls were confined to one side of the railroad tracks that ran down the main street, while the respectable folk lived on the other, insulated from the hell-raising and leading humdrum lives. The cattle towns took a perverse civic pride in their lurid reputations, inflated by eastern reporters in search of "color." Even in their heyday, the cow towns had schools, elections, churches, reform movements, economic conflicts; and after the cattle trade departed, officials repented their wickedness in an effort to attract the once-scorned farmers, who had "stood in the way of progress" by fencing the open range.

In California, the miners who had opened up the state were followed by farmers and town-boomers. Some of the old Spanish pueblos, presidios, and missions grew into towns and cities. A few mining camps acquired stability when industrial mining operations sank shafts to systematically extract ore-veined rock deep beneath the surface. Others were resurrected as agricultural centers.

THE REVOLT FROM THE VILLAGE

By the early twentieth century, the fortunes of country towns were closely tied to national markets. A long-term exodus from the farms, hastened by the agricultural depression after the boom of World War I, and sustained by the mechanization of farming, gradually eroded the traditional economic base of the country towns. The larger towns diversified by attracting industries, but industrialization brought with it city-style problems—pollution, hardening class divisions, the decline of craftsmanship and the advent of mass production, and the replacement of local owners by distant corporate control. Labor unions were banned and local politics was dominated by business elites bent on keeping wages low and "agitators" out.

Attracting industry had other drawbacks. Many growth-obsessed towns offered excessive subsidies in the form of tax concessions and infrastructure improvements to attract new factories. Small-town businesses became dependent on large corporate suppliers that served national markets. In his classic 1923 essay "The Country Town," the iconoclastic economist Thorstein Veblen described small-town shopkeepers as mere "tollgate keepers for the distribution of goods and collection of customs for the large absentee owners of business."

Standardization, industrialization, and the rise of mass culture through radio, movies, and nationally distributed periodicals exposed provincial towns that prided themselves on their self-reliance and resistance to urban ways. The 1920 census was a watershed; it revealed that for the first time in American history more than half of the population dwelled in urban places of 2,500 people and above. And in an increasingly urbanized society, small towns were damned by urban intellectuals (most of them escapees) as backward and provincial.

The reaction was particularly visible in fiction. At the turn of the century, when the influx from the country to the city was accelerating, writers such as Booth Tarkington and Zona Gale celebrated the friendliness and folksiness of small towns; but in the 1910s and 1920s, a new critical realism focused a pitiless gaze on the emotional and cultural aridity of small-town life, giving rise to a literary movement called "the revolt from the village." In 1915, Edgar Lee Masters's *Spoon River Anthology* removed the facade of hypocrisy from small-town lives in terse epigrammatic poems. Sherwood Anderson's *Winesburg, Ohio* (1919), a series of linked, plotless stories tinged by Freudianism, displayed villagers as sexually repressed grotesques. The most stinging indictment was Sinclair Lewis's satirical *Main Street* (1920), which caustically evoked the social and cultural ugliness of Gopher Prairie, Minnesota.

Lewis wrote of his fictional town, "This is America—a town of a few thousand. . . . [I]ts Main Street is the continuation of Main Streets everywhere." To the village rebels, the small town was a metaphor for American culture—its provincialism, fundamentalism, anti-intellectualism, materialism, Fordism. Indeed, in 1922 an anthology edited by Harold E. Stearns appeared under the bland but ironically intended title *Civilization in the United States*. Louis Raymond Reed, the contributor of the essay "The Small Town" wrote: "The civilization of America is predominantly the civilization of the small town" (p. 286).

The intellectuals and urbanites regarded prohibition as small-town morality writ large. The temperance movement had grown from frontier beginnings into a national crusade, culminating in the moral fervor of World War I and the passage of the Eighteenth Amendment. Prohibition pitted rural America against urban America. Walter Lipp-

mann saw it as "a test of strength between social orders. When the Eighteenth Amendment goes down, the cities will be dominant politically and socially as they now are economically." From the ramparts of his *American Mercury,* H. L. Mencken hurled thunderbolts of invective against small-town morality and hypocrisy. To progressive urban intellectuals, small towns stood for nativist opposition to labor unions, foreigners, and radicalism. And there was truth to the indictment, for small-town businessmen embraced the big-business–Republican party credo of laissez-faire and low taxes.

After the village rebels had raked over small-town America, a wave of probing sociologists descended on it. One of the first such studies was Robert and Helen Lynd's *Middletown* (1929), which found in Muncie, Indiana, the conformity and conservatism that the novelists had shown. It was followed by *Middletown in Transition* (1937), analyzing the impact of the Great Depression on Muncie. Other prominent studies included W. Lloyd Warner and associates' five-volume "Yankee City" series about industrialization in Newburyport, Massachusetts, and his *Democracy in Jonesville* (1949), Hollingshead's *Elmtown's Youth* (1949), Blumenthal's *Small-Town Stuff* (1932), and James West's *Plainville USA* (1955). As late as the 1960s, Arthur Vidich and Joseph Bensman, in their *Small Town in Mass Society* (1968), could proclaim that an upstate New York town was "a backwash" and "the last link in America to the nineteenth century and its values." The inhabitants of "Springdale" still proclaimed the old values of individualism, self-help, and autonomy, even though their town had become dependent on state and federal aid. Its politics were dominated by a self-perpetuating elite skilled at extracting subsidies from the state, and its small businessmen were at the mercy of their big corporate suppliers.

TOWNS IN THE INDUSTRIAL ERA

The Great Depression was a watershed, undermining the traditional rural values of self-help and individualism. The 1930s saw an unprecedented intrusion of the federal government into local government. Small-town and rural people had traditionally relied on charity and neighborliness to cope with troubles too big for the individual to handle; poverty was considered a disgrace, and ending one's days at the county poor farm was a fate to be dreaded. And so when unemployment struck, its victims sought to hide their disgrace. A common saying during the Depression was "If I have to be poor I want to be poor in a city where everybody doesn't know I'm broke."

Even in industrial towns the old individualism retained its hold. In Middletown, the Lynds noted, the factory workers were mainly farm boys and "thus close to the network of habits of thought engendered by the isolated, self-contained enterprise of farming." Consequently, they clung to the dream of going into business for themselves and achieving financial success, rather than joining together to assert their economic interests. Similarly, business-dominated, small-town governments, chronically resistant to change and "rocking the boat," averted their eyes from the rising tide of misery among their constituents and chanted the mantra of "Boost, don't knock." But they could not forever ignore the fact that their miserly poor-relief budgets were inadequate to deal with the misery lapping at their doorstep. Eventually, they swallowed their principles and accepted Uncle Sam's helping hand. Federal largess financed a host of public-works projects, from post offices to bridges to new roads. These improvements would never have been made by traditionally parsimonious town fathers.

The Depression brought many people from the cities back to the land, even as the wave of bankruptcies drove others off it. But the countryside was the net loser in this exchange. The rural exodus was temporarily stalled by the agricultural boom of World War II, but it resumed at an even faster pace after the war. More than 8.6 million people departed for cities in the 1940s; the flight continued at the rate of a million per year in the 1950s, and three-quarters of a million annually in the 1960s. The flight of southern blacks from the land was a major component of this human tide, as the mechanization of cotton picking made their labor unnecessary. In 1940 the rural population made up 40 percent of the national population; by 1970 it was only 26.5 percent. In 1975 only 4 percent of the total population was engaged in farming.

Small towns suffered, perforce, from the loss of farmers. A favorite statistic of rural sociologists is the 1:5 ratio—for every five farmers who move away, one business in town goes under. The proof of this theorem was visible in the boarded-up stores along every Main Street. In the 1960s small-town businesses were decimated by a new invader—the shopping mall, often a gallery of stores set down in a former cornfield. The automobile had long been choking Main Street; shopping malls with acres of parking lots and "stripvilles" of establishments catering to the car culture "solved" that problem—at the expense of downtown merchants. Revitalization of central business districts became the challenge of the 1970s. One strategy was restoration of old buildings and the introduction of pedestrian malls and more ample parking facilities.

THE "RURAL RENAISSANCE"

During the 1970s, there was a modest turnaround in the fortunes of rural America. Countering a trend of country-to-city migration nearly as old as the republic, rural counties showed a 15.4 percent gain in population—around four million people in all. The counties with the lowest population densities had the largest increases.

The rush to the countryside sparked a flurry of stories in the press about a "rural renaissance," and demographers scrambled to understand what had happened. Their main conclusions: First, many of the migrants were acting out of the long-standing preference among Americans, consistently shown in opinion polls, for small-town or country living—more for the latter. Second, and a seeming corollary to this, many of the rural immigrants cited "quality of life" as their primary reason for moving. Dissatisfaction with decaying, crime-ridden cities (and overgrown suburbs) was possibly an impetus, but the pull of areas affording natural beauty, space, and privacy was even more decisive. Third, although the usual incentive for moving, economic betterment, was not often cited, the availability of nonfarming jobs—professional, white-collar, and blue-collar—in rural areas made the move feasible for many. This development resulted from diverse causes, including decentralization of industry facilitated by improved communications; the relocation of governmental facilities to low-density areas; the energy boom in the Appalachians, the West, and the "oil patch" states; cheap gasoline; the aging of the general population and a growing number of longer-lived, more affluent retired people who preferred small-town life; the proliferation of community colleges, which alleviated cultural isolation; and the growth of the recreation and nursing-home industries. As commuters to city jobs moved farther out, a new postsuburbia proliferated in the rural fringes of metropolitan areas. The result was clusters of homes that were neither urban nor rural; sociologists christened them "countrified cities" or "linear suburbs" or "plug-in towns."

The migration to rural areas brought problems: environmental degradation, pollution, and the loss of irreplaceable farmland. Some developers did not provide adequate roads or sewage lines; many unincorporated villages tapped groundwater, which was insufficient for their population and polluted by agricultural pesticides. Newcomers roiled the stagnant waters of local politics by demanding urban-style services. The aging machinery of county government creaked under the strain of the demands for services—sewage, paved roads, water.

All this raised a larger question: Would the immigrants seeking quality of life end up degrading that same quality of life? And what of the impact on democratic participation of a diffuse population living in "plug-in cities"? Would the inhabitants shun involvement in local government? Would they take part in community activities in nearby towns? Would they form communities of their own? Or would the open land spawn an alienated population of latter-day outlivers, with no ties to place other than the financial nexus of real estate values?

THE FUTURE OF THE SMALL TOWN

By the mid 1980s, the rural renaissance stalled and the movement to urban areas resumed. Mining regions, hit by falling energy prices, suffered a net loss of 1.7 percent in population; nearly half of all rural counties declined in population. Counties in which manufacturing was the dominant economic activity were shaken by deindustrialization—the restructuring of the national economy from one dominated by manufacturing to one primarily geared to providing services. In Ohio, the heart of the Rustbelt, eighty of eighty-four counties showed a net loss of people.

The economic malaise in the rural areas was starkly etched in unemployment figures. Between May 1985 and May 1986, agricultural employment fell by nearly 4 percent, mining employment by more than 16 percent, and manufacturing employment by 0.6 percent. The rural poor increased by 43 percent between 1978 and 1983, according to the Census Bureau. A Senate subcommittee reported that during the 1980s, net farm income averaged nearly 40 percent less than in the 1970s. More than one thousand rural counties had unemployment rates above 9 percent, compared with the national average of 5.2 percent. Some towns became "rural ghettos."

The farm crisis of the 1980s delivered a devastating blow to agriculturally based towns. More than 270,000 family farms disappeared in a wave of bankruptcies; the land was gobbled up by agribusinesses and consolidated into larger spreads. These corporate farming operations bypassed town merchants and made their bulk purchases in urban centers. They also imported hired laborers who, with no community ties and little hope of acquiring land of their own, formed a permanent underclass.

As town businesses closed their doors, the young and the able fled, leaving behind the poor and the nonaffluent elderly. In some small towns in the farm belt, the median age was over fifty, and many counties showed an excess of deaths over births. The fewer young workers who remained shouldered a heavier tax burden because of the need to provide health care for the oldsters, as well as to maintain schools and basic services.

Manufacturing towns that watched local industries go under to foreign competition or be bought out by conglomerates which cut the work force or shut the plants, found it harder to attract traditionally good-paying factory jobs. In the 1970s and 1980s, the phenomenon of "footloose" industries became more prevalent—establishments that were not tied to any site and left with little concern for the impact on the places they abandoned. Some towns sought to attract service industries, but the jobs often paid less than factory work. And the new factories that did relocate often hired outside workers rather than locals.

All this shuttered stores along Main Street. One study reported that in each decade since 1950 an average of 76 percent of towns of less than 2,500 population suffered a net loss of retail and service establishments—gas stations, grocery stores, lumberyards, hardware, farm implement, and furniture stores. This erosion was not due solely to loss of population; increased competition came from large chains, which offered goods and supplies more cheaply (and were not averse to monopolistic price-cutting). People drove to shopping malls to make their big-ticket purchases rather than buying at home. As a result, some towns could survive only as bedroom communities for cities some 50 miles (80 kilometers) away. Between 1983 and 1986, places outside a Standard Metropolitan Statistical Area (a densely populated area contiguous to a city of fifty thousand or more) suffered the greatest population declines.

Cutbacks in federal aid under the Reagan administration added to the woes of small towns already confronted by a dwindling tax base. They were starved for money to repair bridges and roads, and had to worry about city-style problems like crime, drugs, inadequate schools, air and soil pollution, toxic waste, AIDS, and polluted water tables. Federal crop-support payments to farmers continued, but much of the money went to large operators and the rest did not always help a town's economy, since it was used to pay off the big mortgages assumed during the 1970s rather than to make consumer purchases.

To be sure, many larger towns survived on a solid base of industry and farming and maintained basic services. But even they were hit by the loss of important amenities—a hospital, say, because Medicaid payments are lower for rural areas. The local bank might be taken over by a remote financial conglomerate that was less sensitive to local needs. Deregulation enabled air, rail, and bus lines to halt unprofitable local service, meaning that many towns were cut off from urban centers.

TOWN AND COMMUNITY

Yet, the crisis of the small town is not new; as we have seen, many of the trends are of long standing. The harsh judgment of history is that some small towns are doomed and others will survive only if they adapt to new circumstances. But self-help is often not enough. Governmental policies properly tailored to the needs of the one-quarter of the population in rural areas are needed. Measures designed to shore up the family farm, for example, would slow the small-town death rate in states like Iowa. The festering problem of rural poverty, which has been on the national agenda since at least the 1960s, must be addressed more decisively by the federal government in areas such as health care,

housing, and small business assistance, instead of placing the entire burden on the states.

The picture is by no means uniformly bleak. Many towns are showing adaptability and planning moderate growth strategies. These municipalities, which sociologists call "entrepreneurial towns"—those with newspapers that air local issues, an activist political leadership, schools that emphasize academics rather than sports, and a citizenry willing to spend tax money on infrastructure improvements—have been able to revive fading local businesses or attract new ones to offset their losses.

A contemporary school of "neotraditionalist" city planners draws upon the classic small-town model in laying out new towns with low-traffic streets, local gathering places, sidewalks, pedestrian scale. Even shopping malls—those ravagers of so many small-town businesses—are being torn down and rebuilt as imitation Main Streets with small stores, community centers, and residential areas.

With enlightened leadership and planning, many towns can survive. But survival should not be judged by purely economic criteria or in terms of growth at any price; it should also include invigoration of the town's cultural life and preservation of its history and intangible values of community, smallness and human scale, face-to-face relationships over time, and a sense of place.

So we return to the ideal of community first declared by the early Puritans. John Winthrop described it eloquently in a sermon aboard the *Arbella:* "We must delight in each other, make others' conditions our own, rejoice together, always having before our eyes our commission and community in the work, our community as members of the same bond." New constellations of this old dream must be discovered that are appropriate for a heterogeneous, secular society.

BIBLIOGRAPHY

Atherton, Lewis E. *Main Street on the Middle Border* (1954).

Blumenthal, Albert. *Small-Town Stuff* (1932).

Brownell, Blaine A., and David R. Goldfield, eds. *The City in Southern History: The Growth of Urban Civilization in the South* (1977).

Bushman, Richard L. *From Puritan to Yankee: Character and the Social Order in Connecticut, 1690–1765* (1967).

Critchfield, Richard. *Villages* (1981).

Davidson, Osha Gray. *Broken Heartland: The Rise of America's Rural Ghetto* (1990).

Debo, Angie. *Prairie City: The Story of an American Community* (1944).

Demos, John. *A Little Commonwealth: Family Life in Plymouth Colony* (1970).

Dollard, John. *Caste and Class in a Southern Town*. 3d ed. (1957).

Dykstra, Robert R. *The Cattle Towns* (1968).

Goist, Park Dixon. *From Main Street to State Street: Town, City, and Community in America* (1977).

Greven, Philip J., Jr. *Four Generations: Population, Land, and Family in Colonial Andover, Massachusetts* (1970).

Hilfer, Anthony Channell. *The Revolt from the Village, 1915–1930* (1969).

Hollingshead, August de Belmont. *Elmtown's Youth: The Impact of Social Classes on Adolescents* (1949).

Lesy, Michael. *Wisconsin Death Trip* (1973).

Lingeman, Richard. *Small-Town America: A Narrative History, 1620–the Present* (1980).

Lockridge, Kenneth A. *A New England Town: The First Hundred Years, Dedham, Massachusetts, 1636–1736* (1970).

Lynd, Robert S., and Helen M. Lynd. *Middletown: A Study in Contemporary American Culture* (1929).

————. *Middletown in Transition: A Study of Cultural Conflicts* (1937).

Parker, Tony. *Bird, Kansas* (1989).

Powers, Ron. *Far from Home: Life and Loss of Two American Towns* (1991).

Redfield, Robert. *The Little Community, and Peasant Society and Culture* (1962).

Rifkind, Carole. *Main Street: The Face of Urban America* (1977).

Schwab, Jim. *Raising Less Corn and More Hell: Midwestern Farmers Speak Out* (1988).

Shinn, Charles Howard. *Mining Camps: A Study in American Frontier Government*. Edited by Rodman W. Paul (1965).

Smith, Page. *As a City upon a Hill: The Town in American History* (1966).

Varenne, Hervé. *Americans Together: Structured Diversity in a Midwestern Town* (1977).

Vidich, Arthur, and Joseph Bensman. *Small Town in Mass Society: Class, Power, and Religion in a Rural Community* (1968).

West, James. *Plainville USA* (1955).

SEE ALSO **The City; Community Studies; The Suburbs.**

THE CITY

Steven A. Riess

FROM THE EARLIEST DAYS of colonization to the present, American cities have been central places, providing a focal point for economic development, local government, culture, social reform, and technological innovation, and a site where newcomers clustered and became acculturated. A city is a site with at least twenty-five hundred residents that performs various specialized functions for itself and surrounding smaller communities and supports a cosmopolitan life-style. Organic entities that change over time, cities are composed of three major elements: physical structures (spatial dimensions, demographics, economy, and technology); organizational structures (class, ethnic, and racial groups, social institutions, and government); and value systems (attitudes, ideologies, and behavior). Their evolution can be categorized into four eras: the early American city (1630–1820), which comprised about 5 percent of the population; the walking city (1820–1870), which existed when urbanization occurred at its fastest rate and cities began to provide essential services; the industrialized radial city (1870–1950s), an entity of imposing physical dimensions inhabited by immense populations, a product of industrialization, immigration, and cheap mass transit; and the suburban metropolis (1945–1990s), characterized by the dominance of suburbia, the decline of the urban core, and the emergence of the Sunbelt.

THE EARLY AMERICAN CITY

The first colonial cities, starting with Spanish Saint Augustine, Florida (1565), were clusters of concentrated populations, vanguards of settlement located on bodies of water, whose functions included defense, government, trade, and the support of religion and culture. Their importance transcended population. They were the most dynamic colonial places, and loci of an urbane and cosmopolitan life-style, and sites of key colonial institutions ranging from governments to churches. Their weak and often oligarchic governments provided few public services unconnected to commerce, relying instead on private initiative. Later cities learned from their experience, copying physical layouts, social organizations, and privatism.

Boston was the first English colonial city, founded in 1630 by the Puritans as a model settlement of Visible Saints who shared the same values and beliefs. Boston was an exceptionally homogeneous city, although the Puritan community weakened as the second and third generations were less likely to have a saving experience. By 1690 Boston had a population of seven thousand, which made it the fourth largest city in the British Empire. Philadelphia, New York, Newport, and Charleston, all compact ports, were the other major colonial cities. They were originally overwhelmingly English except for Charleston, which by 1680 had become a haven for French Huguenots, who had first come to South Carolina in 1670, and New York, the cosmopolitan former Dutch colony of New Amsterdam, where eighteen languages were spoken. The early residents of the latter included Sephardic Jews.

Cities became more heterogeneous following Queen Anne's War (1702–1713), as indentured Germans and Scotch-Irish migrated to New York and especially to Philadelphia. After the French and Indian War (1754–1763), there was a substantial immigration of Irish and Scotch-Irish that temporarily halted during the Revolution and resumed afterward. The immigrants shied away from Boston because of its historic intolerance and limited economic opportunities for newcomers.

The colonial cities all had substantial black populations. In the early 1700s, Charleston's black and white populations were equal, and blacks comprised one-fourth of New York and one-sixth of Boston. As late as 1771, 15 percent of New York's adult male work force were slaves.

Colonial cities had a multilayered social structure. Ministers were at the apex of Boston's social structure until they were supplanted in the late seventeenth century by professionals and wealthy merchants who had the biggest homes and the most prominent church pews. Boston's merchants then controlled 40 percent of colonial shipping, but by the mid eighteenth century they had lost their leadership because of an unproductive backcountry and the maturation of aggressive challengers, primarily Philadelphians who shipped wheat from the hinterland to Caribbean and transatlantic markets. Newport emphasized the slave trade; Charleston, rice; and New York, wheat and livestock.

The "better sort" enjoyed a high standard of living and dominated society and public affairs. In 1687 Boston's richest 5 percent controlled 25 percent of the city's taxable wealth, a figure that increased to 44 percent in 1771, about the same ratio as in other cities. The upper class was an open elite, and there were rags-to-riches stories, especially in New York, where 33 to 40 percent of the merchants in 1775 were self-made men. The rich owned elegantly furnished brick homes, rode in carriages, wore expensive clothing and powdered wigs, socialized at the finest coffeehouses, belonged to restrictive voluntary organizations like Philadelphia's Schuylkill Fishing Colony (1732), and married within the elite circle.

The "middling sort" composed about 70 percent of society. They had smaller homes, less property, and cheaper clothes. One-fifth of urban male workers were shopkeepers or other low-level nonmanual workers, and about half were self-employed or highly paid artisans who had a strong self-image as hard working, frugal, and competent.

At the bottom of the social ladder were the impoverished "inferior sorts": unskilled workers, indentured servants, and slaves, comprising 20–30 percent of urbanites in 1770. No permanent white proletariat existed because of opportunities to advance or move on, but the gap between rich and poor was growing. In 1687, 14 percent of Bostonians had no property; the figure had doubled to 29 percent in 1771. The poor mainly lived on the periphery in crowded housing and were increasingly insecure, disaffected, and less deferential.

Municipal governments had limited authority to tax or spend, and outside of New England were regarded as exclusive, elitist, tight-fisted, and insensitive to changing conditions. Their primary duty was to promote commerce rather than to provide essential services or social conformity. Three-fifths of all colonial cities were unincorporated, especially in New England, where they had considerable autonomy. Power there resided in the town meeting, where freemen (only 16 percent at mid century) enacted laws, levied taxes, settled disputes, and elected selectmen to run affairs between meetings. Under the British, New York was originally a royally chartered municipal borough run by a mayor and council dominated by merchants appointed by the governor, but charter reform in 1731 made it an open corporation with annual elections that forced the notables to be more responsive to the growing electorate. Political factions emerged over economic issues and conflicts between rival elite families. Philadelphia, whose government was one of only three closed corporations in the colonies, was run by an oligarchy with long terms, the prerogative to appoint successors, and, except for taxation, other wide-ranging powers. Charleston had no municipal government at all until 1715, when the provincial assembly appointed insensitive commissioners to supervise specific tasks.

Most new laws concerned economic matters because commerce was the cornerstone of urban economies. Municipalities regulated and supervised sites of mercantile activity like the wharfs and markets, and by 1690 all but Boston had a regulated market with standards of quality, weights, and measures. In Boston, however, economic laws comprised a mere 9 percent of all edicts. Bostonians believed that open markets provided opportunities for smaller purveyors and thus did not have a permanent public market until Faneuil Hall was built in 1742.

Cities did a poor job of coping with such public problems as morality, health, poverty, safety, and streets. Homogeneous Boston was the best-governed and most communally responsible city. Its earliest laws included fire-prevention measures, bans on garbage dumping, and penalties for Sabbath breaking and adultery. In 1701 over half of its ordinances dealt with public safety, order, and peace. Public services were paid for by license fees, fines, tariffs, lotteries, rents from public markets and wharves, and, later in the century, by property or poll taxes. There was also heavy reliance on private initiative. Streets received considerable attention because they were essential for commerce, created health hazards by draining poorly, and were dangerous for pedestrians and children at play. Boston had excellent paved streets and sewers, but it took other cities as long as forty years to catch up, mostly through relying on private efforts. Boston had some of the strictest fire regulations and best fire-fighting equipment in the world, yet there were severe fires in 1676, 1679, and 1711, after which the first volunteer fire company was established. The model for the future, however, was Philadelphia's elite Union Fire Company, formed in 1736 by Benjamin Franklin to fight fires and prevent looting.

Chronic poverty, particularly among women and children, materialized by the 1700s and was a major concern by mid century. In Charleston between 1751 and 1774, over 80 percent of people receiving aid were women and children. Impoverishment was frequently caused by the economic dislocations and bloodshed resulting from colonial wars. Thirteen percent of Boston's adult women were widows following King George's War (1744–1748), many of them left without any means of support or marketable skills other than sewing. Assistance to the deserving poor comprised a major portion of municipal expenditures, rising in New York from £250 in 1698 to £5000 in 1770, supplemented by private aid from philanthropists, churches, and voluntary associations. Most assistance was outdoor relief (money, food, clothing, and fuel) rather than indoor relief (institutionalization in almshouses).

Crime was less widespread and less severely punished in the colonies than in England. Homogeneous Puritan communities tried to prevent deviance through social pressure and regulation of public houses, but when necessary they relied on harsher methods such as banishment (the "antinomian" Anne Hutchinson), whipping, and even execution (Quakeress Mary Dyer). As cities became more heterogeneous through the influx of outsiders like sailors, blacks, escaped felons, and runaway servants, the crime rate increased. The rise was accounted for primarily by morals violations, punished by fines and whippings. Policing was originally done by privately organized patrols—as late as 1690 New York was the only city with a paid watch—but by 1720 all the cities had copied the European system of municipally paid daytime constables and night watches to apprehend offenders, report fires, and maintain order against occasional riots caused by such lower-class grievances as impressment and soaring bread prices. Charleston and New York had the added special problem of potential slave insurrections. New York had a slave riot in 1712, and in 1741, when nearly one-fourth of the labor force were bondsmen, rumors of a slave revolt resulted in thirty-one executions.

Little was accomplished in the area of public health. Cities were hard-pressed to cope with the garbage dumped in the streets that attracted hogs and stray animals. Boston had the cleanest streets, yet in 1711 the garbage on the streets caught fire. Infectious diseases were deadly threats, although port officials inspected and quarantined entering ships. Smallpox was particularly dreaded, and there were three outbreaks in Boston between 1666 and 1702. After a fourth episode in 1721 that infected almost 6,000 and killed about 850, Cotton Mather and Dr. Zabdiel Boylston encouraged inoculation. The procedure gained acceptance only slowly, however, and was not widely applied until the 1760s.

Religion was the most important semipublic institution, and a church was usually the city's most prominent physical structure. Religion promoted morality and discipline, a message that became less salient with increased secularization, the worship of money and status, and the popularity of taverns, drinking, gambling, and blood sport. By 1737 Boston had 177 innkeepers and liquor retailers, one for every twenty-five adult males. Religious life was reinvigorated in the 1730s and 1740s by the Great Awakening, which promoted evangelical Protestantism and made thousands of converts. The revival led to higher moral standards and the formation of new churches, denominations, and seminaries that fragmented urban society.

Colonial cities were centers of a cosmopolitan life-style. In Puritan Boston children attended school to learn to read the Bible; future clergymen studied at the publicly supported Boston Public Latin School (1635) and went on to Harvard College (1636). By the mid eighteenth century, education was largely secularized, a mark of status for classically trained elite sons or vocational training for middle-class sons that ranged from apprenticeships to baccalaureate training at the College of Philadelphia (1755, now the University of Pennsylvania). Cities had weekly newspapers, beginning with the *Boston News-Letter* (1704), public and subscription libraries, bookshops, and other institutions like coffeehouses, mechanics' societies, and Philadelphia's American Philosophical Society (1743) that encouraged enlightened discourse.

Cities were instrumental in the coming of the American Revolution because they were the scenes of the greatest oppression and because they had the human resources and communication facilities (inns, coffeehouses, and print shops) to plan and implement resistance. Merchants led the opposition to George III's reassertion of royal authority, particularly following the Stamp Act (1765), to protect their rights as Englishmen. To secure repeal, leading Bostonians drew up petitions, organized boycotts and nonimportation agreements, established committees of correspondence, and allied with other social groups who staged organized riots. The Sons of Liberty subsequently led the opposition to the Townshend Acts (1767) and the Tea Tax (1770), culminating in the Boston Tea Party (16 December 1773). The Coercive (Intolerable) Acts then closed the port of Boston and revoked the charter of Massachusetts, thereby throttling commerce and liberty. Boston's Committee of Correspondence responded by appealing to other cities to organize a continental congress to coordinate collective action against the Crown. After independence and the defeat of the British, urbanites became the leading supporters of a strong national government to facilitate trade and promote economic stability. In 1787, when only 5 percent of Americans lived in cities, twenty of the fifty-five delegates to the Constitutional Convention were urbanites, and these cosmopolites saw the Constitution through to ratification.

The urban population over the next four decades remained at about 5 percent, although the number of cities with over ten thousand residents increased from five in 1790 to twenty-three in 1830. Twenty-five cities obtained more democratic charters, the franchise was liberalized, and most closed corporations like that of Philadelphia (1796) were replaced. An urban frontier emerged on the fringe of a rising national urban network, copying the methods older cities had employed to plat their sites and deal with emerging problems. Towns like Pittsburgh, Louisville, and Cincinnati promoted economic growth at transfer points along navigable waterways like the Ohio River by centralizing and distributing goods and services. These cities also brought the accoutrements of civilization, including institutions of higher learning like Transylvania College (now University) in Lexington, Kentucky.

THE WALKING CITY

The era of most rapid urbanization occurred between 1820 and 1870, when the urban proportion of the national population reached 25 percent, a product of economic growth, the transportation revolution, and immigration. In the period 1830–1860 the number of cities with a population in ex-

cess of ten thousand quadrupled from 23 to 101. New York was the largest in 1860, with 813,600 residents, and eight others surpassed 100,000. These physically small cities seldom extended more than two miles in any direction, and consequently walking was the main form of locomotion. They were still primarily centers of commerce in which land uses were very mixed, although their populations became heterogeneous, divided into ethnic and class subcommunities. Municipal government grew increasingly powerful, often under the control of professional politicians, and began to provide essential public services.

The core of the walking city was the waterfront with its docks, warehouses, business offices, factories, and homes. The economic elite lived nearby in choice locations, particularly the healthier high land, while the poor resided in back lots, alleys, or shanties at the outskirts of town. The biggest cities were densely populated, led by New York with 135.6 persons per acre in 1850; slums were even more packed. Land was extremely valuable, not only in Manhattan, where property tripled in value between 1819 and 1836, but also in instant cities like Chicago. Growth and development were promoted primarily by speculators, businessmen, and politicians who stood to directly profit.

The transportation revolution had a huge impact on urban commerce. New York's emergence as the leading trade center after the War of 1812 was achieved through such innovations as the American Black Ball Line, a regular packet service to Liverpool (1818) that facilitated planning, auctions that cut out middlemen, steamship service via the Atlantic all the way to New Orleans, and the Erie Canal (1825). The city became the nation's financial and communications center, and the home of the finest lawyers, accountants, and other professionals. By 1841 New York controlled 59.1 percent of American foreign trade and dominated the hinterland.

The Erie Canal's success promoted a canal-building mania culminating with the Illinois and Michigan Canal (1848), which connected Chicago to the Mississippi River. Canals were soon surpassed, however, by railroads, introduced by aggressive Baltimoreans who established the Baltimore & Ohio Railroad (1828) to expand the city's nodal zone. Railroads carried freight and passengers rapidly, year-round, and wherever workers could lay tracks. Trackage rose from 2,800 miles in 1840 to 30,600 miles in 1860. The railroad was especially the key to western development. Chicago's emergence as a railroad hub in the 1850s enabled it to overtake conservative Saint Louis as the West's leading city.

The introduction of mass transit in the largest cities encouraged physical expansion by enabling residents to travel longer distances in the same amount of time. In 1827 the omnibus, a large, twelve-passenger vehicle drawn by two horses, was introduced in New York. The slow (three to four miles per hour), uncomfortable ride over fixed routes cost one shilling (12.5 cents), a sum limiting ridership to the middle and upper classes. Nonetheless, by 1853 New York had 683 licensed omnibuses transporting 120,000 riders. The omnibus accustomed people to ride to work, and led to the emergence of the commuter.

In 1832 the superior horse-drawn streetcar was introduced in New York. The forty-passenger vehicles rode on rails, resulting in faster (six miles per hour), cheaper, smoother, and safer rides. They operated under municipal franchises that specified terms of service in return for the right to lay tracks on public streets and long-term contracts. The streetcars were an enormous success, making journeys fast and predictable, and fit in well with a time-driven society. By 1860 at least nine cities had street railroads, led by Philadelphia with 155 miles of track. Philadelphia took advantage of the transportation revolution to annex its surrounding communities in 1854, thereby growing in size from 2 to 129 square miles.

The urban social structure became increasingly unequal. In 1833, Boston's top 4 percent had 59 percent of the city's wealth, and 64 percent in 1848, figures typical of major cities. A few made it from rags to riches, typically in new or smaller industrial cities whose economies were growing rapidly and where there was no entrenched elite. The rich segregated themselves by joining prestigious churches and restricted voluntary associations like the Union Club or a yacht club, and moving toward the periphery, into large mansions with such conveniences as indoor plumbing.

The middle class, 40 percent of the work force, were predominantly white-collar workers who had wide social contacts and belonged to voluntary associations; advocated such values as hard work, self-discipline, and domestic tranquillity; and limited leisure time to useful, moral recreations like baseball. They earned more than blue-collar workers and worked in clean and quiet settings. Under 10 percent were salaried clerks, salesmen, or book-keepers—typically young men who could realistically expect substantially higher future incomes. The middle class lived in good neighborhoods near their jobs, in nicely furnished and carpeted homes with four to six rooms that provided privacy. Their wives shopped at specialty shops until mid century, when an important shift in merchandising occurred with the rise of large department stores with elegant interiors and huge inventories, like A. T. Stewart's in New York, which had two thousand salesclerks.

Blue-collar workers' standard of living declined as wages fell between 1830 and 1850, and it became harder to achieve a competency. Boston's propertyless rose from 44.6 percent in 1830 to 57.3 percent in 1860. At mid century, when the minimum budget for the average New York family of five was nearly $540, tradesmen earned only $300 a year, and wives and children had to work. One-third to one-half of the middle and lower classes were vertically mobile, accumulating property and advancing into better jobs. However, these gains were shaky because of boom-and-bust cycles, and required enormous familial sacrifices. Urbanites, especially young clerks and blue-collar workers, were geographically highly mobile, seeking better opportunities. Only one-third to two-fifths of urban residents remained in the same city for a decade between 1830 and 1860.

Cities were the locus of an emerging working-class community with a shared consciousness of interests, residential propinquity, and a common life-style. Manual workers unaccustomed to time-work discipline maintained an oppositional pre-modern culture largely expressed by leisure-time activities over which, unlike work, they exercised considerable control. These members of the male bachelor subculture enjoyed violent, socially dysfunctional, time-wasting participatory pleasures at gambling dens, groggeries, brothels, cockpits, boxing rings, and raucous theaters.

Manufacturing was mainly small scale in artisan-owned shops, but the rise of a national market at mid century encouraged entrepreneurs to increase production by employing the American system of manufacturing. The earliest factories, in small New England towns like Waltham (1813) and Lowell, Massachusetts (1822), harnessed the energy from fast-running rivers to operate machinery. The textile mills employed single farm girls sixteen to twenty-five years old who lived in a highly regulated and paternalistic community until, in the

1840s, they were replaced by unskilled Irish immigrants. The introduction of steam power enabled industrialists to locate in major cities near cheap labor, transportation, large markets, and sources of credit, information, and technological innovation. However, the urban occupational structure kept a preindustrial flavor because small-scale production lingered on, and many factories did not feature extreme division of labor. New York became the leading manufacturing center, but most plants had fewer than twenty workers. The great industrial boom came during the Civil War, to fulfill military requirements for munitions, food, and clothing.

Privatism slowly gave way to public efforts to deal effectively with urban problems beyond the scope of individual efforts. The movement for municipally sponsored services was advocated by boosters, businessmen, social reformers, and professional politicians. By mid century, state legislatures revised charters to empower municipalities to levy taxes and provide essential services. As local governments gained power, politics became a career for upwardly mobile men who belonged to emerging political machines like Tammany Hall that supported municipalization of services, which meant patronage.

Improved security was a prime requirement. The propertied classes were apprehensive about robberies, assaults, vice, labor unrest, and riots (there were thirty-seven in 1835 alone), which they attributed to lower-class Irishmen unable to cope with urban life; demands grew for deterrence, apprehension, and punishment. Municipalities responded by organizing professional police departments loosely modeled on the London Metropolitan Police (1829). Boston organized the first professional force in the United States (1838), but the prototype was New York's, established in 1844. The police were salaried, appointed and promoted by political connections, worked regular beats, exercised considerable discretion, and by the mid 1850s were armed and uniformed.

Fire protection was originally provided by middle-class volunteer fire companies, but by the 1830s they had become lower-class fraternal and athletic clubs, centers of ethnic, occupational, or neighborhood gangs more interested in racing or in fighting than in quenching fires. Businessmen and fire insurance underwriters lobbied for tougher fire codes, advanced technology, and professionalized fire departments in order to improve fire-fighting capabilities. Most cities established professional fire departments by the 1860s, including Chicago

(1858) and New York (1865)—usually following a disastrous fire.

Physicians, journalists, and health faddists pressured municipalities to take greater responsibility for public health. Key problems included potable water; epidemics (cholera killed 10 percent of the population of Saint Louis in 1849); infant mortality, which surpassed 50 percent in New York at mid century; and clean streets. The first major action occurred in Philadelphia. The city had a history of yellow fever, and in 1798 established its own water system. New York followed suit in 1842, yet as late as 1860, one-fourth of major cities still relied on private water companies that inadequately serviced poor neighborhoods. Cities dealt ineptly with sewers and streets. As late as the 1850s, New York and Chicago still used pigs as scavengers, and only around 1860 were private street cleaning companies hired. Chicago dealt with the sewage problem in the late 1850s by raising street levels so the refuse would flow into Lake Michigan, the source of its water supply. At mid century, one-fourth of city budgets went to paving and cleaning streets, principally major commercial avenues, yet by 1880 only one-half of streets were paved, making street sweeping difficult. Seventy percent of cities had public street cleaning in 1880, but only one-fourth had municipal garbage collection.

The public health movement further advocated that cities provide breathing spaces for moral and health purposes. These needs were first fulfilled by private romantic cemeteries like Cambridge's Mount Auburn (1831), which had landscaped gardens, tree-lined walks, and lakes that provided picnickers an escape from urban hustle and bustle. A municipal park movement emerged in the 1840s to secure fresh air and sites for exercise to make workers healthier, develop choice new neighborhoods, and promote the reputation of cities. New York's secluded 840-acre Central Park (1858), designed by Frederick Law Olmsted and Calvert Vaux with rustic areas and formal gardens, became the model for future suburban parks.

Moral reform was largely in the hands of middle-class voluntary societies motivated by Christian morality and fears about the urban milieu. They advocated public education to promote order by indoctrinating immigrant children with traditional values and behavior and training them for jobs. Boston was the first major city to have a public education system (1818), followed by New York (1832) and Philadelphia (1836), and such systems were commonplace outside the South by 1860. The

Children's Aid Society (1853) publicized the plight of homeless children and sent them to rural foster homes where they would have a good family environment, learn the work ethic, and become healthier. The temperance movement sought to curtail drinking, the reputed root of poverty, unreliable workers, and crime. Penal reformers promoted asylumlike penitentiaries to rehabilitate deviants by separating them from a bad environment and indoctrinating them with Christian morality, a work ethic, and respect for authority. Charity was limited to the deserving poor of high moral character. Thus pregnant women lacking proof of good moral character were turned away from New York's Asylum for Lying-in Women.

Reformers admired the home as the locus of female domesticity and a sanctuary from an increasingly dangerous outside world. Urban families were nuclear and smaller than in the past, but were frequently extended to include unmarried relatives, servants, or boarders. Women were expected to be exclusively homemakers, but poorer wives could not be, and at mid century about one-tenth held jobs, primarily as domestics. They comprised one-fourth of manufacturing workers. Schoolteaching, an extension of the domestic domain, was the only appropriate profession for middle-class young women. In 1860, they comprised nearly four-fifths of teachers in heavily urban Massachusetts. Middle-class women's activities outside the home were largely limited to shopping, often at massive new department stores like A. T. Stewart's in New York, with their elegant interiors and huge inventories; to services at evangelical churches, where they comprised a majority; and to reformist voluntary organizations through which they extended their domestic role.

Cities were major destinations for Irish and German immigrants who came to America at mid century to escape poverty and persecution. More than two-fifths of New Orleans; over half of New York, Boston, and San Francisco; and over three-fifths of Saint Louis, Chicago, and Milwaukee were foreign born. The Irish settled mainly in eastern cities and the Germans in the Midwest, both groups in ethnic villages that helped to ease culture shock. Germans were geographically highly concentrated—in 1860, 83 percent in Milwaukee lived with their own kind, compared with 47 percent of the Irish and 53 percent of the native born. Their neighborhoods provided a full range of Old World institutions, including beer gardens, delicatessens, and turnvereins. Germans arrived with skills, liter-

acy and some capital, and fared far better than the poor, uneducated, and unskilled Irish, who got the lowest-level jobs. At mid century over half of New York's day laborers were Irishmen, and three-fourths of Irishwomen were domestics. They endured deadly riots and other hostility from nativists because of anti-Catholicism, job competition, and political rivalries between native-born Whigs and Know-Nothings and Irish machine Democrats.

Antebellum blacks were the least urban ethnic group. There were sizable free African American communities in southern cities in the 1820s whose residents were relatively more skilled and dispersed than in the North. Three-fourths of free black Charlestonians in 1860 were artisans, primarily barbers, carpenters, and caterers, comprising 16 percent of the city's skilled workers. Northern blacks were overwhelmingly urban, encountered severe prejudice—they could seldom vote or serve on juries, were subject to race riots, and even expulsion—and lived in highly concentrated neighborhoods where segregation encouraged the establishment of a wide-reaching community including churches and mutual aid, educational, and fraternal societies seldom seen in the South except in New Orleans. About one-tenth of slaves lived in cities where they worked as servants, craftsmen, and factory laborers. They comprised over half of the work force in Charleston and Richmond, where feared contacts with freedmen and whites resulted in stringent restrictive laws and, after 1840, a stable slave population.

THE INDUSTRIAL RADIAL CITY

The United States emerged as an urban country in 1920, with over half the population (51.4 percent) residing in cities. The national culture was shaped by urban values, attitudes, and behavior, and cities became a focus of the federal government. Sixty-eight cities had over 100,000 residents, led by New York with 5.6 million. The post–Civil War city differed dramatically from the walking city because it was much bigger, had a larger and more heterogeneous population, enjoyed cheap mass transit, and had highly specialized land uses and industry-based economies. Radial cities were the locus of powerful political machines, impoverished slums, and ethnic villages that encouraged the rise of the Progressive movement to promote political democracy, social justice, economic opportunity, and moral order. These cities promised a better life for poor immigrants, rural dwellers fleeing boring small town society, and African Americans escaping Jim Crow laws.

Urban spatial relationships were reshaped by the emergence of cheap, rapid mass transit. The geographic distribution of businesses, industries, and homes was altered by soaring land costs in the old urban core and expansion toward the periphery made possible by improved transportation. By the mid 1880s, horse-drawn streetcars were used in three hundred cities, supplemented in fourteen major cities by cable cars. In 1888 fast (ten to twelve miles per hour), reliable electric trolleys were introduced, in Richmond, Virginia, and two years later there were 1,260 miles of electrified tracks, compared with 500 miles of cable car tracks and 5,700 miles served by horse-drawn vehicles. In 1902, 22,000 miles of urban tracks were electrified, including elevated routes over crowded downtown streets. Even more advanced were subways, built in Boston (1897), Philadelphia (1908), and especially New York (1904), which had a one-hundred-mile system by 1920. Traction lines required large capital investments for expensive equipment and consolidations, and great political clout (or bribes) to secure necessary franchises and rights of way; nevertheless, they generated substantial profits from millions of five cent rides. Traction lines enhanced real estate values along their routes and facilitated urban sprawl, streetcar suburbs, annexations (Chicago in 1889 grew from 35 to 185 square miles and added 200,000 residents), and consolidations like the merger of Brooklyn and New York in 1898.

Streetcar traffic increased steadily until about 1923, when it began to encounter strong competition from automobiles. Several major cities, particularly Los Angeles and Detroit, dropped plans for subways, opting for better roads instead. By 1930, more than 50 percent of nonfarm families owned a car, typically the cheap Model T, and that ownership had an enormous impact on urban life. Riders traveled independently of fixed streetcar routes and schedules, could live in suburbia, and had greater leisure options, ranging from picnics to necking in the back seat. Furthermore, hundreds of thousands of jobs were created in production, repair, and related industries, and trucks greatly lowered freight costs.

The enhanced mass transit and skyrocketing realty values combined to create central business districts. In Chicago, for example, downtown property values rose by 700 percent between 1877 and 1891, making the old urban core too expensive for housing or factories. The central business district became the locus of administrative, financial, and commercial activities, cultural institutions, and light industry. Suburbanites worked in its office buildings, tourists and business travelers stayed at its hotels, and housewives shopped at its specialty shops and department stores. High land-costs encouraged construction of taller structures, originally built with thick brick or masonry walls limiting interior space. An important improvement was the modern skyscraper. Chicago's ten-story Home Life Insurance Building (1885) was the first, employing a lightweight steel skeleton frame. Tenants of skyscrapers were independent professionals and major companies that centralized large bureaucracies in monumental structures erected for self-advertising, exemplified by Manhattan's fifty-five-story Woolworth Building (1913). New York was the site of nearly half of all American skyscrapers. Its skyline symbolized the city's stature, topped off in the early 1930s by the 102-story Empire State Building.

The central business district was surrounded by concentric rings of residential housing beginning with the slums—impoverished, densely populated, heterogeneous residential areas. Slums had inadequate municipal services and high rates of poverty, substandard housing, infant mortality, communicable diseases, and crime. Housing stock included cellars, shacks, lofts, subdivided warehouses and former mansions, and six-to-eight-story tenements constructed after the Civil War that housed up to 150 individuals—with a single water tap per floor, no ventilation, little light, and outdoor privies. Eighty percent of inner-city families had both parents present and were nuclear, although 20 percent included lodgers to help pay the rent.

Outside the slums were lower-middle and upper-lower-class residential neighborhoods, comprised mainly of modest single-family homes purchased with short-term mortgages from savings and loan associations. Residents included native-born craftsmen and second-generation blue-collar Germans and Irishmen. These urbanites worried about protecting what they had earned and feared the encroachment of slum dwellers into their communities. In the 1920s, they became prime candidates for Ku Klux Klan recruiters. Half of Klan members lived in cities of over fifty thousand, especially in the South and Midwest.

The final concentric ring was the suburban periphery. It was a safe, homogeneous, middle-class

WASP area of large single-family homes with enclosed yards. Residents employed mass transit to travel to work, play, or shopping. Middle-class folk also lived in modest new apartments constructed along major streetcar routes. They were modeled on the luxury apartments of the rich located near the central business district in such exclusive neighborhoods as Chicago's Gold Coast. The rich also had other housing options, ranging from Fifth Avenue mansions to suburban estates.

Industry drove the economy of northeastern and midwestern cities, employing the American system of manufacturing and taking advantage of cheap labor, capital, consumer demand, and support services. Factories relocated to the outskirts or satellite suburbs like Gary, Indiana, where land was cheap, taxes were low, and bosses could exercise more control over their work force, particularly in company towns like Pullman, Illinois. By the 1910s several individual factories, including General Electric (Schenectady), International Harvester (Chicago), and U.S. Steel (Gary) had over fifteen thousand workers, and in the 1920s, sixty-eight thousand worked at Ford's River Rouge plant (Dearborn), the largest in the world.

The huge demand for low-paid unskilled and semi skilled workers was filled by immigrants who earned less than a family of four's minimal needs (fifteen dollars a week), and the entire family had to work at dehumanizing, dangerous, and boring jobs. Wives earned about half as much as their husbands, and children earned one-fourth. Advancement in the late nineteenth century was unlikely. Only one-fifth to one-sixth of manual workers, mainly native-born whites, were vertically mobile. Workers progressed by establishing a savings account and acquiring property. Urbanites were geographically mobile, especially the native-born who moved to better themselves. One in four urban residents moved each year, and the ten-year persistence rate was typically around 50 percent.

The industrial city was a metropolis of immigrants and their children. In 1910, 41 percent of urbanites were foreign-born. Three-fourths of immigrants lived in cities, led by Russian Jews (89 percent), Irish (87 percent), Italians (84 percent), and Poles (80 percent). Milwaukee was nearly 90 percent first- or second-generation immigrant; New York and Chicago, 80 percent. The new immigrants came from traditional societies and were mostly uneducated, unskilled, and indigent, unprepared for urban America. Their goal was not to surpass their fathers but to get a manly job, support their family, and purchase a home as insurance for old age. Jewish migrants were different because they had no homeland, were seldom formerly peasants, were more educated or at least respected scholarship, and had skills (tailoring) and an entrepreneurial tradition. Consequently, they were about two and a half times more likely to end up with a white-collar job than were other new immigrants.

The new immigrants lived in ethnic villages in slum neighborhoods where they reestablished old institutions like churches, maintained high rates of endogamy, and started mutual aid societies, social and athletic clubs, foreign-language newspapers, and parochial schools. Twenty to forty percent of schoolchildren in major immigrant cities attended Catholic schools. Children attended public school briefly because they were uncomfortable, parents feared Americanization, and their labor was needed. Immigrants were marginal people with one foot in each of two different worlds. Daughters were closely supervised but boys were not, and they often grew up tough and street smart. They frequently joined street gangs, hungry for recognition, excitement, money, and a sense of belonging. The gangs provided good training for future boxers and hoodlums.

On the other hand, African Americans, 90 percent of whom resided in the South, were the least urban group. In 1900 only 17 percent of black southerners were urbanites. The great migration north began in 1916, caused by the boll weevil's devastation of cotton fields, the availability of factory work, and aspirations for a safer and better life. Within five years the number of black men in major industrial cities more than doubled, but usually they worked in low-level, dead-end jobs; black women were predominantly domestics. They lived in slums that became ghettos because of white flight, discrimination, blockbusting, and violence against blacks who tried to move into white neighborhoods. African Americans had legal access to schools and public accommodations but encountered prejudice, embarrassment, lower-quality facilities, and brutality if they contested traditional exclusionary customs. Discrimination and ghettoization created opportunities for blacks to service their community's financial, cultural, recreational, and cosmetic needs, resulting in the emergence of such institutions as black insurance firms, newspapers, and baseball leagues. The concentration of black voters increased black political power, and in

1928 Chicago Republican Oscar De Priest became the first northern African American elected to Congress.

The city was the locus of a vibrant culture. A major city was expected to have several newspapers and such institutions of high culture as museums, a symphony, a public library, and universities. Popular recreation was cheap and accessible, enjoyed at such public sites as streets, parks, and beaches; semipublic facilities like amusement parks, arenas, ballparks, racetracks, dance halls, saloons, and vaudeville and movie theaters; and private social and athletic clubs. Urban recreation was largely class based until the 1920s, when higher wages and a shorter workweek democratized leisure. Until Prohibition, the saloon served as the poor man's club; workingmen also favored indoor sports like boxing, bowling, and billiards, and accessible resorts like Coney Island. Thereafter they could afford commercialized spectator sports and had greater access to municipal parks. In the 1920s crowds surpassing fifty thousand attended professional baseball and college football games, boxing championships, horse races, and the Indianapolis 500. However, the most popular entertainment was the movies, which had emerged from inner city nickelodeons in the early 1900s into luxurious, large downtown theaters a decade later.

Lord Bryce (*The American Commonwealth,* 1888) and other early social critics described city government, run by corrupt, self-serving politicians, as the worst American institution. From the 1880s to 1914 nearly 80 percent of the largest cities had machine-run governments, at least for a brief period. They grew stronger over time; in the largest cities during the 1930s, one-third had been in power for over two decades. The boss usually operated from behind the scenes, but a few were also long-term mayors, like Martin Behrman of New Orleans (1900–1920, 1925–1926) and Frank Hague of Jersey City (1917–1947). Machines were not ideologically oriented but cranked out the vote with precision by providing patronage and other services to inner city constituents, or by fixing elections through payoffs or intimidation.

Bosses dispensed personalized government, providing help to people who could turn to no one else, ranging from fixing a traffic ticket to food, relief, and jobs. They sponsored outings, secured preferential treatment from the municipality for business allies, awarded utility franchises and valuable contracts to politically connected entrepreneurs, and gave organized crime a free hand. Boss

Richard Croker of New York (1886–1895, 1898–1902) grew rich on "honest" graft, using inside information to make astute investments or securing stock and contracts from firms seeking city business. His colleague George Washington Plunkitt distinguished this from "dishonest" graft, which was stealing from the city or taking payoffs to protect criminal activity.

Bosses centralized power and decision making, modernized city politics, and promoted urban development, building the urban infrastructure, albeit inefficiently and at a great cost. They were not omnipotent, however, as commonly believed. Tammany Hall, for instance, did not have complete control over New York's Democratic party until 1886, when a disciplined coalition of ward bosses was established on the basis of patronage and election victories. And even under Croker, Tammany did not win every major election, often because of scandals resulting from police corruption.

Furthermore, as David Hammack has pointed out, power in New York was so diffused because of ethnic, religious, and philosophical differences that neither machines nor urban elites could unilaterally postulate a coherent policy, much less act decisively. Finally, rural Republican control of state legislatures made it difficult for machine liberals such as Al Smith and Robert Wagner to repeal restrictive blue laws or enact such reforms as factory regulations or housing codes to improve conditions for their constituents.

Political corruption, urban pathology, growing anomie, and the need for improved public services encouraged the rise of urban reform in the late nineteenth century under the leadership of upper-class mugwumps, investigative journalists, Social Gospelers, the new professionals, and settlement workers. The reform impulse culminated in the Progressive movement (ca. 1900–ca. 1916), which sought to ameliorate life in impersonalized, segmented cities by promoting efficiency, social justice, political democracy, and economic opportunity.

In the 1880s, businessmen seeking efficient and honest government inaugurated the civic reform movement to investigate corruption, elect and promote "the best men," restructure government so as to weaken political machines, and improve sanitation, police, and fire services. They established local good government groups that affiliated into the National Municipal League (1894), which had moderate success electing reform candidates. Certain reform mayors, most notably Hazen Pingree of Detroit (1890–1897), did achieve major accomplishments. Pingree employed business principles to efficiently build parks and schools, reduce utility rates, and cut corruption while making no effort to impose Yankee norms on the new urban folk. Pingree's example was duplicated in the Progressive era by Samuel M. ("Golden Rule") Jones (1897–1904) and Brand Whitlock (1905–1913) in Toledo and Jim Loftin Johnson (1901–1909) in Cleveland.

Since a few good men could not clean up corruption, reformers advocated structural changes including greater home rule, secret ballots, nonpartisan, at-large elections, and stronger administrative schemes, such as the city manager and the commission system in which experts administered urban agencies. Midwestern and western cities secured greater home rule under new charters that took power from councilmen elected from readily corruptible wards and gave greater authority to mayors. The commission system had its first major test in 1900 in Galveston, Texas, following a devastating flood that killed over 7,200 people. It was a success, and by 1917 had been adopted in nearly five hundred mostly small cities. The city manager system was first employed in Staunton, Virginia, in 1908, and within fifteen years 270 largely suburban cities had adopted it.

Settlement workers were among the most liberal Progressives. The first American settlement house was New York's Neighborhood Guild (1886); there were over four hundred by 1910, located in slums and staffed by idealistic middle-class men and women. Volunteers sought to identify neighborhood problems and then arrive at solutions. Settlements offered classes in English, civics, crafts, and job skills; employment bureaus; and recreational facilities ranging from gymnasiums to theaters. In addition, the workers promoted reforms in juvenile justice, playgrounds, housing, public health, and morality.

WASP reformers like Anthony Comstock of the Society for the Suppression of Vice (1873) tried to impose traditional middle-class behavior upon urbanites by fighting immorality. Crusaders expanded temperance into a prohibition movement against the ubiquitous workingman's saloon (New York had seven thousand in 1880), a reputed cause of poverty and broken families, and center of crime and political corruption. Ironically, the Eighteenth Amendment generated a boom in organized crime that had originated in late-nineteenth-century politically protected Irish crime syndicates involved in gambling and prostitution. Vice was rampant in ur-

ban slums and red light districts like Chicago's Levee district, where gambling and prostitution operated freely. Occasional crackdowns followed investigations of police corrupted by gamblers and madams, and hysteric episodes over white slavery. Chicago closed its vice district in 1911, and about one hundred cities followed suit during World War I, most notably New Orleans (Storyville). However, vice soon reemerged in the slums and in working-class suburbs.

Progressive professionals advocated urban planning to address the quality of urban life while creating the efficient city. It began as the City Beautiful Movement that sought to enhance urban life by improving civic design, the impetus coming from Chicago's Columbian Exposition (1893), which influenced public architecture, municipal art, and planning. Fair coordinator Daniel Burnham's comprehensive Chicago Plan of 1909 marked a transition to the City Efficient Movement, directing environmental reform through spatial policies. Planners coordinated mass transit with planned land uses like garden cities, and employed zoning regulations for rational separation of incompatible land uses or buildings and protection of existing areas. New York in 1916 was the first city to introduce comprehensive zoning by establishing specific land use areas, limiting building heights, and restricting lot use to prevent the garment district from expanding toward Fifth Avenue. Ten years later, 591 cities had zoning codes.

The federal government first became deeply involved in the problems of cities during the Great Depression, when urban unemployment skyrocketed from 3.2 percent in 1929 to 15.9 percent in 1931 and 24.9 percent in 1933. In 1932, for instance, 1 million New Yorkers (30 percent), six hundred thousand Chicagoans (40 percent), and far greater proportions in industrial and mining cities (90 percent in Gary, Indiana) were out of work. By the end of 1930, the seventy-five largest municipalities appropriated $420 million for public works. Detroit's relief expenditures rose from $2.4 million in 1929 to $14.9 million in 1931. Cities tried to cope by borrowing, introducing sales taxes, and printing scrip to pay municipal workers. Little assistance came from the Hoover administration, save $300 million from the Reconstruction Finance Corporation.

Urbanites provided the backbone of Franklin Roosevelt's constituency, and the New Deal immediately responded with relief, recovery, and reform programs. Jobs were the biggest problem. The Federal Emergency Relief Administration distributed

$500 million, mainly for work relief. In the winter of 1933–1934 about 8 million families received federal assistance, half from Civil Works Administration minimum-wage projects. The Public Works Administration (1933) promoted recovery through planned public works, especially in New York, where Robert Moses secured one-seventh of its allocations. The majority of Works Progress Administration (1935) grants went to the fifty largest cities, providing work relief (1936–1941) for nearly one-fifth of the work force in public construction projects and in programs like the Writers' Project that supported the arts.

Housing was another major problem. Hundreds of thousands had lost their homes (in 1933 there were one thousand home foreclosures a day), and the construction industry was moribund. The New Deal promoted recovery by establishing the Home Owners' Loan Corporation (1933) to stabilize the mortgage business, and the Federal Housing Administration (1934) to refinance private loans at 4 percent for up to thirty years. The Public Works Administration financed slum clearance and public housing, and the U.S. Housing Authority (1937) helped the neediest with $500 million for loans and grants for slum clearance, and 47,500 new low-cost rental units.

The New Deal instilled public confidence in Washington's ability to cope with major problems and shape the direction of urban development. The federal government provided services once supplied by machines but did not supplant the bosses, who became brokers between Washington and their constituents, doling out jobs, relief, and construction projects.

URBAN AMERICA IN THE SUBURBAN AGE

The postwar metropolis was the locus of enormous change, much of it fostered by federal programs. The most important developments were suburbanization, the expansion of inner city ghettos, the decline of the northeastern and midwestern Rustbelt, and the emergence of the Sunbelt. The postwar city was an exciting and dynamic site of opportunity with industry prospering because of pent-up demand, the needs of baby boomers (consumer goods purchases tripled in fifteen years), and housing shortages. Hundreds of thousands of white veterans moved their growing families to suburbs using their government benefits, while central cities became increasingly black ghettos. By the 1960s, as the economy shifted into a postindustrial phase, the promise of the old industrial cities began to fade as problems mounted with the loss of jobs, fleeing taxpayers, growing impoverishment, spiraling disorder and violence, increasing needs for expensive public services, and an aging infrastructure. Thereafter the most dynamic areas were the suburbs and Sunbelt cities that became the desirable places to live.

As late as 1950, only one of the ten largest cities was located outside the Northeast and Midwest, but by 1980 half were in the booming Sunbelt. New York and Chicago had fewer residents in 1970 than twenty years before, and Saint Louis in 1980 had declined to the level of 1890! Columbus, Ohio, was the only major northern city to grow in the 1970s. The decline in the Rustbelt was tied to white flight to suburbia and the loss of industrial jobs through automation and factory relocation to suburbs and the Sunbelt—and abroad by the 1970s. In the latter decade the number of jobs in the Sunbelt rose by 40 percent, compared with 12.4 percent in the North. New York and Philadelphia alone lost 16 percent of their jobs between 1960 and 1972. The Sunbelt first boomed because of the need during the cold war for military bases and defense-related high-tech industries. It soon attracted an aging population who retired to warm climates (especially after the introduction of air conditioning), and lured industrialists, real estate developers, and entrepreneurs in leisure businesses because of weak unions, low taxes, cheap land, and improved roads and jet travel.

Thirty million Americans lived in suburbia in 1950 and seventy-six million by 1970, when the suburbs surpassed central cities in population (37.6 to 31.4 percent). These were mainly bedroom suburbs made accessible by such federal programs as G.I. loans, FHA mortgage insurance, and highway funding acts (1947, 1956), and by the low cost of cars and gasoline. Mass transit ridership peaked shortly after the war, but the automobile became so ubiquitous that by 1958 ridership on public transportation fell below the rate in 1900. Families left cities for privacy, lower taxes, escape from declining neighborhoods and rising crime, and a higher quality of life that included better schools, parks, and other public services. The new suburbs included totally planned communities like Levittown, New York, and Park Forest, Illinois, where mortgages cost less than rent. Among the fastest growing was Anaheim, California, located at an exit on the Santa Ana Freeway and home to Disneyland, which increased from 17,267 residents in 1952 to 91,100 seven years later.

Urban leaders after World War II encouraged development and the protection of assets by improving highways, ports, and airports, and revitalizing central business districts. Physical expansion was impossible in eastern and midwestern cities because there was no room outside their old boundaries. Pittsburgh and Philadelphia provided a model by employing insurance company capital to refurbish the central business district through cleaning and brightening it up, and enhancing accessibility with buses and underground parking. Pro-development businessmen worked with like-minded politicians, including reformers like De-Lesseps Morrison in New Orleans, bosses like Richard Daley of Chicago, and professional politicians like Robert Wagner of New York, who hired able administrators and secured revenue for capital improvements.

There was far less cooperation from conservative, self-interested business leaders, especially in Sunbelt cities like Dallas, Houston, and Los Angeles, who used their power in publishing, banking, and insurance to shape major policy decisions according to their personal interests. These cities had considerable space available for expansion, mainly through annexation (Phoenix thereby grew from 17 to 187 square miles), that promised greater efficiency and prestige. Consolidations, on the other hand, were quite rare, most notably the Miami/Dade County metropolitan federation (1957), established to avoid duplication of governmental services.

Civic leaders usually focused on the central business district, giving less attention to the needs of residential neighborhoods. One-fifth of urban homes were substandard after the war, and cities began to rely on Washington for assistance. The Housing Act of 1949 sought to eliminate substandard areas and provide decent homes and environments through slum clearance, public housing, and an expansion of FHA mortgage insurance. However, FHA hurt working-class neighborhoods by recommending that developers build homogeneous tracts and redlining inner city areas by refusing to guarantee loans in localities that had older homes or were likely to experience black encroachment. Stable lower-class areas were ruined because mortgages became unavailable, homeowners could not get loans for home improvements,

and merchants had a hard time getting affordable insurance.

Developers were expected mainly to construct low-cost public housing on the cleared sites, but frequently they evaded the spirit of the law by building luxury apartments, parking lots, shopping malls, or even factories that urban boosters applauded, anticipating an enhanced tax base and revitalization of decaying areas. It was expected to take six years to build 810,000 new units, but it took twenty. Meanwhile, about three times as many units were abandoned or razed for highways or urban renewal. The new public housing failed to promote communities as originally planned, and became places to hide the urban poor. Huge multistory developments like Chicago's Robert Taylor Homes, built in the early 1960s, became dangerous places where residents were intimidated by gangs and afraid to leave their apartments.

Working-class communities got another jolt in 1954 when Washington changed its emphasis from redevelopment to urban renewal. The new goal was to fix up decaying neighborhoods to attract more affluent residents, revitalize investment opportunities, and protect the central business district. Neighborhoods that residents considered alive and worth protecting, like Boston's West End, were bulldozed for urban renewal or highways with little concern for dislodged residents. Viable or potentially viable communities were replaced by public or semipublic institutions such as university campuses (University of Illinois on Chicago's Near West Side), baseball parks (Dodger Stadium in Los Angeles's Chavez Ravine), convention centers, and hotels. Displaced residents and small businessmen seldom received adequate assistance.

Major development plans after the 1960s continued to focus on the central business district in hopes of encouraging confidence, investment, resettlement, and tourism. Municipalities improved public transportation with downtown bus malls in Portland and Minneapolis, and subways in San Francisco (1972) and Washington (1976); constructed major symbols of progress like arches, domed stadiums, convention centers, and malls; and supported private restorations of historic but run-down waterfronts like Baltimore's Harborplace and dilapidated markets like Seattle's Pike Place Market. Local governments also supported refurbishment of older inner city housing to attract affluent youthful taxpayers seeking exciting, safe, and convenient neighborhoods. Gentrification began in the 1960s at Philadelphia's Society Hill and Washington's Capitol Hill, and thereafter spread to most major cities, improving their tax base but showing little consideration for those displaced.

The combination of declining industrial employment and the migration of the middle class to suburbia resulted in a major shift in urban demographics and social structure. This was exemplified in the 1970s by the first decline of median family income among urban core residents. The flight of the middle class was crucial because they paid the taxes; supported businesses, cultural institutions, and schools; and promoted social and political reform. Public school demography dramatized the changes: two-thirds of New York's public school students were white in 1957; 14 percent were white in 1987. People had lost their confidence in the city and no longer believed that its problems could be solved. Cities tried to raise taxes to make up for lost revenues and to defer maintenance and services, which encouraged more businesses to leave. New York's infrastructure began to collapse in the late 1960s: buildings were abandoned, and one out of eight residents were on welfare. The outcome was financial collapse in 1975, and a bailout by Washington.

The people left behind and the new in-migrants were increasingly poor people of color. A second great black migration had occurred during World War II, and it continued after the war. By 1970 three-fourths of African Americans lived in cities, comprising the majority in Washington, D.C. (71.1 percent), Newark, Gary, and Atlanta. One decade later, they were a majority in Detroit, Baltimore, New Orleans, and Birmingham as well. Nearly all of the increase between 1950 and 1966 (86 percent) occurred in central cities at a time when 70 percent of white increase was in suburbia. There was also a postwar boom in Spanish-speaking urban populations. New York's Puerto Rican population rose from 61,000 in 1940 to 613,000 in 1960. Ten years later the city was 10 percent Puerto Rican. Substantial Puerto Rican communities have also been established in mid-sized industrial cities in the metropolitan New York region and in Philadelphia, Cleveland, and Chicago. By the late 1980s Miami had a Hispanic majority. It has elected Puerto Rican and Cuban mayors, and the social climate is set by its Cuban immigrants, who have made it the economic capital of the Caribbean. On the West Coast, one-third of Los Angeles in 1980 was Hispanic, and one-tenth Asian.

These newcomers generally ended up in ghettos like New York's Bedford-Stuyvesant, Chicago's West Side, or Los Angeles's Watts, whose popula-

tions greatly increased and whose boundaries expanded. White residents in zones of emergence used various methods to prevent integration, including neighborhood improvement associations that promoted solidarity and political pressure on elected officials, restrictive covenants (illegal since 1947), zoning laws to encourage stability, and violence. The ghetto residents lived in decayed, overcrowded housing, had substandard educational and health facilities, high unemployment, few well-paying jobs with advancement opportunities, and high rates of crime.

Widespread frustrations, epitomized by the black power movement, provided the underpinnings for the eruption of racial hostilities in the summers of 1964 through 1968, when there were about seventy-five "commodity riots." These involved the destruction of neighborhood shops and property, largely white-owned, whereas race riots encompassed interracial conflict over contested turf. About 10 percent of local residents looted white-owned neighborhood stores that symbolized oppression and the unfulfilled expectations of the civil rights movement. The worst violence occurred in Detroit in 1967; forty-three died and two thousand were injured. The riots drew national attention to the problems of the black ghettos and led to increased federal assistance to the inner city.

The black power movement energized the community into grassroots political activity ranging from New York's local school district elections to campaigning for mayors. The first African American mayor of a major city was Carl B. Stokes of Cleveland (1967), who promoted public housing and urban services. By 1970 there were black mayors in fifty cities, primarily those with large African American populations, and by 1990 African Americans had been elected mayor in New York, Chicago, and most of the largest cities, generally because of exceptionally strong black turnouts at the polls.

The riots were an important reason that cities in the 1960s received renewed positive attention from Washington under Democratic administrations already influenced by the "discovery" of poverty in Michael Harrington's *The Other America* (1962). Lyndon Johnson's $390 million Great Society program comprised a variety of initiatives to fight the War on Poverty. In 1964 the Office of Economic Opportunity established such programs as the Job Corps, Head Start, and the community action programs that empowered neighborhood service agencies. Johnson expanded food stamp and urban housing programs and established the Model Cities program (1966), which targeted federal funds for thirty-six neighborhoods, relying on local involvement to coordinate programs to enhance education, housing, health, and jobs. By 1969, total federal expenditures for cities soared to $14 billion, and the number of Americans below the poverty line was cut nearly in half. Under the Nixon administration funds nearly doubled by 1974, but the administration sought to reduce Washington's role in local affairs, first by cutting allocations and reducing or eliminating programs, and later by New Federalism (1972), which gave local governments policy planning responsibilities.

While the federal share of local budgets rose from 15 percent in 1960 to 25 percent in 1975, revenue sharing ended up mainly benefiting suburbia. Ghetto conditions seem to have gotten worse rather than better. African American males have a hard time finding employment (black teenagers' unemployment nearly doubled between 1965 and 1980, to 46.9 percent, reflecting their poor education and lack of access to jobs), and black female-headed households are nearly the norm, rising from about 20 percent in 1960 to 43 percent in 1988. The result is pervasive hopelessness and gang violence among a young and seemingly permanent underclass.

THE FUTURE OF THE CITY

Cities are likely to remain the focal point of economics, government, culture, and innovation for residents of metropolitan districts. Institutions like corporate offices and sports arenas may move to greener pastures, but museums, libraries, and universities are less mobile. Long-term efforts to sustain historic institutions and enterprises by protecting and rebuilding the central business district remain important. Cities will also have to attend to their infrastructure before highways and bridges begin to crumble. These are difficult tasks as revenue sources dry up, historically powerless and voiceless people with their own agendas gain political power, and the gap between the haves and have-nots broadens. Low levels of academic achievement, rising crime rates, and growing proportions of female-headed households provide the potential for a frightening future. Scholars and planners believe there needs to be a balanced metropolitan vision for the future based on a pluralistic symbiotic model with greater shared responsibilities. Yet even more basic is the enormous need for jobs and development in the urban ghettos before conditions become so intolerable and unacceptable that anarchy emerges.

POPULATION OF LEADING U.S. CITIES

1690		1800	
1. Boston	7,000	Philadelphia	69,000
2. Philadelphia	4,000	New York	60,000
3. New York	3,900	Baltimore	26,000
4. Newport	2,600	Boston	25,000
5. Charleston	1,100	Charleston	20,000

1850		1900	
1. New York	515,500	New York	3,437,202
2. Philadelphia	340,000	Chicago	1,698,575
3. Baltimore	169,600	Philadelphia	1,293,697
4. Boston	136,880	Saint Louis	575,238
5. New Orleans	116,375	Boston	560,892
6. Cincinnati	115,435	Baltimore	508,957
7. Brooklyn	96,838	Cleveland	381,768
8. Saint Louis	77,860	Buffalo	352,367
9. Albany	50,763	San Francisco	342,782
10. Pittsburgh	46,601	Cincinnati	325,902
11. Louisville	43,194	Pittsburgh	321,616
12. Buffalo	42,260	New Orleans	287,104
13. Providence	41,573	Detroit	285,704
14. Washington	40,001	Milwaukee	285,315
15. Newark	38,890	Washington	278,718
16. Rochester	36,403	Newark	246,070
17. San Francisco	34,776	Louisville	204,731
18. Chicago	29,963	Minneapolis	202,718
19. Detroit	21,019	Indianapolis	169,164
20. Milwaukee	20,061	Kansas City	163,752

1950		1988	
1. New York	7,891,957	New York	7,352,700
2. Chicago	3,620,962	Los Angeles	3,352,710
3. Philadelphia	2,071,605	Chicago	2,977,520
4. Los Angeles	1,970,358	Houston	1,698,090
5. Detroit	1,849,568	Philadelphia	1,647,000
6. Baltimore	949,708	San Diego	1,070,310
7. Cleveland	914,808	Detroit	1,035,920
8. Saint Louis	856,796	Dallas	987,360
9. Washington	802,178	San Antonio	941,150
10. Boston	801,444	Phoenix	923,750
11. San Francisco	775,357	Baltimore	751,400
12. Pittsburgh	676,806	San Jose	738,420
13. Milwaukee	637,392	San Francisco	731,600
14. Houston	596,163	Indianapolis	727,130
15. Buffalo	580,132	Memphis	645,190
16. New Orleans	570,445	Jacksonville	635,430
17. Minneapolis	521,718	Washington	617,000
18. Cincinnati	503,998	Milwaukee	599,380
19. Seattle	467,591	Boston	577,830
20. Kansas City	456,622	Columbus	569,750

SOURCES: Carl Bridenbaugh, *Cities in the Wilderness: The First Century of Urban Life in America, 1625–1742* (1964), 143; Marshall A. Smelser, *The Democratic Republic, 1801–1815* (1968), 22; Howard P. Chudacoff, *The Evolution of American Urban Society* (1975), 56; *World Almanac and Book of Facts, 1989*, 538–539; *Information Please Almanac, 1991*, 787.

SPACE AND PLACE

BIBLIOGRAPHY

General Works

Chudacoff, Howard P., and Judith E. Smith. *The Evolution of American Urban Society.* 3d ed. (1988).

Goldfield, David R., and Blaine A. Brownell. *Urban America: A History.* 2d ed. (1990).

The Early American City

Bridenbaugh, Carl. *Cities in the Wilderness: The First Century of Urban Life in America, 1625–1742* (1938).

———. *Cities in Revolt: Urban Life in America, 1743–1776* (1955).

Lebsock, Suzanne. *The Free Women of Petersburg: Status and Culture in a Southern Town, 1784–1860* (1984).

Nash, Gary B. *The Urban Crucible: Social Change, Political Consciousness, and the Origins of the American Revolution* (1979).

The Walking City

Blumin, Stuart M. *The Emergence of the Middle Class: Social Experience in the American City, 1760–1900* (1989). Also invaluable on the early American city.

Boyer, Paul S. *Urban Masses and Moral Order in America, 1820–1920* (1978). Also excellent on the industrial city.

Dawley, Alan. *Class and Community: The Industrial Revolution in Lynn* (1976).

Stansell, Christine. *City of Women: Sex and Class in New York, 1789–1860* (1986).

Thernstrom, Stephan. *Poverty and Progress: Social Mobility in a Nineteenth-Century City* (1964).

Wade, Richard C. *The Urban Frontier: The Rise of Western Cities, 1790–1830* (1959).

———. *Slavery in the Cities: The South, 1820–1860* (1964).

Wilentz, Sean. *Chants Democratic: New York City and the Rise of the American Working Class, 1788–1850* (1984).

The Industrial Radial City

Barrett, James R. *Work and Community in the Jungle: Chicago's Packinghouse Workers, 1894–1922* (1987).

Barth, Gunther Paul. *City People: The Rise of Modern City Culture in Nineteenth-Century America* (1980).

Cohen, Lizabeth. *Making a New Deal: Industrial Workers in Chicago, 1919–1939* (1990).

Grossman, James R. *Land of Hope: Chicago, Black Southerners and the Great Migration* (1989).

Hammack, David C. *Power and Society: Greater New York at the Turn of the Century* (1982).

Kantowicz, Edward R. *Polish-American Politics in Chicago, 1888–1940* (1975).

Kasson, John F. *Amusing the Millions: Coney Island at the Turn of the Century* (1978).

Mohl, Raymond A. *The New City: Urban America in the Industrial Age, 1860–1920* (1985).

Nelli, Humbert S. *Italians in Chicago, 1890–1930: A Study in Ethnic Mobility* (1970).

Philpott, Thomas Lee. *The Slum and the Ghetto: Neighborhood Deterioration and Middle-Class Reform. Chicago, 1880–1930* (1978).

Rabinowitz, Howard. *Race Relations in the Urban South, 1865–1890* (1978).

Riess, Steven A. *City Games: The Evolution of American Urban Society and the Rise of Sports* (1989).

Spear, Allan H. *Black Chicago: The Making of a Negro Ghetto, 1890–1920* (1967).

Thernstrom, Stephan. *The Other Bostonians: Poverty and Progress in the American Metropolis, 1880–1970* (1973).

Warner, Sam Bass, Jr. *Streetcar Suburbs: The Process of Growth in Boston, 1870–1900* (1962).

The City in the Metropolitan Era, 1945–1990

Abbott, Carl. *Urban America in the Modern Age, 1920 to the Present* (1987).

Caro, Robert. *The Power Broker: Robert Moses and the Fall of New York* (1974).

Fox, Kenneth. *Metropolitan America: Urban Life and Urban Policy in the United States, 1940–1980* (1986).

Gluck, Peter R., and Richard J. Meister. *Cities in Transition: Social Changes and Institutional Responses in Urban Development* (1979).

Hirsch, Arnold. *Making the Second Ghetto: Race and Housing in Chicago, 1940–1960* (1983).

SEE ALSO **Urbanization**; and various essays in the sections "**Methods and Contexts**," "**Patterns of Everyday Life**," "**Periods of Social Change**," "**Popular Culture and Recreation**," "**Regionalism and Regional Subcultures**," "**Space and Place**," and "**Work and Labor**."

THE SUBURBS

Ann Durkin Keating

IMAGES OF SUBURBS underlie much of American culture today. Television sitcoms from *The Dick Van Dyke Show* to *Roseanne* have made a suburban setting familiar, funny, and resonant with their American audiences. A 1962 Malvina Reynolds song, "Little Boxes," characterized suburbs where

> And the people in the houses
> All went to the university,
> Where they were put in boxes
> And they came out all the same.

In the early 1990s David Byrne sang of a suburban landscape full of Taco Bells and parking lots. Erma Bombeck's *The Grass Is Always Greener over the Septic Tank* (1976) is only one of many imaginatively titled volumes on suburban living that have been published since the 1950s.

American culture is suffused with suburban images because today it is overwhelmingly suburban. Kenneth T. Jackson, in his path-breaking synthesis of American suburban history, *Crabgrass Frontier* (1985), describes how the decades after World War II brought "the suburbanization of the United States." The evidence for such a process is manifold. Suburbs became the predominant home for Americans, with more than 40 percent of the population living in the suburbs, according to the 1980 census. Between 1950 and 1970, more than three-quarters of all new manufacturing and retail jobs were located in suburban areas. Overall between 1950 and 1970, 83 percent of the nation's total growth took place in suburbs. The overwhelming extent of this postwar suburbanization, with its trademark shopping malls, express highways, and industrial parks, leads many to assume that it *began* in 1945—which is not the case. Indeed, settlements on the fringes of cities are as old as the oldest American cities.

EARLY SUBURBS

The earliest suburbs bore little resemblance to the ideal described by the famous landscape architect and planner Frederick Law Olmsted (1822–1903): "the most attractive, the most refined, and the most soundly wholesome forms of domestic life, and the best application of the arts of civilization to which mankind has yet attained" (quoted in Fishman, *Bourgeois Utopias,* p. 198). Before improvements in urban transportation transformed the "walking city," the most highly prized residential locations were close to the center of town. In Europe this was a centuries-old tradition: those with wealth and influence lived in town, while the poor and other outcasts lived outside city walls. In the United States similar forces were at work, and the word "suburb" had definite pejorative connotations. Early-nineteenth-century Philadelphians, for instance, forced unwanted businesses, such as slaughterhouses, and people of lower status to the outskirts of the city.

The suburban villa was an important exception to low-status outlying settlements. It was in many respects the antecedent of the modern suburb. From ancient Greece to eighteenth-century England, the wealthy elites of many societies have had country estates and houses. Such houses were located on the outskirts of cities—far enough away to avoid city problems but close enough for easy travel to and from town. These estates had many of the amenities available in city homes because large retinues of servants ensured the provision of basic comforts such as heated rooms, baths, and lighting. Elite families with many servants operated as self-contained islands—regardless of whether they were in the city or the country. It was not until the development of mechanical systems to provide services and amenities—and all of the socioeconomic changes the elite relied upon—that proximity to neighbors and a community became important to the comfort of a household.

Robert Fishman places the birth of suburbia in late-eighteenth-century London. The tremendous growth of London during that century led to an urban crisis. Some called for reforms such as urban squares and wide streets to alleviate congestion and disorder. However, a growing repulsion toward the city, especially by middle-class merchants, led many to establish weekend villas where their families could escape London's turmoil. These merchants prized "picturesque," naturalistic landscapes. By concentrating villas while still employing picturesque landscaping, they created the first romantic suburbs. As Fishman describes an early suburb at Clapham, outside London, "each property is private, but each contributes to the total landscape of *houses in a park*" (p. 55). Manchester's Victoria Park and Liverpool's Rock Park, both designed in the 1830s, are other examples of early British romantic suburbs.

A similar process took hold in the United States within decades. In antebellum Chicago, the word "suburb" often described an outlying community that was a small agricultural town or an industrial site. There were no commuters in these areas, but the residents were tied more closely to cities than were their more distant counterparts by farming for the city and by coexisting with noxious industries that city dwellers gave rise to but would not tolerate. Frequently, newspaper accounts used the term as an adjective—a "suburban" villa or "suburban" home. For instance, "suburban" served to describe the second home of a wealthy Chicagoan whose family spent summers and holidays away from the congestion and disease of the city. It also characterized the home of a Chicagoan who had retired from an active life in the city to become a gentleman farmer. As time went on, real estate developers planned romantic suburbs such as Chicago's Riverside and Lake Forest; these places combined rural living with urban amenities.

THE SUBURB IN THE INDUSTRIAL ERA

In the nineteenth century, suburban communities developed across the United States as the demands of their residents—often newly transplanted from cities—for services and amenities came to resemble those of urbanites more than those of rural dwellers. Suburbs emerged from new communities as well as older rural settlements. Only after the emergence of uniquely urban services and amenities—which is to say, those unavailable in the countryside—did people feel a need for suburban governments, associations, or developers. Initially, transitional areas between the city and country contained some urban-oriented activities but had no special services to distinguish them from the adjacent countryside. As cities grew, though, they physically impinged upon these formerly outlying communities, causing many to take on the features of a suburb—that is, a place that sought to combine the services and amenities of the city with country living.

The solitary country estate with an army of servants gradually gave way to suburban communities with mechanical service improvements. This transition from human to mechanical supports extended the option of suburban living, formerly reserved for the wealthy, to the middle classes. Lewis Mumford argued that the widening economic base of the suburban movement in Britain in the early nineteenth century, and in the United States later in the century, was the result of transportation innovations. While transportation advances were certainly important in making suburban living possible and affordable for more people, it was the extension of urban amenities to outlying communities that permitted the modern suburb. This is not to say that they negated disparities in wealth, though; transportation improvements did remain essential to the suburban option for all but the wealthiest. Until the 1830s, settlement in and around American cities was largely circumscribed by the distance a person could walk in an hour or so. However, the introduction of the steam ferry (1811) and the omnibus (1830s), the railroad and the horsecar (from the 1840s), the cable car (1870s), and the electric streetcar (1880s) transformed the pattern of settlement within cities. For the first time people could live at some distance from their place of work and commute by means of public transportation.

This separation of work and home was integral to the modernization process in nineteenth-century cities. Facilitated by improving intracity transportation, it gave rise to urban residential areas based on class, ethnicity, or race. These residential areas no longer needed to contain a wide range of economic functions and types of people. Suburbs became an archetype of this segregation into residential areas homogeneous with regard to class. Sam Bass Warner, Jr., has ably explored the agglomeration of

Boston's population by class in late-nineteenth-century streetcar suburbs. At the base of this segregation was a community, not an individual home. As Carol O'Connor explains in "The Suburban Mosaic," "early observers [of suburbs] note the existence of relatively homogeneous local units within heterogeneous suburban regions" (p. 245).

Suburban dwellers were the first to take advantage of ferryboat services. A ferry connection between Manhattan and Brooklyn in 1814 made Brooklyn one of the first commuter suburbs in the United States. Commuters on ferries became a familiar sight by the late nineteenth century. And compact, built-up communities in New York and Philadelphia allowed horse-drawn omnibuses to proliferate in the early nineteenth century. By the second half of the nineteenth century, the railroad, too, had an important impact on suburbs by tying outlying areas more closely to the city center. Thus, the range of areas considered suburban expanded dramatically to include larger towns that served as trading centers for agricultural areas close to the city.

In 1888 the perfection of the electrified street railway (first tested in Richmond, Virginia) led to even more changes in suburban commutation patterns. By 1895, 85 percent of all street railways in the United States had been electrified. The electric streetcar revolutionized mass transit and opened up hundreds of locations for suburban development. No longer restricted to the radial patterns of railroad commuter stops, suburban developers began to fill in the territory between stops.

The automobile took this filling-in process one step further. First visible in cities at the turn of the century, automobiles began to predominate by the 1920s. In 1920 there were over nine million cars in the United States; by 1930 this number had more than tripled to twenty-six million.

It is important to remember that the railroads, streetcars, and automobiles did not *create* these settlements on the outskirts of American cities. Rather, they expanded the area in which suburbs could appear and, as noted earlier, made suburban living affordable for more people. These transportation advances also worked to concentrate suburban settlement along their lines, particularly near railroad and streetcar stations.

Increasingly the term "suburb" was used to designate the settlement surrounding a railroad station. By the 1870s, the frequency and fares of trains to outlying areas were important factors in defining an area as suburban. The availability of relatively inexpensive commuter tickets was crucial for suburban development.

By the 1880s, many of these early suburbs tried to provide urban amenities. Suburbanites did not wish to forsake the society and comforts of the city, so parks, schools, cultural associations, and services like running water and sewer connections became part of the ideal suburban community. These improvements, of course, did not take place overnight. In 1873 the existence of a waterworks in Irving Park, a community outside Chicago, was noted in advertisements for suburban homes. It was an amenity not available in many other suburban communities and was thus cause for special mention. By the 1890s the "model" suburban home was found in a community with paved streets, schools, good transportation, and other services usually available only in the city. This was a far cry from the antebellum picture of a "model" suburban home: an isolated country house to which a wealthy family retired.

This evolution was also evident in changes taking place in established rural towns, as the railroad and population growth pressed suburban expansion further from the city. The increasingly suburban character of many former agricultural towns can be traced in commuter schedules, inclusion of their residents in society registers, and the growing demands for urban services. These demands were met in part by community associations (or real estate developers in new areas), but more and more residents turned to local government for their provision.

In addition to residential development, industry and commerce had been a part of the suburban scene from the beginning. The hinterland was already home to market towns and noxious industries, and suburbanization simply engulfed many of these functions. Also, by the turn of the century, the owners of manufacturing establishments took advantage of relatively inexpensive land along railroad lines to establish suburban plants. For instance, George Pullman established his Pullman car works—and the model town Pullman—in south suburban Chicago in 1882. Glendale, near Cincinnati, was another such planned suburb.

The general trends outlined here were the result of thousands of individual decisions. In his study of Boston's nineteenth-century streetcar suburbs, Sam Bass Warner, Jr., notes "a building process which rested in the hands of thousands of small agents" (p. 117). One set of actors is particularly important to this process: the real estate developers who planned, built, and marketed suburban communities.

The most visible developers were those who created planned suburbs. In the nineteenth century Frederick Law Olmsted was among the most notable designers. He was joined in the twentieth century by developers such as Jessie Clyde Nichols, William Levitt, and James Rouse. Olmsted and his partner, Calvert Vaux, planned sixteen suburbs in the decades after the Civil War, among them Brookline and Chestnut Hill in Massachusetts, Sudbrook and Roland Park in Maryland, Yonkers and Tarrytown Heights in New York, and Riverside in Illinois.

Backed by the Riverside Improvement Company, Olmsted and Vaux sought in designing a suburb in 1868 to "unite at once the beauties and healthy properties of a park with the conveniences and improvements of the city" (Keating, *Building Chicago,* p. 73). Water and sewer mains, individual gas hookups, streetlamps, paved roads, parks, sidewalks, and a railroad depot were just some of the amenities offered. Deeds for lots sold in Riverside included restrictions on building lines, minimum prices for homes and the prohibition of fences; community parkland adjoined all lots. A contemporary account reminded potential residents that "parties buying at Riverside will have the satisfaction of avoiding the demand upon their resources for taxation in the way of improvements, so constant in all towns."

In the nineteenth and twentieth centuries real estate syndicates, land companies, and improvement associations opened thousands of subdivisions in suburban areas across the United States. Through these improvement companies, speculators sought to direct urban growth into the hinterland. Improvements to heighten marketability and attract settlement to particular subdivisions fell into two basic categories: those outside the subdivision and those within it. In the first category were extensions of streetcar and commuter rail lines, the construction of connecting highways, and the development of neighboring parks and boulevards. Among the improvements within subdivisions were commuter rail stations, industries and/or businesses, home construction, and infrastructure such as sidewalks, paved roads, electricity, and water and sewer lines.

While much suburbanization has been unplanned, there are notable exceptions; their influence, however, is debatable. In 1927 Clarence Stein and Henry Wright, under the financial sponsorship of Alexander Bing, planned Radburn, New Jersey, the first garden city in the United States.

During the New Deal the federal government directed the construction of three model suburban communities: Greenbelt, Maryland, near Washington; Greenhills, Ohio, near Cincinnati; and Greendale, Wisconsin, outside Milwaukee. Rexford Tugwell supervised these projects under the Resettlement Administration. Planning began in 1935, and construction was under way for the following three years. The three projects contained housing for 2,267 families. Tugwell believed there should have been not three but three thousand of these projects.

One of the purposes of the program was to demonstrate the advantages of resettling both urban and rural residents in a suburban environment where homes and jobs were located. There was to be plenty of light and many gardens and parks. Urban amenities such as good schools, public utilities, and job opportunities were included in the original plans for each town. But the greenbelt towns never worked out economically, and Congress authorized their sale in 1949 at just over $18 million, half of their $36 million total cost to the federal government.

ORIGINS OF SUBURBAN GOVERNMENT

In the same way that the concept of a suburb evolved over the course of the nineteenth century, its government developed and changed. Early in the century a move to an outlying area was seen as a way of avoiding much of the intrusion of local government on one's life. By the 1870s this changed for many suburban areas, whose residents clamored for more government involvement in the provision of services.

Such demands, though, were not calls for the replication of urban forms. By the mid nineteenth century, city government had acquired an unenviable reputation. An 1869 *Chicago Times* editorial (7 April) commented: "Municipal government in this country is a system of machinery to collect and consume taxes without returning anything like an adequate compensation. It has been refined, and expanded, and compounded to an extent that renders it next to unbearable." Outlying residents sought to obtain and to avoid city government; they needed a form of government somewhere between the urban and the rural.

The contrast between urban and rural government was strong from colonial settlement through the antebellum period. The chartered municipal form, drawn from British antecedents, gave special rights and privileges to urban governments that other local governments did not receive. While the early nineteenth century saw the erosion of the special powers held by chartered cities, their governments were still easily distinguishable from those of rural areas. Suburban government emerged as a new form by the end of the nineteenth century, providing many of the services of chartered urban governments while being shaped by rural governments.

Robert C. Wood examined suburbs and their governments in *Suburbia: Its People and Their Politics* (1958). He felt that while suburbs were home for modern Americans, their governments were decidedly archaic: "They join the other suburban political units around our large cities in clinging persistently to the independence they received when they were isolated villages and hamlets in a rustic countryside" (p. 9). According to Wood and others, suburban government has hindered the development of metropolitan governments that could better serve urban areas. Such an indictment of suburban government goes back to the early years of the twentieth century, when political scientists began to criticize metropolitan governments, often in conjunction with reformers (or *as* reformers) advocating metropolitan consolidation.

CONSOLIDATION AND ANNEXATION

Annexation to the core city was a significant issue for suburbs until the early twentieth century; in some areas, notably those where development and increasing population have been more recent, it remains important. Core cities generally provided superior services and drew many early suburbs within their boundaries as suburbanites sought improvements. In addition, some suburban governments were successful while others were short-lived and soon abandoned; annexation often involved unsuccessful suburban forms.

Studies have identified several important factors in explaining the halt to annexations around the turn of the century. Jon C. Teaford and Kenneth Jackson have provided the most succinct discussions on this subject. Teaford explains:

By 1910 suburban America was a segregated collection of divergent interests, industrial and residential, Protestant and Catholic, truck farmer and commuter, saloon habitué and abstainer. . . . Each of these segments sought to es-

cape from others and to achieve its goals by taking advantage of the state's willingness to abdicate its control over the creation of municipalities. (*City and Suburb*, p. 12)

Jackson notes that this fragmentation heightened racial, ethnic, and class distinctions. Coupled with these divisions was the fact that by the end of the nineteenth century, incorporation as a suburban municipality was an easy process. Suburban municipalities, as well as special districts, dramatically improved the services available outside the city, thus eliminating what had been the strongest drawing card of annexation to the center city—better and less expensive services.

For instance, Brooklyn was incorporated as a city in 1834, and it later annexed two neighboring entities in 1855 and more territory in 1896. This process was spurred on by the introduction of a street railway network and the opening of the Brooklyn Bridge in 1883, both of which encouraged suburban settlement in its nearby rural townships. These townships, like those around Chicago, were composed of multiple settlements that competed for limited town funds. The fledgling suburban communities turned first to the rural townships with their demands for improvements, but they received only limited satisfaction. It was to receive better services and representation that the citizens of these townships agreed to annexation.

In New York the incorporated township and the incorporated village emerged in the closing decades of the nineteenth century to serve an increasing number of suburban communities. The forms were not unlike those found in Chicago: the contiguous townships that were providing suburban services were eventually annexed to the center city. At the same time that the adjacent townships were being absorbed by the city, a number of outlying suburbs began to incorporate as villages. Mount Vernon, just outside the Bronx towns that were annexed to New York City, incorporated in 1892 and avoided annexation. Nearby Bronxville was developed as an exclusive suburb after 1890; it incorporated as a distinct village in 1898, in order to facilitate the orderly development of the area. The end result of these annexations and incorporations was a metropolitan area composed of a central city surrounded by incorporated suburbs.

To the north, as Boston grew to metropolitan status, a similar process was taking place. The major difference was that village incorporation was not an option in Massachusetts. Many of these outlying townships possessed a unique, independent history until the mid nineteenth century, when commuter railroads and streetcar lines drew them into a suburban orbit. Massachusetts's Charlestown, Cambridge, and Roxbury were among the towns that incorporated during the 1840s. Like the towns surrounding Chicago, they were composed of multiple settlements that were joined in a single incorporated government. The town of Cambridge, for instance, was composed of at least three settlements: Old Cambridge, Cambridgeport, and East Cambridge. Some of these modified rural governments became successful suburban forms, and Boston annexed others. As noted earlier, suburbanites created new townships that could more easily provide suburban services and representation. In contrast to New York City, Brooklyn, and Chicago, incorporated townships in Massachusetts became the most familiar suburban type as well as the form of government involved in annexations.

While the township was an important form for suburban governance in the nineteenth century (and beyond for Boston), it played virtually no role in metropolitan areas in the South and the West. For instance, California did not use the township except as a judicial unit. Townships did not serve as intermediate forms while cities like Los Angeles and San Francisco grew. Instead, the county was the basic unit of local government in California. There, as in some other western and southern states, a chartered county form evolved, which was employed in urban areas where more functions were demanded of local government.

The city and county of San Francisco were made coterminous in 1856, after the first spurt of urban growth; but no significant area has subsequently been annexed to San Francisco. Surrounding the city were chartered counties that absorbed further metropolitan growth. Within these counties, however, were incorporated villages and cities similar in scope to those in midwestern and Middle Atlantic metropolitan areas. In the Los Angeles metropolitan area today, numerous chartered counties form the basis of government, with incorporated suburbs and cities—including Los Angeles proper—serving parts of the counties.

STUDENTS OF SUBURBS

Late-nineteenth-century observers heralded the suburban community as the great hope for an in-

dustrializing world. One of the first to describe the suburb was Adna Ferrin Weber, in his 1899 study of urban growth, *Growth of Cities in the Nineteenth Century*. According to Weber, a suburb combined the healthfulness of the country with urban improvements. Weber's suburb had a lower population density than the center city and was distinguished from the surrounding countryside by its city improvements, comforts, and society. Weber saw that the continued deconcentration of urban populations, even in an unplanned fashion, would greatly improve the daily lives of metropolitan residents.

Suburbs were seen by many early social scientists and reformers as a means of humanizing city life. Henry George, the popular nineteenth-century economist and social critic, promoted the benefits of the single tax, arguing that such a government levy on all land rents would make suburban living possible for more of the nation's population. George's 1879 *Progress and Poverty* argued that this would be a dramatic improvement for residents of metropolitan areas:

The destruction of speculative land values would tend to diffuse population where it is too dense and to concentrate it where it is too sparse; to substitute for the tenement house, homes surrounded by gardens, and to fully settle agricultural districts before people were driven far from neighbors to look for land. The people of the cities would thus get more of the pure air and sunshine of the country, the people of the country more of the economics and social life of the city. (p. 147)

Visionary planners such as Ebenezer Howard of London sought to create garden suburbs that would allow as many people as possible to enjoy the benefits of suburban living. In his 1898 study *Garden Cities of To-morrow* (1902; repr. 1945), Howard argued that "town and country *must be married,* and out of this joyous union will spring a new hope, a new life, a new civilization" (p. 48).

Howard's garden-city idea was essentially a plan for moving individuals, as well as industry, out from the city center to provide a more healthful environment. He proposed construction of a town-country magnet that would draw people from cities and rural areas alike. Natural beauty, social opportunities, high wages, and low rents would draw residents to new garden cities. The garden city would be economically self-sufficient yet be at one with nature. Population would be restricted, and all residents would be provided with jobs within the bounds of the community.

Like Weber and George, Howard called for further suburbanization (deconcentration) so that more metropolitan residents could take advantage of the benefits of suburban living. Also in agreement was the urban reformer Frederic C. Howe. In *The City: The Hope of Democracy* (1905), a study of the future of the city in American society, he argued that suburbanization represented the democratic hope of the future.

As the first generation of academic social scientists began to examine and evaluate life in American metropolitan areas, they were struck with the improvements that suburbs brought to metropolitan life. During the 1920s political scientist Harlan Paul Douglass admired suburbs that combined the virtues of city and country: "It [the suburb] is the city trying to escape the consequences of being a city while still remaining a city. It is urban society trying to eat its cake and keep it, too" (*The Suburban Trend,* p. 4).

This is not to say that suburban living was idyllic. It was often lonely—especially for women—and the challenge of maintaining city standards in suburban areas was often overwhelming. William Dean Howells wrote of many of the pitfalls of suburban living in his 1875 *Suburban Sketches:* "In town your fancy would turn to the theaters; in the country you would occupy yourself with cares of poultry or of stock: in the suburb you can but sit upon your threshold, and fight the predatory mosquito."

Other critics of suburbs focused much of their attention on its governance. In 1933 Roderick McKenzie viewed suburban government as "little short of disastrous" and noted that "every great city now has around it a metropolitan area, one with it economically and socially but without political unity" (*The Metropolitan Community,* p. 303). Many critics followed in his footsteps.

More recent historians have added a great deal to our knowledge of suburbs in the late nineteenth and early twentieth centuries. Many case studies have been completed. Warner's *Streetcar Suburbs* stands as a seminal work in the burgeoning subfield of suburban history. As Michael Ebner noted, it was "the first book by an urban historian to examine systematically the suburban tradition" ("Re-Reading Suburban America," p. 228). It served as an important model for subsequent studies.

Several of Warner's arguments were particularly important in setting an agenda for research in suburban history. First, Warner widened the scope of suburban research to include urban neighborhoods that were once suburban. He also felt that nineteenth-century Bostonians' desire for suburban homes was rooted in a rural ideal. In most basic terms, according to this ideal, the country is home to what is good about America, while the city harbors much that is bad. Second, Warner argued that the first suburbs in the United States emerged in the late nineteenth century, with the outward reach of streetcars that enabled the middle class to move from the city center. He argued that the streetcar suburbs were organized along class lines—not by the ethnic enclaves found within neighborhoods closer to the city center. Warner also found that these suburban communities were the result of thousands of individual decisions—not some large-scale plan—to build and settle within the distinct areas of Dorchester, West Roxbury, and Roxbury. Finally, Warner lamented the passing of annexation movements and the rise of politically fragmented metropolitan areas.

Later studies, responding to Warner's arguments, often refined, and sometimes disagreed with, his interpretations. Some found patterns similar to those in Roxbury, Dorchester, and West Roxbury with the arrival of the streetcar and subsequent suburban development. Henry D. Shapiro and Zane L. Miller found that Clifton, a Cincinnati suburb, resembled Warner's suburbs, with growth tied to transportation advances and a subsequent annexation to the city. Joel A. Tarr traced the growing segregation of work and residence in nineteenth-century Pittsburgh, tying this closely to transportation improvements.

By looking at two Boston suburbs, Cambridge and Somerville, Henry C. Binford found that suburban growth took place decades before the arrival of the streetcar. Thus suburbanization there had not depended on the evolution of transportation. While Warner proclaimed the late nineteenth century "the first suburban era," Binford has shown quite convincingly that Cambridge and Somerville were suburbs and commuter havens in the decades before the Civil War.

Another study that focuses on Boston suburbs is *Shaky Palaces* (1984) by Matthew Edel, Elliott Sclar, and Daniel Luria. Taking issue with Warner's view that the building process was the result of thousands of individual decisions, these authors argue that "the building of homes is not the only phase of the building of suburbs. Providing transport access and utilities, and subdividing the farms and woods for small-scale builders to purchase, are also a part of the suburban process." Ronald Dale Karr examined yet another Boston suburb, Brookline, which contrasts strongly with Warner's suburbs. Its residents were wealthier and supported an activist government that rejected annexation. Karr found that the suburban government guided development by selectively withholding services, and that developers used restrictive covenants to shape the communities they were founding. These forces were not apparent in Dorchester, Roxbury, and West Roxbury.

Carol A. O'Connor, in her study of Scarsdale, New York, found that the village government was engaged in actively shaping the community through construction regulations. Zane Miller's study of Forest Park, a twentieth-century Cincinnati suburb, explored the important interaction between developers, local government, and residents in shaping the community.

POST–WORLD WAR II SUBURBS

Although suburbs do have a long history in the context of metropolitan areas across the United States, the explosion in suburban growth after World War II eclipsed much of the earlier growth. Between 1950 and 1970 the suburban population more than doubled, from thirty-six million to seventy-four million. In the fifteen largest metropolitan areas in 1980, the majority of the population lived in suburbs (with the exception of Houston, where only 45 percent of the population lived in suburbs).

There are many reasons for this tremendous growth. As in the earlier periods of suburban growth, transportation innovations spurred new outward expansion from city centers. The automobile and, more important, the superhighway transformed local transportation and settlement patterns across metropolitan areas. Although the federal highway program, including its capstone 1956 Interstate Highway Act, was aimed not at cities, but at connecting them with one another and with rural areas, subsequent highway development transformed the suburban landscape. Public transit went into a permanent decline as the ratio of citizens to registered passenger automobiles dropped from 1,078:1 in 1905 to 4:1 in 1950 to 2:1 in 1970.

Another important reason for the post–World War II suburban boom was the predominance of Federal Housing Administration (FHA) and Veterans Administration (VA) insured-loan programs, which made it less expensive to own a home than to rent in many metropolitan areas. Before the FHA began operation, individuals generally had to put down between one-third and one-half of the property cost. With FHA the down payment necessary for most homes dropped to under 10 percent, lowering a tremendous barrier to home ownership. Between 1934 and 1972 the percentage of American families owning homes jumped from 44 percent to 63 percent. In addition, although the FHA and VA did not lend money to developers, their loan assurances for home buyers allowed developers to borrow the extremely large sums of money necessary to construct large suburban tracts such as those of Levitt and Sons. The FHA also established minimum standards for home construction. Most homes built to FHA and VA standards had central heating, indoor plumbing, telephones, and several major appliances.

Both the FHA and VA insured-loan programs fueled new building in suburban areas. FHA insurance went to new residential developments, primarily in suburban areas (or outlying districts within some cities). In establishing criteria for underwriting home loans, the FHA made it virtually impossible to receive their insurance within older city neighborhoods. Jackson notes that in a sample of 241 new homes insured by the FHA in metropolitan Saint Louis (1935–1939), 91 percent were located in the suburbs.

This dramatic shift from city to suburb in metropolitan areas across the country affected many social and cultural trends. Young white people, through the VA and FHA insured-loan programs, were able to purchase homes far away from their families in city neighborhoods. Women, however, were particularly isolated from the world of work and employment opportunities, as Gwendolyn Wright notes, and this led to many frustrations and problems. Perhaps no one has set out those frustrations more clearly than Betty Friedan in her 1963 book, *The Feminine Mystique.*

Another striking characteristic of suburban growth in the post–World War II period has been its racial segregation. That is, suburbs in metropolitan areas across the United States have been inhabited largely by whites. For instance, during the 1960s in Chicago, 287,000 white families moved to suburban areas; only 13,261 black families obtained residences in a six-county area outside the city. This segregation persisted despite growing numbers of black families in suburban areas during the 1970s and 1980s. In 1980 the proportion of suburban blacks in the United States reached 23.3 percent.

This continuing segregation may stem in part from actions of the federal government. Jackson uncovered important connections between the FHA and VA insured-loan programs and residential segregation in the decades since 1930. He found that FHA underwriters "supported the income and racial segregation of suburbia" (*Crabgrass Frontier,* p. 13). Before racial covenants were outlawed by the U.S. Supreme Court in the 1948 *Shelley* v. *Kraemer* decision, the FHA openly recommended them. The FHA insurers also shied away from any neighborhoods that lacked "economic stability" or "protection from adverse conditions." These were means of redlining whole areas of center cities, many of which were minority occupied.

Compounding this residential segregation has been the shifting nature of occupational structure in metropolitan areas across the United States. While suburbs have been home to industry and business from their beginnings, there was a remarkable shift in manufacturing activity in the years after World War II. Between 1947 and 1967, 293,307 manufacturing jobs (4 percent) were lost by central cities in Standard Metropolitan Statistical Areas (SMSAs—areas with populations greater than one hundred thousand in 1960). At the same time, manufacturing employment in the suburbs increased by 3,902,326 (a 94 percent increase). The suburban share of SMSA manufacturing employment increased from 36 percent in 1947 to 53 percent in 1967. This suburbanization of certain job opportunities has been particularly disadvantageous for the minority groups, who have limited access to suburban residential areas.

A POSTSUBURBAN ERA?

Does "suburb" remain a usable word in the 1990s? Many historians and journalists think not. "Exurbia," "outer city," "edge city," and "technoburb" are among recently coined terms to describe recent varieties of suburbs and/or their predominant trends. The suburb, once a hallmark of modernity, may have become an anachronism.

No one better explores this question than Robert Fishman in *Bourgeois Utopias* (1987). He argues that "suburb" is no longer a useful description of contemporary America: "To me the massive rebuilding that began in 1945 represents not the culmination of the 200 year history of suburbia but rather its end. Indeed, this massive change is not suburbanization at all but the creation of a new kind of city, with principles that are directly opposed to the true suburb" (p. 183). In contrast with suburbs, which were closely tied to central cities, Fishman finds "technoburbs." A technoburb is a peripheral zone, possibly as large as a county, that operates as a viable socioeconomic unit. The boundaries of a technoburb are defined by the locations that can be accessed easily by car:

Spread out along its highway growth corridors are shopping malls, industrial parks, campuslike office complexes, hospitals, schools, and a full range of housing types. Its residents look to their immediate surroundings rather than to the city for their jobs and other needs; and its industries find not only the employees they need but also the specialized services. (p. 184)

While less definitive about the end of a "suburban era," Jackson also sees fundamental changes ahead, perhaps a postsuburban age. With urban gentrification and a rural renaissance, Jackson posits in *Crabgrass Frontier,* "that the long process of suburbanization, which has been operative in the United States since about 1815, will slow over the next two decades" (p. 297).

Whatever the future, the fact remains that the physical shell of suburbanization—including housing, schools, commercial centers, transportation, and other infrastructure improvements—will remain with us for years to come. Suburbanization as a process may come to an end, but we will continue to live with what past generations have built.

In addition, one of the most dramatic characteristics of suburbanization—its ability to create relatively homogeneous local units within larger heterogeneous regions—does not appear to be loosing its hold. The technoburbs that Fishman identifies no longer look to central cities, but they still purposefully exclude those enterprises, peoples, and activities deemed inappropriate by law and custom. Continued political fragmentation further strengthens the power of these relatively homogeneous local units, just as it did in the past. In short, while suburbs have changed dramatically, we will not soon be rid of their physical manifestations; nor has new outlying development abandoned all suburban characteristics.

BIBLIOGRAPHY

General Works

Blumin, Stuart M. "The Center Cannot Hold: Historians and the City." *Journal of Policy History* 2, no. 1 (1990).

Dolce, Philip C., ed. *Suburbia: The American Dream and Dilemma* (1976).

Douglass, Harlan Paul. *The Suburban Trend* (1925).

Ebner, Michael H. "Re-reading Suburban America: Urban Population Deconcentration, 1810–1980." In *American Urbanism: A Historiographical Review,* edited by Howard Gillette, Jr., and Zane L. Miller (1987).

Fishman, Robert. *Bourgeois Utopias: The Rise and Fall of Suburbia* (1987).

Goldfield, David R., and Blaine A. Brownell. *Urban America: From Downtown to No Town* (1979).

Jackson, Kenneth T. *Crabgrass Frontier: The Suburbanization of the United States* (1985).

Mohl, Raymond A. *The New City: Urban America in the Industrial Age, 1860–1920* (1985).

Muller, Peter O. *Contemporary Suburban America* (1981).

O'Connor, Carol A. "The Suburban Mosaic: Patterns of Land Use, Class, and Culture." In *American Urbanism: A Historiographical Review,* edited by Howard Gillette, Jr., and Zane L. Miller (1987).

Stilgoe, John R. *Borderland: Origins of the American Suburb, 1820–1939* (1988).

Tarr, Joel. "From City to Suburb: The 'Moral' Influence of Transportation Technology." In *American Urban History: An Interpretative Reader with Commentaries,* edited by Alexander B. Callow, Jr. 2d. ed. (1973).

Teaford, Jon C. *City and Suburb: The Political Fragmentation of Metropolitan America, 1850–1970* (1979).

Case Studies

Arnold, Joseph L. *The New Deal in the Suburbs: A History of the Greenbelt Town Program, 1935–1954* (1971).

Berry, Brian J. L., Carole A. Goodwin, Robert W. Lake, and Katherine B. Smith. "Attitudes Toward Integration: The Role of Status in Community Response to Racial Change." In *The Changing Face of the Suburbs,* edited by Barry Schwartz (1976).

Binford, Henry C. *The First Suburbs: Residential Communities on the Boston Periphery, 1815–1860* (1985).

Ebner, Michael H. *Creating Chicago's North Shore: A Suburban History* (1988).

Edel, Matthew, Elliott D. Sclar, and Daniel Luria. *Shaky Palaces: Homeownership and Social Mobility in Boston's Suburbanization* (1984).

Gans, Herbert. *The Levittowners: Ways of Life and Politics in a New Suburban Community* (1967).

Karr, Ronald Dale. "Brookline and the Making of an Elite Suburb." *Chicago History* 13, no. 2 (1984).

Kasarda, John D. "The Changing Occupational Structure of the American Metropolis: Apropos the Urban Problem." In *The Changing Face of the Suburbs,* edited by Barry Schwartz (1976).

Keating, Ann Durkin. *Building Chicago: Suburban Developers and the Creation of a Divided Metropolis* (1988).

Miller, Zane L. *Suburb: Neighborhood and Community in Forest Park, Ohio, 1935–1976* (1981).

O'Connor, Carol A. *A Sort of Utopia: Scarsdale, 1891–1981* (1983).

Shapiro, Henry A., and Zane L. Miller. *Clifton: Neighborhood and Community in an Urban Setting* (1976).

Warner, Sam Bass, Jr. *Streetcar Suburbs: The Process of Growth in Boston, 1870–1900* (1962).

SEE ALSO **Landscapes; New England; The New York Metropolitan Region; Racism; Urbanization.**

LANDSCAPES

Wilbur Zelinsky

THE LANDSCAPES OF THE United States are peculiarly American and decidedly unlike those of the nation's ancestral societies. Minimally constrained by the complexities of an Old World past, these man-made, or man-modified, ensembles of terrestrial objects are the purest expression anywhere in our contemporary world of the central dictates of capitalist economics, if modulated somewhat by the singularities of imported and commingled European cultures. In any event, the activities of European settlers and their progeny have transformed a vast territory into something radically different from the aboriginal scene.

ABORIGINAL LANDSCAPES

The newcomers who began entering the future United States more than four centuries ago encountered a land already distinctly humanized over the millennia by some millions of Native Americans. Only locally, in portions of New Mexico and Arizona, were the inhabitants fully sedentary farmers. The great majority of aborigines subsisted by combining cropping systems with hunting, fishing, and gathering along the Pacific Coast and in Alaska; in the more thinly settled tracts west of the 100th meridian (running from the Dakotas to central Texas), they pursued only the latter.

The range and variety of cultural systems were considerable in pre-Columbian America, and the same was true for the resultant landscapes, although our knowledge of their actual appearance is quite fragmentary. House types and village patterns differed markedly from place to place, but most settlement was transient because of the prevailing system of shifting cultivation. The human impact on what appeared wild to the European pioneer was considerable. Substantial evidence indicates that repeated burning, for hunting and other purposes, had created the extensive grasslands of the central United States, while agricultural activity was responsible for the many openings punctuating the eastern forests, those "Indian old fields" that European farmers eagerly exploited. Furthermore, selective harvesting of various trees, shrubs, annuals, and other organisms certainly modified the biota of early America.

Perhaps the most crucial landscape-related factor in aboriginal life, as far as later dealings and misunderstandings with Caucasians were concerned, was a total absence of European concepts of private ownership of land or the precise delineation of property lines. Insofar as there was any thought of proprietorship, it was along communal lines; and boundaries between neighboring communities had always been vaguely defined or nonexistent. Be that as it may, the encounter between invader and aborigine was disastrous for the latter; among the unfortunate results was the near-total obliteration of antecedent landscapes as Native American populations were severely decimated and demoralized, shunted from place to place, and eventually confined to reservations where little of their material culture was left intact. Today perhaps the only remaining aboriginal landscapes with any semblance of authenticity are found in a few New Mexican localities.

THE EUROPEAN TRANSFORMATION

When the first wave of European settlers arrived—in the late sixteenth century in the Southwest, and along the Atlantic seaboard a few decades later—their automatic impulse may have been to re-create the traditional societies and landscapes of their homelands, but pioneer conditions in the New World seldom rendered such faithful transcription feasible. A spectacular abundance of usable land, virtually free for the taking, and the weakness of political and legal controls made it

1289

quite difficult to implement any sort of planning. In place of the orderly, compact, regularly aligned rural and urban settlements envisioned by the various grantees favored by the British, Spanish, Dutch, and French regimes, the actuality turned out to be much messier: scattered, often isolated farmsteads and a string of small seaports and even smaller inland trading centers with little pretense of regularity in layout or elegance in appearance. This statement applies equally well to New England, where, common myth to the contrary notwithstanding, clustered villages were the rare exception before the late eighteenth century. Approximations of European models, such as some of the Hispanic outposts in the Southwest, or New Orleans, Boston, Philadelphia, and Savannah, were few in number.

Building styles in early America tended to be generalized, simplified versions of Old World folk practice. Regional patterns did gradually emerge in the design of houses, barns, churches, cemeteries, and other visible features but, given the frequent mixing of peoples and influences from varied European localities and the impact of a novel environment, simple duplication of any specific Old World scene could hardly occur. Only much later, as wealth and sophistication grew, did individual homes and estates come to resemble what had become fashionable in Europe.

Many a foreign visitor recorded his or her impressions of the early American scene, including the frontier zone, and aside from occasional mild compliments for a major city or two and some of the older, more flourishing farming areas, they were uniformly taken aback by the pervasive physical crudities of town and countryside, a prodigal wastefulness in resource exploitation, and the jarring visual disharmonies in what they generally beheld. As David Lowenthal has noted, what struck them most was the vastness, wildness, and formlessness of a future-oriented land characterized by extravagant extremes. The passage of time has not canceled these early characteristics; indeed, just the reverse has happened in terms of formlessness and incongruous contrasts. As social disparities have widened, as the ranks of both the wealthy and the poor and underprivileged have grown substantially, we often find their two utterly irreconcilable landscapes existing side by side in some of our larger cities.

If the vestiges of aboriginal occupancy were negligible and if the shaping of the colonial and subsequent American scene has been essentially that of European peoples and ideas operating under new, unfamiliar circumstances, there remains one other set of influences, at least in the American South, that is still poorly understood: African influences. Cultural transfers from the Old World in African American church buildings and domestic architecture, yard treatment, agricultural and burial practices are quite plausible in light of the physical evidence despite the paucity of documentation.

The evolution of the American landscape from pioneer days to the present has been largely a matter of applying a series of ever more advanced technologies, along with the necessary investment of capital, to a varied set of places and resources, all in fulfillment of certain cultural and economic drives, as often as not unspoken and unwritten. The former set of forces—the technological and financial—may have altered greatly over the years, but the latter—those internalized imperatives which energize both individuals and the larger society—have remained remarkably consistent over time. As basic a principle as any is the supreme value of individualism and thus a vigorous, if not always productive, competition and the sacredness of private property. In landscape terms this article of faith finds expression in many ways, including the isolated farmstead, the detached, single-family urban or suburban home set on its own lot, the multitude of small burial plots in the countryside, the world's largest proliferation of church denominations and their buildings, weak or nonexistent control of commercial land use, and, consequently, that duplication and excess of facilities so fully embodied in the present-day commercial highway strip. It is the infrequent counterexample, most notably the Mormon communities of Utah with their compact, well-ordered, theocratic landscapes, that reminds us how extreme the general American case really is.

Allied to this powerful streak of individualism is a degree of mobility—obviously spatial, but social as well—that animates American life and landscape to a level no other country can rival. The acceptance—indeed, the celebration—of rapid change quite logically accompanies American individualism and mobility. The landscape results include endless turnover in land use and structures or their remodeling, frequent juxtaposition of building styles from different eras, a high incidence of abandoned farmland, derelict urban neighborhoods and ghost towns, a never-ending series of new highway projects or the relocation or improvement of existing roads, and, except during deepest economic depression, a great amount of construction at various stages of completion in favored localities.

Undergirding so fluid and seemingly anarchic a scene is the most basic principle of all: the sanctity of the profit motive for both individual and business firm. But if a creed common to all of modern Western society happens to be expressed most nakedly in a United States lacking the burden of ancient tradition, there is another facet of the American ethos (one possibly derived from the English cultural system) that is exceptional: an antiurban bias. (The pastoral urges of Americans also find expression in another British heritage, the homeowner's passion for lawns.) Cities may be necessary evils in the furtherance of economic aims, but, unlike the situation in continental Europe, the American metropolis is, with few exceptions, an unloved creature. The results of such disaffection are visually obvious in the cities themselves, as well as in the extraordinary extent of suburbanization and exurbanization. A less direct but nonetheless genuine expression of this mind-set is the propensity to select smaller towns for state capitals and rural or small-town settings for colleges.

Among the environmental circumstances molding the American landscape, few are more noteworthy than the initial superabundance of trees in so much of the eastern half of the country and a good portion of the far West. It was both curse and blessing. Clearing a fifty- or one-hundred-acre (20- or 40-hectare) farm could mean an entire working lifetime of literally backbreaking labor for the homesteader, and the outcome for another generation or so might be unsightly, stump-filled fields and pastures. But the forest also provided absolute necessities: raw materials for house, barn, other outbuildings, fencing, furniture, vehicles, and tools, and, of course, fuel for warmth, cooking, and industrial processes. The fact that so many thousands of sawmills sprang up along the frontier illustrates the centrality of wood and lumber to American life. Rural and much of urban America, early and late, then, has been wood-dominated. Even today the woodlot remains on many farms.

In the past and to a surprising extent today, wood has been the preferred material for houses, churches, school buildings, shops, mills, bridges, and much else. In a land where labor has been dear and lumber cheap, the adoption of brick, stone, and other materials for construction has come about only gradually, locally, and incompletely. So deeply ingrained in the American psyche did the preference for wood become that when the settlement frontier entered the treeless Great Plains, other expedients, such as the sod house, were quite temporary; lumber, even entire prefabricated wooden buildings, were shipped in at considerable expense.

The Impact of Technology In a country of such daunting size, the means for transporting people and goods have always been primary determinants of the material framework of American life and livelihood. The changes over time in the morphology of American cities clearly reflect this fact. For the first two hundred years or so of European settlement—certainly until the 1840s or 1850s—towns were relatively small, compact pedestrian places (with access to horse-drawn carriages limited to the more prosperous) that, with rare exceptions, were tied to waterborne commerce and thus oriented toward wharves and docks. They were also places with minimal spatial segregation of economic functions, classes, or ethnic groups.

The introduction of the steam railroad had a profound impact upon urban form and landscape and, eventually, on the countryside as well. Besides fostering vigorous growth in city size, commerce, and manufacturing, the new mode of transportation transformed the outward appearance of much of the city. There were new depots, freight houses, marshaling yards, maintenance facilities, associated hotels, bridges, and tunnels accompanied by the evisceration of much of the old urban fabric to provide space for tracks and all the other rail-related activities. New factory and warehouse districts arose at rail side, sometimes on a massive scale. By the close of the nineteenth century, the building of commuter and light-rail interurban lines enabled the city to sprawl outward in an unprecedented way, as did the installation of electric trolley service within the expanding metropolis.

Aside from the immediate physical stigmata—the many cuts and fills executed across all but the most subdued of surfaces, defoliation of rights-of-way, creation of parallel telegraph lines and signal systems, and the erection of innumerable small-town depots and ancillary structures—the indirect effects of inserting so many tens of thousands of miles of rail into the countryside were ultimately both visually and socially significant. The presence of an extended "metropolitan corridor" meant availability of city goods, information, and ideas in many formerly isolated villages and hamlets as well as the start of that gradual coalescence, or interdigitation, between town and countryside that has become so prominent an aspect of contemporary America. It is no coincidence that the onset of a standardized way of life became noticeable in the 1850s, just when the railroad began to monopolize long-distance transportation. It was then that some magazines acquired nationwide readership, that a mass market developed for many types of mass-produced merchandise, and that fashions in house design and landscape architecture (including park cemeteries) showed signs of becoming uniform coast to coast thanks to widely circulated manuals and preachments such as those of Andrew Jackson Downing.

Dramatic and pervasive though the effects of the new railroad system may have been, there were many other innovations, less well publicized, that helped modify the American landscape during the latter half of the nineteenth century: barbed-wire fencing, cheap paint, indoor plumbing, mass production of portland cement, the mail-order catalog, the balloon-frame house, electric elevators, and streetlights. Equally important though less celebrated were advances in earth-moving devices and technology and, most especially, the invention and large-scale use of dynamite. In any event, remarkable alterations came about in the topography of American cities. Rough terrain was leveled (as happened in Manhattan), entire surfaces lifted (as in Chicago), dry land created out of swamps (as in Washington), and waterfronts remade (as in New Orleans). In many instances, as in Boston, the changes have been so thoroughgoing that if a seventeenth-century resident were to be resurrected, it is doubtful whether he or she would find any part of the metropolitan area or its harbor recognizable. No major American seaport, and few lake or river ports of consequence, have escaped extensive physical revamping.

Another crucial shaper of the landscape has been the automobile. The easy availability, since the early decades of the twentieth century, of personal vehicles to all but the very poorest, along with great numbers of trucks, buses, motorcycles, and other motorized conveyances as well as access to almost any point, have profoundly reordered the settlement structure and landscapes of America in ways that are still not fully appreciated. As far as the city is concerned, there has been a remarkable outward explosion of population, businesses, and traditional urban functions. In a number of cases, the old urban core has lost its dominance as suburbs, or even virtually autonomous "edge cities," have sprung up

along the periphery. The feasibility of long-distance commuting and the new flexibility in delivering materials and information have facilitated the redistribution of enterprises and employees into what were once remote locations. The urbanization of the countryside is proceeding inexorably. One of the more visible aspects of the phenomenon has been the proliferation of second homes and seasonal housing in environmentally attractive locales within commuting range of major population centers—or, for the airborne affluent, almost anywhere in the country.

Within the more or less contiguous built-up area we still call a city, the imprint of the automobile is hard to ignore. Immense acreage is given over to paved streets and parking lots; multiple-lane, limited-access highways within and around the city with their massive interchanges, bridges, overpasses, and outsize signage and lighting have done more to revise the physiognomy of urban places than even the most imperious of railroad barons could have dreamed of doing. And the interstate highway system and similar projects, with their commercial clusters arising around every interchange, have transformed the face of much of rural America. Every self-respecting modern dwelling has a one- or two-car garage and an ample driveway; along every thriving commercial street we find not just filling stations, auto showrooms, parts dealers, repair facilities, and perhaps some motels but also an endless array of retail establishments geared to the drive-by and/or drive-in trade and a great swarm of often large, garish advertising signs designed to engage the attention and urges of the passing drivers. As symptomatic as anything of the new order is the profusion of auto-oriented shopping malls in city and suburb, a development that gives every indication of becoming the central social institution of our times.

Important as airborne passenger, mail, and freight traffic may have become, the landscape impact of the airplane has been much less profound than that of the automobile or truck. Nevertheless, one of the more striking localized features of present-day America is the airport complex on the outskirts of major metropolises with its mix of office, motel, and high-tech industrial facilities as well as the considerable acreage devoted to the airport proper.

The Impact of Cultural Authority Ultimately rivaling the significance of technology as a shaper of the American landscape have been the workings of central authority, even though it was initially rather weak. A leading item on the agenda of the colonial proprietors and, later, the provincial, state, and national regimes was the rapid disposal of land to settlers through sale or other means. Until the early years of national independence, there was little regularity in the ways real estate was surveyed or bounded. The prevailing pattern throughout the original thirteen states is known as the metes-and-bounds systems, one that relied largely on natural features for designating property lines. The resulting highly irregular mosaic of parcels contrasts with the long-lot system used in areas of early French and some Spanish settlement, one in which long, narrow strips of property ran back at right angles from riverfront or road.

Such relatively casual modes of carving up the American land vanished in the late 1780s when the young republic adopted a rigidly rectangular survey system for the vast, as yet unsettled national domain to which it held title. Moving in advance of permanent settlers, federal surveyors laid out six-by-six-mile townships with straight-line boundaries oriented to the compass. Each township consisted of thirty-six sections, each containing 640 acres, or one square mile (256 hectares, or 2.6 square kilometers). Public roads and virtually all subsequent property lines and field boundaries within sections were aligned north, east, south, and west along or parallel with section lines, and most later urban street layouts followed suit. The result for the nearly 75 percent of American territory so marked off (not counting national parks and forests, early French and Spanish grants, and Indian reservations excluded from the system) is a remarkable geometric repetitiveness in the settlement fabric. It is a checkerboard regularity that can be discerned from the ground but appreciated fully only from the air. The federal example was emulated by several states that controlled unsettled lands not included in the national domain, notably Texas, Georgia, Pennsylvania, New York, and Maine, though their survey methods were not quite as rigorous as in the national case.

The rationale for such a relatively simple method for partitioning the American land was obvious enough: it made good business sense. Henceforth it would be easy to describe, advertise, sell, resell, subdivide, or combine parcels with a minimum of legal fuss and expense. But if the effects of the federal rectangular survey have been deep, widespread, and enduring, other visible evidence of the existence of a relatively underdeveloped central government was scarce during the first several decades of national existence. Perhaps the occasional fort, lighthouse, or customhouse was then the only visible token that some sort of national entity was ruling the land. The visible effects of state and local governments were even more difficult to detect.

The net balance of power and sentiment, as between government and the governed, and thus its landscape expression, began to shift substantially from the time of the Civil War onward, but certain deeply ingrained attitudes persist. Americans have always felt uneasy about centralized governance and the bureaucracy, or indeed any form of external interference with the exercise of property rights or the pursuit of wealth—thus the late, slow, reluctant acceptance of planning and zoning or other land-use regulations. But where controls have been effective, the contrasts between juxtaposed jurisdictions can be quite dramatic—for example, between the landscapes of the District of Columbia and those in its Maryland and Virginia suburbs or the differences between the roadsides of Vermont and those in adjacent states. But even though planners may enjoy their minor triumphs, the larger reality is that entrepreneurs, whether individual or corporate, have been the dominant creators of a landscape whose crevices the homeowner can modify only modestly. Perhaps nothing more vividly illustrates their hegemony than the ways they have contrived suburban housing developments and shopping centers.

However ambivalently Americans may regard control by distant government agencies, there is no escaping its necessity in a modern economy; and with the strengthened central regime a modern citizenry finds itself necessarily imbued with nationalist notions. Inevitably such collective loyalties and such concentrated political power take recognizable form in the landscape. Official architecture is the most obvious point of entry. Governmental edifices in Washington, especially from the 1850s on, and their facsimiles in various state capitals, not to mention the ubiquitous standardized post offices of the twentieth century, set standards that were copied not only by counties and municipalities but also by builders of commercial and residential structures. This is especially striking in the case of the long-lived popularity of various classical revival styles. And even without official sponsorship, nationalist sentiment shows up unmistakably in the persistence of colonial revival designs since the 1880s and all the many buildings reminiscent of Independence Hall.

The federal presence has manifested itself in many ways other than building styles. The American land is punctuated by a great many military installations, some of them quite extensive, and their inevitable offshoots: veterans' clubhouses, Veterans Administration hospitals, and military cemeteries—all readily recognizable. To a marked degree, the historical monuments that began to appear in the 1850s have been as nationalistic in tone as in other lands. But what makes the United States truly exceptional among modern nation-states is the unparalleled profusion of flag display, by private individuals and businesses as well as by official installations, along with a remarkable prevalence of eagles (the national totem) and the national colors (red, white, and blue) in every conceivable venue. A complete inventory of the impress of central authority would require more space than is available here, but certainly one cannot overlook the interstate highway system, the array of rather standardized national parks and forests, the countless accomplishments of the Army Corps of Engineers in their reordering of America's hydrology and much else, and the highly visible feats of the Tennessee Valley Authority and other federal dam projects, some of gargantuan magnitude. Since the New Deal era, we have had the many tangible deeds of the Works Progress Administration, Civilian Conservation Corps, and other agencies and the immediately identifiable federal housing projects in numerous cities.

If the power and prestige of the national regime have generated so many notable signs and symptoms on the American scene, another kind of centralized authority—that of the more successful national or regional business firms—has produced something of a parallel phenomenon. The earliest such expression may well have been the standardized facilities of the major railroad lines, but the trend has fully blossomed more recently with nationally uniform designs for filling stations, hotel and motel chains, and a great assortment of lookalike franchised eating and retail operations.

Salvage and Preservation Although economic, technological, and political forces have been the prime determinants of America's humanized landscapes, certain counterforces have been in evidence. In large part they have been energized by the mistakes and excesses of the past. Exploitation of American soils, waters, forests, and mines for immediate gain was intense, rapid, and all too often totally heedless of ultimate cost or consequence. So thorough has been the assault upon the habitat that, taking plant cover as an example, the survival of any patch of original prairie is improbable, and genuine virgin stands of forest are exceedingly rare, as are streams in anything like their original condition. Virtually everything sylvan that seems wild is actually second- or third-growth forest at best. In some instances one can argue that human intervention may have improved conditions in both substance and appearance. But the contrary situation is much easier to document, a notorious example being the cutover area of northern Michigan, Wisconsin, and Minnesota. The clear-cutting of the once splendid forest in the late nineteenth century, along with many subsequent fires, has yielded a scraggly semidesert of scrub vegetation with no prospect of regeneration for a good many decades.

It was only toward the close of the 1800s that an organized conservation movement was born. It was led by elite members of society who were primarily concerned over the future availability of resources (for both economic and recreational use) and only incidentally, if at all, with the visual aspects of the problem. The same statement applies to the soil conservation programs that began to be implemented seriously in the 1930s. In any event, the question of appearance, of the integrity of man-made or man-modified landscapes, has come to the fore slowly and gradually, in part as a result of the historic preservation movement. From a halting start in the mid nineteenth century with campaigns to safeguard especially memorable single buildings, the movement broadened to embrace entire early settlements and urban neighborhoods of a certain venerability and charm as well as the more significant American battlefields. No doubt sensibilities have been sharpened by such scathing jeremiads against uglification as those by Peter Blake and Ian Nairn, and issues involving both preservation and the look of the land and the works of man have gradually crept onto the political agenda.

Serious problems remain unresolved. Is it possible or desirable to keep these places frozen in a state of suspended animation? Should these localities be museumized or (like Charleston's Historic District or New Orleans's Vieux Carrée) allowed to change ever so slowly? How is genuine authenticity to be attained? How does gentrification of older city neighborhoods fit into the preservation picture?

Another recent movement, the environmental, may have even greater long-term consequences for the American landscape. Pursuing as their most central objective the preservation or restoration of wilderness and various fragile ecosystems, since the 1950s and 1960s the leaders of the movement have gained much popular support and perhaps catalyzed what seems to be a mass conversion to "green," or organic, consciousness. The effect on the landscape is incidental but potentially important. In a parallel development, beautification projects are no longer uncommon in American municipalities, and some cities have gone out of their way to encourage public art.

We must reckon with still another set of forces, those which mold our collective mental landscape images and thus, indirectly but meaningfully, the ways in which we manipulate our environs. Through the media of fiction, verse, landscape painting, calendar art, photography, movies, and television, we have charted a constellation of ideal landscapes in the mind's eye. They include the New England village; the antebellum southern plantation; the idyllic yeoman farm; the Middle American Main Street (so cleverly miniaturized and embalmed in a sanitized Disneyland) with its elm-lined residential streets; the western ranch; the South Sea island paradise; and perhaps others. Much of today's commercial and residential design is a matter of life imitating art.

Scholarly Approaches If an awareness that landscapes or, more generally, the visual aspect of shared spaces are items of common concern were to dawn upon the general public quite belatedly, the academic community has been equally slow in recognizing the value of landscape study. Although for many years geographers in the United States and abroad have debated the definition of the term "landscape," or its equivalent in other languages—with meanings ranging from simple scenery or vista to such abstractions as entire regions — it is only recently that anything resembling a serious school of landscape analysis has emerged. Human geographers have been the most conspicuous members of this loose fraternity, one that also includes historians, landscape architects, and folklorists. The essential premise, eloquently expounded by Henry Glassie and Thomas Schlereth, is that the ensemble of material objects (the relevance of sounds and smells remains moot) we call the landscape represents a priceless archive, a deeply layered palimpsest, the richest sort of means for gaining a deep understanding of human societies past and present. It is interesting and important not just in and of itself but even more for its implicit messages. The

contention is that the documentation furnished by the landscape, including the testimony of those large groups of humanity who leave no written records, offers a much more comprehensive view of human life, thought, and ideals than the paper trail traditionally exploited by historians.

If there has been any central figure in this enterprise, it is undoubtedly John Brinckerhoff Jackson, who through his essays has given the landscape school a certain philosophical coherence and who, through the journal *Landscape,* which he founded in 1951 and edited for many years, has provided practitioners a major forum. The agenda for geographers and other students of the American (and other) landscapes is enormous, a task involving both description, or inventory, and subsequent analysis. More often than not, they have barely begun taking up the challenge, but what has been achieved justifies the claims of the landscape advocates.

At this point one can only briefly sketch what has been done and the long list of future chores. Data and understanding are fullest when it comes to rural houses, farmsteads, barns, and bridges; students of them may have already passed the point of diminishing returns. There has been some progress in studying cemeteries, parks, fencing, roads, roadside architecture, lawns, and gardens, but a great deal remains to be learned. For a large number of other landscape components, our organized knowledge is quite skimpy or entirely lacking. The list includes vernacular church buildings, factories, office buildings and office parks, yard and porch ornaments, field patterns, hospital and school buildings, monuments, shopping malls and commercial structures in general, the entire array of items associated with sport and recreation, trailer parks, abandoned spaces, and, not least, refuse dumps.

Finally, beyond the task of assembling so much needed data there looms the challenge of adequate interpretation of finding and answering the many urgent questions embedded in the many material microworlds we have created or transformed. The potentials of such landscape exegesis appear in Banham's work on Los Angeles, Duncan's account of a Westchester County village, Zelinsky's treatment of the Pennsylvania town, or the essays on the historical geography of the American landscape edited by Michael Conzen.

Such publications suggest that landscape analysis may play an important, perhaps vital role in addressing the grander issues that have begun to engage social historians and social scientists — such as the meaning of community and the operations of power, class, ethnicity, and gender in American life.

In any event, there is little prospect that even the most enterprising set of students can bring to closure any time during the foreseeable future an exciting, ever-expanding research agenda.

BIBLIOGRAPHY

Banham, Reyner. *Los Angeles: The Architecture of Four Ecologies* (1971).

Blake, Peter. *God's Own Junkyard: The Planned Deterioration of America's Landscape* (1964).

Conzen, Michael P., ed. *The Making of the American Landscape* (1990).

Duncan, James S., Jr. "Landscape Taste as a Symbol of Group Identity: A Westchester County Village." *Geographical Review* 63, no. 3 (1973).

Francaviglia, Richard V. *The Mormon Landscape: Existence, Creation and Perception of a Unique Image in the American West* (1978).

Garreau, Joel. *Edge City: Life on the New Frontier* (1991).

Glassie, Henry. *Folk Housing in Middle Virginia: A Structural Analysis of Historic Artifacts* (1975).

Herbers, John. *The New Heartland: America's Flight Beyond the Suburbs and How It Is Changing Our Future* (1986).

Jackson, John Brinckerhoff. *The Necessity for Ruins, and Other Topics* (1980).

———. *Discovering the Vernacular Landscape* (1984).

Jackson, Kenneth T. *Crabgrass Frontier: The Suburbanization of the United States* (1985).

Johnson, Hildegard Binder. *Order upon the Land: The U.S. Rectangular Land Survey and the Upper Mississippi Country* (1976).

Liebs, Chester H. *Main Street to Miracle Mile: American Roadside Architecture* (1985).

Lowenthal, David. "The American Scene." *Geographical Review* 58, no. 1 (1968).

Marschner, Francis J. *Land Use and Its Patterns in the United States* (1959).

Marx, Leo. *The Machine in the Garden: Technology and the Pastoral Ideal in America* (1964).

Meinig, D. W., ed. *The Interpretation of Ordinary Landscapes: Geographical Essays* (1979).

Nairn, Ian. *The American Landscape: A Critical View* (1965).

Nash, Roderick. *Wilderness and the American Mind.* 3d ed. (1982).

Noble, Allen G. *Wood, Brick and Stone: The North American Settlement Landscape* (1984).

Schlereth, Thomas J. *Artifacts and the American Past: Techniques for the Teaching Historian* (1980).

Stilgoe, John R. *Common Landscape of America, 1580–1845* (1982).

———. *Metropolitan Corridor: Railroads and the American Scene* (1983).

Tunnard, Christopher, and Henry Hope Reed. *American Skyline: The Growth and Form of Our Cities and Towns* (1955).

Williams, Michael. *Americans and Their Forests: A Historical Geography* (1989).

Wood, Joseph S. "Village and Community in Early Colonial New England." *Journal of Historical Geography* 8, no. 4 (1982).

Zelinsky, Wilbur. "The Pennsylvania Town: An Overdue Geographical Account." *Geographical Review* 67, no. 2 (1977).

———. *Nation into State: The Shifting Symbolic Foundations of American Nationalism* (1988).

SEE ALSO **Agriculture; Geographic Mobility; National Parks and Preservation; Technology and Social Change; Transportation and Mobility.**

PUBLIC ARCHITECTURE

Craig Zabel

AMERICAN PUBLIC ARCHITECTURE is a physical symbol, often on a monumental scale, of the definition of government and its role in American society. It is within public buildings that the drama of a democratic government has taken place. "Public" architecture can be variously defined. In the broadest sense, any building that is open to all people or contributes to establishing the public face of a city can be considered public. However, the essence of public architecture is composed of those buildings that are built by the people to serve fundamental needs of society, particularly those of government and education. It is these two central categories of public buildings which will be examined here.

COLONIAL BUILDINGS

Before the American Revolution, the goals of public architecture were quite different from what would be sought after 1776. Rather than defining a new nation, public architecture at first was a colonial extension of the imperial ambitions of European governments. The Palace of the Governors in Santa Fe, New Mexico (1610–1614; Fig. 1), was a tiny outpost on the edge of the Spanish world, which sought to provide administrative order to the Christian missionary efforts directed at the Native Americans. This building is atypical among colonial civic buildings in the New World in that the Spanish learned from Native American building techniques and utilized the Pueblo material of adobe. This is in sharp contrast to the public buildings of the English colonies, where native traditions in building were ignored in favor of transplanted European ideas and forms.

In Puritan New England, it was the meetinghouse that first emerged in the seventeenth century as the major public building in a community. These typically large, square, and very plain wooden buildings on the town's common were built pri-

marily for religious services, but they also served as a convenient gathering point for town meetings. A less pious but more convivial setting for holding discussions about the welfare of a community was the local tavern, where government officials often chose to meet. In New Amsterdam, the City Tavern (1641–1642) was even converted in 1653 into the Stadt Huys (city hall), since it was one of the largest and most prominent buildings in the Dutch settlement on the island of Manhattan. This tradition continued into the eighteenth century as can be seen in Williamsburg, Virginia, where the Raleigh Tavern was a center of political discussions second only to the Capitol.

The emergence of a civic architecture beyond meetinghouses and taverns was rather slow and limited during the seventeenth century. Boston's first Town Hall (1657–1658, destroyed 1711) was a rough wooden building with medieval gables exhibiting little architectural pretension other than two belfries that crowned its roof, denoting that the building was a place of assembly. Continuing a medieval tradition, the open first floor of the structure was a market, which added to the importance of the building within the lives of the people of Boston. This market also suggests one of the British government's primary hopes for the colonies as a promising economic venture.

The largest buildings built in the English colonies were colleges, reflecting the importance that education held for colonial society. American colleges throughout their history were often perceived to be ideal communities providing on a small scale a model of what society could be. At first a single building, looking like an enlarged house, was built to contain all of the functions of the college, including dormitories for the students, and sometimes housing for the faculty. The earliest college buildings follow this pattern, such as the Old College at Harvard in Cambridge, Massachusetts (1638–1642, demolished 1678), and the College of William and

Figure 1.   Palace of the Governors, Santa Fe, New Mexico (1601–1614), as it appeared in 1868. COURTESY OF THE MUSEUMS OF NEW MEXICO.

Mary in Williamsburg, Virginia (1695–1699, rebuilt 1705–1715). A common type of college building emerged during the Georgian period of the eighteenth century and is exemplified by Nassau Hall (by Robert Smith and William Shippen, 1754–1756) of the College of New Jersey (later Princeton University). A large symmetrical block is given distinction through a central pavilion and cupola, and stands grandly on a large open, green space, in contrast to the tight, cloistered enclosures of England's Oxford and Cambridge.

When new capital cities were laid out according to a plan, such as Philadelphia (1682), Annapolis (1694), and Williamsburg (1699), care was taken to provide prominent central locations for major public buildings that would create an architectural climax at the end of central avenues. In the plan for the new capital of Virginia, Williamsburg, the College of William and Mary and the Capitol anchor opposite ends of the town's major street, the Duke of Gloucester Street. Adjoining the center of this east-west street is a secondary axis running north: the palace green terminating with the Governor's Palace. At the crossing of these two axes stands Bruton Parish Church. Williamsburg's plan diagrams a balance of the institutions of education, religion, and government with the palace of the crown governor standing at the head of this colonial capital for the British empire.

It was through the Capitol in Williamsburg (1701–1705; rebuilt 1928–1934) that the judgments of royal authority were dispensed to the people of Virginia. The towering two-story cupola asserted

this building as an important landmark. The open arcade at its center provided a welcoming gesture to the public. The **H** plan of the building architecturally expressed the bicameral nature of colonial government, with the House of Burgesses in the east wing and the Governor's Council in the west wing. Another major chamber within the Capitol was the General Court. By colonial American standards, the Virginia Capitol was atypical in its commanding presence and its articulation of its functions. The more common solution for a major civic building (or college building) was to design along the lines of a great house as seen in Richard Munday's Old Colony House at Newport, Rhode Island (1739–1741; Fig. 2), where only the building's size, cupola, and isolated position on a central site set the building apart from the general residential fabric of the town. The most monumental and prominent urban landmarks in colonial cities were church spires. The Old State House in Philadelphia (Independence Hall; Andrew Hamilton and Edmund Woolley, 1731–1753) is a prime example of the dilemma of definition of public architecture in colonial America. A large Georgian block, reminiscent of a house, is fronted by a churchlike tower; however, the building does not appear to be a church since the tower is placed on the broad side, rather than on the traditional narrow end. American society in the English colonies was not one of monumental institutions. The dominant architectural forms of the time were the house and the church. Public and educational buildings tended to be hybrids and transformations of these more prev-

Figure 2. The Colony House, Newport, Rhode Island (1739–1741), as it appeared ca. 1897. FROM THE COLLECTION OF THE NEWPORT HISTORICAL SOCIETY.

alent types. Colonial public architecture suggests that it was built for a society whose ultimate political control lay elsewhere, with the crown and parliament back in England.

BUILDING FOR THE NEW REPUBLIC

With the revolutionary war and the establishment of the United States of America, the role of public architecture had suddenly and dramatically changed. New edifices needed to be conceived to house the just-created democratic institutions of the nascent country. One figure who was especially sensitive to the important role that architecture could play in the definition of a nation and its people was Thomas Jefferson, who was a gentleman-amateur architect, along with his numerous other talents. He played a key role in having the capital of Virginia moved from that symbol of the British crown, Williamsburg, to Richmond, where a fresh start further west could be made. While he was the American minister to France, he designed a new capitol with the assistance of C.-L. Clérisseau. Jefferson modeled his new State Capitol (1785–1798; Fig. 3) after an ancient Roman temple, the Maison Carrée in Nîmes. Jefferson had created a truly monumental and grand structure unlike any American colonial public building. The order, scale, and nobility of a rectangular temple block provided the ideal model of a young nation desiring to establish

instant monuments. Moreover, such a building was invested with romantic associations with the classical past, particularly in the mind of Jefferson: republican Rome. From this building on, the neoclassical temple would be a type repeatedly associated with public buildings and would come to symbolize authority, stability, and culture.

Jefferson's neoclassical buildings were used as models to promote an ideal architectural environment that would ennoble and improve the United States. Nowhere are his architectural ambitions better seen than in his design for the University of Virginia at Charlottesville (1817–1826). In contrast to the large, single institutional block of most colonial colleges, he broke up the university into a series of smaller units and called it his "academical village." His social aim was to create a small, ideal educational community that would encourage intellectual discourse between faculty and students. Faculty lived in two-story pavilions with their living quarters above and classrooms below; each pavilion illustrates a different example of classical architecture. One-story dormitories fronted by colonnades link the pavilions and form two ranges flanking a central quadrangular lawn. More student rooms and six "hotels" (for dining) were located in two outer ranges parallel to the two inner ranges. At the head of the lawn is the Rotunda (originally housing the library), modeled after the ancient Roman Pantheon. Jefferson had replaced the central role given to chapels in colonial college buildings and campuses by placing at the heart of his design a pantheon, dedicated not to religion or pagan gods, but to enlightened thought through books.

During the presidency of George Washington (1789–1797), the government decided to build a new capital city for the nation, reinforcing an often repeated theme during the first century of the United States, a theme of optimistic new beginnings on a generous and ever-enlarging land. A French engineer and architect, Pierre Charles L'Enfant, laid

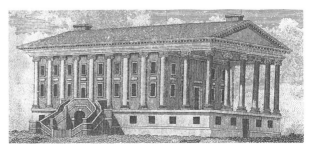

Figure 3. The Capitol in Richmond, Virginia (1785–1798), as it appeared ca. 1802. COURTESY OF THE VIRGINIA STATE LIBRARY AND ARCHIVES.

out the new federal city in 1791. He conceived of it on a truly monumental scale, and it was not until the twentieth century that Washington, D.C., began to approximate L'Enfant's original vision. L'Enfant's design is based upon baroque urban and garden planning, which accentuated sites for major buildings or fountains by use of radial avenues. He adapted principles that in Europe symbolized absolute power (such as in papal Rome or the gardens of Versailles) to create a democratic capital. This was a continual theme in American public architecture: appropriating architectural forms that were used in the past to represent dogmatic authority and recasting them for more republican purposes. At the end of a broad mall, two buildings were to be the centerpieces of this federal city: the President's House and the Capitol (in an arrangement not unlike Williamsburg).

The complicated history of the United States Capitol is one of multiple architects, an evolving design, political division, foreign invasion, civil war, and a key opportunity for a new nation to establish a dominant architectural symbol. A competition for the new building was held in 1792, and the surviving entries make clear the inability of most American architects and builders to think beyond the small scale of colonial examples. However, a late entry by William Thornton pleased the eyes of both Washington and Jefferson. Thornton was encouraged to continue work on a new design and during the mid 1790s the first design for the Capitol was developed. The composition was a hybrid of forms and motifs: a long palacelike block (to provide separate wings for the Senate and House of Representatives) was accentuated in the center with a low Pantheon-like dome and portico facing to the east and a much taller dome and semicircular colonnade on the west (mall) side of the building. How unified the various states wanted to be under a single federal government would be a debate that would continue throughout American society. Nonetheless, from the very start, the dominant architectural symbol for this gathering of the legislators would be the unifying containment of a circular dome (although Thornton in this early design had conceived of two domes).

After Benjamin H. Latrobe was appointed Architect of the Capitol in 1803, the competing domes were reduced to one (the tall, west dome was eliminated from the plans). During the War of 1812, the partially built Capitol and President's House were burned as the British tried to demoralize their former colonial possession by destroying its public buildings. Latrobe returned to rebuild the Capitol (1815–1817; Fig. 4). As a European-trained architect and engineer Latrobe was able to design and build monumental and dignified classical spaces with masonry vaulting of a quality that had previously been unknown in America. He even invented new American orders of columns with capitals decorated with tobacco leaves or cobs of maize, one of the first attempts to create American architectural forms beyond the European tradition.

The Boston architect Charles Bulfinch finally brought the Capitol to completion in 1826. His major addition to the design was to change the building's dome from the low, saucerlike dome of previous designs into a taller, more prominent, and awkward dome. The building was completed, but by 1851 it had grown inadequate for the rapidly growing nation. In the late eighteenth century the future dimensions of the United States were vague and unpredictable. By the mid nineteenth century it was necessary for the nation's major architectural symbol to undergo a radical alteration and expansion to stay in step with the new scale of the United States. The architect Thomas U. Walter added two large wings (1851–1859) to the ends of the original building to provide entirely new and much larger chambers for the House and Senate. To unify the sprawling breadth of the expanded Capitol, Walter built a new and much taller dome (1855–1863). Reminiscent of the domes of Renaissance-baroque churches (particularly Sir Christopher Wren's Saint Paul's Cathedral in London), it secularizes a long-used religious architectural form to symbolize the unity of many states under the single dome of the federal government. The dome was built in iron, reflecting the growing industrial capacity of the nation. Iron was certainly precious to the Union military cause during the Civil War, yet Abraham Lincoln insisted that construction of the dome continue during the war: "If people see the Capitol going on, it is a sign we intend the Union shall go on" (quoted in Hitchcock and Seale, *Temples of Democracy,* p. 141).

No other public building before the Civil War required the enormous size of the United States Capitol. The dominant image for a public building by the early nineteenth century was the classical temple, usually Greek in its inspiration. A Greek temple stimulated romantic thoughts of democracy and the beginnings of Western civilization. Greek Revival buildings were found throughout antebellum America from diminutive temples serving as county courthouses in rural Virginia to boldly scaled capitols in stone to serve the newly created states of the west, as can be seen in Columbus,

Figure 4. The Capitol, Washington, D.C., as it appeared ca. 1870. COURTESY OF THE LIBRARY OF CONGRESS, LC-USZ62-4338.

Ohio, and Nashville, Tennessee. Such buildings proclaimed the arrival of an instant culture evocative of the greatest legacies of antiquity, yet could serve as the context for the workings of a grassroots democracy as exemplified by George Caleb Bingham's painting *The Verdict of the People* (1854–1855), where election results are read to a community from the steps of a classical portico. Greek temples were used in nearly every building type, as seen in Philadelphia, where William Strickland based his design for the Second Bank of the United States (1818–1824) on the Parthenon in Athens, and Thomas U. Walter created a monumental Corinthian temple to serve as the central building at Girard College (1833–1847). Despite this compelling fashion for the Greek, a temple is a rather restrictive form, often poorly lighted because of shadowy colonnades. Both of these Philadelphia examples have interiors vaulted in the Roman manner to make them more functional.

In Washington, D.C., during the 1830s and 1840s several federal buildings were being built in the neoclassical manner by Robert Mills, who in 1836 had also designed the Washington Monument to be built at the heart of the city. This 555.5-foot (169.3-meter) monument (completed by Thomas L. Casey in 1884) in the shape of an ancient Egyptian obelisk is a prime example of the cult worship that arose around President Washington in the nineteenth century as the new nation sought to establish its own history of heroes and myths. This tribute to Washington seeks to outdo the structures of the most monumental builders of all time, the ancient Egyptian pharaohs.

In the mid nineteenth century a major exception to Washington's classical norm for federal buildings was built on a prominent location on the Mall. The architect James Renwick erected the Smithsonian Institution (1846–1855), a dark, brooding, asymmetrical pile of medieval towers and Romanesque arches, appearing like a picturesque cluster of buildings constructed over several generations. The head of the building committee, Congressman Robert Dale Owen published *Hints on Public Architecture* (1849) in which he promoted medieval revival architecture as more flexible, functional, and economical than Greek Revival temples. Other than the late-nineteenth-century Richardsonian Romanesque, classical styles with their civic and public connotations have tended to be preferred over medieval styles for major governmental buildings. Such styles as the Gothic Revival are more associated with religion, natural settings, and individuality.

AN EXPANDING LAND AND THE GILDED AGE

In the early nineteenth century there was an explosive growth in the founding of new colleges, much of it fueled by the desire of various religious groups to have colleges established throughout an ever-growing land. In 1862, Abraham Lincoln signed the Morrill Act providing the means for all states to establish land-grant colleges. Rather than stressing a traditional curriculum of classical or theological education, these new, more democratic institutions were to be built around the pragmatic fields of agriculture, the mechanical arts, and military science. Many of these land-grant colleges would be placed in isolated, rural locations, such as State College, Pennsylvania, and Urbana-Champaign, Illinois. Along with facilitating the agricultural mission of these schools, such a location reflected an often-repeated theme in American higher education; the need to create an ideal learned community of young adults uncorrupted by the temptations of the big city. Another advantage, to the nineteenth-century romantic mind, was life close to nature, with all of its moral and aesthetic advantages. The landscape architect Frederick Law Olmsted was a popular campus planner in the late nineteenth century. He advocated campuses designed like picturesque parks, with small buildings informally grouped. This represented a sharp break from the rigid classical arrangements of the past, which were dominated by a central, large building. Many campuses followed this more naturalistic approach, as can be seen in such diverse places as Smith College and the Kansas State Agricultural College (now Kansas State University); however, most of these colleges were still built with an Old Main dominating the grounds.

For most American children in the nineteenth century the architectural domain of education was the one-room rural schoolhouse. Although there were many variations, the archetypal rural school evoked the higher moral environments of the home and church. A houselike rectangular, gabled block often had such churchlike elements as a belltower, pure white color, and separate entrances for females and males. Most often, children of all ages were taught by one teacher, who encouraged the older children to help the younger. The building became a community gathering point for dispersed rural populations as they congregated for such events as a holiday pageant. To many immigrant families it represented assimilation into American society, for children met people from many backgrounds and were required to learn English. For Native Americans, though, a reservation school teaching only the knowledge, values, and language of white society represented a ruthless effort to eliminate their culture.

In the official realm, the restrictive form of a neoclassical temple often seemed too confining to the growing scale and bureaucracy of government in Victorian America. When the State, War, and Navy Building (1871–1888; now the Old Executive Office Building; Fig. 5) was built in Washington by Alfred B. Mullett (the Treasury Department's Supervising Architect, 1866–1874), it dwarfed its surroundings, including the White House to the east. The chaste, democratic Greek Revival of the early nineteenth century was replaced by the fashionable neobaroque elegance of Napoleon III's Second Empire in France. Mullett's sprawling palacelike block is animated with pavilions, mansard roofs, and a seemingly endless succession of columns.

This enlargement in scale can also be seen in state capitols. The modest Greek Revival Illinois State Capitol in Springfield by John F. Rague, built in the 1830s, was superseded by a much more grandly scaled and ornamented capitol by J. C. Cochrane (1867–1888), reflecting changes in how the people of Illinois thought of themselves. Their state was no longer a western outpost of ill-defined opportunities, but had become a rapidly growing agricultural, commercial, and industrial center for the Midwest, with more sophisticated tastes—as their new capitol made clear. By this time a common type had emerged for state capitols (although there were many individual departures and variations), where wings accommodating the two houses of the legislature flanked a central ceremonial space, usually a domed rotunda, fronted by a portico providing public access. This formula was first suggested by the U.S. Capitol in its various forms and found its first mature expression in a state capitol in Harrisburg, Pennsylvania (Stephen Hills; 1810–1821; now destroyed).

County courthouses, state universities, and capitols often played substantial roles in the competition among cities to predominate in their particular region. The question of which city was to be the county seat or home of the state university often led to major political struggles with long-term economic impact on the winning and losing communities. State capitals often moved in the nineteenth century following changes in population growth and convenience; as a result, capitol buildings often proved to be temporary dwellings of government, echoing the nature of a transient society filling a land of changing boundaries with an unpredictable future. On the other hand, state capitols and county courthouses were monumental symbols in the nineteenth century of the systematic taking of land from the Native Americans for the primary use of white Americans of European descent.

For many citizens direct interaction with the state capitol or Washington, D.C., is minimal. The county courthouse is a more tangible presence of government that is involved in a person's legal relationship to a community, from marriage licenses to court trials. The courthouse is also the archive for the county, where such vital records as land deeds are kept. The workings of a civilized community living under laws is manifested in the county courthouse. It is a place where a community gathers on special occasions and builds memorials to its leaders and military dead. And it is occasionally the stage for landmark legal cases with implications well beyond the county, such as the courtroom struggle of William Jennings Bryan and Clarence Darrow in the 1925 Scopes trial in the Rhea County Courthouse at Dayton, Tennessee.

By the late nineteenth century the courthouse tended to be the dominant architectural landmark in its city. Often standing alone in the central square in town, a tower or dome proclaimed the building's

Figure 5. The State, War, and Navy Building, Washington, D.C. (1871–1881), now the Old Executive Office Building. COURTESY OF THE LIBRARY OF CONGRESS, LC-USZ62-3128.

preeminence over the local architectural environment. This pride-filled symbol of the booster spirit of a county seat was sometimes inflated in size and expense beyond what was truly appropriate for a particular county. One notorious example is the Macoupin County Courthouse (1867–1870) in Carlinville, Illinois, by Elijah E. Myers, the architect of several state capitols. Although the building was budgeted to cost $50,000, the final bill was for $1,380,000 due to graft and the extravagance of its classical design. It took over four decades for the county to pay off the debt.

With the growth of cities in the nineteenth century, the responsibilities of municipal government grew markedly. The design for Philadelphia City Hall (1871–1901) by John McArthur, Jr., reflected a combination of the growing size of local government, city pride, and the excesses of political corruption. Filling the center square of Philadelphia, this heavily ornamented Second Empire masonry pile boasts a tower 511 feet (156 meters) high,

topped by a 37-foot (11-meter) statue of William Penn. During this building's lengthy construction, a seminal public building was built in Pittsburgh: the Allegheny County Courthouse and Jail (1884–1888), designed by America's most prominent architect of the day, Henry Hobson Richardson. Like the Philadelphia City Hall, Richardson's courthouse is a large pavilioned block culminating in a landmark tower. However, Richardson has calmed down the exuberance and eclecticism of Victorian architecture. Unlike the Philadelphia building, ornament and picturesque effects do not dominate. Richardson concentrated on the essential masses, where the forms correspond to the functions within; the rusticated stone walls are articulated by the round arched openings of his distinctive Richardsonian Romanesque style. The Richardsonian romanesque, with its qualities of massiveness, stability, and functional clarity, made it one of the most popular architectural styles for public buildings at the end of the nineteenth century, from the Old Post

Office Building in Washington, D.C. (1891–1899, by W. J. Edbrooke), to numerous courthouses built throughout Texas.

THE AMERICAN RENAISSANCE VERSUS THE SKYSCRAPER

A return to classical order at the end of the Victorian era was heralded by the 1893 World's Columbian Exposition in Chicago. This was a temporary city with white plaster walls organized around a central court of honor. Its classicism, inspired by the teachings of the École des Beaux-Arts in Paris, was one of richness and magnitude suggesting Roman imperialism in contrast to the Greek reserve and severity seen at the beginning of the century. America had moved from a democratic experiment to a world power with imperial aspirations. This world's fair presented a unified ensemble of generously spaced classical buildings that was in sharp contrast to the random development of the emerging skyscraper city in the congestion of downtown Chicago. This illusionary "White City" of the fair would be a compelling model for public architecture for years to come.

Sometimes called the American Renaissance, the turn of the century often saw a desire to reform the center of a city into a unified classical vision, a "City Beautiful." The construction of Washington, D.C., in the nineteenth century had departed sharply from L'Enfant's original intentions. In 1901–1902, a Senate Park Commission advised a return to a modified L'Enfant plan that would be the basis for much of monumental Washington. Many City Beautiful plans were made, but few were fully realized; nonetheless, this planning movement had a major impact upon those model cities for America, the college campus. Cass Gilbert's 1910 master plan for the University of Minnesota, Minneapolis, reflected a revival of interest in Jefferson's plan for the University of Virginia, now greatly monumentalized in the Beaux-Arts classical manner.

Many new state capitols were built during the American Renaissance, most reaffirming the domed, two-winged type, though now academically executed in a more knowing manner of classical and Renaissance sources (in contrast to the innocent simplicity of the Greek Revival and the free eclecticism of the Victorian era). Cass Gilbert's Minnesota State Capitol in Saint Paul (1895–1904) is one of the more refined examples, while Joseph M.

Huston's Pennsylvania State Capitol in Harrisburg (1901–1909) was one of the most excessive (this building's financial scandal eventually landed the architect in jail).

The often-seen tendency of some communities to aggrandize their cities with public buildings of a scale and form associated with more important buildings is well represented by San Francisco's City Hall (1913–1915, by John Bakewell, Jr., and Arthur Brown, Jr.; Fig. 6). Clearly mimicking the domed-palace-block form of Beaux-Arts classical state capitols, this building stands impressively at the heart of a unified civic center of buildings in the City Beautiful manner. However, many Beaux-Arts classical city halls are less dominant in their design, and appear to be just one classical block within a master plan, such as the understated Des Moines City Hall (1910–1911). This city hall was built for a progressive, commission form of city government: a large hall allowed the public to watch the city employees at work (no city bosses would be making deals behind closed doors).

The early development of modern architecture in America was not fought out in the conservative field of governmental architecture. One notable exception was the Woodbury County Courthouse (1915–1918) at Sioux City, Iowa, by the Prairie School firm of Purcell and Elmslie (for William L. Steele). It combines the abstract rectilinear geometry of Frank Lloyd Wright with the organic ornamentation of Louis H. Sullivan. Form follows function as the public offices and courtrooms are contained in the broad base. A skyscraper tower contains more private functions. Despite the radical nature of the building's aesthetic, Purcell and Elmslie did incorporate several traditional features: the series of piers across the front facade is reminiscent of a colonnade, the large lobby is capped with a dome, and the building establishes a landmark presence with its tower.

The skyscraper, that quintessential symbol of the modern American city began to have an impact upon state capitols by the 1920s and 1930s. Rather than the traditional Renaissance Revival dome, Bertram Goodhue's Nebraska State Capitol at Lincoln (1922–1932) is topped with a soaring skyscraper tower. Louisiana governor Huey Long's political ego was monumentalized in a similar skyscraper capitol at Baton Rouge (1931–1932). Even some university campuses started to go vertical: most spectacularly, Charles Z. Klauder's forty-two-story Gothic Revival Cathedral of Learning at the University of Pittsburgh (1924–1937).

Figure 6.   San Francisco City Hall (1913–1915). COURTESY OF THE SAN FRANCISCO PUBLIC LIBRARY.

In the early twentieth century, there was a renewed interest in the Gothic style for college campuses. It offered an alternative to the sometimes cold and monumental classicism of the day. Architects like Ralph Adam Cram and such educators as Woodrow Wilson at Princeton advocated the English Collegiate Gothic and its monastic quadrangles as evocative of the original ideals of college life. This introspective turning toward an elite club of the intellectually and socially select reveling in things English was especially appealing to the private universities of the Ivy League, and is well illustrated by the cloistered confines of Princeton and Yale universities. Many state universities opted for a more open approach of generously spaced buildings, often in the more economical and "American" style of the Georgian revival, as can be seen in the early-twentieth-century architecture of the University of Illinois at Urbana-Champaign.

From the 1920s to the 1950s, most one-room, single-teacher schoolhouses were abandoned in favor of consolidated schools in town, an approach facilitated by the coming of the yellow school bus. The typical urban school of the early twentieth century was a large multiple-classroom building of several stories, where students were now divided by grade level and were taught in a building with a great variety of rooms, allowing for such diverse activities as shop and theater. The nineteenth-century image of a schoolhouse evocative of home and church was replaced by an institutional building whose modular regularity sometimes suggests a factory. Nonetheless, many schools were embellished with the forms and ornament of fashionable architectural styles, making them proud cultural monuments at the center of a community, as can be seen in the neo-Gothic Evanston Township High School in Illinois by Perkins, Fellows and Hamilton

1307

(1923–1924). Elegant school architecture could also symbolize the gross inequities of American society, as was played out on the steps of Central High School in Little Rock, Arkansas, when this exclusively white public school was ordered by the federal government to desegregate in 1957.

Washington, D.C., underwent tremendous growth during the twentieth century, including a number of national shrines as American society continued to sanctify its history. The primary function of Henry Bacon's Lincoln Memorial (1911–1922) and John Russell Pope's Jefferson Memorial (1935–1943) is to contain a larger-than-life statue of a revered president; these structures come much closer than most neoclassical buildings to the original use of classical temples as the abode of a cult figure to a god. While the White House and the Capitol, the quarters for the executive and legislative branches of the federal government, have always been at the core of the plan of Washington and its buildings, the third major branch of government, the judiciary, did not have a building of its own until Cass Gilbert's Supreme Court Building was built (1928–1935) to the east of the Capitol. Since the 1860s the Supreme Court had been meeting in the Old Senate Chamber of the Capitol. Gilbert's white marble temple is one of the most imperial neoclassical buildings in America; to those who pass through its immense portico the building communicates the supreme authority and judgment of the country's laws. Perhaps the greatest impression of twentieth-century Washington, D.C., is not its monuments but the endless number of buildings that have been built for the country's bureaucracy, such as the Federal Triangle, where block after classical block was built during the 1920s and 1930s to accommodate various departments of the nation's government.

FROM THE PWA TO MODERNISM AND BEYOND

Franklin D. Roosevelt's New Deal ushered in a degree of federal involvement in local affairs previously unseen. Such traditional symbols of local pride as a city hall or a public library were now being built by the federal government under New Deal programs such as the Public Works Administration (PWA; 1933–1939). A PWA building often meant a significant upgrading of a local public facility. It was a tangible symbol of governmental stability during the Great Depression, as well as a

symbol that the nation was going back to work. The styles of PWA buildings exhibited great variety, sometimes reassuringly using regional traditions such as a colonial revival post office in Delaware or a Pueblo-style courthouse in New Mexico. Some buildings were more radically modern, such as John Lloyd Wright's Coolspring School in Indiana. However, the style often associated with PWA buildings is stripped classicism, as seen in Charles Z. Klauder's design for Pattee Library at Pennsylvania State University. This austere, more abstract approach to classicism was especially suitable for a nation in a depression desiring to build monumental buildings without ostentation.

In 1939, Ludwig Mies van der Rohe began to create a new plan for the Illinois Institute of Technology on the south side of Chicago. Several city blocks were replaced with a new campus consisting of glass, steel, and brick blocks that looked like carefully designed factories. In the era after World War II, modernism would triumph in American architecture creating a dilemma for public architecture. Civic architecture has often been conservative, reaffirming traditional architectural images of authority such as the portico, dome, or tower. Could a glass box convey such symbolism? Chicago's Richard J. Daley Center (1960–1966) is a steel-and-glass skyscraper containing 121 courtrooms for the city and Cook County. Nothing distinguishes its exterior

Figure 7.   Richard J. Daley Center, Chicago, Illinois (1960–1966). COURTESY OF THE CHICAGO HISTORICAL SOCIETY, HEDRICH-BLESSING PHOTO. HB-29086J.

from a corporate skyscraper other than its isolated location on an entire city block surrounded by an open plaza (Fig. 7).

Some architects deemed the anonymous glass box insufficient as a model for a major public building. A striking alternative was offered by Kallmann, McKinnell, and Knowles's Boston City Hall (1963–1969). Influenced by the brutal concrete forms of Le Corbusier's late buildings, Boston City Hall represents a turning toward a monumentality of heavy masses and geometric shapes. The various functions find separate expression yet all are brought together into a unified whole, appearing a bit like an abstract classical temple. While this building is clearly a monument to modern Boston, other communities have de-emphasized the symbolic role of public architecture. Any functional, no-frills office building is sufficient to house the growing administrative nature of local government. A building that makes a major architectural statement can be construed as a waste of the taxpayers' money. The changing nature of local government can also be seen in city council chambers, which in recent times have tended to emphasize dialogue by having citizens face the council members in modestly scaled rooms, in contrast to the large, formal chambers of the past, where the audience looked down on the proceedings from balconies.

The baby boom years after World War II were naturally boom years for school architecture. The multistory, revival-style educational institutions of the early twentieth century were often replaced with sprawling one-story suburban schools where generously fenestrated modern geometric blocks were distributed in wings appropriate to their functions. An important early precursor to this development is the Crow Island Elementary School in Winnetka, Illinois (1939–1940), by Eliel and Eero Saarinen, and Perkins, Wheeler, and Will. School architecture in recent times has often reflected revisionist attitudes toward curriculum, such as the flexible open plans popular during the 1960s, which allowed for such approaches as team teaching.

At the end of his life, America's most noted modern architect, Frank Lloyd Wright, finally had an opportunity to design a major governmental building, the Marin County Civic Center at San Rafael, California (1957–1972). The building sprawls across its site, addressing the natural context in a manner characteristic of Wright. However, at its center he included a low dome and a separate tower; unlike much of his earlier work, Wright chose to link this building (though in an abstract

Figure 8. Public Service Building, Portland, Oregon (1980–1983). COURTESY OF THE CITY OF PORTLAND.

manner) with the architectural traditions of its type: the American county courthouse.

Postmodernism has brought about a renewed interest in the tradition of building types and historical styles. Michael Graves's Public Service Building in Portland, Oregon (1980–1983; Fig. 8), reflects a partial return to monumental classical forms and symbolic ornament, but with a mannerist manipulation of motifs evocative of the uneasy and disjointed links between contemporary life and the traditions of history. The growth of historic preservation has sought to save the public architecture of the past and to adapt sensitively and add on to existing landmarks. A case in point is the new Civic Center (1982–1990) that Charles Moore and the Urban Innovations Group integrated into the older complex of the 1932 Spanish baroque revival city hall in Beverly Hills, California. Old and new play off of each other as a popular new public place is created.

College architecture has been an arena for all major currents in architecture since 1945. When many new buildings went up to accommodate the explosive growth of colleges and universities from the late 1940s to the 1960s many unified Beaux-Arts classical or Gothic Revival campuses were violated by the ahistorical individuality typical of so many modern buildings. Campus planning became more open-ended where unpredictable growth was expected. Colleges and universities sometimes became the experimental grounds for innovative architects. Charles W. Moore and William Turnbull radically rethought a residential college into a playful village where such communal features as the laundromat were given landmark status in their design for Kresge College (1965–1974) at the University of California, Santa Cruz. Peter Eisenman in his Wexner Center for the Visual Arts (1983–1989) entered into a deconstructionist dialogue with Ohio State University's existing buildings, the aesthetics of demolished buildings, and the conflicting grids of Columbus, Ohio.

The past few decades have been an uneasy time for American monuments. When Venturi and Rauch created Franklin Court in Philadelphia (1972–1976) as a bicentennial tribute to Benjamin Franklin, they chose not to rebuild Franklin's house but to create a ghostly outline of it in stainless steel, with hooded openings in the pavement so that one could see what was left of the foundations. Instead of reconstructing history (like twentieth-century Williamsburg) they clarified what we do and do not know. Maya Lin's Vietnam Veterans Memorial (1981–1982) is the opposite of most of Washington's monuments; it is dark and abstract and recedes into the ground. Its two granite walls (inscribed with the names of the over 58,000 Americans who died in Vietnam) align with the Washington Monument and the Lincoln Memorial as a new example of public building continues the complex symbolizing of American society.

The public architecture of America provides a monumental chronicle of society's changing attitudes toward government and education. At first, colonial public architecture reflected in a diminutive manner the distant institutions of civilization in the homeland. With the founding of a new nation, instant monuments evocative of noble aspirations were sought. As the country grew, so did the scale of government, and the size and constituency of education. Historical forms and styles have often been appropriated for their symbolic associations. The modernist disdain in the mid twentieth century with history in favor of function and structure created the paradox of creating useful buildings devoid of traditional meanings. Many public buildings in recent years have returned to a dialogue with the past, as one sees a renewal of interest in establishing a meaningful architecture for the public realm.

BIBLIOGRAPHY

Allen, William C. *The United States Capitol: A Brief Architectural History* (1990).

American Bar Association and American Institute of Architects. *The American Courthouse: Planning and Design for the Judicial Process* (1973).

Craig, Lois, and Federal Architecture Project. *The Federal Presence: Architecture, Politics, and Symbols in United States Government Building* (1978).

Glazer, Nathan, and Mark Lilla, eds. *The Public Face of Architecture: Civic Culture and Public Spaces* (1987).

Gulliford, Andrew. *America's Country Schools* (1984).

Hitchcock, Henry-Russell, and William Seale. *Temples of Democracy: The State Capitols of the U.S.A.* (1976).

Hoyt, Charles King. *Public, Municipal, and Community Buildings* (1980).

Klauder, Charles Z., and Herbert C. Wise. *College Architecture in America and Its Part in the Development of the Campus* (1929).

Lebovich, William L., and Historic American Buildings Survey. *America's City Halls* (1984).

Lowry, Bates. *Building a National Image: Architectural Drawings for the American Democracy, 1789–1912* (1985).

Maddex, Diane, ed. *Built in the U.S.A.: American Buildings from Airports to Zoos* (1985).

Morrison, Hugh. *Early American Architecture: From the First Colonial Settlements to the National Period* (1952).

Owen, Robert Dale. *Hints on Public Architecture* (1849).

Pare, Richard, ed. *Court House: A Photographic Document* (1978).

Reiff, Daniel D. *Washington Architecture, 1791–1861: Problems in Development* (1971).

Roth, Leland M. *A Concise History of American Architecture* (1979).

Sexton, R. W., ed. *American Public Buildings of Today* (1931).

Short, C. W., and R. Stanley-Brown. *Public Buildings: A Survey of Architecture of Projects Constructed by Federal and Other Governmental Bodies Between the Years 1933 and 1939 with the Assistance of the Public Works Administrations* (1939; repr. 1986).

Turner, Paul Venable. *Campus: An American Planning Tradition* (1984).

U.S. Treasury Department. *A History of Public Buildings Under the Control of the Treasury Department.* Compiled by W. H. Wills and J. A. Sutherland (1901).

Zabel, Craig, and Susan S. Munshower, eds. *American Public Architecture: European Roots and Native Expressions* (1989).

SEE ALSO **The City; Landscapes; Parades, Holidays, and Public Rituals; Urban Cultural Institutions; Village and Town.**

COMMERCIAL ARCHITECTURE

Robert Alan Benson

THE HISTORY OF COMMERCIAL and industrial architecture in the United States is integrally connected with the emergence and development of the most characteristic attitudes, values, and ideals of middle-class Americans. While important facets of the national psyche are reflected in American civic and residential architecture, it is in commercial and industrial building that the most cherished precepts concerning the relationship between private and public enterprise have been dynamically interwoven and expressed.

The Atlantic colonies were established in large part for mercantile purposes. Although many inhabitants had other reasons for settling in the New World, the mercantile impulse was germane to the culture and politics of the new land. Although in 1789 government was constitutionally separated from religion, its fertile relationship to private enterprise, cultivated from the outset of the colonial period, was affirmed. This relationship has remained so vital that in the twentieth century, commercial architecture emphatically represents such national cultural ideals as individualism, ambition, wealth, success, and personal power, as well as social and economic power, the growth of urbanization, and the rise of a market economy.

Freedom, pragmatism, ingenuity, functionalism, and technological progressiveness are among the obvious qualities associated with American commercial and industrial architecture; however, these qualities only began to generate an identifiable architectural expression in the early nineteenth century. Prior to that they had borrowed forms and images from both the civic and residential spheres. Early colonial commercial architecture reflected a mixture of medieval traditions and more urbane seventeenth-century English and continental architectural taste. Retail and small commercial ventures were often managed as family businesses and installed in residences or buildings of residential character, such as the Paul Revere House (1677) in Boston. Trade restrictions imposed by Britain

inhibited the development of mill or industrial building, although European visitors often found American applications of wind- and waterpower in smaller projects to be ingenious and more frequent than in Europe.

Colonial versions of European high-style architecture, based in large part on pattern books, available materials, and incidental local craft, were first introduced in governmental, religious, and residential structures. These eventually lent larger cities such as Boston and Philadelphia a character similar to contemporary London. As the familiar vocabulary was adapted for the agencies of finance and commerce, a uniquely American urban character began to evolve.

One of the earliest examples of such an adaptation is Faneuil Hall (1740), given by Peter Faneuil to the city of Boston to enclose and improve the farmers' market on Dock Square (Fig. 1). The plans were prepared by the portrait painter John Smibert (1688–1751), which indicates the absence of professional architects in mid-eighteenth-century America. It was constructed of red brick with an arcade around the first-floor market space and sash windows admitting light to the second-story public

Figure 1.   Faneuil Hall, Boston (1740). COURTESY OF THE BOSTONIAN SOCIETY/OLD STATE HOUSE.

1313

meeting hall, an arrangement generally derived from European models. The whole block was covered by a gabled roof surmounted by a cupola and loosely resembled the familiar New England meeting-house. The adjacency of market and meeting room reinforced the fact that Faneuil Hall was a popular forum where town worthies informally exchanged opinions on public matters while shopping.

In 1760, land in Newport, Rhode Island, was dedicated to the construction of a market building which, like Faneuil Hall, had an open trading area on the first floor surmounted by two stories of flexible space used for storage, offices, and shops. The Brick Market (1772; Fig. 2) was designed by Peter Harrison (1716–1775), a British-born merchant whose intense interest in architecture had caused him to collect the largest library of treatises and pattern books in the country. His scheme was based on a design by Inigo Jones, who had introduced Italian classicism to England in the late sixteenth century and whose work had been in revival since the early eighteenth century in England.

Although Harrison was no more than a gifted amateur, professional architecture was encouraged and supported by the country's other great amateur, Thomas Jefferson, as a mark of sophistication and wise planning. Commercial architecture began to profit from professional architectural services upon the immigration of Benjamin Henry Latrobe (1764–1820) from England in 1796. The Bank of Pennsylvania (1798–1800; razed 1860s) in Philadelphia is a distinguished example of his early work (Fig. 3). It exhibited masonry construction, including interior vaulting for both structure and architectural effect. Temple porticos fronted both ends of a block supporting a low pantheonic dome, beneath which was

Figure 3. Bank of Pennsylvania (1798–1800; razed 1860s). COURTESY OF THE HISTORICAL SOCIETY OF PENNSYLVANIA, THE PENROSE COLLECTION.

located the banking room, generously illuminated by daylight. The design established a standard of elegance and efficiency that was followed in banking and commercial buildings throughout the country.

William Strickland (c. 1787–1854), who was a talented designer and Latrobe's pupil, won a competition in 1818 for the Second Bank of the United States (1819–1824) in Philadelphia. Faced with Pennsylvania marble, this was the first public building to derive from the Parthenon and signaled the advent of the Greek Revival, the style with which Americans identified nationally after the War of 1812. The Greek Revival style was also employed by Strickland in his design for the Merchants' Exchange (1832) in Philadelphia that converted irregularities of the city plan to advantage. The wedge-shaped site was terminated at its narrower end by a semicircular Corinthian portico surmounted by a lantern modeled on the choragic Monument of Lysicrates of late classical Athens. A similar dependence on classical models characterized the Merchants' Exchange (1836–1842) in New York by Isaiah Rogers (1800–1869). Its exterior Ionic colonnade on a high podium screened a brick-vaulted exchange room 80 feet (24 meters) in diameter.

Such references were certainly signs of sophisticated architectural taste and erudition on the part of designers; but they also directly reinforced pop-

Figure 2. Brick Market, Newport, Rhode Island (1772). FROM THE COLLECTION OF THE NEWPORT HISTORICAL SOCIETY.

ular sentiments about the manifest destiny of the United States as the modern descendant of ancient democratic Greece. This was particularly important during the period of Jacksonian expansionism when the drive westward was envisioned as bringing civilization to the wilderness as well as taking advantage of the limitless natural resources of the Great Plains and western mountains. Towns founded during this period often took Greek names as symbols of this spirit: Athens, Syracuse, Sparta, Utica, Ithaca, Arcadia, Alexandria, Delphos, Troy, Memphis, Corinth. Commercial architecture along the principal streets of these and similar towns was often of a reduced neoclassicism, thus serving as an understated context for more prominent civic, religious, and residential structures in Greek Revival style.

With British restrictions on manufacturing removed by the Revolution, the United States sought to achieve economic independence through the development of industry. In the late eighteenth century, structures based on existing sawmills in New England began to house waterpowered machinery for producing textiles. The earliest mills employed traditional materials and structural techniques, amplified around the turn of the century with the malleability, permanence, and strength of cast iron.

Probably the first building to be planned and constructed as a textile mill was the 1793 spinning mill designed by Samuel Slater (1768–1835) in Pawtucket, Rhode Island (Fig. 4). Based on his experience and familiarity with English textile production, the machinery was housed in a frame structure whose proportions and noble simplicity were consonant with the residential context. The main requirements—large, continuous interior spaces in a two-story block, adequate daylighting, and a structural system rigid enough to stabilize the building against vibrations from the power mechanism and machinery—were all satisfied functionally without sacrificing basic architectural principles or pleasing design. Such a successful integration of social, commercial, and architectural values by manufacturers allayed the fears of many agrarian-minded citizens that industrialization would contaminate the morality of the nation.

The rapid growth of manufacturing in the period between 1810 and 1820 began to alter the size and form of mill buildings. Mills became larger in all dimensions and were increasingly constructed in stone or brick masonry for rigidity and fire protection. They acquired clerestory-light monitors to make their attic spaces more useful, as in the Lippitt Mill (1809–1810) in West Warwick, Rhode Island. With cupolas holding bells to call the workers to their jobs, mills became increasingly important as the focus of community life, especially in small towns.

In the first four decades of the nineteenth century, manufacturing moved beyond the limits of local capital and mechanical skills. To increase output capacity, the textile industry was gradually transformed by an investment and managerial structure geared to efficient production and the organization of a large labor force. Mill buildings evolved to meet new safety needs and production realities. Large lateral towers added for circulation, fire containment, and vertical mechanical runs separated the mill from the meetinghouse typologically, as in the woolen mill by Zachariah Allen (1822; enlarged 1839) in Allendale, Rhode Island. Landscape design, reliance on neoclassical architectural principles to govern a complex of buildings, and a concern for appropriate living quarters for single men and women as well as for families transformed factories from isolated objects into planned communities, sometimes of compelling visual appeal. In the Crown and Eagle mills (1825, 1829, respectively) by Learned Scott in North Uxbridge, Massachusetts, boardinghouses, dormitory structures, and row housing, along with the factory buildings, began to reshape the urban fabric in conjunction with waterways and green areas.

While manufacturing before the Civil War frequently remained rural due to the necessity of locating mills and factories where waterpower could best be harnessed, retail architecture was decidedly urban and more directly responsive to changing technology and economics as well as fashion. The shopping arcade or *passage,* inaugurated in France

Figure 4.   Old Slater Mill (1793). COURTESY OF THE RHODE ISLAND HISTORICAL SOCIETY, PHOTOGRAPH BY H. L. SPENCER, RHIX3328.

in 1790, appeared in the United States in Philadelphia (1827) and Providence, Rhode Island (1828–1829). Designed by John Haviland (1792–1852), the Philadelphia Arcade had street-front arcades while the Providence Arcade, designed by Russell Warren (1783–1860) and James C. Bucklin (1801–1890), had a glass-roofed interior.

The Gothic Revival, a romantic phenomenon that followed on the heels of the Greek Revival, produced a few retail buildings, for example, the step-gabled and pinnacled Oak Hall on North Street in Boston, a frame structure of mid-century date. The use of wood for such highly detailed ornamental buildings was actually facilitated by the invention of the jigsaw during this period, a by-product of the industrial revolution.

In the end, neither the Greek nor the Gothic Revival lent themselves to the economic or spatial exigencies of retail building. Rather, in the late 1840s the Palazzo style began to dominate retail and office buildings, where rows of arched windows separated by engaged columns in the manner of sixteenth-century Venetian palaces defined the stories. Stewart's Downtown Store in New York (1845), executed in white marble, was the first to apply this generalized Renaissance style whose main advantage was its ability to be extended both horizontally and vertically over a large commercial facade.

The rapid spread of the Palazzo style in the 1850s and 1860s was encouraged by the development of cast iron as a finish material as well as a structural component. Pioneered in the United States by James Bogardus (1800–1874), an inventor and foundry owner, iron appeared in the Baltimore Sun Building (1848; Fig. 5), which he designed in collaboration with R. G. Hatfield, and in his design for the Harper Brothers Building in New York (1854). The Sun Building had two iron fronts that had been cast in sections at the Bogardus foundry, shipped to the site, and assembled with bolts as a prefabricated building skin. Iron thus made the repetition of facade units entirely practical as well as far cheaper than building in conventional materials and methods. Cast iron was normally rendered in forms that imitated stone and, because it needed to be painted to protect against weathering, it could be given any color the architect or patron desired. Flexible, practical, and cheap, the popularity of cast-iron components spread rapidly from urban centers to towns and villages to become the first identifiable commercial vernacular architecture.

Perhaps more important, Bogardus used iron as a system of cast columns and wrought beams in the Sun Building. The slender columns, which eliminated the need for heavy masonry-bearing walls, afforded unprecedented interior space as well as lightness and rapid construction by semi-skilled labor. Iron also lent itself to other building components such as stairways and railings. It thus set the stage for the concept of a structural cage in which loads could be carried on continuous columns from top story to foundation. This system was utilized already in the A. T. Stewart Store in New York (1862) by John Kellum, one of the largest cast-iron buildings anywhere. Its central rotunda was surrounded by galleries beneath a skylight and contained a pipe organ for the entertainment of the customers.

Bogardus pushed his system further when he constructed a shot tower for the McCullough Shot and Lead Company of New York (1855). A metal frame served as the structure of the tower with brickwork used merely as infill, thus adumbrating the emergence of the steel skeletal frame in Chicago and New York some thirty years later. In addition to the employment of cast iron, the Haughwout Building (1856) in New York by John P. Gaynor and Daniel Badger incorporated the first passenger elevator. Invented by Elisha Otis, the elevator became the second stimulant of vastly increased height in commercial buildings throughout the country.

Cast iron was also used widely in other commercial-building types. The Crystal Palace (1853) in Bryant Park by Carstensen and Gildemeister

Figure 5. Baltimore Sun Building (1848). COURTESY OF THE MARYLAND HISTORICAL SOCIETY, BALTIMORE.

brought both the materials and the concept of the London Exposition and its Crystal Palace of 1851 to New York. A twenty-minute fire that destroyed the gossamer exposition building in 1858 proved that the major disadvantage of iron was its low melting point. The train shed of the first Grand Central Station (1871) in New York by John B. Snook used a metal skeleton carrying glass panels, as did many other railroad stations. These were superseded by less-combustible steel structures after about 1875 due to the spread of the Bessemer steel process, invented simultaneously in England by Henry Bessemer and in Kentucky by William Kelly in 1856.

Rapid commercial growth after the Civil War produced the most important developments in commercial and industrial architecture. Skyrocketing land values in urban centers demanded that technology address higher density and concentration in commercial buildings. The powerful combination of profit and prestige became the driving motivation for ever-taller buildings. Never before had the largest, tallest, and most dominant buildings in an urban skyline represented the private power of the commercial, financial, and industrial enterprises of a society rather than the power and authority of its religious or governmental institutions.

In New York, the Tribune Building by Richard M. Hunt and the Western Union Building by George B. Post (both built from 1873 to 1875) announced the success of private investment in mass communication. Yet by extending their Victorian masses upward through picturesque clock towers without giving up traditional bearing-wall masonry, they remained only on the cusp of stylistic and technological change. But in the frantic effort to rebuild Chicago after the disastrous fire of 1871, the technological and engineering advances begun by James Bogardus and others came to fruition. Large quantities of concentrated office space were needed to house the growing legions of white-collar workers and secretarial staffs required by the administrations of the vastly expanding business enterprises there. The advantages of metal and glass radically altered the engineering and design of the new fireproof buildings that mushroomed in the Loop to meet the demand.

The first Leiter Building (1879) by William Le Baron Jenney (1832–1907) used cast-iron columns for both interior and peripheral loads, situated columns next to the brick envelope of the facade, and substituted huge plate-glass windows for bearing-walls. Jenney, who had been trained as a civil engineer in France, took the next step towards skeletal

Figure 6. Home Insurance Building, Chicago, Illinois (1883–1885; following the addition of 1891). COURTESY OF THE CHICAGO HISTORICAL SOCIETY, ICHI-00980.

engineering in the Home Insurance Company Building (1883–1885; Fig. 6), which is considered the first skyscraper. Although some bearing masonry continued to support peripheral load in the first two stories, a combination of cast-iron columns and wrought-iron girders established a true skeletal frame for the upper eight stories.

Unfortunately, Jenney's engineering genius far surpassed his abilities in architectural design, where he remained bound to historical precedent and uninspired eclecticism. The question of an appropriate expression for the shell, an expression of contemporary social, economic, and cultural conditions, was taken up by other firms. That Chicago architects were dissatisfied with the initial expression of the new technology in a cloak of revivalist styles is partially attributable to the tradition of practical thinking that began with Thomas Jefferson, Charles Bulfinch, and Benjamin Henry Latrobe, manifesting itself in mill and factory design. It continued under the impulse of sculptor and critic Horatio Greenough who in his writings had called for an organic relationship between the form of a building and its internal realities.

Among those who took up the search for appropriate expression was the firm of Burnham and Root. Although he was in command of the technology at his disposal, John Wellborn Root (1850–1891) was equally concerned with the functional and aesthetic accomplishments of his buildings. The Rookery Building (1885–1886), framed in steel with masonry outer walls, addressed several practical problems by introducing a hollow core in its block-square volume. The resulting light-well permitted the handsome lobby to be brightly illuminated through skylights and insured that all offices on the inside of the upper stories would have the benefit of adequate light and ventilation. The exterior composition was additive and eclectic, a manner that Root rejected in the unornamented Monadnock Building (1889–1891), the first tall building to be treated as a slab in one continuous upward sweep. The steel cage of the Reliance Building (1894–1895) was protected against fire with terra-cotta cladding using Gothic motifs; but its vast expanses of plate glass "Chicago windows" projected the impression that its exterior was truly an expression of the frame and the interior space.

Contemporaneous with the Rookery, Henry Hobson Richardson (1838–1886), one of the foremost architects on the East Coast, designed the Marshall Field Wholesale Store (1885–1887) in Chicago (Fig. 7). The structure consisted of a mix of terra-cotta–clad, cast-iron columns on the first three floors and wood-framing typical of New England mill buildings on the floors above. The understated exterior, however, made an enormous impact on Chicago architects who saw in it an appropriate so-

lution to the form of a modern commercial building. In his religious, civic, and private commissions, Richardson had popularized an energetic neo-Romanesque style. For the Field Wholesale Store, he abandoned all romantic qualities of the revival mode in favor of a severe treatment that projected unity, integrity, economy, and rationality.

Among those most influenced by Richardson were Dankmar Adler and Louis Sullivan (1856–1924) who designed the mixed-use Auditorium Theatre Hotel (1887–1889), an important turning point in their work. Retaining their characteristic finish, ornament, and detail, especially on the interior, in their final scheme they incorporated numerous qualities of the Field Store design, including its solidity, its understatement, and its reliance on the arch as an organizing device. Sullivan developed a personal philosophy about balancing the engineering aspects of the skyscraper with the poetry of ornament derived from geometry and plants. In a series of structures for Saint Louis, Missouri (Wainwright Building, 1890–1891), Buffalo, New York (Guaranty [now Prudential] Building, 1895), and Chicago (Gage Group, 1898–1899) he envisioned tripartite vertical compositions articulated by organic ornament. Perhaps his most notable accomplishment was the Schlesinger and Mayer (now Carson Pirie Scott) Store in Chicago (1899–1904), a celebration of the social aspects of shopping, in which he enclosed the steel cage with a subtle terra-cotta skin that contrasted with an elaborate two-story band of florid wrought-iron ornament enframing the display windows and entrances at pedestrian level. After this tour de force, Sullivan spent his late career designing small banks and thrift institutions as essays in organic ornament for midwestern towns such as Grinnell, Iowa, Owatonna, Minnesota, and Sidney, Ohio.

In 1893, the World's Columbian Exposition opened in Chicago. Planned by Daniel H. Burnham (1846–1912) and landscape architect Frederick Law Olmsted (1822–1903), the Exposition was envisioned as a symbol of American industrial, commercial, and social progress four centuries after the arrival of Columbus. McKim, Mead, and White, Richard Morris Hunt, and other architects from the East Coast were invited to join stylistically conservative Chicago designers such as Burnham to create a complex of classical-revival buildings in the manner of the École des Beaux-Arts in Paris, all in an artificial setting replete with Venetian canals and a lagoon on the lakefront. They succeeded in raising consciousness about architectural and urban-design values, especially among midwesterners of

Figure 7. Marshall Field & Co. Wholesale Store, Chicago, Illinois (1885–1887). COURTESY OF THE CHICAGO HISTORICAL SOCIETY, ICHI-01588.

limited background, who saw in the "White City" a model of urbanity. Yet they also sent a powerful message about the venerability of historical revival architecture derived from Europe—in contrast to the emerging Chicago School of commercial building—as the appropriate vehicle to express commercial, industrial, and social progress as well as national identity.

The impact of the Columbian Exposition can be measured in the spread of the City Beautiful movement, a trend toward improved urban design related to Burnham's master plan for Chicago (1909), and in the continued dominance of revival styles for commercial as well as civic architecture throughout the country. In New York, the technology of steel framing reinforced rising land prices and led to ever higher buildings and more conservative design. When it was erected, the impressive Woolworth Building by Cass Gilbert (1910–1913) in Lower Manhattan was the tallest in the world at 792 feet (238 meters). Its terra-cotta cladding was cast as Gothic ornament, which inspired the nickname "cathedral of commerce" for the corporate headquarters of Frank Woolworth's chain of variety stores.

By contrast, Sullivan's protégé, Frank Lloyd Wright (1867–1959), had designed an innovative office building for the Larkin Soap Company administration in Buffalo, New York (1903; Fig. 8). Avoiding historical references altogether, Wright produced an environment derived not only from the utilitarian realities of the building and the formal precedents of Chicago commercial architecture but also from the need for programming the tasks and duties of a large secretarial staff and managerial team, for social interaction, and for a sense of dignity in the workplace. Nevertheless, apart from the circle of Sullivan and Wright, functionally based architecture without historical ornament remained limited in large part to industrial structures where it could be justified as an expression of economy and efficiency.

Perhaps the clearest indication of this dichotomy is in the architecture produced for the automobile industry. Having experimented with several alternatives to conventional mill construction in the design of factories for automotive production, the Detroit architect Albert Kahn (1869–1942) began to employ reinforced concrete as a structural system in 1905. Commissioned by Henry Ford in 1909, Kahn designed a huge assembly plant in Highland Park, Michigan, in which concrete slabs and steel-girder beams afforded not only strength, safety, and permanence but adequate clearspan space for pro-

Figure 8. Frank Lloyd Wright's Larkin Soap Building, Buffalo, New York (1903). Interior furniture by Wright as well. COURTESY OF THE BUFFALO AND ERIE COUNTY HISTORICAL SOCIETY.

duction. In 1912–1915, the plant incorporated a continuously moving assembly line, the basis of most factory production ever since.

Kahn continued to improve the architecture of factories, creating dramatic forms based on clearly analyzed functional relationships. Vast expanses of glass in industrial framing, jagged roof lines, rows of columnar smokestacks rising out of power plants, and complex truss systems for clearspan space became his trademarks, especially in huge complexes such as the Ford River Rouge Plant in Dearborn, Michigan, begun in 1916. Yet when General Motors commissioned him to design its headquarters in Detroit, Kahn turned out an impressive structure based on classical revivalism.

The General Motors Building (1922; Fig. 9) is an early example of the expression of a corporate culture, rather than the expression of the taste and power of an entrepreneurial individual or family. Rising from an arcade of show windows to display its products at street level, separate tower-like elements are connected to a slab at the back, the whole crowned by a classical colonnade at the top. The location of executive offices at the top level and the general composition of the structure metaphorically suggest the gathering of the five automotive

Figure 9. General Motors Building, Detroit, Michigan (1922). COURTESY OF THE PHOTOGRAPHIC SECTION OF THE GENERAL MOTORS CORPORATION.

companies into one corporate body. Research and development was housed in a lower block just behind the main building, reflecting its supportive but less prominent character.

The extent to which eclectic architectural vocabularies continued to connote grandeur and magnanimity in the minds of patrons can be judged by the Chicago Tribune Tower competition of 1922 in which a neo-Gothic design by John Mead Howells and Raymond Hood took first place over a group of some two hundred entries. Yet the second-place entry by Eliel Saarinen, a tower dynamically telescoping itself skyward with a limited amount of abstract ornamental detail, made its impact on countless office buildings throughout the United States and Canada, even influencing Hood and Howells in their subsequent design work, and paved the way for the important changes in skyscraper design.

The first of those changes was the Art Deco style, which reconciled the continuing taste for ornament and traditional materials with the growing interest in new industrial metals, in technology as a form of power, and in air transportation, electricity, and radio waves as symbols of progress. Art Deco also exploited architecture as a form of advertising, partly in pure verticality and partly in the identifiability of a building profile in the urban skyline. The Union Trust Building by Smith, Hinchman, and Grylls in Detroit (1929) and the Chrysler Building by William Van Alen in New York (1930) both used night illumination to enhance their presence; and the Empire State Building (1931) by Shreve, Lamb,

and Harmon in New York relied on its 101-story height to dominate most of midtown Manhattan. These qualities began to disappear as the impact of the Great Depression cautioned corporation presidents and boards of directors to seek ways of representing fiscal responsibility in architectural form.

The Philadelphia Saving Fund Society building (1933) by George Howe and William Lescaze was the first corporate tower to draw on contemporary German functionalist design in order to make the structure as maintenance-free as possible and to prevent shareholders from suspecting unnecessary expenditure. During the 1930s and 1940s, the Moderne style, a softer version of functionalism influenced by French sources, was especially popular in retail and smaller commercial buildings. In gasoline stations, grocery markets, drugstores, barber shops, beauty salons, and variety stores, it implied an architectural connection with the culture of large-scale business enterprise.

In reaction to European functionalism and the Moderne, Frank Lloyd Wright offered his own solution to the office building and corporate headquarters in the Johnson Wax Administration Building (1939) in Racine, Wisconsin. Its smooth brick surfaces rest on reinforced concrete platforms resembling lilypads and its fenestration consists exclusively of glass tubing held in place by steel spacers. As in the Larkin Building, Wright designed not only the architecture but also the furnishings. The final effect of the whole building was to inspire the work force into a stronger sense of social cohesion.

In an effort to generate electric power, raise living standards in rural areas, provide jobs during the Depression, and implement a policy of long-range regional planning, the federal government initiated a series of hydroelectric dam projects during the 1930s. The most extensive of these, the Tennessee Valley Authority (TVA), begun in 1933, consisted of eight dams along a seven hundred-mile waterway between the Appalachians and the Ohio River (Fig. 10). It was echoed in other projects in the Pacific Northwest, the West, and the Southwest. The architecture of the TVA was cast into the Moderne style and was considered important enough by the Museum of Modern Art in New York to deserve a special exhibit in 1938.

Meanwhile, the rise of the automobile after World War I brought countless other changes to commercial architecture. In the 1930s, freeways had already begun to change the face of Los Angeles. Cross-country travel and truck transport was facili-

Figure 10. Construction of Morris Dam, Tennessee (1933–1936). COURTESY OF THE TEN-
NESSEE VALLEY AUTHORITY.

tated and encouraged by a growing system of state and federal highways, along which service stations and tourist cabins sprang up. The motor lodge or motel was geared to travelers on the move in private vehicles. Motels were accompanied by an entirely new culture of culinary establishments offering low- to medium-priced fare for people of modest means who were in transit. Diners, sometimes literally converted from railroad cars, connoted both the convenience and transitory quality of eating on the road and inadvertently acknowledged the demise of rail transportation that was in

decline after 1914. Public transportation was supplied by the development of bus lines that installed terminals in towns and cities but relied on service stations and stores as stopping places in rural areas. The mobile home also emerged at this time as a kind of updated Conestoga wagon that permitted owners to pull their shelter on the road after them.

The impact of the automobile and the general rise of consumer culture between the world wars was documented by the Chicago World Fair of 1933 and the New York World Fair of 1939. In contrast to

Figure 11.   Country Club Plaza with holiday lights, Kansas City, Missouri (1922–1925).
COURTESY OF J. C. NICHOLS COMPANY SCRAPBOOKS; KC54N55-412; WESTERN HISTORICAL MANU-
SCRIPT COLLECTION—KANSAS CITY.

the Columbian Exposition of 1893, exhibits representing transportation, electrical power, industry, communication, consumer products, and entertainment at both the 1933 and 1939 fairs were contextualized in architectural environments designed with the collective intention of looking stunningly futuristic. This was accomplished in large part by the use of dramatic lighting and water displays and, at the New York fair, by elevated walkways and curvilinear buildings, imparting a sense of free movement. Although the fair buildings were no more than imaginative variations on the Moderne and functionalist styles, they popularized the equation of technology with progress and confirmed the notion of architecture as a vehicle of public relations and advertising.

One of the most important effects of the automobile during this period was its implementation of suburban development. Liberated from having to live near their workplaces, Americans began to move from central cities to newly subdivided neighborhood developments at the edge of or outside city limits. Flourishing central business districts began to be eroded, imperceptibly at first, by decentralized commercial strips and shopping

districts. The Country Club Plaza in Kansas City, Missouri, developed by J. C. Nichols and designed by Edward Beuhler Delk (1922–1925; Fig. 11), offered a master-planned commercial quarter that responded to the rapid growth of the city southward and set a standard for similar developments elsewhere. The use of a neo-Spanish colonial architectural idiom, the concentration of parking in designed areas, and tight controls placed on signage, lighting, and future development, not only preserved the image Nichols planned but made environmental control serve private enterprise in a way that had rarely been seen before.

Suburban shopping strips of less pretension in the 1920s, 1930s, and 1940s offered convenience to motorists who could easily park their cars while doing light shopping. The success of strips eventually led to the development of the supermarket as well as several other concepts, including the drive-in restaurant, drive-in movie theater, and drive-through store. It also led to the shopping center, a concept first articulated in the 1950s by Victor Gruen, an immigrant Austrian architect who saw in it a way to bring a desirable quality of public interaction to the highly decentralized life of the American suburb. Early examples such as Northland Center (1954) in Southfield, Michigan, were treated as elaborate complexes of retail establishments connected by covered sidewalks, interspersed with parklike elements such as fountains, benches, and plantings, and surrounded by parking lots. They thus drew on the imagery of urban and civic life while remaining totally private developments. Their popularity even had the reflexive impact of causing towns such as Richmond, Indiana, and countless others to eliminate automobile traffic from their principal commercial streets and convert them into pedestrian zones in hopes of revitalizing their commercial districts. The enclosure of Southdale Center (1956) in Edina, Minnesota, to avoid inclement weather created the first self-contained shopping concourse.

After World War II, a wave of Modernist influence swept through American business and commercial architecture, due in part to the immigration of several leading European architect-educators to the United States in the late 1930s: Ludwig Mies van der Rohe, Walter Gropius, and Marcel Breuer. Their influence brought about a strong school of commercial building represented by pace-setting structures such as the Lever House by Skidmore, Owings, and Merrill (1952) and the Seagram Building by Mies van der Rohe with Philip Johnson (1957) in New York City. These understated minimalist slabs expressed corporate identity through machine precision and the elegance of tinted glass in a light curtain-wall skin that has no support value and serves only as an insulating envelope. In contrast to earlier complexes such as Rockefeller Center (1931–1933 and later) in New York in which a group of buildings was organized around a public plaza where outdoor activities could be centered, these buildings were conceived as objects isolated

Figure 12.   Vaulted Main Room of Grand Central Terminal, New York City (1913).
COURTESY OF THE NYC MUNICIPAL ARCHIVES.

by set-back plazas, a concept related to the Modernist urban-planning principle of functional separation and zoning.

Modernist concepts likewise dominated such other areas of commercial architecture as transportation. In the Lambert Air Terminal (1956) in Saint Louis, Missouri, Minoru Yamasaki covered large waiting rooms with thin concrete shells whose lightness and curvilinearity for the first time metaphorically suggested aerodynamic forces. Similarly Eero Saarinen engaged the air terminal as a serious architectural problem in his reinforced concrete sculptural design for the Trans World Airlines Terminal at Kennedy Airport (1962) in New York. By contrast, the United Airlines Terminal (1988) by Helmut Jahn at Chicago's O'Hare Airport contextualizes the high technology of air transportation in reminiscences of the rail transportation buildings of the nineteenth century.

In the early 1960s, the main concourse of Grand Central Terminal (1913; Fig. 12) by Reed and Stem with Warren and Wetmore in New York nearly faced demolition when the Pan Am Building (1963) by Emery Roth, Pietro Belluschi, and Walter Gropius was proposed to replace it. The struggle to save Grand Central and the failure to preserve New York's Pennsylvania Station (1910; demolished 1963) by McKim Mead and White were early signs of the conflicts that would continue to emerge in the 1960s and later over the preservation of historic buildings in American cities. In some cases, preservation activities were directed against developers who sought to redevelop the potentially lucrative sites of historic buildings more densely; in others, preservationists fought for historic buildings as the last vestige of history and stability in decaying urban centers.

The preservation movement began just as the sociopolitical base of architectural Modernism came under attack during the postmodern revolution. Postmodernism is associated with broader cultural changes in the United States during the 1960s and 1970s that are also coincidental with the rise of consumerism and late capitalism. In some cases, it fosters the revival of historical styles; in others, it manipulates Modernist architectural language for commercial purposes. The commercial typologies of this period include signature office buildings — whether corporate or speculative — atrium hotels, regional and urban shopping malls, and festival marketplaces: buildings that frequently project the image of public domain but are completely controlled by private interests. They are often gener-

Figure 13. AT&T Building, New York City (1976). COURTESY OF AT&T ARCHIVES.

ated by public/private partnerships in which market success and architectural imagery ambiguously mix with political values.

The earliest example of a postmodern signature office building is the AT&T Building (1976; Fig. 13) by Philip Johnson in New York; it sent shocks of reaction through both architectural and business communities when it was announced. Long the champion of architectural Modernism, Johnson offered AT&T a revivalist granite-clad slab topped by a pediment. In his design for the Humana Building (1985) in Louisville, Kentucky, the winner of a national competition, Michael Graves explored his interest in abstraction fused with classicism through sensuous color and traditional materials. Ironically, the luxurious building denotes health care as a successful business just at the time that health care was in crisis nationally. In these and other cases, the name of the architect and his personal style have become as important an asset as the real estate itself.

The burgeoning suburbs eventually attracted another typology: the office building built on speculation. Found usually along main thoroughfares and often at the exits of interstate freeways, suburban office complexes are predominantly horizontal rather than vertical, often include atrium courts, and are always accompanied by parking decks or surrounded by parking lots. They usually lease space to small businesses, sales personnel, and professional firms, offering them the convenience of suburban location along with an image derived from the signature tower.

The evolution of the regional shopping mall, especially from the late 1960s on, exploited the ambiguity of a private domain open to the public. Excluding whomever its owners wished and elimi-

nating truly civic interaction, malls became paradises of consumerism in contrast to the increasingly empty and dangerous urban centers. Fairlane Town Center (1976; Fig. 14) in Dearborn, Michigan, developed by the Taubman Company, is a consummate example of the interiorization of commercial architecture around atrium courts with corridors of shops strung between large anchor stores. It is also an example of design that alters the users' perceptions of space, time, and movement as retail strategy. Festival marketplaces, an outgrowth of regional malls and open markets, have been developed by James Rouse in Baltimore, New York, Boston, Miami, and many other cities. Usually directed toward leisure activities, these marketplaces often incorporate outdoor dining and entertainment, and are frequently sited on rivers, shores, or harbors.

Commercial architecture had already lent its image to other building types during the twentieth century. The Nebraska State Capitol (1916–1928) in Lincoln by Bertram Grosvenor Goodhue replaced

Figure 14.   Fairlane Town Center, Dearborn, Michigan (1976). Dearborn (*rear*), Town Center with circular parking area (*center*), and Hyatt hotel (*foreground*).

the prevailing classical dome with a vertical tower in the manner of a skyscraper. The Shrine of the Little Flower (1929–1936), a large Roman Catholic church by Henry J. McGill and Talbot F. Hamlin in Royal Oak, Michigan, reflected Art Deco commercial architecture in Detroit and New York. Even more radically, however, the State of Illinois Center in Chicago (1988), a state-office building designed by Helmut Jahn, incorporates a mall into its atrium lobby and encloses it in a curtain-wall structure that rejects all conventional civic imagery and substitutes for it the commercial marketplace. The most public part of the building, the hearing chamber, is buried under the sidewalk near the entrance. Similarly, Philip Johnson's design for the Garden Grove Community Church, the "Crystal Cathedral" (1987), in Garden Grove, California, adopts the reflective-glass skin of nearby suburban office buildings to cover its surfaces.

Historically, the dominant institutions of any culture have determined an architectural language that has been assumed by related or subordinant institutions. On that basis, it may be argued that by the end of the twentieth century, capitalism in the United States is embodied in a variety of related building types possessing a vocabulary that has been assimilated by other sectors of the culture that were formerly considered dominant, especially the religious and the civic. Apparently, this vocabulary stimulates and bears enough meaning, power, and authority that it is an acceptable vehicle to express the values of contemporary religious and political institutions for a large number of citizens of the late capitalist social order. At the least, commercial and industrial architecture have established the visual appearance of American cities and suburbs in the twentieth century; and by the last decade, they have also determined the shape and character of the buildings and spaces in which American public life is formed, ordered, and takes place.

BIBLIOGRAPHY

Andrews, Wayne. *Architecture, Ambition, and Americans: A Social History of American Architecture* (1964).

Condit, Carl W. *The Chicago School of Architecture: A History of Commercial and Public Building in the Chicago Area, 1875–1925* (1964).

Fitch, James Marston. *American Building: The Historical Forces That Shaped It* (1966; 2d ed. 1973).

Gayle, Margot. *Cast-Iron Architecture in New York: A Photographic Survey* (1974).

Gifford, Don, ed. *The Literature of Architecture* (1966). An invaluable anthology of writings on the evolution of architectural theory and practice in nineteenth-century America, drawn from many sources, and made accessible through excellent annotations.

Hamlin, Talbot F. *Greek Revival Architecture in America: Being an Account of Important Trends in American Architecture and American Life . . .* (1944; repr. 1964). This book remains the standard work on the Greek Revival.

Hildebrand, Grant. *Designing for Industry: The Architecture of Albert Kahn* (1974).

Hitchcock, Henry-Russell. *The Architecture of H. H. Richardson and His Times* (1936; rev. ed. 1966). This is neither the first nor the only book on Richardson, but it is scholarly, completely reliable, and probably still the best.

Jencks, Charles. *Late Modern Architecture and Other Essays* (1980).

———. *The Language of Post-Modern Architecture.* 3d rev. enl. ed. (1981). This work is as good an introduction to the subject of postmodernism as any, but no work that is completely clear or unproblematic in its interpretation has appeared yet.

Jordy, William H. *American Buildings and Their Architects.* Vol. 3, *Progressive and Academic Ideals at the Turn of the Twentieth Century* (1972). This series is collectively and individually the finest single study of American architecture that has been published. One volume remains uncompleted, but the quality of scholarship and the authenticity of viewpoint represented by the authors of the other four volumes is extraordinary. See also Pierson titles in this series below.

——. *American Buildings and Their Architects.* Vol. 4, *The Impact of European Modernism in the Mid-Twentieth Century* (1972).

Kirker, Harold and James Kirker. *Bulfinch's Boston, 1787–1817* (1964).

Pierson, William H., Jr. *American Buildings and Their Architects.* Vol. 1, *The Colonial and Neo-classical Styles* (1970).

——. "Part I: The Corporate and the Early Gothic Styles," In *American Buildings and Their Architects.* Vol. 2, *The Corporate and Early Gothic Styles* (1970).

Kaufmann, Edgar, Jr. *The Rise of an American Architecture* (1970).

Twombly, Robert C. *Louis Sullivan: His Life and Work* (1986). Of the many studies of Sullivan, this is the most up-to-date and reliable.

Whiffen, Marcus, and Frederick Koeper. *American Architecture, 1607–1976.* 2 vols. (1981).

SEE ALSO **The City; Landscapes; Material Culture Studies; Public Architecture; The Rise of Mass Culture; The Suburbs; Urbanization; Urban Parks.**

Part VIII

PATTERNS OF EVERYDAY LIFE

FOODWAYS

Peter W. Williams

ARUGULA, BIG MACS, barbecue, C rations, caviar, chitterlings, chop suey, Gerber's strained peaches, jambalaya, johnnycakes, kielbasa, Moon Pies, pemmican, sauerkraut, and Weight Watchers frozen pizzas are all food items that have been consumed at one time or another in the United States of America. Though some foods, such as the humble but omnipresent hamburger, transcend lines of age, class, and geography, preferences for others clearly correlate with historical period, region, social class, gender, age, occupation, race, and ethnicity. Foodways—the manner in which groups of people select, prepare, and ingest edibles—are thus a valuable source of information about the character of the various social groupings of the United States and their interrelations at any given time. Although the term is most commonly used by ethnologists and ethnologically influenced students of folklore and folklife in examining "folk" societies and subcultures, the following essay will focus on the role of food in American society more broadly.

THE COLUMBIAN EXCHANGE

The story of North American foodways begins with the "Columbian exchange," the process that began in 1492 with the European arrival in the New World, through which the natural and human ecologies of the two broad cultural zones began to become inextricably intertwined. European newcomers were faced with the absence of indigenous sources of food—such as wheat bread—to which they had been accustomed. The English "Pilgrims," near starvation after their arrival at Plymouth on coastal New England in 1620, were happy enough to incorporate the maize (corn), beans, and squash offered by the native peoples into their diets, together with the wild turkey, venison, and abundant seafood that the new land offered. The Spanish also reluctantly learned to make do with manioc or cas-

sava as substitutes for wheat in Central and South America until more familiar patterns could be reestablished.

Prior to the coming of the Europeans, the diet of the indigenous North American peoples had varied by region, but was broadly based on locally available fish and game and the three vegetable staples of maize, beans, and squash, together with nuts and berries. As a result of the Columbian exchange this diet also was altered, as were the broader life patterns of the native peoples, who became employed in the cultivation of bananas, sugarcane, rice, and coffee—all of them Old World imports, though now for centuries associated intimately with the Americas. In addition, the Spanish introduced Iberian staples such as wheat, olives, and wine grapes into those areas where they could be successfully cultivated. (Junípero Serra and the Franciscans who organized the California Indians into mission colonies in the late eighteenth century attempted to Europeanize their charges in part through the cultivation of these crops.) A major result of this importation of European food plants and animals and their rapid flourishing was the creation of a living environment both materially and culturally hospitable to succeeding waves of Old World colonists.

Where pre-Columbian native peoples had raised little livestock other than poultry for food, they accepted the introduction of pigs and cattle much more readily than they did most European food plants. Native peoples living near the northern edge of New Spain in what is now the southwestern United States—the Navajo, Pueblo, and Apache— eagerly turned to cattle raising. The horse, previously unknown in the New World, was used more in the raising of cattle and other food animals than for food itself. Its introduction revolutionized the cultures of the Plains peoples through its usefulness for transportation and warfare as well as pursuit of the bison and wild cattle. In the longer run, Spanish cattle and horses paved the way for a western culture featuring latter-day vaqueros (cowboys—sometimes a role ironically played by Indians under the Spanish) and a fierce American appetite for beef. The overall result, according to biohistorian Alfred W. Crosby, Jr., was "so successful ... that ... [it was] probably the greatest biological revolution in the Americas since the end of the Pleistocene era" (*The Columbian Exchange,* p. 66).

ANGLO-AMERICAN COLONIAL PATTERNS

English-speaking colonists began early in the seventeenth century to fashion their own sets of foodways, which combined regional English patterns of cooking and eating successively with locally available foodstuffs, foods transplanted from England, and, eventually, imports from a wide variety of foreign locales. Borrowings from Native American and other neighbors, together, in some cases, with religious and ideological considerations, further influenced Anglo-American patterns. William Bradford describes the earliest patterns of interaction and adaptation in *Of Plymouth Plantation* for the year 1621:

[In April] they began to plant their corn, in which service Squanto stood them in great stead, showing them both the manner how to set it, and after how to dress and tend it. Also he told them except they got fish and set with it (in these old grounds) it would come to nothing.... Some English seed they sowed, as wheat and peas, but it came not to good, either by the badness of the seed, or lateness of the season, or both....

They began now [in September] to gather in the small harvest they had.... Others were exercised in fishing, about cod, and bass, and other fish, of which they took good store, of which every family had their portion. All the summer there was no want. And now began to come in store of fowl, as winter approached, of which this place did abound when they came first (but afterward decreased by degrees). And besides water fowl, there was great store of wild turkeys, of which they took many, besides venison, etc. Besides they had about a peck of meal a week to a person, or now since harvest, Indian corn to that proportion. Which made many afterwards write so largely of their plenty here to their friends in England, which were not feigned, but true reports.

The alternating abundance and want that characterized these and subsequent years in New England gave rise to days both of thanksgiving and of fasting and repentance, the only occasions other than the Sabbath that constituted Puritan collective ritual observance for many decades.

The New England Diet Cattle from England had been introduced into the Plymouth Colony by 1624, thus reducing the necessity for hunting, an occupation or recreation alien to the British "middling" classes. (John Winthrop, the leader of the much larger 1630 settlement of the Massachusetts Bay Colony, was not averse to an occasional expedition with his fowling piece, though.) Wheat and rye supplemented the indigenous maize, and chicken, hogs, and fruit trees were also introduced into New England before long. The Puritan "plain style"—a cultural aesthetic based on a religious objection to overelaborateness, whether in preaching, clothing, or cooking—combined with circumstance to produce what David Hackett Fischer has called "one of the most austere foodways in the Western world" (*Albion's Seed,* p. 135).

The resultant cuisine has endured as part of the New England diet to the present day. After they had overcome their initial aversion to the giant lobsters that abounded in coastal waters, New Englanders appropriated the aboriginal custom of holding clambakes, in which clams, other shellfish, and later accompaniments were cooked while buried in sand with heated rocks. Such affairs were easily turned into communal and, eventually, commercial ventures. Succotash, a mixture of beans and Indian corn, derived both its name and its character from Algonkian usage. Cornmeal yielded various edible products such as samp, a coarse hominy now sold by the Vermont Country Store as a semiexotic, seminostalgic regional item; johnnycake (journey cake), a baked or fried kind of cornbread suitable for taking along on travels; and Indian pudding, made with milk and molasses, and now served at restaurants featuring regional cuisine such as Boston's Durgin Park.

Other aspects of the New England diet that arose from necessity and were later regarded as embodiments of frugal virtue were baked beans, described by Lucy Larcom in the nineteenth century as the "canonical dish of our Forefathers" (Fischer, p. 136), and prepared in advance to avoid cooking on the strictly observed Sabbath; the New England boiled dinner, based on carrots, potatoes, cabbage, and corned beef, that is, meat "corned" with salt as a preservative, then boiled in unseasoned water; and codfish balls or cakes, made from the ubiquitous fish enshrined in a six-foot model at the Massachusetts State House as the "Sacred Cod" in tribute to its role as provider of both food and commercial value. The expansion of trade with Britain, the West Indian colonies, and other ports that did so much to create many coastal mercantile fortunes also enriched the regional diet with molasses, rum, and citrus fruits from the West Indies; tea, coffee, chocolate, spices, and sugar from the East Indies; tapioca from Latin America; dates from the Middle East; wine, brandy, and raisins from the Mediterranean; ginger from China; and rice and corn from the southern colonies. Farther north, those intrepid settlers attempting to eke out a living in the mountains of what would become Vermont and New Hampshire found domestic uses as well as external markets for maple sugar, and a confluence of cultural patterns with nearby French Canada led to other regional adaptations. Pies, an English institution and ubiquitous to all parts of New England, were sometimes fried in Vermont. (Part of Yankee folklore, or perhaps "fakelore," has it that a Yankee is simply anyone who eats pie for breakfast.)

Patterns of food preparation in New England were derived primarily from East Anglia, the region of origin of the majority of the earliest English settlers. Dark English beer was the beverage of choice in the seventeenth century, and was later augmented by fermented apple cider and the universally popular rum, some of it home-brewed from cherries. Pork and beef were the preferred meats. (An abundance of meat and dairy products distinguished the diet of the "middling" classes from their poorer neighbors, and imported products such as tea were at least at first a mark of luxury.) Boiling and baking were the most common means of food preparation. The latter operation could be done in iron kettles or, as circumstances began to permit, in the more elaborate brick ovens that soon became common. Food preparation was strictly gender-typed, and women managed domestic gardens and chicken coops in addition to buying food and preparing meals.

Other British Colonial Foodways New England's culture has received extensive scholarly attention, and provides a useful example of the social and ecological complexities involved in foodways. There were, of course, other sorts of British colonial societies in North America. Virginians also continued English foodways, but more according to the customs of southwestern England. The great planters were the closest thing the colonies produced to an aristocracy, and their ample means and conser-

vative tastes produced the closest the era came to a haute cuisine. "Dining," observed the eminent historian Edmund Morgan, "was a fine art in Virginia," and dinners offered by the plantation elite were major social occasions (*Virginians at Home,* p. 75). In such grand households, kitchens were separate from the main building, and meals were prepared there by slaves or servants. Humbler Virginians had to be content with one-dish "messes" of greens and salt meat seasoned with wild herbs, and ample doses of cornmeal mush. Unlike their more austere New England cousins, Virginians of all classes enjoyed ample seasonings in their foods.

David Hackett Fischer, in *Albion's Seed,* argues that two other cultural zones emerged in the English-speaking colonies that reflected as well the foodways, as well as other folkways, of still other parts of Britain from which they were originally settled. The Delaware Valley Quakers, who hailed primarily from the North Midlands and Wales, were as similar to the New England Puritans in their pragmatic and rigorously antisensual approach to cuisine as they were in their "work ethic." Boiling was the preferred cooking technique, with dumplings and puddings as regional favorites. Sugar came to be shunned, since it was produced by slave labor, a practice abhorrent to Friends' humanitarian principles. Some interchange also developed with the nearby "Pennsylvania Germans" (or, incorrectly, "Dutch") as both groups produced versions of scrapple, a fried mixture of cornmeal and finely chopped miscellaneous parts of the pig or cow.

A more widely spread and perhaps even more enduring approach to food preparation was that of the "backcountry." This was the piedmont and mountain region west of the original coastal zones of settlement, populated originally and primarily by emigrants from the northern British borderlands, many of whom came to be categorized as Scotch-Irish (that is, Scottish lowlanders or transplants in Ulster). These people came culturally prepared to be frontier settlers. Their culinary staples included oats, which in the New World yielded to maize in the form of hominy grits; pigs, which similarly replaced the Old World sheep; potatoes, accepted in Britain only as the fare of simple people; clabber, made from sour milk, curds, and whey; and various sorts of unleavened flat cakes cooked on a griddle. Whiskey—first Scotch, then bourbon—was the backcountry beverage of choice. Vegetables indigenous to North America rounded out the regional diet. It is clear enough how many of these elements combined in various ways to form the bases of a generic southern regional style.

REGIONAL DEVELOPMENTS IN THE NINETEENTH CENTURY

The social and economic polarization of the South was reflected in its foodways as they took shape during the early nineteenth century. Thomas Jefferson was widely known as one of America's first gourmets, a distinction which earned him Patrick Henry's denunciation for unrepublican culinary elitism. Jefferson acquired a firsthand knowledge of continental European foods and techniques for their preparation during his sojourns abroad. A widower at an early age, he employed his daughters, granddaughters, and slaves in the elaborate process of food selection and preparation at Monticello, and utilized inventions of his own such as dumbwaiters to minimize eavesdropping by servants at his frequent elaborate dinners for highly placed guests. His introduction of French chefs and their fare into the White House and the enormous "bar bill" for French wines and champagne—five hundred bottles a year of the latter—generated in the course of official entertaining placed an enormous strain on his resources. Jefferson's largess reflected not only his own expansive temperament but also the tradition of southern hospitality that had originated among the planter class as a means of entertainment among widely scattered plantations, a service to travelers, and a visible means of demonstrating status through conspicuous consumption.

Slave Fare and Its Influence The other side of the southern social spectrum was reflected in the fare of slaves, who frequently subsisted on the three M's—meat (sow belly), meal (corn), and molasses. Several African foodstuffs and descriptive words entered the regional repertoire. Okra (Ashanti, *nkru;* in other West African languages, *nkru, nku, ruma,* or *nkruma*) is a pod containing seeds and a thick, gluey substance eaten fried or in gumbo (Bantu, *ngombo*), a synonym for okra also used in Louisiana Creole and Cajun cuisine to describe a variety of soups or stews thickened with okra or *filé* (French for "threads") powder made from dried sassafras leaves. Goober (Kongo, *nguba*) remains a regional synonym for peanut, transplanted from South America to Africa and then back to the North American colonies. Corn (maize) and yams (a word of mixed African origins) also played a ma-

jor role in southern black fare; like the goober, yams were also introduced from South America to Africa in the sixteenth century by Portuguese traders. The experience many slaves acquired in food preparation facilitated entry into the broader economy after the Civil War; among the few niches in the work force open to them for many decades were jobs as cooks, waiters, and, in the armed forces through World War II, mess stewards. Aunt Jemima and Uncle Ben persist to this day as commercial emblems of nurturing slaves associated with bountiful food service. Interestingly, the Nation of Islam (called Black Muslims), which became influential in many urban black ghettos in the 1950s and 1960s, adopted a dietary code very loosely based on that of traditional Islam, which banned on religious grounds most items associated with soul food; instead, they promoted—ironically, given their ideology—a diet favoring foods characteristic of the white middle-class norm.

The sorts of foods eaten by slaves and, later, sharecroppers were by no means restricted to blacks; rather, a diet based on pork, corn, and such other vegetables as sweet potatoes and cowpeas emerged early as characteristic of the South as a whole, and has persisted with a staying power far in excess of that of most other parts of the country. The earliest stages of settlement saw a heavy reliance on game—deer and bear, as well as smaller animals such as squirrels, opossums (from Virginia Algonkian, *apasum*) and raccoons (Algonkian, *arahkun*). Indian corn rapidly established itself as a primary food, giving rise to innumerable popular derivatives such as hominy (Algonkian, *rockahominie* or *rokahamen*), produced by treating ripe corn with lye; grits (or hominy grits), made of finely ground hominy; cornmeal mush; hush puppies, fried balls of cornmeal and, sometimes, onions; and hoecake and other forms of cornbread. (Wheat bread was eventually introduced into the region, but never displaced cornbread in popularity.) Cowpeas and greens—collard, turnip, and others—were boiled (with frying, a favorite form of preparation) and eaten, with the remaining pot likker (liquor) relished for sopping as well. Chicken was a favored food for special occasions among the poorer classes, while pork was the standby. Little of the pig was wasted, with even such parts as the chitterlings or chitlins (intestines) entering the repertory of blacks in particular. Beef and lamb were not disdained, but the expense, particularly of the latter, relegated them to the wealthier classes. Catfish—fried and served with hush puppies and cole slaw—

remains a favorite among southerners of all sorts and conditions.

Southern Foodways Although these foods have remained popular throughout the South, other foods were abundant more locally and helped to shape a more restrictedly regional cuisine. Seafood was plentiful in coastal areas, and attained a special place in the closely related cuisines of the Creoles (American-born descendants of Europeans or, locally, any residents of New Orleans) and Cajuns (displaced French-speaking Acadians from Nova Scotia who settled amid the bayous of southern Louisiana). New Orleans was particularly a cultural and culinary melting pot, with French, Spanish, African, and Native American elements enhancing its complexity and giving rise to a mixture of spices unacceptable to most Yankees. (Gumbo, mentioned earlier, was built around celery, tomatoes, and bell peppers, with andouille [ANN-dooey] sausage, chicken, or seafood sometimes added.) Cajun foodways built on abundant seafood such as crawfish and redfish; in the 1980s, this hitherto obscure regional culture received national attention through the work of the New Orleans chef Paul Prudhomme, and blackened redfish—as well as blackened almost everything else—began to grace fashionable restaurant menus across the country. (Zydeco music, a similar regional cultural blend, also attained a national following in this period.)

Following the Civil War, the gradual entrance of the South into a national market economy led to mixed consequences. Once antebellum agriculture had become established, according to Joseph R. Conlin, slaves on the better plantations consumed over four thousand calories a day. After the war, though, as Joe Gray Taylor notes, heavily milled corn and fatback (fat meat from the back of the hog) from the Midwest rather than bacon undermined the nutritional value of the diet of rural people. A similar decline in the quantity of fruits and vegetables they consumed further made them vulnerable to malnutrition-related diseases such as pellagra and hookworm. The resultant endemic poor health nurtured the image of a "lazy South" filled with "tobacco roads" of poor, illiterate, disease-ridden sharecroppers.

Though this stereotype was not entirely baseless, reflecting economic circumstances more than character, southerners have expressed a typical ambivalence toward their past in their enshrinement of regional foodways, even as they began to participate fully in a national culture and economy. Coca-Cola (regionally pronounced Koh-KOH-lah)

originated in Atlanta in 1886, and ultimately became an international symbol of American national culture and mass marketing. ("Cocacolonization" has emerged as a synonym for such commercial hegemony.) RC Cola is a more localized taste and is linked with the Moon Pie, a marshmallow sandwich invented in Chattanooga around 1918. Another favorite regional confection is the Goo Goo Cluster (Nashville, 1912). Ice(d) tea is the drink preferred in genteel circles, while corn likker—originally a convenient way of transporting corn in highly condensed and remunerative fashion—is a beverage reflecting another side of regional taste (together with its more sophisticated counterparts, Jack Daniels and Rebel Yell sour mash whiskeys).

National franchising elevated Colonel Sanders' Kentucky Fried Chicken to transregional eminence, making that staple of fine southern cooking an attenuated regional counterpart of the aregional McDonald's and Burger Chef. (Harland Sanders opened his first stand in Corbin, Kentucky, in 1956, but was later bought out by a national syndicate.) Other chains such as Stuckey's, Po' Folks, and Cracker Barrel now market regional cuisine of greater or lesser authenticity along interstate highways within and beyond the South itself, each capitalizing on a "countrified" image in the manner of the Grand Ole Opry and the television program *Hee Haw.* Traditional southern cooking, whether perpetuated through family oral tradition or "yuppified" à la *Southern Living* magazine, retains its hold on the indigenous populace more perhaps than in any other extended cultural region in the United States to this day.

The Great American Steak Religion The crude, pork- and corn-based food habits of the frontier South were also characteristic of the broader frontier of the earlier nineteenth century. European travelers viewed with alarm the monotonous diet of heavy, greasy foods consumed by the locals and offered to these sojourners as well, and noted that dyspepsia—a severe, chronic form of indigestion no longer common—was a widespread problem. (Modern-day truckstops offer similar fare, making it clearer why fast-food franchises have become so popular.) Once family farms had become established, the diet of countryfolk became more varied and salubrious, but continued to be heavy and abundant to generate the energy necessary for strenuous outdoor work. John Mack Faragher, in his *Women and Men on the Overland Trail,* describes a typical midwestern farm family's daily provender at mid century as including two kinds of meat, eggs, cheese, butter, cream, corn, bread, several vegetables, jellies, preserves, relishes, cake, pie, milk, coffee, and tea (p. 52; cited by Conlin, p. 8). Conlin estimates that Americans at the time consumed an average of four thousand calories per day, a startlingly large amount compared with a late-twentieth-century average of about half that, or with the barren diet of contemporary British and Continental laborers and peasants. (Many of the poor, however, consumed far less, often from foods of dubious nutritive value, and malnutrition and its related diseases were scarcely unknown in both rural and urban areas.)

Though corn and pork remained popular especially in the South, it was midwestern beef and wheat that began to rival and eventually surpass them as national dietary staples, especially as the railroads and new agricultural technology made their growth and distribution rapid and economical. The preference for beef, more plentiful in the United States than in any part of the world except perhaps Argentina, would persist as a distinctive character of an emergent national taste, and would later be characterized by food reformer Frances Moore Lappé (*Diet for a Small Planet,* 1971) as the "great American steak religion." The *Statistical Abstract of the United States* (1980) indicated that approximate daily consumption of beef by Americans rose from 2.4 ounces (67 grams) in 1910 to 4.2 ounces (118 grams) in 1976, which accounted in part for a 28 percent increase in fat consumption during that period. (Pork consumption declined slightly from 2.7 to 2.6 ounces [76 to 73 grams] during the same period.) A similar preference for white over whole-grain bread was also in this period emerging as a not entirely wholesome dietary preference. Diurnal alcohol consumption also yielded during the early nineteenth century to coffee and tea, stimulants conducive to the disciplined effort that a nascent national market economy demanded.

Food Reformers This seemingly relentless progress toward a heavy, calorie-laden diet, whether based on pork and corn or beef and wheat, was not without its challengers. A Puritan reformist strain was manifest in the urgings of Catharine Beecher, in *A Treatise on Domestic Economy* (1841), toward a temperate regimen eaten deliberately. She cited physical as well as spiritual health as primary rationales. Beecher's contemporaries also denounced excessive seasonings and fried foods with a similar mixture of motives. One of the most influential reformers of the era was the Presbyterian minister

Sylvester Graham (1794–1851), whose name has ever since been connected intimately with the cracker made from the unbolted flour he promoted. Utopian experiments, ranging from Bronson Alcott's vegetarian Fruitlands (1844–1845) to the herb-loving celibate Shaker communities, similarly practiced variations on the theme of a simple, natural diet that contributed physically to a life-style harmonious with higher laws. (Thoreau's primitive urge to devour a woodchuck raw was only an apparent exception to this tendency.) Religious motives were also prominent in the Seventh-day Adventist movement, which arose out of the Great Disappointment over William Miller's unfulfilled millenarian prophecies in the mid 1840s. Influenced by Graham as well as the Adventists, both John Harvey Kellogg (1852–1943) and C. W. Post (1854–1914) contributed to the quest for a salubrious, natural, precooked food in their respective development of the cornflake and the grape nut. The heavily sugared cold cereals favored by children in the later twentieth century were a far less healthful variation on the Post-Kellogg theme characteristic of the child-oriented consumer culture promoted especially by television commercials.

IMMIGRATION AND ETHNIC FOODWAYS

The quest for a better diet was a primary motive for the vast immigration that altered American society so dramatically during the entire nineteenth century. The potato, another example of the Columbian exchange, was first exported from the highlands of South America to Europe in the sixteenth century, but was originally categorized as an aphrodisiac, a cause of leprosy, and the fare of peasants. Though it eventually became a staple, especially of eastern European folk society, its introduction into Ireland during the later years of the 1500s transformed the diet of that nation and promoted an extraordinary growth in population in the ensuing centuries. This growth came to an abrupt halt in the 1840s, when a devastating blight on the potato crop combined with other political, economic, and demographic factors to result in massive famine and emigration, primarily to the northeastern coastal cities of the United States. (The typical Irish diet had consisted of up to 10 pounds [4.5 kilograms] of potatoes per day, often with little else but milk.) The rapid assimilation of the initially despised but English-speaking Irish militated against the perpetuation of a fare that was basically a variant on a broader northern European peasant theme. Though corned beef and cabbage remains an ethnic favorite on Saint Patrick's Day, this is a residual reminiscence of a vanished folk culture characteristic of many deracinated ethnic groups attached more in nostalgia than in everyday behavior to their ancestral past. (Jiggs's attachment to the dish in the comic strip "Bringing Up Father," however, was a sign of his passive resistance to the hectoring Maggie's attempts at assimilation and social climbing.)

The heavy diet of the German immigrants who streamed into first the middle colonies and then Ohio and other parts of the Old Northwest in the days of the early republic was similarly characteristic of the agrarian folkways of northern Europe. Like the Poles and other Slavs who swelled the ranks of America's newcomers during the latter decades of the century, Germans consumed prodigious quantities of pork together with potatoes, beets, cabbage, and other vegetables that kept well without refrigeration. This fare, which has never gained culinary esteem because of its lack of variety and seasoning (apart from salt, sugar, and vinegar), was developed to its fullest among the misnamed Pennsylvania Dutch. These sturdy people were in fact German Anabaptists drawn to southeastern Pennsylvania through the appeals of their pacifist counterparts, the Quakers, beginning in the late 1600s. Abundance rather than subtlety characterizes this regional cuisine exemplified in such traditional dishes as shoofly pie, chicken corn soup, schnitz (seasoned ham) and apples, scrapple, and the variety of preserved fruits and vegetables that make up the proverbial "seven sweets and seven sours."

New Immigrant Foods The "New Immigration" of the decades from the 1870s through the outbreak of World War I enriched the American diet in a number of ways. Central and eastern European fare, again, did not gain a wide audience outside of a few highly spiced items such as kielbasa (Polish sausage) and Hungarian *gulyas* (goulash). Much more influential beyond the limits of particular ethnic communities was Italian pasta- and tomato-based fare such as spaghetti, lasagna, and, of course, the pizza that has become omnipresent in the mass culture of the later twentieth century. (Tomatoes were also introduced into Europe as a result of the Columbian exchange, but were grown in Britain until the nineteenth century only as an ornamental plant. These "love apples" were feared as poisonous in some places until the turn of the twentieth century.) Ironically in retrospect, many New Immigrants were derided as "garlic eaters" by native-born Americans unaccustomed to highly seasoned foods.

As Evan Jones has pointed out, the presence of Italians in California from the time of the gold rush launched their cuisine into American life through their cultivation of plants and vineyards characteristic of their traditional foodways and also through their involvement in the restaurant business. The durum wheat from which Italian pasta was made began to be grown in Kansas on a large scale through Department of Agriculture encouragement, and the shutting off of European imports by World War I gave further impetus to domestic cultivation. The introduction of the pizza to the United States is a topic of contention perhaps second only to the discovery of America in some circles, but many favor the hypothesis that Wooster Square, New Haven—the old center of that city's strong Italian population—deserves the honor. (Nearby Louie's Lunch is sometimes credited with the introduction of the hamburger as well; other schools of thought give it a German origin, imported via the English Salisbury steak and popularized at the Saint Louis World's Fair in 1904.) The dramatic popularity gained by what was originally known as the "pizza pie" following World War II is a prime example— together with the hamburger, fried chicken, and tacos—of the assimilation of selected items of ethnic diet into the mainstream of popular culture through mass production, franchising, and aggressive advertising and merchandising.

The Greek immigrants who constituted another major wave of the New Immigration have been particularly distinguished as restaurateurs, originally gaining an economic niche through providing food to urban workers seeking a quick lunch on their breaks from the office and factory work that dominated the new economic order of the early twentieth century. Greek proprietors later capitalized on a growing demand for a more distinctive cuisine, providing moussaka, *pastitsio,* and a variety of lamb dishes from the old country in Greektown restaurants and the diners that proliferated in the urban Northeast. A distinctive Greek-American contribution is Cincinnati "five-way" chili, made from ground beef and a complex combination of flavorings (including cumin, allspice, and unsweetened chocolate), served over pasta with grated cheese, kidney beans, and onions. Developed locally in the 1920s, this culinary hybrid later began to encroach on the broader popularity of the Tex-Mex chilis that themselves represent an adaptation and indigenization of Mexican traditions. Though Greek Americans, like most groups of New Immigration provenance, have become increasingly assimilated into the middle-American culinary and broader cultural mainstream, events such as the annual *panegyri* held at many Greek Orthodox churches feature traditional foods—together with music, dancing, and folk costumes—as occasions in which traditional folkways are still honored, if only in the breach.

The Jews who emigrated from the ghettos and shtetls of central and eastern Europe during these tumultuous decades illustrate the complex relationship between ethnicity, cultural adaptation, and religion in their foodways as well as in other aspects of their lives. What has come to be known as Jewish cooking—that characteristic of urban delis—is a variation on the foods of Germany, Romania, Hungary, and the Slavic-speaking countries in which Jewish culture flourished prior to the devastation of the Holocaust, and includes pastrami, corned beef, latkes (potato pancakes), and borscht. Other foods, like matzoh (flat, crisp unleavened bread), are used especially on ritual occasions, and are uniquely Jewish. Also governing the foodways of observant Jews are the kosher (ritually clean) laws, which among other things prohibit the consumption of pork and the mixing of milk and meat products. The maintenance of these customs has been a major issue between Orthodox or Conservative Jews who have chosen to be faithful to tradition, and Reform or secular Jews who reject such practices as obsolete. Roman Catholics, among whom were many Irish, Italian, German, and eastern European immigrants, maintained a similar distance from the dominant American Protestant and secular cultures through their observance of "fish on Fridays," a practice made optional (except during Lent) after the Second Vatican Council of the early 1960s.

Another set of foodways is that of Spanish-speaking peoples—who, in fact, are a wide variety of different groups united mainly by variants on a common language. West Indian (Cuban and Puerto Rican) cuisine varies considerably from that of Mexican Americans, whose poverty, language, and frequent illegal status have helped to preserve traditional foodways longer than those of immediately European origin. In the barrios of southern California and Texas, the tortilla—the traditional flat maize cake—is still a dietary staple, together with salsas (sauces) made from tomatoes and chilis, all reminders of the pre-Columbian regimen. Variations

on these themes have led not only to the simplifications purveyed by Taco Bell and other fast-food chains, but also to the hominy-based *posole* of New Mexico and the barbecue (from West Indian, *barbacoa*) that characterized pre-Anglo California and, in endless varieties, Texas and the South.

FORCES OF STANDARDIZATION

In striking contrast with the diversity of ethnic foodways in the history of American food patterns was the simultaneously emergent force of standardization. A major factor in the growing homogenization of national foodways that began to take shape during the middle decades of the nineteenth century was technology. Beginning in the 1830s, expanding railroad networks provided rapid transportation of goods between city and country, with each being gradually transformed as a result. The availability of a wider and less expensive variety of foodstuffs in urban kitchens and dining rooms was particularly accelerated by the development of the refrigerator car, which permitted the slaughter and processing of animals near where they had been raised and their subsequent distribution virtually anywhere in the world. Large-scale fortunes were made beginning in the 1880s by industrialists such as Gustavus Franklin Swift and Philip Danforth Armour, whose names later attained a nearly generic status as synonymous with meats. Refrigeration also made possible the development of large-scale cultivation of a wide range of vegetables and citrus fruits in Florida and California that had until then played only a limited role in the general American diet, but could now be easily brought to distant markets.

Another technical innovation of long-range importance was quick-freezing. Early in the twentieth century, Clarence Birdseye—better known today as a brand name than as an inventive and eponymous individual—developed a technique for preserving foods through rapid freezing, which precluded decay by not generating the large ice crystals that could destroy cellular walls. Such freezing was the culmination of a whole series of innovations over the course of a century or so, which began with improved canning techniques and continued through Gail Borden's perfection of a condensed form of milk shortly before the Civil War. Corresponding developments in domestic technology, including the refrigerator, the home freezer, and the microwave oven, which permitted rapid defrosting, made possible the widespread use of these preservation techniques from the farm to the kitchen.

By the 1920s, "scientific" advertising had united with aggressive new marketing strategies and techniques of mass distribution to alter national patterns of food selection dramatically. Brand names such as Swift, Birds Eye, and Betty Crocker—a fictional personage whose image is periodically updated—became fixed in shoppers' imaginations as synonymous with uniform, dependable, and reasonably priced products. The supermarket, exemplified by the Great Atlantic and Pacific Tea Company (A&P), began during the 1930s to displace locally owned stores—sometimes by incorporating them into national chains—with new, seemingly giant emporiums featuring self-service and a vast variety of fresh and processed foods and other household goods.

Fast-food chains were a variation on the theme. Their symbiotic relationship with other modernizing forces was exemplified in the monopoly obtained by Howard Johnson's for food service on the Pennsylvania Turnpike, which in 1940 opened as the nation's first interstate highway. HoJo's, as the orange-roofed purveyor of updated versions of traditional New England fare later came to be known, had been founded in 1925; in the 1970s it began to yield to newer, still more efficient chains, such as Ray Kroc's dramatically successful McDonald's. Kroc, the son of a Bohemian immigrant, who rivaled Henry Ford as an archetypal American rags-to-riches entrepreneur, took over a local California drive-in in the 1950s and developed an inordinately successful formula: the easily recognizable golden arches trademark; a national chain of clean, standardized franchised outlets; headquarters at Hamburger Central in Oak Brook, Illinois; a restricted, unsubtle range of products, broadly based in appeal; minimum-wage employees, mainly teenagers; aggressive advertising and public relations campaigns; sophisticated but easily operated standardized equipment; and strategic locations designed to attract travelers, teenagers (since the 1950s, possessed of vast discretionary income), and inner-city dwellers. By the 1990s, ecological and nutritional concerns were successfully prevailing upon McDonald's and other fast-food chains to minimize nonbiodegradable packaging and to decrease the fat content of their usually fried products. The introduction of salad bars at such establishments was also indicative of heightened consumer health consciousness.

The Influence of Government In counterpoint with business and technology as agents of standardization were government, science, and education. The distrust of fresh vegetables and milk that was commonplace through the early decades of the nineteenth century gradually yielded to advances in bacteriology and new processing techniques such as pasteurization. These enabled children especially to take advantage of these vital sources of nutrients, vitamins, and minerals without risk of acquiring mortal diseases spread through improper sanitation. Outrage over widespread unsanitary conditions in food processing was epitomized in the public outcry that followed the publication of Upton Sinclair's *The Jungle* in 1906. The Pure Food and Drugs Act passed by Congress the same year was the first of a long series of measures through which the government sought to regulate the condition of the public diet. This law brought to the federal level the movement among state and local governments to ensure a supply of pure milk that had been in progress since the 1880s. Larger producers, who were in these same years banding together into trade associations, tended to welcome such regulation as enhancing their own efforts to rationalize their industries and squeeze out smaller competitors.

Other governmental involvements played major roles in the standardization of the national diet as well. Just as the Civil War had accelerated the phenomenon of mass production in its demand for rifles with interchangeable parts, it also stimulated demand for vast quantities of edible, palatable, and nutritious foods in standardized form. Gail Borden capitalized on this demand by creating a network of licensed plants throughout the country to provide the Union forces with the condensed milk he had recently perfected. The usual soldier's ration of salt beef or pork and hardtack—a baked mixture of flour and water—was neither appetizing nor salubrious, however. Plentiful coffee was a more popular staple of the military diet. Unpleasant as the regimen of the Union troops may have been, the scarcity of any food at all among their opponents doubtless hastened the collapse of the Confederacy. Growing nutritional knowledge, the "embalmed beef" scandal of the Spanish-American War, and new techniques of food preservation led in subsequent wars to a better and more varied diet, including the C and K rations of World War II, and the once universally reviled Spam, a canned pork product improved in later years.

In addition to war, poverty was a potent factor in mobilizing a variety of institutional forces toward the transformation, the improvement, and, as a by-product, the standardization of the national diet. The muckraking interests that had galvanized public interest in the purity of foods also called attention to the miserable nutritional condition of the poor, especially urban immigrants and the rural native-born, and more especially their children. The Great Depression of the 1930s was a further spur to federal extension and educational work by a number of agencies in promoting better knowledge of preventive nutrition and wholesome techniques of food preparation.

Scientific Housekeeping Still another source of standardization was the "scientific housekeeping" movement that arose among middle-class women in the late nineteenth century. Laura Shapiro, though deploring its bland culinary consequences, interprets it as an attempt by women to attain a new professional dignity and sense of usefulness, while not simultaneously appearing radical. This they attempted by elevating a traditional woman's sphere to a more exalted status. Manifestations of this were the "home economics" movement—the name was first adopted in 1899—which placed many women in university positions, and the cooking schools exemplified by the Boston Cooking School of 1879. The latter, originally aimed at providing working-class girls with commercially and domestically useful skills, soon grew popular with middle-class women as well.

The most distinguished graduate and later director of the Boston Cooking School was Fanny Farmer, whose *Boston Cooking School Cook Book* of 1896 had sold over a third of a million copies by the time of her death in 1915. Although recipe books had been in circulation since the colonial era, Farmer's was the first to approach food preparation with an enthusiastic but no-nonsense practical attitude, utilizing, for example, standardized spoon-and-cup measures that had recently become available commercially. (Farmer's work foreshadowed many later variants, such as Irma S. Rombauer's prodigiously successful *The Joy of Cooking* of 1931.) The overall effect of this movement was the promotion of a nationally standardized cuisine prepared from identical recipes with identical equipment, a development that probably advanced nutrition while certainly abetting the success of brand-name foods and related products in a national market system.

POSTWAR TRANSFORMATIONS

The prosperity that many Americans enjoyed during the decades following World War II made possible suburban life-styles whose followers sought appropriate culinary expression. Outdoor patio living saw new uses for the previously regional barbecue, an adaptation symptomatic of the prestige that California customs now began to exert across the nation. The popularity of the hibachi, a small grill, and of rumaki, an hors d'oeuvre consisting of chicken livers, water chestnuts, and bacon, testified to the new influence of Japanese culture mediated in various ways to North American shores. "Gourmet" cooking, however, was largely synonymous with the culinary Francophilia of a tradition-minded elite, and "American" restaurants tended toward the chophouse, the supper club, the neighborhood family establishment, and the corner bar and grill.

The Politics of Food The social, cultural, and political ferment that swept the nation beginning with the civil rights and antiwar movements of the 1960s had complex ramifications in the realm of foodways. The alarm over the contamination of foods by pesticides sounded by Rachel Carson in her 1962 *Silent Spring* not only led to growing pressure for increased government regulation of agribusiness; it also helped promote a new enthusiasm for organically grown food among counterculturalists and other, more mainstream middle-class Americans concerned with the purity of their diet. For the more radical, the purity of food was not simply rooted in a concern with physical health, but became as well a metaphor for a broader preoccupation with social, political, and spiritual integrity. Macrobiotics, a dietary regimen based on whole grains, beans, and vegetables, attracted many followers, especially in avant-garde enclaves in academic communities and on either coast.

Later twentieth-century food reform, usually based on a call to simplicity of diet, had its roots in the reform movements of the pre–Civil War era. Beginning in the late 1960s, food also became associated with political causes. The feminist movement helped focus attention on both the physical and psychological dimensions of women's health, and promoted a growing awareness among adolescent and younger women in particular of eating disorders such as anorexia—deliberate self-starving in an attempt to attain a fashionably though unhealthily thin figure—and bulimia, consisting of bingeing followed by bouts of self-induced vomiting. A less excessive dieting that found continuing favor among both genders was motivated by a desire to be physically attractive; the irrepressibly American cult of youthfulness as an escape from the ravages of mortality; and a more sensible desire to promote health and longevity through the avoidance of excessive strain on the heart and other organs. Feminism for some has become associated with a vegetarianism based on animal rights, a linkage expounded in Carol J. Adams's *The Sexual Politics of Meat* in 1989. Still other political issues involving food were boycotts of grapes, lettuce, and other crops harvested by migrant workers striving to achieve better pay and working conditions; protests against the sale of infant formula in third-world countries by American firms; and the adequacy of nutrition supplied by school-lunch and other programs in inner-city neighborhoods.

The Expansion of Gourmet Dining   The social and political concerns that focused on food use during these years were paralleled by other developments of somewhat different import. It was this same period that witnessed the transformation of "gourmet" dining from the preoccupation of a small, well-to-do elite into a much broader middle-class phenomenon. Since Lorenzo Delmonico's founding of his celebrated establishment in New York around 1830, French cuisine had enjoyed—with other aspects of that culture—a place of honor among the cognoscenti. *Gourmet* magazine (1941) was the first of what would later become a proliferation of glossy magazines devoted to food and its preparation; it and Julia Child, the Cambridge-based "French Chef" of television fame, helped introduce home preparation of food in the approved manner to growing audiences.

By the early 1970s, something of a revolution had begun to take place in the social functions of food as a mark of status, as well as in its acceptable modes of preparation. Food columns, such as Craig Claiborne's in the *New York Times,* now appeared in life-style rather than women's sections and advocated a wide variety of cooking styles. The introduction of a variety of Chinese regional cuisines, especially those of Szechuan and Hunan provinces, began to displace the primacy of the blander Cantonese and Chinese American dishes that had been the staples of chop suey joints for the previous

century, begun originally by Chinese employed to feed logging and railroad crews. Other cuisines—*nouvelle* French, north Italian, regional Mexican, Vietnamese, Cajun—proliferated bewilderingly as trendy foods among a new consumer culture of "yuppies" eager for novelty and the prestige of seeming to be in on the latest trends. Restaurants, including many formula-following, modish "fern bars," flourished in an industry known for rapid changes of fashion and a correspondingly brief life expectancy for new establishments.

Both regional magazines, such as *Southern Living,* and less sedate rivals of the long-established *Gourmet—Bon Appetit, Food and Wine, Cook's* magazine—aimed at an audience of aspiring upper-middle-class clientele desiring sophistication in the purchase, preparation, and consumption of food as an entree into a breathless new social world. Such glossies aimed at an audience of men as well as women. Formerly associated with professional chefs and gay men, cooking skills now became a necessity both for fathers of young children expected by working wives to share in domestic duties, and for both married and single men wishing to flaunt this newly prestigious social skill. New cooking equipment such as the food processor filled kitchens as well as shops and mail-order catalogs designed for an upscale audience. A cultivated taste for wine—California-produced as well as the traditional French—was an important adjunct to this quest for sensual experience and enhanced status.

AN AMERICAN DIET?

American foodways have often been cited as a particularly good example of the melting pot metaphor once hailed as the essence of American society and culture. The long procession of foods discussed above indicates that this image is not groundless; many Americans today consume regularly a wide variety of edibles reflecting a similarly wide variety of cultures in both their modes of preparation and their ultimate sources. However, some nuances must be added for a more accurate picture.

The food consumption patterns of most Americans in the latter part of the twentieth century reflect a linear progression from the regional British foodways imported during the colonial period to the patterns of mass production and distribution and standardized preparation exemplified in today's supermarkets and fast-food restaurants. In continual tension with this axis have been the variant ethnic, regional, and class-associated foodways that, beginning with the basic crops and game of the aboriginal Native Americans, have interacted with and modified the transition from early modern Britain to the postindustrial United States. Americans today do not so much partake of a common diet as eat within a common matrix, in which certain choices favored by the middle classes are easier to make but others are available as well, though with greater effort or expense. Beef is still plentiful and popular, and the fast-food chains have promoted the consumption of beef, cheese, and wheat flour for hamburger rolls and pizza dough as well as bread. Tea and especially coffee continue as favored daytime beverages suitable to a competitive work force, and their popularity remains strong to the point of addiction. Fresh fruit and vegetables are a still-increasing part of the diet of a health-conscious middle class in which women strongly influence patterns of food selection and preparation.

As the food critic Raymond Sokolov laments, regional foodways are going, but are fortunately not yet gone. Social class and income level push some Americans toward "gourmet" restaurants and others toward government surplus commodities. "Real men" may prefer steak to quiche, and women may choose the salad bar over red meat. Middle-class blacks may occasionally pine for soul food at homecomings, as Italian Americans long for pasta with traditional "gravy" at *feste* and family gatherings. Handmade tortillas may still be the everyday fare of Mexicans isolated in the barrios of southwestern cities. Few, however, are immune to the lure of the hamburger and the pizza. American foodways, in sum, are neither unilinear nor immutable; they are, however, as recognizable as the blue jeans and rock music by which non-Americans, for better or worse, see ours as a distinctive culture.

BIBLIOGRAPHY

Bibliographies and Research Guides

Anderson, Jay Allan. "The Study of Contemporary Foodways in American Folklife Research." *Keystone Folklore Quarterly* 16, no. 4 (Special Food Issue; 1971).

Camp, Charles. "Food in American Culture: A Bibliographic Essay." *Journal of American Culture* 2, no. 3 (1979).

———. "Foodways in Everyday Life." *American Quarterly* 34, no. 3 (1982).

———. *American Foodways: What, When, Why, and How We Eat in America* (1989). Introduction to study of foodways, with most comprehensive bibliography.

———. "Foodways." In *Handbook of American Popular Culture,* edited by Thomas M. Inge (1989).

Mariani, John F. *The Dictionary of American Food and Drink* (1983).

Surveys and Historically Oriented Cookbooks

The American Heritage Cookbook and Illustrated History of American Eating and Drinking (1964). Popular, well-illustrated topical essays with recipes.

Beard, James. *James Beard's American Cookery* (1972). Primarily a cookbook, but with interesting running commentary.

Cummings, Richard Osborn. *The American and His Food: A History of Food Habits in the United States* (1940). Old, but never superseded on some topics.

Hooker, Richard J. *Food and Drink in the United States: A History* (1981). Popular overview.

Jones, Evan. *American Food: The Gastronomic Story* (1975). Popular, but still best historical survey.

FOODWAYS

Regional and Period Studies

Benes, Peter, ed. *Foodways in the Northeast* (1984). Valuable scholarly essays from Dublin Folklife symposium.

Booth, Sally Smith. *Hung, Strung, and Potted: A History of Eating in Colonial America* (1971).

Carson, Barbara G. *Ambitious Appetites: Dining, Behavior, and Patterns of Consumption in Federal Washington* (1990). Exhibit catalog.

Conlin, Joseph R. *Bacon, Beans, and Galantines: Food and Foodways on the Western Mining Frontier* (1986). Provides background beyond rather narrow title topic.

Egerton, John. *Southern Food: At Home, on the Road, in History* (1987). Informal and anecdotal.

Faragher, John Mack. *Women and Men on the Overland Trail* (1979). Occasional discussion of foodways.

Feintuch, Burt. "Foodways, Geography of"; Joe Gray Taylor, "Foodways"; and shorter articles by various authors on foodways topics (e.g., "Moon Pies"). In *Encyclopedia of Southern Culture,* edited by Charles Reagan Wilson and William Ferris (1989).

Fischer, David Hackett. *Albion's Seed: Four British Folkways in America* (1989). Brief, well-annotated foodways sections.

Hilliard, Sam. *Hog Meat and Hoecake: Food Supply in the Old South, 1840–1860* (1972).

Kimball, Marie. *Thomas Jefferson's Cook Book* (1976).

Leonard, Jonathan Norton. *American Cooking: New England* (1970), and other volumes in the Time-Life Foods of the World series. Lushly illustrated; scholarly value of texts varies among volumes.

Low, W. Augustus, and Virgil A. Clift. "Cuisine." In *Encyclopedia of Black America* (1981).

Morgan, Edmund S. *Virginians at Home: Family Life in the Eighteenth Century* (1952).

Taylor, Joe Gray. *Eating, Drinking, and Visiting in the South* (1982).

Weaver, William Woys, ed. *A Quaker Woman's Cookbook: The Domestic Cookery of Elizabeth Ellicott Lea* (1982).

Ethnological and Folkways Studies

Brown, Linda Keller, and Kay Mussell, eds. *Ethnic and Regional Foodways in the United States* (1984). Essays from a variety of disciplinary viewpoints; primarily folkways/ethnological.

Crosby, Alfred W., Jr. *The Columbian Exchange: Biological and Cultural Consequences of 1492* (1972).

"Focus on American Food and Foodways" section in *Journal of American Culture* 2, no. 3 (1979). Variety of articles, stressing fast food and popular culture.

Humphrey, Theodore C., and Lin T. Humphrey, eds. *"We Gather Together": Food and Festival in American Life* (1988).

Jones, Michael Owen, et al., eds. *Foodways and Eating Habits: Directions for Research* (1983).

Sokolov, Raymond. *Fading Feast: A Compendium of Disappearing American Regional Foods* (1981).

———. *Why We Eat What We Eat* (1991).

Mass and Popular Culture

Boas, Max, and Steve Chain. *Big Mac: The Unauthorized Story of McDonald's* (1976). Journalistic but well-informed and perceptive.

Boorstin, Daniel J. *The Americans: The Democratic Experience* (1973). Chapters 35 to 37 on the technology of food processing and distribution since the Civil War.

Dickson, Paul. *Chow: A Cook's Tour of Military Food* (1978).

Green, Harvey. *Fit for America: Health, Fitness, Sport, and American Society* (1986). Discussion of diet reform movements.

Gustafson, Donna, et al. *Art What Thou Eat: Images of Food in American Art* (1991). Exhibit catalogue.

Hirshorn, Paul, and Steven Izenour. *White Towers* (1979). Photographic essay on fast-food architecture.

Langdon, Philip. *Orange Roofs, Golden Arches: The Architecture of American Chain Restaurants* (1986).

Shapiro, Laura. *Perfection Salad: Women and Cooking at the Turn of the Century* (1986). Journalistic but solid treatment of "scientific nutrition" movement.

Stern, Jane, and Michael Stern. *Goodfood* (1983); *Real American Food* (1986); *Square Meals* (1984). Informal explorations of popular diet.

SEE ALSO various essays in the sections "**Ethnic and Racial Subcultures**" and "**Regionalism and Regional Subcultures.**"

MANNERS AND ETIQUETTE

Beth Bailey

To SUGGEST THE FULL significance of etiquette in American history, it is perhaps best to approach the subject obliquely, looking first to one of the central struggles in American history—the struggle over race. D. W. Griffith intended his epic film *The Birth of a Nation* to plead a case: the "birth" he envisioned was the reuniting of North and South, an Anglo-Saxon nation standing against the twin threat of blacks and immigrants. He meant to leave the white middle-class audiences of 1915 cheering as the white-robed Ku Klux Klan rode to the rescue of Anglo-Saxon civilization.

Griffith set up his argument carefully, with predictable scenes that portray black men sexually menacing white women. But Griffith also gave great weight to another scene, clearly intending it to raise the ire of proper audiences. The hero, a southern gentleman, walks along a sidewalk with a lady. They encounter the ambitious mulatto Silas Lynch, who not only does not relinquish the right of way to his "betters" but insists upon being "recognized" by them. While this scene lacks the raw racist charge of a black man sexually threatening a white woman, Griffith clearly intended it as a piece of emotional evidence. Lynch's claims were an egregious breach of etiquette—meant and understood as a challenge to social order. Modern audiences see the "Little Colonel" (the Civil War nickname for our gentleman hero) fuming over this affront and are vaguely puzzled. Audiences in 1915 saw the challenge as significant because they, like Griffith, lived within a system of etiquette that was closely tied to fears about social order and disorder.

The scene does not work with modern audiences partly because we do not know the rules Lynch is breaking. They have passed from our behavior; they have disappeared from the etiquette manuals. The middle-class man or woman today is thoroughly ignorant of the myriad rules of etiquette that would have defined his or her middle-class status fifty or one hundred years ago.

The term "etiquette" itself has fallen out of favor. It sounds quaint—like the system of manners it is most often used to describe. Etiquette, in contemporary American society, most often surfaces in rituals that lay some claim to formality, such as weddings, and in exhortations to politeness based on common good sense. But while the term remains attached to a tradition of rules and manners developed, elaborated, and overelaborated in the nineteenth century, we live within systems of etiquette no less complex and arcane.

Etiquette has played a complex and important role in American history. It is not just that, in Erving Goffman's words, "the gestures which we sometimes call empty are perhaps the fullest things of all" or, in the social historian John Kasson's words, that "the rituals of everyday behavior establish in important measure the structures by which individuals define one another and interact." Both points *are* important: a people's manners—the rituals of their everyday behavior—are full of meaning and of information. We can read manners as ritual and learn much.

But ritual is not the whole story, for manners and etiquette are not interchangeable terms. The term "manners" describes behavior, however unmannerly that behavior might be. Etiquette, on the other hand, is prescriptive. Etiquette is the code of manners, the set of rules, the definition of proper behavior. The relationship between manners and etiquette is complicated and often tense. It is in that tension, which prevents the perfect correspondence of manners and etiquette, that we often learn most.

Etiquette, in addition, is instrumental. In the course of American history, etiquette has often served as a tool—even as a weapon—in struggles over social change in America. Etiquette has often been concerned with drawing lines between people and boundaries between groups—most importantly, between social classes in the nineteenth century and between men and women in the twentieth century (the role of race remains complicated throughout). In observing etiquette, Americans enacted rituals of power and exclusion while claiming them to be natural manifestations of "taste" or of "breeding." But etiquette has also provided means to claim inclusion and served as a forum for testing conflicting claims about the nature and form of civility.

Many different systems of manners and of etiquette have existed in America. A modern high school might have an elaborate but local code of etiquette that, though unwritten, structures daily interactions. Immigrant groups brought the manners and etiquette of their home countries to the United States, and those systems changed through contact with other groups. The fine points of social usage differed between Charleston and New York, Des Moines and Dallas. And in terms of etiquette, the past truly is another country.

Etiquette is a prescriptive system and never fully matches behavior. Even the most universally prescriptive system of etiquette is mediated by factors like religion, race, ethnicity, class, region, gender, and profession. Nonetheless, the observance of appropriate etiquette has been a precondition for participation in public life, and etiquette has worked both to determine social status and to structure relationships between individuals. Of course, what was "appropriate" etiquette was often contested.

While many have claimed otherwise, there is nothing timeless about etiquette—neither the behaviors prescribed and proscribed nor the definitions of the term. A nine-year-old boy in the mid 1960s declared: "I have good manners. I say good night and good morning. I say hello and goodbye, and when I see dead things lying around the house I bury them." His implicit definition and practical interpretation strain the bounds of credulity less than those of many older and better-known advisers. In the pages that follow, I will attempt to offer an overview of the changing definitions of etiquette and to analyze the significance and utility of etiquette in American history.

EARLY CODES

Those who journeyed to the New World carried with them, in addition to the supplies they thought would be useful in the unknown land, a vast store of cultural baggage. They brought to the new continents old ways of seeing, habits of behavior, and systems of manners: sets of assumptions so deeply rooted as to be unconscious and unremarked upon. The culture they transplanted did not flourish unchanged in new soil, but the manners and mores of these new Americans were marked as much by persistence as by change.

The development of American manners is not a story of creative synthesis through cultural contact: the colonists dismissed the aboriginal inhabitants of the new world as "barbarians," and the newly named "Indians," in other languages, thought pretty much the same of the settlers. The Europeans would never have survived in the new landscape without knowledge gained from the Indians, and contact with Europeans radically transformed the lives and culture of Native Americans. But the two groups came from very different worlds and assigned very different meanings to similar acts. What seemed to the Europeans to be trade, for example, was to the tribes of the eastern woodlands often gift-exchange, a ritualized system that served to create and maintain allegiances between tribes. Overall, Europeans tended to describe Native Americans as existing in a state of nature (meaning they were uncivilized), and Native Americans, though drawn into European trade networks and desiring firearms and other European goods, had no desire to wear European-style clothes, live in stuffy houses, or adopt the manners of "Christian people."

The British settlers of North America came from a highly rank-ordered society, and brought with them a belief in the naturalness of hierarchy. Such traditional forms did not serve the settlers of Jamestown well. In England, "gentleman" designated one who did not earn his living through manual labor, and in Jamestown the gentlemen refused to work until John Smith, Gent., subverted proper form and forced them.

For the early settlers in Massachusetts Bay, rank and hierarchy were crucial. The colonists saw their settlements as small and fragile centers of Christian civilization clinging to the edge of a vast and menacing wilderness. The death rate was high, support from England not certain, winters harsh, and food scarce. Order was crucial, so that the community not succumb to chaos within. Order, to these seventeenth-century men and women, entailed hierarchy. John Winthrop, the governor of the colony and a gentleman, wrote in *A Modell of Christian Charity* (1630): "God Almighty in his most holy and wise providence hath so disposed of the condition of mankind as in all times some may be rich, some poor, some high and eminent in power and dignity, others mean and in subjection."

Many of the rules of etiquette transferred to the colonies were concerned with rank and status. The colonists dealt with the issue of hierarchy in ways that seem exceedingly direct to twentieth-century Americans, used to reading class and status in subtler signs. Titles designated status: "Mister" was reserved for gentlemen (a status determined not by behavior but by social position); the wives of gentlemen were addressed as "Madam." Those of commoner clay were called, as in England, "Goodman" and "Goodwife" (or less formally, "Goody"). In America, though, the title of gentleman lost some of its social significance, for a goodman might ascend to the "gentry" if he were elected captain by his peers in the local militia, or if he were chosen to hold a town office such as justice of the peace. In the New World, unlike the Old, a man without substantial fortune, education, or lineage might be addressed as a gentleman.

Rank was assumed as the most natural way of ordering a group of people. Students at Harvard and Yale were listed in order of family standing until 1772, when an alphabetical system was adopted. The change, significantly, seems to have stemmed less from a rise of democratic feelings than from increased difficulty in determining rank and the grumbling of parents who did not agree with the college's determination of their status.

Even in religious services colonists did not assemble as an undifferentiated community of worshipers. Pews were assigned according to community consensus on the social rank of each family, and services offered a ritual enactment of hierarchy and status. Still, rank-order was sometimes contested. Town records tell of shoving matches in the aisles, and of one Goody Elizabeth Randall who claimed the place she believed rightfully hers, pushing and scrambling her way over pews with backs four to five feet tall.

The passing of sumptuary laws in the various colonies also testifies that the boundaries of rank and status were stretched in America. "One end of apparel," according to Urian Oakes (1631–1681), president of Harvard College, "is to distinguish and put a difference between persons according to their places and Condition." But the Massachusetts General Court felt it necessary to register its outrage "that men or women of mean condition, should take upon them the garb of Gentlemen," requiring that one must possess property equivalent to £200

in order to wear "gaudy apparel." The Virginia House of Burgesses had passed similar legislation in its first session. The law was violated, but offenders were rarely convicted.

The general manners of the people can be surmised from their surroundings. While the wealthiest colonists had begun to stock their homes with luxuries imported from Europe, most people lived very humbly. In the Chesapeake Bay area in the seventeenth century, for example, only one-third of the families had chairs or benches in their homes. Homes were small, with little separation of space or function. Few had real beds at first, but those who did kept them in the main room. Families slept together, welcoming travelers into the common bed. Privacy was seen neither as a good or necessary commodity, nor as a requisite for polite behavior.

To eat, common people gathered around a board laid on trestles. Hierarchy remained important: adults and guests sat "above the salt" (the salt cellar placed in the middle of the table) and servants and children below. They shared trenchers and cups, and freely dipped their hands into common serving bowls. European travelers were often appalled at the promiscuous sharing, as common cups became fouled with spit and grease, and bits of tobacco floated in the common drink. As late as 1827, Margaret Hunter Hall wrote home to England, "They are a nasty people, the Americans, at table; there is no denying that fact."

It was not only the common folk or lesser ranks whose concepts of privacy and proper deportment were shocking. The advice offered in the conduct or courtesy books popular in colonial America is telling. "Spit not in the room but in the corner, or rather go out and do it abroad," advises Eleazar Moody's *School of Good Manners,* the most popular of American courtesy books published in the eighteenth century. George Washington, at fifteen, copied out the following in his commonplace book: "Kill no Vermin as Fleas, lice ticks &c in the Sight of Others . . ." and "Being set at meat Scratch not neither Spit Cough or blow your Nose except there's a Necessity for it." Such rules were derived from conduct guides written for nobles at court in the fifteenth and sixteenth centuries; even here we see standards of proper behavior changing, for these versions had dropped proscriptions against "relieving" oneself before the doors of "court chambers"—this advice no longer had to be stated. Still, in colonial and early national America, it was deemed polite to blow one's nose not on the tablecloth but in one's fingers—as long as it was not the hand with which one was eating.

THE SOUTH AND THE NORTH

The manners of colonists differed by region—both because of the accidents of geography and because of the different traditions of polite behavior that served as models. Northern society looked to the moralist strand of English courtesy books, and, in revising them for American consumption, enhanced the religious component. Southerners looked to the landed gentry, reading works in the courtly tradition. Richard Allestree's *The Whole Duty of Man,* first published in London around 1660, was owned by both George Washington and Thomas Jefferson. Allestree presented a model of comportment based on the ideals of chivalry and hierarchy, emphasizing the criteria that made gentlemen. "Gentlemen," he insisted, "sweat only at the Engagement of their Sports," while the lesser ranks must live by the sweat of their brows.

Southern etiquette was based on a chivalric code of honor that was, as Bertram Wyatt-Brown argues in *Southern Honor,* "inseparable from hierarchy and entitlement, defense of family blood and community needs." The code of honor applied to all southern whites, though its proper manifestation differed depending on rank in society and upon gender. The southern code, though never so romantic or so "civilized" as it has been portrayed in retrospect, suffused southern life. In contrast, northern society, with its early emphasis on mercantile pursuits followed by its transformation into an urban-industrial society, developed an ethic and code of manners based on conscience and secular economic concerns.

Honor was enacted, in its most extreme form, through the highly ritualized performance of the duel (which one historian has described as men "killing each other according to strict rules of etiquette"). Dueling was introduced to America by French and British aristocrats serving (on different sides) during the Revolutionary War and was taken up in the ranks of America's military. But dueling became widespread in the postcolonial South, where, in spite of strong opposition, the *code duello* became a part of the gentleman's life.

Duels were fought in defense of honor. If one man insulted another's personal honor, custom and community opinion urged that the matter be resolved through a duel. Duels were governed by a etiquette, though many duelists were not clear on proper form; John Lyde Wilson, a former governor of South Carolina, compiled a "blue book" of dueling etiquette.

Dueling, in keeping with the hierarchical nature of the code of honor, was restricted to gentlemen; one did not challenge or accept a challenge from a social inferior. While a small percentage of southerners qualified as gentlemen in the strictest sense (for example, in 1860, 11,000 families, or 0.75 percent of the southern population, owned fifty or more slaves), a much larger number of white men laid claim to that status as officers in local militias. In a culture noted for its physical violence and hotheadedness, dueling may have served to mediate extremes of violence, for the proper duel offered cooling-off time as the rites of challenge and response were observed, and official intermediaries were sometimes able to settle matters with honor and without violence.

Southern etiquette was also tightly enmeshed with the South's peculiar institution. Deference was expected from slaves. In the physical embodiment of honor, according to Bertram Wyatt-Brown, southern culture linked honor to the body: "the eyes witnessed honor and looked down in deference or shame." Thus a slave who met the gaze of a white person was impudent. Travelers were sometimes confounded by the workings of hierarchy in the South. One young woman, overwhelmingly modest in her relations with white men, undressed freely in the presence of a male slave. His status rendered him unimportant—his race canceled the significance of his sex. The not-uncommon relations between white masters and slave women were also covered by the code of honor. The sexual union itself was no violation of honor or of etiquette, but if someone "violated good taste" and spoke of the liaison directly to any member of the man's family, the entire family was disgraced. In such matters, silence was polite.

While southern manners and etiquette remained rooted in the traditions of hierarchy and honor well into the nineteenth century, in the North both manners and the claims of etiquette had undergone a revolution. The sources of change are two: the rise of democratic sentiment in the wake of the American Revolution, and fundamental changes in the social and economic organization of the nation.

Much of our description of American manners comes from European travelers who were quick to attribute virtually everything to the effects of democracy. "Nothing does democracy more harm than its outward forms of behavior," wrote Alexis de Tocqueville (1805–1859) in a chapter called "Some Reflections on American Manners" in *Democracy in America,* for "many who could tolerate its vices cannot put up with its manners." It was the presumption of equality that rankled the most with Frances Trollope (1780–1863), who made herself very unpopular in America with the publication of her *Domestic Manners of the Americans* (1832). Mrs. Trollope experienced the friendliness of a Cincinnati neighbor as a "violent intimacy," and contact with members of the lower classes was infinitely uncomfortable. "I am very far from intending to advocate the system of slavery," she wrote. "I conceive it to be essentially wrong; but so far as my observation has extended, I think its influence is far less injurious to the manners and morals of the people than the fallacious ideas of equality, which are so fondly cherished by the working classes of the white population in America."

Some Americans rejected the European styles, as did a clergyman who argued that "we have already suffered much by too great an avidity for British customs and manners; it is now time to become independent in our maxims, principles of education, dress, and manners, as we are in our laws and government." Others made the point more directly, as did one Cincinnati lodging-house keeper, who turned Mrs. Trollope away because she did not want to take tea with the other lodgers. When she tried to apologize, explaining that she was not familiar with the manners of the country, he replied, "Our manners are very good manners, and we don't wish any changes from England." Still, travelers told tales of being fawned over by the members of local society, all of whom wanted reassurance that their manners, customs, furnishings, and entertainments matched those of Europe.

Foreign observers cast American etiquette as a drama of democracy, and to some extent it was. What was the proper role in a republic for a system of manners rooted in the chivalric tradition of European court life, of rules of behavior meant to maintain and reinforce hierarchy and fixed place? Formal systems of etiquette, however, did not decline in the face of democratic rhetoric and its limited reality. Instead, etiquette grew in importance as a means of control and a measure of stability in the often confusing and threatening urban-industrial-capitalist society that emerged in nineteenth-century America. An increasingly elaborate code of etiquette mediated the effects of the market economy

and the relative mobility and anonymity felt keenly by our ancestors. This allowed newly useful boundaries to be drawn between the realms of public and private, and between people whose place was no longer fixed and whose status no longer secure.

MIDDLE-CLASS RESPECTABILITY

John Kasson, in his wonderful work *Rudeness and Civility,* argues that the redefinition of the term "genteel" in the nineteenth century "epitomizes enormous changes in economy and society," as the emerging urban-industrial-capitalist system replaced the rank-ordered society of colonial America. "Gentility," in colonial America, designated status; it referred to the well-born. By the 1830s, "genteel" referred to qualities of politeness and grace.

Central to the transformation of the concept of gentility—and to the crucial importance of etiquette in nineteenth-century American society—was the emergence of middle classes. As Kasson emphasizes, the emergence of the industrial-capitalist system did not create a more economically equal society, nor did it offer unlimited mobility. But the diminished importance of inherited rank, along with geographic mobility (especially the move to the rapidly growing cities), combined with the emerging system to offer new possibilities. The new economic system demanded new sorts of workers—clerks and managers, people who did a variety of white-collar work and who, no matter what the reality, defined themselves as upwardly mobile and who sought the trappings and manners of "respectability." While offering many the means to live in comfort, the new industrial-capitalist order left many in desperate poverty. It also created vast fortunes and intense jostling for social position, as money contested name for precedence.

In the ferment of change, all seemed possible. "It is not here, as in the old world," wrote one nineteenth-century adviser, "where one man is born with a silver spoon, and another with a pewter one, in his mouth. You may all have silver spoons, if you will." She was referring not solely to material wealth, but also to the outward signs of gentility. Any man might be a gentleman; any woman a lady. "You may be whatever you will resolve to be," exhorted yet another adviser.

In the flood of writing about society and manners, the "best society" was increasingly defined as middle class—and presented as attainable. "You have it in your power to fit yourselves by the cultivation of your minds, and the refinement of your manners, for intercourse, on equal terms, with the best society in the land," promised the influential writer Catharine Sedgwick (1789–1867). The manners that marked one as a gentleman or lady could be learned. One could master the rules and forms of etiquette and purchase the increasingly available accoutrements of gentility.

The flood of etiquette and advice books that appeared in the nineteenth century offered entree to the world of respectable middle-class behavior. In the 1830s, because of major developments in the technologies of printing and book publishing, books, magazines, and newspapers became much more widely available and much less expensive than before. Etiquette and advice books occupied a prominent place in the offerings of nineteenth-century publishers. According to Arthur Meier Schlesinger, an average of three new etiquette manuals appeared each year between 1830 and the decade of the Civil War, and from the 1870s through World War I, five to six new manuals appeared annually. This staggering number does not include reprints and new editions. Etiquette books were sold by sales agents who went door to door and in direct-mail advertisements in magazines and newspapers. Some were massive and expensive—encyclopedic in form—and others were short and inexpensive "dime books," designed for a mass market. While the forms of etiquette developed in the cities, they were copied by "respectable" folk in small towns and villages throughout the country. The majority of these works were American in authorship and addressed to the middle classes, broadly defined.

These works were very much "how-to" in spirit—self-improvement books—frequently with a heavy dose of moral exhortation. Readers were told, in precise detail, how to sit, how to stand, how to receive a guest, and how to decorate a parlor. No detail was too small for attention: "The general positions for the arms are about the level of the waist, never hanging down or being quite stiff, but being gently bent, the elbow a little raised, the fingers not stretched out stiffly, but also a little bent, and partially separated, or the hands half crossed one over the other, or placed in each other, &c.," offered a volume titled *A Manual of Politeness, Comprising the Principles of Etiquette, and Rules of Behavior in Genteel Society, for Persons of Both Sexes* (1837).

The promise of social mobility and the availability of such helpful advice made gentility, in Kasson's words, "increasingly available as a social desire and a purchasable style and commodity." By the second quarter of the nineteenth century, gentility seemed not so much a product of birth as the result of striving, of solid middle-class effort.

A knowledge of etiquette, no matter how arcane and complex, could serve as a tool for advancement in society. According to the best advisers, the effort involved was considerable, but it paid off. The rituals of etiquette, once mastered, were inclusive. They paved the way to an *attainable* middle-class gentility—and the phrase "middle-class gentility" did not seem contradictory. The importance of etiquette in the nineteenth century, in substantial measure, was a sign of the era's optimism. The rigors of etiquette were born of a sense of possibility.

But nineteenth-century American etiquette had mixed parentage: as it was inclusive, it also worked to exclude; as it grew from optimism, it was also an expression of profound social fears. Karen Halttunen, in her pathbreaking and sophisticated book *Confidence Men and Painted Women,* reads in nineteenth-century urban middle-class culture a "crisis of social identity faced by . . . men and women who were on the move both socially and geographically." As they aspired to gentility and to higher social status, they feared a world where other people were not what they seemed. Halttunen argues that such fears coalesced around the figures of the confidence man and the painted woman, hypocrites who "poisoned polite society with deception and betrayal by dressing extravagantly and practicing the empty forms of false etiquette."

Advice and etiquette books stressed sincerity as the heart of etiquette, insisting that the empty forms were meaningless—even destructive—but nonetheless furnishing detailed instructions on how to comply with those very forms. This paradox, Halttunen argues, was resolved through what she calls a "genteel performance," in which the complexities of etiquette were navigated and performed in a "sincere" manner. The genteel performance was a "polite fiction," presenting "the courtesy of those ladies and gentlemen who adhered to the hundreds of rules governing parlor conduct" as the result of "right feelings and not . . . of the painstaking study of etiquette manuals."

The fiction was fragile; its existence depended upon the collusion of those who participated. Thus its existence depended upon exclusion. Those who threatened the magic of the performance by recognizing it as performance must be excluded. Those who were insufficiently genteel to play their proper roles must be excluded. While a plethora of manuals told people how to be genteel—how to pass—many of the rules they were mastering detailed the art of "polite" exclusion. As Charles William Day's *Hints on Etiquette and the Usages of Society* (1844) explained:

Etiquette is a barrier which society draws around itself as a protection against offences the "law" cannot touch; it is a shield against the intrusion of the impertinent, the improper, and the vulgar,—a guard against those obtuse persons who, having neither talent nor delicacy, would be continually thrusting themselves into the society of men to whom their presence might (from the difference of feeling and habit) be offensive, and even insupportable. (Halttunen, pp. 111–112)

The laws of etiquette provided a series of tests, or measures, of social acceptability. That someone could observe all the complex rules of etiquette and do so "sincerely," seemingly without effort, seemed to be a guarantee of "breeding" or, more accurately, class background, in a society that was both socially and geographically mobile.

In Victorian America, an etiquette of gentility came to be largely synonymous with an exceptional delicacy about matters physical or sexual. Frances Trollope wrote with disgust of American women's "ultra-refinement." Frederick Marryat, another traveler, claimed to have seen, in a seminary for young ladies, a piano with its legs—or limbs—covered by "modest little trousers, with frills at the bottom of them!" Hiram Powers's (1805–1873) statue *The Greek Slave* was dressed in calico blouse and flannel trousers for its exhibit in Cincinnati. Etiquette books advised ladies to avoid questions in polite conversation, for questions might lead to embarrassing subjects. One adviser rather breathlessly told of a lady who inquired of a gentleman what sort of medicine he practiced, only to discover that he was a doctor of "midwifery." This pretentious delicacy is comical in retrospect, but it is important to understand that, as Christopher Mulvey explains in *Transatlantic Manners,* this behavior was meant to demonstrate social status and good breeding as much as or more than to manifest an essential prudery. Refinement was the essential characteristic of respectability.

The formal dinner party was perhaps the greatest test—though of course one had to have passed as "acceptable" in order to be invited. While in the early nineteenth century Americans commonly ate with a two-prong iron or steel fork and a knife, using the rounded blade of the knife to carry food into one's mouth, by the 1830s eating had become a much more complicated business. In the 1830s, Andrew Jackson's White House dinners offered guests a choice of two forks, one silver, one steel. By the 1880s, successful silverware companies like Reed and Barton offered tableware in many patterns—most of which included specialized serving pieces, and up to ten different kinds of knives; twelve different kinds of forks (including those intended specifically for terrapin, for mango, for oyster, and for ice cream); and twenty different kinds of spoons. Knowing which fork to use was not so easy, and making one's way through a formal dinner with no breach of etiquette a formidable task. Washington society commonly noted which new congressmen from the provinces attempted to eat the doilies, and it was said that President Lincoln, when asked by a waiter at his first state dinner whether he would have white wine or red, replied, "I don't know. Which would you?"

"Calling" was the central act of the "genteel performance," and worked most directly to demonstrate social status and to test and reinforce social boundaries. The ritual of calling was controlled by women, who played important roles in advancing families' social status. Most middle- and upper-class women designated a specific day "at home" for receiving callers. Callers presented calling cards to the maid who answered the door, indicating their intentions by the ways the cards were folded. By bending the right-hand corner of the card, one indicated that he or she was only paying respects and did not ask to be received; by bending the whole right-hand side of the card, one asked to be received. The upper left-hand corner, when bent, signaled "congratulations," the lower left-hand corner "condolences." Gender played a role: a man was not to call on a woman without her express invitation. Thus young women had the sole right of initiative in courtship—for it was deemed most important that women be able to exclude unwanted attentions and unsuitable admirers.

Those seeking to be received were either ushered into the parlor or told that the lady of the house was "not at home." This might or might not be strictly true: she might not be receiving that day—or she might be signaling the social unacceptability of the caller. Etiquette books advised their readers to keep strict account of their calls—of whether or not calls were returned, of where they were received and where turned away. Such an accounting offered a clear statement of one's social status (or, in appropriate cases, one's romantic prospects). With characteristic overstatement, the influential writer Mrs. Sherwood (Mary Elizabeth Sherwood, 1826–1903) explained the importance of the calling system in nineteenth-century America: "The [calling] card may well be noted as belonging only to a high order of development. No monkey, no 'missing link,' no Zulu, no savage, carries a card. It is the tool of civilization, its 'field-mark and device.'"

Part of the exclusionary nature of the system stemmed from the competitive struggle for social status. The middling classes meant to demonstrate respectability, but also to advance socially just as they advanced economically. At the same time, those in the upper reaches of society enacted a more stringent form of exclusivity. Caroline Astor, with her aide Ward McAllister, worked to hold the line of society against the claims of the nouveaux riches who flooded New York in the last half of the nineteenth century. Ward McAllister coined the term, "The Four Hundred," in trying to explain why only four hundred were invited to Mrs. Astor's annual Patriarch's Ball (the real reason was space limitation). "There are only about four hundred people in fashionable New York Society," he explained. "If you go outside that number you strike people who are not at ease in a ballroom or else make other people not at ease." Mrs. Astor's invitations determined who belonged to "society," and her insistence on proper form and ritual structured her particular brand of social exclusivity. Still, by the end of the century younger social leaders like Mrs. Stuyvesant Fish and her aide Harry Lehr mocked the strict forms of society, giving dinners that they called "vaudevilles" and that Mrs. Astor publicly called "undignified."

All this genteelly couched jostling for social position lay at the heart of Victorian etiquette. But at the less genteel gut of the system was a great sense of vulnerability. The genteel performance was enacted in controlled spaces—in middle-class parlors with doors kept by maids, in private dinners and balls and parties to which no one came without invitation. This protected world existed in tension with the new world of the industrial city, a city larger, more anonymous, more frightening than before. Money served to cushion existence; those who could afford it kept carriages and drivers, attempting to stretch the boundaries of the private to the public world. But the experience of walking down a city street, subject to the stares of strangers, the importunities of the ill bred, the insults of the com-

mon, the dirt and disorder and chaos—all contributed to the importance of etiquette as a system that stressed strict control of one's own body and emotions and of physical space, in an assertion of the importance of privacy and an emphasis on the ability to exclude the unsuitable.

Of course, the "unsuitable" had their own systems of etiquette. Immigrant groups carried the manners of their old countries, and though no etiquette manual seems directly addressed to immigrants, much of the material that was aimed at Americanization or assimilation dealt with points that might well be described as etiquette. And in the foreign language press, leaders and writers such as Abraham Cahan (1860–1951) of the Yiddish paper, the *Jewish Daily Forward* spoke of the significance of manners and mores. Black leaders advised others of their race on matters of character and etiquette, most notably in a manual called *The Negro in Etiquette: A Novelty* (1899). But while all African Americans were lumped together in common disdain by most whites, blacks were divided by class, by skin color, and by place of origin. Black society, epitomized in the late nineteenth century by the Society of the Sons of New York, guarded its gates against newcomers as carefully as did the originators of the Patriarch's Ball.

While the etiquette of Victorian America seems extremely rigid, changes in social organization continued to strain established forms. New technologies were often the impetus for change in social form. The telephone, for example, fit uneasily into the pattern of calling (the telephone was patented in 1876, and by 1900 approximately 1.5 million were in use in the United States). Advisers agreed that it was a greater assertion of intimacy to telephone than to arrive at the door and present a calling card. If "on a certain footing of intimacy," one explained in 1907, a man might telephone the lady of the house to see if it were all right to call that evening. Eventually, of course, the hierarchy of intimacy would reverse.

The automobile also would present new difficulties as the old system of etiquette tottered. Virginia Scharff argues in *Taking the Wheel* that "the cultural gap between social status and control of technology" caused great concern for the owners of the new machines. Men who drove their own automobiles were cautioned to differentiate themselves from professional drivers (chauffeurs) through dress and manner. Some worried about the amount of power and control vested in a chauffeur, especially when his passenger was a woman. (In French slang, the phrase *chauffer une femme* meant "to make hot love to a woman.") But at the same time, the automobile promised women privacy and protection from unwanted intrusions. The Detroit Electric Car was advertised so: "To the well-bred woman—the Detroit Electric has a particular appeal. In it she can preserve her toilet immaculate, her coiffure intact. She can drive it with all desired privacy, yet safely—in constant touch with traffic conditions around her."

The new technologies of American business also began to transform social etiquette. Typewriters, for example, introduced in the late 1800s, brought a flood of respectable young women into business offices. Women who typed were dubbed "typewriters" after the machines they operated. This label gave rise to the predictable joke ("Here I sit, my typewriter on my knee"), but the increasing presence of women in business complicated other traditional forms. What degree of deference based on gender did an employer owe a secretary? Did the forms of polite society transfer to business relations between the sexes? As more and more "respectable" women entered the public world, attending college, working in offices or stores, moving unchaperoned in public, the existing lines between men and women, public and private, genteel and unacceptable, were necessarily redrawn.

The etiquette of gentility broke down as the entire Victorian worldview, with its insistence on the absolute polarities of civilization and savagery, of good and evil, of men and women, began to crumble. More and more of those who came of age in the late nineteenth century felt stifled by the weight of gentility and the rigidness of form—some rebelling in profound ways and with profound results, others frivolously. But to a great extent, the breakdown of Victorian etiquette and the genteel performance came through those who were not afraid of the city, who found the intense *publicness* of the private world—attending dances with the same people, conducting polite conversations in genteelly appointed parlors—suffocating. They sought the privacy that the public world of the city offered in its anonymity. They sought the excitement of mixing with people of different conditions and backgrounds. And they sought a form of sexual freedom in the companionship of the opposite sex, exploring the new cabarets and restaurants, escaping into the world of the city that had so terrified their parents.

THE ETIQUETTE OF GENDER

If the etiquette of the nineteenth century centered on issues of class, the etiquette of the twentieth century coalesced on issues of sex and gender. The problem of defining relations between the sexes had, in many ways, replaced the problem of defining relations between the classes. Gender etiquette offered a means of controlling the relationships between men and women and of reinforcing the "natural" barriers between the sexes that seemed increasingly under siege in the twentieth century.

We see the shift from class to gender etiquette in the rise of the dating system and the elaboration of dating etiquette in the twentieth century. The calling system, as it operated in courtship, still centered upon class. As an invitation to call was an invitation into one's home, the calling system granted women and their parents the right of initiative, thus allowing them to screen out the unsuitable suitor. Dating transferred initiative to men and shifted the focus of etiquette from the barriers between classes as demonstrated in genteel performance to the roles of the sexes and the importance of gender politics.

The practice of dating originated in American cities in the last decade of the nineteenth century as young people of the working classes, pushed out of overcrowded tenement apartments and drawn to the new urban amusements that catered to them, took flirtations and courtship into the public realm. Their term "date" (which had referred to the temporal liaison with a prostitute) indicated the centrality of money in the relationship: the man paid for entertainment and the woman owed him something in return—flirtatious gaiety, quiet admiration, some degree of sexual intimacy. The practice of dating was taken up, in modified form, by the fast set of "society" youth who were drawn to the possibilities of the city, and filtered its way into middle-class conventionality by the mid 1910s to 1920s.

The new custom was confusing, as dating and calling coexisted for some years. A joke from the 1920s told of the young man who went to call on a young woman of his acquaintance only to find that "she had her hat on." The hat signaled that she expected to go out, and so he took her out, spending his scarce savings on their entertainment. Advisers in mass circulation magazines, such as Mrs. Burton Kingsland, who wrote the column "Good Manners and Good Form" for the *Ladies' Home Journal* in the early years of the twentieth century, attempted to make sense of the new system. The date, these advisers concurred, was an invitation into the man's world. The man was responsible for the expense, and thus claimed the right of initiative: only the man could ask for a date. The system of dating etiquette, as it developed, coalesced on the basic fact of men's money.

Whereas nineteenth-century manuals specified rules of chaperonage or simply assumed them, twentieth-century advisers more and more often discussed the etiquette of sexual relationships. In the 1930s, *Parents* magazine advised parents to deal with the issue of "petting" "dispassionately as being much more a matter of etiquette than of morals." A popular 1930s etiquette book for college women, *Coediquette,* offered information about how a girl should "conduct herself at a football game" and behave at a "rush tea." But the author's credentials were telling: traveling to forty-three universities, she had "dated college men and learned to know them by their lines." Another work linking etiquette and sex, Nina Farewell's *The Unfair Sex* (1953), begins, "Ever since the author's eighteenth birthday, when she surrendered her virginity because she was afraid to seem rude, she has felt a crying need for a handbook for girls—a manual on How to Cope with Men." Others offered very specific information about the etiquette of necking and petting: "for gallantry's sake a man is not in a position to withdraw from petting even should he very much want to," one adviser insisted. Women, according to the laws of etiquette and of nature, were to be the limit setters. Advisers differed in the etiquette of limit-setting: "Dear Abby," in the 1960s article "Blue Jean Biology," suggests a "stereophonic slap" to discourage a "mad lover"; a 1940s advice book suggested "excusing yourself from the room in a flustered way to adjust your hair with a 'Gracious, how I must look!' manner."

While etiquette played a role in the control of nonmarital sex, it was perhaps most important as it came to define qualities of masculinity and femininity. "Good etiquette, for a man, is whatever makes a woman feel more like a woman, without making her feel weakminded. . . . Good etiquette, for a woman, is whatever makes a man feel more like a man, without making him feel more harassed and put upon than he normally does anyway," explained Peg Bracken in *I Try to Behave Myself* (1959). It was the barriers between the sexes that seemed most beleaguered by mid century, and scholarly journals and popular magazines alike were full of analyses of the problems of masculinity and femininity, both allegedly under threat of extinction in modern society. Masculinity and femininity seemed not things inherent, securely linked to one's physical sex, but a set of attributes to be achieved—largely through observing an elaborated and overelaborated gender etiquette.

Advice books, especially those for teenagers and young adults in the postwar years, were full of specific prescriptions, all pointing to the same end. Women, the system of rules made clear, were constantly to demonstrate their submission and need for protection, avoiding acts that they could perform perfectly well (like opening doors or ordering from menus) but that became "aggressive" and "competitive" in the company of a man. Men were to demonstrate control and dominance. As *Esquire Etiquette* declared in 1953: "When she's with you, etiquette renders her helpless. You're It." Not all young people, boys especially, conformed to the rules of etiquette—often much to the disappointment of teenage girls, who expected the conventionalized "perfect" date. But the newly developed teen magazines of the postwar years stressed etiquette (sometimes conflating it with "personality"), and teen advice books for girls spent a good deal of time offering strategies for "subtly" teaching their escorts proper behavior. A 1954 high school etiquette text reminded readers that the boy or man should walk on the outside, closest to the street. "Don't ignore the situation." If he walks on the inside, this book advised girls, "slip around" at the first opportunity.

The etiquette of masculinity and femininity did provide a comfortable script (in that the rules were clear) for a society in which dating was a central ritual that brought together strangers in a fairly intimate situation. The rules of etiquette offered protection, smoothing awkward encounters on those nights better spent washing one's hair, and turning others into the fairy tale stuff of teen magazines. But the etiquette of masculinity and femininity had greater significance than these uses suggest. It was born of deep-seated fears about changing relations between the sexes and served to reject—at least in the "private" world of romantic relationships—women's claims to greater roles in the public world. The etiquette of masculinity and femininity expressed social fears every bit as profound and conservative as the class-based fears that structured the genteel performance of the nineteenth century.

The shift from class to gender in the new etiquette books of the twentieth century does not mean that class lost all importance in American etiquette. The small points of etiquette still serve as signs of "breeding" and background and are easily read by those who seek to exclude others. But as Emily Post discovered from the response to her first etiquette book, published in 1922 under the unwieldy title *Etiquette in Society, in Business, in Politics, and at Home,* her readers were not interested in climbing the social ladder to challenge the ascendancy of the "Worldlys" and the "Wellborns." They were interested in more modest social mobility; they wanted not advice on the protocol of exclusive gentlemen's clubs and entertaining with a staff of twelve, but instead information about the rituals of middle-class inclusiveness—the luncheons and showers and dinners and weddings they intended to invest with grace and propriety.

There was still the threat of exclusion, and advertising played on fears of insufficiency. An advertisement for Doubleday's *Book of Etiquette* read: "Again She Orders—'A Chicken Salad, Please!'" (thus betraying to her date that she could not pronounce the French words that filled the menu). Many a suburban housewife pored over books of etiquette for the table setting that would convince her husband's boss that he had the right social stuff for a promotion. But much writing on etiquette, especially in the post–World War II era, aggressively assumed that America was a middle-class nation, and that all were subject to the same middle-class rules. And the new media taught etiquette in more pervasive fashion than etiquette manuals ever did: advertisements pictured the good life (and justified hiring female "admen" to make sure the ads showed correct table settings, for example); television shows like *Leave It to Beaver* portrayed the polite middle-class family dinner for all to watch and learn.

This middle-class inclusivity masked real barriers in American society, the most obvious, of course, being predicated on race. But the rhetoric of cultural inclusivity through participation in a common middle-class culture was strong, and the forms of etiquette were tightly bound up with this comforting vision. Thus when cultural rebels in the 1960s attacked the forms of politeness and civility, they had found a good target, partly because the etiquette of gender had become increasingly over-elaborated and stifling. Proper etiquette also embodied a respect for authority that necessarily supported the status quo. Some of the prevailing forms of etiquette were tightly bound up with inequality, and some people violated these norms in attempts to create a more democratic society. Others simply rebelled against what they described as "uptight" behavior. However, to cultural conservatives, these attacks on civility seemed to be attacks on civilization itself.

The forms of etiquette have changed drastically in the past half-century. But despite the rejection of much of what passed for polite behavior in earlier decades, Americans have not abandoned the rules of etiquette. Society does require rules or codes, be they informal or formal, for its continued functioning, and many people seek some method of smoothing the travails of social interaction. The enormous popularity of Judith Martin, who writes as "Miss Manners" in a column syndicated in over three hundred newspapers and whose book *Miss Manners' Guide to Excruciatingly Correct Behavior* (1982) has become a classic, witnesses contemporary ambivalence about etiquette. Her authority lies in irony and wit, and while she may refer to "Dear Queen Victoria" her voice and her advice are firmly rooted in the late twentieth century. And, most importantly, her advice is taken seriously.

Prescriptive literature as a serious genre is three decades out of favor in America. But as Miss Manners's surprising success shows, a filter of irony can ease the rigors of etiquette into the modern age. Perhaps even more indicative of the advent of a new system of etiquette in the 1990s is the rise, most notably on college campuses, of whole new codes of civility, codes that are most directly concerned with race, gender, and sexual preference, and that are hotly debated. These codes take up many of the thorny problems of etiquette—the problems that underlie many of our historical systems of etiquette—and this time recognize the problems as political.

BIBLIOGRAPHY

Anderson, Jervis. *This Was Harlem: A Cultural Portrait, 1900–1950* (1988).
Bailey, Beth. *From Front Porch to Back Seat: Courtship in Twentieth-Century America* (1988). Gender etiquette.

Cable, Mary, and the editors of *American Heritage*. *American Manners and Morals: A Picture History of How We Behaved and Misbehaved* (1969). A popular survey.

Carson, Gerald. *The Polite Americans: A Wide-Angle View of Our More or Less Good Manners over 300 Years* (1966). A popular overview.

Cmiel, Kenneth. In *The Sixties: From Memory to History,* edited by David Farber (1992).

Cowles, Virginia. *The Astors* (1979).

Elias, Norbert. *Power and Civility: The Civilizing Process.* Vol. 2. Translated by Edmund Jephcott (1982).

Erenberg, Lewis. *Steppin' Out: New York Nightlife and the Transformation of American Culture, 1890–1930* (1981).

Halttunen, Karen. *Confidence Men and Painted Women: A Study of Middle-Class Culture in America, 1830–1870* (1982).

Hawke, David Freeman. *Everyday Life in Early America* (1988).

Kasson, John. *Rudeness and Civility: Manners in Nineteenth-Century Urban America* (1990). Excellent analysis of nineteenth-century etiquette.

Levine, Lawrence. *Highbrow/Lowbrow: The Emergence of Cultural Hierarchy in America* (1988).

Marchand, Roland. *Advertising the American Dream: Making Way for Modernity, 1920–1940* (1985).

Mulvey, Christopher. *Transatlantic Manners: Social Patterns in Nineteenth-Century Anglo-American Travel Literature* (1990).

Scharff, Virginia. *Taking the Wheel: Women and the Coming of the Motor Age* (1991).

Schlesinger, Arthur Meier. *Learning How to Behave: A Historical Study of American Etiquette Books* (1968).

Wyatt-Brown, Bertram. *Southern Honor: Ethics and Behavior in the Old South* (1982).

SEE ALSO **Courtship, Marriage, Separation, and Divorce; Nightlife; The Rise and Consolidation of Bourgeois Culture; Social Class; The United States as Interpreted by Foreign Observers; Women and Work.**

CLOTHING AND PERSONAL ADORNMENT

Nancy Rexford

CLOTHING AND PERSONAL ADORNMENT are the most immediate means human beings have of communicating personal identity and social position, and the study of dress and appearance leads inevitably to a consideration of the complex and changing relationships of gender, class, and power. Attitudes toward men and women, work and leisure, success and failure, youth and age, health and sickness, beauty and sexuality, are all reflected in America's concern with personal appearance. This concern has from colonial days supported a fashion industry that, in advising us how to acquire the right hair, face, body, and clothes, claims to tell us not only who we can be, but who we ought to be.

NATIVE AMERICANS

When Europeans visited America in the sixteenth and seventeenth centuries, they sent back accounts of a myriad of native peoples with varying customs in dress and adornment. In many regions, Native Americans made clothing from well-dressed skins, but some groups also used woven textiles made from wild cotton (in the Southwest), cedar and spruce bark fiber (in the Northwest), grass, or animal hair. Typical garments included breechclouts (or, for women, short skirts), belts and leggings, moccasins, and robes or mantles, but how much was worn depended on weather and occasion. While utilitarian clothing might be left plain, many garments were elaborately decorated with painted figures, quillwork, feathers, copper disks, beads, or fringe, according to local custom. Some tribes oiled, painted, or tattooed their bodies. Head hair was greased and blackened with charcoal, and, among men, varied widely in cut and style. Body hair was pulled out. Both men and women wore necklaces, earrings, headbands, and other adornments, ornamented with wampum, feathers, animal claws and teeth, turquoise (in the Southwest), or pearls.

European settlers appreciated the comfort and practicality of Indian snowshoes and moccasins, and moccasins became a permanent feature of American dress, not just where other shoes were unavailable but as house slippers, carriage boots, and, in altered form, modern leisure shoes. In a similar vein, the Indians admired European wool and linen textiles, and as their traditional hunting lands were lost, they added more and more woven garments to their wardrobe. But these were integrated into Indian patterns of dress rather than being worn in European style. Blankets (their barter price in beaver skins woven as stripes along the selvage) were used as mantles, for example, and shirts were belted and worn over breechclouts and leggings rather than tucked into trousers. Trade beads were assimilated into traditional Indian ornamentation. Even when the basic garb is European, as it appears in many mid-nineteenth-century photographs, Indian men and women maintained a distinctive culture by adding the blanket mantle and traditional necklaces and headgear.

THE SEVENTEENTH CENTURY

Information about the clothing of colonial Americans is thin compared with the wealth of data available on clothing worn after 1800. We do know what styles were fashionable in England, and it is fair to assume that American dress was similar, since most textiles and many made-up garments were imported from the mother country. Contemporary American portraits (especially of women) provide but equivocal evidence since many sitters were depicted in ambiguous draperies. Where clothing is distinct, there is seldom proof that the sitters were painted in their own clothes. Little actual clothing survives from the colonial period. We have a few accessories owned by seventeenth-century Americans, but nothing like a complete outfit. A number of eighteenth-century dresses and suits exist, but the majority are made of rich materials and have been altered several times. Given the ambiguity of portraits and the scarcity of surviving clothing, scholars interested in early American dress must depend heavily on the written word.

Inventories tell us that the basic garments for seventeenth-century women were (1) the shift (a knee-length white linen undergarment with high or low neck and long or elbow-length sleeves); (2) the skirt (known as a petticoat or "cote"), of which several might be worn, the upper one often tucked up to show another of contrasting color beneath; and (3) a fitted bodice (usually called a doublet or waistcoat), boned when intended for formal wear. With these were worn stockings, garters, and shoes, a cap to cover the hair, and a cloak for warmth. Women of greater means might also own one or more gowns (a one-piece dress). To this basic wardrobe were added white linen neckerchiefs, collars and cuffs, gloves, fans, ribbons to trim the sleeves, masks to protect the complexion from the sun, silk hoods, and jewelry, including rings, necklaces, and earrings.

The typical man's wardrobe consisted of (1) the shirt (a linen undergarment corresponding to a woman's shift); (2) breeches (knee-length pants cut in many variations of fullness but never very tight); and (3) coats, jackets, waistcoats, and doublets (upper-body garments that are difficult to distinguish but that seem to have been worn in layers and that sometimes matched the breeches). To complete the outfit, a man wore stockings with garters, leather shoes or boots, a collar, cuffs, a hat, gloves, and sometimes a muff, cane, and rings.

Except for the linen shirt and shift, the most common material used for clothing was wool of varying weight and quality. Summer garments were sometimes made of linen. For common clothes, solid colors were typical, but utilitarian striped and checked patterns were also used. Printed textiles, however, were still very rare. In more prosperous families, the outer clothing was made of better quality wool or of silk, the latter sometimes woven with complex multicolored designs. Good fabrics were trimmed with gold, silver, or silk braid and ribbon loops and bows. Collars and cuffs of fine linen were trimmed with lace. The wealthiest might own a jeweled hatband. Military men frequently

wore hard-wearing doublets of buff leather, which afforded some protection in battle.

Seventeenth-century Americans wore fabrics of every color, and in the clothing of the well-to-do, glittering braids and lace-edged linens created dramatic contrasts. While the Puritan settlers of Massachusetts disapproved of excess in dress, it is not true that they dressed primarily in black and gray. Tans and browns were probably the most common colors, being practical in a period when outer clothes were seldom washed, but red petticoats, green stockings, and green or blue aprons were a common sight among women of all classes. The "sad" colors often mentioned in inventories do not imply melancholy or gloom. "Sad" is etymologically related to "sated" and signifies being fully saturated with dye, resulting in a dark shade rather than a light one. But a sad (dark) color can be of any hue, and green, purple, orange, and various shades of brown are specifically mentioned.

What diversity there was in colonial dress arose more from class than from region, since Americans everywhere continued to import most of their fabrics and garments from England. Alice Morse Earle does mention a visitor to New York in 1704 who noted that middle-class Dutch women, unlike the English, tended to "go loose," that is, without corsets, and that they liked earrings and wore a different style of cap. Otherwise the differences were chiefly economic.

Surviving correspondence proves that Americans took a lively interest in fashion, but in New England the picture was complicated by Puritan religious principles. Like all seventeenth-century Americans, the Puritans who settled New England brought with them the assumption that fine clothing was an appropriate way of displaying rank and wealth. But for them dress was also a visible sign that revealed the spiritual health of both individual and community. Since the division between rich and poor was part of God's plan, the classes ought to be distinguished by their dress, but since everyone, rich or poor, was supposed to be working toward the good of the community as a whole rather than his own self-aggrandizement, it was not appropriate to compete to see how many luxuries could be acquired nor to spend an inappropriate proportion of one's income on clothing. New fashions were objectionable because they made the old ones unwearable before they were worn out and encouraged competition in wasteful luxury. It was also inappropriate to use clothing as a means of sexual display. Thus the first laws regulating dress, passed in 1634 and 1636, little more than a decade after the first Puritan settlement, targeted "new and immodest fashions" and any garment judged to be "uncomely [meaning inappropriate rather than unattractive] or prejudicial to the common good."

Inappropriate fashions included certain items made with silver, gold, silk, lace, or needlework, and garments that wasted material by being cut with unnecessarily full sleeves or by being slashed. Slashing was a decorative technique in which a garment was slit to allow puffs of the linen shirt or shift beneath to be pulled through the gap. The Puritans tolerated moderate slashing roughly equivalent to leaving a sleeve or bodice seam open. But sometimes fabrics were entirely covered with a pattern of tiny slits. Such fabrics must have ripped and worn out quickly and been difficult to reuse, making them a particularly wasteful example of conspicuous consumption.

The lack of contemporary references to cosmetics or face patches suggests that these European vanities were little known in America. The immodest fashions most often mentioned were women's low necklines and sleeves that left the arm bare below the elbow. Bare arms apparently possessed the erotic attraction that any customarily covered body part may acquire when newly exposed. Female modesty was enjoined by the Bible and felt to be necessary under the Calvinist principle that men and women were predisposed to sin and therefore needed restraints. Modern readers should not confuse this with prudery. In a century when husband, wife, and children all slept together in the same bed, with servants of both sexes in the same room, prudery could hardly exist, while prudence might welcome the support of modesty.

Men were the targets of sumptuary law chiefly in the matter of long hair, which the Bible branded as "shameful." The dislike of long hair extended to the very long and elaborately curled men's wigs that came into widespread use in the 1660s and 1670s. Seventeenth-century preachers racked their brains for words strong enough to express their disapproval (John Eliot called the periwig a "luxurious feminine protexity"), but the fashion gradually spread until wigs were a necessary part of any respectable man's appearance.

In 1651, a new Massachusetts law acknowledged that excess in dress was still a problem, "especially amongst people of mean condition, to the dishonor of God, the scandal of their profession, the consumption of estates, and altogether unsuitable to their poverty." The solution was to forbid silk hoods, thigh-high boots, gold and silver, and other luxuries to any family whose estate was less than £200. Anyone who held public office, who was well educated, or who had been well off in the past was exempt from the ban. Where the earlier laws had touched both rich and poor and been enforced by the churches, this law regulated only the poor and was enforced by the town constables—the temporal authorities were enforcing the privileges of the upper class.

By the middle of the seventeenth century, Puritan society had begun to show signs of change. The rigors of the early years had eased, and increasing prosperity allowed people to acquire more than the bare necessities. The great exodus of Puritans from England had ceased when the Civil War (1642–1652) gave them a cause to fight at home, and the younger generation had difficulty duplicating the same depth and intensity of religious experience known by its parents. Under these conditions, people found it more difficult to accept restrictions in dress. Hannah Lyman of Northampton, Massachusetts, not only wore a forbidden silk hood, but she brassily wore it into court when she was presented to the judge. The last sumptuary laws appeared during the Indian war of the 1670s, an upheaval perceived as divine punishment for a spiritual decay visibly symbolized by the inclination toward luxurious dress. But in spite of bare arms and silk hoods, ribbons and wigs, the Indian threat was turned back, and after the middle 1680s the laws seem no longer to have been enforced.

THE EIGHTEENTH CENTURY

In the seventeenth century, rich and elaborate clothing had often appeared in startling contrast to the relatively primitive living conditions. But in the growing culture of consumption in the eighteenth century, fine clothing found a more fitting setting in fine houses with elaborate furnishings, and the importance of being in fashion became a recurring theme in American social life. The Puritan paradigm whereby both rich and poor dressed with restraint but according to their condition had been replaced in the later seventeenth century by the older and simpler idea that costly dress was a privilege vested only in people of wealth and rank. After 1700, that privilege began to be perceived as an obligation to dress well. Taking pains with one's dress (and suffering them too) was a way both of showing respect and of receiving it.

The importance of clothing and fashion in eighteenth-century society resonates throughout the personal diary of Samuel Sewall. In 1720, his third wife having died, Sewall (then aged sixty-eight) began to court a wealthy widow, Madam Winthrop. On 12 October, he found her barricaded behind a piece of black needlework, but when at last it was taken away, "I got my Chair in place, had some converse, . . . [and] Ask'd her to acquit me of Rudeness if I drew off her glove. Enquiring the reason, I told her 'twas great odds between handling a dead goat, and a living Lady. Got it off." It is hard not to smile at Sewall's note of triumph, but Madam Winthrop wore gloves indoors not primarily to keep suitors at a distance but to prove that she could afford servants to do all but the most refined and unnecessary needlework. On another visit Sewall was pleased to receive courteous treatment but noted that Madam Winthrop was "not in Clean Linen as sometimes." The implication is that she had not taken any special care in her dress to please or impress him—not a good sign. Madam Winthrop was apparently embarrassed by Sewall's personal appearance: "she spake somthing of my needing a Wigg." Sewall abominated wigs and told her that since God, his "best and greatest Friend," had given him the hair he had, he had no heart to go to some lesser person for a wig. Madam Winthrop, countering with an argument from a book Sewall himself had given her, "quoted him saying 'twas inconvenient keeping out of a Fashion commonly used." Few of Madam Winthrop's contemporaries would have considered her point of view inappropriate or frivolous—even "Col. Townsend spake to me of my Hood: Should get a Wigg." Sewall continued to visit Madam Winthrop for a time, but by 7 November "I did not bid her draw off her glove as sometime I had done. Her Dress was not so clean as somtime it had been." And with these eloquent messages in the language of costume, Samuel Sewall's courtship came to an end.

Wigs in a myriad of styles were worn by every man with any pretense to fashion or respectability until late in the century. The voluminous wig of Sewall's day diminished only slowly. By the 1780s, many men merely powdered and curled their own hair to make it look like a wig, and in the next decade powder was gradually abandoned; but some conservative men wore wigs into the nineteenth century. Women's hair was relatively simple until

about 1770, when elaborately built-up styles came into fashion. Anna Green Winslow described hers in her diary for May 1773: "I had my HEDDUS roll on, Aunt Storer said it ought to be made less, Aunt Deming said it ought not to be made at all. It makes my head itch, & ach, & burn like anything." This "head roll" was made of cow tail, horsehair, and human hair carded together and formed into a cushion. Anna's natural hair was combed up over it, pomaded, and probably powdered and augmented with extra curls. From hairline to the top of her cap, twelve-year-old Anna's hairstyle measured an inch longer than her face. In Europe, elaborate powdered hairstyles appeared above faces enameled with dangerous white lead paints and cheeks flaming with rouge. This extreme of artificiality was probably rare in America, but rouge, pearl powder, and patches were known.

The adoption of wigs in the later seventeenth century coincided with a broader change in men's clothing. The doublet disappeared, and the ancestor of the modern three-piece suit—breeches, coat, and vest (waistcoat)—came into use. As the century passed, the knee-length vest shortened, the coat became slimmer, and the breeches tighter. The formal coat was cut so as to require a very straight posture, with shoulders drawn back. For less formal occasions, the looser and more comfortable frock coat was worn, and for private moments at home, coat and wig could be replaced by a loose dressing gown and cap. Farmers protected their clothing with a large, shirtlike linen or wool coverall (also called a frock), while laborers doffed their coats and waistcoats in hot weather.

Women's clothing also changed around 1700. Over the linen shift, a woman now put on separate boned stays that created a stiff, cone-shaped torso. One or more petticoats were worn, the top one meant to show, and for most of the century, fashion required that these be supported by a hoop. Over these garments, the fashionable woman wore an unboned gown open down the center front from neck to hem and made so that the front edges did not meet. The gap was filled at the bottom by the petticoat, and at the top by the stomacher, a triangular piece of material, often elaborately decorated. Working women omitted both hoop and gown and instead wore a hip- or thigh-length, front-opening bodice. Some were formfitting and were worn over stays. Others, called bed gowns or short gowns, were cut loose enough to require no stays, allowing the freedom of movement necessary for heavy work.

The chief materials continued to be linen for undergarments and wool or silk for suits and gowns. Where summers were hot, people wore unlined linen, and as the century progressed, printed cottons were increasingly fashionable for gowns. Silk weaving reached high levels of sophistication in the eighteenth century, and fine silk dresses were so highly prized that they were remade and passed down for generations. Men's suits for special occasions were beautifully embroidered in colored silks, and the buttonholes were outlined with metallic braid. None of these stylish materials were made in America. Northern colonial communities did raise sheep and cultivate flax, producing woolens and linens suitable for sheets, towels, blankets, and common clothing. Virginia cloth, a southern-made cotton fabric, was used to clothe slaves. But silk, fine linen, broadcloth, and other quality wools had to be imported.

Along with imported fabrics came imported fashions. Some Americans kept their measurements with London agents, but most depended on local tailors and dressmakers to keep them in the mode. Imported shoes, silk stockings, hats, gloves, fans, and laces rounded out the American wardrobe. The desire to be in fashion was an entirely respectable concern for both sexes. Since men took care of business and were more likely to travel to London or correspond with London agents, they were often the ones who selected fabrics and accessories for their families. When shopping was done by proxy, personal taste was difficult to consult, and Americans tended instead to stipulate that whatever was purchased be in the latest fashion. This, coupled perhaps with the fear of appearing provincial, resulted in Americans' dressing even more elaborately than their counterparts abroad, a fact noted by many travelers. In 1784 Abigail Adams wrote from London, "I am not a little surprised to find dress, unless on public occasions, so little regarded here. The gentlemen are very plainly dressed, the ladies much less so than with us. . . . There is not that neatness in their appearance which you see in our ladies" (quoted in Earle, *Two Centuries of Costume*, p. 733).

Americans recognized their dependency on foreign manufactures as a weakness, especially when England began to tax them. From the 1760s through the 1780s, it became patriotic to spin and wear homespun rather than enrich England by wearing imported fabrics. Anne Hollingsworth Wharton's 1897 biography of Martha Washington mentions visitors to Mrs. Washington in 1777 who "felt rebuked by the plainness of her apparel and her example of persistent industry, while we were extravagantly dressed idlers, a name not very creditable in these perilous times" (p. 117).

The eighteenth-century day was divided into morning and afternoon. Relatively informal and comfortable clothing was permitted until dinner, but genteel folk dressed formally for the afternoon. The midday change of clothes is recorded by a London merchant who, visiting Mount Vernon in 1785, found George Washington coming from his farm in morning "undress" (plain blue coat, white cassimere waistcoat, black breeches, and boots). After chatting, the General excused himself. He returned dressed for his three o'clock dinner wearing a clean shirt, a drab coat (probably a good deal tighter than his blue one), a white waistcoat, white silk stockings, and powdered hair. Another Mount Vernon story related by Wharton describes some visiting young girls who neglected to dress for this midday meal, only to be surprised by the arrival of several young French officers. Hastily requesting leave to go up and dress properly, they were mortified to be told by Mrs. Washington to "remain as you are, what is good enough for General Washington is good enough for any guest of his." The girls' morning dress was probably loose and cool (it may not even have required a corset), while to dress formally meant to look attractive but feel uncomfortable, a combination that signified both self-respect and a desire to please others. To eyes accustomed to the rigidly controlled body shapes of corseted women, the loose look appeared slatternly and undisciplined. Thomas Jefferson wrote to his daughter Patsy on 22 December 1783:

Some ladies think they may under the privileges of the dishabille be loose and negligent of their dress in the morning. But be you from the moment you rise till you go to bed as cleanly and properly dressed as at the hours of dinner or tea. A lady who has been seen as a sloven or slut in the morning will never efface the impression she then made with all the dress and pageantry she can afterwards involve herself in.

Children's Clothing Children's clothing underwent a number of changes during the eighteenth century. In the seventeenth century, infants were swaddled for the first four to six weeks and thereafter were dressed very much like their mothers until age five or six, when boys changed their skirts for breeches. Beginning in the early eighteenth century, however, swaddling was replaced with diapers and dresses made too long to be kicked off. These were shortened when the baby began to walk. At two or three, children were put in adult clothing, but, as before, there was no distinction of gender until the boys were breeched. Even little children's dresses had stiffened bodices or were worn over stays. Padded caps called puddings protected the head from falls, and leading strings attached to the shoulders kept little ones from straying.

The influence of Jean-Jacques Rousseau's *Émile* (1762) brought a gradual relaxation in the style of children's clothing. Young children were allowed loose muslin dresses sashed at the waist, a style that was eventually extended to older girls as well. Boys old enough to be breeched were put in "skeleton suits," consisting of a tight jacket with two rows of buttons on the front rising over the shoulders and a pair of ankle-length pants.

THE NINETEENTH CENTURY

The early nineteenth century saw significant changes in both men's and women's dress. For men the most visible were the replacement of knee breeches by trousers and the loss of ornamentation and color. Black gradually replaced other dark and neutral colors until, by 1860, all business and formal coats and trousers were black wool and waistcoats were limited to black and white. The monotony was relieved somewhat by the new casual sack suits, made of pronounced checks and plaids in the 1850s and 1860s and of tan and brown tweeds toward the end of the century. Nineteenth-century masculine models included two opposing figures. The first was the businessman (a gaunt Yankee early on, later a portly entrepreneur), whose conservative clothes reflected his success through expensive materials and tailoring, and his obsession with work in their avoidance of color and ornament. The second was the dandy or masher, who specialized in conspicuous and time-consuming dressing and other behaviors redolent of idleness. The desirable male look was clean-shaven except for sideburns in the early nineteenth century, but by the 1860s beards and moustaches were becoming indispensable, suggesting that the ideal had shifted toward older men.

Women's clothing about 1800 permitted a new degree of naturalness and comfort inspired by classical models. Whereas eighteenth-century dress had imposed a highly artificial shape on the body, now the body gave its shape to the clothes. Hoops were discarded, along with the large-scale floral silks that had spread over them. Stiff stays were replaced with lighter corseting, and softly gathered white cotton dresses revealed the moving body beneath. High-heeled buckled shoes gave way to flat sandals, and hairstyles so diminished that some women cropped their hair. The new fashions required little material and less trimming, so they were available to nearly all classes. Some Americans deplored the new styles as immodest, others criticized any emulation of foreign fashions as unbefitting a free nation, but these skimpy, high-waisted dresses were nevertheless universally worn and are the first garments that commonly survive with American documentation and minimal alteration.

The freedom of classical styles did not last very long. Shortly after 1820, the waistline dropped, tight lacing returned, and skirts became fuller. Over the succeeding decades fashionable dresses managed to restrict movement through every possible means: sleeves or skirts too wide for doorways and hats to match, armholes cut so that one could not raise the arms, sleeves too tight to bend the arms, sleeves that dragged in the soup, bonnet brims so deep one could see only straight ahead, layers of heavy petticoats, bulky trains that swept the streets, tied-back skirts in which it was difficult to take a normal step, bodices so heavily boned and tightly fitted that they became second corsets.

Burdensome fashions persisted in ironic contrast to the improvement in women's condition in other areas. By century's end, many women enjoyed the benefits of secondary and college education, and the traditional occupations of domestic service and needlework had expanded to include teaching, factory and clerical work, social work, and nursing. Women had increasing impact on public life through their participation in the abolition, temperance, and women's rights movements, community social work, and women's clubs. But most women clung doggedly to the latest fashion, no matter how uncomfortable. In 1851 feminist leaders introduced the bloomer, a kind of Turkish trouser worn under a matching dress of ordinary style except for being knee-length. It provoked a storm of abuse, as if women in trousers were ready to expropriate the entire male domain, leaving emasculated men home with squalling babies. The bloomer was soon abandoned for public wear, but it continued a covert existence in the health dress worn at spas and the gym suits girls wore for single-sex sports. Later reformers advocated lightening or discarding corsets, redesigning underwear, and reducing the oppressive weight of clothing. "Aesthetic dress" advocates rejected the fashionable stiff bodice and draped skirt in favor of softly gathered classical dresses with Pre-Raphaelite details.

Most women did not benefit from these new ideas until the twentieth century, but other changes did find widespread acceptance. The thin footwear of the early nineteenth century gave way to more substantial leather boots after 1860. In the 1890s young women adopted the shirtwaist, a white, tailored blouse worn with a simple skirt and optional tailored jacket, which allowed greater freedom of movement than the heavily boned fashionable bodice. This style, based on men's suits, was associated with "The Gibson Girl," a new and distinctive American type with freer manners and a more active life-style than her mother. Shirtwaist suits were worn on the street, by clerical workers at the office, and while participating in the new fads for tennis, golf, and bicycling.

The nineteenth century continued to observe the division between tight-fitting public and more comfortable private forms of dress. Women wore loose wrappers at breakfast, while doing housework in the morning, and in their own rooms (a refuge women often sought in the summer heat); and from the 1880s a tighter version called a tea-gown could be worn at home in the afternoon. But a corset and fitted bodice were required when receiving visitors or appearing in public, for loose clothing out of its limited sphere suggested immorality, slovenliness, or lack of self-respect. As the century progressed, etiquette became even more complex, and different activities required different clothes. The latest canvas shoes, chic at Newport, had no place on the street in New York, and attention to such distinctions were as much a symbol of wealth and leisure as were more ostentatious kinds of display. Dressing well, which in the eighteenth century had been an upper-class obligation, now became a female obligation, partly because men's clothing had become so dull.

Middle-class women were also strongly admonished by etiquette books and popular magazines to take pains with their dress. Clean, well-fitting, becoming, and above all appropriate clothing was an important part of female attractiveness, and being attractive was the source of a woman's power (or "influence," as it was called in the nineteenth century). Only beauty could draw men, inclined by nature to "baser passions," into a domestic circle where they could be "influenced" by wives and mothers stronger than they in moral sensibility and religious sentiment. According to the magazine *De-morest's* in 1883, "many a man's heart has been kept from wandering by the bow on his wife's slipper." Beauty was duty, and the lesson was taught from earliest childhood. Jefferson had warned his six-year-old daughter Maria "not to go out without your bonnet because it will make you very ugly and then we should not love you so much" (20 September 1785). Pale skin, considered beautiful and ladylike everywhere, acquired additional importance in the South, where children of mixed blood lived on every plantation. Obvious rouging of the cheeks ended soon after 1800, but the English traveler Frances Trollope noted in *Domestic Manners of the Americans* (1832) that in the late 1820s the ladies of Cincinnati "powder themselves immoderately, face, neck, and arms, with pulverised starch; the effect is indescribably disagreeable by day-light, and not very favourable at any time" (1949 ed., p. 300). Later in the century, skin washes and lotions were used, but other cosmetics were supposed to be unobtrusive.

There was little regional variation in women's dress within the United States, partly because all new fashions emanated from one source—Paris. If anything, this fixation on Paris intensified through the century with the rise of highly publicized designers like Charles Worth and Jacques Doucet, to whom rich American style-setters went for their clothes. Conformity to fashion was encouraged by a growing system of transatlantic and coastal packet ships and a network of canals and railroads that sped new textiles, accessories, and fashion information to increasingly remote areas. Beginning with *Godey's Lady's Book* in 1830, American magazines began to include fashion plates (copies of French designs, not indigenous American styles), and their wide circulation helped bring all classes into the fashion mainstream.

The great exception, of course, was field slaves, who were provided coarse cotton clothing of extremely simple cut. House slaves, being more visible in public, tended to be better dressed and were more likely to receive castoff clothing as gifts. Some slaves were able to buy bright accessories to help individualize their holiday dress. Among free people, what deviation there was from mainstream fashion was found chiefly among sects like the Quakers, Shakers, and Mennonites, who dressed "plain" on religious principle. People in California and other parts of the Southwest that were under Spanish or Mexican rule also wore distinctive styles until those regions were overrun by American culture in the 1840s. Otherwise most differences reflected economic class and, to some degree, climate. Immigrants, encouraged to adopt American customs as quickly as possible to speed their assimilation, rarely retained elements of national dress beyond the first generation. Only very close-knit groups such as the Hasidic Jews kept distinctive garments in daily wear.

Although the United States continued to look to Europe for new fashions, it became increasingly independent in its manufactures. The cotton gin (1793) made southern cotton profitable, encouraged slavery, and supplied the New England textile mills founded after the Revolution. Some mills specialized in coarse "Negro cloth" to clothe field slaves, and most emphasized quantity rather than quality. Not until April 1863 did *Godey's Lady's Book* note that "in previous seasons [Lowell calicoes] have been very nice, common, cheap goods, not remarkable for beauty. But this season they are equal to any English prints." Repeated attempts to establish silk culture were unsuccessful, and silk weaving took hold only after heavy duties were levied on imported silks during the Civil War.

The sewing machine transformed the early ready-made clothing industry in the 1850s and was widely used by dressmakers and in homes by the 1860s. It was also the first step in mechanizing the shoe industry, which by century's end not only provided this continent with footwear of every grade but was a significant exporter as well. Pattern drafting systems simplified and standardized the art of cutting out clothing and made paper patterns in graduated sizes available to the general public by the late 1870s. By 1900 most American men were wearing ready-made clothes. Women could buy ready-made cloaks, underwear, wrappers, and accessories, but because fashion required an exact fit in the bodice, most dresses were still custom-made.

Children's Clothing Nineteenth-century children did not wear fully adult styles until their teens, suggesting it was now desirable to prolong childhood. Little boys were given suits with skirts, and older ones wore suits with knee pants before graduating to adult trousers. Girls' dresses were gradually made longer as the wearer approached maturity.

THE TWENTIETH CENTURY

The acceptance of loose, unstructured clothing in the 1910s permitted the success of ready-made dresses and made the private dressmaker obsolete.

The new styles also eliminated the traditional division of the day into private and public times according to whether loose or tight clothing was worn. Evening wear was signaled instead by fabric, decoration, décolleté, or archaic elements such as long skirts that were no longer found in daytime clothing.

The twentieth century was the first to see the development of a specifically American style, emphasizing sportswear. It grew out of an increasingly informal life-style and found its models in the movies. In the 1930s, New York stores began to recognize and feature American designers (who had been working incognito for years), a development given further impetus when World War II cut New York off from its fashion sources in Paris. The century was also noteworthy for the use of artificial fibers and materials. Rayon came into wide use by the 1930s, and nylon stockings became a staple at the end of World War II. These were followed by acrylics, polyesters and related fibers, tubular jerseys, bonded knits, and permanent-press fabrics. In spite of domestic technological advances, many textile and apparel industries were lost to foreign countries with less expensive labor.

Regional differences in dress, never very distinct, were further discouraged in the twentieth century by the explosion of nationally distributed images in movies, television, and magazines and by the mobility of the population. The clearest exception occurs in the western hats, boots, and fancy belt buckles men wear in Texas and the Southwest, but there are also subtle differences in taste elsewhere in the country. These have less to do with cut than with what styles are chosen for what occasions. Life in New York and Washington requires more formal clothing than in Boston. Like Boston, California is informal, but it is far more flamboyant and experimental in color and style.

Men's business and formal suits changed only in detail in the twentieth century, gaining minimal variety through the use of wide or narrow trousers with or without cuffs, double- or single-breasted coats with wide or narrow lapels, and more or less shoulder padding. Richard Martin and Harold Koda suggest that while men's basic garments are not subject to dramatic seasonal style changes, there are persistent stylistic types that fall into twelve categories (including jock, nerd, businessman, and rebel). Although reinterpreted over time, these types remain recognizable from decade to decade.

More important than changes in cut has been the creeping informality in dress. As early as 1900, women's magazines inveighed against the "shirt-sleeve habit" indulged in by men who went coatless at home and even on the street, looking slovenly beside their corseted wives. By century's end, many businesses that once would have expected their male employees to appear in three-piece suits now required only trousers, buttoned shirt, and tie. Non-matching coats and trousers became acceptable and vests were increasingly omitted altogether. Sportswear cut loose from traditional khakis and tweeds and was made in every bright color, a trend echoed faintly in formal clothes as well. Early in the century and into the 1920s, men wore knickers and knee socks (often bright tartans) for sports, with perhaps a sweater replacing the vest. Informal shirts were often colored and patterned, and the collar gradually became lower and softer. Beginning in the 1930s, men began to wear swimsuits without tops, shorts that bared the leg, and short-sleeved, knitted "sport shirts." From the knit sport shirt, the next step was the "T-shirt," which by the 1960s was made in colors and by the 1970s and 1980s was printed with mottoes and pictures so that it looked less like underwear.

Not only did women enjoy greater informality in the twentieth century, they saw the basic cut of their clothing change radically as well. The first steps were to loosen the bodice and to shorten the skirt to the knee. Once a skintight fit was abandoned, corsets became less necessary for creating the fashionable line. The introduction of pantyhose gave the coup de grace to the gartered foundation garment and made possible the miniskirts of the 1960s. These changes allowed real freedom of movement but were offset by the persistent fashion for extremely high heels. Women's hats, a necessary component of decency for two centuries, fell out of use in the 1960s except for functional headgear. In the 1930s, pants and shorts came into common use, at first for sports and loungewear but gradually for more occasions, until they went nearly everywhere by 1975. The wearing of trousers, so controversial in the nineteenth century, simply seemed practical after two world wars in which women had worn them while employed in war industries. The 1970s and 1980s saw revivals of 1920s and 1930s styles, with a growing emphasis on broad shoulders and narrow hips that was interpreted by some as an attempt to minimize the waist, by others as an attempt to ape masculine body lines. The "dress for success" books for businesswomen of the period recommended masculine-style jackets worn with skirts and heels to establish the wearer's gender,

suggesting that symbolism in dress was still far more important than practicality.

When women bobbed their hair in the 1920s, they symbolically discarded the burden of traditional femininity in favor of boyish freedom. But our culture is not nearly so disturbed by women borrowing masculine traits as by men taking on feminine qualities. Thus when young men adopted long hair in the 1960s, middle America was outraged. In that same decade many black Americans stopped straightening their hair and wore it in natural "Afro" styles. These styles were widely imitated by whites in the 1970s, reflecting the new acceptance by both races that "black is beautiful."

Aside from the tendency toward informality and the adoption by women of men's garments, the most important long-term trend in the twentieth century is the fashion emphasis on body rather than clothes. The roots of this development are complex. The moral superiority claimed for women in the nineteenth century had justified many advances in women's position, but it also required eschewing personal indulgence and putting family (or substitutes like schoolchildren or the urban poor) before self. As middle-class women spent less time immured at home and more time in the world, such restraints perhaps came to seem unfair. At any rate, moral superiority was rarely claimed or conceded by the 1920s. This allowed women greater freedom in a climate of self-indulgence, but it also left personal attractiveness as the chief criterion of female distinction. Whereas in the nineteenth century the essential female grace lay in the inner character, and careful grooming and dress were recommended chiefly as means of attracting men to the benign domestic sphere of female moral influence, now physical attractiveness was an end in itself. The cultivation of beauty became for women a means of personal aggrandizement, and the acquisition of beautiful women became for men a symbol of status and wealth. The growing prevalence of divorce may well have put pressure on women to preserve a youthful and attractive appearance.

An attractive appearance came to be defined less in terms of clothing than of the body itself. This was encouraged by the tendency toward informality in dress and the relaxation of etiquette, so that clothes simply became less important, and also by the tendency to wear fewer and scantier clothes for many occasions. As short skirts, sleeveless and backless dresses, and increasingly brief bathing suits revealed more and more of the body, the body itself inevitably became the focus of attention.

Beauty parlors had already become common by the 1890s, specializing not only in hair care but in manicures, wrinkle removal,. massages, face peeling, and even rudimentary plastic surgery. Makeup began to come out of the closet soon after 1900, and by the 1920s lipstick and powder were applied in public. With the popularity of short skirts, sheer stockings, and sleeveless dresses, women of the 1920s routinely began to shave leg and underarm hair.

After 1900, a new generation of women's magazines, including *Vogue* at the couture end and *Ladies' Home Journal* for the middle class, depended for their survival more on advertising than on subscriptions, and at present women's magazine advertising is dominated by perfumes and skin- and hair-care products. This change grows partly out of the emphasis on beautiful bodies, but it also reflects the fact that makeup, unlike clothing, is not really essential, so that manufacturers must market not only the product but the need for it. Doing this requires massive advertising. Thus a symbiotic relationship developed between women's magazines and beauty product manufacturers that conspired to teach women that unembellished looks were ugly and that "natural" beauty is possible only with the aid of art. During this same period, photographs gradually replaced drawings in both fashion articles and advertising. At first the new images of real bodies with their ordinary waistlines and big feet clashed with the idealized drawings. This conflict was solved not by moderating the ideal but by idealizing the models. Real women, chosen for their height and slenderness, carefully posed, and cleverly photographed, create an exemplar more powerful than any drawing because they prove that the ideal can actually be attained and thus impose on women the obligation to attain it.

Feminists have protested the exploitation of women in advertising as in pornography, but Rita Freedman in *Beauty Bound* suggests that by teaching personal control through assertive behavior, feminism may have encouraged women to reshape their lives by reshaping their bodies. Certainly by the 1980s, the traditional emphasis on dieting had expanded to include physical fitness, and women are now expected to develop their muscles like men. This change is often described as a liberation from traditional models of dependent femininity, but the implication that natural female bodies are unacceptable still entraps all too many young women in masochistic behaviors such as anorexia and compulsive fitness training.

Men have not escaped this growing emphasis on the beautiful body, although it has taken longer to show pernicious effects. Twentieth-century models of male attractiveness have in general been more athletic than those fashionable in previous centuries. Portliness went out in the 1890s, and now a slim, athletic build implies health and strength. Transient models such as the hippie radical or the sensitive male of the 1960s and 1970s did not counter the general expectation of physical fitness in men. By the 1980s, a barrage of images of heavily muscled cartoon heroes, movie stars, and athletes created such pressure for a powerful body that young men felt obligated to spend hours working out with weights, and many took drugs to build their muscles artificially, a kind of self-destructive behavior formerly associated with women. The pressure on both sexes to have lean and muscular bodies has inflated the market for diet programs, special foods, expensive equipment, and special clothing for exercise. As a result, "attractively fit" bodies have become a status symbol, along with overdesigned, high-priced athletic shoes and tight exercise leotards and bicycling pants whose elastic materials allow freedom of movement and yet reveal every nuance of muscle.

Children's Clothing Children's clothing has also changed dramatically in the twentieth century, reflecting the prevailing trend toward increased informality. In the early twentieth century, rompers became available to toddlers of both sexes, and dresses were abandoned by boys out of infancy. In the last several decades, children's dress has become increasingly gender-specific. For fancy occasions, even tiny boys wear suits and girls dresses. Everyday clothes differ less in cut, but a rigid color code, beginning with pink for girls and blue for boys, was established by 1950. In spite of the interest in unisex dress in the 1970s, children's clothing clearly reflects contemporary concern with establishing gender identity from a very early age.

CLOTHING AND PERSONAL ADORNMENT

BIBLIOGRAPHY

General Works

Banner, Lois. *American Beauty* (1983).

Corson, Richard. *Fashions in Hair: The First Five Thousand Years* (1965).

———. *Fashions in Makeup: From Ancient to Modern Times* (1972).

Cunnington, Phillis, and Anne Buck. *Children's Costume in England from the Fourteenth to the End of the Nineteenth Century* (1965).

Earle, Alice Morse. *Two Centuries of Costume in America, 1620–1820* (1903; repr. 1974).

Kidwell, Claudia Brush. *Suiting Everyone* (1978).

Kidwell, Claudia, and Valerie Steele. *Men and Women: Dressing the Part* (1989). Essays on gender symbols in dress, including children's.

McClellan, Elisabeth. *History of American Costume, 1607–1870* (1937; repr. 1977). Outdated but not yet superseded.

Montgomery, Florence. *Textiles in America, 1650–1870* (1984).

Waugh, Norah. *The Cut of Men's Clothes, 1600–1900* (1964).

———. *The Cut of Women's Clothes, 1600–1930* (1968).

Native Americans

Conn, Richard. *Robes of White Shell and Sunrise: Personal Decorative Arts of the Native American* (1974).

Maxwell, James A. *America's Fascinating Indian Heritage* (1978).

Seventeenth Century

Trautman, Patricia. "When Gentlemen Wore Lace: Sumptuary Legislation and Dress in Seventeenth-Century New England." *Journal of Regional Cultures* 3, no 2 (1983).

———. "Dress in Seventeenth-Century Cambridge, Massachusetts: An Inventory-based Reconstruction." *Dublin Seminar for New England Folklife: Annual Proceedings* (1987).

Eighteenth Century

Baumgarten, Linda. *Eighteenth-Century Clothing at Williamsburg* (1986).

Los Angeles County Museum of Art. *An Elegant Art: Fashion and Fantasy in the Eighteenth Century* (1983).

Wright, Merideth. *Put On Thy Beautiful Garments: Rural New England Clothing, 1783–1800* (1990).

Nineteenth Century

Blum, Stella, ed. *Victorian Fashions and Costumes from "Harper's Bazar,"* 1867–1898 (1974).

Cunnington, C. Willett, and Phillis Cunnington. *Handbook of English Costume in the Nineteenth Century* (1959). Good coverage of men's clothing.

Gernsheim, Alison. *Victorian and Edwardian Fashion: A Photographic Survey* (1982).

Majer, Michele. "American Women and French Fashion." *The Age of Napoleon: Costume from Revolution to Empire, 1789–1815* (1989).

Rexford, Nancy. *Shoes.* Vol. 1 of *Women's Clothing in America, 1795–1930* (1992). Social history, etiquette, and dating/identification.

Severa, Joan. *Dressed for the Photographer: Ordinary Americans and Fashion, 1840–1900* (1992).

Twentieth Century

Blum, Stella. *Everyday Fashions of the Thirties, as Pictured in Sears Catalogs* (1986).

———, ed. *Everyday Fashions of the Twenties, as Pictured in Sears and Other Catalogs* (1981).

Ewing, Elizabeth. *History of Twentieth-Century Fashion* (1986).

Freedman, Rita. *Beauty Bound* (1986).

Martin, Richard, and Harold Koda. *Jocks and Nerds: Men's Style in the Twentieth Century* (1989).

Milbank, Caroline Rennolds. *New York Fashion: The Evolution of American Style* (1989). Also includes a short chapter on the nineteenth century.

O'Donnol, Shirley. *American Costume, 1915–1970: A Source Book for the Stage Costumer* (1982).

SEE ALSO **Gender; Gender Roles and Relations; Material Culture Studies.**

HOUSING

Elizabeth Collins Cromley

Americans' need for housing has been satisfied by an impressive diversity of house forms. This essay will identify some characteristic configurations of housing, consider what kinds of households used particular kinds of dwellings, and look at the ways that climate, materials, designers, builders, and construction methods created these houses. The diversity of ethnic heritages, the range of resources available for building, the historical moment, and the class position of dwellers all have affected the form of American housing.

This overview of American housing is organized chronologically. The first section, on seventeenth- and eighteenth-century houses, emphasizes regional differences, since both climate and European settlement patterns strongly influenced the shape of early houses. The second section, on the nineteenth century, focuses on new national trends, emerging class demarcations, and the effects of industrialization on house forms. The twentieth-century section considers the diversity of house forms within each income level, and closes with some indications of future directions in housing.

THE COLONIAL PERIOD

The future United States was colonized independently by several European nations in the late sixteenth and seventeenth centuries. Spanish, French, Dutch, and English colonists were sent to the New World to secure parts of North America for their home countries' economic benefit. They arrived to find a landscape inhabited by Native Americans speaking a wide variety of languages, living in a variety of structures, and with unfamiliar community organizations.

New England and the Chesapeake region were the focus of English colonization. The shelters the colonists made upon first arrival were rude constructions: tree branches, twigs, and bark created a wigwam; a hollow in the earth protected new arrivals from the weather. Colonial efforts at creating housing depended primarily on settlers' knowledge of house types, room arrangements, and building practices brought with them from their countries of origin, combined with the building materials available on New World sites. When woodworking skills and tools imported from England combined with a ready supply of wood in New England, timber-framed houses sheathed in overlapping clapboards and roofed in shingles resulted.

Many one-room houses were erected in New England and the Chesapeake by and for ordinary farmers and townspeople. A common type had wood posts planted directly in the ground—called earth-fast construction—supporting a pegged-together timber frame. Sheathed and roofed in wood, unpainted, often with a clay-covered wooden chimney, such houses could easily last for at least a decade or two. Owners of such structures may have planned to move on when agricultural opportunities called them elsewhere, or to return to the mother country after improving their fortunes. Such dwellings constituted the largest number of Anglo dwellings in the seventeenth and eighteenth centuries.

A one-room house had to contain all the persons and activities of the household that required shelter. When feasible, some activities were pushed outdoors. For example, a cooking fire with a tripod-suspended pot served as outdoor kitchen. Sleeping, socializing, and work spaces all could occupy a single room, activities changing with times of day. A one-room house might have extra space under the roof—a rough attic reached by a ladder served many people as a bedroom. For the poorest, one-room structures continued to provide housing through the nineteenth century both on the traditionally understood frontier, and in urban settings where poverty allowed no other choice.

New Englanders intending to create permanent towns built wooden houses on stone footings to protect the wood from decay; they constructed stone or brick fireplaces and chimneys to secure the wood structure from fire. They carefully cut mortises, tenons, and a variety of other timber joints to create a lasting structure, and added onto the house as family size and resources expanded. The hall-parlor plan represents a well-known organization of the main spaces in a seventeenth-century New England house. The main floor was divided into two rooms set left and right of a front door. The hall was the all-purpose room in which cooking and daily meals, spinning, and small-scale household production took place. Furniture was sparse, and tables and benches could be pushed against the walls to allow multiple activities to take place. The parlor was reserved for the finer household goods, special meals, visiting, and the parents' bed.

The exterior of the New England hall-parlor house reflected its internal organization. A massive chimney rose through the middle of the roof, signaling the presence of one chimney core opening into fireplaces in the hall, in the parlor, and perhaps toward the rear if there was a kitchen across the back of the house. Such a kitchen was often the first addition made by a growing family, and the extended roof that covered it gave New England houses their characteristic saltbox profile. On the floor above the hall and parlor might be additional rooms, named "hall chamber" and "parlor chamber" for their location, and used both as sleeping spaces for the children and servants or apprentices living in the household and for storage.

The middle states of New York, New Jersey, and Pennsylvania were early homes for German and Dutch settlers as well as the English. Dutch settlers occupied New York's Hudson Valley, and nearby New Jersey and Long Island in the mid seventeenth century. Houses were constructed of wood, framed with heavy timber anchor-beams visible on the interior. These knee-braced beams supported the high ceilings of rooms often arranged in linear fashion, each room having its own front door. Limestone or brick sheathed the exterior; dates, initials, or geometric patterns were sometimes introduced into the brick courses. Increasing prosperity allowed the Dutch to expand originally one- or two-room houses into multiroom long bar, L shape, or square plans.

In Pennsylvania, German immigrants arrived in the later seventeenth and eighteenth centuries. They built freestanding houses in farmstead set-

Reconstructed planter's house, Saint Mary's City, Maryland (c. seventeenth century). COURTESY OF THE COLONIAL WILLIAMSBURG FOUNDATION.

tings. The preferred exterior wall materials for German house builders were stone or exposed timber framing with clay or masonry infill. The characteristic house form had as its principal ground-floor rooms the kitchen with a cooking fireplace and the *stube,* or entertaining room, with a heating stove and built-in seats along the walls. Like the early Anglo houses, German houses had exposed ceiling beams. Second-floor chambers complemented one or two ground-floor bedrooms. Stone cellars contained insulated storage rooms for food, and sometimes, a spring. In the eighteenth century, German settlers migrated south into Maryland, the Valley of Virginia, and North Carolina, where they continued to build stone and half-timbered houses.

Settlers in Maryland and Virginia built houses to suit a warmer climate. While the earliest established planters erected large houses with many rooms, by the eighteenth century it was common for a prosperous planter to construct multiple buildings clustered together instead of a single house. These forms were influenced by the southern commitment to an agricultural economy based on slave and indentured labor. One building provided a home for the planter and his immediate family. Slaves and servants had separate outbuildings in which to sleep. The kitchen, with its overheated atmosphere and hazardous sparks, occupied a building of its own. Additional storage and utility buildings dotted the near landscape, such that travelers described the planter's house as looking like a little village.

The houses erected for slaves in the South tended to provide minimum space for each household group—usually a single room for a family. The slaves built their housing with materials that were inexpensively acquired; sometimes leftovers from a more important piece of construction were handed along to them. A slave house might contain two or more households, each with one room on the main floor and an attic space above, the several households separated by partitions. A small window or two let in light; a door could create cross-ventilation; the fields served as privy. The slaves' scanty possessions were sometimes secreted in storage holes in the earthen floor.

Slave houses were located close to the work sites; a small cluster would be built near the fields where the slaves worked, creating a quarter apart from the owner's house. Sometimes slave houses were lined along a drive near the master's house, contributing to the townlike appearance of the planter's domain. If near the main house, slave dwellings were likely to have a coat of paint or other exterior finish, to give visual appeal to the planter's home grounds. If located at a greater distance, slave houses were made weatherproof but otherwise left unfinished on the exterior.

Ambitious families built houses in brick on both rural and town sites in Maryland, Virginia, and the Carolinas. They created symmetrical structures of two or three stories, sometimes extended laterally with wings or dependencies. The wealthiest looked to England for stylistic potential, adapting late Renaissance classical details for exterior door and window ornament, and for interior mantelpieces, moldings, door and window frames, elaborated staircases, and paneling. But they still relied on the aggregation of mostly wooden buildings to contain all the functions of the agricultural year, as did the majority of less prosperous planter households.

The French settlers arrived on the eastern shores of Canada and moved westward to the Great Lakes in the seventeenth century. Settlements followed the path of the Mississippi River; two of the original French foundations are the modern cities of Detroit and Saint Louis. Driven from Canada, French-speaking Acadians became Cajuns in the New Orleans–Delta region of Louisiana.

The French building traditions brought to America include the tall roof of northern Europe, the exterior veranda used for circulation, exterior staircases to the second story, and timber building methods such as *poteaux sur solle*—squared-off logs standing on a horizontal sill of wood. The spaces between the vertical logs were filled with clay and a binder such as hair or straw, or stones and mortar.

In the warm and wet Delta region, the raised creole cottage provided a convenient ground floor for services, relatively crudely finished, able to withstand an occasional flood, and a principal floor one level above ground where finely crafted woodwork would stay dry. A surrounding veranda that served the principal rooms was reached by a broad flight of steps in the country or smaller exterior stairs in urban settings.

Spanish settlers first colonized Florida in the late sixteenth century, then California, New Mexico, and the rest of the Southwest. Houses set flush with the street helped to create an urban clarity of definition for plazas and rectilinear street grids—features of the Spanish town plan prescribed by guidelines for the creation of colonial towns, the 1873 Laws of the Indies. In Florida, simple houses of two rooms, expanded by adding rooms in single file, were built of wattle and daub or boards and roofed in thatch. More sophisticated builders used coquina, a local stone made up of compacted seashells, or "tabby," a kind of cement mixture of shells, sand, lime, and water. Favored building materials in the Southwest were adobe (sundried brick) combined with local wood for ceiling beams, door and window frames, and veranda framing. In a dry climate, adobe was long-lasting, cheap to build with, and easily repaired with a periodic coat of clay to seal the surface.

Single Brothers' House, Salem, North Carolina (1769). COURTESY OF OLD SALEM, RESTORATION, WINSTON-SALEM, NORTH CAROLINA.

The Spanish house was often a single range of rooms wrapped around a courtyard, sometimes with a second story. Extended roofs sheltered verandas and patios, characteristic of hot-climate architecture; outdoor courtyards and indoor rooms were equally essential in providing for the household's space needs. Elaborated wooden screens and grilles allowed Florida builders to encourage the passage of breezes through houses. The Spanish tradition of tile as a surfacing material gave color to the more expensive houses.

Climate played an important role in forming the configurations of colonial-era houses. In warm-climate areas, greater use was made of outdoor spaces than in the colder regions. Thus outdoor kitchens in separate buildings were used by French builders in the lower Mississippi Valley, Spanish settlers in Florida, and Anglo settlers in Virginia. Hispanic houses of the Southwest and Florida displayed a similar attitude to outdoor spaces with their second-story porches and courtyards. Outdoor passages from one part of the home grounds to another were common; one walked outdoors from the planter's main house to a subsidiary library or schoolhouse, often with bedrooms above; or one went onto the veranda of a creole cottage to get to the next room instead of using an interior hallway. Colder-climate architecture tended toward steep roofs, small window areas, and entranceways that faced south. Additional space in the attic above the parlor and hall was used as a sleeping area for household members and for storage.

THE NINETEENTH CENTURY: IMMIGRATION AND INDUSTRIALIZATION

The coastal settlements of the early period expanded as a growing population moved inland, after the 1785 survey of western lands, to find new farmland, to found new towns, and to exploit new resources. The original settlers were joined by immigrants from Germany, Scandinavia, Ireland, Russia, and elsewhere. Land made available to settlers by the United States government through the Homestead Act of 1862 and other legislation drew new arrivals west of the Appalachians and across the Mississippi.

Well established before the nineteenth century, the single-family house continued to serve American households. For new arrivals on the fron-tier, migrant or immigrant, one-room houses satisfied the need for speedily erected and economical shelter, just as they had for seventeenth- and eighteenth-century settlers. In the longer-settled areas, prosperous planters, farmers, and merchants built showplace single-family houses with many rooms.

Houses were directly affected by industrialization, which added many new possibilities to the nineteenth-century repertoire of house ideas. New materials were mass-produced and shipped around the country by rail; these included sawn lumber, nails, ornament in wood or cast iron, and prefabricated dwellings. New town forms developed with characteristic new housing types: the company town added tenements and boardinghouses, communitarian utopias developed collective dwellings, and commuter suburbs served the burgeoning middle class with variations on the single-family home at all prices.

A long-mythologized house form of this period was the log house, associated with the self-reliant economy of the frontier. The log construction method was indeed widely used during the period of western migration as a conveniently and quickly erected, inexpensive house that made use of on-site materials. It afforded housing to rural people with small resources. While an individual, casually built log house might not last more than a generation, the tradition of building them persisted for many generations in rural areas. Small, one-room log houses could be assembled quickly with round logs, the gaps between them chinked with mud and straw.

By the early nineteenth century, water-powered mills were turning out mass-produced sawn lumber, nails, textiles, and other goods; mill workers settled near these workplaces, creating new towns and giving rise to new housing needs. One such new form was the company town. Housing produced by companies to house their workers ran from single-family cottages to two- and three-story houses for managers and tenements for single workers or for poorer families. Management-owned housing was rented to workers, and sometimes the rent was subtracted from the paycheck before payday.

At Lowell, Massachusetts, in the 1820s, the cotton company built boardinghouses where single women workers lived communally, sharing bedrooms and eating centrally prepared meals in group dining rooms; there was a housemother to guarantee propriety. Next to the cotton mills in

HOUSING

Baltimore's Jones Valley, mill workers could live in company-sponsored two-family houses; each household had two rooms on each floor of a two-story house located within a block or two of the mill.

The elaborate and much-publicized company town of Pullman, Illinois, built in the 1880s, provided single-family, two-family, and four-family houses, tenements, boardinghouses, and a hotel. Workers at the vast Pullman railroad car plant lived in these many housing types, according to their means, across the street from the factory buildings in a nicely landscaped town with public market buildings, church, stables, and a park. Exorbitant rents caused the state to divest George Pullman of his interest in the town. The houses remain in good condition and are still inhabited. The town, now part of Chicago, is a historic site.

In cities of the industrial era, multifamily housing rather than houses for single families became the norm. At the turn of the nineteenth century, older houses that had been built for single families "filtered down" and were subdivided for renters at rates affordable to workers. The demolition and rebuilding that characterized urban centers in the 1830s and 1840s decreased this housing stock, leaving poor families in need of specially designed cheap rental quarters—tenements. The name "tenement" was applied to any house in which three or more households shared a common roof but lived in separate quarters. As urban housing after about 1830 took on distinctive class differences, "tenement" came to refer to a building for working-class, immigrant, or poor tenants; the term "apartment" came into use as the name for a middle-class family unit in a multifamily dwelling.

In the second and third quarters of the nineteenth century, thousands of tenement dwelling units were erected in New York, Philadelphia, and other growing cities. The physical form of early tenements was varied. Often built of wood, some resembled private houses, while others reminded contemporaries of huge barracks. Tenement landlords rarely supplied their tenants with pure water or sanitary facilities. Wood construction made tenement living a fire hazard, one not alleviated by the tendency to make fire escapes out of wood. High death rates in tenement districts drew attention to the health problems created by their unsanitary conditions, leading to legislative efforts to control their design in the 1850s, 1860s, and 1870s.

A typical tenement built for profit in the last quarter of the nineteenth century in New York was sited on a lot 25 feet by 100 feet (7.5 by 30 meters). It was called a dumbbell tenement after the shape of the plan: the plan narrowed in the center to create a light well, while at the front and back it spread to the full-lot width. Each tenement house had five floors with four units on each floor. Family units in such buildings usually had no more than three rooms—a living room used for cooking, eating, washing, income-producing work, and socializing, and two bedrooms, used for sleeping but also for income-producing piecework. Families frequently took in unrelated boarders to help pay the rent, so parents, children, and boarders all slept in proximity to each other—a lack of privacy that early social workers found threatening to morality. When there were indoor toilet facilities, they were limited to water closets in the public halls; bathtubs were not supplied in tenements. However, for those who wanted to bathe, public baths were common in larger cities after 1900.

Only two or three apartments per floor rather than the standard four was a variant of the tenement for tenants who could afford higher rents. Fewer units per floor meant that each family gained square footage. Two apartments per floor in a 25-foot-wide (7.5-meter) building each ran from front to back in a long string of rooms. When these apartments had no interior hallways, a space-saving device, they were called railroad flats because one walked from room to room as if going through the cars on a train.

Charitable organizations and individual philanthropists participated in the building of workers' housing. Alfred Tredway White promoted "5% philanthropy," the idea that public-spirited investors could put their money into progressively conceived workers' housing projects and still make a modest 5 percent return on the investment. White assembled large plots of land the size of an entire city block, and built model tenements such as the Tower and Riverside buildings, in Brooklyn, which provided three- or four-room units in two-room-deep perimeter-type buildings. These structures were built to wrap around the edge of the lot, leaving the land inside free to be used for recreation, laundry, and children's play. Every apartment had cross-ventilation and ample sunshine from both the street and courtyard sides. Unlike privately sponsored tenements, whose owners were bent on saving money, philanthropic housing often included bathtubs in the basement and private water closets within each household space.

The mid nineteenth century saw the definition

of an American middle class with boundaries in part articulated by housing form. Farmers, the backbone of the American economy, built improved farmhouses with the aid of advice in agricultural journals. The modern farm included a house with heating and cooking stoves, a pump drawing running water into the kitchen sink, and many rooms to differentiate receiving company from work-related tasks or from the family's sitting and sleeping rooms. The activities of the farm, and therefore the specific spaces of the farmhouse and its linked, work-related buildings, were often divided by gender between husband and wife, their male and female children, and their farmhands. The women's sphere included the kitchen, the dooryard, and adjunct spaces for readying butter and eggs for market; the men's sphere was the barn, the barnyard, and adjunct spaces for tending to farm animals and crops.

Some farm families built larger and more refined log structures with several rooms. Building techniques such as finely cut corner notching, found throughout the Midwest and the South, exhibit highly developed building skills exercised with elaborate tool kits. In the upland South a double-pen log house (the dogtrot form) comprised two one-room log structures separated by an open passage and joined under a single roof. The open-air passage served as circulation (that is, the path of movement for residents), as an outdoor protected sitting area, and for the ventilation needed in hot southern summers. Nineteenth-century "improvements" led to sheathing log houses in clapboards or some other modern finish and enclosing the open-air passage, creating a center hall, often with stairs to an added second story. Such alterations sometimes made the log house look like a framed central-passage house.

In the northern Midwest, immigrant Finns, Swedes, and Norwegians brought northern European, refined corner-notching techniques to build houses of one and two stories with logs. As their farms prospered, their houses grew to several rooms, with interior walls notched into the exterior log structure. Often a porch was part of the basic plan. Logs for these houses were carefully squared off and the bark removed before the corner joints were cut. The logs were closely fitted and the internal walls plastered for a smooth finish.

Another new housing idea of the nineteenth century emerged from the flourishing utopian and religious communities in which the believers often lived in large collective dwellings rather than single-family houses. The Shaker community at Hancock, Massachusetts, created a large, collective dwelling form, the Brothers' and Sisters' House, which contained rooms for all the males and rooms for all the females of the group, spatially segregated from each other. The Shaker dwelling house included sophisticated built-in cupboards and drawers to accommodate the residents' need for storage and to free the floor from extra pieces of furniture. At Salem, North Carolina, a settlement of Moravians created large, gender-segregated collective dwellings for their single members, constructed using German half-timbering with brick infill. Married church members moved into single-family houses for raising families, and ultimately went to their final rest in gender-segregated cemeteries.

More middle-class families took up living in suburbs from the 1850s on. The first suburbs arose with the first transportation lines. Railroads and ferry boats linked urban downtowns with new residential districts created as bedroom communities for middle- and upper-middle-income households. Commuting husbands went to city workplaces while homemaking women and children spent the day in the healthy fresh air and greenery of the suburb. A profusion of illustrated architectural books from the 1840s on promoted ornamental cottages in landscaped settings as the American single-family ideal.

By the 1880s trolley lines reached out from many American downtowns to open up new residential areas for middling families whose budgets might allow them to live in half of a two-family house or one floor of a triple (three-flat) house in a "streetcar suburb." The wide availability of factory-cut lumber gave rise to a proliferation of moderately priced wooden houses for members of the emerging middle class in towns and suburbs.

Apartment houses for middle-class tenants provided another version of the collective dwelling in mid-nineteenth-century cities. This type first appeared under the name "hotel" in Boston about 1860. The conveniences provided by a hotel, including meals, maid service, central heating, gas or electric light, and security, tempted the well-to-do to renounce private houses and turn to apartment living. First called "flats," "French flats," or "Parisian dwellings," because they reminded early observers of the apartment-house tradition of middle-class Parisians, apartment houses designed expressly to preserve family privacy yet provide the pleasant ser-

Central Park Apartments, New York City (c. 1881).

vices of a hotel were under construction in the late 1860s in New York, and in the 1870s in Washington, Chicago, and elsewhere.

Apartment houses for the middle class developed first as smaller buildings not too different in external appearance from large private houses. Inside, each floor was built to be a separate family unit. Early (1870–1880) apartment house designs of four or five stories made use of staircases rather than elevators. Servants slept on the topmost floor, and rents were adjusted so that those who had to climb the most stairs paid the least.

Much larger apartment houses of eight to ten stories appeared in the 1880s along with elevators, elaborate lobbies, doormen, and other service staff. Tall apartment houses in Chicago, Washington, Boston, and New York presented a new architectural image to passersby—one poised among the architectural conventions for a private house, a hotel, and an office building of the period. These buildings were constructed using new steel-cage engineering techniques, and were decorated on the exterior with stylish historical ornament in stone and terra-cotta.

The interior planning of an apartment unit was grounded in middle-class standards of family privacy and the sociable display of consumer goods. A formal parlor provided the space for receiving guests and placing the best furniture. Apartments for the wealthy, such as the 1883 Central Park Apartments in New York, had additional reception rooms—a library, a drawing room, and even a bil-

liard room. Dining rooms were standard for all middle-class apartments. Family bedrooms ranged from one or two to eight or more; in addition there were always servants' rooms, either within the family unit or in attic or basement spaces. Apartment buildings set the standard for central heating, gas and electric lighting, telephones, refrigerators, and other technological household advances in the 1890s.

Private houses of the wealthy in the early-nineteenth-century city were often four or five stories high, with a basement half aboveground. In the basement were a kitchen and family dining room. It was important for the kitchen to have immediate access to the backyard, where a cistern or pump was located and where garbage could be dumped. On the first floor, raised somewhat above sidewalk level by a flight of steps, were the reception rooms—a front and back parlor, and perhaps a formal dining room. The upper floors contained bedrooms and family sitting rooms. At the top, in the attic, were servants' rooms, storage, and workrooms.

Some early houses also contained a "counting room" or office in which the male head of the household conducted business. However, one aspect of improvement in house design of the nineteenth century was purging the house of explicit business and income-producing activities, so the counting room did not persist. Of course, the house served to enhance a family's income-producing potential because it secured extended family and social connections so necessary for the successful conduct of business, certified the social rank of the inhabitants, and itself increased in value.

At the same time, the home was increasingly mythologized as a refuge completely separated from work. A middle-class woman was told—in household magazines, manners manuals, and fiction—that her primary role was to be the moral force in the household, educator of her children, and example to her husband. She represented honorable values untainted by the commerce that weakened the moral fiber of the working world beyond the home. This framing of women mystified the real work that went on inside the household and the cash relations that underpinned the existence of servants and housewives.

Wealthy families continued to live in private houses in the cities of the later nineteenth century, but often possessed at least one country house as well. Philadelphians built summer homes on the Atlantic coast of New Jersey in towns such as Elberon; a winter home in Manhattan was complemented by a summer home at Newport, Rhode Island, or Asheville, North Carolina. Country houses for the well-to-do displayed familiarity with European architectural styles, which were inventively interpreted in wood, brick, or stone. Popular styles were the Greek revival in the 1830s and 1840s, Italianate and Gothic revival in the 1840s and 1850s, French Second Empire in the 1860s and 1870s, Victorian in the 1870s, and Queen Anne in the 1880s. Information on up-to-date architectural styles was available to architects, clients, and builders in mass-distributed books—another influence of industrialization. All these styles allowed American builders to display ornamental vocabularies, both inside and outside, adjusting the use of lavish materials to suit the wealth of the patron.

The spaces provided for a wealthy family in a country house of the later nineteenth century included several reception rooms—drawing room, library, parlor, sitting room, billiard room, boudoir; a dining room and perhaps a separate breakfast room; family bedrooms, typically grouped together on the second floor; a service suite of rooms including the kitchen, several pantries, food storage rooms, laundry rooms, servants' dining room, servants' bedrooms; several bathrooms, located separately for family members and for servants; and additional services located in the basement, stable, and carriage house.

The kinds of activities and meanings the American house had to support changed with time, climate, ethnicity, gender, and economics. Such changes were evident even on the simple level of function. For example, the late-nineteenth-century middle-class urban dwelling, whether in a single-family or multifamily configuration, tended to include a kitchen and a bathroom, and to exclude the income-producing work site. In a Virginia farmhouse of the early nineteenth century, the reverse was the case: separate kitchens were in independent back buildings, frequent baths were not part of people's behavior, and income was produced by work done in the house and its immediate landscape.

TWENTIETH-CENTURY DWELLINGS

The twentieth century continued to use many of the nineteenth century's innovations—apartment houses, suburbs, and multiroom single-family houses. The automobile affected both the location of houses and their design: garages became part of the home. Most influential was the increased role of the state in housing production and distribution, seen in areas as diverse as zoning law, publicly subsidized housing for the poor, and federal mortgage insurance. The state's negligence was also visible in the rise of homeless individuals and families.

Regional and climate characteristics so evident in houses of the eighteenth century continually diminished in the wake of industrialization. Modern building materials such as steel and concrete were used in every region, and inventions such as air-conditioning made climate-specific design solutions unnecessary. Manufactured housing increased rapidly since the 1970s, providing already-built houses that were trucked to sites all over the country and priced for households with very modest incomes. Such houses were designed for generic buyers; only after installing them were climate-specific adjustments made.

The twentieth century saw the distribution and incorporation of utilities into houses on a scale never before experienced. Most Americans since World War II lived in dwellings that had electricity for lighting and appliances, gas for cooking, stoves or furnaces for heating, indoor plumbing and sanitary facilities, and hot and cold running water. Before 1850 many of these conveniences were unavailable; some could be had only by the wealthiest households. Middle- and upper-class households that once had servants to light fires and lamps, cook meals, and empty slops now had plumbing and heating systems, power tools, and appliances to accomplish these housekeeping tasks. These same systems, tools, and appliances came to be a normal part of low-cost housing.

As immigrant populations moved into American cities, older generations, now Americanized, sought new homes, either in apartments or in single-family houses built for low-income households. Small houses priced to meet low-to-middling budgets and sized for the economy of servantless housekeeping were offered in diverse markets. In the first decade of the twentieth century, a house could be contracted for with a builder, or purchased already built from a developer. Mail-order houses such as Sears, Roebuck's could be purchased either as a set of plans and specifications that a local builder would follow, or as a complete house shipped as precut parts with instructions, to be erected on the site of one's choice, perhaps with one's own labor. Small, one-story houses with four rooms, called bungalows, were built nationwide, popularized by specialized magazines and even in songs. A living room, a kitchen, a bathroom, and one or two bedrooms provided lower-income families with homes of their own. Financing assisted those without savings to achieve independence. Manufacturers or developers offered special rates and installment payments at the turn of the century, a financial support system taken up later by banks and other thrift institutions, and subsidized by the federal government.

Early-twentieth-century housing also included multifamily alternatives located away from the center of the city in peripheral or suburban settings. Garden apartments emerged as a popular form of low-rise, three-to-five-story housing, set back from the street in landscaped grounds. Generous courtyards provided residents with recreational and even gardening possibilities. Apartment units were placed so that every one had generous light and cross ventilation; occupants of several units shared laundry equipment, garages, and storage rooms. Such apartment developments were sponsored by businesses that wanted sound investments, such as insurance companies, or by organizations working to improve the lot of their membership, such as labor unions.

Downtown housing accommodated households that did not fit the standard American family model. Single people, both male and female, found city housing to their taste in hotels or single-room-occupancy apartments. One or two rooms with a private bath located close to cultural attractions and downtown workplaces satisfied those who had no need for larger apartments and who rejected the life-style of the suburbs. At the turn of the century many "bachelor flats" were built for this group, whose special needs were not much acknowledged at the end of the century.

Company towns sponsored by corporations and erected for their workers continued in the twentieth century. Companies located away from population centers had to make special provisions for bringing workers to the job site; a new town near the site was an obvious solution. An example is Copperton, Utah, built in the 1920s by a copper mining company next to a vast open mine. The town of several square blocks contained schools and playgrounds, public meeting spaces, and single-family houses built according to five different plans.

Exterior gables, porches, and window details combined with varied colors and material finishes to give the houses a good deal of individuality. Four-car garages at the rear corners of four contiguous lots were the only collective features; each house had its own front and back yards, clothesline, and driveway.

Suburban homes were widely believed to be superior places to bring up children for both physical and moral health reasons. The outer edges of cities were built up as automobile-era suburbs in the 1920s and 1930s, each house with its own garage, front yard, and back yard. The model suburban town of Radburn, New Jersey, was built in 1929 to demonstrate the latest in planning theory for the automobile era. A commuter suburb, the town was located near railroad lines but was also structured around the private car. Modest three-bedroom houses were finished in brick, wood, and stucco using half-timbered and other historical motifs. Houses faced onto two circulation systems: the back of the house and its garage faced an automobile street; the front of the house and its entrance faced a paved pedestrian route. Car traffic near houses used cul-de-sac streets with a low speed limit; larger collector streets took traffic through town and linked it to highways. All the pedestrian paths crossed automobile paths by means of bridges and underpasses, to protect pedestrians (especially children) from accidents. Every house was linked by a network of walking paths to the school and to a small shopping district.

The expansion in population after World War II gave rise to a demand for more single-family housing subsidized by federal loan programs. Huge numbers of houses were erected by developers such as the Levitt brothers, whose Levittowns in New York, Pennsylvania, and New Jersey became synonymous with repetitive and homogeneous suburban housing developments. Their houses, built by the thousands using traditional masonry and carpentry techniques, had minimum square footage, maximized the appliances and services that made for modern housekeeping, and were intended for future expansion. The company provided ideas to transform carports into garages, and garages and attics into bedrooms.

In the 1930s public housing began to redress problems created by the Great Depression. Poor but employed families were preferred as the tenants in federally produced row houses and low-rise apartments built all over the country. The best of these included playgrounds and landscaping; family unit sizes were kept to the minimum, and low-rise configurations meant that districts of subsidized housing did not reach the high densities that more prosperous neighborhoods found threatening.

After World War II, migrations of formerly rural Americans, especially southern African Americans, into cities pointed up the need for increased modern urban housing. Decades of suburban housing production had taken attention away from inner-city conditions. There, tenement buildings that had been constructed in the 1870s and 1880s still served poorer families in densely spaced, ethnically homogeneous enclaves. Houses once built for single families after the Civil War continued to serve as inner-city housing, subdivided to create two, three, or more apartments. Such housing lacked up-to-date plumbing and wiring and was often in serious disrepair. Neighborhoods, once identified as slums, were not thought worthy of the investment necessary for upgrading. The oldest, most decayed housing had always been inherited by those least able to pay; to city administrators and urban planners of the 1950s, this old housing looked too decayed to serve anyone. "Urban renewal" policies were formulated to demolish and replace it, rebuilding center-city neighborhoods with the most up-to-date dwelling units equipped with modern plumbing, heating, lighting, and other services. The tower form was preferred because it used less land and initially appeared to be cheaper to build.

The replacement housing planned in these years was government-sponsored, but the state had never been widely supported as a housing initiator. Many critics still felt that housing was the rightful province of private enterprise, and in the absence of full commitment, public moneys did not achieve the amount of replacement housing originally intended. Building costs far exceeded estimates, and high-rise housing turned out to be far more costly than the low-rise units developed in the 1930s. Such small row and single-family houses continued to be erected in rural and suburban settings under federal programs, such as the 1950s and 1960s housing found on Indian reservations.

An example of public housing erected in this era is the 1958 Pruitt-Igoe redevelopment neighborhood in Saint Louis. Dwelling units were organized in thirty-three towers, each eleven stories high. Family units included large windows, several rooms, and fully equipped kitchens and bathrooms. Apartments were reached by elevators which stopped on every third floor. The fresh paint and services seemed to create the atmosphere for successful home life, but the project as a whole was ill managed.

Housing such as Pruitt-Igoe concentrated large numbers of poor households in too limited an area rather than mixing varied income households or dispersing smaller housing projects for the poor in several neighborhoods. So many people without resources could not keep their dwelling units in good repair, and city officials did not invest in the necessary maintenance of the public spaces—halls and elevators, parking lots and playgrounds—that should have been their responsibility. Pruitt-Igoe was finally demolished in 1972 after it proved unrepairable. In many cities, tower public housing has been closed awaiting reuse plans or has been sold to middle-class buyers as condominiums; some projects are being reduced in height to create more domestically scaled environments.

Housing for the wealthy in the twentieth century has few characteristics besides size and location that differentiate it from that of the middle-income and the poor. A full array of services has been a feature of expensive housing since 1900, but has been available to middling and poor households as well since World War II. Since the 1930s, architect-designed modernist houses of one story with an open plan and walls of glass have satisfied wealthy clients willing to take an artistic risk. Suburban houses in historical styles, popular in the nineteenth century, have remained the most popular in well-to-do, exclusive suburbs outside many American cities. Zoning laws have been used to require very large lot sizes and costly houses in neighborhoods allocated to the wealthy. The phenomenon called gentrification characterized efforts to reclaim inner-city buildings for housing in the 1970s and 1980s. The historic preservation movement, having raised appreciation of historic architecture among the upwardly mobile, provided a counter to urban renewal by demolition. Late-nineteenth-and early-twentieth-century houses were sold to willing renovators who treasured the urbanity and historic character of aging city neighborhoods. Preserved blocks of such houses, now inhabited by wealthier owners, drove up real estate prices in areas previously deemed slums. In urban downtowns housing commanding high rents or sale prices has been created from underutilized older office and factory buildings, and sometimes even philanthropic tenements have been converted to high-priced condominiums.

High-rise towers have also been used for expensive apartments across the country, located in urban neighborhoods associated with social success. The sizes of household units for the wealthy can be much larger than units in middle-class or publicly subsidized apartment towers, and the material finishes are finer; the construction techniques and utilities and service systems use the same technologies. As in the nineteenth century, well-to-do people often possess more than one home, and a small urban apartment often suits their needs when combined with a large country house. The cost of renting or owning even a small apartment, however, depends significantly on location. Two rooms in the "best" building may cost as much as a dozen rooms in a less desirable place.

Since the 1970s some shifts in house form have suggested that developers and legislators acknowledge that household form is more diverse than the single-family standard. Municipalities recognized the need for families to incorporate an elderly parent into the household by structuring zoning laws to allow "mother-in-law" apartments attached to single-family houses. Apartment buildings were designed to allow two unrelated individuals to share one unit while each maintained a separate social life. Both bore the costs of rent on a shared kitchen and living room, services and utilities, and each had a personal bedroom and bathroom. Recognizing that many families were headed by a single parent, some multifamily dwellings were organized around collective day care for children. Housing forms were needed that recognize the many alternatives to a standard family that comprised households.

Near the end of the twentieth century, striking similarities between house forms for all classes and regions pointed up the triumph of modern construction techniques and services over ethnic and regional variants. Tall apartment towers served all income levels; they were just erected in different neighborhoods to serve different classes. The costliness and quality of materials and the square footage distinguished a single-family suburban house for a wealthy client from one for a poor client, but both were likely to have paved roads and driveway, gas and electric power, appliances, heat, cooking equipment, and indoor plumbing.

What Americans lacked was equal access to these house forms and to the comfortable and secure life they promise. Regional imbalances in price led to mansion price tags on four-room bungalows in some areas. Young middle-class or poor people could never expect to amass a down payment to buy their own house in inflated real estate markets. Low-income families who could only afford to be tenants found that income tax breaks were given to those who buy housing but not to those who rent. Racial discrimination in housing, although illegal, still prevented some from living in the district or the building of choice. The success of constructing and servicing houses must be followed up by economic and social structures that give everyone access to housing.

BIBLIOGRAPHY

General Histories

Bishir, Catherine W., Charlotte V. Brown, Carl R. Lounsbury, and Ernest H. Wood III. *Architects and Builders in North Carolina: A History of the Practice of Building* (1990).

Blackmar, Elizabeth S. *Manhattan for Rent, 1785–1850* (1989).

Clark, Clifford E., Jr. *The American Family Home 1800–1960* (1986).

Cromley, Elizabeth. *Alone Together: A History of New York's Early Apartments* (1990).

Cummings, Abbott Lowell. *The Framed Houses of Massachusetts Bay, 1625–1725* (1979).

Glassie, Henry. *Folk Housing in Middle Virginia: A Structural Analysis of Historic Artifacts* (1975).

Gottfried, Herbert, and Jan Jennings. *American Vernacular Design, 1870–1940: An Illustrated Glossary* (1988).

Hayden, Dolores. *Seven American Utopias: The Architecture of Communitarian Socialism, 1790–1975* (1976).

Hubka, Thomas C. *Big House, Little House, Back House, Barn: The Connected Farm Buildings of New England* (1984).

Larkin, Jack. *The Reshaping of Everyday Life, 1790–1840* (1988).

McMurry, Sally. *Families and Farmhouses in Nineteenth-Century America: Vernacular Design and Social Change.* (1988).

Nabokov, Peter, and Robert Easton. *Native American Architecture* (1989).

Plunz, Richard. *A History of Housing in New York City* (1990).

Upton, Dell, ed. *America's Architectural Roots: Ethnic Groups That Built America* (1986).

Upton, Dell, and John Michael Vlach, eds. *Common Places: Readings in American Vernacular Architecture* (1986).

Welfeld, Irving. *Where We Live: A Social History of American Housing* (1988).

Wright, Gwendolyn. *Moralism and the Model Home: Domestic Architecture and Cultural Conflict in Chicago, 1873–1913* (1980).

———. *Building the Dream: A Social History of Housing in America* (1981).

Housing Policies and the Future

Davis, Sam, ed. *The Form of Housing* (1977).

Franck, Karen A., and Sherry Ahrentzen, eds. *New Households, New Housing* (1989).

Goetze, Rolf. *Rescuing the American Dream: Public Policies and the Crisis in Housing* (1983).

Hayden, Dolores. *Redesigning the American Dream: The Future of Housing, Work, and Family Life* (1984).

Nutt-Powell, Thomas E. *Manufactured Homes: Making Sense of a Housing Opportunity* (1982).

Sternlieb, George, James Hughes, and Robert Burchell, eds. *America's Housing: Prospects and Problems* (1980).

SEE ALSO **Immigration; Urbanization;** and various articles in **"Space and Place."**

THE CULTURE OF CONSUMPTION

Christopher Lasch

DURING THE EARLY stages of industrialization, the provision of basic necessities absorbed most of the nation's productive capacity. Railroads, iron and steel, foundries and machine shops, lumber, textiles, and meat packing ranked among the leading industries in 1900. By the middle of the twentieth century, however, the shift from heavy industry to consumer goods—automobiles, household appliances, radios and television sets, ready-made clothing, prepared food—was unmistakable. At the height of the postwar boom, consumer debt (excluding real estate loans) increased from $27.4 billion to $41.7 billion (52 percent) in the four years from 1952 to 1956 alone. Half of the families in the middle-income range carried installment payments.

Their ancestors had been taught that "he that goes a borrowing goes a sorrowing," in the saying of Benjamin Franklin's Poor Richard. In the "affluent society," as John Kenneth Galbraith called it in 1958, this homespun philosophy seemed as archaic as homespun clothing. The morality of thrift, it seemed, was hopelessly misplaced in an economy based on immediate gratification. "Buy now, pay later" sounded like a more appropriate axiom. Who could object to a little everyday extravagance when it helped to sustain unprecedented prosperity, an outpouring of goods? In supermarkets, shoppers chose from "thousands of items on the high-piled shelves," according to an excited report in *Life* magazine, "until their carts became cornucopias filled with an abundance that no other country in the world has ever known."

The growing acceptance of indebtedness provides one measure of the degree to which a culture of consumption has come to shape Americans' habits and expectations. The consumption of goods and services that do not contribute to the bare maintenance of life goes on in every society, of course, and as soon as a society accumulates a surplus beyond subsistence, consumption often assumes riotous proportions. In the book of Revelation (18:12–13), we read of ancient Babylon with its "merchandise of gold, and silver, and precious stones, and of pearls, and fine linen, and purple, and silk, and scarlet, and all thyine wood, and all manner vessels of ivory, and all manner vessels of most precious wood, and of brass, and iron, and marble, and cinnamon, and odours, and ointments, and frankincense, and wine, and oil, and fine flour, and wheat, and beasts, and sheep, and horses, and chariots, and slaves, and souls of men." As this recital reminds us, however, a luxurious way of living usually rests on the back of a degraded laboring class, servile in condition if not always in law. It is only when the masses become consumers in their own right, entitled, as they see it, to the comforts formerly monopolized by the few—entitled even to an occasional taste of genuine luxury—that we can properly speak of a whole culture pervaded by the ideal of consumption.

THEORIES OF CONSUMPTION

In the United States, a mass market in consumer goods began to take shape in the 1920s, collapsed in the Great Depression, and finally became the dominant fact of economic life in the 1940s and 1950s, thanks to the combined effects of government spending and the improvements in workers' standard of living achieved by labor unions. But the hope that mass consumption would generate economic growth and prosperity on an unprecedented scale had a much longer history. It figured prominently in the political economy of the eighteenth century, especially in the writings of Bernard Mandeville, David Hume, and Adam Smith. Mandeville (1670–1733) disputed the long-accepted idea that luxury led to corruption and civic decline. Hume (1711–1776) insisted that a refinement of taste, even when it led to sensual gratification, was a mark not of decadence but of social and economic progress. According to Smith (1723–1790), the "effort of every man to better his condition" was the "principle from which public and national, as well as private opulence is originally derived" (*Wealth of Nations*, vol. 1, p. 348). Smith admitted that ordinary people had an exaggerated respect for wealth and for the "vain and empty distinctions of greatness"; but even if worldly goods could not buy happiness or peace of mind, it was "well that nature imposes upon us in this manner," he thought (*Theory of Moral Sentiments*, pp. 182–183). Ambitious men and women worked harder, as long as they had some prospect of success, than those who lacked the acquisitive impulse.

Insatiable desire, formerly condemned as a source of social instability and spiritual corruption, thus acquired the sanction of economic theory. The appetite for better things, once these things were placed within reach of the common people, would lead to the indefinite expansion of the productive forces necessary to satisfy it. In the United States, a country blessed with an abundance of land and a shortage of labor that made for high wages, the democratic implications of the new political economy were spelled out by reformers who identified social improvement with a revolution of rising expectations. "Improvement" rested on a general expansion of the taste not just for material comforts but for amenities and refinements of every kind, moral and mental as well as material. The Unitarian clergyman Theodore Parker (1810–1860), by way of contrasting slavery with free labor, argued that "every farmer and day-laborer" in Connecticut was a "consumer" of "tea, coffee, sugar, rice, molasses, salt, and spices; of cotton, woolen, and silk goods, ribbons and bonnets; of shoes and hats; of beds and other furniture; of hardware, tinware, and cutlery; of crockery and glassware; of clocks and jewelry; of books, paper, and the like." The effects of this consumption stimulated the "mechanic and the merchant" to improve production and distribution; their efforts stimulated the farmer and laborer "in return, all grow up together; each has a market . . . continually enlarging and giving vent to superior wares" ("A Letter on Slavery," p. 65).

In the flush times following the Civil War, the equation of improvement with democracy no longer appeared as plausible as it had to antebellum reformers like Parker. The rich set a high, some would have said an obscene, standard of consumption; but it was no longer clear that hard-pressed farmers and wage earners were in any

position to follow their example or to aspire to anything, indeed, beyond sheer survival. In a nation polarized between extremes of wealth and poverty, social theorists began to argue that progress and poverty went hand in hand. Henry George (1839–1897) took the position that the accumulation of wealth widened the gap between the rulers and the ruled; that advanced civilizations had to devote more and more of their resources to the maintenance of an idle ruling class; and that they finally collapsed, top-heavy, of their own weight. Thorstein Veblen's (1857–1929) attack on the leisure class could be cited in support of the same conclusions. Defenders of American capitalism, meanwhile, retreated from the claim that economic growth would benefit everyone in the long run. Instead they justified inequality on the grounds that it represented the "survival of the fittest." Increasingly worried about overproduction, they despaired of expanding the domestic market. Overseas expansion, they believed, was the only way to absorb the American economy's excess capacity. Charles A. Conant (1861–1915), a leading imperialist, estimated that the "creation of new demands at home" would continue "as long as human desires continue expansible," but he pointed out, rather gloomily, that "there has never been a time before when the proportion of capital to be absorbed was so great in proportion to possible new demands" ("The Economic Basis of 'Imperialism,'" p. 337).

THE CASE FOR CONSUMPTION

Faced on the one hand with agitation for a radical redistribution of wealth and on the other with an aggressive imperialism (which invoked the same Darwinian ideology that was used to justify inequality at home), spokesmen for what came to be known as the Progressive movement revived the argument, in a bolder and more sweeping form, that the only hope for democracy lay in mass consumption. Some of these Progressives harked back to Adam Smith, whose economic theory contained a democratic undercurrent, according to the sociologist Albion Small (1854–1926), that was usually overlooked by his latter-day disciples. If Smith had lived until the end of the nineteenth century, Small maintained, he would have welcomed democratic reforms that increased the demand for goods and led to a general improvement in the standard of living. Simon Patten (1852–1922), a leading economist, attempted to refute pessimists like Henry

George by arguing that consumer spending annulled the "ancient tragic model" of growth and decay, progress and poverty. "Those who would predict to-morrow's economic states from a study of the economic states of Rome or Venice," according to Patten, overlooked the unprecedented abundance made possible by the modern productive system, which placed civilization on a "new basis" (*The New Basis of Civilization,* pp. 9, 14). Walter Weyl, one of the editors of the influential weekly *The New Republic,* invoked Patten's "brilliant" analysis of the "transition from a pain economy to a pleasure economy" in support of the contention that abundance, which generated a growing demand for a "full life for all members of society," represented the best "hope of a full democracy" (*The New Democracy,* pp. 191, 197). Another admirer and protégé of Patten, the political scientist Rexford Tugwell, later a member of Franklin D. Roosevelt's brain trust, likewise identified democracy with higher wages, more leisure, and better recreation. But it was left to John Maynard Keynes (1883–1946), whose theory of deficit spending guided the economic policies of the New Deal, Harry Truman's Fair Deal, John F. Kennedy's New Frontier, and Lyndon Johnson's Great Society, to work out the most sophisticated rationale for mass consumption as the key to full employment and economic growth. Orthodox economists had exaggerated the value of abstinence and thrift, Keynes argued. The expectation of profits, not abstinence, was the engine that drove economic enterprise, and profits in turn presupposed a rising standard of living in the population as a whole and a general desire for a more abundant existence.

Social and economic theories that tied democracy to abundance and consumption not only influenced public policy—chiefly by making full employment, high wages, and the management of consumer demand important priorities—but also helped to undermine the weight of moral traditions that condemned extravagance and self-indulgence. Both the biblical and the republican tradition saw nothing but trouble in the excess of wants over needs. Theorists of consumption, on the other hand, celebrated this same excess as a "superlative machine," in Patten's words, ". . . for the quickening of progress" (p. 55). This is not to say that economic theory alone was enough to discredit the austere ethic of plain living and high thinking or that a culture of consumption was the outcome envisioned by all those who condemned the old "puritanical" morality of scarcity. In the years immediately pre-

ceding World War I, inherited moral traditions came under attack from a variety of critics advancing quite different and often incompatible programs.

Some of these critics wanted to replace religion with a new religion of art. Others took their cue from science—a more reliable guide to the conduct of life, in their view, than moral precepts founded on religion. Avant-garde intellectuals, sometimes appealing to the authority of Freud, proclaimed the liberation of personality from repression. Feminists proclaimed the emancipation of women. Professional healers began to articulate a therapeutic ethic that was more concerned to make people healthy than to make them wise or good. Social workers questioned the value of self-reliance in a complex, interdependent society in which people had to rely on others. In general, the expansion of professional authority had the effect of discouraging people from relying on their own resources—on their local communities, their neighborhoods, and their churches. The churches themselves, influenced by liberal theology and the Social Gospel, redefined their mission as a form of therapy designed to assure peace of mind, not to activate a slumbering sense of sin.

THE CELEBRATION OF WASTE

All these developments tended to weaken moral traditions that stressed the value of hard work and self-command, cautioned against extravagant expectations of a trouble-free existence, and held individuals strictly accountable for their actions. In the 1920s, permissive moralities spread from elites to the masses. The postwar "revolution in manners and morals," much discussed at the time, in retrospect can be understood as the flowering of a consumer culture. The advertising industry, which first achieved prominence in the 1920s, allied itself with movements of cultural liberation or at least exploited liberationist ideologies for its own purposes. Edward Bernays, one of the founders of modern advertising and public relations, boasted of having broken the taboo that kept women from smoking in public. Seizing on cigarettes as "torches of freedom" and invoking the memory of prewar parades for woman suffrage, he persuaded a contingent of women to join New York's Easter parade in 1929, ostentatiously smoking "as a protest against women's inequality," as he put it (Stuart Ewen, *Captains of Consciousness,* pp.

160–161). The flapper, who personified both the emancipation of women and the revolt of youth, appealed to advertisers as the personification of consumption as well. She embodied the spirit of change, the restless craving for novelty and excitement recognized by advertisers as the most important stimulus to consumption. Since young people were presumably more receptive to change than adults, advertising psychologists stressed the importance of introducing innovations by addressing them to the young. The rapid pace of change made even children more knowledgeable about the new world of commodities than their parents. "Were it not for the children, some of you parents would not know even now what a tremendous change for the better Paramount has [made] in motion pictures" (Ewen, p. 148). Such advertisements had the effect of elevating the young to arbiters of taste, whose consumer preferences had to be respected by adults struggling to keep up with the changing times.

Advertisers made no secret of their intention to promote novelty for its own sake, in the hope that consumers would exchange perfectly serviceable goods for goods that conformed to the latest fashions. Earnest Elmo Calkins (1868–1964), one of the first to grasp the principle of "artificial obsolescence," distinguished between goods "we *use*" and "those we *use up*." It was the second category that fascinated advertisers and the manufacturers who followed their lead. "Artificial obsolescence," Calkins explained, meant the continual redesign of products, "entirely apart from any mechanical improvement, to make them markedly new, and encourage new buying, exactly as the fashion designers make shirts longer so you can no longer be happy with your short ones." The taste for "better things," as William L. Day pointed out, required an "ideal of beauty that happens to be current." "The world depends on obsolescence and new merchandise," said the industrial designer John Vassos (Jeffrey L. Meikle, *Twentieth-Century Limited,* pp. 16, 70, 83).

Resistance to Creative Waste

This open celebration of waste, so obviously incompatible with the ideals of thrift and saving in which most Americans had been raised, met with a good deal of initial resistance in the business world. Henry Ford (1863–1947), a pioneer in the technology of mass production, took an unfashionably narrow view of consumption. In 1926, he declared that Ford owners represented the "vast majority [who] cling to the old-fashioned idea of living within their incomes."

A year later, he brought out the Model A and immediately froze its design, to the dismay of the advertising industry. His intention, he said, was to manufacture a car "so strong and so well-made that no one ought ever to have to buy a second one." But Ford's rival Alfred P. Sloan (1875–1966) had already pointed the way to the future by introducing annual model changes at General Motors. By 1927, his Chevrolet was outselling the Model T; the introduction of the Model A, notwithstanding Ford's hatred of extravagance, was itself a concession to the principle of "creative waste," as the advertising consultant Christine Frederick called it (Roland Marchand, *Advertising the American Dream,* pp. 157–159). Eventually Ford capitulated to fashion and allowed his designers to introduce new models every year, like his increasingly successful competitors.

The Great Depression forced millions of Americans to spend less freely than before, but it did not revive respect for the simple life. Walter B. Pitkin (1878–1953), a Columbia professor, warned advertisers that hard times might encourage a "return to the primitive, a back-to-the-soil type of living" (Marchand, pp. 300–301). Instead of deploring such a prospect, a handful of prominent figures actually welcomed it. Senator John H. Bankhead (1872–1946) of Alabama called for an agrarian revival, a "restoration of that small yeoman class which has been the backbone of every great civilization." Ford himself, still unreconciled to the culture of consumption, launched an abortive movement back to the land in 1932: "The land! That is where our roots are. No unemployment insurance can be compared to an alliance between a man and a plot of land" (Schlesinger, *The Age of Roosevelt: The Coming of the New Deal,* pp. 361–363).

Spending for Prosperity

But nothing came of these appeals. Those who set the terms of public discussion argued that spending, not saving, held out the best hope of prosperity. Advertisements and motion pictures continued to admire the rich, dwelling in loving detail on their pearls, yachts, and luxurious mansions. Advertisements designed to exploit the "whole ground of feminine longing and feminine envy," as the Hoover Company explained to its salesmen, encouraged middle- and working-class women to aspire to opulence and ease. "You see her wearing a plain little house dress, but she sees herself someday in velvet and ermine." In the meantime, she used a vacuum cleaner "that the richest woman in the world can't outdo her in." The idea behind its advertising campaign, Hoover pointed out, was to picture the "woman of wealth and the woman of little means," to "contrast their situation" and reveal the "gulf" between them, and then to "bridge that gulf" by showing that both owned a Hoover. A trade journal, *Advertising and Selling,* held up the Hoover campaign as the epitome of psychological insight. "Ordinary folks are always pleased to know they can have the products good enough for Vanderbilts, Astors, Huttons, Mellons, and Fords" (quoted in Marchand, pp. 292–295).

World War II, in spite of shortages and rationing, did nothing to reduce the social prestige of goods or the appeal of consumption. On the contrary, wartime propaganda explained the war essentially as a defense of the high standard of living Americans were privileged to enjoy. The "American way of life" was now identified so closely with the American standard of living, and freedom with a wide choice of competing consumer goods, that appeals to any larger war aims seemed almost superfluous—unlikely to succeed in any case. The postwar migration to the suburbs, even more clearly than the war effort, indicated how completely the consumerist ideal had eclipsed older conceptions of the American dream. Any lingering sense of a common civic identity was unlikely to flourish in communities populated by rootless, transient individuals and organized around the pursuit of private pleasures. Single-family dwellings and private motorcars, not to mention the absence of civic amenities, made this commitment to privacy unmistakable. Physically removed from the workplace, suburbs were devoted to leisure by definition, and the vast housing tracts that grew up on their fringes, pushing farther and farther into the countryside, announced in every detail of their design that leisure was to be enjoyed in private—more often than not, in front of a television set.

In 1946, only six thousand television sets were manufactured in the United States. By 1953, the figure had risen to seven million. The number of sets in use rose from seventeen thousand in 1946 to ninety million in 1971. This seductive new medium promoted consumption not merely in advertising but in programs that typically showed suburban families surrounded by their possessions. Its imagery of abundance, however fantastic and dreamlike, had a firm basis in fact. In the 1950s, the number of Americans owning their dwellings surpassed the number of renters for the first time in the twentieth century. By 1960, a quarter of those dwellings had been built during the previous decade—striking evidence of the postwar housing boom. Only 12 percent of them lacked a bathtub or shower, as compared to 39 percent in 1940. Ninety-eight percent had a refrigerator. Thirteen percent had air conditioning, and by 1968 this figure had risen to 37 percent.

In the 1920s, most industrial workers still enjoyed neither paid holidays nor vacations. By 1963, eight holidays and a two-week vacation were the norm. Leisure spending accounted for 15 percent of the gross national product by 1950. The emergence of a youth market further testified to the shift from a production to a consumption ethic. In 1963 American adolescents spent $22 billion—an amount, as William E. Leuchtenburg points out, that was double the gross national product of Austria (*A Troubled Feast,* p. 65).

It was no wonder that America was now admired—when it was not hated or feared—less for its democratic institutions or its championship of democratic revolutions abroad, as in the old days, than for its vast and seemingly inexhaustible wealth. A lavish display of American products in a Swiss department store, accompanied by the injunction to "live like an American," left no doubt about the meaning of that slogan. When Vice President Richard M. Nixon and Soviet Premier Nikita Khrushchev debated the merits of capitalism and communism at the American National Exhibition in Moscow in 1959, it was entirely fitting that their argument took place in a model kitchen full of labor-saving appliances. What Nixon and Khrushchev said on that occasion was of no importance; the goods spoke for themselves.

The Affluent Society Consumer goods spoke so loudly, in fact, that social critics began to fear that the voice of moderation and sobriety was in danger of being completely submerged in the clamorous invitation to buy, to borrow, and to spend without a second thought, and to indulge every whim as quickly as it came to mind. When Dwight Eisenhower engaged an advertising firm to promote his campaign for the presidency in 1952, many commentators objected to this packaging of a candidate by Madison Avenue—a practice that threatened to replace political discourse with advertising slogans. Mass promotion, it was now clear, would not stop with the marketing of washing machines and refrigerators. In *The Image* (1962), Daniel Boorstin pointed out that images of reality threatened to replace reality itself, so that politics came to revolve not around events but around "pseudo-events" staged for the benefit of the mass media. Paul

Goodman argued that American youth were "growing up absurd," unable to look forward to useful, honorable work that made some lasting contribution to society instead of producing goods no one really needed. Galbraith's *Affluent Society* (1958) called attention to the contrast between "private affluence and public squalor." According to Galbraith, neither economists nor politicians and administrators admitted the "diminishing urgency of wants" in the age of abundance. Instead they sought to engineer a constantly rising level of private consumption, while public services and amenities were allowed to decay.

The family which takes its mauve and cerise, air-conditioned, power-steered, and power-braked automobile out for a tour passes through cities that are badly paved, made hideous by litter, blighted buildings, billboards, and posts for wires that should long since have been put underground. They pass on into a countryside that has been rendered largely invisible by commercial art.... They picnic on exquisitely packaged food from a portable icebox by a polluted stream and go on to spend the night at a park which is a menace to public health and morals.... Is this, indeed, the American genius? (Galbraith, pp. 146, 253)

CRITICS OF CONSUMPTION

In the 1960s, criticism of consumption figured prominently in the rhetoric of the New Left. The 1962 Port Huron Statement, founding charter of the Students for a Democratic Society, condemned marketing techniques intended to "create pseudo-needs in consumers" and to make "wasteful 'planned obsolescence'... a permanent feature of business strategy" (Miller, *"Democracy Is in the Streets,"* p. 339). This was a familiar line of criticism by that time; but spokesmen for the New Left soon began to elaborate it into a more sweeping condemnation of American society. Not content merely to repeat the indictment already drawn up by liberals like Boorstin and Galbraith, they maintained that mass consumption was part of a larger strategy of "social control" deliberately designed to tranquilize the public and to prevent discontent from finding political expression. The "new authoritarianism," as Herbert Marcuse called it, provided "satisfaction in a way which generates submission and weakens the rationality of protest." Instead of using forcible repression to keep people in line, it relied on "repressive desublimation" and "repressive tolerance." Theodore Roszak, building on Marcuse's work, explained: "The strategy chosen... is not

harsh repression, but rather the *Playboy* version of total permissiveness.... The business of inventing and flourishing treacherous parodies of freedom, joy, and fulfillment becomes an indispensable form of social control" (*Making of a Counter Culture,* pp. 14–15). Radical theorists of the sixties turned criticism of affluence on its head. In their view, "symbolic sexual stimulation" and other "attenuated forms" of pleasure, in Philip Slater's words, served to maintain the illusion of scarcity in the midst of abundance. "Our society has become so affluent," Slater wrote, "that it threatens to give the show away—to disclose the absurdity of the scarcity assumptions in which it is based." Capitalist production could now maintain itself only by getting people "to substitute products for real satisfactions"—by "generating esoteric erotic itches that cannot be scratched outside the world of fantasy, but lend themselves well to marketing" (*The Pursuit of Loneliness,* pp. 90–92). Americans did not really think of themselves as an affluent society at all; if they did, they would come to see that they already had everything they needed in the way of material goods.

Consumption as Social Control Consumption thus came to be understood by the New Left as a system of total control, more insidious than harsher forms of totalitarianism because it rested not on violence but on the semblance of hedonism and self-indulgence. If totalitarian states terrorized their subjects into submission, the culture of consumption allegedly achieved the same result by gentler methods. Advertising was a more sophisticated and therefore more effective method of thought control than torture, by means of which totalitarian regimes brainwashed political prisoners into confessions of political nonconformity. In America, conformity was assured by a type of brainwashing unrecognizable as such (except to those equipped with theoretical insight into its operation), since consumers were supposedly free to make their own decisions. In reality, their capacity for independent judgment, according to theorists of the New Left, was systematically destroyed by the propaganda of commodities.

This indictment contained a core of truth, which could not be dismissed on the grounds that consumers seldom buy mindlessly what they are told to buy. Those who replied to the New Left by questioning the efficacy of advertising, often citing spectacular marketing failures like the Edsel or the Nehru suit, never managed to counter the more important point that advertising serves not just to promote a given product but to promote consumption as a way of life. The importance of advertising is not that it invariably succeeds in its immediate purpose, much less that it lobotomizes the consumer into a state of passive acquiescence, but simply that it surrounds people with images of the good life in which happiness depends on consumption. The ubiquity of such images leaves little space for competing conceptions of the good life. A society in which the market is the central institution, moreover, is quite different from a society that restricts the operation of the market to ascertainable limits—for example, by regulating wages and prices, by setting aside certain lands or facilities for common use, by passing sumptuary laws and other impediments to consumption, or simply by declaring that some things are not for sale. Such restrictions are by no means unknown even today, but they seem destined to wither away as the market inexorably expands.

The Commercialization of Life Mass markets do not easily coexist with institutions that operate according to principles antithetical to the market—schools and universities, newspapers and magazines, charities, families. Sooner or later, it tends to absorb them all. It puts an almost irresistible pressure on every activity to justify itself in the only terms recognized by the market—to become a business proposition, to pay its own way, to show black ink on the bottom line. It turns news into entertainment, scholarship into professional careerism, social work into the scientific management of poverty. Even the family, widely regarded as the last bastion of spontaneous fellow feeling, comes to be modeled on the market. It becomes a little factory for turning out a distinctive product, the well-adjusted child. Parents are encouraged to consume great quantities of expert advice in order to improve the product. Professional helpers advise and intimidate them, correct their mistakes, or replace them altogether when the occasion seems to warrant this ultimate form of interference. The child-care industry itself competes for control of the child with the mass media and the advertisers, who regard children not as products but as consumers, endlessly demanding and entitled to immediate gratification.

The impact of mass communications on the world of ideas provides another example of the expansion of the market at the expense of activities initially resistant to commercialization. Improved technologies of communication would seem to make it possible for artists and intellectuals to reach a wider audience than they ever dreamed of. By transforming the certification of literary and artistic excellence, however, the new media turn ideas into commodities. Their appetite for novelty (that is, for old formulas in new packages), their reliance on immediate recognition of the product, and their need for ideological revolutions at regular intervals make "visibility" the overriding test of intellectual merit. The first judgment of a book or an idea becomes the last; a book either becomes a best-seller or drops out of sight; and the book in any case takes a back seat to the article or interview it occasions. Here, as elsewhere, journalism no longer reports events; it creates them. It refers less and less to actual events and more and more to a circular and self-validating process of publicity. It no longer presupposes a world that exists independently of the images made about it.

The self-referential character of mass media usually defeats attempts to hold them up to high standards of objectivity, for example by enforcing "truth in advertising." Movements intended to protect consumers against false or misleading advertisements, to organize consumers' lobbies, or to exploit collective buying power for constructive political ends once seemed to hold out some promise. Collective action by consumers, however, has proved almost impossible to achieve. Consumers have no interests in common, except perhaps for a common stake in truthful communication; and the campaign against flagrant falsehood does not confront the real difficulty. The mass media seldom traffic in outright lies. Their effect is more subtle: to obliterate the very distinction between truth and falsehood. They conjure up a world in which it is hard to tell the difference between fantasy and actual events—a world that bears a certain resemblance to the world of everyday experience but resists moral or epistemological judgment. The only mode of judgment that seems appropriate to the mass media is aesthetic—whether an advertisement or a news program is sufficiently dramatic, amusing, or otherwise appealing to compel attention and to get high ratings from the agencies that monitor audience response.

For the same reasons, the influence of consumerism on politics is not confined to the packaging of candidates. The mass media gradually replace political parties as the agents of political education. The media define the issues, select the candidates, and announce the outcome of elections in advance by continually polling the electorate. Opinion surveys help to shape opinion instead of merely recording it. Indeed they make the concept of public opinion increasingly anachronistic by destroying collective memory, by replacing accountable authorities with media-selected "spokesmen" and political celebrities, and by treating all ideas, all programs, all controversies and disagreements, as equally newsworthy, equally deserving of fitful attention, and therefore equally inconsequential and forgettable. In a culture of consumption, political life ceases to be guided by controversies about the common good and becomes another exercise in mass promotion. The citizen disappears into the consumer of political imagery, and the pressure to please and entertain the electorate makes it increasingly unlikely that political leaders will speak truthfully, make hard choices, or call for sacrifices in the general interest.

THE REVISIONIST DEFENSE OF CONSUMPTION

Historical studies of the culture of consumption have not always distinguished very carefully between the erosion of citizenship and public culture, on the one hand, and the allegedly totalitarian implications of consumption on the other. The first studies, which began to appear in the 1970s, were heavily influenced by the New Left and specifically by Herbert Marcuse (1898–1979) and other members of the Frankfurt school of social theory. The works of Stuart Ewen, for example, leave the impression that consumption is part of an all-embracing, quasi-conspiratorial system of control, which eliminates every form of autonomous activity and renders the consumer incapable of independent judgment. Such at least is the standard criticism of Ewen's and other early interpretations, which have been challenged in several ways by a growing body of revisionist scholarship. A number of studies have objected to the passivity these interpretations attribute to consumers.

According to the new way of thinking, consumers should be understood as active participants in the culture of consumption, choosing the goods they please and endowing them with significance not always anticipated by those who sell them. Charles F. McGovern, Daniel Miller, Elizabeth Wilson, Michael Denning, and George Lipsitz, among others, have claimed that consumers' ability to "recontextualize" commodities makes it impossible to

regard consumption as a monolithic system of exploitation and domination. Often drawing on literary theories associated with "postmodernism" (which displace attention from the author to the reader and see the reader as a creator of meanings unintended by the author), these historians insist that consumers arrive at "negotiated" or even "subversive" readings of commodities and mass culture. In this way they allegedly escape the control of their would-be controllers.

A second line of revisionism takes issue with the contention that consumption is exploitive or oppressive even in the intention of its promoters. Warren Susman was one of the first historians to claim that consumerism often has a liberating intent and certainly that it has liberating effects. Many other scholars have followed him in arguing that the culture of consumption generates a new sense of possibility, encourages subject populations to demand their share of good things, and thus leads just as easily to a radical politics of redistribution as to a politics of acquiescence. The emancipatory potential of consumerism is emphasized, in varying ways and degrees, by Fredric Jameson, Andrew Ross, Richard King, Roy Rosenzweig, Kathy Peiss, John Kasson, Ronald Edsforth, and William R. Leach.

A third strategy of revision alters the chronology of consumer culture by extending it backward in time. Whereas earlier interpretations treated it strictly as a twentieth-century phenomenon, Colin Campbell traces its roots to nineteenth-century romanticism, while Neil McKendrick goes back to the expansion of consumption in eighteenth-century England. Chandra Mukerji insists that the origins of consumer culture can be traced all the way back to the sixteenth century, when the English nobility began to cultivate a taste for luxuries and refinements unimagined by their ancestors. Like other revisionists, Mukerji emphasizes the symbolic and communicative aspect of objects. The goods so eagerly consumed by the nobility, she argues, carried with them a new appreciation of the art of living and prompted a search for a more efficient system of production. Consumption, formerly seen as a by-product of capitalism (of late capitalism at that), thus comes to be understood as one of its principal causes.

This is not the place to comment on the strengths and weaknesses of these revisionist interpretations of consumption. One point needs to be made in conclusion, however. By depicting the culture of consumption in a genial light and by vastly extending its chronological scope, revisionism makes it seem more inescapable than ever. Critics of consumption in the 1960s and 1970s, even though they probably exaggerated the "cultural hegemony" of those who controlled and directed it, wrote in hopes that it might eventually give way to a more satisfying way of life—to a participatory democracy as opposed to a democracy of consumption. As these hopes recede, consumption takes on a certain air of inevitability. If we believe the revisionists, a culture of consumption has been with us for a long time and shows no sign of disappearing. Consumption is now experienced, by historians no less than by the general public, as the "very element in which we all breathe," in Michael Denning's words (Agnew, "Coming Up for Air," p. 12). These words testify, if nothing else, to its powerful grip on the contemporary imagination.

BIBLIOGRAPHY

Primary Materials Cited

Boorstin, Daniel J. *The Image: The Guide to Pseudo-Events in America* (rev. ed. 1972).

Conant, Charles A. "The Economic Basis of 'Imperialism.'" *North American Review* 167 (1898).

Galbraith, John Kenneth. *The Affluent Society* (1958).

Miller, James. *"Democracy Is in the Streets": From Port Huron to the Siege of Chicago* (1987). Contains the complete text of the Port Huron Statement.

Parker, Theodore. "A Letter on Slavery" (1847). In *The Slave Power,* edited by James K. Hosmer (n.d.).

Patten, Simon. *The New Basis of Civilization* (1907; repr. 1968).

Roszak, Theodore. *The Making of a Counter Culture: Reflections on the Technocratic Society and Its Youthful Opposition* (1969).

Schlesinger, Arthur M., Jr. *The Age of Roosevelt: The Coming of the New Deal* (1959). Contains material on back-to-the-land movements in the 1930s.

Slater, Philip. *The Pursuit of Loneliness: American Culture at the Breaking Point* (1970).

Smith, Adam. *The Theory of Moral Sentiments* (1759). Edited by D. D. Raphael and A. L. Macfie (1976).

———. *The Wealth of Nations* (1776). Edited by Belfort Bax. 2 vols. (1908).

Weyl, Walter. *The New Democracy* (1912).

Historical Studies of Consumption

Agnew, Jean-Christophe. "Coming Up for Air: Consumer Culture in Historical Perspective." *Intellectual History Newsletter* 12 (1990).

Bronner, Simon J., ed. *Consuming Visions* (1989).

Campbell, Colin. *The Romantic Ethic and the Spirit of Modern Consumerism* (1987).

Denning, Michael. *Mechanic Accents: Dime Novels and Working-Class Culture in America* (1987).

Edsforth, Ronald. *Class Conflict and Cultural Consensus: The Making of a Mass Consumer Society in Flint, Michigan* (1987).

Ewen, Stuart. *Captains of Consciousness: Advertising and the Social Roots of the Consumer Culture* (1976).

Horowitz, Daniel. *The Morality of Spending: Attitudes Toward the Consumer Society in America, 1875–1940* (1985).

Jameson, Fredric. "Reification and Utopia in Mass Culture." *Social Text* 1 (1979).

Kasson, John. *Amusing the Million: Coney Island at the Turn of the Century* (1978).

King, Richard. *The Party of Eros: Radical Social Thought and the Realm of Freedom* (1972).

Leach, William R. "Transformations in a Culture of Consumption: Women and Department Stores, 1890–1925." *Journal of American History* 71 (1984).

Lears, T. J. Jackson, and Richard Wightman Fox, eds. *The Culture of Consumption: Critical Essays in American History, 1880–1980* (1983).

Leuchtenburg, William E. *A Troubled Feast: American Society Since 1945* (rev. ed. 1979).

Lipsitz, George. *Time Passages: Collective Memory and Popular Culture* (1989).

McCracken, Grant. *Culture and Consumption: New Approaches to the Symbolic Character of Consumer Goods and Activities* (1988).

McKendrick, Neil, John Brewer, and J. H. Plumb. *The Birth of a Consumer Society: The Commercialization of Eighteenth-Century England* (1982).

Marchand, Roland. *Advertising the American Dream: Making Way for Modernity, 1920–1940* (1985).

Meikle, Jeffrey L. *Twentieth-Century Limited: Industrial Design in America, 1925–1939* (1979).

Miller, Daniel. *Material Culture and Mass Consumption* (1987).

Mukerji, Chandra. *From Graven Images: Patterns of Modern Materialism* (1983).

Peiss, Kathy. *Cheap Amusements: Working Women and Leisure in Turn-of-the-Century New York* (1986).

Rosenzweig, Roy. *"Eight Hours for What We Will": Workers and Leisure in an Industrial City, 1870–1920* (1983).

Ross, Andrew. *No Respect: Intellectuals and Popular Culture* (1989).

Susman, Warren. *Culture as History: The Transformation of American Society in the Twentieth Century* (1984).

Wilson, Elizabeth. *Adorned in Dreams: Fashion and Modernity* (1987).

SEE ALSO **Communications and Information Processing; Mass Culture and Its Critics; Modern America: The 1960s, 1970s, and 1980s; Modernization Theory and Its Critics; The Postwar Period Through the 1950s; The Rise and Consolidation of Bourgeois Culture; The Suburbs; Technology and Social Change; Television.**

Part IX

WORK AND LABOR

AGRICULTURE

Nan Elizabeth Woodruff

THE EUROPEAN INVASION of North America grew out of the social dislocation wrought by the transition from feudalism to capitalism in seventeenth- and eighteenth-century European, especially English, society. Land enclosure drove people from the countryside into the cities and left those remaining on the land in a state of impoverishment. The commercialization of agriculture in the English countryside was paralleled in the cities by an emerging bourgeoisie and a growing class of paupers. English society in the seventeenth century was increasingly characterized by class conflict and religious and political strife. The settlement of North America originated in this caldron of privilege and dispossession. Many who came to the colonies sought to escape the ravages of capitalism while benefiting from its successes. Thus the history of early American agrarian life was shaped by contradictory actions as the settlers sought to reap the rewards offered by the Atlantic economy while avoiding some of its harsher aspects.

When the first English settlers arrived in Jamestown, Virginia, they began a process of conquest that would take three centuries to complete. When it was over, the boundaries of the United States would stretch across the Pacific to Hawaii, reach toward the Arctic as far as Alaska, and south into the islands of the Caribbean. Whether carried out by the southern slave-owner, the sturdy pioneer family, the gold rusher, or the rancher or cattleman, the conquest of this vast territory brought with it genocide, slavery, indentured servitude, and peonage. It was a process marked by violence and greed coupled with hope for a better life, and it brought into sharp conflict different notions of property, liberty, and individualism.

The free labor society that had emerged in seventeenth-century England was not immediately transplanted to the New World. Instead, as Eugene Genovese has argued, the transition from feudalism to capitalism and the rise of free labor in Western Europe led, ironically, to the creation of various forms of unfree labor in the New World. With the exception of the early New England Puritans, the majority of those who came to America in the seventeenth and eighteenth centuries came as indentured servants, redemptioners, convicts, or slaves. And as the settlers moved farther west, they encountered the labor systems of an earlier conquest—the Spanish haciendas that employed various forms of tribute, peonage, and slavery.

Thus the history of American agriculture reflects less the traditional story, chronicled in school textbooks, of a free people conquering a wilderness and liberating primitive natives from their backward cultures and economies. Instead, the development of American agriculture must be understood within the context of the emergence of Western capitalism and the process of making a nation-state. Its history was embedded in the expansion of a world-market economy, even though many regions retained noncapitalist forms of production until after the Civil War. The rise of American capitalism, then, was not a unilinear process but involved the transformation of different kinds of subsistence and labor systems that spanned the hunter and gatherer societies of Native Americans as far north as Alaska, the haciendas of the Southwest, the southern slave plantations, and the partially subsistence households of the northern colonies and the southern backcountry. It was a process marked by resistance and at times by violence.

One of the first problems encountered by the colonists was the hundreds of thousands, probably millions, of native peoples, who had inhabited North America for over ten thousand years. The numerous tribes that peopled the coasts of North America practiced various forms of subsistence agriculture or lived as hunters and gatherers. During the early years, colonists in all regions traded and often maintained good terms with the many tribes.

However, as the demand for reliable labor increased, many Europeans, especially in the southern colonies, turned to the enslavement of the native peoples. The attempts at enslavement were not generally successful, though South Carolinians managed a rather profitable Indian slave trade with the Caribbean.

The invasion of America had disastrous consequences for the Indians. Disease killed thousands while others perished in the many wars that characterized the first decades. And the intrusion of the Atlantic economy, especially the trade in furs, hides, guns, and liquor, undermined the subsistence economy of the preconquest years. As the Indians came to realize that the settlers intended not only to stay but to occupy most of the land, they increased their opposition to what was no longer an invasion but a conquest.

The extermination of the native peoples was crucial to the growth of the colonial economy, for without land the northern family farms and the southern plantations could not survive. Indeed, as events in Virginia revealed, the lack of land could lead to major class conflict. During the seventeenth century, Virginia had developed a staple-crop economy based on tobacco and worked by indentured servants. By the 1660s, the number of servants completing their contracts increased. Plantation owners, faced with a labor shortage, illegally extended the terms of their laborers' contracts and worked them as hard as slaves. Freedom became an equally difficult struggle for those who managed to survive the terms of their indenture. Physically worn out from their years as field laborers and often deprived of their legal claim to land, money, and tools, most became landless and poverty-stricken.

By the late seventeenth century, Virginia experienced increasing class conflict as a growing group of landless white men demanded land and opportunity. However, their aspirations were stymied in the east by plantation owners who did not welcome small landowners, and in the west by Indians. These growing class tensions erupted in Bacon's Rebellion in 1676, when property owners on the frontier defeated the Indians and opened up new lands for the landless. Virginia, like other southern colonies, was characterized by a slave economy bordered by a backcountry yeomanry. The cost of yeomen's freedom, then, was borne by the enslavement of Africans and the extermination of the Indians.

On the eve of the American Revolution, the colonies had developed into regional economies that were defined as much by the labor employed as by the crops produced. The New England and Middle Atlantic colonies consisted of small family farms that produced grains and livestock. In sharp contrast, the Hudson River valley estates employed a mixture of tenants, indentured servants, hired hands, and slaves, while in the South, a staple-crop economy emerged that was based on African slavery.

During the late eighteenth century, these regional economies experienced dramatic growth. Population increases in the new nation and in Europe during the 1790s created a demand for foodstuffs both at home and abroad. In the northern colonies, rural society was increasingly transformed by an expanding market that reached into the rural households, and in the southern colonies, the invention of the cotton gin, combined with a growing market for cotton, breathed new life into a flagging slave economy. The growing commercialization of the northern agrarian society and the expansion of the southern slave economy led to increasing class conflict over questions of land and its relationship to the broader issues of political and economic rights. Whether it was the Regulators of the Carolinas, the anti-rent rioters in the Hudson Valley, or participants in Shays's Rebellion in western and central Massachusetts, at issue was the right of small-scale producers to have access to land and protection from the vagaries of the market. Yeomen's struggles to retain control over their property and production would continue in the North until the Civil War, and in the South and West until the late nineteenth century. Rural capitalism was met in the countryside with ambivalence as households sought the benefits of the market without the exploitation. The republican ideology of the Revolution gave meaning to their struggles, as Thomas Jefferson and others argued that democracy rested on the ability of small producers to control their property and the means of production.

Thus, the petty commodity producers of rural America entered the nineteenth century armed with an ideology that encouraged them to participate in commercial production while warning them against debt and the vagaries of the market. However, few households could survive without the commodities that the market offered. Their struggles to balance their household economy with capitalist penetration defined the lives of rural families until 1860. In the North, a rapidly expanding industrial order shaped the response of households, while in the plantation South, yeomen found themselves hedged in by a slave economy. Thus the stages and ways in which small farmers entered the market were contoured by the dominant productive relations of the societies in which they lived.

Most antebellum northern farmers sought to maintain some degree of autonomy over a household economy that was based on a local exchange of mutuality and reciprocity. Neighboring households traded their labor and their produce for needed goods or services. Within the household itself, the division of labor was along gender lines. The men were responsible for the cultivation of the crops while women maintained the home and cared for the children. Yet both often shared in making candles, soap, and textiles, and either might tend the barn or the garden, usually with the help of their children. The survival of the household depended in part on the ability of children to inherit land.

The farms that dotted the northern countryside were embedded in a growing industrial capitalist market that increasingly undermined the autonomy of the households. By the 1820s, declining fertility rates and land shortages, combined with an expanding textile industry in the towns, led to a growth in rural wage labor and an increase in household manufacturing. Farm women participated directly in a larger market as they traded their handmade textiles to local merchants for household commodities and luxury items. On one level, the penetration of industrial capitalism into the countryside allowed women to earn wages that sustained the household and prevented family members from having to migrate to the factories or to the West. Yet on another level, the outwork system undermined the old ways of subsistence and barter. Thus, the rise of industrial capitalism transformed the countryside by incorporating it into the wage labor and consumer markets. In turn, household labor played a crucial role in the rise of northern industry.

An emerging capitalist North based on free labor and political democracy contrasted sharply with the southern slave economy that vested property rights in both land and humans. As Eugene Genovese has argued, after 1820 a mature slave-owning class had developed that rejected the principles of economic and political liberalism. It was a society that was decidedly noncapitalist, participating in a national and global market while maintaining a world based on slave labor.

The slave economy had major implications for the yeomen who lived on the periphery of the plantations. Unlike their northern counterparts, southern yeomen had more limited access to a market economy. Planters refused to provide the internal improvements necessary to link the plantations with the backcountry subsistence farms. Thus, in contrast with Europe and the North, yeomen were limited in their ability to participate as small commodity producers in a regional commercial economy. Instead, they existed as semi-subsistence farmers until the consequences of the Civil War forced them into an emerging capitalist economy.

Both the free labor North and the slave South depended upon the vast lands of the western territories for the survival of their economies. Northern farmers escaping the encroachments of a capitalist market joined southern backcountrymen and aspiring slave owners in search of more and better land. The Louisiana Purchase in 1803 and the defeat of Native Americans following the War of 1812 opened the Missouri and Ohio territories, with slave owners generally moving into the region south of Missouri and the small landowners taking the lands in what became Illinois and Indiana. Settlement in the West, however, was laden with ideological significance, for the millions of acres of public domain held the key to the nation's economic and political survival.

The settlement of the western territories was connected to the national policies of the newly created American republic. For Thomas Jefferson and his successors, an abundance of land made possible the realization of a citizenry of independent small property owners unimpeded by the class divisions of the Old World. Without the shackles of servitude or wage labor, these small commodity producers would sustain the republican virtues of independence and hard work. Thus, the national land policies from the Northwest Ordinance of 1787 to the Homestead Act of 1862 sought in principle to provide cheap land to family farmers. However, the reality of land distribution and labor relations on the frontier often fell short of this democratic vision.

The settlement of the ever-extending frontier in the nineteenth century must be understood within the context of the emergence of capitalism in the Northeast. With the rise of factories and towns came a demand for agricultural products, and by the eve of the Civil War, a network of roads, railways, and canals had connected the hinterlands to the northeastern markets. Thus, the first generation of settlers lived initially as subsistence households. But by the 1840s, agrarian life on the frontier increasingly resembled the harsher realities of the commercial world many had sought to escape.

What kinds of communities did the pioneers create during the antebellum years? The answer to this question depended upon time and place. For example, the initial settlements in Illinois differed from those in the Southwest, California, or Hawaii. Access to land and the market depended upon the kinds of labor and tenure relations encountered in the different regions.

Sugar Creek, a community in central Illinois that was settled in 1818 by families from the southern up-country, represented one kind of frontier community. Unable to plow the hard sod, most families cleared the trees and planted where the soil was softer. Family labor and neighborly reciprocity sustained Sugar Creek until the 1850s, for most lacked income to hire wage labor. However, as in New England, households could not survive completely outside of the market. It took money to move west, and many had to borrow from loan sharks at exorbitant rates. Farm improvements also required money, as did necessities such as gunpowder, crockery, and coffee. Farmers searched for ways to obtain cash by trying to sell hogs and garden products. However, Sugar Creek was isolated from the roads that fed into the expanding area of Springfield, Illinois. Farm women, as they had in New England, earned much of the money for the household by selling their eggs, butter, and textiles to local merchants.

Family farm owners were only half of the population in Sugar Creek. The other part of the community consisted of squatters who built log cabins on unclaimed lands, grazed their livestock on the commons, and hooked timber from the Congress lands. During the 1830s and 1840s, however, these squatters were displaced as the expansion of the eastern market through railways and roads brought land speculators. Inspired by technological innovations such as the steel plow, horse-powered corn planters, mowers, reapers, and machine threshers, speculators carved up the common lands and sold them to local farmers looking to expand their operations or to newly arrived settlers. With the destruction of public lands for woodcutting and the abolition of a commons for grazing, the squatters lost any chance of becoming landowners.

By 1850, Sugar Creek had become a community divided along class lines as the landowners extended their holdings and hired the former squatters as wage hands or tenants. Thus farmers now became landlords and employers, while the squatters lost any rights to the land and became wage workers or tenants. Subsistence households, whether of squatters or of freeholders, represented the transitional form of agricultural society until the expanding northeastern economy pulled the outlying regions into its orbit.

By 1860 the prairie cornbelt had been established and integrated into the spreading market economy. And, if Sugar Creek was any example, only a few families prospered. Most either moved farther west, onto the Great Plains, or followed the Overland Trail into Oregon and California. Still others became hired laborers or tenants with little hope of obtaining land of their own. The Jeffersonian vision of a nation based on an independent yeomanry removed from debt and oppression was not often the reality of the frontier.

The yeoman's dream certainly floundered in the Southwest, where settlers encountered the Spanish land system that dated back to the sixteenth-century conquest. In southwest Texas, Mexican hacendados used peon labor to raise cattle in a system that resembled the paternalistic slave-owning South. Property existed not for individual ownership but for the inheritance and continuation of lineages. The livestock was raised not for the market but to sustain the hacienda. In 1836, the hacendados were defeated when the Republic of Texas was created. Entailed notions of property were quickly replaced by those of private property when the republic declared all Mexican livestock public property. With the help of the Texas Rangers and cowboys, ranches were raided and the landowners were forced through violence and intimidation to sell or abandon their lands. However, the Texas conquest did not go unchallenged. In 1859–1860, Juan Cortina led many displaced peons in raids against the Texans and briefly held the Rangers at bay. In the end, the Anglos prevailed, attached themselves to the Mexican hierarchy through intermarriage, and continued as ranchers.

The Mexican-American War brought in additional domains that stretched from Texas to California. Within these new territories were landowning elites who employed various forms of unfree labor. For example, in New Mexico the *partidaro* system existed, whereby a patron loaned land and sheep to the head of a household, who owed payment in the form of ewes. Under this system, over twenty families controlled the economy of New Mexico in the nineteenth century. As late as 1900, one patron had access to over twenty-seven thousand ewes through the *partidaro*.

When the gold rushers and land seekers reached the coast of California, they encountered a Spanish tenure arrangement that included haciendas and missions that employed Indian labor to raise cattle. After 1848, California entered a period of transformation, especially after the 1860s when railroads connected the region with markets in the East. However, California did not produce a land of yeomen farmers; rather, the large Spanish estates were transferred to the American owners, who used vagrancy laws to impress Indian labor. By the 1850s, the agricultural economy was characterized by bonanza farms that produced wheat and other cereals until the Civil War. However, labor continued to be a problem, and many migrants from the South argued for the adoption of African slavery. When that possibility was lost, landowners turned to Chinese contract labor until the 1880s. The roots of the large-scale agribusiness economy that dominated California in the late nineteenth and twentieth centuries were planted in the early years of conquest.

Historians have traditionally discussed the American West within the context of expansion to California. However, there were two other quite different regions that would eventually become states. In Alaska, the Aleutian peoples lived as hunters and fishermen, while across the Pacific, native Hawaiians worked plots of land under various chiefdoms. Both societies differed considerably from that of Sugar Creek.

The first American sugar planters arrived in Hawaii in the 1830s. They justified their invasion by arguing that they were emancipating a backward people from an oppressive chiefdom. Instead, native peoples lost their land and were turned into plantation wage laborers who were paid in scrip. Landowners never had enough labor, however, because the majority of native peoples had been killed by diseases introduced by explorers and traders in the late eighteenth and early nineteenth centuries. And of those who remained, few were willing to work on the terms established by their new conquerors. Consequently, the planters were forced to recruit Chinese contract laborers who worked the processing mills while natives sweated in the sugar fields.

The sugar plantation economy accelerated in 1848–1850, when land tenure laws were changed to allow non-natives to purchase property. In addition, the California gold rush created a market not only for sugar but also for vegetables, turkeys, and swine. Near the end of the century, five American companies controlled the political economy of the islands.

By the time of the Civil War, the rapidly expanding capitalist economy of the Northern states had reached as far as Hawaii to encompass many different land and labor systems that produced a wide variety of products. This growth was fueled by state policies that subsidized railroads and land speculators, and privileged commercial production over other forms of agriculture. Technological changes also contributed to the commercialization of agriculture and to further concentration of land and capital as fewer farmers had the money to purchase additional land or to mechanize.

While the territorial limits of the continental United States were established by 1860, the actual incorporation of these regions and their peoples into a nation remained to be accomplished. The defeat of the slave South paved the way for the final expansion of capitalism and the creation of a nation-state based on the principles of economic and political liberalism. Yet the incorporation of regional elites and labor systems entailed new definitions of liberty, property, and citizenship that clashed with views rooted in republican notions of free labor or, in the case of Native Americans, in a communal vision of property. In any case, the expansion of capitalist agriculture in the late nineteenth century brought in its wake violence and social dislocation. Its triumph was not without challenge.

The American Civil War destroyed the noncapitalist slave South and emancipated more than three million slaves. However, the meaning of that newly won freedom was a contested issue that was not settled for decades. Nor could the struggle over the meaning of freedom for the freed men and women be understood outside the context of the white yeomen or the former slave owners. Above all, the destruction of slavery required new definitions of property and citizenship. The postbellum South was shaped by constant class conflict as planters, freedmen, and yeomen clashed over the issues surrounding landownership and labor. At issue were the rights of the freedmen to have access to land and to control their own labor. This notion of freedom collided with that of the former masters who sought to retain a dependent labor force, at first through coercion and force, then through the legal power of the state.

As soon as Yankee troops liberated portions of the plantation South, former slaves asserted their independence. Initial efforts of northern planters and missionaries to discipline the freedmen as free workers encountered tremendous resistance. Nor did freedmen heed their former masters' orders to work on what they considered unfair terms. They challenged planter efforts to impose gang labor and other forms of coercion by withdrawing women and children from the fields, by joining Union League Clubs, by boycotting and striking for decent working conditions, and by disputing crop settlements. Planters responded to such militancy by passing vagrancy and apprentice laws and other forms of coercion designed to force freedmen back to work on landowners' terms.

The struggle over land and labor in the post-bellum South centered on different notions of freedom and property. During slavery, many slaves had insisted on and secured the right to maintain their own gardens and livestock, to fish and to hunt. After the war, they avoided working for the planters by continuing these subsistence activities. By the 1870s, planters employed the legal instruments of the state to control their labor force. Through fishing, game, and fence laws, freedmen lost access to their subsistence and were left with no alternative but to work on the plantations in what had emerged as the system of sharecropping. Growing out of the refusal of blacks to work as gang laborers, sharecropping allowed freedmen to retain limited access to the land. As Harold Woodman has shown, it was a form of wage labor whereby the worker received his wages in the form of a share of the crop—usually one-half or one-fourth. The planter provided housing, food, clothing, tools, and the means of production. Credit was issued at the commissary, where workers had to purchase all of their necessities at high prices and an interest rate that was as high as 20 percent. After the harvest, accounts were settled and the cropper families almost always came out deeper in debt. In its most extreme form, the new plantation economy led to debt peonage.

While freedmen fought over rights to the land and their labor, the up-country yeomen struggled to retain their semi-subsistence households that were based on local exchange, reciprocity, and common rights to the land. After the war, railroads and merchants moved into the upper piedmont and backcountry hills, bringing with them the cotton economy. The rapidly expanding market, combined with fencing and game laws, transformed the subsistence farmers into cotton producers who relied heavily on merchant credit. Poor harvests and the crop-lien system drove many into bankruptcy and

tenancy. Yeomen and freedmen alike learned the meaning of freedom in the emerging capitalist order. For both it spelled dispossession and powerlessness.

The freedmen's struggles over landownership and decent wages, the transformation of the yeomanry, and the expansion of the market economy led to the southern agrarian movements of the late nineteenth century. The National Farmers' Alliance and Industrial Union, or the Southern Farmers Alliance, was formed in the late 1870s in the Cross Timbers section of Texas to combat the economic woes of southern farmers. The southern alliance was one of three such alliances. A "northern" alliance was organized in 1880 in Chicago as the National Farmers' Alliance and gained considerable support in the Midwest. A third, the Colored Farmers' National Alliance, was formed in 1886 in Texas as the segregated counterpart to the southern alliance. Of these, the southern alliance was the largest and played the most significant role in what would become the Populist party in the 1890s. The Alliance movement embodied the republican ideology of small semi-subsistence farmers who believed that democracy rested in the right of small producers to control the fruits of their own labor. Their demands for a subtreasury system and public ownership of railroads and telegraph companies, represented their efforts to democratize the growing centralization of economic and political power. As Steven Hahn has argued, they sought the creation of a "cooperative commonwealth" similar to the vision advocated by the Knights of Labor and the Greenback Labor party.

The Alliance movement swept into the Midwest as well, where farmers were caught in a web of indebtedness, rising rates of tenancy, and exploitation by middlemen, bankers, and railroads. In spite of the Homestead Act of 1862, farmers found it difficult to secure 160 acres of good land, for most of the public domain had been parceled out to railroads and mining companies. While midwestern farmers did not have to compete with a plantation system, they had a similar problem with the large bonanza corn farms in Illinois and Indiana, and the wheat estates in the Red River valley of North Dakota. These concerns were run like modern businesses with managers, accountants, and wage labor.

In the Populist challenge, small producers waged a rearguard battle against the encroachments of capitalism. Drawing from a republican heritage that stressed a society of small farmers, artisans, and

1398

businessmen, the Populists sought to democratize both the polity and the economy. The subtreasury system, the nationalization of railroads and telegraph companies, the direct primary, and many other of their reforms aimed to return government and the economy to the world of the petty producers. The Republican party's victory in the 1896 presidential election signaled the triumph of the corporate order and removed a large number of Americans from the political arena.

The Populists failed in part because of limitations within the movement. Their base consisted of classes of farmers whose interests were not always compatible. By stressing the credit and marketing side of farming, leaders avoided confronting the issue of land distribution and the related question of tenancy, sharecropping, and casual labor. Both large and small landowners and their tenants suffered the ravages of the market and middlemen, and thus could rally around a platform that called for their regulation. But to call into question the actual productive relations in the countryside would have focused attention on other aspects of class conflict that landowners sought to avoid.

Thus, that wing of populism which belonged mainly to the larger landowners and town businessmen saw its goals accomplished during the Progressive Era. Congress provided funds for cooperatives, agricultural credit, and the establishment of the Agricultural Extension Service and an expansion of funding for the land-grant colleges. These reforms combined with the highest farm prices in American history to create boom times for American farmers until World War I.

However, these good times were not shared by all. In the South, for example, the defeat of populism resolved the struggle over the meaning of freedom that was raised with the abolition of slavery. The plantation economy actually expanded in the first two decades of the twentieth century and was undergirded by segregation and disfranchisement. In the Arkansas and Mississippi deltas there emerged large-scale business plantations that were often owned by corporations from the North and England; were run by professional managers and accountants; and were advised by county agents who stressed scientific farming. Thousands of black sharecroppers and wage hands labored under close supervision, often working in gangs. Antienticement laws that prohibited the recruitment of labor by employers outside the country, peonage, and planter control of the local authorities ensured that few would find other employment. Not until the great migration of World War I would southern African Americans find genuine alternative opportunities.

Plantation agriculture was only part of the modern southern economy. In the older cotton and tobacco regions, small farmers and tenants eked out an existence amid a declining world market, the boll weevil, and soil erosion. The twentieth-century rural South, with its large-scale plantations and an impoverished class of sharecroppers and tenant farmers, resembled the underdeveloped regions of a colonial world. Its wrenching poverty was manifested in high rates of illiteracy and death from preventable diseases combined with the lowest standard of living in the country—a condition that bore testimony to the success of the capitalist revolution initiated by the Civil War.

The rise of business agriculture in the South and Midwest following the Civil War mirrored developments in the Southwest and the West as the expansion of capitalist agriculture led to a growing concentration of land and capital coupled with a rise in indebtedness and tenancy. As in the South, the incorporation of the West involved resolving questions of land and labor.

The development of the West involved far more than the trek of pioneers and corporations, for in defeating the slave South, radical Republicans had raised the issue of citizenship and had vested it with promises of education, political participation, and landownership. While southerners of all classes and races struggled throughout the late nineteenth century over the questions surrounding citizenship and landownership, a similar conflict occurred in the West over the status of Native Americans. Federal policymakers joined northeastern reformers, land-hungry settlers, and corporations in a battle over the future of the Indians. When it was over, Native Americans found themselves in much the same situation as southern blacks—segregated and disfranchised. Reservations were not plantations, but the power relations that governed their creation and operation were not very different.

As the growing number of homesteaders realized that most of the public lands had been taken by larger business concerns, they turned to the Indian lands for relief. Corporations also had their eyes on those lands, for some of them contained rich sources of minerals and others blocked the expansion of railroad lines. Thus, by the 1870s the "Indian problem" became a major issue for American policymakers, who linked the question of Indian citizenship and landownership to economic expansion. Strengthened by scientific theory, reformers, intellectuals, and politicians argued that Indian lands stood in the way of progress and the march of civilization. No people, they insisted, had the right to live on undeveloped property. And according to leading anthropologists, the only salvation for native peoples lay in displacing them from the tribal lands which they held sacred and which were connected to "primitive" rituals. If Indians were settled on individual farms, their ties to their sacred land and rituals would be severed. Whether couched in the lofty terms of uplift and reform or the language of corporate self-interest, the federal policies as they related to Indians had the same effect—displacement and further impoverishment.

The solution devised incorporated notions of citizenship with economic expansion. Indians would be civilized through ownership of small plots and through education. Once they had been integrated into a booming economy, their success would be reward enough for the loss of their lands. Reformers assumed that the engine propelling civilization was private property. Their views found expression in the passage of the Dawes General Allotment Act in 1887, which provided for individual allotments giving citizenship to all Indians who took an allotment as well as to those who moved off reservations. Once Indians had proven their ability to manage their own farms, they would be granted citizenship. The surplus lands were to be sold to the public with tribal consent.

The allotment plan failed to meet the demands for more land. By the turn of the century, the population and economy of the western states had rapidly expanded as railroads united agricultural markets in the Midwest with the Pacific Coast. Urbanization placed further demands on agricultural production. In the face of increasing demands for acreage, most tribes refused to sell their surplus lands, especially when they were not offered the market price for them. Frustrated by this obstinacy, politicians and businessmen appealed to the Supreme Court to gain access to tribal holdings. The Court granted their wish by allowing Congress to negate treaties and to sell Indian lands without tribal approval. The first decades of the twentieth century saw the seizure and sale of millions of tribal acres. In addition, Congress used the funds from these sales to launch massive irrigation projects on the reservations. Since the concept of beneficial use governed access to water, any Indians who did not farm their irrigated lands stood to lose them to their more aggressive white neighbors who obtained government leases. Thousands of acres of tribal lands were leased to mining and corporate agricultural interests. As Frederick E. Hoxie has shown, by the twentieth century, a campaign to assimilate the Indians as citizens had turned into one to integrate their natural resources into the national economy, with the Indians taking the hindmost.

Corporate agriculture also swept across southwest Texas, transforming the cattle haciendas of the border region and the cowboy culture of the Panhandle. The removal of the Apaches and Comanches in the 1870s opened up new lands in the central and northern plains of Texas. Initially independent ranchers and cowboys grazed their livestock on the open range. However, in the 1880s, English, Scottish, and northeastern capital moved into the region, formed cattlemen's associations to fight the homesteaders and cowboys, and enclosed the range. The fence wars of the 1880s represented the last struggle of homesteaders and independent ranchers to survive in the Panhandle, for they viewed their access to open ranges and water supplies as a common right. At issue was a redefinition of property rights that shifted the balance of power from small producers to corporate operators.

The development of the Texas frontier, then, consisted of claiming land, livestock, and water as private property. Thus, the world of the independent rancher and cowboy gave way to the corporate holdings such as the famous King Ranch. Consisting in 1885 of 500,000 acres, Richard King's ranch operated like a Mississippi Delta plantation with its own commissary, homes for five hundred workers, wagon sheds, blacksmith shops, and stables. By 1932, it had grown to encompass almost 1.25 million acres. The Texas cattle industry could match any industrial concern in the East with its millions of acres of cattle supervised by cowboys who lived in bunkhouses and worked as wage laborers. And cowboys often behaved like the proletariat they had become by engaging in strikes for better wages and working conditions.

Farther south, along the Mexican border, the expansion of capitalist agriculture destroyed the remnants of a cattle hacienda system, replacing it with large-scale vegetable and cotton farms worked by Mexican migrant labor. By 1900 the ranch societies of both the border and parts of central Texas gave way to commercial farming. Overgrazing, northern quarantine laws, and world overproduction, combined with the development of refrigerated cars and the refinement of irrigation technology, made vegetable and cotton production a profitable business. In addition, the rapid exhaustion of free lands in the plains led farmers from that region into Texas in search of greater profits. However, the invading capitalists did not always acquire their lands through the most ethical means, often using violence and intimidation to obtain the property of reluctant Mexican American landowners.

Capitalist penetration of the border regions did not go unchallenged. As David Montejano has shown, the Mexican American peons and small ranchers, who were displaced when the hacendados left, fought their decline into wage labor. Social tensions culminated in 1915–1916 in the Plan de San Diego when bands of displaced peons and rancheros raided farms, burned bridges, derailed trains, and sabotaged irrigation pumps. For five months they held the landowners in captive fear. In the end, they were defeated by the Texas Rangers, who used the rebellion as an excuse to invade Mexican American communities, murdering innocent people and forcing others to sign over their lands. By the 1920s, the agricultural economy of southwest Texas had developed into a class system that placed Anglos in control of production while Mexican Americans were relegated to the status of wage laborers.

Of all the regional agricultural economies that emerged after the Civil War, California stood as the most spectacular symbol of corporate agriculture. The expansion of the transcontinental railroads created markets for California fruits and vegetables throughout the country. Improvements in irrigation technology allowed the cultivation of thousands of acres of semiarid lands.

A persistent concern of the California growers centered on the issue of labor. Citrus and vegetable crops required large quantities of unskilled labor during the harvest. Thus, landowners sought to secure the cheapest seasonal wage workers. After the Chinese Exclusion Act (1882) was passed, they turned to Japanese workers. However, the Japanese proved far too independent for the corporate farmers. Using their own contractors, they bargained for lower wages and thereby became the dominant labor pool. Then they withheld their labor until owners paid them decent wages. Even worse, their goal was to become landowners. Their success in achieving this end resulted in 1910 in legislation restricting their rights to own land. Growers did not tolerate any competition, even that of small commodity producers like the Japanese.

From 1910 until the eve of World War I, California growers relied on a predominantly white labor force as people were driven back to the land during the economic hard times that preceded the war. These years also saw the first efforts to organize California agricultural workers; both the conservative American Federation of Labor and the radical Industrial Workers of the World (IWW) launched unsuccessful organizing campaigns. Not until the 1930s would farmworkers mount a major challenge to the landowners' power.

After World War I, California growers turned to a predominantly Mexican migrant labor force. Like southern plantation owners, the fruit and citrus companies of California exercised unparalleled control over their workers. Remembering the influence of the IWW during the war, landowners in the 1920s established cooperative labor bureaus in conjunction with the Farm Bureau Federation, the chambers of commerce, and the farm employers' associations. Utilizing local law-enforcement officials, the labor bureaus enforced wage agreements and eliminated competition for workers. Above all, these measures made labor organizing more difficult, for no longer could workers strike on a single farm. Instead, they would have to organize an entire region. Thus, as Cletus Daniel has argued, as industry in the 1920s saw the rise of welfare capitalism, in the fields of California, corporate farmers sought to cut costs by further reducing their laborers' standard of living.

As in industry, the development of agriculture in the United States from the end of the Civil War until World War I was marked by growing consolidation and specialization. The formation of growers' associations in California, Texas, Hawaii, and the South revealed that large-scale producers viewed themselves as part of the emerging corporate world. Their connections to the research wings of the U.S. Agricultural Extension Service and the state agricultural universities placed them in the forefront of scientific knowledge as it related to agricultural modernization and efficiency.

The agrarian unrest of the late nineteenth and early twentieth centuries, then, must be understood within the context of the rise of corporate agriculture. Whether it was in the form of the Southern Alliance members, Grangers, Populists, or the strikers on the sugar plantations of Hawaii, the ranches of Texas, and the Delta cotton fields, or in the form of bloody Indian wars, at issue were the rights of small producers to land and of wage workers to decent working conditions. The social upheavals of these years made it clear that farmers were not an undifferentiated mass united by their ties to the soil. Rather, the violence and human misery that accompanied the advance of capitalism in the countryside revealed that class divisions distinguished agrarian life, as they did that in the factories.

In the late nineteenth and early twentieth centuries, regional agricultural elites solved the land and labor problems. In the South, after the defeat of populism, segregation and disfranchisement assured a plantation labor force of poor and unskilled blacks, whereas most whites were confined to tenancy. In the Southwest and in California, corporate agriculture depended on a cheap, controllable, and powerless labor force of Mexican and Chicano labor. And throughout the West, Native Americans lost their lands and were confined to marginal areas that were called reservations. Like African Americans, Chicanos, and Mexicans, they were removed from the realm of citizenship and thus lacked the power to challenge their plight successfully.

Agrarian unrest did not end with populism, for as tenancy continued to rise in the southwestern states, the antimonopoly wing of the Populists in that region merged with the Socialist party to form renters' unions. And along the border in Texas, small farmers, renters, and migrant workers formed the Mexican Protective Association in opposition to the large-scale agriculture that had emerged there. And still farther west, the IWW organized the harvest stiffs in the wheat fields of the Midwest and the migrant workers on the Pacific Coast. In short, the failure of the populist movement did not end dissent. Rather, rural people continued to struggle against the large-scale interests that were destroying their lives.

The antimonopoly strain of populism reached its fullest expression in the Midwest, where it emerged as a significant component of progressivism. One of the major political movements of the twentieth century developed in North Dakota and Minnesota with the creation of the Farmer-Labor party. From its inception, the movement was torn by internal ideological disputes that reflected the different approaches to agricultural problems in the first decades of the twentieth century.

Farmers in the Midwest were surrounded by an industrial world of agricultural processing corporations that deprived producers of a fair share of their crops. A reformist wing, drawing from the Populists, sought to regulate the grain elevators, railroads, warehouses, and banks. These farmers organized into the Equity Cooperative Exchange, which became a model for cooperatives in the twentieth century. As supporters of Theodore Roosevelt's Bull Moose party, they sought enactment of legislation to provide federal support for agricultural credit and cooperatives. During Woodrow Wilson's administration, many of their objectives were realized in the Federal Farm Loan Act (1916). Eventually the cooperatives of the Midwest competed with large companies like Pillsbury and General Mills.

Another wing of the farmer-labor movement grew out of the North Dakota Socialist party. Known as the Nonpartisan League, it sought to form an alliance with labor and to nationalize the banks, railroads, and grain elevators. Its strategy centered on seizing the Republican party and enacting a social democratic platform through the party machinery. The Nonpartisan League achieved success in South Dakota, where in 1919 the legislature created a state-owned bank and flour mill. However, because many of its members opposed America's entry into World War I, the League suffered from wartime antiradical hysteria. Nevertheless, in 1918 the Farmer-Labor party was created and remained a force in midwestern politics until the 1940s (even later in Minnesota), electing several governors, congressmen, and senators.

By far the most important farmers' organization in the twentieth century was the American Farm Bureau Federation. Created in 1920 from a network of local bureaus, it became the major lobbying group for commercial farmers, particularly those in the Midwest and the South. The Farm Bureau stressed the business side of agriculture and sought legislation to secure better farm prices and to improve marketing, transportation, and credit facilities. Another major organization, the Farmers' Union (1927), invested its efforts in forming cooperatives.

All of these farm organizations entered the debates over production and prices that sharpened after 1920 as the wartime boom years gave way to the bust period of the 1920s and 1930s. American agriculture entered a depression as declining world markets led to low prices, the collapse of the rural credit structure, increasing indebtedness, and foreclosures. Following the dictates of the Agricultural Extension Service, farmers had purchased tractors and farm implements, thus increasing their indebtedness. Nor did farm income keep up with costs, for by 1933 farm prices had dropped 63 percent while the costs of implements and motor vehicles had declined only 6 and 16 percent, respectively.

Thus, many commercial growers supported the McNary-Haugen Bill (1928), which called upon the federal government to bring farm prices into parity with those of industry.

Not all sectors of the agricultural economy experienced the depression equally. For example, the plantation South saw the complete collapse of its economy as cotton fell to six cents a pound. Embattled by floods, drought, soil erosion, and the boll weevil, planters reduced the meager earnings of their workers even more. In contrast, large-scale enterprises specializing in vegetables and fruits expanded in the 1920s. Spurred by increasing urbanization, mechanization, better varieties of seeds, and improved irrigation, intensive truck farming increased in the North Atlantic and Pacific Coast states and in the Carolinas, Florida, Texas, and the Great Lakes region.

Thus, the economic crisis of the 1920s did not fall evenly on everyone. Southern sharecroppers and tenant farmers watched as their access to credit and food dwindled and their children died from preventable diseases. And as the Great Depression came, thousands of southern families followed those from other parts of the country into the migrant labor stream, driving out the Mexican Americans, thousands of whom were illegally deported by the federal government. Refugees from federal policies, mechanization, and the Dust Bowl, these black and white families drove west in worn-out cars and trucks in search of work in the giant fields of California. None of the farmers' organizations addressed the desperation of these people.

When the American economy collapsed in the early 1930s, many rural peoples hardly noticed a difference. However, as the Depression deepened, grass-roots agrarian movements emerged all over the nation as workers sought to defend themselves against increasing exploitation resulting from the economic hard times. Still others found themselves worse off due to New Deal reforms. Thus, structural changes combined with federal policies in the 1930s to create massive agrarian unrest.

Federal policymakers held conflicting views about how best to solve the agrarian problem. One group, headed by the American Farm Bureau Federation and the Federal Extension Service, saw the solution in production control and parity payments. For these people, the problem with farming centered on its inability to keep up with the modernizing pace of industry. Others saw farming as a way of life deserving of preservation. For these experts, like Rexford Tugwell, rural society must be reformed to save the small family farmer while elevating the sharecroppers and tenant farmers to the status of landowners.

These opposing views derived from different visions of the role of agrarian life in a democracy. The first saw agriculture as a business and sought to equalize its competitive edge with other sectors of the industrial economy. The second drew from the long-standing republican vision that stressed the importance of small-scale farming to the survival of democracy. They reflected the different directions that American agriculture had followed since the opening of the frontier, and both battled for power in the administration of Franklin Roosevelt.

New Deal agricultural policies reflected these polar ideas. The centerpiece of Roosevelt's agricultural program, the Agricultural Adjustment Administration (AAA), embodied the goals of the Farm Bureau and businessmen. Concerned with boosting prices, the AAA paid farmers to plow under one-third of their crops and to slaughter one-third of their pigs. It favored large-scale producers over smaller ones and actually displaced sharecroppers and tenant farmers. Yet Tugwell and the social planners secured support for their programs in the creation of the Resettlement Administration in 1935 and of the Farm Security Administration (FSA) in 1937, both of which sought to address the needs of small farmers, tenants, and croppers. Under the FSA, farmers were resettled on marginal lands that they purchased at low interest rates. Others lived in cooperatives that combined industrial with agricultural work. The FSA also sought to aid migrants by building government camps for families.

Other New Deal programs sought to integrate rural life into the national economy and society. In a sense, the agrarian problem of the 1930s centered on definitions of modernity and progress. Much of rural America in the early twentieth century had become an eyesore in a nation that was characterized by suburbs, automobiles, department stores, and a vast array of consumer goods and gadgets, radios, and the talking movies. Households and communities came to measure themselves against the ads they saw in magazines or the Sears Roebuck catalog. Pictures of shining kitchens with all of the modern conveniences contrasted sharply with homes that still drew their water from a well, burned kerosene for light, cooked on wood stoves, and scrubbed clothes on washboards.

Thus, many government programs aimed at equalizing rural society with urban, industrial

America. Federal agencies built a massive dam system that brought rural electrification and possibilities for future economic development. Public health programs sought to eradicate hookworm, pellagra, typhoid, malaria, and many other diseases that plagued the countryside. Credit was extended to allow farm improvements as well as home ownership. Soil conservation became a major aspect of agricultural policy as reforestation and grasslands bills sought to replenish the worn-out soils and to prevent future droughts and the Dust Bowl tragedy.

Yet major New Deal measures that granted industrial workers Social Security, a minimum wage, maximum hours, collective bargaining, and the right to organize denied those benefits to the agrarian working class. Indeed, some measures actually worsened their plight. As a result, the 1930s witnessed massive grass-roots mobilization in the countryside. From the southern plantations to the citrus and vegetable fields of California, hundreds of thousands of sharecroppers, tenant farmers, migrants, and wage hands called upon the federal government to grant them economic and political rights. Unfortunately, policymakers turned their ears to the voices of the large landowners.

Some of the most violent strikes in the 1930s occurred in the fields of California, where workers saw their wages reduced drastically. Filipino vegetable and fruit workers and Mexican cotton-pickers organized major strikes in the early 1930s that were met with evictions and violence. California growers, backed by local officials and chambers of commerce, refused to negotiate and gained a reputation for brutal repression. Despite the blatant violation of civil liberties and some murders, the federal government refused to grant a minimum wage to the workers. Not until the 1960s, with the rise of César Chávez and his United Farm Workers Union, would migrant laborers obtain a minimum wage, abolition of child labor, and rights to decent housing and health conditions.

In the plantation South, the AAA displaced thousands of sharecroppers as landowners plowed under their tenants' land and stole their parity checks. In the Arkansas Delta the Southern Tenant Farmers' Union (STFU) was organized in 1934 to obtain the workers' share of the agricultural program. Planters employed the state and local authorities to evict some union members, and to beat and murder others. The terror that swept across the Delta revealed the complete lack of protection for southern rural blacks, as well as many whites, and

made it clear just how far outside the realm of citizenship they were.

The STFU forced a debate within the AAA and the Department of Agriculture over how to deal with southern poverty. Chester Davis, the head of the AAA and a close ally of the plantation owners, argued that conditions were not as bad as the union had presented them. President Roosevelt, fearful of losing his southern support in Congress, sided with Davis and the planters. Thus, the major agricultural legislation of the administration actually worsened rather than relieved the plight of the plantation workers. Those sympathetic to the poor secured the creation of the Farm Security Administration to help croppers and tenants purchase their own farms with low-interest government loans. However, planter opposition, underfunding, and restrictions within the agency meant that few benefited from the FSA.

The 1930s, then, witnessed the collapse of the plantation system of sharecropping and tenant farming as New Deal programs initiated crop diversification, land consolidation, and mechanization. By the 1960s, the agricultural South had made the transition from a labor-intensive to a capital-intensive economy. However, the human costs were high, as thousands were driven from the land, including small family farmers who could not afford to mechanize or who could not compete with the increasingly large estates.

In the long run, the policies underlying the AAA prevailed over those of the social planners. Indeed, the Farm Bureau and its partners on the West Coast lobbied to restrict funding for the FSA and succeeded in destroying it during World War II. Parity and production control remained the essence of agricultural policy for the rest of the twentieth century. After the 1930s, agriculture consolidated into larger concerns, branched out to include processing and marketing in the citrus and poultry businesses, and was based more than ever on scientific management and efficiency. These developments, combined with federal policies that encouraged farmers to invest more in technology, led to the demise of the family farmer.

By the end of the twentieth century, the chicken or beef one purchased in a grocery store more likely came from a subsidiary of Gulf and Western than from a family farm. The business side of agriculture had finally defeated the agrarian vision of farming as a way of life. Thus, family operators of the late twentieth century shared many of the burdens of their ancestors: indebtedness, competition from corporations, and exploitation by middlemen, often in the form of cooperatives supposedly designed to protect their interests. The only difference was that the family farmers, who had played so central a role in American ideology since its inception, were rapidly disappearing, destined to take their place next to the McCormick reaper and the southern sharecroppers in the museums.

BIBLIOGRAPHY

Barron, Hal. *Those Who Stayed Behind: Rural Society in Nineteenth-Century New England* (1984).

Chan, Sucheng. *This Bittersweet Soil: The Chinese in California Agriculture, 1860–1910* (1986).

Clark, Christopher. *The Roots of Rural Capitalism: Western Massachusetts, 1780–1860* (1990).

Cronon, William. *Changes in the Land: Indians, Colonists, and the Ecology of New England* (1983).

Danhof, Clarence H. *Change in Agriculture: The Northern United States, 1820–1870* (1969).

Daniel, Cletus. *Bitter Harvest: A History of California Farmworkers, 1870–1941* (1981).

Daniel, Pete. *Breaking the Land: The Transformation of Cotton, Tobacco, and Rice Cultures Since 1880* (1985).

Faragher, John Mack. *Sugar Creek: Life on the Illinois Prairie* (1986).

Fields, Barbara Jeanne. "The Nineteenth-Century American South: History and Theory." *Plantation Society in the Americas* (April 1983).

———. *Slavery and Freedom on the Middle Ground: Maryland During the Nineteenth Century* (1985).

Fite, Gilbert. *American Farmers: The New Minority* (1981).

Foner, Eric. *Nothing but Freedom: Emancipation and Its Legacy* (1983).

Fox-Genovese, Elizabeth, and Eugene D. Genovese. *The Fruits of Merchant Capital: Slavery and Bourgeois Property in the Rise and Expansion of Capitalism* (1983).

Gates, Paul. *The Farmers Age: Agriculture, 1815–1860* (1960).

Genovese, Eugene D. *The Political Economy of Slavery: Studies in the Economy and Society of the Slave South* (1965).

———. *Roll, Jordan, Roll: The World the Slaves Made* (1974).

Gjerde, Jon. *From Peasants to Farmers: The Migration from Balestrand, Norway, to the Upper Midwest* (1985).

Grubbs, Donald H. *Cry from Cotton: The Southern Tenant Farmers' Union and the New Deal* (1971).

Hahn, Steven. *The Roots of Southern Populism: Yeoman Farmers and the Transformation of the Georgia Upcountry, 1850–1890* (1983).

Hahn, Steven, and Jonathan Prude, eds. *The Countryside in the Age of Capitalist Transformation: Essays in the Social History of Rural America* (1985).

Hicks, John D. *The Populist Revolt: A History of the Farmers' Alliance and the People's Party* (1931).

Hoxie, Frederick E. *A Final Promise: The Campaign to Assimilate the Indians, 1880–1920* (1984).

Jamieson, Stuart. *Labor Unionism in American Agriculture* (1946).

Jensen, Joan. *Loosening the Bonds: Mid-Atlantic Farm Women, 1750–1850* (1986).

Kelley, Robin D. G. *Hammer and Hoe: Alabama Communists During the Great Depression* (1990).

Kirby, Jack Temple. *Rural Worlds Lost: The American South, 1920–1960* (1987).

Kulikoff, Allan. "The Transition to Capitalism in Rural America." *William and Mary Quarterly* 3rd ser., vol. XVI, no 1 (January 1989): 120–142.

Montejano, David. *Anglos and Mexicans in the Making of Texas, 1836–1986* (1987).

Morgan, Edmund S. *American Slavery, American Freedom: The Ordeal of Colonial Virginia* (1975).

Takaki, Ronald. *Pau Hana: Plantation Life and Labor in Hawaii, 1835–1920* (1983).

Webb, Walter Prescott. *The Great Plains* (1931).

Woodman, Harold D. "Post–Civil War Southern Agriculture and the Law." *Agricultural History* 53, no. 1 (January 1979): 319–337.

———. "Postbellum Social Change and Its Effects on Marketing the South's Cotton Crop." *Agricultural History* 56, no. 1 (January 1982): 215–230.

Woodruff, Nan Elizabeth. *As Rare as Rain: Federal Relief in the Great Southern Drought of 1930–31* (1985).

Woodward, C. Vann. *Origins of the New South, 1877–1913* (1951).

Worster, Donald. *Dust Bowl: The Southern Plains in the 1930s* (1979).

SEE ALSO **Foodways; Transients, Migrants, and the Homeless;** and various essays in the sections "**Ethnic and Racial Subcultures**," "**Periods of Social Change**," "**Regionalism and Regional Subcultures**," and "**Space and Place**."

SLAVERY

James Oakes

TAKE AWAY ALL someone's freedom and you have a slave. It is that simple: slavery is the complete denial of freedom. Unlike the feudal serf, the indentured servant, the battered wife, or the imprisoned thief, the slave is completely unfree, totally subordinate to the authority of the master. This means that the slave cannot enter into any of the commonly recognized social relationships that define people as human beings—marriage, work, citizenship, even parenthood—except to the extent that the master allows it. Because marriage involves formal rights and responsibilities between husbands and wives, for example, a legally married slave is something of an anomaly, since the spouse would have obligations to someone other than the master, thus undermining the essence of slavery. The slave, in short, is "socially dead," formally barred from participation in any social relationships that might interfere with his or her total subordination to the master. And since participation in society defines people as human beings, slavery is the most thoroughly dehumanizing of all forms of subordination.

To dehumanize a human being is not only to perpetrate an abomination—it is also to construct an inherent contradiction. It has often been said, at least since Hegel, that the contradictions arising from the dehumanization of the slave virtually define the system of bondage. Much of the history of American slavery can be reviewed by tracing these contradictions through the day-to-day interactions of master and slave. But concentrating on the contradictions means that a good deal that is historically specific to slavery in the American South will be lost. After all, slave systems have appeared in all parts of the globe, from antiquity onward. If to be human is to participate in society, the meaning of dehumanization must vary with the form of society within which slavery appears. To distinguish the slavery of ancient Rome from that of the Old South, therefore, is to appreciate not only the contradictions intrinsic to slavery itself but also the specific tensions arising from slavery's relationship to a liberal political structure, a capitalist world system, and a racist cultural framework. Above all, we need to understand the implications of the fact that in the modern world, the histories of slave labor and free labor are inextricably intertwined.

THE SOUTH AS A SLAVE SOCIETY

The wealth of the Old South derived not from the corn and pork it produced in abundance to feed itself but from the "surplus" commodities—tobacco, rice, sugar, and especially cotton—generated by the slaves and sold largely outside the South. We may therefore speak of the Old South as a slave economy or, more generally, as a slave society. In so doing, however, we are making a distinction of tremendous historical importance. For although dozens of societies have had slaves, by some counts there have been only five genuine slave societies in all of human history: Greece, Rome, Brazil, the Caribbean, and the American South. Where slaves in most times and places counted for little more than 5 or 10 percent of the population, full-scale slave societies were perhaps one-fourth to one-half slaves. But these numbers are misleading insofar as they divert our attention from the more important qualitative characteristics of a true slave society. For in slave societies slaves were not merely present in large numbers; their presence dominated the economic, social, and political history of their age.

One way to envision a slave society is to construct what economic historians call a counterfactual. Imagine the Old South without slaves. Everything is different. The social pyramid—slaveholders on top, nonslaveholders in the middle, slaves on the bottom—does not simply change with the hypothetical removal of slaves; it collapses altogether. However oversimplified the pyramid undoubtedly is, its mere plausibility demonstrates how thoroughly slavery defined the entire structure of southern society before the Civil War. Do the same thing with the northern colonies of British North America in the middle of the eighteenth century, and the results are very different. In every colony slavery was legal, and in places like New York City slaves were at times surprisingly numerous. In colonial New England a substantial proportion of the most prominent leaders were slaveholders. Yet if all the slaves had been removed from the northern colonies, the structure of society would not have been fundamentally altered. The basis of the economy, the organization of politics, and the social hierarchy might have changed somewhat, but they would not have been radically transformed. The difference between the northern and southern colonies in the eighteenth century was the difference between a society with slaves and a slave society.

In the antebellum South social standing was determined by whether one was slave or free and, if free, whether one owned or did not own slaves. "It is in truth the slave labour in Virginia which gives value to her soil and habitations," Thomas R. Dew explained in 1832; "take away this and you pull down the atlas that upholds the whole system" (Drew Gilpin Faust, ed., *The Ideology of Slavery*, p. 30). So overwhelming was slavery's presence in the economy and society that the preservation of the slaveholders' power became, directly or indirectly, the guiding force of the most significant political activities.

THE ORIGINS OF SOUTHERN SLAVERY

The origins of plantation slavery can be traced to a dramatic social transformation that radically increased the purchasing power of western Europeans on both sides of the Atlantic. The first phase of the Atlantic slave trade, from roughly 1450 to 1650, preceded this consumer revolution; it therefore appears in retrospect to have been a mere expansion of slavery's geographic scope. After about 1650, however, commercial expansion became substantive economic change. Slaves were no longer merely present in European outposts; rather, European colonies became slave societies—the first in Western history since the decline of Rome. Early attempts to exploit the labor of indigenous Indian populations or to encourage the migration of a European work force were largely abandoned as one New World colony after another switched to the labor of imported Africans. Around the mid seventeenth century the slave trade expanded dramatically, and it did so largely in response to an equally dramatic increase in the demand for consumer goods.

Throughout the seventeenth century a rapidly growing proportion of English working people sold their labor for wages and purchased the basic commodities they needed to survive. Above the wage laborers there grew a prosperous new middle class of men and women who began to purchase items once deemed luxuries, items that far surpassed their subsistence needs. But consumer demand mostly grew out of more pressing concerns. For quick comfort and inexpensive calories, for relaxation and for warmth, the new wage-earning classes of London and elsewhere, together with prosperous farmers in Old and New England, generated an unprecedented demand for tobacco, sugar, cocoa, coffee, rice, and cotton. New World slave societies came into existence to serve the needs of this exploding population of consumers stretched along the rim of the North Atlantic basin.

The colonial South was inescapably swept up in all these changes. By 1620 Virginians had discovered that Europeans could afford to develop an addiction for tobacco. All the colonists had to do was to get the land and labor to cultivate it. As part of the headright system Virginia planters were rewarded with a fifty-acre tract for each indentured servant brought to America. (Indentured servants were those who promised to work for five to seven years in return for all or part of the cost of their passage to America.) This system facilitated the growth of a tobacco economy in the seventeenth century by allowing settlers to build up large plantations and at the same time providing them with the necessary workers. Thus the colonial South's dependence on the growing demand for tobacco was established at a time when the bulk of the labor was performed by British servants.

But indentured servitude could only be a short-term solution to the labor problem of the seventeenth century. Over the long run the system put itself out of business—in general because laborers were released from their indentures after completing their years of service and, in Maryland and Virginia in particular, because so many servants died before their service was completed. In these circumstances the labor shortage would never disappear and could actually intensify over time. There was, however, an alternative.

Even as tobacco plantations developed with an

indentured labor force, free Virginians steadily acquainted themselves with the resources of the Atlantic slave trade. Slowly they established the legal distinction between slave and free, reconstructing absolute bondage in their own world. The first Africans had arrived in Virginia in 1619, but their numbers were small and grew only erratically until the closing decades of the seventeenth century. After 1680, when the flow of British indentured servants slowed down, Virginians began the changeover that would transform their colony from a society with slaves into a slave society in about a generation. Slave imports to Virginia and Maryland skyrocketed; South Carolina quickly followed suit; and by 1750 even Georgia—whose founders had initially prohibited slavery—was fully dependent on the plantation system that by then characterized the North American slave economy.

If southern slavery was linked at birth to a developing capitalist society with a seemingly insatiable demand for slave-produced goods, it does not follow that slavery itself was "capitalist." For all the slave system's affinities with the consumer revolution and private property, master and slave confronted one another in ways that differed profoundly from the social relations of a free labor system. The results for the southern economy as a whole were, in the long run, devastating. Slavery's short-term profitability is now widely acknowledged, and for some scholars the mere fact that southern planters drew a healthy return on their investment is all that needs to be said. But critics of the Old South, beginning with the abolitionists, were not entirely mistaken in their conclusion that slavery was responsible for the increasing economic backwardness of the region's economy. Slavery encouraged the exhaustion of the soil, discouraged savings, and retarded technological development. Without a free market in labor power, the slave South lacked not only capitalism's incentives to industrious labor but also the capacity to develop a robust home market in consumer goods. So while slavery was shaped by capitalism, it nonetheless lacked many of capitalism's salient features.

The letters and diaries of antebellum slaveholders reveal the distinctive fusion of slavery and capitalism that characterized daily life in the Old South. If double-entry bookkeeping had yet to reach the antebellum plantations, the irrational pursuit of quick riches that nearly destroyed the earliest settlement at Jamestown had long since given way to a more calculating ethic that alone could ensure the survival of a slave economy in a capitalist world. Every tedious journal entry recording the weather, the condition and whereabouts of the field hands, or the numbers of rows planted, weeds dug, or bales packed was sparked by the capitalist world's demand for cotton. Behind every task assigned to every slave every day stood the mill owners and factory hands of Old and New England. At the root of every systematic attempt to sustain the slaves' productivity—including the bribes, the whippings, and the crude efforts to encourage breeding—was the growing consumer demand of the free laborers, dependent and independent, on farms and in cities on both sides of the Atlantic. Thus was the rationalizing force of capitalism fused with the nonrational substance of slavery.

The hybrid nature of the Old South—its combination of slavery and capitalism—presents special problems. Slavery is what distinguished southern society; its particular economic tendencies separated the South from the North, pushing southern history along its own path of development. Yet capitalism is what set New World slave societies apart from their predecessors in antiquity. American masters were among the first in history whose power depended on commercial relations with a capitalist world that was ultimately more powerful than all the slave societies put together.

THE POLITICS OF SLAVERY

If slavery was the denial of freedom, in liberal societies that meant, primarily, the denial of rights. Difficult as it is to define liberalism, the best shorthand definition must acknowledge the primacy of rights. Whereas medieval society recognized the rights of certain groups within a hierarchical social order, liberalism made rights universal; rights were the primary device by which the social order was established. A liberal political structure is dedicated to the preservation of rights. Thus, if liberalism defines social life as a series of rights, it defines social death—slavery—as the denial of rights.

In the simplest cases this appeared in the law as the mere "exception" of the slave from the rights of free citizens. A 1638 "act for the liberties of the people" of Maryland located the slaves, literally, in parentheses: "[A]ll Christian inhabitants (slaves excepted) to have and enjoy all such rights, liberties, immunities, privileges and free customs, within this province, as any natural born subject of England hath or ought to have or enjoy in the realm of England" (John Codman Hurd, *The Law of Freedom and Bondage in the United States* [1858; repr. 1968], vol. 1, p. 248). By the nineteenth century the statutes regulating slavery had become far more specific. The Louisiana slave code of 1824 was a quite detailed list of the rights that, in their explicit denial, defined the essence of slavery. Much of the statute reads as a series of negations. The slave was "incapable" of making contracts, owned no possessions, could bequeath nothing, could not hold public office or engage in any civil procedures, could neither sue nor be sued, and could marry only with the consent of the master (slave marriages "could not produce any of the civil effects which result from such contract"). Alabama's slave code of 1852 did much the same thing when it defined slavery, in effect, by turning the Bill of Rights upside down.

There was a curious irony in this, for slavery actually revealed the boundaries of freedom by specifying what it meant to be unfree. Southerners could define slavery only in the terms they used to define freedom. That is what Thomas R. R. Cobb, one of the antebellum South's best legal scholars, did when he declared: "Of the three great absolute rights guaranteed to every citizen by the common law, viz., the right of personal security, the right of personal liberty, and the right of private property, the slave, in a state of pure or absolute slavery, is totally deprived" (*An Inquiry into the Law of Negro Slavery in the United States of America* [1858], p. 83). Only in a society where freedom was understood as the primacy of rights could "absolute or pure slavery" be defined in simple Lockean terms as "the condition of that individual, over whose life, liberty, and property another has the unlimited control" (*An Inquiry,* p. 3). This is how southern law put the slave outside of society. Without rights, the slave could form none of the basic economic, political, or personal relationships that together bring society into existence.

Liberalism had a robust variety of linguistic devices for imagining the slave's place outside of society. The first was the "state of nature," where no one's rights were secure and where life degenerated into a Hobbesian nightmare, a perpetual state of war. The "social compact" invoked by state constitutions all across the South presumed the existence of a world where no compact had been made prior to man's entrance into society. Where there was no compact there was no society, and without society no one's rights were secure. Here was the perfect place for the slave—outside society, banished forever to a state of nature that had degenerated into the chaos of perpetual war. Locke defined slavery as "the state of war continued" (*Two Treatises of Government*).

More commonly, liberalism recognized the master-slave relationship by retaining a language of property rights stripped of its origins in the state of nature. Notwithstanding the enormous moral and political difficulties raised by the definition of humans as property, southern states fell into the habit of such definition from their earliest slave codes. Virginia's 1705 statute declared that all slaves "shall be held to be real estate and not chattels and shall descend unto heirs and widows according to the custom of land inheritance" (A. Leon Higginbotham, Jr., *In the Matter of Color,* p. 52). Other colonies followed Virginia's lead by defining slaves as either real or personal property. Once this was done, the way was clear for a defense of slavery on the grounds of property rights. The "right of property is before and higher than any constitutional sanction," one southern state constitution declared in 1850, adding quickly that "the right of the owner of a slave to such slave and its increase is the same and as inviolable as the right of the owner of any property whatever" (Hurd, *Law of Freedom and Bondage,* vol. 2, p. 18). In such ways the language of liberalism provided masters with a justification for slavery that was compatible with liberal political culture.

By defining slaves as property, masters facilitated the reduction of their labor force to the status of a commodity—items to be bought and sold on the open market as freely and profitably as the cotton and tobacco and sugar the slaves labored to produce. This degree of commodification helps explain why the South could simultaneously embrace the practice of human slavery and the principle of human equality. For it is in the nature of commodity exchange that it *appears* to be equitable. It was no accident that the secular ideal of human equality emerged in Western history at the moment when consumer society was born. For with the spread of the commodity form based on the "universal equivalent" of money, it was possible for the first time to imagine that the most important relationships among men and women were grounded on the principle of equal exchange. The fact that modern slavery not only arose in this setting but also extended the commodification of society by defining human beings as salable goods, goes a long way toward explaining the paradox of slavery and freedom in American history.

But there were problems in defining slavery in terms of property and commodity. It was easy enough to invoke the right of property in defense of slavery or to demonstrate that the Bible and historical precedent sanctioned slavery. What the master class had to do, however, was to justify the specific enslavement of one particular group of human beings—dark-skinned Africans and their descendants. Here the liberal distinction between "natural" and "artificial" inequality proved crucial, for it provided slaveholders with a powerful justification for distributing or withholding rights differentially throughout society. Racism—the proposition that blacks are by nature, and not by law, a distinct and inferior race of people—emerged in the late eighteenth century almost as a counterweight to the developing doctrine of human equality. Drawing on a host of European prejudices against blackness, heathenism, cultural difference in general, and the lower classes in particular, racism distinguished itself by unifying these prejudices under the framework of a pseudoscientific geneticism specific to the Enlightenment. In short, the eighteenth century invented the modern concept of "race," and with it a relentlessly deterministic dogma that justified the enslavement of an inherently, and so perpetually, inferior "Negro."

By the late eighteenth century the state's awesome power to define who should and should not be enslaved occasioned almost no comment, given the consensus within which white Americans operated: slaves should be Negroes and Negroes should be slaves. "White persons may not be enslaved," one southern legal scholar explained. "The presumption of freedom arises from the color," just as "the black color of the race raises the presumption of slavery" (Thomas R. R. Cobb, *An Inquiry*, pp. 66–67). By 1860 racism had become the single most important means by which masters attempted to reconcile the contradiction between slavery and freedom in their society.

THE RULING RACE

Racism served also to mask the powerful divisions slavery had created among free southerners. At any given time the majority of free men in the South did not own even a single slave. Within the slaveholding class itself the majority of masters owned a relatively small fraction of the slaves. The richest 10 percent of the owners—2 or 3 percent of the South's free men—held 50 percent of the slaves. Half the masters owned no more than five slaves each; only one in four owned more than ten. And

since landownership and slave ownership patterns tended to coincide, those with the most slaves had the best lands with the highest proportions of improved acreage.

By participating in the invention of a category called race, and by employing that category as a way of distinguishing slave from free, the slaveholders sought to define themselves as something other than the ruling class they were. In the words of one southern politician, "we are the governing race." Although nearly universal among slaveholders, the idea of a ruling race falsely suggested that membership in the South's dominant class depended on biology rather than the more prosaic processes of social reproduction. In fact, the social hierarchy of the Old South had to be re-created with each new generation. The answer to the question of how a slave society reproduced itself in a liberal capitalist world must come from somewhere other than racist ideology.

The great challenge for slaveholding parents was to raise their children to the exercise of despotic rule and, at the same time, to a world of individual freedom and political equality. The source of this ambiguity is easy enough to trace: slaveholding families were strongly influenced by new Anglo-American ideas about how to order domestic life properly, as well as by the presence of slaves within the household. The result was a master class whose culture was at once recognizably American and yet distinctively southern. Standing at the intersection of slavery and liberal capitalism, planter families were a paradigm in miniature of the larger history of the antebellum South.

At first glance there is nothing distinctively southern about the "enlightened" attitudes toward marriage and child rearing that made their appearance among planter families sometime in the middle-to-late eighteenth century. As early as 1750 Virginia planters began to express unprecedented concern for privacy, to idealize the affectionate companionship of husband and wife, and to sentimentalize children. With the elevation of her role as nurturing mother, the plantation mistress increasingly nursed her own children, abandoning the aristocratic tradition of wet-nursing that still prevailed on the European continent. Plantation homes were constructed with a newfound concern for the solitude of the individual. The evocative symbolism of southern family portraiture was transformed: the father, no longer aloof and above his family, instead assumed a loving pose beside his wife and among his children. Gone, or at least substantially diminished, was the image of the family as the domestic reflection of patriarchal government, with its emphasis on hierarchy and subordination, obedience, and intergenerational continuity. The new understanding demanded that children be nourished on love more than on filiopietism, reared to individual autonomy rather than hierarchical interdependence. In this emerging image of the family, the world was remade with each generation.

Certainly the Old South was no stronghold of sexual equality. Male-dominated families prevailed throughout nineteenth-century America, and perhaps more firmly in the South than elsewhere. Property laws continued to disadvantage women. Given the dangers of childbirth, large families continued to place southern women's lives and health in jeopardy. And, of course, to be a slaveowner was to be, nine times out of ten, a male. Nevertheless, relatively egalitarian inheritance patterns, female literacy, property rights for women, and the legal recognition of the distinctive interests of wives and children represented major inroads of liberal political culture among slaveholding families.

Without entailed estates, with no tradition of primogeniture, and with none of the elaborate legal mechanisms that preserved the integrity of noble privilege in Europe, the slaveholders developed child-rearing and inheritance patterns that reflected the powerful force of liberalism. In the late eighteenth century every southern state abolished primogeniture, long after it had been abandoned in practice. Planters broke up their estates with each passing generation, distributing their property differentially but broadly among their children. Eldest sons could expect to take possession of the family home, but land and slaves were distributed among sons and daughters. The diaries and letters of slaveholders make it clear that by the nineteenth century the advantages of the well-born, although considerable, were by themselves insufficient to ensure that the child would live in the same degree of comfort as the parents. Every young man was expected to make his own contribution to the social reproduction of the slaveholding class. Self-discipline, hard work, and the systematic acquisition of wealth became central ideals passed down from father to son in slaveholding families.

Given the prevalence of the bourgeois ideals of equal opportunity and individual achievement, each new generation of slaveholders faced the challenge of reconstructing a society that distributed its wealth very unevenly. For this pattern of inequality to remain constant in a society in which estates were divided up every generation, at least some of the children of wealthy planters had to rebuild their parents' fortunes, and many others had to fail in that endeavor. Because the children of small slaveholders usually began their adult lives as slaveless farmers, most of them had to reenter the slaveholding class on their own, and some had to remain outside the master class throughout their productive lives. The statistical evidence bears this out. Upward—and downward—mobility were, almost by definition, characteristic of the life cycle within the master class. Because slave ownership was something that came later in life, upward mobility was a normal experience for successful masters. Nor was this a rare experience in the Old South, for in 1860 one out of every four free families owned at least one slave, and the proportion had usually been higher than that. Most often, slave ownership rates ranged from 30 to 35 percent, and in many parts of the South they were higher still, even in 1860. Over the course of a free man's lifetime there was probably a fifty-fifty chance of becoming a slaveholder for some period of time.

Yet it would be a mistake to conclude from all of this that the history of the slaveholding class was a mere variation on a larger liberal theme. The South was, at bottom, a slave society, and the significance of slavery extended well beyond the relationship of master and slave. The ownership of even a single slave affected all the other relationships that made up the master's world. Slavery reshaped the ties between farmers and merchants; it transformed the relationship between slaveholders and their neighbors; and it profoundly influenced the bonds of marriage and the patterns of child rearing within the master's family. For all liberalism's influence, slavery nevertheless reproduced itself in distinctive ways, beginning with the organization of family life.

Consider what could happen to the rhythm of daily life when a free farmer acquired a slave. We know that slaveless farmers relied extensively on the labor of their own families, that they divided work in patterns based on age and gender, and that these patterns changed over time as the family grew and matured. The ownership of only a few slaves, perhaps even one, could subtly but profoundly alter these patterns. No doubt the effects multiplied as the number of slaves in the household increased. But the consequences appeared, and were perhaps most pronounced, with the ownership of the first few.

With a slave on the farm, particularly a male, a father could more easily afford the labor lost by sending his son to school or by having his daughters tutored. Not surprisingly, the slaveholders' children were absent from school less frequently than were the children of slaveless yeomen farmers. Despite the fact that public education in the South advanced more slowly than in the North, the children of slaveholders, girls as well as boys, were almost always educated. So widespread was literacy within the slaveholding class that the overall literacy rate among free southerners was one of the highest in the Western world.

A female slave, perhaps only one, could relieve the mistress of some of the most onerous chores of housekeeping, from cooking and cleaning to gathering wood and tending the family's vegetable garden. Whereas nine out of ten women on slaveless farms did their own chores at home, less than a third of small slaveholders' wives did. And only 7.7 percent of the mistresses on large plantations performed their own household chores, for as the number of slave laborers grew, the mistress was transformed into a domestic manager.

As free children reached adulthood, slave labor could make it easier for parents to subsist and prosper without the help of their own offspring. Bound labor often replaced child labor in the life cycle of the slaveholding family. Free men were most likely to own slaves when they were in their forties and fifties, when their children came of age and moved out on their own. Thus slavery loosened the bonds of intergenerational dependency that made older parents traditionally reliant on their grown children. In turn, children benefited from the age structure of the slaveholding class. The average number of slaves a master owned peaked in middle age but declined among those who reached their sixties. Slavery thus allowed the most prosperous parents to transfer some of their wealth to their grown children in the critical years of early adulthood.

As with relationships within the family, the ties between family and society began to change with the purchase of a single slave. Most masters were farmers for whom the cost of a slave was a significant expense, in fact a major investment. Whether farmers borrowed the money to buy a slave or saved the cash, they naturally expected the fruits of slave labor to repay the initial expense. Property taxes on slaves added to the burden. Since slaveholders monopolized the most productive soils, the taxes on their lands were often higher than those of yeomen farmers. To own even a single slave, therefore, was to be subject to periodic payments and yearly taxes that slaveless farmers did not have to meet.

Simply put, slavery required production for the market. In most cases this meant that the slave's labor would be devoted primarily to producing crops for which there was a relatively predictable consumer demand in the market. Statistical evidence shows a fairly clear correlation between slave ownership and production of staples such as cotton, tobacco, sugar, and rice. The more slaves a master owned, the more land he was likely to devote to marketable crops.

But slavery also made market production easier. By some estimates the average slave produced at least twice as much as was necessary for his or her subsistence, thus making slave ownership a source of considerable profit to masters for as long as the market in staples was flourishing. It was not that slave labor was intrinsically more productive than free labor—evidence of slavery's efficiency is subject to tremendous dispute. But it is clear that a slave was normally expected to work longer and harder than were any members of the master's family. Slave children went to work in the fields at a younger age than did free children; slave women were expected to do fieldwork, which few free women did except at harvest time. Slave men worked longer hours and had fewer holidays than did free men. In the slave quarters of large plantations, cooking and baby-sitting were frequently communal chores, often reserved for elderly slaves, and this, too, increased the labor power available in the work force. Slaves usually produced most of their own food, provided much of the diet for the master's family as well, and at the same time increased the farm's production of marketable staples.

For all the economic obligations slave ownership entailed, it also liberated masters from the heavy reliance on neighbors that was essential to successful yeoman communities. Slave ownership eased the settlement process by fulfilling at least some of the demands for labor that all farmers experienced. Slaves could clear the fields, build the barns, perfect the crafts, and perform the labors that normally impelled yeomen farmers into cooperation with their neighbors. At the same time, superior access to markets made it easier to purchase inexpensive goods from distant manufacturers than from a local class of artisans, craftsmen, and merchants. Just as slave labor eased settlers' reliance on neighbors, so did the combination of plantation self-sufficiency and dependence on international markets effectively limit the slaveholders' economic links to their own communities. The larger the plantation, the more removed it was likely to be from the commercial activities of the locality.

Slavery undermined community attachments in many ways that contemporary observers could scarcely fail to notice. Neighbors complained about the social isolation of local planters. Slaveholders' wives were tortured by their husbands' incessant readiness to uproot their families and abandon their communities. Travelers were astonished by the high rates of turnover of plantation ownership. And they had good reason to be. Only a small minority of planter families, as few as 20 percent, lived in the same place for more than two decades. The reasons for the relentless migration of the slave-holding class lie in the social consequences of slavery itself.

Take away a master's land and he was still a master; take away his slaves and his entire social identity was transformed. By definition, slavery gave the master the power not simply to dispose of the slave but to transport the slave to and fro at will. This meant that the slaveholder's power, unlike the feudal lord's, was not tied to a specific landed estate. Slavery required relatively few ties to place and community. As a class the masters had a far greater interest in protecting their slaves than in protecting their soils—which the slaveholders in fact exhausted far more than was necessary. Thus slavery not only facilitated migration; it also encouraged farming methods that spurred movement.

In the end physical expansion was the only way the slave economy could grow enough to sustain the social reproduction of the master class. It was possible to introduce more efficient farming techniques that might enhance the productivity of the slave plantations. But given the masters' paramount interest in slaves rather than in land, the advantage of reforming agriculture was never as clear to the masters as it was to their critics. Even with such techniques, the productive potential intrinsic to slave labor was probably limited. The indisputable growth of the southern economy before the Civil War, in particular the rise in per capita incomes, depended almost entirely on the expansion of slavery onto new western lands. It was no accident that the issue which, more than any other, precipitated the sectional crisis was the expansion of slavery.

THE MASTER-SLAVE RELATIONSHIP

Slavery in the United States "was above all a labor system," as Kenneth Stampp pointed out in *The Peculiar Institution* (p. 34), and the bulk of the slaves' labor was performed on rural plantations. To be sure, slaves in southern society served in many other capacities that were common to slavery elsewhere. They were a source of prestige and an indication of wealth; they worked as domestic servants on family farms, in plantation houses, and in urban residences. They were skilled craftsmen, factory operatives, nurses, and sometimes plantation managers. On the other hand, they did not serve in the military, they were not teachers, and they did not staff the government bureaucracy as slaves did in other times and places. Rather, slaves in North America were primarily field hands on farms and plantations.

The unparalleled level of consumer demand for slave-produced goods emanating from the capitalist world sustained a competitive environment in which masters had little choice but to impose some system of labor management, however ineffective or informal, on their slaves. Seventy-five percent of the slave population was concentrated on farms with ten or more slaves, and for most of them systematic management of some sort was all but impossible to avoid. By 1860—with four million slaves, almost four hundred thousand masters, and commodity prices that guaranteed few quick fortunes—the most successful farms were those that sustained the highest levels of productivity over the long term.

Nevertheless, slavery actually provided little room for significant improvement in productivity. As laborers, the slaves had little incentive to care very much or to work very hard. They had nothing like the feudal serf's powerful claim to rights in the land. Slaves also lacked the incentives built into a wage-labor economy: the sheer need to go to work to survive, the promise of more pay for more work, and the added enticement of upward mobility in the future. They had nothing to gain from working hard on cash crops that did not add to their basic subsistence. The limited hierarchy within the slave community offered no real possibility of social advancement. Slave parents could work neither for their own nor for their children's eventual independence. No institutionalized promise of future freedom provided an incentive for slaves to work hard. So, while countless slaves took justifiable pride in their skills as nurses, managers, cooks, or artisans, the vast majority of slave laborers, the field hands, had no motivation to care very much about the success of the master's efforts to produce a good crop.

Thus southern masters tried to rationalize the labor of slaves who had every reason to resent such efforts, and this proved a major source of tension within the master-slave relationship. Work was what the slaves did all day, and so work was what provoked many of the conflicts between master and slave. The rules of the workplace set the daily, seasonal, and yearly rhythms of life on farms throughout the slave economy. Yet the very effort to impose a system that would increase worker output appeared to slaves as a direct reminder of the master's arbitrary power.

On the well-managed plantation order was ideally maintained by a hierarchy of the work force—extending from field hands to drivers to overseers to the master—and an often elaborate set of rules and regulations. There were general rules of the plantation and special rules for field hands, children, and women, particularly "breeders" and "sucklers." There were different rules for winter and summer, and rules for different days of the week. There were even rules requiring that rules be enforced uniformly. Slaves were to wake up and go to sleep according to the rules, and rules determined when they ate, how much they ate, and how their meals were prepared. Rules governed the slaves' intercourse with other slaves as well as with whites, on and off the plantation. Additional instructions described in detail how each job was to be performed, how far apart rows should be planted, how many bales should be picked by each hand, and how quickly slave songs should be sung in the field. By 1860 the accumulated list of suggested rules published in dozens of articles on plantation management could have filled volumes.

As the existence of such rules suggests, the subordination of the slaves to the master's authority extended well beyond the control of labor. Because slaves were a source of wealth separate from the crops they produced, their care and feeding, and ultimately their sexual reproduction, were as important to masters as the productive cultivation of crops and soil. Many owners therefore distinguished the management of slaves from the rational organization of their labor, and they often insisted that slaves were at least as important as what they produced. No comparable interest in serf management appears in the manorial documents that survive from medieval Europe, nor can this aspect of slave management be equated with the problem of labor control in capitalist enterprises. When the masters contemplated the management of slaves, they were reflecting on the appropriate exercise of powers that extended far beyond those of a factory owner or a feudal lord.

Just as masters boasted of their success in improving the productivity of slave labor, so did they emphasize the material rewards of maintaining a healthy slave population. Yet the very detail with which masters explored the subject of slave management inadvertently reveals that the essence of slavery was not treatment at all but, rather, the master's power over the intimate details of slave life. The masters cared about the treatment of slaves not simply because they had an interest in them but because they had the power to control the slaves' private lives. Masters could decide whether slaves would get married, where they would live, what they would eat, when they would wake up and go to bed, and how they would dress. What the masters exposed in their detailed examinations of slave treatment was not that they were uniquely humane but that they were extraordinarily powerful.

They exposed more than that. Owners addressed the treatment question by trading suggestions about how best to arrange the most mundane aspects of slave life, things free men and women assumed were private affairs. It seemed perfectly ordinary for one master to require that slaves not overcook their vegetables, for another to insist that slave women "have a change of *drawers* for the winter," and for still others to set rules determining at what time and in what manner the slaves could eat their supper. This was not the language of uninhibited greed but of rational calculation.

Nevertheless, it was a rationalism that exposed the distinctive character of slavery. That distinctiveness derived in large part from the fact that the slave family subsisted within the master's household. The family remained the procreative unit, but the economic functions of the household were under the control of the masters, giving them power to make many of the domestic decisions denied to the slave family. Every time the masters extended their control over another aspect of the slave's daily life, they demonstrated in precise and highly personal terms what it meant to be unfree. For slaves there was no such thing as a right of privacy. To be a slave could mean filing past the master for receipt of weekly rations or to be examined for cleanliness or torn clothing. Slave cabins were not simply built to the masters' specifications; they were open to periodic inspections.

If total subordination meant that masters could demand much more than hard work and obedience from their slaves, the denial of rights had similarly practical consequences for day-to-day treatment of slaves. Masters took it for granted that they had every right to choose which ministers the slaves would hear, when slaves could attend church services, and which sermons were appropriate. Slaveholders enforced the laws restricting the slaves' freedom of movement by prohibiting them from "strolling about" or leaving the plantation without permission. Others denied slaves permission to trade commodities they cultivated on their own. Some were so intent on restricting trade that they did not allow slaves to plant their own gardens.

The slaveholders' power was nowhere more evident than in slave families. Masters often reserved the right to veto a proposed marriage. On large units they sometimes prevented slaves from marrying anyone off the plantation. Masters set the rules about how much work pregnant women could perform, when nursing mothers should return to the fields, how small children were to be cared for while the parents were at work, and the age at which slave children should begin labor. Even the personal relations of husband and wife were subject to the owner's arbitration. And masters never relinquished their power to break up a marriage.

Hence the fatal paradox: what masters defined as issues of treatment, as problems of management, appeared to slaves as extreme assertions of the master's power. The most trivial rules—making sure slaves got to bed on time, for example—were among the most palpable symbols of unfreedom. For, unlike the periodic shock of family breakup or the brutal beating of a particularly unruly field hand, the day-to-day treatment of slaves was a relentless and perpetual reminder of how far the master's power extended and how completely the freedom of the slaves was denied. This was, with labor control, the second of the two great sources of conflict between masters and slaves.

THE SLAVE FAMILY

The tensions intrinsic to the master-slave relationship arose most commonly out of a contradiction perhaps distinctive to slavery in the Old South:

the same families that had no recognition under the law had nonetheless become essential to slavery's survival. The "peculiar institution" could not reproduce itself without slave families. As early as 1750 southern slavery was becoming uniquely dependent upon the physical reproduction of the slave population, and with the withdrawal of the United States from the Atlantic slave trade in 1808, the masters no longer had a dependable alternative source of slaves. The system could survive only with slave families. And yet these families lacked all legal standing; they were neither the primary units of economic productivity nor the chief mechanism for the redistribution of power in society.

Without the civil recognition that distributes legal and property rights among husbands, wives, and children, the slave family was neither patriarchal nor matriarchal—for neither spouse had the formal powers that normally justify the use of such terms. If all slaves had no legal rights, then husbands could have no more rights than wives. If slaves could own no property, the family could not be the vehicle for the transmission of estates. If slavery was perpetual, slaves could not rear their children for the eventual assumption of power or independence. The family structure that emerged from such conditions was unique in American social history.

Gender distinctions that prevailed in free families, for example, were undermined by the slave labor system. The work each slave was expected to perform was limited primarily by physical capacity, and women could do most of the jobs men could do. From early childhood all slaves—boys and girls, men and women—mostly did the same kinds of tasks. If men concentrated on plowing and digging where women focused on hoeing and weeding, what distinguished slavery was the fact that the majority of slaves, men and women, spent their days doing field work. Thus, while certain gender differences were maintained, there was no sense that the labor of slave women was primarily domestic, or that their work should be confined to meeting the subsistence needs of their families.

Nevertheless, many of the distinctions associated with family life did emerge within the slave community. Masters assigned communal cooking and child-rearing tasks to women, while traditional artisanal crafts were reserved for male slaves. Domestic service in the master's house was largely restricted to females. Above all, as bearers of children, as nursing mothers, slave women assumed roles and obligations different from those of slave men.

This made women uniquely vulnerable to their masters' interest in sexual reproduction, but it also gave them a kind of leverage unavailable to slave men. In the master's dependence upon her fertility the slave woman found and exercised a degree of influence—a bargaining chip—in her dealings not only with her master but also within her own family. Slave women thereby assumed a degree of influence within their families that helped to counteract the formal powerlessness of both husbands and wives.

With the modicum of influence they recovered through their reproductive capacities, slave women protected the integrity and emotional life of their families as best they could, and with surprising success. The slave family was notoriously subject to the disruptive intrusions of the master and at the same time profoundly important to the cultural stability of the slave community. Above all, the slave family was a creative adaptation to the anarchic realities of slavery. Although it was a legal nonentity, the slave family's existence was tolerated by masters who could respect or destroy it as their interests and inclinations determined. But as a cultural anchor within the slave community, the family developed in ways that compensated for its intrinsic vulnerability.

Kinship, for example, radiated outward from the slave family, embracing cousins and nieces, nephews and in-laws, as close rather than distant relatives. Fictive kin—"aunts" and "uncles" with no blood ties—further extended the lines of family outward until they blended smoothly and indistinguishably into the slave community as a whole. In a world where nuclear families were intrinsically vulnerable to the master's power to break them apart, the extended relations of the slave community preserved a sense of family stability in the wake of otherwise wrenching dislocations. One of the largest forced migrations in history, the slave trade within the antebellum South was so widespread that the average slave could expect to be sold at least once in a lifetime and would likely witness the sale of half a dozen close relatives. Yet the family provided an anchor for the larger community of slaves, and the slave community in turn nourished a sense of self-worth and solidarity that helped sustain each member of the family.

At the same time, the slave family gave masters a potent weapon in the perpetual struggle with their slaves. Owners clearly recognized that the strength of slavery rested in large measure on the strength of the slave family. The stronger the family attachments, the less likely a slave was to run away. Thus most escapees were young men who had grown beyond the protective umbrella of their childhood families and had not yet established new families of their own. A wife and child were powerful restraints on a slave who yearned to escape but who could not face the prospect of leaving his family behind. The slaves had taken full advantage of the contradictions of the system to create a family life, a community, and a culture that could generate, support, and justify the acts of resistance that the master's demands provoked. But the more successfully the slaves protected their families, the more fully they realized their community life, the more effectively their culture explained their circumstances—the more bearable, and peaceful, slavery became.

SLAVE RESISTANCE

But life was not always peaceful on antebellum plantations. Overt tensions between master and slave repeatedly erupted in the workplace. Slaveholders complained that their bondsmen were impudent because they very often *were* impudent; masters complained that their slaves were lazy because they rarely exhibited any zest for their labors. By deliberate lassitude, by running away, by sabotage, slaves withheld their labor from the master. By planning their individual and collective acts of day-to-day resistance as deliberate responses to particular grievances, the slaves made known their objections to mistreatment, neglect, and overwork.

If forced labor inevitably generated resistance, it was often the strength of family ties that determined the strength of a slave's militancy. Pushed too hard by an overseer, whipped once too often by the master, a field hand's decision to strike back or not was most often made in consultation with family members and in consideration of family attachments. In more direct ways resistance was commonly tied to family life. Women ran away with their children to prevent their families from being broken up; husbands fled to find relatives from whom they had been separated. Acts of resistance were often provoked by the master's abuse of a slave's spouse or child, or by a particularly galling intrusion into the slave's personal affairs.

It was, then, a precarious peace that rested on the security of the slave community and the vibrancy of African American culture. The slaveholders saw the advantages of family stability, but there was no way for the master class to maintain itself without disrupting and destroying slave families on a massive scale. To "manage negroes" was to interfere inevitably in the personal lives of slave families and thereby to provoke hostility. To discipline a slave was to anger and horrify that slave's husband, wife, parent, or child. To own slaves was to enjoy the right to break up a family, but to exercise that right was to rekindle within the slave community a passionate hatred of bondage. Family life made slavery bearable, it held slaves to their plantations, it gave slaves something whose integrity was not worth risking. But children gave parents a powerful incentive to struggle for freedom, while the family in general gave all slaves something worth protecting. In the end the legal kinlessness of the slaves made slavery the inveterate enemy of the very families it created. And so the slaves resisted.

BIBLIOGRAPHY

Censer, Jane Turner. *North Carolina Planters and Their Children: 1800–1860* (1984).

Clinton, Catherine. *The Plantation Mistress: Woman's World in the Old South* (1982).

Davis, David Brion. *The Problem of Slavery in Western Culture* (1966).

———. *The Problem of Slavery in the Age of Revolution, 1770–1823* (1975).

Faust, Drew Gilpin, ed. *The Ideology of Slavery: Proslavery Thought in the Antebellum South, 1830–1860* (1981).

Finley, M. I. *Ancient Slavery and Modern Ideology* (1980).

Fox-Genovese, Elizabeth. *Within the Plantation Household* (1988).

Franklin, John Hope. *The Militant South, 1800–1861* (1956).

Freehling, William. *The Road to Disunion.* Vol. 1, *Secessionists at Bay 1776–1854* (1990).

Genovese, Eugene D. *The Political Economy of Slavery: Studies in the Economy and Society of the Slave South* (1965).

———. *Roll, Jordan, Roll: The World the Slaves Made* (1974).

Higginbotham, A. Leon, Jr. *In the Matter of Color: Race and the American Legal Process, The Colonial Period* (1978).

Isaac, Rhys. *The Transformation of Virginia, 1740–1790* (1982).

Kulikoff, Allan. *Tobacco and Slaves: The Development of Southern Cultures in the Chesapeake, 1680–1800* (1986).

Lewis, Jan. *The Pursuit of Happiness: Family and Values in Jefferson's Virginia* (1983).

Miller, Joseph C. *Way of Death: Merchant Capitalism and the Angolan Slave Trade, 1730–1830* (1988).

Morgan, Edmund S. *American Slavery, American Freedom: The Ordeal of Colonial Virginia* (1975).

Oakes, James. *The Ruling Race: A History of American Slaveholders* (1982).

———. *Slavery and Freedom: An Interpretation of the Old South* (1990).

Patterson, Orlando. *Slavery and Social Death: A Comparative Study* (1982).

Smith, Daniel Blake. *Inside the Great House: Planter Family Life in Eighteenth-Century Chesapeake Society* (1980).

Stampp, Kenneth M. *The Peculiar Institution: Slavery in the Ante-bellum South* (1956).

SLAVERY

Thornton, J. Mills, III. *Politics and Power in a Slave Society: Alabama, 1800–1860* (1978).

Wright, Gavin. *The Political Economy of the Cotton South: Households, Markets and Wealth in the Nineteenth Century* (1978).

Wyatt-Brown, Bertram. *Southern Honor: Ethics and Behavior in the Old South* (1982).

SEE ALSO **African American Music; African Migration; Antebellum African American Culture; The Deep South; The Plantation; Postbellum African American Culture; Race; Racial Ideology; Racism; The Southern Tidewater and Piedmont.**

HOUSEHOLD LABOR

Judith Babbitts

EVER SINCE THE first settlements in the seventeenth century, the vast majority of women in this country have performed household tasks on a regular basis throughout their adult lives. Indeed, housework is perhaps the single most common work experience shared by women around the world. Yet household labor has become a significant topic of research and analysis only in the last few decades. Before women's history achieved legitimacy within the historical profession, most historians considered the lives of ordinary women and the unpaid work they did at home unworthy of scholarly inquiry. Those who did undertake such research discovered that, although household tasks appear commonplace and routine, the study of housework is complex. In the United States it involves examining cultural ideals about the home and family, ethnic and gender ideologies about the division of household labor, beliefs about paid and unpaid work in a capitalist economy, and the dependence of household processes on larger economic and social systems, such as energy sources and municipal services. The tools people use to perform household tasks, generally referred to as "household technology," further link the study of housework to larger industrial systems and to manufacturers' strategies in producing, advertising, and distributing new appliances and products. Understanding the relationship of household labor to the larger economy also involves looking at the home as a workplace, for paid domestic service has been an important source of income for generations of immigrant, working-class, and African American women.

Moreover, unlike many other historical topics, the question of who does the housework is a widely discussed and debated issue today. The increasingly large number of working mothers with small children has created a "second shift" for wage-earning women across the economic spectrum and shaken old assumptions in many families and among government policymakers about who should provide child care and other housekeeping services. And ever since the women's movement of the 1970s raised issues about equity for men and women in all areas of life, including housekeeping and child rearing, decisions about who cooks dinner and who diapers the baby have taken on political overtones, especially in two-career families. Whether or not historians personally wrestle with such dilemmas, they are aware of the public debate. Historical studies on household labor invariably throw light on the current discussion about the allocation of domestic tasks today. The study of housework, then, involves not only documenting and interpreting the changes and continuities in household labor over time, but also in understanding the ideas and attitudes, deeply embedded in the culture, about how it should be done and who should do it.

PREINDUSTRIAL HOUSEHOLDS

Seventeenth-century New Englanders did not use the term "housework" to describe the tasks they performed to maintain the household. Instead the word "housewifery" differentiated the tasks women did from those done by men. In the rural preindustrial conditions that characterized the early colonies, every family member worked around and in the house to produce most of the products and perform many of the services necessary for the family's survival. The family's level of self-sufficiency varied depending on whether it lived on the frontier or close to a settled area, but some generalizations can nevertheless be made. Women were responsible for a wide range of duties that began at sunrise and ended after nightfall. To the repetition of tasks that filled each day—preparing and cooking meals, caring for young children, managing the hearth, hauling water, spinning, tending livestock, cleaning utensils—was added the weekly or monthly chores of laundering, brewing hard cider and beer, mending clothing, churning butter, and making candles. The changing of the seasons engaged women in still another round of activities: pickling and preserving fruits, vegetables, and meats; planting gardens; making lye and soap; and weaving linen and sewing new clothes for the coming season to replace those garments worn or outgrown in the previous year. Of all these tasks, spinning required the most complex skills and filled many of the extra minutes in a woman's day, for it could be done with one eye on small children and another on the hearth. Women also performed the tasks that contributed to the community's health and well-being. They concocted medicines from herbs, cared for the sick and aged, assisted each other at childbirth, and prepared the dead for burial.

Men and boys carried out essential steps in many of the labor processes that culminated with women's efforts. Males of the household felled trees and split wood for the hearth; they cultivated crops and cared for livestock; and they, as well as women, hauled water for cleaning and laundering. Men took grain to the mills for grinding, and usually made regular trips to the nearby town for tools and foodstuffs that the family could not produce itself. They hunted for animals and fished to add variety to the family table. Women spun and sewed cloth, but men worked leather for shoes and whittled wood into kitchen implements or made furniture.

A common household inventory would have included a loom, a butter churn, a wooden bucket for hauling water, a spinning wheel, mortars, pestles, candle molds, salt barrels, iron kettles, quilts, assorted wooden implements for cooking, and wooden trenchers for eating. To acquire many of these tools, a relatively self-reliant household had to be connected to a larger market economy that provided products made by skilled artisans, such as iron pots, axes, or guns, and to have surplus food or other objects to barter or sell. As probate records show, whether household utensils were bought or homemade, they were very valuable and often bequeathed to the next generation.

The gender-segregated, but mutually dependent, division of labor that characterized the New England colonies was nearly universal. The proper and expert use of household tools and the acquisition of craft skills required the mastery of complicated processes. Young girls and boys acquired the

skills necessary for adult life by imitating their mothers or fathers or through apprenticeship with a relative or adult of the same sex. In times of illness or the absence of her husband, a wife could step in and take over a man's chores and was then called a "deputy husband," but in normal circumstances men and women infrequently exchanged roles. Historians disagree over how rigid the sexual division of labor was or whether there was rhyme or reason to who did what task, but the decision of who would cook dinner or care for the baby was less a personal one than a traditionally prescribed role.

Both men and women acquired their senses of self-identity and self-worth from this clear delineation of roles. Yet, although the work was reciprocal, it was not equally valued. New England families existed in a patriarchal society in which the law and religious doctrine upheld the father's position as head of the household and as the family's public representative. The economic value of women's work did not increase their autonomy or authority within the family or their status in the community. Husbands controlled the family's resources, and in most cases even the possessions their wives brought into the marriage. Men and women knew that they could not easily maintain a household without the special skills of the other, but larger cultural and religious ideas about women's "nature" and their subordinate and dependent status lessened the value placed on women's domestic tasks.

In the seventeenth-century Chesapeake Bay colonies of Maryland, Virginia, and the Carolinas, an initial scarcity of women in the early years of settlement meant that men were forced to do some domestic chores and women to work in the fields to help produce the cash crops that justified their indentured status. When stable nuclear families became the norm in the late 1600s, more rigidly defined sex roles developed and women took over responsibility for household chores. Slaves or indentured servants might help lighten some women's work by providing an extra pair of hands and female companionship, but more often such women worked in the fields, leaving the domestic tasks to their mistress. She tended the garden, the livestock, and the dairy; prepared food and clothing, raised her children, and cared for the sick. As the economy expanded and the number of plantations grew, affluent women increasingly supervised and managed the domestic work of slaves within their households, but the vast majority still clothed and nursed all the members of their households, including slaves. Without denying the benefit and privilege that white women derived from owning slaves, historians have shown that all women in the early colonies worked long and hard at domestic tasks to sustain their largely self-sufficient households.

THE RISE OF THE DOMESTIC IDEAL

Women's routine domestic activities took on political significance during the colonies' struggle for independence from Great Britain. Without women's refusal to buy imported goods and their willingness to increase their production of homespun, the economic boycott against British products might have failed. But instead of acquiring for them the full rights of citizenship after the war, women's patriotism was rewarded with only a heightened appreciation of their roles as mothers. In this function, women were the most important educators of their young children and could best serve their new nation by dedicating themselves to teaching republican virtues to the next generation. Historian Linda Kerber has called the new image that emerged the "Republican Mother." Instead of exercising the rights of citizenship themselves by voting or holding political office, the republican mother would raise virtuous, responsible male citizens who would govern the nation in the future. Although there were benefits to the title and the role—both strengthened the argument for the expansion of women's education, for example—in general the redefinition of women as primarily mothers subordinated their role as housewives.

In the northeastern part of the United States, these new ideas about the importance of motherhood coincided with the growth of cities and industry at the end of the eighteenth and the beginning of the nineteenth centuries and helped to rationalize and give meaning to the changing nature of women's household work. The new market economy that began to develop by the mid eighteenth century made manufactured products such as textiles, clothing, baked goods, and other foodstuffs readily available to families living in urban areas. As the family produced fewer of the necessities of daily life, the need for both female and male labor to maintain the household diminished. Young daughters and sons, unmarried sisters, and husbands left the household to work in factories, mills, and offices for the wages the family needed to buy the new consumer goods. About the same time,

family size began to diminish. More widespread use of birth control methods, combined with the realization that children were not economic assets in an urban environment, had, by 1850, reduced the average family size to four or five children, compared to seven or eight a century earlier.

These economic and demographic changes contributed to a new ideology about the home. In popular magazines and literature, religious sermons, advice books, and manuals, the household was transformed into a private refuge. It became a haven from the dangerous, competitive world of the capitalist marketplace. Left behind in the home when others went "out to work," the wife and mother preserved what some remembered as the virtues and morality of an older era. The woman presumedly did not "work," for in an economy that defined value by wages she was not paid for the activities she performed within the privacy of her home. Instead, popular images showed the ideal housewife creating a pleasant and cultured environment for her family, educating her children in Christian and republican principles, entertaining graciously, and easing the emotional cares and worries of her work-weary husband. The home had become women's special sphere and she a "lady" within it. Some historians have labeled this vision of the domestic, pious, and submissive female the cult of true womanhood, and have used the ideology of gender spheres to designate the nineteenth-century notion that men's natural place was in the public world of wage labor and politics, women's within the sanctuary of the home.

Most women, whether they were wealthy or poor, immigrant or African American, were affected by the cultural expectation that they should strive to become ladies. Class distinctions throughout the nineteenth and early twentieth centuries make generalizations difficult, but overall, the reality of most women's lives made achieving the ideal a virtual impossibility. Although more prosperous women might have hired help to assist them, the majority of middle- and working-class women continued to perform arduous, demanding household tasks, as had their mothers and grandmothers before them. Housework was as vital to the well-being of the family as it had ever been, but in the popular culture its importance was ignored, if not denied. Advertisements for the new household products that were beginning to appear in abundance at the turn of the century pictured servants, not the mistress of the house, performing most of the hard physical labor in the home. For the women from poor and working-class families who could not even dream of hiring servants, cooking, cleaning, and laundering had not disappeared from their daily routine, but were now devalued as menial chores. Moreover, by pronouncing women's true place to be at home, the doctrine of gender spheres rendered wage work inappropriate for women. Those women forced to leave their homes to work as laundresses, domestic servants, vendors, or even prostitutes to help their families survive could never hope to achieve the American middle-class ideal of womanhood.

SOUTHERN PLANTATION SOCIETY

Southern households differed from northern ones mainly in that they existed in a rural, slave society that remained largely self-sufficient for a longer time did than the commercial, urbanizing northeast. With less access to larger economic markets than women in the north, southern women and their slaves produced more of the necessities of daily living. They spun and wove cloth for most of the plantation's needs; grew, preserved, baked, stored, and cooked almost all their food throughout the year; tended gardens and livestock; and nursed the sick.

Slaves relieved slaveholding women of many of their daily housekeeping chores, but not of the major tasks of managing the house servants, storing and inventorying supplies that were purchased in bulk, supervising and participating in fall and spring cleaning and, on smaller plantations, repairing and sewing clothes for their own families and their slaves. Some plantation mistresses also cared for sick slaves and assisted them at childbirth.

Depending on the size of the plantation, a slave might be assigned specific tasks, but generally slave women who worked within the plantation house did the full range of domestic chores. They cleaned, hauled water, cooked, laundered, ironed, cared for children, tended the garden and livestock, and helped the mistress cure, salt, and preserve the family's meats and other foods. Many also prepared herbal remedies to cure illnesses and nursed the sick. Slave women sewed for the white household and for themselves, but rarely alongside their mistresses.

While in the North the hearth was the center of the kitchen and the home, in the South the kitchen and the heat it produced in summer were separated from the house and presided over mostly by slave women. These women apparently took pride in their cooking skills, and good cooks were respected by both African Americans and whites.

Early in the morning or late at night, slave women performed a second set of domestic chores in their slave quarters. On some plantations slaves ate in communal kitchens, but most slave women cooked meals for their own families. They supplemented their daily rations of food with vegetables grown in small garden plots, food pilfered from their mistresses' kitchen, or with fish or game their husbands brought to the table. Both slave men and women possessed skills, passed on from the community's elders, that made them as resourceful and self-reliant as colonial families had been. Slave men, for example, chopped wood for fires, constructed and repaired furniture and other wooden implements, and sewed leather items for clothing and household use.

The gender division of labor that existed during slavery endured as freedmen and -women reconstituted their families after the Civil War. Domestic duties then fell to women; the men worked in the fields, with the women joining them when needed in the harvest or planting seasons. Most historians conclude that if many African American women seemed eager to embrace the duties of housewife and mother after slavery, this may have been because they found it a relief to devote their energies and domestic skills solely to the well-being of their own families after generations of working in white women's households.

PROFESSIONALIZING HOUSEWORK

In the late nineteenth century, the home economics or domestic science movement attempted to regain society's respect for women's domestic labor and to relieve the unrelenting drudgery of housework by introducing notions of professionalism, order, and efficiency into the home. Catharine Beecher, a precursor of the home economics movement and an early advocate of the idea that housewives required training in proper household management, published *A Treatise on Domestic Economy, For the Use of Young Ladies at Home, and at School* in 1841 and a second edition of the book in 1869 coauthored with her sister, Harriet Beecher Stowe, entitled, *The American Woman's Home, or, Principles of Domestic Science; being a guide to the formation and maintenance of economical, healthful, beautiful, and Christian homes.*

In encyclopedic fashion, both volumes instructed women in the care of their homes and families, including chapters on home decoration, exercise, care of babies and the disciplining of children, baking, cooking, and nutrition, consumer advice, and suggestions for the most efficient arrangement of kitchens and the best designs for toilets. The Beechers' intent was to recapture for the American housewife the place she lost in the economy when she ceased to produce the necessities of daily life for her family. The Beechers were steeped in the domestic ideal, however, and their goals were to make women better housewives, not relieve them of their domestic chores. Nevertheless, their efforts later helped initiate domestic science classes in women's colleges and state universities in the Midwest and West. Cooking schools and privately owned training institutions in northern cities offered similar instruction in housekeeping to employers of domestic servants, those servants themselves, and to young women embarking on marriage or work in settlement houses where such skills were needed. During the Progressive Era (1870–1900), urban reformers also advocated offering courses in home economics in the elementary and high schools, arguing that girls prepared to do sewing, cooking, and cleaning would later find respectable employment in middle- and upper-class homes and acquire useful habits of industry. Teaching housekeeping skills seemed a particularly effective way to indoctrinate immigrant girls with the American values of thrift, order, cleanliness, and efficiency. Reformers who saw the participation of immigrant women in the labor force as the cause of many urban problems believed that training them in the "domestic arts" would keep them at home or working in the homes of other women and out of the industrial marketplace.

Those middle-class women who worked to redefine housework as a professional, scientific occupation formed the Home Economics Association in Lake Placid, New York, in 1899. This association emphasized the importance of a sanitary, healthful, well-managed home environment and urged homemakers to accept the advice of "experts" on nutrition, time management, budgeting, and consumption to ensure the physical and moral wellbeing of their families. Although formal training in homemaking skills justified the expansion of higher education for women, the association's goals were to make women content to remain in the home by equating domesticity with challenging professional work outside. Home economists reached housewives around the country through women's magazines, housekeeping manuals, and cookbooks and by endorsing household products that purportedly saved time and energy. The experts set ideal standards for the home, frustratingly elusive even for those middle-class women who could afford to hire help. In evaluating the influence of the home economics movement, some historians believe that the association's emphasis on time-budgeting activities and its reliance on experts undermined women's traditional ways of sharing information and support across generations and within neighborhood communities.

Charlotte Perkins Gilman, like Catharine Beecher an important theorist in rethinking women's work in the home, promoted communal alternatives to the image of the ideal household. Writing in 1898 in *Women and Economics* and later in 1903 in a book called simply *The Home: Its Work and Influence,* Gilman equated the solitary woman laboring to maintain her own household with a primitive stage in the evolution of work. She proposed a more progressive vision that included industrialized kitchens and collective child care. But Gilman and women like her, such as Melusina Fay Pierce, who founded the Cambridge Cooperative Housekeeping Society in 1869 to organize a cooperative bakery, store, and laundry for housewives, were in the minority in their desire to reform America's households. When they wrote at the turn of the century, most women were still full-time housewives. The demand for commercially prepared meals, group child care, and other household services would not arise until more women with children entered the labor force in the 1960s and 1970s.

PAID HOUSEHOLD HELP

In the seventeenth century, one-third of colonial households included domestic help. Often they were young immigrant women and men who arrived in the New England colonies as indentured servants, bound or indebted to a family for five to seven years in exchange for passage to the New World and room, board, and clothing. Generally, female servants performed the same tasks as their mistresses, cleaning, tending the garden and the animals, and spinning, weaving, and sewing. Young girls from poorer families might also join a household as apprentices, learning more complicated household chores such as spinning or weaving from their mistresses in exchange for labor of all kinds. So acceptable and widespread was the practice of young women living and working in households other than their own that no stigma was attached to the position. These forms of domestic service continued until after the American Revolution.

By the 1830s, however, the expanding urban middle class was buying many of the household commodities it needed and no longer required young women to help it prepare textiles, butter, cheese, or other products for the family or to sell in a nearby town. City families wanted women primarily to do housework. By then a pool of predominantly immigrant women was available, as native-born women began to earn wages in newly opened factories, shops, and offices. Many Irish, Scandinavian, German, and Slavic women came to the United States to work as domestic servants rather than do brutally hard farm work in their native lands. For the most part, domestic servants continued to live in the homes of their employers, but they now received wages as well as room and board. According to historian Faye Dudden, by mid-century approximately 15 to 30 percent of all urban households had live-in domestic help, and by 1870, the first year the U.S. Census documented women's employment, nearly one-half of all women who worked for wages were domestic servants. Whether in their own homes or in those of others, women's most important occupation in the nineteenth century was household labor.

Live-in servants in cities usually did not work alongside their mistresses as servants had done in self-sufficient colonial households, but their chores were similar to those all housewives did. As nurse-maids, laundresses, cooks, cleaning women, waitresses, and seamstresses, domestic servants often worked ten to twelve hours per day, seven days a week. Many relationships between domestics and their mistresses were amicable. Still, the imbalance of power between employer and employee was frequently made even more difficult by the prejudice that grew out of different ethnic, religious, or racial backgrounds between the two women. Employers complained about their "unwashed Irish immigrant servants" who were ignorant of the most rudimentary cleaning processes and if left unsupervised might debase the family's children with their Roman Catholicism. Domestics complained of loneliness and isolation, long hours, low pay, backbreaking chores, lack of privacy, unreasonable and exploitative employers, and the stigma of having a

menial, low-status job. Proponents of domestic service for working-class and immigrant girls argued that, compared to factory employment, domestics worked in an environment that would protect their health and morals and would prepare them for their future roles as mothers and wives. And for some immigrant women, doing housework in middle-class homes may have quickened the pace of acculturation, for they thus learned English rapidly and were exposed to an American way of life they could teach their own children.

Whether they liked domestic service or not, for many women it was the only wage work they could find. Not until the decades just prior to the twentieth century, and only in some areas of the country, did alternative employment opportunities begin to appear. Then even immigrant women had more options and the paucity of domestics created what popular women's magazines referred to as "the servant problem," or a scarcity of "good help." At the same time, African American women began to migrate northward to become the dominant source of paid household labor in urban areas. These women preferred day work, which allowed them the flexibility to care for their own families and households in the evenings and on weekends. Day workers had largely replaced live-in help in most cities around the country by as early as 1920. Sufficient numbers of African American women remained as domestic workers in the South, however, that southern white women did not experience a scarcity of help until the 1940s and 1950s, when a second large migration of African Americans to northern cities occurred.

In 1900, African American women made up one-third of the servant population in the United States; by 1930 they constituted half of all servants. By then few worked full-time for a single employer. Usually they were hired on a weekly basis for only a day or two to do a specific task. During World War II, many African American women found higher-paying jobs in war-related industries, but after the demobilization most were forced to return to domestic work. In 1950, domestic workers constituted 41 percent of all wage-earning African American women. During the first half of the twentieth century, racial discrimination often combined with a lack of education to prevent African American women from finding work other than as domestic workers or laundresses. Unlike many white women, African American women remained in that occupation most of their lives.

HOUSEHOLD TECHNOLOGY

The only household innovations that eased women's work in the nineteenth century, according to historian Susan Strasser, were the eggbeater, which replaced the fork for beating egg whites, and the coal or wood stove, which eliminated the hours women spent every day tending the hearth. With these two exceptions, food preparation took virtually the same amount of time and effort for a granddaughter as it had for her grandmother. Then in the four decades that spanned the turn of the twentieth century, a number of household machines and products changed the nature of housework, at least for the women who could afford them. Gas and electric stoves, vacuum cleaners, washing machines, irons, and prepared foods were mass produced and distributed and dramatically reduced the heavy, hard labor women had heretofore expended in housework. But before women could replace their manual labor with mechanical power, they had to have access to gas and electricity.

Utilities such as gas and electricity, water and sewerage, garbage collection, and central heating all required municipal expenditures. The uneven distribution of these services within a city or to outlying areas illustrated the political as well as economic nature of urban planning. Piped household water was generally available in wealthy homes by the end of the nineteenth century, but hot and cold running water were not found in many middle-class homes until the beginning of the 1930s. Rural and poor urban families continued to haul their water until after World War I, and some families had to wait for tap water until after World War II, when rural electrification and municipal water systems were fully developed. Most people did not have indoor plumbing until the 1930s.

Having indoor running water ended the back-breaking chore of lugging water, sometimes up several flights of stairs, heating it, hauling it to where the work was to be done, and eventually disposing of it. With tap water came higher standards of domestic and personal hygiene and an unexpected change in the most onerous household chore, doing laundry. Coupled with the washing machine, plumbing brought the family's dirty laundry back into the home.

Women had always dreaded washday and had found alternatives whenever possible to doing the laundry themselves, either by hiring washerwomen or using commercial laundries. Before 1920, almost all upper-class and many urban middle-class families, as well as a substantial percentage of working-class families, sent their laundry out to be done. Only three thousand washing machines were manufactured in 1909; by 1919 more than half a million were produced, and by 1925 that number had grown to 880,000. As washing machines appeared in more households, commercial laundries began to disappear, and for the first time in almost a century middle-class women became their own laundresses again.

Electricity produced the most dramatic changes in women's lives during the 1920s and 1930s. Electric current was available in many urban areas by the 1880s and by 1925 more than half the homes in America had access to it. By 1900, women could own electric irons and vacuum cleaners; but they had to wait until the 1920s and 1930s for other small appliances, such as toasters and coffee makers. The invention and widespread distribution of electric refrigerators did not occur until almost 1940. Before then the icebox, an insulated container for storing ice and food, was the norm for most families.

The story of the development of home refrigerators illustrates the complex interconnections between housework and larger economic factors. Historian Ruth Schwartz Cowan in *More Work for Mother* (1983) documents the support that electric utility companies gave major manufacturers of compression refrigerators, such as General Electric, by promoting both refrigerators and the idea of mechanical refrigeration to their customers. Smaller companies that sold gas absorption refrigerators eventually disappeared from the marketplace, because they could not compete with the aggressive marketing and national distribution capabilities of giants such as GE, General Motors, Kelvinator, and Westinghouse. Cowan offers other examples of alternative household appliances that never reached the stores—even though they were superior to existing products—because the companies that produced them believed they could not make a profit on their manufacture and sale. Even those who produced labor-saving devices, she notes, did not have saving the labor of housewives as their number-one concern.

Electricity removed some of the hard physical labor from household chores, but did not eliminate it. Electric irons, for example, replaced heavy, stove-heated flatirons but failed to change the process of ironing. Portable vacuum cleaners left cleaner carpets but required a greater expenditure of energy to operate than a carpet sweeper. Advertisements for electrically powered household equipment assured women that they need not lament the lack of hired help; with their "electrical servants" they could do all the work themselves. After World War I most advertisements for household products depicted housewives doing their own work; domestic servants had literally disappeared from the picture.

Even more than the availability of new energy sources and appliances, the packaging and preparation of foodstuffs outside the home eased women's household chores. National companies such as Van Camp, Campbell, and Heinz were offering canned foods for sale by the latter half of the nineteenth century. By 1910, even the urban working class relied on packaged baked goods. The purchase of canned goods rose with income levels, and as the century wore on consumers increasingly bought more of their food from stores rather than growing or making it themselves. Frozen foods were available as early as the 1930s, but it was not until after World War II, with the expansion of electrical service and the improvement of refrigerators, that frozen foods became commonplace in many American homes. In 1954 "TV dinners" appeared on the market, and two decades later the first meal packaged for the microwave oven was in the supermarket freezer ready for sale.

Technological innovations and unevenly distributed city services accentuated class and regional divisions among women. Poor immigrant women caring for their families in the tenements and basement flats of large cities in the early twentieth century struggled against dirt and squalor without running water or indoor toilets. If running water was available, several families often shared the tap, which meant that someone, usually the housewife, carried water in buckets for the family's needs a considerable distance. A large percentage of families used communal toilets located in the cellar or yard. Overcrowding and the presence of boarders to bring in extra money added to the clutter and noise and ultimately to the work. Middle-class social workers attributed slovenly housekeeping habits and incompetent child-rearing practices to immigrant women, often without understanding the difficult circumstances under which these women labored to feed, shelter, and clothe their families. Urban reformers urged foreign-born women to adopt "American" standards of nutrition, cleanliness, and infant care, demeaning the methods and beliefs immigrants had learned from their mothers

and grandmothers. Without adequate living space, sufficient income, running water, garbage collection, and central heating, such advice only helped to increase the distance between the two groups of women.

The industrialization of the home, as some historians have described the changes brought about by new household technologies and products, eased the most onerous aspects of women's domestic chores but did not shorten the time housework took. Time-budget studies conducted from 1900 to 1930 showed that housework remained a full-time job in spite of new energy sources and mechanical aids. In 1930, as it had been in 1900, the average work week for housewives was over forty-five hours, with rural women spending more time in laundering, cleaning, and meal preparation than urban women. By 1930 women of all classes used similar equipment and utilities and strove to achieve the same standards of efficient housework. By 1970 the number of hours per week that women spent on housework had risen to fifty-five, but if the women also worked outside the home that number was reduced to twenty-six. How could this be? How could labor-saving machines not save labor?

A shift in the standard of living, and above all in cultural expectations about cleanliness, nutrition, and the activities women performed in the home helps explain why the new labor-saving machines did not reduce the time spent in housework. For some middle-class women a decline in the servant population meant they were doing their own housework. For those with a rising standard of living, this meant that a family had moved into larger living quarters and the housewife had more rooms to clean. Some women used the time they saved on washing clothes by hand to spend with their children or on beautifying their homes. But in general the American family now had higher standards and greater expectations about the finished product that resulted from all these new machines in the home. Vacuum cleaners meant carpets could be gotten cleaner and cleaned more frequently; washing machines meant people could change their clothes more often and expect to wear cleaner clothes than scrub boards alone could produce.

Two of the major shapers of these new expectations were the household products and appliances industries. Using guilt, shame, fear, and even competition with other housewives, manufacturers worked to reshape the image of the ideal wife and mother in order to sell their products. In their advertisements, manufacturers sold a message about homemaking along with their merchandise. The measure of the good American housewife, the companies declared, was brighter wash, cleaner floors, tastier meals, lighter cakes, and better-nourished children than her neighbor's. By the second decade of the twentieth century, women's magazines such as *Ladies Home Journal* and *McCall's* were filled with ads for labor-saving devices and products that would help housewives do everything better, quicker, and easier. By the 1920s the number of ads had doubled, as had the range of electrical goods and prepared foods on the market. The mass-circulation magazines helped spread the idea in the 1920s, and again in the 1950s, that home and marriage were a woman's highest calling and that her choosing among the myriad of consumer goods available expressed her judgment and creativity as a homemaker. Whatever time and energy a woman spent preparing meals, cleaning the bathroom, and decorating her home was an investment in her family's physical and emotional well-being.

Some historians argue that technology, rather than improving women's lives, increased their domestic responsibilities and impoverished their community interactions. Appliances, they say, were designed so that women could do all the household chores themselves without the assistance of other family members or hired help. Isolated and confined to their homes with their electric washing machines, refrigerators, stoves, and irons, women traded what historian Susan Strasser calls "craft satisfaction, intimacy, and community" for the illusion that in choosing consumer goods they were exercising autonomy and individualism.

During the Depression and the war years, many households took on some of the qualities of self-reliance they had abandoned decades earlier. To cope with unemployment and diminished household resources during the 1930s, families resorted to making what they might previously have bought. Many women revived old skills of knitting, canning, baking, and sewing, while others supplemented their family's income by dressmaking, cleaning, or taking in laundry. During World War II, food rationing encouraged women's gardening skills and the pickling and preserving of homegrown foods. Women learned to repair broken appliances or to substitute manual labor for mechanical energy. As riveters, welders, and workers in war industries women proved they could be both housewives and wage laborers. Nevertheless, for most young married women and mothers, the new role of wage earner was only temporary. When the war was over,

traditional cultural stereotypes of women's proper place reemerged. The majority of women who remained in the labor force after the war were older, many of whom had been working before the war began. Dismissed from their wartime positions, most found low-status, low-paying jobs in traditionally female-dominated occupations. And the domestic ideal reasserted itself in new guises.

THE NEW DOMESTICITY

Often referred to as the decade of the new Victorian domesticity or the decade of the family, the 1950s were filled with contradictions. The popular media portrayed the ideal woman as a happy blend of "Supermom" and "Mrs. Consumer," spending her days in suburbia, shopping and chauffeuring her children from one activity to another. The portrait of the ideal family invariably showed dad cooking over a barbecue in the backyard while mom, wearing heels, skirt, and sweater, pearls and an apron, stood smiling at the doorway of their one-family home as their 2.5 children played with their pet cocker spaniel. Women seemed to delight in maintaining the family's emotional equilibrium while submerging their own individuality for the good of their children and husbands. As in the nineteenth-century family image, the actual labor of cleaning, cooking, laundering, and running the household seemed to have been cropped from the picture.

Studies showed, in actuality, that in spite of new household technologies and growing affluence, women of all classes spent an average of four hours a day doing housework and an additional three and a half hours a day caring for children. Housework remained a full-time job even for women who worked for wages outside their homes. And in spite of the celebration of full-time motherhood and suburban living, increasing numbers of women were leaving home to work for wages outside it. Twenty-nine percent of the total work force was female in 1950, but by the late 1960s women's participation in the labor force was considered essential for working-class families to enter the middle class and for middle-class families to retain their comfortable standard of living. By the end of the 1960s, for the first time in American history women who did not work for wages were in the minority. In 1965, women represented 33 percent of the work force and by 1975 they accounted for 40 percent.

During the women's movement of the 1970s, housework became a prime target for feminists demanding changes in the nuclear family. In one widely read article, "The Politics of Housework," Pat Minardi wrote, "[Men] recognize the essential fact of housework right from the beginning. Which is that it stinks." Feminist Margaret Benston advocated communal kitchens, child care, and laundries, arguing as Charlotte Perkins Gilman had, at the beginning of the century, that only when the private work of housekeeping became public labor would women achieve equality with men. Some groups of individuals did form cooperative buying clubs or lived communally with equitable housekeeping arrangements for a while, but with the exception of cooperative child care few such efforts survived for long. For a brief time, an organization called Wages for Housework advocated paying women for the work they did at home, but the movement received little support from the majority of feminists. Although feminists raised fundamental questions about the division of labor in the family, virtually no major structural or institutional changes occurred in the society to support those changes. With the exception of the Displaced Homemakers' Bill (1977), which created training centers to help divorced or widowed women acquire skills to enter the job market, and the law's acknowledgment that a woman's past homemaking services had monetary value in arriving at a divorce settlement, housekeeping remained the most invisible and unappreciated labor of American women. The women's movement eventually focused its efforts on securing political and economic gains for women, and the New Right stepped in to champion, not to change, the traditional nuclear family and women's role as housewife within it.

In recent years, however, changes in the economy and in the makeup of American families have transformed many women's lives. By 1980, about 51 percent of all adult women worked outside the home, and by 1985 about 53 percent of women with preschool children were in the labor force. There also have been increases in the divorce rate, the number of women in poverty, the number of households without a husband or male living in them, and the creation of single-person households and single-child families. The large number of mothers in the work force has rendered old fashioned the ideal of the full-time homemaker and made many nonwage-earning women apologetic about being "just a housewife." In spite of these changes, women's roles in the home seem to have remained virtually intact. In the late 1980s, sociologist Arlie Hochschild surveyed two-income families across the economic spectrum and learned that women were still responsible for the home, as they had been for the last three centuries. Housework by men had barely increased, despite women's increasing wage-work. Studies even showed that women living without men did less housework, with and without children; the presence of men in the household seemed to create about eight hours of additional housework for a woman each week.

The explanations, like the study of housework itself, are complex. Some historians believe the housewife's role, although unremunerated and often unacknowledged, is crucial to the success of a capitalist economy. Capitalism depends on women's work in the home, they say, to reproduce the labor force in both the literal sense of bearing and rearing children and in the sense of feeding, clothing, and providing decent living quarters for wage laborers. Historically, employers offered men what they called "a family wage," and cultural norms—the persistence of the separate spheres ideology—reinforced the notion that husbands should be the sole supporters of their families. In the past, this cultural image that women belonged at home affected the kinds of jobs available to them when they did go out to work. Segregated in low-status, low-paying, female-dominated occupations such as clerical work, teaching, nursing, and sales, women continued to think of their wage work as only temporary and as a supplement to a husband's salary. Women defined themselves foremost as wives and mothers, and secondarily as workers. These historians believe that the inequities women encounter in the paid labor force are a result of their role as housewives. Some historians add the uneven power relations between men and women to this explanation, arguing that men's superior earning power in the marketplace and the cultural image that women should be subservient reinforces the gender division of labor in the home.

Others have disputed the notion that patriarchy and capitalism alone account for the persistence of traditional family life and the idea that women should be primarily responsible for work done in the home. Instead, they point to deeply engrained cultural values that lead individuals to choose privacy and autonomy above collective living arrangements or commercial solutions to household tasks. Women, they say, prefer to do their own housework and care for their children themselves, because they believe that doing so best contributes to the well-being of their families. Although the proponents of this theory concede that the allocation of housework to women is a social convention, they argue that, because new household technologies or women's participation in the wage labor force have not dramatically changed assumptions about who does what at home, only a conscious effort to equitably share housework on the part of individual families will make a difference.

Regardless of whether one accepts an economic or a cultural explanation for current beliefs about who does what in the household, the historical record offers useful insights for devising strategies for change. Contrary to the nineteenth-century ideal of the home as a haven from the capitalist marketplace, the record shows a continuous and increasing interconnection between the two spheres. Whether through the creation of new products and appliances, alternative employment options for immigrant and African American domestic servants, or the establishment of ideal standards of housekeeping, American economic interests have affected the work women do at home since the early nineteenth century. Images of the ideal housewife and American family that have been portrayed in the popular media and promulgated by advertisers of consumer products continue to influence contemporary beliefs about housework. This link between the home and the larger economy has led some historians to believe that until housework is acknowledged not as a service to family members or others but as a contribution to the well-being of society in general, those who do it will continue to be undervalued and undercompensated.

BIBLIOGRAPHY

Boydston, Jeanne. *Home and Work: Housework, Wages, and the Ideology of Labor in the Early Republic* (1990).

Cowan, Ruth Schwartz. *More Work for Mother: The Ironies of Household Technology from the Open Hearth to the Microwave* (1983).

Dudden, Faye E. *Serving Women: Household Service in Nineteenth-Century America* (1983).

Hartmann, Heidi. "Capitalism and Women's Work in the Home, 1900–1930." Ph.D. dissertation (1974).

Hayden, Dolores. *The Grand Domestic Revolution: A History of Feminist Designs for American Homes, Neighborhoods, and Cities* (1981).

Hochschild, Arlie. *The Second Shift: Working Parents and the Revolution at Home* (1989).

Jensen, Joan M. *Loosening the Bonds: Mid-Atlantic Farm Women, 1750–1850* (1986).

Katzman, David M. *Seven Days a Week: Women and Domestic Service in Industrializing America* (1981).

Matthews, Glenna. *"Just a Housewife": The Rise and Fall of Domesticity in America* (1987).

Ogden, Annegret. *The Great American Housewife: From Helpmate to Wage Earner, 1776–1986* (1986).

Palmer, Phyllis. *Domesticity and Dirt: Housewives and Domestic Servants in the United States, 1920–1945* (1989).

Strasser, Susan. *Never Done: A History of American Housework* (1982).

Ulrich, Laurel Thatcher. *Good Wives: Image and Reality in the Lives of Women in Northern New England, 1650–1750* (1980).

Vanek, Joann. "Household Technology and Social Status: Rising Living Standards and Status and Residence Difference in Housework." *Technology and Culture* 19 (Jan. 1978): 361–375. See table 3, p. 374.

SEE ALSO **Clothing and Personal Adornment; Feminist Approaches to Social History; Foodways; Gender; Gender Roles and Relations; Housing; The United States as Interpreted by Foreign Observers; Women and Work.**

LABOR: COLONIAL TIMES THROUGH 1820

Sharon V. Salinger

LABOR IN EARLY America is a topic that covers more than two hundred years and involves multiple economies and regional diversity. However, labor in all of the North American colonies shared two primary characteristics: the importance of the household and the scarcity of workers.

The household was the primary productive unit whether it was located in an urban or a rural setting, whether in the northern, southern, or middle colonies. A focus on the household not only provides a fuller understanding of the economy but also enables us to integrate the primary labor of women, housework, in order to assess its contribution to the economy, as well as its relationship to the emerging industrial order and to the production of surplus value and capital.

Scarcity describes labor everywhere. Until well into the eighteenth century, the supply of free laborers was both unreliable and expensive. Governor William Leete of Connecticut wrote in 1680, "there is seldom any want relief; because labor is deare" (Richard Morris, *Government and Labor in Early America,* p. 45). William Byrd II of Virginia echoed the lament. He abandoned a scheme to introduce the production of hemp in Virginia because "Labour being much dearer than in Muscovy, as well as Freight, we can make no Earnings of it" (Morris, p. 46). While one could argue with the rosy picture painted by these writers, the perceived labor scarcity was a problem to be reckoned with in each of the colonies. Whether the complaint came from tobacco producers in the Chesapeake or from craftsmen in the port cities, potential employers regularly complained about the chronic shortage of laborers.

The origins of labor scarcity are found in the nature of the imperial economy. The mother country, while rich in capital and labor, had very limited natural resources. The colonies, in contrast, were without capital and labor, but their natural resources were plentiful, especially land. No colonist needed to work for someone else when land was so readily available. In regions where staple crop production dominated, land was abundant and the demand for labor was particularly intense because it was the ability to control large numbers of laborers that separated the successful planter from the unsuccessful.

The port cities and agricultural regions of the northern and middle colonies solved some of the problems of labor scarcity by blending bound and free workers. Free labor continued to operate in a precapitalist mode. Most tradesmen, for example, until late in the eighteenth century paid their laborers with a combination of wages and goods. Merchant seaman were the only exception; they, by the early eighteenth century, were free and fully waged laborers. Unfree labor was best characterized by paternalism, a system that combined mutuality with the constant reminder that society was ordered vertically and masters controlled virtually all aspects of servants' lives.

Plantation owners of the southern and Chesapeake colonies responded to the shortage of workers by depending on unfree laborers to produce staple crops. Virginia and Maryland planters, for example, cultivated tobacco initially with white indentured servants, later replaced by black slaves. While Carolina planters also relied on unfree labor, slaves were present in the region from the beginning, and by the middle of the eighteenth century, the majority of workers were black.

Toward the end of the eighteenth century, labor systems diverged dramatically. In the cities and in the rural economies of New England and the middle colonies, the labor scarcity, which had created incentives for the use of unfree labor, was replaced by labor surplus, which began to render the system obsolete. Labor surplus was the result of a variety of factors. Most important, urban populations grew in the midst of unevenly developing economies. For the first time, substantial unemployment occurred that ushered in a new phase of labor relations. Employers turned less often to the labor of unfree workers, the paternalistic order disappeared, and a system of capitalist wage relations emerged. Staple crop producers, on the other hand, experienced no reduction in their needs for labor, nor did the middle of the eighteenth century usher in a period of labor surplus. Rather, they remained committed to slavery. Thus, in the northern and middle colonies unfree labor disappeared and free wage labor dominated, while in the Chesapeake and southern colonies, institutions of unfree labor became more firmly entrenched.

As a result of the relationship between production and labor, this essay focuses on three primary economic systems and their differing labor forms—agriculture, staple crop and mixed; the household, urban and rural; and the cities, skilled and unskilled. While it is uncontroversial to define labor in terms of production, I adopt a slightly amended, less traditional conception. In "Servants and Slaves" Richard Dunn defines the colonial laborer as any woman or man who performed manual labor for a head of a household either with or without wages: a slave, servant, apprentice, wage laborer, or dependent family worker. This excludes many manual workers who were independent or semi-independent producers: self-employed farmers, tenant farmers, or craftsmen; nevertheless, the men and women included constituted the majority of the population of early America.

This essay explores two primary aspects in the lives of laboring people in early America. Foremost, it investigates the nature of their tasks and the organization of their labors, and the impact of the various labor systems on workers' lives.

THE CHESAPEAKE

When the first ships touched shore at Jamestown in 1607, labor was not the central concern. Planners and immigrants assumed that American Indians would be molded into a labor force that would be compelled to do all manner of work. In addition, skilled craftsmen, recruited for the Virginia enterprise, would transform the region's natural resources into wealth. The majority of the colonists would be called upon to make key decisions and could spend their extensive leisure time counting their money.

The settlers' hopes for easy riches were dashed precipitously. Rather than wealth, the Jamestown settlers were greeted by the specter of death. In addition, American Indians refused to labor for Europeans; and even had the craftsmen survived the fevers of the Chesapeake, Virginia lacked the precious minerals like gold and silver that would either keep them busy or make them rich. The dismal picture brightened somewhat by 1612 when John Rolfe (1585–1622) discovered that the lands of Virginia were well suited for the cultivation of tobacco. Tobacco was used in England primarily for medicinal purposes until regular shipments arrived from the New World. As a result, the demand began to rise and people increasingly smoked for pleasure. The "jovial weed," while seeming to offer a solution to the colony's financial woes, had a hidden problem—its cultivation required intensive labor. Thus, the recruitment of labor became a critical issue.

In order to solve the problems caused by the shortage of workers, the Chesapeake colonists imported laborers. The Virginia Company of London, the joint stock company charged with promoting and developing Virginia, attempted to fill the immediate need for laborers by enticing young Englishmen to labor for them as indentured servants.

Indentured Labor Virginians used three primary forms of indentured labor. From the perspective of the laborer, sharecropping tenants were perhaps in the best position. They were transported to the colony by the Virginia Company and plantation owners, were assigned land to work, were supervised by company agents, and were entitled to half of what they produced. After seven years their tenancy ended and they received fifty acres of land. For each tenant whose transport he paid, a planter received a bonus of fifty acres.

Apprenticeship was the second form of unfree labor; from the individual's vantage point it was the worst extreme. The origins of apprenticeship are found in the Middle Ages, when the institution was devised by members of craft guilds to ensure proper training and to limit the numbers of individuals who could enter the trades. Apprentices contracted with masters for a specified number of years, to be trained in the "art and mystery of the craft" in exchange for clothing, food, and shelter. The Virginia variation only slightly resembled its English origins; it was fashioned less as a system of education than as a means to recruit agricultural laborers. Apprentices were transported to the colony and were bound for seven years to the planter who purchased them. At the end of the term, they became tenants for an additional seven years. If at any time during their service they were convicted of a crime, their term as a servant was to begin again for seven more years.

Indentured servitude, the final form, was a variation on contract labor, but the innovation in Virginia included the practice of selling servants. The first group of servants entered contract agreements with the Virginia Company of London. In exchange for transportation to Virginia, food, shelter, and clothing, they would labor for four to seven years and receive "shares in the venture's anticipated profits" (Warren Billings, "The Law of Servants and Slaves," p. 47). When the company's solvency became precarious, rather than continue to buy servants, it instituted a headright system that encouraged individuals to pay the costs of shipping servants to Virginia. For each servant brought into the colony, masters received fifty acres of land; servants were promised that at the end of their service, they too would be rewarded with land. By 1625, according to the first Virginia census, over 40 percent of the colony's residents were indentured servants, almost all of them from England.

Individuals became indentured servants in a number of ways. Most entered into servitude because they were too poor to pay their own passage to the colonies, and they were willing to exchange two to nine years of their labors for the hopes of more prosperous futures. Others were kidnapped. "Spirits" roamed the docks of seventeenth-century London, plying adults with alcohol and children with sweets to lure them onto ships bound for America. Although individual "spirits" claimed thousands of victims, their practices were short-lived and accounted for only a small proportion of the servants who emigrated. Still others were a part of "His Majesty's Seven Year Passengers," the mocking description for transported convicts or political prisoners exiled to do labor in America. Of as many as thirty thousand convict servants who were transported from British jails between 1718 and 1775, two-thirds went to Virginia and Maryland.

Although workdays in the New World plantations were from sunrise to sunset, during even the most intense growing seasons "field laborers were permitted five hours rest during the heat of the day, Saturday afternoon off, and the 'old Holidayes . . . observed'" (Lois G. Carr and Lorena S. Walsh, "Economic Diversification," p. 154). During the winter months, little was done except hunting and cutting firewood. The laws of Maryland and Virginia "required only that masters provide 'sufficient' food, clothing, and shelter; a Sunday free of hard labor; and moderation in correction" (Carr and Walsh, p. 155). To a very great extent, servants' lives de-

pended most on the personalities of individual masters. If a master were humane, servitude might be tolerable; if not, life was a nightmare.

A legal system gradually developed to regularize the system of indentured labor. Some of the laws enacted by the Virginia legislature acknowledged how difficult it was to force servants to work. If a servant ran away, the law provided "added service, whippings, hair croppings, or, in the instance of habitual offenders, brandings" (Billings, p. 50). The laws also identified servants as chattel, and thus masters could handle them just as they did other forms of property like clothing or livestock. Finally, the laws licensed masters to use "reasonable" force to control their servants. The courts also provided recourse for those unlucky servants whose masters were cruel. Lois Carr and Lorena Walsh note, "servants might be forced to eat unfamiliar food, but they could not go unfed; they might be worked to exhaustion five or six days a week, but, on Sunday, they could rest" (p. 155).

Indentured servants in the Chesapeake were the human machines with which planters produced staple crops. In Virginia and Maryland, servants' labors were devoted primarily to the cultivation of tobacco. Tobacco was labor intensive—after seedlings were planted and thinned, the fields had to be weeded, and worms had to be removed continuously from the plants. Harvesting was also time consuming: the mature leaves were picked first, bundled, and transported for curing. As the smaller leaves grew, they were harvested. All of this work occurred in climates that varied from hot and steamy to steamy and unbearable.

Chesapeake planters appeared to have had such an insatiable appetite for servants that they enticed thousands of Englishmen to come to Virginia to grow tobacco for them. Over the course of the seventeenth century, improved techniques increased the amount of tobacco an individual could produce; and by putting more laborers into the fields, output grew even more rapidly: "About seventy-five thousand whites immigrated to the Chesapeake colonies from Britain between 1630 and 1680, and from half to three-quarters of them arrived as indentured servants" (Allan Kulikoff, *Tobacco and Slaves*, p. 32). Planters wanted men who could be put to work in the tobacco fields; not surprisingly, more than six times as many men as women served indentures.

In the last decades of the seventeenth century, the supply of English servants declined. More men and women were able to find jobs in England, and the push to America lessened. In addition, with the founding of Pennsylvania and other colonies, English servants had a choice. In the early half of the seventeenth century, servants had only the option of remaining unemployed in England or risking their lives in the fever-ridden Chesapeake or West Indies. After 1682, the year Pennsylvania was founded, individuals who wanted to serve indentures in the New World could continue to fill the demand in the humid climates of Virginia and Maryland, Jamaica or Barbados, or sign on with a master who grew wheat or flax in Pennsylvania or made chairs or shoes in Philadelphia. Not surprisingly, fewer and fewer men and women were available to labor in the plantation colonies.

Black Slaves   While the supply of servants declined, the demand for labor did not. According to Richard Dunn, "During the 1680s and 1690s in the Chesapeake, black slaves from West Africa began to replace English servants as the mainstay of the labor force" ("Servants and Slaves," p. 164). The shift from white servants to black slaves started slowly at the end of the seventeenth century. In 1660, there were at most seventeen hundred blacks residing in Virginia and Maryland; by 1680 this number had increased to four thousand. Slaves entered the colony in small numbers, primarily from the West Indies, and planters used them to supplement rather than replace their labor force. However, as white servants became difficult to obtain and a more regularized trade in slaves developed, planters began to purchase slaves in larger numbers.

The increasing supply of West African slaves for the English colonies was due to the opening of the slave trade. From 1663 to 1698, the exclusive rights to the English trade belonged to Adventures to Africa, a group that reorganized and rechartered its name in 1672 to Royal Africa Company. When its hold was broken, private slavers rushed into business, and for the first time a regular trade existed to supply North American planters with slaves. Between 1695 and 1700, three thousand Africans were enslaved, equal to the number in the previous twenty years. As a result, the racial composition of Chesapeake labor shifted, and by 1700 from two-thirds to three-quarters of the unfree laborers were black.

Other impulses besides timing highlight the switch from white to black unfree labor in the Chesapeake. Virginia and Maryland planters experienced a temporary supply shortage of servants during the English Civil War, but by the late seventeenth century the diminishing supply of English servants was permanent. In addition, mortality declined dramatically, thereby creating financial in-

centives to invest in slaves. For the first fifty years of the Virginia colony, the chances of anyone's surviving were extremely unlikely. Thus, owning a man for life was not a sound investment, especially since a slave cost twice as much as a servant. In his *American Slavery,* Edmund Morgan notes that "if the chances of a man's dying during his first five years in Virginia were better than fifty-fifty—and it seems apparent that they were—and if English servants could be made to work as hard as slaves, English servants for a five-year term were the better buy" (pp. 297–298). By the end of the seventeenth century, "the price of a lifetime slave became competitive with the price of a short-term servant" (Dunn, p. 164). Since slaves served for life, they became the cheapest form of labor.

Declining mortality contributed to an altered social constellation in the Chesapeake that hastened the substitution of black slaves for white servants. Death during the first fifty years of settlement was indiscriminate—masters and servants died young. However, just as everyone began to live longer and increasing numbers of servants completed their terms, achieved freedom, and demanded land, the economic climate in Virginia worsened. Land became difficult to get and tobacco prices plummeted. As a result, tensions heated up and erupted, in 1676, in Bacon's Rebellion. Bacon's Rebellion defies a simple narrative. The fighting pitted white settlers against Indians, and white settlers against each other. Of the hundreds who joined with Nathaniel Bacon to fight Indians, many were frustrated frontiersmen whose hopes for acquiring cheap lands were stymied by an agreement forged after the 1644 war, which prohibited white settlement north of the York River. Planters calculated that a move to a slave system would solve some of the labor problems because slaves served for life and thus would not become discontented freedmen.

Seventeenth-century planters were involved primarily in a transatlantic trade in tobacco; by the early eighteenth century, tobacco production ceased to dominate. As a result, labor was redirected as well. The origins of this shift are many. However, among the most important impulses were depressed tobacco prices after 1680, disruption in the trade as a result of the many colonial wars, increasing competition as more and more immigrants and newly freed servants entered the market, and soil exhaustion from too many tobacco crops.

The shift in production and the move from white to black unfree labor altered the character of the work system. Slaves were not protected by the laws of servitude that required masters to provide adequate food, clothing, or housing. Colonial lawmakers gradually chipped away at the vestiges of the slave's humanity. They began by distinguishing blacks from whites in the right to carry arms. Ultimately the status of black adults and their children was comparable with chattel, all rights stripped from them, including marriage, education, and, of course, freedom. The law gave masters the right to determine how much force was appropriate to punish various breaches of conduct. These laws assumed that no master would harm or injure his property without just cause.

As black slaves came to dominate unfree labor, work discipline changed for both servants and slaves. Saturday became a full workday, and there were only three holidays a year. In Virginia, by the 1730s only skilled servants who arrived under indenture retained a free Saturday afternoon. For slaves the work regimen was extremely constricted, and one day was very much like the next. They could not even depend on Sundays off. House slaves prepared meals for endless rounds of guests regardless of the day. Night-work was often added to field hands' chores: beating corn into meal or stripping tobacco leaves. Lois Carr and Lorena Walsh point out that in the 1770s, for example, Landon Carter had his slaves "tie up ninety tobacco plants into hands each night" (p. 159). Diversification also created additional work. Little had happened on a tobacco plantation during the months from December to February; this changed. More timber had to be cut and carted to meet the demands for more casks. Pastures were cleared and swamps were grubbed. Ultimately diversification worked to separate the labor of whites and blacks. Increasingly tasks requiring skills were reserved for white laborers while the cultivation of tobacco and corn fell to slaves.

Chesapeake labor altered dramatically over the course of two centuries. Initially it was organized to produce tobacco in exhange for European goods, and white indentured servants performed the bulk of the labor. Tobacco was grown into the nineteenth century, but now it was cultivated by black slaves and it no longer dominated production. Additional agricultural products and economic diversity changed work roles. Male and female slaves no longer worked together or performed the same jobs. Chesapeake labor had changed from white to black, from servant to slave.

Change in Gender Roles Diversification in production altered gender roles of both white and black workers. From 1760 to 1820, as Virginia and Maryland planters abandoned tobacco cultivation in favor of wheat, other grains, and livestock, tasks became more varied and the gender division of labor became more marked. When tobacco was the primary crop, work routines for male and female slaves varied very little. The new tasks however, required a certain level of skill—"sowing and mowing grains, plowing, harrowing, carting, ditching, lumbering, fishing, and milling" (Carr and Walsh, p. 176)—jobs carried out primarily by men. Slave women continued to work in the fields, performing unskilled manual labor and separate from the men. They were assigned the less desirable chores: "building fences, grubbing swamps in the dead of winter, cleaning winnowed grain of weed seed, breaking up new ground too rough or weedy to plow, cleaning stables, and loading and spreading manure" (Carr and Walsh, p. 177).

The shift away from tobacco affected the labor of free men and women as well. The men and women with small holdings worked together to grow tobacco because labor was scarce and expensive. On the small number of wealthy plantations, the work roles of men and women diverged from the beginning. The men focused on the production and marketing of tobacco; the wives of planters were responsible for supervising household labor.

With diversification, men and women devoted their time to a larger range of activities and labor tasks separated more clearly along gender lines. Men continued to market crops, and "some planters began to raise a little wheat, rye, or beans and peas for variety in their diets" (Carr and Walsh, p. 145). Women had time for vegetable gardens; they made cheese and butter, preserved meat, and spun yarn. Home manufacturing increased, spurred in part by the nonimportation agreeements during the Revolution. Planters' wives and daughters continued to card wool, hackle flax, spin, weave, knit, sew, mold candles, make cider, and salt meat. Wives and daughters of tenant farmers did piecework for planters and often made clothing for slaves.

CAROLINA

The economies of the Deep South were as dependent upon staple crop production and unfree labor as that of the Chesapeake, yet its original population and the development and nature of its labor systems differed greatly. In contrast with most of the American colonies that were populated by English, European, and African immigrants, Carolina's settlers came by way of the West Indies—planters and their slaves. Rather than an unfree labor system that evolved from white to black, black slaves were present in the colony from its inception.

The earliest Carolina population consisted of a mixture of Africans and Europeans who had been forced out of Barbados. These emigrants were either sons of lesser planters or small landowners. The sons of lesser planters had very little likelihood of inheriting any land; thus, they took their inheritance in the form of servants and slaves. The small landowners had been forced from their holdings. In terms of settlement and labor in the Carolinas, among the most important features of the push away from Barbados was that enslaved Africans were part of almost every outgoing contingent.

Thus in the earliest years of settlement (after 1670), the Carolina population was a mixture of black slaves and white planters. The proprietors, faced with virtually unlimited land supplies, sought a product or products that would bring them wealth and enable them to enter the transatlantic market. Livestock emerged as the first, if temporary, solution. With land abundant and settlement sparse, cattle could graze freely. In addition, the British West Indies provided a ready market because the settlers' obsession to grow sugar required that they import food. As a result, Carolina planters employed many of their slaves as cowboys—they moved with the herds into the remote interior of the colony, tending and protecting them. Carolina slaves often labored alone, beyond the view of overseers or bosses, and reappeared when the cattle were ready for market. Cattle production provided planters with a number of advantages: it enabled them to amass capital, it used relatively few laborers, and it made the larger part of the labor force available for the immense task of clearing the dense Carolina forests.

For the first two decades following the settlement of the colony, no labor form dominated, nor did any single economic activity occupy the work force. However, during the second generation, production shifted to rice, which altered labor relations. Although the English had known about rice since the seventeenth century, it was neither consumed nor traded with any regularity. However, southern Europeans had adopted rice as a dietary staple, and Carolina's proprietors recognized its trade potential. Early attempts to grow the grain failed, not because the soil and climate were unsuitable but because none of the planters knew exactly what they were doing. Rice production was successful in the Carolinas only after sufficient numbers of West Africans were present, because they were familiar with rice cultivation. Rice has shallower roots than tobacco, and the boggy soils of the Carolinas were ideal for it. Thus the labor organization of rice production in the Carolinas was not, as in other regions of staple crop production, a system imposed by Europeans on Africans. The style of planting and hoeing, the cooking, and the work songs that provided the rhythms of production were transported to the colony by West Africans. This is not to imply that slaves' playing an active role in determining the nature of production somehow mitigated the effects of slavery. Rather, ironically, as Peter Wood convincingly argued, rice cultivation was introduced by West Africans and "rice culture turned planters increasingly toward slave labor" (*Black Majority,* p. 37).

In addition to rice, Carolina settlers developed one other major export crop, indigo. Although indigo grew wild in some areas of the South, the most desirable variety, deep blue, came from the West Indies. During the 1740s, the war with France halted English importation of the West Indian variety, and Carolina planters began to develop the crop in earnest. Eliza Lucas (Pinckney), a Caribbean immigrant, deserves much of the credit. She was born in Antigua where she learned indigo cultivation from her father. She was brought to South Carolina in 1738 and by 1741 was experimenting with West Indian indigo seeds. Lucas's initial crops were cultivated specifically to produce seed, which she distributed to local planters. West African skills contributed greatly to the success of indigo cultivation, since slaves working the fields used only slight variations on their rice techniques.

With the successful cultivation of rice and indigo, labor demand increased and planters sought laborers from a number of sources. As in the Chesapeake, American Indians were unwilling to work for them. Indentured servants were imported into the Carolinas, but the demand for them was so great that servants could contract for very short periods of time. More important, servants never came to the Carolinas in sufficient numbers to affect the size of the work force and, as in other regions of intensive agricultural production, indentured servants lacked sufficient incentives to work.

African labor provided the most reasonable alternative. A systematic slave trade had developed, which kept transportation costs lower than for white servants. Since a master owned slaves for their lifetime, slavery would solve some of the difficulties caused by servitude: short indentures and continual turnover. In addition, Africans were reputed to work more efficiently in the subtropical Carolinas.

Finally, West Africans did considerably more than provide labor. They brought with them to the New World the skills that contributed both to the adoption of rice as one of the region's staple crops and to a wide range of labors they performed. One critical problem confronting early Carolina settlers was clearing the forests. Slaves provided the labor and a three-stage technique: black men and adolescents felled and split the trees; slave women and children removed the brush and hauled the wood; and at night, the best time to avoid the winds, the slaves burned the fields.

Through the eighteenth century, blacks dominated labor in the Carolinas. The colony got off to a rocky start, and only after sufficient numbers of West African slaves were present did planters in the region produce sufficient quantities of rice and indigo for those crops to be profitable. These two export products, as well as the general economic health of the colony, owed much to the West African heritage of Carolina slaves.

THE NORTH

In the middle and New England colonies, the configuration of labor was different as a result of the nature of agricultural production and the existence of cities. No crops in these colonies required the intensive labor of tobacco or sugar, nor were there cities in the Chesapeake or the South that resembled the seaports of Boston, New York, and Philadelphia.

Rural production in the northeastern and middle colonies was characterized by mixed agriculture, in part as a result of the nature of settlement. Immigrants to New England organized into townships and divided lands among individual family units. New York settlement varied greatly, from the vast patroonships worked by tenants to smaller family holdings in newer areas. In Pennsylvania families joined together around churches and villages and farmed rich soil. Sizes of landholdings varied by social and economic status, but most founding families were given ample acreage and produced a wide range of crops, from grains and flax to apples and cherries. Most farmers sold or exchanged their surplus, but these transactions rarely involved cash.

The colonists who traveled from England to New England during the 1630s belonged for the most part to households that had been prosperous enough to own servants. They transported these servants to the New World in numbers far surpassing the proportion of families with servants in England—or, in fact, the proportion of families that would own bound labor in future generations. For example, about 13 percent of the households in England had servants, whereas more than 20 percent of emigrating families transported servants. These families had no illusions about the nature of the work required to found new settlements and, as Edward Johnson warned, it required "every one that can lift a hawe" (Daniel Vickers, "Working the Fields," p. 54).

However, once the servants who accompanied the earliest settlers were freed, they were not systematically replaced. Indentured labor never played a significant role in New England. Indeed, only 4 percent of the families in Essex County, Massachusetts, had servants. The owners of the largest estates, individuals like John Pynchon of Springfield, Massachusetts, continued to have servants. Pynchon, for example, employed his servants "to raise wheat, cattle and timber for shipment abroad" (Vickers, p. 54). Yet Samuel Symonds, who at his death owned seventeen hundred acres and was among the wealthiest landholders in seventeenth-century Massachusetts, had only two manservants in his home. Estimates suggest that only one-quarter of all Massachusetts families owned servants of either gender. New England farm families did need additional labor at various times—during harvesting, house building, and birthing—but they preferred, if possible, to use their own offspring. If their requirements for labor exceeded what their families could provide, they exchanged or hired labor for specific tasks or days.

Similarly, Pennsylvania's founding generation was well aware of the scarcity of labor in the colonies; the Free Society of Traders, the joint stock company in charge of promoting and organizing the colony, planned to import both servants and slaves. As in the colonies to the north, unfree labor was important for the founding generation, primarily in agriculture. However, Pennsylvanians continued to rely on unfree labor until well into the eighteenth century, primarily as an urban work force. Establishing farms required intensive labor, and as James Claypoole, the secretary of the Free Society of Traders revealed, he would use slaves "for cutting down trees, building, plowing or any sort of labor that is required in the first planting of a country" (Sharon V. Salinger, *"To Serve Well and Faithfully,"* p. 22). While precise figures are unavailable, at least 271 individuals signed indentures to serve in Pennsylvania during the 1680s; estimates of the slave population in the early decades place it somewhere between four hundred and five hundred.

Like their counterparts in the Chesapeake, New Englanders and Pennsylvanians successfully put into place a gendered division of labor in which women had primary responsibility for the house, children, and garden while men worked in the fields. The exceptions to this were during peak labor demand. July in Pennsylvania, for example, was the time for the rye harvest. Farmers with sizeable acreage might hire a dozen or more day laborers to assist. However, most farmers hired one or two workers, and everyone in the family old enough to help did so. Women formed teams with the men and, using a slightly lighter scythe, helped reap and pile the grain. Haying followed. The scythes for this operation were heavier, so the women followed behind the men to spread the grass to dry. Afterward, everyone worked to load the hay onto the wagons.

Household economies in the seventeenth century were characterized by mixed enterprises in which the roles of men and women were interdependent. Household textile production provides a clear example of the many layers of family labor. Men "sowed, turned, and broke flax; the women weeded, pulled, combed, spun, reeled, boiled, spooled, warped, quilled, wove, bucked and bleached it" (Laurel Ulrich, "Martha Ballard and Her Girls," p. 75). For knitting and sewing, men's labor also provided the raw materials. Then the adult female and her daughters created a wide range of items including cotton wool, and linen hose, woolen "leggins" and "buskins," and shifts, skirts, aprons, and petticoats for the women, trousers and jackets for the men. However, men's coats and breeches and women's dresses were often made by the tailor or dressmaker.

Although women in all types of households had a comparable range of chores that needed to be accomplished, focusing for the most part on food preparation and child care, the economic status of the household dictated to a large extent the amount of time spent on various tasks. For example, women in middling families spent more time than their counterparts in other classes in food preparation and preservation. They had more equipment and a wider range of food available than

poor women but, unlike wealthy women, they had no servants to supervise. Middling wives were required to do the work themselves or with the assistance of their daughters. Wives in poorer rural families lacked access to the varieties of food and equipment, and certainly had no servants to share the labor. They weeded gardens or gathered vegetables for others in exchange for food or a bit of money. Their city counterparts took in washing or sewing. Clearly the economic status of the household determined to a large extent the ways in which women spent their time. All were involved with the chores of the household. But in addition, wives of middling households could trade or barter for items they needed. Wealthy women were more likely to purchase these goods. Poorer women were involved in a complicated system of barter, labor, and scavenging.

Women also were responsible for milking cows, feeding the swine and chickens, and nursing sick animals. They were especially busy during slaughtering time, helping cut and salt, dealing with all of the parts—cleaning the tripe, dressing the calf's head or pig's feet, preparing sausage casings, and cooking organ meats. Their gardening chores occupied them from early spring, when the seeds were sown or seedlings transplanted, until late October, when the cabbages were stored in the root cellar and the seeds were gathered for next year's planting.

Besides the household tasks women performed, they participated in an often hidden but essential network of exchange of goods and services that rarely involved cash but contributed to surplus value and capital accumulation. Female neighborliness and social networks meant that women would help a sick neighbor or assist at a birth. They would meet to pull flax together or share recently caught fish. And the products women created were bartered in an informal economic network. Preserves might be exchanged for cheese, surplus cherries or cheese for candles.

During the seventeenth century, New England Puritans valued women's work highly and men acknowledged that their labors contributed greatly to the success of the household. In 1630, for example, the Massachusetts Court of Assistance allotted twenty shillings to each man whose family had not yet arrived from England. The money was to be used to hire the services ordinarily performed by their wives. In 1645, the Massachusetts Court of Elections reimbursed tavern keepers Richard Sherman and "ye wife of Richard Sherman" for the charges accrued by the colony's deputies and governor for room and board. Richard and his wife were paid separately and in different amounts. The court's payment made a distinction between male and female labor within the tavern and reflected, by assigning a monetary value to each, the economic legitimacy of both claims.

While women's work remained virtually unchanged throughout the eighteenth century and family production remained focused within households that continued to be primarily agricultural and not self-sufficient, the value of female labor eroded. This decline reflected not the nature or economic value of housework but the perception of housewifery. Many factors contributed to the devaluing of housework, but perhaps most critical was the gradual transformation of the economy during the eighteenth century into one in which men were the exclusive economic agents. In the colonial period, although women did not have equal social status with men, their position did not undermine their economic role in the household. However, as the role of money increased and market consciousness expanded, the economic realm became extra-household and the exclusive domain of men. And women, who continued to be relegated to the home and who realized no external cash value for their labors, were denied labor value. The emerging formulation of the economy as a complex of activities that could occur only outside the household made it impossible for women to "lay claim to the status of 'worker,'" and they ceased to be considered as part of the "real economy" (Jeanne Boydston, *Home and Work,* p. 21).

The value of women's work in the household experienced a brief resurgence during the American Revolution. American victory appears to have been dependent in part on women's home manufacturing. However, the effect was ephemeral, and at war's end the household once again lost much of its economic agency. In agricultural households, the growth of the market affected men and women differently. Women continued to spend most of their time converting raw materials into usable items, but the interdependence of male and female household labor ended. Rather than bringing their surplus or raw materials home, men were more likely to exchange them in the marketplace for cash. Women were not totally removed from the market, but their involvement increased as consumers rather than as producers. The political and economic orders in the new republic were based on the work performed by men, which increasingly

was done outside the household. Domestic labor had become marginalized.

URBAN LABOR AND REVOLUTIONARY POLITICS

Although Boston, Philadelphia, and New York contained only a small minority of the colonial population—never more than about 10 percent—these seaports played a far more important role in the social, economic, and political life of the colonies than their size would suggest. In addition, their changing labor relations portended the industrial order in nineteenth-century America. With Boston the oldest and Philadelphia the youngest, their growth and sizes remained relatively constant until the middle of the eighteenth century, when Philadelphia's population surpassed those of the other two. These cities were the hub in a system of maritime commerce, commercial interchange, and petty commodity production. Boston, Philadelphia, and New York provided entry to the huge numbers of immigrants—primarily English, European, and African—who arrived in an almost continuous stream throughout the colonial period. The urban laboring classes processed the products that linked the colonies to the international chain of labor and markets. The cities also served the populations of the hinterland—as markets for their agricultural produce and as places to procure manufactured goods from home and abroad.

The majority of urban laborers were employed in commerce and petty commodity production. They included the skilled and the unskilled, the unfree and the free. Unskilled laborers worked primarily as "porters, wood choppers, sawyers, scavengers, chimney sweeps, washerwomen, and waterside and construction workers who stowed and unloaded ship cargoes, excavated cellars, drained swamps, hauled materials, and the like" (Gary B. Nash, Billy G. Smith, and Dirk Hoerder, "Labor in the Era of the American Revolution," p. 416). Merchant seamen belonged to this group, a reflection of their wage rates rather than of levels of skill.

Merchant seamen, or Jack Tars, were the largest group of free wage laborers in the eighteenth century, numbering somewhere between twenty-five thousand and forty thousand in the period from 1700 to 1750. They are important beyond the size of their group because their experiences provide a window on the emerging capitalist wage relations. Their labor task was to move cargo; their primary place of business, the docks and the ships that plied the Atlantic trade. The common seaman provided the labor that linked the colonies to the vast transatlantic world.

The ship has been described as a forerunner of the factory. On it, seamen were confined within an enclosed setting, had specific tasks, and were required to work cooperatively. Although mariners tended to stay with one ship only for the length of the voyage, the basic division of labor from ship to ship was the same; what may have varied was the size of the crew. Writing in *Between the Devil and the Deep Blue Sea* (1987), Marcus Rediker notes that each ship had "a master, a mate, a carpenter, a boatswain, a gunner, a quartermaster, perhaps a cook, and four or five able or ordinary seamen" (p. 83). A larger ship or one more heavily manned might include a "second mate, a carpenter's mate, and four or five more common tars." (Rediker [1987], p. 83).

Jack Tar performed a wide range of tasks that were determined primarily by whether the ship was in port or at sea. At sea, he worked the sails and rigging, repaired the ship's machinery, and performed navigational tasks. He learned to read the winds and weather. While rank dictated to a very large extent the tasks while in transit, the chores involved while docked were performed and known by everyone. Cargo required loading, maneuvering, and securing; and once the ship reached its destination, cargo had to be unloaded. It was a dangerous life. Merchant seamen suffered all of the ills of their contemporaries—yellow fever, typhus, skin diseases, and so on—but many of their afflictions were peculiar to their work. It was not unusual to lose a finger while rolling a cask, suffer a hernia while lifting a heavy load, or get a rope burn from the rigging. Shipboard life was dangerous, and men died from being swept overboard by high seas, from falling from the rigging, or from being struck by falling or shifting cargo.

Laborers and merchant seamen traditionally were on the lowest rung of the social and economic ladders in the cities. Economic necessity often forced them into these jobs, and while in them, their occupational and economic mobility was restricted. As a group they shared the lowest standard of living and status of any of the laboring classes of the port cities.

Artisans were the colonies' skilled craftsmen; while some tramped through the rural areas to ply their trades, most were concentrated in the cities. Artisans, known also as tradesmen, mechanics, artificers, and leather apron men, accounted for "between one-third and one-half of all city taxpayers during the late colonial and revolutionary period" (Steven Rosswurm, *Arms, Country and Class,* p. 14). They owned property that included their tools, skills, and produced commodities. Artisans occupied the middling and upper ranks of the laboring people. They ranged in status from the apprentice to the master, and in wealth from the tailors and shoemakers who clustered on the bottom of the economic heap to tanners and silversmiths, who often occupied the upper end.

Unlike England and Europe, in which the hierarchy of skills was adhered to fairly strictly, the crafts in the colonial cities were organized loosely, and within each craft there were gradations of status. Apprentices were the low extreme. They signed to serve a master for approximately seven to nine years in exchange for being taught the "art and mystery" of the trade. In the middle were journeymen. They had served an apprenticeship, owned their own tools, and hired themselves out. Masters were at the top. They were generally older and worked for themselves. In theory, serving an apprenticeship and a comparable amount of time as a journeyman assured the way to master.

Most of the seaports' trades were organized in this traditional way. In addition, Philadelphia's artisans, more than their counterparts in the other port cities, relied on unfree labor: indentured servants and slaves. They preferred servants but were willing to buy slaves when servants were unavailable. Most craftsmen produced "bespoke" work (items that were custom ordered) in small shops with five to ten workers, one or two of whom were unfree. The notable exceptions were shipyards and ropewalks, which often had up to twenty-five workers.

The work cycle depended on the vagaries of the weather and the seasons. When the port froze, shipping halted. In the winter of 1728–1729, for example, "36 ships lay frozen at dockside in Philadelphia; several decades later a visitor counted 117 ships icebound in the Delaware" (Gary B. Nash, *The Urban Crucible,* p. 10). A winter freeze not only put maritime laborers like stevedores and mariners out of work, it prevented the cooper from shaping the barrel staves outside, or the housewright from digging the cellar. Work time was in part controlled by the seasons, since most work could be done only by the light of day. The seasons affected wage rates as well. No standardized wage system existed in the eighteenth-century city; Philadelphia's master mechanics were paid both by the piece and by time. Often the newest journeyman in the shop received a piece rate until his productivity warranted payment by the day. However, master craftsmen used different pay schedules to their advantage to mitigate seasonal differences. In the 1790s, journeymen received a flat rate during the long days of summer, when production was higher, and a piece rate during the winter, when shorter days meant more limited production.

During most of the colonial period, craftsmen were aligned, regardless of status, on the basis of their craft and vague promises that they would rise through the ranks. Indeed, labor was fluid, and considerable mobility was possible both horizontally, from craft to craft, and vertically, from apprentice to master. Due to the scarcity of skilled labor in the colonies and an absence of guilds, craftsmen often developed many marketable skills: "The blacksmith was a toolmaker, a soap boiler, a tallow chandler" (Rediker [1982], p. 131) and although legislation was passed to prevent tanners from acting as curriers or shoemakers, they often did so. The Bostonian Paul Revere provides the classic example of the multitalented craftsman. He distinguished himself primarily as a silversmith, yet he engraved also copperplates, was "a dentist who set false 'foreteeth,'" manufactured "clock faces for clockmakers," "branding irons for hatters," and "spatulas and probes for surgeons" (Rediker [1982], p. 132).

Labor relations in the early American port towns were relatively harmonious. However, after the Revolution, labor in the cities changed. "Merchant capitalists and master craftsmen restructured the social relations of production, [and] transformed wage labor into a market commodity" (Sean Wilentz, *Chants Democratic,* p. 5). This established a new set of labor relations and led to conflict. During the colonial period, craftsmen tended to make products on custom order and to rely mostly on household labor. As the size of the operation grew and the shop produced a surplus, the master might take on an apprentice, hire a journeyman, or buy the time of a servant or slave. In the period of the American Revolution, as free workers became more plentiful and less expensive, master craftsmen moved to the position of employers and merchant capitalists. Skilled laborers were hired and fired as economic necessity dictated.

The result was considerable labor unrest. In Philadelphia, for example, cracks appeared in the once cohesive community of work. In 1786, journeymen printers organized and went out on strike to protest a reduction in their wages. Carpenters were next. In 1791, journeymen united as employers attempted to cut wages. The cabinetmaking and chairmaking trades erupted next; beginning in 1794, the battle lines were drawn over prices and wages. Their quarrel spread, and they appealed to journeymen in a wide range of crafts, and to the public, in Philadelphia and in other cities. The journeymen won. Together with the masters, they agreed to guaranteed prices for all work. Labor conflict reached its peak with the city's shoemakers. The interests of masters and workmen began to diverge and in 1799 approximately one hundred journeymen walked out on strike to protest an attempted wage reduction. Although calm reigned for a short time, in 1805 journeymen demanded a wage increase. Masters rejected the raise, which propelled journeymen to strike once more; this time they stayed out of work for six weeks. The finale occurred with the 1806 Conspiracy Trial in which masters accused workmen of collusion. For masters, journeymen were simply one element in a complex system of costs that affected profit; journeymen pointed to the fortunes masters had made from their labors while they could barely put food on the table.

Capitalist wage relations usually associated with industrialization were in place in the mid-Atlantic and New England regions by the early national period. Population pressures on land supplies, especially in the older settlements of New England, forced men and women to seek work elsewhere, and they migrated to the cities in search of jobs. However, the urban economies were faltering. In Boston, by the mid eighteenth century, "it was no secret that for men of the laboring classes it was difficult to live as one's father" (Gary B. Nash, Billy G. Smith, and Dirk Hoerder, "Labor in the Era of the American Revolution," p. 422). Philadelphia's economy remained strong until about a decade and a half before the Revolution. Then, "wages of laborers and merchant seamen began in the early 1760s a decline which, interrupted only by a brief resurgence after 1765, continued until the outbreak of the Revolution" (Nash et al., p. 423). The urban laboring classes were accustomed to work interruptions caused by inclement weather. What was new were periods of unemployment brought by business slumps. Jobs, especially in the cities, became increasingly harder to find. Because of this labor surplus, men and women were forced to sell their labor cheaply. Thus, employers were provided with an inexpensive labor force which helped fuel the shift to the industrial order of the nineteenth century.

BIBLIOGRAPHY

General

Dunn, Richard S. "Servants and Slaves: The Recruitment and Employment of Labor." In *Colonial British America: Essays in the New History of the Early Modern Era,* edited by Jack P. Greene and J. R. Pole (1984).

Morris, Richard. *Government and Labor in Early America* (1946).

Rediker, Marcus. "'Good Hands, Stout Heart, and Fast Feet': The History and Culture of Working People in Early America." *Labour/Le Travailleur* 10 (Autumn 1982): 123–144.

Thompson, E. P. "Eighteenth-Century English Society: Class Struggle Without Class?" *Social History* 3 (May 1978): 133–165.

The Chesapeake

Billings, Warren M. "The Law of Servants and Slaves in Seventeenth-Century Virginia." *Virginia Magazine of History and Biography* 99, no. 1 (1991): 45–62.

Carr, Lois Green, and Lorena S. Walsh. "Economic Diversification and Labor Organization in the Chesapeake, 1650–1820." In *Work and Labor in Early America,* edited by Stephen Innes (1988).

Kulikoff, Allan. *Tobacco and Slaves: The Development of Southern Cultures in the Chesapeake, 1680–1800* (1986).

Menard, Russell. "From Servants to Slaves: The Transformation of the Chesapeake Labor System." *Southern Studies* 16, no. 4 (1977): 355–390.

Morgan, Edmund S. *American Slavery, American Freedom: The Ordeal of Colonial Virginia* (1975).

Women and Labor

Boydston, Jeanne. *Home and Work: Housework, Wages, and the Ideology of Labor in the Early Republic* (1990).

Jensen, Joan. *Loosening the Bonds: Mid-Atlantic Farm Women, 1750–1850* (1986).

Ulrich, Laurel Thatcher. "Martha Ballard and Her Girls: Women's Work in Eighteenth-Century Maine." In *Work and Labor in Early America,* edited by Stephen Innes (1988).

Unfree Labor

Dunn, Richard S. *Sugar and Slaves: The Rise of the Planter Class in the English West Indies, 1624–1713* (1972).

Galenson, David W. *White Servitude in Colonial America: An Economic Analysis* (1981).

Horn, James. "Servant Emigration to the Chesapeake in the Seventeenth Century." In *The Chesapeake in the Seventeenth Century: Essays on Anglo-American Society,* edited by Thad Tate and David L. Ammerman (1979).

Salinger, Sharon V. *"To Serve Well and Faithfully": Labor and Indentured Servants in Pennsylvania, 1682–1800* (1987).

Silver, Timothy. *A New Face on the Countryside: Indians, Colonists, and Slaves in South Atlantic Forests, 1500–1800* (1990).

Smith, Abbot Emerson. *Colonists in Bondage: White Servitude and Convict Labor in America, 1607–1776* (1947).

Ulrich, Laurel Thatcher. "Martha Ballard and Her Girls: Women's Work in Eighteenth-Century Maine." In *Work and Labor in Early America,* edited by Stephen Innes (1988).

Wood, Peter H. *Black Majority: Negroes in Colonial South Carolina from 1670 Through the Stono Rebellion* (1974).

Urban Labor and Revolutionary Politics

Lemisch, Jesse. "Jack Tar in the Streets: Merchant Seamen in the Politics of Revolutionary America." *William and Mary Quarterly* 3d ser., 25 (1968): 371–401.

Lynd, Staughton. "The Mechanics in New York Politics, 1774–1788." *Labor History* 5, no. 3 (1964): 225–246.

Nash, Gary B. *The Urban Crucible: Social Change, Political Consciousness, and the Origins of the American Revolution* (1979).

Nash, Gary B., Billy G. Smith, and Dirk Hoerder. "Labor in the Era of the American Revolution: An Exchange." *Labor History* 24 (Summer 1983): 414–439.

Olton, Charles S. *Artisans for Independence: Philadelphia Mechanics and the American Revolution* (1975).

Rediker, Marcus. *Between the Devil and the Deep Blue Sea* (1987).

Rock, Howard. *Artisans of the New Republic: The Tradesman of New York City in the Age of Jefferson* (1979).

Rosswurm, Steven. *Arms, Country, and Class: The Philadelphia Militia and the "Lower Sort" in the American Revolution, 1765–1783* (1987).

Smith, Billy G. "The Material Lives of Laboring Philadelphians, 1750 to 1800." *William and Mary Quarterly* 3rd ser., 38, no. 2 (1981): 163–202.

———. *The "Lower Sort": Philadelphia's Laboring People, 1750–1800* (1990).

Vickers, Daniel. "Working the Fields in a Developing Economy: Essex County, Massachusetts, 1630–1675." In *Work and Labor in Early America,* edited by Stephen Innes (1988).

Wilentz, Sean. *Chants Democratic: New York City and the Rise of the American Working Class, 1788–1850* (1984).

Young, Alfred. "The Mechanics and the Jeffersonians: New York, 1789–1801." *Labor History* 5, no. 3 (1964): 247–276.

SEE ALSO The American Colonies Through 1700; The American Colonies from 1700 to the Seven Years' War; The American Colonies from the Seven Years' War Through the Revolution; The Deep South; The Early National Period; New England; The Plantation; The Southern Tidewater and Piedmont.

LABOR: THE JACKSONIAN ERA THROUGH RECONSTRUCTION

Richard Oestreicher

IN 1820, FREE wageworkers were still a minority in a society where the dominant labor systems were slavery and independent family proprietorship (family farms, small craft-shops). Half a century later that minority had become a decisive majority. A society of independent farmers and craftsmen, slave-owners and slaves had become a society of employees and bosses. By 1870, two-thirds of all Americans earned their livings as manual wage earners. Some workers believed that abundant opportunities to climb the social ladder still existed, but a large majority would in fact remain wage earners all of their lives.

From morning to night, from birth to death, this new wage-earning majority lived differently from their grandparents. They rose to clocks, which had once been all but unknown except in church towers, village squares, or upper-class drawing rooms. They dressed (quickly) in store-bought clothes and donned machine-made shoes, quite different from their grandparents' homespun and homemade apparel. And then, quite unlike their grandparents who had worked at home (although even then in gender-specific tasks), the men left for the commercial world of factories, construction sites, or offices. Women, unless they were young and unmarried, or widowed or abandoned, remained home in their now-separate sphere of housekeeping, child rearing, and domestic production. Their grandparents had pondered the incomprehensible whims of a sometimes angry God who withheld rain or spread disease in unpredictable ways. To such mysteries now had been added new worries—the vagaries of a market that sometimes threatened employment just as unpredictably as the weather, and the all-too-comprehensible power of the boss upon whose whims that employment depended.

The relationship between employers and employees governed the lives of the majority of Americans directly and set the social and economic context for the rest. Farmers grew cash crops destined for urban markets. Merchants and shopkeepers sold the goods made by wage laborers. Bookkeepers recorded the sales and profits. Ministers and politicians praised the nobility of honest labor at the same time that, without any apparent sense of irony or contradiction, they also lauded the virtues of frugality and temperance as the sure path to upward mobility out of the wage class. A new economic class, a working class, had been formed in one lifetime, and the consequences of that event affected more Americans in more ways than any other event of the nineteenth century.

Working-class formation was so intertwined with a great many other social changes—agricultural improvements; virtual revolutions in transportation, communication, and finance; changing attitudes about work, family, gender, religion, and leisure; a new political party system; and technological innovations—that historians often subsume working-class formation under a larger process of societal transformation. For classical Marxists, working-class formation was the inexorable consequence of capitalist development: the history of class formation is essentially equivalent to the history of capitalism. For modernization theorists, proletarianization was merely one aspect of more fundamental processes of centralization, bureaucratization, and social differentiation. In retrospect, the dominance of capitalism in western Europe and North America, and the resulting European conquest of the rest of the globe, has made it seem almost inevitable that these changes took a capitalist form. But we need only to consider that capitalist hegemony in the United States was finally determined by the bloodiest war of the nineteenth century to recognize that economic development could have taken many forms. Over the last century and a half, working-class formation has taken place everywhere in the developed world, but always in different ways.

The particular way it happened in America has shaped American politics, culture, and institutions ever since. Three peculiarities of American working-class formation were especially important. First, the United States was the first democratic republic in which working-class formation took place. Elsewhere, workers' initial attempts to organize and improve conditions were mingled with struggles to abolish legally enshrined upper-class privileges, overturn sharply defined class boundaries, and establish political rights. In the United States, for most white males, such rights predated industrialization and working-class formation. American working people, in their initial industrial conflicts, were protesting usurpation of legally guaranteed equality rather than trying to overturn an Old Regime and establish a new political order.

Second, far more than in most countries, working-class formation in the United States was multiethnic, the result of the largest mass migration in human history. Between 1840 and 1930 close to forty million immigrants entered the United States, and the majority of them entered as workers. As a result, class conflict overlapped with ethnic, religious, and racial conflict. Bosses disproportionately tended to come from the culturally and politically dominant caste of white, native, Anglo-Saxon Protestants, while the majority of working people were outsiders—members of ethnic, racial, or religious minorities. While some immigration and interethnic conflict took place in nearly every industrializing country, American class relations mirrored those of a colonial regime to an extent unmatched in western Europe.

Third, the initial working-class formation took place in the United States at a time when the country was convulsed by the political conflict between free and slave labor. In that conflict, bosses and northern white workers found themselves on the same side: their differences seemed less important than their common struggle for freedom. However, once the supremacy of free labor was unequivocally established, both white employers and white working people were ambivalent about the status of the four million former slaves who outnumbered white non-agricultural manual workers in 1865. We still suffer from the consequences of that ambivalence.

The cumulative effects of republican traditions, ethnic diversity, and the heritage of slavery produced a particular pattern of class relations. Until well into the twentieth century the working class was so divided by ethnicity, race, religion, and regionalism that it is easier to talk about various working-class subcultures and ethnic fragments than about a common working-class culture. Nonetheless, American class relations were characterized by sustained conflict, bitterness, and often ferocious violence. Yet, despite the intensity of conflict, the dominant trends within the labor movement were usually reformist and ideologically moderate. Efforts were oriented more toward preventing the development of clear class boundaries, which threatened to undermine social and political equality, than toward sharpening those boundaries in order to mobilize workers for revolutionary reconstruction.

PATHS TO PROLETARIANIZATION

Across the vast territory of antebellum America, people became workers in many ways. Each occupation changed at a different pace, and the same occupations developed differently in different places. Well into this period, the process of transition from earlier labor systems was still far from complete. The differences in how this change occurred are important for understanding the experiences and attitudes of each group of workers, but within the patchwork of variations we can identify three common paths, three ways that most people who became workers did so. Shoemakers, tailors, leather workers, printers, and hatters were among the many traditional craftsmen reduced from independent craftsmen to wage earners. Second, recruitment into new, large-scale, capital-intensive industries such as textile and paper mills, railroads, and iron foundries, swelled the ranks of workers. Finally, the numbers in such traditional occupations as domestic servants, laborers, wagon drivers, longshoremen, and sailors all grew as well.

Reorganization of the Crafts Despite the variations in the work cultures of individual crafts, nearly all functioned under a similar artisanal regime until the late eighteenth century. Production took place in small workshops organized by master craftsmen. Masters and journeymen performed the same tasks, and each made the entire product from start to finish. Craftsmen collectively maintained a monopoly over craft knowledge by limiting access to the craft to apprentices who completed training with existing craftsmen. Since journeymen were full parties to this control over craft knowledge, since they owned their own tools, and since the minimum capital entry requirements for proprietorship were modest, journeymen had considerable independence, and most journeymen could expect to become masters.

As merchant-capitalists and entrepreneurial masters slowly reorganized the crafts in the early nineteenth century, these businessmen increasingly departed from the artisanal model. They divided the production process into steps, with each worker performing only one task. While some tasks still required considerable skill, others could be performed by unskilled or semi-skilled labor. Simple hand-operated machinery—such as treadle sewing machines for sewing shoes and clothing, hand-operated presses for shaping materials to molds and patterns and so on—could be adapted to some of these tasks. The cost savings from division of labor drove down the prices of finished goods, undermining the competitive position of traditional craftsmen. Master craftsmen either adapted to the new system of labor and to technological innovations or were forced into the emerging class of wageworkers themselves. In the most radically transformed trades, even skilled workers now possessed full knowledge of only selected steps in production. Skilled labor was still crucial to nearly all of the craft-based industries, but the roles of skilled workers had changed. What had been the collective knowledge of all producers passed slowly to the newly emerging class of managers and bosses who now alone were capable of organizing production in its entirety.

As successfully reorganized firms expanded, the minimum firm size necessary for effective competition increased dramatically. In Philadelphia in 1850, the mean industrial-firm size was 12.9 workers per firm, and 59 percent of all industrial workers worked in firms of twenty-six or more workers. This represented a dramatic change from only thirty years before, when 86 percent of the city's industrial workers worked in firms with less than ten employees and over 99 percent in firms with less than twenty workers. The Philadelphia pattern was typical of national trends: in virtually every place historians have studied, they have discovered similar changes in the old craft industries.

Increased firm size dramatically raised the capital requirements for proprietorship and cut journeymen off from access to the means of production even in those crafts that had not yet introduced any new machines. Workers now depended on bosses for employment and survival. The usual citywide price lists of the artisanal era, under which individual masters paid journeymen for each completed product a price that reflected both the market value of the product and traditional community norms of fair remuneration, gave way to unilaterally determined piece rates and daily wages. For craftsmen who were now paid wages, a term heretofore restricted to day laborers, the linguistic change reflected a profound psychological change. A journeyman cordwainer who was paid the established price for his shoe retained his republican sense of independence: he sold his product, not himself. A craftsman who was paid wages, even a well-paid craftsman like a shoe cutter, had sold himself for a day. A craft hierarchy characterized by common knowledge, in which each producer performed the same tasks and in which rank was a function of stage of life cycle, had evolved into a class system of employers and employees.

In only a few of the reorganized craft industries did new machines or technology have a revolutionary influence, at least in their early stages of development. In such trades as shoe, hat, and saddle production, and clothing manufacture, machines sped up particular steps in the production process but did not alter the essential structure of production before the 1850s. Nor did the larger firm size usually offer decisive economies of scale beyond the minimum necessary for effective division of labor. The competitive advantage of reorganization stemmed from three critical factors: substitution of cheaper labor for more expensive labor, closer supervision of labor, and intensification of pace. Reorganization of the crafts was thus inherently an adversarial process. Employers gained competitive advantage primarily by undermining the skills of craft workers or pushing them to work harder, steadier, or faster.

Before the 1840s, women were by far the largest source of cheap labor for entrepreneurs who wanted to take advantage of new craft divisions of labor. In 1832, a third of the industrial workers in the Northeast (over 40 percent in Massachusetts, the most industrialized state) were women and girls. Gender barriers still restricted the use of female labor, even in some crafts where division of labor stimulated demand for low-cost unskilled labor. Cultural conceptions of appropriate gender roles were as important as economic forces in determining the sexual division of labor, but a gender-based division of labor provided the economic basis for most of the sweated crafts. Shoemaking and clothing manufacture are two examples: the predominance of subcontracting to small garret shop owners and of outwork—a system in which pieces precut in a shop are assembled by workers in their homes into finished pieces, which are returned to the shop—exerted a sharp downward pressure on wages. Most women who entered American industries before 1825 went to work in the new textile mills; after that time, with the expansion of crafts reorganized around a gender-based division of labor, more women entered craft industries. By 1850, the majority of female industrial workers in the United States worked in the reorganized crafts.

Closer supervision, which made acceleration of the work pace possible, complemented the cost advantages gained by division of labor. As Moses Brown, the Providence merchant-capitalist who helped finance the first successful cotton mill, established in 1790 by Samuel Slater, and who helped pioneer establishment of a variety of infant industries, explained, "one hundred looms in families will not weave so much cloth as thirty . . . constantly employed under the immediate inspection of a workman" (Gordon, Edwards, and Reich, p. 58).

Employers who sought to realize the advantages of Brown's insight faced a concerted struggle. While preindustrial artisans had always worked long hours, an intermittent work pattern with frequent breaks and holidays was deeply embedded in their work culture. Employers who demanded steadier work were thus forcing workers to abandon widespread traditions and expectations, expectations that not only made work less dreary and physically taxing but also had significance as symbols of republican independence. It is perhaps for this reason that manufacturers played crucial roles in antebellum moral-reform movements designed to alter public morality and increase individual restraint, such as temperance and sabbatarianism; manufacturers were also disproportionately overrepresented in evangelical Protestant revivalism, which usually emphasized attitudes and behavior conducive to good work habits.

The Industrial Revolution: Mill Hands and Factory Workers In the craft industries, proletarianization destroyed the independent status of the male artisan and expanded the roles of women as substitutes for more expensive male labor. By mid century, pockets of outworkers and craft manufactories were scattered throughout the rural economies of the Northeast, and the economies of large cities like New York, Philadelphia, and Cincinnati

depended heavily on the reorganized crafts. In 1855, nearly half of New York City's labor force worked in these industries.

But in the Massachusetts towns of Lowell, Lawrence, Waltham, Fall River, and in dozens of lesser-known mill and factory towns, industrialization revolved around the large-scale, capital-intensive industries that captured the imagination of (and caused alarm among) contemporaries and subsequent scholars. Since the 1820s, new towns had sprung up as giant multistory brick mills lined fast-flowing New England streams, railroad repair shops mushroomed at unoccupied rail junctions, and mine shafts burrowed into Pennsylvania hillsides. Where farms and villages had recently dotted quiet landscapes, now the churning of waterwheels and the noises of leather belts, gearshifts, and power looms echoed over the roofs of boardinghouses and tightly packed alleys. Smoke from iron and glass furnaces or locomotive boilers darkened the skies. "When I went out at night," wrote a Lowell millhand in 1844 "the sound of the mill was in my ears, as of crickets, frogs, and jewsharps, all mingled together in strange discord. . . . You know that people learn to sleep with the thunder of Niagara in their ears, and a cotton mill is no worse, though you wonder that we do not have to hold our breath in such a noise" (as quoted in Bode, p. 33).

The size of such enterprises and their tight concentration around sources of waterpower, raw materials, and convenient transportation made them seem more economically important than they were. In 1850 agriculture still dominated the American economy: 55 percent of the labor force worked in agriculture. Within the industrial sector, the reorganized crafts and traditional unskilled occupations still employed a large majority of workers. There were more than twice as many tailors, milliners, seamstresses, and dressmakers (217,000) as cotton mill workers (92,000). There were twice as many carters, wagon drivers, and teamsters (39,700) as railroad workers (20,000). Cotton, iron, coal, metal fabricating, machine- and shipbuilding, railroads, glass, paper, and brewing together accounted for no more than 5 percent of the American labor force in 1850. But the immediate landscape-transforming power and the wider economic and cultural ripples of such industries seemed indeed to merit the term "Industrial Revolution." Nothing quite like it had happened before.

These industries had never been based on an artisanal model. They did not develop by reorganizing the work processes of an existing body of producers. The technological histories of these industries varied, belying any simplistic conceptions of a unified industrial revolution; but all used machinery, all operated on a larger scale than the artisanal crafts, all employed a variety of skilled and unskilled labor, all depended on the extensive division of labor precluding any artisanal sense of holistic responsibility for the final product, and all had always required a level of capitalization too high for even the most frugal and industrious craftsmen to raise without outside investors or government assistance.

The knowledge of skilled workers was critical to the success of these firms, but their recruitment and training, expected career paths, and relationships with both managers and unskilled workers were quite different from those of skilled workers in the craft-based industries. In the craft-based industries, most entrepreneurs had prior shop-floor experience. Outside investors who were attracted to the large-scale, capital-intensive industries because their mercantile experience alerted them to untapped potential markets often had no such knowledge about the industries in which they were investing. The Boston Associates who founded the cotton mills at Waltham and Lowell were all merchants. Given this lack of practical experience among managers and the costly consequences of mistakes in capital-intensive industries, skilled workers had considerable leverage. Mule spinners (textile thread machinists), glassblowers, and iron puddlers were among the most highly paid workers in America.

But workers learned their trades on the shop floor of enterprises they knew they had very little chance of ever owning. Training emphasized the day-to-day knowledge necessary to make production. Skilled workers trained their helpers and work crews; younger members of the work gang hoped gradually to work themselves up shop-floor promotional ladders based on the division of labor—from helper to gatherer to glassblower; or from railroad brakeman to fireman to engineer. Where factory crafts successfully maintained control over apprenticeship, apprenticeship had a different meaning than the prelude to proprietorship implicit in the craft shop. Iron puddlers' and glassblowers' struggles to control apprenticeship reflected the adversarial realities of the factory, where controlling access to skills helped protect craft power.

Nor did completion of apprenticeship necessarily carry with it the same life-cycle significance as in the craft shop. For the artisanal apprentice, apprenticeship marked graduation from unpaid to paid labor, entrance into the egalitarian fraternity of fellow mechanics, and accession to manhood. In the factory, the puddler's helper had been a paid member of a functioning work crew from the start, and completion of his apprenticeship did not guarantee a fundamental change in status. Opportunities to move into more highly paid tasks depended on turnover among the skilled workers or expansion of production.

All of the large-scale, capital-intensive industries employed both unskilled and skilled labor in multistage production processes that usually involved more complex division of labor than the reorganized craft industries. The artisanal crafts, the world of the craftsman before craft reorganization, had been a largely male world that sharply distinguished itself from the "lower orders" of laborers, dockhands, sailors, and servants. When reorganization brought women, untrained male immigrants, and country boys into the closely guarded preserve of the craftsmen, they were seen as threatening interlopers. Even in the eighteenth century, though, iron furnaces, glasshouses, shipyards, and paper mills had needed woodcutters to cut wood for charcoal furnaces, miners, rag sorters, wagon drivers, and a wide variety of helpers. The social, familial, and cultural relationships between the different kinds of workers necessary for these enterprises varied, but in no case were their worlds as clearly and self-consciously segregated as the mechanics were from the laborers of the preindustrial city.

In the textile mills, until the 1850s, gender marked the dividing line between skilled and unskilled labor. Men worked as overseers, mule spinners, carders, machinists and machine repairers, dyers, finishers, and skilled weavers (in woolens and worsteds)—all high-wage jobs that needed some combinations of physical strength, technical training, and mechanical experience. Women tended drawing frames and spinning machines and ran power looms and other machines that did not demand great strength or mechanical knowledge. Until the arrival of new waves of impoverished immigrants from Ireland in the mid 1840s (and a few years later from French Canada), gender barriers were sharp and distinct. Except for a few watchmen, virtually no adult males worked in jobs defined as unskilled, and even the most skilled women worked at tasks paid below the minimum for adult males. Gender segregation even extended, to some degree, into the tasks performed by children. While young boys and girls were equally divided among the "doffers" who replaced bobbins on spinning throstles as they filled with yarn (perhaps because the adults they worked with were all women), boys worked as piecers, tying up loose threads, for the male mule spinners. By their mid teens, girls and boys were consistently assigned gender-specific tasks.

Unskilled and skilled male workers worked together in many of the other large-scale industries. In the early and mid nineteenth century, in industries like glass, iron, and metal casting, where skilled blowers, puddlers, and molders directed work crews of helpers and assistants, work gangs were often based on kin and familial ties. The blowers, puddlers, and molders were middle-aged men; their crews included sons, nephews, neighbors, and children of friends. By the 1850s and 1860s, the hierarchy of such work crews also reflected the ethnic hierarchy of successive waves of immigration, but as each ethnic group attained footholds in the skilled ranks, it used its position to re-create kin and family work networks among relatives and fellow countrymen.

While there were many exceptions, the rapid expansion of large-scale, capital-intensive industries after 1825 generally represented a potential opportunity for many workers, a magnet that attracted willing recruits—in contrast to craft reorganization, which threatened the status and livelihood of a preexisting mechanic population. Life for early factory workers was heavy, hard, and hazardous, but for many workers, the life they had left behind was even worse.

Expansion of Preindustrial Labor: Laborers, Servants, and Farm Hands The term "industrialization" conjures up images of noisy steam engines, complicated machines, and "dark, satanic" mills, but the expansion of markets for industrial goods, the increasing pace of new transportation networks, mushrooming urban populations, and the commercialization of agriculture needed to feed city dwellers also created enormous new demands for very traditional forms of unskilled labor. Canals, railroads, factories, and tenements were built mainly with human muscle. In the genteel households of the new urban middle class, an emerging cult of female domesticity established new standards of cleanliness, order, and conspicuous consumption and declared for middle-class women new proprieties that could be fulfilled only with the help of domestic servants. Millions of acres of prairies had to be cleared away and sown with

wheat, corn, and other crops to feed factory owners, millhands, and the burgeoning urban middle class and its servants.

The physical realities of shoveling dirt, scrubbing pots, or harvesting grain had not changed very much between the late eighteenth century and the mid nineteenth century. But the place of these occupations within the structure of American society, their social meaning and significance, had changed. In preindustrial society, the field labor that farmers had not done themselves, the domestic labor that wives and daughters had not done for their own households, and even much of the digging and lifting in the seaport cities or commercial villages had been performed either by people outside the polity—slaves, indentured servants, apprentices, free blacks, and other marginalized individuals—or by young people as part of preparation for marriage and setting up an independent household. Forced labor was not on a wage basis. Many of those who worked for wages did so intermittently, and few expected to do so all their lives. Their employers were often relatives, neighbors, or friends, and non-economic considerations of neighborliness, communal loyalty, and generational obligation influenced the relationship between employers and employees.

By 1850 most of the people who dug canals, laid railroad tracks, and cleaned houses earned wages paid by strangers; they had become a permanent segment of the emerging working class. An Irish construction laborer went from one canal or railroad to another or from the railroad to the mill. His daughter was not "help" for a neighboring farmer's wife but the live-in, full-time scullery maid for the wife of a merchant. When she left the merchant's household, it was most likely to run a tenement household where she would cook and clean for a laboring husband and several boarders.

The situation of free agricultural laborers in 1850, by far the largest group of traditional wage earners, was more ambiguous than that of urban laborers, canal boatmen, or servants. Many were young people still connected by non-economic bonds—family, kinship, and community—to the people who employed them. But many were now also immigrants, newcomers, or migrants. Nineteenth-century observers and generations of historians from Frederick Jackson Turner to recent economic historians have argued that most of these laborers were farmers in the making who worked for wages for a few years while either waiting to inherit the family farm or saving the relatively modest sum necessary to begin farming on the frontier. Such arguments, however, draw as much from the ideology and wishful thinking of latter-day Jeffersonians as from empirical investigation: despite the overwhelming evidence of persistent inequality in acquisition and ownership of land, social mobility via farm ownership has long been viewed as one of the bases of American democracy. More sophisticated versions of the Turner thesis do grant that there were serious impediments to a simple laborer-to-proprietor scenario. For many agricultural laborers in settled areas, a job in a nearby factory or on a railroad track gang seemed less risky and perhaps even more lucrative than migration to distant farming country where cheap land was available. For those willing to consider such moves, prime farmland was not easy to acquire, even in newly settled regions. The best lands and those most accessible to transportation went quickly, and thereafter newcomers had either to settle for more marginal lands or to pay premium prices. According to the estimate of an 1832 Illinois settler, even if a would-be farmer acquired government lands at the minimum price of $1.25 per acre, the costs of fencing, preparing the land for planting, building a house, and buying seed, livestock, and tools drove the start-up costs for a 160-acre farm up to $976 (Schob, *Hired Hands and Plowboys,* pp. 260–266). With annual wages for agricultural laborers no more than $150 per year in most eastern states, $976 was a large sum.

Optimistic scenarios that imagine sturdy and virtuous farmboys working for a few years before they assumed their Jeffersonian heritage as independent yeomen are certainly exaggerated. The optimistic scenario fits best for the first wave of settlers in newly settled areas. Early arrival did translate into greater opportunities; and while such frontier opportunities influenced migration patterns and helped to shape American culture, they hardly represent the situation of most mid-nineteenth-century rural laborers. Most people lived far from the frontier, and even in frontier regions, with each new arrival after the first cohort, the area came to be less and less a frontier.

The abundance of cheap land certainly provided opportunities for a great many nineteenth-century Americans. But with each decade, the westward march of settlement moved the sites of available land farther and farther from developed population centers, making them less accessible to the landless populations of long-established farming regions. As new areas were settled, they duplicated the dilemma that New England had faced by the late 1700s: too little land to allow all the increased population of the next generation to support themselves as farmers.

Abundant land helped American workers. Some laborers did become farmers; the pull of cheap land drove up the wages of the rest. But even a vast continent was not big enough to provide farms for everyone who might want one. Surplus rural populations would have to find work elsewhere. At mid century, with substantial portions of the Midwest still not fully settled, perhaps that was not completely clear. It would become so in the next generation.

LABOR ORGANIZATION AND WORKING-CLASS DEVELOPMENT

In the half-century from the 1820s to the 1870s, workers' efforts to organize were at the same time a story of recurring failure and of extraordinary success. From a purely bureaucratic or organizational point of view, most labor organization was temporary. Unions repeated a distressing cycle of initial success, expansion, optimistic hopes for dramatic improvement, and then virtual collapse after the next financial panic and depression. After a flurry of strikes (many victorious), some surprisingly successful forays into labor politics (including the world's first labor parties—the workingmen's parties, which appeared in several dozen cities at the end of the 1820s), the development of an impressive array of citywide labor federations of local craft unions and even embryonic national organization in the 1830s, nearly all labor organizations collapsed after the panic of 1837. Massive shorter-hours campaigns in the 1840s were followed by new and revived unions in the late 1840s and early 1850s, but many fell apart again after the panic of 1857. In the mid and late 1860s, several national unions finally seemed headed for permanence as national union membership reached several hundred thousand, but after the panic of 1873, most organizations disappeared once again. Fewer than ten national unions survived the mid-decade depression with even a skeleton crew intact, and stable labor organization seemed no closer than it had forty years before.

But the number of membership cards and the longevity of union charters are not the only measures of success. While labor activists between the 1820s and 1870s mostly failed to establish durable organizations or stable systems of collective bargaining, they succeeded at something as important: they convinced a substantial portion of their fellow workers to accept their critique of the emerging wage system and to accept their vision of a collective morality for coping with it. The language of labor, the symbolic collective embodiment of an emerging class, entered the vernacular. By the close of the era, every politician, regardless of what policies he actually advocated, proclaimed his sympathy for the rights of labor and asserted that his program was labor's only true salvation. Every worker knew what a strike was. Every craft had developed norms of appropriate output and acceptable work practices. And most Americans accepted the notion that the concept of liberty and justice for all was morally inconsistent with the lives of grinding poverty and underpaid toil so many of its citizens were now leading. Working-class activists could not yet provide convincing answers to the question of how to solve that problem, but few workers any longer had illusions that their situation was temporary, or that the problem would solve itself.

IMMIGRANTS

Before 1840 most workers had been native rural whites who migrated out of the countryside into nearby towns and cities. After 1840 immigration rates rose so quickly and immigrants concentrated so heavily in working-class occupations that they quickly exceeded the still considerable flow of native rural migrants. The Irish came in great numbers after the potato famine of the early 1840s. Less drastic but similar pressures began to affect the peasantry of the German-speaking regions of central Europe about the same time. By the 1850s an even larger flood of Germans followed on the heels of the Irish. Every city had its "Corktown" or "Little Germany." Boston's Irish outnumbered the population in every city in Ireland except Dublin. New York's Kleindeutschland was bigger than all but two or three German cities.

In scarcely more than a decade, foreign-born workers and their native-born children outnumbered workers of native rural origins in nearly every large American city or major mill town. Renowned as a destination for Yankee farm girls, Lowell, Massachusetts, had until almost mid century a working population that was mostly native Protestants. Only 3.7 percent of the work force of Lowell's Hamilton Manufacturing Company was foreignborn in July 1836. By August 1850, immigrants constituted 38.6 percent of the Hamilton workers; by June 1860, 61.8 percent. In Fall River in the 1820s, only 6 percent of local mill operatives named in two contemporary lists were foreign-born; by 1845, nearly half of the employees of a local iron works had Irish surnames, and in 1850, 59 percent of Fall River's factory workers and laborers were immigrants. In New York City in 1855, 70.4 percent of the workers in twenty leading blue-collar occupations were foreign-born. In Pittsburgh in 1850, 69.5 percent of the people in working-class occupations were immigrants.

Contrary to popular mythology, those who emigrated to America were rarely among the poorest or most oppressed in their own countries. People pressured by economic changes were more likely to consider leaving farm or homeland and to seek new ways of making a living, but those who did were also responding to other motives. They were rarely compelled to leave out of sheer necessity.

The most obvious exception might be the post-famine Irish, but John Bodnar has noted that studies of Irish emigration show that "the poorest were not the first to leave" (*The Transplanted,* p. 6). The heaviest flow out of the Irish countryside in the famine years came from the wealthier and more developed eastern and central counties rather than from the poorest counties of the west with the highest proportion of landless residents. When the very poor did leave rural Ireland, they were more likely to be able to manage the passage to nearby England than to America. The Irish who did emigrate were much poorer than migrants from Yankee farms, but the preponderance of young, single people among the newcomers suggests that their motives for emigration may not have been so different from the motives of native migrants. For more than a generation before the famine, Irish young people had been leaving in increasing numbers. By the 1870s less than 16 percent of Irish immigrants to America were married. The rural young faced a more extreme version of the dilemma confronting developed agricultural regions in America. Because of dense rural populations, high and increasing land rents, evictions of tenants by modernizing landlords, very small family landholdings, and many children, rural Irish families could not provide the minimum livelihood their children would need before they could marry and establish their own families. For single adults faced with postponing marriage for many years, emigration may have looked appealing.

Among the other nationalities who emigrated to America in substantial numbers in the antebellum years, relatively few emigrants had been completely impoverished. Both British and German emigration came mainly from more developed and commercialized regions. In Scotland, for example, emigrants from the more urbanized and industrialized Lowlands outnumbered those from the Highlands by seventeen to one. Emigrants from both Britain and the German states came disproportionately from two groups adversely affected by capitalist development: traditional handcraft producers unable to compete with cheaper machine-made goods, and marginal agriculturalists who faced declining living standards because meager lands could not sustain more commercialized and competitive forms of agricultural production.

A substantial proportion of the immigrants did differ from native rural migrants in one crucial respect. Even those who had been artisans or small landholders had exhausted most of their resources to pay for the transatlantic passage. They arrived nearly penniless, and they had no nearby home or farm to return to if conditions in the city were worse than they had expected. A variety of immigrant aid societies organized by fellow countrymen tried to help them, but the enormous flood of immigrants into the major eastern ports after 1845 was so large that voluntary organizations could at best provide only token assistance to a fraction of the immigrants. Chain migration of kin and village cohorts helped ease the transition. Immigrants usually had a relative or former resident of the same village who had learned something about American ways to help them find work. But work they had to find, and quickly. They clustered in the most low-paying and unattractive jobs. Economic necessity may not have been essential to their decision to emigrate, but necessity shaped their job options once they arrived.

As they settled in, the initial networks of family, kin, and village acquaintances became the basis of organized ethnic communities. Because of their own preferences for association with people of their own language and background, on the one hand, and the hostility of natives, on the other, immigrant workers not only stuck together but raised their American-born children with clear ethnic identities. When unskilled construction workers organized into laborers' unions in New York in the 1850s, they did so quite consciously as Irish organizations. When German bakers, cigarmakers, and cabinetmakers met in newly organized craft unions in American cities in the 1850s and 1860s, they kept their minutes in German. Most union organizers professed interethnic unity, but for the most part their unions in these years were ethnically segmented nonetheless.

Where their native-born counterparts organized in the 1840s and 1850s, they often did so separately from the Irish and the Germans. Indeed, the movement that probably captured the most enthusiasm among native-born urban craftsmen of those decades was nativism. Using a populist and laboristic rhetoric that bore more than a superficial similarity to the language of 1830s labor organizers, nativist politicians denounced the immigrants as tools of the monopolistic corrupters of American liberty. Combining these appeals to the disgruntlement of hard-pressed craftsmen in the reorganized urban crafts with a heavy dose of anti-Catholicism, nativist politicians captured the mayorships of New York, Philadelphia, and Pittsburgh, and nativism emerged as a national political force in the 1856 presidential campaign of ex-President Millard Fillmore on the American ("Know-Nothing") party ticket.

With this heritage of ethnic identity and organized hostility among native workers, the American working class that emerged in the second half of the nineteenth century was something like a building with three massive columns. Native, Irish, and German workers each formed crucial segments of the industrial labor force, but segments separated from each other. Bridging the gaps between them would be a difficult problem for American labor organizers for several generations afterward.

FORCED LABOR

Early America was built by forced labor. At the time of the American Revolution, nearly one-quarter of the population of the thirteen colonies was African American; since all slaves except the very young worked, slaves represented a disproportionate part of the labor force. In addition, the majority of the whites who came to America before 1800 came in bondage as redemptioners: people who agreed to allow ship owners to auction them to the highest bidder for a period of years in payment for their ship's passage, as convicts who exchanged American bondage for a hangman's noose, or as debtors who traded servitude for debtors' prison.

At the end of the eighteenth and the beginning of the nineteenth centuries, a combination of economic and moral pressures seemed to be undermining servitude. In an increasingly commercialized economy, those who sought to buy labor recognized that hiring people on short-term wage contracts was often more flexible and less risky than assuming the large expense of purchasing a slave or a long-term indenture. The rapid expansion of waged labor gave those who sought opportunity in America a far more appealing alternative than indentured servitude. As improving transportation cut the time for transatlantic passage from months to weeks and, by the 1860s, to days even, the expense and danger fell correspondingly. Indentured servitude, already declining in the late 1700s, disappeared completely as the rising tide of free immigrants replaced the bonded labor of the previous century.

The idealism generated by the American Revolution also aroused serious opposition to black slavery. In all of the northern states, slavery was either outlawed or gradually abolished in the generation after the Revolution. Anti-slavery advocates at the Constitutional Convention were forced to compromise with slave-owners who threatened to torpedo American nationhood if slavery was outlawed, but they did win agreement for a clause prohibiting further importation of slaves into the United States starting twenty years after the Constitutional Convention. American slavery, never as profitable as in the sugar colonies of the West Indies or the plantations of Central and South America, looked like it might be slowly phased out.

Ironically, while the rise of the factory system sealed the final doom of other forms of servitude, it gave black slavery in the American South a rebirth. The explosive growth of the textile mills of New England and the English Midlands created a virtually insatiable demand for cotton. Before the cotton gin and mechanized production of cotton cloth, cotton had been a luxury good. Now it rivaled sugar as the world's great cash crop. Even though abolition of the American slave trade (in 1808) helped to drive up the price of slave labor, the cotton boom made slavery immensely profitable. After 1815, slave labor, high cotton prices, and the rich virgin bottomlands of the Gulf Coastal Plain turned American plantation cotton production into a great get-rich-quick scheme. The plantation elite, now unapologetic advocates for expanding the source of their wealth, was on a collision course with the equally enthusiastic advocates of capitalist commercial development in the North.

Only in these closing decades of the antebellum era did southern plantation slavery approach the *Gone With the Wind* stereotype of American popular culture. The majority of the last two generations of American slaves did work in the cotton fields of a few thousand wealthy planters and lived in the shadows of their mansions. Quantitative historians have squabbled about the exact composition of the plantation slave-labor force, but in the 1840s and 1850s, at least three-quarters—perhaps up to or over 90 percent—of American slaves worked as field hands. Most of the remainder were household servants or artisans such as carpenters, blacksmiths, or coopers. In the aftermath of slavery, most of the first small African American middle class—the initial cohort of ministers, teachers, professionals, and skilled workers—were the descendants of the house servants and artisans of the last slave generation.

Those who had been field hands entered emancipation poorly equipped to compete in a wage-labor economy. Not only were most illiterate, but, equally important, they lacked essential experience in negotiation or handling money. They had no resources or marketable assets other than their capacity for physical labor.

Even those who did have skills, such as the former plantation artisans or the small numbers who had worked as slaves for hire in southern cities, encountered unremitting hostility from most white employers and white workers in both North and South. While some white workers had joined the abolitionist crusade on moral grounds, the majority of the northern public had been won to the anti-slavery cause because they had become convinced that the competition of slave labor threatened free labor. They did not look upon job competition from ex-slaves any more favorably than they had greeted competition with slavery.

This combination of white hostility and lack of marketable assets kept most of the ex-slaves out of the emerging industrial economy for two more generations. They remained in southern agriculture until the twentieth century. Yet given the constraints they faced, their story is not one of total failure. Within a generation, the majority had escaped gang labor on their former plantations. They worked as small farmers, tenants, and sharecroppers—still for most a life of hard labor and poverty, but a life that allowed for far more independence and sense of achievement than had the lives of their parents.

CONCLUSION

The question of free versus slave labor had postponed a full reckoning with the contradictions of wage labor. But it was no coincidence that Boston machinist and labor organizer Ira Steward demanded, according to David Montgomery, at the end of 1865 that Radical Reconstruction be directed at the plight of wage workers as well as the former slaves: "So must our dinner tables be reconstructed, our dress, manners, education, morals, dwellings, and the whole Social System" (quoted in *Beyond Equality,* p. ix). No sooner had the question of free versus slave labor been settled than Americans were forced to recognize that they faced a new labor question: the relationship between labor and capital. Those who were slow to appreciate this fact had the point forcefully driven home to them in the summer of 1877. Just as Reconstruction symbolically ended with the withdrawal of the last federal occupying troops from the South, railroad workers, protesting wage cuts and increased workloads, virtually shut down the nation's entire transportation system. When hundreds of thousands of other working people in dozens of cities joined striking railroad workers in their battles with police, national guardsmen, and finally federal troops, they turned the 1877 railroad strike into the largest strike anywhere in the world in the entire nineteenth century.

In its aftermath followed mass-marketed popular exposés, a senatorial investigation into the conditions of labor and capital, sudden expansion of labor organization culminating in the explosive growth of the Knights of Labor in the middle of the next decade, and calls by nervous defenders of property for urban police reform, armory construction, and national guard reorganization. No one had a clear or convincing prescription for solving the central dilemma posed by this new labor problem: How to reconcile the democratic political culture that defined what it was to be an American with the social and economic hierarchies of capitalism. But for more than half a century thereafter, the labor problem and all of its ramifications persistently occupied center stage. The making of an American working class—even one so divided against itself by the cleavages of race, ethnicity, religion, region, and economic sector—had permanently and fundamentally altered American society.

BIBLIOGRAPHY

Bode, Carl. *American Life in the 1840s* (1967).

Bodnar, John. *The Transplanted: A History of Immigrants in Urban America* (1985).

Commons, John R., et al. *History of Labour in the United States.* Vol. 1 (1918).

Dawley, Alan. *Class and Community: The Industrial Revolution in Lynn* (1976).

Dublin, Thomas. *Women at Work: The Transformation of Work and Community in Lowell, Massachusetts, 1826–1860* (1979).

Dudden, Faye E. *Serving Women: Household Service in Nineteenth-Century America* (1983).

Faler, Paul G. *Mechanics and Manufacturers in the Early Industrial Revolution: Lynn, Massachusetts, 1780–1860* (1981).

Fogel, Robert W., and Stanley L. Engerman. *Time on the Cross: The Economics of American Negro Slavery* (1974).

Foner, Philip S. *History of the Labor Movement in the United States.* Vol. 1, *From Colonial Times to the Founding of the American Federation of Labor* (1947).

Gerber, David A. *The Making of an American Pluralism: Buffalo, New York, 1825–1860* (1989).

Gordon, David M., Richard Edwards, and Michael Reich. *Segmented Work, Divided Workers: The Historical Transformation of Labor in the United States* (1982).

Gutman, Herbert G. *Work, Culture, and Society in Industrializing America: Essays in American Working-Class History* (1976).

Handlin, Oscar. *Boston's Immigrants: A Study in Acculturation* (1941).

Hirsch, Susan E. *Roots of the American Working Class: The Industrialization of Crafts in Newark, 1800–1860* (1978).

Hugins, Walter. *Jacksonian Democracy and the Working Class: A Study of the New York Workingmen's Movement, 1829–1837* (1960).

Katz, Michael B., Michael J. Doucet, and Mark J. Stern. *The Social Organization of Early Industrial Capitalism* (1982).

Laurie, Bruce. *Working People of Philadelphia, 1800–1850* (1980).

Lebergott, Stanley. *Manpower in Economic Growth: The American Record Since 1800* (1964).

———. "Labor Force and Employment, 1800–1960." In *Output, Employment, and Productivity in the United States After 1800.* Vol. 30, *Studies in Income and Wealth* (1975).

Levine, Bruce, et al. *Who Built America?* (1992).

Licht, Walter. *Working for the Railroad: The Organization of Work in the Nineteenth Century* (1983).

McGaw, Judith A. *Most Wonderful Machine: Mechanization and Social Change in Berkshire Paper Making, 1801–1885* (1987).

Montgomery, David. *Beyond Equality: Labor and the Radical Republicans, 1862–1872* (1981).

———. *The Fall of the House of Labor: The Workplace, the State, and American Labor Activism, 1865–1925* (1987).

Pessen, Edward. *Most Uncommon Jacksonians: The Radical Leaders of the Early Labor Movement* (1967).

Prude, Jonathan. *The Coming of Industrial Order: Town and Factory Life in Rural Massachusetts, 1810–1860* (1983).

Ransom, Roger L., and Richard Sutch. *One Kind of Freedom: The Economic Consequences of Emancipation* (1977).

Ross, Stephen J. *Workers on the Edge: Work, Leisure, and Politics in Industrializing Cincinnati, 1788–1890* (1985).

Schob, David E. *Hired Hands and Plowboys: Farm Labor in the Midwest, 1815–1860* (1975).

Shelton, Cynthia J. *The Mills of Manayunk: Industrialization and Social Conflict in the Philadelphia Region, 1787–1837* (1986).

Stansell, Christine. *City of Women: Sex and Class in New York, 1789–1860* (1986).

Walkowitz, Daniel J. *Worker City, Company Town: Iron- and Cotton-Worker Protest in Troy and Cohoes, New York, 1855–1884* (1978).

Wallace, Anthony F. C. *Rockdale: The Growth of an American Village in the Early Industrial Revolution* (1980).

Ware, Norman. *The Industrial Worker, 1840–1860* (1924).

Wilentz, Sean. *Chants Democratic: New York City and the Rise of the American Working Class, 1788–1850* (1984).

SEE ALSO **Minorities and Work; Quantification and Its Critics; Slavery.**

LABOR: THE GILDED AGE THROUGH THE 1920s

John B. Jentz

THE HISTORY OF the American working class from the 1870s through the 1920s is characterized more by its disjunctures than its coherence. Radical and conservative labor organizations rose and fell. The greatest waves of immigration in American history redefined the American working class, and the entrance of women and blacks into the work force did the same. New industrial cities grew over the tops of hamlets and market towns along the Great Lakes and in the South. American corporate capitalism emerged in the 1890s out of the ruins of that decade's depression, the country's worst to date.

The new corporations of the early twentieth century made the assembly line the standard of the American factory, and they created a mass commercial culture that, particularly during the 1920s, reshaped the way American workers lived and thought about themselves. Growing bureaucracies in business and government created new kinds of white-collar labor, expanding the definition of work and the working class to include people such as telephone operators. Amidst the prosperity of the "roaring twenties," manufacturing workers reached their historically highest proportion of the American work force.

American politics changed almost as dramatically, shifting from an era of intense party competition in the Gilded Age, or the last third of the nineteenth century, to an era of Republican party dominance after 1896. Only Woodrow Wilson broke the Republican hold on the presidency between 1896 and Franklin D. Roosevelt's victory in 1932. In the first two decades of the twentieth century, a middle-class progressive reform movement provided an occasional ally for organized labor and positively reshaped the context of public opinion in which some labor issues were addressed. Yet the progressive movement declined in the 1920s along with the fortunes of labor. In the midst of all this social and economic change America fought the Spanish-American War in 1898 and entered the First World War in 1917. The country emerged from both as a world power with an empire and a foreign policy that was hostile to a Russian revolution that was made in the name of liberating the working classes of the world.

There were nonetheless patterns amidst the complexities and disjunctures. Some order was imposed from above by the changing American economy and political system. Workers struggled to define an order of their own from below, and their efforts shaped not only the American labor movement but also American society and culture. To understand the full dimensions of American labor history in these sixty years one needs to place the struggles of organized labor within the larger context of the history of the American working class, most of which was never incorporated within labor institutions. In turn, the history of the working class needs to be seen within the context of the phases of the American industrial revolution, the history of immigration, and the character of the political system of the late nineteenth and early twentieth centuries.

GILDED AGE WORKERS AND THE TRIUMPH OF CORPORATE CAPITALISM

The last third of the nineteenth century was the classic period of American industrialization, when the country built its heavy industry and a national railroad system. Although the American industrial revolution had begun in the 1820s and 1830s, industrialization before the Civil War was restricted to a narrow sector of the economy—the production of light consumer goods such as cloth, boots and shoes, and clocks. In an overwhelmingly agricultural society the market for these goods was dependent on the prosperity of rural America. After the Civil War the growth of cities and the railroads helped create a market for industrial goods, such as iron and steel, that was not so dependent on a rural market. At the same time the railroad system gave access to a truly national market that stimulated the growth of all types of manufacturing.

Basic industry grew exponentially. The production of bituminous coal, the main energy source for smokestack America, expanded over ten times between 1870 and 1900. The production of rolled iron and steel grew over twelve times in the same period. The whole American economy developed with such rapidity that the gross national product in 1900 was approximately six times what it had been in 1869. By the turn of the century America was the preeminent industrial economy in the world with an output greater than its closest rivals combined.

The explosive growth of manufacturing capacity meant a similar expansion of the work force. The people employed in manufacturing jumped from over 2.6 million in 1870 to almost 7.2 million in 1900. Immigrant men filled much of the demand for industrial labor in America's cities, but women and children were also drawn into the work force in unprecedented numbers. In 1890, one-fifth of the children between the ages of ten and fifteen held jobs. By 1900 women made up one-quarter of the nonfarm work force, although they were not primarily in manufacturing. In Pittsburgh at the turn of the century less than one-quarter of employed women were in manufacturing; most were servants, waitresses, saleswomen, clerks, teachers, nurses, or midwives. Working-class families, especially those with unskilled breadwinners, needed income from women, and sometimes children, to survive; but wage labor was not the only source of income. Housewives took in boarders, for example, one of the many kinds of work they performed outside the wage economy. In a large sample of all types of Pennsylvania households in 1901, one-fifth of the families took in boarders.

The Gilded Age economy was unstable during this rapid expansion. America experienced two severe depressions in the mid 1870s and the mid 1890s, as well as sharp contractions in 1884 and 1888. Both the economy at large and people's everyday lives seemed out of control. Economic instability—in addition to inequality and the growth of big business—helps explain the appeal of mass protest movements in the 1880s, such as those led by the Populists and the Knights of Labor. Both tried to use politics and the government to define a new order controlled from below, based on local institutions such as cooperatives. The Populists and the Knights were mass movements with diverse constituencies that included substantial numbers of wage earners. The Populists were concentrated among farmers and farm workers in the rural West and South, while the core constituency of the Knights was among workers and small businessmen in cities and towns. The economic instability of the Gilded Age also helps explain why skilled workers—such as machinists, iron molders, carpenters, printers, and cabinetmakers—were attracted to unions in their crafts: these unions offered stability and concrete benefits in return for the high dues they charged. Craft unions provided another kind of control from below. Such unions were the backbone of the American Federation of Labor (AFL) founded in 1886.

Gilded Age workers lived with an almost constant threat of unemployment, and their organizations frequently disintegrated from insolvency and disinterest during depressions. The depression of the 1890s was the first one survived by a significant number of American trade unions, an organizational feat too seldom appreciated. It was, however, usually purchased at the price of limiting union membership to skilled workers who could pay their dues. This organizational achievement built on an unequal distribution of income within the American working class: on the average, America's skilled workers were better off than even their British counterparts, but America's unskilled workers were no better off than their British compatriots, and perhaps less so.

The distinction between the skilled and unskilled had even wider implications. In America unskilled workers were more likely to be recent immigrants, while the skilled were more typically immigrants of longer residence, the children of such immigrants, or Yankees—that is, the native-born of Anglo-American parents. As the European origins of immigrants to the United States shifted in the late nineteenth century, the craft workers were commonly from northwestern Europe, while the unskilled workers came from eastern, central, and southern Europe. The Yankees were especially prominent in the most skilled jobs in metal fabrication and in the best railroad occupations, such as train engineers. A typical Gilded Age production facility in heavy industry, a steel rolling mill, for example, had a work force with a sizable core of skilled northern European craft workers directing a larger group of laborers and helpers. The craft workers often acted as subcontractors within the plant, who reached agreements with management and hired laborers themselves to fulfill the tasks.

A long-term decline in prices lent a harsh and uncompromising character to the relations between capital and labor in the Gilded Age. The index of wholesale prices declined by 50 percent between 1870 and 1896, as new technologies increased productivity and lowered costs per unit. Businessmen also were able to lower costs by bringing previously unexploited, rich natural resources into the market for the first time, such as the iron ore of the Mesabi range in Minnesota. Often called the great depression before the cataclysm of the 1930s usurped the name, this price deflation was also caused by intense business competition. Businessmen constantly cut costs to outsell their competitors, and labor was frequently one of the costs they tried to cut.

The labor history of the late nineteenth century was punctuated by frequent, bitter, and often violent strikes in which neither side felt it could give much ground. From the railroad strike of 1877—America's first national strike—through the pitched battles of the Homestead strike in 1892 and the Pullman strike in 1894, conflicts between labor and capital took on a violent and volatile character. The larger conflicts spilled over into the wider community and usually involved state and national intervention by the courts and troops. Class conflict became a stark reality for Americans in the late nineteenth century. Declining profits also often became a stark reality for businessmen, who were frequently unable to cut labor costs due to working-class resistance. This resistance was usually led by the skilled workers who were also most able to form lasting unions.

The solution to the instability and declining prices of the Gilded Age economy came out of the private economy, not from the government, as the Populists and Knights of Labor had advocated. Leading the corporate merger movement between 1897 and 1904, investment bankers under the leadership of J. P. Morgan brought "fair" competition to industry by combining smaller companies into huge corporations which, if not monopolies, were large enough to shape the market in which they operated by influencing prices and dividing up market share. A notable achievement of the new corporate economy was a rising rate of prices. The wholesale price index increased by 50 percent between 1896 and 1913, just before the outbreak of World War I in Europe. These years were also marked by unprecedented prosperity and relatively mild swings in the business cycle. Led by investment bankers, American business had begun building a new order from above, a process that culminated in the 1920s.

Successful new corporations—and not all were successful—combined their increases in size and structure with new managerial techniques that provided greater control over their far-flung enterprises. Developed by the railroads in the late nineteenth century, modern management techniques meant creating departmentalized bureaucratic structures, usually broken down into functional units and coordinated by a strong central bureaucracy to which the middle managers regularly fed information. These middle managers were frequently innovators in their fields of responsibility, and they tried to increase their control by changing the ways workers performed their tasks. The subsequent struggles between managers and workers for control on the shop floor defined much of American working-class history in the early twentieth century. The main target of the new managers was the substantial power of skilled workers within the production process, a legacy of the Gilded Age. Also pitted against the new managers was a working class expanded by the "new" immigration of the Ellis Island era between the late 1890s and World War I. Immigrants often new to industrial work and urban life faced some of the most sophisticated and powerful business organizations in the world.

Applying mass production to heavy industry had occupied business in the previous era. The new corporations applied mass-production techniques in making consumer goods, such as cigarettes, electrical appliances, and cars. The new corporations also pioneered the application of electricity in the factory, so that it became the predominant industrial power source by the 1920s. So profound were these changes that some historians speak of a second industrial revolution, although it was, in fact, another stage in a process that had begun in the early nineteenth century. Changes in managerial structure and the application of new technologies produced huge increases in labor productivity—and corporate profits—in the 1920s. Between 1919 and 1929 labor productivity increased 2.2 percent annually, in contrast to 1.5 percent in the preceding decade.

The mass production of consumer goods in the early twentieth century could only be sustained if the products were successfully marketed on a scale never before achieved. Advertising reached new levels of sophistication and influence in the 1920s. Business reached a wider public through electronic technologies, such as the radio; and advertisers helped define new images of everyday life in order to market everything from washing machines to cigarettes. American merchandisers and financial institutions also pioneered installment buying so that masses of Americans, including workers, could buy into a definition of the American dream through an unheard-of abundance of consumer goods. Installment buying was needed in part because the wages of American workers did not keep pace with increases in productivity or profits in the 1920s, although real wages did increase. This relatively slow increase in wages helped ensure that markets were inadequate for the flood of new consumer goods, one of the inner weaknesses of the American economy during the boom of the 1920s.

IMMIGRANTS, BLACKS, AND ORGANIZED LABOR IN THE PROGRESSIVE ERA

Historians have usually distinguished the "old" immigration originating in northwestern Europe from the "new" immigration from eastern and southern Europe. The 1880s, when 5.2 million immigrants arrived, witnessed the historic pinnacle of the old immigration from Scandinavia, Germany, and the British Isles; but a rapid shift to the new immigration also began in the same decade. The numbers of new immigrants from places like Italy, Austria-Hungary, and Russia surpassed even the volume of the 1880s to make the first ten years of the twentieth century the unparalleled immigrant decade in American history. Over eight million entered the country, and Ellis Island became fixed in the American imagination as the gateway to a new life. Looking at these two decades separately obscures a larger fact, however: two-thirds of the thirty-three million immigrants who arrived in America between 1820 and 1920 entered the country after 1880. In one sense, the great majority of these immigrants did not enter America, they entered the American working class; and their arrival profoundly reshaped the hierarchies within it and its labor institutions.

Research by Peter R. Shergold sheds new light on the status divisions among American workers at the turn of the century. Comparing workers in Pittsburgh and Birmingham, England, Shergold found that, contrary to conventional wisdom, American

workers did not necessarily have a higher standard of living. The main characteristic of the American working class was a sharp inequality between the skilled and unskilled. Divisions within Birmingham's working class were comparatively narrow. Pittsburgh's skilled craft workers were much better off than their Birmingham counterparts, earning in some cases up to twice as much. Pittsburgh's unskilled workers may have had slightly better wage rates, but their overall standard of living was hardly higher than their counterparts in Birmingham, in part because the community facilities available to Birmingham's unskilled workers were considerably better.

Skilled workers in Pittsburgh could live according to the "American standard" of which Samuel Gompers, president of the AFL, was so proud. They could purchase a small home, perhaps even with indoor plumbing, buy cigars, subscribe to a labor newspaper, and pay for tickets to watch professional baseball. This composite skilled worker in turn-of-the-century Pittsburgh would have found much in common with a German upholsterer in Chicago, described in a government report in 1884 (Illinois Bureau of Labor, *Third Biennial Report*):

Family members 5—father, mother, and three children . . . The house they occupy contains four cozy rooms, all nicely carpeted. Family comparatively healthy. Wife quite intelligent, and children neat and well dressed. Father belongs to trades union, and carries some life insurance. He states that he has run in debt during the past year somewhat, but principally for groceries. Father works but about forty weeks during the year. . . . If he had work the entire year he would not now be in debt.

For breakfast they commonly had "coffee, meat, bread and butter," for supper "coffee, bread, potatoes and meat." The family's annual budget included expenditures for "books, and papers, etc." in addition to union dues and life insurance premiums.

The contrast with unskilled laborers was stark. Pittsburgh's common laborers at the turn of the century lived in rickety wooden tenements near the noise and stench of the blast furnaces where so many of them worked. Children played on unpaved streets, and leisure consisted of sleep and perhaps a drink at a local saloon. Particularly during the era of the new immigration, common laborers often came to America unaccompanied by families and lived in ramshackle boardinghouses near the plants where they worked or near railroad junctions from which they could more easily travel to their next job. The sharp contrast between the earning power and living standard of skilled and unskilled workers in America was compounded by ethnic and racial cleavages. In turn-of-the-century Pittsburgh, common laborers were typically Italians, Slavs, Poles, or Austro-Hungarians, whose cultural traits compounded the contrasting living standards of the skilled and unskilled. These new immigrants also had different agendas from the German, Scandinavian, British, and Irish skilled workers who occupied the upper echelons of the blue-collar work force. Recently arrived, the new immigrants commonly intended to save money in order to return home to their old villages as "rich" men. While hoarding what they could save from their meager wages, they lived in material squalor, which they hoped was temporary.

The Italians were a case in point. In the early twentieth century they replaced the Irish as America's typical unskilled construction laborers. Arriving as single men or without their families, Italian men worked in gangs of fellow countrymen, intending to go home when the opportunity arose. This helps explain why 3.8 million Italians arrived between 1899 and 1924, and 2.1 million left in the same period. And some of them returned to the United States a second or third time for the same reasons. When the new immigrants, such as Italian laborers, started to stay, bring their families over, and build urban neighborhoods, they started a new chapter in the social history of the American working class.

The new immigration ended abruptly with the beginning of World War I in 1914, and it did not resume in its prewar volume mainly because of the immigration quota laws passed in the early 1920s. In the absence of massive immigration, the increasing demand for labor that came with the wartime boom, and then with the prosperity of the 1920s, was met first by blacks and women. To an ever-greater extent Hispanics, especially Mexicans, also helped meet the need, since they were not covered by the immigration quota laws. Women occupied a special niche in the manufacturing economy, which will be discussed in the last section of this essay. Blacks from the South began to fill the ranks of common laborers, helpers, and unskilled machine tenders that had been the positions of the new immigrants. The racial hatred permeating American working-class life has obscured the extent to which the history of blacks in the American working class is analogous to that of the new immigrants.

Blacks were practically the only native-born Americans in the unskilled working class of Pittsburgh in the early twentieth century, and their numbers increased dramatically during World War I. Before the war the black American population was concentrated overwhelmingly in the rural South. Although there were pockets of black settlement in a few northern cities, dating in some cases to pre–Civil War times, there was no sustained migration from the South to northern cities. World War I changed the situation dramatically as corporations, led by the railroads, recruited thousands of black workers. Once the process began, blacks moved north on their own, as news of opportunities spread by word of mouth and through personal letters. The letters sent home by black laborers had an impact similar to the "immigrant letters" that were read in European peasant villages by family and friends.

With the black migration north during World War I a new era began in black American and working-class history. For the first time blacks made up substantial elements of the work forces of northern industries from steel and meatpacking to railroads and construction. They also started forming their own urban communities, reinforced in their size and homogeneity by racial prejudice that hindered black dispersal. The arrival of blacks in cities was marked by some of the largest race riots in American history. Racial prejudice also typified the reaction of organized labor, despite a few pronouncements from AFL leadership opposing provisions in union charters excluding people on the basis of race. Although there were some successful interracial organizing efforts, there were just as many cases where, understandably distrustful of unions, blacks served as strikebreakers. The history of such events is usually interpreted in the context of American race relations, but they also need to be seen in the light of the disparity between the different levels of the American working class and the impact that disparity had on organized labor.

The history of organized labor in the late nineteenth and early twentieth centuries had an almost schizophrenic character, typified on the one hand by conservative craft unionism incorporated into the AFL, and on the other by episodic flashes of militance embodied in massive strikes that often ended in violence and labor defeat. While the AFL moved cautiously in politics and kept its organizational efforts largely confined to craft workers, the Industrial Workers of the World (IWW) tried to organize one big union of all workers. The IWW led unskilled workers in dramatic and often violent strikes. Appropriately, the AFL was founded in the

1880s, a decade marked not only by massive labor unrest but also by the shift from the old to the new immigration. The AFL craft unions included in their membership, and were often founded and led by, immigrants from northwestern Europe. Samuel Gompers, founder and early president of the AFL, was of Dutch Jewish heritage, but he was raised in London, where he learned the ways of modern labor unions. The IWW was founded in Chicago in 1905 during the height of the new immigration. The IWW appealed to the lowest levels of the American working class, and it was particularly adept at organizing the single men who lived in the harsh and isolated logging camps and mining towns of the West.

This rooting of different types of labor organization in the differing strata of the working class is a necessary but insufficient explanation of the complex history of the organized American labor movement. The character of the national political system, for example, also profoundly shaped the history of organized labor, and not simply in its forays into electoral politics. A review of the history of organized labor can help illustrate the wider import of labor's social history and aid in defining questions and refining hypotheses about how social change influenced the subsequent history of the labor movement. In general, during the Progressive Era—the first two decades of the twentieth century—the most conservative elements of organized labor could extract modest gains from the political system, after extensive efforts. But these gains, such as the Clayton Antitrust Act, too often proved disappointing in their result for labor. The radical side of organized labor met with sustained hostility from business and government, and it was repressed during and after World War I.

In the 1890s, Gilded Age America seemed to be at a dead end of violence, disorder, and political ossification. Agrarian protest, represented by the Populists, shook the major parties, especially the Democrats in the South and West. Unemployed workers filled the streets of urban America. In the Pullman railroad strike of 1894, Grover Cleveland, a Democratic president, used federal troops against striking workers—just as a Republican president, Rutherford B. Hayes, had used them in the nationwide railroad strike of 1877. The class conflict of the 1890s was so extensive that it changed the thinking of important segments of American political and corporate leadership. Middle-class Progressives, such as Jane Addams, tried to make democracy meaningful to the immigrants crowding American

industrial cities, cooperating with organized labor on issues like child-labor laws and factory inspection. Both middle-class reformers and enlightened conservatives in America's corporate business leadership also felt that a new and more productive way of managing the conflicts between capital and labor had to be developed. They formed the National Civic Federation to bring together representatives of business, labor, and the public, which usually meant urban middle-class reformers. Samuel Gompers participated actively in the organization, which promoted the use of arbitration in labor disputes, and generally worked to create a spirit of accommodation across the divide separating management and labor. Along with other reform groups, it helped create a more favorable public opinion on labor issues than had been the case in the Gilded Age.

Labor had new room to maneuver in the first two decades of the twentieth century, but this room was clearly circumscribed. During the anthracite coal strike of 1902, for example, Theodore Roosevelt—future candidate of the Progressive party in 1912—cajoled the mine owners into an arbitrated settlement with the United Mine Workers, instead of sending troops. Aided by the return of prosperity, a wide range of unions besides the miners gained significant organizational victories in the late 1890s and first few years of the century. In these years Chicago was probably the most unionized city in the world after London. By 1904 American unions had organized 20 percent of the workers in manufacturing, mining, transportation, and construction. This was an unparalleled union achievement, based in many cases on the cooperation on the local level between experienced labor leaders, who were usually old immigrants, and unskilled workers, who were frequently among the new immigrants. Hostility and misunderstanding were not the only relationships between the differing strata of the working class. In a huge 1904 strike, Chicago packinghouse workers of different income levels and ethnic backgrounds were able to work together because of their common experience on the shop floor and their cooperation with strong community organizations in nearby neighborhoods.

The Progressive movement and the National Civic Federation notwithstanding, business greeted the union successes of the early twentieth century with an unprecedented, and largely successful, anti-union "open shop" drive that was aided by a recession in 1904. Despite cooperation between old and new immigrants in a major strike in the Chicago packinghouses during that year, the packinghouse owners won and the workers there remained unorganized. Business also attacked organized labor in the courts during the first decade of the century, and it was so successful that Gompers led the AFL out of its usual political passivity to make demands on the major political parties for legislation giving unions relief from the results of several Supreme Court decisions. Significant gains for labor had to wait, however, until Woodrow Wilson needed labor support to help secure his tenuous hold on the presidency.

Wilson owed his narrow victory in 1912 to Theodore Roosevelt's campaign as leader of the Progressive party, which drew votes from William Howard Taft, the Republican nominee. Further to the left of the Progressives, the Socialist Party of America, under the leadership of Eugene Victor Debs, polled an unprecedented 6 percent of the presidential vote, an achievement never again equaled. Wilson needed to appeal to these reform constituencies to stay in the White House for a second term, since he had won with only 41 percent of the popular vote in the election of 1912. In Wilson's first term there were several legislative victories for labor, the most significant being the Clayton Antitrust Act, which labor had advocated to limit the use of court injunctions against unions. The courts had been using the Sherman Antitrust Act (1890) to justify injunctions against strikes, calling them conspiracies in restraint of trade prohibited under the Sherman law. The Clayton Act amended the Sherman law to limit this use of the injunction as a measure to suppress strikes. As happened so frequently, however, this legislation—Gompers called it "labor's Magna Charta"—proved hollow because of its narrow interpretation by the courts.

World War I proved more beneficial to the conservative wing of organized labor than the programs of the first Wilson administration. Union membership increased substantially between 1914 and American entrance in the conflict in 1917, and it increased even more with American involvement in the war. During the war, membership in AFL unions reached an all-time high of about three million, up from about 1.6 million in 1910. The government needed labor's cooperation to maintain war production, which was threatened by a wave of strikes after America entered the war. The Wilson administration responded by including labor leaders and spokesmen in policy-making circles and granting most of labor's demands for wage increases and benefits. In return the administration

demanded a no-strike pledge from labor. Never before had labor leaders been involved in the power circles of America, and Gompers became a member of the trusted inner circle of government policy. At the same time, the federal government cracked down on labor radicals, whom it accused of undermining the war effort. Since the Socialist party opposed the war, it suffered severely and Debs went to jail in 1919 for a violation of the Espionage Act. This crackdown on the Left foreshadowed what was to come.

When the war ended, so did government management of the economy that had given unions a new power in the American economic system. Workers, both organized and unorganized, sought to preserve their wartime gains against a determined effort by business to win back its old freedom of action. During 1919 more workers went on strike than in any year in American history. Major strikes in steel, bituminous coal, and among the Boston police set the pattern for a period of labor conflict—and labor retreat—that lasted through a sharp economic downturn in 1922. Government on all levels intervened against strikes, supported by a public mood aroused against radicalism and communism. Fears inspired by both the Russian Revolution and labor's postwar assertiveness produced America's red scare of 1919–1920. In 1919 and 1920 Attorney General A. Mitchell Palmer launched a wide-ranging and thorough attack on Left-leaning organizations. He decimated an American Left already weakened by internal divisions over how to respond to the Russian Revolution. Fears of foreign radicals also helped ensure the passage of immigration restriction laws in the early 1920s.

The red scare and union defeat began more than a decade of labor decline that did not end until the organizing drives of the Congress of Industrial Organizations (CIO) in the mid 1930s. Organized labor had gone from unparalleled success to a defeat that seemed permanent by the mid 1920s. The fact that its organizational and political successes in the second decade of the century depended on the unusual Democratic victory under Wilson and then on a world war had been obscured by the bright light of long-sought victories. With men like Calvin Coolidge and Herbert Hoover in the White House, corporate America claimed, with temporary credibility, to have the will and means to meet workers' needs for higher wages, job security, and greater benefits through what has come to be called "welfare capitalism." Corporations started providing a set of programs for their employees ranging from company sports teams through life insurance to profit sharing, all of which were designed to prove that unions were no longer needed. With unions weak or nonexistent, immigration a mere trickle, the Left practically impotent, and America awash in consumer goods, an era had ended in the history of the American working class. The death of Gompers in 1924 accentuated the point. Except for one year he had been president of the AFL since its founding in 1886.

For labor the 1920s marked a return to the "normalcy" of its hostile relation with the state. The formative years of the modern American labor movement took place at a time when achieving power in the political system seemed remote and other options for exercising power could easily appear more realistic. Seen in this light, the local cooperative communalism of the Knights, the conservative trade unionism of the AFL, and the revolutionary unionism of the IWW shared the common endeavor of founding a base for exercising power outside the established party system. Given this political environment, labor's organizational failures need less analysis than the working-class roots of its successes, and the limitations these roots carried with them.

SHAPING CITIES BY BUILDING WORKING-CLASS NEIGHBORHOODS

Both the successes and defeats of the labor movement have to be related to the distinctive character of working-class formation in the late nineteenth and early twentieth centuries, particularly to the urbanization of the working class and its reconstitution by immigration from Europe and migration from the South. For sixty critical years, as America became the world's preeminent industrial power, American workers were engaged in two fundamental projects—building urban communities and becoming Americans. The construction of labor institutions was part of, but subordinate to, these two primary endeavors.

The urbanization of the American working class was one of the most important developments in American history. Between 1870 and 1910 the urban industrial core of the nation expanded from the East to include the Old Northwest. New industrial cities emerged, such as Cleveland, Pittsburgh, and Detroit, each of which had at least 450,000 people by 1910. Chicago came to dominate the entire midwestern industrial region with a population in 1910

of over 2.1 million. Medium-sized industrial cities developed rapidly as well. In 1910 there were fifty-nine cities with populations between fifty thousand and one hundred thousand, and forty-two of them were in the industrial East and Midwest. Cities like Rockford, Illinois, South Bend, Indiana, Youngstown, Ohio, and Johnstown, Pennsylvania, formed part of the urban and industrial expansion of the country. They were also sites for the formation of its immigrant industrial working class, just like Chicago and New York.

Urbanization was part of the redistribution of economic and social resources that marked the industrial revolution. Urbanization, manufacturing growth, and gains in labor productivity moved in tandem; all three increased most rapidly in two decades of unusual prosperity, the 1880s and the first decade of the twentieth century. These decades also included the historic peaks of immigration to the United States. The immigrants of these decades settled disproportionately in American cities, and particularly in cities with rapidly expanding industrial economies—in the New England, mid-Atlantic, and midwestern states. In 1870 America's cities with at least twenty-five thousand residents averaged 34 percent foreign-born, although such cities in the South and West were consistently below this mean figure. The same regional distribution held true in 1910, when the average percentage of foreign-born in all large cities had declined somewhat to 29 percent, but the proportion of the urban population made up of the children of immigrants had increased considerably. Although these children were American-born, they were not yet part of the American mainstream. In the last quarter of the nineteenth century two-thirds or more of the populations of the cities in America's industrial core were composed of immigrants and their children. The fact that these urban immigrants were also overwhelmingly working-class is too frequently overlooked.

Foreign-born men, women, and children set about building a community life for themselves in American cities, and in the process they profoundly shaped the character of urban life. Numerous scholars have studied the formation of these ethnic working-class communities, documenting the strength and diversity of the institutions they created, from the churches, schools, and fraternal orders to singing societies, theater companies, and banks. The immense resources of time, energy, and money put into creating and maintaining these institutions can be understood by looking at any one of the massive churches that still mark the skylines of so many of the residential neighborhoods in America's midwestern industrial cities. The similar efforts of blacks to build urban communities in the North after World War I are too seldom compared to the construction of immigrant neighborhoods and social institutions. The building of black communities on Chicago's South Side and in New York's Harlem, for example, was part of the history of the American working class, as well as a critical chapter in the history of black America.

Before the depression of the 1890s, when the scale of so much American business was smaller, immigrant communities were often complemented by a substantial number of ethnic businesses capable of employing a significant portion of the immigrant work force. In fact, labor conflict often took on an intraethnic character, when German furniture workers struck the shops of German furniture manufacturers, or when east European Jewish workers struck Jewish-owned garment shops. The depression of the 1890s destroyed many ethnically owned businesses, and the corporate reorganization of the economy afterwards absorbed many others into larger corporations owned by native-born Americans. As the power and significance of ethnic businesses declined in the twentieth century, urban immigrant neighborhoods encompassed less of the lives of immigrant workers. The ability of labor organizers to use community pressure against employers declined as well.

Unions and political machines were two important parts of the building of working-class America. Both performed different mediating functions between workers and the larger society. Too often political machines are seen only as manipulators of their foreign-born constituents. In fact, immigrants were able to influence the machines to provide concrete benefits. Through political machines urban workers could have some say in directing public resources to themselves through jobs on public construction projects or through the paving of streets in working-class neighborhoods. The machines, of course, had their cost, and it was not simply the corruption for which they were famous. Since the machines were the primary political vehicles for urban workers, they usurped a vote that unions, and especially Left political parties, claimed for themselves. Machines were especially sharp competitors for the political left, in part simply because they had integrated workers into American political life before parties of the Left were on the scene. Workers thus felt an allegiance to them, as

well as receiving benefits and favors from them. The machines also co-opted working-class leaders with the jobs, money, and power at their disposal.

The creation of unions, benefit societies, mechanics institutes, socialist singing societies, and labor parties was part of this larger process of the formation of America's urban working class. Local unions after the Civil War were frequently analogous to fraternal orders, as well as to the craft associations from which so many derived. The Knights of Labor offer the best illustration of the use of fraternal ritual to build a labor institution. Uriah S. Stephens, the most important leader in the founding of the Knights in 1869, was a native-born Philadelphia tailor. The secret fraternal ritual he advocated helped the organization survive the depression of the 1870s, unlike most labor institutions; the fraternal ritual offered a wider basis for uniting workers of differing nationalities than the cultures of particular crafts.

Fraternalism, however, aroused the opposition of the Catholic church and limited the ability of the Knights to organize openly and effectively amidst the labor unrest of the late 1870s and 1880s. Terence V. Powderly, the son of Irish Catholic immigrants, took over as Grand Master Workman in 1879, ended the secrecy, and opened up the Knights to all working people. An ideology of radical republicanism with deep roots in the American Revolution replaced fraternalism as its unifying culture. The Knights became the most important labor organization of the 1880s by transcending their local and fraternal origins, while at the same time adopting a loose structure based on local and district assemblies that integrated a diverse multitude of local organizations into a larger whole. The Knights' complicated organizational structure sheds light on the tasks facing all labor institutions in the era: they had to draw on local institutions and separate national cultures while transcending their limitations. Yet the weak central authority of the Knights also limited their ability to control their own members and contributed to their demise.

The cigar makers offer a contrasting example. The Cigar Makers' International Union (CMIU) was the power base for Samuel Gompers and helped form the AFL in 1886. The AFL competed with and then supplanted the Knights in the late 1880s and early 1890s. When Gompers arrived in New York as a thirteen year old from London, the local cigar industry was based in small craft shops and dominated by central Europeans, primarily Germans and Bohemians. Gompers made his way as a leader in the cigar makers' union in alliance with Adolph Strasser, a German-speaking Hungarian immigrant. In the midst of the depression of the 1870s, they organized a local union on the basis of high dues, strong benefits, and abolition of special-language sections. They were not only trying to build on solid dues-paying members but also to form an organization to compete with the ethnic and fraternal groups that supplied their members with benefits and social activities. The German and Bohemian ethnic culture of New York's Lower East Side supplied Gompers and Strasser with organizational models, even when they worked to found unions that would compete with ethnic associations.

After a huge cigar makers' strike following the great railroad upheaval of 1877, Gompers and Strasser decided that their local in the CMIU had to have more centralized authority and more discipline, along with its high dues and benefits package, to survive and prosper. By the early 1880s they had achieved these organizational reforms, which provided models for other unions in the AFL. By then their main competitors among the cigar makers' union were immigrant socialists who disliked the limited goals of the union and wanted to appeal to a broader base of workers. Socialists remained a powerful force within the CMIU and the AFL into the twentieth century, despite the triumph of the policies of Gompers and Strasser. The price of the cigar makers' victory, however, was to limit their union to a narrow sector of their own industry. By the turn of the century their union organized primarily the makers of the most expensive cigars, while most workers in the industry, who were increasingly women, made cheap ones. The cigar makers refused to organize the women.

Although the organizational tactics of the CMIU had succeeded in creating a stable union, success cut it off from the vitality of American working-class life, which was deeply rooted in urban, ethnic, working-class neighborhoods, such as the Lower East Side in New York City where Gompers and Strasser had first organized. The strength and creativity of such communities was demonstrated again in 1909 and 1910 when the International Ladies' Garment Workers' Union (ILGWU) organized its industry on the Lower East Side. The industry was for the most part small-scale and immigrant owned, in contrast to the general trend in American industry toward large corporate organization. The ILGWU became one of America's few successful industrial unions, organizing all workers in an industry irrespective of skill. This union was as much a creation

of the Jewish and Italian working-class communities on the Lower East Side as of the union movement. Community support helped give the striking garment workers, female and male, Jewish and Italian, a strength that invigorated the ILGWU and made it into one of America's strongest and most militant unions.

There are numerous examples of the strength and creativity of immigrant working-class neighborhoods. Polish communities were the staunchest supporters of several coal strikes in the anthracite mining region of Pennsylvania. Neighborhoods of new immigrants united behind strikers in the Chicago packinghouse strike of 1904. Immigrant communities held out longest in the steel strike of 1919. Yet these local, usually ethnic, sources of support and solidarity also limited the formation of strong centralized labor institutions that could contest with the likes of U.S. Steel. At the same time unions drew on community support but had to compete with ethnic leaders and organizations that divided their members and claimed their resources. This tension between local working-class communities and the labor movement was inherent in the contemporary situation of American workers. The American industrial working class was still centrally engaged in building the local urban communities that would sustain it. The greatest wave of immigration in American history had only ended with the outbreak of World War I. The urbanization of the American working class, and the building of urban working-class communities, were still under way throughout the 1920s.

SHAPING AMERICAN CULTURE BY BECOMING AMERICANS

Becoming Americans was the other major project of America's immigrant workers between the 1870s and the 1930s. The traditional image of assimilation pictured a process in which immigrants were acted upon by American society—a process in which they surrendered their original culture and received another one, along with at least a modicum of prosperity. A generation of social historians have struggled to show how assimilation was a two-way process in which accommodations were made on both sides. As they became Americans, immigrants helped redefine who Americans were, even while the dominant society struggled, with mixed success, to impose its definition upon them.

LABOR: THE GILDED AGE THROUGH THE 1920s

The struggle to become American defined the culture of the working class, even when the struggles were not over questions that the labor movement considered critical to the interests of workers. Conflicts over temperance or religion in the schools were central to defining what it meant to be an American worker.

Immigrants—whether old or new—brought with them a variety of local and regional cultures, and usually dialects, which they used to build their communities. The Italian neighborhoods of a large city could encompass within them the folkways of Sicilian peasants and the anarchism of Italian industrial workers. The "little Germanies" of American cities were led by solid and conservative German-American businessmen—brewers, furniture manufacturers, clothing retailers—but they also included socialists exported in the 1880s as a result of Otto von Bismarck's antisocialist laws, and farm laborers from the landed estates east of the Elbe River. These immigrant enclaves could unite in crises, in opposition to temperance laws, for example, or in response to tragedies such as the 1911 fire at the Triangle Shirtwaist Company in New York City. That fire killed almost 150 young female garment workers, most of whom were first or second generation Jewish immigrants. The Triangle Shirtwaist fire galvanized the Lower East Side behind labor legislation in New York State and was critical in the history of the ILGWU. In such ways these immigrant enclaves helped shape the urban political liberalism of twentieth-century America.

These same enclaves supported within them oppositional subcultures that shaped the way immigrant workers reacted to American industrial society. Peasants-turned-industrial workers not only found the discipline of routinized factory labor alienating—as many historians have documented—but they also brought with them concepts of a "just price" for food that could lead immigrant women to march on grocery stores in opposition to high bread prices. Immigrant socialists and anarchists, radicalized in the old country, founded political parties and radical unions, such as those that opposed Gompers and Strasser in New York City in the 1880s. The Chicago anarchists, made notorious by the Haymarket riot of 1886, represented the largest among several interrelated anarchist communities in American cities. People circulated among them, sometimes with traveling radical theater troupes, and the radical communities were bolstered by new recruits from European repressions. The German anarchists of Chicago were only

a memory by the early twentieth century, but Italian anarchists revived the anarchist tradition, and the Sacco and Vanzetti trial of the 1920s showed again how radical politics could frighten the American public into supporting miscarriages of justice.

Before the depression of the 1890s these radical subcultures were sustained by enclaves of immigrant craftsmen in American factories. Still essential to the production process in the Gilded Age, these craftsmen were the workers most likely to regularly attend union meetings, subscribe to labor newspapers, and attend fundraising events, such as picnics. The craftsmen in factories complemented and helped sustain the ethnic enclaves of immigrant working-class communities in American cities. Even if they were not radicals, and most were not, such craftsmen helped create and maintain institutions and cultures that a wide range of native-born Americans considered alien and threatening. The Pledge of Allegiance was first published in a children's magazine in 1892, and school systems around the country rapidly adopted it as part of daily educational routine. Its popularity was stimulated by immigration and labor unrest such as the Pullman strike during America's worst depression until that time. The Pledge was clearly designed to indoctrinate at least the children of immigrants with American values, which too many of their parents apparently lacked. As the immigrant generation fought for its place in American society, it argued that its inherited culture was a legitimate part of America, protected by American constitutional freedoms. Necessity made the immigrants cultural pluralists, while the Pledge of Allegiance tried to integrate their children into a homogeneous political culture.

The children of immigrants are known for abandoning the culture of their parents and adopting American ways, but this is a stereotype that masks a more subtle reality. Members of the second generation enthusiastically adopted a particular segment of American culture—its popular urban variety—that they in turn helped to define, and which the established arbiters of American culture considered "low" and debasing. Herbert Gutman, one of America's premier labor historians, has asked (in *Power and Culture,* p. 387) what it meant for American culture, both popular and elite, when the children of immigrants became the largest group of American workers in the late nineteenth century: "What does the concept of 'assimilation' mean in the context of rapid capitalist development *and* the emergence of new popular urban culture?"

1469

The easiest answer is that second generation immigrants participated in defining the terms of their assimilation by helping create the culture they adopted. They worked to redefine what it meant to be an American so that the new definition would encompass them. The prominence of second generation immigrants in creating popular music is one of the most obvious examples. Tin Pan Alley was dominated by second generation immigrants in twentieth century America. The same could be said of the movie industry. The creation of jazz, one of America's most distinctive art forms, by urban black America can be seen in a similar light. Blacks in the 1920s were engaged in building their own urban working-class communities after the great migration to the North had begun during World War I. Although blacks were not immigrants, they were new arrivals in urban America, and jazz was part of their effort to create black communities there. The cultural flowering of the Harlem Renaissance in the 1920s—a period marked by prohibition and a revival of the Ku Klux Klan—was not only an effort to create a new black culture but also to redefine American culture, to make it wide and supple enough to include black Americans, just as immigrants and their children were trying to define the terms of their assimilation. The results of both endeavors created a vital and powerful popular culture.

Corporate America also had its say about the character of the American working class and popular culture. As business tried to sell the flood of consumer goods it was producing, its sophisticated advertising redefined the American dream to include the availability of a cornucopia of commodities. Intellectuals reacted to the success of this new commercialism with cries against homogenization, but they were only half right. Before the advent of the television networks, the new radio stations in the 1920s were controlled to a surprising extent by local ethnic communities that used them to sustain their own cultures and institutions as well as to advertise the products created by America's second industrial revolution. The Chicago Federation of Labor even had its own station. Yet those who railed against homogenization were correct in seeing how commercialism was defining a new national standard for how Americans should live. This standard may have helped General Electric sell appliances, but it also helped unions argue that their immigrant members were satisfied with too little: Americans lived better than they dared demand. Popular com-

mercial culture also built bonds between working Americans that were not based on ethnicity or craft. Similar bonds were being defined on the job, and a new culture in the workplace also contributed to defining what it meant to be a working-class American in the twentieth century.

Corporate America also systematically changed the process of production and the nature of work within it. New technologies were introduced that made the semi-skilled machine tender the most common type of factory worker, not the unskilled casual laborer. Although the work was routine, it required training and experience; and business discovered that the high rate of employee turnover that typified unskilled labor in the nineteenth century was too costly in the twentieth. Industry also discovered that women made good employees, precisely in such semi-skilled jobs. Women filled whole departments at General Electric and Westinghouse, producing coils for motors or light bulbs. Business showed even more preference for women in low-level white-collar jobs, and occupations such as secretary, bookkeeper, clerk, and telephone operator were almost completely feminized in the 1920s. The proportion of working-age women in the labor force rose from 20.6 percent in 1900 to 24.8 percent in 1930, with the greatest expansion in white-collar jobs. Not until well after World War II would the labor movement address the issues involved in organizing women in the white-collar work force. Women in the factories were harder for labor to avoid.

Scientific management techniques, usually identified with Frederick Winslow Taylor, became popular among businessmen around World War I as solutions to labor control, particularly for semi-skilled workers, whether male or female. Taylor's famous time and motion studies were used to define how tasks should be performed and at what speed. Taylorism also helped undermine the enclaves of craft labor that had been so critical to industrial production, and to the labor movement, in the Gilded Age. Taylorism was not as successful as its advocates had hoped it would be, but it was part of a thorough redefinition of work that made it more homogeneous—and under greater supervision—than it had been before. Both Taylorism and the benefits offered by welfare capitalism were efforts to keep and control semi-skilled workers. Scientific managers set production goals designed to maximize output through rewards to individuals. Workers were supposed to maximize their pay by surpassing their production goals, but they soon learned that the goals increased along with increased output.

Workers in departments informally joined together to limit production in a way that was more tolerable and did not induce higher production quotas. New workers were quickly educated by their fellows about what was expected and what punishments the group could inflict on those who violated workplace norms. A new shop-floor culture developed not based on craft or ethnicity but on workplace solidarities. As business hired more and more women in the 1920s to fill in for the immigrants excluded from the country by the new immigration restriction laws, solidarities among women supplemented the new workplace culture, just as rituals of masculinity played so prominent a place among men on the job. These new solidarities were more inclusive than the old ones of ethnicity and craft. They helped redefine who working-class Americans were, even as the institutions of the labor movement were in retreat.

The 1920s were an end and a beginning in American working-class history. The labor institutions created largely by the old immigrant generation in the Gilded Age and the Progressive Era were defeated or pushed to the periphery of the American economy. These institutions also never met the challenge posed by the entrance of women and blacks into the working class. At the same time, immigrants were rapidly becoming Americans, blacks were becoming urbanites, and women were becoming permanent wage earners. No homogeneous working class emerged from the 1920s, but a new generation of workers did emerge, one that held new ideas about what it meant to be both an American and a worker. These ideas were being shaped by the children and the grandchildren of immigrants, and by blacks from the South. These people were secure enough in their sense of being Americans to want to change American society rather than to build enclaves within it or accommodate themselves to it. Their day would come in the next decade.

BIBLIOGRAPHY

General Works

Bodnar, John. *The Transplanted: A History of Immigrants in Urban America* (1985). Synthesizes contemporary scholarship on immigrants in urban America.

Brownlee, W. Elliot. *Dynamics of Ascent: A History of the American Economy.* 2d ed. (1988). An accessible introduction to American economic history.

Dulles, Foster Rhea, and Melvyn Dubofsky. *Labor in America: A History.* 2d rev. ed. (1984). Focuses on the organized labor movement.

Gordon, David M., Richard Edwards, and Michael Reich. *Segmented Work, Divided Workers: The Historical Transformation of Labor in the United States* (1982). Political economists place labor within the history of class relations and the economy.

Kessler-Harris, Alice. *Out to Work: A History of Wage-earning Women in the United States* (1982).

Montgomery, David. *The Fall of the House of Labor: The Workplace, the State, and American Labor Activism, 1865–1925* (1987). The best labor history of the whole era; interrelates the social, economic, and political dimensions of labor history.

Tomlins, Christopher L. *The State and the Unions: Labor Relations, Law, and the Organized Labor Movement in America, 1880–1960* (1985).

Ward, David. *Cities and Immigrants: A Geography of Change in Nineteenth-Century America* (1971).

Monographs and Essays on Labor History

Barrett, James R. *Work and Community in the Jungle: Chicago's Packinghouse Workers, 1894–1922* (1987). Particularly useful on the relations between the old and new immigrants in a major industry.

Bernstein, Irving. *The Lean Years: A History of the American Worker, 1920–1933* (1960).

Brody, David. *Steelworkers in America: The Nonunion Era* (1960). Good on the new immigrants in an industrial setting.

———. *Workers in Industrial America: Essays on the Twentieth-Century Struggle* (1980). Includes synthetic essays on major periods.

Cohen, Lizabeth. *Making a New Deal: Industrial Workers in Chicago, 1919–1939* (1990). Includes the best social history of workers in the 1920s.

Cooper, Patricia A. *Once a Cigar Maker: Men, Women, and Work Culture in American Cigar Factories, 1900–1919* (1987).

Fink, Leon. *Workingmen's Democracy: The Knights of Labor in American Politics* (1983).

Grossman, James R. *Land of Hope: Chicago, Black Southerners and the Great Migration* (1989).

Gutman, Herbert G. *Work, Culture, and Society in Industrializing America: Essays in American Working-Class and Social History* (1976). Includes essays that have redefined historians' views of Gilded Age America.

———. *Power & Culture: Essays on the American Working Class,* edited by Ira Berlin (1987). Path-breaking essays that complement those in the work cited above.

Hall, Jacquelyn D., et al. *Like a Family: The Making of a Southern Cotton Mill World* (1987). A case study of southern industry that is excellent on the role of women.

Hoerder, Dirk, ed. *"Struggle a Hard Battle": Essays on Working-Class Immigrants* (1986). Treats immigrant workers active in the labor movement by ethnic group.

Kaufman, Stuart Bruce. *Samuel Gompers and the Origins of the American Federation of Labor, 1848–1896* (1973).

Keil, Hartmut, and John B. Jentz. *German Workers in Chicago: A Documentary History of Working-Class Culture from 1850 to World War I* (1988). Translated documents illustrating the history of an immigrant working-class group, primarily in the Gilded Age.

Laslett, John H. M. *Labor and the Left: A Study of Socialist and Radical Influences in the American Labor Movement, 1881–1924* (1970).

Montgomery, David. *Workers' Control in America: Studies in the History of Work, Technology, and Labor Struggles* (1979). Includes essays that have shaped subsequent discussion about culture and politics in the workplace.

Moody, J. Carroll, and Alice Kessler-Harris. *Perspectives on American Labor History: The Problem of Synthesis* (1989). An introduction to the debate among labor historians about interpreting recent research in their field and linking it to other developments in American history.

Nelson, Bruce C. *Beyond the Martyrs: A Social History of Chicago's Anarchists, 1870–1900* (1988). Analyzes an oppositional labor subculture in Chicago.

Oestreicher, Richard Jules. *Solidarity and Fragmentation: Working People and Class Consciousness in Detroit, 1875–1900* (1986). Defines the idea of oppositional labor subculture and analyzes the phenomenon in Detroit.

LABOR: THE GILDED AGE THROUGH THE 1920s

Salvatore, Nick. *Eugene V. Debs: Citizen and Socialist* (1982). The best biography of America's most important socialist.

Schatz, Ronald W. *The Electrical Workers: A History of Labor at General Electric and Westinghouse, 1923–1960* (1983). An excellent study on workplace culture in the 1920s.

Schneirov, Richard, and Thomas J. Suhrbur. *Union Brotherhood, Union Town: The History of the Carpenters' Union of Chicago, 1863–1987* (1988). A social history of a local union movement, particularly strong on the interrelation of ethnic and class issues.

Shergold, Peter R. *Working-Class Life: The "American Standard" in Comparative Perspective, 1899–1913* (1982). A quantitative analysis of the living standards of workers in the United States and Great Britain.

Zunz, Olivier. *The Changing Face of Inequality: Urbanization, Industrial Development, and Immigrants in Detroit, 1880–1920* (1982). A social and urban history strong on the changing dimensions of class and ethnicity.

SEE ALSO various essays in "**Processes of Social Change**" and "**Regionalism and Regional Subcultures**."

LABOR: THE GREAT DEPRESSION TO THE 1990s

Mary E. Frederickson
Timothy P. Lynch

THE SIX DECADES between 1930 and 1990 dramatically affected the lives of American workers in ways that varied according to race, ethnicity, gender, region, and occupation. Americans have had to redefine the nature and meaning of their work over this period in response to changing economic conditions, often outside their control. Despite numerous redefinitions, however, the primacy of work in American society has remained constant. As Robert and Helen Lynd wrote in their classic study of Muncie, Indiana, in 1935, "One's job is the watershed down which the rest of one's life tends to flow." During this period of labor history, community-based groups of workers united by race, ethnicity, and region, became a fragmented work force, identifying less with each other, and more as individuals living and working within a mass consumer culture.

Wearing collars of different hues—blue, white or pink—workers have tried to direct their work lives, individually and collectively throughout the period. Vying for control with a powerful corporate elite, Americans, whether members of trade unions or not, came to expect the federal government to be responsible for protecting their rights as employees. During the Great Depression, when workers exerted a new level of political power, protesting their conditions in ways that captured the attention of both government and business, protection came from the labor legislation of the New Deal. As the New Deal era gave way to war-generated prosperity, a growing numbers of Americans in the United States saw themselves as part of a labor force that shared a common work ethic, a political ideology grounded in freedom and individualism, and the promise of economic prosperity reflected in a high standard of living. As the nation's economic dominance waned in the 1970s, workers became more vulnerable to control by corporations. By the 1990s, wages were on the decline, jobs were scarce, the government was endorsing an antilabor platform, and economic security eluded a steadily increasing percentage of the labor force.

THE GREAT DEPRESSION AND THE NEW DEAL

Campaigning for the presidency in the autumn of 1928, Herbert Hoover proclaimed: "We are nearer today to the ideal of the abolition of poverty and fear from the lives of men and women than ever before in any land." One year later, the stock market came crashing down with ruinous effect, making a mockery of Hoover's words. Within three weeks, beginning in late October 1929, a total of $30 billion in paper value was lost in the collapse of the market and credit structure. The depression that followed devastated the nation, sowing poverty and despair.

Hoover's optimism, as misplaced as it appears in retrospect, was grounded in the growth of the nation's economy in the 1920s, years that witnessed record production levels. The steel, rubber, and glass industries boomed as Americans built new homes and purchased automobiles, small appliances, refrigerators, and telephones. High protective tariffs increased the demand for domestic goods over expensive imports, but despite sharp increases in production by American factories, the percentage of the U.S. labor force that was engaged in agriculture, mining, and manufacturing fell from 58 to 47 percent by 1930. Automation, heralded by corporations and scorned by workers, was taking its toll. The greatest increases in employment occurred in the white-collar sectors: clerical and service-industry jobs multiplied dramatically. Many of these new positions were filled by women, who made up a quarter of the nation's work force by 1930. Female employment grew by more than 27 percent during the decade (from 8.5 million in 1920 to 10.7 million by 1930). The flood of immigrant workers entering the country between 1890 and 1920 slowed to a trickle after restrictive quotas, the result of laws passed in 1921 and 1924, sharply curtailed entry. While African Americans continued their migration from southern farms to northern cities, racial and gender discrimination forged a segmented labor market.

Real wages, which had remained virtually constant from 1890 to 1915, increased by 40 percent from the beginning of World War I to 1929. But the bulk of this jump had occurred by 1923. When compared to the enormous increase in production, real wages had not kept pace. As the 1920s drew to a close, production was growing at a far greater pace than real wages, and overproduction plagued industries like textiles, garments, and small appliances. By 1929, unsold goods accumulated on stockroom shelves across the nation. Unemployment, which had generally remained below 5 percent of the work force throughout most of the decade, rose; by 1930 the figure had climbed to 8.9 percent.

In an economic climate newly dependent on consumer buying, unskilled and semi-skilled American workers found themselves easily replaceable and their job security more and more tenuous. After a record number of strikes in the years immediately following World War I, the 1920s witnessed a period of relative quiescence. This was not the result of contentment. The problems that had fostered labor unrest after the war remained. Union membership fell over the course of the 1920s, the American Federation of Labor (AFL) dropping from about 5 million members in 1919 to about 3 million in 1933. Industries that had burgeoned during the decade—auto, steel, electrical, glass—remained almost completely unorganized. Workers had few benefits, no means for voicing grievances, and no protection against unemployment. The once-militant United Mine Workers Union was quieted to an echo of labor's victories past. The industrial work force, divided along occupational, regional, racial, gender, and ethnic lines, could not speak in one voice. Dominated by white male craftworkers, the AFL could not command, and in fact shunned, this new industrial labor force.

At this point, the worst economic collapse in American history brought the economy to its knees. By the fall of 1930, unemployment had risen to 15 percent; it would hit almost 25 percent by 1933. Many workers saw their wages and/or hours cut.

Each round of cuts diminished the nation's buying power and set off another round of cuts. Apple sellers and breadlines became the symbols of economic hard times. Many of the twelve million workers unemployed in 1932 hit the road, abandoning families and loved ones, but most stayed put. For many, the Depression forced a reliance on family. In an effort to weather the storm together, the most recent immigrants, especially those of southern and eastern European stock, drew on the same support systems they had used to sustain themselves when they first came to America.

Public relief was quickly overwhelmed by the severity of the situation. Hoover's philosophy of "rugged individualism" put the burden of assistance on state, and especially, local governments. The social consequences of this sharp economic downturn were widespread: malnutrition, high rates of infant mortality, increased rates of alcoholism and petty crime. Marriage and birthrates plunged as a generation of young Americans waited for prosperity to return.

In a society that stressed the values of hard work and thrift, many blamed themselves for being out of work. Others responded in angry protests against rapidly declining economic conditions. The Communist party organized Unemployed Councils in many major cities, staging protests and demonstrations. The "Ford Hunger March" in Dearborn, Michigan, in 1932 became the most infamous of these, when riots left four dead and dozens injured. Throughout the nation workers gathered for spontaneous anti-eviction protests and relief riots as demands for government intervention reached a frenzied pitch. Radicals hoped for the anticipated mass movement, but as the Depression worsened, none developed.

The single most dramatic mass political action came at the polls on 8 November 1932 when Hoover and the Republicans were soundly repudiated by working-class voters. Franklin Delano Roosevelt won the election by a landslide, winning all but seven states—not so much due to an articulated ideology or program, but more because Americans felt abandoned by Hoover. In the four "lame duck" months between FDR's election and inauguration the economy grew even worse: unemployment in industrial cities like Pittsburgh and Birmingham, Alabama reached 50 percent. Bank failures became commonplace, and breadlines and soup kitchens multiplied. Fear gripped American workers, those still employed, and those searching for a job.

LABOR: THE GREAT DEPRESSION TO THE 1990s

The economic crisis reached its low watermark on Inauguration Day, March 1933 with a nationwide bank panic. President Roosevelt met it with the now-famous phrase from his inaugural address, "the only thing we have to fear is fear itself." He then proceeded to demand and be given unprecedented powers to change the monetary system and to create an army of federal agencies, which provided jobs for millions on government-sponsored projects. The New Deal president infused Americans with new hope. Banks had been failing at the rate of 921 per year since 1921. Nine days after his inauguration, and the Monday after the first of his Sunday evening "fireside chats" over the radio to the American people, banks across the country began to reopen. Over 75 percent of all banks were operating again by the end of March.

The Roosevelt administration also pushed for regulation of private industry, and on 16 June 1933, Congress passed the National Industrial Recovery Act, which established codes of fair competition to stabilize business and created the National Recovery Administration (NRA). Section 7a of the legislation guaranteed workers the right "to organize and bargain collectively through representatives of their own choosing," thereby advancing the legitimacy of unions. By linking the popularity of FDR to unionization, labor leaders counteracted the notion that unions represented radical, foreign ideologies, and urged workers to sign on with the slogan, "the President wants you to join the union." In reality, neither Roosevelt nor NRA head Hugh S. Johnson were pro-union. Nonetheless, Section 7a provided badly needed support for the labor movement in its darkest days. After Congress legalized collective bargaining, workers responded to union drives with unprecedented enthusiasm.

That summer of 1933 the United Mine Workers (UMW), with John L. Lewis at the helm, launched a massive campaign among coal miners with great success. In the needle trades both the International Ladies Garment Workers Union (ILGWU) headed by David Dubinsky and the Amalgamated Clothing Workers Union (ACWU) under Sidney Hillman also staged major recruiting drives. AFL unions signed on workers in industries as diverse as fruit picking and stage acting, claiming two million new members by 1934. These gains within the ranks of the AFL had the conflicting effects of strengthening the Federation while creating dissension within the organization. Significantly, many of the new members recruited after 1933 were in jobs classified as either semi-skilled or unskilled; thousands were women; many belonged to ethnic or racial minorities. This suddenly diverse membership actively challenged how the AFL was run, raised questions about the power held by the leadership, and advocated organizing workers on an industrywide basis without regard to trade, skill, or job classification.

At the AFL's 1935 convention, Lewis led the charge, fighting for more vigorous unionization of the mass-production industries. The AFL leadership, with William Green as president, resisted reform. The following month, on 9 November 1935, Lewis, together with Dubinsky, Hillman, and Charles Howard of the International Typographical Union (ITU), and four presidents of small AFL affiliates, formed the Committee for Industrial Organization (CIO). (In 1938 this CIO became the Congress of Industrial Organizations, also the CIO.) Green condemned the mavericks, but compromise was not in his repertoire. Once set in motion, the CIO approach to unionism could not be stopped.

Throughout the nation, workers in mass-production industries joined the CIO by the thousands. Steel, rubber, and auto workers who long had been ignored by the craft-oriented unionists in the AFL, flocked into newly organized locals from Pennsylvania to Georgia to Illinois. The CIO also broke new political ground in 1936 by making substantial contributions to FDR's reelection campaign. CIO-Political Action Committees helped the Democratic landslide that November, returning FDR to the White House, with the largest presidential vote cast up to that time. Scores of prolabor candidates also won federal, state and local offices.

The CIO victories continued into 1937 with an epic confrontation in Flint, Michigan, where the United Auto Workers sustained the first major sit-down strike: for several weeks they controlled Fisher Body Plant No. 2, turning back police, and facing down the National Guard to finally win recognition from General Motors on February 3. Autoworker solidarity was fueled by the Woman's Emergency Brigade, which marched outside the plants and got provisions through the police blockades to the strikers inside. Local citizens helped, and music composed and sung by strikers kept up morale. Victory over the corporate giant GM emboldened workers in other industries. For example, later in the same year, after months of Steel Worker Organizing Committee (SWOC) organizing in mills, U.S. Steel finally came to terms with the labor union. Victories in the auto and steel industries encouraged workers in industries and trades of all types to don CIO buttons and carry membership cards.

By the end of 1937 over 200,000 had joined the UAW and over 300,000 came into the SWOC.

Industrial unionism gave workers new power in shops and plants across the nation. Voicing grievances, organizing nonunion workers, utilizing labor's political clout, unionism transformed the meaning of American labor. The CIO, unlike the AFL, was eager to recruit black workers. CIO leaders knew that success in many industries required across-the-industry organization. To this end they organized the kill floors of Chicago's meat-packing industry, the coke ovens in steel, the foundries in metalworking, all workplaces with large numbers of African American workers. CIO organizers stressed the importance of organizing black workers and sold the idea to white workers reluctant to belong to an interracial union by appealing to their pragmatism: bringing black workers into the union reduced the chance of their being used as strikebreakers. Many in the CIO endorsed the political left and the interracial ideology of socialists and communists. The CIO was willing to use political radicals, many of whom were experienced organizers whose expertise in the field was unparalleled. This made the CIO susceptible to the red-baiting that would plague it in the decade after 1938.

Workers in the 1930s militated against corporate giants in the nation's largest industries, and labor used its power as an effective political tool. Overall in the depressed 1930s, union membership tripled, growing from over 3 million in 1932 to almost 9 million in 1939. There were setbacks—Ford Motor Company remained unorganized, Little Steel proved elusive, and few government employees and other white-collar workers in the expanding clerical sector were organized. Nevertheless, the unparalleled success of industrial unionism permanently changed the American labor movement and the self-image of American workers. The idea of membership open to all workers, without regard to race, gender, or occupation, theoretically, although not always in practice, meant that workers, organized and unorganized, could see themselves moving from the margins of society into the economic and social mainstream of American life.

The New Deal played a decisive role in labor's ascendancy, creating a climate that protected workers' rights and encouraged union organization. The government's role worried many labor leaders who began to see the fate of labor tied too closely to Roosevelt's administration, federal legislation, and generally, forces outside their control. This concern intensified as the administration shifted its focus away from a singular emphasis on economic recovery toward preparation for war.

RETURNING PROSPERITY: THE WAR YEARS

American war production began more than two years prior to the U.S. declaration of war. President Roosevelt started off the year of 1939 by recommending a $535 million defense program. Both Congress's authorization for rearmament and the demands for munitions by European countries at war with the Axis powers brought prosperity and growth to American manufacturers and industries. In the wake of this boom, unions continued to organize workers and push for higher wages, resulting in thousands of work stoppages between 1939 and 1941. Labor's effort to secure its share of the long-awaited economic recovery, recovery that New Deal programs had not fully accomplished, caused the government to prod the AFL and CIO unions to sign no-strike pledges once the nation entered the war.

In 1941, 2.3 million workers—70 percent of them CIO unionists—took part in over 4,200 work stoppages. Though less militant than earlier ones, this strike wave ranked among the most decisive in American labor history. One-and-a-half million American workers joined the union ranks between June 1940 and December 1941. Strong in numbers, unions were also now able to present a "solid front" in such industries as steel and autos, and that strengthened their hand in wage negotiations and contract provisions for favorable grievance procedures, benefits, seniority rights, and work rules. Protracted labor struggles threatened production timetables, so while the nation rushed to war overseas, employers sought to keep peace at home in order to win lucrative government and military contracts. The fervency of management's desire for prompt completion fed both the rapid growth of unions and the success of strikes during this relatively short period. Eventually, after the Japanese bombing of Pearl Harbor on 7 December 1941 catalyzed the nation to join the Allies, the AFL and CIO officially agreed to submit labor disputes to a federal mediation board, rather than to strike, for the duration of the war.

Meanwhile, successful labor organization intensified the battles between the AFL and CIO, and heated up the race to organize workers in the electrical, aircraft, paper, textiles, food-processing, and woodworking industries. Millions of Americans joined the armed forces, and unemployment, at record levels in the 1930s, finally diminished in the boom of industrial production. The influx of new workers into industry to replace men entering military service boosted union membership. To meet the increased demand for war materials, women became a larger portion of the work force, entering industrial production jobs previously held by men.

By 1945, nineteen million female laborers were part of a civilian work force of fifty-four million. Many of these women had been working before the war, but after 1940, as more industrial jobs became available, they moved from lower-paying positions, usually in the service or clerical sectors, into newly available higher paying industrial jobs. As the nation depended increasingly on women's labor, the government launched a media campaign in newspapers, magazines, and newsreels, urging women to serve their country as part of the "industrial army." These bulletins and advertisements always presumed the temporary nature of women's war work, stating pointedly that industrial jobs were really "men's work" to be filled by women only "for the duration." Millions of American women took advantage of the demand for their labor, moving into higher paying and full-time jobs, seeking specialized training to improve their chances of permanent industrial employment. Women comprised two-thirds of the twelve million workers who entered the labor force during the war; the majority of these women had been unemployed or underemployed prior to the war.

American women quickly proved themselves. They performed wartime jobs with all the diligence of their male counterparts and achieved the same levels of production and quality. Yet they were routinely paid less for the same work. Government directives opposed differential pay, but employers frequently manipulated job descriptions to suit their own ends to the disadvantage of female employees. Although female union membership increased dramatically during World War II, labor leaders were not really supportive either. In 1943, UAW president R. J. Thomas called differential wages for female workers "a women's problem." Unions, like governmental officials, the media, and most employers, considered women a temporary addition to the work force.

By the war's end, the government was waging a new propaganda campaign, this time one designed to get women out of the work force. Women industrial workers were reminded that they were "taking a man's place," and that he was about to return home having sacrificed for his country. Even though women held jobs across the traditional sexual division of labor, their entry into the job market during the war years was viewed by many as simply an extension of woman's role as helpmate. Regarded this way, their employment posed no threat to traditional gender roles. Meanwhile, government and industry turned a blind eye toward women's domestic responsibilities during the war, ignoring the crucial issues of adequate day care for children, and the increased burden of home and family duties borne by working women whose husbands, fathers, and brothers were overseas. Suddenly, women were being chastised, told that they were needed at home. Some government officials even implied that women workers were responsible for a perceived rise in juvenile delinquency. Increasingly, advertisements showed wives in the kitchen preparing meals for husbands returning home after a long day at work.

The notion that if women left the workplace men could have jobs did not match the reality of the immediate postwar economy in which manufacturing positions were being eliminated. With nine million servicemen returning from overseas, government officials feared another recession and consequently endorsed policies designed to avoid high unemployment. The G.I. Bill, for example, encouraged returning soldiers to go to school as a means of augmenting future employment prospects, rather than to look for a job immediately. Some industries reimposed Depression-era restrictions that had been lifted during the war, and once again mandated maximum age limits for female employees and the ban against hiring married women. Indeed, women lost their jobs at a rate 75 percent greater than that of their male counterparts. Even more significantly, as Ruth Milkman argues, the female-employment pattern set at that time established the paradigm for women's work that would continue for many decades after the war.

World War II also provided industrial opportunities for blacks as well as for white women, and they too fought against constant discrimination in the workplace. During the Depression, 50 percent of skilled blacks lost their jobs between 1930 and 1936. Even when the war upped the demand for workers, blacks were largely excluded from skilled jobs in the defense industry. Labor-starved plants in Connecticut, Maryland, and California imported whites from other parts of the country rather than hire local blacks for even unskilled work. The situation for African Americans grew so grim, with employers making public pronouncements they would consider blacks only for menial jobs, that A. Philip Randolph, president of the Brotherhood of Sleeping Car Porters, threatened President Roosevelt with a march of fifty thousand blacks on Washington, D.C., in 1941. When African Americans were first upgraded to skilled jobs in the auto industry, there were many wildcat strikes in defiance of union leaders and management alike. The worst eruption came after the influx of 300,000 southern whites and blacks into the area surrounding Detroit's war plants. Race riots exploded on 20 June 1941, with thirty-five killed and six hundred wounded, mostly blacks. At the end of two days, police had arrested fifteen hundred people; among them, less than three hundred were white.

The Detroit race riots, along with Randolph's threat, moved Roosevelt to ban employment discrimination by companies filing defense contracts, and later to create the Fair Employment Practices Commission (originally established as the Fair Employment Practice Committee on 25 June 1941) in order to enforce his executive order.

The percentage of black males in skilled jobs nearly doubled from 4.4 in 1940 to 7.3 in 1944, as they experienced more diversification in employment than they had in the previous seventy-five years. The number of black government employees, fifty thousand in 1937, had quadrupled by 1946. Nonetheless, as with women workers, the ideal and the reality of equality were two very different things. Blacks' greatest economic gains came between 1940 and 1950 as a result of world conflict, but the war at home of racial tensions flared, too. In many plants, whites refused to stay on the job with blacks, sometimes staging "hate" strikes. Many unions, including independent railroad brotherhoods, the International Association of Machinists, and the Boilermakers, continued to discriminate severely against black members or to bar them entirely. At war's end 95 percent of all professional jobs were held by whites.

Still, some gains were made. The median annual income for black full-time workers rose 45 percent between 1939 and 1955 (it rose 57 percent for white workers during the same period). Migrating north to escape marginal labor as sharecroppers and domestics, thousands of blacks settled in northern cities with available war production jobs. African Americans entered workplaces where there had been few if any minority employees previously. Industries organized by the CIO showed the great-

est advances, if only because black workers had been virtually unheard of in these work forces before. In any case, black employment rose especially in steel, metals, and meat-packing, as well as in midwestern auto plants producing military vehicles, in California aircraft companies, and in shipbuilding southeastern coastal towns such as Norfolk and Newport News.

Full employment during the war years helped white women and African Americans in gaining better-paid manufacturing jobs which in turn enabled them to provide for their families and save for the future. Yet despite these new opportunities and higher wages, each year of war brought an increase in strikes: in 1942 there were 2,968 work stoppages involving 840,000 workers; in 1943 walkouts jumped to over 3,700 and involved almost 2 million workers, an upsurge due largely to a half-million UMW soft-coal miners walking off the job. In 1944, living costs rose nearly one-third, and by 1945 many of the nearly 3.5 million striking workers took action spontaneously in walkouts staged without the authority of union leadership. Wildcat strikes were only a gross measure of widespread worker discontent. Hiring novice workers, work speedups, fatigue from extended shifts, and unfamiliar machinery resulted in a marked increase in industrial accidents. Casualties from the war were both on the front lines and the production lines. The industrial army, just as soldiers in the war zones of Europe and Asia, grew weary of fighting. Rumors of massive wartime profits accruing to industrialists and entrepreneurs frustrated workers who were struggling to meet production on the shop floor. The high hourly wages so attractive to Depression-ravaged workers in 1939 and 1940 began to lose their appeal as wartime inflation, industrial accidents, and regular double shifts spent away from home and family made workers resentful and uneasy.

World War II was a major turning point in the history of American labor. Industrial workers, women, and African Americans gained some autonomy and power, foreshadowing major changes through the civil rights and women's liberation movements of the postwar era. But before those movements gained momentum in the 1950s and 1960s, the work force demobilized and in the process two things happened: white male workers, many of them war veterans, reestablished their hegemony over the workplace, and U.S. corporations, no longer hampered by full-employment levels, reasserted their control over American workers.

LABOR IN THE POSTWAR ERA

World War II gave new strength to American workers and to the labor movement. At war's end in 1945, more Americans than ever before had money in their pockets and a list of material goods they wanted to purchase. Industries converted as quickly as possible from war production to goods for personal consumption. The nation focused its attention on domestic issues. Concerns about jobs, wages, home, and family dominated the agendas of most American workers. Many feared another depression as returning servicemen flooded the job market and millions of workers looked to the labor movement for security and protection.

By 1945, union membership rose to an all-time high of almost fifteen million workers organized, over 35 percent of the nonagricultural labor force. The AFL maintained its dominance as the larger of the two federations with over 10 million members. Although relatively smaller with its 4.5 million members, the CIO controlled core industries such as auto and steel. After the war both the AFL and CIO had difficulty keeping their membership from participating in widespread strikes. In fact, 1946 was the most strike-ridden year in American history. Striking workers were no longer concerned about obtaining the right to collectively bargain under the union banner or about the existence of unions. Postwar workers walked out to protest layoffs and shortened hours.

Labor leaders, emboldened by the movement's new power, spoke up for more control over the industrial process, while industrialists attempted to reassert their authority in the workplace where they believed management had conceded too much control to workers in order to meet high production quotas during the war years. Union contracts negotiated in the war's immediate aftermath presaged the increasing control industry would exert in the succeeding decade. Some unions accepted the responsibility of disciplining members who defied contract agreements; many others, given little choice, bowed to terms set by employers seeking to circumscribe union power and contain the labor movement's role in industrial decision-making.

The limits of organized labor's power were further diminished by the Taft-Hartley Act. Impatient with the rash of strikes, a Republican-controlled Congress passed the law on 23 June 1947 over President Truman's veto. Revising the National Labor Relations Act (also known as the Wagner Act) of 1935, the Taft-Hartley Act established "unfair" labor practices, including secondary boycotts, jurisdictional strikes, refusal to bargain in good faith, and contributing to political campaigns. In addition, Taft-Hartley banned the closed shop, thereby allowing employers to hire nonunion workers. The law required newly hired workers to join the union in union shops, but it also permitted states to enact "right to work laws" that outlawed union shops. Taft-Hartley also required union leaders to sign affidavits stating that they were not Communists. It also changed the National Labor Relations Board (NLRB) from an advocate for labor into a neutral intermediary. Employers discovered they could drain a union's financial resources by engaging in lengthy NLRB proceedings.

United Mine Workers leader John L. Lewis and CIO and U.S. Steel Workers of America president Philip Murray refused to sign the anticommunist affidavits; but most union leaders could not afford to risk losing access to the NLRB by not signing. To combat Taft-Hartley, both the AFL and the CIO vigorously campaigned to elect a prolabor Congress. While during the 1930s and early 1940s some unionists envisioned a prolabor third party, by the late 1940s labor most often supported the Democratic party. In the 1948 election workers' votes and dollars returned Truman to the White House and restored a Democratic majority to both houses of Congress. Such effort brought limited benefits, however, for the new Congress failed even to revise the Taft-Hartley Act, let alone repeal it.

The reformist approach to politics that typified union political activity during the late 1940s was buttressed by the expulsion of a number of Communists from the CIO. Even though the Soviet Union had been an ally during World War II, American foreign policy became doggedly anti-Soviet, and suspicion about labor leaders and unions sympathetic to the left intensified. Red-baiting within unions resulted in the purging of radicals and the tempering of activism. More and more, labor leaders acquiesced to the general principles of capitalism, following the dictates of industrialists and the two-party political system. By 1950, although unions had established themselves as a fixture within the American political and economic system, their role in providing a counterbalance to industrial power was severely diminished.

For both organized and nonunion workers, the 1950s and 1960s were decades of seeming affluence. Real wages grew at an unprecedented pace. At first glance working men and women had joined the nation's burgeoning middle class. Enjoying the material benefits of postwar prosperity, more American families than ever before owned their own homes—60 percent by 1960. Working-class families sought their share of the American dream in the suburbs, moving from older neighborhoods in large industrial cities. The blue-collar work force was being assimilated into middle-class life; class distinctions, some said, were becoming blurred. Indeed, by 1956 white-collar workers had for the first time in United States history outnumbered blue-collar Americans—the first indicator that the nation was moving from an industrial to postindustrial economy.

During these years collective bargaining proved a potent tool for advancing wages for both white and black union members. Despite inflation, real earnings increased over 40 percent from the late 1940s through the 1960s. Union workers began to secure cost-of-living adjustments in their contracts, and automatic annual increases tied to rising productivity. Yet, workers failed to secure protection of their income against unexpected fluctuations in the economy. Employers successfully resisted the worker-management planning that many laborites advocated. Granted, unemployment compensation cushioned the blow of layoffs for many, but few enjoyed the kind of security won by UAW workers: supplementary employment benefits that, combined with government benefits, could provide up to 95 percent of an employee's weekly wages. Even under the UAW-negotiated provisions, supplementary unemployment benefits were paid only so long as the union's funds were solvent. As beneficial as these plans were, they did not engage the unions in production-planning.

In the 1950s and 1960s, in addition to bargaining for higher wages, workers sought "fringe" benefits. Pensions, health care, group insurance, vacations, and the like figured more prominently in the packages negotiated between labor and management. This created a mixed system of benefits with some—health care, for example—provided by industry, and others, such as social security, by the government. Forced to include these items in union contracts, many employers reversed their position on government spending for social security. In their minds, it was better for the government to pay the bill than the corporation. Critics noted that control of pension funds for investment was left in the hands of employers, not workers. These arrangements shifted labor-generated funds out of the hands of workers into the control of the bank-

ing establishment, in effect endorsing and buttressing the priorities of finance capitalism.

Some unions did direct their own pension funds and a few invested in cooperative housing projects, worker-managed industrial ventures, or other forms of innovative social investment. Others, the International Brotherhood of Teamsters under president James R. (Jimmy) Hoffa, for example, used pension funds in a number of highly questionable ventures. Benefit packages negotiated by unions also had the effect of accentuating the rift between the stronger unions in core industries, such as steel and auto, and those in the service sector and light manufacturing.

Nonunion workers often received improved wages and benefits as a result of successful collective bargaining by unionized workers within an industry. Keeping step with the unions was one way an employer could hope to remain free of unionization. Yet, although both unionized and unorganized workers made considerable gains in wages and other benefits as a result of collective bargaining, labor still had not gained entry into managerial decision-making. Workers sometimes did attempt to exert such control through slowdowns, wildcat strikes, and similar strategies. But overall, management maintained and even solidified its authority over production decision-making in the two decades after 1945.

THE 1960S AND 1970S: YEARS OF CHANGE AND REACTION

During the 1930s the labor movement seemed to hold the potential for a profound transformation of American society. Militant workers called for radical changes in the political and economic system. During the 1960s, however, the majority of unions stayed away from the protest front. Taking labor's place on the front lines, the civil rights, antiwar, and women's liberation movements called for a reordering of social and economic priorities. To be sure, the boycotts against grapes, iceberg lettuce, and Gallo wines led by Cesar Chavez on behalf of Hispanic farm workers in California played a part in the protests of the 1960s. But generally, American workers did not support those demanding fundamental change. While many members of the Old Left were laborites advancing the cause of workers under the banner of the CIO, members of the New Left were seldom associated with unions. In fact, the long-standing support of American foreign policy by the AFL and CIO positioned them as but another facet of the American establishment, especially during the Vietnam War.

For example, George Meany, president of the AFL-CIO (which merged in 1955), publicly supported the war policy of the administration of President Lyndon B. Johnson, and criticized those unionists who argued against the war. At the 1967 AFL-CIO national convention, an antiwar resolution was defeated by a vote of two thousand to six! And in 1972, the AFL-CIO's Executive Council refused to endorse Democratic candidate George McGovern for president because of his antiwar position, despite his prolabor record in Congress.

With respect to issues of race, too, the AFL-CIO failed to meet the challenges of the times. Only one African American, A. Philip Randolph, served on the twenty-seven member executive council even though 25 percent of the AFL-CIO's membership was black. In 1960 the Negro American Labor Council was formed to promote the interests of blacks in the unions. Although the AFL-CIO had long supported civil rights legislation, the leadership seemed unresponsive to blacks' demands for greater representation in leadership positions, and access to skilled jobs. Even in a traditionally progressive union like the UAW where African Americans comprised one-third of the membership, they held few leadership positions. Young militant blacks in a number of the auto plants in Detroit formed radical organizations to promote their interests, and while this movement was short-lived, involving only a small core within the UAW, it reflected a deep and widespread discontent.

For all African Americans there were both signs of gains and reasons for concern. Opportunities in public employment and federal benefits had improved family income for blacks from about 40 percent of that of whites in 1940 to over 64 percent in 1970. During the 1960s, as employment opportunities improved in the clerical sector and the computer and aerospace industries, the centers of employment shifted away from industrial urban areas, leaving many black workers isolated in urban ghettos. Poor educational opportunities kept blacks from obtaining the requisite training in new technologies. Even in the unions, where black workers had made great strides, continued occupational segregation kept black employees in lower grade jobs. Even the Equal Employment Opportunity Commission (EEOC), created to investigate com-

plaints under the antibias mandate of Title VII of the Civil Rights Act of 1964, helped little, due to inadequate funding and slow procedures.

Meanwhile, women workers entered the labor force in unprecedented numbers. Passage of the Equal Pay Act (1963), Title VII of the Civil Rights Act (1964), and Executive Order 11246 (1964) led women to reassess their roles in the workplace and in their unions. The UAW's Women's Department and the Education and Social Action Department of the International Union of Electrical Workers (IUE) led the way by endorsing the elimination of discriminatory state laws, advocating job protection during maternity leaves as well as the establishment of child-care facilities. Workers' education programs in New York and Michigan began to offer seminars for union women, staff, leaders, and rank-and-file workers. Union women organized conferences to address issues of concern to female workers across the country: improving job conditions, gaining equal opportunity under the law, and increasing participation by women in their unions.

Female employment was a key factor in the material success of the American working class during the relatively affluent decades of the 1950s and 1960s. The twenty years between 1950 and 1970 witnessed unparalleled growth in the percentages of women in the work force—from roughly 31 percent in 1950 to 43 percent in 1970. During the entire half century from 1900–1950 it had increased only 10 percent. Significantly, the greatest increase occurred among married women. In 1940 only one out of seven married women worked outside the home; in 1950 this figure was one out of five, and by 1970 two out of five. Clearly, the prosperity and higher standard of living enjoyed by American workers was purchased in part with the wages of women.

In the postwar decades women were heavily recruited into the burgeoning service, clerical, and government employment, which comprised half the labor force by 1950. At the same time, mechanization in mining, agriculture, and factories kept the number of jobs relatively stable though production levels skyrocketed. The number of employees in mining and agriculture actually declined, from over 25 percent of the work force in 1940 to about 5 percent by 1970. For those remaining on the job, mechanization made the work ever more dull and monotonous. Whether on the assembly line or in the office, work failed to provide a sense of personal fulfillment. In the white-collar sector, the largest increase in positions was in sales and clerical work, jobs offering relatively low pay and little or no opportunity for autonomy or advancement.

These changes in the work force had little effect on the distribution of wealth. In both 1950 and 1970, the top fifth of the population enjoyed over 40 percent of the nation's income while the bottom fifth received less than 5 percent. In 1970 a full 60 percent of American workers and their families fell below the U.S. Bureau of Labor Statistics own line for an "intermediate" standard of living ($10,700 in 1970).

In the early 1970s, women established two new organizations designed to improve the status of female employees. In 1973 the National Association of Working Women (known as Nine to Five) was formed to organize clerical workers, and six months later, the Coalition of Labor Union Women (CLUW). The latter, an umbrella organization of union women, explicitly sought to increase the number of women in trade-union leadership positions, to support legislation on women's concerns, to elect women to political office, and to organize the millions of nonunion female workers. Nine to Five created chapters across the country, gained a membership of over twelve thousand and made impressive gains in banks, offices, and insurance companies, while raising the consciousness of nonunion clerical workers across the nation. CLUW grew rapidly as well, constituting sixty-five chapters and fifteen thousand members by 1984. Paralleling the structure of most unions, CLUW established a convention format to pass resolutions and set policies to guide local chapters.

Though very different in their approach to organizing these two groups changed the labor movement's orientation toward female employees. Recognizing the importance of women within unions, the AFL-CIO endorsed the Equal Rights Amendment in 1973. During the next decade, many unions addressed "women's issues" such as affirmative action, child care, and pay equity. More women were elected to leadership positions, especially on the local level, and in 1980 CLUW president Joyce Miller was the first woman to sit on the AFL-CIO's Executive Council.

Despite the progress, relatively few women became national labor leaders, even in unions such as the Amalgamated Clothing and Textile Workers' Union or the Communication Workers of America, both with a majority of female members. Indeed, the dearth of female leaders is startling given the increased proportion of unionized women. As au-

tomation, deindustrialization, and overseas employment increased, eliminating manufacturing jobs, male union membership declined. Almost all of the labor movement gains of the 1970s derived from increases in female membership, as unions sought to offset the general decline in membership by targeting specific occupational groups: teachers, hospital personnel, and public-sector clerical and service workers.

In the years after the 1955 AFL-CIO merger, public employees comprised the one new area of unionization to emerge. President John F. Kennedy gave it a boost when he issued Executive Order 10988 encouraging union membership among federal workers. Between 1955 and the early 1970s, the number of organized public employees increased tenfold, to over four million. In this period, the American Federation of State, County, and Municipal Employees (AFSCME), the American Federation of Teachers (AFT), the National Education Association (NEA), and unions of policemen, fire fighters, civil servants, nurses, and postal workers grew rapidly. By the early 1970s, AFSCME had become one of the AFL-CIO's largest affiliates.

Ironically enough, the success of organized labor's early radicalism contributed to its subsequent conservative image during the turbulent 1960s. From a position of respectability, labor wielded considerable political power during the 1950s and 1960s. Democratic candidates were well aware of the importance of the labor vote, and liberal legislation, during the Kennedy and Johnson administrations continued the work begun by the New Deal. But there were limits to what could be achieved by this marriage of organized labor and the Democratic party. Despite many attempts, the most hated elements within the Taft-Hartley Act were not repealed. Furthermore, when Richard M. Nixon narrowly defeated Hubert H. Humphrey in the 1968 presidential election, the death knell of labor's political influence was sounded.

Labor's political influence at the national level declined, but its role in state and local politics did not follow the same pattern. In fact, throughout the 1960s and 1970s and even into the decade of the 1980s and beyond, labor organizations operating at the grass-roots level exercised political influence by lending support to specific local issues, raising funds for political candidates, and fostering an informed electorate among their memberships.

Labor's enduring ability to wield power in local politics underscores the importance of rank-and-file commitment and raises the issue of participatory democracy within unions themselves. During the 1930s when workers struggled to gain recognition of their unions for collective bargaining, rank-and-file members actively participated in the fight. But with the entrenchment of unions in many industries during the postwar years, the relationship between leadership and membership changed. Contract negotiations with employers generally involved only a small cadre of union leaders. The decision to accept or reject what had been negotiated involved little more than a perfunctory vote by the rank and file, following the recommendations of their leaders. In some unions, such an atmosphere of disengagement bred negligence, nepotism, and corruption. Members tried to make leaders more responsive to their needs. Such a spirit of intra-union reform infused the Miners for Democracy movement, the Steelworkers Fight Back drive, and the Teamsters for Democratic Union. As the rank and file struggled to regain control over the decision-making process, management was figuring out ways to undermine labor's gains and make unions the scapegoat for America's economic problems.

DEINDUSTRIALIZATION AND AMERICAN LABOR

Throughout the 1970s, unionized manufacturing jobs declined, American industrial production was downscaled, and major industrial sites closed, most significantly in the iron, steel, automobile, rubber, and textile industries. At the same time in a nation where the majority of American workers held or aspired to white-collar jobs, lived in suburbs away from urban industrial centers, and participated in the educational boom of the 1960s by sending their children to college, there was dwindling public support for the labor movement.

The real economic growth that Americans enjoyed during the 1960s averaged over 4 percent per year; the nation's Gross National Product (GNP) expanded by 50 percent over the ten years; and the average American family had one-third more spendable income by the decade's end. The 1970s, however, told a different story. GNP growth slowed to 2.9 percent per year, and by 1980 American families had only 7 percent more real purchasing power than in 1970. Furthermore, all of this growth came between 1970 and 1973. After 1973 there was *no* real income increase. By the end of the 1970s the inflation rate, which had remained at a low 2.3

percent throughout the 1960s, averaged 12.5 percent. Unemployment, which hovered around 5 percent during the 1960s, averaged 7 percent of the labor force at the end of the 1970s. By 1980, the American standard of living, so touted in the 1960s, had dropped from first among the world's industrialized nations to tenth.

Moreover, during the 1970s the U.S. share of global manufactured exports fell from more than 25 percent (in the early 1960s) to less than 17 percent (in the early 1980s). Trade deficit figures soared during these years, and a close look at major exports reveals the fact that the United States, at least in comparison to Japan, has become an exporter of raw goods—soybeans, corn, and wheat—and an importer of cars, iron, steel, and electrical consumer goods.

The basic problem with the U.S. economy in the 1970s, 1980s, and on into the 1990s can be traced to deindustrialization. The impact on American workers and organized labor has been overwhelming. As economists Barry Bluestone and Bennett Harrison argue in *The Deindustrialization of America,* this process has involved the "widespread, systematic disinvestment in the nation's basic productive capacity." Capital has been "diverted from productive investment in our basic industries into unproductive speculation, mergers and acquisitions, and foreign investment." U.S. corporations have continued to invest their resources but not in the basic industries of the United States.

Examples of deindustrialization abound. Faced with aging equipment during the 1970s, U.S. Steel chose not to rebuild steel capacity but rather to spend five billion dollars to acquire Marathon Oil of Ohio. General Electric expanded its capital stock in the 1970s by investing outside the nation. GE's worldwide payroll increased by five thousand workers during the period—thirty-thousand foreign jobs were added while twenty-five thousand Americans lost their jobs. RCA Corporation and Ford Motor Company followed similar strategies, cutting U.S. employment, increasing their foreign work force, and spending their capital—in Ford's case more than 40 percent of its total budget—outside the country.

The impact of such capital mobility on organized labor has been profound. Beginning in the 1970s, the nation's core industries—auto, steel, and rubber—used the strategy of capital mobility, threatened or real, to demand smaller wage increases or actual wage rollbacks along with reductions in business taxes and cuts in community and social services. As Bluestone and Harrison argued, "corporate demands for wage concessions (givebacks) became the most prominent feature of industrial relations in the 1980s." By 1980, twenty states had passed "right-to-work" legislation that made paying union dues voluntary, undermining the financial strength of the unions.

During the 1970s, newly developed anti-union tactics continued to weaken the trade-union movement. A new generation of "union busters" sported gray-flannel suits and leather briefcases. They bore little resemblance to the company police, labor spies, or "goon squads" of earlier eras when physical violence characterized most labor-management conflicts, but they were no less effective. By the late 1970s, more than one thousand specialized consulting firms were advising corporations on how to keep union organizers and sympathizers out of the workplace, on how to defeat a union when elections could not be avoided, or, in cases where unions had won elections, on how to decertify them.

Paradoxically, while corporate deindustrialization strategies were demobilizing the labor movement, corporate officers managed to convince the public that American industry's problems stemmed not from executive decision making but from overpaid American workers protected by union contracts. Focusing on the gains that labor had made to secure a living wage deflected attention from the process of capital mobility and let labor stand as the scapegoat for the deindustrialization of the United States.

During the 1970s, the number of unfair labor practices recorded by the National Labor Relations Board against American businesses increased by 300 percent. The reason for this increase was that hundreds of companies, following the advice of anti-union consultants, found it more profitable to break the law and pay a small fine than to allow a union to organize their employees. The chances of a union winning a representation election fell by half between 1970 and 1978. At the same time, the number of annual decertifications multiplied from fewer than 240 to over 800. By 1978, unions were consistently losing elections—at a rate of three to one—in workplaces where there had been prior union victories.

Finally, the 1970s witnessed an assault on labor in the political arena. Trade unions, already confronted with capital mobility strategies, right-to-work legislation, sophisticated anti-union advisers,

and blatant violations of fair labor practices had lost momentum. To deliver the knockout punch, American corporations formed nonprofit political action committees (PACs) designed to circumvent federal laws that prohibited private corporations from donating money directly to political candidates, and their growth was staggering. Corporate PACs proved effective in defeating labor law reform and maintaining the probusiness climate that enhanced profits and limited worker autonomy.

By the 1980s, new technology made the option of capital mobility from one region to another, or from one nation to another, a reality for most large U.S. corporations. Corporate access to wide-body jet transport, for shipping equipment and goods, to satellite-linked telecommunications systems, and to powerful computer networks for instantaneous coordination of worldwide operations shifted bargaining power in favor of capital to an unprecedented degree. Corporations used their enhanced power to demand more labor concessions within the United States. Their ability to move, to another community or another country, enabled corporations to make "take it or leave it" propositions to American workers, organized and unorganized. Interregional rivalry to attract capital intensified. American states and localities competed to provide businesses with incentive packages, including reduced corporate taxes and access to low-wage, nonunion labor. Clearly, there has been a close correlation between deindustrialization and deunionization.

But organized labor has not been the only target of corporate "reform" initiatives. By 1980 only one in four American workers belonged to a trade union. Consequently, changing the terms for organized workers alone would not be enough to bring about the significant, long-term decreases in labor costs that corporations were seeking. In order to achieve the level of worker "flexibility" they desired, corporations sought to hire nonunion labor, decertify existing unions, and dismantle the "safety net" that had protected American workers since the New Deal era. Increasingly throughout the 1970s and 1980s, private corporations made bold demands on state governments to foster low levels of workmen's compensation insurance, to reduce unemployment benefits per worker, and to set low minimum wages. States were encouraged to curtail programs that endorsed affirmative action and protected workers' health and safety. State laws providing income maintenance were also targeted as undesirable: food stamps, welfare, and job-training programs. Many of these programs were the result of past political victories by workers and their unions. These programs have served over the years to protect workers from the insecurity that comes from being totally dependent on the demands of capital. By 1980 it was clear that the labor movement's past gains were at risk. Moreover, collective bargaining proved an ineffective tool against capital mobility, for its case by case approach reaches few workers, and no amount of bargaining can provide for rebuilding a local economic base once a large corporation has pulled out of a particular community.

By the time Ronald Reagan entered the White House in 1981, the stage was set for another major shift in labor's political fortunes. Seven months into his first term, with significant budget and tax-cut victories to his credit, Reagan responded to a strike by the nation's air-traffic controllers with a forty-eight-hour ultimatum, followed by the massive firing of twelve thousand Professional Air Traffic Controllers Organization (PATCO) members. Briefing the press from beneath a portrait of Calvin Coolidge, whose election followed his ironfisted handling of the 1919 Boston police strike, Reagan insisted that "Dammit, the law is the law . . . if they strike, they quit their jobs." Refusing to negotiate while the strike continued, Reagan demanded that there be no amnesty for those who had walked out.

Organized labor reeled from the blow; the president's message to the labor movement was unmistakable. Furthermore, a majority of Americans, 57 percent, approved the president's abrupt action, believing that the air controllers, as public employees with a no-strike clause in their contract, were wrong to go on strike. Government action against PATCO, a union of relatively well-paid, white-collar supporters of Reagan in the 1980 election, did not stop with the firings. The FAA announced that disciplinary action would be taken, even against strikers who returned to work; the Justice Department prosecuted PATCO leaders; and a Federal judge penalized PATCO with staggering fines of $4.4 million for violation of a back-to-work order. Felony charges were filed against seventy-two PATCO leaders in twenty cities across the country. Robert E. Poli, PATCO president, threatened with a jail sentence and fined a thousand dollars per day for leading the strike, was stunned by the severity of the response and accused the administration of "brutal overkill." Not since the days of the Palmer raids in

1919 had the government waged such a massive assault against organized labor. Destroyed as a union, PATCO survives only as a new and powerful symbol of anti-union government policy.

During Reagan's first administration, union membership plummeted from 24.7 percent in 1980 to 18 percent in 1985 (see chart). Never had there been such a steep decline in the number of workers belonging to a trade union. Moreover, the Reagan administration ordered the Bureau of Labor Statistics to cease publishing data collected about union affiliation. Published government data on American unions were reduced from a range of categories that included types of unions and membership by gender and race to a single column that reported the number of "work stoppages" in a given year. However, unpublished data in the bureau's Washington office tell the story of the decimation of small unions, and the loss of hundreds of thousands of union members from the United Steel Workers, the United Automobile Workers, and the Teamsters, in the recession of the early 1980s. By Reagan's election in 1984, labor's political power seemed to have evaporated; unions appeared to have been relegated to the margins of public life.

In the mid 1980s, labor scholars and economists refocused attention on the positive political role that organized labor should play in a democratic society. Thomas B. Edsall's 1984 study, for example, finds that "the collapse of labor's legislation power facilitated the adoption of a set of economic policies highly beneficial to the corporate sector and to the affluent." He argues that the implications of labor's decline go far beyond the fate of the unions and their membership for "without a strong labor movement there is no broad-based institution in American society equipped to represent the interests of those in the working and lower-middle class in the formulation of economic policy." With the voice of labor effectively muted, corporate and business interests could continue to dominate the American political system unchallenged.

In this context, American workers face the daunting tasks of reorganizing workers, unifying an increasingly diversified American labor force, and attaining the political power required to influence, in fact to formulate, economic policy. The present leadership at the top levels of organized labor, labeled "the bald old men in Bal Harbour, Florida," by Thomas Geoghegan, resembles the AFL hierarchy of the late 1920s more than a dynamic, visionary cadre capable of leading American workers into

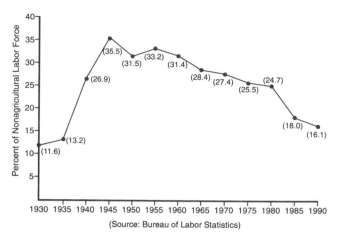

Fig. 1.   Union Membership, 1930–1990

a hopeful future. In 1990, just as in the early 1930s and the late 1940s, American workers stood at a crucial crossroads.

Without a fundamental redistribution of economic power, the working people of the 1990s would inherit a legacy of low-wage jobs, anti-union government policies, and an NLRB that ensures that almost every organizing drive and contract renegotiation turns into a lawsuit. American women and minorities, most of whom hold low-wage, service-sector jobs, will comprise a majority of the 1990s work force. Like the industrial workers of the Depression era, these Americans have few ways to voice their concerns. The community or factory-based labor forces of the 1920s and 1930s have given way to a fragmented work force divided against itself in a multiplicity of segments: blue-versus white-collar, African American versus white versus Hispanic, male versus female. This fragmentation works against the mobilization and political action of American workers.

CONCLUSION

In the 1930s Americans suffered from an economic collapse that spawned high unemployment and necessitated government intervention. The militancy of American labor in that decade, measured in part by a meteoric rise in union membership, reached a level unsurpassed in the twentieth century. Full economic recovery from the Depression came only with the nation's entry into World War II, a period when the scarcity of workers on the home front meant premium wages and powerful unions, but these were only for the war's duration. The

need for wartime workers translated into a short-term redistribution of industrial jobs to women and African Americans previously excluded from the factory. The war's end changed the relationship between labor and management as both vied for power and control in postwar American society. Economic prosperity, fueled by consumer purchases and the demand for housing, raised hopes as well as real wages. Increasingly, American cultural life became consumer driven, and the desire for material well-being found more workers leaving traditional, urban blue-collar neighborhoods in favor of suburban comfort. Community changes reflected shifts in the labor force itself, for 1956 marked the first year a majority of American workers held white-collar jobs.

American workers faced years of change and reaction in the 1960s. African Americans sought equal rights in the voting booth and the workplace. Following the lead of black civil rights activists, American women laid claim to rights ranging from equal pay for equal work to gender-neutral hiring. White workers felt threatened by black militancy on the job and in white working-class suburbs where housing and school integration efforts were focused. Male workers felt threatened by the demands of working women and retaliated by reviving a domestic ideology reminiscent of that used to rationalize the displacement of female workers at the end of World War II.

As various groups contested their rights in the larger society and on the shop floor, industries such as textiles, shoes, and steel, continuing a quest for cheaper labor that dated from the late nineteenth century, shifted a greater percentage of their operations from older northeastern and midwestern plants to newly built facilities in the Southeast and Southwest, the region dubbed the "Sunbelt." This decentralization of American industry, which accelerated after the oil crisis of the early 1970s raised corporate costs and squeezed profits. Soon, Sunbelt perks—low-cost utilities, nonunion labor, and tax breaks—could not bridge the profit gap, and American companies looked overseas for workers willing to accept rates of pay far below those necessary for a living wage in the United States.

By the 1980s, widespread deindustrialization of American industry was under way, rapidly eliminating the number of high-wage, union-protected jobs. Recessions plagued the economy in 1970, 1973, 1979, and 1982; real wages declined; and workers struggled to make ends meet. Families became more dependent than ever on dual incomes as women moved into the work force in unprecedented numbers. By 1980 only 15 percent of American families resembled the 1950s ideal in which 70 percent of families claimed father as breadwinner and mother as homemaker.

As the 1990s began American workers faced increased vulnerability and difficulty in maintaining their standard of living. Unionization is one indicator of worker economic and political strength. By that measure, Americans have slipped badly in recent years. Organized labor claimed one out of seven nonagricultural workers at the end of the 1980s, basically the same percentage of the industrial work force that unions held in the late 1920s, before the great organization drives of the New Deal era. Thus, in the years between 1930 and 1990, American workers have come full circle (see Fig. 1), having survived the Depression-ridden economy of the 1930s, benefited from war-induced prosperity, and returned to an economically vulnerable position as the twentieth century draws to a close.

BIBLIOGRAPHY

Historiographical Essays

Brody, David. "Labor History in the 1970s: Toward a History of the American Worker." In *The Past Before Us: Contemporary Historical Writing in the United States*, edited by Michael Kammen (1980).

Kimeldorf, Howard. "Bringing Unions Back in (Or Why We Need a New Old Labor History)." *Labor History* 32 (1991): 91–103; and responses by Michael Kazin, Alice Kessler-Harris, David Montgomery, Bruce Nelson, and Daniel Nelson. "The Limits of Union-Centered History: Responses to Howard Kimeldorf." *Labor History* 32 (1991): 104–127.

Montgomery, David. "To Study the People: The American Working Class." *Labor History* 21 (1980): 485–512.

Moody, J. Carroll, and Alice Kessler-Harris, eds. *Perspectives on American Labor History: The Problem of Synthesis* (1989).

Ozanne, Robert W. "Trends in American Labor History." *Labor History* 21 (1980): 513–521.

Zieger, Robert H. "Workers and Scholars: Recent Trends in American Labor Historiography." *Labor History* 13 (1972): 245–266.

General Works

Brody, David. *Workers in Industrial America: Essays on the Twentieth-Century Struggle* (1979).

Buhle, Paul, and Alan Dawley, eds. *Working for Democracy: American Workers from the Revolution to the Present* (1985).

Davis, Mike. *Prisoners of the American Dream: Politics and Economy in the History of the U.S. Working Class* (1986).

Dubofsky, Melvyn. *American Labor Since the New Deal* (1971).

Filippelli, Ronald L. *Labor in the United States* (1984).

Fraser, Steve, and Gary Gerstle, eds. *The Rise and Fall of the New Deal Order, 1930–1980* (1989).

Gordon, David M., et al. *Segmented Work, Divided Workers: The Historical Transformation of Labor in the United States* (1982).

Green, James R. *The World of the Worker: Labor in Twentieth-Century America* (1978).

Green, James R., ed. *Workers' Struggles, Past and Present: A "Radical America" Reader* (1983).

Hall, Burton, ed. *Autocracy and Insurgency in Organized Labor* (1972).

Montgomery, David. *Workers' Control in America: Studies in the History of Work, Technology, and Labor Struggles* (1979).

Tomlins, Christopher L. *The State and the Unions: Labor Relations, Law, and the Organized Labor Movement in America, 1880–1960* (1985).

Zieger, Robert H. *American Workers, American Unions, 1920–1985* (1986).

———. *Organized Labor in the Twentieth-Century South* (1991).

Worker Culture

Aronowitz, Stanley. *False Promises: The Shaping of American Working-Class Consciousness* (1973).

Blauner, Robert. *Alienation and Freedom: The Factory Worker and His Industry* (1964).

Burger, Bennett. *Working-Class Suburbia: A Study of Auto Workers in Suburbia* (1960).

Chonoy, Eli. *Automobile Workers and the American Dream* (1955).

Frisch, Michael H., and Daniel J. Walkowitz, eds. *Working-Class America* (1983).

Gans, Herbert J. *The Levittowners: Ways of Life and Politics in a New Suburban Community* (1982).

Garson, Barbara. *All the Livelong Day: The Meaning and Demeaning of Routine Work* (1977).

Gerstle, Gary. *Working-Class Americanism: The Politics of Labor in a Textile City, 1914–1960* (1989).

Hall, Jacquelyn D., et al. *Like a Family: The Making of a Southern Cotton Mill World* (1987).

Halle, David. *America's Working Man: Work, Home, and Politics Among Blue-Collar Property Owners* (1984).

Howe, Irving, ed. *The World of the Blue-Collar Worker* (1973).

Howell, Joseph T. *Hard Living on Clay Street: Portraits of Blue-Collar Families* (1973).

Kirby, Jack T. *Rural Worlds Lost: The American South, 1920–1960* (1986).

Komarovsky, Mirra. *Blue-Collar Marriage* (1964).

Kornblum, William. *Blue-Collar Community* (1974).

Leggett, John C. *Class, Race, and Labor: Working-Class Consciousness in Detroit* (1968).

Levison, Andrew. *Working-Class Majority* (1974).

Levitan, Sar A., ed. *Blue-Collar Workers: A Symposium on Middle America* (1971).

May, Elaine T. *Homeward Bound: American Families in the Cold War Era* (1988).

Mills, Nicolaus, ed. *Culture in an Age of Money: The Legacy of the 1980s in America* (1990).

Rubin, Lillian B. *Worlds of Pain: Life in the Working-Class Family* (1976).

Sexton, Brendan, and Patricia C. Sexton. *Blue Collars and Hard Hats* (1971).

Shostak, Arthur B., and William Gomberg, eds. *Blue-Collar World* (1964).

Terkel, Studs. *Hard Times: An Oral History of the Great Depression* (1970).

————. *Working: People Talk About What They Do All Day and How They Feel About What They Do* (1972).

Widick, B. J., ed. *Auto Work and Its Discontents* (1976).

Whyte, William H., Jr. *The Organization Man* (1956).

Zweig, Ferdynand. *The Worker in an Affluent Society* (1962).

Gender, Race and Ethnicity

Baron, Ava, ed. *Work Engendered: Toward a New History of American Labor* (1991).

Benson, Susan P. *Counter Cultures: Saleswomen, Managers, and Customers in American Department Stores, 1890–1940* (1986).

Bracey, John H., August Meier, and Elliott Rudwick, eds. *Black Workers and Organized Labor* (1971).

Deutsch, Sarah. *No Separate Refuge: Culture, Class, and Gender on an Anglo-Hispanic Frontier in the American Southwest, 1880–1940* (1987).

Foner, Philip S. *Women and the American Labor Movement* (1980).

————. *Organized Labor and the Black Worker, 1619–1981* (1982).

Gabin, Nancy F. *Feminism in the Labor Movement: Women and the United Auto Workers, 1935–1975* (1990).

Goldin, Claudia. *Understanding the Gender Gap: An Economic History of American Women* (1989).

Groneman, Carol, and Mary Beth Norton, eds. *To Toil the Livelong Day: America's Women at Work, 1780–1980* (1987).

Harris, William H. *The Harder We Run: Black Workers Since the Civil War* (1982).

Howe, Irving. *The World of Our Fathers* (1976).

Jacobson, Julius, ed. *The Negro and the American Labor Movement* (1968).

Jensen, Joan M., and Sue Davidson, eds. *A Needle, a Bobbin, a Strike: Women Needleworkers in America* (1984).

Kelley, Robin D. G. *Hammer and Hoe: Alabama Communists During the Great Depression* (1990).

Kenneally, James J. *Women and American Trade Unions* (1978).

Kessler-Harris, Alice. *Out to Work: A History of Wage-earning Women in the United States* (1982).

Kornbluh, Joyce L., and Mary Frederickson, eds. *Sisterhood and Solidarity: Workers' Education for Women, 1914–1984* (1984).

Meier, August, and Elliott Rudwick. *Black Detroit and the Rise of the UAW* (1979).

Melosh, Barbara. *The Physician's Hand: Work Culture and Conflict in American Nursing* (1982).

Milkman, Ruth, ed. *Women, Work and Protest: A Century of U.S. Women's Labor History* (1985).

O'Sullivan, Judith, and Rosemary Gallick. *Workers and Allies: Female Participation in the American Trade Union Movement, 1824–1976* (1975).

Van Raaphorst, Donna L. *Union Maids Not Wanted: Organizing Domestic Workers, 1870–1940* (1988).

Wertheimer, Barbara M. *We Were There: The Story of Working Women in America* (1977).

Biographies

Anderson, Jarvis. *A. Philip Randolf: A Biographical Portrait* (1973).

Barnard, John. *Walter Reuther and the Rise of the Autoworkers* (1983).

Dubofsky, Melvyn, and Warren Van Tine. *John L. Lewis: A Biography* (1977).

Fraser, Steve. *Labor Will Rule: Sidney Hillman and the Rise of American Labor* (1991).

Goulden, Joseph. *Meany* (1972).

————. *Jerry Wurf: Labor's Last Angry Man* (1982).

Larrowe, Charles P. *Harry Bridges: The Rise and Fall of Radical Labor in the United States* (1977).

Phelan, Craig. *William Green: Biography of a Labor Leader* (1988).

Robinson, Archie. *George Meany and His Times: A Biography* (1981).

Sloane, Arthur A. *Hoffa* (1991).

Velie, Lester. *Desperate Bargain: Why Jimmy Hoffa Had to Die* (1977).

Individual Industries, Unions, and Strikes

Billings, Richard N., and John Greenya. *Power to the Public Worker* (1974).

Braun, Robert J. *Teachers and Power: The Story of the American Federation of Teachers* (1972).

Brody, David. *Butcher Workmen: A Study of Unionization* (1964).

Brooks, Robert R. *As Steel Goes: Unionism in a Basic Industry* (1940; repr. 1970).

Brooks, Thomas R. *Communications Workers of America: The Story of a Union* (1977).

Clark, Paul F. *The Miners' Fight for Democracy* (1981).

Daniel, Cletus E. *Bitter Harvest: A History of California Farmworkers, 1870–1941* (1981).

Fine, Sidney. *The Automobile Under the Blue Eagle: Labor, Management, and the Automobile Manufacturing Code* (1963).

————. *Sit-Down: The General Motors Strike of 1936–1937* (1969).

Fink, Leon, and Brian Greenberg. *Upheaval in the Quiet Zone: A History of Hospital Workers' Union Local 1199* (1989).

Fitch, John A. *The Steel Workers* (1989).

Friedlander, Peter. *The Emergence of a UAW Local, 1936–1939: A Study in Class and Culture* (1975).

Gaventa, John. *Power and Powerlessness: Quiescence and Rebellion in an Appalachian Valley* (1980).

Herling, John. *Right to Challenge: People and Power in the Steelworkers Union* (1972).

Hume, Brit. *Death and the Mines: Rebellion and Murder in the United Mine Workers* (1971).

Leab, Daniel J. *A Union of Individuals: The Formation of the American Newspaper Guild, 1933–1936* (1970).

Schatz, Ronald W. *The Electrical Workers: A History of Labor at General Electric and Westinghouse, 1923–60* (1983).

Schwartz, Harvey. *The March Inland: Origins of the ILWU Warehouse Division, 1934–1938* (1978).

Zieger, Robert H. *Madison's Battery Workers, 1934–1952: A History of Federal Labor Union 19587* (1977).

————. *Rebuilding the Pulp and Paper Workers' Union, 1933–1941* (1984).

The Great Depression

Bernstein, Irving. *The Lean Years: A History of the American Worker, 1920–1933* (1960; repr. 1972).

————. *The Turbulent Years: A History of the American Worker, 1933–1941* (1969).

Galenson, Walter. *The CIO Challenge to the AFL: A History of the American Labor Movement, 1935–1941* (1960).

Morris, James O. *Conflict Within the AFL: A Study in Craft Versus Industrial Unionism, 1901–1938* (1958).

Preis, Art. *Labor's Giant Step: Twenty years of the CIO* (1964; 2d rev. ed. 1972).

World War II and Its Aftermath

Anderson, Karen. *Wartime Women: Sex Roles, Family Relations, and the Status of Women During World War II* (1981).

Foster, James C. *The Union Politic: The CIO Political Action Committee* (1975).

Glaberman, Martin. *Wartime Strikes* (1980).

Gluck, Sherna B. *Rosie the Riveter Revisited: Women, the War, and Social Change* (1988).

Gregory, Chester. *Women in Defense Work During World War II* (1974).

Gross, James A. *The Reshaping of the National Labor Relations Board: National Labor Policy in Transition, 1937–1947* (1982).

Harris, Howell J. *The Right to Manage: Industrial Relations Policies of American Business in the 1940s* (1982).

Lee, R. Alton. *Truman and Taft-Hartley: A Question of Mandate* (1966).

Levenstein, Harvey A. *Communism, Anti-Communism, and the CIO* (1981).

Lichtenstein, Nelson. *Labor's War at Home: The CIO in World War II* (1983).

Marcus, Maeva. *Truman and the Steel Seizure Case* (1977).

Oshinsky, David M. *Senator McCarthy and the American Labor Movement* (1976).

Seidman, Joel. *American Labor from Defense to Reconversion* (1953).

From the 1950s to the 1990s

Aronowitz, Stanley. *Working Class Hero: A New Strategy for Labor* (1983).

Bluestone, Barry, and Bennett Harrison. *The Deindustrialization of America: Plant Closings, Community Abandonment, and the Dismantling of Basic Industry* (1982).

Bowles, Samuel, David M. Gordon, and Thomas E. Weisskopf. *Beyond the Waste Land: A Democratic Alternative to Economic Decline* (1983).

Edsall, Thomas Byrne. *The New Politics of Inequality* (1984).

Ehrenreich, Barbara. *Fear of Falling: The Inner Life of the Middle Class* (1989).

————. *The Worst Years of Our Lives* (1990).

Freeman, Richard B., and James L. Medoff. *What Do Unions Do?* (1984).

Geoghegan, Thomas. *Which Side Are You on?: Trying to Be for Labor When It's Flat on Its Back* (1991).

Harrison, Bennett, and Barry Bluestone. *The Great U-Turn: Corporate Restructuring and the Polarizing of America* (1988).

Horowitz, Irving Louis, John C. Leggett, and Martin Oppenheimer, eds. *The American Working Class: Prospects for the 1980s* (1979).

Kuttner, Robert. *The Economic Illusion: False Choices Between Prosperity and Justice* (1984).

Lawrence, Robert Z. *Can America Compete?* (1984).

Levy, Frank. *Dollars and Dreams: The Changing American Income Distribution* (1987).

Thurow, Lester C. *The Zero-Sum Society: Distribution and the Possibilities for Economic Change* (1980).

Tolchin, Susan J., and Martin Tolchin. *Dismantling America: The Rush to Deregulate* (1983).

SEE ALSO **The Culture of Consumption; Minorities and Work; Socialist and Communist Movements; Women and Work;** and various essays in the sections "**Periods of Social Change**," "**Processes of Social Change**," and "**Science, Medicine, and Technology**."

BUSINESS CULTURE

John Lauritz Larson

JOHN LOCKE BLAMED it all on money. In the beginning, in America, as in a state of nature, the "want of people and money gave men no temptation to enlarge their possessions." Individuals enjoyed liberty and formed governments without fear of injustice or tyranny. But money fostered accumulation and stimulated greed, while "ambition and luxury . . . taught princes to have distinct and separate interests from their people" (*Second Treatise on Government,* sections 108, 111). The result was corruption, born of wealth and the freedom to pursue it.

Colonists in British North America thought they saw themselves in Locke's treatise on government, because they lived in something like a state of nature. Freely they entered into compacts to govern themselves; freely they made their own livings. Then, just as Locke predicted, corrupt princes, their hands filled with money, conspired from a distance to enslave them. With great righteousness, Americans took up the work of rebellion, determined to eliminate corruption while protecting wealth and freedom.

From this peculiar starting point, self-creating Americans fashioned a business culture in the nineteenth century that liberated private ambition, celebrated innovation, and helped usher in a worldwide capitalist revolution. Practical entrepreneurs in a mercantilist world, they rejected imperial frameworks and adopted limited republican governments. Because they found the origins of corruption in government, early Americans held their princes at bay and expected developing markets to sort out inevitable clashes of interests. At first their approach fostered freedom of enterprise, but eventually competition gave rise to new princes in the form of giant monopolistic enterprises. After a century of liberation, Americans found themselves possessed of a rich but distorted economy, and no less worried about freedom and riches than the founders of the republic had been. Another century made

them masters of a global economy—and yet more fretful than ever about the maintenance of their prosperity.

THE BUSINESS ENVIRONMENT IN 1800

In 1800, Americans were farmers. Only 6 percent of the 5.3 million population resided in thirty-three "urban" places. Cities sheltered the majority of merchants, artisans, and laborers—figures most often associated with the business world. Everyone else lived on farms and plantations, or in small towns where the rhythms of agricultural life established community values. The overwhelmingly rural character of this economy seems almost to preclude discussion of a business culture at the beginning of the nineteenth century. But in 1800, the business of Americans was agriculture.

Agriculture The great staple-crop planters dominated agriculture in the southern United States. With few tenants to farm their land, large and small planters decided for themselves which crops to plant, how best to employ vacant land, when and where to sell commodities, and what to take in exchange. If they were slaveowners, they assumed the additional responsibility of managing the lives of their laborers. Their pose as gentry notwithstanding, American planters worked hard to manage their complex enterprises.

A much larger number of American husbandmen worked smaller family farms. Best characterized as semisubsistence farmers, these landowners met most of their immediate needs directly or by trading goods and services with their neighbors. Middling farmers commonly planted patches of tobacco, wheat, barley, rye, flax, or hemp, intended for sale in commercial markets. Farm families located near urban centers also specialized in dairy products, vegetables, fruits, and meat. Many farms raised sheep for wool, from which the women of

1495

the household produced their family's clothing. How much farmers produced expressly for the market depended largely on their distance from centers of exchange, although individual customs, ambitions, and the availability of credit also played a part.

At the bottom of the agricultural social pyramid, a class of farm laborers worked for some kind of "wage." The adolescent sons of white farm owners fell into this category. White females might be employed in the farmhouse or dairy until they married. Inevitably some individuals labored all their lives on other people's farms. Genuine subsistence farmers infringed as squatters on frontier land, scraping out livings for their families but never accumulating tangible wealth. Most of the one million African American slaves labored in their masters' businesses, with no real economic freedom. Free blacks found their opportunities almost as closely circumscribed.

The Manufacturing Trades Ancillary to the agricultural economy, artisans and tradesmen often lived in rural communities, where their work became embedded in the agrarian cultural framework. Truly urban places in early America, however, exhibited artisanal cultures reminiscent of the European craft tradition. The standard unit of enterprise for skilled artisans in America was the independent workshop. Owned (and usually occupied) by the master craftsman, the independent shop employed one or more journeymen working for wages as well as apprentices bound for a term of years in exchange for room and board and initiation into the mysteries of the trade. Together this group of laborers produced finished goods from raw materials, usually without power equipment. Craftsmen sold their products directly to consumers, purchased their materials directly from suppliers, and supervised all aspects of their enterprises. In such shops, the master worked *and* managed the work of others; customarily he was the most skillful artisan in the establishment.

Certain preindustrial trades required larger and more specialized facilities and locations. Tanning yards often were banished to suburban fringes because of the filth and smell they created. Mills of all kinds necessarily stood where falling water offered a power source. Heat-using industries (liquor, turpentine, candles, glass, iron) required large equipment or fuel supplies that influenced their location and organization. Iron "plantations," for example, typically were built in hardwood forests where the furnace's appetite for charcoal could be met. Yet even in these relatively capital-intensive enterprises, working masters directed the activity and trained the apprentices while simultaneously tending their accounts.

Much of what Americans owned and used in 1800 was produced in the home. Sometimes homemade furniture, flatware, candles, and shoes substituted for fancier products a farm family could not afford. Other items, such as textiles, issued primarily from the household. Farm women produced most clothing and bed and table linens, using hand carders, spinning wheels, and hand looms. Some specialists, both men and women, wove coverlets at home, and where the markets sustained them, skillful weavers might work full time in the "putting out" system, producing cloth for yarn manufacturers.

American communities suffered from chronic shortages of skilled labor, and market conditions fostered high wages, easy mobility, and a fair degree of instability within the artisan community. Apprentices abandoned their obligations with impunity, and masters just as casually ignored their obligations to nurture and educate their charges. Half-trained journeymen found employment in rapidly growing cities long before they perfected their skills. While the cultural values of the traditional artisans — cooperative work, honor to the trade, and a competence for all practitioners — found ready expression in America, the foundations of that culture were compromised from a very early date.

Merchants and Shopkeepers The markets to which both farmers and artisans directed their productive ambitions were tended in 1800 by a small class of merchants and shopkeepers. At the bottom end of this network, nearest the great majority of farmers and consumers, stood the small town or country storekeeper. A general-purpose merchant offering all kinds of hardware, soft goods, and imported "groceries" (spirits, coffee, tea), the country storekeeper bought his stock from a mercantile house in the city. He retailed goods on credit (keeping his own detailed books); received farm produce in trade; brokered goods, services, debts, and credits among his customers; exported the accumulated surplus of his neighborhood; and hoped in the end to make a profit for himself.

In port cities, both large and small merchants engaged in a high-stakes speculative game of import-export trade. The size and organization of mercantile operations depended on each merchant's capital stock and strategy for making money.

Some tied up huge sums in shipping, then scrambled to gather cargoes to keep their vessels filled. Others leased space for discrete "adventures," hoping to profit from buying cheap and selling dear. Some merchants specialized in a few transactions at which they became acknowledged experts; others played all markets promiscuously. Some sold on credit to the network of interior retailers, while others dumped their goods at dockside auctions in order to return their capital immediately to the Atlantic trade. One thing united these merchants in a community of business: they played a risky game filled with uncontrollable variables, in which lucky newcomers often got rich and wealthy veterans sometimes went broke with the turning of the evening tide.

Credit tied the whole system together. Long denied the right to coin their own money, colonists early learned to substitute merchant paper, book credits, and simple barter as their media of commercial exchange. Rural residents traded goods and services with each other, often documenting debts with paper notes or entries on the storekeeper's ledgers. Storekeepers purchased stocks of goods on long credits which they hoped to extinguish with what little cash and surplus produce they collected from their customers. Urban wholesalers extended credit to their buyers while accepting credit from their sellers, hoping that the markup and quick sales would cover all debts and yield a profit. Importers bought on credit from their overseas connections, who demanded payment in cash or good bills of exchange, usually acquired in unrelated export transactions.

Supporting this pyramid of debt, the output of American land and labor increased so that American business probably was solvent (if highly illiquid) even while it teetered on the brink of disaster. Lacking uniform systems of banking, insurance, collections, and exchange, merchants depended on their own confidence and the good faith of others. Lapses of either produced sudden panics, which ruined certain players (usually the weak) and profoundly restructured the game. Country storekeepers protected themselves to some extent by owning land and keeping a hand in the local rural economy; urban merchants invested in real estate and consumer durables as a hedge against uncertainties in trade—and as proof of their success.

Was It Capitalism? Was business in 1800 already a modern capitalist game? Historians disagree sharply on the answer to this question. Clearly, most Americans at that time depended on themselves and their local communities for most of their daily needs. Relatively few worked for cash wages, and few employers followed strictly rational calculations. Rural Americans engaged in market transactions at least occasionally, yet they did not depend on markets for survival, nor did they surrender their sense of values to iron laws of supply and demand.

Because these early Americans responded primarily to perceived family or community needs, rather than to some analytical goal of profit maximization, they appear to some historians to have been guided by a sense of "moral economy." Other scholars (and insightful contemporaries) have pointed to widespread competitive behavior and a tendency to embrace (or repel) changes according to selfish interest as proof of a modern, liberal, capitalistic outlook in the founding generation. However motivated, this first generation of Americans did not impede the rise of complicated markets. Neither did their rhetoric and understanding condemn the economic liberty from which capitalist principles evolved. As colonists, Americans had grown up in a mercantilist network closely bounded (in theory) by government structures and regulations. While this large imperial framework protected and even promoted colonial enterprises, Americans more often noticed barriers to innovation and private gain. Strong competitive forces, stemming from abundant land, scarce labor, and unsatisfied colonial consumer demand, frustrated mercantilist theory and influenced American economic ambitions, even among the most traditionally minded farmers and artisans. Lacking a scholarly explanation for their economic system, Americans tended to describe what they wanted as freedom from outside control.

Whether Americans consciously embraced mercantilist orthodoxy or the radical liberal doctrines published in Adam Smith's *Wealth of Nations* (1776), the world in which they lived exhibited elements of both ideals. Some principles belonging to the past they took for granted and preserved; novel tenets of liberal capitalism they often seized as rights in tradition or natural law. The business culture they created never perfectly reflected any single system.

THE REVOLUTIONARY LEGACY

The American Revolution redefined the business culture of the early United States, but that was not its expressed intention. Conceived in political terms of "republicanism," the Revolution promised freedom and equality to people who supplied their own shades of meaning to these powerful concepts. Therefore, while revolutionary republicanism did not dictate the rise of capitalism in America, the promise of the Revolution empowered and encouraged individuals to pursue wealth and innovation in ways which fostered that result.

Revolutionary Ideology American radicals diagnosed a sickness—"Old Corruption"—in eighteenth-century English society, against which they mounted their rebellion. New money, gained in speculative trade, had greased the wheels of English politics, bathed aristocrats in decadent luxury, and subverted the landed basis of the English constitution—or so complained the English "country" Whigs. This old-fashioned critique ill suited American elites, who were themselves really entrepreneurs; but it helped justify American frustrations with the imperial regime, and it laid the foundations for revolutionary republicanism.

Republicanism appealed to American elites because it promised relief from the prerogatives of alien governors. In a republic, only the people at home—not some distant ruling class—could control the governing agenda. Provincial societies seemed uniquely made up of "common" people. Widespread landownership qualified most Americans as independent citizens. With the largest number of dependent laborers encapsulated within the system of black slavery, revolutionary enthusiasts could imagine the "whole people" of the colonies as independent householders sharing common interests in property, security, and personal liberty.

Republicanism appealed to the "lower orders" in America because it promised relief from the pretensions of elites whose claims to power and respect had never been proved. Freed from restraint by privileged classes in England or at home, ordinary Americans could imagine an open political culture that more nearly matched the open environment in which they lived. Thus the rhetoric engendered different postwar images in the minds of urban artisans, who followed the class-based radicalism of Thomas Paine; in the minds of country farmers, for whom self-government often meant a return to rural tradition; and in the minds of lesser planters, merchants, and manufacturers, who wished to share the prerogatives of power with their "betters."

If revolutionary republicanism failed to harmonize these visions of the new republic, it never-

theless mobilized whole communities to throw off the British yoke and embark upon the experiment. As soon as independence was secured by the Treaty of Paris (1783), however, American politics unraveled. It was then that revolutionaries discovered the irretrievable force of the promises they had made: liberty and equality, once tendered, were not easily abridged within the framework of republican ideals. In post-Revolution America, the future belonged to those who called for freedom. In business and economic matters, the result was a culture that increasingly favored innovation and development at the expense of traditional rights.

Law and the Role of Government The decline of tradition in the face of restless ambition can be seen in the changing uses of law and government in the early United States. European traditions placed responsibility for prosperity and welfare squarely in the hands of government; and although in America controls over prices, wages, and market transactions never operated effectively, new governments still set out to guide economic behavior. Republican theory obligated government to protect and promote the "general welfare." Exploiting this language in the federal Constitution, Treasury Secretary Alexander Hamilton laid down fiscal and banking policies in the 1790s that quickly revived the public credit and facilitated national commerce. Given control over money and trade, the new national government practically guaranteed that economic policies would be uniform (and probably congenial) for commercial and developmental interests.

Hamilton's program sparked political opposition, especially in Virginia and the South, but this reflected local fears of federal power and a preference for agriculture more than popular doubts about the wisdom of economic legislation. State governments in all regions passed their own laws to improve transportation, create banks and issue currency, stimulate commerce, control product quality, fix weights and measures, open up new land, and encourage capital development. Municipalities retained time-honored powers to regulate prices and wages—although they usually found them inexpedient to use. Ordinary citizens habitually turned to their governments to protect their livelihoods, adjudicate their conflicts, and enhance the environment for seeking wealth.

What changed at first, then, was not the traditional role of government in the economy but the effects of such intervention. American courts, for example, gradually enlarged the freedom of entrepreneurs by favoring innovation over tradition in cases of conflicting property rights. In 1805 (*Palmer* v. *Mulligan*), the New York Supreme Court upheld a mill builder's interference with the rights of downstream proprietors, even though he proved no prior common law right. Gradually, American courts began rejecting as "obstructionist" the claims of vested interests who resisted change. Such a legal bias fed on itself, undermining ancient habits whenever ambition challenged the status quo. Before long, judges found themselves forced to rule in favor of new claimants against parties who, once favored, now sought protection from further innovation. In 1837 (*Charles River Bridge* v. *Warren Bridge*), the U.S. Supreme Court embraced the doctrine of "creative destruction," systematically favoring growth over vested rights. More to the point, judges increasingly looked to market forces, not the rule of law, to allocate society's resources.

Legislators discovered similar limits to their capacity for making economic laws. The evolution of business corporations illustrates a steady retreat from regulatory tradition by lawmakers faced with ever-more popular electoral demands. Early corporate charters established a unique relationship between the government and private "incorporators," who were engaged to provide a public benefit in exchange for special privileges. Traditionally limited to charitable trusts, hospitals, schools, and asylums, such charters were adapted in the early United States to establish bridges, turnpikes, banks, and occasionally industrial concerns. Conceived in traditional terms, to accomplish a public good with private resources, these early American corporations proved useful for capitalizing large, expensive enterprises — especially capital-intensive public works like canals and, later, railroads. Legislators found themselves besieged with applications. To escape the unenviable task of bestowing privileges on some while denying others, democratic lawmakers adopted general incorporation laws, first in New York (1811) and then throughout the nation as markets developed. Thereafter corporations lost much of their special policy orientation and became simply business instruments.

Liberation and Improvement Neither entrepreneurs nor lawmakers began the nineteenth century determined to eliminate the role of the state or establish the doctrine of laissez-faire as the centerpiece of American policy. It was their shared desire, however, to foster prosperity, encourage innovation, eliminate arbitrary preferments, knock down barriers, open up opportunities, and cultivate

the "better sort" of private ambitions. All these objectives were thought of as "improvement," and improvement — whether private gain or the advancement of humankind — seemed to many early Americans to be the very proof of the virtue of liberty.

How did improvement relate to enterprise? At a rhetorical level, the terms often seemed to be synonymous; in practice, however, Americans often disagreed about the "improvement" accomplished by particular examples of enterprise. Innovations usually displaced earlier systems in which some persons sought their livings. Bridges destroyed ferry operators; new roads routed traffic away from the establishments of tavern keepers; improvements in rivers eliminated the need for haulers and warehouse operators who lived off breaks in traffic. Later, steamboats injured keelboats, railroads hurt canals, and steam engines threatened waterpower. In industry, machines displaced skilled workers; in farming, new lands outproduced old; on the plantation, the cotton gin inexorably tightened the noose of slavery around the necks of African American laborers.

Within the framework of American liberty, these problems of distributive justice took on heightened importance in the first decades of the nineteenth century. Originally, the elite founders of the new nation confidently believed they could design and direct improvements for the benefit of the whole people. But competing interests and insistent demands, from the middling and lower classes, to participate on their own behalf rendered it increasingly hazardous for men in office to take firm, positive action. Many entrepreneurs — especially visionary advocates of canals, railways, and large factories — clung to government preferment and endorsement, but an emerging majority of people embraced freedom *from* public policy as more likely to suit their needs. Thus in 1825, when President John Quincy Adams challenged Congress to seize boldly the task of improvement, the lawmakers demurred. Were they "palsied by the will of their constituents," he asked. They answered, proudly, Yes.

Liberation, promised in a revolution set forth in republican terms, produced democracy and entrepreneurial freedom in the new United States. What emerged as liberal, capitalist America over the course of the nineteenth century was not the design of the founding elites. Neither was it the product of sinister forces at work subverting the republican experiment. The American business culture resulted from the activities of individuals who were already entrepreneurs (in custom if not in self-concept), in a field of abundant resources, under a political regime that could not justify erecting barriers to private ambitions.

EXPANSION OF ANTEBELLUM MARKETS

Armed with a culture of liberation, American entrepreneurs in the nineteenth century remodeled a continent and revolutionized everything about the means of production. The first step required expanding and perfecting the market as the primary institution of resource allocation and economic exchange over a fast-growing geographic field that soon stretched from sea to sea. The annihilation of spatial and temporal distances, the rationalization of work, and the triumph of cash transactions took place within a single generation and sprang from such indigenous American roots that the most strident critics found the transformation practically irresistible.

Transportation and Communication Simple distance and the difficulty of getting around in the new United States kept markets local and oriented to the Atlantic trade. Port cities communicated more readily with London and Le Havre than with their own hinterlands. Members of the new federal Congress complained bitterly about traveling to sessions in New York and Philadelphia, and news traveled so poorly that during sessions they made little effort to stay in touch with constituents back home.

To address this communications problem, investors in the port cities as well as leaders in state and national governments quickly turned to public works of transportation improvement. Beginning in the 1790s, turnpikes improved main routes between cities or into urban hinterlands. Canals promised greater improvements, but they posed much greater technical and financial challenges. Only in the 1820s and 1830s were important works such as the Erie, the Chesapeake and Ohio, the Wabash and Erie, and the Dismal Swamp Canal opened for traffic.

Steamships introduced a fundamentally different category of change based on fossil fuel energy. After 1807, when Robert Fulton demonstrated the *Clermont* on the Hudson River, steamboats quickly mastered two-way navigation on America's rivers.

By 1830, steam navigation on the Mississippi and Ohio rivers, the Great Lakes, and the coastal waterways offered steadily improving access to the trans-Appalachian frontier. New roads and canals — many built or projected by states as public works—augmented the river system. In the states of the Old Northwest, great schemes of internal improvement collapsed in the Panic of 1837 and the depression years that followed. Nevertheless, by mid century this network of highways, rivers, and three thousand miles (4,800 kilometers) of canals had brought a regional population of about eleven million into the market.

No sooner had the steamboat capped this impressive waterborne network than the railroad appeared to overwhelm it. Experimental lines such as Baltimore and Ohio, the Boston and Providence, and the Camden and Amboy proved successful in the early 1830s; rapid technical evolution during the next decade placed increasingly powerful locomotives on heavy "T" rails, pulling eight-wheeled cars and coaches at unbelievable speeds (over 30 miles, or 48 kilometers, per hour) just as the capital market righted itself for a mid-1840s burst of expansion. By the outbreak of the Civil War, American railroads had laid some thirty thousand miles (48,000 kilometers) of track.

The railroad's unique contribution was speed. Ten times faster than canal boats and wagons, railroads set new standards of impatience for a generation that soon craved instantaneous communications. Postal railroad cars, introduced in 1837, cut delivery time for many letters from days to hours. The same year, Samuel F. B. Morse invented the electric telegraph and the fantasy came true. Virtually instantaneous communication of news, orders, prices, and inventories awaited only the erection of transmission lines. Railroads quickly adopted the telegraph for their own traffic control, sharing rights-of-way to string the wires.

The magnitude of these changes in transportation and communication rendered old environments practically incomparable with the new. Average freight rates fell by nine tenths, but this misses the point: the vast majority of freight hauled in 1850 would not have entered the market without these improvements. The same was true of the circulation of news and information. Of course, not every place received equal treatment in the emerging networks, and earlier systems of transportation and communication played important (and profitable) roles long after shiny innovations appeared.

Domestic Marketing Networks Important social consequences attended the creation of interregional markets. After 1820 the development of export markets, particularly for grain and cotton, lured new settlers into the West in record numbers. Within a year or two of relocation, most pioneer farmers found new markets for their produce; after 1850, railroads actually overtook the westering settlers and began purposefully colonizing new lands. Federal land sales boomed; twenty new states entered the Union by 1860; exports of cotton, grain, and other farm produce approached $1 billion.

To pay remittances to exporting farmers, streams of manufactured goods flowed into the countryside, tended by merchants and carriers whose number, scale of operations, and sophistication steadily increased. Cities such as Cincinnati and Saint Louis took shape as exporting centers, then quickly acquired processing industries (pork packing, distilling, milling) and manufacturing trades. As transportation improved, competition between local producers and more distant vendors drove down consumer prices and rewarded more efficient suppliers. The increasing volume of trade allowed merchants to specialize in cotton, wheat, hardware, groceries, insurance, or forwarding services. New agents called "jobbers" helped local merchants navigate among large specialty houses by breaking down large lots into smaller retail stocks. Such specialization and expertise enhanced the efficiency of market transactions.

The extension of complex markets across half a continent brought most Americans into more regular dependency on the money economy. Barter economies survived on the frontier as temporary expedients, not as alternatives to the larger commercial networks. Once in place, markets fostered their own elaboration. Innovative merchants and manufacturers bought goods in larger lots, built more efficient steamboats, invented machines, adopted telegraphic communication, extended credit in novel ways (or exploited credit extended to them), incorporated railroad companies and banks, lobbied governments, occasionally lied and cheated each other—all seeking competitive advantages in this burgeoning market economy.

The spiraling velocity of transactions required constant infusions of new "money," for which antebellum entrepreneurs turned to federal and state governments, private and incorporated banks, canals, railroads, insurance companies, cotton warehouses, merchant paper, personal promissory notes—anything to circulate as currency in impersonal, long-distance transactions. Although the Second Bank of the United States, established in 1816, foundered in 1833 on the rocks of political opposition, lesser banks and private networks of credit (assisted after 1850 by the credit reporting services of the Bradstreet Agency and later R. G. Dun and Company) kept the money supply buoyant, if not always safe. Panics shook financial markets in 1819, 1837, and 1857, ruining the overextended and reminding everyone how unpredictable the game could be.

Nobody could cling for long to the old pace of life—or business—in these rapidly developing markets, and the relentlessness of these changes disappointed individuals who pinned their hopes on the status quo. Farmers in Michigan in the 1830s, for example, gained high-speed access to markets but had to fence their pastures to keep livestock off the tracks. Forwarding merchants and local middlemen everywhere found their markets invaded by better-heeled distant competitors. In the 1830s, Hudson River farmers complained that the Erie Canal brought unfair competition from wheat farmers in the Genesee Valley; two decades later Genesee Valley farmers complained that railroads brought the same from Michigan and Illinois. Bankers and debtors found their notes appearing for payment more quickly. Confidence men and speculators watched their "float," the delay of information, disappear. A generation of Americans confronted, for the first time, the bewildering complex of reinforcing changes they chose to call "progress."

Nowhere was the potential for cumulative change more clearly realized than in New York City. Gifted with excellent natural waterways, New York merchants plunged their state into debt in 1817 to build the spectacular Erie Canal, which served to reorganize the commerce of the country. New York merchants pioneered sailing on schedule to England; organized coastal service to the cotton ports; perfected the system of dockside auctions; and multiplied banking, insurance, investment, information, and credit facilities until they offered the quickest and cheapest services, the freshest news, the latest prices, and the widest selection of buyers, sellers, and merchandise of any city on the continent. They gained such dominance over American markets that even the railroads, which ignored existing patterns of trade in so many places, confirmed the rise of the port of New York.

The Transformation of Workshops Expanding and quickening markets revolutionized the structure of American manufacturing in the first half of the nineteenth century. New factories filled with big machines impressed everyone with the abruptness of their novelty, but far subtler changes in artisans' workshops started the making of an American working class. To meet rising demand or seize novel opportunities, master craftsmen experimented with systems of production that tended to enlarge the shop, capitalize techniques, subdivide tasks, routinize work, and return to the master a larger share of the fruits of labor. In this way, the vast majority of American workers, who before 1850 never entered a factory, joined the ranks of people who worked all their lives for wages.

The deterioration of workshop traditions stands out in the experience of booming canal towns such as Rochester, New York. In 1823, when the Erie Canal arrived, this sleepy country town virtually exploded with entrepreneurial changes. Giant flour mills on the Genesee River anchored an export trade that canal transportation made possible. Farmers turned to growing wheat for export and consuming more "store-bought" goods, which local merchants and artisans scrambled to provide. To meet the extraordinary demand for barrels, coopers subdivided their craft, hiring farmers to cut rough staves which journeymen finished into barrels in the shop. Shoemakers rationalized the cutting and fitting of shoes, then hired women at piece rates to sew the uppers and soles together. Apprentices became runners, delivering pieces and collecting finished articles but learning nothing about the craft. Journeymen, lured by ready employment, found wages but not "positions" in Rochester.

Market forces thus altered economic and social relations without the influence of big machines. Innovative masters invested more in tools, materials, and facilities, and then sought to reduce the wage bill. Alternatively, merchant investors with cash and credit gained control of markets and supplies, and then dictated new conditions in the workplace. Collegiality within the shops disappeared, and profits for the owner no longer implied upward mobility for apprentices and journeymen. Rochester's successful manufacturers moved into new homes in different parts of town, leaving their employees to neighborhoods (and aspirations) that could not share in their proprietary values. Terms of employment once appropriate to the temporary status of the journeyman did not provide a living for workers with families—yet such were the wages the market offered. Frustration, jealousy, and alienation mounted as workers watched the innovations of their masters undermine the quality of life to which they thought they, as free men and women, were entitled.

The degradation of the artisans' culture produced political as well as social tensions. In New York City, rapidly becoming the nation's premier manufacturing center, workingmen's parties and trade union movements tried repeatedly to discipline the masters, block the influence of merchant investors, and preserve the rights of labor within the Painite republican tradition. All over America, however, a strategic dilemma pitted artisans who would resist the progress of capitalization against those who aimed more narrowly at better wages and shorter hours within the framework of class employment.

Dark Satanic Mills Nothing evoked more American pity and scorn at the end of the eighteenth century than the abject poverty and hopeless dependency of Europe's industrial classes. In 1791, Treasury Secretary Alexander Hamilton had tried to promote industrial growth in his *Report on the Subject of Manufactures;* but negative voices silenced Hamilton, and most Americans seemed content to leave factories (and factory workers) in Europe. Yet at precisely the same moment, American industrialization began at a small water-powered mill in Rhode Island.

In 1789, an English textile mechanic named Samuel Slater teamed up with Providence merchant Moses Brown to build the first American spinning mill. Slater's first mill (1791), and the dozens like it that quickly followed, exploited small sources of waterpower in southern New England to drive carding and spinning machines that spewed miles of cotton yarn into easily glutted markets. Confined primarily to rural settings by the location of the streams, employing the surplus labor of women and children while men worked at technical jobs (or farmed nearby company land), and limited in size by the power available and the number of neighborhood hand-loom weavers recruited to fashion the yarn into cloth, Slater-style mills at first seemed to complement the rural economy by generating incomes for poor families. As a result, the textile revolution was well established in America before many people acknowledged the importance of the factory system.

It was Francis Cabot Lowell's large-scale, fully integrated textile factory that drew all the attention in 1814, when the Boston Manufacturing Company first produced cotton cloth. Lowell combined in a single building all the processes from "picking" raw cotton to weaving finished cloth (and later dyeing and printing as well), integrating the machinery for efficiency, subdividing work into simple (and repetitive) tasks, capturing transaction costs and economies of scale lost to Slater-style firms, and turning out yard after yard of cheap cloth especially suited to clothing the southern planters' slaves.

A corporate charter sustained Lowell's first industrial venture, and by 1822 the dividends encouraged the same investors to develop a huge source of waterpower on the Merrimack River. At this site, named Lowell, Massachusetts, over the next twenty years the Merrimack Manufacturing Company developed five enormous cotton mills worth $5 million, employing 1,800 workers and producing 250,000 yards of cloth per week. Eight additional corporations, owned largely by the same investors, compounded operations at Lowell into the nation's largest industrial complex. Sensitive to the alien appearance of their giant enterprise, Lowell and his followers had stressed the public service that their corporations performed by stimulating the regional economy and creating employment for young unmarried women. Model boardinghouse environments theoretically protected Lowell operatives from the evils that degraded European workers; besides, according to the owners, Lowell "girls" saw factory work as a temporary prelude to a traditional domestic life. But market forces soon replaced such talk of social benefits with concern for efficiency, competition, and the profit margin.

This phenomenal success notwithstanding, few American manufacturers before the Civil War copied the system of the Lowell corporations. Even in textiles, where all the largest firms appeared, most companies remained private concerns or partnerships. After 1828 the use of steam power in factories freed manufacturers to locate anywhere they pleased, but this did not produce dramatic concentrations of capital. Textile magnates such as Samuel Slater multiplied their holdings by adding firms or joining complex webs of partnerships. Most industrialists managed their businesses as separate proprietary firms, and few fully mastered systems of cost accounting or managed to dominate their primary markets. Nobody sought the social experimentation suggested by the Lowell boardinghouses.

Free Labor Ideology Between the gradual transformation of traditional workshops and the radical alternatives of cotton mill employment, most antebellum workers found that the world in which they worked kept changing. Technological

innovations embedded more capabilities in machines that required less talent or experience to operate. The "American system of manufacturing" with interchangeable parts, developed by Eli Whitney, Samuel Colt, and other manufacturers of small machines, further removed the artistry of the maker from the utility of the product. Social perquisites long respected on the job — drams of liquor or impromptu suspensions of work to attend the circus, toast a birthday, or engage in political debates—fell before the rational calculations of employers who now paid wages by the hour and measured productivity in marketable output.

Because these changes in the world of work came at the hands of thousands of autonomous employers, they did not generate the kind of sympathy that might have followed the sudden spread of English-style "dark satanic mills" (the phrase is William Blake's). As long as most white Americans still owned farms, as long as skilled artisans nursed proprietary hopes, as long as most wage earners still knew "the boss" face to face and "mill girls" returned to hearth and home, the progress of capitalization seemed indistinct. Articulating a "free labor ideal" by mid century, middle-class people in the North insisted that as long as they were free from government corruption and class rule, their independence would survive in the marketplace. Objective measures did not entirely justify their confidence; but because the strident critics of free labor ideology—labor radicals and southern slaveholders — clearly spoke a language of class interest, most Americans entered the Civil War era believing that independence, free markets, and democratic politics still guaranteed personal liberty.

RISE OF BIG BUSINESS

Americans' delight in freedom of the marketplace reflected their belief that governments, not businesses, distorted the results of competition. John Locke had implied, and Adam Smith clearly had written, that no player in the game of capitalism could long sustain an unfair advantage, except through artificial preferment. Although many antebellum artisans found reason to wonder if the marketplace really "played fair," it was after the Civil War that the rise of big business introduced truly shocking contradictions to the liberal ideal. Under certain circumstances, free markets rewarded efficiency by favoring enormous enterprises that could sustain their productive advantages only by controlling or suppressing competition. This phenomenon surprised businessmen as much as consumers, and the rise of big business in America is best seen as both a problem *for* business and a problem *about* business in society.

Bureaucracy and the Railroads   The key to operating very large businesses lay in bureaucratic systems of management, and these techniques emerged as antebellum railroads struggled to control complex operations. From the beginning, railroads developed as technologically integrated systems, with one enterprise owning the roadway, selecting the equipment, operating trains, and handling the freight. Monopolistic operations worked even better when railroads integrated service over long lines or complex networks. Accordingly, after 1850, railroads began to combine into systems such as the Erie, New York Central, and Pennsylvania railroads, which managed about five hundred miles (800 kilometers) each and influenced policies on hundreds more, stretching from the Atlantic to Chicago and beyond.

Twenty times more expensive than the largest cotton mills, these trunkline railroads by 1860 employed more workers and engaged in more complicated transactions over a vastly larger geographical field than any other business in the country. In a cotton mill, everybody worked in a single complex of buildings, and almost nobody handled money. But train crews moved across the landscape, station hands worked in isolated spots, machinists repaired equipment, track gangs fixed the roadway, and conductors, agents, and paymasters handled money. No enterprise before had tried to coordinate so many different activities over great distances with exacting accuracy.

To control this complex business, managers on the Baltimore and Ohio, the Western Railroad, the Erie, and the Pennsylvania pioneered line-and-staff command structures; separated finance and business strategy from traffic and operations; further divided operations, maintenance, and machinery; and broke their lines into divisions of approximately fifty miles (80 kilometers). Statistical records made it possible to check the performance of one division against that of another. Auditors tracked down income and disbursements, guaranteeing faithful service from a legion of "middle managers" (who carried out transactions for entrepreneurs but earned wages themselves). Superintendents assumed operating responsibility for their divisions as if they were independent railroads; however, their performance was judged—and their salaries set—not by the market but by upper management.

Bureaucratic structures made it possible for American railroads to deliver relatively convenient and efficient services across a network that after 1869 spanned the continent. Capitalization for major lines reached into the hundreds of millions while total system mileage approached two hundred thousand (320,000 kilometers) at century's end. Easily expanded or subdivided, bureaucratic management techniques functioned roughly like machines in a workshop: they fixed the nature and dimensions of each task and required of the servant only the faithful execution of routine operations.

Bureaucratic complexity and rapidly changing markets taught railroad managers to discourage competition wherever possible. Driven to run full trains every day, in order to minimize the burden of high fixed costs, competing railroads often took business at less-than-profitable rates. They recovered any lost revenue through higher charges on noncompeting service, presenting consumers with a wildly distorted market in which identical goods might travel on the same train to the same destination, at rates that differed by a factor of ten. Railroad owners blamed distortions on cutthroat competition, which resulted when consumers forced the carriers to bid against each other. To eliminate such hurtful competition, railroads leased or purchased competitors' lines, formed pools to divide the traffic, and—like sovereign nations—forged strategic alliances to maintain peace and prosperity. Consumers denounced these efforts to restrain free trade.

Economies of Scale   As the nation's first big businesses, railroads introduced the problems of cutthroat competition and monopolistic influence into the American marketplace. Their success as big businesses made it possible for certain manufacturing and distribution industries to pursue strategies of giantism. In the 1870s and 1880s, economies of scale, rooted in technological advantages, prohibitive capital requirements, transportation discounts, or perhaps secret (and dishonorable) deals, catapulted certain firms into commanding positions from which they proceeded, like the railroads, to manipulate the game of competition.

Technology drove Andrew Carnegie's conquest of the steel industry. By quickly adopting the Bessemer process in the early 1870s, running his mills at maximum output, cutting costs, and selling steel as cheaply as possible, Carnegie seized a spiral of advantages. Quality and price gave him an edge with which he forced competitors to sell out; greater capacity improved his leverage in coal, iron ore, and labor markets; lower costs yielded cheaper steel, a larger share of the market, more takeovers, and greater control over the cost of materials and labor. Carnegie's furnaces burned out faster than those of more careful producers, but new equipment incorporated the latest innovations.

Oil baron John D. Rockefeller started with a secret railroad contract that lowered his transport costs and paid him kickbacks on competitors' shipments as well. Rockefeller undersold his Cleveland competition and took over the regional business. With volume under his control, he demanded greater transportation concessions, took over pipelines, forced down crude oil prices, built efficient new refineries, made his own tin cans, and pinched every penny in the process. His aptly named "Standard" brand of kerosene became practically the only one on the shelves.

Wholesale and retail merchants captured economies of scale by combining larger markets (reached by the railroads) with volume discounts. Manufacturers of clothing, housewares, tools, furniture, toys, and other mass consumer products gladly discounted large lots (and the railroads discounted shipping) to vendors, such as Marshall Field in Chicago, who opened huge retail department stores designed for "one-stop shopping" and customer satisfaction. Economies of scale allowed these giant merchants to beat local outlets on price, quality, and selection. Once established, these firms always commanded special terms and sometimes developed exclusive product lines, invested in manufacturing, and extended networks of branch stores. Marshall Field and Company's huge capital base supported money-back guarantees that would easily bankrupt a small shopkeeper trading with only his own capital.

According to classical theory, monopolists sold shoddy goods at artificially high prices, yet here were Carnegie, Rockefeller, and Field selling first-rate products at bargain prices. Vertical integration (controlling processes from raw material to retail sale) and horizontal combination (buying out the competition) explained their ability to do this. Railroads provided the expanding mass markets; bureaucratic systems made such firms manageable; consumer benefits kept them appealing to the great body of private customers. But interlocking economies of scale allowed a few players to dominate the market, while vast sums of capital tied up in plant, equipment, and inventories encouraged these high-stakes gamblers to protect themselves from competition. The giant firms of the Gilded Age were built by vigorous entrepreneurs, but a system of oligopoly was curtailing natural market forces. More

alarming, a small number of very rich men held interlocking investments in giant firms that potentially controlled the economy of the country.

A National Capital Market Andrew Carnegie built a $480 million empire by investing retained earnings from companies he owned alone or with selected partners. His was the exception to the rule, however, for most Gilded Age capitalists took advantage of new corporate structures and a rapidly developing securities market to marshal the capital of many investors behind the efforts of a few entrepreneurs. Once again, railroads led the way. First organized as franchise corporations, railroads sold shares to raise money but quickly pioneered the use of corporate mortgage bonds that borrowed funds against a pledge of future earnings and the value of the capital plant being built. When railroads paid off, which they did handsomely during and after the Civil War, passive investors often found these securities more attractive than risky enterprise or public debt. Limited liability, which after 1860 protected most corporate stockholders from individual responsibility for the debts of the firm, rendered passive investment even more attractive.

Stocks and bonds generated capital only if convenient markets traded them. Big-city stock exchanges filled the need, dominated from the 1870s by the New York Stock Exchange. First railroad securities, then in the 1890s industrial stocks and bonds, flooded Wall Street; brokers, investment bankers, and corporation lawyers appeared (as if by magic) to assist this new business of financing business. These instruments of capital formation separated ownership from entrepreneurship. Corporate leaders played with other people's money, not just their own; investors piled up wealth not from productive work but from securities manipulation. As a result, ambitious entrepreneurs such as Rockefeller wielded much more financial power than their private fortunes implied (especially early in their careers), while quick profits from stock operations introduced speculation as a separate career.

Corporations generated capital and structured these giant new firms, but booming capital markets exaggerated problems of cutthroat competition as mass markets approached saturation. Fabulous profits born of economies of scale lured more investors than the railroads and other center industries could support. Price-cutting strategies destroyed the weak, but too much competition took the profit out of everybody's business. Integration and combination removed some of the danger for innovative firms, but what could stop ruinous competition among the handful of giant survivors? The custodians of large corporations, originally owners but increasingly professional managers responding to boards of directors, seized every opportunity to protect their masters' capital by controlling costs and wages, binding customers with special terms, securing favorable government policies, incorporating technological advantages, and suppressing price competition.

In this manner what Alfred D. Chandler has called the "visible hand of management" challenged the invisible hand of Adam Smith's markets for control of America's economic resources. Railroads tried pooling—formal agreements that set rates between competing cities and divided the proceeds according to agreed-upon market shares. In 1882 John D. Rockefeller invented the "trust," in which leading shareholders surrendered control of competing firms to trustees who then managed the whole industry on cooperative terms. Still other enterprises joined trade associations designed to fix prices, limit production, manipulate labor, or discourage new entrants into crowded fields. All these solutions met with angry opposition from the American people, who wondered in increasing numbers if corporations were corrupting their free markets.

Antitrust and the Problem of Monopoly

The antitrust critique of American business always reflected a fundamentally liberal or Smithian foundation. Free markets were supposed to work best, and combinations to restrain competition by definition were ruled out of order. Since the 1850s, when the eastern railroads first manipulated their rates to accommodate trunkline competition, local businesses had bitterly condemned pricing policies that built up or destroyed whole communities without regard for their economic right to exist. Railroad managers insisted that if they gave up rate-making power, they would become mere public utilities. To compete as businesses—and therefore deliver cheap and efficient transportation according to Smithian principles—railroads demanded economic freedoms that significantly compromised the freedom of others.

This dilemma existed because large railroad systems now controlled the networks in which other businesses found their markets. Competition among carriers dictated one set of strategies while competition between shippers and carriers encouraged others. Building on common law traditions that recognized the capacity for common carriers to distort commodities markets, Gilded Age shippers begged their governments for relief from railroad oppression. State legislatures responded sympathetically, especially in the Midwest during the 1870s Granger Movement; but interstate corporations sought refuge from rate regulation under the "equal protection" clause of the Fourteenth Amendment. Industry leaders proposed that legalized pooling or cartelization might generate more uniform and stable rates, but skeptical voters and lawmakers clung to their faith in competition. The 1887 Interstate Commerce Act outlawed pooling as well as discriminatory rates. As a result, railroad companies merged into larger systems, labored vigorously to frustrate the enforcement of the law, and tried to find a niche between ruinous competition and illegal collusion.

As giant firms appeared in steel, oil, sewing machines, farm equipment, beef, jute bags, and other industries, popular agitation against monopoly spread. Congress responded in 1890 with the Sherman Antitrust Act, which outlawed all "restraints of trade" but left the prosecutors and judges considerable room to interpret the principle in practice. Sensitive to the economic power of the corporations (major sources of bribes and campaign contributions), neither the executive branch nor the courts rushed to impose the Sherman ideal. With unmeasured cynicism, American justices in the 1890s could find serious restraints of trade only in the activities of organized labor.

Antitrust legislation did little to dismantle America's big businesses at the end of the nineteenth century, but it did restate in clarion terms that century's confidence in free markets and the liberal ideal. Antitrust advocates seldom addressed the fact that many of their foes performed more efficiently than smaller firms. In fact, most antimonopoly rhetoric issued from injured interest groups—small merchants and manufacturers, rural middlemen, and organized labor. At issue, they insisted, were not current prices, wages, or rates but accumulations of power that threatened the fundamental liberty of all entrepreneurs. Not yet ready to adjust theory to changing realities, most Americans still hoped that conspirators could be punished and the automatic system of competition restored to its natural glory.

What antitrust legislation did accomplish in American business was another tremendous round of consolidations, known to historians as the "great merger movement." Federal proscriptions on all forms of collusion forced closely allied firms into outright consolidation. Over two thousand individual firms disappeared in corporate mergers between 1895 and 1904. Unbelievable giants, such as the $1.4 billion United States Steel, concentrated power in American industry more narrowly than ever before. Investment bankers such as J. P. Morgan played crucial roles in arranging these mergers and placed themselves on the new boards of directors. Thus, because of antitrust pronouncements designed to restore entrepreneurial liberty, control of America's center economy shifted further away from the entrepreneurs.

HEROIC OR
MONOPOLISTIC ENTERPRISE?

Wholly unprepared for the rise of big business, Gilded Age Americans celebrated the progress of industrialization, with its consumer benefits and rising living standard, at the same time denouncing their betrayal by cynical monopolists and "bloodless" corporations. Nothing in their views on civil liberty or economics explained the triumph of monopolistic firms, and nothing preoccupied the culture quite like the problem of economic justice in the age of the business titans. On the one hand, self-made captains of industry fulfilled the grandest American myth; on the other hand, their networks of corporate power seemed to block the aspirations of all who would follow in their steps. In a search for self-understanding that formed a bridge to the coming century, this generation struggled to reconceive the revolutionary promise of liberty in a harsh new corporate world.

Triumphant Capitalist Values Despite the rise of the "visible hand" in the Gilded Age business community, traditional liberal values absolutely dominated the thinking of the business culture. Even while they struggled to control market forces, businessmen (and they were almost exclusively men) praised the "natural selection" process that gave them wealth and power. Charles Elliott Perkins, president of the Chicago, Burlington, and Quincy Railroad, for example, pontificated endlessly on the folly of lawmakers bending the laws of trade, never admitting that half his days were consumed in trying to do the same. After bribing politicians, corrupting the courts, falsifying records, swindling investors, and breaking competitors through all manner of extortions, the robber barons never tired of praising natural markets, individual liberty, and freedom of enterprise.

Business values received academic sanction at the hands of social Darwinists such as William Gra-

ham Sumner, who explained "scientifically" why some grew rich while many drifted toward poverty. Only the fittest survived, according to a tautological formula in which fitness was measured in well- or ill-gotten wealth. By such a standard, no social failures could be blamed on the business classes. No capitalist could threaten the public interest, because business success defined appropriate social results. Trapped in a cruel parody of earlier values, American entrepreneurs in the Gilded Age found liberal principles turned against them until it seemed that mass dependency and abject poverty were the natural results of a free society.

For those who found sociological justification a bit too harsh, Christian clergymen such as Russell Conwell explained business triumph as the work of the Lord. "To make money honestly is to preach the gospel," proclaimed this Philadelphia Baptist. Furthermore, "ninety-eight out of one hundred of the rich men in America are honest. That is why they are rich" ("Acres of Diamonds," quoted in Ray Ginger, *Age of Excess,* p. 281). Some extraordinary characters sincerely believed in this gospel of wealth; Carnegie wrote books on the theme and poured much of his fortune into philanthropies that alone, he argued, justified riches. Yet the most pious of the moguls stubbornly ignored the parts they played in creating conditions of squalor about them.

For lighter diversion, Horatio Alger cranked out over one hundred popular novels in which heroes like "Ragged Dick" propelled themselves from "rags to riches." These remarkable celebrations of the self-made man invariably keyed the heroes' success to benevolent sponsorship or outrageous good fortune—a plot device that mimicked reality all too accurately. Astonishingly, considering the ambivalence with which Americans beheld their business leaders, Alger's readers seemed not to recognize the irony in stories that elevated one (and only one) lucky boy to the top of the heap.

Class and Conspicuous Consumption In reality, neither natural selection nor pluck and luck determined who got rich and who did not in late-nineteenth-century business. Except for Andrew Carnegie (always the exception), the very rich of the Gilded Age came mostly from a preexisting class of elites who enjoyed family connections, capital assets, education, and leisure reaching back to the Civil War. Rockefeller and certain railroad schemers, such as Jay Gould and Jim Fisk, multiplied their original, modest, assets through dishonest (or dishonorable) gambits. Most business leaders, however, hurried to cultivate respectable appearances. The unfortunate Gould, who seemed particularly nasty, found himself ostracized by peers who sacrificed him to the sharks of popular criticism.

Criticism mounted, too, as millionaires flashed their money. Ideologically prepared to doubt the honesty of railroad magnates and industrial monopolists, Americans watched in amazement as the superrich built extraordinary town houses in New York, bought extravagant furniture and clothing, threw lavish parties, served outrageous delicacies, and built fabulous summer "cottages" by the shore. Multimillion-dollar dwellings lined the sea walk at Newport, Rhode Island, the "castles" of the Vanderbilts, Rockefellers, and others of this new American royalty.

In 1899, Thorstein Veblen blasted such "conspicuous consumption," and the entire business culture, in his *The Theory of the Leisure Class.* His was not the first critical voice, by any means: for a generation of activists and essayists—Henry George, Eugene V. Debs, and Henry Demarest Lloyd, to name just three—had been denouncing the excesses of "wealth against commonwealth." Veblen, however, broke free of contemporary rhetoric, stripping bare his subjects with anthropological detachment, driving home a functional analysis of the economic system and the class structure that echoed John Locke's appreciation for the state of nature.

Veblen's writings punctured the capitalists' self-satisfaction and exposed the distortions of language and perception that inhibited cultural criticism. Yet nothing seemed to change as a result. Established economists and sociologists rushed to minimize the damage, and businessmen simply ignored Veblen. Political radicals continued to hope that sheer numbers in a democratic culture would eventually bring power to the people. The middle classes beheld the spectacle of Gilded Age capitalism with a mixture of envy and admiration. As long as liberal values survived in the minds of middling proprietors, the glitter of Newport and uptown Manhattan kept petty capitalists in the game.

How Narrow the Portal? In retrospect we can see that the window of opportunity in American business grew narrower throughout the nineteenth century. By the exercise of liberty and innovation in relatively unrestricted markets, individuals accumulated property and power, which brought others into increased dependency. At times such gains were illegitimate, even by the standards of the day,

and once ahead, people often cheated to protect their positions; but much of the economic hierarchy resulted from successful competition in the marketplace. When giant firms in the Gilded Age began to prey upon the business class itself, critics inside the business culture began to ask if the age of enterprise was passing. If so, was the experiment of liberty endangered?

Women, blacks, and American Indians no doubt could see the question coming, because the promise of liberty never had extended fully to these dependent, "inferior" classes. Women had entered the story as "surplus labor" in Alexander Hamilton's *Report on the Subject of Manufactures,* and while many individual women played business roles and whole troops of women labored in the work force, women never gained equal rights as entrepreneurs. African Americans found entrepreneurial opportunities strictly limited by universal race discrimination. Black entrepreneurs often thrived in special industries or sectors that catered to the black community, but always the frontiers of opportunity were bounded by the interests of the dominant culture. As wards of the federal government under the reservation system, most American Indians were "protected" (read "excluded") from the enterprise system. The 1887 Dawes Act, intended to integrate them into the commercial economy as proprietors, cruelly exposed new Indian landholders to unscrupulous white speculators.

American Jews participated more successfully in business, yet Anglo-Saxon capitalists never failed to stereotype their character. Some of the most successful New York bankers endured personal insults and social exclusion because they were Jews. In the final decades of the nineteenth century, when eastern European Jews poured in through the gates of immigration, anti-Semitism grew significantly more ugly. In fact, Americans harbored prejudices against a wide variety of ethnic groups. In *How the Other Half Lives* (1890), Jacob Riis, himself a Scandinavian immigrant and a reformer out to improve the lot of New York's urban poor, nevertheless published nasty caricatures of "Shylock" Jews, drunken Irishmen, and passionate, knife-wielding Italians.

Even white Anglo-Saxon Protestants paused to wonder, by 1900, if opportunities were declining. Main Street entrepreneurs felt besieged by huge suppliers, carriers, and competitors who dictated the terms of business. Middle managers by the thousands carried out millions of transactions on behalf of corporate directors who seemed increasingly powerful and few in number. Even consumers, whose preference for cheap, plentiful goods had helped "elect" the new captains of industry, found that once established, monopolistic firms could disregard their interest in quality, style, or price. The people still elected their governors, but business orthodoxy admitted no legitimate role for government in business. If business set the terms of most people's lives, and if the visible hand of management took over business systems, how could liberty—or even enterprise—prevail?

EPILOGUE: THE AMERICAN CENTURY

How could liberty and enterprise prevail? This question stalked Americans relentlessly in the second century of national existence. In the twentieth century Americans perfected a consumer economy and a widespread popular mythology that, by the 1950s, offered the "American Dream" as the very definition of human freedom. Three themes illustrate the evolution of the American business culture in the twentieth century. First, to tame the business cycle, politicians and private bankers gradually developed systems of monetary and fiscal policy designed to mediate the forces of the marketplace. Second, in pursuit of profits, individual firms grew large and bureaucratic, diversified their lines, expanded overseas, and articulated professional management systems. Third, to make a living, more and more Americans surrendered their farms, small shops, and domestic duties in favor of wage or salaried positions, swelling the "labor" pool to include middle- and upper-class men and women. What bound this nation of employees together was not so much the earning as the spending of money. In the popular mind, capitalism became of system of buying goods and services. By the end of another century of business evolution, Americans found themselves unbelievably affluent by world standards, yet frustrated by inequalities, dangerously unsure of how their economic system functioned, disappointed in the performance of both government and business, and profoundly insecure.

Taming the Business Cycle The first achievement of the twentieth century, that redounded to everybody's benefit, was the relative taming of the business cycle. Throughout the nineteenth century, financial panics sparked by crises in the monetary system had pitched the economy into serious depressions. Uncertain how to create an elastic but sound form of currency, American bankers and en-

trepreneurs clung to the gold standard and weathered storms that produced more social misery with each repetition. By 1907 private bankers such as J. Pierpont Morgan had found that they could prop up the financial pyramid during moments of business anxiety, and in 1913 Congress created the Federal Reserve System to do the same. This network of twelve regional bankers' banks created a common reserve currency that could be loaned to member banks to stem emergencies. Part fiscal agency, part central bank, the new "Fed" acquired in the course of a generation both the power and expertise to manage the American money supply, but not without some painful failures along the way.

The Fed was too new, or too perversely wedded to "hard money" doctrines, to prevent the 1929 crash of American—and world—capitalism. For years Wall Street's bull market vacuumed up investment cash and bank credits, drawing even country banks and small town investors into high-risk speculative purchases. When confidence collapsed, the value of securities evaporated and the downward spiral drained the banking system of money—most painfully the savings accounts of frugal, hardworking people. Contrary to everyone's expectations, the Great Depression grew more severe for three full years. Unemployment rose to a high of 25 percent, the quoted value of all Wall Street stocks plummeted 83 percent, stores and factories closed or cut their hours; yet no automatic mechanism checked the unfolding disaster. Beginning in 1933, President Franklin D. Roosevelt's New Deal measures—the Bank "Holiday," the Federal Deposit Insurance Corporation, the Gold Reserve Act, the Securities and Exchange Commission, all kinds of relief and public works programs, and finally the Social Security Act—dramatically (if often accidentally) expanded the money supply and rekindled confidence among business and household consumers. Strong recovery marked the years 1933–1937, but so great was the damage that full confidence in economic growth did not return until the mobilization for World War II.

The lessons of mobilization during two world wars, together with the experience of interwar boom and bust and the fear of renewed stagnation, convinced postwar American politicians that the automatic workings of the gold standard, the business cycle, and even free competition did not guarantee acceptable levels of social welfare. Postwar demobilization programs, such as the G.I. Bill of Rights, aimed at reconverting the wartime economy without shocks to domestic prosperity. Partial remobilization for the cold war kept the federal government in the marketplace as an enormously important consumer, while the Truman and Eisenhower administrations cautiously manipulated social security benefits and taxes for countercyclical purposes. Beginning with the 1964 Kennedy Tax Cut and Lyndon Johnson's Great Society programs, the hand of government boldly maneuvered money and credit policies, public works, entitlements and transfers, taxes, and all kinds of subsidies and incentives, always seeking to stimulate growth, relieve inequities, encourage enterprise, preserve consumer and investor confidence, improve the quality of life, and protect Americans from enemies (real and imagined) at home and abroad.

The results of these countercyclical government policies proved frustrating, especially as the cold war arms race, a shooting war in Vietnam, and external shocks such as the 1973 Arab oil embargo inflated the costs of these experiments without achieving the desired effects. A popular backlash, encouraged in the 1980s by President Ronald Reagan, brought significant deregulation to the banking system, airlines, telecommunications, and other businesses, as well as a natiowide taxpayers' revolt. Most recently, corrupt practices on Wall Street, savings and loan bankruptcies, rising unemployment, and consumer malaise have reminded Americans how much they depend on regulatory agencies, federal deposit insurance, and other modern tools of economic management for their confidence in the capitalist system.

Bureaucracy and the Modern Firm Corporate strategies, a second theme illustrating major trends in twentieth-century business, favored more growth and bureaucratization to handle complex operations. Besides practicing the vertical integration and the horizontal combination perfected during the Gilded Age, center firms in the new century began to diversify into new product lines that exploited similar processes, materials, or technologies. Highly efficient new management structures, pioneered in the 1920s at DuPont and General Motors, decentralized operations among nearly autonomous divisions, while top management kept control of finance and strategic planning. Elaborate statistical controls made it possible for cost accountants to measure the efficiency of every step in a complex manufacturing process, while decentralized command identified those to hold accountable among hundreds of corporate servants.

Diversified companies triggered no antitrust watchdogs because they did not monopolize any one line of products; still, giant multidivisional, multifunctional corporations gained internal control over many transactions that would have taken place in open markets, thereby suppressing competition where it mattered most. Full-time research and development laboratories fed new product and process ideas into such companies, while increasingly professional (and effective) advertising analyzed and stimulated markets for finished products. By the 1950s, experts in finance and organization began building huge conglomerates out of companies with almost nothing in common. Beatrice, for example, a Nebraska creamery that in the 1890s pioneered brand name butter, eventually diversified into eight thousand product lines! Of course the leaders of such corporations knew more about stocks, bonds, and bank loans than they knew about butter (or any product). Finance capitalism, a game of speculative harvest invented by Gilded Age titans such as Jay Gould, and played so disastrously in the Roaring Twenties, experienced glorious reincarnation during the merger mania of the late 1960s, and the junk bond scams of the 1980s.

Overseas expansion of American business followed naturally from the growth of the firm, the decentralization of management, and the rise of American influence in the markets of the world. The earliest multinational firms (Singer Sewing Machine, Standard Oil) moved overseas to better serve distribution, sales, and service of their products. In the twentieth century, American companies invested overseas to help finance expanding sales, to rebuild war-torn trading partners, to develop resources such as oil, rubber, or fruits, and to exploit populations of low-paid workers. American companies invested most heavily in industrialized Canada and Europe, and in nearby Latin America; but with the decline of formal empires after World War II, American firms moved quickly into Middle Eastern, African, Indian, and Asian markets. Liberal economists such as Walt W. Rostow (whose *The Stages of Economic Growth: A Non-Communist Manifesto* first appeared in 1960) declared a new capitalist millennium, that promised to place "third world" peoples on the sure road to modernization and prosperity.

Unfortunately, the potential for corruption in foreign investment proved enormous, especially when undemocratic regimes eagerly traded valuable franchises, unique resources, or the welfare of their people for American dollars and military hardware. Cold war competition between Marxist and capitalist countries and the rising tide of postcolonial revolutions encouraged the United States government to support and protect business investments that secured friendly relations, protected strategic resources, or thwarted the enemy's influence around the globe. Thus cloaked in patriotic rhetoric, terribly exploitative deals were struck in the name of democracy and the "free world." Government and business alike deflected criticism of their unholy collaborations in Guatemala, Iran, or Venezuela (to name three) as "communist propaganda." By 1970, however, even scholars at the Harvard Business School had begun to question the character of multinational enterprise, and some abuses had been exposed.

If business seemed to be running the world, it became less clear in the twentieth century who was running American business. Back in the Gilded Age, everybody knew the names of leading business tycoons; but by the 1930s a class of professional managers — men (rarely women) who did not own the firm or even necessarily understand the business, but who managed the assets for salaries — had taken control of corporate boardrooms. Herbert Hoover early noticed that public corporations technically were owned by thousands of individual shareholders, a "democratic" tendency he celebrated in a 1922 booklet entitled *American Individualism.* In 1932, more critical analysts Adolf A. Berle and Gardiner C. Means published a detailed study, *The Modern Corporation and Private Property,* that documented the separation of ownership and control. Passive shareholders increasingly left managerial decisions to salaried executives and became mere constituents, like consumers of products, to be satisfied with quarterly dividends. Such an arrangement encouraged executives to favor security over risk and to adopt strategies that paid high salaries and dividends regardless of market conditions. Today, critics as diverse as junk-bond wizard Michael Milken, billionaire entrepreneur H. Ross Perot, and management specialist W. Edwards Deming all charge that American executives have paid themselves millions to mismanage other people's property and destroyed American competitiveness in the process.

Working for a Living If there has been a decline of entrepreneurship among American business leaders, it has been more than matched by the transformation of almost everybody into employees. In 1900, about half the American work force worked for pay; the other half owned their own businesses (mostly farms). By 1970, 85 percent of the entire work force (93 percent of the nonfarm sector) turned up on somebody's payroll! Americans in the twentieth century increasingly faced the marketplace not as capitalists but as workers. Yet this nation of workers did not develop a working-class view of the world or the business system. Even organized labor, which gained a powerful bargaining position during and after World War II, never seriously attacked the capitalist system. Although twentieth-century Americans no longer owned the means of production, they continued to think like proprietors, and they sought through income the security and comfort they used to enjoy as entrepreneurs.

Ethnic and racial diversity contributed in part to this bourgeois outlook. Before 1920, the worst cutthroat competition for jobs took place inside urban immigrant communities while native-born Americans still owned farms or practiced skilled trades. The flood of new immigrants, averaging about one million per year from 1905 to 1914, frightened the natives and sparked restrictive legislation in the 1920s that abruptly reduced this flow. At the same time, up to two million persons annually left farms for America's cities, adding new black and white workers with varying skills to the burgeoning urban workforce. Better education, English language skills, and racial discrimination generally lifted Anglo-Saxon whites to the top of labor markets, while prejudicial attitudes and settlement patterns sharply divided communities of workers into hostile competitive subgroups. Spurred by civic reformers to seek respectability in frugal habits and property, successful laborers bought homes and quickly attached (or transferred) proprietary values to this new form of family estate. Almost nothing in this process of individual striving fostered a culture of solidarity or alternative working-class values.

Mechanization, automation, and the evolution of wholly new industries spelled opportunity for these ambitious, urbanizing masses (even while it dislodged established workers from skilled or semiskilled positions). Average real income of employees increased steadily after 1900, and in the 1920s wage-earners gained another 30 percent, while consumer prices remained essentially static. Not everybody enjoyed average income, of course, and a great proportion of profits remained in the hands of the capitalists; but for a majority of workers before the Great Depression, prospects had improved and promised to continue. Not surprisingly, union membership actually dropped after 1920 and remained unchanged until the rise of industrial unions in the middle 1930s.

The Great Depression blasted the high hopes of American workers and called into question the capacity of business to provide jobs for the population. National unemployment figures masked disastrous conditions in major industrial cities: unemployment in Toledo, Ohio, topped out at 80 percent! Angry workers denounced the capitalists whose recklessness had produced such misery, and labor organizers encountered their most receptive American audience in a generation. Local governments and New Deal programs distributed millions in relief; but President Roosevelt (like most conservative businessmen) hated doling out money, and federal legislation tried to focus on getting people back to work. Section 7a of the National Industrial Recovery Act (1933) encouraged the formation of industrial unions powerful enough to bargain with organized capital, and the Wagner Act (1935), creating the National Labor Relations Board, admitted big labor to the national policy table. Between 1937 and 1939, Congress of Industrial Organization (CIO) affiliates won recognition for steel workers, miners, and auto workers — most dramatically in sit-down strikes at General Motors, violently at Ford Motor Company and Republic Steel. Overall, union membership doubled between 1935 and 1937, then doubled again by 1953, to an all-time high of 25 percent of the labor force.

The success of big labor during and after World War II, coupled with rising progressive income taxes and social security transfers affected a slight redistribution of wealth from the top to the middle classes of American society — not as great as wounded conservatives in the 1950s pretended, but enough to help reestablish middle-class aspirations among the majority of American workers. The real bonus came from unprecedented economic growth: from 1945 to 1970, the American gross national product doubled, as did average household consumption (despite a 46 percent increase in population). American business seemed miraculously cured of whatever ailed it in the 1930s. Important causes of the postwar boom could be found in defense outlays (rising to 9 percent of GNP) and government welfare spending (almost 15 percent of GNP by 1970) for housing, education, medical care, job training, and family income support. Nobody fully understood this complex economy, but as long as it grew and tried to include the lower classes, not very many complained.

Rising expectations more than matched rising incomes as postwar families swelled the American middle class. Buying and trading homes, buying and trading cars, and shopping for goods and furnishings became favorite pastimes in themselves. Enclosed malls sprang up near suburban sub-

divisions, where major retail department stores together with dozens of shops, restaurants, boutiques, and movie theaters beckoned customers to enjoy evening and Sunday shopping, in air-conditioned comfort, with acres of free parking. This latest consumer revolution stimulated both construction and retail service sectors in nearly every local economy (often ruining downtown business districts in the process). A new generation, the "baby boomers," knew nothing of the Great Depression but came of age at a time when jobs seemed secure, incomes *always* rose, and spending came too easily. Such was the American way of life at the height of the cold war, and unless attacked by maniacal Russian communists, American business seemed capable of perpetuating the fun indefinitely.

Affluence and Insecurity. In the 1960s, women staged a feminist revolt, demanding equal pay and equal access to careers traditionally pursued by men; blacks turned up the heat of their attack on racial segregation; and college students mounted angry assaults on business and government for involvement in the Vietnam War. Besieged with contradictory demands, the federal government under presidents Kennedy and Johnson tried to finance guns *and* butter out of economic growth. After 1965, the resulting inflation began to erode prosperity; but the feminist movement brought millions of women into paid employment in time for their earnings to help counteract downward pressures on many people's standard of living. Single-income households, working mothers with children, unskilled or marginal workers (among whom blacks and minorities were represented disproportionately) suffered steady degradation. Unemployment (except during certain war years) persisted throughout the postwar expansion at between 4 and 7 percent, and this stubborn level of joblessness excluded a subclass of chronically unemployed persons no longer looking for work. Everyone ignored the frustrating hardships of the working poor — upwards of fifty million people in what Michael Harrington as early as 1962 called "the other America." In a modern nation of employees, a rising number of individuals and families not only held no property, but they could not find a job.

According to Harrington, poverty in modern America was more pernicious for being "invisible." Because of the postwar boom, America's masses no longer were poor, and it became easier for business, government, and ordinary taxpayers to blame the victims of chronic poverty. Economist John Kenneth Galbraith once warned in *The Affluent Society* (1958) that economic theories designed around classic conditions of scarcity might ill-serve an age of abundance; however, it remained unclear by the 1990s whether economic thought or abundance itself had failed to sustain the American Dream. A decade of "Reaganomics"—recycled versions of supply-side policies first recommended to President Kennedy—had not produced desired levels of real growth or retired the national debt. If the collapse of worldwide communism yielded a "peace dividend" at home, it remained to be seen where and how to redeploy those resources. Confronting public debts in the trillions of dollars, burdened with consumer charges, frustrated by the cruel failure of antipoverty and welfare programs, staggered by health care inflation, frightened by a rising underclass at home and stiff competition from abroad (especially Japan), and bombarded by shrill voices of criticism at every gesture, Americans slipped into a blue mood as they contemplated the end the "American century."

Advice abounded from all perspectives. In *Workforce 2000,* published by the conservative Hudson Institute (1987), William B. Johnson and Arnold H. Packer predicted a steady deindustrialization of the economy, with a corresponding rise in service jobs, presistent unemployment for the unskilled and a graying and increasingly female work force. Productivity gains in service industries, they argued, were the key to future growth. For the liberal Brookings Institution, Robert Z. Lawrence asked *Can America Compete?* (1984). His answer was yet, because America was *not* deindustrializing. Reduce the federal deficit to correct trade imbalances, he argues, and growth would follow. W. Edwards Deming, in *Out of the Crisis* (1986), blamed the American management system for demoralizing workers, rewarding inept bureaucrats, and corrupting corporate executives. Where these and other prophets, armed with alternative histories and theories, would lead American business in the twenty-first century cannot yet be discerned. Our historical commitment to liberty and enterprise seemed likely to endure, yet in their affluence Americans remained not happy but insecure.

BIBLIOGRAPHY

General Works

Blackford, Mansel G., and K. Austin Kerr. *Business Enterprise in American History,* 2d ed. (1990).

Chandler, Alfred D., Jr. *The Visible Hand: The Managerial Revolution in American Business* (1977).

Hall, Kermit L. *The Magic Mirror: Law in American History* (1989).

Hounshell, David A. *From the American System to Mass Production, 1800–1932* (1984).

Hurst, James Willard. *Law and Markets in United States History: Different Modes of Bargaining Among Interests* (1982).

Laurie, Bruce. *Artisans into Workers: Labor in Nineteenth-Century America* (1989).

Scheiber, Harry N. "Federalism and the American Economic Order, 1789–1910." *Law and Society Review* 10 (1975): 57–118.

Business in 1800

Clark, Christopher. "Household Economy, Market Exchange and the Rise of Capitalism in the Connecticut Valley, 1800–1860." *Journal of Social History* 13 (1979): 169–189.

Doerflinger, Thomas M. *A Vigorous Spirit of Enterprise: Merchants and Economic Development in Revolutionary Philadelphia* (1986).

Jensen, Joan. *Loosening the Bonds: Mid-Atlantic Farm Women, 1750–1850* (1986).

Mitchell, Robert D. *Commercialism and Frontier: Perspectives on the Early Shenandoah Valley* (1977).

Tryon, Rolla M. *Household Manufactures in the United States, 1640–1860* (1917).

Ulrich, Laura Thatcher. *A Midwife's Tale: The Life of Martha Ballard, Based on Her Diary, 1785–1812* (1990).

Revolutionary Ideology

McCoy, Drew R. *The Elusive Republic: Political Economy in Jeffersonian America* (1980).

McDonald, Forrest. *Novus Ordo Seclorum: The Intellectual Origins of the Constitution* (1985).

Matson, Cathy D., and Peter S. Onuf. *A Union of Interests: Political and Economic Thought in Revolutionary America* (1990).

Nelson, John R., Jr. *Liberty and Property: Political Economy and Policymaking in the New Nation, 1789–1812* (1987).

Antebellum Business

Albion, Robert Greenhalgh. *The Rise of New York Port, 1815–1869* (1939; repr. 1961).

Blewett, Mary H. *Men, Women, and Work: Class, Gender, and Protest in the New England Shoe Industry, 1780–1910* (1988).

Clark, Christopher. *The Roots of Rural Capitalism: Western Massachusetts, 1780–1860* (1990).

Cochran, Thomas C. *Frontiers of Change: Early Industrialism in America* (1981).

Faragher, John Mack. *Sugar Creek: Life on the Illinois Prairie* (1986).

Hammond, Bray. *Banks and Politics in America, from the Revolution to the Civil War* (1957).

Handlin, Oscar, and Mary Flug Handlin. *Commonwealth: A Study of the Role of Government in the American Economy: Massachusetts, 1774–1861.*(Rev. ed. 1969).

Johnson, Paul E. *A Shopkeeper's Millennium: Society and Revivals in Rochester, New York, 1815–1837* (1978).

Scranton, Philip. *Proprietary Capitalism: The Textile Manufacture at Philadelphia, 1800–1885* (1983).

Stansell, Christine. *City of Women: Sex and Class in New York, 1789–1860* (1986).

Tucker, Barbara M. *Samuel Slater and the Origins of the American Textile Industry, 1790–1860* (1984).

Wilentz, Sean. *Chants Democratic: New York and the Rise of the American Working Class, 1788–1850* (1984).

Era of Big Business

Fine, Sidney. *Laissez-Faire and the General Welfare State* (1964).

Ginger, Ray. *The Age of Excess: The United States from 1877 to 1914.* 2d ed. (1975).

Kirkland, Edward C. *Dream and Thought in the Business Community, 1860–1900* (1956).

Lamoreaux, Naomi. *The Great Merger Movement in American Business, 1895–1904* (1985).

Larson, John Lauritz. *Bonds of Enterprise: John Murray Forbes and Western Development in America's Railway Age* (1984).

Livesay, Harold C. *Andrew Carnegie and the Rise of Big Business* (1975).

McCraw, Thomas K. *Prophets of Regulation* (1984).

Porter, Glenn. *The Rise of Big Business, 1860–1910* (1973).

Sklar, Martin J. *The Corporate Reconstruction of American Capitalism, 1890–1916* (1988).

Thomas, John L. *Alternative America: Henry George, Edward Bellamy, Henry Demarest Lloyd and the Adversary Tradition* (1983).

Twentieth Century

Barnet, Richard J., and Romand E. Müller. *Global Reach: The Power of the Multinational Corporations* (1974).

Berle, Adolph A., and Gardiner C. Means. *The Modern Corporation and Private Property* (1933; rev. ed., 1968).

Bernstein, Michael A. *The Great Depression: Delayed Recovery and Economic Change in America, 1929–1939* (1987).

Boesky, Ivan. *Merger Mania: Arbitrage, Wall Street's Best Kept Money-making Secret* (1985).

Chandler, Alfred D., Jr. *Strategy and Structure: Chapters in the History of the American Industrial Enterprise* (1962).

Collins, Robert M. *The Business Response to Keynes, 1929–1964* (1981).

Deming, W. Edwards. *Out of the Crisis* (1986).

Dengen, Robert A. *The American Monetary System: A Concise Survey of Its Evolution Since 1896* (1987).

Galbraith, John Kenneth. *The Affluent Society* (1958; rev. ed. 1984).

Harrington, Michael. *The Other America: Poverty in the United States* (1962; rev. ed. 1981).

Kindleberger, Charles P. *Multinational Excursions* (1984).

Rostow, Walt W. *The Stages of Economic Growth: A Non-Communist Manifesto* (1960; 2d ed. 1971).

Schwartz, John E. *America's Hidden Success: A Reassessment of Public Policy from Kennedy to Reagan* (1988).

Vernon, Raymond. *Sovereignty at Bay: The Multinational Spread of U.S. Enterprises* (1971).

SEE ALSO **The Rise and Consolidation of Bourgeois Culture; The Gilded Age, Populism, and the Era of Incorporation; Industrialization; Labor; Technology and Social Change; Wealth and Income Distribution.**

WEALTH AND INCOME DISTRIBUTION

Lee Soltow

SINCE THE COLONIAL period, observers of the American scene have commented on the distribution of wealth and income in this country.

In 1772, Benjamin Franklin contrasted the inequality of Europe with the "happy mediocrity" of the colonies:

Whoever has travelled through the various parts of Europe, and observed how small is the proportion of people in affluence or easy circumstances there, compared with those in poverty and misery; the few rich and haughty landlords, the multitude of poor, abject, rack-rented, tithe-paying tenants and half-paid and half-starved ragged laborers; and views here the happy mediocrity that so generally prevails throughout these States, where the cultivator works for himself and supports his family in decent plenty, will, methinks, see abundant reason to bless Divine Providence for the evident and great difference in our favor, and be convinced that no nation known to us enjoys a greater share of human felicity. (Benjamin Franklin, *The Works of Benjamin Franklin.* Edited and compiled by John Bigelow [1904], vol. 10, p. 398)

Foreign writers have generally tended to minimize differences, perhaps because they have met only certain types of individuals. Crèvecoeur observed in 1782:

Here . . . are no aristocratical families, no courts, no kings, no ecclesiastical dominion, no invisible power giving to a few a very visible one; no great manufacturers employing thousands, no great refinement of luxury. The rich and the poor are not so far removed from each other as they are in Europe. (Michel-Guillaume Jean de Crève-coeur, *Letters of an American Farmer* [1782], in *America in Perspective,* ed. edited by Henry Steele Commager [1947], p. 4)

Native-born writers with panaceas for the economy have been likely to exaggerate inequalities. In the early republic Langston Byllesby stated: "The tendency of the existing systems to an oppressive *Inequality of Wealth,* together with its unstable character and disorders arising therefrom, have fre-

quently undergone the discussion of able men" (*Observations on the Sources and Effects of Unequal Wealth* [1826; repr. 1961], p. 22).

A quarter-century later the financial reformer Edward Kellogg suggested:

Let those who doubt whether two and a half per cent of the population own one-half of the property of the nation, select in their own neighborhood, or in a village containing, say, four thousand inhabitants, the twenty most wealthy men, and see if the twenty are not worth as much as all the rest. (*Labor and Other Capital* [1849; repr. 1971], p. xix)

A contemporary of Kellogg's, Alexander Campbell, noted:

Labor has improved our farms, built our cities, constructed our ships, canals and railroads, erected our factories, furnaces and mills; all intellectual development and moral culture are likewise the result of labor, yet the greater portion of the American people toil day by day for a mere subsistence and are destitute of the time and means necessary for social and intellectual culture. Look where you will upon society, you will see those who build palatial residences living in hovels, those who manufacture the finest cloths are clothed in the coarsest fabrics, those who produce in abundance the most wholesome and delicate food are subsisting on the poorest diet, and all to a great extent destitute of the ordinary comforts and conveniences of life. While another class, few in number, and not physically, intellectually or morally better than the average of society, acquire the larger portion of the products of labor. All candid men will acknowledge that the wealth is not distributed in accordance with either the physical, mental or moral usefulness of those who obtain it. ("The True Greenback," in Edward Kellogg, *Labor and Other Capital* [1849; repr. 1971], pp. 6, 7)

Forty years later James Bryce found, "There are no struggles between privileged and unprivileged orders, not even that perpetual strife of rich and poor which is the oldest disease of civilized states" ("The Faults and Strengths of American Democracy"

[1888], in *America in Perspective,* ed. Henry Steele Commager [1947], p. 224).

Some may have been considering consumption; others, income; and yet others, wealth. Individuals tend to look for those consumer goods or services of high utility to themselves.

A century after Bryce, George D. Lundberg, editor of the *Journal of the American Medical Association,* emphasized the inequalities that exist in the availability of a strategic economic service in late-twentieth-century American society:

It is not a coincidence that the United States of America and the Republic of South Africa ... [are] the only two developed, industrialized countries that do not have a national health policy.... The problem is manifested in a higher percentage of people who are black and Hispanic being unemployed and thus having less employment-related health insurance ... [S]urely we in this rich and successful country can manage to provide basic medical care because it is the right thing to do, and the time has come. ("National Health Care Reform: An Aura of Inevitability Is upon Us," *Journal of the American Medical Association* 265, no. 19 [1991]: 2566, 2567)

Reading the range of opinion from Franklin to Lundberg, one might conclude—and people do perceive—that there is greater inequality in the United States today than there was two centuries ago, a completely erroneous conclusion, as the evidence presented here will show. The perception of equality or inequality never can be determined for all times, all places, and all people. The perception of the degree of inequality considered to be excessive is usually influenced by an individual's lifetime experience. Franklin considered Europe and America as they existed two centuries ago. Lundberg's statement concerns a world that has undergone vast economic and technological changes since Franklin's time, but even in today's world there exist substantial inequalities in standards of living. Nostalgia may lead us emotionally astray, in part, because life appeared to be simpler and less gadget-filled and because the differences between, say, one dollar and ten dollars and one hundred dollars seemed greater than in a period of higher nominal and real incomes.

Disconcerting as the variation of outlook in these quotations may be, they do suggest that a nation should be concerned with the variability in the pattern of the distribution of economic benefits—wealth (how much people have) and income (how much people receive within a given period of time)—among its people. Should economic goods be divided rather equally among families, or should the rich be rewarded with shares of value worth hundreds or thousands of times those of the poor? How much attention should be given to incentive rewards and how much to basic needs for all? Can middle classes be neglected by focusing narrowly on the conditions of the rich and the poor—only on the upper and lower tails of the skewed distributional curves of income and wealth?

The shares of total income received by the rich and the poor in any given year obviously are quite disparate in a capitalistic society and often surprisingly disparate in controlled-market societies. This means that analysts usually focus on the extent of change in these shares from year to year, from decade to decade, and even from century to century. Investigations must be quantitative in order to determine the shares of national wealth received by individuals and economic units within the economy. This entails using such statistical tools as Lorenz curve charts, Gini coefficients, the familiar bell-shaped normal curve, and skewed shapes, particularly the lognormal curves, for various income years. Unfortunately, studies of specific income characteristics of people often are known for only one year. Thus, knowledge of income and wealth inequality in the United States since its inception is often quite limited, and in no sense have we been able to develop a continuous image of the changes in distributions that have taken place.

COMPARISONS BETWEEN COUNTRIES

One way to judge inequality within a country is to compare how rich that nation is relative to others—an observation that goes back to Franklin. Decision makers in a poor nation may feel it cannot afford much inequality, whereas decision makers in a rich nation can allow disparity if they so choose because levels for the poor may be deemed adequate by world standards. World Bank estimates for 109 countries in 1990 show that the United States, with a population of 246 million, had a gross national product of $4.88 trillion; 109 countries (including the United States, and China and India, but excluding much of eastern Europe) with a population of 4.462 billion, had a gross national product of $15.86 trillion. That is, the United States had 5 percent of the population and 31 percent of the product, a share that has been at least that large since World War II. Indeed, per capita wealth among the free in the United States as early as 1798 may have been almost as large as in England and

Wales, at that time the world's leader. In comparison with other countries, then, the United States could always have allowed substantial inequality.

The World Bank's distribution for the United States is depicted by considering six shares presented in Table 1, four for the lowest four quintile ranges and two for the top decile ranges. Are these out of line relative to the other "high-income" economies in 1990? Probably not, as judged by shares of the top groups. Table 1 states that the top 10 percent of households in the United States had 25.0 percent of aggregate income, while in the leading twenty countries (column 2), the top 10 percent averaged 24.8 percent. It may be significant, however, that the share for the lowest 20 percent was 4.7 percent for the United States and 6.2 percent for the leading twenty countries. In this sense, the poor receive a smaller proportion of national income in our society.

The six shares given in Table 1 can be cumulated and plotted as a Lorenz curve (Figure 1). Note that the shares of the quintiles are cumulated: the first point represents the share of the lowest 20 percent, the second point the share of the lowest 40 percent, and so on. Toward the right side of the figure are points showing the share of the lowest 90 percent; for the United States, this point is 75 percent. Were there perfect equality, the lowest 90 percent would have 90 percent of income, and the Lorenz curve would appear as the diagonal line on the chart. The Gini coefficient of relative inequality is the area formed by the actual Lorenz curve and the diagonal line, divided by the area of the triangle (gray line) under the diagonal. (The triangle is the area formed by the diagonal, the base line at zero percent of income, and the vertical line at 100 percent of persons.) The coefficient is zero if all households have the same income, and unity (1.0) if one person has all the income, that is, the lower the Gini coefficient, the greater the equality of whatever is being measured. In the case of the United States, the Gini coefficient is 0.36.

The rather staggering inequality of product among the 4.46 billion people in all 109 countries is also estimated in Table 1 and depicted in Figure 1, considering that the six shares for known countries in four partitioned sectors (low-, middle-, upper-middle-, and high-income economies) are representative of all the 109 countries partitioned among those four sectors. The Lorenz curve of the world's income distribution shows an extreme sweep, with a shallow and then a steep slope. It encompasses a large area of inequality when compared with the diagonal line of equality, giving a Gini coefficient of almost .80.

We would like to have a Lorenz curve of income for the United States for every year since its inception, say, from 1789 or 1776, or even earlier. Ideally, we would like such a distribution for all other countries in the same period so we could see

TABLE 1 Percentage Share of Household Income, 1990, by Percentile Group of Households

	United States (1)	Average, 20 High-Income Countries (2)	Average, 6 Low-Income Countries (3)	Average, 41 Countries (4)	109 Countries (5)
Lowest 20 percent	4.7	6.2	7.6	6.2	0.7
Second quintile	11.0	12.0	11.4	11.1	1.4
Third quintile	17.4	17.4	15.3	15.9	2.5
Fourth quintile	25.0	23.9	21.1	22.5	7.6
Highest 20 percent	41.9	40.6	44.7	44.3	87.7
Highest 10 percent	25.0	24.8	30.3	28.8	68.1
Gini coefficient within country, average† within 109 countries	.362	.352	.332	.364	.795

Source: World Bank, *World Development Report 1990.* Tables 1 and 30.

*Among the 109 countries, percentile shares are stated for 6 or 36 low-income economies, 8 of 34 middle-income, 7 or 14 upper-middle-income, and 20 of 25 high-income economies. I have employed unweighted averages of known shares within each of the four sectors in determining the world Lorenz curve in column (5).

†The Gini coefficient for each country is unadjusted for continuity considerations, that is, each has been computed considering only the six stated shares.

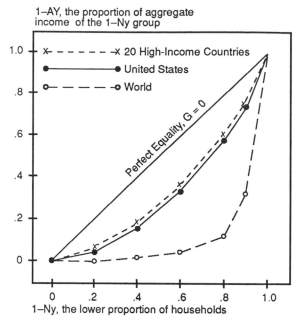

1–AY, the proportion of aggregate
income of the 1–Ny group

Figure 1. Lorenz curves of the distribution of household income in 1990 in the United States, 20 upper-income countries, and in the world (109 countries)

in what ways our concept of equality or inequality has emerged relative to that in other societies. Unfortunately, data are sparse, and little is known for various countries for years prior to World War II, except for a few select years in a few areas of the world. Annual income distributions for the United States, to be presented shortly, are not available until 1946 or 1947.

We would also like distributions not only for income but also for wealth in real estate, various forms of personal property, and the value of rights in other assets. It is not strange that records of the past often reveal more concerning asset values than concerning income because asset items were more likely to be either taxed or inherited (or both), and people generally had a better understanding of what they possessed at a given time than of what their earnings were in the form of an income stream over a period of time. In the following sections I will discuss consumption, wealth distribution, and income distribution, and I will offer some observations on health as a measure of equality.

CONSUMPTION: NECESSITIES AND LUXURIES

Significant distributions depict the degree of inequality for consumer items such as necessities

(food, clothing, and shelter), luxuries, and savings. In general there is greater equality of expenditures among persons and households for necessities such as salt, sugar, and potatoes, and less equality—almost by definition—for luxuries such as videocassette recorders, travel, or even medical expenditures and insurance. Statistics generally support the proposition that expenditures for food display the least inequality, followed by those for clothing. Shelter, measured by rental values, occupies a middle inequality position, between the categories of food and savings, with a Lorenz curve and Gini coefficient in the 1990s about the same as those for income (with a G for the United States of about .40). Both clothing and shelter are more significant in cold and severe climates.

Watches and Clocks The main difficulty in focusing on the distribution of any specific item historically is that what was likely to have begun as a luxury evolved into a necessity, or at least something much more commonly purchased. Consider a watch or a clock, an item possessed by only 10 percent of adult males in Connecticut in 1779. In the next generation, possession of timepieces increased sixfold (4.4 percent a year), while population in the state was increasing by only .70 percent a year. (The Gini coefficient of the distribution of timepieces among the state's inhabitants dropped precipitously from nearly .90.) The impetus was derived from Eli Terry (1772–1852) of Connecticut, who started mass-producing wooden clocks after 1792.

There are probably many examples in the United States of items that were initially luxuries but tended to evolve into necessities. Considering them in their totality, the nation has probably become more egalitarian in the long run, particularly in the twentieth century. Yet the economic evidence for this supposition for the years since 1789 is sparse. The arguments I present in the remainder of this article support, at best, a working hypothesis of decreased inequality.

Food Evidence suggests that levels of food consumption were probably comparatively high in the United States even by 1789, relative to consumption in Europe. Thus, inequality in the distribution of food expenditures was low and has changed little over the last two centuries. Admittedly, the evidence is somewhat tangential because it is based on the heights of all army recruits (not a sample of the population and not an indicator for women who did not serve) centered on the years 1812, 1864, and 1918, as well as on a sample of all adult males for 1976 to 1980. Some feel that food and nutritional standards do affect height at the median, mode, and first and other quartiles. At least the data are available and must be examined from the standpoint of changes in shares of aggregate height for various quartile ranges at different times.

Did short men (or recruits) lose in socioeconomic position relative to tall men (or recruits) in the three half-century periods delineated above? I find that relative inequality in stature figures—the Lorenz curves in these years—approximately duplicate each other at the fifty-year intervals. That is, there is no evidence of improvement or deterioration among lower or upper groups, which proves positively that nutrition and food consumption do affect height distributions. While there is evidence that taller recruits were more literate than those below median height in 1812, by the middle of the century this relationship no longer held, and there is some minimal evidence among some groups that the relationship was reversed.

Clothing In *Capital,* Karl Marx chose to highlight the plight of factory workers during the industrial revolution, a process he surely viewed as increasing degradation and inequality. Yet he chose not to explore the rising standards of consumption in clothing for middle and lower groups even as he cited tenfold increases in output of textiles in England.

I suspect that the shift in clothing production after 1825 from the home manufacturing to the factory very fundamentally altered the relative distribution of expenditures for clothing in America. The decrease in prices and the manifold increase in yardage production may have meant a decrease in inequality.

Data pertaining to clothing expenditures out of income in the period of home production are best illustrated with statistics for New York State, where state censuses of 1825, 1835, and 1845 clearly demonstrate that yardage manufactured at home declined in this period, as was true in England. The earliest data are shown in Table 2. The startling fact emerges that there was great inequality in this year, an era of relative self-sufficiency. Admittedly, production was not synonymous with consumption, and the latter would have shown less inequality. Yet a Gini coefficient of .50 or .40 is substantial, judged by present-day standards that can be determined from the 1990 inequality levels stated in Table 1.

Housing Dwellings often are considered to be the best expression of well-being of a country's population. The distribution of rental values, actual or implicit, often can serve as the best simple proxy

TABLE 2 Homewoven Yardage of Households in New York (1825)

Total Yards of Households, ✕	Number of Households
1,000 and over	1
500 – 999	2
200 – 499	56
100 – 199	257
50 – 99	493
20 – 49	479
10 – 19	143
1 – 9	41
0	303
	1,775

Gini coefficient	
✕ ≥ 0	.52
✕ > 0	.42

Source: Lee Soltow, "Inequalities in the Standard of Living in the United States, 1798 to 1875," Table 17.

for the distribution of income. Such proved to be the case in the 1980 census, in which both the income and the dwelling-value distributions were approximately lognormal in shape, with the same Lorenz curves and Gini coefficients, about .40. A student of family budgets in the early twentieth century and in the nineteenth century notes that about 10 percent of a household's expenditures consisted of rent and that rent was about 10 percent of house value; this general pattern appears to hold for both low- and middle-income groups, and often for high-income groups as well.

In general, what can be said about dwelling distributions in the past? Did the mansions that arose among a predominance of log cabins, shanties, and huts signal a land of relative equality or inequality compared with 1980 or 1990 as shown by Lorenz curves? Was American society as homogeneous as some guess it was, or were the mansions a sign of a great range in wealth and income? Fortunately, we have data from the first decade of the republic that can be compared with data from 1980. In 1798, a census of real estate in the United States was conducted as the basis of a graduated tax on the value of dwellings. This remarkable investigation produced one of the distributions shown in Table 3.

The frequency table forms an almost exact lognormal distribution, with great range and inequality. The mansion of highest value was built by Elias Hasket Derby (1739–1799) of Salem, Massachusetts; some of its furnishings are displayed in the fine arts museums of Boston and Philadelphia. What a con-

TABLE 3 Share of Housing Value (A_{HV}) of the Top Proportion of Dwellings (N_{HV}) in the United States in 1798 and 1980

N_{HV} Proportion of Dwelling (1)	1798		1980	
	A_{HV} Share of Housing Value (2)	$A_{HV\cdot5}$ Square Root Housing Values (3)	A_{HV} Share of Housing Value (4)	A Share of Income (5)
.01	.187	.056	.058	.050
.02	.272	.092	.087	.086
.05	.421	.183	.179	.170
.10	.565	.295	.286	.280
.20	.734	.465	.447	.452
.30	.831	.595	.575	.589
.40	.896	.701	.675	.701
.50	.939	.789	.758	.791
.60	.966	.855	.831	.865
.70	.981	.907	.898	.921
.80	.991	.948	.946	.961
.90	.997	.979	.982	.988
1.000	1.000	1.000	1.000	1.000
N	576,798	576,798	69,300,000	87,440,000
Mean value	$262	$12	$43,900	$19,900
Gini coefficient	.706	.416	.388	.417

Source: Lee Soltow, *Distribution of Wealth and Income in the United States in 1798*, p. 55.

Note: The top 2 percent of dwellings accounted for 27.2 percent of housing value in 1798 and 8.7 percent in 1980. The top 2 percent of families and unrelated individuals in 1980 had 8.6 percent of income, as shown in (5). Consider the square roots of housing values in 1798; the top 2 percent had 9.2 percent of the aggregate of these transformed values, as shown in (3).

trast between this edifice and the shanties worth but a few dollars at most, with dirt floors and perhaps only a hole in the roof to vent smoke from the fire!

The contrast between relative inequality then and now is displayed in Table 3. The Gini coefficient of the distribution of housing values drops from .70 in 1798 to almost .40 in 1980. Taking the square root of housing value in 1798 produces a distribution whose relative dispersion is similar to that of the distributions of housing values and income in 1980: a ratio of 100 to 1 in the difference between housing values of $10,000 and $100 in 1798 thus approximates a ratio of 10 to 1 involved in housing values of $500,000 and $50,000 in 1980. There has been a revolution in housing, a revolution transcending that in clothing or watches and clocks. The 90 percent of dwellings consisting of logs have been destroyed. People in the late twentieth century do not experience as great a relative difference in building materials. Few, for example, live in houses with dirt floors.

This brief survey concerning food (heights), clothing (yardage), and housing (dwelling values)

is but an initial statement of living conditions. One could investigate other indicators of consumption, drawing up a frequency table concerning, say, furniture values in 1814 or personal carriages (chariots, chaises, sulkies, etc.) in 1798 in order to buttress an argument that there was substantial inequality in the past. And one need not limit the argument to tangible economic goods. For example, adult males at specific ages were less likely to be married if they had no wealth, as revealed in the federal censuses of 1850 to 1870. The married poor in any specific age group had fewer children, on the average, than did married persons with wealth; and the children of the poor were less likely to attend school.

WEALTH

Possessions One of the most fundamental assets an individual could possess in the early nineteenth century was the ability to read and write. Literacy was achieved by less than half of adult males and by an even smaller proportion of females in the eighteenth century. Only after the significant surge in public schooling in the 1830s did the ability to read and write become more universally distributed, with a consequent drop in economic inequality. In general, one can construct an attribute model (a model that allows attributes — characteristics of a population — to be analyzed) using literacy, or a television set, or any particular good that a proportion of the population possesses in any given year. Before personal computers existed, no one owned one. When they first became available, a few people were able to buy one; later many people were able to buy one. Suppose the population possessing personal computers increases from 0 to .10, and .50, to .90 over a period of years. The coefficient of variation (the standard deviation divided by the mean and a measure of relative dispersion like the Gini coefficient) continuously decreases from infinity to almost 0; the Gini coefficient thus decreases from 1 to almost 0; only if there is deterioration in the attribute coverage would inequality increase. Examples of this might be the proportion of women receiving prenatal care or the proportion of persons owning land in an agricultural society.

The above attribute model obviously is inadequate if one considers quantities and values. The same proportion of people might own land, but a few great landowners might obtain increasing amounts of the best land while those formerly owning forty acres might be left with only ten. One individual could own thousands of books while another had only a Bible.

Distribution of Wealth Most people in the nineteenth century knew approximately what their wealth position was; indeed, those who were enumerated were asked this specific question for the census of real estate in 1798 and for the general censuses in 1850, 1860, and 1870. The crucial period between 1798 and 1850 leaves a data gap that can be filled in part by the distribution of 164,962 properties found in the Ohio "tax duplicate" of 1835. This strategic new state, settled by people from the older states to the east, had 17 percent of the country's population in 1840. The proportion of its population with real estate in 1835 was in line with that in the United States as a whole. These distributions provide a most valuable measure of the differences between economic classes at the five dates. They show that about 41 to 43 percent of adult free males (twenty years and older) owned land in the middle of the century, down somewhat from the 50 percent with real estate in 1798. Yet this drop generally might have been expected because

the country was shifting from an overwhelmingly rural economy to an economy undergoing the industrial revolution.

The five wealth distributions are analyzed in Figure 2 and in Table 4. They illustrate the important proposition that wealth inequality changed very little in the seventy-two-year span. Indeed, the estimates made by Alice Hanson Jones for the colonies in 1774 show inequality of similar magnitudes; her study was based on 919 estates of deceased persons. The five wealth sets shown in the table demonstrate the fact that the Lorenz curves of wealth distribution among those having wealth were similar, with Gini coefficients a little over .60; considering both those with and without wealth, the Gini coefficients were about .80 in all five years. The overall Gini coefficient (.80) equals the proportion with wealth (.50) times its Gini coefficient (.60) plus the proportion without wealth (.50) times a Gini coefficient of 1.0.

Let us add one data set for wealth in the twentieth century, the real estate proportion of wealth in 1983, in order to give historical perspective to the nineteenth-century data. Here there is evidence of a little softening in the degree of inequality, with an overall Gini coefficient equation of $.73 = .67 \times .59 + .33 \times 1$. A larger proportion of families and single individuals owned real estate, partly a result of the stimulus for home ownership derived from

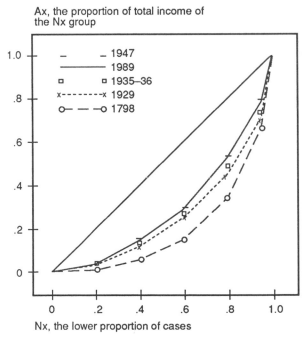

Figure 2. Lorenz curves of income distribution in the United States in selected years

TABLE 4 Summary Table of the Degree of Relative Inequality of the Distribution of Wealth in Real Estate Among Free Adult Males in the United States in 1798, 1835 (Ohio), 1850, 1860, 1870 (Whites), and 1983

	Wealth > 0			Wealth ≥ 0			Straight-line model		
	G*	Mean	Number (000)	G	Mean	Number (000)	b	R²	Number of Points†
Real estate									
1983 U.S.	.594	76,700	53,500	.727	51,340	79,800	1.61	.975	103
1870 whites, U.S.	.624	4,150	3,700	.833	1,850	8,300	1.79	.981	24
1860 free, U.S.	.649	3,500	3,000	.845	1,540	6,800	1.77	.995	31
1850 free, U.S.	.643	2,470	2,000	.848	1,046	4,800	1.83	.996	29
1835, Ohio	.637	530	139	.799	294	250	1.73	.993	32
1798 free, U.S.	.632	1,434	433	.818	708	878	1.78	.982	30
Income, dwelling-derived									
1860 free, U.S.				?			?		
1798 free, U.S.				.631	878		1.26	.996	26

*G is the Gini coefficient of relative inequality; b is the slope of the line on lognormal probability shown in Figure 2.

†Point below $5,000 in 1983 and, generally, below $200 in 1850–1870 are not considered here and in Figure 2.

Sources: 1983 data from G. Elliehausen, Federal Reserve Board; they are essentially for families and unrelated individuals. Remaining sources and details are from Lee Soltow, "Inequalities in the Standard of Living in the United States, 1798 to 1875," Table 1.

the income-tax deduction for mortgage interest. In addition, the greater income equality and the graduated income-tax rate structure in 1983 exerted influence. A prominent study by the Federal Reserve Board in 1962–1963 for the United States produced a distribution for *overall* wealth with a Gini coefficient of only .76; in 1870, the Gini coefficient was .83 for total wealth (real estate plus personal property). The Federal Reserve data for 1983 yield a Gini coefficient of .80 for total wealth.

Charts of wealth distributions in European countries at the beginning of the eighteenth century reveal greater inequality among wealth holders, particularly where royalty and aristocracy were present, than in the United States. For the early twentieth century, there exists an excellent wealth census comparison with Australia, a land without an aristocracy. This distribution shows amounts of wealth held by various groups and the absence of positive wealth among the bottom 20 percent of people. This 1915 census of Australia and its states demonstrates the same relative inequality that existed in the United States among the free in the 1850 to 1870 period.

The Poor and Destitute A fundamental weakness in the otherwise splendid wealth distributions we have for the United States is that they tell us *nothing* about the economic conditions of those without wealth: the propertyless, including the poor and the destitute.

Table 4 and Figure 2 further elaborate the estimate of income distribution in 1798 in an attempt to depict conditions among lower classes relative to classes above them by using housing data adjusted to known totals. The approximate straight line presented in Figure 2 indicates that income was lognormal in shape and that those in the lower 40, 20, and 10 percent of the income spectrum fell logically in order relative to those above them in terms of incomes ranked by size. There was an important quantitative principle at work at the time. The Gini coefficient of wealth distribution just among those possessing wealth was the same as that for income for all persons: .60; the Lorenz curves for these two sets were similar.

A further index of relative deprivation in America perhaps can be stated with housing figures from the census for Ontario in 1851. There, 12 percent of dwellings were classified as "shanties," as distinguished from those which were log, frame, brick, or stone. Studies for South Carolina farms with little acreage and value—the more marginal farms—reveals little; these farmers and part-time farmers usually did own a horse, a cow, and other farm animals. Studies in 1835 of Ohio townships and counties in which low proportions of the population possessed land revealed that fairly substantial numbers of children attended school.

The federal censuses of 1850–1870 include rough estimates of paupers in each state who re-

TABLE 5   Shares of Total Income Received by Top Groups in the United States, 1913–1948

Year	Top 1%	Top 5%	Year	Top 1%	Top 5%	Year	Top 1%	Top 5%
1913	15		1925	14	25	1937	13	24
1914	13		1926	14	25	1938	11	23
1915	14		1927	14	26	1939	12	23
1916	16		1928	15	27	1940	12	23
1917	14	25	1929	15	26	1941	11	22
1918	13	23	1930	14	26	1942	10	19
1919	13	23	1931	13	26	1943	9	18
1920	12	22	1932	13	27	1944	9	17
1921	14	25	1933	12	25	1945	9	17
1922	13	25	1934	12	25	1946	9	18
1923	12	23	1935	12	24	1947	8	17
1924	13	24	1936	13	24	1948	8	18

Note: Numbers have been rounded.

Source: U.S. Bureau of the Census, Historical Statistics of the United States, p. 302.

ceived support during the year (see Table 5). In spite of the large degree of measurement error that must exist in these figures, the number of those receiving support never exceeded 1 percent of the population. This is in contrast with the 5 percent of destitute households in Sweden; those needing help in 1850 or the 16 percent so classified in 1805. The United States proportion was far less than those on poor relief rolls in England and Wales, covered by poor laws, where the proportion was 7.5 percent in 1850 and 13.6 percent in 1803. Nevertheless, Herman Melville could observe in 1854:

The native American poor never lose their delicacy or pride; hence, though unreduced to the physical degradation of the European pauper, they yet suffer more in mind than the poor of any other people in the world. Those peculiar social sensibilities nourished by our own peculiar political principles, while they enhance the true dignity of a prosperous American, do but minister to the added wretchedness of the unfortunate. ("Poor Man's Pudding and Rich Man's Crumbs," Harper's New Monthly Magazine 9 [June 1854], p. 98)

Housing as an Indicator of Inequality   Since we have wealth distributions for only one-half of the people, at best, we seek any expression of a distribution that covers all the people in any year. New York State conducted a census of housing values from 1855 to 1875; values for 1875 have been tallied and can be compared with values in 1798 and in 1980. The most fundamental fact stems from all areas in the state, excluding New York and Kings counties: the lower 40 percent of housing values accounted for 7 percent of aggregate housing value in 1798, 8 percent in 1875, and 18 percent in 1980. (If there were perfect equality in housing values, 40

percent of housing values would account for 40 percent of aggregate value, meaning that this fundamental distribution essentially did *not* change during the industrial revolution.) There was a dramatic movement toward equality in the next hundred years, with the lower 40 percent attaining 18 percent of value, almost half the share (20 percent) it could attain under conditions of perfect equality. The overriding conclusion is that relative inequality did not change in the nineteenth century but decreased significantly by the late twentieth century.

These aggregate statistics are difficult to translate into the lives of people, and it is worthwhile to present extreme examples to make the point. Was Elias Hasket Derby's 1798 mansion a mirage? Probably not. Consider wards 10 and 13 in Buffalo in 1875, a rich ward and a poor ward. The former included a mansion costing five hundred thousand dollars, built between 1868 and 1870 by William Fargo, president of the American Express Company. The latter included a house worth fifty dollars, occupied by John Madigan, laborer, and his family. The ratio of the two values is 10,000 to 1, a most extreme ratio for a democracy such as the United States.

INCOME DISTRIBUTIONS

Little is known about income distribution in the nineteenth century, but there is reason to believe that inequality may have been quite large in 1798. My preferred estimate for that year is illus-

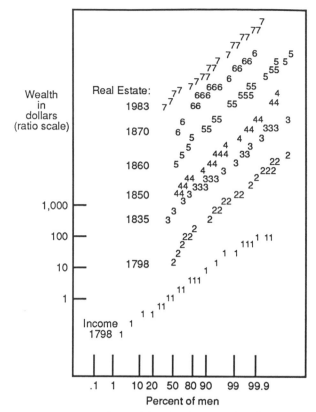

Figure 3. A tier chart of the distribution of real estate among adult free males in the United States in 1798, 1850, 1860 (Whites), 1870, 1983, and in Ohio in 1835 (a logonormal probablity chart)

trated as a Lorenz curve in Figure 3, and in Figure 2 it is demonstrated to be essentially lognormal in shape. This frequency curve for 1798 is based on the census of real estate dwellings in that year and shows substantial inequality, with a Gini coefficient of .60 or above, considerably more than for any other year to be discussed in this section. (For instance, the projected coefficient is .49 for the year 2000.) There was large regional variation in 1798 and an especially large variation between counties and townships. The standard of living, from this point of view, revealed extreme inequality, and the averages or aggregates shown in national accounts that are usually presented as depicting the economy at the time seem far removed from reality for most individuals.

Is the dwelling-derived estimate of income inequality in 1798 too large? I believe it is reasonable, considering the fact that the relative distribution of the sizes of families was substantial at the time, with a Gini coefficient of about .30. There was strong

variation in the average income for counties and smaller area units that stemmed in part from lower prices for farm products in the West. Adjustment for this area variation decreases the Gini coefficient from .60 to .55. Consider also that the economy at the time was dominated by seasonal movement in a rural setting subject to floods, drought, insects, fires, sickness, and the remainder of the disruptions due to war. There were great differences attributable to farm size, fertility, and terrain. The effects of inheritance on wealth holdings, dependent on past accumulation, were large. Traces of the influence of primogeniture persisted in several states. And slavery strengthened inequality of income among the free.

It is especially the lower income groups about which little is understood. The censuses of 1890 and 1900 show that 16 percent and 22 percent of the gainfully employed, respectively, experienced at least some unemployment. Considering all days lost in the year among the gainfully employed produces an annual rate of 4.0 percent for the civilian labor force in 1890. It climbed to 14 percent in 1895, then dropped to 5 percent in 1900. The unemployment rate remained relatively low until 1930 (except for 1921), then began to rise to a devastating annual rate of 25 percent in 1933.

Surveys of incomes of poor, middle, and affluent groups have been conducted annually in the United States in detail since 1946, and in lesser detail for 1929, 1935–1936, 1941, and 1944. Simon Kuznets developed estimates of the shares of the top 1 and 5 percent of the population from 1913. There is an unfortunate silence about income shares for the whole of the nineteenth century and earlier. An estimate of income distribution in 1798 will be presented that is based on the census of housing values in that year.

TABLE 6   The Gini Inequality Coefficient (G) for Money or Personal Income of Households in the United States, Selected Years

1988–1988	G	Year	G
1798	.60 (?)	1964	.40
1929	.48	1947	.40
1935–1936	.45	1970	.39
1947	.39	1989	.42

Sources: U.S. Bureau of the Census, *Historical Statistics of the United States,* pp. 293, 301; and *Money, Income, and Poverty Status . . . 1989.* Table 6; Lee Soltow, *Distribution of Wealth and Income in the United States in 1798,* p. 273 (3).

WEALTH AND INCOME DISTRIBUTION

TABLE 7   The Indigent in the United States, 1850–1870

Year	White population	Number supported	Proportion supported
1850	19,553,000	134,972	.007
1860	26,443,000	221,665	.008
1870	33,589,000	116,102	.003

Source: U.S. Bureau of the Census, Compendium of the Ninth Census, pp. 531–535.

Lorenz curves for income distributions and Gini coefficients stemming from these Lorenz curves are presented for selected years in Figure 3 and in Table 6. A larger Gini coefficient means a larger degree of relative inequality, with the actual Lorenz curve in general being farther removed from the line of equality. The onset of World War II brought a dramatic increase in employment levels, and materially boosted the relative income shares of the lowest income groups by the end of the war and the immediate postwar period. Inequality then remained remarkably low until about 1970. Since that time, inequality has risen some, and is predicted to rise more. The average income in the top quintile class has risen, especially relative to incomes in lower classes. We saw in Table 1, using some alternative data, that inequality in 1990 is a little high when compared with European countries.

One multiple-regression analysis for the years 1947 to 1985 shows that increases in the Gini coefficient are most significantly related to shifts in industry (from better-paying manufacturing employment to lower-paying service employment) as well as to recent increases in female employment among high-income families. Downward shifts in Gini coefficients have been related to strengthened Social Security payments and earlier increases in female employment among low-income families. One prognosis from this type of analysis leads to an increase of the Gini coefficient from .43 in 1985 to .49 in the year 2000, and this is without considering the significant cut in marginal income-tax rates in the late 1980s.

The Kuznets data (shares of total income of the top 1 and 5 percent) present some perspective on inequality earlier in the twentieth century (Table 7). These shares remained constant, to a certain extent, for the entire generation prior to World War II; they then dropped rather dramatically during the decade prior to the strong postwar recession in 1949.

HEALTH

There are other measures of change in equality than dollar values of consumption, wealth, and income. As the quotation from George D. Lundberg in the early part of this article suggests, health may be a significant alternative measure.

Sickness   Little or nothing is known about sickness rates in the United States in the nineteenth century or the early twentieth century. A most intriguing report presented in the *Compendium of the 1850 Census* records the proportion of sick persons among members of Friendly Societies in the United States from 1843 to 1852 who received payments as 16 percent; that is, sixteen of every one hundred received at least some assistance in any given year on the average. Unfortunately, age-specific rates are not given, so that this proportion may understate the incidence relative to England, where 23 percent of members (22 percent if ad-

TABLE 8   Distribution of the Number of Years Lived After Age 20, as Revealed in Period Life Tables for Males in the United States, 1900 and 1980

Age, selected years	Adult years lived	Of 100,000 at age 20, number dying in age year	
		1900	1980
20 – 20.99	.5	642	190
21 – 21.99	1.5	697	201
25 – 25.99	5.5	726	202
30 – 30.99	10.5	778	189
50 – 50.99	30.5	1,180	724
70 – 70.99	50.5	2,109	2,624
100 – 100.99	80.5	11	131

All ages 20 and up		1900	1980
Mean adult years lived		41.73	51.69
Gini coefficent		.245	.159

	Gini coefficent			
	20 and older		15 and older	
	Males	Females	Males	Females
1900	.245	.242	.235	.233
1920	.222	.225	.215	.216
1940	.184	.168	.174	.159
1960	.164	.134	.154	.126
1980	.159	.128	.151	.120
2000	.148	.123	.140	.115

Source: J. F. Faber and A. H. Wade, *Life Tables for the United States: 1900–2050.* Tables 3a–3k.

justed to 1851 census populations) received assistance in the years 1856 to 1860.

Life Expectancy A final measure of inequality is the number of years of adult life lived by a male from age twenty, as revealed in the life expectancy tables for the ten-year intervals from 1900 to 1980 and by projections to the year 2000. The fundamental thrust toward equality embodied in these figures is quite dramatic, and underlines the evolving concept that all human beings must be treated with dignity, respect, and ever-increasing equality.

The distribution presented in Table 8 shows the number of years lived in the United States in 1900, highlighting dispersion in life spans. The Gini coefficient for years lived drops dramatically, by 33 to 40 percent in the case of males, and by half in the case of females. The Lorenz curve for the distribution of the number of adult years lived by males moves ever closer to the line of equality. It has moved almost halfway toward the equality diagonal from 1900 to the projected year 2000 for males, and exactly halfway in the case of women.

CONCLUSION

The evidence reviewed in this article concerning who receives how much of society's resources has involved examining distributions of consumption (timepieces, food, clothing, and shelter), wealth (possessions and housing), income, and health. The evidence points to the fact that inequality changed very little in the late eighteenth century and throughout the nineteenth century, except for the dramatic events associated with the emancipation of the slaves.

There was a very significant shift toward equality in the twentieth century, particularly in the 1940s, that is, after the Great Depression in the 1930s. It is not tangential to economic forces at work that this movement encompassed the period of World War II, an effort demanding the direct services of one-third of the adult male labor force, one in which men from *all* economic classes offered their lives by serving in the armed forces.

There seems to be an ever-widening thrust toward greater equality, particularly for vast numbers of middle- and lower-income groups. These movements encompass Social Security, child care, medical care, women's rights, and the right to life itself. There have been, and will continue to be, countermovements toward the end of the twentieth century as emphasis is placed on free-market economies and on incentives for those in the top quintile of income and wealth. But the very long-run trend seems to indicate movement toward further equality.

BIBLIOGRAPHY

Technical Resources
Aitchison, J., and J. A. C. Brown. *The Lognormal Distribution* (1957).
Porter, Theodore M. *The Rise of Statistical Thinking, 1820–1900* (1986).
Sen, Amartya. "Poverty: An Ordinal Approach to Measurement." *Econometrica* 44, no. 2 (1976): 219–231.

General and Economic History
Bailyn, Bernard. *Voyagers to the West: A Passage in the Peopling of America on the Eve of Revolution* (1986).
Hufton, Olwen H. *The Poor of Eighteenth-Century France, 1750–1789* (1974).
Jones, Alice Hanson. *Wealth of a Nation to Be: The American Colonies on the Eve of the Revolution* (1980).
Lis, Catharina. *Social Change and the Labouring Poor: Antwerp, 1770–1860* (1986).
Main, Jackson Turner. *Society and Economy in Colonial Connecticut* (1985).

Martin, Edgar W. *The Standard of Living in 1860: American Consumption Levels on the Eve of the Civil War* (1942).

Marx, Karl. *Capital: A Critique of Political Economy.* Translated by Ben Fowkes (1887; repr. 1977).

Nash, Gary B. *The Urban Crucible: Social Change, Political Consciousness, and the Origins of the American Revolution* (1979).

Riley, James C. *Sickness, Recovery, and Death* (1989).

Smith, Billy G. *The "Lower Sort": Philadelphia's Laboring People, 1750–1800* (1990).

Soltow, Lee, and Edward Stevens. *The Rise of Literacy and the Common School in the United States: A Socioeconomic Analysis to 1870* (1981).

Tocqueville, Alexis de. *Democracy in America* (1966). The Henry Reeve text.

Treatises on Equality

Brown, Henry Phelps. *Egalitarianism and the Generation of Inequality* (1988).

Fogel, Robert William. "Nutrition and the Decline in Mortality Since 1700: Some Preliminary Findings." In *Long-Term Factors in American Economic Growth,* edited by Stanley L. Engerman and Robert E. Gallman, National Bureau of Economic Research Studies in Income and Wealth, 51 (1986).

Jouvenal, Bertrand de. *The Ethics of Redistribution* (1952; repr. 1990).

Maxwell, Nan L. *Income Inequality in the United States, 1947–1985* (1990).

Williamson, Jeffrey G., and Peter H. Lindert. *American Inequality: A Macroeconomic History* (1980).

Data Sources

Canada. *Appendix to Census of Canada, Upper Canada* (1851–1852). National Archives of Canada, Microfilm C11712 to C11762.

Davenport, Charles B., and Albert G. Love. *Statistics: Army Anthropology,* vol. 15, pt. 1 (1921).

David, Paul A., and Peter Solar. "A Bicentenary Contribution to the History of the Cost of Living in America." In *Research in Economic History,* edited by Paul Uselding, vol. 2 (1977).

Faber, J. F., and A. H. Wade. *Life Tables for the United States: 1900–2050,* U.S. Department of Health and Human Services, Social Security Administration, Actuarial Study no. 87 (1982).

Gould, Benjamin Apthorp. *Investigations in the Military and Anthropological Statistics of American Soldiers* (1979). Reprint of U.S. Sanitary Commission, *Memoirs of the War of the Rebellion,* vol. 2 (1869).

Kidwell, Claudia B., and Margaret C. Christman. *Suiting Everyone: The Democratization of Clothing in America* (1974).

Knibbs, George Handley. *The Private Wealth of Australia and Its Growth as Ascertained by Various Methods, Together with a Report of the War Census of 1915* (1918).

U.S. Bureau of the Census. *Compendium of the 1850 Census* (1854). Seventh census.

———. *Compendium of the Ninth Census* (1872). 1870 census.

———. *Historical Statistics of the United States, Colonial Times to 1970, Part 1* (1975).

————. Money, Income and Poverty Status in the United States, 1989. Current Population Reports, Series P-60, no. 168 (1990).

World Bank. *World Development Report 1990* (1990).

Historical Studies

Komlos, John. "The Height and Weight of West Point Cadets: Dietary Change in Antebellum America." *Journal of Economic History* 47 (1987): 897–927.

Kuznets, Simon. *Shares of Upper Income Groups in Income and Savings,* National Bureau of Economic Research Publications no. 55 (1953).

Lampman, Robert J. *The Share of Top Wealth-Holders in National Wealth, 1922–1956,* National Bureau of Economic Research Publications no. 74 (1962).

Lemon, J., and G. Nash. "The Distribution of Wealth in Eighteenth-Century America: A Century of Change in Chester County, Pennsylvania, 1693–1802." *Journal of Social History* 2, no. 2 (1968): 1–24.

Lis, Catharina, and Hugo Soly. *Poverty and Capitalism in Pre-Industrial Europe* (1979).

Main, Gloria L. "Probate Records as a Source for Early American History." *William and Mary Quarterly* 3d ser., 32, no. 1 (1975): 89–99.

————. *Tobacco Colony: Life in Early Maryland, 1650–1720* (1982).

Main, Jackson Turner. "The Distribution of Property in Post-Revolutionary Virginia." *Mississippi Valley Historical Review* 41, no. 2 (1954–1955): 241–258.

Menard, Russell R., P. M. G. Harris, and Lois Green Carr. "Opportunity and Inequality: The Distribution of Wealth on the Lower Western Shore of Maryland, 1638–1705." *Maryland Historical Magazine* 69, no. 2 (1974): 169–184.

Margo, Robert A., and Richard H. Steckel. "Heights of Native-Born Whites During the Antebellum Period." *Journal of Economic History* 43 (1983): 167–174.

Nash, Gary B. "Urban Wealth and Poverty in Pre-Revolutionary America." *Journal of Interdisciplinary History* 6, no. 4 (1975–1976): 545–584.

Pope, Clayne L. "Households on the American Frontier: The Distribution of Income and Wealth in Utah, 1850–1900." In *Markets in History,* edited by David W. Galenson (1989).

Soltow, Lee. "The Censuses of Wealth of Men in Australia in 1915 and in the United States in 1860 and 1870." *Australian Economic History Review* 12, no. 2 (1972): 125–141.

————. *Men and Wealth in the United States, 1850–1870* (1975).

————. "Distribution of Income and Wealth." In *Encyclopedia of American Economic History,* edited by Glenn Porter (1980). This article includes an extensive bibliography.

————. "Watches and Clocks in Connecticut, 1800: A Symbol of Socioeconomic Status." *Connecticut Historical Society Bulletin* 45, no. 4 (1980): 115–122.

————. "The Distribution of Income in the United States in 1798: Estimates Based on the Federal Housing Inventory." *Review of Economics and Statistics,* 69, no. 1 (1987): 181–185.

————. *Distribution of Wealth and Income in the United States in 1798* (1989).

————. "The Rich and the Destitute in Sweden, 1805–1855: A Test of Tocqueville's Inequality Hypotheses." *Economic History Review* 2d ser., 1, no. 42 (1989): 43–63.

————. "Inequalities in the Standard of Living in the United States, 1798 to 1875." Forthcoming in National Bureau of Economic Research series, *Amer-*

ican Economic Growth and the Standard of Living Before the Civil War, edited by Robert Gallman and John Wallis (1992).

Steckel, Richard H. "Height and Per Capita Income." *Historical Methods* 16, no. 1 (1983): 1–7.

Yule, George U. "Notes on the History of Pauperism in England and Wales from 1850, Treated by the Method of Frequency Curves." *Journal of the Royal Statistical Society* (June 1896).

SEE ALSO **The Aristocracy of Inherited Wealth; The Culture of Consumption; The U.S. as Interpreted by Foreign Observers.**

THE ARISTOCRACY OF INHERITED WEALTH

Ronald Story

WHILE SEVENTEENTH-CENTURY Virginia and Maryland have sometimes seemed the antithesis of Puritan New England, the availability of productive land and the rise of a strong European tobacco market initially produced significant equality of circumstance and opportunity in the Chesapeake area, similar to that in New England. This was partly because many people vital to the colonies—royal administrators, London creditors, and shippers—lived in England, not America; partly because Chesapeake life in this age of primitive accumulation was so grim that large landholders often worked as hard and lived as sparsely as those of lower economic status, mostly because a planter working alone could profitably produce a thousand pounds of tobacco from three acres of land. Those who could buy large acreage and indentured servants predominated, to be sure. In the mid seventeenth century the median wealth of the top fifth of the white Chesapeake population was forty times that of the bottom fifth, and many in the top fifth came from English gentry or merchant families. But a factor of forty between top and bottom is actually low for the modern world, and most landholders were not well born. Similarly, although officeholding, despite a rudimentary system of representation, was the monopoly of the propertied, one-third of new mid-seventeenth-century officeholders were either illiterate or former indentured servants, and a truculent factionalism inhibited the evolution of these and other politicians into a cohesive ruling elite.

Several factors increased the living standards of the rich and the distance between rich and poor in the late seventeenth and early eighteenth centuries. One was the acquisition of large tracts of land beyond the tidewater; another was chronically low tobacco prices, which rewarded economies of scale. Most important was the introduction of African slaves. Slaves were more permanent and productive farm laborers than indentured servants—meaning that slave ownership would bring a decisive competitive advantage, especially in clearing and working the large tracts. And slaves cost more—meaning that ownership was likely to be concentrated among the better-off. By the early eighteenth century, wealthy planters owned two-thirds of all Chesapeake slaves, thus putting real distance between themselves and those below, who now possessed property worth less than a hundredth of the property of the top fifth. With significant wealth in land and slaves, moreover, came easily transmissible estates and hence a hereditary planter elite capable of consolidating itself through intermarriage and political alliances and of establishing an upper-class standard of living centering on the country estate, the county seat, and the colonial assembly. As the eighteenth century progressed, holdings in land and slaves brought access to English credit and cultural amenities and preferment for imperial appointments and naval contracts, all reinforcing the system of hereditary privilege wrought ultimately by slavery.

Puritan New England sought to combat the materialism and economic conflict of the seventeenth century by constructing "Christian commonwealths" centering on church life and such humble occupations as subsistence farming and traditional crafts. Initial land distributions were remarkably even, and colony officials frequently imposed either wage or price controls to prevent sudden accumulations from conditions of scarcity or glut. For this reason and also because New England provided few ways to amass wealth compared with England or the early Chesapeake, and therefore attracted fewer people determined to gain wealth at any cost, the distance between rich and poor was generally smaller during the first two generations of settlement—on the order of five to one—than for any other private property system of the modern era. Both the church and the town polity were broadly participatory, moreover, and most land-owners could expect to hold at least local office at one time or another.

A five-to-one ratio is not equality, however. A more or less permanent "standing order" of ministers and better-off landholders existed from the start; they were gradually joined by thriving coastal merchants. Initially, religious fervor assured ministers predominance of place in this elite. But ministers could neither bequeath their pulpits nor prevent the diversity and secularism that weakened the role of the church. They therefore relinquished their place to the merchants, who benefited from colonial growth and could bequeath their wealth easily and in highly flexible form. During the eighteenth century this mercantile ascendance intensified as a result of expanding opportunities for imperial trade and preferment, a seaboard population boom that multiplied urban land values, and strategic marital alliances that preserved capital and connections. Except in its rarefied imperial reaches, commerce remained easier to enter than plantation agriculture, particularly for prosperous craftsmen and others familiar with trade. Nevertheless, in the commercial towns the proportion of wealth owned by the top tenth of the population rose steadily from 40 percent in the late seventeenth century to over 50 percent in the 1770s; the wealth of the top 5 percent—the imperial mercantile establishment—rose from 25 percent to 40 percent. Ministers capitalized on their status to become in-laws to and spokesmen for the merchants, intertwining with them socially but losing autonomy. Farmers, scattered and isolated save for a few big timber suppliers, remained a part of the standing order only by virtue of the votes they still mustered in the colonial assemblies, which continued to draw members from a broader socioeconomic net than in Maryland and Virginia.

The largest middle colonies followed divergent paths. In New York the Dutch and later the first English governors bestowed vast Hudson River estates on favored families. During the eighteenth century, tenants gradually occupied this land on long leases. Some used the profits from fur trapping and wheat production to purchase their farms outright. Most, however, remained tenants, leaving to their landlords not only the profit from milling and marketing the grain but also the capital gains and rents from owning the land. Landowners therefore remained an important element of the New York elite in a way that New England landowners did not. But neither was this the Chesapeake. The Hudson River funneled all production through the harbor of New York City, which became a notable shipping town and, eventually, a major port of settler debarkation. As the city grew, so did its merchant community, which cemented its position through intermarriage and joint investments with the great landowners. While New York's elite included Huguenots and Dutch Reformed families, the Anglican attachment was very strong, as was the connection to England and English institutions generally. Perhaps reflecting the manorial tradition, wealthy New Yorkers owned more African slaves than did other northern elites.

Pennsylvania, too, had a manorial presence—the Penn family not only owned the colony initially but also retained ownership of all undistributed land throughout the colonial era. Most grants went outright to actual settlers, however, so that eighteenth-century Pennsylvania, blessedly fertile, consisted chiefly of freehold family farms producing grain and other commodities for Atlantic markets rather than great holdings on the New York pattern; as late as 1760 the upper tenth of wealthy farmers and middlemen controlled just 30 percent of rural wealth. The only significant Pennsylvania elite was therefore in Philadelphia, where an aggressive merchant community made itself the chief colonial carrier and merchandiser of the British empire. This merchant elite had two wings. The smaller was Anglican in the New York fashion, with strong attachments to England (from which it drew credit) and extensive involvement in politics (from which it gained contracts and protection). The larger was, like the Penns, Quaker. Apolitical by creed, self-reliant by choice, Quaker merchants relied heavily on the transatlantic Friends network for commercial contacts and credit, and on the social life of the Quaker meetings to shape the marriages of their children in ways that consolidated wealth. By 1770 some 150 Quaker and Anglican merchants controlled 70 percent of Philadelphia's trade, while the top tenth of the population, with interests in shipbuilding, distilling, and real estate as well as commerce, owned 65 percent of the city's wealth.

THE FEDERAL AND NATIONAL PERIODS

The withdrawal of British authority affected elite formation in several ways. Most immediately, it shook the pro-British Tory establishment that most relied on imperial connections and protection, and opened the way, particularly in the North, to men eager to raid British shipping, supply the Continental Army, open nonimperial markets, and develop alternative commodities. Many prominent Boston, New York, and Philadelphia families trace their "arrival" to this crucial period. Second, since the conflict with Britain disrupted British financing, there was both a need and an opportunity to develop domestic sources of credit. Alexander Hamilton's promotion of a national bank and a national debt were responses to this need, but more serviceable were the elite-sponsored, state-chartered banking and property insurance corporations that arose in every region, together with a swarm of savings banks, life insurance companies, investment banking firms, and stock markets, all working to convert accumulated funds into venture capital. Third, independence focused attention on the North American continent as well as on the Atlantic Ocean. This led on the one hand to efforts, eventually successful, to erect protective tariffs against manufactured goods, and on the other to the creation, chiefly by federal and state governments at the instigation of the northern elite, of a rudimentary wagon and water transportation system reaching not only from state to state but also far into the trans-Appalachian West.

Historians once assumed that the development of economic infrastructure within the context of territorial expansion and democratic government must have produced a churning and leveling that shattered the seaboard elites. This appears not to have happened. While certain southerners, especially in Virginia, dissipated their fortunes by clinging to public service and worn-out land, most wealthy planters benefited from westward expansion by, if they were mobile, purchasing and clearing the richest Gulf cotton lands or, if they were not mobile, selling slaves to those who were. As cotton and slave prices rose, so did the wealth of the old planters as well as of the new ones. In 1860 the top 10 percent of white families owned half of the South's property and two-thirds of its slaves, and possessed, as it had a century earlier, more than a hundred times as much property as the bottom 40 percent.

Northern elites, too, adapted well. The landed wing of elite New York State was badly damaged by the British departure. The commercial wing did better, in part because New York City's strategic location, enhanced by the opening of the Erie Canal in 1825, enabled merchants to remain merchants. Commercial profits accumulated so rapidly that by mid century New York was a major financial center as well, providing capital for the expansion of the cotton kingdom and the early canal and railroad system. Merchant capital from Boston flowed into textiles, railroads, and insurance; profit from these ventures then flowed into rudimentary trust companies and cultural institutions designed to combine and preserve family fortunes. Philadelphians invested in coal, iron, chemicals, and machine-tool production as well as banking and railroads. In all locales there was a shift in professional careers from the ministry to medicine and especially to law, a crucial new adjunct to success in a nation of "laws, not men." Partly for these reasons, the maldistribution of northern wealth increased steadily, particularly in urban areas. In the seaboard cities a tenth of the population owned three-fourths of all property by 1860; the top 1 percent owned nearly half.

Despite these patterns, prior to the Civil War the various regional elites did not resolve themselves into a Hamiltonian national upper class, able to reap the benefits of continental hegemony while remaining insulated from democratic control. There were two principal reasons for this. First and more important, the issue of slave labor versus free labor opened a vast chasm between the southern elite, whose prosperity rested on huge investments in forced agricultural labor, and their northern counterparts, who prospered by investing in labor-saving industrial machinery. National financial and cultural institutions of genuine power might have bridged this division for a while. In the event, the Civil War destroyed the basis of the division by destroying the slave wealth and political power of the great planters, and therefore their relevance to the process of national elite formation.

Besides this fundamental regional schism, the older seaboard elites, while they persisted well enough, found it difficult to absorb and control the decentralizing forces thrown up by the new order—the railroad boomers and commodity traders of the West, the lawyers and politicians spawned by electoral politics, particularly in the cities and the Midwest; and the swarming parvenu manufacturers and retailers of the early industrial era. Fewer wealthy Americans were self-made than was once thought, but they were more numerous than ever before. In the upper Mississippi Valley, where these trends converged during the 1850s, property ownership tended to be egalitarian, politics middle-class, loyalties fragmented. Fortunately for the easterners—like Stephen Douglas and Long John Wentworth—midwestern politicians were promoters, not redistributionists, and midwestern businessmen—like Cyrus McCormick and Charles Ogden—though autonomous, generally emulated and cooperated with eastern institutions instead of assailing them. Northern politics and manners acquired a decidedly western hue; northern economic and cultural life, somewhat less so.

AFTER THE CIVIL WAR

The next major phase of elite development coincided with the emergence between 1870 and 1930 of a mature industrial economy built around transcontinental railroads and urban transit systems, large-scale extractive industries and electric-power generation, and mass-produced, mass-distributed industrial and consumer goods and services from steel to telegrams to newspapers to automobiles. Industrialization produced a very high rate of economic growth and therefore both higher average family income and more opportunities for new business activity, especially in the industrial heartland. Yet the key to this new industrial order proved to be its immense physical and organizational scale—physical because the bigger the factories and rail systems, the more productive they were; organizational because such vast enterprises necessitated both huge capitalization and complex managerial controls. As it turned out, the readiest tool for capitalizing and controlling such ventures was the giant corporation, a form of business organization that also facilitated the consolidation of firms vertically, in order to control materials, and horizontally, in order to control markets. And whereas industrialization per se brought income and opportunity to many Americans, the industrial corporation brought a more extreme concentration of ownership, even after antitrust legislation broke up some monopolies, than had existed in American business since the mid eighteenth century. The same is true of family wealth. The tenth of the population that had owned over half of everything in 1860 owned 65 percent by the early twentieth century, and drew a third of the national income as well. At the apex, just 1 percent of American families owned two-fifths of America's wealth, including all its federal bonds; 70 percent of its corporate stock; and an astonishing one-fifth of its real estate. The distance between the top and bottom of society, once a serviceable comparative measure, was now all but infinite.

There were significant centrifugal forces within this corporate elite. Many new industries not only were located outside the East but also were run by aggressive, contentious men whose loyalties ran as much to locale and industry as to big business generally. Chicago meat packing is one example; Detroit automobiles, Minneapolis flour milling, and Ohio rubber are others. In contrast with earlier periods, moreover, some leading capitalists were Catholic—like Thomas Fortune Ryan and William Grace—rather than Protestant, or Jewish—like James Loeb and Felix Warburg—rather than Christian. There was no fissure comparable with the slavery-nonslavery division because the basic patterns of investment and accumulation were everywhere the same. But the captains of industry controlled powerful, almost feudal, enterprises. Subsurface tensions over corporate behavior or political attitudes could therefore become debilitating rifts between regions or individuals or, more likely, industrial combinations, as eventually happened in Germany.

Developments in three areas of elite life—society, finance, and culture—pushed the new order in the direction of a national business class rather than of warring industrial fiefdoms. Of these, society was perhaps the most noticeable if the least significant. A striking feature of this industrial elite was its unprecedented conspicuous consumption: bejeweled attire, palatial residences, travel by private train or fleets of luxury automobiles, culture (art collections and opera houses), and sport (yachting, polo, and golf). The object of such expenditure, besides coarse pleasure and the mimicry of Europe, was to demonstrate success in accumulation and social standing. Every newspaper had its society columnist, every community its society leader, every city its *Social Register* of those who had "made it." The charity ball, a spectacular example of carefully chronicled conspicuous display, became the main social event of the year, followed closely by the debutante ball signaling the marriage availability of upper-class daughters. High society thus organized had divisive features because it rested in part on envy and exclusion. But by inducing new money to emulate and chase old money, it united as well. It also united because New York, with more millionaires than elsewhere and more nouveaux riches, captured society's center stage, thus setting trends that other elites, particularly in the Midwest, soon imitated.

In finance the chief figures were the investment bankers, most notably J. P. Morgan, who grew concerned about "cutthroat competition" that might bring industrial collapse and speculative excesses that might shatter credit. Morgan's solution to the problem of competition was to create European-style cartels either by forming quasi monopolies, as with the steel industry in 1900, or by influencing firms through financial leverage and interlocking directorates, as occurred by 1915 with over a hundred giant corporations, including American Telephone, Westinghouse, and Standard Oil as well as several rail systems and big commercial banks. His solution to the problem of speculation was to demand sound practices from the companies he dealt with and to conduct himself with visible integrity and restraint. Other combinations arose to challenge the Morgan interests, and the founding of the Federal Reserve System in 1913 partly undercut the influence of investment banking. Finance capitalism was in any case not adequate to handle the enormous imbalances that led finally to the Great Depression. But Morgan and the financiers who followed his lead in the proper uses of capital did induce greater cooperation among industrialists. Since Morgan's home, New York, was the nation's chief financial center, this, too, worked to pull the business system back into an eastern orbit.

Society and finance had more short-term than long-term impact. The reverse was true of culture. A kind of cultural curriculum emerged at the turn of the century consisting of the experience to be gained by passing through a constellation of exclusive institutions. The Episcopal church, which became the denomination of choice for successful people (including some erstwhile Catholics and Jews) was a part of this curriculum, as were resorts such as Newport, Rhode Island, and Bar Harbor, Maine. So were the right schools (chiefly a cluster of New England boarding schools with a half-dozen Episcopal schools at their core), the right colleges (chiefly the Ivy League institutions centering on Harvard, Yale, and Princeton), and the right clubs (chiefly downtown establishments with yacht and country clubs at the periphery). The curriculum provided a means of absorbing wealthy parvenus and their children into elite ranks, and of providing elite youth generally with a body of common knowledge, some useful career training, proper role models, and, it was hoped, suitable marriage partners, badges of affiliation, and business contacts. Elite Boston, though still economically robust, contributed to upper-class formation principally through the New England elements of the curriculum.

The new class had three other features of note. First, in politics the class operated largely as a Republican party patriciate, occasionally holding office but more commonly influencing politicians through co-optation, party organizations through campaign contributions, and governments by filling top judicial and administrative posts. Second, in occupational terms the sheer size of the great industrial firms meant that management was a more important career alternative than in the nineteenth century. While in theory this rewarded ability instead of wealth, and thus diminished the ability of the rich to guarantee positions (instead of mere money) to their children, in practice managers of this era came chiefly from those with connections to capital or with the right college credentials, thus enhancing the career prospects of elite children. The Forbses of Boston, the Welds of Boston and New York, and the Aldriches of New York and Providence exemplify this change. Third, the class was intensely tribal, particularly in the East—wholly exclusionary as to race, partially exclusionary as to religion and gender. Jews, though prominent in business and the elite colleges, were not admitted to key schools, clubs, and resorts or to certain industries, including commercial banking and oil. Upper-class women could spend and marry money but not make it. Jews developed Jewish schools, resorts, and clubs in part because they were excluded from those of the Christian upper class. Women developed women's schools, colleges, and social organizations because the upper class was male dominated, if not misogynist.

THE TWENTIETH CENTURY

In the late twentieth century, the elite evolved in new directions. Within the corporate economy, the new prominence of petrochemicals, aerospace industries, electronics, and consumer services, much of it driven by an enlarged federal government, shifted economic initiative from older industrial areas to the Sunbelt regions of Florida, California, and the Southwest, producing large numbers of new elite families, including some Asian Americans, as well as arriviste corporate managers, many of them from state universities or provincial versions of the upper-class cultural curriculum. Partially offsetting these trends was a long wave of mergers, conglomerations, takeovers, and buy-outs that, in the manner of a century earlier, further concentrated corporate ownership and control and also increased the influence of the New York investment bankers who financed the deals and the Washington regulators who favored them. But since many of the investment bankers and regulators were themselves new men, many of them from Irish, Italian, and Jewish backgrounds, it is not clear that the eastern establishment reasserted its authority in quite the earlier fashion. Nationwide, a third of the five hundred richest families of the 1980s did not inherit substantial wealth, while two-thirds of top corporate managers were of middle-class origins. Upper white-collar professional and managerial families in Boston and Philadelphia may have skidded into lower socioeconomic categories more than they had a hundred years earlier; many leading lawyers, managers, and financiers in these cities were in fact transplants from the Midwest.

On the other hand, the combination of new trust devices to preserve family fortunes and the effective working of the cultural curriculum meant that most members of the national upper white-collar class persisted across generations. Moreover, 80 percent of the one hundred richest families inherited great wealth, while 70 percent of key individuals holding four or more corporate directorships and 60 percent of the directors of major banks were members of the upper class. A chief distinguishing feature of the contemporary upper class, besides its modest ethnic and religious diversity, may be that it includes more top corporate executives (most of them large company stockholders) than at the turn of the century. It seems also, as befits a government-driven bicoastal-Sunbelt economy, to be less local and more national in orientation. In 1976 local *Social Registers* were consolidated into a single national volume. "Society" itself, based initially on exclusivity and formality, is now celebrity oriented, attaching itself to a remarkable degree to personalities from sports, the arts, and especially television. The handful of upper-class African American families have come predominantly from these areas, especially television, as have a few of the small number of autonomous corporate women.

The rise of television, a politically effective but enormously expensive medium, has meant that those with money are more dominant, particularly in national elections, than they were even during the patrician era at the turn of the century. Partly for this reason, federal policy since the 1970s has favored the corporate rich in numerous ways: regressive taxation, decreased corporate regulation, high military spending, large-scale, high-interest deficit financing. By the end of the 1980s, income and wealth had reached their highest concentration ever. The top 10 percent of the population, which had owned 60 percent of all wealth in 1860 and 65 percent in 1910, now owned 70 percent; the top 1 percent owned 45 percent of total wealth. There were now 1,300,000 American millionaires; there were 50 billionaires. The 400,000 wealthiest households owned 27 percent of net American worth; the 500 richest families owned 170 billion dollars of net business worth and thus controlled 40 percent of all nonresidential private capital. Income from rents, dividends, and interest surpassed income from wages and salaries for the first time, with the result that the top 20 percent of the population—the broad managerial and professional elite—made 45 percent of all after-tax American income, or 50 percent if capital gains are included. The top 1 percent—the corporate upper class—made 11 percent of all after-tax income, or 15 percent including capital gains.

A final notable development is the internationalization of wealth in the late twentieth century. American corporations have greatly increased their investment abroad, so that overseas operations now contribute substantially and disproportionately to overall corporate earnings. American branch managers abroad are often members of the host country's elite if they reside there long enough. Yet the U.S. share of world output has fallen almost to its pre-1914 level of 25 percent, while its total national assets have fallen behind Japan's by a sizable amount. Foreign, especially English and Japanese, companies have invested heavily in the United States and have purchased government bonds in order to take advantage of high American interest rates. Multinational corporations also have multinational management more than ever before. It is nonetheless suggestive that of the twenty-five richest men in the world as of 1989, nine were Japanese and seven were west European. Four were from the United States.

BIBLIOGRAPHY

Aldrich, Nelson W., Jr. *Old Money: The Mythology of America's Upper Class* (1988).

Bailyn, Bernard. *The New England Merchants in the Seventeenth Century* (1964).

Baltzell, E. Digby. *Philadelphia Gentlemen: The Making of a National Upper Class* (1958).

Benjamin, Philip. *The Philadelphia Quakers in the Industrial Age, 1865–1920* (1976).

Chandler, Alfred, Jr., and Richard S. Tedlow, eds. *The Coming of Managerial Capitalism: A Casebook on the History of American Economic Institutions* (1985).

Domhoff, G. William. *Who Rules America Now? A View for the '80s* (1983).

Gilbert, Dennis, and Joseph A. Kahl. *The American Class Structure: A New Synthesis* (1982).

Hall, Peter D. *The Organization of American Culture, 1700–1900: Private Institutions, Elites, and the Origins of American Nationality* (1982).

Henretta, James A., and Gregory H. Nobles. *Evolution and Revolution* (1987).

Jaher, Frederic C. *The Urban Establishment: Upper Strata in Boston, New York, Charleston, Chicago, and Los Angeles* (1982).

Miller, Elinor, and Eugene D. Genovese, eds. *Plantation, Town, and Country: Essays on the Local History of American Slave Society* (1974).

Morgan, Edmund. *American Slavery, American Freedom: The Ordeal of Colonial Virginia* (1975).

Pessen, Edward. *Riches, Class, and Power Before the Civil War* (1973).

Phillips, Kevin. *The Politics of Rich and Poor: Wealth and the American Electorate in the Reagan Aftermath* (1990).

Rutman, Darrett B., and Anita H. Rutman. *A Place in Time: Middlesex County, Virginia, 1650–1750* (1984).

Thernstrom, Stephan. *The Other Bostonians: Poverty and Progress in the American Metropolis, 1880–1970* (1973).

Thernstrom, Stephan, and Richard Sennett, eds. *Nineteenth-Century Cities: Essays in the New Urban History* (1969).

SEE ALSO **Business Culture; Marxism and Its Critics; Social Class; Socialist and Communist Movements; Wealth and Income Distribution.**

WOMEN AND WORK

Nancy F. Gabin

THE HISTORY OF WOMEN and work in the United States is woven of change and continuity. The shift from an agrarian to a commercial and industrial economy in turn transferred the location of much of women's work from the domestic to the public sphere. The demography of the female labor force changed, too, as the working girl of the nineteenth century gave way to the working mother of the mid to late twentieth century. The class composition of the female labor force also diversified, especially as the tertiary sector expanded. Despite the sometimes dramatic evidence of change, long threads of continuity reach back into the seventeenth century and forward to the present. Women remain principally responsible for work in the home despite their ever-growing presence in jobs outside the home. The gender division of labor also endures in the public sphere. Gender distinctions and gender hierarchies have always defined occupations, wages, and working conditions and have shaped women's employment opportunities.

The history of women and work in the United States has grown apace with the larger field of women's history. Like much early women's history, women's labor history was "contributory" in character. As the title of one notable survey of working women in America announced, historians sought to prove that "we were there" in the labor force and the labor movement from the beginning. In time the goals and purposes of historians became more interesting and sophisticated. Historians of women and work, for example, have emphasized the importance of defining work broadly to include unpaid labor as well as the more conventional remunerated work outside the home. Based on a male model of behavior, an emphasis on paid involvement in the public sphere overlooks or undervalues women's many contributions to family survival. Whether they produced goods in their homes, took in and cared for boarders or other women's children, engaged in the unpaid work of family nurture, or took jobs outside the home,

women have always worked. Challenging the tendency to accept at face value the division of spheres, scholars have evaluated both the significance of, and public attitudes toward, all these activities. Historians also have moved from narrative descriptions to analyses of the indirect, uneven, and complex impact of industrialization on women. The consequences of work for women have provoked lively debate among historians, who ask to what extent it reduced the differences between the sexes or advanced the cause of gender equality. Other questions raised by historians of women and work concern the significance of class, race, and ethnicity for women's labor experience, the role of the state in regulating and defining women's work, and the individual and collective efforts of women workers to direct their own lives.

This essay draws on the growing secondary literature to examine the history of women and work from the seventeenth century to the present. Describing the varied character of women's work and assessing the extent and sources of change and continuity, it is organized chronologically in four sections. The first examines the preindustrial era in colonial America. The second describes the relationship of women to the commercialization of agriculture and the beginning of industrialism in the years between the Revolution and the Civil War. The third part focuses on the Gilded Age and the Progressive Era, a period when women's place in the economy grew as the economy itself expanded significantly. The last section explores the changes and continuities of the modern era from World War I to the present.

THE PREINDUSTRIAL ERA, 1600–1800

In the seventeenth and eighteenth centuries, the vast majority of women lived on farms. Although tasks were divided on the basis of gender, men's and women's spheres were both complementary and overlapping. Men were responsible for work in the fields and the outbuildings; women were responsible for work inside the house and for dairying and gardening. Women's work was skilled, complex, and arduous; with the exception of the cultivation of grain and supervision of livestock, they were responsible for the production of nearly all food and clothing. The colonial American housewife was expected to possess the knowledge of a flax spinster, wool spinster, weaver, dyer, fuller, tailor, knitter, miller, brewer, baker, gardener, dairy maid, chandler, and soapmaker. Dependence defined women's place in the colonial economy and society. But although married women themselves owned no property and had no legal right to their own earnings, they engaged in barter or trade of the goods they produced to obtain other items. Scholars debate the extent and significance of this economic activity, but there is evidence that colonial families supplemented homegrown products with textiles, flour, butter, and meat bought from tradesmen, peddlers, and neighboring producers, often with women's income. Women also traded or bought such household necessities as soap, candles, and herbal medicine. Moreover, just as men hired hands to assist in the production of grain, women sought assistance with their own work, partly by relying on craftspeople for various steps in the production process. Even before the Revolution there was a primitive putting-out system in New England in which women sold yarn to storekeepers who then put it out to knitters or weavers; women also might have paid to have the fabric whitened or fulled. Not only did some women in this way buy themselves freedom from the most onerous work, but the women with whom the merchant contracted for the work gained a means of support as well. The system was sufficiently developed that by the 1770s many women, especially those in towns, did not themselves produce cloth.

Despite the power of patriarchy in colonial America, women occasionally assumed male responsibilities and engaged in the public sphere as economic actors. If a husband was absent or incapacitated, a wife might assume the role of "deputy husband" and act as farmer, weaver, or merchant, all male-defined roles. As long as such behavior was only temporary, it was tolerated by colonial society. Denied access to formal apprenticeship and unable to sign contracts or own property, women were excluded from the skilled trades. But women were not entirely without their own resources. There is evidence from the eighteenth century of women engaged in business, although usually on a partnership basis with their husbands or as an auxilliary job to housewifery. Women customarily operated taverns and boarding houses; others had small shops selling pastries, dry goods, hardware, or liquor; some women opened schools. Many more, especially single women, hired themselves out as domestic servants. Midwifery was another employment engaged in by women; payment came in the form of goods or cash. A very few exceptional women were lawyers, landowners, and merchants.

Not all women in colonial America, of course, were free. In New England, white women usually arrived with their families, but in the middle and southern colonies, they more often came alone as indentured servants or prospective wives for male settlers. Although most indentured servants were male, women also bound themselves for a period of time, usually several years, in return for transportation and room and board. Some did agricultural work, but most performed the domestic work expected of white women. Indentured servants had little freedom; they could not marry or bear children, they—or, more properly stated, their terms of service—could be bought, traded, or sold, and they had limited rights to redress of grievances against their masters. But indentured servants, who were white, had something that slaves, who were black, did not: the promise of freedom after the contract expired. The only difference between female servants when their indentures ended and white women who never served an indenture was later age at marriage and first birth. Race, however, mattered. Beginning in the late seventeenth century, African men and women were bought and sold in the colonies. Slavery spread in the southern colonies, where landowners engaged in the production of labor-intensive cash crops. It is indicative of the racist dimension of white gender ideology that slave women were expected to perform not only domestic but also agricultural work.

The work of Native American women also differed in several important respects from that of free white women in colonial America. The tribes were unified by a subsistence economy that generally assigned to women the work of gathering and processing food and caring for children and to men the tasks of hunting and warfare. There were, however, many tribes with diverse ways of organizing labor. Indian societies differed in both the definition of appropriate tasks for women and men and the degree of flexibility or rigidity in applying each definition. The Iroquois Confederacy, for example, provided women with considerably more economic and political power than Europeans considered possible or preferable. Indifferent to the dynamics of gender politics among the Indians, European observers saw only a division of labor that assigned to women tasks that their culture assigned to men. They therefore perceived Indian women as mere drudges or slaves of Indian men. The irony was that as they chopped wood, built houses, carried heavy loads, and engaged in agriculture and trade, native American women actually enjoyed much greater freedom and autonomy than did European women. Although a few colonists considered or hailed the Indian alternatives, the counterexamples of gender-role definitions and gender relations offered by Indian societies were overlooked by most Europeans.

The American Revolution marked something of a turning point for women and work. During the war, women's work acquired a new political value. Whether they boycotted British tea, spun yarn and wove cloth to avoid purchasing British goods, or performed the work of men who were in the military, patriot women endowed their prosaic production with great importance. The spur that the Revolution gave to domestic manufacturing of consumer goods formerly purchased from British producers also expanded economic and employment opportunities for American women, particularly the growing number of poorer women—notably widows with children—responsible for their own and their families' support. The ideology of republican motherhood, the political philosophy that defined women's place in the new nation, expanded women's traditional role to include the training of children for citizenship. The legacy of the Revolution for women and work, however, was ambiguous. The higher esteem in which American women were held during the Revolution was not translated into equality or independence after the war. The social changes demanded by war were regarded as temporary, and women's dependent and inferior status was codified in the new Constitution and in state regulations. Republican motherhood reconfirmed rather than challenged the gender division of labor. And in asserting women's distance from the public sphere, it also suggested a new gendered definition of labor that would make equivocal the women's place in the economy of the early national period.

EARLY INDUSTRIALISM AND NATIONAL EXPANSION, 1790–1860

The period between the Revolution and the Civil War has always attracted the interest of historians of women in the United States. The growth of commerce and industry as the nation emerged from colonial status irrevocably changed people's lives. Much attention has been paid to the putative separation of home from work and the rise of a middle class. For their part, historians of women's role in labor have shifted attention from middle-class women to those who could not afford to emulate the bourgeois ideal of the leisured woman. Although much scholarship has focused on women and the textile industry, the story recently has grown more complex. Historians have uncovered the continued importance of domestic manufacturing throughout the nineteenth century. They also have emphasized the extent to which race and ethnicity as much as gender shaped women's relationship to work.

Even as the nation's economy changed and diversified, agriculture continued to be the principal occupation of most Americans. For women who continued to live in rural and agricultural settings in all regions, the daily content and rhythms of life varied remarkably little from that of their foremothers in colonial America. The westward movement uprooted people but not values; by and large, behavior, not attitudes, changed as Americans crossed the Allegheny and Appalachian mountains to homestead on the westward-moving frontier. But despite the continuity in gender roles, farm families, particularly those in New England, experienced change. Population growth, urbanization, and the rapidly developing transportation system promoted the commercialization of agriculture. In the hinterlands of larger towns and cities, farm women increased their involvement with the marketplace by expanding their butter-making enterprises. But only larger farms close to urban markets could take advantage of the demand for dairy products. As land prices in New England skyrocketed and people contemplated the high cost of moving westward, many farm families sought other sources of cash. Additionally, there were more consumer goods available for purchase, which enhanced the quality of life not only aesthetically but practically, as it cost less to buy than to produce cloth, furniture, and other items.

Outwork was one answer to the cash needs of farm families in the antebellum period. Some goods were manufactured in homes. Beginning in the 1820s, for example, Boston merchants imported palm leaf from the Caribbean and distributed it to country storekeepers in central Massachusetts and southern New Hampshire. The storekeepers split the leaf and put it out to local people, mostly women, who braided hats for sale in the South and Midwest. Payment often took the form of credit on store accounts. Tens of thousands of people earned money this way from the 1820s to the 1850s. In several industries some steps in the production process remained hand operations while others were mechanized. Women in their homes would perform one or two steps in the process of production, while others working in shops or factories did the rest, often using machinery. Home manufacture thus complemented and indeed facilitated factory manufacture.

The boot and shoe industry developed in this way in the nineteenth century. Men in cities such as Lynn, Massachusetts, cut the leather, using hand tools early in the century and later operating machines. The pieces were shipped to the countryside, where women working in their homes sewed together the uppers of the shoe; their work was not mechanized and shifted from homes to factories until the 1870s. Once sewn together, the pieces were shipped back to Lynn, where men and women working in shops and factories completed the process. In its early stages, the textile industry also integrated home work with mill work. Beginning in the 1790s, spinning was the first step to move from the home into mills. Rather than drive textile production out of the household, spinning mills actually created greater demand for household labor as women were sought to weave on consignment for local mill merchants.

Despite the significance of the so-called Rhode Island system for the production of cloth and the sustenance of the rural family economy, its days were numbered as a method of organizing textile production. Power looms were introduced in textile mills in the 1820s. Once weaving was mechanized, all the principal steps in the production of cloth were integrated under one roof. The scale of operation increased dramatically. In contrast to the relatively small-scale spinning mills employing just several hundred people, by the 1830s the eight major textile firms in Lowell, Massachusetts, together employed six thousand workers. And in contrast to the composition of the spinning-mill labor force, which consisted largely of children and adult men, the people who worked in the new textile factories were the daughters, usually between fifteen and twenty-five years old, of farm families. The commercialization of agriculture and the increasing reliance by farm families on goods produced off their own farms, therefore, not only increased the need for cash but also created the free, mobile labor supply required by American industry. As the need for their labor in maintaining the home diminished, they followed their work out of the home into the factory, leaving rural communities too small or too remote to sustain much cottage industry.

The hiring policies of textile manufacturers beginning in the 1820s made women the first factory work force in the United States. Two decades later, in 1840, 37 percent of American workers earned their living outside agriculture. Of these half-million people, 9 percent were in manufacturing; women still made up half of all workers in manufacturing. In some factories, women comprised 90 to 95 percent of the work force. The labor-recruitment strategy was novel enough but not completely unfamiliar or unexpected. In the early republic, advocates of industrialism urged the employment of women as a means to ensure the survival and dominance of American agriculture. Alexander Hamilton (1755–1804) argued that factory work would provide the farmer with a new source of profit and support "from the increased industry of his wife and daughters," while women and children would be "rendered more useful, and the latter more early useful, by manufacturing establishments, than they would otherwise be." Tench Coxe (1755–1824) was even more explicit. "Female aid in manufactures," he remarked, "prevents the diversion of men and boys from agriculture." The decision to hire young, native-born women thus met the labor requirements of textile manufacturers, but it also satisfied the interest of farm daughters in employment and addressed the concerns of farm families particularly and society generally about the future of agriculture in the new nation.

The parallel and overlapping intents and purposes of the various participants make it impossible to frame a simple analysis of the impact of economic change on women in the antebellum period. The Yankee farm girls who entered the textile factories confounded conventional attitudes about proper female behavior. Many were impelled not by poverty but by the desire for independence, the chance to enjoy urban amenities, and the opportunity to earn money for their own purposes. They evidently sought and appreciated the independence and freedom of living and working away from home. At least at the outset, they were not viewed and did not view themselves as an inferior or lower class. Indeed their sense of class equality with their employers as well as the importance of their employment prompted their collective resistance to what they perceived as the degradation of their labor. As manufacturers responded to increased competition by speeding up the pace of work, reducing wages, and intensifying discipline, women workers reacted by striking against wage cuts in the 1830s and mobilizing a movement for ten-hour laws in the 1840s.

There is also evidence that this group of American women experienced as much exploitation as liberation. The jobs generally were an interlude before marriage to a farmer rather than a long-term route to female independence. Most women took their first factory jobs in their late teens; most stayed less than five years, returning home to marry and become farm wives. The paternalistic labor-relations policies of the mill owners replicated and reinforced patriarchal family relations. Work itself was hierarchically gendered. All supervision in the factory was male; the occupational structure was organized according to a strict sexual division of labor; there was no upward mobility for women within the factory. Although factory jobs paid more than any other form of female employment in the antebellum period, women received lower wages than men, even if they performed the same work. The rationale for women's low wages drew on old ideas, such as the notion that without employment, women might otherwise be idle; therefore, the public service performed by the factory owners for the community justified low wages.

The women working in the textile factories also were regarded not as heads of households but rather as supplementary wage earners not requiring more than the soon-to-be proverbial "pin money." Women's work, moreover, always had been regarded as intrinsically less valuable than men's, if only because women were not perceived as producing for the market. Despite the fallacious reasoning, the devaluation of women's work sustained the wage-determination policies of factory owners. The potential of factory work to liberate women from parental or male control was further blunted when it became stigmatized as unsuitable employment for middle-class women. Unwilling to redress the grievances of the Yankee farm girls, manufacturers replaced the departing and dwindling supply of native-born workers with Irish women and men in the late 1840s and 1850s. Once the factory labor force was predominantly foreign-born, the work was no longer acceptable for native-born women with certain class aspirations.

Descriptions of other women's work in the antebellum period further indicate the limited and ambiguous impact of economic change on women.

The situation of female garment makers illuminates the persistent vulnerability of women. Before the advent of the sewing machine in the 1850s, the garment industry emphasized the outwork system in such cities as New York. After the sewing machine was invented, the location of production began to move "inside" to a factory setting, but outwork persisted, especially for such finishing steps as button-holing and button-sewing. As was the case in the boot and shoe industry during this period, inside garment workers were unmarried women and out workers were married women, often heads of households. The garment industry became one of the most important sources of employment for urban women. By 1860, one-quarter of the 100,000 employed women in New York City worked in manufacturing, and two-thirds of these worked in the garment trades alone. The work, however, was extremely low paid, required constant effort, and involved children as well as adults. As early as 1830, labor reformer Mathew Carey called out workers' wages and working conditions "harrowing truths." By the 1850s, the exploitation of these women had become firmly entrenched as contractors forced already low wages lower by unscrupulously cutting rates and withholding wages for allegedly inferior work. That the starving seamstress became something of a Victorian sentimentality indicates both growing class divisions in the United States and the class-specific character of female employment.

By the 1850s, most forms of female employment were considered inappropriate for middle-class women and girls. Not only did this Victorian gender ideology differentiate experience by sex, but it defined each sphere, domestic and public, by virtue of its separation from the other. Woman was defined as the embodiment of all that was contrary to the values and behavior of men in the marketplace, and thus, to the marketplace itself. The "pastoralization of housework," as Jeanne Boydston terms it, rendered invisible the economic dimension of women's work. Women performed their labor for reasons other than profit. For middle-class women, the ideology of separate spheres, therefore, proscribed their paid employment and reinforced their dependence on men. The exigencies of working-class life, however, meant that working-class women actually violated ideological injunctions. Unable or unwilling to remain in their homes, women ventured into the public sphere as seamstresses, vendors, washerwomen, servants, and prostitutes. In so doing, they encountered reformers, the majority of whom were female, who declared them poor mothers. Those who worked at home were even more vulnerable. Responsible for their own and their children's survival, desperate, and isolated, they developed neither the gender-consciousness nor class-consciousness that might have served as a resource against economic exploitation. As Mary Blewett has shown, divisions among working-class women were just as, if not more, important than divisions between working-class women and men. Unmarried inside workers often had a very different perspective on industry than did married out workers, and their clashes, such as during the 1860 shoemakers' strike, demonstrated another of the diverse and insidious consequences of economic development and ideological changes in antebellum America.

The experience of black women before the Civil War offers additional insight into the difficulty of assessing the subject of women and work in the antebellum period. The vast majority lived as slaves in the South. Although they lived on farms of varying size, they all generally did agricultural work as well as domestic work in their own quarters and in the Big House. In this regard, white masters did not respect any gender division of labor in African societies or in African American society. They also denied to their slaves the right or privilege of equal treatment: black women were expected to do work that white women were not. Black women as a result regarded their work differently depending on whether it benefited their masters or their own families and the slave community. The willingness and eagerness of black people before and after emancipation to act according to the precepts of Victorian gender ideology must not be understood (or dismissed) as mere mimicking of elite whites. Black women's attitudes toward domesticity actually did not indicate capitulation as much as resistance.

At the other end of the occupational spectrum from women in manufacturing and domestic service were women who taught, wrote, or sought entry into the male professions. The common-school reform movement created job opportunities for women with some education. Taking advantage of gender notions of appropriate wages, boards of education consistently paid women teachers one-third to one-half less than men. As new job opportunities opened for men and as teachers earned less money, women increasingly filled the gap. Comprising 25 percent of all teachers in 1860, women represented 60 percent of the labor force in 1880. The devel-

opment of publishing offered some women work as writers in the middle period. Sarah Josepha Hale (1788–1879) edited *Godey's Lady's Book;* Catharine Beecher (1800–1878) and others wrote domestic-management treatises; and a host of novelists, including Harriet Beecher Stowe (1811–1896) and Catherine Sedgwick (1789–1867), gained a popular audience. The professionalization of medicine gradually diminished the role played by women as healers; male doctors took over areas of medicine customarily practiced by women, most notably obstetrics, and erected institutional barriers to women's efforts to continue the practice of medicine. Although all these occupations were generally closed to working-class women and thus were deemed acceptable for unmarried middle-class women, they, too, were shaped in significant ways by the mid nineteenth century's gender definition of labor.

WOMEN'S WORK IN THE GILDED AGE AND THE PROGRESSIVE ERA

The changes that occurred in the history of women and work between the Civil War and World War I are evident in statistics. In 1860, nearly all black women worked and approximately 10 percent of all white women held paying jobs. By 1880, 16 percent of all women were in the labor force. Twenty years later, the figure was 21 percent, and by 1920, 23 percent of all women were employed. The rising trend is clear, but there were important differences in women's labor force participation rates with respect to race and nativity. Black women's labor force activity was much greater than that of either native- or foreign-born white women until well into the twentieth century; 40 percent of black women in 1890 and 44 percent by 1920 were employed. In comparison, 15 percent of native-born white women and 20 percent of foreign-born white women held paying jobs in 1890. By 1920, white women's labor force participation had changed, too, although it is important to recognize that the work performed by many immigrant wives inside the home as well as the work of women on farms may not have been fully recorded by census enumerators. The proportion of foreign-born white women in the labor force remained about the same as in 1890, but the figure for native-born white women jumped to 23 percent, an increase that reflects the growth of white-collar and professional employment for women.

Several factors account for the increased extent of female labor force participation between 1860 and 1920. The increasing mechanization of the labor process in manufacturing created new and more job opportunities for women. The growth of business also increased the demand for women to fill clerical, retail, and other service jobs. Immigration increased dramatically between 1880 and 1915, while the birthrate among native-born whites decreased, enlarging the size of a working class dependent on female as well as male wage earning. The emergence of the women's professions created vocational space for middle- and upper-class women and further diversified, and divided, the female labor force along class lines.

In the late nineteenth and early twentieth centuries, the American working class was a large and diverse group. Millions of native-born whites, the majority of whom were female, migrated from farms and rural communities to towns and cities in search of work. Living largely in the South until World War I and denied access to manufacturing jobs on account of racism and the structure of the economy, blacks constituted another important component of the working class; black women generally worked as agricultural laborers or as domestic servants. First- and second-generation immigrants swelled the ranks of the working class in these decades, dominating the population of major northern cities and holding a variety of cultural attitudes toward female employment. Regardless of race, nativity, and geography, however, the American working-class family formed a wage-earning unit because the wages paid adult men were wholly inadequate to support a family. Low wages, unstable and seasonal employment, illness, and accidents all made more than one wage earner absolutely necessary to the survival of the working-class family in the Gilded Age and the Progressive Era. The importance of wage work for working-class women in this period is reflected in women's increasing share of the labor force. In 1820, women represented a mere 6 percent of all workers; in 1870, the proportion was nearly 14 percent; and by 1910, the figure had grown to 25 percent.

Working-class women worked in a variety of jobs. In manufacturing, the mechanization and subdivision of the labor process created jobs for women in such male-dominated trades as printing; in the growing industries of food processing and paper box making, which already employed women; and in wholly new industries like electrical-goods production. The service sector also expanded in this period. The growth of business required larger clerical staffs. At the same time, a technological revolution in office equipment and procedures introduced machines into the labor process, subdividing the work of the all-around clerk, reducing wages, and undermining the status of the job as a route to upward mobility in a firm. As men left clerical work, women filled the gap. Representing just 2.6 percent of all office workers in 1870, women increased their share of the clerical labor force to 19.4 percent in 1890 and 37.7 percent in 1910. The feminization of clerical work was paralleled by a similar process in retail trade. The growth of cities and the development of the department store created new space for women; women's share of the sales work force grew from barely 4 percent in 1870 to 25 percent in 1910. The growth in telephone communications mirrored developments in manufacturing, clerical work, and sales. By World War I, the feminization of work in the industry was so complete that women had come to account for almost 99 percent of the nation's more than 140,000 switchboard operators.

The new job opportunities in the manufacturing and service sectors of the economy prompted the decline of the relative importance of domestic and personal service for women. In 1870, three of every five employed women in the United States were domestic servants. By 1910, just one in four was so employed. The higher wages and greater freedom of nonservice jobs were important factors in the reorganization of the female labor force. Also significant were new living arrangements in the growing cities and new household technology that simplified housekeeping. Apartments were smaller than single-family homes, and well-off urban residents benefited most immediately from such improvements as gas lines, electricity, running water, and heated water, which reduced the need for servants. Ironically, because washing machines required steam heat and huge facilities until the 1910s, middle-class urban households commonly made use of commercial laundries; female employment in laundries multiplied several times over between 1870 and 1910, even as the demand for domestic servants to do such work declined.

Despite the increasing opportunities for employment, occupational segregation by sex continued to define and delimit the place of women in the American economy. A very high degree of job concentration in the female labor force characterized this period. In 1900, five million women worked in 294 of 303 occupations, but only 43 of these jobs had more than 5,000 women. By contrast, an impressive 90 percent of all working women were in jobs in which women predominated. Women were concentrated in low-paid unskilled or semi-skilled jobs in textile mills, garment centers, food-processing plants, tobacco factories, and commercial laundries; men were concentrated in mining, construction, transportation, and heavy industrial production. Even the jobs newly available to women in offices and department stores were soon feminized. Within industries, too, male and female jobs were differentiated. In the garment industry, women sewed, and men cut and pressed. In canneries, men processed the food, shipped the goods, and managed the operations; women washed bottles, scrubbed floors, sorted food, and labeled and filled jars. The gender division of labor defined women's work not only as fundamentally different than men's but also as less skilled or less difficult or less valuable. For these reasons, as well as the intense competition among women for a small number of jobs, women's wages always were lower than men's.

Although the dual labor market denied women access to jobs in all but a few occupational categories, there were in absolute terms more opportunities than ever before. The diversity within the female labor force has prompted debate about the kinds of choices women made about employment and how they made them. For example, although the proportion of married women in the labor force increased in these years, from 4.6 percent in 1890 to 10.7 percent in 1910, married women generally did not work for wages outside the home. The force of circumstances, however, could send married women out to work. Because of black men's limited employment opportunities, persistent poverty, and racism, black married women had high rates of labor force activity. In seven southern cities in 1880, 35 percent of married black women but only 7 percent of married white women were employed outside the home. Similarly, in cotton-textile towns, where male wage rates were very low and there was a tradition of female hiring, many married white women worked, comprising as much as one-third of the female labor force in the mills. Large urban areas with mixed economies offered women a variety of options. Married women could take in boarders or do piecework without leaving the home to work. The importance of the structure of opportunity makes it difficult to weigh or determine precisely the role of ethnic traditions.

The behavior of single and married Italian women, whose labor force participation rates were lower than those of other immigrant women, suggests the power of cultural conventions. Irish women's expectations of late marriage and economic independence help explain their seeming preference for domestic work.

The impact of work on women themselves also has been the souce of much debate among historians of women and work in this period. The power and authority of occupational segregation by sex, some argue, meant that employment was not at all liberating for women and was actually a conservative experience that confirmed rather than challenged gender inequality. It was difficult for women to regard wage work as a route to independence and equality: wages generally were too low to support a woman living by herself, let alone a family; there was little if any upward mobility in the female labor market; and marriage and childrearing became an escape from onerous and unappealing work rather than a form of female oppression. Not disputing or minimizing the low wage and occupational status of working women, other scholars criticize the model of female victimization implicit in such interpretations. They emphasize instead the extent to which women's culture in and out of the workplace served as a resource rather than a trap for working women, enabling them to engage in many forms of resistance that ranged from individual and small group actions to union organizing, strike activity, and collective bargaining.

Generalizations about the impact of economic change and employment on middle-class women are also difficult to make or sustain. Because clerical jobs required a level of education that poorer women, particularly those who were foreign-born or black, likely did not have, they were deemed especially suitable for native-born or middle-class white women in the years between high school and marriage. Also significant was the development of the women's professions: teaching, nursing, library work, and social work. Either older vocations already feminized and now elevated to the status of professions, such as teaching, or new vocations shaped and staffed by educated women, like social work, the women's professions emerged in part because the male professions of law, religion, and medicine resisted the entrance of women. Women made some gains in medicine, but the male bastions of the ministry and the law remained relatively secure. In 1920, only 3 percent of American attorneys were female. By contrast, in 1900, women comprised 10 percent of the medical profession, although that was a peak figure that soon declined. The women's professions, however, also developed as an outlet for women who by talent, training, and inclination wanted to do something outside the domestic sphere. This was especially true for the first generation of college-educated women, who dominated the ranks of professional women in this period.

Although middle-class women were more fully integrated into the labor force in the late nineteenth and early twentieth centuries, they also felt the restrictions of occupational segregation by sex and gender hierarchy. Marriage and vocation, for example, were still regarded as incompatible and mutually exclusive for middle-class women. The women's professions defined themselves by extending women's sphere, "by suggesting that women were naturally inclined and equipped to care for the young, sick, or poor, or to serve as guardians of culture, or to guide young women on the path to adulthood." The women's professions usually were practiced in places that were homelike: hospitals, schoolrooms, libraries, colleges, and settlement houses. Described and justified as extensions of conventional notions of femininity, the women's professions were defined as the helping professions. For women, vocation meant service, not profit. Women professionals, therefore, received less pay, had limited upward occupational mobility, and their work was accorded less prestige than that of men professionals. By creating a lower-level professional caste, the women's professions helped by contrast to define the distinctive qualities of men's professions: high status, profit, and expertise.

The growing interest of the state in female employment indicates the persistence of Victorian gender ideology as a factor shaping the relationship of women to work. The positions taken by legislators and judges on the subject of state regulation of female employment illuminate attitudes toward gender, work, and politics—central concerns in the Gilded Age and the Progressive Era. Two Supreme Court decisions illustrate the political economy of gender in this period. The Illinois State Supreme Court rejected an appeal by Myra Bradwell of her exclusion from the Illinois bar in 1869 on the grounds that she was a married woman and therefore not a fully free agent capable of acting in the interest of clients in courts of law. The court, moreover, declared that the "hot strife of the bar, in the presence of the public," would destroy her femininity. The United States Supreme Court upheld the lower-court ruling in 1873, agreeing that the timidity and delicacy of the female sex "unfit it for many of the occupations of civil life." *Bradwell* v. *Illinois* was widely used thereafter to defend the exclusion of women from professional careers. In *Muller* v. *Oregon* in 1908, the Supreme Court ruled that an Oregon law limiting the number of hours women could be employed was constitutional because "the physical well-being of women becomes an object of public interest and care in order to preserve the strength and vigor of the race." In contrast to *Bradwell, Muller* could not reasonably call for the exclusion of women from wage labor. But like the earlier decision, the court's 1908 ruling affirmed the fundamental inequality of the sexes. Grounded in a gender conception of labor, both decisions rejected similar regulations of men's employment.

Protective legislation for women had complex consequences. In an era when organized labor was weak and not particularly friendly toward women workers, the state appeared to be the only ally in the effort to challenge their exploitation by employers. Working women themselves endorsed and sought female-labor laws as a means of improving the conditions of employment. Some women, however, were hurt by protective legislation: their income decreased or their work was speeded up; they were dismissed from jobs requiring night work or overtime; and employers (and unions) used the laws to deny women access to better-paying men's jobs. Once codified, the notion of female weakness and dependence embedded in the laws and the court decisions was difficult to extirpate.

The experience of working women during World War I revealed both how far they had come since the Civil War and how far they had yet to go. Women did gain access to men's jobs, although not on the scale that they would during World War II. The concept of equal pay for equal work gained some legitimacy as the National War Labor Board stipulated its incorporation into some agreements. The creation of the wartime Women in Industry Service of the Department of Labor, which was granted permanent status in 1920 as the Women's Bureau of the Department of Labor, institutionalized an advocate for women wage earners inside the federal government. And insofar as women's efforts during the war secured for them the elective franchise, then the period marked an advance. But the war also accelerated long-term trends in occupational segregation by sex and exacerbated tensions and conflict between women and men in workplaces. The limits of change during World War I indicate the power of tradition and continuity.

1920 TO THE PRESENT

Despite its uneven rhythms, change rather than continuity appears most significant in the period since 1920. Broken up by the Great Depression and World War II, the trend toward greater female labor force participation by married women seems inevitable in light of social and demographic changes on the one hand and long-term developments in the structure of the economy on the other. The greater presence of women in professional jobs, another hallmark of the modern era, seems a less foregone conclusion and due as much to the politics of feminism as to objective factors and structural forces.

Historians debate the timing and causes of married women's massive entrance into the paid labor force. Some highlight the years between World War I and World War II, and especially the 1920s, offering evidence of the rising standard of living among middle-class Americans and their now-greater need for additional income. Others emphasize the impact of women's employment experience during World War II in changing attitudes about married women's work outside the home. Still other scholars stress post-1945 developments, particularly the tremendous expansion of the service sector, in explaining the transition from the working girl to the working mother. The preoccupation of historians with middle-class women has prompted recent efforts to examine diversity within the female labor force and to generate a specifically working-class history of women and work. In general, however, scholarship on women and work in the post–World War I period does not yet look much beyond 1950. Even the secondary literature on the period from 1920 to 1950 is less extensive quantitatively and qualitatively than for earlier historical periods. There is much room for new work on the modern era.

The image of the flapper dominates our view of the 1920s. The public's flirtation with her reveals a great deal about perceptions of and attitudes toward women and work at the onset of the modern era. Glamorous, economically independent, sexually free, and single, the flapper reflected the wide approval of employment for young, single women regardless of class. Indeed the flapper was typically represented as a middle-class office worker. But the reality of clerical work with its low wages and limited horizons meant that the flapper also reflected the widespread lack of support for female independence and married women's employment. The class-specific character of the flapper denied the extent to which working-class women had initiated the same behavior before World War I and then drew on the motifs of youth, consumption, and independence to mobilize labor militancy in southern textile towns during the 1920s. The middle-class orientation of the flapper also masked the exigencies of wage earning for working-class females in the 1920s. The atmosphere of consumerism and optimism that pervaded the seemingly prosperous 1920s obscured continuing realities of economic hardship for rural women and working-class families. The 1920s, then, consolidated prewar trends such as the feminization and expansion of clerical work and updated the image of the working woman rather than introducing any significant changes.

The Great Depression reversed, if only temporarily, whatever change might have been underway by 1930 in social attitudes toward women jobholders. Although women as well as men lost jobs, they remained nearly invisible. Public attention instead focused on men and the psychological consequences for them of the inability to fulfill the expected male role of provider. The extent of concern for the battered male ego meant that wives who worked felt responsible for their own husbands' trauma. Women also became society's scapegoat for unemployment. This view found expression in the popular opinion that women should not work and deprive men of jobs. "There are approximately ten million people out of work in the United States today," wrote Norman Cousins in 1939. "There are also ten million or more women, married and single, who are jobholders. Simply fire the women, who shouldn't be working anyway, and hire the men. Presto! No unemployment. No relief rolls. No depression." A few leaders and policy makers challenged these views, pointing out that men would not want the jobs held by women, that most married women who worked were supporting families as heads of households or members of two-income families, and that if the right to work was to be based on need, then single men should be fired, too. But their counterarguments were ineffective.

The view of women as illegitimate competitors in the labor market sustained campaigns throughout the 1930s to eliminate married women from the work force. The 1932 Federal Economy Act decreed that in the event of layoffs, married employees should be fired first if the spouse also held a job with the federal government. Although written in gender-neutral terms, in practice the act penalized women; some 1,600 married female employees were dismissed within a year of implementation of the act. Federal employees were not the only women vulnerable to discriminatory treatment. State and municipal governments pressed married women to leave civil-service jobs beginning in 1930 and 1931. Three-quarters of the school systems in the United States refused to hire married women as teachers during the 1930s; half the systems fired female teachers who married. Employers in the private sector fired women who married or introduced a means test for women workers seeking to obtain or retain jobs. As late as 1939, twenty-six state legislatures were considering bills that would explicitly bar married women from state jobs.

Yet whatever society did or tried to do, women did not give up their jobs or stop searching for work. Despite private and public policy and notwithstanding the persistent unemployment problem, women's proportion of the work force inched up slightly to 25.1 percent in 1940 rather than declined from their 24.3 percent share in 1930. Three factors account for this seeming anomaly. First, women were largely absent from industries that suffered most from the Depression. Construction, transportation, autos, and steel lost heavily and only slowly recovered, but light industry, where female manufacturing workers were concentrated, recovered more rapidly than heavy industry. Similarly, clerical and social-service jobs, in which women predominated, not only recovered more rapidly but actually expanded during the decade. Finally, jobs in domestic service, another female-dominated category, started to become available again as early as 1932 and 1933. Women like men lost their jobs and found it difficult to obtain reemployment, but the gender division of labor created different experiences for women and men.

No assessment of the 1930s is complete without consideration of the New Deal. On balance, New Deal legislation improved working conditions and labor standards and advanced the idea of gender equality but at the same time offered new official sanction to gender discrimination. The New Deal's relief efforts generally ignored women because they focused on the notion of a principal—male—breadwinner. Also, the public-works projects that generally characterized work relief benefited men to a much greater extent than women. The labor-standards provisions of the National Recovery Administration's industry codes codified sex-differentiated wage rates. After the National Industrial Recovery Act (1933) was declared unconstitutional in 1935, the principle of federal labor-standards was incorporated into the Fair Labor Standards Act (FLSA, 1938). Although the act's wage and hour provisions were gender neutral, it exempted groups, including farm workers, domestic servants, and food-service workers, that contained many women. The FLSA's prohibition of homework sought to eliminate exploitation and raise the wages of factory workers, but it also disadvantaged married women who sought to contribute to the family income while staying at home with their children. These and other New Deal policies demonstrate the invisibility of women workers generally and married women workers particularly in the 1930s. The Depression and its unemployment may have given new official sanction to married women's work outside the home if the family needed their wages. But women were still defined in relation to the family, not as individuals.

Made to feel guilty about their labor force activity during the Great Depression, women were encouraged, indeed exhorted, to enter the labor force and were made to feel guilty for not working outside the home during World War II. The dramatic change from blame to praise prompted many at the time to assert that the war would be a turning point in women's history, marking the beginning of a new era of female independence and gender equality. The significance of World War II for American women remains a central question in analyses of the female experience in this century. With one eye on the entrance of married women into the paid labor force and another on the resurgence of feminism in the 1960s, historians have evaluated the short- and long-term impact of the war, debating the extent of change and continuity in social, political, and economic terms. There is much grist for the mill. Nearly half of the eleven million women employed in the United States in 1940 worked in low-paid, low-status clerical, sales, and service jobs. Similarly, the 20 percent who worked in manufacturing were concentrated in a few low-paid industries, such as textiles and clothing. The demand for labor to meet the nation's wartime needs led to the greater employment of women in all areas of the economy. At the peak of women's wartime employment in 1944, the percentage of the female labor force in clerical, sales, and service jobs had declined to 36 percent, while the proportion employed in manufacturing had increased to 34 percent. Although the entrance of over 3 million women into manufacturing represented a significant 140 percent increase over the figure for 1940, perhaps the most striking change occurred in male-dominated basic industries, where the number of women increased by 640 percent. Other notable developments involved the entrance of married women, particularly those with young children, into the labor force and the upward occupational mobility of black women, who moved out of domestic work and into manufacturing jobs for the first time. Although many of these changes were only temporary, their impact on the attitudes and behavior of women and men, unionists and employers, and policy makers and political activists has been hotly contested.

The treatment accorded women workers during the war conveyed a double message. Women were supposed to work but only temporarily. The war was not supposed to institute any revolutionary or long-term changes in ideology and practice. Stressing patriotism as the sole motive for taking jobs, the War Manpower Commission and the Office of War Information glamorized war work to suggest that women would not lose femininity even if they took male jobs. The federal government for the first time assumed responsibility for constructing and operating facilities for the care of children of women working in defense industries, but programs were inefficiently administered, too few centers were constructed, and funds were canceled at the end of the war. Employers only reluctantly recruited women for jobs that were not traditional women's work. Faced with the inevitable, they tried to feminize the work, redrawing rather than subverting the boundaries of the gender division of labor and justifying lower wage rates as well. Employers, moreover, had no plans to retain wartime women employees after the war, as seniority provisions denying women rights to wartime jobs after reconversion to domestic production made clear.

The federal government's policy on equal pay reinforced the limited character of change during World War II. In November 1942, the National War Labor Board (NWLB) declared that women were to receive pay equal to men's if placed in the same or substantially similar jobs. In disputed cases, the board demanded the elimination of sex labels on jobs to more fairly determine wage rates. Many women received wage increases as a result of the order and the vigilance of unions in seeking its application. But the NWLB also allowed loopholes by which employers evaded the more radical implications of the government's equal-pay policy: the terms "heavy" and "light" were permitted as substitutes for "male" and "female" in job classifications; equal work was defined narrowly to avoid a general equalization of men's and women's wage rates and inevitable conflict over the idea of comparable worth. Although there were important exceptions, unions generally shared the view that women would be—or should be—only temporarily employed "for the duration."

Reconversion confirmed the temporary character of most wartime gains for working women. Voluntarily and involuntarily, many women left the labor force in 1945. Nationally, the proportion of women among all workers employed in basic industries fell from a wartime high of 25 percent in October 1944 to 13 percent in April 1947, a figure only four percentage points higher than that for 1939. Although the number of women in the labor force never fell to prewar levels and eventually exceeded wartime figures, the occupational distribution of women resembled that before 1941. Of the 17 million women working outside the home in 1950, 58 percent were employed in the clerical, retail, and service sectors; and the majority of the 19 percent employed in manufacturing worked in the textile and clothing industries. The war years left some indelible marks. The movement for pay equity survived and the wartime women's movement in unions regrouped and began pressing for the elimination of all forms of gender discrimination in employment. Although it had no singular or uniform impact, wartime employment also affected the attitudes and behavior of women and their families. The resurgence in the immediate postwar period of domesticity and conventional ideas about the proper place of women and men, however, all but overwhelmed the few challenges that survived the ravages of reconversion.

Economic and demographic forces, however, undermined all efforts to prevent change. After World War II, the size of the female labor force increased dramatically, the woman who did not work for wages became the exception rather than the rule, and the working wife became a standard feature of American life. Statistics illustrate the trends. In 1940, 25 percent of women over the age of sixteen worked outside the home. In 1960, 40 percent of women were working. By 1980, 51.5 percent of all adult women held jobs outside the home. Women's share of the labor force grew as well. Women were 29 percent of the work force in 1950, 35 percent in 1965, and 40 percent by 1975; in the 1980s, more than half of all workers were female. Equally significant was the growing importance of employment for married women. In 1940, just 15 percent of all married women worked for wages outside the home. In 1950, when married women represented half of all women in the labor force for the first time since the Census Bureau recorded such information, 21 percent of wives were employed. The percentage of married women at work increased another 10 percent in each of the next three decades; by 1980, 50 percent of all married women were employed outside the home. At first, most of the new married women workers were over the age of forty or forty-five, past the years when they would normally have children living at home. But the proportion of women with school-age children who held jobs also increased. Of women with children between the ages of six and seventeen, 25 percent in 1948, 40 percent in 1960, and 60 percent by 1980 were employed outside the home. In the past twenty years, women with preschool-age children also have established a significant presence in the labor force. At the end of the 1960s, one-third of women with preschool-age children worked outside the home. In 1980, 45 percent of women with children under the age of six were employed. By 1985, the figure already had increased to 53.4 percent, and it continued to rise.

Supply and demand explain the post–World War II trends. On the one hand, the greatest growth in the economy after World War II occurred in the service sector, creating ever-increasing numbers of white- and pink-collar jobs that were already defined as women's work. On the other hand, postwar inflationary trends increasingly made a second income necessary for families to achieve and, eventually, to maintain a middle-class life-style. These factors also account for the ideological shift that justified women's new role. As long as married women's labor-force activity could be considered supplementary and dispensable and in familial rather than individual terms, then it was deemed compatible with traditional notions of female dependence and domesticity. Many women considered themselves only temporarily employed until specific items were paid for—a home, a second car, a vacation, a child's college education. The gender division of labor reinforced the view of married women's wage earning as marginal and episodic.

The traditionally low-paid, dead-end jobs available to women not only kept their contribution to family income low but were unlikely to inspire confidence as routes to independence.

As women realized that their lives would be shaped by a permanent relationship to work, however, they began to reevaluate their status in the labor market. Their interest in higher wages, upward occupational mobility, and greater job satisfaction was addressed in legislation forbidding discrimination on the basis of sex. Women's entrance into the skilled trades at one end of the occupational spectrum and their increasing share of the professions of law, medicine, and business at the other end illustrate the significance of the changes that have occurred in women's relationship to work since World War II. Having acquired identities as workers, women began to assess critically the obstacles to their achievement in the labor market. Their confrontation with gender inequality in the workplace occurred at the same time as gender relations came under scrutiny. For all these reasons, the extent of change in the past fifty years appears far greater than that which occurred over the course of the preceding century.

Yet the fundamental changes coexist with seemingly intractable dilemmas. The idea that women belong in the home has lost much of its material base, but women still are principally responsible for housework. The passage of antidiscriminatory legislation and the massive entrance of women into the labor force has not eliminated gender segregation in the labor market. Most women still work in female-dominated, low-paid jobs. Acknowledging occupational segregation by sex but rejecting the principle of gender hierarchy on which the division of labor is based, advocates of working women advance comparable worth as a strategy for redressing the persistent disparity between the wages of women and men. Pay equity, however, remains a distant goal for the mass of women in clerical and service jobs because the cost of closing the gap between men's and women's wages is great. Comparable worth also seems to offer little relief to women employed in industries characterized by intense competition, low profits, and low capital investment. Women in business and the professions complain that there is a "glass ceiling" that limits their access to the highest ranks. As the very term suggests, it will be difficult to break that invisible barrier until it has become visible, until women's complaints are recognized as legitimate. The final chapter in the history of women and work in America has not yet been written.

WORK AND LABOR

BIBLIOGRAPHY

Surveys and Overviews

Evans, Sara M. *Born for Liberty: A History of Women in America* (1989).

Kessler-Harris, Alice. *Out to Work: A History of Wage-earning Women in the United States* (1982).

Kleinberg, S. Jay. "Women in the Economy of the United States from the American Revolution to 1920." In *Retrieving Women's History: Changing Perceptions of the Role of Women in Politics and Society,* edited by S. Jay Kleinberg (1988).

Matthaei, Julie A. *An Economic History of Women in America: Women's Work, the Sexual Division of Labor, and the Development of Capitalism* (1982).

Weiner, Lynn Y. *From Working Girl to Working Mother: The Female Labor Force in the United States, 1820–1980* (1985).

Wertheimer, Barbara Mayer. *We Were There: The Story of Working Women in America* (1977).

Monographs and Essay Collections

Baron, Ava, ed. *Work Engendered: Toward a New History of American Labor* (1991).

Benson, Susan Porter. *Counter Cultures: Saleswomen, Managers, and Customers in American Department Stores, 1890–1940* (1986).

Blewett, Mary H. *Men, Women, and Work: Class, Gender, and Protest in the New England Shoe Industry, 1780–1910* (1988).

Boydston, Jeanne. *Home and Work: Housework, Wages, and the Ideology of Labor in the Early Republic* (1990).

Cantor, Milton, and Bruce Laurie, eds. *Class, Sex, and the Woman Worker* (1977).

Cowan, Ruth Schwartz. *More Work for Mother: The Ironies of Household Technology from the Open Hearth to the Microwave* (1983).

Davies, Margery W. *Woman's Place Is at the Typewriter: Office Work and Office Workers, 1870–1930* (1982).

Diner, Hasia R. *Erin's Daughters in America: Irish Immigrant Women in the Nineteenth Century* (1983).

Dublin, Thomas. *Women at Work: The Transformation of Work and Community in Lowell, Massachusetts, 1826–1860* (1979).

Dudden, Faye E. *Serving Women: Household Service in Nineteenth-Century America* (1983).

Gabin, Nancy F. *Feminism in the Labor Movement: Women and the United Auto Workers, 1935–1975* (1990).

Greenwald, Maurine W. *Women, War, and Work: The Impact of World War I on Women Workers in the United States* (1980).

Groneman, Carol, and Mary Beth Norton, eds. *"To Toil the Livelong Day": America's Women at Work, 1780–1980* (1987).

Hall, Jacquelyn Dowd, et al. *Like a Family: The Making of a Southern Cotton Mill World* (1987).

Harris, Barbara J. *Beyond Her Sphere: Women and the Professions in American History* (1978).

Jensen, Joan M. *Loosening the Bonds: Mid-Atlantic Farm Women, 1750–1850* (1986).

————. *With These Hands: Women Working on the Land* (1981).

Jensen, Joan M., and Sue Davidson, eds. *A Needle, a Bobbin, a Strike: Women Needleworkers in America* (1984).

Jones, Jacqueline. *Labor of Love, Labor of Sorrow: Black Women, Work, and the Family from Slavery to the Present* (1985).

Kessler-Harris, Alice. *A Woman's Wage: Historical Meanings and Social Consequences* (1990).

Melosh, Barbara. *"The Physician's Hand": Work Culture and Conflict in American Nursing* (1982).

Milkman, Ruth. *Gender at Work: The Dynamics of Job Segregation by Sex During World War II* (1987).

————, ed. *Women, Work, and Protest: A Century of Women's Labor History* (1985).

Morantz-Sanchez, Regina M. *Sympathy and Science: Women Physicians in American Medicine* (1985).

Stansell, Christine. *City of Women: Sex and Class in New York, 1789–1860* (1986).

Tentler, Leslie Woodcock. *Wage-earning Women: Industrial Work and Family Life in the United States, 1900–1930* (1979).

Ulrich, Laurel Thatcher. *Good Wives: Image and Reality in the Lives of Women in Northern New England, 1650–1750* (1982).

Walsh, Mary Roth. *"Doctors Wanted: No Women Need Apply": Sexual Barriers in the Medical Profession, 1835–1975* (1977).

SEE ALSO **Feminist Approaches to Social History; Gender; Social Reform Movements; Women's Organizations;** and various essays in the section "**Work and Labor.**"

MINORITIES AND WORK

Robert L. Harris, Jr.

From its colonial origins to the present, the United States labor market has been segmented along racial, ethnic, class, and gender lines. There has especially been a racial/ethnic hierarchy of labor, with people of color (Africans, Asians, Chicanos, and Latinos) clustered at the lower rungs in poorly paid, unskilled, and semi-skilled positions, with little prospect of job mobility. Minority workers have often entered the labor market as "unfree" laborers, that is, as slaves, contract workers, or peons. They have performed the least desirable and lowest paying types of work, usually receiving less compensation for the same jobs held by whites under a dual-wage system.

Minority workers have been a reserve labor force, the last-hired and the first-fired, a buffer for employers during periods of expansion or contraction. They have also been used to discipline labor, to keep wages low, and to impede the organization of workers into labor unions. Minority workers supplied much of the hard labor that created the agricultural base and the transportation infrastructure for industrialization and modernization in the United States.

The labor market for most of the twentieth century has consisted of primary, secondary, and tertiary sectors. The primary labor market carries high wages, steady employment, and upward mobility. At the upper end, it is occupied by white-collar salaried or self-employed workers with high status, autonomy, and often supervisory duties. At the lower end are positions with high salaries but less autonomy. These are usually blue-collar skilled and unionized positions. The secondary labor market provides low wages, few or no benefits, little mobility, and unsteady employment. Work is often casual, that is, part-time, seasonal, and temporary. Until the 1970s a job in the primary sector generally yielded sufficient earnings to support a family. The secondary sector, however, where most minority workers were located, did not pay enough to sus-

tain a family. The tertiary sector of the labor market includes the underground economy of crime, prostitution, gambling, and drug trafficking, as well as labor by undocumented workers and in sweatshops. This type of work is risky, often leading to incarceration or deportation. Because of limited opportunities in the primary and secondary sectors of the labor market, minority workers, especially in the barrios and ghettos, have found the underground economy a means of survival.

SLAVERY

The colonists, who settled what later became the United States, initially relied on white indentured servants as a source of labor to clear the fields, tend livestock, and cultivate crops. The supply of white indentured servants was fairly abundant until the 1660s, when political and economic improvements in England reduced the number of individuals willing to risk the possibility of progress abroad in return for three to seven years of labor. Moreover, white landowners, particularly in the South, became concerned about potential disruption from the presence of a land-hungry class of white men. Bacon's Rebellion in 1676 confirmed their fears, when Nathanial Bacon, Jr. (1647–1676), a recent settler in Henrico County, Virginia, led a band of frontiersmen against the Indians, despite the disapproval of Governor William Berkeley. Bacon also sided with white settlers who complained about a restricted franchise, excessive taxation, inadequate protection against the Indians, and favoritism in the distribution of offices and tax exemptions. Although quickly suppressed after Bacon's death, the rebellion had a disquieting effect on the planters.

Slavery evolved gradually in the South after the mid seventeenth century and became entrenched by the beginning of the eighteenth century. Approx-

TABLE 1   Definition of Labor Market Segments, 1980
___

UPPER-TIER PRIMARY:
-managerial and professional specialty occupations, except health assessment and
    treating
-supervisors and proprietors, sales occupations
-sales representatives, commodities, and finance
-farm operators and managers

LOWER-TIER PRIMARY:
-health assessment and treating
-technologists and technicians, except health
-protective service
-precision production, craft, and repair
-transportation occupations
-material moving equipment operators

UPPER-TIER SECONDARY:
-health technologists and technicians
-other sales
-administrative support occupations, including clerical
-machine operators and tenders
-fabricators, assemblers, inspectors

LOWER-TIER SECONDARY:
-private household occupations
-service occupations, except protective and household
-handlers, equipment cleaners, helpers, and laborers
-farming, forestry, and fishing, except farm operators and managers
___

imately a half million Africans were enslaved in the British colonies of North America; about 60 percent of them were imported between 1720 and 1780. During the seventeenth century, slaves were used to perform a variety of tasks from clearing the land, tending livestock, and planting crops to serving as skilled artisans. Large plantations were the exception during the eighteenth century, as most bondsmen worked on small farms with few slaves. Bondswomen generally did domestic work until harvest time, when all available hands were needed in the fields.

As plantations developed and grew larger, they became more complex and labor became more specialized. Plantations with thirty or more slaves had the greatest degree of specialization. A white overseer, employed by the planter to manage the labor force, usually relied on one slave as foreman and a few others as drivers to supervise the work of a gang of five or six slaves. On larger plantations, some slaves might devote full time to ditching, cultivating vegetables, tending livestock, driving wagons, and working as blacksmiths, carpenters, coopers, millers, sawyers, shoemakers, stonemasons, and weavers. Domestic slaves on larger plantations might be divided into butlers, coachmen, cooks, footmen, laundresses, maids, nurses, and seamstresses.

During the revolutionary war era, slavery stagnated as the colonies curtailed the slave trade and colonists, with the exception of those in the Carolinas and Georgia, enlisted slaves in the military with a promise of freedom. Slavery never took full root in the North, where there was a sufficient supply of European labor for most of the colonial period. Between 1780 and 1804, each northern state took measures to abolish slavery, and bondage virtually disappeared by the 1830s. Even some southerners, moved by the "Rights of Man" rhetoric of the period, manumitted slaves. Agricultural recessions in the 1780s and 1790s together with a shift in the Upper South from tobacco to wheat cultivation resulted in a slave surplus.

Several developments during the late eighteenth century, however, led to a renewed demand for slaves and the expansion of slavery into the Deep South. By 1780, there had been a revolution in cotton-cloth production in England due to several inventions and refinements, such as James Hargreaves's spinning jenny, Richard Arkwright's waterframe, and Samuel Crompton's mule. Population growth in Europe, which expanded by a third between 1750 and 1800, swelled demand for raw cotton. In 1793 Eli Whitney (1765–1825) improved the old roller gin to make separation of cotton lint from seed easier and cotton cultivation therefore more profitable. Improvements in cotton production coincided with similar changes in sugar refining. Moreover, refugees from the Haitian Revolution (1791) fled to Louisiana with their slaves and established sugar plantations. Although slaves cultivated a variety of crops, such as wheat and tobacco in Maryland and Virginia, tobacco in North Carolina and Kentucky, rice on the sea islands of South Carolina and Georgia, hemp in Kentucky, and foodstuffs like corn, sweet potatoes, and peas throughout the South, most slaves cultivated cotton.

From 1790 to 1860, slaveholders resettled about one million blacks in the Deep South. Most slaves were taken in family units from the upper South. In the Deep South, they once again cleared the land, built homes, and prepared the area for settlement. In 1850, the Federal Census reported 2.5 million slaves in southern agriculture, with 2 percent in hemp production, 5 percent in rice cultivation, 6 percent in sugar production, 14 percent in tobacco cultivation, and 73 percent in cotton production. About one-fourth of the slaves belonged to owners with less than ten slaves, more than half lived in units of twenty slaves or more, and about one-fourth worked on plantations with more than fifty slaves.

Cotton was the United States' most important commercial crop and leading export, and slaves worked year round, from sunup to sundown, to bring in the crop. The cotton season began about March with plowing and sowing seed, as did planting corn and cultivating vegetables. By May, it was time to chop cotton and kill the weeds around the new shoots. This work continued throughout the summer until about September, when the cotton was picked, ginned, and pressed for shipment. From September to December, the slaves picked and shucked corn and harvested vegetables. With the start of the new year, there were hogs to be slaughtered and meat to be cured, wood to be cut and hauled, ditches cleaned, tools repaired, fences mended, and manure spread. There was always work to be done, in season and out.

More acres in the South were planted in corn than in cotton, because corn could be grown at little additional cost to cotton planters. About one-half of the corn crop was used for animal feed. In 1860, the South raised two-thirds of the nation's hogs. By 1860, the value of hogs and other butchered livestock was greater in the South than in the North. In those instances where slave-owners had extra hands, they hired them to work in the cities or in industry for short periods or for a year.

About 10 percent of the slave population—approximately 400,000 by 1860—lived in cities and towns. Slaves as well as free blacks worked in practically every skilled and unskilled occupation in the South. Blacks were more likely to enjoy skilled positions in the South than in the North. In 1860, there were about 250,000 free African Americans in the South and the same number in the North. Whether North or South, free African Americans faced segregation in transportation, accommodations, education, housing, and employment. Free blacks had a slight advantage in the North, where they could learn to read and write, form their own organizations, especially churches, and vote, although on the same basis as white men in only four states. While free African Americans possessed more rights in the North, they also had less occupational mobility and worked primarily as unskilled laborers or as servants. In the South, free blacks as well as slaves were likely to work as skilled artisans.

By the 1840s, about 5 percent of the slave population worked in industry, where they were either owned by companies or hired from the slave-owner. Slave labor was cheaper than wage labor and profitable to slaveholders, who received a return on investment equal to or greater than the average returns on other ventures. About four-fifths of industrial slaves were owned directly by industrial entrepreneurs. Slaves worked in textile mills, tobacco factories, and hemp manufacturing. They were barbers, blacksmiths, cabinetmakers, carpenters, coopers, sawyers, seamstresses, shoemakers, tailors, tanners, weavers, and wheelwrights. They worked in fisheries, gristmills, lumbering, quarries, sawmills, shipbuilding, and the turpentine industry. They built and repaired streets, turnpikes, and canals. Almost every railroad in the South was constructed in part with slave labor. Coal-mining and the iron industry made greater use of slaves over a longer period of time than any other business. Slaves were the chief labor force in Upper South ironworks. In 1861, the Tredegar Iron Company in Richmond, Virginia, employed nine hundred workers, half of them slaves. Tredegar was the South's leading iron mill, and it employed the third largest iron-working force in the United States. In total, about ten thousand slaves worked in southern ironworks before the Civil War.

Industrial slaves worked from sunrise to sunset, six days a week, every week of the year, much like plantation slaves. They usually performed the hot, dirty, and hazardous work. Tobacco, hemp, and textile mills favored slave women and children for labor in which sprightliness and nimbleness were more important than strength. Slave labor in the main was as efficient as wage labor. Slaves were not used more widely in southern industry for fear they would undermine the institution of slavery. In cities and towns, they had examples of black men and women who were free, opportunities to become literate, and access to political news. The potential for disaffection, unrest, escape, and even rebellion was ever present under such circumstances.

ASIANS, HISPANICS, BLACKS: 1865–1915

While most African Americans toiled in agriculture, primarily cotton, even after the Civil War and emancipation, Chinese men entered the labor force as plantation workers in Hawaii, gold miners in California, and railroad construction workers in the West. A dramatic decline in Hawaii's indigenous population, from approximately 300,000 in 1778 to about 44,000 a century later, due to forced labor and European disease, caused planters to look elsewhere for labor.

In 1849, a major flood in southeastern China drove hundreds of thousands of Chinese men from their villages in search of work in China and overseas. Both Hawaiian and United States employers favored Chinese workers who, as single men or as married men without wives and children, were ideal for migrant farm labor, mining, and railroad construction. They could be housed inexpensively and transported easily to places where their labor was needed. Chinese workers first came to the United States in large numbers during the gold rush of the late 1840s. Two-thirds of the Chinese in the 1850s were miners. By 1860, they were 10 percent of California's population and 25 percent of its work force. Between 1850 and 1882, over 100,000 Chinese men entered the United States. They worked on the most dangerous segments of the transcontinental railroad as it was built through the Rocky Mountains. Ninety percent of the work force on the Central Pacific Railroad was Chinese in 1867. They cleared the trees, laid track, operated power drills, and handled explosives for boring tunnels. Thousands lost their lives.

Chinese men also worked in citrus and celery harvesting and in fisheries. After completion of the transcontinental railroad in 1869, most Chinese settled in California. Almost half the workers in San Francisco factories in 1872 were Chinese. Because of a shortage of women in the West, Chinese men were employed in domestic service, food service, and laundries. A dual-wage scale prevailed, especially in the garment industry where, in 1870, Chinese men averaged $300 to $400 per year, while white women earned $600 to $900 per year, and white men were paid $900 to $1,200.

Chinese men traveled to the United States as sojourners, with the intention of returning home after several years abroad. During the interval, they would send some of their wages to families back home and would seek to save enough to purchase land in China. Although more than 100,000 Chinese men immigrated to the United States between 1850 and 1882, only 8,848 Chinese women came during the same period. Family patriarchs assumed that by keeping wives and children in China, the men were more likely to send money home. The few Chinese women brought to the United States were usually purchased from destitute families in China for prostitution in the United States. By 1870, two-thirds of the Chinese women in San Francisco worked as prostitutes. When business was slack, they were forced to do subcontracted sewing work. For the most part, they labored under slavelike conditions.

As the Chinese appeared in the West, Chicanos—people of Indian and Spanish heritage—were no longer needed in the labor force and pushed off their lands into Mexico. After the Mexican American War in 1848, the United States acquired almost half of Mexico's territory, including the area that became the states of Arizona, California, Colorado, Nevada, New Mexico, and Utah. There were about 80,000 Spanish-speaking people and some quarter of a million Indians living on those lands. A combination of restrictive legislation, litigation, vigilantism, beatings, and murder forced many of them out; whites taking over the mines, the cattle boom of the 1860s, and railroad expansion in Texas drove others off their lands. By the late nineteenth century, the social, economic, political, and numerical displacement of Mexicans and Indians was evident. For example, in 1860, 30.5 percent of the Chicano population in San Diego worked as ranchers and farmers, 39.1 percent as skilled workers, and 15.9 percent as unskilled laborers. By 1880, less than 2 percent were involved in ranching, 4.8 percent held skilled jobs, and 80.9 percent were unskilled laborers.

After the Civil War, new labor arrangements replaced slavery. Many white planters did not believe that African Americans would work without coercion after emancipation. The planters required black workers to sign contracts that restricted their freedom of movement, required obedience to the landowner, and asserted the landowner's right to regulate their working hours. The freedmen preferred arrangements that gave them greater autonomy, removed them from the former slave quarters near the owner's home, and allowed them to work on their own rather than in gangs under the supervision of a driver, similar to slavery. Given the shortage of cash in the South after the war, planters were willing to try a system that did not depend on wages while offering incentive to the freedmen to work hard without strict supervision.

Planters and freedmen reached a mutual accommodation whereby the former slaves cultivated cotton for a share of the crop. By working for a share of the crop, the freedmen theoretically could earn more if they worked harder. They could also determine the extent to which family members would labor in the fields. Initially, women were withdrawn from the fields for domestic work as wives and mothers. However, at harvest time, the most labor-intensive point in the growing season, both women and children assisted in picking the cotton.

Two types of share arrangements developed in the South. If freedmen owned a mule, farm implements, and had sufficient capital until harvest, they became tenant farmers and paid the owner one-quarter of the crop for use of the land. If they did not have enough resources, landowners supplied everything except food and clothing in return for half the crop, and the freedmen became sharecroppers. To subsist until harvest, sharecroppers had to purchase goods on credit, with interest rates as high as 60 percent. Most sharecroppers ended the year in debt, and many tenant farmers became sharecroppers. Although cotton production doubled in the South from 1869 to 1889, the price fell by almost half due to competition from cotton grown abroad and a decline in global demand. Those circumstances made it even more difficult for sharecroppers to escape the burdens of debt peonage. Despite these obstacles, by 1880, one-fifth of black farmers owned their own land, although their farms, about 47.3 acres (18.9 hectares), were less than one-third the size of the average white farm.

To discipline black labor and to make black agricultural workers more pliant, white plantation owners recruited Chinese, Italian, and Mexican workers after emancipation. Chinese men who had worked constructing the Southern Pacific Railroad were brought into Louisiana and Mississippi during the 1870s. The largest group of Chinese in any southern state settled in the Delta region of Mississippi. Soon after their arrival, the Chinese left the cotton fields to become small grocers. They could not earn enough as sharecroppers to achieve their objective of saving money to retire in China. With a small amount of capital, the Chinese would rent a room to open a store and sell groceries. The Delta Chinese filled a niche left open by southern whites, who considered it demeaning to operate a store in a black neighborhood and to serve black patrons. Black men in the main were not able to fill that niche because they lacked the same access to credit as whites and Chinese. As outsiders, the Chinese were not concerned about their social status in the United States; they worried about saving enough money to secure their position in China.

The Chinese grocers did not have the same expectations placed on them for credit and special favors to friends as did black grocers. The Chinese could be more friendly toward their customers than whites in the racially hierarchical South. They offered greater services and were able to sell goods at lower prices because their family labor cut their costs. They did not require the deferential behavior demanded by whites, and their stores were often one of the few integrated public spaces in the South. As other Chinese entered the Delta, they worked first with relatives, where they learned enough English to survive and the fundamentals of business operation. With a combination of savings, loans from relatives, and credit from wholesalers, they opened stores in other areas. The Chinese maintained excellent credit. When a Chinese merchant defaulted on a debt, relatives usually made up the loss to keep their good credit standing.

After the fall of Radical Reconstruction and removal of African American men from politics, white planters saw no further need to import foreign labor. They preferred black laborers who worked harder, could be dismissed or disciplined with greater ease, and could be exploited economically with little fear of retribution or protest from a foreign government.

Often out of necessity, black women participated in the labor force at a much higher rate than any other racial or ethnic group. Black houseservants were usually young girls rather than older women. Once married and with a family, black women often switched to taking in laundry, allowing them to stay home with their children. In 1890, 85 percent of employed black men and 96 percent of employed black women worked in agriculture or domestic service. About one-quarter of married black women were in the labor force, eight times the proportion of U.S.–born married white women. By 1900, 44 percent of black women workers were in agriculture and 44 percent in private household service, mostly as servants and laundresses. Only 3 percent were in manufacturing and about 1 percent in professions, primarily as teachers. Although black women were one-third of southern female workers in 1890, they were only 3 percent of textile workers. The textile industry that emerged in the South after the Civil War was confined almost exclusively to white workers. In South Carolina, state law prohibited African Americans from working in the same room, using the same stairway, or even sharing the same factory window with white textile workers.

Although they did not have a foreign government to protect them, black workers did organize in the South to improve their condition. Black women in Atlanta formed the Washerwomen's Association in 1881 and struck for higher wages. About 3,000 women participated in the strike, which was put down by white landlords and the city government. Black agricultural workers in 1888 started the Colored Farmers' National Alliance and Cooperative Union. At its peak in 1891, the organization had 1.2 million members in twelve states. The group supported cooperatives, published newspapers, raised money for longer school terms for black children, and assisted members who faced hard times with their mortgages. The organization sponsored a cotton pickers' strike in 1891 that led to its demise. Cotton picking was grueling labor. To earn $1.20 per day, a cotton picker had to gather about two hundred pounds (90 kilograms) of cotton, working in the field from dawn to dusk, in excruciating heat. The strike for higher wages met brutal and successful opposition from the white cotton growers. Many black farmers joined the Populist party, formed in 1891, which for a time sought to unite black and white farm workers. Because it posed a threat to the status quo and brought black men more actively into politics, southern white landowners defeated the Populist party and barred black men from southern politics for more than half a century.

Although black men could vote for a time in the South, Chinese immigrants were denied that privilege until after World War II. The Naturaliza-

tion Law of 1790 specified that naturalized citizenship was limited to "whites," a law that remained in effect until 1952. Moreover, according to the Cable Act of 1922, any American woman who married an alien ineligible for citizenship lost her own citizenship. Asians from the Indian subcontinent were generally classified as caucasian; however, the U.S. Supreme Court in 1923 ruled that Asian Indians were not "white," and therefore could not be naturalized as citizens. For a long time, the United States was a country whose citizens were almost exclusively of European ancestry.

Because of pressure from white workers, the U.S. Congress passed the Chinese Exclusion Act in 1882 that terminated Chinese immigration. Between 1850 and 1882, some 330,000 Chinese had entered the country. As they were pushed out of agricultural and factory work, the Chinese became laundry operators. In 1900, one-quarter of the employed Chinese males in the United States were laundrymen. Operating a laundry required little capital and little command of English. Similar to the Delta Chinese grocers, this was a niche left by others that the Chinese, especially on the West Coast, developed for themselves. After the Chinese Exclusion Act was renewed in 1892 and made indefinite in 1902, the Chinese population declined to about 62,000 by 1920. Approximately 47 percent of the Chinese who had immigrated to the United States returned to China.

After the Chinese Exclusion Act was passed, farm owners in the United States and Hawaii recruited Japanese workers. As contract workers, the Japanese could earn four to six times the wages paid in Japan. Between 1885 and 1924, 200,000 Japanese immigrated to Hawaii and about 180,000 immigrated to the United States. Almost 90 percent of the Japanese labored as agricultural or domestic workers. Like the Chinese, the Japanese came to the United States as sojourners. Japanese men outnumbered women by about twenty-five to one. In 1907, the so-called Gentlemen's Agreement between the United States and Japan barred the immigration of unskilled Japanese. Unlike the Chinese Exclusion Act, which prohibited the immigration of wives and relatives, the Gentlemen's Agreement permitted wives and relatives to join husbands who decided to remain in the states. Between 1909 and 1923, about 23,000 Japanese women entered the United States as "picture brides," whose marriages had been arranged by mail. After African American women, Japanese women had the highest labor force participation. Half of them worked in agriculture. By 1920, Japanese workers produced one-third of the truck crops in California.

Almost 70 percent of the Japanese population lived in California by 1930. Initially, they were migratory workers who labored on farms, railroads, and in canneries. During the fishing season, for example, they were shipped to Alaska and then back to California. Through ethnic solidarity and enterprise, the Japanese rose from field-workers to farmers. They formed credit-rotating associations, or *tanomoshi* to pool capital and to assist members in purchasing land and equipment. Through their farmers' organizations, they shared information about agricultural techniques and crop prices. Racist legislation impeded but failed to stop their progress. For example, California in 1913 passed a law denying land ownership to Japanese immigrants. Twelve other states enacted similar legislation. Under the law, they could lease land for terms not longer than three years. To skirt the law, Japanese put land in the names of children or relatives born in the United States. The Japanese became farmers at a propitious moment, when industrialization and urbanization during the late nineteenth century created a demand for fresh produce in the cities. Irrigation projects in California, completion of the railroad, and introduction of refrigerator cars opened new markets for fruit distribution. Japanese farmers concentrated on short-term crops like berries and truck vegetables. By 1940, they grew almost 95 percent of California's snap beans and celery.

Almost as a form of ethnic succession, Koreans, Filipinos, Asian Indians, and Mexicans replaced the Chinese and Japanese as agricultural workers. Korean immigrants were more likely to come from urban areas and almost 40 percent were Christians. They assimilated more easily, but their numbers were small. Only about 8,000 Koreans immigrated to the United States between 1903 and 1920. Most Koreans were farm workers, although in the cities, they worked in restaurants and as gardeners, janitors, and domestic servants. Like the Japanese, they organized credit-rotating associations, or *kae* to help them purchase land. After Japan declared Korea a protectorate in 1905, it cut off Korean immigration to Hawaii and the United States.

With Japanese and Korean immigration restricted, Hawaiian sugar planters turned to the Philippines for cheap labor. By 1932, Filipinos were 70 percent of the plantation labor force in Hawaii. Almost 110,000 had settled in Hawaii and some 40,000 settled in the United States; they were nearly all male, and all but entirely confined to agricultural work and domestic service. Farm owners in the West held stereotypical views of Filipino men, who supposedly were well adapted to stoop labor because of their short stature. Nonetheless, the 1934 Independence Act halted Filipino immigration to the United States and the American Federation of Labor (AFL) sought legislation to pay Filipinos to return to the Philippines on condition that they would never return to the states. Under the Repatriation Act of 1935, about 20 percent of Filipinos returned home.

In 1907, Asian Indians began arriving on the West Coast. Only about 6,400 entered the United States; 99 percent of them were male. Families generally sent the second or youngest sons to earn money to pay off debts at home. Initially they worked on the railroads and in lumber mills but they were driven from those jobs by white workers and forced into agriculture. Most of the Asian Indians lived in California. In 1917, Congress enacted legislation that prohibited new immigration, and between 1920 and 1940, almost half the immigrants returned to India.

As Asian immigration declined, the number of unskilled Mexican workers in the United States grew rapidly. During the late nineteenth century, there was little difference economically between the United States and Mexico. By the beginning of the twentieth century, a gap developed that widened over time. By 1905, a Mexican family could make several times more money picking cotton in Texas than they could earn in Mexico. Mexican workers replaced Asian laborers on railroad construction and maintenance in southern California, New Mexico, and Nevada. They suffered from a differential pay scale under which Asian workers received $1.50 per day, Greeks $1.60 per day, but Mexicans only $1.25.

Mexicans became a critical labor force in the growth of agribusiness, which depended on a large mobile work force. By World War I, they were the most important ethnic group of agricultural workers in the Imperial Valley of California. A Mexican family might live in more than five places during the year as they followed the ripening crops. They picked tomatoes in Indiana, a job that required constant stooping and carrying heavy crates in the hot sun. Next, they might harvest sugar beets in Michigan, which was monotonous and difficult work with long hours, often in inclement weather. Large farmers considered Mexicans as particularly suited to drudgery in the fields and could exploit their labor because of worsening economic conditions in Mexico.

WORLD WAR I–WORLD WAR II

The United States experienced a severe labor shortage during World War I, as the nation restricted immigration from Europe and as large numbers of Europeans returned to protect their homelands during the war. The labor shortage provided an opportunity for minority workers in general and African Americans in particular to enter northern industry in large numbers for the first time. While the North needed workers, the South had a labor surplus due to boll weevil infestation and devastating floods in 1916 that wiped out crops in the Black Belt. In 1910, three-quarters of all African Americans lived in the South, where almost two-thirds worked in agriculture. Between 1910 and 1930, about 1.2 million African Americans migrated North, where they found employment in meat-packing, steel, automobiles, shipbuilding, and other areas of manufacturing.

African Americans were confined to so-called Negro jobs, positions that whites generally avoided, where the work was heavy, hot, dangerous, and dirty. Although the pay for the same jobs in plants was equal, black men were usually lumped into specific job categories with lower salaries. Black women were also barred from most good jobs. White women often refused to work beside black women and demanded separate eating and sanitary facilities; white customers objected to black saleswomen, receptionists, and secretaries. It was difficult for black women workers to secure employment in manufacturing, so that only 8 percent of them were in manufacturing by 1930, compared with 25 percent of black men. More than a third of black female industrial workers were in the garment industry. Black women generally worked in factories, not as machine operatives but as service workers who cleaned factory buildings and equipment. The proportion of black women in domestic service grew from 44 percent in 1900 to 54 percent by 1930; it was one of the few areas of work open to them.

During World War I, black workers took over the unskilled positions that were previously held by European immigrants. Even unskilled jobs were attractive to black workers, who could earn three times as much in the North as in the South. Black workers were often introduced into northern industry as strikebreakers to discipline white labor. When white steelworkers in Pittsburgh went on strike in 1875, mill owners sought experienced workers to replace them and recruited black steelworkers from Richmond, Virginia. White steelworkers, similar to white workers in general, resisted the entry of black workers into the industry. In 1890, the Amalgamated Association of Iron, Steel, and Tin Workers in Pittsburgh went on strike to protest the presence of black workers. From 1881 to 1900, there were more than thirty strikes throughout the country against the employment of black workers in industry.

Initially, black workers in the iron and steel industry of western Pennsylvania occupied a range of positions from unskilled to white-collar jobs. During the late nineteenth century, race was not the barrier to job mobility it would later become. Immigrants from southern and eastern Europe at first trailed African Americans in skilled positions because of language barriers and limited industrial experience. In 1910, in western Pennsylvania, black steelworkers earned a weekly average of $14.98, while Slovak workers made $12.39, and Polish workers only $12.21.

At the time, black men made up about 3 percent of the work force in western Pennsylvania. They did not predominate in any department or critical area. Soon Germans gained control of the carpentry division, Poles the hammer shop, and Serbs the blooming mill at the Jones and Laughlin Steel plant in Pittsburgh. When black migrants arrived in large numbers between 1916 and 1930, they entered lower echelon jobs with limited opportunities for advancement, contrary to their earlier status. By 1920 in the Pittsburgh area, 13.6 percent of native-born whites held unskilled positions; 31.7 percent of the foreign-born whites and 54.4 percent of African Americans worked at unskilled jobs. Most black workers shunned unions because of hostile white labor. In western Pennsylvania, as in most parts of the country, they were barred from such craft unions as electrical workers, plumbers, and sheet metal workers. At the Homestead Steel Works, of 1,737 black workers, only 8 joined the steelworkers' union. During the strike of 1919, only one of them cooperated with the walkout. Steel companies in Illinois, Indiana, and Pennsylvania brought in about 30,000 black workers to break the strike. After the steel companies broke the strike, the number of black steelworkers dropped dramatically.

MINORITIES AND WORK

The introduction of black workers as strike-breakers in the metal industry in East Saint Louis, Illinois, in 1917 sparked labor unrest and major race riots. During the summer of 1919, race riots erupted in some twenty-five cities and towns across the country. Competition for jobs, housing, transportation, education, political power, and recreational facilities generated racial hostility and conflict. Racial tension continued during the 1920s as African Americans were confined to bulging ghettos of major American cities.

The prosperity of the 1920s eluded many African Americans who lost ground due to unionization and exclusion from skilled positions. Black labor force participation, which was higher than that for whites in 1910, declined by 1920 and became lower by 1930. The Great Depression struck the black population sooner, cut deeper, and lasted longer than for the rest of the country. During the early twentieth century, the number of black men in the building trades as carpenters and brickmasons dropped, while the number of white men in these occupations rose. From 1928 to 1949, the railroad unions prevented the hiring of black men as firemen, brakemen, trainmen, or yardmen. Prior to that time, most of the firemen and brakemen in the South were black.

During the Depression, African Americans lost a third of the positions they held in industry. White workers began to take jobs shunned before as "Negro work," especially in restaurants and service areas. White male railroad workers beat and even murdered black firemen to take over their jobs. By 1935, 30 percent of the black population depended on government relief for its survival. Other minority workers, particularly Chicanos, faced a similar situation. White workers replaced many Chicano field workers in California, and the United States government deported almost half a million people of Mexican origin during the 1930s, including tens of thousands who were U.S. citizens. Most New Deal legislation adversely affected minority workers. Payments to planters and large farm owners to plow under their crops and to reduce farm acreage pushed many sharecroppers and tenant farmers off the land. Landowners did not share federal payments with agricultural workers. Social security, workmen's compensation, and minimum-wage legislation did not cover agricultural workers, cooks, domestic servants, and yard workers. Minority workers were forced to rely more on the welfare programs of the New Deal than on job creation projects.

During the Depression and World War II years, black workers organized sharecropper unions, boycotted white businesses that did not hire them in the North, demonstrated against organized labor, and threatened a march on Washington against discrimination in defense industries. Their efforts produced improvements by 1945 for black workers in particular and for minority workers in general. After World War II, black workers achieved more progress in their labor status than at any other time, except the abolition of slavery. Labor demand during World War II, executive, legislative, and judicial action, as well as changes in racial attitudes in the fight against fascism led to dramatic improvements in the work status of black and other minority workers.

In New York and other northern cities, black boycotts led to employment as retail clerks, office workers, and bus drivers. Black workers in different parts of the country staged some twenty-two strikes against limited promotion opportunities, wage differentials based on race, and other forms of discrimination. The U.S. Supreme Court ruled in October 1940 that states could no longer use race as a basis for paying different salaries to black and white teachers. During the 1940s, more than 1.5 million African Americans migrated from the South to the North and West. More than half the black population lived in urban areas by 1950. Changes in the work force helped black women to escape domestic household service. The number of black female domestic workers declined as the number of black female manufacturing workers increased.

A. Philip Randolph (1889–1979), who organized the Brotherhood of Sleeping Car Porters in 1925 and won union recognition by 1937, announced in January 1941 that he would lead a march on Washington for fair employment in defense industries and desegregation of the armed services. To prevent a potentially embarrassing event as the United States mobilized for war, President Franklin D. Roosevelt issued Executive Order #8802 on June 25, 1941, in a successful effort to stop the demonstration, which was scheduled for July 1. Executive Order #8802 established a Fair Employment Practices Committee to encourage equal employment opportunities in companies with defense contracts. The establishment of the FEPC helped to improve the status of black workers through public hearings, publicity, and persuasion.

Black union membership increased tenfold during the 1930s, especially as the Congress of Industrial Organizations (CIO) conducted a massive unionizing campaign. The CIO organized industries as a whole rather than organizing individual crafts, as the AFL did. The CIO actively recruited black workers, who were important in organizing the automobile, meat-packing, and steel industries. Also, manpower shortages during World War II had the greatest effect in opening job opportunities for African Americans. In 1942, the CIO established the Committee to Abolish Racial Discrimination. Although the union helped to improve the general condition of black workers, it did little to change the status of black labor relative to white labor, especially in employment training and promotion.

Because of labor shortages on the mainland during World War II and depressed economic conditions on the island, large numbers of Puerto Ricans entered the labor force for the first time. About 81 percent of the U.S. Puerto Rican population lived in New York City. Puerto Rican men toiled in the garment industry, hotel and restaurant work, and in cigar manufacturing, while women generally did piecework at home, sewing and embroidering, and making lampshades, hats, and artificial flowers. Some Puerto Ricans came to the United States on temporary contracts to work on farms in New Jersey and New York.

Mexican workers during World War II received temporary visas to toil in the agricultural fields of the Southwest. Under the Bracero Program, the U.S. Farm Security Administration signed contracts with individual workers who agree to labor in the United States for a specific time period in a certain occupation, such as farming. In return, the U.S. government provided transportation to and from the United States and guaranteed the prevailing wage, adequate housing, and medical services. Employers applied to the government to hire *braceros*. The program, which lasted from 1942 to 1964, aroused criticism on both sides of the border. The Catholic church in Mexico complained that the program broke up families and introduced Mexicans to immoral practices in the United States. Mexican employers denounced the program for depriving them of able workers. American labor charged that the program basically benefited agribusiness and kept wages low.

Except for Japanese, Asians' status improved during World War II. In 1943, Congress repealed the Chinese Exclusion Act, provided for Chinese naturalization, and gave China a small annual immigration quota. Asian Indians were also granted naturalization rights. These changes occurred because of the strategic importance of China and In-

dia to the war effort. Executive Order #8802 opened industry to Filipino workers on the West Coast. During the war, the California attorney general reinterpreted the land laws to allow Filipinos who were not citizens to lease and to purchase land. After the Japanese attack on Pearl Harbor, President Franklin D. Roosevelt signed an executive order to evacuate 110,000 Japanese to internment camps. The Japanese Americans sent to the camps worked primarily in the agriculture fields established in the camps. They grew vegetable crops and raised poultry and cattle for their own consumption and for military posts, and earned one-third the wages that they would have been paid outside the camps. Japanese Americans lost almost $400 million in property because of their internment. Ironically, the Japanese in Hawaii, who were 37 percent of the population, with few exceptions, were not interned during the war. They were more critical to the island's economy than Japanese workers were to the economy of the West Coast.

FROM THE 1950S TO THE 1990S

The civil rights movement of the late 1950s and early 1960s together with the Immigration Act of 1965 affected minority workers as profoundly as the changes during World War II. In 1961, President John F. Kennedy issued Executive Order #10925 requiring federal contractors to file periodic reports indicating compliance with nondiscrimination in employment and establishing the principle of affirmative action. Title VII of the 1964 Civil Rights Act set up the Equal Employment Opportunity Commission with power to seek legal remedy against discrimination by companies or unions.

With mechanization of farming and the growth of agribusiness, there was less demand for agricultural workers. Most minority workers by the 1960s were in clerical, manufacturing, and service positions. They started to move into the primary labor market, but at the lower end. At a time when greater opportunity existed for those minority workers able to find employment, their labor-force participation rates declined. In 1920, for example, 81.1 percent of African American men were in the labor force, but they comprised only 66.7 percent of the labor force by 1980. A similar decline occurred for Chinese and Filipino men who had labor-force participation rates of 87 percent and 96.5 percent respectively in 1920, but only 74.3 percent and 77.6 percent by 1980. While the labor force participation rates for minority males decreased, they increased for all women, especially white women. In 1920, 19.5 percent of white women were in the labor force, a figure that grew to 49.4 percent by 1980. Greater competition for jobs, especially with the entry of more women into the labor force, has led to a decline in minority labor force participation. Moreover, the loss of traditional unskilled and semi-skilled positions has also affected minorities in the labor force. The rate of labor force participation for African American women has continued to rise, but it has been outstripped by Japanese, Chinese, and Filipino women, who bring higher educational qualifications to the market.

Minority workers since the 1960s have experienced contradictory trends. Between 1970 and 1986, the proportion of black families with incomes over $35,000 per year has grown but the percentage of black families with incomes under $10,000 per year has also increased. A man or a woman, regardless of race or ethnicity, with high-quality education or skills generally enjoys equal access at least to entry level and mid-range positions in the primary sector of the labor market. Many Asian immigrants after the 1965 Immigration Act, which eliminated racial and ethnic quotas, came from the professional class and immigrated as families.

Filipinos, who are now the largest Asian group in the United States, have the most highly educated women in the country. Forty-one percent of them have college or advanced degrees. They are heavily concentrated in the health-diagnosing and treatment occupations and work as doctors, dentists, pharmacists, and nurses. Filipino women also had the highest median income level of all women in 1980.

Forty-nine percent of recent Chinese immigrants, the second largest Asian group, have been managers, professionals, and technical workers. In 1980, a larger percentage of Chinese American men and women (44 percent and 30 percent) had college degrees than white men and women (21 percent and 13 percent).

Japanese are the third largest Asian group and have one of the highest family income levels, due primarily to the high labor force participation of Japanese women (exceeded only by Filipino women).

Vietnamese, the fourth largest Asian group, came to the United States in two waves. The first immigrants arrived in 1975, after the fall of South Vietnam. The earlier immigrants were generally well educated, could often speak English, were Christian, and they had worked closely with the Americans in South Vietnam during the war years. The second wave's were more diverse, many of them peasants and fishermen. They have been employed in the United States in agriculture, craft, operative, fishing, and service positions.

Koreans make up the fifth largest Asian group. They, too, have been highly educated at home and find themselves underemployed in the United States. Many Korean nurses and physicians have had to work as orderlies and medical assistants, while improving their language skills and studying to pass professional licensing examinations. According to a 1983 study, 78 percent of the Korean greengrocers in New York City had college degrees. They found a niche in the retail produce business, replacing older white merchants who retired or moved to the suburbs. In New York City, by 1980, Koreans owned three-quarters of the greengrocery stores. Most brought capital with them to start businesses or borrowed it from Korean American credit-rotating organizations.

Asian Indians, the sixth largest Asian group, increased their population in the United States from 10,000 in 1965 to more than half a million by 1985. The new Asian Indian immigrants come primarily from the professional class. Among Asian groups, they have the lowest percentage working in services and the highest percentage in professional and managerial positions. They have found a niche in the hospitality industry; in 1980, they owned almost a third of the hotels and motels in the United States.

Similar to African Americans, Asian American communities have become bipolar with a growing entrepreneurial-professional middle class and a stagnating underclass in the secondary and tertiary sectors of the labor market. In 1980, 51 percent of employed Chinese immigrants worked in menial service and low-skilled blue-collar jobs. They generally live in the Chinatowns of the big cities, where unemployment and impoverishment run high. In 1980, 25 percent of New York's Chinatown population lived in poverty. Although Filipinos have a high proportion of college graduates, Filipino-Americans have twice the high school dropout rate and lower enrollments in higher education than other Asian Americans.

A similar profile exists for the Latino population in the United States. Chicanos form the largest Latino group. They are concentrated primarily in the Southwest but also live in the Midwest. Because

Chicanos move easily between the United States and Mexico, they have remained a reserve employment army. As Chicano agricultural laborers have organized unions to press for better pay and working conditions, growers have turned increasingly to Southeast Asian and Caribbean workers. Locked in the barrios of the Southwest, Chicanos in the main have become casual laborers, hired for part-time and seasonal work. Only about a third of Chicanos graduate from high school in the United States and less than 4 percent complete four years or more of college.

The second largest Latino group, Puerto Ricans, present a comparable picture. Perhaps because of their easy and frequent movement between the island and the mainland, they too have remained a reserve army of labor. While agriculture has diminished as the major employer, over half the island's work force is semi-skilled or unskilled. Most Puerto Ricans in the United States live in New York City, which had a Puerto Rican population of 1 million in 1983. They toil largely in the garment industry and as service workers. Over one-third of U.S. Puerto Rican families live in poverty, a higher rate than for any minority group. Next to Chicanos, they have the worst high school dropout rate.

The most prosperous Latinos, Cubans, are the third largest group. After the Cuban Revolution in 1958, approximately 10 percent of Cuba's population left the country. Professionals made up almost half the immigrants in the United States. Cuban immigrants to the United States after 1960 resembled western European immigrants more than Latinos. A disproportionately high number of businessmen, entrepreneurs, and professionals left Cuba. They were more urban than rural. Although about three-fifths of Cuba's population was considered white, almost 95 percent of the Cubans in the United States by 1970 classified themselves as white. By 1980, there were over 800,000 Cubans in the United States; Miami became the second largest Cuban city after Havana. In Miami, Cubans started numerous businesses, such as grocery stores, restaurants, banks, furniture manufacturing plants, garment plants, and cigar factories. The number of businesses owned by Cubans in Miami grew from 919 in 1967 to 18,000 by 1980. Cubans had the highest median family income of all Latinos and higher family incomes than African Americans. Initially Cubans came to the United States as sojourners, similar to Asian immigrants before World War II. Cubans left as families, however, not as single men. As of 1970, only 10 percent of Miami's Cubans were

citizens, but by 1980, the figure rose to a third, with 86.4 percent of the noncitizens indicating that they planned to become citizens. Not all Cubans enjoyed prosperity; 17 percent of Cuban families were below the poverty line in 1980, with most impoverished Cubans living in the New York City area.

Chicanos, Puerto Ricans, and Cubans have been joined by Latinos from Central America, who came to the United States in large numbers only after 1950. Civil unrest and economic conditions increased immigration, both legal and illegal, of El Salvadoreans, Dominicans, Panamanians, Guatemalans, and Hondurans. By the mid 1980s, almost half a million Salvadoreans lived on the West Coast, primarily in Los Angeles. About half a million Dominicans resided on the East Coast, with 90 percent in New York City. Four-fifths of the Dominicans worked in semi-skilled and unskilled jobs in textile mills, as machine operators, in restaurants and hotels, and as janitors, domestic servants, and maintenance workers.

The relative prosperity of some minority workers and their entry into job categories previously closed to them might suggest the end of a labor market segmented along racial and ethnic lines. Los Angeles in 1940, for example, did not have a single Japanese American employed as a fireman, policeman, mailman, or public school teacher. Today, it is in the public sector that minority workers have found greatest access to employment. The shift of the United States economy from an industrial to a technological base has had as great an effect on minority workers as the change from an agricultural to an industrial economy. Unskilled and semi-skilled minority workers have suffered from the exodus of big business to the suburbs. The central cities have become more dependent on a service economy that requires professional qualifications. Even with professional qualifications, however, race and ethnicity remain salient aspects of employment. Asian American men have joined the primary sector of the labor market but generally in mid-range and lower tier jobs. They hold more technical than managerial or executive positions. While white women are more likely to work as secretaries, women of color are more apt to be typists, keypunch operators, and file clerks.

African American male college graduates have higher unemployment rates and lower median incomes than their white counterparts. In 1989, the unemployment rate for college-educated black men aged twenty-five to sixty-four was about three times that of white men. Black male college gradu-

TABLE 2 Distribution of Workers Across Labor Market Segments, by Racial-Ethnic Group and Gender, 1980

	Upper-Tier Primary	Lower-Tier Primary	Total Primary	Upper-Tier Secondary	Lower-Tier Secondary	Total Secondary
WOMEN						
American Indian	18	8	26	45	28	73
Chicana	11	7	18	52	30	82
European American	23	8	31	51	18	69
African American	15	7	22	46	32	78
Japanese American	23	9	32	48	20	68
Chinese American	24	10	34	51	15	66
Filipina American	15	19	34	46	19	65
Island Puerto Rican	24	8	32	51	18	69
U.S. Puerto Rican	13	8	21	60	19	79
MEN						
American Indian	19	39	58	19	23	42
Chicano	12	33	45	24	31	55
European American	34	34	68	19	13	32
African American	14	32	46	26	28	54
Japanese American	41	25	66	16	17	33
Chinese American	43	17	60	16	25	41
Filipino American	24	25	49	26	24	50
Island Puerto Rican	24	33	57	22	21	43
U.S. Puerto Rican	14	28	42	33	25	58

Source: Teresa Amott and Julie Matthaei, *Race, Gender, and Work: A Multicultural Economic History of Women in the United States,* 1991, pp. 339, 340.

ates were also more likely to be underemployed than whites; almost a third of black men with college degrees were in occupations that do not require a college education compared with 14 percent of white men. Nearly half of white male professionals worked in higher paying primary jobs, while only a third of black male professionals held similar positions. The idea that the economic gap between blacks and whites is closing holds true more for women than for men, that is, when we compare black with white women. Part of the reason for such difference is that the labor market remains segmented along gender lines, with women, like men of color, holding lower paying positions in the primary sector. All women are likely to face a dual-wage scale for work similar to that performed by all men. Black women in 1984, for example, earned 97 percent of the weekly wages of white women, 78 percent of those of black men, but only 53 percent of those of white men.

Since the mid 1970s, employment has shifted to industries in which minority participation, especially African American and Latino, has been and remains low. Additionally, businesses have moved to areas of the country, especially the Sunbelt, where wages are lower, fringe benefits are less, and

unions are absent or weak. Black family median income, after rising from 54 percent of white family median income in the 1950s to 61.5 percent in 1975, fell to 57 percent by 1986. Latino family median income, 66.9 percent of white family median income in 1975 dropped to 65.2 percent by 1985.

For many African Americans and Latinos, the military has been an alternative to poor employment opportunities in civilian life. In 1986, 30 percent of the army, 20 percent of the Marines, 17 percent of the air force, and 14 percent of the navy was African American; 32 percent of the female enlistees in the army were African American. Black enlistees in the army had a higher educational level than whites and reenlisted more frequently. When recent veterans were asked to compare military and civilian life, African Americans rated the military more positively than whites. With the thawing of Cold War tensions, this employment option will probably become less viable for minority workers.

In 1988, 14 percent of all adults and 20 percent of all children under the age of seventeen were people of color. By the year 2000, one-third of all school-age American children and one-third of the net additions to the U.S. labor force will be people of color. The U.S. economy will become more dependent on minority workers in the primary sector of the labor market. The bipolarization of the minority work force into those with educational achievement and marketable skills and those with little education and few skills will pose as great a challenge to the labor market as its segmentation along racial, ethnic, and gender lines, which restricted occupational and economic mobility for most of the twentieth century.

BIBLIOGRAPHY

Amott, Teresa, and Julie Matthaei. *Race, Gender, and Work: A Multicultural Economic History of Women in the United States* (1991).

Baron, Harold M. "The Demand for Black Labor: Historical Notes on the Political Economy of Racism." *Radical America* 5, no. 2 (1971): 1–46.

Boles, John B. *Black Southerners, 1619–1869* (1983).

Bonacich, Edna. "A Theory of Ethnic Antagonism: The Split Labor Market." *American Sociological Review* 37, no. 5 (1972): 547–559.

———. "Abolition, the Extension of Slavery, and the Position of Free Blacks: A Study of Split Labor Markets in the United States, 1830–1863." *American Journal of Sociology* 81, no. 3 (1975): 601–628.

———. "Advanced Capitalism and Black/White Race Relations in the United States: A Split Labor Market Interpretation." *American Sociological Review* 41, no. 1 (1976): 34–51.

Dickerson, Dennis C. *Out of the Crucible: Black Steelworkers in Western Pennsylvania, 1875–1980* (1986).

Gann, L. H., and Peter J. Duignan. *The Hispanics in the United States: A History* (1986).

Harris, William H. *The Harder We Run: Black Workers Since the Civil War* (1982).

Jaynes, Gerald David, and Robin M. Williams, Jr., eds. *A Common Destiny: Blacks and American Society* (1989).

Jones, Jacqueline. *Labor of Love, Labor of Sorrow: Black Women, Work, and the Family from Slavery to the Present* (1985).

Lewis, Ronald L. *Coal, Iron, and Slaves: Industrial Slavery in Maryland and Virginia, 1715–1865* (1979).

Loewen, James W. *The Mississippi Chinese: Between Black and White* (1971).

Loewenberg, Bert James. "Efforts of the South to Encourage Immigration, 1865–1900." *South Atlantic Quarterly* 33, no. 4 (1934): 363–385.

Meisenheimer, Joseph R., II. "Black College Graduates in the Labor Market, 1979 and 1989." *Monthly Labor Review* 113, no. 11 (1990).

Mirandé, Alfredo. *The Chicano Experience: An Alternative Perspective* (1985).

One Third of a Nation: A Report of the Commission on Minority Participation in Education and American Life (1988).

Stampp, Kenneth M. *The Peculiar Institution: Slavery in the Antebellum South* (1956).

Starobin, Robert S. *Industrial Slavery in the Old South* (1970).

Takaki, Ronald. *Strangers from a Different Shore: A History of Asian Americans* (1989).

Trotter, Joe William, Jr., ed. *The Great Migration in Historical Perspective: New Dimensions of Race, Class, and Gender* (1991).

Wade, Richard C. *Slavery in the Cities: The South, 1820–1860* (1964).

SEE ALSO **Health Care**; **Racism**; and various essays in the sections "**Ethnic and Racial Subcultures**" and "**Periods of Social Change**."

THE PROFESSIONS

Samuel Haber

THE PROFESSIONS are a disputed category because they are not inert or passive objects, like preserved butterflies under a lepidopterist's gaze, to be calmly classified, labeled, and considered. Rather, they are active, changing, influential social groups that energetically classify, label, and consider themselves—they take an important part in their own definition. Originally the term "profession" referred to any occupation, and this is still its primary meaning in most Romance languages. The word goes back to the practice of the Roman tax collector, who called upon taxpayers to declare publicly (to profess) their occupation so that they might be properly assessed. By the eighteenth century its primary meaning had narrowed in the Anglo-Saxon world to refer more particularly to clergymen, lawyers, and physicians (and often to military officers). These were occupations endowed with honor and authority: they were worthy of a gentleman.

In nineteenth- and twentieth-century America this definition was extended in various overlapping ways—through resemblance, differentiation, self-definition, and social designation. A driving force behind such extension was ambition. To enter a profession or to transform one's occupation into a profession was a way of rising in life. The resemblance of the professions to one another, even in the eighteenth century, when there were few, was of a loose sort. It would be difficult to isolate a single feature that essentially defined a profession. The professions were occupations of gentlemen, but there were gentlemanly pursuits—superintending one's landed estate, for example—that were not considered professions; and the lower ranks of the professions of medicine and law (surgeons and solicitors) were often not considered gentlemanly. A classical education was a common preparation for the upper ranks of most professions, though clearly less common among military officers. Subordination to exogenous requirements diminished within the professions but was much praised among the clergy of the Church of England. The similarities that helped define the professions in the eighteenth century, and more decidedly afterward, were like family resemblances, shared by many members but rarely by all.

Differentiation was also important in defining the professions. In the eighteenth century, a profession stood in contrast with a trade, something usually considered beneath the dignity of a gentleman. Mercantile pursuits for profit and handicrafts were clearly not professions. In nineteenth-century America, such disdain for working with one's hands rapidly disappeared, although as late as the end of the twentieth century even a highly skilled blue-collar worker would not be regarded as a professional. That some American craftsmen won the appellation "professional" owed much to their energetic campaigns of self-definition. Dentists and pharmacists (the latter both mechanical and mercantile) were disdained by the medical profession, and they in response mimicked the physicians with a vengeance: they too formed associations to declare themselves professionals and to lobby legislatures for such recognition. Dentists even beset the Census Bureau until it classified them as professionals.

Not all such campaigns of self-definition succeeded. If the resemblances to the traditional professions was too incongruous, social designation would often be withheld. When in the late nineteenth and early twentieth centuries librarianship and public-school teaching came to be dominated by women, and the women were placed in clearly subordinate positions, these occupations declined in status and lost much of their earlier public recognition as professions. In that era a woman was rarely granted authority over anyone except children, and her honor was defined by her chastity. A profession made up largely of women seemed to be an anomaly. The definition of the professions is a social and historical matter, shifting but still bearing some relation to the qualities of the traditional professions.

GENERAL HISTORIOGRAPHICAL TRENDS

The first writings on the history of the professions were by the professionals themselves. These were usually commemorative works about a ministerial, medical, or bar association, extolling the leadership and the achievements of the particular group. In such works the well-being of the practitioners and the progress of their science were usually assumed to be indistinguishable. They therefore provided justification for the authority and honor that the profession had or should have achieved. However, the scholarly studies of the histories of the relevant disciplines—medicine, law, and religion—in their usually brief discussions of their organized professions sometimes provided a refreshing contrast to the apologetic works written by practitioners.

An important turning point in the historiography of the professions was the publication of a work by two Englishmen. This study, *The Professions* (1933), written by A. M. Carr-Saunders and P. A. Wilson, placed the discussion of these occupational groups into a broader social setting than had been envisioned in the earlier scholarship. Though they drew extensively upon the special histories of diverse professions, the authors tried to extract from those narratives a social role for the professions that they believed had great contemporary importance. They argued that the professions provided the social leaven that might raise society to a new era of "freedom, dignity, and responsibility."

The essential characteristic of the professions, Carr-Saunders and Wilson argued, was the application to the ordinary business of life of intellectual techniques acquired through long training. Since the industrial revolution, such intellectual techniques were preeminently those of the natural sciences. This made the professions both progressive and stabilizing, for the advance of the natural sciences seemed obviously progressive and the requirements of extensive training prescribed the sustaining of institutions. This argument worked best with the scientific professions like medicine and less well with what the authors called the "institutional professions," such as law. Significantly, they omitted the ministry altogether. Modern soci-

ety, they asserted, had entered an era of large-scale organizations, and this had affected the professions. But what differentiated professional organization from the rest, they thought, was that it provided for both cooperation and autonomy. It also provided the means of bringing "the expert into service of democracy." Their hope was that the modalities of professional organization would spread to society at large.

Writing early in the Great Depression, when the social order in most Western nations was badly shaken, Carr-Saunders and Wilson proposed the professions as a third way between the anarchic laissez-faire capitalism of the United States and the oppressive statism of the Soviet Union. Such a vision was strikingly similar to pronouncements of some of the professionals themselves, but rarely had it been put forward so boldly and comprehensively. The work of Carr-Saunders and Wilson gave impulse and direction to much of the scholarly writing on the professions in the generation that followed, yet those studies were seldom as ideologically explicit as their influential predecessor.

An advantageous way of looking at some of the changes in the literature on the professions brought about by the scholars of the generation that followed would be to compare the Carr-Saunders and Wilson article on the professions in the *Encyclopaedia of the Social Sciences* (1934) with that on the same subject by Talcott Parsons in the *International Encyclopedia of the Social Sciences* (1968). While many of the ideas of Carr-Saunders and Wilson are retained in Parsons's analysis, clearly Parsons's argument is more systematic and coherent, for he casts his discussion within the framework of Max Weber's methodology, theory, and general worldview. This makes the subject of the professions even more momentous than it had been in the work of Carr-Saunders and Wilson. In Parsons's analysis, the professions become the embodiment of "cognitive rationality" and instruments in "the main historical trend" of the extension of "the range of rationally ordered organization" in the world. If Parsons seems more audacious than Carr-Saunders and Wilson, his empirical supports are much slighter. Most often he does not refer to any profession in particular, and when he does, it is usually medicine. Nonetheless, he maintains and develops many of the themes found in the earlier literature. The element of intellectual training is central to his discussion, and he places great stress upon the role of the universities in providing cognitive and technical proficiency. He also looks to the professional association as the "institutional means of putting competence to socially responsible use." In this particular, like Carr-Saunders and Wilson in others, he accepts the professionals at their own valuation.

Whatever the shortcomings of Carr-Saunders and Wilson's as well as of Parsons's work on the professions, they gave the subject a kind of excitement that made it an attractive meeting ground for sociologists and historians. Carr-Saunders and Wilson's study had notable influence upon the writing about the professions before World War II, and Parsons's idea held sway after the war, but by the 1960s and 1970s the new scholarship turned sharply critical of both. Some of this development owed much to Parsons's efforts to make available the writings of Max Weber to American audiences. For Weber not only described the "rationalization" of the world, he also gave an account of growing monopolization (with its restrictive and malefic effects) as a special rational response to market uncertainties.

The New Critical scholarship of the 1960s and 1970s emphasized the monopolistic aspects of the professions, their interest in limiting the supply of practitioners in order to increase their income. Moreover, these scholars charged that Parsons had taken the professions' "ideology of service" at face value. The new studies tried to treat the professions as one would any occupation, except that they had a remarkably successful sales talk which enabled them to win monopolistic powers from the government. The upshot was "right-wing" and "left-wing" Weberian scholarship—the former emphasizing professional expertise and granting professional privileges some legitimacy, the latter emphasizing professional monopolistic and restrictive practices and discrediting the legitimacy of those privileges. Alongside the left-wing Weberians stood some Marxist critics who also stressed the monopolistic practices of the professions and, in addition, treated "professional posturing" as false consciousness and predicted the future proletarianization of "mental labor in advanced capitalism."

More recently, the description of modernization as the spread of "cognitive rationality" and "extending the range of rationally ordered organization" has come under attack from many writers as being too one-sided. Theodor Adorno and Herbert Marcuse, for example, have argued provocatively that the advance of this kind of rationality and the advance of neurosis go hand in hand. The Weberian analysis of the professions also has come to

seem one-sided in both motives and effects. Rather than portray the professions as the epitome of modernization, I have argued elsewhere that the special importance of the professions is their success in maintaining much that is precapitalist and predemocratic in the modern world. The present article is written from that perspective.

Before discussing the historical development of the professions, it will be helpful to engage in a brief survey of the major turns and events of that development.

The American professions were born in the mid eighteenth century. In this era the colonies were brought closer politically and economically to the mother country, and the rapid social differentiation in the cities and the southern colonies created an upper class that ardently mimicked British gentlemanly ways. It also provided some basis for the adoption of gentlemanly usages by those engaged in occupations that were considered professions in Britain.

By 1830 it had become evident that a powerful egalitarian impulse in America was sweeping before it many of the marks of a society that had been run by finished gentlemen. This was an ambivalent egalitarianism, combining a vague eagerness for leveling in the social order with a distinct desire to remove all restraints upon the ambitious and the capable. The professions, both in their style and in their science that seemed to support their style, came under attack. Though diminished in reputation, privileges, and self-assurance, they managed to enclose and preserve the authority and honor of the traditional gentleman in their relationships to their clients if not to society at large.

The years 1880 to 1900 were ones of economic expansion and consolidation, as well as of rapid increase in social stratification and what were considered persuasive justifications for that stratification. The professions' traditional claim of authority and honor also found new supports that helped the associations win new licensing legislation. Those laws distinguished between rightful and wrongful practitioners and ostensibly granted monopoly powers to the legitimate ones.

After the 1880s the professions increased and extended their powers and numbers. This was particular true in the first decades of the twentieth century. If, nonetheless, the discussion of twentieth-century developments may seem somewhat abbreviated in this article, that follows from one of its principal arguments—that the last decades of the nineteenth century were the formative era of the modern professions. Their models of aspiration and achievement were fashioned in the 1880s and 1890s. Much of the professions' earlier history culminated in the late nineteenth century, and much of their later history derived from that era. However, in the 1960s and 1970s, the professions again came under attack in a manner reminiscent of the egalitarian assaults of the mid nineteenth century. These new attacks were far less consequential, and by the 1980s the expanding professions had recovered their momentum. The professions today are prominent models for a singular kind of social position. They seem to offer an escape from vexing supervision at work as well as from some of the depersonalization and uncertainty of markets and bureaucracies.

THE RISE OF THE PROFESSIONS, 1750–1830

The first wave of professionalization consisted largely of the acquisition of the proprieties and learning of the upper ranks of the British professions by men of lower standing in the colonies who did similar work. The learning itself was a propriety, for today much of it would seem to have little immediate and practical relevance. One of the important marks of an eighteenth-century professional was a liberal arts education. Being almost exclusively a privilege of the upper classes, classical learning conferred dignity and social status upon those who acquired it. Instruction in the classical languages and authors, it was said, engendered a refinement, embellishment, and enlargement of mind that contrasted sharply with the narrowness and even coarseness of the tradesman and mechanic, who had access only to apprenticeship training. Therefore, one of the characteristic features of the professionalization of American occupations in this era was the increasing proportion of practitioners who boasted a liberal arts education. In the ministry that percentage had always been high, but in medicine and law this development was remarkable. By 1771, the Suffolk bar demanded a liberal education for admission to practice, and somewhat earlier the bar association in New York City agreed to accept only college graduates as clerks. Those with bachelor's degrees were favored in most jurisdictions. Later writers were to wonder at the many professionals in this era with such degrees. Between 1800 and 1830 more than 90 percent of Massachusetts lawyers were college graduates.

Alongside this desire to make a gentleman's education a qualification for these occupations in America, the professionals demonstrated their interest in appropriating the science cultivated by the upper ranks of their callings in England. Actually, the Americans were often more resolute and formal about this than their English counterparts. American physicians set up medical schools along the pattern of those in Scotland, where many early leaders of the profession studied. American lawyers sponsored lectures on law, borrowing from Sir William Blackstone's Vinerian Lectures, then expanded and regularized these into proto–law schools, usually attached to established colleges. (Before the Revolution, some of the foremost colonial lawyers had attended the Inns of Court and were actually called to the English bar.) By the early nineteenth century American ministers had established theological seminaries, something that had almost no parallel in England.

Other features of the English gentlemanly professions translated less well. The eminent Dr. John Morgan (1735–1789) on his return from his grand tour of the Continent, tried to establish honoraria rather than fixed fees as the proper mode of payment, but to no avail. Nor was he more successful in setting up ranks within the profession. A few of the more distinguished American physicians refused to practice surgery or to compound drugs, but most doctors ignored those punctilios of the London physician. Lawyers were somewhat more successful in setting up ranks in their profession. The rank of barrister (sometimes called counsel) in a number of colonies was separated from the attorneys, and members of the new rank were given a monopoly on practice in the superior courts. New Jersey in addition set up the rank of serjeant, and Massachusetts provided three grades: attorney, counselor, and barrister. Often a lawyer might rise through the ranks and practice in them simultaneously, thereby gaining entry to all courts.

Such laxity was characteristic of the monopoly powers granted to the professions. These powers, the professionals expected, would help secure them a suitable income—a competence. That was a favorite term. It meant both the sufficiency of means for comfortable living and the distinctive skills that those easy circumstances could advance and sustain. It was the income with which a gentleman could preserve his proper "port and carriage," his honor and authority; but the notion of maximization of income was lacking. This, in part, explains the looseness of the monopoly powers granted by the professional licensing laws and the meager force behind them. They did, however, clearly distinguish between reputable and disreputable practitioners. By 1800, three-quarters of the states had such laws governing the practice of law, and by 1830 only three states were without them for medicine. Licensed professionals flaunted the public recognition of their competence. They were authoritative and respected, and stood at the head of their professions.

The most important feature of the English gentlemanly professions adopted by their American counterparts was the special relation of professional and client. In the English setting, this was the interjection of the general relation between gentlemen and those below them into the world of occupations. While a tradesman or mechanic gave his customer what he wanted, the professional gave his client what he needed. This was a relation of authority and dependence. It had its origins in the traditions of feudal Europe as well as in the transference of feelings from parent-child relationships to class ties—a shift not uncommon in aristocratic societies. The relation of professional and client characteristic of the upper ranks of the English professions became an ideal for their American imitators.

That relation received explicit expression in the codes of medical ethics adopted by the medical societies of this era; later it appeared in the code of the American Medical Association, where it remained throughout the nineteenth century. All these codes derived from that of Dr. Thomas Percival of Manchester, England. Percival was an ardent admirer of the great eighteenth-century London physicians. But what could be taken for granted in London had to be expounded and explicated in Manchester—and even more so in America. Percival's initial purpose had been to set off the domain of the physician and to protect it from the intrusive upstart surgeons. Percival called his work a code of medical ethics, yet for the most part it dealt with etiquette. The confusion of ethics and etiquette was an important characteristic of gentlemanly culture. The salient point of the code was its description of the relationship between the physician and his patient.

Percival bade doctors "so to unite *tenderness* with *firmness,* and *condescension* with *authority,* as to inspire the minds of their patients with gratitude, respect and confidence" (Leake, ed., *Percival's Medical Ethics,* p. 27). This was the epitome of gentlemanly bearing. The virtues of the gentlemanly doctor were mastery delicately balanced by compassion; the virtues of the deferential patient were

unmitigated respect for the physician and compliance with his directions. If in this formula we today bridle at the word "condescension," it is because our more egalitarian age has coarsened the meaning of what the eighteenth century took to be a subtle moral imperative. Condescension was a form of humility that could counterbalance authority (Dr. Samuel Johnson called it a "voluntary humiliation: descent from superiority") and was exercised by those of elevated mind and social station. It was the humane act of a superior who, while he condescended, remained superior, for he was performing an act of grace toward those on whose level he was placing himself.

Ministers and lawyers, without such a code, had other devices with which to strengthen the professional relationship of authority and dependence. Perhaps as important as the relationship between the professional and his client was the relationship among the professions themselves. The ministry, the preeminent profession in seventeenth-century New England played a special role in giving particularity to the concept and ideal of the professions much beyond their time and place. The years 1750–1830, however, were not only the era of the establishment of the gentlemanly professions, they were also the years in which the ministry clearly declined from preeminence in America and the lawyers rose to a paramount position. This shift owed much to developments within these professions as well as to changes in society at large. It was primarily in seventeenth-century New England that the ministry held an exalted position in society, and the effects of that prominence were felt in varying degrees in the other colonies. The decline of the ministry from that prominence has been often linked to secularization, a term perhaps somewhat indefinite but still useful in describing the diminishing importance of religious ideas and experience for the ordering of the broader society.

Protestantism's special emphasis on the inwardness of religion as well as its propensity for dissension contributed to this secularization, as did the growing economic and social diversification of the society in which Protestantism flourished. In addition, the Great Awakening in the second quarter of the eighteenth century, which fostered religion of the heart—religion at a high emotional temperature— endangered and weakened the authority of some of the most commanding ministers. In this era of relative decline, the rapidly growing body of Anglican clergy in the colonies set in motion a brief countercurrent in the mid eighteenth century in their campaign to bring a bishop to America and to augment their priestly powers. This endeavor closely paralleled the efforts of colonial lawyers and doctors to assume professional standing. Because they backed what proved to be the losing side in the Revolution, however, the priests' hopes were dashed. By 1830 the ministry had declined in power, yet its influence was still great. At the least, the ministers were the philosophers of the multitude, supplying a foundation of moral belief and behavior as well as a scheme of general purposes and ends that helped give meaning to life. Without this, the amazing practical accomplishments of Americans would have been less likely.

The lawyers quickly rose to preeminence among the professions. In broadest terms, this can be seen as part of a prevailing cultural shift from the world outlook of John Calvin (1509–1564) to the world outlook of John Locke (1632–1704), from the preoccupation with sin to the preoccupation with rights. The lawyer was the priest of rights. It is not at all surprising, therefore, that the lawyers played such an extraordinary role in the Revolution and in the establishment of the new government. The Constitution, which embodied the fundamental principles of American government, defined itself as law. That meant those principles could be determined in the courts through the ordinary practice of litigation. This was the lawyer's domain. William Wirt (1772–1834), son of a tavern keeper who rose to the post of attorney general of the United States, described the esteem of the profession through which he himself had been raised: "Men of talents in this country have generally been bred in the profession of law," he wrote in 1803, "and indeed throughout the United States, I have met with few persons of exalted intellect whose powers have been directed to any other pursuit. The bar in America is the road to honor" (Robert A. Ferguson, *Law and Letters in American Culture* [1984], p. 12).

THE EGALITARIAN INTERREGNUM, 1830–1880

Although the ideal of the profession, developed and elaborated in America between 1750 and 1830, showed surprising durability, some of its institutional fixtures constructed during this era were swiftly dismantled in the years that followed. The years from about 1830 to 1880, from the standpoint of organizational power and effectiveness, were the nadir of the professions in America; in this period a widespread and powerful egalitarian impulse that had been latent in much of American culture became manifest and demolished the underpinnings of a society that had previously been run by gentlemen. Clearly it was an equivocal egalitarianism, in that it mixed a sentiment for leveling with a distinct eagerness for rising in the world. That volatile mixture was compounded in varying proportions in different sections of the country and segments of society.

Among the principal sources of this egalitarianism were the expanding political democracy, market capitalism, and evangelical Protestantism. Each took on new force and momentum in this era, pressing against different kinds of exclusiveness for the sake of dissimilar sorts of opportunity and exhibiting distinctive styles of leveling. Suffrage extension, and the new political devices that accompanied it, to all appearances made most white males—irrespective of social standing, religious belief, merit, and even virtue—members of the ruling class. Government by gentlemen, often vociferously attacked, gave way to government by political machine, in which democrats equally acquiesced.

Market capitalism, quickened by the rapid improvement of transportation and more generally invigorated by public support for the construction of social-overhead capital, unwittingly furnished an extraordinary corrosive for the prescriptive and decorous ranks in society. Ambitious businessmen entered markets that had been based upon local connections, traditional restraints, and various insular forms of monopoly. In the world of commerce and industry, authority and honor took on new connotations. Special recognition was granted to success in the marketplace as in the past success in war, politics, and art had been given distinctive approbation. The honor granted to commercial success helped to justify the increasingly unequal distribution of wealth that characterized the major cities. However, in the rural North, where most of the American population lived, commercial agriculture and smallholdings prevailed. There markets worked with fewest restraints and the distribution of wealth was probably brought closer to some sort of equality than at any other time or place in the nation's history.

Evangelical Protestantism, the third component of the equivocal egalitarian impulse of the era, embodied an attack upon authority but could also provide a justification of existing conditions. Two principal and interrelated developments within the evangelical Protestantism of these years were the gradual erosion of the Calvinist distinction between God's predestined elect and all others, and the emergence of the seasonal revival, with its unique spiritual technology, as a central institution of Protestant piety. This turned evangelical Protestants away from church establishments, hierarchies, ritual, elevated and learned clergy, creeds, and sometimes separate denominations. It turned them toward such vagaries as perfectionism and millenarianism, latent with social disruption. Strictly speaking, evangelical Protestant egalitarianism extended to the realm of salvation and not to the scheme of creation. In nineteenth-century America, however, those categories became increasingly porous.

In this setting, the traditional distinction between gentlemen and ordinary folk dissolved rapidly. There was no clamor for the replacement of that honorific title with a more egalitarian term; rather, the bulk of the white male population, without much fuss, simply took on and was granted the designation "gentleman." This posed a threat to the distinction between professions and ordinary occupations. The classical education, the science, and even the technical education of the professional came under attack. Classical learning, once an indicium of gentlemanly status, was now widely derided as exclusive and useless. After 1830, a growing number of young men bypassed the colleges, the fortresses of classical education, on their way to the professions. The laymen's charge that the vaunted science of the professions was useless and encumbering found acceptance within the professions themselves.

In this era, the sciences of the professions—their systematized knowledge based upon theoretical understanding—were beset with difficulties. The resulting doubts weakened the professionals' resolve in response to the attacks upon their elevated standing and privileges. The science of the physician in the eighteenth and early nineteenth centuries was a humoral "system" explaining in comprehensive terms the cause and cure of disease. Benjamin Rush (1745–1813), for example, declared that there was but one disease, its cause the irregular convulsive action of blood vessels and its primary treatment bloodletting. Some doctors held fast to such systems and the heroic treatment they required (usually bleeding, mercurials, and narcotics); others, though, shaken by their melancholy experience and the unsettling findings of the French clinician Pierre Louis (1787–1872)—who through rigorous statistical studies demonstrated that venesection had few beneficial effects—were led to conclude that medicine was an uncertain science. It was not surprising, therefore, that the simple (but patented) "botanic medicine" of Samuel Thomson (1769–1843), and the recondite homeopathy of Samuel Hahnemann (1755–1843) would find acceptance—botanic medicine by the commonalty, and homeopathy by the upper classes.

The science of law in late-eighteenth- and early-nineteenth-century America derived from a long and venerable accumulation of custom, judicial decision, and legislation, most of which, to the disgust of some patriots, had been received from England. The substantive law was intricately entangled with procedure and confined within the various common-law forms of action. Ironically, William Blackstone's attempt to give a connected and rational account of the whole legal system helped lead Americans willy-nilly away from the forms and fictions that he cherished. The comprehensiveness and clarity of his work raised the hope among his American imitators that law might be freed from inherited modes in order to deal more directly with justice in a democratic society. In addition to such theoretical considerations there were some practical embarrassments. To the extent that Americans accepted the common-law rule of stare decisis, the many American courts with their many rulings threatened to confuse even the most learned lawyers. The legal profession therefore was divided and weakened by its doubts when faced with the resolute campaign of David Dudley Field (1805–1894) for the reform of law. Field contended that the law could be so simplified and codified that its basic principles might easily be grasped by all, and the number of lawyers reduced. In the Jacksonian era, the movement for legal reform often combined with a drive against the legal profession.

The theological science of the majority of American ministers in the eighteenth and early nineteenth centuries had been one of the various forms of modified Calvinism. Its basic doctrines, however, seemed to deny that man could be active in his own salvation. Yet in times of declining religious fervor some ministers brushed aside this dogma and appealed to their congregations to "make a new heart and spirit." The apparent successes of the religion of the heart, breaking forth in a series of great revivals, led some of the most renowned Calvinist theologians to becloud fundamental issues and the leading revivalists to downgrade doctrine altogether. What was the recourse of the gentlemanly ministry, guardians of orthodox doctrine, when the revivalists attacked the traditional notion that a valid ministry was an educated one? And what was it when the lowly revivalists joined the patrician statesmen of Enlightenment persuasion to disestablish the already discredited Anglican church after the Revolution as well as the Standing Order in Massachusetts and Connecticut some time later?

The disestablishment of the clergy was a foreshadowing. When the licensed doctors tried to use governmental powers against the medical sects, the latter struck back with Samuel Thomson in the lead and various Evangelicals as allies. When the dust had cleared, ten states had repealed their laws giving the medical societies the right to examine candidates and grant licenses. At the same time, bar associations that had arisen in the late eighteenth and early nineteenth centuries were deprived of their powers to admit new lawyers to practice. The Indiana state constitution went so far as to provide that "every person of good moral character who is a voter is entitled to practice law in any of the courts of the state" (Roscoe Pound, *The Lawyer from Antiquity to Modern Times* [1953], p. 233).

With the relinquishment of their classical learning and the downgrading of their science, some professionals began to place more emphasis upon their craft. After 1830, two seemingly opposite tendencies in technical education for the professions came to light: a widespread disparagement of training for the professions in favor of giving free play to natural talent-gained currency, and a booming market appeared for technical instruction, resulting from a rush of young men into the professions once they seemed accessible. The outcome was the rapid proliferation of proprietary schools for awarding professional degrees. In medicine, competition was brisk, and quite soon entry into these schools became exceedingly easy and graduation a matter of course. Between 1830 and 1845 the number of medical colleges doubled.

The legal profession was rife with propriety schools as well, but these were of less consequence. For in law such schools competed not only with apprenticeship preparation but also with do-it-yourself training, Blackstone's *Commentaries* in hand. The most reputable proprietary school, at Litchfield, Connecticut, which usually catered to young men with bachelor's degrees, closed in 1833. The small number of college-connected law schools that survived had no fixed entry requirements. Most lawyers in this era did not get their training through formal education. This seems to have been true of the ministers as well. The first

theological seminaries, formed in the early nineteenth century to ensure the inculcation of Calvinist doctrine and to ward off threatening Enlightenment notions then gaining influence in the colleges, were later supplemented by seminaries with the more limited purpose of upholding denominational standards and imparting homiletic skills. The seminary catalogs often listed a bachelor's degree as prerequisite for admission, but their students more often came directly out of the revivals than out of the colleges. Among the Methodists and the Baptists, the two largest denominations by mid century, most ministers had avoided the seminaries altogether.

Yet for those ministers who attended the seminaries, the experience was one of the most important sources of camaraderie and colleagueship that their profession afforded. The seminary alumni associations were often the most vital professional associations of ministers in this era. As for the doctors, their state and local medical societies aimed to serve more diverse purposes. During the period 1830–1880, the number of those societies grew, though they were often factious and unstable. One of the leaders of the New York State society, Dr. Nathan Smith Davis (1817–1904), who had been able to enter the profession because many of the traditional requirements had been abandoned, was unwilling to see his own achievement devalued by further laxity and want of distinction. He gathered about him a band of zealous doctors whose common cause was raising the profession to its former standing. This group became the basis for the American Medical Association (founded 1847), whose chief concerns were the struggle against "irregular" medicine and the improvement of medical education. In a manner characteristic of the outlook of professionals, these doctors sought those measures that would make their duty and their interest the same. They would benefit practitioners, but in ways they believed would improve the quality of medical services. The glut of poorly trained and "irregular" doctors was harmful to the public as well as to the well-trained and proficient practitioners. "Numbers should be restricted," wrote Davis, "by adding to the standard of requirements" (*History of Medical Education and Institutions in the United States* [1851], p. 227). In this interim period the AMA accomplished little; it persisted, nonetheless, and so became the saving remnant that carried the memory and ambition of earlier days into a later, more favorable era.

Perhaps the most salutary medical organizations of this era were the nascent specialty associations. Humoral pathology held back specialization because it was based upon the belief that the causes of disease were general, and the studying of organs meant studying symptoms rather than causes. From this standpoint, only quacks who were ignorant of medical science or charlatans who pandered to popular superstition for profit would be specialists. The first ophthalmologists and laryngologists were given both these labels. But when humoral pathology was refuted, "Baconian" inductive principles were defined as the true scientific method—and the customary scorn for specialists was more difficult to maintain. A motion recognizing specialties as legitimate fields of practice was tabled at an AMA convention in 1854 and not passed until fifteen years later.

Specialization served not only to subdivide medical practice but also led to the establishment of new healing professions. The humbling of the medical profession encouraged those who had done its most menial work to aspire to equal standing with doctors. Apothecaries, traditionally the lowest rank in medicine, laid the groundwork of the new profession of pharmacy in this era. In addition, men who had combined the crudest minor surgery of the mouth with skillful cosmetic embellishments now began to call themselves dentists. These dentists, owing to their rudimentary medical training, were unwelcome at the medical society meetings and quickly set up their own associations. Soon it would no longer be a disgrace to be called a dentist, promised the first president of the American Society of Dental Surgeons, and the organization provided that each and every member "shall be entitled to a diploma, or degree of Doctor of Dental Surgery" (Charles R. E. Koch, *History of Dental Surgery,* vol. 1 [1909], p. 173). The founding of the Baltimore College of Dental Surgery in 1839 afforded a somewhat more reputable form of credentialing, and the school became one of the principal centers of the new profession.

The profession of law resisted specialization and occupational division. Moreover, compared with doctors, lawyers showed less interest in professional organization. They had less need of such devices. The work of the lawyers brought them together in the county courthouses and the appellate courts, where they could fraternize and confer on common concerns. The most spirited lawyers' organizations of this era were the law library associations, usually with headquarters and facilities in the county courthouse. The leading lawyers joined these organizations to collectively purchase and own the enginery of their work—the law treatises, court reports, reference works—that enabled them to pepper their arguments with copious precedents, lofty allusions, and indisputable information. Those organizations usually provided the bases for the local bar associations formed in a later era.

Without any more elaborate organizational structures, the law in this era remained the most eminent of the professions. The most fundamental issues of government—constitutional questions, the very ends of dominion and sovereignty, as lawyers were wont to assert and many Americans to grant—were within the practitioner's ken. To the extent that lawyers could extol the law and the Constitution as a national holy of holies, to that degree they became honored Levites of that shrine. While the lawyers' authority and honor may have dimmed somewhat in this period compared with the previous era, lawyers nonetheless adapted more easily than ministers and physicians to the new deliverances and constraints of these years.

Yet all three traditional professions maintained gentlemanly authority and honor within their work setting though they surrendered some of both in society at large. They adopted a strategy of attempting to strengthen what they took to be the centers of professional distinctiveness and coherence when they found the boundaries increasingly undefendable. The central fact of this era for the professions was that they were able to maintain the distinction between the specially honored and authoritative professions and the ordinary occupations. That prodigious accomplishment invites attention to the factors that made it possible.

First of all, as has been suggested, the leveling attack upon the professions was peculiarly equivocal. While some Americans wanted to bring all barriers down and looked upon the distinctiveness of the professions as pure humbug, others wanted to make entry less restrictive but keep the dominion and esteem of the professions intact. Less obvious but still important was the local sheltered-market situation that the professions enjoyed. The client usually chose a professional through personal connections, and that meant the market for professional services was local, personal, and differentiated. Professionals, therefore, could usually avoid the sharp rivalry and price competition that might have undermined their authoritative standing with their clients. Furthermore, the professions, with all the difficulties in their sciences during this era, remained significantly the work of the intellect—which, notwithstanding the corrosive effects of revivalism, was still often intertwined with spirit and placed above the mundane. And intellect retained some of its association with elevated standing in the community.

Finally, the three traditional professions dealt with men and women who were in peril or pain, leaving them dependent and sometimes childlike. The structure of the situation brought to light the circumstantial inequality between the bestower and the recipient of the service. The professional relationship of authority and dependence echoed the reciprocal relationship of protection and subordination that pervaded earlier eras in Europe. It is not surprising, therefore, that the professional found the various usages of the traditional gentlemanly class particularly congenial.

THE REESTABLISHMENT OF THE PROFESSIONS: 1880–1900

By the 1880s important changes were apparent in the organizational momentum and direction of the professions. New professions appeared more rapidly, and both old and new professions took on a fresh spirit, moving toward legislative enactments that once again gave them public recognition and some governmental support for their efforts to raise educational standards and restrict entry into their ranks. Such legislation, it was hoped, would assure professional competence (in both senses of the word) and strengthen the authoritative relationship between the professional and his client. State legislatures passed a great variety of licensing laws, but these enactments were not secure until the Supreme Court, in *Dent* v. *West Virginia* (1888), upheld a model licensing law that enabled a board of health composed of regular doctors to deprive Dr. Marmaduke Dent, who held a diploma from the American Eclectic College of Medicine, of the right to practice. As if to make amends for past humiliations, this victory worsted a doctor trained in one of the offshoot schools of the Thomsonian movement that had led the successful campaign to set aside medical practice laws in the 1830s.

Justice Stephen Field, who just fifteen years earlier had upheld a citizen's "inalienable right to pursue his own calling," now found, along with the rest of the court, that "no one has the right to practice a profession without having the necessary qualifications" determined by "an authority competent to judge." That authority turned out to be the organized profession itself. This decision was a signal blow to the prestige of the "irregular" and unconforming practitioners. (Its practical effects in West Virginia were less drastic than might be imagined, however, because the irregulars quietly pushed an enactment through the legislature setting up licensing boards parallel to those of the regulars that would admit them to practice.)

What is striking about this new wave of legislation that reestablished the professions is how readily it was accepted by the public. This acquiescence in turn owed much to broader changes in American society. Contemporaries often called attention to the rapid expansion as well as the consolidation and new restrictions in the economy and the social order. The railroads in the 1880s became prototypes of centralization, hierarchy, rapid expansion, and new types of restriction. In this decade railway expansion astonished even some of its most sanguine promoters, adding at least a hundred thousand miles of track, a greater amount than the total previously in use. This increase was accompanied by the appearance of hierarchical and centralized bureaucracies, the growth of cartels, and nationwide railroad systems. Similar changes arose in other industries, and parallel development of expansion and restriction appeared in other areas: immigration, labor organization, urbanization, race relations, and the civil service. Those forces which had promoted the equivocal egalitarianism of an earlier era—political democracy, evangelical Protestantism, and market capitalism—now exhibited similar tendencies toward expansion as well as new kinds of constraints and restrictions of their own.

This new strengthening of social and economic hierarchies was accompanied by significant shifts in social thought. Open and self-confident attacks upon "the dogma of equality" became more acceptable. "Inequality appears to be the divine order," wrote Charles Dudley Warner ("Equality," *Atlantic* 45 [1880]: 24), and many Darwinians found it to be the natural order as well. The notion of science also shifted. In the eighteenth and early nineteenth centuries the professions spoke proudly of their science, but it usually meant simply a body of systematized knowledge. It was placed in contrast with art: "A science teaches us to know, and an art to do" (William Stanley Jevons, *Elementary Lessons in Logic* [1870], vol. 1, p. 7). But by the 1880s, "science" more often meant "natural science" (what the eighteenth century called "natural philosophy"), which was thought to be the most rigorous form of truth. Moreover, after the mid nineteenth century, "science" was applied more extensively to technology. It taught not only to know but also to do. In addition, within natural science there was a shift of attention from the descriptive sciences like botany and geology, in which lay collectors played a role, to experimental sciences like chemistry and physics, in which amateurs had less importance.

Linked to these changes was the new preeminence of medicine among the traditional professions—it was based upon natural science, whereas law rested upon an "institutional" science—and the astonishingly rapid growth of engineering among the more recent professions. Germ theory gave the doctor a convincing explanation of the causes of disease, and advances in physiology provided some understanding of how the body and various remedies responded to such ailments. The diphtheria antitoxin seemed to be the decisive instance. What had been a frightening and horrible disease that could choke a child to death before one's eyes now yielded to the new "serum therapy." The outcome was an enormously increased self-confidence among doctors and a growing popular respect for them.

The new preeminence of medicine was part of a broader intellectual shift, a new understanding of human nature and the requisites of human happiness. The rise of law had been linked to the Enlightenment, the blurring of the sense of human sin, and the sharpening of the sense of human rights. The rise of medicine was linked to the blurring of the sense of human rights and a sharpening of the sense of human needs. The preeminence of law had reflected the decline of Calvin and the rise of Locke as guide to human affairs; the preeminence of medicine reflected the decline of Locke and the rise of Darwin as the interpreter of the human condition. Of course this outline may be helpful only in suggesting the direction of change. In 1990 Calvin was alive for Princeton Seminary at least, and Locke inhered in many Supreme Court decisions. Surely the sense of sin and the demand for rights were powerful and moving forces in the late nineteenth century; yet now they were mitigated by the insistence of the students of the rapidly advancing physiological sciences that man must also be seen as a complex biological organism, and that much of his conduct could best be understood in those terms.

The capital of scientific medicine in this era was the Johns Hopkins Medical School (opened 1893). The school was generously endowed and therefore only loosely linked to economic considerations in forming its curriculum, hiring its faculty, and determining its very high entrance requirements. It led in American medical education for the next half-century. The brilliant pathologist William Henry Welch (1850–1934), the first dean of the school, assumed the role of evangelist of the methods and teachings of the German medical laboratory. It was in response to a call from Johns Hopkins that the Association of American Medical Colleges was formed (1890) with the purpose of reforming medical education. The association laid the groundwork for the decisive changes that followed the famous Flexner Report (1910). The outcome of that report was the closing of those schools whose facilities for training doctors capable of keeping up with new scientific discoveries were inadequate. The resulting restriction upon entry into the medical profession did not seem to be sinister.

While the physicians' authority and esteem rose more rapidly in this era than did those of the other professions, the rate of growth of the engineers in sheer numbers clearly outpaced that of their fellow professionals. Three national associations of engineers—mining, mechanical, and electrical—were established and joined the formerly less-specialized society of civil engineers to represent the profession. This specialization reflected the growth of particular markets for technical skills as well as the increasing application of science to technology. Leaders in the profession were usually the consulting engineers and educators, whose situation resembled that of the members of the older professions. But the bulk of the engineers were lesser employees in the bureaucracies of large organizations. The discrepancy between the preachments of the presidents of the engineering societies and the work experience of those engineering employees brought to the surface some signs of restiveness among the latter. They had little of the right to command and not much of the regard and approbation they had been led to believe were appropriate to professional standing. Eventually, the expanding corporations were able to alleviate such disquiet through vertical-line promotions and horizontal honorific distinctions within the firm. Nonetheless, the image of a profession among these low-ranking engineers was a much diminished one.

The neo-Weberian analysis of the professions, with its emphasis upon cognitive rationality, monopoly, and bureaucracy (the rational ordering of "social action"), can be quite helpful in the discussion of the foremost and the most rapidly growing professions of the late nineteenth century—medicine and engineering. However, these were but two of the professions that quickened, strengthened, and grew in the late nineteenth century. The ministry and law, for example, among the traditional professions, and architecture as well as college teaching, among the newer ones in America, also took on new vigor and attained new influence and stature in this era. For these professions, among others, the Weberian concepts are less illuminating. Even in medicine, the prime instance for the neo-Weberian analysis, there is an extraordinary dimension that is obscured from such a perspective. That is the presence of the past: the power of the English gentlemanly ideal to find new supports and to flourish in differing circumstances.

The epitome of that dimension in American medicine of the late nineteenth century was William Osler (1849–1919), who, along with William Henry Welch, shed luster upon Johns Hopkins's first medical school faculty. If anything, Osler was the more illustrious. He was a clinician and did scientific work, but his reputation did not rest upon any of his discoveries. Rather, he is remembered for his eloquent reassertion of English gentlemanly ways to the galaxy of his brilliant students and before the meetings of the various medical societies in which he took an active part. The doctor, taught Osler, must be the carrier of high culture, learned, affable, and humane. Osler reaffirmed the importance of the personal rapport between the physician and the patient based upon a relationship of authority and dependence. The authority of the doctor was to rest upon the new medical sciences, the physician's culture and bearing, and what seemed to be the intrinsic inequality in the relationship between the healer and the sufferer.

Gentlemanly ideals also flourished in the rapidly growing profession of college teacher, one of whose important tasks was still passing civic culture on to the coming generation. Like the engineers, these professionals increasingly found themselves working in bureaucratic settings. However, the business corporations, in which the engineers worked, pursued narrow objectives and their success could readily be measured in dollars. The objectives of the university, by contrast, were broad and diverse, and the measure of success was uncertain. The professor, unlike the engineer (but much like the physician in the hospital), helped to set the objectives and gauge the success of the organization in which he worked. Under these conditions the professor could more readily maintain authority and honor.

Among the architects and the military, the quest for authority and honor was evident as well. Both reflected and utilized the conditions of the late nineteenth century that were favorable to all professions. For the architects, the rapid growth of cities and the rise of a class of newly rich with a zest for lavish spending created a boom market for civic, commercial, and residential building. The leading American architects responded to these favorable circumstances by striving to remold their occupation into an honorable and circumscribed profession. For much of the nineteenth century most of the designing of buildings was done by carpenter-builders using architectural handbooks. Most of the men who called themselves architects had little formal architectural education. The American Institute of Architecture had been founded in 1857, and though its requirements for membership were not exacting, its membership remained small until the 1880s. The most important impetus for elevating the standing of the profession came from the Society of Beaux-Arts Architects, founded in 1894. This was truly the elite of the profession, made up of Americans who had studied at that famous Paris school. Until the 1880s, England with its craft tradition in architecture was the chief influence upon American practice. In the last decades of the century, the French tradition, which held that architecture was both a fine art and a science, became dominant. That shift brought with it the ideal image of the French architect, who combined the temperament of an artist with the authority of a scientist. That ideal image did much to help the American architect assert himself with regard to his client, and it also contributed to the drive for the educational reforms, the licensing laws, and the professional codes of ethics adopted in the years that followed.

A change of European models was also important to the American military in the last decades of the nineteenth century. Prior to the Franco-Prussian War the American army had borrowed many of its patterns and practices from the French, but by the 1880s German organization was gradually replacing them. The military attitudes and manners of American officers derived from the earlier model of the English gentleman-officer. This was the eighteenth-century version of the ancient ideal of the gentleman-warrior whose virtues were courage and courtesy, and whose honor was appropriate to his rank. Sequestered at West Point, this tradition withstood the powerful leveling assaults of the Jacksonian era. West Point at that time had been attacked as aristocratic and "wholly inconsistent with the spirit of our liberal institutions" (Stephen E. Ambrose, *Duty, Honor, Country: A History of West Point*

[1966], pp. 64–65). By the 1880s, America's rapidly growing industrial might have led many to believe that the nation's era of isolationism was drawing to a close and that its military had taken on a new importance. In addition, the hierarchies that spread through American society made military organization and authority less anomalous. The junior officers entered upon a wide-ranging discussion about their professional standing and how to improve it. Raising educational standards for officers and barring entry to the incompetent were recurrent themes. In addition, they occasionally contrasted the professional ideals of the military with the commercial character of civilian life. The officer's code rejected money-making, selfish gain, and luxurious living. Oddly, the gentleman officer could easily slip into a disdainful attitude toward the society he had vowed to protect.

Although this attitude was clearly not characteristic of the professional of this era, gentlemanly authority and honor nonetheless had taken on new meaning in the polarized society of the late nineteenth century. The professional now asserted that he was neither a capitalist nor a worker; rather, he stood in some third position with an outlook arising from that standing. He was not a capitalist because his authority and honor were not derived from wealth and the dollar was not usually the best indication of his achievement. He was not a worker, though he was employed, because he worked from a position of authority and was therefore never wholly at the bidding of those who employed him. He maintained precapitalist presumptions. He was not self-denying, but his self-interest was directed and constrained by the requirements of his vocation. For him, duty guided self-interest; this duty arose from an abiding relationship between persons and entailed action that one's position required. This ideology was later reflected in Carr-Saunders and Wilson's arguments and hopes for the professions.

SINCE 1900

While much of the modern conception and self-understanding of the professions rapidly took shape in the last decades of the nineteenth century, many of the more remarkable organizational achievements occurred in the first decades of the twentieth. The American Medical Association, which previously had been national largely in name only, now set up a substantial organization with an able staff to coordinate and invigorate the activities of the state medical societies. The American Bar Association, which had been a gentlemen's club of eminent lawyers who cooled themselves at Saratoga every summer and, amid innocent dissipations, discussed selected legal issues, rapidly moved away from that splendorous spa; they met instead in the major cities of the nation and reached out to lawyers who had previously been ignored. Not only did the national organizations of doctors and lawyers attract an increasing proportion of practicing doctors and lawyers, but the national organizations of architects, dentists, engineers, and pharmacists absorbed a growing portion of their practitioners as well. The state organizations pushed more effective licensing laws through their legislatures. In this, the Progressive Era, when the use of legislation to regulate markets in the interests of morality, general prudence, and social beneficence was widely accepted, professional licensing laws could be seen as serving those interests. Moreover, as the catchwords "efficiency" and "uplift" became Progressive slogans, accountancy and social work put forward their claims to professional status. Pediatrics established itself as a specialty in medicine in these years, with considerable help from the crusading Children's Bureau. The first two decades of the century was an era of reform, but it was reform with few egalitarian proclivities. The professions prospered in such circumstances.

Little noticed in these years was the beginning of a shift in American economic life that was to have a far-reaching influence during the rest of the century. This was the rise of the service economy. It involved the transfer of the American labor force from agriculture, mining, and manufacturing to leisure industries, civil service, and education; and within manufacturing, from direct production to planning, allocation, and distribution. This shift produced new jobs, some better and some worse than those they replaced. Most of the new jobs were less susceptible to the rigorous work discipline characteristic of the factory. It is not surprising that many workers in such jobs reached toward the modes of professionalism. The conspicuous appetite for professional status in the service sector is one of the unmistakable elements in the growth of this important part of the American economy.

One of the results of these developments was the appearance of what Amitai Etzioni called the "semi-professions"—occupations whose workers adopted many of the devices of the professions but were not generally accorded the authority or honor of the traditional professions. A noteworthy characteristic of some of these semi-professions — for example, nursing, public school teaching, social work, and librarianship—was that they were composed largely of women. Some of them clung fervently to the usages of the professions, others adopted the methods of trade unions, and still others chose the instrumentalities of both. It is for these semi-professions that the Marxist discussion of the "proletarianization" of educated labor had some relevance.

However, in the period from the 1960s to the late 1970s, under the impact of a new egalitarian movement, it seemed that the traditional professions might well be leveled or at least be drastically transformed. Young doctors were setting up hospital meetings with nurses, social workers, occupational therapists, physical therapists, and even orderlies to discuss patients' progress. Young lawyers were giving up practice to write books showing how almost anyone could do her or his legal work without a lawyer. Young nuns and priests were shedding their distinctive dress and rushing out to social confrontations without attempting to say anything distinctive about the spiritual significance of those encounters. For all that, unlike the egalitarian onslaught of the mid nineteenth century, these tumults had few lasting effects upon the professions. Reformers of the 1960s and 1970s did not provide much of a persuasive critique of the science or praxis of the professions, and most practitioners maintained their self-confidence and stood their ground. One important change of this era was the opening of the major professional associations to blacks and to increasing numbers of women. During the process of reestablishing the professions in the nineteenth century, they had been excluded, not because they posed much of an economic threat but because blacks (like women) were not granted a white man's authority and honor in society at large. Admitting them would have threatened the standing of the other members of the professional association. The civil rights movement and advancing feminism mitigated that threat.

Historically, the market economy in America has provided an impressive growth of industrial productivity as well as a notable rise in living standards. Yet this has not been achieved without cost. Intrinsic to that achievement was the development of less-gratifying work and the exclusion of a larger, more elevated purpose for economic endeavor. The leading professions in bringing ideals and predispositions of an earlier era into the modern world strove to retain what the market economy relinquished. Professions, of course, are occupations and therefore can be understood, in part, as economic interest groups. Yet they offer much more than economic betterment—they offer a way of life. This is the power of their attraction.

BIBLIOGRAPHY

Statistical Information

United States Bureau of the Census. *Comparative Occupation Statistics for the United States 1870–1940* (1943).

———. *Historical Statistics of the United States, Colonial Times to 1970* (1975).

Historiographical Discussion

Abbott, Andrew. *The System of Professions: An Essay on the Division of Expert Labor* (1988). Chapter 1 examines the sociological literature; there is an extensive bibliography.

Berlant, Jeffrey. *Profession and Monopoly: A Study of Medicine in the United States and Great Britain* (1975). A Neo-Weberian perspective.

Carr-Saunders, A. M., and P. A. Wilson. *The Professions* (1933; repr. 1964).

———. "Professions." In *Encyclopaedia of the Social Sciences*. Vol. 12 (1934).

Geison, Gerald, ed. *Professions and Professional Ideologies in America* (1983).

Haber, Samuel. *The Quest for Authority and Honor in the American Professions, 1750–1900* (1991). A full exposition of the standpoint of this article.

Larson, Magali S. *The Rise of Professionalism: A Sociological Analysis* (1977). A Neo-Marxist study.

Parsons, Talcott. "Professions." *International Encyclopedia of the Social Sciences,* Vol. 12 (1968).

The Era of Establishment, 1750–1830
Bell, Whitfield J. *The Colonial Physician and Other Essays* (1975).

Haber, Samuel. "The Professions and Higher Education in America: A Historical View." In *Higher Education and the Labor Market,* edited by Margaret S. Gordon (1974).

Hudson, Winthrop. "The Ministry in the Puritan Age." In *The Ministry in Historical Perspectives,* edited by H. Richard Niebuhr and Daniel D. Williams (1956).

Leake, Chauncey, ed. *Percival's Medical Ethics* (1927).

Murrin, John M. "The Legal Transformation: The Bench and Bar of Eighteenth-Century Massachusetts." In *Colonial America,* edited by Stanley Katz (1971; rev. ed. 1987).

Youngs, John William Theodore. *God's Messengers: Religious Leadership in Colonial New England, 1700–1750* (1976).

The Egalitarian Interregnum 1830–1880
Atack, Jeremy, and Fred Bateman. *To Their Own Soil: Agriculture in the Antebellum North* (1987). Statistical study of equality of condition.

Beck, Dorothy Fahs. "The Development of the Dental Profession in the United States." Master's thesis, University of Chicago (1932).

Bloomfield, Maxwell. *American Lawyers in a Changing Society, 1776–1876* (1976).

Ferguson, Robert A. *Law and Letters in American Culture* (1984).

Gallman, Robert E. "'The Egalitarian Myth,' Once Again." *Social Science History* 5 (1981). One installment in the important exchange between Gallman and Edward Pessen indicating that Pessen's "hard facts" are quite impressionistic.

Kett, Joseph F. *The Formation of the American Medical Profession: The Role of Institutions, 1780–1860* (1968).

Mead, Sidney E. "The Rise of the Evangelical Conception of the Ministry in America: 1607–1850." In *The Ministry in Historical Perspectives,* edited by H. Richard Niebuhr and Daniel D. Williams (1956).

Pessen, Edward. *Riches, Class, and Power Before the Civil War* (1973). Social stratification in eastern cities.

Pound, Roscoe. *The Lawyer from Antiquity to Modern Times* (1953).

Scott, Donald M. *From Office to Profession: The New England Ministry, 1780–1850* (1978).

Warner, John Harley. *The Therapeutic Perspective: Medical Practice, Knowledge, and Identity in America, 1820–1885* (1986).

Reestablishment, 1880–1900
Bacon, Mardges. *Ernest Flagg: Beaux-Arts Architect and Urban Reformer* (1985).

Calvert, Monte. *The Mechanical Engineer in America, 1830–1910: Professional Cultures in Conflict* (1967).

Hobson, W. K. "Symbol of the New Profession: Emergence of the Large Law Firm, 1875–1915." In *The New High Priests: Lawyers in Post–Civil War America,* edited by Gerard W. Gawalt (1984).

Huntington, Samuel P. *The Soldier and the State: The Theory and Politics of Civil-Military Relations* (1957).

Matzko, John A. "The Early Years of the American Bar Association, 1878–1928." Ph.D. diss., University of Virginia (1984).

Moldow, Gloria. *Women Doctors in Gilded-Age Washington: Race, Gender, and Professionalization* (1987).

Osler, William. *Counsels and Ideals from the Writings of William Osler,* C. N. B. Camac, comp. (1906).

Rothstein, William G. *American Physicians in the Nineteenth Century: From Sects to Science* (1972).

Veysey, Laurence R. *The Emergence of the American University* (1965).

Since 1900

Etzioni, Amitai, ed. *The Semi-Professions and Their Organization: Teachers, Nurses, Social Workers* (1969).

Freidson, Eliot. *Professional Powers: A Study of the Institutionalization of Formal Knowledge* (1986).

Gerstl, Joel, and Glenn Jacobs, eds. *Professions for the People: The Politics of Skill* (1976). Reflects the spirit of the 1960s.

Ginzberg, Eli, and George J. Vojta. "The Service Sector of the U.S. Economy." *Scientific American* 244 (March 1981): 48–55.

Halpern, Sydney. "Segmental Professionalization Within Medicine: The Case of Pediatrics." Ph.D. diss., University of California–Berkeley (1982).

Lipset, Seymour Martin. "White Collar Workers and Professionals—Their Attitudes and Behavior Towards Unions." In *Readings in Industrial Society,* edited by William A. Faunce (1967).

Morais, Herbert M. *The History of the Negro in Medicine* (1967).

Morantz-Sanchez, Regina Markell. *Sympathy and Science: Women Physicians in American Medicine* (1985).

Morello, Karen Berger. *The Invisible Bar: The Woman Lawyer in America, 1638–1986* (1986).

Starr, Paul. *The Social Transformation of American Medicine* (1982).

SEE ALSO various essays in the sections "Education, Literacy, and the Fine Arts," "Methods and Contexts," and "Science, Medicine, and Technology."